POSTCARDS

FROM

SPAIN

D0448352

Driving through Andalusia, you may come across bucolic scenes like this one of a shepherd tending his flock. See chapter 7. © Anthony Cassidy/Tony Stone Images.

Just inland from the overdeveloped beach resorts of the Costa del Sol is lovely unspoiled country-side and farmland. © *Thomas Kanzler/The Viesti Collection, Inc.*

The little town of Ronda, one of the oldest and most aristocratic in Spain, is a fantastic place to explore. See chapter 7. © Thomas Kanzler/The Viesti Collection, Inc.

Córdoba's whitewashed dwellings boast flower-filled patios and balconies. See chapter 7. © A.S.K./Viesti Associates, Inc.

Visit one of Jerez's bodegas (wineries) to taste the golden sherry that has been called the lifeblood of Spain. See chapter 7. © Degas-Parra/ Ask Images/Viesti Collection, Inc.

A woman sells crafts on Plaza de España in Seville. See chapter 7. © Kindra Clineff Photography.

Follow the sounds of castanets to Seville's Club Los Gallos for an evening of flamenco dancing. See chapter 7. © Kelly/Mooney Photography.

At Seville's landmark square, the Plaza de España, you can rent rowboats for excursions. See chapter 7. © P & G Bowater/The Image Bank.

If you visit only a few Spanish cities in your lifetime, make beautiful, romantic Toledo one of them. See chapter 4. © P & G Bowater/The Image Bank.

The running of the bulls at Pamplona's Fiesta de San Fermín is one of the most popular events in Europe. See chapter 14. © Oliver Benn/Tony Stone Images.

From Easter until late October, some of Spain's best bullfighters appear at the Maestranza bullring in Seville. See chapter 7. © J. Du Boisberran/The Image Bank.

The Mezquita (mosque) in Córdoba is a fantastic labyrinth of red-and-white peppermint-striped pillars. See chapter 7. © Bill Wassman/The Stock Market.

The Alhambra, a lavish palace in Granada, is one of the most exotic settings in Europe. See chapter 7. © Nik Wheeler Photography.

On a hiking tour, you might discover a forgotten village nestled into the valleys of the Pyrenees. See chapters 1 and 2. © Ric Ergenbright Photography.

Gaudí's La Sagrada Familia in Barcelona is a bizarre wonder that has yet to be completed. See chapter 10. © Kindra Clineff Photography.

Street entertainers, flower vendors, café patrons, and strollers congregate on Barcelona's Les Rambles, the most famous promenade in Spain. See chapter 10. © Robert Frerck/Odyssey/Chicago.

Drink in Madrid's vibrant nightlife surrounded by the elaborately tiled walls of historic Los Gabrieles. See chapter 3. © Robert Frerck/Odyssey/Chicago.

Picasso's famous anti-war masterpiece, Guernica, now rests in Madrid's Museo Nacional Centro de Arte Reina Sofía. See chapter 3. © Nik Wheeler Photography.

Filled with taverns and bars, the Plaza Mayor is the heart of Old Madrid. See chapter 3. © Robert Frerck/Odyssey/Chicago.

With its 12th-century walls and fishing boats, Tossa de Mar makes a delightful base for a Costa Brava vacation. See chapter 12. © Tom Benoit/Tony Stone Images.

The arid plains of New Castile are visible from Toledo's lofty hilltop position. See chapter 4.
© Nik Wheeler Photography.

Segovia's glorious 12th-century El Alcázar has been the residence of Spanish monarchs since
the days of Ferdinand and Isabella. See chapter 4. © Michael Busselle/Tony Stone Images.

Harborside houses reflected in the water on the island of Majorca. See chapter 18. © David C. Tomlinson/Tony Stone Worldwide.

Set against a backdrop of olive-green mountains, the area around Deià in Majorca is beautiful and serene. See chapter 18. © Michael Defreitas Photography.

When should I travel to get the best airfare?
Where do I go for answers to my travel questions?
What's the best and easiest way to plan and book my trip?

frommers.travelocity.com

Frommer's, the travel guide leader, has teamed up with **Travelocity.com**, the leader in online travel, to bring you an in-depth, easy-to-use resource designed to help you plan and book your trip online.

At **frommers.travelocity.com**, you'll find free online updates about your destination from the experts at Frommer's plus the outstanding travel planning and purchasing features of Travelocity.com. Travelocity.com provides reservations capabilities for 95 percent of all airline seats sold, more than 47,000 hotels, and over 50 car rental companies. In addition, Travelocity.com offers more than 2,000 exciting vacation and cruise packages. Travelocity.com puts you in complete control of your travel planning with these and other great features:

> **Expert travel guidance from Frommer's** - over 150 writers reporting from around the world!
>
> **Best Fare Finder** - an interactive calendar tells you when to travel to get the best airfare
>
> **Fare Watcher** - we'll track airfare changes to your favorite destinations
>
> **Dream Maps** - a mapping feature that suggests travel opportunities based on your budget
>
> **Shop Safe Guarantee** - 24 hours a day / 7 days a week live customer service, and more!

Whether traveling on a tight budget, looking for a quick weekend getaway, or planning the trip of a lifetime, Frommer's guides and Travelocity.com will make your travel dreams a reality. You've bought the book, now book the trip!

Other Great Guides for Your Trip:

Frommer's Barcelona, Madrid & Seville

Spain For Dummies

Frommer's Spain's Best-Loved Driving Tours

Frommer's Europe

Frommer's Europe from $70 a Day

Frommer's Gay & Lesbian Europe

Frommer's Europe's Greatest Driving Tours

Europe For Dummies

Hanging Out in Europe

Frommer's Road Atlas Europe

Here's what the critics say about Frommer's:

"Amazingly easy to use. Very portable, very complete."

—*Booklist*

♦

"The only mainstream guide to list specific prices. The Walter Cronkite of guidebooks—with all that implies."

—*Travel & Leisure*

♦

"Complete, concise, and filled with useful information."

—*New York Daily News*

♦

"Hotel information is close to encyclopedic."

—*Des Moines Sunday Register*

♦

"Detailed, accurate and easy-to-read information for all price ranges."

—*Glamour Magazine*

Spain
2001

by Darwin Porter & Danforth Prince

IDG Books Worldwide, Inc.
An International Data Group Company
Foster City, CA • Chicago, IL • Indianapolis, IN • New York, NY

ABOUT THE AUTHORS

Veteran travel writers **Darwin Porter** and **Danforth Prince** have written numerous best-selling Frommer's guides, notably to France, Italy, England, Germany, and Spain. Porter, who was bureau chief for the *Miami Herald* when he was 21, wrote the first-ever Frommer's guide to Spain while still a student. Prince, who began writing with Porter in 1982, worked for the Paris bureau of the *New York Times*.

IDG BOOKS WORLDWIDE, INC.

An International Data Group Company
909 Third Avenue
New York, NY 10022

Find us online at **www.frommers.com**

ISBN 0-7645-6170-7
ISSN 1091-2827

Editor: Matthew Garcia
Production Editor: Todd A. Siesky
Photo Editor: Richard Fox
Design by Michele Laseau
Cartographer: Elizabeth Puhl
Production by IDG Books Indianapolis Production Department

SPECIAL SALES

For general information on IDG Books Worldwide's books in the U.S., please call our Consumer Customer Service Department at 1-800-762-2974. For reseller information, including discounts, bulk sales, customized editions, and premium sales, please call our Reseller Consumer Service Department at 1-800-434-3422.

Manufactured in the United States of America.

5 4 3 2 1

Contents

List of Maps   ix

1   The Best of Spain   1

1 The Best Travel Experiences   1

2 The Best Small Towns   3

3 The Best Beaches   4

4 The Best Castles & Palaces   5

5 The Best Museums   6

6 The Best Cathedrals & Churches   7

7 The Best Vineyards & Wineries   9

8 The Best Festivals   12

9 The Best Paradors   13

10 The Best Luxury Hotels   14

11 The Best Hotel Bargains   16

12 The Best Restaurants   17

2   Planning Your Trip: The Basics   19

1 The Regions in Brief   19

2 Visitor Information, Entry Requirements & Customs   25

3 Money   27

The Spanish Peseta   28

4 When to Go   29

Spain Calendar of Events   30

5 Special-Interest Vacations   34

6 Health & Insurance   38

7 Tips for Travelers with Special Needs   39

8 Getting There   42

Fly for Less: Tips for Getting the Best Airfares   44

9 Getting Around   49

Riding the Rails in Style   52

10 Tips on Accommodations   54

Fast Facts: Spain   56

Planning Your Trip: An Online Directory   60

3   Madrid   75

1 Orientation   76

Neighborhoods in Brief   78

2 Getting Around   79

Fast Facts: Madrid   82

3 Where to Stay   84

Family-Friendly Hotels   96

4 Where to Dine   102

An Early-Evening Tapeo   106

5 Seeing the Sights   125

Frommer's Favorite Madrid Experiences   134

6 Shopping   138

7 Madrid After Dark   144

The Sultry Sound of Flamenco   145

4   Side Trips From Madrid   156

1 Toledo   156

   The Siege of the Alcázar   164

2 Aranjuez   170

3 San Lorenzo de El Escorial   172

4 Segovia   176

5 Alcalá de Henares   181

6 El Pardo   183

7 Chinchón   184

8 Ávila   185

   A Saint & Her City   187

9 Cuenca   191

5   Old Castile & León   195

1 Ciudad Rodrigo   195

2 Salamanca   198

3 Zamora   206

4 León   208

5 Valladolid   213

6 Burgos   217

6   Extremadura   223

1 Guadalupe   223

   Land of the Conquistadors   226

2 Trujillo   227

3 Cáceres   230

4 Mérida   233

5 Badajoz   237

6 Zafra   239

7   Andalusia   242

1 Jaén, Baeza & Úbeda   242

2 Córdoba   250

3 Seville   262

   The Legacy of al-Andalus   283

4 Jerez de la Frontera   285

5 Cádiz   292

6 Costa de la Luz   295

7 Ronda   297

8 Granada   302

8   The Costa del Sol   318

1 Algeciras   319

   Beaches: The Good, the Bad & the Ugly   321

2 Tarifa   322

3 Estepona   322

4 San Pedro de Alcántara   324

5 Puerto Banús   325

6 Marbella   326

   A Marbella Tasca *Crawl*   336

7 Fuengirola & Los Boliches   337

8 Mijas   339

9 Torremolinos   340

10 Málaga   347

11 Nerja   355

9   Valencia & the Costa Blanca   359

1 Valencia   359

   The Disappearing Barracas   371

2 Benidorm   372

3 Alicante   375

4 Elche   379

5 Murcia   381

10 Barcelona 384

1 Catalonian Culture 385

2 Orientation 387

    The Barcelona Card 390

    Neighborhoods in Brief 391

3 Getting Around 393

    Fast Facts: Barcelona 395

4 Where to Stay 397

    Family-Friendly Hotels 404

5 Where to Dine 409

    Family-Friendly Restaurants 419

6 Seeing the Sights 425

    Frommer's Favorite Barcelona Experiences 430

7 Active Pursuits 438

8 Shopping 439

9 Barcelona After Dark 444

10 Side Trips from Barcelona 451

11 Catalonia 454

1 Montserrat 455

    A Journey to Andorra 456

2 Tarragona 458

    The Beaches of the Costa Dorada 463

3 Sitges 464

    Rusiñol: The Enigmatic Figure of Modernisme 467

12 Girona & the Costa Brava 472

1 Girona 472

2 Lloret de Mar 479

3 Tossa de Mar 482

4 Figueres 485

    The Mad, Mad World of Salvador Dalí 486

5 Cadaqués 489

13 Aragón 491

1 Zaragoza 491

2 Tarazona 498

3 Calatayud 499

4 Nuévalos/Piedra 500

5 Sos del Rey Católico 501

14 Navarre & La Rioja 502

1 Pamplona (Iruña) 504

    The Running of the Bulls 507

2 Olite 511

3 Tudela 513

4 Sangüesa 515

5 Logroño 517

6 Haro 519

15 The Basque Country 521

1 San Sebastián (Donostia) 523

2 Fuenterrabía (Hondarribía) 535

3 Guernica 537

4 Bilbao 538

5 Vitoria (Gasteiz) 546

16 Cantabria & Asturias   550

1 Laredo   552
2 Santander   553
3 Santillana del Mar & Cuevas de Altamira   557
4 Los Picos de Europa   560
5 Gijón (Xixón)   565
6 Oviedo (Uviéu)   568

17 Galicia   573

1 La Coruña   573
2 Santiago de Compostela   579
   The World's Oldest Hotel   584
3 Rías Altas   587
4 Rías Bajas   589
5 Pontevedra   591
6 Lugo   594
7 El Grove & La Toja   596
8 Túy (Túi)   597

18 The Balearic Islands   599

1 Majorca   601
2 Ibiza   630
3 Formentera   647
4 Minorca   650

Appendix A: Spain in Depth   668

1 Spain Today   669
2 History 101   670
   Dateline   670
3 Architecture Through the Ages   674
The Spectacle of Death   676
4 Spanish Art   679
5 A Taste of Spain   681

Appendix B: Useful Terms & Phrases   685

1 Basic Vocabulary   685
2 Numbers   687
3 Transportation Terms   687

Index   689

List of Maps

Spain's Regions   20

Madrid Metro   80

Accommodations in Central
   Madrid   86

Dining in Central Madrid   104

Central Madrid Attractions   126

Madrid Environs   157

Toledo   158

Old Castile & León   197

Salamanca   199

Extremadura   225

Andalusia   243

Córdoba   251

Seville   263

Granada & the Alhambra   303

The Costa del Sol   319

Marbella   327

The Costa Blanca   361

Valencia   363

Barcelona Metro   394

Barcelona Accommodations   398

Barcelona Dining   410

The Barri Gòtic   427

Barcelona Attractions   428

Catalonia   455

Girona & the Costa Brava   473

Aragón   493

Navarre & La Rioja   503

Pamplona   505

Basque Country   522

San Sebastián   525

Bilbao   539

Cantabria & Asturias   551

Galicia   575

Santiago de Compostela   581

The Balearic Islands   600

Majorca   603

Palma de Majorca   605

Ibiza   631

Ciudad de Ibiza   634

Minorca   651

AN INVITATION TO THE READER

In researching this book, we discovered many wonderful places—hotels, restaurants, shops, and more. We're sure you'll find others. Please tell us about them, so we can share the information with your fellow travelers in upcoming editions. If you were disappointed with a recommendation, we'd love to know that too. Please write to:

Frommer's Spain 2001
IDG Books Worldwide, Inc.
909 Third Avenue
New York, NY 10022

AN ADDITIONAL NOTE

Please be advised that travel information is subject to change at any time—and this is especially true of prices. We therefore suggest that you write or call ahead for confirmation when making your travel plans. The authors, editors, and publisher cannot be held responsible for the experiences of readers while traveling. Your safety is important to us, however, so we encourage you to stay alert and be aware of your surroundings. Keep a close eye on cameras, purses, and wallets, all favorite targets of thieves and pickpockets.

WHAT THE SYMBOLS MEAN

✪ Frommer's Favorites

Our favorite places and experiences—outstanding for quality, value, or both.

The following abbreviations are used for credit cards:

AE	American Express	ER	enRoute
CB	Carte Blanche	JCB	Japan Credit Bank
DC	Diners Club	MC	MasterCard
DISC	Discover	V	Visa

FIND FROMMER'S ONLINE

www.frommers.com offers up-to-the-minute listings on almost 200 cities around the globe—including the latest bargains and candid, personal articles updated daily by Arthur Frommer himself. No other Web site offers such comprehensive and timely coverage of the world of travel.

The Best of Spain

Spain is one of the most diverse and visually stunning nations of Europe. As you begin to plan your trip, you may find yourself overwhelmed with so many fascinating sights, beautiful landscapes, and charming towns to fit into your limited time. So let us give you a hand. We've scoured the country in search of the best places and experiences, and we've chosen our very favorites below, admittedly very personal and opinionated choices.

Seek out a Picasso masterwork. Check out the "hanging houses" in cliff-top Cuenca. Run from a charging bull down the cobblestone streets of Pamplona (Scratch that: From the safety of protective barricades, watch the *locals* elude the bulls). Enjoy fresh seafood paella in a picture-perfect fishing village. We hope that our picks, everything from the sultry sound of flamenco to tapas tasting, will get you started on the road to planning the trip that's right for you.

1 The Best Travel Experiences

- **Sitting in *Sol* or *Sombra* at the Bullfights:** With origins as old as pagan Spain, the art of bullfighting is the expression of Iberian temperament and passions. Detractors object to the sport as cruel, bloody, and savage. Fans, however, view bullfighting as a microcosm of death, catharsis, and rebirth. These philosophical underpinnings may not be immediately apparent, but if you strive to understand the bullfight, it can be one of the most evocative and memorable events in Spain. Head for the *plaza de toros* (bullring) in any major city, but particularly in Madrid, Seville, or Granada. Tickets are either *sol* (sunny side) or *sombra* (in the shade); you'll pay more to get out of the sun. Observe how the feverish crowds appreciate the ballet of the *banderilleros,* the thundering fury of the bull, the arrogance of the matador—all leading to "death in the afternoon."
- **Feasting on Tapas in the *Tascas:*** Tapas, those bite-size portions washed down with wine, beer, or sherry, are reason enough to go to Spain! Tapas bars, called *tascas,* are a quintessential Spanish experience. Originally tapas were cured ham or *chorizo* (spicy sausage). Today they are likely to be anything—*gambas* (deep-fried shrimp), anchovies marinated in vinegar, stuffed peppers, a cool, spicy gazpacho, or hake salad. These dazzling spreads will hold you over until the fashionable 10pm dining hour.

- **Getting Caught Up in the Passions of Flamenco:** It's best heard in some old tavern, in a neighborhood like the Barrio de Triana in Seville. From the lowliest *taberna* to the poshest nightclub, you can hear the staccato foot stomping, castanet rattling, hand clapping, and sultry guitar sound. Some say its origins lie deep in Asia, but the Spanish gypsy has given the art form, which dramatizes inner conflict and pain, an original style. Performed by a great artist, flamenco can tear your heart out with its soulful, throaty singing.

- **Seeing the Masterpieces at the Prado:** One of the world's premier art museums, it's home to some 4,000 masterpieces, many of them acquired by Spanish kings. The wealth of Spanish art is staggering—everything from Goya's *Naked Maja* to the celebrated *Las Meninas* (*The Maids of Honor*) by Velázquez (our favorite). Masterpiece after masterpiece unfolds before your eyes: You can imagine your fate in Hieronymus Bosch's *Garden of Earthly Delights* or recoil from the horror of Goya's *Disasters of War* etchings. When the Spanish artistic soul gets too dark, escape to the Italian salons and view canvases by Caravaggio, Fra Angelico, and Botticelli. See chapter 3.

- **Sipping Sherry in Jerez de la Frontera:** In Spain, sherry is called Jerez, and it's a major industry and subculture in its own right. Hispanophiles compare its complexities to the finest wines produced in France and make pilgrimages to the *bodegas* (wineries) in Andalusia that ferment this amber-colored liquid. More than 100 *bodegas* are available for visits, tours, and tastings, and most open their gates to visitors interested in a process that dates from the country's Roman occupation. See chapter 7.

- **Wandering the Crooked Streets of Barcelona's Gothic Quarter:** Long before Madrid was founded, the kingdom of Catalonia was a bastion of art and architecture. Whether the Barri Gótic, as it's called in Catalán, is truly Gothic is the subject of endless debate, but the Ciutat Vella, or old city, of Barcelona is one of the most evocative neighborhoods in Spain. Its richly textured streets, with their gurgling fountains, vintage stores, and ancient fortifications, inspired such artists as Pablo Picasso (a museum of his work is found here) and Joan Miró (who was born in this neighborhood). See chapter 10.

- **Going Gaga Over Gaudí:** No architect in Europe was as fantastical as Antoni Gaudí y Cornet, the foremost proponent of Catalán *modernisme*. Barcelona is studded with the works of this extraordinary artist—in fact, UNESCO now lists all his creations among World Trust Properties. This eccentric genius conceived buildings as "visions." A recluse and a celibate bachelor, as well as a fervent Catalán nationalist, he lived out his own fantasy. Nothing is more stunning than his Sagrada Familia, Barcelona's best-known landmark, a cathedral on which Gaudí labored for the last 43 years of his life before he was killed tragically by a tram in 1926. The landmark cathedral was never completed, but believe it or not, they're still working on it. If it's ever finished, "The Sacred Family" will be Europe's largest cathedral. See chapter 10.

- **Running with the Bulls in Pamplona:** Okay, maybe it's smarter to watch, not actually participate in, the running of the bulls. The Fiesta de San Fermín in July is the most dangerous ritual in Spain, made even worse by copious amounts of wine consumed by participants and observers. Broadcast live on TV throughout Spain and the rest of Europe, and originally introduced to North American audiences by Ernest Hemingway, the festival features herds of furious bulls that charge down medieval streets, sometimes trampling and goring some of the hundreds of people who run beside them. Few other rituals in Spain are as breathtaking and foolhardy. And few others as memorable. See chapter 14.

Impressions

Three Spaniards, four opinions.

—Old Spanish proverb

- **Following the Ancient Pilgrim Route to Santiago:** Tourism as we know it began during the Middle Ages, as thousands of European pilgrims journeyed to the shrine of Santiago (Saint James) in Galicia in northwestern Spain. Even if you're not motivated by faith, you should come to see some of the most dramatic landscapes and the grandest scenery in Spain by crossing the northern tier of the country—all the way from the Pyrenees to Santiago de Compostela. Some of the country's most stunning architecture can be viewed along the way, including gems in Roncevalles, Burgos, and León. The deluxe Hostal de Los Reyes Católicos in Santiago awaits the weary pilgrim at the end of the journey. See chapter 17.

2 The Best Small Towns

- **Cuenca:** Set amid a landscape of rugged limestone outcroppings at the junction of two rivers, Cuenca is a fascinating combination of medieval masonry and cantilevered balconies that seem to float above the steep gorges below. The angularity of the architecture here is said to have inspired early versions of cubism, a fact commemorated in Cuenca's Museo de Arte Abstracto Español. This museum is considered to be one of the finest modern art museums in Spain. See chapter 4.
- **Zafra:** Zafra's 15th-century castle is the largest and best preserved in the region. It is set within the angular, stark white architecture of Zafra, which is also said to have inspired the cubists. See chapter 6.
- **Baeza:** After it was wrenched away from the Moors in 1227, Baeza became a frontier town between the Christian and Moorish worlds, and a diehard symbol of the Catholic ambition to occupy all of Iberia. Today a wealth of architecture survives as evidence of the splendor of Iberian history. See chapter 7.
- **Carmona:** Pint-sized, sleepy Carmona—usually visited as a side trip from Seville—packs a historical wallop, evoking the Roman occupation of Iberia. The town claims an architectural legacy from every occupying force dating from 206 B.C., when the Romans defeated the resident Carthaginian army. See chapter 7.
- **Arcos de la Frontera:** Parts of Andalusia are very overcrowded, so you may want to stretch out and relax when you arrive at this ancient Arab town. Now a historical monument, Arcos de la Frontera is 20 miles (32km) east of Jerez de la Frontera—the town that sherry put on the map. The place to stay is the Parador Casa del Corregidor (an old vicar's home). From there you can set out to explore this lofty town, hemmed in on three sides by the Guadalete River. The parador is perched along the edge of a cliff, and walks from there in almost any direction offer spectacular views of this *pueblo blanco* (white village) of whitewashed Andalusian houses. See chapter 7.
- **Ronda:** The site appears inhospitable—a gorge slices through the town center and its twin halves are interconnected with bridges that are antiques in their own right. But the winding streets of this old Moorish town are perfect for wandering, and the views of the surrounding Andalusian countryside are stupendous. Ronda is also revered by bullfighting fans, both for its bullring (the oldest and most beautiful in Spain) and the region's skill in breeding the fiercest bulls in the country. See chapter 7.

- **Mijas:** Wander through streets and alleys once trod by the Phoenicians, the Celts, and the Moors. Today, the town offers a welcome dose of medieval flair on the Costa del Sol, a region otherwise filled with modern, anonymous, and often ugly resort hotels. See chapter 8.
- **Nerja:** On the Costa del Sol at the *Balcón de Europa* (Balcony of Europe) lies this Mediterranean gem, with a palm-shaded promenade jutting out into the sea. Lined with antique iron lampposts, the village overlooks a pretty beach and fishing fleet. The resort town is on a sloping site at the foot of a wall of jagged coastal mountains. You can snuggle up in the parador or lodge in one of the little inns on the narrow streets. See chapter 8.
- **Elche:** Although famed as a charming medieval village, Elche is best known as the excavation site of one of the premier sculptures of the Roman Empire in Iberia, *La Dama de Elche,* now exhibited in Madrid's archaeological museum. These days, you can still see date palms planted originally by the Phoenicians and a mystery play celebrating the Assumption of the Virgin, which has been performed in the village church every year since the 1300s. See chapter 9.
- **Sitges:** South of Barcelona is Spain's most romantic Mediterranean beach town, with a 1½-mile-long sandy beach and a promenade studded with flowers and palm trees. Sitges is a town with a rich connection to art; Picasso and Dalí both spent time here. Wander its little lanes and inspect the old villas of its *Casco Antiguo,* the old quarter. When not at the beach, you can view three good art museums, including one in the former studio of artist Santiago Rusiñol (1861–1931). Nowadays, thousands of gay men and lesbians flock to Sitges, but there's a wide spectrum of visitors of all persuasions. See chapter 11.
- **Cadaqués:** The 16th-century church that dominates this town from a nearby hilltop isn't particularly noteworthy, but Cadaqués—on the Costa Brava near the French border—still charms with whitewashed, fishing-village simplicity. The azure waters of the Mediterranean appealed to surrealist master Salvador Dalí, who built a suitably bizarre villa in the adjoining hamlet of Lligat. See chapter 12.
- **Santillana del Mar:** Jean-Paul Sartre called it "the prettiest village in Spain." Only 6 blocks long and just 3 miles (5km) from the sea, Santillana del Mar perfectly captures the spirit of Cantabria. It's also near the Cuevas de Altamira, often called "the Sistine Chapel of prehistoric art." Romanesque houses and mansions line the ironstone streets. People still sell fresh milk from their stable doors, as if the Middle Ages had never ended, but you can live in comfort at one of Spain's grandest paradors, Parador de Santillana, a converted 17th-century mansion. See chapter 16.
- **Deià:** On the island of Majorca, you'll find this lovely old village (also spelled Deyá), where the poet Robert Graves lived until his death in 1985. Following in his footsteps, artists and writers flock to this haven of natural beauty, 17 miles (27km) northwest of Palma. The views of the sea and mountains are panoramic. Gnarled and ancient olive trees dot the landscape. You can book into cozy nests of luxury like La Residencia or Es Molí. See chapter 18.

3 The Best Beaches

Spain may be flanked to the east by France and the Pyrenees and to the west by Portugal, but most of the country is ringed with sand, rock, and seawater. That, coupled with almost year-round sunshine, has attracted many millions of beachgoers.

- **Costa de la Luz:** This stretch of coastline in southwestern Andalusia boasts long stretches of sand and almost-constant sunshine. The blue, sometimes rough,

Atlantic waters are enticement enough, as is the region's proximity to several historic cities. Foremost among coastal cities is Cádiz, with Seville just a short drive inland. This area is less developed than the more popular Costa del Sol. See chapter 7.

- **Costa del Sol:** Stretching east from Gibraltar along the southernmost coast of Spain, the Costa del Sol is the most famous, party-hearty, and overdeveloped string of beaches in Iberia. The beaches feature superb sand, and the Mediterranean waters are calm and warm throughout most of the year. But these charms have brought throngs of visitors, making this the most congested string of coastal resorts in Europe. The most important resorts here are Marbella, Torremolinos, Málaga, and Nerja. Look for soaring skyscrapers; eye-popping bikinis; sophisticated resorts and restaurants alongside hotels that cater to tour groups; lots of sunshine; and interminable traffic jams. See chapter 8.
- **Costa Blanca:** This southeastern coast embraces the industrial city of Valencia, but its best-known resorts, Benidorm and Alicante, are packed with northern-European sun-seekers every year. The surrounding scenery isn't particularly dramatic—flat, sunbaked terrain bathed in a stark white light. But the water is turquoise, the sand is white, and a low annual rainfall virtually guarantees a sunny vacation. See chapter 9.
- **Costa Brava:** Rockier, more serpentine, and without the long stretches of sand that mark the Costa Blanca, the cliff-edged Costa Brava stretches from Barcelona to the French border. Look for the charming, sandy-bottomed coves that dot the coast. Although there are fewer undiscovered beaches here than along Spain's Atlantic coast, the Costa Brava still retains a sense of rocky wilderness. One of the more eccentric-looking villas along this coast belonged to the late Salvador Dalí, the region's most famous modern son who lived much of his life near Cadaqués. See chapter 12.
- **Costa Verde:** Radically different from the dry and sunbaked coastline of Andalusia, the rocky Costa Verde (Green Coast) resembles a sunny version of Ireland's western shore. It's temperate in summer, when the rest of Spain can be unbearably hot. Much of the coast is within the ancient province of Asturias, a region rife with Romanesque architecture and medieval pilgrimage sites—and one that has not yet been overwhelmed with tourism. Premier resorts include some districts of Santander, Gijón, and, a short distance inland, Oviedo. See chapter 16.
- **The Balearic Islands:** Just off the coast of Catalonia and a 45-minute flight from Barcelona, this rocky, sand-fringed archipelago attracts urban refugees seeking the sun, jet-set glitterati, and exhibitionists in scanty beachwear. The Mediterranean climate is warmer here than on the mainland. Majorca in particular has been targeted by northern Europeans, many of whom have bought vacation homes there. The city of Palma de Majorca has the greatest number of high-rises and the most crowded shorelines. Much of Ibiza is party central for young people and gay visitors during the summer. Sleepy Minorca offers more isolation. See chapter 18.

4 The Best Castles & Palaces

- **Palacio Real** (Madrid): No longer occupied by royalty, but still used for state occasions, the Royal Palace sits in the heart of Madrid on the bank of the Manzanares River. It was built in the mid–18th century over the site of a former palace. It's not Versailles, but it's still mighty impressive, with around 2,000 rooms. No one has lived here since the king fled in 1931, but the chandeliers, marble columns, and ornate, gilded borders, paintings, and objets d'art, including Flemish tapestries and Tiepolo ceiling frescoes, are still well preserved. The empty thrones of King Juan Carlos and Queen Sofia are among the highlights of the tour. See chapter 3.

- **El Alcázar** (Segovia): Once the most impregnable castle in Spain, it rises dramatically from a rock spur near the ancient heart of town. Isabella married Ferdinand at this foreboding site, surrendering rights that eventually led to the unification of Spain. Today, it's the single most photographed and dramatic castle in Iberia. See chapter 4.
- **Palacio Real** (Aranjuez): Built at enormous expense by the Bourbon cousins of the rulers of France, it was designed to emulate the glories of Versailles in its 18th-century neoclassicism. The gardens are even more fascinating than the palace. The gem of the complex is the Casita del Labrador, an annex as rich and ornate as its model—Marie Antoinette's Petit Trianon at Versailles. See chapter 4.
- **Alhambra** (Granada): One of Spain's grandest sights, the Alhambra was originally conceived by the Muslims as a fortified pleasure pavilion. Its allure was instantly recognized by Catholic monarchs after the Reconquest. Despite the presence of a decidedly European palace in its center, the setting remains one of the most exotic (and Moorish) in all of Europe. See chapter 7.
- **Alcázar** (Seville): The oldest royal residence in Europe still in use was built by Peter the Cruel (1350–69) in 1364, 78 years after the Moors left Seville. Ferdinand and Isabella once lived here. One of the purest examples of the Mudéjar, or Moorish, style, its decoration is based on that of the Alhambra in Granada. A multitude of Christian and Islamic motifs are combined architecturally in this labyrinth of gardens, halls, and courts, none more notable than the Patio de las Doncellas (Court of the Maidens). See chapter 7.

5 The Best Museums

The spectacular **Prado** in Madrid is no mere museum, but a travel experience. It's worth a journey to Spain just to visit it (see "The Best Travel Experiences" above).

- **Museo Lázaro Galdiano** (Madrid): This rare collection demonstrates the evolution of enamel and ivory crafts from the Byzantine era to 19th-century Limoges. Of almost equal importance are displays of superb medieval gold and silver work along with Italian Renaissance jewelry. The museum also contains galleries with rare paintings, everything from Flemish primitives to works by Spanish masters of the golden age, including El Greco, Murillo, and Zurbarán. There are also paintings from Goya's "Black Period" and from the English and Italian masters Constable and Tiepolo. See chapter 3.
- **Thyssen-Bornemisza Museum** (Madrid): Madrid's acquisition of this treasure trove of art in the 1980s was one of the greatest coups in European art history. Amassed by a central European collector beginning around 1920, and formerly displayed in Lugano, Switzerland, its 700 canvasses are arranged in chronological order in a way that rivals the legendary holdings of the queen of England herself. Works by artists ranging from El Greco to Picasso decorate the walls. See chapter 3.
- **Museo de Arte Abstracto Español** (Cuenca): The angular medieval architecture of the town that contains it is an appropriate foil for a startling collection of modern masters. A group of some of Spain's most celebrated artists settled in Cuenca in the 1950s and 1960s, and their works are displayed here. They included Fernando Zobel, Antoni Tápies, Eduardo Chillida, Luis Feito, and Antonio Saura. See chapter 4.

- **Museo de Santa Cruz** (Toledo): Built as a hospital for the poor and orphaned by the archbishop of Toledo, this is the most important museum in New Castile. The Santa Cruz museum is known for its plateresque architecture, notably its intricate facade, and for the wealth of art inside. Among its noteworthy collection of 16th- and 17th-century paintings are 18 works by El Greco. Especially evocative is his *Altarpiece of the Assumption,* completed in 1613 during his final period. The gallery also contains a collection of primitive paintings. See chapter 4.
- **Museo Nacional de Escultura** (Valladolid): The greatest collection of gilded polychrome sculpture—an art form that reached its pinnacle in Valladolid—is on display here in the 15th-century San Gregorio College. Figures are first carved in wood, then painted with great artistry to achieve a lifelike appearance. The most remarkable exhibit is an altarpiece designed by Alonso Berruguete for the Church of San Benito. Be sure to see his *Martyrdom of St. Sebastian.* See chapter 5.
- **Museo Nacional de Arte Romano** (Mérida): A museum that makes most archaeologists salivate, this modern building contains hundreds of pieces of ancient Roman sculpture discovered in and around this dried-out, sunbaked Extremaduran town. The Roman treasures included theaters, amphitheaters, racecourses, and hundreds of tombs full of art objects, many of which are on display here. In 1986 the well-known and award-winning architect Rafael Moneo created a stir in architectural circles when he designed this ambitious and innovative brick building. Designing the building on a grand scale, he freely borrowed from Roman motifs and daringly incorporated an ancient Roman road, which was discovered when the foundations were dug. See chapter 6.
- **Museo Provincial de Bellas Artes de Sevilla** (Seville): The Prado doesn't own all the great Spanish art in the country. Located in the early 17th-century convent of La Merced, this Andalusian museum is famous for its works by such Spanish masters as Valdés Leal, Zurbarán, and Murillo. Spain's golden age is best exemplified by Murillo's monumental *Immaculate Conception* and Zurbarán's *Apotheosis of St. Thomas Aquinas.* See chapter 7.
- **Museu Picasso** (Barcelona): Picasso, who spent many of his formative years in Barcelona, donated some 2,500 of his paintings, drawings, and engravings to launch this museum in 1970. It's second only to the Picasso Museum in Paris. Seek out his notebooks, which contain many sketches of Barcelona scenes. Here is a rare chance to see the development of Picasso's genius in his early works; since the pieces are arranged in rough chronological order, you'll discover that he completely mastered traditional representational painting before tiring of it and beginning to experiment. Watch for numerous portraits of his family, as well as examples from both his Blue Period and Rose Period. His obsessive *Las Meninas* series—painted in 1959—offers exaggerated variations of the theme of the famous picture by Velázquez hanging in Madrid's Prado Museum. See chapter 10.
- **Teatre Museu Dalí** (Figueres): The eccentric Salvador Dalí is showcased here as nowhere else. The surrealist artist—known for everything from lobster telephones to *Rotting Mannequin in a Taxicab*—conceived of his art partly as theater. But be warned: As Dalí's final joke, he wanted the museum to spew forth "false information." See chapter 12.

6 The Best Cathedrals & Churches

- **Catedral de Ávila:** One of the earliest Gothic cathedrals in Castile, this rugged and plain edifice was called "a soldier's church." A brooding, granite monolith, which in some ways resembles a fortress, it is the centerpiece of a city that produced St. Teresa, the most famous mystic of the Middle Ages. In contrast with the foreboding exterior, the interior of the cathedral, with its High Gothic nave, is filled with notable works of art, including many plateresque statues. See chapter 4.

- **Catedral de Toledo:** Ranked among the greatest of all Gothic structures, this cathedral was built on the site of an old Arab mosque. A vast pile from the 13th through the 15th centuries, it has an interior filled with masterpieces—notably an immense polychrome retable carved in flamboyant style and magnificent 15th- and 16th-century choir stalls. In the treasury is a splendid 16th-century silver and gilt monstrance, weighing about 500 pounds. See chapter 4.

- **Real Monasterio de San Lorenzo de El Escorial** (near Madrid): Philip II, who commissioned this monastery in the 1530s, envisioned it as a monastic fortress against the distractions of the secular world. Frightening in its severe dignity, and more awesome than beautiful, it's the world's best example of the religious devotion of Renaissance Spain. This huge granite fortress, the burial place for Spanish kings, houses a wealth of paintings and tapestries—works by everyone from Titian to Velázquez. See chapter 4.

- **Catedral de León:** Filled with more sunlight than any other cathedral in Spain, it was begun in 1250 with a design pierced by 125 stained-glass windows and 57 oculi, the oldest of which date from the 13th century. This architectural achievement, unique in Spain, is stunning but also dangerous. The sheer mass endangers the resistance of the walls. Architects fear that an urgent restoration is needed to strengthen the walls to prevent collapse. The well-preserved cloisters are also worth a visit. See chapter 5.

- **Catedral de Santa María** (Burgos): After its cornerstone was laid in 1221, this cathedral became the beneficiary of creative talent imported from England, Germany, and France. It is the third-largest cathedral in Spain, after Seville and Toledo. Art historians claim that among medieval religious buildings, it has the most diverse spectrum of sculpture in Gothic Spain—so diverse that a special name has been conjured up to describe it: the School of Burgos. El Cid is buried here. See chapter 5.

- **Catedral de Sevilla:** The Christians are not the only occupants of Seville who considered this site holy; an enormous mosque stood here before the Reconquista. To quote the Christians who built the cathedral, they planned one "so immense that everyone, on beholding it, will take us for madmen." They succeeded. After St. Peter's in Rome and St. Paul's in London, the cathedral of this Andalusian capital is the largest in Europe. Among its most important features are the tomb of Columbus, the *Patio de los Naranjos* (Courtyard of the Orange Trees), the Giralda Tower, and the *Capilla Real* (Royal Chapel). See chapter 7.

- **Mezquita-Catedral de Córdoba:** In the 1500s, the Christian rulers of Spain tried to gracefully convert one of the largest and most elaborate mosques in the Muslim world, the Mezquita, into a Catholic cathedral. The result, a bizarre amalgam of Gothic and Muslim architecture, is an awesomely proportioned cultural compromise that defies categorization. In its 8th-century heyday, the Mezquita was the crowning Muslim architectural achievement in the West, rivaled only by the Mosque at Mecca. See chapter 7.

- **Catedral de Barcelona:** Completed in 1450, this cathedral grew to represent the spiritual power of the Catalán empire. With its 270-foot facade and flying buttresses and gargoyles, it is the Gothic Quarter's most stunning monument. The interior is in the Catalán Gothic style with slender pillars. See chapter 10.

- **Montserrat** (near Barcelona): Since its inauguration in the 9th century by Benedictine monks, Montserrat has been the preeminent religious shrine of Catalonia and the site of the legendary statue of *La Moreneta* (the Black Madonna). Its glory years ended abruptly in 1812, when it was sacked by the armies of Napoléon. Today, sitting atop a 4,000-foot mountain, 7 miles long and 3½ miles wide, it is one of the three most important pilgrimage sites in Spain and the most popular day excursion from Barcelona. See chapter 11.
- **Catedral de Santiago de Compostela:** During the Middle Ages, this verdant city on the northwestern tip of Iberia attracted thousands of religious pilgrims who walked from as far away as Italy through hostile terrain to seek salvation at the tomb of St. James. The cathedral itself shows the architectural influences of nearly 800 years of religious conviction, much of it financed by donations from exhausted pilgrims. Its two most stunning features are its Obradoiro facade, a baroque masterpiece, and its carved Doorway of Glory behind the facade. An enormous silver censor called the *Botafumeiro* swings from the transept during major liturgical ceremonies. Although the original need for this swinging incense ceremony is no longer necessary—to overpower the stench of faithful pilgrims not known for their excessive bathing habits—tradition lives on. See chapter 17.

7 The Best Vineyards & Wineries

Spanish wines are some of the best in the world and are remarkably affordable here. Here's a list of *bodegas* (wineries) that receive visitors—some old favorites as well as some bright newcomers that are quickly gaining international recognition. For more information about the 10 wine regions—and the 39 officially recognized wine-producing *Denominaciones de Origen* scattered across those regions—contact **Wines from Spain,** c/o the Commercial Office of Spain, 405 Lexington Ave., 44th Floor, New York, NY 10174-0331 (☎ **212/661-4959**).

RIBERA DEL DUERO

Halfway between Madrid and Santander, this region near Burgos is the fastest developing wine district in the country and the beneficiary of massive investments in the past few years. Cold nights, sunny days, the highest altitudes of any wine-producing region in Spain, and a fertile alkaline soil produce flavorful, award-winning wines. Among the noteworthy individual vineyards is:

- **Bodegas Señorío de Nava** (Nava de Roa; ☎ **987-20-97-12**): This is one of the region's best examples of a once-sleepy and now-booming vintner. Merlot and Cabernet Sauvignon grapes are cultivated, as are more obscure local varieties such as *Tinta del país* (also known as *Tempranillo*) and *Garnacha* (or *Grenache,* as it's called across the border in France). Some of the wines bottled here are distributed under the brand name Vega Cubillas.

JEREZ DE LA FRONTERA

This town of 200,000 (most of whom work in the wine trade) is surrounded by a sea of vineyards, which thrive in the hot, chalky soil. Ninety-five percent of the region is planted with the hardy and flavorful *Palomino fino* to produce sherry, a wine fortified by high-alcohol additives, which has long been one of the most beloved products of Spain. Few other regions contain so many *bodegas,* any of which can be visited as part of active public relations programs that are the most accommodating in Spain. See chapter 7 for more information, but some of the outstanding choices include:

- **Hijos de Agustín Blazquez** (Jerez de la Frontera; ☎ **956-15-15-00**): Established in 1795, its products have been judged among the finest in the region since the 1980s. Connoisseurs consider this sherry a perfect accompaniment for tapas, for which the town of Jerez is also well known.
- **Emilio Hidalgo** (Jerez de la Frontera; ☎ **956-34-15-97**): This *bodega* was established in 1896 by a local lawyer, and ever since it has produced exotic forms of sherry snapped up as collectors' items by aficionados everywhere.
- **Antonio Barbadillo** (Sanlúcar de Barrameda; ☎ **956-36-08-94**): This firm controls 70% of the sherry produced in the region around Sanlúcar, a town just 15 miles (24km) north of Jerez. Venerable and respected, it boasts one of the most impressive headquarters of any distillery in the south—a palace originally conceived as a residence for a local bishop. Although established in 1821, it remained a small-time player until the 1960s, when production and quality zoomed upward. Some of its wine is distributed in Britain as Harvey's of Bristol.
- **González Byass** (Jerez de la Frontera; ☎ **956-35-70-00**): Flourishing since 1835, this *bodega* has gained enormous recognition from one of the most famous brand names and the world's best-selling sherry, Tío Pepe. It isn't as picturesque as you might have hoped, since modernization has added some rather bulky concrete buildings to its historic core. Nonetheless, it's one of the most visible names in the industry.
- **Pedro Domecq** (Jerez de la Frontera; ☎ **956-15-15-00**): The oldest of all the large sherry houses was established in 1730 by Patrick Murphy, an Irishman. Its *bodega* contains casks whose contents were once destined for such sherry lovers as William Pitt, Lord Nelson, and the duke of Wellington. If you visit this sprawling compound, look for *La Mezquita bodega,* whose many-columned interior somewhat resembles the famous mosque in Córdoba.

PENEDÉS

In ancient times, thousands of vessels of wine were shipped from this region of Catalonia to fuel the orgies of the Roman Empire. Much of the inspiration for the present industry was developed in the 19th century by French vintners, who found the climate and soil similar to those of Bordeaux. The region produces still wines, as well as 98% of Spain's sparkling wine (*cava*), which stands an excellent chance of supplanting French champagne in the minds of celebrants throughout the world. In fact, Freixenet is the largest selling sparkling wine in the world.

- **Cordoníu** (Sant Sadurní d'Anoia; ☎ **93-818-32-32**): With a history dating from the mid-1500s, this vineyard became famous after its owner, Josep Raventós, produced Spain's first version of sparkling wine. During the harvest, more than 2.2 million pounds of grapes, collected from about 1,000 growers, are pressed daily. The company's headquarters, designed around the turn of the century by Puig i Cadafalch, a contemporary of Gaudí, sits above the 19 miles of underground tunnels where the product is aged.
- **Freixenet** (Sant Sadurní d'Anoia; ☎ **93-891-70-00**): Cordoníu's largest and most innovative competitor began in 1889 as a family-run wine business that quickly changed its production process to incorporate the radical developments in sparkling *cava.* Today, although still family owned, it's an awesomely efficient factory pressing vast numbers of grapes, with at least a million cases sold to the United States every year. Award-winning brand names include Cordon Negro Brut and Carta Nevada Brut. The company now operates a vineyard in California, which produces the sparkling wine Gloria Ferrer, which has won awards in the United States.

- **Miguel Torres** (Vilafranca del Penedés; ☎ **93-817-74-27**): This winery was established in 1870 by a local son (Jaime Torres), who returned to his native town after making a fortune trading petroleum and oil in Cuba. Today, you can see what was once the world's largest wine vat (132,000 gallons); its interior was used as the site of a banquet held in honor of the Spanish king. Thanks to generations of management by French-trained specialists, it is now one of the most sophisticated and advanced vineyards in the region. Like the others, it's also close enough to Barcelona, the beach resort of Sitges, and the ancient monastery of Montserrat to permit a side trip.

LA RIOJA

Set in the foothills of the Pyrenees close to the French border, La Rioja turns out what most people have in mind when they think of Spanish wines. The region produced millions of gallons during the regime of the ancient Romans, and it boasts quality-control laws promulgated by a local bishop in the 9th century. Here are some of the best vineyards for a visit:

- **Héderos de Marqués de Riscal** (Elciego; ☎ **941-60-60-00**): This vineyard was founded around 1850 by a local entrepreneur who learned wine-growing techniques after a prolonged exile in France. The modern-day enterprise still bases most of its income on the 492 acres acquired by the organization's founding father. Despite several disappointing years between 1975 and 1985, it is still one of the most respected in the region.
- **Bodegas Riojanas** (Cenicero; ☎ **941-45-40-50**): Set on the main street of the wine-growing hamlet of Cenicero, this century-old *bodega* expanded massively in the 1980s, and upgraded its visitor information program. You'll be received in a mock-feudal tower where you can learn the nuances of the wine industry.
- **Bodegas Muga** (Haro; ☎ **941-31-18-25**): This *bodega* adheres more to the 19th-century old-world craftsmanship than any of its competitors. The winery contains an assortment of old-fashioned casks made from American or French oak. Production is small, eclectic, and choice.
- **La Rioja Alta** (Haro; ☎ **941-31-03-46**): Another *bodega* in the wine-growing community of Haro, La Rioja Alta is set near the railway station. Founded in 1890, it has the dank and atmospheric cellars you'd expect, and was graced in 1984 by a visit from Spain's royal family. About 85% of the production at this small but quality outfit is bottled as *reservas* (aged at least 3 years) and *gran reservas* (aged at least 5 years).

GALICIA

This Celtic outpost in the northwestern corner of Spain produces white wines that connoisseurs praise as the perfect accompaniment to local seafood. The marketing name for the product, appropriately, is "El Vino del Mar" ("Sea Wine"), although the *Denominación de Origen* includes the appellations "Rias Baixas" and "Ribeiro." Per capita wine consumption in Galicia is the highest in Spain, and formerly a majority of the wine produced here was consumed locally. Massive investments during the 1980s changed all that, as you'll note after visits to the region's most viable wineries, such as:

- **Bodega Morgadio** (Albeos-Crecente; ☎ **986-66-61-50**): This vineyard, near Pontevedra, launched the Denominación de Origen "Rias Baixas" in 1984. Four friends whom locals referred to as "madmen" bought 70 acres of land that, with the Albariño grape, they transformed into one of the most respected and award-winning vineyards in the district. Fertilizers for each year's crop comes from the *bodega*'s own flock of sheep. The success of old-fashioned farming methods coupled with state-of-the-art fermentation tanks is a model of entrepreneurial courage in an otherwise economically depressed outpost of Spain.

8　The Best Festivals

- **The Autumn Festival** (Madrid; ☎ **91-580-25-75**): Held in October and November, the Festival de Otoño is the best music festival in Spain, with a lineup that attracts the cream of the European and South American musical communities. The usual roster of chamber music, symphonic pieces, and orchestral works is supplemented by a program of *zarzuela* (musical comedy), as well as Arabic and Sephardic pieces composed during the Middle Ages. See chapter 2.
- **Feria del Caballo** (Jerez de la Frontera; ☎ **956-33-11-50**): Few events show off Spain's equestrian traditions in such flattering light. Costumes are appropriately ornate; riders demonstrate the stern, carefully controlled movements developed during countless medieval battles; and the entire city of Jerez (otherwise famous for its sherry) becomes one enormous riding ring for the presentation of dressage and jumping events. Horse buying and trading is commonplace at this May event; especially coveted is a graceful type of white horse (*Cartujanos*) first bred by the Moors. See chapter 2.
- **Las Hogueras de San Juan** (Alicante; ☎ **96-520-00-00**): Bonfires blaze through the night on June 20 as a celebration of a festival revered by the Celtic pagans and Romans alike—the summer solstice. Stacks of flammable objects, including discarded finery and cardboard replicas of sinners and witches, are set ablaze in a ceremony that reminds some observers of the *auto da fés* during the Inquisition. The bonfire signals the beginning of 5 days of nightly fireworks and daily parades during which normal business comes virtually to a standstill. See chapter 2.
- **Moros y Cristianos** (Alcoy, near Alicante; ☎ **96-520-00-00**): The agonizing, century-long process of evicting the Moors from Iberia is re-created during 2 days of simulated, vaudeville-style fighting between "Moors" and "Christians" every April (dates vary). Circus-style costumes worn by the Moors are as absurdly anachronistic as possible. When the Christians win, a statue of the Virgin is carried proudly through the city as proof of Alcoy's staunchly passionate defense of its role as a bastion of Christianity. See chapter 2.
- **La Tomatina** (Buñol, Valencia): Held every year on the last Wednesday in August, nearly everyone in the town along with thousands from neighboring towns and villages join this 2-hour-long tomato war (11am to 1pm). The local government organizes and sponsors the festival, bringing in four truckloads of tomatoes totaling more than 88,000 pounds of vegetable artillery. Two local bands provide the music for dancing and singing and plenty of drinking. Portable showers are installed for the participants. See chapter 2.
- **A Rapa das Bestas—The Capture of the Beasts** (San Lorenzo de Sabuceno, Galicia; ☎ **986-85-08-14**): In the verdant hills of northwestern Spain, horses graze at will, oblivious to boundary markers and borders. On the first weekend of July, they are rounded up and herded into a corral, in a ritual that evokes the Wild West. Here, each is branded and then released back into the wild after a few days of medical observation. For information, contact the Office of Tourism in Pontevedra. See chapter 2.
- **Misteri d'Elx** or "**The Mystery Play of Elche**" (Elche; ☎ **96-545-38-31**): Based on the reputed mystical powers of an ancient, black-faced statue of the Virgin,

the citizens of Elche have staged a mystery play in the local church every year for more than 6 centuries. The chanting and songs that accompany the plot line are in an archaic dialect that even the Castilians can barely understand. Competition is fierce for seats during the August event, and celebrations precede and follow the play. See chapter 9.

9 The Best Paradors

Funded and maintained by the government, Spain's paradors (*paradores* in Spanish) are hostelries that showcase a building or setting of important cultural and historic interest. Some are, admittedly, much older, grander, and more interesting than others. Here are the country's most interesting and unusual.

- **Parador de Ávila** (Ávila; ☎ **920-21-13-40**): Built as an enlargement of a 15th-century palace (Palacio de Piedras Albas, also known as the Palacio de Benavides), this parador features gardens that flank the northern fortifications of this well-preserved 11th-century walled city. While only some of the comfortable, airy bedrooms are in the original palace, it's still the region's most intriguing hotel. In the parador restaurant, try the roast suckling pig, a regional specialty. See chapter 4.

- **Parador de Turismo de Cuenca** (Cuenca; ☎ **969-23-23-20**): This 16th-century building, once a Dominican convent, is one of the newer paradors in Spain. Like the medieval houses for which Cuenca is famous, the balconies here jut out over rocky cliffs, overlooking swift-moving rivers below. The sight of the *casas colgadas*, or "suspended houses," is unforgettable. An adjoining restaurant specializes in seasonal wild game. See chapter 4.

- **Parador Nacional de Conde Orgaz** (Toledo; ☎ **925-22-18-50**): Although this is a relatively modern building, the architecture subtly evokes much older models. Views from the windows, boasting a faraway glimpse of the city's historic core, evoke the scenes El Greco painted in his *View of Toledo*. A swimming pool comes as a welcome relief in blistering Toledo. Such regional dishes as stewed partridge are featured in the hotel restaurant. See chapter 4.

- **Parador San Marcos** (León; ☎ **987-23-73-00**): Originally home to the Order of Santiago—a group of knights charged with protecting pilgrims who journeyed across northern Spain in the 12th century—the building was expanded and embellished into a monastery some 400 years later. These days, set beside the Bernesga River and with a lavishly decorated church on the grounds, it's one of Spain's most deluxe paradors. The public areas are pure medieval grandeur: a dramatic lobby, grand entranceway, huge cast-iron chandelier, and stone staircases. See chapter 5.

- **Parador Turístico de Zamora** (Zamora; ☎ **980-51-44-97**): This one-time Moorish fortress-turned-Renaissance palace is among the most beautiful and richly decorated paradors in Spain. A medieval aura is reflected in the details: armor, coats-of-arms, tapestries, and attractive four-poster beds. A swimming pool enhances the tranquil back garden. Castilian fare such as stuffed roast veal typifies the restaurant's offerings. See chapter 5.

- **Parador de Cáceres** (Cáceres; ☎ **927-21-17-59**): Live like royalty at this palace, built in the 1400s on the site of Arab fortifications. The parador is in the city's old quarter, recently declared a World Heritage Site. The spacious public areas are decorated with soft cream shades and rough-hewn ceiling beams. Venison with goat cheese and roast kid with rosemary are typical of the varied Extremaduran cuisine served in the parador restaurant. See chapter 6.

- **Parador Nacional de Trujillo** (Trujillo; ☎ **927-32-13-50**): A parador set in the inviting 16th-century convent of Santa Clara, this was originally built in a combination of medieval and Renaissance styles. The building was transformed into a hotel in 1984 and the bedrooms are considerably more lavish than they were during their stint as nuns' cells. The cuisine is the best in town. See chapter 6.
- **Parador Vía de la Plata** (Mérida; ☎ **924-31-38-00**): A 16th-century building that was at various times a convent and a prison, this parador once hosted a meeting between the much-hated dictators of Spain (Franco) and Portugal (Salazar) in the 1960s. Mudéjar, Roman, and Visigothic elements adorn the interior in unusual but stunning juxtaposition. The inner courtyard and Mozarabic gardens add a grace note. The kitchen serves the best of the area, including gazpacho, *calderetas extremeñas* (stews), and the famous Almoharin figs. See chapter 6.
- **Parador Castillo de Santa Catalina** (Jaén; ☎ **953-23-00-00**): In the 10th century, Muslims built this foreboding fortress on a cliff high above town. After the Reconquista, the Christians added Gothic vaulting and touches of luxury, which remain in place thanks to a renovation by the government. Bedrooms provide sweeping views over Andalusia. A swimming pool is a welcome retreat from the burning sun. Sample such dishes as cold garlic soup and partridge salad in the panoramic restaurant. See chapter 7.
- **Parador de Santillana** (Santillana del Mar; ☎ **942-81-80-00**): This bucolic parador recalls the manor houses that dotted northern Spain's verdant hillsides more than 400 years ago. Composed of thick stone walls and heavy timbers, it's pleasantly isolated and elegantly countrified. An added bonus is its proximity to what has been called "the Sistine Chapel of prehistoric art"—the Caves of Altamira. See chapter 16.
- **Parador del Molino Viejo** (Gijón; ☎ **98-537-05-11**): As the name implies, this hotel grew up around the decrepit remains of a *molino,* a cider mill (and the antique presses are still on hand). Close to San Lorenzo Beach, it's the only parador in the northern province of Asturias. The dining room serves up typical Asturian cuisine, including the famous *fabada,* a rich white bean and pork stew. See chapter 16.
- **Parador Nacional Casa del Barón** (Pontevedra; ☎ **986-85-58-00**): The building is a 16th-century Renaissance palace built on foundations that are at least 200 years older than that. It's famous as one of Spain's first paradors. Inaugurated in 1955, its success led to the amplification of the parador program. The hotel is still alluring today, with its delightful terrace garden and stately dining room, which serves the fresh fish and seafood for which Galicia is known. See chapter 17.
- **Hostal de Los Reyes Católicos** (Santiago de Compostela; ☎ **981-58-22-00**): The best is saved for last—this is one of the most spectacular hotels in Europe. Originally a hospice for wayfaring pilgrims, it boasts a lavish 16th-century facade, four open-air courtyards, and a bedchamber once occupied by Franco. Today the hotel is a virtual museum, with Gothic, Renaissance, and baroque architectural elements. There are four cloisters of immense beauty, elegant public areas, and spectacular bedrooms. See chapter 17.

10 The Best Luxury Hotels

- **Park Hyatt Villa Magna** (Madrid; ☎ **91-587-12-34**): Although it looks like a House of Parliament, this elegant hotel is regal and sedate, giving off the aura of a country estate. Fine furnishings, beautiful linen, and such designer toiletries as fragrant Maja soaps are part of the exquisite guest rooms. The hotel is surrounded by beautiful gardens. See chapter 3.

- **The Ritz** (Madrid; ☎ **91-521-28-57**): Flawless service is the hallmark of Madrid's most distinguished hotel. Antiques, gracious marble bathrooms, and elegant detailing characterize the bedrooms. This Edwardian grand hotel is more relaxed than it once was, the old haughtiness of former management gone with the wind—it long ago rescinded its policy of not allowing movie stars as guests. You still may have to wear a coat and tie, however. See chapter 3.

- **Hotel Alfonso XIII** (Seville; ☎ **95-422-28-50**): This is where the royal family stayed when the Infanta Elena, daughter of Juan Carlos, married in Seville in 1995. Built to house visitors for the Iberoamerican Exposition of 1929, this grand hotel features Moorish-style rooms, with doors opening onto little balconies overlooking a Spanish courtyard with a bubbling fountain and potted palms. Set in front of the city's fabled Alcázar, the Alfonso XIII is one of the most legendary hotels of Spain. See chapter 7.

- **La Bobadilla** (Loja; ☎ **958-32-18-61**): The most luxurious retreat in the south of Spain, this secluded oasis lies in the foothills of the Sierra Nevada, an hour's drive northeast of Málaga. Whitewashed *casas* (small individual villas) cluster around a tower and a church. Each individually designed *casa* is complete with a roof terrace and balcony overlooking olive groves. Guests live in luxury within the private compound of 1,750 acres. See chapter 8.

- **Marbella Club** (Marbella; ☎ **95-282-22-11**): Built during the golden age of the Costa del Sol (the 1950s), this bastion of chic is composed of ecologically conscious clusters of garden pavilions, bungalows, and small-scale annexes. The luxurious rooms are modeled after pages of a European design magazine. It has many competitors but remains an elite retreat. See chapter 8.

- **Puente Romano** (Marbella; ☎ **95-282-09-00**): On manicured and landscaped grounds facing the beach, Puente Romano evokes a highly stylized Andalusian village. Exotic bird life flutters through lush gardens planted with banana trees and other vegetation. Villas are spacious and beautifully furnished, with marble floors and bathrooms, big mirrors, and tasteful wood furnishings. In the summer, flamenco dancers entertain here. See chapter 8.

- **Hotel Ritz** (Barcelona; ☎ **93-318-52-00**): A 1919 *grand luxe* hotel formerly known as the Palace, this is one of the finest hotels in Spain, if not all of Europe. Guests are enveloped in dazzling elegance, with all the gilt, marble, and fresh flowers they would ever want. Classic belle époque detailing extends to the plush guest quarters, many of which have high, ornate ceilings and gold bathroom fixtures. See chapter 10.

- **Hotel María Cristina** (San Sebastián; ☎ **943-42-49-00**): One of the country's great belle époque treasures, this old-world seafront hotel has sheltered discriminating guests since 1912. Oriental rugs, antiques, potted palms, high ceilings, formal lounges, marble pillars, and marble floors show off a turn-of-the-century glamour. The bedrooms are traditional with wood furnishings and tasteful pastel fabrics. Nothing else in the Basque country quite measures up to this old charmer. See chapter 15.

- **La Residencia** (Deià, Majorca; ☎ **971-63-90-11**): Set amid 30 acres of citrus and olive groves, this tranquil hotel was converted from two Renaissance-era manor houses. Jasmine-scented terraces open onto panoramic views of the surrounding villages and mountains. Pampered guests are served a creative cuisine that features local produce. Leisure facilities include a swimming pool fed by mountain spring water. Many of the bedrooms have regal four-poster beds. It's a haven from the rest of overcrowded Majorca. See chapter 18.

11 The Best Hotel Bargains

- **Hostal del Cardenal** (Toledo; ☎ 925-22-49-00): The summer residence of Toledo's 18th-century Cardinal Lorenzano, built right into the walls of the old city next to the Bisagra Gate, this just happens to be Toledo's best restaurant. But the setting—rose gardens, cascading vines, and Moorish fountains—makes it an ideal place to stay as well. Spanish furniture and a scattering of antiques recapture the aura of old Castile. See chapter 4.
- **Posada de San José** (Cuenca; ☎ 969-21-13-00): This hotel, located in the oldest part of medieval Cuenca, is a remarkable bargain. In the 17th century it was a convent, but the rooms have been converted to receive guests and are now decorated in rustic style. The posada sits atop a cliff, overlooking the forbidding depths of a gorge and the river below; views are superb. See chapter 4.
- **Hostería Real de Zamora** (Zamora; ☎ 980-53-45-45): Once the dreaded headquarters of the local Spanish Inquisition, today this hotel offers a far friendlier welcome. Guests enjoy coffee on the patio and the pleasure of a garden planted along the city's medieval fortifications. Imagine if these 15th-century walls could talk. See chapter 5.
- **Hotel Doña María** (Seville; ☎ 95-422-49-90): Near the fabled cathedral, this hotel boasts a rooftop terrace with unmatched views of the Andalusian capital. A private villa that dates from the 1840s, the Doña María has a swimming pool ringed with garden-style lattices and antique wrought-iron railings. Bedrooms are uniquely designed with tasteful Iberian antiques. See chapter 7.
- **Hotel Reina Victoria** (Ronda; ☎ 95-287-12-40): This country-style hotel is best known as the place where the German poet Rainer Maria Rilke wrote *The Spanish Trilogy*. Its terrace, perched on a dramatic precipice, offers commanding views of the countryside. An Englishman built this Victorian charmer in 1906 to honor his recently deceased monarch, Queen Victoria. See chapter 7.
- **Hotel América** (Granada; ☎ 958-22-74-71): This one-time private villa, within the walls of the Alhambra, is one of the most popular small hotels in Granada. Its cozy bedrooms are filled with reproductions of Andalusian antiques. Plants cascade down the white plaster walls and the ornate grillwork onto the shady patio. Good-tasting, inexpensive meals are served in the hotel restaurant. See chapter 7.
- **Hotel Mijas** (Mijas; ☎ 95-248-58-00): This is the most charming of affordable hotels along the Costa del Sol. It's designed in typical Andalusian style, with flowering terraces, wrought-iron accents, and sun-flooded bedrooms. Although built in the 1970s, it blends in perfectly with the region's gleaming white buildings. See chapter 8.
- **Huerto del Cura** (Elche; ☎ 96-545-80-40): From your bedroom you'll have a panoramic view of Priest's Grove, a formidable date-palm forest. Between Alicante and Murcia, this is one of the choice addresses in the south of Spain. Bedrooms are handsomely maintained and beautifully furnished, and a swimming pool separates the palm grove from the rooms. The regional cuisine in the hotel's restaurant is excellent. See chapter 9.
- **Mesón Castilla** (Barcelona; ☎ 93-318-21-82): This two-star charmer with an art nouveau facade is right in the heart of Barcelona. It is well maintained and well managed, with prices that are blessedly easy on the wallet. Comfortable

rooms often come with large terraces. Only breakfast is served, but there are many nearby taverns with excellent food. See chapter 10.

- **Hotel Pampinot** (Fuenterrabía; ☎ **943-64-06-00**): The Infanta María Teresa stayed at this 16th-century aristocratic mansion on a journey to France for her eventual marriage to the Sun King, Louis XIV. Now a stately hotel, it's on a quiet side street in this Basque seaside resort near the French border. Behind a richly textured stone facade and Renaissance detailing are bedrooms furnished with both antiques and reproductions. See chapter 15.

12 The Best Restaurants

- **El Amparo** (Madrid; ☎ **91-431-64-56**): In the old days of Franco, gastronomes flocked to Jockey or Horcher. Today their savvy sons and daughters head to El Amparo, the trendiest of Madrid's gourmet restaurants. It serves haute Basque cuisine against a backdrop of cosmopolitan glamour. Patrons sample everything from cold marinated salmon with a tomato sorbet to ravioli stuffed with seafood. See chapter 3.
- **Sobrino de Botín** (Madrid; ☎ **91-366-42-17**): Since 1725, this restaurant has been celebrated for its roast suckling pig, prepared in a 200-year-old tile oven. Hemingway even mentioned it in *The Sun Also Rises*. The roast Segovian lamb is equally delectable. There is little subtlety of flavor here—only food prepared by time-tested recipes that have appealed to kings as well as Castilian peasants. The aromas waft clear across Madrid's old town. See chapter 3.
- **Mesón de Cándido** (Segovia; ☎ **921-42-59-11**): Foodies from around the country flock to this 19th-century Spanish inn, "The House of Cándido," for one dish: roast suckling pig, acclaimed the best in Spain (even by Hemingway, who might otherwise be seen at Botín in Madrid). In Spanish it's called *cochinillo asado,* and it's delectable—prepared according to a century-old recipe. Here's a secret: The *cordero asado,* or roast baby lamb, is equally flavorful. See chapter 4.
- **Mesón Casa Colgadas** (Cuenca; ☎ **969-22-35-09**): Without a doubt, this is the most spectacularly situated restaurant in Spain—a "hanging house" suspended over a precarious precipice. The food is Spanish and international, with an emphasis on regional ingredients. The dishes can be ingenious, but the culinary repertoire usually reflects proven classics that might have pleased your grandparents. See chapter 4.
- **Chez Victor** (Salamanca; ☎ **923-21-31-23**): In the historic center of this university town, this is the most glamorous continental restaurant around. Chef Victoriano Salvador gives customers terrific value for their pesetas with his imaginative, oft-renewed menus. The freshly prepared fish and his traditional version of roast lamb are especially tempting. Regionally rooted but modern in outlook, Salvador has a finely honed technique and isn't afraid to be inventive on occasion. See chapter 5.
- **El Caballo Rojo** (Córdoba; ☎ **957-47-53-75**): Begin your evening with a sherry in the popular bar, followed by a visit to the traditional dining room. Not only Andalusian dishes are served here; some classics are based on ancient Sephardic and Mozarabic specialties. Most guests begin with a soothing gazpacho and wash everything down with sangría. Finish off the meal with one of the homemade ice creams—we recommend pistachio. See chapter 7.
- **El Plat** (Valencia; ☎ **96-374-12-54**): No Spanish dish is more famous than paella, and Valencia is where this culinary delight originated. Locals maintain that it tastes better on its home turf than anywhere else in the world, and we

concur. In Valencia, El Plat is known as *"El Rey del Arroz"* (The Rice King). Each day of the week chefs prepare a different version of this succulent dish, often studded with shellfish. See chapter 9.

- **Jaume de Provença** (Barcelona; ☎ 93-430-00-29): The Catalán capital has more great restaurants than even Madrid. At the western end of the Eixample district, this Catalán/French restaurant is the domain of one of the city's most talented chefs, Jaume Bargués. He serves modern interpretations of traditional Catalán and southern French cuisine—such dishes as pigs' trotters with plums and truffles or crabmeat lasagna. His personal cooking repertoire is distinctive, and he has been known to create new taste sensations when he's feeling experimental. See chapter 10.
- **Botafumeiro** (Barcelona; ☎ 93-218-42-30): The city's finest seafood is prepared here, in a glistening, modern kitchen visible from the dining room. The King of Spain is a frequent patron, enjoying paellas, *zarzuelas,* or any of the 100 or so ultra-fresh seafood dishes. The chef's treatment of fish is the most intelligent and subtle in town—but don't expect such quality to come cheap. See chapter 10.
- **Los Caracoles** (Barcelona; ☎ 93-302-31-85): Locals say this restaurant is so old it was around to welcome the Roman armies. Actually it's been feeding hungry Cataláns only since 1835, but any restaurant that has thrived that long must be doing something right. These days, a young, sophisticated crowd of food lovers has discovered the full array of hearty Catalán and Spanish dishes served here. The namesake snails are always worth a try. See chapter 10.
- **Empordá** (Figueres; ☎ 972-50-05-62): Although ordinary on the outside, this hotel restaurant is one of the finest on the Costa Brava. It was a favorite of Salvador Dalí, who once wrote his own cookbook. Haute Catalán cuisine is the specialty—everything from duck foie gras with Armagnac to suprême of sea bass with flan. The flavors are refined yet definite. See chapter 12.
- **Akelare** (San Sebastián; ☎ 943-21-20-52): The Basques are renowned for their cooking, and the owner-chef of this San Sebastián restaurant, Pedro Sabijana, pioneered the school of *nueva cocina vasco* (modern Basque cuisine). His restaurant has attracted gourmets from around Europe. Sabijana transforms such seemingly simple dishes as fish cooked on a griddle with garlic and parsley into something magical. No other eatery in northern Spain comes close to equaling the superb viands dispensed here. There are those (and we are among them) who consider Subijana the best chef in Spain. See chapter 15.

Planning Your Trip: The Basics

In this chapter, you'll find everything you need to plan your trip, from a sketch of Spain's various regions to tips on when to go and how to get the best airfare.

1 The Regions in Brief

Three times the size of Illinois, with a population of approximately 40 million, Spain faces the Atlantic Ocean and the Bay of Biscay to the north and the Mediterranean Sea to the south and east. Portugal borders on the west, with the Pyrenees separating Spain from France and the rest of Europe. The southern coastline is only a few sea miles from the north coast of Africa. It's difficult to generalize about Spain because it is composed of so many regions—50 provinces in all—each with its own geography, history, and culture. The country's topography divides it into many regions: The Cantabrian mountains in the north, those of Cuenca in the east, and the Sierra Morena in the south mark off a high central tableland that is itself cut by hills.

MADRID & ENVIRONS

Set on a high, arid plateau near the geographic center of Iberia, Madrid was created by royal decree in the 1600s, long after the much older kingdoms of León, Navarre, Aragón, and Catalonia, and long after the final Moor was ousted by Catholic armies. Since its birth, all roads within Spain have radiated outward from its precincts, and as the country's most important airline and railway hub, it's likely to be your point of arrival (although many international flights and European trains now arrive in Barcelona as well).

Despite the city's increasingly unpleasant urban sprawl, its paralyzing traffic jams, and skyrocketing prices, Madrid remains one of Europe's great cities. Take in the Prado, the Thyssen-Bornemisza Museum, and perhaps the Royal Palace. Walk through historic neighborhoods around the Plaza Mayor (but beware of muggers). Devote time to one of the city's greatest pastimes, a round of tapas tasting.

Plan on at least 2 days to explore the city and another 3 for trips to the attractions beyond the capital. Perhaps as important as a visit to Madrid is a day trip to the imperial city of **Toledo,** which brims with monuments and paintings by El Greco and is home to one of Spain's greatest cathedrals. Other worthy excursions include a view of the

Spain's Regions

Roman aqueduct at **Segovia,** tours through such monuments as **El Escorial,** and a visit to the "hanging village" of **Cuenca,** site of a world-class museum of modern art.

OLD CASTILE & LEÓN

The proud kingdoms of Castile and León in north-central Iberia are part of the core from which modern Spain developed. Some of their greatest cathedrals and monuments were erected when each was staunchly independent. But León's annexation by Queen Isabella of Castile in 1474 (5 years after her politically advantageous but unhappy marriage to Ferdinand of Aragón) irrevocably linked the two regions.

Even Spaniards are sometimes confused about the terms *Old Castile* (see chapter 5, "Old Castile & León") and *New Castile,* a modern linguistic and governmental concept that includes a territory much larger than the medieval entity known by Isabella and her subjects. Although it's easy to take a train to and from Madrid, we don't recommend you try to see the regions' highlights as day trips from Madrid; it's better to treat them as overnight destinations in their own right.

Highlights include **Burgos** (the ancient cradle of Castile), **Salamanca** (a medieval Castilian university town), and **León** (capital on the northern plains of the district bearing its name and site of one of the most unusual cathedrals in Iberia). If time remains, consider an overnight stay at the extraordinary parador in **Ciudad Rodrigo,** as well as trips to **Zamora,** known for its stunning Romanesque churches, and **Valladolid.**

EXTREMADURA

Far from the mainstream of urbanized Spain, fascinating Extremadura lives in a time warp where hints of the Middle Ages and ancient Rome crop up unexpectedly beside sun-baked highways. Many of the conquistadors who pillaged native civilizations in the New World came from this hard, granite land.

Be prepared for hot, arid landscapes and smoking diesel trucks carrying heavy loads through this corridor between Madrid and Lisbon. You can see a lot in about 2 days, stopping off at such sites as **Guadalupe,** whose Mudéjar monastery revolves around the medieval cult of the Dark (or Black) Virgin, and **Trujillo,** where many of the monuments were built with gold sent home by native sons like Pizarro, Peru's conqueror. **Cáceres** is a beautiful, fortified city with one foot planted firmly in the Middle Ages, while **Zafra** displays greater evidence of the Moorish occupation than anywhere in Spain outside of Andalusia.

ANDALUSIA

In A.D. 711 Muslim armies swept into Iberia from strongholds in what is now Morocco. Since then, Spain's southernmost district has been enmeshed in the mores, art, and architecture of the Muslim world. During the 900s, *Andalucía* blossomed into a sophisticated society—advanced in philosophy, mathematics, and trading—that far surpassed a feudal Europe still trapped in the Dark Ages. Moorish domination ended completely in 1492, when Granada was captured by the armies of Isabella and Ferdinand, but even today the region offers echoes of this Muslim occupation. Andalusia is a dry district that isn't highly prosperous, despite such economically rejuvenating events as Seville's Expo.

The major cities of Andalusia deserve at least a week, with overnights in **Seville** (hometown of Carmen, Don Giovanni, and the barber); **Córdoba,** site of the Mezquita, one of history's most versatile religious edifices; and **Cádiz,** the seaport where thousands of ships embarked on their colonization of the New World. Perhaps greatest of all is **Granada,** a town of such impressive artistry that it inspired many of the works by the 20th-century romantic poet Federico García Lorca.

THE COSTA DEL SOL

The Costa del Sol sprawls across the southernmost edge of Spain between Algeciras to the west—a few miles from the rocky heights of British-controlled Gibraltar—and Almería to the east. Think traffic jams, suntan oil, sun-bleached high-rises, and near-naked flesh. The beaches here are some of the best in Europe, but this can also be an overly crowded, crime-filled region.

Unless you travel by car or rail from Madrid, chances are you'll arrive by plane via **Málaga,** the district's most historic city. The coast's largest resort town is distinctive, Renaissance-era **Marbella,** the centerpiece of 17 miles of beaches. Today it's a chic hangout for the tanned and wealthy. **Nerja** is just one of the booming resorts that has kept its out-of-the-way, fishing-village feel. The most overcrowded and action-packed resort is **Torremolinos.** One modern development that has managed to remain distinctive is **Puerto Banús,** a neo-Moorish village curving around a sheltered marina where the wintering rich dock their yachts.

VALENCIA & THE COSTA BLANCA

Valencia, the third-largest city in Spain, is rarely visited by foreign tourists because of the heavy industry that surrounds its inner core. More alluring are such resorts as **Alicante** and **Benidorm** or the medieval town of **Elche** (where some of the world's most famous ancient Roman statues were discovered). Unless you opt to skip Valencia completely, plan to see the city's cathedral, the exterior of its Palacio de la Generalidad, and as many of its three important museums as you can fit into a 1-day trip. For the Costa Blanca, allow as much or as little time as you want to spend on the beach.

BARCELONA & CATALONIA

Barcelona's history is older than that of its rival, Madrid, and its streets are filled with Gothic and medieval buildings that Spain's relatively newer capital lacks. During the 1200s it rivaled the trading prowess of such cities as Genoa and Pisa, and it became the Spanish city that most resembled other great cities of Europe. Allow yourself at least 3 days to explore the city, with stops at the Picasso Museum, the Joan Miró foundation, the Gothic quarter, and a crowning triumph of early *modernista* architecture, the Eixample District, where you'll find many of Antoni Gaudí's signature works. Make time for a stroll along Les Rambles, one of the most delightful outdoor promenades in Spain.

Don't overlook Catalonia's other attractions, all within easy reach of Barcelona. A short drive to the south is **Sitges,** a stylish beach resort that caters to a diverse clientele ranging from freewheeling nudists and gay party crowds to fun-seeking families. Other destinations are **Tarragona,** one of ancient Rome's district capitals, and **Montserrat,** the "Serrated Mountain," site of one of Europe's best-preserved medieval monasteries.

THE COSTA BRAVA

It's Spain's other Riviera, a region with a deep sense of medieval history and a topography that's rockier and more interesting than that of the Costa del Sol. The "Wild Coast" stretches from the resort of Blanes, just north of Barcelona, along 95 miles (153km) of dangerously winding cliff-top roads that bypass peninsulas and sheltered coves on their way to the French border. Despite hordes of Spanish and Northern European midsummer visitors, the Costa Brava resorts still manage to feel less congested and less spoiled than those along the Costa del Sol.

Sun worshippers usually head for the twin beachfront resorts of **Lloret de Mar** and **Tossa de Mar.** Travelers interested in the history of 20th-century painting go to **Figueres;** Salvador Dalí was born here in 1904, and a controversial and bizarre museum of his design is devoted exclusively to his surrealist works.

ARAGÓN

Except for Aragón's association with Ferdinand, the unsavory, often unethical husband of Queen Isabella, few foreign visitors ever thought much about this northeastern quadrant of Iberia. A land of noteworthy Mudéjar architecture and high altitudes that guarantee cool midsummer temperatures, it's also one of the foremost bull-breeding regions of Spain.

Aragón is best visited as a stopover between Barcelona and Madrid. Stay overnight in **Zaragoza,** the district capital, and take a series of day trips to **Tarazona** ("The Toledo of Aragón"), **Calatayud,** and **Daroca,** all important Moorish and Roman military outposts, and **Nuévalos/Piedra,** the site of an extraordinary riverside hotel built in 1194 as a Cistercian monastery. Also worth a trip is **Sos del Rey Católico,** the rocky, relatively unspoiled village where Ferdinand was born.

NAVARRE & LA RIOJA

This strategic province, one of the four original Christian kingdoms in Iberia, shares a border, and numerous historical references, with France. One of France's Renaissance kings, Henri IV "de Navarre," was linked to the province's royal family. Many Navarre customs, and some of its local dialect, reflect the influence of its passionately politicized neighbors, the Basques. Celtic pagans, Romans, Christians, and Arabs have all left architectural reminders of their presence. The province contains nine points where traffic is funneled into and out of Spain, so if you're driving or riding the train, say, from Paris to Madrid, chances are you'll get a fast overview of Navarre. The province's best-known destination is **Pamplona,** the district capital and annual host for the bull-running Fiesta de San Fermín.

One small corner of Navarre is composed of **La Rioja,** the smallest *autonomía* (semiautonomous province) of Spain. Irrigated by the Ebro River, it produces some of the country's finest wines. If wine tasting appeals to you, head for the town of **Haro** and drop in on several *bodegas* (wineries) to sample local vintages.

THE BASQUE COUNTRY

This is the native land of Europe's oldest traceable ethnic group. The Basque people have been more heavily persecuted than any other group within Spain, by Madrid regimes determined to shoehorn their unusual language and culture into that of mainstream Spain. The region of rolling peaks and fertile, sunny valleys hugs the Atlantic coast adjacent to the French border. It also boasts the best regional cuisine in Spain.

Unless you want to spend more time relaxing on the beach, allow 3 leisurely days for this unusual district. Visit **San Sebastián** (Donostia) for its international glamour, **Fuenterrabía** (Hondarribía) for its medieval history, **Guernica** for a sobering reminder of the Spanish Civil War, and Lekeitio for its simple fishing-village charm.

CANTABRIA & ASTURIAS

Positioned on Iberia's north-central coastline, these are the most verdant regions of Spain. In the Middle Ages pilgrims passed through here on their way to **Santiago de Compostela**—a legacy evident from the wealth of Romanesque churches and abbeys in the vicinity. Come for beaches that are rainier, but much less crowded, than those along Spain's southern coasts.

Enjoy such beach resorts as **El Sardinero** and **Laredo,** as well as the rugged beauty of **Los Picos de Europa,** a dramatic mountain range that is home to rich colonies of wildlife. Sites of interest include the **Caves of Altamira** (called "the Sistine Chapel of prehistoric art," although admission is strictly regulated), the pre-Romanesque town of **Oviedo,** and the architecturally important old quarter of **Gijón.** The region's largest city, **Santander,** lies amid a maze of peninsulas and estuaries favored by boaters. In summer it becomes a major beach resort, although **San Sebastián** is more fashionable.

GALICIA

A true Celtic outpost in northwestern Iberia, Galicia's landscape is often compared to rainy, windswept Ireland. Known for a spectacularly dramatic coastline, the region is wild and relatively underpopulated. Spend at least 2 days here enjoying some of the most scenic drives in Iberia. Stop at historic and religious sites like **Santiago de Compostela** or the ancient Roman outpost of **Lugo.** Perhaps the region's greatest city is **La Coruña,** the point of embarkation for Spain's tragic Armada, sunk by the English army on its way to invade Britain in the late 16th century.

THE BALEARIC ISLANDS

"Discovered" by English Romantics in the early 19th century, and long known as a strategic naval outpost in the western Mediterranean, these islands are sunny, subtropical, mountainous, and more verdant than the Costa del Sol. They have their pockets of style and posh, although **Majorca** and **Ibiza** are overrun in summer, especially by British and German travelers on package tours. Ibiza also attracts a large gay crowd. **Minorca** is more fashionable, although more inconvenient to get to.

2 Visitor Information, Entry Requirements & Customs

VISITOR INFORMATION

The official Web site for the Spanish tourist office is **www.okspain.org.** See **"Planning Your Trip: An Online Directory"** following this chapter for tips on where to find lots of other help and information on the Internet.

IN THE UNITED STATES   For information before you go, contact the **Tourist Office of Spain,** 666 Fifth Ave., 35th Floor, New York, NY 10103 (☎ 212/265-8822), which can provide sightseeing information, calendars of events, train and ferry schedules, maps, and much, much more. Elsewhere in the United States, branches of the Tourist Office of Spain are located at 8383 Wilshire Blvd., Suite 956, Beverly Hills, CA 90211 (☎ 323/658-7188); 845 N. Michigan Ave., Suite 915 E., Chicago, IL 60611 (☎ 312/642-1992); and 1221 Brickell Ave., Suite 1850, Miami, FL 33131 (☎ 305/358-1992).

IN CANADA   Contact the **Tourist Office of Spain,** 102 Bloor St. W., 34th Floor, Toronto, ON M5S 1M9 (☎ 416/961-3131).

IN GREAT BRITAIN Contact the **Spanish Tourist Office,** 22–23 Manchester Square, London WIM 5AP (☎ 020/7486-8077).

ENTRY REQUIREMENTS

Visas are not needed by U.S., Canadian, Irish, Australian, New Zealand, or British citizens for visits of less than 3 months. You do need a valid passport unless you're a citizen of another EU country (in which case you need only an identity card, although we always recommend you carry a passport anyway).

Safeguard your passport in an inconspicuous, inaccessible place like a money belt. If you lose it, visit the nearest consulate of your native country as soon as possible for a replacement.

CUSTOMS

You can take into Spain most personal effects and the following items duty-free: two still cameras and 10 rolls of film per camera, tobacco for personal use, 1 liter each of liquor and wine, a Walkman or portable CD player, a tape recorder, a laptop, a bicycle, sports equipment, fishing gear, and two hunting weapons with 100 cartridges each.

WHAT YOU CAN BRING HOME TO THE U.S. Returning U.S. citizens who have been away for 48 hours or more are allowed to bring back, once every 30 days, $400 worth of merchandise duty-free. You'll be charged a flat rate of 10% duty on the next $1,000 worth of purchases. Be sure to have your receipts handy. On gifts, the duty-free limit is $100. You cannot bring fresh foodstuffs into the United States; tinned foods, however, are allowed. For more information, contact the **U.S. Customs Service,** 1301 Constitution Ave. (P.O. Box 7407), Washington, DC 20044 (☎ 202/927-6724) and request the free pamphlet *Know Before You Go.* It's also available on the Web at **www.customs.ustreas.gov/travel/kbygo.htm**.

WHAT YOU CAN BRING HOME TO THE U.K. Citizens of the United Kingdom who are returning from a European Community (EC) country will go through a separate Customs Exit (called the "Blue Exit") especially for EC travelers. In essence, there is no limit on what you can bring back from an EC country, as long as the items are for personal use (this includes gifts), and you have already paid the necessary duty and tax. However, customs law sets out guidance levels. If you bring in more than these levels, you may be asked to prove that the goods are for your own use. Guidance levels on goods bought in the EC for your own use are 800 cigarettes, 200 cigars, 1 kilogram smoking tobacco, 10 liters of spirits, 90 liters of wine (of this, not more than 60 liters can be sparkling wine), and 110 liters of beer. For more information, contact **HM Customs & Excise,** Passenger Enquiry Point, 2nd Floor Wayfarer House, Great South West Road, Feltham, Middlesex, TW14 8NP (☎ 020/8910-3744; from outside the U.K. 44/020-8910-3744), or consult their Web site at **www.open.gov.uk**.

WHAT YOU CAN BRING HOME TO CANADA For a clear summary of Canadian rules, write for the booklet *I Declare,* issued by **Revenue Canada,** 2265 St. Laurent Blvd., Ottawa K1G 4KE (☎ 613/993-0534). Canada allows its citizens a $750 exemption, and you're allowed to bring back duty-free 200 cigarettes, 2.2 pounds of tobacco, 1.5 liters of liquor, and 50 cigars. In addition, you're allowed to mail gifts to Canada from abroad at the rate of Can$60 a day, provided the gifts are unsolicited and don't contain alcohol or tobacco (write on the package "Unsolicited gift, under $60 value"). All valuables should be declared on the Y-38 form before departure from Canada, including serial numbers of valuables you already own, such as expensive foreign cameras. *Note:* The $750 exemption can be used only once a year and only after an absence of at least 7 days.

WHAT YOU CAN BRING HOME TO AUSTRALIA The duty-free allowance in Australia is A$400 or, for those under 18, A$200. Personal property mailed back from England should be marked "Australian goods returned" to avoid payment of duty. Upon returning to Australia, citizens can bring in 250 cigarettes or 250 grams of loose tobacco, and 1,125 milliliters of alcohol. If you're returning with valuable goods you already own, such as foreign-made cameras, you should file form B263. A helpful brochure, available from Australian consulates or Customs offices, is *Know Before You Go.* For more information, contact **Australian Customs Services,** GPO Box 8, Sydney NSW 2001 (☎ 02/9213-2000).

WHAT YOU CAN BRING HOME TO NEW ZEALAND The duty-free allowance for New Zealand is NZ$700. Citizens over 17 can bring in 200 cigarettes, or 50 cigars, or 250 grams of tobacco (or a mixture of all three if their combined weight doesn't exceed 250 grams); plus 4.5 liters of wine and beer, or 1.125 liters of liquor. New Zealand currency does not carry import or export restrictions. Fill out a certificate of export, listing the valuables you are taking out of the country; that way, you can bring them back without paying duty. Most questions are answered in a free pamphlet available at New Zealand consulates and Customs offices: *New Zealand Customs Guide for Travellers, Notice no. 4.* For more information, contact **New Zealand Customs,** 50 Anzac Ave., P.O. Box 29, Auckland (☎ 09/359-6655).

3 Money

CURRENCY

THE PESETA The basic unit of Spanish currency is the **peseta** (abbreviated **pta.**), currently worth about 6/10 of a cent in U.S. currency. Coins come in 1, 5, 25, 50, 100, 200, and 500 pesetas. Notes are issued in 500, 1,000, 5,000, and 10,000 pesetas.

All world currencies fluctuate, so you should be aware that the amounts appearing in this book are not exact. Currency conversions are presented only to give you a rough idea of the price you'll pay in U.S. dollars. There is no way to predict exactly what the rate of exchange will be when you visit Spain. Check the newspaper or ask at your bank for last-minute quotations.

Be advised that rates of exchange vary, depending on where you convert your money. In general, you'll get the best exchange rate by using your credit card or withdrawing cash from an ATM. Banks also offer competitive rates, but keep in mind they charge a commission for cashing traveler's checks. You'll get the worst rates of exchange at your hotel, as well as at point-of-entry sites like an airport or train station.

THE EURO The **euro,** the new single European currency, became the official currency of Spain and 10 other countries on January 1, 1999, but not in the form of cash. (There are still no euro banknotes or coins in circulation—payment in euros can be made only by check, credit card, or some other bank-related system.)

The Spanish peseta will remain the only currency in Spain for cash transactions until December 21, 2001, when more and more businesses will start posting their prices in euros alongside those in pesetas, which will continue to

The Spanish Peseta

For American Readers   At this writing, $1 = approximately 165 pesetas (or 1 peseta = ⁶/₁₀ of 1 U.S. cent). This was the rate of exchange used to calculate the dollar equivalents given throughout this edition.

For British Readers   At this writing, £1 = approximately 265 pesetas (or 1 peseta = ⁴/₁₀ of 1 pence). This was the rate of exchange used to calculate the pound values in the table below.

The Euro   At this writing, 1 euro equaled approximately 166 pesetas, a rate that is likely to remain constant throughout the life of this edition. Although it wasn't in particularly widespread use at the time of the compilation of this chart, look for an increasing emphasis on the euro and its applicability to daily life in Spain.

Note: Because the exchange rate fluctuates from time to time according to a complicated roster of political and economic factors, this table should be used only as a general guide.

Peseta	U.S.$	U.K.£	Euro	Peseta	U.S.$	U.K.£	Euro
50	0.30	0.20	0.30	20,000	120	80	120
100	0.60	0.40	0.60	25,000	150	100	150
300	1.80	1.20	1.80	30,000	180	120	180
500	3.00	2.00	3.00	35,000	210	140	210
700	4.20	2.80	4.20	40,000	240	160	240
1,000	6.00	4.00	6.00	45,000	270	180	270
1,500	9.00	6.00	9.00	50,000	300	200	300
2,000	12.00	8.00	12.00	100,000	600	400	600
3,000	18.00	12.00	18.00	125,000	750	500	600
4,000	24.00	16.00	24.00	150,000	900	600	900
5,000	30.00	20.00	30.00	200,000	1,200	800	1,200
7,500	45.00	30.00	45.00	250,000	1,500	1,000	1,500
10,000	60.00	40.00	60.00	500,000	3,000	2,000	3,000
15,000	90.00	60.00	90.00	1,000,000	6,000	4,000	6,000

exist for a while longer. Over a maximum 6-month transition period, peseta banknotes will be withdrawn from circulation.

This is the symbol of the euro €; its official abbreviation is EUR.

Although at this time very few, if any, Spanish hotel and restaurant bills are actually paid in euros, there will be an increasing emphasis on the new pan-European currency during the lifetime of this edition.

ATM NETWORKS

PLUS, Cirrus, and other networks connecting automated-teller machines operate in Spain. If your bankcard has been programmed with a PIN, it's likely you can use your card at ATMs abroad to withdraw money directly from your home bank account. Check with your bank to see if your PIN code must be reprogrammed for use in Spain. Before leaving, always determine the frequency limits for withdrawals and what fees, if any, your bank will assess. For **Cirrus** locations abroad, call ☎ **800/424-7787;** also, Cirrus ATM locations

in selected cities are available on MasterCard's Internet site (www.
mastercard.com). For **PLUS** use abroad, contact your local bank or check
Visa's page on the World Wide Web (www.visa.com).

TRAVELER'S CHECKS

Traveler's checks are something of an anachronism from the days before the
ATM made cash accessible at any time. These days traveler's checks seem less
necessary, but some people still prefer the security of knowing they can recover
their money if it's stolen.

You can get traveler's checks at almost any bank. American Express offers
denominations of $10, $20, $50, $100, $500, and $1,000. You'll pay a service
charge ranging from 1% to 4%. You can also get **American Express traveler's
checks** over the phone by calling ☎ **800/221-8472;** by using this number,
Amex gold and platinum cardholders are exempt from the 1% fee. AAA members can obtain checks without a fee at most AAA offices.

Visa offers traveler's checks at Citibank locations nationwide, as well as several other banks. The service charge ranges from 1.5% to 2%; checks come in
denominations of $20, $50, $100, $500, and $1,000. **MasterCard** also offers
traveler's checks. Call ☎ **800/223-9920** for a location near you.

If you opt to carry traveler's checks, be sure to keep a record of their serial
numbers, separately from the checks of course, so you're ensured a refund in
just such an emergency.

CREDIT CARDS

Credit cards are invaluable when traveling. They are a safe way to carry money
and provide a convenient record of all your expenses. You can also withdraw cash
advances from your credit cards at any bank (but you'll start paying hefty interest on the advance the moment you get the cash, and you won't receive frequent-flyer miles on an airline credit card). At most banks, you don't even need to go
to a teller; you can get a cash advance at the ATM if you know your PIN.

Note, however, that at press time some credit card companies were discussing
plans to increase fees for foreign currency transactions. Citibank, in particular,
was considering adding a whopping 4% fee onto the 1% to 2% fee already
charged by Visa or MasterCard. Ask your bank about fees before you go.

4 When to Go

CLIMATE

Spring and fall are ideal times to visit nearly all of Spain, with the possible
exception of the Atlantic coast, which experiences heavy rains in October and
November. May and October are the best months, in terms of both weather
and crowds.

In summer it's hot, hot, and hotter still, with the cities in Castile (Madrid)
and Andalusia (Seville and Córdoba) heating up the most. Madrid has dry
heat; the average temperature can hover around 84°F in July and 75° in September. Seville has the dubious reputation of being about the hottest part of
Spain in July and August, often baking under average temperatures of 93°.

Barcelona, cooler in temperature, is often quite humid. Midsummer temperatures in Majorca often reach 91°. The overcrowded Costa Brava has
temperatures around 81° in July and August. The Costa del Sol has an
average of 77° in summer. The coolest spot in Spain is the Atlantic coast from
San Sebastián to La Coruña, with temperatures in the 70s in July and August.

August remains the major vacation month in Europe. The traffic from France, the Netherlands, and Germany to Spain becomes a veritable migration, and low-cost hotels along the coastal areas are virtually impossible to find. To compound the problem, many restaurants and shops also decide it's time for a vacation, thereby limiting the visitors' selections for both dining and shopping.

In winter, the coast from Algeciras to Málaga is the most popular, with temperatures reaching a warm 60° to 63°. Madrid gets cold, as low as 34°. Majorca is warmer, usually in the 50s, but it often dips into the 40s. Some mountain resorts can experience extreme cold.

HOLIDAYS

Holidays include January 1 (New Year's Day), January 6 (Feast of the Epiphany), March 19 (Feast of St. Joseph), Good Friday, Easter Monday, May 1 (May Day), June 10 (Corpus Christi), June 29 (Feast of St. Peter and St. Paul), July 25 (Feast of St. James), August 15 (Feast of the Assumption), October 12 (Spain's National Day), November 1 (All Saints' Day), December 8 (Immaculate Conception), and December 25 (Christmas).

No matter how large or small, every city or town in Spain also celebrates its local saint's day. In Madrid it's May 15 (St. Isidro). You'll rarely know what the local holidays are in your next destination in Spain. Try to keep money on hand, because you may arrive in town only to find banks and stores closed. In some cases, intercity bus services are suspended on holidays.

Spain Calendar of Events

The dates given below may not be precise. Sometimes the exact days are not announced until 6 weeks before the actual festival. Check with the National Tourist Office of Spain (see "Visitor Information, Entry Requirements & Customs," earlier in this chapter) if you're planning to attend a specific event.

January

- **Granda Reconquest Festival,** Granada. The whole city celebrates the Christians' victory over the Moors in 1492. The highest tower at the Alhambra is open to the public on January 2. For information, contact the Tourist Office of Granada (☎ **958-22-66-88**). January 2.
- **Día de los Reyes (Three Kings Day),** throughout Spain. Parades are held around the country on the eve of the Festival of the Epiphany. Various "kings" dispense candy to all the kids. January 6.
- **Día de San Antonio (St. Anthony's Day),** La Puebla, Majorca. Bonfires, dancing, revelers dressed as devils, and other riotous events honor St. Anthony on the eve of his day. January 17.

February

- **ARCO** (Madrid's International Contemporary Art Fair), Madrid. One of the biggest draws on Spain's cultural calendar, this exhibit showcases the best in contemporary art from Europe and America. At the Crystal Pavilion of the Casa de Campo, the exhibition draws galleries from throughout Europe, the Americas, Australia, and Asia, who bring with them the works of regional and internationally known artists. To buy tickets contact El Corte Ingles at ☎ **91-418-88-00,** or Madrid Rock at ☎ **91-547-24-23.** The cost is between 5,000 ptas. ($30) and 6,000 ptas. ($36). You can get schedules from the tourist office closer to the event. Dates vary, but usually mid-February.

- **Bocairente Festival of Christians and Moors,** Bocairente (Valencia). Fireworks, colorful costumes, parades, and a reenactment of the struggle between Christians and Moors mark this exuberant festival. A stuffed effigy of Mohammed is blown to bits. Call ☎ **96-290-50-62** for more information. February 4 to 7.
- **Carnavales de Cádiz,** Cádiz. The oldest and best-attended carnival in Spain is a freewheeling event full of costumes, parades, strolling troubadours, and drum beating. Call ☎ **956-21-13-13** for more information. Late February or early March.
- **Madrid Carnaval.** The carnival kicks off with a big parade along the Paseo de la Castellana, culminating in a masked ball at the Círculo de Bellas Artes on the following night. Fancy-dress competitions last until February 28, when the festivities end with a tear-jerking "burial of a sardine" at the Fuente de los Pajaritos in the Casa de Campo. This is followed that evening by a concert in the Plaza Mayor. Call ☎ **91-429-31-77** for more information. Dates vary.

March

- **Fallas de Valencia,** Valencia. Dating from the 1400s, this fiesta centers around the burning of papier-mâché effigies of winter demons. Burnings are preceded by bullfights, fireworks, and parades. Call ☎ **96-351-04-17** for more information. March 13 to 19.

April

- ✪ **Feria de Sevilla (Seville Fair).** This is the most celebrated week of revelry in all of Spain, with all-night flamenco dancing, entertainment booths, bullfights, horseback riding, flower-decked coaches, and dancing in the streets. You'll need to reserve a hotel early for this one. For general information and exact festival dates, contact the Office of Tourism in Seville (☎ **95-422-1404**). April 30 to May 7.
- ✪ **Semana Santa (Holy Week),** Seville. Although many of the country's smaller towns stage similar celebrations (especially notable in Zamora), the festivities in Seville are by far the most elaborate. From Palm Sunday until Easter Sunday a series of processions with hooded penitents moves to the piercing wail of the *saeta,* a love song to the Virgin or Christ. *Pasos* (heavy floats) bear images of the Virgin or Christ. Again, make hotel reservations way in advance. Call the Seville Office of Tourism for details (☎ **95-422-14-04**). April 16 to 23.
- **Moros y Cristianos (Moors and Christians),** Alcoy, near Alicante. During 3 days every April, the centuries-old battle between the Moors and the Christians is restaged with soldiers in period costumes. Naturally, the Christians who drove the Moors from Spain always win. The simulated fighting takes on almost a circuslike flair, and the costumes worn by the Moors are always absurd and anachronistic. Call ☎ **96-520-00-00** for more information. April 23 to 25.

May

- **Festival de los Patios,** Córdoba. At this famous fair residents decorate their patios with cascades of flowers. Visitors wander from patio to patio. Call ☎ **957-47-12-35** for more information. May 4 to 16.
- **Romería del Rocío (Pilgrimage of the Virgin of the Dew),** El Rocío (Huelva). The most famous pilgrimage in Andalusia attracts a million people. Fifty men carry the statue of the Virgin 9 miles to Almonte for consecration. May 14 to 24.

⚙ **Fiesta de San Isidro,** Madrid. Madrileños run wild with a 10-day celebration honoring their city's patron saint. Food fairs, Castilian folkloric events, street parades, parties, music, dances, bullfights, and other festivities mark the occasion. Make hotel reservations early. Expect crowds and traffic (and beware of pickpockets). For information, write to Oficina Municipal de Información y Turismo, Plaza Mayor, 3, 28014 Madrid, or call ☎ **91-429-31-77.** May 12 to 21.

⚙ **Feria del Caballo (Horse Fair),** Jerez de la Frontera. "Horses, wine, women, and song," according to the old Andalusian ditty, make this a stellar event at which some of the greatest horses in the world go on parade. Call ☎ **956-33-11-50** for more information. May 14 to 21.

June

• **Veranos de la Villa,** Madrid. This program presents folkloric dancing, pop music, classical music, zarzuelas, and flamenco at various venues throughout the city. Open-air cinema is a feature in the Parque del Retiro. Ask at the tourist office for complete details (the program changes every summer). Sometimes admission is charged, but often these events are free. Mid-June until the end of August.

• **Corpus Christi,** all over Spain. A major holiday on the Spanish calendar, this event is marked by big processions, especially in Toledo, Málaga, Seville, and Granada. June 6.

⚙ **International Music and Dance Festival,** Granada. Celebrating its 50th year in 2000, Granada's prestigious program of dance and music attracts international artists who perform at the Alhambra and other venues. It's a major event on the cultural calendar of Europe. Reserve well in advance. For a complete schedule and tickets, contact El Festival Internacional de Música y Danza de Granada (☎ **958-22-18-44**). June 20 to July 6.

⚙ **Las Hogueras de San Juan (St. John's Bonfires),** Alicante. During the summer solstice, bonfires blaze through the night to honor the event, just as they did in Celtic and Roman times. The bonfire signals the launching of 5 days of gala celebrations with fireworks and parades. Business in Alicante comes to a standstill. Call ☎ **96-520-00-00** for more information. June 20 to 24.

• **Verbena de Sant Joan,** Barcelona. This traditional festival occupies all Catalans. Barcelona literally lights up—with fireworks, bonfires, and dances until dawn. The highlight of the festival is the fireworks show at Montjuïc. June 23 to 24.

July

• **La Rapa das Bestas (The Capture of the Beasts),** San Lorenzo de Sabuceno, Galicia. Spain's greatest horse roundup attracts equestrian lovers from throughout Europe. Horses in the verdant hills of northwestern Spain are rounded up, branded, and medically checked before their release into the wild again. For more information, phone ☎ **986-85-08-14.** July 1 to 3.

• **Festival of St. James,** Santiago de Compostela. Pomp and ceremony mark this annual pilgrimage to the tomb of St. James the Apostle in Galicia. Galician folklore shows, concerts, parades, and the swinging of the *botafumeiro* (a mammoth incense burner) mark the event. July 15 to 30.

• **San Sebastián Jazz Festival,** San Sebastián. Celebrating its 35th year (2000), this festival brings together the jazz greats of the world at the pavilion of the Anoeta Sport Complex. Other programs take place alfresco at the Plaza de Trinidad in the old quarter. The Office of the San

Sebastian Jazz Festival (☎ 943-48-11-79) can provide schedules and tickets. July 21 to 26.

✪ **Fiesta de San Fermín,** Pamplona. Vividly described in Ernest Hemingway's novel *The Sun Also Rises,* the running of the bulls through the streets of Pamplona is the most popular celebration in Spain. It also includes wine tasting, fireworks, and, of course, bullfights. Reserve many months in advance. For more information, such as a list of accommodations, contact the Office of Tourism, Duque de Ahumada, 3, 31002 Pamplona (☎ 948-20-65-40). July 7 to 14.

August

- **Santander International Festival of Music and Dance,** Santander. The repertoire includes classical music, ballet, contemporary dance, chamber music, and recitals. Most performances are staged at the Plaza de la Porticada. For further information, contact Festival Internacional de Santander (☎ 942-210-508). Throughout August.

- **Fiestas of Lavapiés and La Paloma,** Madrid. These two fiestas begin with the Lavapiés on August 1 and continue through the hectic La Paloma celebration on August 15, the day of the Virgen de la Paloma. Thousands of people race through the narrow streets. Apartment dwellers hurl buckets of cold water onto the crowds below to cool them off. There are children's games, floats, music, flamenco, and zarzuelas, along with street fairs. For more information, call ☎ 91-429-31-77. August 1 to 15.

- **The Mystery Play of Elche.** This sacred drama is reenacted in the 17th-century Basilica of Santa María in Elche (near Alicante). It represents the Assumption and the Crowning of the Virgin. For tickets, call the Office of Tourism in Elche (☎ 96-545-38-31). August 11 to 15.

- **Feria de Málaga (Málaga Fair).** One of the longest summer fairs in southern Europe (generally lasting for 10 days), this celebration kicks off with fireworks displays and is highlighted by a parade of Arabian horses pulling brightly decorated carriages. Participants are dressed in colorful Andalusian garb. Plazas rattle with castanets and wine is dispensed by the gallon. For information, call ☎ 95-221-34-45. August 11 to 20.

✪ **La Tomatina (Battle of the Tomatoes),** Buñol (Valencia). This is one of the most photographed festivals in Spain, growing in popularity every year. Truckloads of tomatoes are shipped into Buñol, where they become vegetable missiles between warring towns and villages. Portable showers are brought in for the cleanup, followed by music for dancing and singing. Last Wednesday in August.

September

- **Diada,** Barcelona. This is the most significant festival in Catalonia. It celebrates the region's autonomy from the rest of Spain, following years of repression under the dictator Franco. Demonstrations and other flag-waving events take place. The *senyera,* the flag of Catalonia, is everywhere. Not your typical tourist fare, but interesting. September 11.

- **Fiestas de la Merced,** Barcelona. This celebration honors Nostra Senyora de la Merced, the city's patron saint, known for her compassion for animals. Beginning after dark, and after a mass in the Iglesia de la Merced, a procession of as many as 50 "animals" (humans dressed like tigers, lions, and horses) proceeds with lots of firecrackers and sparklers to the Cathedral of Santa Eulalia, then on to the Plaza de Sant Jaume, and eventually into The Rambles, Plaza de Catalunya, and the harbor-front. For more information, call ☎ **93-478-47-04.** September 24.

- **International Film Festival,** San Sebastián. The premier film festival of Spain takes place in the Basque capital, often at the Victoria Eugenia Theater, a belle époque masterpiece. Retrospectives are often featured, and weeklong screenings are held. For more information, call ☎ **943-48-12-12.** September 21 to 30.

October

- **St. Teresa Week,** Ávila. Verbenas (carnivals), parades, singing, and dancing honor the patron saint of this walled city. Dates vary.

✪ **Autumn Festival,** Madrid. Both Spanish and international artists partic-ipate in this cultural program, with a series of operatic, ballet, dance, music, and theatrical performances from Strasbourg to Tokyo. This event is a premier attraction, yet tickets are reasonable. Make hotel reservations early. For tickets, contact Festival de Otoño, Plaza de España, 8, 28008 Madrid (☎ **91-580-25-75**). Late October to late November.

- **Grape Harvest Festival,** Jerez de la Frontera. The major wine festival in Andalusia honors the famous sherry of Jerez, with 5 days of processions, flamenco dancing, bullfights, livestock on parade, and, of course, sherry drinking. For information, call ☎ **956-333-11-50.** Mid-October (dates vary).

November

- **All Saints' Day,** all over Spain. This public holiday is reverently cele-brated, as relatives and friends lay flowers on the graves of the dead. November 1.

December

- **Día de los Santos Inocentes,** all over Spain. This equivalent of April Fools' Day is an excuse for people to do loco things. December 28.

5 Special-Interest Vacations

Spain is one of the best destinations in Europe for enjoying the outdoors. Lounging on the beach leads the list of activities for most travelers, but there's lots more to do. Spain's mountains lure thousands of mountaineers and hikers, and fishing and hunting are long-standing Iberian obsessions. The Pyrenees of Catalonia and Aragón, plus the Guadarramas outside Madrid, attract devoted skiers in the winter. Watersports ranging from sailing to windsurfing are prime summer attractions.

In addition to sports and adventures, we've also detailed some of the best educational and cultural programs below.

Note: The inclusion of an organization in this section is in no way to be interpreted as a guarantee. This information is presented only as a preview, to be followed by your own investigation.

BIKING

The leading U.S.-based outfitter is **Easy Rider Tours,** P.O. Box 228, Newburyport, MA 01950 (☎ **800/488-8332** or 978/463-6955). Their tours average between 30 and 50 miles a day; and the most appealing follows the route trod by medieval pilgrims on their way to Santiago. The bike tours offered by **Backroads,** 801 Cedar St., Berkeley, CA 94710 (☎ **800/ GO-ACTIVE**), take you through the verdant countryside of Galicia and into Portugal's Minho region. Companies that specialize in bike tours of Camino de Santiago include **Camino Tours,** Seattle, WA 98115 (☎ **800/938-9311** or 206/523-1764), and **Saranjan Tours,** 18665 NE St., Suite 102, Kirkland, WA 98033 (☎ **800/858-9594** or 425/869-8636).

In England, the **Cyclists' Touring Club,** 60 Meadrow, Godalming, Surrey GU7 3HS, UK (☎ **01483/417-217**), charges £25 a year for membership; part of the fee provides for information and suggested cycling routes through Spain and dozens of other countries.

GOLF

In recent decades, thousands of British retirees have settled in Spain, and their presence has sparked the development of dozens of new golf courses. Although the Costa Blanca has become an increasingly popular setting for golf, more than a third of the country's approximately 160 courses lie within its southern tier, within a short drive of the Costa del Sol.

Packages that include guaranteed playing time on some of the country's finest courses, as well as airfare and accommodations, can be arranged through such firms as **Golf International** (☎ **800/833-1389** in the U.S.), **Spanish Golf Adventures** (☎ **800/772-6465** in the U.S. and Canada), **Central Holidays** (☎ **800/935-5000** in the U.S. and Canada), **PGA Travel** (☎ **800/283-4653** in the U.S., or 770/455-8019), and **Comtours** (☎ **800/ 248-1331** in the U.S.).

What are the two most talked-about golf courses in Spain? The well-established **Valderrama** on the Costa del Sol, a Robert Trent Jones–designed course carved out of an oak plantation in the 1980s, and Hyatt's new **La Manga Club** on the Costa Blanca near Murcia. It's the site of three golf courses, one of which was recently remodeled by Arnold Palmer. The Ryder Cup between Spain and the United States was held in 1997 at Valderrama, Apt. de Correos, 1, 11310 Sotogrande (☎ **956-795-775**), on the western tip of the Costa del Sol, near Gibraltar.

HIKING & WALKING

If you're drawn to the idea of combining hiking with stopovers at local inns, contact **Winetrails,** Greenways, Vann Lake, Ockley, Dorking EH5 5NT, UK (☎ **01306/712-111**). This U.K.-based company conducts 10-day treks through northern Spain's wine districts.

To venture into the more rugged countryside of Catalonia, Andalusia's valley of the Guadalquivir, or the arid, beautiful Extremaduran plains, contact **Ramblers Holidays,** P.O. Box 43, Welwyn Garden AL8 6PQ, UK (☎ **01707/331-133**). Walking tours through the Pyrenees, the region around Alicante, and across the eerie volcanic expanses of the Canary Islands are conducted by **Waymark Holidays,** 44 Windsor Rd., Slough SL1 2EJ, UK (☎ **01753/516-477**).

An outfit known for its luxurious and pricey tours is **Abercrombie & Kent International,** 1520 Kensington Rd., Oak Brook, IL 60521 (☎ **800/ 323-7308** or 630/954-2944). They conduct a 9-day "Walking the Pyrenees" tour on the Spanish side of the mountainous border with France. Special emphasis is placed on the medieval churches that provided rest and hope to 10th-century pilgrims on their way to Santiago.

HORSEBACK RIDING

You can take a tour that winds across Asturia and Galicia on your way to the medieval religious shrine at Santiago de Compostela. Lodging, the use of a horse, and all necessary equipment are included in the price. For information and reservations, contact the **Centro Hípico "O Castelo,"** calle Urzáiz, 91, no. 5-A Vigo, Spain (☎ **986-42-59-37**).

A well-known equestrian center that conducts tours of the Alpujarras highlands is **Cabalgar,** Rutas Alternativas, Bubión, Granada (☎ **958-76-31-35**). The farm is best known for its weekend treks through the scrub-covered hills of southern and central Spain, although longer tours are available.

SAILING

Alventus, an agency based in Seville, offers weeklong cruises along the coast of Andalusia and the Algarve. Its three-masted, 42-foot sailing yacht departs from the Andalusian port of Huelva. For reservations and information, contact Alventus at calle Imagen, 6, 41003 Sevilla (☎ **95-421-00-62**).

In northern Spain, consider a journey with **Voyages Jules Verne,** 21 Dorset Sq., London NW1 6QG, UK (☎ **0171/616-1000**). Its guided vacations take in Galicia, its Portuguese neighbors, Trás-os-Montes and the Minho district, and Porto, the second-largest city in Portugal. The trips end with a boat ride up the Douro River back into Spain.

SKIING

You wouldn't think there'd be good skiing in a country that's often so blazing hot, but Iberia's mountain ranges provide some surprising opportunities for schussing. And because skiers in Spain tend to keep the same late hours at resorts, slopes are noticeably less crowded between 9 and 11am and between 1 and 3pm—presumably the times when skiers are sleeping off a night of clubbing or enjoying a late breakfast.

Besides the usually crowded facilities in Andorra, Spain's most successful and best-equipped resorts include **Sierra Nevada,** an Andalusian ski resort that was formally launched in the 1960s; **Baqueira-Beret** in the Pyrenees, a favorite of Spain's royal family; and **Alto Campo** in Cantabria.

For information about how and where to ski, call the **Ski Resort's Association of Spain (ATUDEM)** in Madrid (☎ **91-350-20-20**). For information from Spain's oldest ski club, contact the **Sierra Nevada Club,** Edificio Cetursa, Plaza de Andalucía, 18196 Sierra Nevada, Granada (☎ **958-24-91-11**). For information on the slopes in Andorra, contact **Andorra's Oficina de Turismo,** Dr. Vilanova (☎ **00376/820214**).

LEARNING VACATIONS

See "Tips for Travelers with Special Needs," later in this chapter, for details on Interhostel and Elderhostel programs for seniors.

STUDYING SPANISH Salminter, calle Toro, 34–36, 37002 Salamanca (☎ **923-21-18-08;** fax 923-26-02-63), conducts courses in conversational Spanish, with optional courses in business Spanish, translation techniques, and Spanish culture. Classes contain no more than 10 persons. There are courses of 2 weeks, 1 month, and 3 months at seven progressive levels. The school can arrange housing with Spanish families or in furnished apartments shared with other students.

Another good source of information about courses in Spain is the **American Institute for Foreign Study (AIFS),** 102 Greenwich Ave., Greenwich, CT 06830 (☎ **800/727-2437** or 203/399-5000). This organization can set up transportation and arrange for summer courses, with bed and board included. It can help you arrange study programs at either the University of Salamanca, one of Europe's oldest academic centers, or the University of Granada.

The biggest organization dealing with higher education in Europe is the **Institute of International Education (IIE),** 809 United Nations Plaza, New York, NY 10017 (☎ **212/883-8200;** www.iie.org). A few of its booklets are free, but for $44.95, plus $6 for postage, you can purchase the more definitive *Vacation Study Abroad.* To order the book, call ☎ **800/445-0443.**

One well-recommended clearinghouse for academic programs throughout the world is the **National Registration Center for Study Abroad (NRCSA),** 823 N. 2nd St., P.O. Box 1393, Milwaukee, WI 53201 (☎ **414/278-0631;** www.nrcsa.com). The organization maintains language-study programs throughout Europe, including at about 10 cities throughout Spain. Most popular are the organization's programs in Seville, Salamanca, and Málaga, where language courses last between 4 and 6 hours a day. With lodgings in private homes included as part of the price and part of the experience, tuition begins at around $615 for an intensive 2-week language course. Courses accept participants aged 17 to 80.

A clearinghouse for information on at least nine different Spain-based language schools is **Lingua Service Worldwide,** 216 E. 45th St., 17th Floor, New York, NY 10017 (☎ **800/394-5327** or 212/867-1225). Maintaining information about learning programs in 10 languages in 17 countries outside the United States, it represents organizations devoted to the teaching of Spanish and culture in 11 cities of Spain, including one in the Canary Islands.

One well-recommended language school that manages to combine a resort setting with intensive linguistic immersion is the **Escuela de Idiomas Nerja,** calle Almirante Ferrándiz, 73, 29780 Nerja, Málaga (☎ **952-52-16-87**). It offers a 2-week Spanish course for 48,000 ptas. ($288) and a 4-week course for 80,000 ptas. ($480). Also offered are one-on-one courses, refresher courses for teachers, and Spanish for business. Classes are limited to a maximum of 10 students each.

For more information about study abroad, contact the **Council on International Educational Exchange (CIEE),** 205 E. 42nd St., New York, NY 10017 (☎ **800/ 226-8624** or 212/822-2700; www.counciltravel.com).

"EARTHWATCHING" **Earthwatch,** 680 Mount Auburn St., P.O. Box 403, Watertown, MA 02272-9924 (☎ **617/926-8200**), is a nonprofit organization that recruits ordinary people to work as paying volunteers for university professors on field expeditions throughout the world. Volunteers are almost never specialists in any particular field but interested intergenerational participants. Note that only 10% of volunteers are students; many are senior citizens. Ongoing projects in Spain include monitoring the S'Albufera wetlands on the island of Majorca, excavating a prehistoric cluster of Copper Age villages on Majorca, researching the remains of a Bronze Age Iberian village near Borja in Aragón, and participating in the Spanish dolphin project off the southern coast.

Participation in Earthwatch's 2-week Spanish projects involves a tax-deductible contribution of between $1,600 and $2,000, depending on the project, plus airfare to Spain. Living arrangements, as well as all meals and drinks at the organization's Saturday-night beer parties, are provided.

BIRDING The Iberian Peninsula lies directly across migration routes of species that travel with the seasons between Africa and Europe. Some of the most comprehensive studies on these migratory patterns are conducted by Spain's **Centro de Migración de Aves,** SEO/BirdLife, Carretera de Humera 63–1, 28224 Pozuelo, Madrid (☎ **91-434-09-10**). Based at a rustic outpost near Gibraltar, their summer work camps and field projects appeal to participants who want to identify, catalog, and "ring" (mark with an identifying leg band) some of the millions of birds that nest on Spanish soil every year. Participants are expected to pay for their "tuition," room, and board, but can often use the experience toward university credit, especially in such fields as zoology and ecology.

BOTANIC TOURS   Travel specialist **Cox & Kings,** Gordon House, 10 Green Coat Place, London SW7P 1PH, UK (☎ **020/7873-5006**), leads 2-week treks in search of wild orchids, unusual ferns, and samples of the varied flora that grow in the damp but sunny foothills of the Pyrenees in Aragón. The firm also conducts other organized tours through Spain.

6   Health & Insurance

STAYING HEALTHY

Spain should not pose any major health hazards. The rich cuisine—garlic, olive oil, and wine—may give some travelers mild diarrhea, so take along some antidiarrhea medicine, moderate your eating habits, and even though the water is generally safe, drink mineral water only. Fish and shellfish from the horrendously polluted Mediterranean should only be eaten cooked.

If you are traveling around Spain (particularly southern Spain) over the summer, limit your exposure to the sun, especially during the first few days of your trip and, thereafter, from 11am to 2pm. Use a sunscreen with a high protection factor and apply it liberally. Remember that children need more protection than adults do.

If you suffer from a chronic illness, consult your doctor before your departure. For conditions like epilepsy, diabetes, or heart problems, wear a **Medic Alert Identification Tag** (☎ **800/825-3785;** www.commedicalert.org), which will immediately alert doctors to your condition and give them access to your records through Medic Alert's 24-hour hotline. Membership is $35, plus a $15 annual fee.

Pack prescription medications in your carry-on luggage. Carry written prescriptions in generic, not brand-name form, and dispense all prescription medications from their original labeled vials. Also bring along copies of your prescriptions in case you lose your pills or run out.

Contact the **International Association for Medical Assistance to Travelers (IAMAT)** (☎ **716/754-4883** or 416/652-0137; www.sentex.net/~iamat). This organization offers tips on travel and health concerns in the countries you'll be visiting and lists many local English-speaking doctors. In Canada, call ☎ **519/836-0102.**

INSURANCE

There are three kinds of travel insurance: trip-cancellation, medical, and lost luggage coverage.

Trip-cancellation insurance is a good idea if you have paid a large portion of your vacation expenses up front, say by purchasing a tour. Trip-cancellation insurance should cost approximately 6% to 8% of the total value of your vacation. (Don't buy it from your tour operator, though—talk about putting all your eggs in one basket!)

Your existing health insurance should cover you if you get sick while on vacation (but if you belong to an HMO, you should check to see whether you are fully covered when away from home). If you need hospital treatment, most health insurance plans and HMOs cover out-of-country hospital visits and procedures, at least to some extent. However, most make you pay the bills up front at the time of care, and you get a refund after you've returned and filed all the paperwork. Members of **Blue Cross/Blue Shield** can now use their cards at select hospitals in most major cities worldwide (☎ **800/810-BLUE** or www.bluecares.com for a list of hospitals). **Medicare** covers only U.S. citizens traveling in Mexico and Canada. For independent travel health-insurance providers, see below.

Check your existing policies before you buy additional insurance you might not need. But if you do require additional insurance, try one of the following: **Access America** (☎ **800/284-8300**), **Travel Guard International** (☎ **800/ 826-1300**), and **Travelex Insurance Services** (☎ **800/228-9792**). In the United Kingdom, there's **Columbus Travel Insurance** (☎ **020/7375-0011** in London; www.columbusdirect.co.uk). Companies specializing in accident and medical care include **MEDEX International** (☎ **888/MEDEX-00** or 410/453-6300; fax 410/453-6301; www.medexassist.com), and **Travel Assistance International** (Worldwide Assistance Services; ☎ **800/821-2828** or 202/828-5894; fax 202/828-5896).

7 Tips for Travelers with Special Needs

TIPS FOR TRAVELERS WITH DISABILITIES

Because of Spain's many hills and endless flights of stairs, visitors with disabilities may have difficulty getting around the country, but conditions are slowly improving. Newer hotels are more sensitive to the needs of those with disabilities, and the more expensive restaurants, in general, are wheelchair-accessible. (In Madrid, there's even a museum designed for the sightless and sight impaired, called the **Museo Tiflológico**—see chapter 3, "Madrid.") However, since most places have limited, if any, facilities for people with disabilities, you might consider taking an organized tour specifically designed to accommodate travelers with disabilities.

There are more resources out there than ever before. *A World of Options,* a 658-page book of resources for travelers with disabilities, covers everything from biking trips to scuba outfitters. It costs $35 ($30 for members) and is available from **Mobility International USA,** P.O. Box 10767, Eugene, OR 97440 (☎ **541/343-1284,** voice and TDD; www.miusa.org). Annual membership for Mobility International is $35, which includes their quarterly newsletter, *Over the Rainbow.*

The **Moss Rehab Hospital** (☎ **215/456-9600**) has been providing friendly and helpful phone advice and referrals to travelers with disabilities for years through its **Travel Information Service** (☎ **215/456-9603;** www. mossresourcenet.org).

You can join the **Society for the Advancement of Travel for the Handicapped (SATH),** 347 Fifth Ave. Suite 610, New York, NY 10016 (☎ **212/ 447-7284;** fax 212-725-8253; www.sath.org), for $45 annually, $30 for seniors and students, to gain access to their vast network of connections in the travel industry. They provide information sheets on travel destinations and referrals to tour operators that specialize in traveling with disabilities. Their quarterly magazine, *Open World for Disability and Mature Travel,* is full of good information and resources. A year's subscription is $13 ($21 outside the U.S.).

Travelers with disabilities may also want to consider joining a tour that caters specifically to them. One of the best operators is **Flying Wheels Travel,** 143 West Bridge (P.O. Box 382), Owatonna, MN 55060 (☎ **800/535-6790**). They offer various escorted tours and cruises, with an emphasis on sports, as well as private tours in minivans with lifts. Other reputable specialized tour operators include **Access Adventures** (☎ 716/889-9096), which offers sports-related vacations; **Accessible Journeys** (☎ 800/TINGLES or 610/521-0339), for slow walkers and wheelchair travelers; **The Guided Tour** (☎ 215/782-1370); and **Directions Unlimited** (☎ 800/533-5343).

Vision-impaired travelers should contact the **American Foundation for the Blind,** 11 Penn Plaza, Suite 300, New York, NY 10001 (☎ 800/232-5463), for information on traveling with guide dogs.

British travelers with disabilities can contact **Radar (Royal Association for Disability and Rehabilitation),** Unit 12, City Forum, 250 City Rd., London EC1V 8AF (☎ 020/7250-3222), for useful annual holiday guides. *Holidays and Travel Abroad* costs £5, *Holidays in the British Isles* goes for £7, and *Long Haul Holidays and Travel* is £5. RADAR also provides holiday information packets on such subjects as sports and outdoor holidays, insurance, and financial arrangements for people with disabilities. Each of these fact sheets is available for £2. All publications can be mailed outside the United Kingdom for a nominal fee.

Another good British service is the **Holiday Care Service,** 2nd Floor Imperial Buildings, Victoria Road, Horley, Surrey RH6 7PZ (☎ 01293/774-535; fax 01293/784-647), which advises on accessible accommodations. Annual membership costs £15 (U.K. residents) and £30 (abroad) and includes a newsletter and access to a free reservations network for hotels throughout Britain and, to a lesser degree, Europe and the rest of the world.

TIPS FOR GAYS & LESBIANS

In 1978, Spain legalized homosexuality among consenting adults. In April 1995, the parliament of Spain banned discrimination based on sexual orientation. Madrid and Barcelona are the major centers of gay life in Spain, and the most popular resorts for gay travelers are Sitges (south of Barcelona), Torremolinos, and Ibiza.

The **International Gay & Lesbian Travel Association (IGLTA)** (☎ 800/448-8550 or 954/776-2626; fax 954/776-3303; www.iglta.org) links travelers up with the appropriate gay-friendly service organization or tour specialist. With around 1,200 members, it offers quarterly newsletters, marketing mailings, and a membership directory that's updated quarterly. Membership often includes gay or lesbian businesses but is open to individuals for $150 yearly, plus a $100 administration fee for new members. Members are kept informed of gay and gay-friendly hoteliers, tour operators, and airline and cruise-line representatives. Contact the IGLTA for a list of its member agencies, who will be tied into IGLTA's information resources.

General gay and lesbian travel agencies include **Family Abroad** (☎ 800/999-5500 or 212/459-1800; gay and lesbian) and **Above and Beyond Tours** (☎ 800/397-2681; mainly gay men).

We're biased, of course, but we recommend you pick up *Frommer's Gay & Lesbian Europe,* which is packed with sightseeing tips, hotel and restaurant reviews, shopping, and lots of nightlife suggestions for Madrid, Barcelona, Sitges, and Ibiza.

There are also two good, biannual English-language gay guidebooks, both focused on gay men but including information for lesbians as well. You can get the *Spartacus International Gay Guide* or *Odysseus* from most gay and lesbian book stores, or order them from **Giovanni's Room** (☎ 215/923-2960) or **A Different Light Bookstore** (☎ 800/343-4002 or 212/989-4850). Both lesbians and gays might want to pick up a copy of *Gay Travel A to Z* ($16).

The *Ferrari Guides* (www.q-net.com) is yet another very good series of gay and lesbian guidebooks.

Out and About, 8 W. 19th St. no. 401, New York, NY 10011 (☎ **800/ 929-2268** or 212/645-6922), offers guidebooks and a monthly newsletter packed with good information on the global gay and lesbian scene. A year's subscription to the newsletter costs $49. *Our World,* 1104 N. Nova Rd., Suite 251, Daytona Beach, FL 32117 (☎ **904/441-5367**), is a slicker monthly magazine promoting and highlighting travel bargains and opportunities. Annual subscription rates are $35 in the United States, $45 outside the United States.

TIPS FOR SENIORS

Don't be shy about asking for discounts, but always carry some kind of identification, such as a driver's license, that shows your date of birth. Also, mention the fact that you're a senior citizen when you first make your travel reservations. For example, many hotels and airlines offer senior discounts. In most cities, people over the age of 60 qualify for reduced admission to theaters, museums, and other attractions, and discounted fares on public transportation.

Members of the **American Association of Retired Persons (AARP),** 601 E St. NW, Washington, DC 20049 (☎ **800/424-3410** or 202/ 434-2277), get discounts not only on hotels but on airfares and car rentals, too. AARP offers members a wide range of special benefits, including *Modern Maturity* magazine and a monthly newsletter.

The **National Council of Senior Citizens,** 8403 Colesville Rd., Suite 1200, Silver Spring, MD 20910 (☎ **301/578-8800**), a nonprofit organization, offers a newsletter six times a year (partly devoted to travel tips) and discounts on hotel and auto rentals; annual dues are $13 per person or couple. **Golden Companions,** P.O. Box 5249, Reno, NV 89513 (☎ **800/392-1256** or 631/454-0880), helps travelers 45-plus find compatible companions through a personal voicemail service. Contact them for more information.

Another helpful publication is *101 Tips for the Mature Traveler,* available from **Grand Circle Travel,** 347 Congress St., Suite 3A, Boston, MA 02210 (☎ **800/221-2610** or 617/350-7500).

Grand Circle Travel is also one of the hundreds of travel agencies specializing in vacations for seniors. Many of these packages, however, are of the tour-bus variety, with free trips thrown in for those who organize groups of 10 or more. Seniors seeking more independent travel should probably consult a regular travel agent. **SAGA International Holidays,** 222 Berkeley St., Boston, MA 02116 (☎ **800/343-0273**), offers inclusive tours and cruises for those 50 and older. SAGA also sponsors the more substantial "Road Scholar Tours" (☎ **800/621-2151**), which are fun but with an educational bent.

If you want something more than the average vacation or guided tour, try **Elderhostel** (☎ **877/426-8056;** www.elderhostel.org) or the University of New Hampshire's **Interhostel** (☎ **800/733-9753**), both variations on the same theme: educational travel for senior citizens. On these escorted tours, the days are packed with seminars, lectures, and field trips, and the sightseeing is all led by academic experts. **Elderhostel,** 75 Federal St., Boston, MA 02110-1941 (☎ **877/426-8056;** www.elderhostel.org), arranges study programs for those aged 55 and over (and a spouse or companion of any age). Most courses last about 3 weeks and many include airfare, accommodations in student dormitories or modest inns, meals, and tuition. Write or call for a free catalog, which lists upcoming courses and destinations. Interhostel takes

Planning Basics

travelers 50 and over (with companions over 40), and offers 2- and 3-week trips, mostly international. The courses in both these programs are ungraded, involve no homework, and often focus on the liberal arts. They're not luxury vacations, but they're fun and fulfilling.

British travelers can contact **Wasteels,** Victoria Station, opposite Platform 2, London SW1V 1JY, UK (☎ **0207/834-7066**), for a Rail Europe Senior pass, sold to British residents 60 years of age and older for £5. The pass entitles seniors to discounted rail tickets on many of the rail lines of Europe. To qualify, British residents must present a valid British Senior Citizen rail card, available for £16 at any BritRail office if proof of age and British residency are presented.

TIPS FOR FAMILIES

Several books on the market offer tips to help you travel with kids. Most concentrate on the United States, but two, *Family Travel* (Lanier Publishing International) and *How to Take Great Trips with Your Kids* (The Harvard Common Press), are full of good general advice that can apply to travel anywhere. Another reliable tome with a worldwide focus is *Adventuring with Children* (Foghorn Press).

Family Travel Times is published six times a year by **TWYCH (Travel with Your Children)** (☎ **888/822-4388** or 212/477-5524), and includes a weekly call-in service for subscribers. Subscriptions are $39 a year for bimonthly editions. A free publication list and a sample issue are available by calling, or by sending a request to 40 Fifth Ave., New York, NY 10011.

The University of New Hampshire runs **Familyhostel** (☎ **800/733-9753**), an intergenerational alternative to standard guided tours. You live on a European college campus for the 2- or 3-week program, attend lectures, seminars, go on lots of field trips, and do all the sightseeing—all of it guided by a team of experts and academics. It's designed for children (aged 8 to 15), parents, and grandparents.

The best deals for British families are often package tours, especially those offered by **Thomsons Travel** (☎ **020/7387-9321**). It offers dozens of air/land packages to Spain that have a predesignated number of airline seats reserved for free use by children under 18 who accompany their parents. To qualify, parents must book airfare and hotel accommodations lasting 2 weeks or more, and book as far in advance as possible. Savings for families with children can be substantial.

8 Getting There

BY PLANE

FROM NORTH AMERICA Flights from the U.S. east coast to Spain take 6 to 7 hours. The national carrier of Spain, **Iberia Airlines** (☎ **800/772-4642;** www.iberia.com), has more routes into and within Spain than any other airline. It offers daily nonstop service to Madrid from New York, Chicago, and Miami. In addition, Iberia has service to Madrid from Toronto (through Montréal) two and three times a week, depending on the season. Also available are attractive rates on fly-drive packages within Iberia and Europe; they can substantially reduce the cost of both the air ticket and the car rental.

A good money-saver to consider is **Iberia's EuroPass.** Available only to passengers who simultaneously arrange for transatlantic passage on Iberia and a minimum of two additional flights, it allows passage on any flight within Iberia's European or Mediterranean dominion for $250 for the first two flights and $125 for each additional flight. This is especially attractive for passengers wishing to combine trips to Spain with, for example, visits to such far-flung destinations as Cairo, Tel Aviv, Istanbul, Moscow, and Munich. For details, ask Iberia's phone representative. The EuroPass can be purchased as a part of an Iberian Air itinerary from your home country only.

Iberia's main Spain-based competitor is **Air Europa** (☎ 888/238-7672), which offers nonstop service from New York's JFK Airport to Madrid, with continuing service to major cities within Spain. Fares are usually lower than Iberia's.

The latest Spanish airline in the market is **Spanair** (☎ 888/545-5757), which is the only airline to service the Washington, D.C., area. Spanair flies directly from Washington's Dulles Airport to Madrid 7 days a week, with services continuing on to many of the main cities in Spain.

American Airlines (☎ 800/433-7300; www.aa.com) offers daily nonstop service to Madrid from its massive hub in Miami.

Delta (☎ 800/241-4141; www.delta.com) runs daily nonstop service from Atlanta (its worldwide hub) and New York (JFK) to both Madrid and Barcelona. Delta's Dream Vacation department offers independent fly-drive packages, land packages, and escorted bus tours.

United Airlines (☎ 800/538-2929; www.ual.com) does not fly into Spain directly. It does, however, offer airfares from the United States to Spain with United flying as far as Zurich, and then using another carrier to complete the journey. United also offers fly-drive packages and escorted motor coach tours.

Continental Airlines (☎ 800/231-0856; www.continental.com) offers daily nonstop flights, depending on the season, to Madrid from Newark, New Jersey.

US Airways (☎ 800/428-4322; www.usairways.com) offers daily nonstop service between Philadelphia and Madrid. The carrier also has connecting flights to Philadelphia from more than 50 cities throughout the United States, Canada, and the Bahamas.

FROM THE UNITED KINGDOM   British Airways (BA) (☎ 0345/222-747, or 020/8759-5511 in London) and **Iberia** (☎ 020/7830-0011 in London) are the two major carriers flying between England and Spain. More than a dozen daily flights, on either BA or Iberia, depart from London's Heathrow and Gatwick airports. The Midlands is served by flights from Manchester and Birmingham, two major airports that can also be used by Scottish travelers flying to Spain. There are about seven flights a day from London to Madrid and back and at least six to Barcelona (trip time: 2 to 2½ hours). From either the Madrid airport or the Barcelona airport, you can tap into Iberia's domestic network—flying, for example, to Seville or the Costa del Sol. The best air deals on scheduled flights from England are those requiring a Saturday night stopover.

British newspapers are always full of classified advertisements touting "slashed" fares to Spain. A good source is *Time Out*. London's *Evening Standard* has a daily travel section, and the Sunday editions of most papers are full of charter deals. A travel agent can always advise what the best values are at the time of your intended departure.

Charter flights to specific destinations leave from most British regional airports (for example, Málaga), bypassing the congestion at the Barcelona and Madrid airports. Figure on saving approximately 10% to 15% on regularly scheduled flight tickets. But check carefully into the restrictions and terms; read the fine print, especially in regard to cancellation penalties. One recommended company is **Trailfinders** (☎ 020/7937-5400 in London) which operates charters.

Fly for Less: Tips for Getting the Best Airfares

1. Keep your eyes peeled for **sales.** Check your newspaper for advertised discounts or call the airlines directly and ask if any promotional
rates or special fares are available. You'll almost never see a sale
during the peak summer vacation months of July and August, or
during the Thanksgiving or Christmas seasons, but in the off-season,
there have been astoundingly low European fares in the past few
years. If you already hold a ticket when a sale breaks, it might even
pay to exchange your ticket, which usually incurs a $50 to $75
charge.

2. **Ask the reservations agent lots of questions.** If your schedule is flexible, ask if you can secure a cheaper fare by staying an extra day or by
flying midweek. Many airlines won't volunteer this information, so
you've got to be persistent on the phone.

3. **Consolidators,** also known as bucket shops, are a good place to find
low fares. Consolidators buy seats in bulk from the airlines and then
sell them back to the public at prices below even the airlines' discounted rates. Their small boxed ads usually run in the Sunday travel
section at the bottom of the page. Before you pay a consolidator,
however, ask for a record locator number and confirm your seat
with the airline itself. Be prepared to book your ticket with a different
consolidator—there are many to choose from—if the airline can't
confirm your reservation. Also be aware that bucket shop tickets are
usually nonrefundable or rigged with stiff cancellation penalties, often
as high as 50% to 75% of the ticket price.
   Council Travel (☎ 800/226-8624; www.counciltravel.com) and
STA Travel (☎ 800/781-4040; www.sta.travel.com) cater
especially to young travelers, but their bargain-basement prices are
available to people of all ages. **Travel Bargains** (☎ 800/AIR-FARE;
www.1800airfare.com) was formerly owned by TWA but now offers
the deepest discounts on many other airlines, with a 4-day advance
purchase. Other reliable consolidators include **1-800/FLY-CHEAP**
(www.1800flycheap.com); **TFI Tours International** (☎ 800/
745-8000 or 212/736-1140), which serves as a clearinghouse for
unused seats; or rebators such as **Travel Avenue** (☎ 800/333-3335 or
312/876-1116).

In London there are many bucket shops around Victoria Station and Earls
Court that offer cheap fares. Make sure the company you deal with is a member of the IATA, ABTA, or ATOL. These umbrella organizations will help you
out if anything goes wrong.

CEEFAX, the British television information service, runs details of package
holidays and flights to Europe and beyond. Just switch to your CEEFAX channel and you'll find travel information.

FROM AUSTRALIA   From Australia, there are a number of options to fly
to Spain. The most popular is Qantas/British Airways (☎ 13-13-13), which
flies daily via Asia and London. Other popular and cheaper options are
Qantas/Luftansa via Asia and Frankfurt, Qantas/Air France via Asia and Paris,

4. **Surf the Web for bargains** (but always check the lowest published fare before you shop for flights online, so you know if you're getting a deal). See "Planning Your Trip: An Online Directory" following this chapter for lots of advice on how to use the Internet to its fullest; it goes into much greater detail than we can here. However, just to mention a couple of sites briefly, good bets include **Arthur Frommer's Budget Travel** (www.frommers.com), **Microsoft Expedia** (www. expedia.com), **Yahoo's Travel Page** (www.yahoo.com), **Travelocity** (www.travelocity.com), and **Trip.com** (www.trip.com). Several major airlines offer a free e-mail service known as **E-Savers,** via which they'll send you their best bargain airfares on a regular basis. It's a service for the spontaneously inclined. But the fares are cheap, so it's worth taking a look. See the Web addresses given above for each airline.

5. **Consider a charter flight.** Discounted fares have pared the number available, but they can still be found. Most charter operators advertise and sell their seats through travel agents, thus making these local professionals your best source of information for available flights. Before deciding to take a charter flight, however, check the restrictions on the ticket: You may be asked to purchase a tour package, to pay in advance, to be amenable if the day of departure is changed, to pay a service charge, to fly on an airline you're not familiar with (this usually is not the case), and to pay harsh penalties if you cancel—and be understanding if the charter doesn't fill up and is canceled up to 10 days before departure. Summer charters fill up more quickly than others and are almost sure to fly, but if you decide on a charter flight, seriously consider cancellation and baggage insurance.

   Among charter-flight operators is **Council Travel,** a subsidiary of the Council on International Educational Exchange (CIEE), 205 E. 42nd St., New York, NY 10017 (☎ **212/822-2700**). This outfit can arrange charter seats to most major European cities, including Madrid, on regularly scheduled aircraft. Another big charter operator is **Travac,** 989 Sixth Ave., 16th Floor, New York, NY 10018 (☎ **800/TRAV-800** or 212/563-3303).

   Be warned: Some charter companies have proved unreliable in the past.

and Alitalia via Bangkok and Rome. The most direct option is on Singapore Airlines, with just one stop in Singapore. Alternatively, there are flights on Thai Airways via Bangkok and Rome, but the connections are not always good.

BY TRAIN

If you're already in Europe, you might want to go to Spain by train, especially if you have a EurailPass. Even without a pass, you'll find that the cost of a train ticket is relatively moderate. Rail passengers who visit from Britain or France should make couchette and sleeper reservations as far in advance as possible, especially during the peak summer season.

Since Spain's rail tracks are of a wider gauge than those used for French trains (except for the TALGO and Trans-Europe-Express trains), you'll probably have to change trains at the border unless you're on an express train (see below). For long journeys on Spanish rails, seat and sleeper reservations are mandatory.

The most comfortable and the fastest trains in Spain are the TER, TALGO, and Electrotren. However, you pay a supplement to ride on these fast trains. Both first- and second-class fares are sold on Spanish trains. Tickets can be purchased in the United States or Canada at the nearest office of Rail Europe or from any reputable travel agent. Confirmation of your reservation takes about a week.

If you want your car carried aboard the train, you must travel Auto-Expreso in Spain. This type of auto transport can be booked only through travel agents or rail offices once you arrive in Europe.

To go from London to Spain by rail, you'll need to change not only the train but also the rail terminus in Paris. In Paris it's worth the extra bucks to purchase a TALGO express or a "Puerta del Sol" express—that way, you can avoid having to change trains once again at the Spanish border. Trip time from London to Paris is about 6 hours; from Paris to Madrid, about 15 hours or so, which includes 2 hours spent in Paris just changing trains and stations. Many different rail passes are available in the United Kingdom for travel in Europe. Call or stop in at **Wasteels** at Victoria Station opposite platform 2, London, SW1V 1JZ (☎ **020/7834-7066**). They can help you find the best option for the trip you're planning.

BY BUS

Bus travel to Spain is possible but not popular—it's quite slow (service from London will take 24 hours or more). But coach services do operate regularly from major capitals of western Europe, and once in Spain, usually head for Madrid or Barcelona. The major bus lines running from London to Spain are **Eurolines Limited,** 52 Grosvenor Gardens, London SW1W 0AU, UK (☎ **0990/143-219** or 020/7730-8235), and **Aerolineas** (☎ **93-490-40-00** in Barcelona or 01582/40-4511 in Britain).

BY CAR

If you're touring the rest of Europe in a rented car, you might, for an added cost, be allowed to drop off your vehicle in a major city such as Madrid or Barcelona.

Highway approaches to Spain are across France on expressways. The most popular border crossing is near Biarritz, but there are 17 other border stations between Spain and France. If you're planning to visit the north or west of Spain (Galicia), the Hendaye-Irún border is the most convenient frontier crossing. If you're going to Barcelona or Catalonia and along the Levante coast (Valencia), take the expressway in France to Toulouse, then the A-61 to Narbonne, and then the A-9 toward the border crossing at La Junquera. You can also take the RN-20, with a border station at Puigcerdá.

If you're driving from Britain, make sure you have a cross-Channel reservation, as traffic tends to be very heavy, especially in summer.

The major ferry crossings connect Dover and Folkestone with Dunkirk. Newhaven is connected with Dieppe, and the British city of Portsmouth with Roscoff. To take a car on the ferry from Dover to Calais on P & O Stena Lines (☎ **087/0600-0611**) costs £118 ($200.60) and takes 1 hour, 15 minutes. This cost includes the car and two passengers.

One of the fastest crossings is by Hovercraft from Dover to Boulogne or Calais. It costs more than the ferry, but it takes only about half an hour. For reservations and information, call **Hoverspeed** (☎ 800/677-8585 for reservations in North America or 08705/240-241 in England). The Hovercraft takes 35 minutes and costs £105 to £169 ($178.50 to $287.30) for the car and two passengers. The drive from Calais to the border would take about 15 hours.

You can take the Chunnel, the underwater Channel Tunnel linking Britain (Folkestone) and France (Calais) by road and rail. **Eurostar** tickets, for train service between London and Paris or Brussels, are available through Rail Europe (☎ 800/4-EURAIL for information). In London, make reservations for Eurostar at ☎ 0990/300003 (accessible in the United Kingdom only); in Paris at ☎ 01-44-51-06-02; and in the United States at ☎ 800/EUROSTAR. The tunnel also accommodates passenger cars, charter buses, taxis, and motorcycles, transporting them under the English Channel from Folkestone, England, to Calais, France. It operates 24 hours a day, 365 days a year, running every 15 minutes during peak travel times, and at least once an hour at night. Tickets may be purchased at the toll booth at the tunnel's entrance. With "Le Shuttle," gone are the days of weather-related delays, seasickness, and advance reservations.

The cost is £254.20 ($432.15) for the car and up to seven passengers. Once you land, you'll have about a 15-hour drive to Spain.

If you plan to transport a rental car between England and France, check in advance with the rental company about license and insurance requirements and additional drop-off charges. And be aware that many car-rental companies, for insurance reasons, forbid transport of one of their vehicles over the water between England and France.

BY ESCORTED TOUR

An escorted tour may not be the option for you if you like to strike out on your own and you value spontaneity. But some people love escorted tours. They let you relax and take in the sights while a bus driver fights traffic for you; they spell out your costs up front; and they take you to the maximum number of sights in the minimum amount of time with the least amount of hassle.

If you do choose an escorted tour, you should ask a few simple questions before you buy:

1. What is the cancellation policy? Do they require a deposit? Can they cancel the trip if they don't get enough people? Do you get a refund if they cancel? If you cancel? How late can you cancel if you are unable to go? When do you pay in full?
2. How busy is the schedule? How much sightseeing do they plan each day? Do they allow ample time for relaxing by the pool, shopping, or wandering?
3. What is the size of the group? The smaller the group, the more flexible the itinerary, and the less time you'll spend waiting for people to get on and off the bus. Tour operators may be evasive about this, but they should be able to give you a rough estimate. Some tours have a minimum group size and may cancel the tour if they don't book enough people.
4. What is included in the price? Don't assume anything. You may have to pay for transportation to and from the airport. A box lunch might be included in an excursion, but drinks might cost extra. Beer might be included, but wine might not. Can you opt out of certain activities, or does the bus leave once a day, with no exceptions? Are all your meals planned in advance? Can you choose your entree at dinner, or does everybody get the same chicken cutlet?

Note: If you choose an escorted tour, think strongly about purchasing travel insurance from an independent agency, especially if the tour operator asks you to pay up front. See the section on insurance, earlier in this chapter. One final caveat: Since escorted tour prices are based on double occupancy, the single traveler is usually penalized.

There are many escorted tour companies to choose from, each offering transportation to and within Spain, prearranged hotel space, and such extras as bilingual tour guides and lectures. Many of these tours to Spain include excursions to Morocco or Portugal.

Some of the most expensive and luxurious tours are run by **Abercrombie & Kent International** (☎ **800/323-7308** or 630/954-2944; www.abercrombie kent.com), including deluxe 13- or 19-day tours of the Iberian Peninsula by train. Guests stay in fine hotels, ranging from a late medieval palace to the exquisite Alfonso XIII in Seville.

American Express Vacations (☎ **800/241-1700** in the U.S. and Canada) offers many options in Spain and can also arrange non-escorted package deals.

Trafalgar Tours (☎ **800/626-6604** or 212/689-8977; www.trafalgartours. com) offers a number of tours of Spain. One of the most popular offerings is a 16-day trip called "The Best of Spain" (this land-only package is $1,335; with land and air, it's $1,905 to $2,115).

Insight Vacations "Highlights of Spain" is a 10-day tour that begins in Madrid, sweeps along the southern and eastern coasts, and concludes in Madrid. The company offers the tour for $1,863 to $2,023 including airfare, accommodations, and some meals. For information, contact your travel agent or Insight International (☎ **800/582-8380**).

Alternative Travel Group Ltd. (☎ **01865/310-399**) is a British firm that organizes walking and cycling vacations, plus wine tours in Spain, Italy, and France. Tours explore the scenic countryside and medieval towns of each country. If you'd like a brochure outlining the tours, call ☎ **01865/315-663.**

Petrabax Tours (☎ **800/634-1188;** www.petrabax.com) attracts those who prefer to see Spain by bus, although fly/drive packages are also offered, featuring stays in paradors. A number of city packages are also available, plus a 10-day trip that tries to capture Spain in a nutshell, with stops in places ranging from Madrid to Granada. **Dolmen Europa** (☎ **888/527-0110**) escorts visitors to the Basque country and the highlights of the northern coast, including stopovers in Bilbao to see the Guggenheim Museum. **Escapade Vacations** (☎ **800/942-2114;** www.escapadevactions.com) sells both escorted and package tours to Spain. It can book you on bus tours as well as land and air packages. Its grandest offering is "Ultimate Spain" with a private driver and guides. Naturally, only Spain's best hotels are used by this upmarket outfitter.

Recently, more and more special-interest tours to Spain are being offered, including tours by **Archetours, Inc.** (☎ **800/770-3051;** www.archetours.com), which features tours devoted to Spanish architecture. These tours encompass Barcelona's **Modernise,** plus the art and architecture of Bilbao and Barcelona. On the other hand, **Camino Tours** (☎ **800/938-9311;** www.caminotours. com) will take you across the country on foot or by bike. Walking tours cross the Pyrenees and the Picos de Europa, and biking tours go through the south of Spain or La Rioja wine country. Tours are limited to groups of 6 to 20 people.

BY PACKAGE DEAL

Package tours are not the same thing as escorted tours. They are simply a way to buy airfare and accommodations at the same time. For popular destinations like Spain, they can save you a ton of money. In many cases, a package that includes airfare, hotel, and transportation to and from the airport costs you less than just the hotel alone would have, had you booked it yourself. That's because packages are sold in bulk to tour operators—who resell them to the public at a cost that drastically undercuts standard rates.

Packages, however, vary widely. Some offer a better class of hotels than others. Some offer the same hotels for lower prices. Some offer flights on scheduled airlines, while others book charters. In some packages, your choice of accommodations and travel days may be limited. Some packages let you choose between escorted vacations and independent vacations; others will allow you to add on just a few excursions or escorted day trips (also at lower prices than you could locate on your own) without booking an entirely escorted tour. Each destination typically has one or two packagers that are cheaper than the rest because they buy in even greater bulk. If you spend the time to shop around, you will save in the long run.

The best place to start your search is the travel section of your local Sunday newspaper. Also check the ads in the back of national travel magazines like *Travel & Leisure, National Geographic Traveler,* and *Condé Nast Traveller.* One of the biggest packages in the Northeast, **Liberty Travel** (☎ 888/271-1584; www.libertytravel.com), usually boasts a full-page ad in Sunday papers. You won't get much in the way of service, but you will get a good deal. **American Express Vacations** (☎ 800/241-1700; www.americanexpresscom) is another option.

Another good resource is the airlines themselves, which often package their flights with accommodations. Among the airline packagers, **Iberia Airlines** (☎ 800/772-4642; www.iberia.com) leads the way. Other packages for travel in Spain are offered by **TWA** (☎ 800/221-2000; www.twa.com), **United Airlines** (☎ 800/538-2929; www.ual.com), **American Airlines FlyAway Vacations** (☎ 800/321-2121; www.aa.com), and **Delta Dream Vacations** (☎ 800/872-7786; www.delta.com).

Solar Tours (☎ 800/388-7652; www.solartours.com) is a wholesaler that offers a number of package tours to Madrid, Barcelona, and Seville, as well as to major beach resorts. Self-drive packages through Andalusia and other areas are also featured. A 9-day "Moorish Escapade" tour of Andalusia is its most popular jaunt. **Spanish Heritage Tours** (☎ 800/456-5050; www.shtours.com) is known for searching for low-cost airfare deals to Spain—round-trips to Madrid for $449 or to Málaga for $509. The tour agent also features both air and land packages to Barcelona and Madrid. **Travelplan, Inc.** (☎ 888-SPAIN99; www.g-air-europa.es) compiles a moderately priced series of package tours to some of the most visited places in Spain, especially Costa del Sol resorts. Packages generally feature airfare from New York to Málaga. **Discover Spain Vacations** (☎ 800/227-5858; www.centralholidays. com), the marketing arm of Iberia, is the most reliable tour operator and the agency used for air and land packages to some of the highlights of Spain, including Madrid, Córdoba, Seville, Granada, and the Costa del Sol. Naturally, round-trip airfares on Iberia are included in the deal. Several fly/drive packages are also offered.

9 Getting Around

BY PLANE

Two affiliated airlines operate within Spain: Iberia and its smaller cousin, Aviaco. (For reservations on either of these airlines, call ☎ 800/772-4642 in the U.S.) By European standards, domestic flights within Spain are relatively inexpensive, and considering the vast distances within the country, flying between distant points sometimes makes sense.

If you plan to travel to a number of cities and regions, Iberia's "Visit Spain" ticket, priced between $240 and $260 ($299 and $349 to include the Canary Islands), depending on the season, can be a good deal. Sold only in conjunction with a transatlantic ticket and valid for any airport within Spain and the Balearic Islands, it requires that you choose up to four different cities in advance, in the order you'll visit them. Restrictions forbid flying immediately back to the city of departure, instead encouraging far-flung visits to widely scattered regions of the peninsula. Only one change within the preset itinerary is permitted once the ticket is issued. The dates and departure times of the actual flights, however, can be determined or changed without penalty once you arrive in Spain. Also, passengers who want to exceed the designated number of stops (four) included within the basic ticket can add additional cities to their itineraries for $50 each. Children under 2 travel for 10% of the adult fare, and children 2 to 11 travel for 50% of the adult fare. The ticket is valid for up to 60 days after your initial transatlantic arrival in Spain.

BY TRAIN

Spain is crisscrossed with a comprehensive network of rail lines. Hundreds of trains depart every day for points around the country, including the fast TALGO and the newer, faster AVE trains, which reduced rail time between Madrid and Seville to only 2½ hours.

If you plan to travel a great deal on the European railroads, it's worth buying a copy of the ***Thomas Cook Timetable of European Passenger Railroads.*** It's available exclusively in North America from **Forsyth Travel Library,** 226 Westchester Ave., White Plains, NY 10604 (☎ **800/FORSYTH**), at a cost of $27.95, plus $4.95 postage priority airmail in the United States plus $2 (U.S.) for shipments to Canada.

The most economical way to travel in Spain is on the Spanish State Railways (RENFE). Most main long-distance connections are served with night express trains having first- and second-class seats as well as beds and bunks. There are also comfortable high-speed daytime trains of the TALGO, TER, and Electrotren types. There is a general fare for these trains; bunks, beds, and certain superior-quality trains cost extra. Nevertheless, the Spanish railway is one of the most economical in Europe; in most cases, this is the best way to go.

RAIL PASSES   RENFE, the national railway of Spain, offers the **Spain Flexipass,** a discounted rail pass. Flexipasses permit a designated number of travel days within a predetermined time block—for example, 3 or 5 days in 1 month or 10 days in 2 months. You must buy these passes in the United States prior to your departure. For more information, consult a travel agent or **Rail Europe** (☎ **800/4-EURAIL**).

Iberojet Travel, Inc. offers a computerized link to RENFE with its "instant purchase ticketing." By calling ☎ **800/222-8383,** travelers can reserve seats for travel between various cities within Spain and on journeys on RENFE to neighboring countries. The network includes access to the Intercity, Estrella, and Tren Hotel lines, as well as access to the AVE, Spain's high-speed network.

The Eurailpass   The Eurailpass is one of Europe's greatest travel bargains, offering unlimited first-class travel in any country in western Europe, except the British Isles (good in Ireland). You must buy these passes in the United States before your departure; call your travel agent or **Rail Europe** (☎ **800/ 4-EURAIL**).

The Eurailpass also entitles you to discounts on some bus and steamship lines. Passes are available for 15 days to as long as 3 months and are strictly nontransferable. Children under 4 travel free, provided they don't occupy a seat of their own (otherwise, they're charged half fare); children 4 to 12 pay half fare. If you're under 26, you can purchase a Eurail Youthpass, which entitles you to unlimited second-class travel for 15 days, 1 month, or 2 months.

The **Eurail Saverpass** provides discounted 15-day travel for groups of three people traveling continuously together between April and September or two people between October and March. The price of a Saverpass, valid all over Europe, is good for first class only.

The **Eurail Flexipass** allows passengers to visit Europe with more flexibility. It's valid in first class and offers the same privileges as the Eurailpass. However, it provides a number of individual travel days that can be used over a much longer period of consecutive days. That makes it possible to stay in one city and yet not lose a single day of travel. The pass entitles you, within a 2-month period, to 10 or 15 days of travel.

With similar qualifications and restrictions, travelers under 26 can purchase a **Eurail Youth Flexipass.** It also allows, within a 2-month period, for 10 or 15 days of travel.

The Europass   Like the Eurailpass, the Europass offers the most favorable rates only to buyers who purchase it outside Europe. Europasses can be purchased from any travel agent, or arranged over the phone by dialing ☎ **800/ 4-EURAIL.**

Depending on the fee, the Europass allows unlimited rail travel within and between three and five European countries with shared (contiguous) borders, arranged into several different price tiers. The countries participating in the Europass plan include Italy, France, Germany, Switzerland, and Spain. The terrain covered by the Europass plan is deliberately less broad-based than that honored by the 17 countries within the Eurail network.

If you opt for 5 to 7 days of first-class train travel in three of the above-mentioned countries (Italy plus two contiguous countries on the list), you'll have up to 2 months to complete your travel.

If you opt for 8 to 10 days of travel within any 2-month period, you'll be able to add a fourth country from the above-cited list, and if you opt for 11 to 15 days of travel within any 2-month period, you can travel through all five of the countries while using the pass.

You can reduce costs with this means of transport by sharing your trip with another adult, who will receive a 50% discount on each of the above-mentioned fares.

Note: You can add what Europass refers to as an "associate country" (Austria, Benelux, Greece, or Portugal) to the reach of your Europass by paying a surcharge.

BY CAR

A car offers the greatest flexibility while you're touring, even if you're just doing day trips from Madrid. Don't, however, plan to drive in Madrid or Barcelona for city sightseeing; it's too congested. Theoretically, rush hour is Monday to Saturday from 8 to 10am, 1 to 2pm, and 4 to 6pm. In reality, it's always busy.

CAR RENTALS   Many of North America's biggest car-rental companies, including Avis, Budget, and Hertz, maintain offices throughout Spain. Although several Spanish car-rental companies exist, we've gotten lots of letters from readers of previous editions telling us they've had a hard time resolving billing irregularities and insurance claims, so you might want to stick with the U.S.-based rental firms.

Riding the Rails in Style

Al Andalus Expreso (or simply Al Andalus) is a restored vintage train that travels through some of the most historic destinations in Andalusia. The train retains an atmosphere and level of service you just don't see very often these days. The passenger and dining cars boast panels of inlaid marquetry, hardwoods, brass fittings, and etched glass that could well be found in the Edwardian parlor of a private mansion; beneath the antique veneers, state-of-the-art engineering maintains comfortably high speeds. The train offers fine dining and such amenities as individual showers on wheels.

Al Andalus consists of 13 carriages manufactured in Britain, Spain, or France between 1929 and 1930. These carriages were collected and restored by railway historians at RENFE. Included are two restaurant cars, a games and lounge car, a bar car where live piano music and evening flamenco dances are presented, five sleeping carriages, and two shower cars. All carriages (except the shower cars) are air-conditioned and heated.

For reservations, contact your travel agent. For additional brochures and information, contact **Marketing Ahead,** 433 Fifth Ave., New York, NY 10016 (☎ **800/223-1356** or 212/686-9213).

Note that tax on car rentals is a whopping 15%, so don't forget to factor that into your travel budget. Usually, prepaid rates do not include taxes, which will be collected at the rental kiosk itself. Be sure to ask explicitly what's included when you're quoted a rate.

Avis (☎ **800/331-1212;** www.avis.com) maintains about 100 branches throughout Spain, including about a dozen in Madrid, eight in Barcelona, a half dozen in Seville, and four in Murcia. If you reserve and pay your rental by telephone at least 2 weeks before your departure from North America, you'll qualify for the company's best rate, with unlimited kilometers included. You can usually get competitive rates from **Hertz** (☎ **800/654-3001;** www. hertz.com) and **Budget** (☎ **800/472-3325;** www.budget.com); it always pays to comparison shop. Budget doesn't have a drop-off charge if you pick up in one Spanish city and return to another. All three companies require that drivers be at least 21 years of age and, in some cases, not older than 72. To be able to rent a car, you must have a passport and a valid driver's license; you must also have a valid credit card or a prepaid voucher. An international driver's license is not essential, but you might want to present it if you have one; it's available from any North American office of the American Automobile Association (AAA).

Two other agencies of note include **Kemwel Holiday Autos** (☎ **800/ 678-0678;** www.kemwel.com) and **Auto Europe** (☎ **800/223-5555;** www. autoeurope.com).

Many packages include airfare, accommodations, and a rental car with unlimited mileage. Compare these prices with the cost of booking airline tickets and renting a car separately to see if these offers are good deals. Internet resources can make comparison shopping easier. **Microsoft Expedia** (www.expedia.com) and **Travelocity** (www.travelocity.com) help you compare prices and locate car rental bargains from various companies nationwide. They will even make your reservation for you once you've found the best deal. See "Planning Your Trip: An Online Directory" following this chapter for tips.

INSURANCE   Before you drive off in a rental car, be sure you're insured. Hasty assumptions about your personal auto insurance or a rental agency's additional coverage could end up costing you tens of thousands of dollars—even if you are involved in an accident that was clearly the fault of another driver.

The basic insurance coverage offered by most car-rental companies, known as the **Loss/Damage Waiver (LDW)** or **Collision Damage Waiver (CDW),** can cost as much as $20 a day. It usually covers the full value of the vehicle with no deductions if an outside party causes an accident or other damage to the rental car.

Americans who have their own car insurance policies are most likely covered in the United States for loss of or damage to a rental car, and liability in case of injury to any other party involved in an accident. Coverage probably doesn't extend outside the United States, however. Be sure to find out whether you are covered in the area you are visiting, whether your policy extends to all persons who will be driving the rental car, how much liability is covered in case an outside party is injured in an accident, and whether the type of vehicle you are renting is included under your contract. (Rental trucks, sports utility vehicles, and luxury vehicles may not be covered.)

Most major credit cards provide some degree of coverage as well— provided they were used to pay for the rental. Terms vary widely, however, so be sure to call your credit card company directly before you rent. If you are uninsured for driving abroad, your credit card provides primary collision coverage as long as you decline the rental agency's insurance. This means that the credit card will cover damage or theft of a rental car for the full cost of the vehicle. If you already have insurance, your credit card will provide secondary coverage— which basically covers your deductible.

Credit cards will *not* cover liability, or the cost of injury to an outside party and/or damage to an outside party's vehicle. If you do not hold an insurance policy, or if your policy doesn't cover you outside the United States, you may want to seriously consider purchasing additional liability insurance from your rental company. Be sure to check the terms, however: Some rental agencies cover liability only if the renter is not at fault; even then, the rental company's obligation varies according to the policy.

DRIVING RULES   Spaniards drive on the right side of the road. Drivers should pass on the left; local drivers sound their horns when passing another car and flash their lights at you if you're driving slowly (slowly for high-speed Spain) in the left lane. Autos coming from the right have the right-of-way.

Spain's express highways are known as *autopistas,* which charge a toll, and *autovías,* which don't. To exit in Spain, follow the *salida* sign, except in Catalonia, where the word to get off is *sortida.* On most express highways, the speed limit is 75 m.p.h. (120kmph). On other roads, speed limits range from 56 m.p.h. (90kmph) to 62 m.p.h. (100kmph). You will see many drivers far exceeding these limits.

The greatest number of accidents in Spain are recorded along the notorious Costa del Sol highway, the Carretera de Cádiz.

If you must drive through a Spanish city, try to avoid morning and evening rush hours. Never park your car facing oncoming traffic, as that is against the law. If you are fined by the highway patrol (*Guardia Civil de Tráfico*), you must pay on the spot. Penalties for drinking and driving are very stiff.

MAPS   Start by checking out the free color fold-out map at the back of this book.

For one of the best overviews of the Iberian Peninsula (Spain and Portugal), get a copy of Michelin map number 990 (for a folding version) or number 460 for the same map in a spiral-bound version. For more detailed looks at Spain, Michelin has a series of six maps (nos. 441 to 446), showing specific regions, complete with many minor roads.

For extensive touring, purchase *Mapas de Carreteras-España y Portugal,* published by Almax Editores and available at most leading bookstores in Spain. This cartographic compendium of Spain provides an overview of the country and includes road and street maps of some of its major cities as well.

The American Automobile Association (☎ **800/222-4357**) publishes a regional map of Spain that's available free to members at most AAA offices in the United States. Also available free to members is a guide of approximately 60 pages, *Motoring in Europe,* that gives helpful information about road signs and speed limits, as well as insurance regulations and other relevant matters. Incidentally, the AAA is associated with the **Real Automóvil Club de España,** José Abascal, 10, Madrid 28003 (☎ **91-594-74-00**). This organization can supply helpful information about road conditions in Spain, including tourist and travel data. It will also provide limited road service, in an emergency, if your car breaks down.

BREAKDOWNS   These can be a serious problem. If you're driving a Spanish-made vehicle, you'll probably be able to find spare parts, if needed. But if you have a foreign-made vehicle, you may be stranded. Have the car checked out before setting out on a long trek through Spain. On a major motorway you'll find strategically placed emergency phone boxes. On secondary roads, call for help by asking the operator to locate the nearest Guardia Civil, which will put you in touch with a garage that can tow you to a repair shop.

As noted above, the Spanish affiliate of AAA can provide limited assistance in the event of a breakdown.

BY BUS

Bus service in Spain is extensive, low priced, and comfortable enough for short distances. You'll rarely encounter a bus terminal in Spain. The station might be a cafe, a bar, the street in front of a hotel, or simply a spot at an intersection.

A bus may be the cheapest mode of transportation, but it's not really the best option for distances of more than 100 miles. On long hauls, buses are often uncomfortable. Another major drawback might be a lack of toilet facilities, although rest stops are frequent. It's best for 1-day excursions outside a major tourist center such as Madrid. In the rural areas of the country, bus networks are more extensive than the railway system; they go virtually everywhere, connecting every village. In general, a bus ride between two major cities in Spain, such as from Córdoba to Seville or Madrid to Barcelona, is about two-thirds the price of a train ride and a few hours faster.

10 Tips on Accommodations

From castles converted into hotels to modern high-rise resorts overlooking the Mediterranean, Spain has some of the most varied hotel accommodations in the world—with equally varied price ranges. Accommodations are broadly classified as follows:

ONE- TO FIVE-STAR HOTELS

The Spanish government rates hotels by according them stars. A five-star hotel is truly deluxe, with deluxe prices; a one-star hotel is the most modest accommodation officially recognized as a hotel by the government. A four-star hotel offers first-class accommodations; a three-star hotel is moderately priced; and a one- or two-star hotel is inexpensively priced. The government grants stars based on such amenities as elevators, private bathrooms, and air-conditioning. If a hotel is classified as a *residencia,* it means that it serves breakfast (usually) but no other meals.

HOSTALS

Not to be confused with a hostel for students, a *hostal* is a modest hotel without services, where you can save money by carrying your own bags and the like. You'll know it's a hostal if a small *s* follows the capital letter *H* on the blue plaque by the door. A hostal with three stars is about the equivalent of a hotel with two stars.

PENSIONS

These boarding houses are among the least expensive accommodations, but you're required to take either full board (three meals) or half board, which is breakfast plus lunch or dinner.

CASAS HUÉSPEDES & FONDAS

These are the cheapest places in Spain and can be recognized by the light-blue plaques at the door displaying *CH* and *F,* respectively. They are invariably basic but respectable establishments.

YOUTH HOSTELS

Spain has about 140 hostels (*albergues de juventud*). In theory, those 25 or under have the first chance at securing a bed for the night, but these places are certainly not limited to young people. Some of them are equipped for persons with disabilities. Most hostels impose an 11pm curfew. For information, contact **Red Española de Alberques Juveniles,** calle José Ortega y Gasset, 71, 28006 Madrid (☎ **91-543-74-12**).

PARADORS

The Spanish government runs a series of unique state-owned inns called paradors (*paradores* in Spanish), which now blanket the country. Deserted castles, monasteries, palaces, and other buildings have been taken over and converted into hotels. Today there are 86 paradors in all, and they're documented in a booklet called *Visiting the Paradors,* available at Spanish tourist offices (see "Visitor Information, Entry Requirements & Customs" at the beginning of this chapter).

At great expense, modern bathrooms, steam heat, and the like have been added to these buildings, yet classic Spanish architecture, where it existed, has been retained. Establishments are often furnished with antiques or at least good reproductions and decorative objects typical of the country.

Meals are also served in these government-owned inns. Usually, typical dishes of the region are featured. Paradors are likely to be overcrowded in the summer months, so advance reservations, arranged through any travel agent, are wise.

The government also operates a type of accommodation known as ***albergues:*** these are comparable to motels, standing along the roadside and usually built in hotel-scarce sections for the convenience of passing motorists. A client is not allowed to stay in an *albergue* for more than 48 hours, and the management doesn't accept reservations.

In addition, the government runs *refugios,* mostly in remote areas, attracting hunters, fishers, and mountain climbers. Another state-sponsored establishment is the *hostería,* or specialty restaurant, such as the one at Alcalá de Henares, near Madrid. *Hosterías* don't offer rooms; decorated in the style of a particular province, they serve regional dishes at reasonable prices.

The central office of paradors is **Paradores de España,** Requeña, 3, 28013 Madrid (☎ **91-516-66-66**). The U.S. representative for the Paradores of Spain is **Marketing Ahead,** 433 5th Ave., New York, NY 10016 (☎ **800/223-1356** or 212/686/9213). In the United Kingdom, contact **Keytel International,** 402 Edgeware Rd., London W2 1ED (☎ **020/7402-8182**). Travel agents can also arrange reservations. In the United States, you can make a reservation at any parador by calling **Fourth Dimension Tours,** 7101 SW 99th Ave., Suite 105, Miami 33173 (☎ **800/343-0020**).

RENTING A HOUSE OR APARTMENT

If you rent a home or an apartment, you can save money on accommodations and dining and still take daily trips to see the surrounding area.

Apartments in Spain generally fall into two different categories: hotel *apartamentos* and *residencia apartamentos.* The hotel apartments have full facilities, with chamber service, equipped kitchenettes, and often restaurants and bars. The residencia apartments, also called *apartamentos turísticos,* are fully furnished with kitchenettes but lack the facilities of the hotel complexes. They are cheaper, however.

One rental company to try is **Hometours International** (☎ **800/367-4668** or 865/690-8484), which mainly handles properties in Andalusia. Call them and they'll send you a 40-page color catalog with descriptions and pictures for $5 to cover postage and handling. Units are rented for a minimum of 7 days.

Another agency is **ILC (International Lodging Corp.)** (☎ **800/SPAIN-44** or 212/228-5900), which rents privately owned apartments, houses, and villas, for a week or more. It also offers access to suites in well-known hotels for stays of a week or longer, sometimes at bargain rates. Rental units, regardless of their size, usually contain a kitchen. The company's listings cover accommodations in Madrid, Barcelona, Seville, Granada, and Majorca.

Fast Facts: Spain

Business Hours Banks are open Monday to Friday 9:30am to 2pm and Saturday 9:30am to 1pm. Most offices are open Monday to Friday 9am to 5 or 5:30pm; the longtime practice of early closings in summer seems to be dying out. In restaurants, lunch is usually 1 to 4pm and dinner 9 to 11:30pm or midnight. There are no set rules for the opening of bars and taverns, many opening at 8am, others at noon; most stay open until 1:30am or later. Major stores are open Monday to Saturday 9:30am to 8pm; smaller establishments, however, often take a siesta, doing business 9:30am to 1:30pm and 4:30 to 8pm. Hours can vary from store to store.

Climate See "When to Go," earlier in this chapter.

Currency See "Money," earlier in this chapter.

Customs See "Visitor Information, Entry Requirements & Customs," earlier in this chapter.

Driving Rules See "Getting Around," earlier in this chapter.

Drugstores To find an open pharmacy outside normal business hours, check the list of stores posted on the door of any drugstore. The law requires drugstores to operate on a rotating system of hours so that there's always a drugstore open somewhere, even Sunday at midnight.

Electricity Most hotels have 220 volts AC (50 cycles). Some older places have 110 or 125 volts AC. Carry your adapter with you, and always check at your hotel desk before plugging in any electrical appliance. It's best to travel with battery-operated equipment or just buy a new hair dryer in Spain.

Embassies/Consulates If you lose your passport, fall seriously ill, get into legal trouble, or have some other serious problem, your embassy or consulate can help. These are the Madrid addresses and hours: The **United States Embassy,** calle Serrano, 75 (☎ **91-587-2200;** metro: Núñez de Balboa), is open Monday to Friday 9am to 6pm. The **Canadian Embassy,** Núñez de Balboa, 35 (☎ **91-423-32-50;** metro: Velázquez), is open Monday to Friday 8:30am to 5:30pm. The **United Kingdom Embassy,** calle Fernando el Santo, 16 (☎ **91-319-02-00;** metro: Colón), is open Monday to Friday 9am to 1:30pm and 3 to 6pm. The **Republic of Ireland** has an embassy at Claudio Coello, 73 (☎ **91-576-35-00;** metro: Serrano); it's open Monday to Friday 9am to 2pm. The **Australian Embassy,** Plaza Diego de Ordas 3, Edificio Santa Engracia 120 (☎ **91-441-93-00;** metro: Rios Rosas), is open Monday to Thursday 8:30am to 5pm and Friday 8:30am to 2:15pm. Citizens of **New Zealand** have an embassy at Plaza de la Lealtad, 2 (☎ **91-523-02-26;** metro: Banco de España); it's open Monday to Friday 9am to 1:30pm and 2:30 to 5:30pm.

Emergencies The national emergency number for Spain (except the Basque country) is ☎ **006;** in the Basque country it is ☎ **088.**

Language The official language in Spain is Castilian (or *Castellano*). Although Spanish is spoken in every province of Spain, local tongues reasserted themselves with the restoration of democracy in 1975. After years of being outlawed during the Franco dictatorship, Catalán has returned to Barcelona and Catalonia, even appearing on street signs; this language and its derivatives are also spoken in the Valencia area and in the Balearic Islands, including Majorca (even though natives there will tell you they speak *Mallorquín*). The Basque language is widely spoken in the Basque region (the northeast, near France), which is seeking independence from Spain. Likewise, the Gallego language, which sounds and looks very much like Portuguese, has enjoyed a renaissance in Galicia (the northwest). Of course, English is spoken in most hotels, restaurants, and shops.

The best phrasebook is *Spanish for Travellers* by Berlitz; it has a menu supplement and a 12,500-word glossary of both English and Spanish.

Liquor Laws The legal drinking age is 18. Bars, taverns, and cafeterias usually open at 8am, and many serve alcohol to 1:30am or later. Generally, you can purchase alcoholic beverages in almost any market.

Mail Airmail letters to the United States and Canada cost 120 ptas. (70¢) up to 15 grams, and letters to Britain or other EU countries cost 75 ptas. (45¢) up to 20 grams; letters within Spain cost 35 ptas. (20¢). Postcards have the same rates as letters. Allow about 8 days for delivery to North America, generally less to the United Kingdom; in some cases, letters take 2 weeks to reach North America. Rates change frequently, so check at your local hotel before mailing anything. As for surface mail to North America, forget it. Chances are you'll be home long before your letter arrives.

Police The national emergency number is ☎ **006** throughout Spain, except in the Basque country, where it is ☎ **088.**

Rest Rooms In Spain they're called *aseos* and *servicios* or simply *lavabos* and labeled *caballeros* for men and *damas* or *señoras* for women. If you can't find any, go into a bar, but you should order something.

Safety Pickpockets and purse snatchers flourish throughout Spain, particularly in Madrid, Barcelona, Seville, and the Costa del Sol. In the wake of so many robberies, visitors have taken to leaving their passports at their hotel. But here's a catch-22 situation: Identification checks are common by Spanish police, who are actually cracking down on illegal immigrants. Police officers or plainclothes agents can stop you at any time of the day or night and demand to see your passport. You can be arrested, as many visitors are, if you can't produce yours. Carry your passport with you but carefully conceal it on your body, perhaps in a safety belt.

Taxes The internal sales tax (known in Spain as IVA) ranges between 7% and 33%, depending on the commodity being sold. Food, wine, and basic necessities are taxed at 7%; most goods and services (including car rentals) at 13%; luxury items (jewelry, all tobacco, imported liquors) at 33%; and hotels at 7%.

If you are not a European Union resident and make purchases in Spain worth more than 15,000 ptas. ($90), you can get a tax refund. To get this refund, you must complete three copies of a form that the store will give you, detailing the nature of your purchase and its value. Citizens of non-EU countries show the purchase and the form to the Spanish Customs Office. The shop is supposed to refund the amount due you. Inquire at the time of purchase how they will do so and discuss in what currency your refund will arrive.

Telephones If you don't speak Spanish, you'll find it easier to telephone from your hotel, but remember that this is often very expensive because hotels impose a surcharge on every operator-assisted call. In some cases it can be as high as 40% or more. On the street, phone booths (known as *cabinas*) have dialing instructions in English; you can make local calls by inserting a 25-peseta coin for 3 minutes.

In Spain many smaller establishments, especially bars, discos, and a few informal restaurants, don't have phones. Further, many summer-only bars and discos secure a phone for the season only, then get a new number the next season. Many attractions, such as small churches or even minor museums, have no staff to receive inquiries from the public.

In 1998, all telephone numbers in Spain changed to a nine-digit system instead of the six- or seven-digit method used previously. Each number is now preceded by its provincial code for local, national, and international calls. For example, when calling to Madrid from Madrid or another province within Spain, telephone customers must dial 91-123-4567. Similarly, when calling Valladolid from within or outside the province, dial 979-123-4567.

To call Spain from another country, first dial the international long-distance code (011) plus the country code (34), followed by the 9-digit number. Hence, when calling Madrid from the United States, dial (011-34) 91-123-4567.

To make an international call from Spain, you must dial 07, followed by the country code, the area code, and the telephone number.

When in Spain, the access number for an **AT&T** calling card is ☎ **1-800-callATT.** The access number for **Sprint** is ☎ **800/888-0013.**

More information is also available on the Teléfonica Web site at **www.telefonica.es**.

Time   Spain is 6 hours ahead of eastern standard time in the United States. Daylight saving time is in effect from the last Sunday in March to the last Sunday in September.

Tipping   Don't overtip. The government requires restaurants and hotels to include their service charges—usually 15% of the bill. However, that doesn't mean you should skip out of a place without dispensing some extra pesetas. The following are some guidelines:

Your hotel porter should get 75 ptas. (45¢) per bag and never less than 100 ptas. (60¢), even if you have only one suitcase. Maids should be given 150 ptas. (90¢) per day, more if you're generous. Tip doormen 125 ptas. (75¢) for assisting with baggage and 50 ptas. (30¢) for calling a cab. In top-ranking hotels the concierge will often submit a separate bill, showing charges for newspapers and other services; if he or she has been particularly helpful, tip extra. For cab drivers, add about 10% to the fare as shown on the meter. At airports, such as Barajas in Madrid and major terminals, the porter who handles your luggage will present you with a fixed-charge bill.

In both restaurants and nightclubs, a 15% service charge is added to the bill. To that, add another 3% to 5% tip, depending on the quality of the service. Waiters in deluxe restaurants and nightclubs are accustomed to the extra 5%, which means you'll end up tipping 20%. If that seems excessive, you must remember that the initial service charge reflected in the fixed price is distributed among all the help.

Barbers and hairdressers expect a 10% to 15% tip. Tour guides expect 200 ptas. ($1.20), although a tip is not mandatory. Theater and bullfight ushers get from 50 to 75 ptas. (30¢ to 45¢).

Planning Your Trip: An Online Directory

by Lynne Bairstow

Lynne Bairstow is the coauthor of *Frommer's Mexico* and the editorial director of *e-com* magazine.

Day by day, the Internet becomes more integrated into our lives—including the way we plan and book our travel. By early 2000, 1 in every 10 trips was being booked online, a trend that's sure to accelerate.

The Internet not only provides a wealth of destination information but also gives you the chance to compare experiences with fellow travelers, ask experts for pretrip advice, seek out discounted fares once accessible only to travel industry insiders, and stay in touch via e-mail while you're away. The instant communication and storehouse of information have revolutionized the way travel is researched, reserved, and realized.

This Online Directory will help you take better advantage of the travel planning information available online, and it's best used in conjunction with this book. Part 1 lists general Internet resources that can make any trip easier, such as sites for finding the best possible prices on airline tickets. In Part 2 you'll find some top online guides for Spain, organized by region.

Keep in mind this isn't a comprehensive list, but a discriminating selection to get you started. Recognition is given to sites based on their content value and ease of use and aren't paid for—unlike some Website rankings, which are based on payment. Finally, remember this is a press-time snapshot of leading Web sites—some undoubtedly will have evolved, changed, or moved by the time you read this.

1 Top Travel Planning Web Sites

While the Internet was once a conglomerate of sites for researching places to visit, several key companies have emerged that offer comprehensive travel planning and booking. In addition to Frommer's Online (see box, above), we list the other top online travel agencies below, along with some more specialized services.

WHY BOOK ONLINE?

Online agencies have come a long way over the past few years, now providing tips for finding the best fare and giving suggested dates or times to travel that yield the lowest price if your plans are flexible. Other sites even allow you to establish the price you're willing to pay, and they check the airlines' willingness to accept it. However, in some cases, these sites might not always yield the best price. Unlike a travel agent, for example, they may not have access to charter flights offered by wholesalers.

What You'll Find at the Frommer's Site

We highly recommend **Arthur Frommer's Budget Travel Online** (**www.frommers.com**) as an excellent travel planning resource. Of course, we're a little biased, but you'll find indispensable travel tips, reviews, monthly vacation giveaways, and online booking. Among the site's most popular features is the regular "Ask the Expert" bulletin boards, which feature one of the Frommer's authors answering your questions via online postings.

Subscribe to Arthur Frommer's Daily Newsletter (**www.frommers.com/newsletters**) to receive the latest travel bargains and inside travel secrets in your e-mailbox every day. You'll read daily headlines and articles from the dean of travel himself, highlighting last-minute deals on airfares, accommodations, cruises, and package vacations. You'll also find great travel advice by checking our Tip of the Day or Hot Spot of the Month.

Search our Destinations archive (**www.frommers.com/destinations**) of more than 200 domestic and international destinations for great places to stay, tips for traveling there, and what to do while you're there. Once you've researched your trip, the online reservation system (**www.frommers.com/booktravelnow**) takes you to Frommer's favorite sites for booking your vacation at affordable prices.

Online booking sites aren't the only places to reserve airline tickets; all major airlines have their own Web sites and often offer incentives—bonus frequent-flyer miles or Net-only discounts, for example—when you buy online or buy an e-ticket.

The new trend is toward conglomerated booking sites. By mid-2000, a consortium of U.S. and European airlines are planning to launch an as-yet unnamed Web site that will offer fares lower than those available through travel agents. United, Delta, Northwest, and Continental have initiated this effort, based on their success at selling airline seats at their own online sites.

The best of the travel planning sites are now highly personalized; they store your seating preferences, meal preferences, tentative itineraries, and credit card information, allowing you to plan trips or check agendas quickly.

In many cases, booking your trip online can be better than working with a travel agent. It gives you the widest variety of choices, control, and the 24-hour convenience of planning your trip when you choose. All you need is some time—and often a little patience—and you're likely to find the fun of online travel research will greatly enhance your trip.

WHO SHOULD BOOK ONLINE?

Online booking is best for travelers who want to know as much as possible about their options, those who have flexibility in their travel dates and are looking for the best price, and bargain hunters driven by a good value who are open-minded about when they travel.

One of the biggest successes in online travel for both passengers and airlines is the offer of last-minute specials, such as American Airlines' weekend deals or other Internet-only fares you must purchase online. Another advantage is that you can cash in on incentives for booking online, such as rebates or bonus frequent-flyer miles.

More people still look online than book online, partly due to fear of putting their credit card numbers out on the Net. Secure encryption and increasing experience buying online have removed this fear for most travelers. In some cases, however, it's simply easier to buy from a local travel agent who can deliver your tickets to your door (especially if your travel is last minute or you have special requests). You can find a flight online and then book it by calling a toll-free number or contacting your travel agent, although this is somewhat less efficient. To be sure you're in secure mode when you book online, look for a little icon of a padlock (in Netscape or Internet Explorer) at the bottom of your Web browser.

Business and other frequent travelers also have found numerous benefits in online booking, as the advances in mobile technology provide them with the ability to check flight status, change plans, or get specific directions from handheld computing devices, mobile phones, and pagers. Some sites will even e-mail or page passengers if their flights are delayed.

Online booking is increasingly able to accommodate complex itineraries, even for international travel. The pace of evolution on the Net is rapid, so you'll probably find additional features and advancements by the time you visit these sites. What the future holds for online travelers is ever-increasing personalization, customization, and reaching out to you.

TRAVEL PLANNING & BOOKING SITES

Below are listings for sites for planning and booking travel. The sites offer domestic and international flight, hotel, and rental-car bookings, plus news, destination information, and deals on cruises and vacation packages. Free (one-time) registration is required for booking.

✪ Travelocity (incorporates Preview Travel). **www.travelocity.com; www.frommers.travelocity.com**

Travelocity is Frommer's online travel planning/booking partner. Travelocity uses the SABRE system to offer reservations and tickets for more than 400 airlines, plus reservations and purchase capabilities for more than 45,000 hotels and 50 car-rental companies. An exclusive feature of the SABRE system is its **Low Fare Search Engine,** which automatically searches for the three lowest-priced itineraries based on a traveler's criteria. Last-minute deals and consolidator fares are included in the search. If you book with Travelocity, you can select specific seats for your flights with online seat maps and view diagrams of the most popular commercial aircraft. Its hotel finder provides street-level location maps and photos of selected hotels. With the **Fare Watcher** e-mail feature, you can select up to five routes and receive e-mail notices when the fare changes by $25 or more.

Travelocity's **Destination Guide** includes updated information on some 260 destinations worldwide—supplied by Frommer's.

Note to AOL Users: You can book flights, hotels, rental cars, and cruises on AOL at keyword: Travel. The booking software is provided by Travelocity/Preview Travel and is similar to the Internet site. Use the AOL "Travelers Advantage" program to earn a 5% rebate on flights, hotel rooms, and car rentals.

Expedia. www.expedia.com

Expedia is Travelocity's major competitor. It offers several ways of obtaining the best possible fares: **Flight Price Matcher** service allows your preferred airline to match an available fare with a competitor; a comprehensive **Fare Compare** area shows the differences in fare categories and airlines; and **Fare Calendar** helps you plan your trip around the best possible fares. Its main limitation is that like many online databases, Expedia focuses on the major airlines and hotel chains, so don't expect to find too many budget airlines or one-of-a-kind B&Bs here.

TRIP.com. www.trip.com

TRIP.com began as a site geared toward business travelers, but its innovative features and highly personalized approach have broadened its appeal to leisure travelers as well. It is the leading travel site for those using mobile devices to access Internet travel information.

TRIP.com includes a trip-planning function that provides the average and lowest fare for the route requested, in addition to the current available fare. An on-site "newsstand" features breaking news on airfare sales and other travel specials. Among its most popular features are Flight TRACKER and intelliTRIP. **Flight TRACKER** allows users to track any commercial flight en route to its destination anywhere in the United States, while accessing real-time FAA-based flight monitoring data. **intelliTRIP** is a travel search tool that allows users to identify the best airline, hotel, and rental-car rates in less than 90 seconds.

In addition, the site offers e-mail notification of flight delays, plus city resource guides, currency converters, and a weekly e-mail newsletter of fare updates, travel tips, and traveler forums.

Yahoo! Travel. www.travel.yahoo.com

Yahoo! is currently the most popular of the Internet information portals, and its travel site is a comprehensive mix of online booking, daily travel news, and destination information. The **Best Fares** area offers what it promises, plus provides feedback on refining your search if you have flexibility in travel dates or times. There is also an active section of Message Boards for discussions on travel in general and specific destinations.

SPECIALTY TRAVEL SITES

Although the sites listed above provide the most comprehensive services, some travelers have specialized needs that are best met by a site catering specifically to them.

For adventure travelers, **iExplore (www.iexplore.com)** is a great source for information and for booking adventure and experiential travel, as well as related services and products. The site combines the secure Internet booking functions with hands-on expertise and 24-hour live customer support by seasoned adventure travelers, for those interested in trips off the beaten path. The company is a supporting member of the Ecotourism Society and is committed to environmentally responsible travel worldwide.

Another excellent site for adventure travelers is **Away.com (www. away.com),** which features unique vacations for challenging the body, mind, and spirit. Trips may include cycling in the Loire Valley, taking an African safari, or assisting in the excavation of a Mayan ruin. For those without the time for such an extended exotic trip, offbeat weekend getaways are also available. Services include a customer service center staffed with experts to answer calls and e-mails, plus a network of over 1,000 prescreened tour

Airline Web Sites

Below are the Web sites for the major airlines serving Spain. These sites offer schedules and flight booking, and most have pages where you can sign up for e-mail alerts for weekend deals and other late-breaking bargains.

Air Europa. www.easyspain.com
American Airlines. www.aa.com
British Airways. www.british-airways.com
Continental Airlines. www.flycontinental.com
Delta. www.delta.com
Iberia. www.iberia.com
Qantas. www.qantas.com
TWA. www.twa.com
United Airlines. www.ual.com
US Airways. www.usairways.com

operators. Trips are categorized by cultural, adventure, and green travel. Away.com also offers a Daily Escape e-mail newsletter.

GORP (Great Outdoor Recreation Pages; **www.gorp.com**) has been a standard for adventure travelers since its founding in 1995 by outdoor enthusiasts Diane and Bill Greer. Tapping into their own experiences, they created this Web site that offers unique travel destinations and encourages active participation by fellow GORP visitors through the sophisticated menu of online forums, contests, and discussions.

For travelers who prefer more unique accommodations, **InnSite** (**www.innsite.com**) offers listings for inns and B&Bs in all U.S. states and dozens of countries around the globe. Find an inn at your destination, have a look at images of the rooms, check prices and availability, and then send e-mail to the innkeeper if you have further questions. This is an extensive directory of bed-and-breakfast inns but includes listings only if a proprietor submitted one (*Note:* It's free to get an inn listed). The descriptions are written by the innkeepers, and many listings link to the inn's own Web sites, where you can find more information and images.

Another good resource for mostly one-of-a-kind places in the United States and abroad is **Places to Stay** (**www.placestostay.com**), which focuses on resort accommodations.

"Have Kids, Still Travel!" is the motto of the **Family Travel Forum** (FTF; **www.familytravelforum.com**), a site dedicated to the ideals, promotion, and support of travel with children. FTF is supported by memberships, which are available in flexible prices from a $2.95 monthly fee to a heftier annual fee for more comprehensive services. Since no advertising is accepted, FTF provides its members with honest, unbiased information, informed advice, and practical tips designed to make traveling with children a healthier, safer, hassle-free experience, not to mention a better value.

TOP VACATION PACKAGE SITES

Both **Expedia** and **Travelocity** (see above) offer excellent selections and searches for complete vacation packages. Travelers can search by destination and desired dates coupled with how much they're willing to spend. Travelocity has a valuable "Cruise Critic" function, to help would-be cruisers find firsthand accounts of the quality and details of a cruise from recent passengers.

Travel wholesalers, like **Apple Vacations** (www.applevacations.com) and **Funjet** (www.funjet.com) are also good starting points, but they still require that the final booking be handled through a travel agent.

As travel agents tend to be more expert at sorting through the values in vacation packages, you might find **Vacation.com** (www.vacation.com) helpful in previewing packages and finding an appropriate agent to help you book the deal. This site represents a nationwide network of 9,800 local travel agencies that specialize in finding the best values in cruises, vacation packages, tours, and other leisure travel services. To find a Vacation.com member agency, enter your ZIP code and the Vacation.com Agency Finder will locate a nearby office.

LAST-MINUTE DEALS & OTHER ONLINE BARGAINS

There's nothing airlines hate more than flying with lots of empty seats. The Net has enabled airlines to offer last-minute bargains to entice travelers to fill those seats. Most of them are announced on Tuesday or Wednesday and are valid for travel the following weekend, but some can be booked weeks or months in advance. You can sign up for weekly e-mail alerts at airlines' sites (for their Web sites, see "Airline Web Sites," above) or check sites that compile lists of these bargains, such as **Smarter Living** or **WebFlyer** (see below). To make it easier, visit a site that'll round up all the deals and send them in one convenient weekly e-mail. But last-minute deals aren't the only online bargains; other sites can help you find value even if you haven't waited until the eleventh hour. Increasingly popular are services that let you name the price you're willing to pay for an air seat or vacation package and travel auction sites.

⭐ **1travel.com. www.1travel.com**
Here you'll find deals on domestic and international flights, cruises, hotels, and all-inclusive resorts like Club Med. 1travel.com's **Saving Alert** compiles last-minute air deals so you don't have to scroll through multiple e-mail alerts. A feature called "Drive a little using low-fare airlines" helps map out strategies for using alternate airports to find lower fares. And **Farebeater** searches a database that includes published fares, consolidator bargains, and special deals exclusive to 1travel.com. *Note:* The travel agencies listed by 1travel.com have paid for placement.

Cheap Tickets. www.cheaptickets.com
Cheap Tickets has exclusive deals that aren't available through more mainstream channels. One caveat about the Cheap Tickets site is that it'll offer fare quotes for a route and later show this fare isn't valid for your dates of travel—most other Web sites, such as Expedia, consider your dates of travel before showing what fares are available. Despite its problems, Cheap Tickets can be worth the effort because its fares can be lower than those offered by its competitors.

Bid for Travel. www.bidfortravel.com
Bid for Travel is another of the travel auction sites, similar to Priceline (see below), which are growing in popularity. In addition to airfares, Internet users can place a bid for vacation packages and hotels.

Go4less.com. www.go4less.com
Specializing in last-minute cruise and package deals, Go4less has some excellent offers. The **Hot Deals** section gives an alphabetical listing by destination of super-discounted packages.

LastMinuteTravel.com. www.lastminutetravel.com
Suppliers with excess inventory come to this online agency to distribute unsold airline seats, hotel rooms, cruises, and vacation packages. It's got great

deals, but you have to put up with an excess of advertisements and slow-loading graphics.

Moment's Notice. www.moments-notice.com

As the name suggests, Moment's Notice specializes in last-minute vacation and cruise deals. You can browse for free, but if you want to purchase a trip you have to join Moment's Notice, which costs $25. Go to **World Wide Hot Deals** for a complete list of special deals in international destinations.

✪ Priceline.com. travel.priceline.com

Even people who aren't familiar with many Web sites have heard about Priceline.com. Launched in 1998 with a $10-million ad campaign featuring William Shatner, Priceline lets you "name your price" for domestic and international airline tickets and hotel rooms. In other words, you select a route and dates, guarantee with a credit card, and make a bid for what you're willing to pay. If one of the airlines in Priceline's database has a fare lower than your bid, your credit card will automatically be charged for a ticket.

But you can't say when you want to fly—you have to accept any flight leaving between 6am and 10pm on the dates you selected, and you may have to make a stopover. No frequent-flyer miles are awarded, and tickets are non-refundable and can't be exchanged for another flight. So if your plans change, you're out of luck. Priceline can be good for travelers who have to take off on short notice (and thus unable to qualify for advance-purchase discounts). But be sure to shop around first, because if you overbid, you'll be required to purchase the ticket—and Priceline will pocket the difference between what it paid for the ticket and what you bid.

Priceline says that over 35% of all reasonable offers for domestic flights are being filled on the first try, with much higher fill rates on popular routes (New York to San Francisco, for example). They define "reasonable" as not more than 30% below the lowest generally available advance-purchase fare for the same route.

Smarter Living. www.smarterliving.com

Best known for its e-mail dispatch of weekend deals on 20 airlines, Smarter Living also keeps you posted about last-minute bargains on everything from Windjammer Cruises to flights to Iceland.

SkyAuction.com. www.skyauction.com

This auction site has categories for airfare, travel deals, hotels, and much more.

Travelzoo.com. www.travelzoo.com

At this Internet portal, over 150 travel companies post special deals. It features a Top 20 list of the best deals on the site, selected by its editorial staff each Wednesday night. This list is also available via an e-mailing list, free to those who sign up.

Know When the Sales Start

While most people learn about last-minute weekend deals from e-mail dispatches, it can be best to find out precisely when these deals become available. Because the deals are limited, they can vanish within hours—sometimes even minutes—so it pays to log on as soon as they're available. Check the pages devoted to these deals on airlines' Web pages to get the info. An example: Southwest's specials are posted at 12:01am Tuesdays (Central time). So if you're looking for a cheap flight, stay up late and check Southwest's site to grab the best new deals.

One of the best sources of travel information is word-of-mouth from someone who has just been there. Internet discussion groups are offering an unprecedented way for travelers around the globe to connect and share experiences. The **Frommer's Online** site (**www.frommers.com**) offers these message boards and also areas where you can pose questions to the guidebook writers themselves in the section "Ask the Expert." **Yahoo! Travel, Expedia,** and **Travelocity** are other good sources of online travel discussion groups.

The granddaddy of specialized discussions on particular topics is **Usenet,** a collection of over 50,000 newsgroups. You'll find a comprehensive listing at **Deja News** (**www.dejanews.com/usenet/**) or at **www.liszt.com**.

WebFlyer. www.webflyer.com
WebFlyer is a comprehensive online resource for frequent flyers and also has an excellent listing of last-minute air deals. Click on **Deal Watch** for a round-up of weekend deals on flights, hotels, and rental cars from domestic and international suppliers.

ONLINE TRAVELER'S TOOLBOX
Veteran travelers usually carry some essential items to make their trips easier. The following is a selection of online tools to smooth your journey.

ATM Locator: Visa. www.visa.com/pd/atm/
ATM Locator: MasterCard. www.mastercard.com/atm
Use these sites to find ATMs in hundreds of cities in the United States and around the world. Both include maps for some locations and both list airport ATM locations, some with maps. *Tip:* You'll usually get a better exchange rate using ATMs than exchanging traveler's checks at banks, but check in advance to see what kind of fees your bank assesses for using an overseas ATM.

CDC Travel Information. www.cdc.gov/travel/index.htm
Health advisories and recommendations for inoculations from the U.S. Centers for Disease Control and Prevention. The CDC site is good for an overview, but it's best to consult your personal physician to get the latest information on required vaccinations or other health precautions.

✪ **Foreign Languages for Travelers. www.travlang.com**
Here you can learn basic terms in more than 70 languages and click on any underlined phrase to hear what it sounds like. (*Note:* Free audio software and speakers are required.) It also offers hotel and airline finders with excellent prices and a simple system to get the listings you're looking for.

Intellicast. www.intellicast.com
Here you'll find weather forecasts for all 50 states and cities around the world. Note that temperatures are in Celsius for many international destinations, so don't think you'll need that winter coat for your next trip to Athens.

✪ **Mapquest. www.mapquest.com**
The best of the mapping sites lets you choose a specific address or destination, and in seconds it returns a map and detailed directions. It really is easier than calling, asking, and writing down directions. The site also links to special travel deals and helpful sites.

Net Cafe Guide. www.netcafeguide.com/mapindex.htm
Stop here to locate Internet cafes at hundreds of locations around the globe. Catch up on your e-mail, log on to the Web, and stay in touch with the home front, usually for just a few dollars per hour.

Tourism Offices Worldwide Directory. www.towd.com
This is an extensive listing of tourism offices, some with links to these offices' Web sites.

Travelers' Tales. www.travelerstales.com
Considered the best in compilations of travel literature, Travelers' Tales are an award-winning series of books grouped by destination (Mexico, Italy, France, China) or by theme (Love & Romance, The Ultimate Journey, Women in the Wild, The Adventure of Food). It's a new kind of travel book that offers a description of a place or type of journey through the experiences of many travelers. It makes for a perfect traveling companion.

The Travelite FAQ. www.travelite.org
Here you'll find tips on packing light, choosing luggage, and selecting appropriate travel wear—helpful if you always tend to pack too much or are a compulsive list maker.

Universal Currency Converter. www.xe.net/currency
Come here to see what your dollar or pound is worth in more than a hundred other countries.

U.S. Customs Service Traveler Information.
www.customs.ustreas.gov/travel/index.htm
Wondering what you're allowed to bring in to the United States? Check at this thorough site, which includes maximum allowance and duty fees.

U.S. State Department Travel Warnings. travel.state.gov/travel_warnings. html
You'll find reports on places where health concerns or unrest might threaten U.S. travelers. Keep in mind that these warnings can be somewhat dated and conservative. You can also sign up to receive State Department briefings via e-mail.

Web Travel Secrets. www.web-travel-secrets.com
If this list leaves you yearning for more travel-oriented sites, Web Travel Secrets offers one of the best compilations around. One section offers advice and tips on how to find the lowest prices for airlines, hotels, and cruises. The other section provides a comprehensive listing of Web travel links for airfare deals, airlines, booking engines, cars, cruise lines, discount travel and best deals, general travel resources, hotels and hotel discounters, search engines, and travel magazines and newsletters.

2 The Top Web Sites for Spain

Information updated by Matthew Garcia

GENERAL GUIDES FOR SPAIN
✪ **All About Spain. www.red2000.com**
Take a region-by-region, city-by-city photo tour of Spain online, or check out each city-specific guide to sights, excursions, dining, nightlife, festivals, and the like. This user-friendly site also features an ample travelers' yellow pages with listings of Spain's transportation and tour operators, accommodations, restaurants, job listings, and real estate.

Checking E-mail at Internet Cafes

Until a few years ago, most travelers who checked their e-mail while traveling carried a laptop—an expensive and often technologically problematic option. Thankfully, Web-based free e-mail programs have made it much easier to check your mail.

Just open an account at any one of the numerous "freemail" providers—the original leaders continue to be **Hotmail** (hotmail.com), **Excite** (www.excite.com), and **Yahoo! Mail** (mail.yahoo.com), but many are available. AOL users should check out **AOL Netmail,** and **USA.NET** (www.usa.net) comes highly recommended for functionality and security. You can find hints, tips, and a mile-long list of freemail providers at **www.emailaddresses.com**. Then all you'll need to check your mail is a Web connection, easily available at Net cafes and copy shops around the world. After logging on, just point the browser to your freemail's Internet address, enter your username and password, and you'll have access to your mail. From these sites, you can download all your e-mail—even from office accounts—or your local or national Internet Service Provider address. There'll be a section generally called "check other mail" that allows you to add the names of other e-mail servers.

The downside is that most Web-based e-mail sites allow a maximum of only 3MB capacity per mail account, which can fill up quickly. Also, message sending and receiving isn't immediate; some messages may be delayed by several hours or even days.

Internet cafes have become ubiquitous, so for a few dollars an hour you'll be able to check your mail and send messages from virtually anywhere in the world. Interestingly, these cafes tend to be more common in very remote areas, where they may offer the best form of access for an entire community, especially if phone lines are difficult to obtain.

Online Directory

Cybersp@in. www.cyberspain.com

Whether you want to see some Picassos or get a feel for Spanish *fútbol* fanaticism, this site offers a taste of a colorful Spain. Get a quick flamenco lesson. Peek at the major cities' top tourist attractions. Try out some recipes. One drawback: Cybersp@in is short on specifics, such as addresses, phone numbers, and timetables.

Fine Products of Spain. www.tienda.com

If you've returned from a visit to Spain and simply cannot forget the taste of chorizo, the smell of Spanish soap, or the beauty of Spanish textiles, you're in luck. Tienda.com is an American site that sells and ships all manner of Spanish products, from foodstuffs (wine, olive oil, cheeses) to painted tiles and cigars.

Tourist Office of Spain. www.okspain.org

Stake out a campsite, or find out how to see the country from the back of a horse or the seat of a bicycle. The less rustic traveler can use this guide to make reservations at hotels and villas, explore Spain's culinary possibilities, or plan a cultural vacation.

✪ TuSpain (Your Spain). tuspain.com

Appealing to everyone from weekend museum hoppers and summer villa owners to ecotourists and language students, this site has it all. Your Spain covers real estate, arts and culture, news, embassies, residency, education programs, transportation, food and wine, museums, businesses, heritage, and translators. You can even read interviews with foreigners living in Spain.

MADRID

Madrid by All About Spain. www.red2000.com/spain/madrid

Along with facts about the history and geography of Spain's capital city, this guide gives basic information on sightseeing, monuments, museums, nightlife, fiestas, cuisine, local folklore, and day trips. The site includes a photo tour and searchable hotel and restaurant directories.

✪ Madridman. www.madridman.com

A passionate (bordering on fanatical) American fan of the Spanish city, Madridman is eager to help you plan a trip, offering travel tips, hotel recommendations, transportation facts, photos, museum information, and weather reports. For a multisensory experience, check out the live Madrid radio broadcasts, video clips of Spanish TV shows, audio clips of popular Spanish songs, and video tours.

Museo del Prado. museoprado.mcu.es

The art museum's site leads you by the hand on a virtual visit, explaining how to look at a painting, showing samples of Rembrandts and Goyas, and pointing you to the museum's 50 most important works. You can also find out about conferences, guided tours, hours, tickets, and the Prado's history.

✪ Soft Guide Madrid. www.softguides.com/index_madrid.html

It's not much to look at, but this vast, easy-to-use site will tell you virtually everything you need to know about Madrid: how to get around, where to stay, what to eat, what to do for fun, where to shop, and so on. Big pluses: detailed city maps, information on local customs, and an ample lodging guide with breakdown of prices.

Web Madrid. www.webmadrid.com

This graphics-filled site has weather reports, a restaurant directory, bar and disco listings, an electronic entertainment magazine, and a "Foreign Guide" with all the usual basics on transportation, exchange rates, and tourist offices.

OLD CASTILLE & LEÓN

Salamanca Guide. www.guiasalamanca.com/sal.htm

Although in Spanish only, this barebones guide will give you some quick views of the city, plus information on history, food, and local businesses.

ANDALUSIA

Altur: Travel and Tourism in Andalucia, Spain. www.altur.com

Looking for a relaxing sojourn in the countryside of southern Spain? Stop by this site, which directs visitors to beaches and natural areas, rural tourism, culture, and food in the sunny provinces of Seville, Granada, Málaga, Córdoba, Cádiz, Almeria, Jaén, and Huelva. You can also reserve hotel rooms and buy train or plane tickets online.

Andalucia: There's Only One. www.andalucia.org

There's more than one way to see the region of Andalusia. Each week, this site suggests a new travel route through the area. Better yet, there's a searchable directory of hotels, restaurants, leisure activities, tourist services, and transportation. For an overview of the region's history, geography, and culture, check out the guide's "Touristing in Andalucia" section.

✪ **Andalucia.com. www.andalucia.com**
The Andalucia.com folks provide heaps of information about southern Spain's outdoorsy offerings: camping, hiking, climbing, sailing, hot-air ballooning, bullfighting. For less adventurous tourists, the site covers museums, festivals, restaurants, flamenco, and the like. There's even a handy village-by-village guide.

Sevilla On Line. www.sol.com
Not only can you find a barber in Seville with help from this site, you can track down business conventions, hotels, bars, restaurants, museums, post offices, and city buses. It also includes a nice listing of fiesta days and other events.

THE COSTA DEL SOL

Absolute Marbella. www.absolute-marbella.com
Read the current issue of this Costa del Sol magazine, which includes restaurant reviews, horoscopes, an events calendar, and feature stories. There's also an A-to-Z phone directory of local businesses.

**Costa del Sol: Everything Under the Mediterranean Sun.
www.costasol.com**
At this commercial site, you can book a room, hire a car, or find package deals on golf vacations and resort holidays.

Costa Guide. www.costaguide.com
This guide's tourist section points visitors to consulates and transportation schedules, and provides an online yellow pages listing local shops and services. You can search for a restaurant by cuisine, find out where the good golf courses are, and read a short history of each town on the coast.

Fuengirola: Un Sol de Ciudad. www.pta.es/fuengirola
Calling Fuengirola the heart of Costa del Sol, this online brochure introduces the town's cuisine, art, culture, attractions, sports, and famous golf courses. There aren't a lot of details or interactive components, but the site does list hotels and their amenities, bus and train schedules, and useful phone numbers.

**Marbella Scene: The Essence and Style of Marbella. www.marbella-scene.
com**
A British writer relocated in Marbella shares his impressions of the place "where Europe meets Africa" and recommends his favorite bar, restaurant, hotel, and spots for quiet contemplation. Not much on information, but there are some beautiful photos.

VALENCIA & THE COSTA BLANCA

Benidorm. www.athenea.com/benidorm
Take a photo tour of Benidorm, a city famous for its beaches, or get the lowdown on lodging, dining, transportation, and travel agencies. If you can't make it to this little corner of Spain, you can still sample Benidorm from home through regional recipes and virtual postcards.

Valencia: A Virtual Trip. www.upv.es/cv/valbegin.html
For those who enjoy a walking tour, this site provides a map on which all major sites are marked. It also describes and shows photos of the Mediterranean city's history, festivals, cuisine, nightlife, monuments, museums, sports, business, gardens, shops, hotels, and transportation.

Online Directory

BARCELONA

Barcelona: A Different Point of View. members.xoom.com/barcy
A Barcelona native offers a quirky insider's view of the city, sharing historical tidbits and observations alongside photos of oft-overlooked details. The lovely presentation of the site reveals the emotion, the life force, the spirituality, and the sensory pleasures of Barcelona.

Barcelona Prestige. www.bcn-guide.com
This online companion to a print guide holds a lot of practical information—price-specific restaurant listings, museum hours, bus and subway routes, and descriptions of local shops. There's something for the dreamy cybertraveler, too: a photo tour of Barcelona's fabulous monuments.

Poble Espanyol. www.poble-espanyol.com
Duck into a little Barcelona attraction. Illustrated with enticing photos, this site guides visitors to the Poble Espanyol district's architecture, galleries, Internet cafes, and convention centers. A calendar lists festivals and other events.

Time Out: Barcelona. www.timeout.com/barcelona
As always, Time Out's guide is thorough and easily navigable. Along with an entertainment guide, weather reports, online travel booking, and a currency converter, the site provides a wealth of information on accommodations, dining, sightseeing, kids' stuff, gay and lesbian culture, shopping, and more.

✪ Transports Metropolitans de Barcelona. www.tmb.net/weleng.htm
If the actual public transportation system in Barcelona is nearly as snazzy as its site, you're in for a treat. Amid chic, color-coded graphics and animated vehicles, you can learn how to navigate the city's bus lines and Metro (subway) system, get ticket information, read the latest TMB news, and absorb all sorts of tourist tips.

CATALONIA

✪ Castello d'Empuries. www.castellodempuries.net
A veritable multimedia extravaganza, this guide to the small Spanish town features numerous video clips, a virtual-reality tour of an ancient church, and interactive maps. Lower-tech travelers can use the events calendar and photo-illustrated text, describing, in detail, Marshes National Park, the bustling Empuriabrava area, and the town's many hotels, restaurants, and tourist attractions.

Catalonia Tourism Guide. www.travelcat.com
Click on any Catalonian town listed in the margin for facts on transportation, news, events, culture, and history. For lodging, check out the guide's recommendations for two-star to five-star hotels; links take you right to their sites.

Hoteles Catalonia. www.hoteles-catalonia.es
Make reservations online to stay at a hotel in Spain's Catalonia region. This serviceable site lists three- to five-star hotels and their amenities, services, prices, and locations.

**Railways of the Autonomous Government of Catalonia. www.fgc.
catalunya.net**
The name is a mouthful, but the site is a simply and attractively designed guide to Catalonia's transportation system. Find maps, ticket information, fares, news, a description of each train line, and customer service.

Tourism Catalonia. tourism.catalonia.net
Find out about vacation rentals, farmhouses, hostels, and other accommodations in Spain's Catalonia region. Also see what the area has to offer in the way

of festivals and adventure sports. This well-prepared guide's food-and-drink section includes a lesson in Catalán eating habits and a course-by-course description of the local fare. There's also a section on local humor and a glossary of common words and phrases.

NAVARRE & LA RIOJA

Hoteles Rurales de Navarra. www.hotelesruralesnavarra.es
A view of autumn leaves and waterfalls introduces this guide to rural lodging in Spain's Navarre region. You can make reservations online to stay in a quaint country inn. The site provides photos and a full description of each establishment as well as a brief but appealing guide to each town's attributes.

Sansol. www.arrakis.es/~melgar
This little guide to the "most beautiful" village of Sansol shows historic works of art and architecture, plays audio clips of local musicians singing auroras, gives brief history and geography lessons, and provides a chat room.

THE BASQUE COUNTRY

Agritourism in Basque Country. www.encomix.es/nekazal
For a low-stress and low-cost vacation, take a look at this guide to rural travel in north-central Spain. The site lists accommodations by region, describes the amenities of each establishment, and gives specific prices.

San Sebastián International Film Festival. www.sansebastianfestival.com
If you time your visit right, you can catch this annual international film festival in Basque country. The site lists entry requirements, schedules, ticket information, prizes, and so on. There's a section about transportation and lodging as well as a history of the festival.

Sarean: Internet and the Basque Country. www.cd.sc.ehu.es/Sarean
Although entirely free of frills, this site virtually overflows with links. The online directory leads to Basque tour guides, individual city and village sites, activities listings, sports clubs, universities, government pages, music, and more.

GALICIA

A Coruña. www.turismocoruna.com
You'll see the Coruña tower, where Picasso held his first exhibition, on the opening page of this site. Inside you can read up on this beach town's history and sample the many multiperiod art offerings. Look through a list (some with links) of 22 recommended restaurants and their prices and find out how to get two-for-one rates on accommodations. There is a photo gallery and an online map.

Costa da Morte. www.finisterrae.com
Romp through more than two dozen coastal villages, and see their ancient artifacts, quaint hotels, and sea festivals. In this site's "Tales" section, you can learn about legendary shipwrecks and local figures. Check out the lodgings segment for recommended hotels, restaurants, campsites, and rural inns.

THE BALEARIC ISLANDS

Ciutadella de Menorca. www.infotelecom.es/ciutadella
Meander through the burial tombs, caves, and other ancient wonders of the island of Menorca under this site's guidance. A map directs visitors to the island's many beaches. A very good calendar lists cultural events, and special sections show the old town, stone quarries, and signs of urbanization.

Guia de Formentera. www.guiaformentera.com

Along with tips on getting to Formentera, this site gives facts on the island's history and geography. For biology buffs, there's a photo-illustrated guide to plant and animal life. Sun worshipers can find a map to the best beaches, complete with a legend deciphering beach signs (a blank sign indicates a nude beach).

Ibiza Hotels. www.ibiza-hotels.com

As its name suggests, this site lists hotels in Ibiza and offers online reservation services. Additional perks: You can rent a car, buy a ferry ticket, check the weather report, use the currency converter, and see a virtual-reality panoramic view of the Ibiza harbor.

Ibiza Night. www.ibizanight.com

A hint of English-as-a-second-language, coupled with graphics that are equal parts artful and cheesy (a shopping cart on the moon?!), lend an exotic atmosphere to this site's descriptions of Ibiza's art scene, beaches, fashions, music venues, accommodations, restaurants, and other cultural offerings. For the practical traveler, Ibiza Night lists local public services and emergency phone numbers.

Madrid 3

Madrid was conceived, planned, and built when Spain was at the peak of its confidence and power, and the city became the solid and dignified seat of a great empire stretching around the world. Monumental Madrid glitters almost as much as Paris, Rome, or London—and parties more than any other city on the continent. Although it lacks the spectacular Romanesque and Gothic monuments of older Spanish cities, Madrid never fails to convey its own sense of grandeur.

Madrid has the highest altitude of any European capital, and its climate is blisteringly hot in summer but often quite cold in winter. Traffic roars down wide boulevards that stretch from the narrow streets of the city's 17th-century core to the ugly concrete suburbs that have spread in recent years.

Don't come to Madrid expecting a city that looks classically Iberian. True, many of the older buildings in the historic core look as Spanish as those you might encounter in rural towns across the plains of La Mancha. However, a great number of the monuments and palaces mirror the architecture of France—an oddity that reflects the link between the royal families of Spain and France.

Most striking is how the city has blossomed since Franco's demise. During the '80s Madrid was the epicenter of *la movida* (the movement), a resuscitation of the arts after years of dictatorial creative repression. Today, despite stiff competition from such smaller cities as Barcelona and Seville, Madrid still reigns as the country's artistic and creative centerpiece.

More world-class art is on view in the central neighborhood around the stellar Prado Museum than within virtually any concentrated area in the world. You can see Caravaggios and Rembrandts at the Thyssen-Bornemisza; El Grecos and Velázquezes at the Prado itself; and the Dalís and Mirós—not to mention Picasso's wrenching *Guernica*—at the Reina Sofía. Ironically, much of the city's art was collected by 18th-century Spanish monarchs whose artistic sense was frequently more astute than their political savvy.

Regrettably, within the city limits you'll also find sprawling expanses of concrete towers, sometimes paralyzing traffic, growing street crime, and entire districts that, as in every other metropolis, bear virtually no historic or cultural interest for a temporary visitor. Many long-time visitors to the city find that its quintessential Spanish feel has subsided somewhat in the face of a Brussels-like "Europeanization" that has occurred since Spain's 1986 induction into the European Union. The city's gems remain the opulence of the Palacio Real, the bustle of El Rastro's flea market, and the sultry fever of late-night flamenco. When urban commotion starts to overwhelm, seek respite in the Parque del Retiro, a vast, verdant oasis in the heart of the city just a stone's throw from the Prado.

If your time in Spain is limited, a stopover in Madrid coupled with day trips to its environs can provide a primer in virtually every major period and school of Spanish art and architecture dating from the Roman occupation. No fewer than nine world-class destinations are within 100 miles. They include Toledo, one of the most success-ful blends of medieval Arab, Jewish, and Christian cultures in the world; Segovia, site of a well-preserved ancient Roman aqueduct and monuments commemorating Queen Isabella's coronation in 1474; and Ávila, the most perfectly preserved medieval fortified city in Iberia, with its 11th-century battlements and endless references to Catholicism's most down-to-earth mystic, St. Teresa. El Escorial, El Pardo (Franco's favorite hangout), and the palace and monuments at Aranjuez, reveal the tastes and manias that inspired rulers of Spain throughout history. The neofascist monument at *El Valle de los Caídos* (the Valley of the Fallen) is a powerful testament to those who died in the Spanish Civil War. To see rural Iberia at its most charming, head for Chinchón or, better yet, the cliff-top village of Cuenca, where a lavish homage to modern art and music has recently been installed. For more information on these day trips, see chapter 4, "Side Trips from Madrid."

1 Orientation

ARRIVING

BY PLANE   Madrid's international airport, **Barajas,** lies 9 miles east of the center and has two terminals—one for international traffic, the other for domestic—connected by a moving sidewalk. For Barajas Airport information, call ☎ 91-305-83-43.

Air-conditioned yellow airport buses can take you from the arrival terminal to a bus depot beneath the central Plaza de Colón. You can get off at stops along the way, provided that your baggage isn't stored in the hold. The fare is 385 ptas. ($2.30); buses leave every 15 minutes, either to or from the airport.

By taxi, expect to pay 2,500 ptas. ($15) and up, plus surcharges, for the trip to the airport and for baggage handling. If you take an unmetered limousine, make sure you negotiate the price in advance.

A subway connecting Barajas Airport and central Madrid was completed in 1999, allowing additional ground transportation options. However, the ride involves a change: Take line 8 to Mar de Cristal and switch to line 4; the one-way trip costs 130 ptas. (80¢).

BY TRAIN   Madrid has three major railway stations: **Atocha** (Avenida Ciudad de Barcelona; metro: Atocha RENFE), for trains to Lisbon, Toledo, Andalusia, and Extremadura; **Chamartín** (in the northern suburbs at Augustín de Foxá; metro: Chamartín), for trains to and from Barcelona, Asturias, Cantabria, Castilla-León, the Basque country, Aragón, Catalonia, Levante (Valencia), Murcia, and the French fron-tier; and **Estación Príncipe Pío** or Norte (Paseo del Rey 30; metro: Norte), for trains to and from northwest Spain (Salamanca and Galicia). For information about connections from any of these stations, call RENFE (Spanish Railways) at ☎ 91-328-90-20, daily 7am to 11pm.

For tickets, go to the principal office of **RENFE,** Alcalá 44 (☎ 91-328-90-20; metro: Banco de España). The office is open Monday to Friday 9:30am to 8pm.

BY BUS   Madrid has at least eight major bus terminals, including the large **Estacíon Sur de Autobuses,** calle Méndez Alvaro (☎ **91-468-42-00;** metro: Méndez Alvaro). Most buses pass through this station.

BY CAR   All highways within Spain radiate outward from Madrid. The following are the major highways into Madrid, with information on driving distances to the city:

Highways to Madrid

Route	From	Distance to Madrid
N-I	Irún	315 miles (507km)
N-II	Barcelona	389 miles (626km)
N-III	Valencia	217 miles (349km)
N-IV	Cádiz	388 miles (625km)
N-V	Badajoz	254 miles (409km)
N-VI	Galicia	374 miles (602km)

VISITOR INFORMATION

The most convenient **tourist office** is near the American Express office, on Duque de Medinaceli 2, Banco de España (☎ 91-429-31-77; metro: Plaza de España); it's open Monday to Friday 9am to 7pm and Saturday 9:30am to 1pm. Ask for a street map of the next town on your itinerary, especially if you're driving. The staff here can give you a list of hotels and hostals but cannot recommend any particular lodging.

CITY LAYOUT

All roads lead to Madrid, which has outgrown its previous boundaries and is branching out in all directions.

MAIN ARTERIES & SQUARES   Every new arrival must find the **Gran Vía,** which cuts a winding pathway across the city beginning at the **Plaza de España,** where you'll find one of Europe's tallest skyscrapers, the Edificio España. This avenue is home to the largest concentration of shops, hotels, restaurants, and movie houses in the city, with **calle de Serrano** a close runner-up.

South of the Gran Vía lies the **Puerta del Sol,** the starting point for all road distances within Spain. However, its tourism significance has declined, and today it is a prime hunting ground for pickpockets and purse snatchers. **Calle de Alcalá** begins here at Sol and runs for 2½ miles.

The **Plaza Mayor** lies at the heart of Old Madrid and is an attraction in itself with its mix of French and Georgian architecture. (Again, be wary of thieves here, especially late at night.) Pedestrians pass under the arches of the huge square onto the narrow streets of the old town, where you can find some of the capital's most intriguing restaurants and *tascas,* serving tasty tapas and drinks. The colonnaded ground level of the plaza is filled with shops, many selling souvenir hats of turn-of-the-century Spanish sailors or army officers.

The area south of the Plaza Mayor—known as *barrios bajos*—is made up of narrow cobblestone streets lined with 16th- and 17th-century architecture. From the Plaza, take **Arco de Cuchilleros,** a street packed with markets, restaurants, flamenco clubs, and taverns, to explore this district.

Gran Vía ends at calle de Alcalá, and at this juncture lies the grand **Plaza de la Cibeles,** with its fountain to Cybele, "the mother of the gods," and the main post office (known as "the cathedral of post offices"). From Cibeles, the wide **Paseo de Recoletos** begins a short run north to Plaza de Colón. From this latter square rolls the

---

Finding an Address

Madrid is a city of both grand boulevards and of cramped meandering streets. Finding an address can sometimes be a problem, primarily because of the way buildings are numbered. On most streets, the numbering begins on one side and runs consecutively until the end, resuming on the other side and going in the opposite direction. Thus, number 50 could be opposite number 250. But there are many exceptions to this system. That's why it's important to know the cross street as well as the number of the address you're looking for. To complicate matters, some addresses don't have a number at all. What they have is the designation *s/n,* meaning *sin número* (without number). For example, the address of the *Panteón de Goya* (Goya's Tomb) is Glorieta de San Antonio de la Florida, s/n. Note that in Spain, as in many other European countries, the building number comes after the street name.

---

serpentine central artery of Madrid: **Paseo de la Castellana,** flanked by expensive shops, apartment buildings, luxury hotels, and foreign embassies.

Heading south from Cibeles is **Paseo del Prado,** where you'll find Spain's major attraction, the Museo del Prado, as well as the *Jardín Botánico* (Botanical Garden). The *paseo* leads to the Atocha Railway Station. To the west of the garden lies **Parque del Retiro,** a magnificent park once reserved for royalty, with restaurants, nightclubs, a rose garden, and two lakes.

STREET MAPS　Arm yourself with a good map before setting out. Falk publishes the best, and it's available at most newsstands and kiosks in Madrid. The free maps given away by tourist offices and hotels aren't really adequate for more than general orientation, as they don't list the maze of little streets that is Old Madrid.

Neighborhoods in Brief

Madrid can be divided into three principal districts—Old Madrid, which holds the most tourist interest; Ensanche, the new district, often with the best shops and hotels; and the periphery, which is of little interest to visitors.

Plaza Mayor/Puerta del Sol　This is the heart of Old Madrid, often called the tourist zone. Filled with taverns and bars, it is bounded by Carrera de San Jerónimo, calle Mayor, Cava de San Miguel, Cava Baja, and calle de la Cruz. From the Plaza Mayor, the Arco de Cuchilleros is filled with Castilian restaurants and taverns; more of these traditional spots, called *cuevas,* line the Cava de San Miguel, Cava Alta, and Cava Baja. To the west of this old district is the Manzanares River. Also in this area, Muslim Madrid is centered on the Palacio de Oriente and Las Vistillas. What is now the Plaza de la Paja was actually the heart of the city and its main marketplace during the medieval and Christian period. In 1617 the Plaza Mayor became the hub of Madrid, and it remains to this day the nighttime center of tourist activity, more so than the Puerta del Sol.

The Salamanca Quarter　Ever since Madrid's city walls came tumbling down in the 1860s, the district of Salamanca to the north has been the fashionable address. Calle de Serrano cuts through this neighborhood and is lined with stores and boutiques. Calle de Serrano is also home to the U.S. Embassy.

Gran Vía/Plaza de España　Gran Vía is the city's main street, lined with cinemas, department stores, and the headquarters of banks and corporations. It begins at the

Plaza de España, with its bronze figures of Don Quixote and his faithful squire, Sancho Panza.

Arquélles/Moncloa   The university area is bounded by Pintor Rosales, Cea Bermúdez, Bravo Murillo, San Bernardo, and Conde Duque. Students haunt its famous ale houses.

Chueca   This old, decaying area north of the Gran Vía includes the main streets of Hortaleza, Infantas, Barquillo, and San Lucas. It is the center of gay nightlife, with dozens of clubs and cheap restaurants. It can be dangerous at night, although police presence is usually notable.

Castellana/Recoletos/Paseo del Prado   Not a real city district, this is Madrid's north-south axis, its name changing along the way. The Museo del Prado and some of the city's more expensive hotels are found here. Many restaurants and other hotels are located along its side streets. In summer its large medians serve as home to open-air terraces filled with animated crowds. The most famous cafe is the Gran Café de Gijón (see "Where to Dine," later in this chapter).

2 Getting Around

Getting around Madrid is not easy, because everything is spread out. Even many Madrileño taxi drivers, often new arrivals themselves, are unfamiliar with their own city once they're off the main boulevards.

BY SUBWAY

The metro system is quite easy to learn and use. The fare is 145 ptas. (85¢) for a one-way trip, and the central converging point is the Puerta del Sol. The metro operates 6am to 1:30am, and you should try to avoid rush hours. For information, call ☎ 91-429-31-77. You can save money on public transportation by purchasing a 10-trip ticket known as a *bonos*—it costs 680 ptas. ($4.10).

BY BUS

A bus network also services the city and suburbs, with routes clearly shown at each stop on a schematic diagram. Buses are fast and efficient because they travel along special lanes. Both red and yellow buses charge 145 ptas. (85¢) per ride. For 680 ptas. ($4.10) you can purchase a 10-trip *bonos* ticket (but without transfers) for Madrid's bus system. It's sold at **Empresa Municipal de Transportes,** Alcantara, 24 (☎ 91-406-88-00), where you can buy a guide to the bus routes. The office is open daily 8am to 2pm.

BY TAXI

Cab fares are pretty reasonable. When you flag down a taxi, the meter should register 180 ptas. ($1.10); for every kilometer thereafter, the fare increases by 89 ptas. (55¢). A supplement is charged for trips to the railway station or the bullring, as well as on Sundays and holidays. The ride to Barajas Airport carries a 400 ptas. ($2.40) surcharge, and there is a 160 ptas. (95¢) supplement from railway stations. In addition, there is a 160 ptas. (95¢) supplement on Sundays and holidays, plus a 160 ptas. (95¢) supplement at night. It's customary to tip at least 10% of the fare.

Warning: Make sure the meter is turned on when you get into a taxi. Otherwise, some drivers assess the cost of the ride, and their assessment, you can be sure, will involve higher mathematics.

Madrid Metro

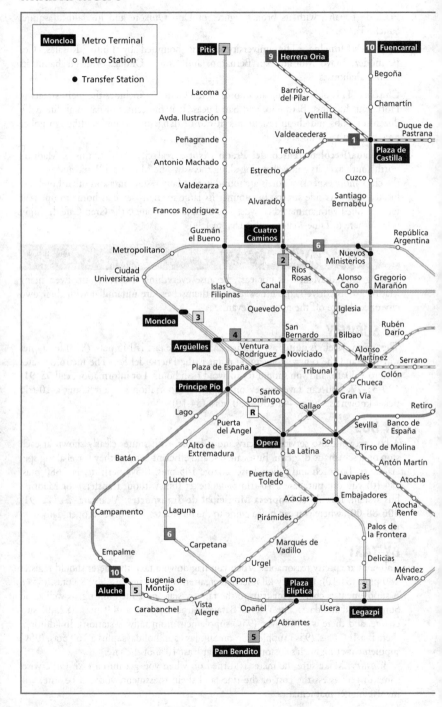

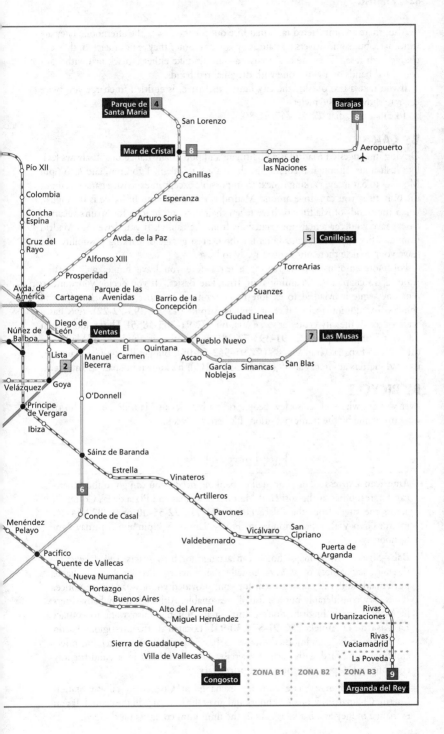

Parque de Santa María **4**
San Lorenzo
Barajas **8**
Aeropuerto ✈
Mar de Cristal **8**
Campo de las Naciones
Pío XII
Colombia
Canillas
Concha Espina
Esperanza
Cruz del Rayo
Arturo Soria
Avda. de la Paz
5 Canillejas
Alfonso XIII
Prosperidad
TorreArias
Avda. de América
Cartagena
Parque de las Avenidas
Barrio de la Concepción
Suanzes
Núñez de Balboa
Diego de León
Ciudad Lineal
Ventas
Pueblo Nuevo
7 Las Musas
Lista
El Carmen
Quintana
Manuel Becerra
Ascao
García Noblejas
Simancas
San Blas
2
Velázquez
Goya
O'Donnell
Príncipe de Vergara
Ibiza
Sáinz de Baranda
Estrella
Vinateros
6
Artilleros
Menéndez Pelayo
Conde de Casal
Pavones
Vicálvaro
San Cipriano
Pacífico
Valdebernardo
Puerta de Arganda
Puente de Vallecas
Nueva Numancia
Portazgo
Buenos Aires
Alto del Arenal
Miguel Hernández
Rivas Urbanizaciones
Sierra de Guadalupe
Rivas Vaciamadrid
Villa de Vallecas
La Poveda
1
Congosto
ZONA B1
ZONA B2
ZONA B3
9
Arganda del Rey

Also, there are unmetered taxis that hire out for the day or the afternoon. They are legitimate, but some drivers operate as gypsy cabs. Since they're not metered, they can charge high rates. They are easy to avoid—always take either a black taxi with horizontal red bands or a white one with diagonal red bands.

If you take a taxi outside the city limits, the driver is entitled to charge you twice the rate shown on the meter.

To call a taxi, dial ☎ **91-447-51-80.**

BY CAR

Driving in congested Madrid is a nightmare and potentially dangerous. It always feels like rush hour, although theoretically, these are 8 to 10am, 1 to 2pm, and 4 to 6pm Monday to Saturday. Parking is next to impossible except in expensive garages. About the only time you can drive around Madrid with a minimum of hassle is in August, when thousands of Madrileños have taken their cars and headed for Spain's vacation oases. Save your car rentals for excursions from the capital. If you drive into Madrid from another city, ask at your hotel for the nearest garage or parking possibility and leave your vehicle there until you're ready to leave.

For more information on renting a car before you leave home, see "Getting Around" in chapter 2, "Planning Your Trip: The Basics." If you decide you want to rent one while in Madrid to explore its environs or to move on, you have several choices. In addition to its office at Barajas Airport (☎ **91-393-72-22**), Avis has a main office in the city center at Gran Vía, 60 (☎ **91-305-4855**). Hertz, too, has an office at Barajas Airport (☎ **91-393-72-28**) and another in the heart of Madrid in the Edificio España, Gran Vía, 88 (☎ **91-542-58-05**). Budget Rent-a-Car maintains its headquarters at Gran Vía, 49 (☎ **91-393-7216**). It's known in Spain as **Interrent.**

BY BICYCLE

Ever wonder why you see so few people riding bicycles in Madrid? Those who tried were overcome by the traffic pollution. It's better to walk.

Fast Facts: Madrid

American Express   For your mail or banking needs, you can go to the American Express office at the corner of Marqués de Cubas and Plaza de las Cortés, 2, across the street from the Palace Hotel (☎ **91-322-55-00** or 91-322-54-24; metro: Gran Vía). Open Monday to Friday 9am to 5:30pm and Saturday 9am to noon.

Baby-Sitters   Most major hotels can arrange for baby-sitters, called *canguros* (literally, kangaroos) or *niñeras.* Usually the concierge keeps a list of reliable nursemaids and will contact them for you, provided you give adequate notice. Rates vary considerably but are usually reasonable. Although many baby-sitters in Madrid speak English, don't count on it. You may also want to contact **La Casa de la Abuela** (☎ **91-574-30-94**). Located in the prestigious Barrio Salamanca, this "grandmother's house" is basically a children's hotel and offers childcare combined with creative exercises and workshops in a child-friendly environment. Open year-round and prices vary.

Currency Exchange   The currency exchange at Chamartín railway station (metro: Chamartín) is open 24 hours and gives the best rates in the capital. If you exchange money at a bank, ask about the minimum commission charged.

Many banks in Spain still charge a 1% to 2% commission with a minimum charge of 500 ptas. ($3). However, branches of **Banco Central Hispano** charge no commission. Branches of **El Corte Inglés,** the department store chain, offer currency exchange facilities at various rates. You get the worst rates at street kiosks such as Chequepoint, Exact Change, and Cambios-Uno. Although they're handy and charge no commission, their rates are very low. Naturally, **American Express** offices offer the best rates on their own checks. ATMs are plentiful in Madrid.

Dentist   For an English-speaking dentist, contact the **U.S. Embassy,** Serrano, 75 (☎ **91-587-22-00**); it maintains a list of dentists who have offered their services to Americans abroad. For dental services, also consult **Unidad Médica Anglo-Americana,** Conde de Arandá, 1 (☎ **91-435-18-23**). Office hours are Monday to Friday 9am to 8pm and Saturday 10am to 1pm, and there is a 24-hour answering service.

Doctor   For an English-speaking doctor, contact the **U.S. Embassy,** Serrano, 75 (☎ **91-587-22-00**).

Drugstores   For a late-night pharmacy, dial ☎ **098** or look in the daily newspaper under *Farmacias de Guardia* to learn which drugstores are open after 8pm. Another way to find one is to go to any pharmacy, which even if closed always posts a list of nearby pharmacies that are open late that day. Madrid has hundreds of pharmacies, but one of the most central is **Farmacia Gayoso,** Arenal, 2 (☎ **91-521-28-60;** metro: Puerta del Sol). It is open Monday to Saturday 9:30am to 9:30pm.

Embassies/Consulates   See "Fast Facts: Spain" in chapter 2.

Emergencies   A centralized number for fire, police, or ambulance is ☎ **112.**

Hospitals/Clinics   **Unidad Médica Anglo-Americana,** Conde de Arandá, 1 (☎ **91-435-18-23;** metro: Usera), is not a hospital but a private outpatient clinic offering the services of various specialists. This is not an emergency clinic, although someone on the staff is always available. The daily hours are 9am to 8pm. For a real medical emergency, call ☎ **112** for an ambulance.

Internet Access   Head for **Net Café,** San Bernardo, 81 (☎ **91-595-0999;** e-mail: netcafe@netcafe.es), open daily 11am to 2am, if you've just gotta check your e-mail (800 pesetas per hour).

Newspapers & Magazines   The Paris-based *International Herald Tribune* is sold at most newsstands in the tourist districts, as is *USA Today,* plus the European editions of *Time* and *Newsweek. Guía del Ocio,* a small magazine sold in newsstands, has entertainment listings and addresses, but in Spanish only.

Police   Dial ☎ **112.**

Post Office   Madrid's central office is in the Palacio de Comunicaciones at Plaza de la Cibeles (☎ **91-396-20-00**).

Rest Rooms   Some public rest rooms are available, including those in the Parque del Retiro and on Plaza de Oriente across from the Palacio Real. Otherwise, you can always go into a bar or *tasca,* but you should always order something. All the major department stores, such as Galerías Preciados and El Corte Inglés, have good, clean rest rooms.

Safety   Because of an increasing crime rate in Madrid, the U.S. Embassy has warned visitors to leave valuables in a hotel safe or another secure place when

going out. Your passport may be needed, however, as the police often stop foreigners for identification checks. See "Safety" under "Fast Facts: Spain" in chapter 2 for more details about this requirement. The embassy advises against
carrying purses and suggests that you keep valuables in front pockets and carry
only enough cash for the day's needs. Be aware of those around you and keep a
separate record of your passport number, traveler's check numbers, and credit-
card numbers.

Purse snatching is common, and criminals often work in pairs, grabbing
purses from pedestrians, cyclists, and even cars. A popular scam involves one rob-
ber smearing the back of the victim's clothing, perhaps with mustard, ice cream,
or something worse. An accomplice then pretends to help clean up the mess, all
the while picking the victim's pockets.

Every car can be a target, parked or just stopped at a light, so don't leave anything in sight in your car. If a vehicle is standing still, a thief may open the door
or break a window to snatch a purse or package, even from under the seat. Place
valuables in the trunk when you park and always assume that someone is watching to see whether you're putting something away for safekeeping. Keep the car
locked while driving.

Taxes   There are no special city taxes for tourists, except for the value-added tax
(VAT; known as IVA in Spain) levied nationwide on all goods and services, ranging from 7% to 33%. In Madrid the only city taxes are for home and car owners,
which need not concern the casual visitor.

Telephone   To make calls in Madrid, follow the instructions in "Fast Facts:
Spain" in chapter 2. However, for long-distance calls, especially transatlantic
ones, it may be best to go to the main telephone exchange, **Locutorio Gran Vía,**
Gran Vía, 30, or **Locutorio Recoletos,** Paseo de Recoletos, 37–41. You may not
be lucky enough to find an English-speaking operator, but you can fill out a simple form that will facilitate the placement of a call.

Transit Information   For metro information, call ☎ **91-305-8656.**

3 Where to Stay

Although expensive, Madrid's hotels are among the finest in the world. More than
50,000 hotel rooms blanket the city—from *grand luxe* bedchambers fit for a prince to
bunker-style beds in the hundreds of neighborhood *hostales* and *pensiones* (low-cost
boarding houses). Three-quarters of our recommendations are modern, yet many
guests prefer the landmarks of yesteryear, including those grand old establishments,
the Ritz and the Palace (ca. 1910–12). *But beware:* Many older hotels in Madrid
haven't kept up with the times and a handful haven't added improvements or overhauled bedrooms substantially since the 1960s.

Traditionally, hotels are clustered around the Atocha Railway Station and the Gran
Vía. In our search for the most outstanding hotels, we've downplayed these two popular but noisy districts. The newer hotels have been built away from the center, especially on residential streets jutting off from Paseo de la Castellana. Bargain seekers,
however, will still find great pickings along the Gran Vía and in the Atocha district.

Note: In inexpensive hotels, be warned that you'll have to carry your bags to and
from your room. Don't expect bellboys or doormen in cheaper hotels.

PARKING   This is a serious problem, as so few hotels have garages; many buildings
turned into hotels were constructed before the invention of the automobile. Street
parking is rarely available, and even if it is, you run the risk of having your car broken

into. If you're driving into Madrid, most hotels (and most police) will allow you to park in front of the hotel long enough to unload your luggage. Someone on the staff can usually pinpoint the location of the nearest garage in the neighborhood, often giving you a map showing the way. Be prepared to walk a few blocks to your car. Parking charges given in most hotel listings are the prices these neighborhood garages charge for an average-size vehicle. Don't plan on renting a car for your time in Madrid. If you're moving on to explore the countryside, just pick up your rental when you're ready to set out.

NEAR THE PLAZA DE LAS CORTÉS
VERY EXPENSIVE

✪ **Hotel Villa Real.** Plaza de las Cortés, 10, 28014 Madrid. ☎ **91-420-37-67.** Fax 91-420-25-47. www.derbyhotels.es. E-mail: info@derbyhotels.es. 115 units. A/C MINIBAR TV TEL. 48,000 ptas. ($288) double; from 75,000 ptas. ($450) suite. AE, DC, MC, V. Parking 1,600 ptas. ($9.60). Metro: Sevilla, Banco de España.

Until 1989, the Villa Real was little more than a run-down 19th-century apartment house across a three-sided park from the Spanish parliament (*Congreso de los Diputados*) between Puerta del Sol and Paseo del Prado. Since then, developers have poured billions of pesetas into renovations to produce this stylish hotel patronized by the cognoscenti of Spain. The facade combines an odd mix of neoclassical and Aztec motifs and is guarded by footmen and doormen. Rooms at the Villa Real are more consistent in quality than those offered by its neighbor, the Palace (see below), but lack the latter's mellow charm and patina. The interior contains a scattering of modern paintings amid neoclassical detailing.

Each of the accommodations offers a TV with video movies and satellite reception, a safe for valuables, soundproofing, a sunken salon with leather-upholstered furniture, and built-in furniture accented with burl-wood inlays. Although rooms aren't imaginative, they're mostly large, with separate sitting areas and big, bright, well-equipped bathrooms with hair dryers.

Dining/Diversions: The social center of the hotel is its high-ceilinged bar. The hotel's formal restaurant, Europa, serves both lunch and dinner, with Spanish and international cuisine.

Amenities: 24-hour room service, laundry/valet, baby-sitting, express checkout, sauna, foreign currency exchange, business center.

The Palace. Plaza de las Cortés, 7, 28014 Madrid. ☎ **800/325-3535** in the U.S., 800/325-3589 in Canada, or 91-360-80-00. Fax 91-360-81-00. www.palacemadrid.com. 460 units. A/C MINIBAR TV TEL. 56,000–79,000 ptas. ($336–$474) double; from 100,000 ptas. ($600) suite. AE, DC, MC, V. Parking 2,500 ptas. ($15). Metro: Banco de España.

The Palace is an ornate Victorian wedding cake known as the "grand *dueña*" of Spanish hotels. It had an auspicious beginning, inaugurated personally by King Alfonso XIII in 1912, and covers an entire city block in the historical and artistic area. It faces the Prado and Neptune Fountain and lies within walking distance of the main shopping center and best antiques shops. Some of the city's most intriguing *tascas* and restaurants are a short stroll away.

A Note on Making Hotel Reservations

The telephone area code for Madrid is 91 if you're calling from within Spain. If you're calling from the United States, dial 011, the country code (34), Madrid's city code (91), and then the local number.

Accommodations in Central Madrid

Anaco **24**
Aristos **13**
Casón del Tormes **6**
Castellana Inter-Continental Hotel **13**
Conde Duque **9**
Crowne Plaza Madrid City Centre **7**
Cuzco **13**
Emperatriz **13**
Eurobuilding **13**
Gran Hotel Colón **15**
Gran Hotel Reina Victoria **33**
Grand Hotel Velazquez **14**
Green Hotel El Prado **32**
Hostal Cervantes **27**
Hostal La Macarena **2**
Hostal La Perla Asturiana **19**
Hostal Nuevo Gaos **23**
Hostal Residencia Americano **20**
Hostal Residencia Don Diego **14**
Hotel Chamartín **13**
Hotel Claridge **16**
Hotel Escultor **11**
Hotel Francisco I **3**
Hotel Husa Princesa **9**
Hotel Inglés **30**
Hotel Mercátor **17**
Hotel Opera **4**
Hotel Orense **10**
Hotel Paris **21**
Hotel Puerta de Toledo **1**
Hotel Residencia Cortezo **18**
Hotel Residencia Lisboa **29**
Hotel Santo Domingo **5**
Hotel Villa Magna, a Park Hyatt **13**
Hotel Villa Real **28**
Meliá Castilla **13**
Meliá Madrid Princesa **8**
Miguel Angel **12**
NH National **26**
The Palace **31**
Residencia Liabeny **22**
The Ritz **25**
Santo Mauro **11**
Tirol **9**
Tryp Ambassador **4**
Wellington **14**

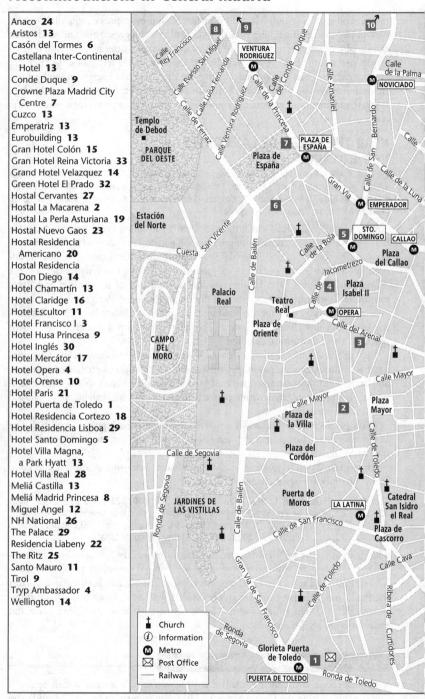

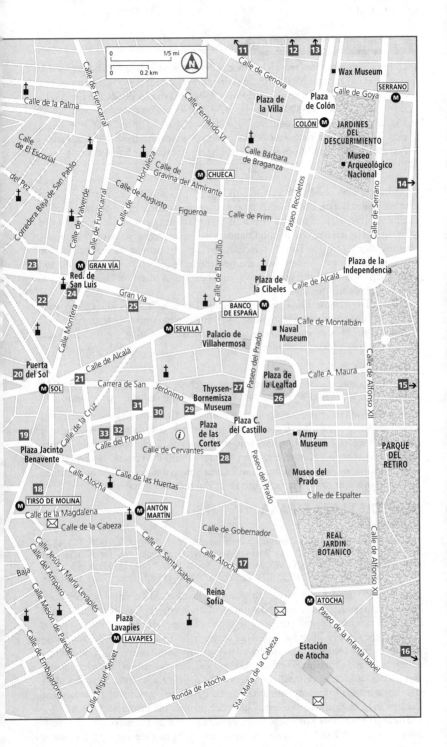

If You Have an Early Flight

Unless absolutely necessary, it's worth making the journey into Madrid rather than staying at rather bleak Barajas, where the airport is located. If you find that you have to stay here, the least expensive option is the **Best Western Villa de Barajas,** av. De Logroño, 331 (☎ **91-329-2818;** fax 91-329-2704), where double rooms go for 15,000 ptas. ($90). Each room has TV and telephone, and offers 24-hour room service. There is also a restaurant offering traditional Spanish food. The hotel runs a free shuttle bus to and from the airport. The trip takes about 5 minutes.

Architecturally, the Palace captures the grand pre–World War I style, with an emphasis on space and comfort. Although it doesn't achieve the snob appeal of its nearby siblings, the Ritz and the Villa Real, it's one of the largest hotels in Madrid and offers first-class service. The air-conditioned hotel has conservative, traditional rooms, boasting plenty of space, large bathrooms, and lots of amenities such as hair dryers. Accommodations vary widely, with the best rooms found on the fourth, fifth, and sixth floors. Rooms on the side are noisy and lack views. Many rooms appear not to have been renovated for some time.

Dining/Diversions: The elegant La Cupola serves Italian specialties along with Spanish cuisine highlights. Piano music and other entertainment are featured.

Amenities: 24-hour room service, laundry/valet, baby-sitting, express checkout, foreign currency exchange, business center.

INEXPENSIVE

Hostal Cervantes. Cervantes, 34, 28014 Madrid. ☎ **91-429-27-45.** Fax 91-429-83-65. 12 units. TV. 6,500 ptas. ($39) double. MC, V. Metro: Banco de España.

One of Madrid's most pleasant family-run hotels, the Cervantes has been appreciated by our readers for years. You'll take a tiny birdcage-style elevator to the immaculately maintained second floor of this stone-and-brick building. Each room contains a comfortable bed, spartan furniture, and a tiny bathroom with shower stall. No breakfast is served, but the owners, the Alfonsos, will direct you to a nearby cafe. The establishment is convenient to the Prado, Retiro Park, and the older sections of Madrid.

NEAR THE PLAZA ESPAÑA
EXPENSIVE

Crowne Plaza Madrid City Centre. Plaza de España, 28013 Madrid. ☎ **800/465-4329** in the U.S., or 91-454-85-00. Fax 91-548-23-89. www.crowneplaza.es. E-mail: reservas@crowneplaza.es. 306 units. A/C MINIBAR TV TEL. From 39,167 ptas. ($235) double; from 53,410 ptas. ($320) suite. AE, DC, MC, V. Parking 1,600 ptas. ($9.60). Metro: Plaza de España.

Built in 1953 atop a city garage, the Crowne Plaza could be called the Waldorf-Astoria of Spain. A massive rose-and-white structure soaring upward to a central tower 26 stories high, it's one of the tallest skyscrapers in Europe. Once one of the best hotels in Spain, the Crowne Plaza has long since ceased to be a market leader. Its accommodations include conventional doubles as well as luxurious suites, each containing a sitting room and abundant amenities, such as a safe, luxury mattress, bedside controls, and trouser press, even in some cases alcoves for sitting. Each room, regardless of its size, has a marble bathroom with a hair dryer. Furniture is usually of a standardized modern style, in harmonized colors. The upper floor rooms are quieter.

Dining/Diversions: Los Lagos is the breakfast room of the hotel, and the main restaurant, Mirador de la Plaza de España, offers a tempting regional Spanish cuisine nightly. The Plaza cocktail bar is a major gathering point for business people.

Amenities: Room service, laundry, money exchange, medical service, hairdresser, shopping arcade, gym, whirlpool, sauna.

MODERATE

Casón del Tormes. Calle del Río, 7, 28013 Madrid. ☎ **91-541-97-46.** Fax 91-541-18-52. 63 units. A/C TV TEL. 15,000 ptas. ($90) double; 18,000 ptas. ($108) triple. MC, V. Parking 1,600 ptas. ($9.60). Metro: Plaza de España.

This attractive three-star hotel is around the corner from the Royal Palace and Plaza de España. Behind a four-story red-brick facade with stone-trimmed windows, it overlooks a quiet one-way street. A long, narrow lobby contains a marble floor and a bar opening into a separate room. Guest rooms are generally roomy and comfortable with color-coordinated fabrics and dark wood, including mahogany headboards. Bathrooms are very small but with adequate shelf space and stall showers. Motorists appreciate the public parking lot near the hotel. Laundry service is provided.

✪ Hotel Santo Domingo. Plaza Santo Domingo, 13, 28013 Madrid. ☎ **91-547-9800.** Fax 91-547-5995. 120 units. A/C MINIBAR TV TEL. Mon–Thurs 28,000 ptas. ($168) double; Fri–Sun 21,000 ptas. ($126) double. Breakfast free Sat–Mon mornings; otherwise, 1,450 ptas. ($8.70) extra. AE, DC, MC, V. Parking 2,500 ptas. ($15). Metro: Santo Domingo.

This stylish, carefully decorated hotel rises from a position adjacent to the Gran Vía, a 2-minute walk from the Plaza de España. It was inaugurated in 1994, after an older building was gutted and reconfigured into the comfortable modern structure you'll see today. Rooms are decorated individually, each in a style a wee bit different from that of its neighbor, in pastel-derived shades. Some contain gold damask wall coverings, faux tortoiseshell desks, and striped satin bedspreads. Bathrooms are generally spacious and outfitted with ceramics and marble slabs. The best units are the fifth-floor doubles, especially those with furnished balconies and views over the tile roofs of Old Madrid. Each is soundproofed to guard against noise from the street and from its neighbors and contains personal answering machines. There's a bar and a restaurant in the hotel's lobby serving lunch and dinner every day.

ON OR NEAR THE GRAN VÍA
EXPENSIVE

Hotel Gaudí. Gran Vía, 9, 28013 Madrid. ☎ **91-531-2222.** Fax 91-531-5469. www.hoteles-catalonia.es. E-mail: catalon@hoteles-catalonia.es. 88 units. A/C MINIBAR TV TEL. 26,900 ptas. ($161.40) double; 40,000 ptas. ($240) suite. AE, DC, MC, V. Metro: Gran Vía.

In a turn-of-the-century building in the heart of Madrid, this hotel is located in a beautifully restored landmark Modernist building. It was constructed in 1898 by Emilio Salas y Cortes, one of the teachers of the great Barcelona architect Gaudí, and was overhauled in 1998. Some of the most important attractions of Madrid are within an easy walk, including the Prado, the Thyssen Museum, and the Plaza Mayor with its rustic taverns. The bedrooms come in a number of sizes, but each is comfortably furnished and beautifully maintained with hair dryers and safes.

Dining: The hotel restaurant serves Spanish and international food, and there's a separate snack bar.

Amenities: Fitness center, whirlpool, sauna.

MODERATE

Residencia Liabeny. Salud, 3, 28013 Madrid. ☎ **91-531-90-00.** Fax 91-532-74-21. 222 units. A/C MINIBAR TV TEL. 16,000 ptas. ($96) double; 18,000–23,000 ptas. ($108–$138) triple. AE, MC, V. Parking 1,500 ptas. ($9). Metro: Puerta del Sol or Gran Vía.

The Liabeny, behind an austere stone facade, is in a prime location midway between the Gran Vía and Puerta del Sol. It has seven floors of comfortable, contemporary rooms, which are newly redecorated but a bit pristine. They are of a good size and functionally furnished with comfortable beds and neatly organized bathrooms, mainly with shower stalls. The cocktail bar is warming, although in a rather macho style, and the dining room is strictly for convenience. Added pluses include personal attention from the staff, a coffee shop, and good laundry service.

INEXPENSIVE

Anaco. Tres Cruces, 3, 28013 Madrid. ☎ **91-522-46-04.** Fax 91-531-64-84. 39 units. A/C TV TEL. 10,000–12,500 ptas. ($60–$75) double; 14,000–17,000 ptas. ($84–$102) triple. AE, DC, MC, V. Parking 1,500 ptas. ($9). Metro: Gran Vía, Callao, or Puerta del Sol.

Modest yet modern, the Anaco is just off the Gran Vía but opens onto a tree-shaded plaza. It's for those who want a clean resting place for a good price, and don't expect much more. The rooms are compact and contemporary, with built-in headboards, reading lamps, and lounge chairs. Each has a comfortable bed with a firm mattress, plus a compact tiled bathroom with a shower stall. *A useful tip:* Ask for one of the five terraced rooms on the top floor, which rent at no extra charge. The hotel has a bar/cafeteria/restaurant open daily, and English is spoken here. Nearby is a municipally operated garage.

Green Hotel El Prado. Calle Prado, 11, 28014 Madrid. ☎ **91-369-0234.** Fax 91-429-2829. E-mail: prado@green-hoteles.com. 45 units. 16,200–21,750 ptas. ($102.05–$137.05) double. AE, MC, V. Metro: Plaza Santa Ana.

You might get the feeling this hotel is both overbooked and understaffed. But it has comfortable rooms, relatively reasonable rates, and a well-scrubbed interior less than a decade old. You'll register in a somewhat claustrophobic lobby, then head upstairs to a room that's cozy and sleekly outfitted with contemporary-looking, full-grained walls and partitions. Other than breakfast, no meals are served.

Hostal Nuevo Gaos. Calle Mesonero Romanos, 14, 28013 Madrid. ☎ **91-532-71-07.** 23 units. A/C TV TEL. 7,500–8,500 ptas. ($45–$51) double. AE, DC, MC, V. Parking 1,500 ptas. ($9). Metro: Callao or Gran Vía.

On three floors of a 1930s building just off the Gran Vía, this residencia offers the chance to enjoy simple comfort at bargain prices. Rooms are humble and small with plain, livable furnishings and a firm mattress. Bathrooms are adequate, with stall showers. The place lies directly north of Puerta del Sol, across the street from the popular flamenco club Torre Bermejas. Breakfast can be taken at a nearby cafe.

NEAR THE PUERTA DEL SOL
EXPENSIVE

Gran Hotel Reina Victoria. Plaza Santa Ana, 14, 28012 Madrid. ☎ **91-531-45-00.** Fax 91-522-03-07. www.trypet.com. 201 units. A/C MINIBAR TV TEL. 28,000 ptas. ($168) double; from 65,000 ptas. ($390) suite. AE, DC, MC, V. Metro: Tirso de Molina or Puerta del Sol.

This hotel is as legendary as the famous bullfighter Manolete who used to stay here, giving lavish parties and attracting mobs in the square below. Since the recent renovation and upgrading of this property by Spain's Tryp Hotel Group, it's less staid and more impressive than ever.

Built in 1923, the hotel sits behind an ornate stone facade, which the Spanish government protects as a historic monument. Although it's located in a congested and noisy neighborhood in the center of town, the Reina Victoria opens onto its own sloping plaza, usually filled with flower vendors, older people reclining in the sun, and young people resting between bouts at the dozens of neighborhood tapas bars.

The soundproof accommodations are midsize and fairly standard, with private safes and quality mattresses, plus tidily organized bathrooms with hair dryers and marble vanities.

Dining/Diversions: Guests enjoy the hotel's stylish and popular lobby bar, the Manuel Gonzalez Manolete, filled with lavishly displayed bullfighting memorabilia. The in-house restaurant is El Ruedo.

Amenities: 24-hour room service, concierge, baby-sitting. Because of the hotel's position in one of Madrid's most interesting neighborhoods, almost anything is available within a few minutes' walk.

Tryp Ambassador. Cuesta Santo Domingo, 5 and 7, 28013 Madrid. ☎ **91-541-6700.** Fax 91-559-1040. E-mail: ambassador@trypnet.com. 182 units. A/C MINIBAR TV TEL. 28,000 ptas. ($168) double; from 38,000 ptas. ($228) suite. AE, DC, MC, V. Metro: Opera or Santo Domingo.

In the early 1990s the Tryp hotel chain renovated and enlarged this late 19th-century palace of the dukes of Granada. The result is a lavishly restored, four-story historic hotel with grand public areas that's interconnected via a sunny lobby to a six-story annex containing about 60% of the establishment's rooms. Regardless of location within the premises, all rooms are conservatively modern, and outfitted in white and salmon accented with mahogany. Most are large and soundproofed and come with private safes and twin beds fitted with luxury mattresses. Bathrooms are outfitted in marble with hair dryers, robes, and deluxe toiletries.

Dining/Diversions: The restaurant on the premises, El Madroño, includes a greenhouse-style bar lavishly filled with plants and caged exotic birds.

Amenities: Room service, dry cleaning/laundry, concierge, baby-sitting.

MODERATE

✪ **Hotel Opera.** Cuesta de Santo Domingo, 2, 28013 Madrid. ☎ **91-541-2800.** Fax 91-541-6923. E-mail: hotelopera@phoenix.net. 79 units. A/C TV TEL. 15,000 ptas. ($90) double. AE, DC, MC, V. Parking 2,000 ptas. ($12). Metro: Opera.

Don't judge this little discovery by its dreary facade or its narrow windows; it livens up considerably once you enter. Set close to the royal palace and the opera house, this hotel isn't regal but offers first-rate comfort and a warm welcome from its English-speaking staff. Guest rooms range from medium to surprisingly spacious, each with first-rate furnishings, including twin or double beds. Bathrooms are excellent, clad in marble with dual basins. The hotel's lovely El Café de la Opera is a popular rendezvous point, even if you're not a guest. It's adorned with fabric-covered walls and horse-y art. The Opera remains one of Madrid's relatively undiscovered boutique hotels.

INEXPENSIVE

Hostal la Macarena. Cava de San Miguel, 8, 28005 Madrid. ☎ **91-365-92-21.** Fax 91-364-27-57. 25 units. TEL. 8,000 ptas. ($48) double; 10,000 ptas. ($60) triple; 13,000 ptas. ($78) quad. MC, V. Metro: Puerta del Sol, Opera, or La Latina.

Known for its reasonable prices and praised by readers for its warm hospitality, this unpretentious hostal is run by the Ricardo González family. A 19th-century facade with belle époque patterns stands in ornate contrast to the chiseled simplicity of the ancient buildings facing it. The location is one of the hostal's assets: it's on a street (a noisy one) immediately behind Plaza Mayor near one of the best clusters of *tascas* in Madrid. Rooms range from small to medium and are all well kept, with modest furnishings and comfortable beds. Windows facing the street have double panes. Bathrooms are tiny and contain stall showers.

Hostal la Perla Asturiana. Plaza de Santa Cruz, 3, 28012 Madrid. ☎ **91-366-46-00.** Fax 91-366-46-08. www.perlaasturiana.com. E-mail: perlaasturiana@mundivia.es. 33 units. TV TEL. 5,800 ptas. ($34.80) double; 7,800 ptas. ($46.80) triple. MC, V. Metro: Puerta del Sol.

Ideal for those who want to stay in the heart of old Madrid (1 block off Plaza Mayor and 2 blocks from Puerta del Sol), this small family-run place has courteous staff at the desk 24 hours a day for security and convenience. You can socialize in the small, comfortable lobby adjacent to the reception area but stay here for the cheap prices and location, not grand comfort. Each of the small rooms comes with a comfortable bed plus a simple and adequate bathroom with a stall shower. Many inexpensive restaurants and tapas bars are nearby. No breakfast is served.

Hostal Residencia Americano. Puerta del Sol, 11, 28013 Madrid. ☎ **91-522-28-22.** Fax 91-522-11-92. 44 units. TV TEL. 6,500 ptas. ($39) double; 8,500 ptas. ($51) triple; 9,500 ptas. ($57) quad. AE, MC, V. Metro: Puerta del Sol.

Americano, on the third floor of a five-floor building, is suitable for those who want to be in the thick of Puerta del Sol. Most of the guest rooms are outside chambers with balconies facing the street and all have been refurbished. Although the rooms are small, especially when three or four guests are crowded in, the beds are good. Bathrooms are bleak, clean cubicles with showers. No breakfast is served.

Hotel Francisco I. Arenal, 15, 28013 Madrid. ☎ **91-548-43-14.** Fax 91-542-28-99. 58 units. TV TEL. 12,000 ptas. ($72) double. Rates include breakfast. AE, DC, MC, V. Metro: Puerta del Sol or Opera.

The Francisco offers clean, modern rooms. It has a pleasant lounge and bar, and, on the sixth floor, you'll find a comfortable, rustically decorated restaurant. Considerably modernized in 1993, the hotel added new bathrooms as well as air-conditioning in most of the rooms, which range from small to medium. All the bathrooms are small but the beds are comfortable with frequently renewed mattresses. The hotel provides limited room service as well as laundry and valet service.

Hotel Inglés. Calle Echegaray, 8, 28014 Madrid. ☎ **91-429-65-51.** Fax 91-420-24-23. 58 units. TV TEL. 13,000 ptas. ($78) double; 16,000 ptas. ($96) suite. AE, DC, MC, V. Parking 1,300 ptas. ($7.80). Metro: Puerta del Sol or Sevilla.

You'll find this little hotel (where Virginia Woolf used to stay) on a central street lined with *tascas*. Behind the red-brick facade is a modern, impersonal hotel with contemporary, well-maintained rooms. The lobby is air-conditioned, but guest rooms are not; guests who open their windows at night are likely to hear noise from the enclosed courtyard, so light sleepers beware. Rooms come in a variety of shapes, most of them small, and some in the back are quite dark. Twin and double beds have fine mattresses and linens. Tiled bathrooms are cramped but tidily maintained, with shower stalls. The hotel operates its own 24-hour cafeteria as well as a TV lounge with comfortable armchairs.

Hotel Paris. Alcalá, 2, 28014 Madrid. ☎ **91-521-6496.** Fax 91-531-0188. 121 units. A/C TV TEL. 13,000 ptas. ($78) double. Rates include breakfast. AE, DC, MC, V. Metro: Puerta del Sol.

Originally built in grandiose style in the 1870s when it was undoubtedly more chic than it is today, this hotel occupies a prime location adjacent to the hysterical traffic of the Puerta del Sol. It contains five floors of simple but clean and comfortable rooms, each with parquet floors, white walls, and views that extend either over the surrounding neighborhood or over a quiet courtyard. Rooms are generally small but with comfortable good beds. Bathrooms are also small with shower stalls. Something about the dark-paneled lobby might remind you of the old-fashioned, hot, and somnolent Spain of long ago. There's a high-ceilinged dining room one floor above lobby level, serving wholesome, uncomplicated meals every day at lunch and dinner. This hotel is a good bargain if your tastes aren't too demanding, if you're not a budding decorator, or if you just want a central location.

Hotel Residencia Lisboa. Ventura de la Vega, 17, 28014 Madrid. ☎ **91-429-98-94.** Fax 91-429-46-76. 27 units. A/C TV TEL. 7,500 ptas. ($45) double. AE, DC, MC, V. Parking 2,200 ptas. ($13.20). Metro: Puerta del Sol.

Our only complaint about the Lisboa, on Madrid's most famous restaurant street, is that it can be a bit noisy. The hotel is a neat, modernized townhouse with compact rooms and a staff that speaks five languages. Most of the rooms, on four floors of this old building, are small but a few are comfortably larger. Most come equipped with a double bed, some with twins; all are fitted with firm mattresses. Bathrooms are small, mainly with shower stalls. The Lisboa does not serve breakfast, but budget dining rooms, cafes, and *tascas* surround the neighborhood.

NEAR ATOCHA STATION
EXPENSIVE

NH Nacional. Paseo del Prado, 48, 28014 Madrid. ☎ **91-429-6629.** Fax 91-369-1564. E-mail: nhnacional@nh-hoteles.es. 214 units. A/C MINIBAR TV TEL. 24,100 ptas. ($151.85) double; 55,000 ptas. ($346.50) suite. AE, DC, MC, V. Metro: Atocha.

This stately hotel was built around 1900 to house the hundreds of passengers flooding into Madrid through the nearby Atocha railway station. In 1997 a well-respected nationwide chain, NH Hotels, ripped out much of the building's dowdy interior, reconstructing the public areas and bedrooms into a smooth, seamless decor that takes maximum advantage of the building's tall ceilings and large spaces. In the bedrooms the belle époque trappings of another day have been replaced with modern designer decor, even avant-garde art, giving the units a welcoming ambience. Today it's a destination for dozens of corporate conventions. On site are a restaurant and a simple bistro-style coffee shop, along with a staff well versed in dealing with the demands of international clients.

INEXPENSIVE

Hotel Mercátor. Calle Atocha, 123, 28012 Madrid. ☎ **91-429-05-00.** Fax 91-369-12-52. 89 units. MINIBAR TV TEL. 13,500 ptas. ($81) double; 14,500 ptas. ($87) suite. AE, DC, MC, V. Parking 1,740 ptas. ($10.45). Metro: Atocha or Antón Martín.

Only a 3-minute walk from the Prado, Centro de Arte Reina Sofía, and the Thyssen-Bornemisza Museum, the Mercátor is orderly, well run, and clean, with enough comforts to please the weary traveler. Its public rooms are simple, outfitted in modern minimalism. Some of the guest rooms are more inviting than others, especially those with desks and armchairs. Twenty-one units are air-conditioned. Beds have firm mattresses and fine linen. Bathrooms are usually cramped although they are equipped with good showerheads. The Mercátor is a *residencía*—that is, it offers breakfast only and does not have a formal restaurant for lunch and dinner; however, it has a bar and cafeteria serving light meals, such as *platos combinados* (combination plates). The hotel has a garage and is within walking distance of American Express. Laundry service is provided, plus room service 7am to 10pm.

Hotel Residencía Cortezo. Doctor Cortezo, 3, 28012 Madrid. ☎ **91-369-01-01.** Fax 91-369-37-74. 90 units. A/C MINIBAR TV TEL. 15,000 ptas. ($90) double; 18,000 ptas. ($108) suite. AE, DC, MC, V. Parking 2,000 ptas. ($12). Metro: Tirso de Molina.

Just off calle de Atocha, which leads to the railroad station of the same name, the Cortezo is a short walk from Plaza Mayor and Puerta del Sol. The accommodations are comfortable but simply furnished, with contemporary bathrooms. Beds are springy and the furniture is pleasantly modern; many rooms have sitting areas with a desk and armchair. The public rooms match the guest rooms in freshness. The hotel was built in 1959 and last renovated in 1997.

NEAR RETIRO/SALAMANCA
VERY EXPENSIVE

✪ **Park Hyatt Villa Magna.** Paseo de la Castellana, 22, 28046 Madrid. ☎ **800/ 223-1234** in North America, or 91-587-12-34. Fax 91-431-22-86. www.madrid.hyatt.com. E-mail: hotel@villamagna.es. 182 units. A/C MINIBAR TV TEL. 65,000 ptas. ($390) double; from 95,000 ptas. ($570) suite. AE, DC, MC, V. Parking 3,000 ptas. ($18). Metro: Rubén Darío.

One of the finest hotels in Europe, the nine-story Park Hyatt is faced with slabs of rose-colored granite set behind a bank of pines and laurels on the city's most fashionable boulevard. It's an even finer choice than the Palace or Villa Real and is matched in luxury, ambience, and service only by the Ritz, which has a greater patina since it's much older. Separated from the busy boulevard by a parklike garden, the hotel has contemporary lines. In contrast, its interior recaptures the style of Carlos IV, with paneled walls, marble floors, and bouquets of fresh flowers. Almost every film star shooting on location in Spain stays here. This luxury palace has plush but dignified rooms decorated in Louis XVI, English Regency, or Italian provincial style. Each comes with a TV with video movies and satellite reception (including news broadcasts from the United States).

Dining/Diversions: A pianist provides entertainment in the lobby-level champagne bar. In his restaurant, LeDivellec, French chef Jacques le Divellec serves international food in a glamorous setting with a summer terrace overlooking the garden. For the more exotic flavors of Chinese cuisine, there is the Tse Yang Restaurant.

Amenities: 24-hour room service, concierge, same-day laundry and dry cleaning, limousine service, baby-sitting, business center, car rentals, barber and beauty shop, the boutique "VillaMagna," availability of both tennis and golf (15 and 25 minutes from the hotel, respectively).

✪ **The Ritz.** Plaza de la Lealtad, 5, 28014 Madrid. ☎ **800/225-5843** in the U.S. and Canada, or 91-701-67-67. Fax 91-701-67-67. www.ritz.es. E-mail: reservas@ritz.es. 158 units. A/C MINIBAR TV TEL. 60,000–85,000 ptas. ($360–$510) double; from 150,000 ptas. ($900) suite. AE, DC, MC, V. Parking 4,000 ptas. ($24). Metro: Banco de España.

The Ritz is the most legendary hotel in Spain. With soaring ceilings and graceful columns, it offers all the luxury and pampering you'd expect of a grand hotel. Although the building has been thoroughly modernized, great effort was expended to retain its belle époque character and architectural details.

No other Madrid hotel, except the Palace, has a more varied history. One of *Les Grand Hôtels Européens,* the Ritz was built in 1908 by King Alfonso XIII with the aid of César Ritz. It looks out onto the circular Plaza de la Lealtad in the center of town, near 300-acre Retiro Park, facing the Prado, the Palacio de Villahermosa, and the Stock Exchange. The Ritz was constructed when costs were relatively low and when spaciousness and luxury were the standard. Its facade has even been designated a historic monument. The glory days of 1910 live on in the rooms with their spacious closets, luxury mattresses, antique furnishings, and hand-woven carpets. Bathrooms are spacious, with robes, dual basins, deluxe toiletries, and hair dryers. The hotel requests that male guests wear a jacket and tie after 11am in the public areas. Nonetheless, casual wear, even blue jeans, is seen at the hotel, but such guests are conspicuous by their lack of what the Spanish call *gracia.*

Dining: The hotel maintains a formal dining room, called Restaurante Goya, lined with mirrors and 16th-century Flemish tapestries. The international menu features the most elaborate paella in Madrid. In time-honored Spanish tradition, guests tend to dress up here, sometimes even for breakfast. (Management stresses that this is not a resort hotel.) Guests looking for a more casual eatery usually head for the Jardín Ritz.

Amenities: 24-hour room service with everything from good nutty Jabugo ham to fresh hake, laundry/valet, express checkout, fitness center, car-rental kiosk, business center, foreign currency exchange.

EXPENSIVE

Emperatriz. López de Hoyos, 4, 28006 Madrid. ☎ **91-563-80-88.** Fax 91-563-98-04. 158 units. A/C MINIBAR TV TEL. 26,500 ptas. ($159) double; 65,000 ptas. ($390) suite. AE, DC, MC, V. Metro: Rubén Darío.

This hotel lies just off the wide Paseo de la Castellana. Built in the 1970s, it has been recently renovated in a combination of Laura Ashley and Spanish contemporary by Madrid's trendiest firm, Casa & Jardin. Rooms are comfortable and classically styled in cheery yellows and salmons, and come with TVs that get many different European channels. Ask for a room on the seventh floor, where you get a private terrace at no extra charge.

Dining/Diversions: Guests gather in the cozy lobby bar before planning their assault on Madrid for the evening. Standard Spanish and international cuisine is served in the hotel's restaurant, followed by a substantial breakfast buffet in the morning. There is a moderately priced fixed-price lunch.

Amenities: Beauty salon, barbershop, laundry/valet service, concierge, room service.

Wellington. Velázquez, 8, 28001 Madrid. ☎ **91-575-44-00.** Fax 91-576-4164. www. hotel-wellington.com. E-mail: wellin@genio.infor.es. 288 units. A/C MINIBAR TV TEL. 38,000 ptas. ($228) double; from 52,000 ptas. ($312) suite. AE, DC, MC, V. Parking 2,750 ptas. ($16.50). Metro: Retiro or Velázquez.

The Wellington, with its somber antique-tapestried entrance, is one of Madrid's more sedate deluxe hotels, built in the mid-1950s but substantially remodeled since. Set within the Salamanca residential area near Retiro Park, the Wellington offers redecorated but staid guest rooms, each with cable TV and movie channels, music, two phones (one in the bathroom), and a combination safe. Units are furnished in English-inspired mahogany reproductions, and the bathrooms are modern and immaculate, with marble sheathing and fixtures. Doubles with private terraces (at no extra charge) are the most sought-after accommodations.

Dining/Diversions: An added bonus here is the El Fogón grill room, styled like a 19th-century tavern, where many of the provisions for the typically Spanish dishes are shipped in from the hotel's own ranch. The pub-style Bar Inglés is a hospitable rendezvous. Lighter meals are served in the Las Llaves de Oro (Golden Keys) cafeteria.

Amenities: 24-hour room service, same-day dry cleaning and laundry, outdoor swimming pool in summer, garage, beauty parlor.

MODERATE

Gran Hotel Colón. Pez Volador, 11, 28007 Madrid. ☎ **91-573-59-00.** Fax 91-573-08-09. 359 units. A/C MINIBAR TV TEL. 19,800–23,800 ptas. ($119 –$143) double. AE, DC, MC, V. Parking 2,000 ptas. ($12). Metro: Sainz de Baranda.

East of Retiro Park, Gran Hotel Colón is just a few minutes from the city center by subway. Built in 1966, it offers comfortable yet reasonably priced accommodations in a modern setting. More than half of the accommodations have private balconies, and all contain traditional furniture, much of it built-in. Rooms vary in size but most offer

---

ⓘ   Family-Friendly Hotels

Meliá Castilla *(see p. 100)*   Children can spend hours and all their extra energy in the hotel's swimming pool and gymnasium. On the grounds is a showroom exhibiting the latest European automobiles. Hotel services include baby-sitting, providing fun for kids and parents too.

Crowne Plaza Madrid City Centre *(see p. 88)*   Safe and reliable, and located at the very heart of Madrid, this 26-story hotel offers roomy accommodations and good beds and attracts a large family trade to its precincts. It's got location, reasonable prices, and all the services, including laundry, that most family travelers need.

The Tirol *(see p. 102)*   This centrally located three-star hotel is a favorite of families seeking good comfort at moderate price. It has a cafeteria.

---

roomy comfort, with firm mattresses, dark wood beds, and adequate closet space. Bathrooms are small, with stall showers, but with suitable shelf space. Other perks include two dining rooms, a covered garage, and bingo games. One of the Colón's founders was an interior designer, which accounts for the unusual stained-glass windows and murals in the public rooms and the paintings by Spanish artists in the lounge.

Gran Hotel Velázquez. Calle de Velázquez, 62, 28001 Madrid. ☎ **91-575-28-00.** Fax 91-577-5131. 146 units. A/C MINIBAR TV TEL. 21,970 ptas. ($131.80) double; from 32,000 ptas. ($192) suite. AE, DC, MC, V. Parking 2,200 ptas. ($13.20). Metro: Velázquez.

This is one of the most attractive medium-size hotels in Madrid, with plenty of comfort and convenience. Opened in 1947 on an affluent residential street near the center of town, it has a 1930s-style art deco facade and a 1940s interior filled with well-upholstered furniture and richly grained paneling. Several public rooms, including a bar, lead off a central oval area. As in many hotels of its era, the rooms vary, some large enough for entertaining, with a small separate sitting area for reading or watching TV. All contain piped-in music, walk-in closets, and private safes. Bathrooms are decorated in marble or tiles, with either stall showers or tubs. The in-house restaurant, Roceo, features both international and Spanish cuisine. There's also room service (8am to midnight), a beauty salon, dry cleaning, and laundry service.

INEXPENSIVE

Hotel Claridge. Plaza Conde de Casal, 6, 28007 Madrid. ☎ **91-551-94-00.** Fax 91-501-03-85. 150 units. A/C TV TEL. Mon–Thurs 12,800 ptas. ($76.80), Fri–Sun 10,000 ptas. ($60) double; Mon–Thurs 20,000 ptas. ($120), Fri–Sun 18,000 ptas. ($108) suite. AE, MC, V. Metro: Conde de Casal.

This contemporary building, last renovated in 1994, is beyond Retiro Park, about 5 minutes from the Prado by taxi or subway. The rooms are well organized and pleasantly styled: small and compact, with coordinated furnishings. They include excellent beds and small well-organized bathrooms. You can take your meals in the hotel's cafeteria and relax in the modern lounge.

SOUTH OF THE PLAZA MAYOR
INEXPENSIVE

Hotel Puerta de Toledo. Glorieta Puerta de Toledo, 4, 28005 Madrid. ☎ **91-474-7100.** Fax 91-474-0747. E-mail: hpto@hotel-puertodetoledo.es. 160 units. A/C MINIBAR TV TEL. 12,600–13,960 ptas. ($79.40–$87.95) double. AE, DC, MC, V. Metro: Puerta de Toledo.

One of the largest buildings on its square, this red-brick hotel was constructed in 1968 in a contemporary design that doesn't detract from the monument it faces. Public areas are outfitted with stone floors, angular and low-slung *moderno* furniture, and an unfrilly decor that might remind you of the waiting lounge in a large international airport. Bedrooms are small, but with big windows—most of them overlooking the square—and comfortable contemporary furniture. Overall, this hotel's low prices more than compensate for its rather banal look. On the premises only breakfast is served, but the staff will direct you to a nearby restaurant, about a block away, that's under separate management.

CHAMBERÍ
VERY EXPENSIVE

Castellana Inter-Continental Hotel. Paseo de la Castellana, 49, 28046 Madrid. ☎ **800/ 327-0200** in the U.S., or 91-310-02-00. Fax 91-319-58-53. 306 units. A/C MINIBAR TV TEL. 48,000–62,000 ptas. ($288–$372) double; from 76,500 ptas. ($459) suite. AE, DC, MC, V. Parking 2,600 ptas. ($15.60). Metro: Rubén Darío.

Solid, spacious, and conservatively modern, this is one of Madrid's most reliable hotels. Originally built in 1963, the Castellana Inter-Continental lies behind a barrier of trees in a neighborhood of apartment houses and luxury hotels. Its high-ceilinged public rooms are gorgeous, with terrazzo floors and giant abstract murals pieced together from multicolored stones and tiles. Most of the accommodations have private balconies and traditional furniture, each with a color TV with in-house videos and channels from across Europe. Most rooms have generous living space with safes and very large beds, often king size. Bathrooms are tiled and well equipped with robes, phones, and hair dryers.

Dining/Diversions: The La Ronda Bar offers drinks near the elegant Los Continentes Restaurant, serving a creative Mediterranean cuisine. In addition, El Jardín is a retreat in summer, with candlelit dinners and live soft background music. Another restaurant, El Sarracin, provides good food at thrifty prices.

Amenities: There's a helpful concierge and a travel agent who will book theater tickets, rental cars, and airline connections; there's also 24-hour room service, laundry, baby-sitting, kiosks and boutiques, hairdresser/barbershop, business center, top floor gym with sauna and outdoor solarium.

✪ **Santo Mauro Hotel.** Calle Zurbano, 36, 28010 Madrid. ☎ **91-319-6900.** Fax 91-308-5477. E-mail: santo-mauro@itelco.es. 37 units. A/C MINIBAR TV TEL. 46,000 ptas. ($276) double; from 60,000 ptas. ($360) suite. AE, DC, MC, V. Parking 1,950 ptas. ($11.70). Metro: Rubén Darío or Alonso Martínez.

This hotel opened in 1991 in what was once a neoclassical villa built in 1894 for the duke of Santo Mauro. Set within a garden and done in a French style, it's decorated with rich fabrics and deco art and furnishings. Staff members outnumber rooms by two to one. Each of the rooms contains an audio system with a wide choice of tapes and CDs as well as many lovely details, like raw silk curtains, Persian carpets, antique prints, and parquet floors. Rooms are large and come in combinations ranging from studios to duplex suites.

Dining/Diversions: An elegant bar is located off the main lobby, and tables are set up beneath the garden's large trees for drinks and snacks.

Amenities: 24-hour room service, laundry/valet, reception staff trained in the procurement of practically anything, indoor swimming pool, health club with sauna and massage.

EXPENSIVE

Conde Duque. Plaza Conde Valle de Súchil, 5, 28015 Madrid. ☎ **91-447-70-00.** Fax 91-448-35-69. www.hotelcondeduque.es. E-mail: condeduque@hotelcondeduque.es. 143 units. A/C MINIBAR TV TEL. 28,000 ptas. ($168) double; from 34,000 ptas. ($204) suite. AE, DC, MC, V. Parking 1,800 ptas. ($10.80). Metro: San Bernardo.

The modern four-star Conde Duque, near a branch of El Corte Inglés department store, opens onto a tree-filled plaza in a residential neighborhood near the Glorieta Quevado. The hotel is 12 blocks north of the Plaza de España, off calle de San Bernardo, which starts at the Gran Vía. Furnishings include modern headboards and reproductions of 19th-century English pieces, plus bedside lights. Rooms contain a lot of thoughtful extras, including private safes, quality mattresses, fax facilities, a tea/coffeemaker, and a digital fire warning system. Bathrooms contain scales, phones, hair dryers, hydromassage showers (suites only), and magnifying mirrors.

Dining: The hotel operates a tearoom and cafeteria, plus a full-service restaurant serving regional and international dishes.

Amenities: Concierge, laundry/dry cleaning, baby-sitting.

Miguel Angel. Miguel Angel, 29–31, 28010 Madrid. ☎ **91-442-81-99.** Fax 91-442-53-20. 270 units. A/C MINIBAR TV TEL. 30,000–40,000 ptas. ($180–$240) double; from 50,000 ptas. ($300) suite. AE, DC, MC, V. Parking 2,500 ptas. ($15). Metro: Gregorio Maranon.

Just off Paseo de la Castellana, the sleek, modern Miguel Angel opened its doors in 1975 and has been renovated periodically ever since. It has a lot going for it: ideal location, contemporary styling, good furnishings, an efficient staff, and plenty of comfort. There's an expansive sun terrace on several levels, with clusters of garden furniture surrounded by paintings of semitropical scenes. The soundproof rooms are done in color-coordinated fabrics and carpets, and in many cases reproductions of classic Iberian furniture, each with a superbly comfortable bed.

Dining/Diversions: The Farnesio bar is decorated in a Spanish Victorian style, with piano music beginning at 8pm. A well-managed restaurant on the premises is the Florencia. Dinner is served until around 3am in the Zacarías Boîte restaurant, where you can dine while watching an occasional cabaret or musical performance.

Amenities: 24-hour room service, same-day laundry/valet, indoor heated swimming pool, saunas, hairdressers, drugstore. Art exhibitions are sponsored in the arcade of boutiques.

MODERATE

Hotel Escultor. Miguel Angel, 3, 28010 Madrid. ☎ **91-310-42-03.** Fax 91-319-25-84. 61 units. A/C MINIBAR TV TEL. From 15,000 ptas. ($90) double; from 23,000 ptas. ($138) suite. AE, DC, MC, V. Parking 2,300 ptas. ($13.80) nearby. Metro: Rubén Darío.

This comfortably furnished hotel built in 1975 provides fewer services and facilities than others within its category, but it compensates with larger rooms, each with its own charm. Fully air-conditioned, the hotel has a knowledgeable staff, a small bar open nightly, and a traditional restaurant, the Señorio de Erazu, which closes on Saturday at lunchtime and all day on Sunday. Room service is offered at breakfast only, 7 to 10:30am.

Hotel Orense. Pedro Teixeira, 5, 28020 Madrid. ☎ **91-597-1568.** Fax 91-597-1295. E-mail: comercial@hotelorense.com. 130 units. A/C MINIBAR TV TEL. Mon–Thurs 20,750–23,250 ptas. ($130.75–$146.50) double; Fri–Sun 12,500 ptas. ($78.75) double. AE, DC, MC, V. Metro: Santiago Bernabeu.

At first glance, you might mistake this silver-and-glass tower for one of many upscale condominium complexes surrounding it on all sides. Stylish and streamlined, with a design inaugurated in the late 1980s and renovated in 1996, it offers reproduction Oriental carpets and conservatively contemporary furniture that's comfortable, tasteful, and upscale. Accommodations are appropriate for a stay of up to several weeks, equipped along the lines of a private apartment. (In fact, management rents some of them to international corporations for long-term lodging and office space.) On the premises are a bar and a restaurant, the Orense, that's open daily for lunch and dinner.

INEXPENSIVE

Hostal Residencia Don Diego. Calle de Velázquez, 45, 28001 Madrid. ☎ **91-435-07-60.** Fax 91-431-42-63. 58 units. A/C TV TEL. 11,235 ptas. ($67.40) double; 14,000 ptas. ($84) triple. MC, V. Metro: Velázquez.

On the fifth floor of an elevator building, Don Diego is in a combination residential/commercial neighborhood that's relatively convenient to many of the city monuments. The vestibule contains an elegant winding staircase with iron griffin heads supporting its balustrade. The hotel is warm and inviting, filled with leather couches and comfortably angular but attractive furniture. Rooms are a bit small but comfortable for the price, with excellent beds. Bathrooms are cramped but adequate, with shower stalls. The staff is very service oriented and keeps the place humming along efficiently. A bar stands at the far end of the main sitting room. The hotel's cafeteria serves breakfast 7:45 to 11am. From 7 to 11pm daily, you can order drinks and snacks, especially sandwiches and omelets. Laundry service is provided, and room service is available daily 8am to midnight.

CHAMARTÍN
EXPENSIVE

The Cuzco. Paseo de la Castellana, 133, 28046 Madrid. ☎ **91-556-06-00.** Fax 91-556-03-72. 328 units. A/C MINIBAR TV TEL. 26,000 ptas. ($156) double; from 33,000 ptas. ($198) suite. AE, DC, MC, V. Parking 2,100 ptas. ($12.60). Metro: Cuzco.

Popular with businesspeople and tour groups, the Cuzco lies in a commercial neighborhood of big buildings, government ministries, and the main Congress Hall. The Chamartín railway station is only a 10-minute walk north, so this is a popular and convenient place to stay. The 15-floor structure, set back from Madrid's longest boulevard, has been redecorated and modernized many times since it was completed in 1967. The rooms are spacious, with separate sitting areas, video movies, modern furnishings, and good beds; bathrooms have hair dryers.

Dining/Diversions: There is a bilevel snack bar and cafeteria. The lounge is a forest of marble pillars and leather armchairs, its ambience enhanced by contemporary oil paintings and tapestries.

Amenities: Beauty parlor, sauna, massage, health club.

Eurobuilding. Calle Padre Damián, 23, 28036 Madrid. ☎ **91-345-45-00.** Fax 91-345-45-76. 520 units. A/C MINIBAR TV TEL. 32,000 ptas. ($192) double; from 36,000 ptas. ($216) suite. AE, DC, MC, V. Parking 2,500 ptas. ($15). Metro: Cuzco.

Even while the Eurobuilding was on the drawing boards, the rumor was that this five-star sensation of white marble would provide "a new concept in deluxe hotels." It is actually two hotels linked by a courtyard, away from the city center but right in the midst of apartment houses, boutiques, nightclubs, first-class restaurants, and the modern Madrid business world.

The more glamorous of the twin buildings is the main one, named Las Estancias de Eurobuilding; which contains only suites, all recently renovated in pastel shades. Ornately carved gold-and-white beds, large terraces for breakfast and cocktail entertaining—all are tastefully coordinated. Across the courtyard the neighbor Eurobuilding contains less-impressive, but still very comfortable, double rooms, many with views from private balconies of the formal garden and swimming pool below. All the accommodations have TVs with video movies and satellite reception, security doors, and safes.

Dining: Le Relais Coffee Shop is suitable for a quick bite, and Le Relais Restaurant offers buffets at both breakfast and lunch. For more formal dining, La Taberna at both lunch and dinner features a selection of Spanish and international cuisine, specializing in seafood and paella dishes.

Amenities: Laundry/valet, concierge, 24-hour room service, baby-sitting, health club with sauna, outdoor swimming pool.

Meliá Castilla. Calle Capitán Haya, 43, 28020 Madrid. ☎ **800/336-3542** in the U.S., or 91-567-50-00. Fax 91-567-5051. www.solmelia.com. E-mail: melia-castilla@solmelia.com. 915 units. A/C MINIBAR TV TEL. 31,500 ptas. ($189) double; from 59,500 ptas. ($357) suite. AE, MC, V. Parking 2,950 ptas. ($17.70). Metro: Cuzco.

This mammoth hotel is one of the largest in Europe. Loaded with facilities and built primarily to accommodate conventions, Meliá Castilla also caters to the needs of the individual traveler. Everything is larger than life here: You need a floor plan to negotiate the place. The lounges and pristine marble corridors are vast—there is even a landscaped garden as well as a showroom full of the latest-model cars. Each good-size room comes with excellent twin beds and contemporary furniture. Note that some lower rooms are quite noisy. Meliá Castilla is in the north of Madrid, about a block west of Paseo de la Castellana, and a short drive from the Chamartín railway station.

Dining/Diversions: The hotel has a coffee shop, a seafood restaurant, a restaurant specializing in paella and other rice dishes, cocktail lounges, and the Trinidad nightclub. In addition, there's the restaurant/show Scala Meliá Castilla.

Amenities: 24-hour room service, hairdresser/barbershop, concierge, baby-sitting, laundry/valet, swimming pool, shopping arcade with souvenir shops and bookstore, saunas, gymnasium, parking garage.

MODERATE

The Aristos. Avenida Pío XII, 34, 28016 Madrid. ☎ **91-345-04-50.** Fax 91-345-10-23. 24 units. A/C TV TEL. 21,000–23,000 ptas. ($126–$138) double. AE, DC, MC, V. Parking 1,500 ptas. ($9). Metro: Pío XII.

This three-star hotel is in an up-and-coming residential area of Madrid not far from the Eurobuilding (see above). Its main advantage is a garden where you can lounge, have a drink, or order a complete meal. The hotel's restaurant, Aristos Bar, offers breakfast, snacks, and informal meals, including local specialties, in a pleasant, relaxed atmosphere. Each of the medium-sized rooms has a small terrace and modern furniture.

Hotel Chamartín. Estacíon de Chamartín, 28036 Madrid. ☎ **91-323-30-87** or 91-334-49-00. Fax 91-733-02-14. www.husa.es. E-mail: chamartin@husa.es. 396 units. A/C MINIBAR TV TEL. 29,000 ptas. ($174) double; from 44,000 ptas. ($264) suite. AE, DC, MC, V. Metro: Chamartín. Bus: 5.

This brick-sided hotel soars nine stories above the northern periphery of Madrid. It's part of the massive modern shopping complex attached to the Chamartín railway station, although once you're inside your soundproofed room, the noise of the railway station will seem far away. The owner of the building is RENFE, Spain's government railway system, but the nationwide chain that administers it is HUSA Hotels. The hotel lies 15 minutes by taxi from both the airport and the historic core of Madrid and sits atop one of the capital's busiest metro stops. The well-appointed rooms are good size, with private safes, quality mattresses, and cushiony furnishings, along with orderly bathrooms with stall showers and hair dryers. Especially oriented to the business traveler, Chamartín offers a currency exchange kiosk, a travel agency, a car-rental office, and a lobby video screen that posts the arrival and departure of all of Chamartín's trains.

Dining/Diversions: A coffee bar serves breakfast daily, and room service is available 7am to midnight. The hotel restaurant, Cota 13, serves international cuisine. A short walk from the hotel lobby, within the railway-station complex, are a handful of shops and movie theaters, a roller-skating rink, a disco, and ample parking.

ARGÜELLES/MONCLOA
VERY EXPENSIVE

Hotel Husa Princesa. Princesa, 40, 28008 Madrid. ☎ **91-423-500.** Fax 91-423-501. www.husa.es. E-mail: husaprincesa@husa.es. 275 units. A/C MINIBAR TV TEL. 36,300 ptas. ($228.70) double; 71,900–83,200 ptas. ($452.95–$524) suite. AE, DC, MC, V. Metro: Argüelles.

This 14-story member of a nationwide chain (HUSA) was originally built around 1973 and renovated frequently several times since then. Set in the heart of monumental Madrid, with a design that focuses on a soaring public area, lots of sunlight, and contemporary furnishings, it's favored by conventioneers, business travelers, groups, and lots of individual travelers, many of them European. Bedrooms are tastefully outfitted in cool colors—a welcome antidote for the Madrileño heat—and soft fabrics. Each has a separate writing table, a stone-trimmed bathroom, and all the conveniences you'd expect in a large-scale big-city hotel.

Dining/Diversions: There's both a full-fledged restaurant (El Rincón de Argüelles) and a buffet-style cafeteria (Triángulo Coffee Shop) that remains open 24 hours a day. The Royal Bar features a live pianist. La Terraza Garden Bar, surrounded by greenery and flowering shrubs, is open only May to October.

Amenities: Concierge, fitness center with indoor pool, 24-hour room service, steam bath, massage and beauty facilities, squash courts, saunas.

Meliá Madrid Princesa. Princesa, 27, 28008 Madrid. ☎ **800/336-3542** in the U.S., or 91-541-82-00. Fax 91-541-19-05. www.solmelia.com. E-mail: melia.madrid@solmelia.es. 265 units. A/C MINIBAR TV TEL. 38,000 ptas. ($228) double; from 39,900–67,000 ptas. ($239.40–$402) suite. AE, DC, ER, MC, V. Metro: Rodríguez.

Here you'll find one of the most modern yet uniquely Spanish hotels in the country. Its 23 floors of wide picture windows have taken a permanent position in the capital's skyline. Each of the bedrooms is comfortable, spacious, and filled with contemporary furnishings, including excellent beds, plus a TV with video movies and many channels from across Europe. Most offer views over the skyline of Madrid. The chalk-white walls dramatize the flamboyant use of color; the bathrooms are sheathed in marble and come with hair dryers.

Dining/Diversions: Restaurante Princesa is elegant and restful; equally popular is Don Pepe Grill. The cuisine in both restaurants is international and includes an array of Japanese and Indian dishes. There are three bars and a coffee shop.

Amenities: 24-hour room service, concierge, baby-sitting, hairdresser/barber, laundry, gallery with souvenir shops and bookstores, health club with sauna and massage.

MODERATE

The Tirol. Marqués de Urquijo, 4, 28008 Madrid. ☎ **91-548-19-00.** Fax 91-541-39-58. www.hotel-tirol.com. 95 units. A/C TV TEL. 13,800 ptas. ($82.80) double. Rates include buffet breakfast. MC, V. Metro: Argüelles. Bus: 2 or 21.

A short walk from Plaza de España and the swank Meliá Madrid Princesa hotel (see above), the Tirol is a good choice for clean, unpretentious comfort. Furnishings in this three-star hotel are simple and comfortable. Eight of the guest rooms have private terraces. A cafeteria and a parking garage are within the hotel.

4 Where to Dine

Madrid boasts the most varied cuisine and the widest choice of dining opportunities in Spain. At the fancy tourist restaurants, prices are just as expensive as in New York, London, or Paris, but there are lots of affordable taverns and family restaurants as well.

It's the custom in Madrid to consume the big meal of the day from 2 to 4pm. After a recuperative siesta, Madrileños then enjoy tapas, and indeed, no culinary experience would be complete without a tour of the city's many tapas bars (see "An Early Evening *Tapeo*," below, and "Our Favorite *Tascas*," later in this chapter). All this nibbling is followed by light supper in a restaurant, usually from 9:30pm to as late as midnight. Many restaurants, however, start serving dinner at 8pm to accommodate visitors from other countries who don't like to dine so late.

Many of Spain's greatest chefs have opened restaurants in Madrid, energizing the city's culinary scene. Gone are the days when mainly Madrileño food was featured, which meant Castilian specialties such as *cocido* (a chickpea-and-sausage stew) or roast suckling pig or lamb. Now you can take a culinary tour of the country while remaining in Madrid—from Andalusia with its gazpacho and braised bulls' tails to Asturias with its *fabada* (a rich pork stew) and *sidra* (cider) to the Basque country, which has the most sophisticated cuisine in Spain. There is also a host of Galician and Mediterranean restaurants in Madrid. Amazingly, although Madrid is a landlocked city surrounded by a vast arid plain, you can order some of the freshest seafood in the country here.

Follow the local custom and don't overtip. Theoretically, service is included in the price of the meal, but it's customary to leave an additional 10%.

One way to save money is to order the *menú del día* (menu of the day) or *cubierto* (fixed price)—both are fixed-price menus based on what is fresh at the market that day. They are the dining bargains in Madrid, although often lacking the quality of more expensive à la carte dining. Usually each includes a first course, such as fish soup or hors d'oeuvres, followed by a main dish, plus bread, dessert, and the wine of the house. You won't have a large choice. The *menú turístico* is a similar fixed-price menu, but for many it's too large, especially at lunch. Only those with large appetites will find it to be the best bargain.

In most cases service can seem perfunctory by U.S. standards. Waiters are matter-of-fact, do not fawn over you, nor do they return to the table to ask how things are. This can seem off-putting at first, but if you observe closely you'll see that Spanish waiters typically handle more tables than American waiters and that they generally work quickly and efficiently.

NEAR THE PLAZA DE LAS CORTÉS
MODERATE

El Espejo. Paseo de Recoletos, 31. ☎ **91-308-23-47.** Reservations required. *Menú del día* 3,000 ptas. ($18). AE, MC, V. Daily 1–4pm and 9pm–midnight. Metro: Colón. Bus: 27. INTERNATIONAL.

Here you'll find good food and one of the most perfectly crafted art nouveau decors in Madrid. If the weather is good, you can sit at one of the outdoor tables and be served by uniformed waiters who carry food across the busy street to a green area flanked with trees and strolling pedestrians. We prefer a table inside, within view of the tile maidens with vines and flowers entwined in their hair. Upon entering, you'll find yourself in a charming cafe/bar, where many visitors linger before heading toward the spacious dining room. Dishes include grouper ragout with clams, steak tartare, guinea fowl with Armagnac, and lean duck meat with pineapple. Try profiteroles with cream and chocolate sauce for dessert.

Errota-Zar. Jovellanos, 3, 1st floor. ☎ **91-531-2464.** Reservations recommended. Main courses 2,800–3,000 ptas. ($16.80–$18); *menu completo* 5,000 ptas. ($30). AE, DC, MC, V. Mon–Sat 1–4pm and 9pm–midnight. Closed Aug 15–30. Metro: Banco España and Sevilla. BASQUE.

Next to the House of Deputies and the Zarzuela Theater, Errota-Zar means "old mill," a nostalgic reference to the Basque country, home of the Olano family, owners of the restaurant.

A small bar at the entrance displays a collection of fine cigars and wines, and the blue-painted walls are adorned with paintings of Basque landscapes. The restaurant has only about two dozen tables, which can easily fill up. The Basque country is long known as the gastronomic capital of Spain, and Errota-Zar provides a fine showcase for this kitchen cuisine.

The deliciously prepared food is an array of sun-kissed bounty from the fields and rivers of Spain. Try such appetizers as the rare tolosa kidney bean or fried anchovies. Many Basques begin their meal with a *tortilla de bacalao* or salt cod omelet. For main dishes, sample the delights of *chuleton de buey* or oxtail, along with grilled vegetables, or *kokotxas de merluza en aceite,* the latter the cheeks of the hake fish cooked in the finest virgin olive oil. Hake cheeks may not sound appetizing, but Spaniards and many foreigners praise this dish. You might opt instead for *foie al Pedro Jimenez* or duck liver grilled and served with a sweet wine sauce. The best homemade desserts are *cuajada de la casa,* a thick yogurt made from sheep's milk, or *tarta de limon,* a lemon cake. You might also try, as an oddity, rice ice cream in prune sauce.

NEAR PLAZA DE LA CIBELES
MODERATE

✪ **Bocaito.** Calle Libertad, 4–6 (2 blocks north of *Las Cibeles*). ☎ **91-532-1219.** Reservations recommended. Main courses 2,000–2,800 ptas. ($12–$16.80). MC, V. Mon–Fri 1–4pm and 8:30pm–midnight; Sat 8:30pm–midnight. Closed last 2 weeks Aug. Metro: Banco de España. SPANISH/TAPAS.

Inside this 150-year-old house, four original columns of wood encircle the high ceiling, and bullfighting posters adorn the white-tile walls. Behind a bar shaped into two horseshoes, the staff cooks and prepares some of the most appreciated tapas in Madrid. The selection of tapas ranges from simple delights such as *ajos tiernos en aceite* (tender garlic in olive oil), cured Serrano ham, *gambas fritas* (fried shrimp), and green asparagus in scrambled eggs to some very sophisticated delicacies, such as *bacalao con caviar* (salt cod pâté with caviar). The famous *mejimecha* (mussels marinated with ham and onions in béchamel sauce) is sublime, as are the anchovies of the house and tasty croquettes. The prices for the tapas range from 900 to 1,200 ptas. ($5.40 to $7.20). Don Miguel Benavente, the chef and owner for more than 3 decades, recommends the *plato combinado* (a combination platter of all tapas), which, together with a glass of their very palatable Rioja house wine, is available at a cost of 1,500 ptas. ($9). A selection of the culinary treats on offer includes the *plato de cuchara* (daily specials), lentils

Dining in Central Madrid

Alkalde **27**
Amparo **27**
Arce **31**
Bocaito **33**
Bola **7**
Cabo Mayor **10**
Café Balear **16**
Cairpen **8**
Casa Alberto **41**
Casa Lucio **1**
Casa Mingo **9**
Casa Vallejo **12**
Cenador del Prado **42**
Cervecería Alemania **39**
Cervecería Santa Bárbara **15**
Chata **1**
Ciao Madrid **14**
Cosaco **2**
Errota-Zar **45**
Espejo **28**
Esquina del Real **5**
Foster's Hollywood **25**
Fuencisla **11**
Gamella **48**
Goizeko Kabi **20**
Gran Café de Gijón **29**
Horcher **48**
Jockey **17**
Lhardy **43**
Mad Madrid **35**
Mentidero de la Villa **30**
Museo de Jamon **38**
Nabucco **13**
O'Pazo **10**
Olivo Restaurant **20**
Paellería Valenciana **36**
Paloma **24**
Pedro Larumbe **26**
Pescador **22**
Posasa de la Villa **3**
Principe de Viana **20**
Restaurante Salvador **34**
Ríofrio **18**
San Carlo **46**
Schotis **1**
Sobrino de Botin **4**
Suntory **19**
Taberna Carmencita **32**
Taberna del Alabardero **6**
Taberna Toscana **44**
Teatriz **23**
Terraza **37**
Tocororo **40**
Trainera **21**
Viridiana **47**
Zalacaín **16**

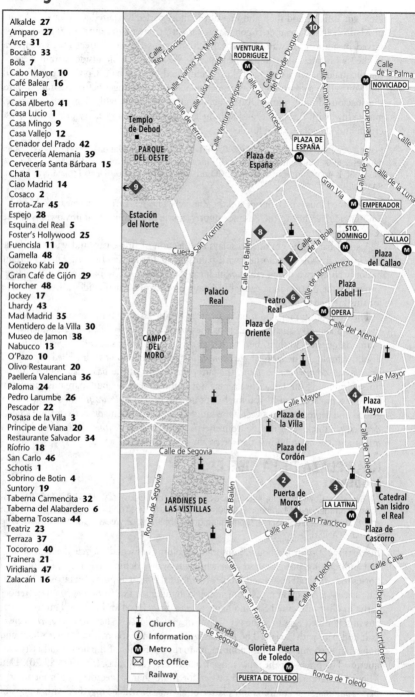

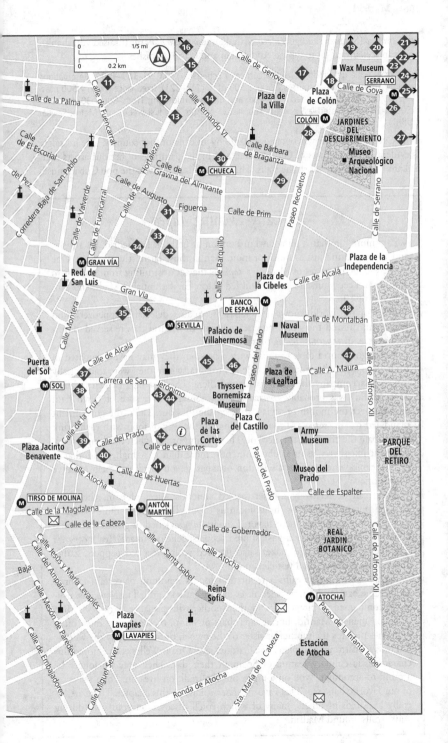

with *chorizo* (Spanish sausage), *merluza* (hake), *osso bucco al horno* (braised veal shank), and a miscellany of more typical Andalusian and Castilian dishes.

Tocororo. Calle del Prado, 3 (at the corner of Echegaray). ☎ **91-369-4000.** Reservations required Thurs–Sat. Main courses 2,500–3,500 ptas. ($15–$21); fixed-price menu 1,500 ptas. ($9). AE, DC, MC, V. Tues–Wed 1:30–4pm and 8:30pm–midnight; Thurs–Sun 1:30–4pm and 8:30pm–1:30am. Closed last 2 weeks Feb, last week Aug, and first week Sept. Metro: Sevilla. CUBAN.

This Cuban restaurant was opened in 1998 by an exile of that country. The nostalgia is evident in the pictures of Old Havana, and in the paintings of famous artists such as Lam y Mattos that adorn the walls. The waitstaff is as lively as the pop Cuban music

An Early-Evening *Tapeo*

What's more fun than a pub crawl in London or Dublin? In Madrid, it's a *tapeo*, and you can drink just as much or more than in those far northern climes. One of the unique pleasures of Madrid, a *tapeo* is the act of strolling from one bar to another to keep yourself amused and fed before the fashionable Madrileño dining hour of 10pm.

Most of the world knows that tapas are Spain's delectable appetizers, and restaurants around the world now serve them. In Madrid they're served almost everywhere, in *tabernas, tascas,* bars, and cafes.

Although Madrid took to tapas with a passion, they may have originated in Andalusia, especially around Jerez de la Frontera, where they were traditionally served to accompany the sherry produced there. The first tapa (which means a cover or lid) was probably *chorizo* (a spicy sausage) or a slice of cured ham perched over the mouth of a glass to keep the flies out. Later, the government mandated bars to serve a "little something" in the way of food with each drink to dissipate the effects of the alcohol. This was important when drinking a fortified wine like sherry, as its alcohol content is more than 15% higher than that of normal table wines. Eating a selection of tapas as you drink will help preserve your sobriety.

Tapas can be relatively simple: toasted almonds; slices of ham, cheese, or sausage; potato omelets; or the ubiquitous olives. They can be more elaborate too: a succulent veal roll; herb-flavored snails; *gambas* (fried or grilled shrimp); a saucer of peppery *pulpo* (octopus); stuffed peppers; delicious *anguila* (eel); *cangrejo* (crabmeat salad); *merluza* (hake) salad flavored with sweet red peppers, garlic, and cumin; and even bull testicles.

Each bar in Madrid gains a reputation for its rendition of certain favorite foods. One bar, for example, specializes in very garlicky grilled mushrooms, usually accompanied by pitchers of sangría. Another will specialize in *gambas*. Most chefs are men in Madrid, but at tapas bars or *tascas,* the cooks are most often women—perhaps the mother or sister of the owner, or more usually the wife.

Louis Armstrong, Manolete, Ava Gardner, and Orson Welles each enjoyed this characteristic culinary feature of Spain in their day. They may no longer be around to accompany you on a *tapeo*, but the tradition lives on. For a selection of our favorite bars, see "Our Favorite *Tascas,*" later in this chapter. There are literally hundreds of others, many of which you'll discover on your own during your strolls around Madrid.

playing on the stereo. The dishes are typical Caribbean dishes, such as *ceviche* (marinated fish), *ropa vieja* (shredded meat served with black beans and rice), or lobster enchilada. If you prefer a simpler repast, try a selection of *empanadas y tamales* (fried potato pasties and plantain dough filled with onions and ground meat). Special cocktails of the house include *mojito* (rum, mint, and a hint of sugar) and daiquiris. In winter there is live Cuban music. With a discreet but pleasant ambience, this restaurant is located in the zone of *La Marcha* (most of the bars and discos are in this area) and enjoys limited competition as there are only six other Cuban restaurants in the whole city.

ON OR NEAR THE GRAN VÍA
EXPENSIVE

Arce. Augusto Figueroa, 32. ☎ **91-522-59-13.** Reservations recommended. Main courses 2,800-5,750 ptas. ($16.80–$34.50). AE, DC, MC, V. Mon–Fri 1:30–4pm; Mon–Sat 9pm–midnight. Closed the week before Easter and Aug 15–31. Metro: Colón. BASQUE.

Arce has brought some of the best modern interpretations of Basque cuisine to Madrid, thanks to the enthusiasm of owner/chef Iñaki Camba and his wife, Theresa. Within a comfortably decorated dining room, you can enjoy dishes made of the finest ingredients using flavors designed to dominate your taste buds. Examples include a salad of fresh scallops and an oven-baked casserole of fresh boletus mushrooms, seasoned lightly so the woodsy vegetable taste comes through. Look for unusual preparations of hake and seasonal variations of such game dishes as pheasant and woodcock.

San Carlo. Barquillo, 10. ☎ **91-522-7988.** Reservations recommended. Main courses 2,600–3,000 ptas. ($15.60–$18); menu deluxe 6,000 ptas. ($36); fixed-price menu 2,500 ptas. ($15). AE, DC, MC, V. Tues–Sat 1:30–4pm and 9pm–midnight; Sun 1:30–4pm. Closed Aug 14–19. Metro: Banco de España. ITALIAN.

In the center of Madrid, this winning choice is located in a 19th-century building whose interior evokes the Teatro San Carlo in Naples. Walls are adorned with paintings and photographs of famous artists who have appeared here. On weekends there is live musical entertainment. The restaurant aspires to fill a gap in the Madrid market for quality Italian food at affordable prices, and succeeds admirably. If you want only a light pizza, opt for the front room. But if you desire more authentic Italian cuisine, head for the rear. Here you find the cutting edge in Italian cuisine, using local products to create unique dishes. Try pasta with prawns and mushrooms or delectable lasagna with fresh eggplant and basil. One of the finest meat dishes is fillet of veal with fresh asparagus and a mushroom known as *colmenillas*. Among the fish selections, sample *lubina con tomato seco al vino blanco*, or whitefish perfectly prepared with sundried tomatoes in a white wine sauce. Finish with an Amaretto tiramisu.

MODERATE

El Mentidero de la Villa. Santo Tomé, 6. ☎ **91-308-12-85.** Reservations required. Main courses 1,950–2,540 ptas. ($11.70–$15.25); *menú del día* 2,200 ptas. ($13.20). MC, V. Mon–Fri 1:30–4:30pm; Mon–Sat 9pm–midnight. Closed last 2 weeks of Aug. Metro: Alonso Martínez, Colón. Bus: 37. SPANISH/FRENCH.

The Mentidero ("Gossip Shop" in English) is a truly multicultural experience. The owner describes the cuisine as "modern Spanish with Japanese influence and a French cooking technique." That may sound confusing, but the result is an achievement; each ingredient manages to retain its distinct flavor. The kitchen plays with such adventuresome combinations as veal liver in sage sauce, a spring roll filled with fresh shrimp and leeks, noisettes of veal with tarragon, fillet steak with a sauce of mustard and brown sugar, and médallions of venison with puree of chestnut and celery. One notable dessert is the sherry trifle. The postmodern decor includes trompe l'oeil ceilings, exposed wine racks, ornate columns with unusual lighting, and a handful of antique carved merry-go-round horses.

INEXPENSIVE

Paellería Valenciana. Caballero de Gracia, 12. ☎ **91-531-17-85.** Reservations recommended. Main courses 1,250–2,800 ptas. ($7.50–$16.80); fixed-price menu 1,600 ptas. ($9.60). AE, MC, V. Mon–Sat 1:30–4:30pm. Metro: Gran Vía. SPANISH.

This lunch-only restaurant ranks as one of the best values in the city. The specialty is paella, of course, which you must order by phone in advance. Once you arrive, you might begin with a homemade soup or the house salad, then follow with the rib-sticking paella served in an iron skillet for two or more only. Among the desserts, the chef's pride is razor-thin orange slices flavored with rum, coconut, sugar, honey, and raspberry sauce. A carafe of house wine comes with the set menu, and after lunch the owner comes around dispensing free cognac.

NEAR THE PUERTA DEL SOL
VERY EXPENSIVE

Lhardy. Carrera de San Jéronimo, 8. ☎ **91-521-33-85.** Reservations recommended in the upstairs dining room. Main dishes 6,500–9,000 ptas. ($39–$54). AE, MC, V. Mon–Sat 1–3:30pm and 8:30–11pm. Closed Aug. Metro: Puerta del Sol. SPANISH/INTERNATIONAL.

Lhardy has been a Madrileño legend since opening in 1839 as a gathering place for the city's literati and political leaders. (In 1846 it even entertained Dumas—father, not son.) At street level is what may be the most elegant snack bar in Spain. Within a dignified antique setting of marble and hardwood, cups of steaming consommé are dispensed from silver samovars into delicate porcelain cups, and rows of croquettes, tapas, and sandwiches are served to stand-up clients who pay for their food at a cashier's kiosk near the entrance. The ground-floor deli and take-out service is open daily 9am to 3pm and 5 to 9:30pm.

The real culinary skill of the place, however, is on Lhardy's second floor, where you'll find a formal restaurant decorated in the ornate belle époque style of Isabel Segunda. Specialties of the house include fish, pork, veal, tripe in a garlicky tomato and onion wine sauce, and *cocido*, the celebrated chickpea stew of Madrid. *Soufflé sorpresa* (baked Alaska) is the dessert specialty.

Terraza. Alcala, 15. ☎ **91-521-8700.** Main courses 3,500–4,000 ptas. ($21–$24); fixed-price menu 9,000 ptas. ($54). AE, DC, MC, V. Mon–Fri 1–3:30pm and 9–11:30pm; Sat 9–11pm. Closed Aug. Metro: Sevilla. SPANISH/INTERNATIONAL.

Glamorous in its neo-baroque casino location, and with a mouthwatering menu, this restaurant is a perfect example of postmodern Spanish cuisine. The fifth-floor restaurant provides a panoramic view of the heart of Madrid and can be reached by an elevator or by a sweeping 19th-century staircase designed to impress. The decor is classically restrained with high ceilings and crystal chandeliers. The delicious food uses fresh seasonal ingredients and reinterprets Spanish dishes. An example is raya in oil and saffron with parsley puree and nuts on a bed of finely diced fries. More traditional dishes include the succulent *merluza a la Gallega* (Galician hake), *crema de la fabada asturiana* (creamed Asturian bean soup), and the steeply priced *jamon jabugo* (cured ham from acorn-fed pigs) served with a *menestra* (mixed vegetables) al dente. Only French champagne and Spanish wines are listed, and one of the best is the rounded woody red, the Ribeira de Duero from the province of Valladolid.

EXPENSIVE

Caripén. Plaza de la Marina Española, 4. ☎ **91-541-1177.** Reservations recommended on weekends. Main courses 3,500–4,000 ptas. ($21–$24). MC, V. Mon–Sat 9pm–3am. Closed Aug. Metro: Opera/Santo Domingo. ITALIAN/FRENCH.

In a historic district near the Royal Opera House and the Spanish Senate, this restaurant was once El Tablao, the flamenco club of Lola Flores, one of the most famous of all Spanish dancers. Its art deco decor has been restored, and instead of flamenco, you get the inspired French bistro cookery of Daniel Boute. At his little 25-table restaurant, diners sample some of the finest French bistro fare in the Spanish capital. The restaurant is especially popular with the *gatos,* or cats, of Madrid because it serves until 3am when most other quality establishments are shuttered. (Local residents are called *gatos* because they like to roam about at night.) Go for the *mejillones de roca* (mussels in white wine and cream sauce) or a perfectly prepared steak tartare. The pasta is homemade, and one excellent dish is foie with setas or duck liver and mushrooms. The skate in black butter is one of the finest choices, and you can finish off with such desserts as tiramisu, freshly made fruit tarts, or crêpes.

MODERATE

Casa Paco. Plaza Puerta Cerrada, 11. ☎ **91-366-31-66.** Reservations required. Main courses 1,200–3,800 ptas. ($7.20–$22.80); fixed-price menu 3,800 ptas. ($22.80). DC. Mon–Sat 1–4pm and 8:30pm–midnight. Closed Aug. Metro: Puerta del Sol, Opera, or La Latina. Bus: 3, 21, or 65. STEAK.

Madrileños defiantly name Casa Paco, just beside the Plaza Mayor, when someone dares to denigrate Spanish steaks. They know that here you can get the thickest, juiciest, tastiest steaks in Spain, priced according to weight. Señor Paco was the first in Madrid to sear steaks in boiling oil before serving them on plates so hot that the almost-raw meat continues to cook, preserving the natural juices. Located in the Old Town, this two-story restaurant has three dining rooms but reservations are imperative. If you face a long wait, while away the time sampling the tapas at the bar in front. Around the walls are autographed photographs of notables.

Casa Paco isn't just a steakhouse; you can start with fish soup and proceed to grilled sole, baby lamb, or *Casa Paco cocido,* the house version of Madrid's famous chickpea and pork soup. You might top it off with one of the luscious desserts, but know that Paco no longer serves coffee. It made customers linger, keeping tables occupied while potential patrons had to be turned away.

Cornucopia. Calle Flora, 1. ☎ **91-547-6465.** Reservations recommended. Main courses 1,800–2,600 ptas. ($10.80–$15.60); fixed-price lunch (Tues–Fri only) 1,600 ptas. ($9.60). AE, DC, MC, V. Tues–Fri 1:30–4pm and Tues–Sun 8:30–11:30pm. Closed 1 week in Aug. Metro: Opera or Callao. EURO-AMERICAN.

Set on a narrow side street adjacent to the medieval Plaza de Descalzas Reales, this restaurant occupies the mezzanine level of what was originally a 19th-century private palace. Its glamour and allure derive from its ownership by four partners, two of whom (North Carolina–born Jennifer Cole and her cohort, Kimberly Manning) are American; the others include French-born François and Spanish-born Fernando. Within a pair of elegant and airy dining rooms whose gleaming parquet floors remain from the original decor, you can admire the frequently changing paintings, all available for sale. Menu items include mussels with fennel and a roasted red pepper sauce over black fettuccini; grilled baby hen with mushrooms and sherry sauce; and grilled pork tenderloin stuffed with brie and bacon, and served with a pomegranate-apple compote and a red wine reduction sauce. Desserts are sumptuous and might include a dollop of such original homemade ice creams as *morito.* Named after a traditional

Cuban cocktail, it's flavored with mint, lemon, and rum. All the food is well prepared, the ingredients are fresh, and the staff is among the most inviting in Madrid.

✪ **El Cenador del Prado.** Calle del Prado, 4. ☎ **91-429-15-61.** Reservations recommended. Jackets and ties are recommended for men. Main courses 1,500–2,600 ptas. ($9–$15.60); fixed-price menu 3,350 ptas. ($20.10). AE, DC, MC, V. Mon–Fri 1:45–4pm; Mon–Sat 9pm–midnight. Closed Aug 12–19. Metro: Sevilla. INTERNATIONAL.

In this deceptively elegant restaurant's anteroom, an attendant will check your coat and packages into an elaborately carved armoire before the maître d' ushers you into one of a trio of rooms. Two of the rooms, done in peach and sepia, have cove moldings and English furniture, as well as floor-to-ceiling gilded mirrors. A third room, the most popular, is ringed with lattices and flooded with sun from a skylight.

The imaginative food reflects the French influence with an occasional Asian flourish. You might enjoy such specialties as crêpes with salmon and Iranian caviar, a salad of red peppers and salted anchovies, a casserole of snails and oysters with mushrooms, a ceviche of salmon and shellfish, potato-leek soup studded with tidbits of hake and clams, sea bass with candied lemons, veal scaloppini stuffed with asparagus and garlic sprouts, or médaillons of venison served with pepper-and-fig chutney.

La Esquina del Real. Calle Unon, 18. ☎ **91-559-4309.** Reservations recommended on weekends. Main courses 2,300–2,800 ptas. ($13.80–$16.80). AE, V. Mon–Fri 2–4pm and 9pm–midnight; Sat 9pm–midnight. Closed last 2 weeks of Aug. Metro: Opera/Sol. FRENCH.

Next to the Teatro Real you'll find this restaurant in an impressive 17th-century building with an ancient stone facade, thick granite walls, and the original wooden beams supporting old ceilings. This place has a sophisticated atmosphere yet prices are very reasonable. One Madrid food critic recently called this place one of the city's "best kept" culinary secrets. The hospitable owner and chef, Marcel Magossian, extends a hearty welcome to patrons and feeds them well. Fresh ingredients are transformed into even tastier concoctions, like large prawns with a delicate flavoring of raspberry vinaigrette or the roast oxtail with mashed potatoes and fresh mushroms that taste of the woods. A rather common dish, veal fricassée in mushroom sauce, is transformed into something sublime here. To end your repast, you might opt for a combination platter of warm cheese, as many habitués do, or else go for the tart tatin, ice cream with a crunchy caramel sauce brought to the table for a flambé.

INEXPENSIVE

Casa Alberto. Huertas, 18. ☎ **91-429-93-56.** Reservations recommended. Main courses 1,000–2,500 ptas. ($6–$15). AE, DC, MC, V. Tues–Sat 1–4pm; Tues–Sun 8:30pm–midnight. Metro: Antón Martín. CASTILIAN.

One of the oldest *tascas* in the neighborhood, Casa Alberto was established in 1827 and has thrived ever since. On the street level of a house where Miguel de Cervantes lived briefly in 1614, it contains an appealing mixture of bullfighting memorabilia, engravings, and reproductions of Old Master paintings. Many visitors opt only for the tapas, continually replenished from platters on the bar, but there's a sit-down dining area for more substantial meals. Specialties include fried squid, shellfish in vinaigrette sauce, *chorizo* (sausage) in cider sauce, and several versions of baked or roasted lamb.

✪ **Mad Madrid.** Calle Virgin de los Peligros, 4. ☎ **91-532-6228.** Reservations recommended. Main courses 1,600–2,100 ptas. ($10.70–$14.05); fixed-price menu (at lunch only) 1,500 ptas. ($10.05). AE, DC, MC, V. Mon–Wed 1–4pm and 9:30pm–3am; Thurs–Sat 1–4pm and 9:30pm–4am. Dinner served until 12:30am. Metro: Sevilla, Gran Vía. INTERNATIONAL.

This restaurant bar in the very center of Madrid is a hot spot. Done in red and gray minimalism (sort of a tongue-in-cheek Soviet style), there's also a garden where you can enjoy a cocktail on a summer night. Taking her inspiration from around the Mediterranean, chef Belen Laguía changes the menu every 3 months. Staples, however, include starters such as goat cheese on caramelized onions and corral salad, composed of wild chicken marinated in vinegar and cream on four types of lettuce. Other dishes to savor are marinated salmon with dill and golden caviar, which is black, from an inland sea in the dry southern province of Murcia. This is served with Japanese seaweed and fresh seasonal vegetables presented al dente. Desserts include an apple tart, not too sweet, topped with egg yolk.

Museo del Jamón. Carrera de San Jerónimo, 6 (1 block east of Puerta del Sol). ☎ **91-521-0346.** Menu del día 950–1,600 ptas. ($5.70–$9.60); platos combinados 500–750 ptas. ($3–$4.50). MC, V. Daily 8:30am–1am. Metro: Puerta del Sol. SPANISH/TAPAS.

The displays on the walls of this unique establishment explain the bewildering name: "The Museum of Ham." As in an art exhibition, large amounts of different kinds of hams—cured by a variety of methods—hang from the ceilings. The popular *chorizos* are hooked in rows reminiscent of one of those scenes in Golden Age paintings. This is indeed a real museum of the most celebrated fast food in Spain. On certain nights the tavern offers live entertainment in the dining area upstairs, often a guitarist. The *paella* for two is reasonably priced. The aged *jamon Serrano*, or Serrano ham, is a great delicacy now highly prized at tapas bars throughout Spain, Europe, and North America. You might try it in small sandwiches known as *bocattas* or as an always available tapa. The daily menu is varied and served in generous portions. Service is efficient if not too friendly, but customers don't seem to mind.

Taberna del Alabardero. Felipe V, 6. ☎ **91-547-25-77.** Reservations required for restaurant only. Bar: tapas 450–1,500 ptas. ($2.70–$9); glass of house wine 200 ptas. ($1.20). Restaurant: main courses 1,900–2,500 ptas. ($11.40–$15). AE, DC, MC, V. Daily 8am–1am. Metro: Opera. BASQUE/SPANISH.

In close proximity to the Royal Palace, this little Spanish classic is known for its selection of tasty tapas, ranging from squid cooked in wine to fried potatoes dipped in hot sauce. Photographs of famous former patrons, including Nelson Rockefeller and the race-car driver Jackie Stewart, line the walls. The restaurant in the rear is said to be one of the city's best-kept secrets. Decorated in typical tavern style, it serves a savory Spanish and Basque cuisine with market-fresh ingredients.

RETIRO/SALAMANCA
EXPENSIVE

Alkalde. Jorge Juan, 10. ☎ **91-576-33-59.** Reservations required. Main courses 2,000–5,300 ptas. ($12–$31.80); fixed-price menu from 6,000 ptas. ($36). AE, DC, MC, V. Daily 1:15–4pm and 8:30pm–midnight. Closed Sat–Sun in July–Aug. Metro: Retiro or Serrano. Bus: 8, 20, 21, or 53. BASQUE.

For decades Alkalde has been known for serving top-quality Spanish food in an old tavern setting. Decorated like a Basque inn, it has beamed ceilings with hams hanging from the rafters. Upstairs is a large *típico* tavern; downstairs is a maze of stone-sided cellars that are pleasantly cool in summer (although the whole place is air-conditioned).

Basque cookery is the best in Spain, and Alkalde honors that noble tradition. Begin with the cream of crabmeat soup, followed by *gambas a la plancha* (grilled shrimp) or *cigalas* (crayfish). Other recommended dishes include *mero salsa verde* (brill in green sauce), trout Alkalde, stuffed peppers, and chicken steak. The dessert specialty is *copa Cardinal* (ice cream topped with fruit).

✪ **El Amparo.** Callejón de Puigcerdá, 8 (at corner of Jorge Juan). ☎ **91-431-64-56.** Reservations required. Main courses 2,950–4,500 ptas. ($17.70–$27). AE, MC, V. Sun–Fri 1:30–3:30pm; daily 9–11:30pm. Closed week before Easter and in Aug. Metro: Serrano. Bus: 21 or 53. BASQUE.

Behind the cascading vines on El Amparo's facade is one of Madrid's most elegant gastronomic enclaves. Inside this converted carriage house, three tiers of rough-hewn wooden beams surround tables set with pink linens and glistening silver. A sloping skylight floods the interior with sun by day; at night, pinpoints of light from the high-tech hanging lanterns create intimate shadows. Polite, uniformed waiters serve well-prepared nouvelle cuisine versions of cold marinated salmon with a tomato sorbet, cold cream of vegetable and shrimp soup, bisque of shellfish with Armagnac, ravioli with crayfish dressed with balsamic vinegar and vanilla-scented oil, roast lamb chops with garlic puree, breast of duck, ragout of sole, steamed fish of the day, roulades of lobster with soy sauce, and steamed hake with pepper sauce.

El Pescador. Calle José Ortega y Gasset, 75. ☎ **91-402-12-90.** Reservations required. Main courses 6,000–15,000 ptas. ($36–$90); fixed price menu 6,500 ptas. ($39). MC, V. Mon–Sat noon–4pm and 8pm–midnight. Closed Aug. Metro: Lista or Diego de Leon. SEAFOOD.

El Pescador is a popular spot packing in crowds with more than 30 kinds of fish served, all prominently displayed in a glass case. Many of them are unknown in North America, and some originate off the coast of Galicia. The management air-freights them in and prefers to serve them *a la plancha* (grilled). You might start off with spicy fish soup and accompany it with one of the many good wines from northeastern Spain. If you're not sure what to order (even the English translations might sound unfamiliar), try one of the many varieties and sizes of shrimp. They go under the names *langostinos, cigalas, santiaguinos,* and *carabineros.* Many of them are expensive and priced by the gram, so be careful when you order.

Horcher. Alfonso XII, 6. ☎ **91-532-35-96.** Reservations required. Jackets and ties for men. Main courses 3,500–8,000 ptas. ($21–$48). AE, DC, MC, V. Mon–Fri 1:30–4pm; Mon–Sat 8:30pm–midnight. Metro: Retiro. GERMAN/INTERNATIONAL.

Horcher originated in Berlin in 1904. In 1943, prompted by a tip from a high-ranking German officer that Germany was losing the war, Herr Horcher moved his restaurant to Madrid. For years it was known as the best dining room in the city, but fierce competition has lately stolen that crown. Nevertheless, the restaurant has continued its grand European traditions, including excellent service.

You might try the skate or shrimp tartare or the distinctive warm hake salad. Both the venison stew with green pepper and orange peel and the crayfish with parsley and cucumber are typical of the elegant fare served with style. Spanish aristocrats often come here in autumn to sample game dishes, including venison, wild boar, and roast wild duck. Other main courses include veal scaloppini in tarragon and sea bass with saffron. For dessert, the house specialty is crêpes Sir Holden, prepared at your table with fresh raspberries, cream, and nuts.

✪ **La Gamella.** Alfonso XII, 4. ☎ **91-532-45-09.** Reservations required. Main courses 2,300–4,500 ptas. ($13.80–$27). AE, DC, MC, V. Mon–Fri 1:30–4pm; Mon–Sat 9pm–midnight. Closed 2 weeks around Easter and 2 weeks in Aug. Metro: Retiro. Bus: 19. CALIFORNIAN/CASTILIAN.

La Gamella established its gastronomic reputation shortly after it opened several years ago in another part of town. In 1988, its Illinois-born owner Dick Stephens moved his restaurant into the 19th-century building where the Spanish philosopher Ortega y Gasset was born. The prestigious Horcher, one of the capital's legendary restaurants (see above), is just across the street, but the food at La Gamella is better. The russet-colored, high-ceilinged design invites customers to relax. Mr. Stephens has prepared his delicate and light-textured specialties for the king and queen of Spain, as well as for Madrid's most talked-about artists and merchants, many of whom he knows and greets personally between sessions in his kitchen.

Typical menu items include a ceviche of Mediterranean fish, sliced duck liver in truffle sauce, a dollop of goat cheese served over caramelized endive, duck breast with peppers, and an array of well-prepared desserts, including an all-American cheesecake. Traditional Spanish dishes such as chicken with garlic have been added to the menu, plus what has been called "the only edible hamburger in Madrid." Because of the intimacy and the small dimensions of the restaurant, reservations are important.

La Trainera. Calle Lagasca, 60. ☎ **91-576-8035.** Reservations recommended. Main courses 3,000–6,000 ptas. ($18–$36). AE, DC, MC, V. Mon–Sat 1–4pm and 8pm–midnight. Metro: Serrano. SEAFOOD.

This restaurant is more expensive, and more chic, than its sprawling, paneled interior might imply. Suitable for up to 300 diners at a time, it occupies a quartet of dining rooms within a turn-of-the-century building in the glamorous shopping neighborhood of Serrano. Look for vaguely Basque-inspired platters of very fresh seafood, which arrive steaming hot and drizzled with subtle combinations of herbs, wines, and olive oils. No meat of any kind is served here. Instead, you'll find spicy and garlic-enriched versions of fish soup, an *escabeche of bonita* served as an appetizer, fillet of sole prepared in any of several different versions, Cantabrian crayfish, and well-conceived versions of a *salpicon de mariscos* (a platter of shellfish). Other fish include red mullet, swordfish with capers, monkfish, and virtually anything else that swims. Any of them can be preceded with a heaping platter of shellfish set atop a bed of artfully arranged seaweed. Succulent shellfish, including lobster, shrimp, crab, and mussels, plus an array of other items, is market-priced by weight.

Pedro Larumbe. Serrano, 61. ☎ **91-575-1112.** Reservations required. Main course 2,800–3,000 ptas. ($16.80–$18); *menu completo* 6,500 ptas. ($39). AE, DC, MC, V. Mon–Fri 1:30–4pm and 9pm–midnight; Sat 9pm–midnight. Closed Aug 15–30. Metro: Ruben Dario and Nuñez de Balboa. BASQUE/FRENCH.

In an opulent section of La Castellana very close to Plaza de Colón, this century-old building was once the headquarters of the famous newspaper *ABC.* Today it is the elegant restaurant of National Gastronomic Award winner Pedro Larumbe. There are three dining areas, each as elegant as the others: the classic Salon Pompeyano, the art deco Salon Fundador, and the beautifully tiled Patio Andalus. This Navarrese chef not only likes a fin-de-siècle decor, he prefers turn-of-the-century cookery as well. His specialties are often from the tried-and-true recipes of yesterday, as evoked by his *solomillo a la mostaza,* or steak with mustard sauce. He also specializes in hake in green sauce with mussels, a favorite dish of the Basque country. One of his specialties is *ensalada de bocavante con salsa de almendras,* or lobster salad with almond dressing, a true delight. The service is impeccable, the wine list well chosen, and the desserts something to write home about: tiramisu with a sweet wine and caramel sauce or "tear drops" of chocolate—that is dark and rich tear-shaped chocolate pieces.

Suntory. Paseo Castellana, 36. ☎ **91-577-3734.** Reservations recommended. *Menu completo* 6,500 ptas. ($39). AE, DC, MC, V. Mon–Sat 1:30–3:30pm and 8-11pm. Metro: Rubén Dario. JAPANESE.

Already acclaimed for its chain restaurants around the world, Suntory has invaded an attractive section of La Castellana and is winning converts to its impeccably prepared cuisine. Decorated in a minimalist style evocative of other Japanese restaurants around the world, this is the domain of Ken Sato, acclaimed as the finest Japanese chef in Spain. There are three dining areas, including the Teppan Yaki, the Shabu-Shabu, and a sushi bar. The finest and freshest of fish and shellfish is served here. Visiting Japanese praise the quality of fish found in Spanish waters. Try some of the exquisite sushi or the Mediterranean prawn tempura. The red tuna sashimi is our favorite. Finish these delicacies with a tempura helado or cake with vanilla icing.

✪ **Viridiana.** Juan de Mena, 14. ☎ **91-531-5222.** Reservations recommended. Main courses 3,000–4,500 ptas. ($18–$27). AE, MC, V. Mon–Sat 1:30–4pm and 9pm–midnight. Closed 1 week at Easter and 2 weeks in Aug. Metro: Banco. INTERNATIONAL.

Viridiana—named after the 1961 Luis Buñuel film classic—is praised as one of the up-and-coming restaurants of Madrid, known for the creative imagination of its chef and part-owner, Abraham García, who has lined the walls with stills from Buñuel films. (He is also a film historian, not just a self-taught chef.) Menu specialties are contemporary adaptations of traditional recipes, and they change frequently according to availability. Examples of the individualistic cooking include a salad of exotic lettuces served with smoked salmon, a chicken pastilla laced with cinnamon, baby squid with curry served on a bed of lentils, roasted lamb served in puff pastry with fresh basil, and the choicest langostinos from Cádiz. The food is sublime, and the inviting ambience makes you relax as you sit back to enjoy dishes that dazzle the eye, notably venison and rabbit arranged on a plate with fresh greens to evoke an autumnal scene in a forest.

MODERATE

Gran Café de Gijón. Paseo de Recoletos, 21. ☎ **91-521-54-25.** Reservations required for restaurant. Main courses 3,000–5,000 ptas. ($18–$30); fixed-price menu 1,800 ptas. ($10.80). AE, DC, MC, V. Sun–Fri 7am–1:30am; Sat 7am–2am. Metro: Banco de España, Colón, or Recoletos. SPANISH.

Each of the old European capitals has a coffeehouse that traditionally attracts the literati—in Madrid it's the Gijón, which opened in 1888 in the heyday of the belle époque. Artists and writers still patronize this venerated old cafe, many of them spending hours over one cup of coffee. Open windows look out onto the wide paseo and a large terrace is perfect for sun worshippers and bird-watchers. Along one side of the cafe is a stand-up bar; on the lower level is a restaurant. Food is prepared the way it used to be in Madrid. In summer, sit in the garden to enjoy a *blanco y negro* (black coffee with ice cream) or a mixed drink.

CHAMBERÍ
VERY EXPENSIVE

✪ **Jockey.** Amador de los Ríos, 6. ☎ **91-319-24-35.** Reservations required. Main courses 3,500–6,750 ptas. ($21–$40.50). AE, DC, MC, V. Mon–Fri 1–4pm and Mon–Sat 9pm–midnight. Closed Aug. Metro: Colón. INTERNATIONAL.

For decades this was the premier restaurant of Spain. A favorite of international celebrities, diplomats, and heads of state, it was once known as the Jockey Club, although "Club" was eventually dropped because it suggested exclusivity. The restaurant, with tables on two levels, isn't large. Wood-paneled walls and colored linen provide a cozy ambience. Against the paneling are a dozen prints of jockeys mounted on horses—hence the name.

Since Jockey's establishment shortly after World War II, each chef who has come along has prided himself on coming up with new and creative dishes. You can still order Beluga caviar from Iran, but might settle happily for the goose-liver terrine or slices of Jabugo ham. Cold melon soup with shrimp is soothing on a hot day, especially when followed by grill-roasted young pigeon from Talavera or sole fillets with figs in Chardonnay. Stuffed small chicken Jockey style is a specialty, as is *tripa Madrileña*, a local dish. Desserts are sumptuous.

EXPENSIVE

La Fuencisla. San Mateo, 4. ☎ **91-521-6186.** Reservations recommended. Main courses 2,500–2,800 ptas. ($15–$16.80); *menu completo* 6,000 ptas. ($36). AE, MC, V. Mon–Sat 2–4pm and 9pm–1am. Closed Aug. Metro: Tribunal. SPANISH.

Near El Museo Romantico is this small but comfortable restaurant that for nearly half a century has been serving meals in the traditional Spanish style. A family business, La Fuencisla (named as an offering to the Virgin of Segovia) is run by Señor and Señora de Frutos. Señor de Frutos greets the visitors in the front while the Señora creates tasty homemade meals in the kitchen. The dishes are typical of the Segovian kitchen, and ingredients are prepared according to time-tested recipes. No dish is more typical than the grilled chops of milk-fed lamb, praised by gastronomes. Begin with fresh asparagus in country butter and aromatic garlic or savory mussels in a marinara sauce. Fillet of tuna freshly baked in the oven is another pleaser. For desserts, the cooks always prepare homemade tarts, which are especially good when the fresh fruit comes in. Otherwise, you might opt for the rice pudding or *flan de coco* (coconut pudding).

La Paloma. Jorge Juan, 39. ☎ **91-576-8692.** Reservations recommended. Main courses 2,800–3,200 ptas. ($16.80–$19.20); *menu completo* 7,500 ptas. ($45). AE, DC, MC, V. Mon–Sat 1:30–4pm and 9pm–midnight. Metro: Vergara. BASQUE/FRENCH.

In the exclusive Barrio Salamanca, this small but comfortable restaurant is the showcase for the culinary talents of chef-owner Segundo Alonso, who made a stellar reputation at the more exclusive El Amparo. Many of his fans followed him here and have since become regulars. His restaurant is in a nostalgic old restored house with high ceilings and wooden beams. His French and Basque dishes are some of the finest of their kind in Madrid. His food is robust, and he's known for what is called "variety meats," especially pigs' trotters. Even if you have never sampled this dish before, dare to here. You might be glad you did. You could settle instead for his equally celebrated wood pigeon stuffed with foie gras. He also does an excellent lasagna with crab meat, spinach, and leeks, and a fine *rabo de toro*, or bull's tail stewed in red wine sauce. The best fish dish is grilled turbot with tomato paste and thyme or sea urchin gratinéed and served with quail eggs. For dessert, try fresh dates with Chantilly cream or a velvety almond mousse with cinnamon ice cream.

✪ **Las Cuatro Estaciones.** General Ibémñez Ibero, 5. ☎ **91-553-63-05.** Reservations required. Main courses 2,100–5,000 ptas. ($12.60–$30); fixed-price dinner 6,500 ptas. ($39). AE, DC, MC, V. Mon–Fri 1:30–4pm; Mon–Sat 9–11:30pm. Closed Easter and Aug. Metro: Guzmán el Bueno. MEDITERRANEAN.

Las Cuatro Estaciones is placed by gastronomes and horticulturists alike among their favorite Madrid dining spots, and is neck-and-neck with the prestigious Jockey. In addition to superb food, the establishment prides itself on the masses of flowers that change with the season. Depending on the time of year, the mirrors surrounding the multilevel bar near the entrance reflect thousands of hydrangeas, chrysanthemums, or poinsettias. Even the napery matches whichever colors the resident florist has chosen as the seasonal motif. Each person involved in food preparation spends a prolonged apprenticeship at restaurants in France before returning home to try their talents on the taste buds of aristocratic Madrid.

Representative specialties include crab bisque, a petite marmite of fish and shellfish, a salad of eels, fresh asparagus, and mushrooms in puff pastry with parsley-butter sauce, and a nouvelle cuisine version of blanquette of monkfish so tender it melts in your mouth. The desserts include daily specials brought temptingly to your table.

MODERATE

La Bola. Calle de la Bola, 5. ☎ **91-547-69-30.** Reservations required. Main courses 2,000–4,000 ptas. ($12–$24). No credit cards. Mon–Sat 1–4pm and 9pm–midnight; Sun 1–4pm. Metro: Santo Domingo. Bus: 1 or 2. MADRILEÑA.

This is *the* taberna in which to savor the 19th century. Just north of the Teatro Real, it's one of the few restaurants (if not the only one) left in Madrid with a blood-red facade; at one time, nearly all fashionable restaurants were so coated. La Bola hangs on to tradition like a tenacious bull. Time stands still inside this restaurant with its traditional atmosphere, gently polite waiters, Venetian crystal, and aging velvet. Ava Gardner, with her entourage of bullfighters, used to patronize this establishment, but that was long before La Bola became so well known to tourists. Grilled sole, fillet of veal, and roast veal are regularly featured. Basque-style hake and grilled salmon are well recommended. Refreshing dishes to begin your meal include grilled shrimp, red-pepper salad, and lobster cocktail.

Teatriz. Calle Hermossila, 15. ☎ **91-577-5379.** Reservations recommended. Main courses 2,000–2,400 ptas. ($12–$14.40); *menu completo* 4,500 ptas. ($27). AE, DC, MC, V. Daily noon–3am. Closed Aug. Metro: Serrano. ITALIAN.

Decorated by the famed French architect and designer Philippe Starck, this old theater has been transformed into a top-notch Italian restaurant. Theater seats have long given way to dining tables, but Starck kept many of the elements of the old theater. As you head for the rest rooms, you encounter a stunning fountain of marble, silver, and gold, everything bathed in a bluish light, making you think you're in a night club. The kitchen closes at midnight, but the bar remains open until 3am. The dishes are genuine and cleverly crafted. Launch yourself with fresh mozzarella with tomatoes in virgin olive oil or raw salmon and turbot flavored with fresh dill. One of the best pastas is a tortellini filled with Parmesan-flavored ground meat. The desserts are worth saving room for, including cannelloni stuffed with dark chocolate or a fresh cheese mousse with mango ice cream. There is also a velvety smooth tiramisu.

INEXPENSIVE

Foster's Hollywood. Velázquez, 80. ☎ **91-435-61-28.** Main courses 950–2,950 ptas. ($5.70–$17.70). AE, DC, MC, V. Sun–Thurs 1pm–midnight; Fri–Sat 1pm–2am. Metro: Serrano. AMERICAN.

When Foster's opened its doors in 1971, it was not only the first American-style restaurant in Spain, but one of the first in Europe. Since those early days, it has grown to 15 restaurants in Madrid and has even opened branches in Florida. A popular hangout for both locals and visiting Yanks, it offers a choice of dining rooms, ranging from classical club to a faux film studio with props. The varied menu includes Tex-Mex selections, ribs, steaks, sandwiches, freshly made salads, and, as its signature product, hamburgers grilled over natural charcoal. The *New York Times* once claimed that it had "probably the best onion rings in the world."

Other locations include Paseo de la Castellana, 116–118 (☎ **91-564-63-08**), and Princesa, 13 (☎ **91-559-19-14**), near Plaza de España.

Ríofrío. Centro Colón, Plaza de Colón, 1. ☎ **91-319-29-77.** Main courses 700–3,200 ptas. ($4.20–$19.20); fixed-price menu 2,500 ptas. ($15); sandwiches 525–900 ptas.

($3.15–$5.40). AE, DC, MC, V. Daily 7:30am–2am. Metro: Colón. Bus: 5, 14, 21, 27, or 45. INTERNATIONAL.

Overlooking Madrid's Columbus Circle, this is an all-purpose place for drinking, eating, or nightclubbing. The least-expensive way to eat here is at one of two self-service cafeterias where average meals run from 1,200 to 1,800 ptas. ($7.20 to $10.80). There's also a larger restaurant with international cuisine, serving meals averaging 3,500 ptas. ($21), plus yet another dining room for informal lunches, dinners, snacks, or aperitifs. The spacious glassed-in terrace, open year-round, is known for serving some of the best paella in Madrid. Finally, there's even a nightclub, El Descubrimiento, should you desire to make an evening of it. The club serves dinners from 4,500 ptas. ($27), which includes not only the meal but a show to follow. Sandwiches are available throughout the day if you'd like just a light bite in the hot Madrid sun.

NEAR ALONSO MARTÍNEZ
MODERATE

Café Balear. Calle Sagunto, 18. ☎ **91/447-9115.** Reservations recommended. Main courses 1,600–5,500 ptas. ($9.60–$33). AE, MC, V. Daily 1:30–4pm; Tues–Sat 8:30–11:30pm. Metro: Iglesia. PAELLA/SEAFOOD.

Only a handful of other restaurants in Madrid focus as aggressively as this one on the national dish of Spain, paella, which here comes in 14 different versions with permutations that might surprise even the most jaded aficionado. Within a yellow-and-white dining room loaded with potted plants, you can order any of several *calderas* (casseroles) that bubble with all kinds of fish and shellfish. Paella here includes versions with shellfish, with chicken and shellfish, with pork, with crabs, with lobster, and an all-black version that's tinted with squid ink for extra flavor. There's even a vegetarian version if you absolutely, positively hate fish. Your fellow diners represent many of the creative arts of Spain, with lots of journalists, writers, poets, and artists who seem to have adopted the place.

Casa Vallejo. Calle San Lorenzo, 9. ☎ **91-308-6158.** Reservations recommended. Main courses 1,600–4,000 ptas. ($9.60–$24); fixed-price menu (available Mon–Fri only) 1,800 ptas. ($10.80). MC, V. Mon–Sat 2–4pm; Tues–Sat 9:30pm–midnight. Metro: Tribunale or Alonso Martínez. SPANISH.

This hardworking bistro with a not terribly subtle staff has less exposure to international clients than some of its competitors. Despite that, you'll find a sense of culinary integrity that's based on a devotion to fresh ingredients and a rigid allegiance to time-tested Spanish recipes. Occupying a turn-of-the-century building, it contains room for only 42 diners at a time. Menu items include garlic soup; tartlets layered with tomatoes, zucchini, and cheese; a ragout of clams and artichokes; croquettes of chicken; breast of chicken garnished with a fricassee of fresh wild mushrooms; pork fillet; duck breast in orange or prune sauce; and creamy desserts. Budget gourmands in Madrid praise the hearty flavors here, the robust cookery, and the prices.

Ciao Madrid. Calle Apodaca, 20 (☎ **91-447-0036;** metro: Tribunal), and calle Argensola, 7 (☎ **91-308-2519;** metro: Alonso Martínez). Reservations recommended. Pastas 1,200–1,600 ptas. ($7.20–$9.60); main courses 1,600–2,500 ptas. ($9.60–$15). AE, DC, MC, V. Mon–Fri 1:30–3:45pm and Mon–Sat 9:30pm–midnight. The branch at calle Apodaca is closed in Sept; branch at calle Argensola is closed in Aug. ITALIAN.

These two highly successful Italian restaurants are run by members of the extended Laguna family. The older of the two is the branch on calle Apodaca, established about a dozen years ago; its cohort entered the scene in the early 1990s. Both maintain the same hours, prices, menu, and a decor inspired by the tenets of minimalist Milanese decor, with good-tasting food items that include risottos and pastas, such as ravioli or tagliatelle with wild mushrooms. No one will mind if you order a pasta as a main course (lots of clients here do, accompanying it with a green salad). If you're in the mood for a more substantial main course, consider osso bucco, veal scaloppini, chicken or veal parmigiana, and any of several kinds of fish.

CHAMARTÍN
VERY EXPENSIVE

✪ **Zalacaín.** Alvarez de Baena, 4. ☎ **91-561-48-40.** Reservations required. Main courses 9,500–12,000 ptas. ($57–$72). AE, DC, MC, V. Mon–Fri 1:15–4pm; Mon–Sat 9–11:45pm. Closed week before Easter and in Aug. Metro: Rubén Darío. INTERNATIONAL.

Outstanding in both food and decor, Zalacaín opened in 1973 and introduced nouvelle cuisine to Spain. It is reached by an illuminated walk from Paseo de la Castellana and housed at the garden end of a modern apartment complex. In fact, it's within an easy walk of such deluxe hotels as the Castellana and the Miguel Angel. The name of the restaurant comes from the intrepid hero of Basque author Pío Baroja's 1909 novel, *Zalacaín El Aventurero.* Zalacaín is small, exclusive, and expensive. It has the atmosphere of an elegant old mansion: The walls are covered with textiles, and some are decorated with Audubon-type paintings. Men should wear jackets and ties.

The menu features many Basque and French specialties, often with nouvelle cuisine touches. It might offer a superb sole in a green sauce, but it also knows the glory of grilled pigs' feet. Among the best dishes are oysters with caviar and sherry jelly; crêpes stuffed with smoked fish; ravioli stuffed with mushrooms, foie gras, and truffles; bouillabaisse; and veal escalopes in orange sauce. For dessert, we'd suggest one of the custards, perhaps raspberry or chocolate.

EXPENSIVE

✪ **El Olivo Restaurant.** General Gallegos, 1. ☎ **91-359-15-35.** Reservations recommended. Main courses 2,950–3,800 ptas. ($17.70–$22.80); fixed–price meals 3,850–5,800 ptas. ($23.10–$34.80). AE, DC, MC, V. Tues–Sat 1–4pm and 9pm–midnight. Closed Aug 15–31 and 4 days around Easter. Metro: Plaza de Castilla. MEDITERRANEAN.

Locals praise the success of a non-Spaniard (in this case, French-born Jean Pierre Vandelle) in recognizing the international appeal of two of Spain's most valuable culinary resources: olive oil and sherry. Designed in tones of green and amber, this is the only restaurant in Spain that wheels a cart stocked with 40 regional olive oils from table to table. From the cart, diners select a variety to soak up with chunks of rough-textured bread that is, according to your taste, seasoned with a dash of salt.

Menu specialties include grilled fillet of monkfish marinated in herbs and olive oil, then served with black-olive sauce over compote of fresh tomatoes, and four preparations of codfish arranged on a single platter and served with a *pil-pil* sauce. (Named after the sizzling noise it makes as it bubbles on a stove, pil-pil sauce is composed of codfish gelatin and herbs that are whipped into a mayonnaiselike consistency with olive oil.) Dessert might be one of several different chocolate pastries.

Note: Many clients deliberately arrive early as an excuse to linger within El Olivo's one-of-a-kind sherry bar. Although other drinks are offered, the bar features more than 100 brands of vino de Jerez, more than practically any other establishment in Madrid. Priced at 250 to 750 ptas. ($1.50 to $4.50) per glass, they make the perfect aperitif.

✪ **Principe de Viana.** Calle Manuel de Falla, 5. ☎ **91-457-15-49.** Reservations required. Main courses 1,800–3,200 ptas. ($10.80–$19.20). AE, DC, MC, V. Mon–Fri 1–4pm and 9–11:30pm; Sat 9–11:30pm. Closed in Aug. Metro: Lima. BASQUE.

You Paid What?

47,000 hotels, 700 airlines, 50 rental car companies. And a few million ways to save money.

Travelocity.com
A Sabre Company

Go Virtually Anywhere.

AOL Keyword: Travel

Will you have enough stories to tell your grandchildren?

Yahoo! Travel

This place has gotten rave reviews. Fish is of course the most important staple of Basque cuisine, and there is a wide selection from which to choose. You might go the traditional route, with *bacalao ajoarriera* (cod with red peppers and tomatoes) and *merluza en salsa verde* (hake in parsley, garlic, and olive oil sauce). There are more adventurous modern concoctions, such as a salad with *chipirones* (baby squid) and *mojellas* (sweet meats) in a soya viniagrette. Those with a sweet tooth will be more than satisfied with the dessert of cream cheese and mango sorbet. From the many Spanish and occasional foreign wines to choose from, the Albirino from Galicia is particularly recommended.

MODERATE

✪ **El Cabo Mayor.** Juan Ramón Jiménez, 37. ☎ **91-350-87-76.** Reservations recommended. Main courses 2,800–3,900 ptas. ($16.80–$23.40). AE, DC, MC, V. Mon–Fri 1:30–4pm; Mon–Sat 8:45–11:45pm. Closed 1 week at Easter and Aug 25. Metro: Cuzco. SPANISH.

Near Chamartín train station, this is one of the best, most popular, and most stylish restaurants in Madrid, attracting on occasion the king and queen of Spain. An openair staircase leading to the entranceway descends from a manicured garden on a quiet side street where a battalion of uniformed doormen stands ready to greet arriving taxis. The restaurant's decor is nautically inspired, with hardwood panels, brass trim, pulleys and ropes, a tile floor custom-painted with sea-green and blue replicas of waves, and hand-carved models of fishing boats. Some dozen bronze statues honoring fishers and their craft are displayed in brass portholes in illuminated positions of honor.

Menu choices include paprika-laden peppers stuffed with fish, a salad composed of Jabugo ham and foie gras of duckling, Cantabrian fish soup, stewed sea bream with thyme, asparagus mousse, salmon in sherry sauce, and loin of veal in cassis sauce. Desserts include a rice mousse with pine-nut sauce.

✪ **Goizeko Kabi.** Comandante Zorita, 27. ☎ **91-533-0185.** Reservations recommended. Main courses 1,800–5,000 ptas. ($10.80–$30). AE, DC, V. Mon–Sat 1–4pm and 8:30pm–midnight. Metro: Alvarado. BASQUE.

This restaurant serves some of the best Basque dishes in Madrid in an intimate, understated interior. Particularly delicious is the starter of *boquerones*, almost sweet anchovies marinated in garlic and olive oil. We loved the *bacalao pil-pil vizcaina* (cod in a Basque garlic sauce) and the wonderfully juicy king prawns. Dessert lovers will revel in the orange mousse with a coating of bitter chocolate or the more experimental black bread ice cream with coffee sauce.

✪ **O'Pazo.** Calle Reina Mercedes, 20. ☎ **91-553-23-33.** Reservations required. Main courses 2,200–5,350 ptas. ($13.20–$32.10). MC, V. Mon–Sat 1–4pm and 8:30pm–midnight. Closed Aug. Metro: Nuevos Ministerios or Alvarado. Bus: 3 or 5. GALICIAN/SEAFOOD.

This deluxe Galician restaurant is viewed by local cognoscenti as one of the top seafood places in the country. The fish is flown in daily from Galicia and mostly priced by weight at market rates. In front is a cocktail lounge and bar, all polished brass, with low sofas and paintings. Carpeted floors, cushioned Castilian furniture, soft lighting, and colored-glass windows complete the picture.

The fish and shellfish soup is delectable, although others gravitate to the seaman's broth as a beginning course. Natural clams are succulent, as are *cigalas* (a kind of crayfish), spider crabs, and Jabugo ham. Main dishes range from baby eels to sea snails, from Galician style scallops to *zarzuela* (a seafood casserole).

CHUECA
INEXPENSIVE

Nabucco. Calle Hortaleza, 108. ☎ **91-310-06-11.** Reservations recommended. Pizza 755–1,000 ptas. ($4.55–$6); main courses 950–1,600 ptas. ($5.70–$9.60). AE, DC, MC, V. Daily 1:30–4pm; Sun–Thurs 8:45pm–midnight; Fri–Sat 8:45pm–1am. Metro: Alonso Martínez. Bus: 7 or 36. ITALIAN.

In a neighborhood of Spanish restaurants, the Italian trattoria format here comes as a welcome change. The decor resembles a postmodern update of an Italian ruin, complete with trompe l'oeil walls painted like marble. Roman portrait busts and a prominent bar lend a dignified air. Menu choices include cannelloni, a good selection of veal dishes, and such main courses as osso bucco. You might begin your meal with a selection of antipasti.

Restaurante Salvador. Calle Barbieri, 12. ☎ **91-521-4524.** Reservations recommended. Main courses 1,600–3,200 ptas. ($9.60–$19.20). AE, MC, V. Mon–Sat 1:30–4pm and 9–11:30pm. Closed Aug. Metro: Chueca. SPANISH/BASQUE.

The owner of this bustling restaurant, José Blasquez Garcia, configured it as a mini-museum to his hobby and passion, the Spanish art of bullfighting. Inside, near a bar that stocks an impressive collection of sherries and whisky, you'll find the memorabilia of years of bull-watching, including photographs of great matadors beginning in the 1920s, and agrarian artifacts used in the raising and development of fighting bulls. The menu is as robust and two-fisted as the decor, featuring macho-sized platters of oxtail in red wine sauce; different preparations of hake, one of which is baked delectably in a salt crust; stuffed peppers, fried calamari and shrimp; and the local version of a dessert-based comfort food, *arroz con leche,* which most of the regular clients here seem to order by habit.

✪ **Taberna Carmencita.** Libertad, 16. ☎ **91-531-66-12.** Reservations recommended. Main courses 1,800–2,800 ptas. ($10.80–$16.80); fixed-price menu 1,500 ptas. ($9) available only at lunch. AE, DC, MC, V. Mon–Fri 1–4pm; Mon–Sat 9pm–midnight. Metro: Chueca or Banco de España. SPANISH/BASQUE.

Carmencita, founded in 1840 and exquisitely restored, is a street-corner enclave of old Spanish charm filled with 19th-century detailing and tile work. It was a favorite hangout for the poet Federico García Lorca, as well as a meeting place for intelligentsia in the pre-Civil War days. Meals might include entrecôte with green pepper sauce, escalope of veal, braised mollusks with port, fillet of pork, codfish with garlic, and Bilbao-style hake. Every Thursday the special dish is a complicated version of Madrid's famous *cocido.* Patrons wax lyrical over this regional stew and the chefs have had decades to get it right.

OFF THE PLAZA MAYOR
MODERATE

Casa Lucio. Cava Baja, 35. ☎ **91-365-32-52.** Reservations recommended. Main courses 2,500–3,600 ptas. ($15–$21.60). AE, DC, MC, V. Sun–Fri 1–4pm, daily 9pm–midnight. Closed Aug. Metro: La Latina. CASTILIAN.

Set on a historic street whose edges once marked the perimeter of Old Madrid, this is a venerable *tasca* with all the requisite antique accessories. Dozens of cured hams hang from hand-hewn beams above the well-oiled bar. Among the clientele is a stable of sometimes surprisingly well known public figures—perhaps even the king of Spain. The two dining rooms, each on a different floor, have whitewashed walls, tile floors, and exposed brick. A well-trained staff offers classic Castilian food, which might include Jabugo ham with broad beans, shrimp in garlic sauce, hake with green sauce, several types of roasted lamb, and a thick steak served sizzling hot on a heated platter, called *churrasco de la casa.*

El Schotis. Cava Baja, 11. ☎ **91-365-32-30.** Reservations recommended. Main courses 1,200–2,900 ptas. ($7.20–$17.40); fixed-price menu 3,250 ptas. ($19.50). AE, DC, MC, V. Daily 1–4pm; Mon–Sat 8:30pm–midnight. Metro: Puerta del Sol or La Latina. SPANISH.

El Schotis was established in 1962 on one of Madrid's oldest and most historic streets. A series of large and pleasingly old-fashioned dining rooms is the setting for an animated crowd of Madrileños and foreign visitors, who receive ample portions of conservative, well-prepared vegetables, salads, soups, fish, and above all, meat. Specialties of the house include roast baby lamb, grilled steaks and veal chops, shrimp with garlic, fried hake in green sauce, and traditional desserts. Although one reader found everything but the gazpacho ho-hum, this local favorite pleases thousands of diners annually. There's a bar near the entrance for tapas and before- or after-dinner drinks.

La Posada de la Villa. Cava Baja, 9. ☎ **91-366-1860.** Reservations recommended. Main courses 1,850–3,000 ptas. ($11.10–$18). AE, MC, V. Daily 1–4:30pm; Mon–Sat 8pm–midnight. Closed Aug. Metro: La Latina. SPANISH/GRILLED MEATS.

This historic inn founded in 1642 offers a modern, more sanitized version of the earthy, grilled cuisine that fed the stonemasons who built the thick walls around you. Within a trio of dining rooms whose textured plaster and old stonework absolutely reeks of Old Castile, you'll find a hardworking staff and a menu that focuses on a time-honored specialty—roasted baby lamb—that's ordered more often than anything else on the menu. Other excellent choices include different versions of hake; Madrid-style tripe, and the rich, savory stew (*cocida Madrileño*) that many local residents remember fondly from the days of their childhood. Notice that many of the chairs have brass plaques bearing the names of famous patrons—we saw one labeled "Janet Jackson" last time!

✪ Sobrino de Botín. Calle de Cuchilleros, 17. ☎ **91-366-42-17.** Reservations required. Main courses 1,000–3,200 ptas. ($6–$19.20); fixed-price menu 4,000 ptas. ($24). AE, DC, MC, V. Daily 1–4pm and 8pm–midnight. Metro: La Latina or Opera. SPANISH.

Ernest Hemingway made this restaurant famous. In the final two pages of his novel, *The Sun Also Rises,* Jake invites Brett to Botín for the Segovian specialty of roast suckling pig, washed down with Rioja Alta.

As you enter, you step back to 1725, the year the restaurant was founded. You'll see an open kitchen with a charcoal hearth, hanging copper pots, an 18th-century tile oven for roasting the suckling pig, and a big pot of soup whose aroma wafts across the tables. Painter Francisco Goya was once a dishwasher here. Your host, Antonio, never loses his cool—even when he has 18 guests standing in line waiting for tables.

The two house specialties are roast suckling pig and roast Segovian lamb. From the à la carte menu, you might try the fish-based "quarter-of-an-hour" soup. Good main dishes include baked Cantabrian hake and filet mignon with potatoes. The dessert list features strawberries (in season) with whipped cream. You can accompany your meal with Valdepeñas or Aragón wine, although most guests order sangría.

INEXPENSIVE

El Cosaco. Plaza de la Paja, 2. ☎ **91-365-3548.** Reservations recommended. Main courses 850–1,975 ptas. ($5.10–$11.85). AE, MC, V. Daily 9pm–midnight; Sun 1:30–3:30pm. Metro: La Latina. RUSSIAN.

One of the few Russian restaurants in Madrid sits adjacent to one of the most charming and evocative squares in town. Inside, you'll find a trio of dining rooms outfitted with paintings and artifacts from the former Soviet Union. Menu items seem to taste

Picnic, Anyone?

On a hot day, do as the Madrileños do: Secure the makings of a picnic lunch and head for Casa de Campo (metro: El Batón), those once-royal hunting grounds in the west of Madrid across the Manzanares River. Children delight in this adventure, as they can also visit a boating lake, the Parque de Atracciones, and the Madrid zoo.

Your best choice for picnic fare is **Rodilla,** Preciados, 25 (☎ **91-522-57-01;** metro: Callao), where you can find sandwiches, pastries, and take-out tapas. Sandwiches, including vegetarian, meat, and fish, begin at 95 ptas. (55¢). It's open Monday and Tuesday 8:30am to 10:30pm; Wednesday, Thursday, and Sunday 9am to 11pm; and Friday and Saturday 9am to 11:30pm.

best when preceded with something from a long list of vodkas, many of them from small-scale distilleries you might not immediately recognize. Items include rich and savory cold-weather dishes that seem a bit disjointed from the sweltering heat of Madrid, but which you might find as satisfying alternatives from the all-Spanish restaurants in the same neighborhood. Examples include beef Stroganoff; quenelles of pike-perch with fresh dill; and thin-sliced smoked salmon or smoked sturgeon that's artfully arranged with capers, chopped onions, and chopped hard-boiled eggs. Red or white versions of borscht make a worthy debut, and blinis, stuffed with caviar or paprika-laced beef, are always excellent.

La Chata. Cava Baja, 24. ☎ **91-366-14-58.** Reservations recommended. Main dishes 1,600–2,300 ptas. ($9.60–$13.80). AE, MC, V. Daily 12:30–5pm; Mon–Sat 8pm–midnight. Metro: La Latina. SPANISH.

The cuisine here is Castilian, Galician, and northern Spanish. Set behind a heavily ornamented tile facade, the place has a stand-up tapas bar at the entrance and a formal restaurant in a side room. Many locals linger in the darkly paneled bar, which is framed by hanging Serrano hams, cloves of garlic, and photographs of bullfighters. Full meals might include such dishes as roast suckling pig, roast lamb, *calamares en su tinta* (squid in its own ink), grilled fillet of steak with peppercorns, and omelets flavored with strips of eel.

IN THE ARTURO SORIA DISTRICT
MODERATE

Nicomedes. Moscatelar, 18. ☎ **91-388-7828.** Reservations recommended. Main courses 2,000–2,300 ptas. ($12–$13.80). AE, DC, MC, V. Tues–Sat 1:30–4pm and 9:30pm–midnight; Sun 1:30–4pm. Closed Aug. Metro: Esperanza and Arturo Soria. EXTREMADURAN.

This colonial-style building has been completely refurbished by the charming Suárez sisters into a modern-looking château of five floors with beautiful, tall bay windows covering the full height of this impressive edifice. The immensity of the windows allows copious amounts of natural light to flood into the dining areas. The pervading atmosphere is one of openness combined with friendly hospitality. Customers often dine out in fine weather on a summer terrace. The modernity of the building is reflected in the style of the cuisine as well. The dishes from the western province of Extremadura are given a Madrid showcase here. Goat cheese with glazed onions is a tasty opener, as are *bolsitas rellenas de gamba y queso fresco* (crispy pasta balls stuffed with shrimp and freshly made cheese). *Rapa al horno con habitas y ajetes* (baked monkfish with beans and tender garlic) is a savory offering, although *solomillo de buey,* or fondue of ox steak, is more typical of the region. For dessert, try the homemade cake of the day or a special sweet "biscuit" made with prunes and served with a caramel sauce. The house wine is Marti de la Costa from 1996.

NEAR PLAZA REPÚBLICA ARGENTINA
MODERATE

Casa Benigna. Benigno Soto, 9. ☎ **91-413-3356.** Reservations required. Main courses 3,500–4,000 ptas. ($21–$24); *menu sorpresa* 6,500 ptas. ($39). AE, DC, MC, V. Mon–Sat 1:30–3:30pm and 9–11pm; Sun 1:30–4pm. Closed Aug 7–21. Metro: Concha Espina. MEDITERRANEAN/SCANDINAVIAN.

This small bistro in the northern sector of Madrid has been run by the family of Jorge Garcia for more than a decade. It is decorated in typically inviting Mediterranean style with blue walls and with murals of rural landscapes, even a library of books. The restaurant is the only one in Madrid that blends the cuisine of the far north of Europe with that of the sunny Mediterranean countries. The family has a close relative in Norway who contributes to their Scandinavian recipes. The dishes are exquisitely prepared and based on the finest ingredients. Here you can order everything from Norwegian herring in delectable marinades to *arroz abanda,* a variation of traditional paella using different varieties of seafood. One especially good dish is *mamoncillo de cordero mechado,* or roast ribs of tender baby lamb. Many vegetarians and others appreciate their *parillada de verduras,* or grilled fresh vegetables. For dessert opt for the Norwegian cookies with wild berries or freshly made crêpes with apple sauce.

Príncipe y Serrano. Serrano, 240. ☎ **91-458-8676.** Reservations recommended. Main courses 1,700–3,500 ptas. ($10.20–$21); *menu completo* 6,500 ptas. ($39). AE, DC, MC, V. Mon–Fri 1:30–4pm and 8:30pm–midnight; Sat 8:30pm–midnight. Closed Aug. Metro: Colombia and Concha Espino. CASTILIAN.

In an exclusive area of the Serrano district, this classic restaurant exudes distinction. Its sophisticated dining areas on both floors offer a warm and cozy atmosphere, and the outside lawns and flowered patios (one of them resembling a miniature golf course with small swimming pools) make you forget you are in the center of a big city. There is the big *salon central,* two small dining areas for more private dinners, plus a bar downstairs. The cooking is simple yet cosmopolitan and always done under the close supervision of the two daughters of the famed Salvador Gallego, who is known as the master of haute Spanish cuisine in the Sierra of Madrid. The cookery is classic but inventive, as evoked by an especially good dish—roast potatoes with mussels. Based on the sea's bounty, try the *merluza al estilo abuela Salvadora* (baked hake with onions gratinée and ham) or the *manitas de Iberico rellenas de morcilla* (pork filled with chorizo, that spicy Spanish sausage). We take delight in the freshly made apple tart with prune sauce or the crêpes filled with mango and served in a fancy caramel cream sauce.

INEXPENSIVE

La Atalaya. Joaquin Costa, 31. ☎ **91-562-8745.** Reservations recommended. Main courses 2,300–2,600 ptas. ($13.80–$15.60); fixed-price menu 1,600 ptas. ($9.60). AE, DC, MC, V. Tues–Sat 1:30–4pm and 9pm–midnight; Sun 1:30–4pm. Closed Aug. Metro: República de Argentina. CANTABRIAN.

The owner of this pleasant restaurant, Gena Sanchez, hails from Santander in Northern Spain and, in the typical style of her hometown, has decorated the yellow walls of her establishment with a plethora of modern paintings. The food is also typical of Spain's green northern coast, with an emphasis on fresh fish. Every Thursday and Saturday the chefs prepare the most typical dish of Santander, a hearty cabbage soup. Called *cocido montanés,* it is also made with sausage, green beans, and black pudding.

Caracoles marucas, or clams Santander style, prepared in a spicy sauce, is another good offering, as is *sopa de pescado,* or fish soup, one of the finest of its kind in Madrid. You might opt for a *torta de queso caliente,* a warm cheese soufflé. For dessert, traditional regional puddings are served.

NEAR CIUDAD UNIVERSITARIA
EXPENSIVE

San Mamés. Bravo Murillo, 88. ☎ **91-534-5065.** Reservations recommended. Fixed-price menus 5,000–6,000 ptas. ($30–$36). AE, DC, MC, V. Mon–Fri 1:30–4pm and 8:30–11:30pm; Sat 1:30–4pm. Closed Aug. Metro: Cuatro Caminos. BASQUE/MADRILEÑA.

Situated in the north of the city in a historic building, this restaurant has been in the hands of the Garcia family more than 50 years. The *tasca* (tavern) is decorated with colorful ceramic tiles and photographs of the celebrities who have dined here over the years. It is considered something of a secret address. Only two rooms, it has an atmosphere of intimacy and good cheer, almost homelike. The style of cookery offers some of the best cuisine from both the Madrid and Basque kitchens. The owners shop carefully for the ingredients to prepare a repertoire of very tasty and well-flavored dishes. Their most typical dish is *callos a la Madrileña,* a tripe stew with meat and chickpeas, beloved by their habitués. Otherwise, you might opt for *bacalao aquarido,* salt cod prepared with green peppers, tomatoes, and onions. Another dish favored in the Basque country is *cocochas de merluza,* which are the cheeks of the hake fish served with a bread sauce. For dessert, the owners recommend their *requeson con pasas,* or cheesecake with raisins, or a hearty pudding called *tocino de cielo.*

INEXPENSIVE

Las Batuecas. Avenida Reina Victoria, 17, 28033. ☎ **91-554-0452.** Reservations required. Main courses 1,800–2,200 ptas. ($10.80–$13.20); fixed-price menu 1,300 ptas. ($7.80); *menu completo* 3,000 ptas. ($18). No credit cards. Mon–Fri 1–4pm and 9–11pm; Sat 1–4pm. Closed Aug. Metro: Guzmán El Bueno and Cuatro Caminos. SPANISH.

This restaurant unpretentiously calls itself *a casa de comidas,* or "meal house." Since 1954, the little restaurant of José Pascual and his family has been located near the *ciudad universitaria.* Many of their customers originally came here as students, and over the years have become devotees of the homemade Spanish food, which is wholesome and good without being pretentious. The decoration is plain, with old paintings and newspaper articles intermixed with cartoons and reviews by travel and food magazines in different languages. It has two floors with tables, all in the rustic style. But no one comes here for decor; the food is the attraction. Come here with a big appetite and launch yourself into a fine meal with such dishes as *tortilla de callos,* or omelet with tripe, perhaps squid cooked in its ink. You can try their fresh artichokes cooked with white wine and ham or *berenjenas rebosadas* (sliced eggplant batter-fried). One of the tastiest main dishes is shoulder flank of lamb roast, perfectly done. Desserts include cakes made from almonds, chocolate, or vanilla, or a fine selection of puddings.

OUR FAVORITE *TASCAS*

Don't starve waiting around for Madrid's fashionable 9:30 or 10pm dinner hour. Throughout the city you'll find *tascas,* bars that serve wine and platters of tempting hot and cold hors d'oeuvres known as tapas: mushrooms, salads, baby eels, shrimp, lobster, mussels, sausage, ham—and, in one establishment at least, bull testicles. Below we've listed our favorite tapas bars. Keep in mind that you can often save pesetas by ordering at the bar rather than occupying a table.

Casa Mingo. Paseo de la Florida, 2. ☎ **91-547-79-18.** Main courses 550–1,200 ptas. ($3.30–$7.20). No credit cards. Daily 11am–midnight. Metro: Norte, then 15-min. walk. SPANISH.

Casa Mingo has been known for decades for its cider, both still and bubbly. The perfect accompanying tidbit is a piece of the local Asturian *cabrales* (goat cheese), but the roast chicken is the specialty of the house, with a large number of helpings served daily. There's no formality here, since customers share big tables under the vaulted ceiling in the dining room. In summer, the staff sets up tables and wooden chairs out on the sidewalk. This is not so much a restaurant as a *bodega/taverna* that serves food.

Cervecería Alemania. Plaza de Santa Ana, 6. ☎ **91-429-70-33.** Beer 200–400 ptas. ($1.20–$2.40); tapas 300–2,000 ptas. ($1.80–$12). No credit cards. Sun–Thurs 11am–12:30am; Fri–Sat 11am–2am. Metro: Alonso Martín or Tirso de Molina. TAPAS.

This place earned its name because of its long-ago German clients. Opening directly onto one of the liveliest little plazas in Madrid, it clings to its turn-of-the-century traditions. Young Madrileños are fond of stopping in for a mug of draft beer. You can sit at one of the tables leisurely sipping beer or wine since the waiters make no attempt to hurry you along. To accompany your beverage, try the fried sardines or a Spanish omelet. Many of the *tascas* on this popular square are crowded and noisy—often with blaring loud music—but this one is quiet and a good place to have a conversation.

Cervecería Santa Bárbara. Plaza de Santa Bárbara, 8. ☎ **91-319-04-049.** Beer 150–300 ptas. ($.90–$1.80); tapas 350–4,000 ptas. ($2.10–$24). MC, V. Daily 11:30am–midnight. Metro: Alonzo Martínez. Bus: 3, 7, or 21. TAPAS.

Unique in Madrid, Cervecería Santa Bárbara is an outlet for a beer factory, and the management has spent a lot to make it modern and inviting. Hanging globe lights and spinning ceiling fans create an attractive ambience, as does the black-and-white checkerboard marble floor. You go here for beer, of course: *cerveza negra* (black beer) or *cerveza dorada* (golden beer). The local brew is best accompanied by homemade potato chips or by fresh shrimp, lobster, crabmeat, or barnacles. You can either stand at the counter or go directly to one of the wooden tables for waiter service.

Taberna Toscana. Manuel Fernandez y Gonzales, 10. ☎ **91-429-60-31.** Beer 140 ptas. (85¢), glass of wine 110 ptas. (65¢); tapas 250–4,000 ptas. ($1.50–$24). MC, V. Tues–Sat noon–4pm and 8pm–midnight. Closed Aug. Metro: Puerta del Sol or Sevilla. TAPAS.

Many Madrileños begin their nightly *tasca* crawl here. The ambience is that of a village inn that's far removed from 20th-century Madrid. You sit on crude country stools, under sausages, peppers, and sheaves of golden wheat that hang from the age-darkened beams. The long, tiled bar is loaded with tasty tidbits, including the house specialties: *lacón y cecina* (boiled ham), *habas* (broad beans) with Spanish ham, and *chorizo* (a sausage of red peppers and pork)—almost meals in themselves. Especially delectable are the kidneys in sherry sauce and the snails in hot sauce.

5 Seeing the Sights

THE TOP ATTRACTIONS

In the heart of Madrid, near the Puerta del Sol metro stop, the **Plaza Mayor** is the city's most famous square. It was known as the Plaza de Arrabal in medieval times, when it stood outside the city wall. The original architect of Plaza Mayor itself was Juan Gómez de Mora, who worked during the reign of Philip III. Under the Hapsburgs, the square rose in importance as the site of public spectacles, including the abominable *autos-da-fé*, in which heretics were burned. Bullfights, knightly tournaments, and festivals were also staged here.

Central Madrid Attractions

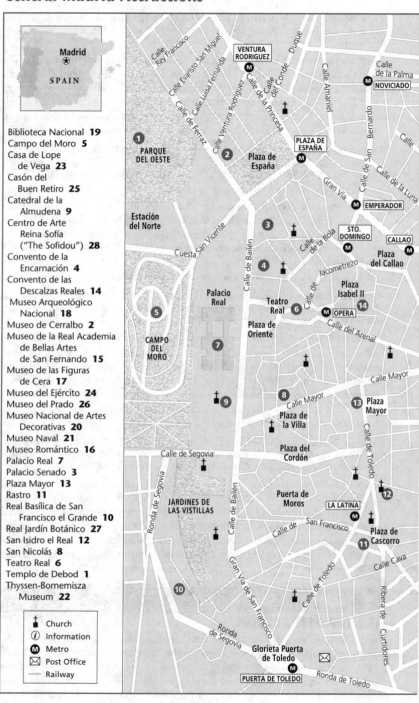

Biblioteca Nacional **19**
Campo del Moro **5**
Casa de Lope
 de Vega **23**
Casón del
 Buen Retiro **25**
Catedral de la
 Almudena **9**
Centro de Arte
 Reina Sofía
 ("The Sofidou") **28**
Convento de la
 Encarnación **4**
Convento de las
 Descalzas Reales **14**
Museo Arqueológico
 Nacional **18**
Museo de Cerralbo **2**
Museo de la Real Academia
 de Bellas Artes
 de San Fernando **15**
Museo de las Figuras
 de Cera **17**
Museo del Ejército **24**
Museo del Prado **26**
Museo Nacional de Artes
 Decorativas **20**
Museo Naval **21**
Museo Romántico **16**
Palacio Real **7**
Palacio Senado **3**
Plaza Mayor **13**
Rastro **11**
Real Basílica de San
 Francisco el Grande **10**
Real Jardín Botánico **27**
San Isidro el Real **12**
San Nicolás **8**
Teatro Real **6**
Templo de Debod **1**
Thyssen-Bornemisza
 Museum **22**

† Church
ⓘ Information
Ⓜ Metro
⊠ Post Office
⋯⋯ Railway

Madrid
★
SPAIN

PARQUE DEL OESTE

VENTURA RODRIGUEZ
NOVICIADO
PLAZA DE ESPAÑA
Plaza de España
Gran Via
EMPERADOR
Estación del Norte
STO. DOMINGO
CALLAO
Plaza del Callao
Cuesta San Vicente
Palacio Real
Plaza Isabel II
Teatro Real
Plaza de Oriente
OPERA
Calle del Arenal
CAMPO DEL MORO
Calle Mayor
Plaza Mayor
Plaza de la Villa
Plaza del Cordón
Calle de Segovia
JARDINES DE LAS VISTILLAS
Puerta de Moros
LA LATINA
Plaza de Cascorro
Glorieta Puerta de Toledo
PUERTA DE TOLEDO
Ronda de Toledo

126

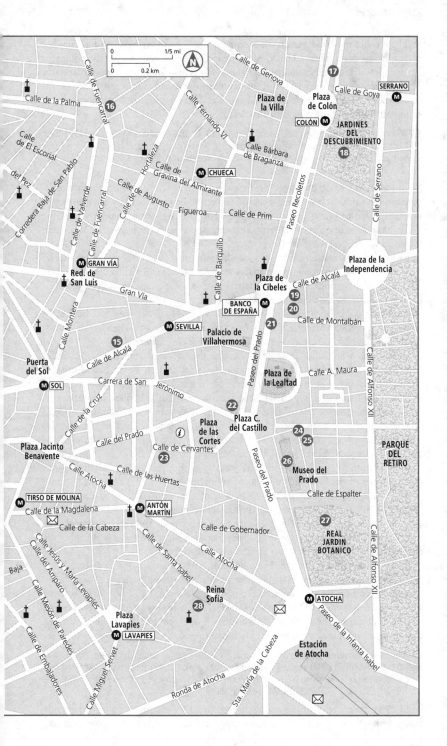

Three times the buildings on the square burned—in 1631, 1672, and 1790—but each time the plaza bounced back. After the last big fire it was completely redesigned by Juan de Villanueva. Nowadays a Christmas fair is held around the equestrian statue of Philip III (dating from 1616) in the center of the square. On summer nights, the Plaza Mayor becomes the virtual living room of Madrid, as tourists sip sangría at the numerous cafes and listen to street musicians.

✪ **Museo del Prado.** Paseo del Prado. ☎ **91-330-28-00.** Admission 500 ptas. ($3) adults, 250 ptas. ($1.50) students and seniors. Tues–Sat 9am–7pm; Sun and holidays 9am–2pm. Closed Jan 1, Good Friday, May 1, and Dec 25. Metro: Banco de España or Atocha. Bus: 10, 14, 27, 34, 37, or 45.

With more than 7,000 paintings, the Prado is one of the most important repositories of art in the world. It began as a royal collection and was enhanced by the Hapsburgs, especially Charles V, and later the Bourbons. For paintings of the Spanish school, the Prado has no equal; on your first visit, concentrate on the Spanish masters (Velázquez, Goya, El Greco, and Murillo).

Major Italian works are exhibited on the ground floor. You'll see art by Italian masters—Raphael, Botticelli, Mantegna, Andrea del Sarto, Fra Angelico, and Correggio. The most celebrated Italian painting here is Titian's voluptuous Venus being watched by a musician who can't keep his eyes on his work.

The Prado is a trove of the work of El Greco (ca. 1541–1614), the Crete-born artist who lived much of his life in Toledo. You can see a parade of "The Greek's" saints, Madonnas, and Holy Families—even a ghostly *John the Baptist.*

You'll find a splendid array of works by the incomparable Diego Velázquez (1599–1660). The museum's most famous painting, in fact, is his *Las Meninas,* a triumph for its use of light effects. The faces of the queen and king are reflected in the mirror in the painting itself. The artist in the foreground is Velázquez, of course.

The Flemish painter Peter Paul Rubens (1577–1640), who met Velázquez while in Spain, is represented by the peacock-blue *Garden of Love* and by the *Three Graces.* Also worthy is the work of José Ribera (1591–1652), a Valencia-born artist and contemporary of Velázquez whose best painting is the *Martyrdom of St. Philip.* The Seville-born Bartolomé Murillo (1617–82)—often referred to as the "painter of Madonnas"—has three versions of the Immaculate Conception on display.

The Prado has an outstanding collection of the work of Hieronymus Bosch (1450?–1516), the Flemish genius. *The Garden of Earthly Delights,* the best-known work of "El Bosco," is here. You'll also see his *Seven Deadly Sins* and his triptych *The Hay Wagon. The Triumph of Death* is by another Flemish painter, Pieter Breughel the Elder (1525?–69), who carried on Bosch's ghoulish vision.

Francisco de Goya (1746–1828) ranks along with Velázquez and El Greco in the trio of great Spanish artists. Hanging here are his unflattering portraits of his patron, Charles IV, and his family, as well as the *Clothed Maja* and the *Naked Maja.* You can see the much-reproduced *Third of May* (1808), plus a series of Goya sketches (some of which, depicting the decay of 18th-century Spain, brought the Inquisition down on the artist) and his expressionistic "black paintings."

✪ **Thyssen-Bornemisza Museum.** Palacio de Villahermosa, Paseo del Prado, 8. ☎ **91-369-01-51.** Admission 700 ptas. ($4.20) adults, 400 ptas. ($2.40) students and seniors, free for children 11 and under. Tues–Sun 10am–7pm. Metro: Banco de España. Bus: 1, 2, 5, 9, 10, 14, 15, 20, 27, 34, 45, 51, 52, 53, 74, 146, or 150.

Until 1985 the contents of this museum overflowed the premises of a legendary villa near Lugano, Switzerland; it was a hugely popular attraction there. The collection had been laboriously amassed over a period of about 60 years by the wealthy Thyssen-Bornemisza family, of Holland, Germany, and Hungary. Experts had proclaimed it one of the world's most extensive and valuable privately owned collections, rivaled only by the holdings of Queen Elizabeth II. For tax and insurance reasons, and because the collection had outgrown the boundaries of its lakeside villa, the collection was discreetly put on the market in the early 1980s to the world's major museums. Amid endless intrigue, glamorous supplicants from eight different nations came calling. Among them were Margaret Thatcher and Prince Charles; trustees of the Getty Museum in Los Angeles; the president of West Germany; and the duke of Badajoz, brother-in-law of King Carlos II. Even emissaries from Walt Disney World came! Eventually, the collection was awarded to Spain for $350 million. Controversies over the huge public cost of the acquisition raged for months. Despite the brouhaha, various estimates have placed the value of this collection between $1 and $3 billion.

To house the collection, an 18th-century building adjacent to the Prado, the Villa-hermosa Palace, was retrofitted with appropriate lighting and security devices, and renovated at a cost of $45 million. Rooms are arranged numerically so that by following the order of the various rooms (numbers 1 through 48, spread out over three floors), a logical sequence of European painting can be traced from the 13th through the 20th centuries. The nucleus of the collection consists of 700 world-class paintings. They include works by, among others, El Greco, Velázquez, Dürer, Rembrandt, Watteau, Canaletto, Caravaggio, Hals, Memling, and Goya.

Unusual among the world's great art collections because of its eclecticism, the Thyssen group also contains 19th- and 20th-century paintings by many of the notable French impressionists, as well as works by Picasso, Sargent, Kirchner, Nolde, and Kandinsky—artists who had never been well represented in Spanish museums. In addition to European paintings, major American works can be viewed here, including paintings by Thomas Cole, Winslow Homer, Jackson Pollock, Mark Rothko, Edward Hopper, Robert Rauschenberg, Stuart Davis, and Roy Lichtenstein. There is an agreeable and moderately priced cafeteria and restaurant on site.

✪ **Museo Nacional Centro de Arte Reina Sofía.** Santa Isabel, 52. ☎ **91-467-50-62.** Admission 500 ptas. ($3), free after 2:30pm on Sat and all day Sun. Mon and Wed–Sat 10am–9pm; Sun 10am–2:30pm. Free guided tours Mon and Wed at 5pm, Sat at 11am. Metro: Atocha.

What the Prado is to traditional art, this museum is to modern art. Madrid's "MoMA" (Museum of Modern Art) is the greatest repository of 20th-century works in Spain. Set within the echoing, futuristically renovated walls of the former General Hospital, originally built between 1776 and 1781, the museum is a sprawling, high-ceilinged showplace. Once designated "the ugliest building in Spain" by Catalán architect Oriol Bohigas, the Reina Sofía has a design that hangs in limbo somewhere between the 18th and the 21st centuries. It incorporates a 50,000-volume art library and database, a cafe, a theater, and a bookstore.

Special emphasis is paid to the great artists of 20th-century Spain: Juan Gris, Salvador Dalí, Joan Miró, and Pablo Picasso (the museum has been able to acquire a handful of his works). What many critics feel is Picasso's masterpiece, *Guernica,* now rests at this museum after a long and troubling history of traveling. Banned in Spain during Franco's era (Picasso refused to allow it to be displayed here anyway), it hung until 1980 at New York's Museum of Modern Art. The fiercely antiwar painting immortalizes the town's shameful blanket bombing by the German Luftwaffe, who were fighting for Franco during the Spanish Civil War. Guernica was the cradle of the Basque nation, and Picasso's canvas made it a household name around the world.

✪ **Museo Lázaro Galdiano.** Serrano, 122. ☎ **91-561-60-84.** Admission 500 ptas. ($3). Tues–Sun 10am–2pm. Closed holidays and Aug. Metro: Rubén Darío or Núñez de Balboa. Bus: 9, 16, 19, 27, 45, 51, 61, 89, or 114.

Imagine 37 rooms in a well-preserved 19th-century mansion bulging with artworks—including many by the most famous old masters of Europe. Most visitors take the elevator to the top floor and work down, lingering over 15th-century handwoven vestments, swords and daggers, royal seals, 16th-century Limoges crystal, Byzantine jewelry, Italian bronzes from ancient times to the Renaissance, and medieval armor.

One painting by Bosch evokes his own peculiar brand of horror, the canvas peopled with creepy fiends devouring human flesh. The Spanish masters are the best represented: El Greco, Velázquez, Zurbarán, Ribera, Murillo, and Valdés-Leal.

One section is devoted to works by the English portrait and landscape artists Reynolds, Gainsborough, and Constable. Italian artists exhibited include Tiepolo and Guardi. Salon 30—for many, the most interesting—is devoted to Goya and includes paintings from his "black period." This off-the-beaten track museum is a gem and usually enjoyably underpopulated, a nice contrast to the overcrowded Prado, Thyssen, and Reina Sofía.

✪ **Palacio Real (Royal Palace).** Plaza de Oriente, Calle de Bailén, 2. ☎ **91-454-8700.** Admission 850 ptas. ($5.10) adults, 350 ptas. ($2.10) students and children. Mon–Sat 9am–6pm; Sun 9am–3pm. Metro: Opera or Plaza de España.

This huge palace was begun in 1738 on the site of the Madrid Alcázar, which burned to the ground in 1734. Some of its 2,000 rooms—which that "enlightened despot" Charles III called home—are open to the public; others are still used for state business. The palace was last used as a royal residence in 1931 before King Alfonso XIII and his wife, Victoria Eugénie, fled Spain.

Highlights of a visit include the Reception Room, the State Apartments, the Armory, and the Royal Pharmacy. The Reception Room and State Apartments should get priority here if you're rushed. They embrace a rococo room with a diamond clock; a porcelain salon; the Royal Chapel; the Banquet Room, where receptions for heads of state are still held; and the Throne Room.

The rooms are literally stuffed with art treasures and antiques—salon after salon of monumental grandeur, with no apologies for the damask, mosaics, Tiepolo ceilings, gilt and bronze, chandeliers, and paintings.

If your visit falls on the first Wednesday of the month, look for the changing of the guard ceremony, which occurs at noon and is free to the public.

In the Armory, you'll see the finest collection of weaponry in Spain. Many of the items—powder flasks, shields, lances, helmets, and saddles—are from the collection of Carlos V. From here, the comprehensive tour takes you into the Pharmacy. Afterward, stroll through the Campo del Moro, the gardens of the palace.

Panteón de Goya (Goya's Tomb). Glorieta de San Antonio de la Florida, s/n. ☎ **91-542-07-22.** Admission 300 ptas. ($1.80), free on Wed and Sun. Tues–Fri 10am–2pm and 4–8pm; Sat–Sun 10am–2pm (in summer daily 10am–2pm only). Metro: Norte. Bus: 41, 46, 75, or C.

In a remote part of town beyond the Norte train station lies Goya's tomb, containing one of his masterpieces: an elaborately beautiful fresco depicting the miracles of St. Anthony on the dome and cupola of the little hermitage of San Antonio de la Florida. This has been called Goya's Sistine Chapel. Already deaf when he began the painting, Goya labored dawn to dusk for 16 weeks, painting with sponges rather than brushes. By depicting common street life—stone masons, prostitutes, and beggars—Goya raised the ire of the nobility who held judgment until the patron, Carlos IV, viewed it. When the monarch approved, the formerly outrageous painting was deemed acceptable.

The tomb and fresco are in one of the twin chapels (visit the one on the right) that were built in the latter part of the 18th century. Discreetly placed mirrors will help you see the ceiling better.

✪ **Monasterio de las Descalzas Reales.** Plaza de las Descalzas Reales, s/n. ☎ **91-542-00-59.** Admission 650 ptas. ($3.90) adults, 350 ptas. ($2.10) children. Sat and Tues–Thurs 10:30am–12:30pm and 4–5pm; Fri 10:30am–12:30pm; Sun 11am–1:15pm. Bus: 1, 2, 5, 20, 46, 52, 53, 74, M1, M2, M3, or M5. From Plaza del Callao, off Gran Vía, walk down Postigo de San Martín to Plaza de las Descalzas Reales; the convent is on the left.

In the mid–16th century, aristocratic women either disappointed in love or wanting to be the "bride of Christ" stole away to this convent to take the veil. Each brought a dowry, making this one of the richest convents in the land. By the mid–20th century, the convent sheltered mostly poor women. True, it still contained a priceless collection of art treasures, but the sisters were forbidden to auction anything, so they were literally starving. The state intervened, and the pope granted special dispensation to open the convent as a museum. Today the public can look behind the walls of what was once a mysterious edifice on one of the most beautiful squares in Old Madrid.

An English-speaking guide will show you through. In the Reliquary are the noble-women's dowries, one of which is said to contain bits of wood from Christ's Cross; another, some of the bones of St. Sebastian. The most valuable painting is Titian's *Caesar's Money.* The Flemish Hall shelters other fine works, including paintings by Hans de Beken and Breughel the Elder. All the tapestries were based on Rubens's cartoons, displaying his chubby matrons.

Real Fábrica de Tapices (Royal Tapestry Factory). Fuenterrabía, 2. ☎ **91-434-0551.** Admission 250 ptas. ($1.50). Mon–Fri 9am–2pm. Closed Aug and holidays. Metro: Menéndez Pelayo. Bus: 10, 14, 26, 32, 37, C, or M9.

In this factory the age-old process of making exquisite (and very expensive) tapestries is still carried on with consummate skill. Nearly every tapestry is based on a cartoon of Goya, the factory's most famous employee. Many of these patterns, such as *The Pottery Salesman,* are still in production today. (Goya's original drawings are in the Prado.) Many of the other designs are based on cartoons by Francisco Bayeu, Goya's brother-in-law.

THE BULLFIGHT

Madrid draws the finest matadors in Spain. If a matador hasn't proved his worth in the **Plaza Monumental de Toros de las Ventas,** Alcalá, 237 (☎ **91-356-22-00;** metro: Ventas), he just hasn't been recognized as a top-flight artist. The major season begins during the Fiestas de San Isidro, patron saint of Madrid, on May 15. This is the occasion for a series of fights with talent scouts in the audience. Matadors who distinguish themselves in the ring are signed up for Majorca, Málaga, and other places.

The best way to get tickets to the bullfights is at the stadium's box office (open Friday to Sunday 10am to 2pm and 5 to 8pm). Alternatively, you can contact one of Madrid's most competent ticket agents, **Localidades Galicia,** Plaza del Carmen, 1 (☎ **91-531-27-32;** metro: Puerto del Sol). It's open Tuesday to Saturday 9:30am to 1:30pm and 4:30 to 7:30pm, and Sunday 9:30am to 1:30pm; in May, it's open Monday to Saturday 9:30am to 8pm and Sunday 9:30am to 2pm. Regardless of where you buy them, tickets to bullfights range from 2,000 to 20,000 ptas. ($12 to $120), depending on the event and the position of your seat within the stadium. Concierges for virtually every reputable upper-bracket hotel in Madrid can acquire tickets, through inner channels of their own, to bullfights and other sought-after entertainment. Front-row seats at the bullfights are known as *barreras*. *Delanteras* (third-row seats) are available in both the *alta* (high) and the *baja* (low) sections. The cheapest seats sold, *filas,* afford the worst view and are in the sun (*sol*) during the entire performance. The best seats are in the shade (*sombra*). Bullfights are held on Sunday and holidays throughout most of the year, and every day during certain festivals, which tend to last around 3 weeks, usually in the late spring. Starting times are adjusted according to the anticipated hour of sundown on the day of a performance, usually 7pm from March to October and 5pm during late autumn and early spring. Late-night fights by neophyte matadors are sometimes staged under spotlights on Saturday around 11pm.

IF YOU HAVE MORE TIME
MUSEUMS

Museo Arqueológico Nacional. Serrano, 13. ☎ **91-577-79-12.** Admission 500 ptas. ($3), free for children and adults over 65. Free on Sat 2:30–8:30pm and Sun. Tues–Sat 9:30am–8:30pm; Sun 9:30am–2:30pm. Metro: Serrano or Retiro. Bus: 1, 9, 19, 51, 74, or M2.

This stately mansion is a storehouse of artifacts from the prehistoric to the baroque. One of the prime exhibits here is the Iberian statue *The Lady of Elche*, a piece of primitive carving (from the 4th century B.C.) discovered on the southeastern coast of Spain. Finds from Ibiza, Paestum, and Rome are on display, including statues of Tiberius and his mother, Livia. The Islamic collection from Spain is outstanding. There are collections of Spanish Renaissance lusterware, Talavera pottery, Retiro porcelain, and some rare 16th- and 17th-century Andalusian glassware.

Many of the exhibits are treasures that were removed from churches and monasteries. A much-photographed choir stall from the palace of Palencia dates from the 14th century. Also worth a look are the reproductions of the Altamira cave paintings (chiefly of bison, horses, and boars), discovered near Santander in northern Spain in 1868.

Museo de América (Museum of the Americas). Avenida de los Reyes Católicos, 6. ☎ **91-549-2641.** Free admission. Tues–Sat 10am–3pm; Sun 10am–2:30pm. Metro: Moncloa.

This museum, situated near the university campus, houses an outstanding collection of pre-Columbian, Spanish-American, and Native American art and artifacts. Various exhibits chronicle the progress of the inhabitants of the New World from the Paleolithic period to the present day. One exhibit, "Groups, Tribes, Chiefdoms, and States," focuses on the social structure of the various peoples of the Americas. Another display outlines the various religions and deities associated with them. Also included in the museum is an exhibit dedicated to communication, highlighting written as well as nonverbal expressions of art.

Museo del Ejército (Army Museum). Méndez Núñez, 1. ☎ **91-522-89-77.** Admission 100 ptas. (60¢) adults, free for children under 18 and adults over 65. Tues–Sun 10am–2pm. Metro: Banco de España or Retiro. Bus: 10, 19, 27, or 34.

This museum in the Buen Retiro Palace houses outstanding exhibits from military history, including El Cid's original sword. In addition, you can see the tent used by Charles V in Tunisia, relics of Pizarro and Cortés, and an exceptional collection of armor. Look for the piece of the cross that Columbus carried when he landed in the New World. The museum had a notorious founder: Manuel Godoy, who rose from relative poverty to become the lover of María Luisa of Parma, wife of Carlos IV.

Museo de la Real Academia de Bellas Artes de San Fernando (Fine Arts Museum). Alcalá, 13. ☎ **91-522-1491.** Admission 400 ptas. ($2.40) adults, 200 ptas. ($1.20) students.

Free for children 17 and under. Tues–Fri 9am–7pm; Sat–Mon 9am–2pm. Metro: Puerta del Sol or Sevilla. Bus: 15, 20, 51, 52, 53, or 150.

An easy stroll from Puerta del Sol, the Fine Arts Museum is located in the restored and remodeled 17th-century baroque palace of Juan de Goyeneche. The collection—more than 1,500 paintings and 570 sculptures, ranging from the 16th century to the present—was started in 1752 during the reign of Fernando VI (1746–59). It emphasizes works by Spanish, Flemish, and Italian artists. You can see masterpieces by El Greco, Rubens, Velázquez, Zurbarán, Ribera, Cano, Coello, Murillo, Goya, and Sorolla.

Museo Municipal. Fuencarral, 78. ☎ **91-588-86-72.** Admission 300 ptas. ($1.80) adults, 150 ptas. (90¢) seniors and children under 18. Free Wed and Sun. Tues–Fri 9:30am–8pm; Sat–Sun 10am–2pm. Metro: Bilbao or Tribunal. Bus: 3, 21, 40, 147, or 149.

After years of restoration, the Museo Municipal again displays collections on local history, archaeology, and art, with an emphasis on the Bourbon Madrid of the 18th century. Paseos with strolling couples are shown on huge tapestry cartoons. Paintings from the royal collections are here, plus period models of the best-known city squares and a Goya that was painted for the Town Hall.

Museo Nacional de Artes Decorativas. Calle de Montalbán, 12. ☎ **91-532-64-99.** Admission 400 ptas. ($2.40) adults, 200 ptas. ($1.20) students, children, and seniors. Tues–Fri 9:30am–3pm; Sat–Sun 10am–2pm. Metro: Banco de España. Bus: 14, 27, 34, 37, or 45.

In 62 rooms spread over several floors, this museum near the Plaza de la Cibeles displays a rich collection of furniture, ceramics, and decorative pieces. Emphasizing the 16th and 17th centuries, the eclectic collection includes Gothic carvings, alabaster figurines, festival crosses, dollhouses, baroque four-poster beds, a chapel covered with leather tapestries, and even kitchens from the 18th century. Two new floors focusing on the 18th and 19th centuries have recently been added to the museum.

Museo Naval. Paseo del Prado, 5. ☎ **91-379-52-99.** Free admission. Tues–Sun 10:30am–1:30pm. Closed Aug. Metro: Banco de España. Bus: 2, 14, 27, 40, 51, 52, or M6.

The history of nautical science and the Spanish navy, from the time of Isabella and Ferdinand until today, comes alive at the Museo Naval. The most fascinating exhibit is the map made by the *Santa María*'s first mate to show the Spanish monarchs the new discoveries. There are also souvenirs of the Battle of Trafalgar.

Museo Romántico. San Mateo, 13. ☎ **91-448-10-71.** Admission 400 ptas. ($2.40) adults, 200 ptas. ($1.20) students and children, free for seniors over 65 years. Tues–Sat 9am–3pm; Sun 10am–2pm. Closed Aug. Metro: Alonso Martínez.

Geared toward those seeking the romanticism of the 19th century, this museum is housed in a mansion decorated with numerous period pieces: crystal chandeliers, faded portraits, oils from Goya to Sorolla, opulent furnishings, and porcelain. Many exhibits date from the days of Isabella II, the high-living, fun-loving queen who was forced into exile and eventual abdication.

Museo Sorolla. General Martínez Campos, 37. ☎ **91-310-15-84.** Admission 400 ptas. ($2.40). Tues–Sat 10am–3pm; Sun 10am–2pm. Metro: Iglesia or Rubén Darío. Bus: 5, 16, 61, 40, or M3.

From 1912, painter Joaquín Sorolla and his family occupied this elegant Madrileño townhouse off Paseo de la Castellana. His widow turned it over to the government, and it is now maintained as a memorial. Much of the house remains as Sorolla left it, right down to his stained paintbrushes and pipes. The museum wing displays a representative collection of his works.

⊙ Frommer's Favorite Madrid Experiences

Tasca **Hopping.** This is the quintessential Madrid experience and the fastest way for a visitor to tap into the local scene. *Tascas* are Spanish pubs serving tapas, those tantalizing appetizers. You can go from one to the other, sampling each tavern's special dishes and wines.

Eating "Around Spain." The variety of gastronomic experiences is staggering: You can literally restaurant-hop from province to province without ever leaving Madrid.

Viewing the Works of Your Favorite Artist. Spend an afternoon at the Prado, savoring the works of your favorite Spanish artist, devoting all your attention to his work.

Bargain Hunting at El Rastro. Madrid has one of the greatest flea markets in Europe, if not the world. Wander through its many offerings to discover that hidden treasure you've been searching for.

Enjoying a Night of Flamenco. Flamenco folk songs (*cante*) and dances (*baile*) are an integral part of the Spanish experience. Spend at least one night in a flamenco tavern listening to the heart-rending laments of gypsy sorrows and dreams.

Outdoor-Cafe Sitting. This is a famous experience for the summertime, when Madrileños come alive again on their terrazas. The drinking and good times can go on until dawn. From glamorous hangouts to lowly street corners, the cafe scene takes place mainly along the axis formed by the Paseo de la Castellana, Paseo del Prado, and Paseo de Recoletos (all of which make up one continuous street).

Although Sorolla painted portraits of Spanish aristocrats, he was essentially interested in the common people, often depicting them in their native dress. On view are the artist's self-portrait and the paintings of his wife and their son. Sorolla was especially fond of painting beach scenes of the Costa Blanca.

Museo Taurino (Bullfighting Museum). Plaza de Toros de las Ventas, Alcalá, 237. ☎ **91-725-18-57.** Free admission. Mar–Oct, Tues–Fri and Sun 9:30am–2:30pm; Nov–Feb, Mon–Fri 9:30am–2:30pm. Metro: Ventas. Bus: 12, 21, 38, 53, 146, M1, or M8.

This museum will serve as a good introduction to bullfighting for those who want to see the real event. Here you'll see the death costume of Manolete, the *traje de luces* (suit of lights) that he wore when he was gored to death at age 30 in Linares's bullring. Other memorabilia evokes the heyday of Juan Belmonte, the Andalusian who revolutionized bullfighting in 1914 by performing close to the horns. Other exhibits include a Goya painting of a matador, as well as photographs and relics that trace the history of bullfighting in Spain from its ancient origins to the present day.

Museo Tiflológico. La Coruña, 18. ☎ **91-589-42-00.** Free admission. Tues–Fri 10am–2pm and 5–8pm; Sat 10am–2pm. Metro: Estrecho. Bus: 3, 42, 43, 64, or 124.

This museum is designed for sightless and sight-impaired visitors. Maintained by Spain's National Organization for the Blind, it's one of the few museums in the world that emphasizes tactile appeal. All the exhibits are meant to be touched and felt; to that end, the museum provides audiotapes, in English and Spanish, to guide visitors as they move their hands over the object on display. It also offers pamphlets in large type and Braille.

One section of the museum features small-scale replicas of such architectural wonders as the Maya and Aztec pyramids of Central America, the Eiffel Tower, and the Statue of Liberty. Another section contains paintings and sculptures created by blind artists, such as Miguel Detrel and José António Braña. A third section outlines the status of blind people throughout history, with a focus on the sociology and technology that led to the development of Braille during the 19th century.

Real Basílica de San Francisco el Grande. Plaza de San Francisco el Grande, San Buenaventura, 1. ☎ **91-365-38-00.** Admission 50 ptas. (30¢). Tues–Sat 11am–1pm and 4–6:30pm. Metro: La Latina or Puerta del Toledo. Bus: 3, 60, C, or M4.

Ironically, Madrid, the capital of cathedral-rich Spain, does not possess a famous cathedral—but it does have an important church, with a dome larger than that of St. Paul's in London. This 18th-century church is filled with a number of ecclesiastical works, notably a Goya painting of St. Bernardinus of Siena. A guide will show you through.

Templo de Debod. Paseo de Rosales. ☎ **91-366-76-15.** Admission 300 ptas. ($1.80) adults, 150 ptas. (90¢) children under 16; free on Wed and Sun. Apr 1–Sept 30, Mon–Fri 10am–2pm and 6–8pm; Oct 1–Mar 31, Mon–Fri 9:45am–1:45pm and 4:15–6:15pm; Sat–Sun 10am–1pm year-round. Metro: Plaza de España or Ventura Rodríguez. Bus: 25, 33, 39, 46, or 74.

This Egyptian temple near Plaza de España once stood in the Valley of the Nile, 19 miles from Aswan. When the new dam threatened the temple, the Egyptian government dismantled and presented it to Spain. Taken down stone by stone in 1969 and 1970, it was shipped to Valencia and taken by rail to Madrid, where it was reconstructed and opened to the public in 1971. Photos upstairs depict the temple's long history and there is a lovely park looking out over the western suburbs of the city (great for a nighttime summer stroll).

PARKS & GARDENS

Casa de Campo (metro: Lago or Batán) is the former royal hunting grounds—miles of parkland lying south of the Royal Palace across the Manzanares River. You can see the gate through which the kings rode out of the palace grounds, either on horseback or in carriages, on their way to the tree-lined park. A lake contained within Casa de Campo is usually filled with rowers. You can have drinks and light refreshments around the water or go swimming in a city run pool. Children will love both the zoo and the Parque de Atracciones (see "Especially for Kids," below). The Casa de Campo can be visited daily 8am to 9pm.

Parque de Retiro (metro: Retiro), originally a royal playground for the Spanish monarchs and their guests, extends over 350 acres. The huge palaces that once stood here were destroyed in the early 19th century; only the former dance hall, the Cáson del Buen Retiro (housing the modern works of the Prado) and the building containing the Army Museum remain. The park boasts numerous fountains and statues, plus a large lake. There are two exposition centers, the Veláquez and Crystal palaces (built to honor the Philippines in 1887), and a lakeside monument, erected in 1922 in honor of King Alfonso XII. In summer the rose gardens are worth a visit, and you'll find several places for inexpensive snacks and drinks. The park is open daily 24 hours, but it is safest from 7am to about 8:30pm.

Across calle de Alfonso XII, at the southwest corner of Parque de Retiro, is the **Real Jardín Botánico** (Botanical Garden; ☎ **91-420-30-17;** metro: Atocha; bus: 10, 14, 19, 32, or 45). Founded in the 18th century, the garden contains more than 104 species of trees and 3,000 types of plants. Also on the premises are an exhibition hall and a library specializing in botany. The park is open daily from 10am to 8:30pm; admission is 200 ptas. ($1.20).

LITERARY LANDMARKS

Casa de Lope de Vega. Cervantes, 11. ☎ **91-429-92-16.** Admission 200 ptas. ($1.20). Mon–Fri 10am–2pm; Sat 10am–1:30pm. Closed Aug. Metro: Anton Martín.

Felix Lope de Vega, a prolific Madrid-born author, dramatized Hapsburg Spain as no one had before, earning a lasting position in Spanish letters. A reconstruction of his medieval house stands on a narrow street—ironically named for Cervantes, his competitor for the title of the greatest writer of the golden age of Spain. The dank, dark house is furnished with relics of the period, although you can't be sure that any of the furnishings or possessions actually belonged to this 16th-century genius.

Chicote. Gran Vía, 12. ☎ **91-532-67-37.** Beer 550 ptas. ($3.30), whiskey and soda 1,000 ptas. ($6). Mon–Sat 8am–3am (till 3am Fri–Sat). Metro: Gran Vía.

Ernest Hemingway used Chicote as a setting for his only play, *The Fifth Column.* He would sit here night after night, gazing at the *putas* (it was a famed hooker bar back then) as he entertained friends with such remarks as "Spain is a country for living and not for dying." The bar still draws a lively crowd.

Sobrino de Botín. Cuchilleros, 17. ☎ **91-366-42-17.**

In the final two pages of Hemingway's novel *The Sun Also Rises,* Jake invites Brett here for roast suckling pig and red wine. In another book, *Death in the Afternoon,* Hemingway told his mythical "Old Lady": "I would rather dine on suckling pig at Botín's than sit and think of casualties my friends have suffered." Since that time, thousands upon thousands of Americans have eaten at Botín (see "Where to Dine," earlier in this chapter, for details), a perennial favorite of all visiting Yankees.

AN ARCHITECTURAL HIGHLIGHT

Puerta de Toledo. Metro: Puerta de Toledo.

The Puerta de Toledo is one of the two surviving town gates (the other is Puerta de Alcalá). Constructed during the brief and unpopular rule of Joseph I Bonaparte, this one marks the spot where citizens used to set out for the former imperial capital of Toledo. On an irregularly shaped square, it stands at the intersection of the Ronda de Toledo and calle de Toledo. Its original purpose was a triumphal arch to honor Napoléon Bonaparte. In 1813, it became a symbol of Madrid's fierce independence and the loyalty of its citizens to their Bourbon rulers, who had been restored to the throne in the wake of the Napoleonic invasion.

ESPECIALLY FOR KIDS

Museo de Cera de Madrid (Wax Museum). Paseo de Recoletos, 41. ☎ **91-319-26-49.** Admission 1,500 ptas. ($9) adults, 1,000 ptas. ($6) children, children 3 and under free. Daily 10am–2pm and 4–8pm. Metro: Colón. Bus: 27, 45, or 53.

The kids will enjoy seeing a lifelike wax Columbus calling on Ferdinand and Isabella, as well as Marlene Dietrich checking out Bill and Hillary Clinton. The 450 wax figures include heroes and villains of World War II. Two galleries display Romans and Arabs from the ancient days of the Iberian Peninsula; a show gives a 30-minute recap of Spanish history from the Phoenicians to the present.

Parque de Atracciones. Casa de Campo. ☎ **91-463-29-00.** Admission 600 ptas. ($3.60). Apr–May, Tues–Fri noon–8pm, Sat–Sun noon–10pm; June–Aug, Tues–Fri 6pm–1am, Sat 6pm–2am, Sun noon–1am; Sept, Tues–Sun (variable hours; call to check before going);

Oct–Mar, Sat noon–8pm (sometimes 9pm), Sun 11am–8pm (sometimes 9pm). Take the Tele-férico cable car (see below); at the end of this ride, microbuses take you the rest of the way. Alternatively, take the suburban train from Plaza de España and stop near the entrance to the park (Entrada de Batán).

The park was created in 1969 to amuse the young at heart with an array of rides and concessions. The former includes a toboggan slide, a carousel, pony rides, an adventure into outer space, a walk through a transparent maze, a visit to jungle land, a motor-propelled series of cars disguised as a tail-wagging dachshund puppy, and a gyrating whirligig clutched in the tentacles of an octopus named El Pulpo. The most popular rides are a pair of roller coasters named 7 Picos and Jet Star.

The park has many diversions for adults. See the listing for the Auditorio del Parque de Atracciones, under "Madrid After Dark," later in this chapter, for details.

Teleférico. Paseo del Pintor Rosales, s/n. ☎ **91-541-74-50.** Fare 375 ptas. ($2.25) one way, 520 ptas. ($3.10) round-trip. Apr–Sept, daily 11am–9pm; Oct–Mar, Sat–Sun noon–9pm. Metro: Plaza de España or Argüelles. Bus: 74.

Strung high above several of Madrid's verdant parks, this cable car was originally built in 1969 as part of a public fairgrounds (Parque de Atracciones) modeled vaguely along the lines of Disneyland. Today, even for visitors not interested in visiting the park, the teleférico retains an allure of its own as a high-altitude method of admiring the cityscape of Madrid. The cable car departs from Paseo Pintor Rosales at the eastern edge of Parque del Oeste (at the corner of calle Marqués de Urquijo) and carries you high above two parks, railway tracks, and over the Manzanares River to a spot near a picnic ground and restaurant in Casa de Campo. Weather permitting, there are good views of the Royal Palace along the way. The ride takes 11 minutes.

Zoo Aquarium de la Casa de Campo. Casa de Campo. ☎ **91-512-37-70.** Admission 1,600 ptas. ($9.60) adults, 1,300 ptas. ($7.80) seniors and children 3–8, free for children 2 and under. Daily 10am–sunset. Metro: Batán. Bus: 33.

This modern, well-organized facility allows you to see wildlife from five continents, with about 3,000 animals on display. Most are in simulated natural habitats, with moats separating them from the public. There's a petting zoo for the kids and a show presented by the Chu-Lin band. The zoo/aquarium complex includes a 520,000-gallon tropical marine aquarium, a dolphin aquarium, and an array of colorful parrots.

ORGANIZED TOURS

A large number of agencies in Madrid book organized tours and excursions to sights and attractions both within and outside the city limits. Although it won't exactly be spontaneous, some visitors appreciate the convenience and efficiency of being able to visit so many sights in a single well-organized day.

Many of the city's hotel concierges, and all of the city's travel agents, will book anyone who asks for a guided tour of Madrid or its environs with one of Spain's largest tour operators, **Pullmantours,** Plaza de Oriente, 8 (☎ **91-541-18-07**). Regardless of their destination and duration, virtually every tour departs from the Pullmantour terminal at that address. Half-day tours of Madrid include an artistic tour priced at 5,250 ptas. ($31.50) per person, which includes entrance to a selection of the city's museums, and a panoramic half-day tour for 3,000 ptas. ($18).

Toledo is the most popular full-day excursion outside the city limits. Trips cost 8,700 ptas. ($52.20). These tours (including lunch) depart daily at 9:45am from the above-mentioned departure point, last all day, and include ample opportunities for wandering at will through the city's narrow streets. You can, if you wish, take an abbreviated morning tour of Toledo, without stopping for lunch, for 5,600 ptas. ($33.60).

Another popular tour stops briefly in Toledo and continues on to visit both the monastery at El Escorial and the Valley of the Fallen (*Valle de los Caídos*) before returning the same day to Madrid. With lunch included, this all-day excursion costs 12,000 ptas. ($72).

The third major destination of bus tours from Madrid's center to the city's surrounding attractions is Pullmantour's full-day guided excursion to Ávila and Segovia, which takes in a heady dose of medieval and ancient Roman monuments that are really very interesting. The price per person with lunch included is 9,000 ptas. ($54).

The hop-off, hop-on **Madrid Vision Bus** lets you set your own pace and itinerary. A scheduled panoramic tour lasts a half hour, provided that you don't get off the bus. Otherwise, you can opt for an unlimited number of stops, exploring at your leisure. The Madrid Vision makes four complete tours daily, two in the morning and two in the afternoon; on Sunday and Monday buses depart only in the morning. Check with **Trapsa Tours** (☎ **91-767-17-43**) for departure times, which are variable. The full-day tour with unlimited stops costs 2,200 ptas. ($13.20). You can board the bus at the Madrid tourist office.

6 Shopping

THE SHOPPING SCENE

Spain has always been known for its craftspeople, many of whom still work in the time-honored and labor-intensive traditions of their grandparents. It's hard to go wrong if you stick to the beautiful handcrafted objects—hand-painted tiles, ceramics, and porcelain; handwoven rugs; handmade sweaters; and intricate embroideries. And, of course, Spain produces some of the world's finest leather. Jewelry, especially gold set with Majorca pearls, represents good value and unquestioned luxury.

Some of Madrid's art galleries are known throughout Europe for discovering and encouraging new talent. Antiques are sold in highly sophisticated retail outlets. Better suited to the budgets of many travelers are the weekly flea markets.

Spain continues to make inroads into the fashion world. Its young designers are regularly featured in the fashion magazines of Europe. Excellent shoes are available, some highly fashionable. But be advised that prices for shoes and quality clothing are generally higher in Madrid than in the United States.

GREAT SHOPPING AREAS

THE CENTER   The sheer diversity of shops in Madrid's center is staggering. Their densest concentration lies immediately north of Puerta del Sol, radiating out from calle del Carmen, calle Montera, and calle Preciados.

CALLE MAYOR & CALLE DEL ARENAL   Unlike their more stylish neighbors to the north of Puerta del Sol, shops in this district to the west tend to be small, slightly dusty enclaves of coin and stamp dealers, family owned souvenir shops, clock makers, sellers of military paraphernalia, and an abundance of stores selling musical scores.

GRAN VÍA   Conceived, designed, and built in the 1910s and 1920s as a showcase for the city's best shops, hotels, and restaurants, the Gran Vía has since been eclipsed by other shopping districts. Its art nouveau/art deco glamour still survives in the hearts of most Madrileños, however. The bookshops here are among the best in the city, as are outlets for fashion, shoes, jewelry, furs, and handcrafted accessories from all regions of Spain.

EL RASTRO   It's the biggest flea market in Spain, drawing collectors, dealers, buyers, and hopefuls from throughout Madrid and its suburbs. The makeshift stalls are at their most frenetic on Sunday morning. For more information, see the "Flea Markets" section, below.

PLAZA MAYOR   Under the arcades of the square itself are exhibitions of lithographs and oil paintings, and every weekend there's a loosely organized market for stamp and coin collectors. Within 3 or 4 blocks in every direction you'll find more than the average number of souvenir shops.

ON CALLE MARQUÉS   Viudo de Pontejos, which runs east from Plaza Mayor, is one of the city's headquarters for the sale of cloth, thread, and buttons. Also running east, on calle de Zaragoza, are silversmiths and jewelers. On calle Postas, you'll find housewares, underwear, soap powders, and other household items.

NEAR THE CARRERA DE SAN JERÓNIMO   Several blocks east of Puerta del Sol is Madrid's densest concentration of gift shops, crafts shops, and antiques dealers—a decorator's delight. Its most interesting streets include calle del Prado, calle de las Huertas, and Plaza de las Cortés. The neighborhood is pricey, so don't expect bargains here.

NORTHWEST MADRID   A few blocks east of Parque del Oeste is an upscale neighborhood that's well stocked with luxury goods and household staples. Calle de la Princesa, its main thoroughfare, has shops selling shoes, handbags, fashion, gifts, and children's clothing. Thanks to the presence of the university nearby, there's a dense concentration of bookstores, especially on calle Isaac Peral and calle Fernando el Católico, several blocks north and northwest, respectively, from the subway stop of Argüelles.

SALAMANCA DISTRICT   It's known throughout Spain as the quintessential upper-bourgeois neighborhood, uniformly prosperous; its shops are correspondingly exclusive. They include outlets run by interior decorators, furniture shops, fur and jewelry shops, several department stores, and design headquarters whose output ranges from the solidly conservative to the high-tech. The main streets of this district are calle de Serrano and calle de Velázquez. The district lies northeast of the center of Madrid, a few blocks north of Retiro Park. Its most central metro stops are Serrano and Velázquez.

HOURS & SHIPPING

Major stores are open (in most cases) Monday to Saturday 9:30am to 8pm. Many small stores take a siesta between 1:30 and 4:30pm. Of course, there is never any set formula, and hours can vary greatly from store to store, depending on the idiosyncrasies and schedules of the owner.

Many art and antiques dealers will crate and ship bulky objects for an additional fee. Whereas it usually pays to have heavy objects shipped by sea, it might surprise you that in some cases it's almost the same price to ship crated goods by airplane. Of course, it depends on the distance your crate will have to travel overland to the nearest international port, which, in many cases for the purposes of relatively small-scale shipments by individual clients, is Barcelona. Consequently, it might pay to call two branches of **Emery Worldwide** from within Spain to explain your particular situation and get comparable rates. For information about sea transit for your valuables, call **Emery Worldwide Ocean Services** at its only Spanish branch, Barcelona (☎ 93-479-30-50). For information about **Emery Worldwide Air Freight,** call its main Spanish office in Madrid (☎ 91-747-56-66) for advice on any of the dozen of air freight pickup stations they maintain throughout Spain. They include, among many others, Barcelona, Alicante, Málaga, Bilbao, and Valencia. For more advice on this, and the formalities that you'll go through in clearing U.S. customs after the arrival of your shipment in the United States, call **Emery Worldwide** in the United States at ☎ **800/488-9451.**

For most small and medium-size shipments, air freight isn't much more expensive than ocean shipping. **Iberia's Air Cargo Division** (☎ **800/221-6002** in the U.S.) offers air-freight service from Spain to either New York, Chicago, Miami, or Los Angeles. What will you pay for this transport of your treasured art objects or freight? Here's a rule of thumb: For a shipment under 220 pounds (100 kilos), from either Barcelona or Madrid to New York, the cost is approximately 734 ptas. ($4.40) per pound. The per pound price goes down as the weight of the shipment increases, declining to, for example, 254 ptas. ($1.50) per pound for shipments of more than 1,100 pounds (500 kilos). Regardless of what you ship, there's a minimum charge of 8,500 ptas. ($51).

For an additional fee, Iberia or one of its representatives will pick up your package. For a truly precious cargo, ask the seller to build a crate for it. For information within Spain about air-cargo shipments, call Iberia's cargo division at Madrid's Barajas Airport (☎ **91-748-1010**) or at Barcelona's airport (☎ **93-401-3426**).

Remember that your air-cargo shipment will need to clear Customs after it's brought into the United States. This can involve additional paperwork, costly delays, and in some cases a trip to the airport where the shipment first entered the United States. It's usually easier (and in some cases, much easier) to hire a commercial customs broker to do the work for you. Emery Worldwide, a division of CF Freightways, can clear most shipments of goods for around $138, which you'll pay in addition to any applicable duty you owe your home government. For information, you can call ☎ **800/443-6379** within the United States.

SHOPPING A TO Z
ANTIQUES

In addition to the shops listed below, the flea market (see **El Rastro,** below) is a source of antiques.

Centro de Anticuarios Lagasca. Lagasca, 36. No phone. Metro: Serrano or Velázquez.

You'll find about a dozen antiques shops here, clustered into one covered arcade. They operate as individual businesses, although by browsing through each you'll find an impressive assemblage of antique furniture, porcelain, and whatnots. Open Monday to Saturday 10am to 1:30pm and 5 to 8pm.

Galeria de Arte del Lubre. Serrano, 5. ☎ **91-576-96-82.** Metro: Retiro. Bus: 9 or 15.

Housed in a mid–19th-century building are several unusual antiques dealers (and a large carpet emporium as well) many of whom specialize in antique, sometimes monumental paintings. Each establishment maintains its own schedule, although the center itself has overall hours. Open Monday to Saturday 10am to 2pm and 5 to 8:15pm.

ART GALLERIES

✪ **Galería Kreisler.** Hermosilla, 8. ☎ **91-431-42-64.** Metro: Serrano. Bus: 27, 45, or 150.

One successful entrepreneur on Madrid's art scene is Ohio-born Edward Kreisler, whose gallery, now run by his son Juan, specializes in figurative and contemporary paintings, sculptures, and graphics. The gallery prides itself on occasionally displaying and selling the works of artists who are critically acclaimed and displayed in museums in Spain. Open Monday to Saturday 10:30am to 1pm and 5 to 9pm. Closed Saturday afternoon July 15 to September 15 and August.

CAPES

Capas Seseña. Cruz, 23. ☎ **91-531-68-40.** Metro: Sevilla or Puerta del Sol. Bus: 5, 51, or 52.

Founded shortly after the turn of the century, this shop manufactures and sells wool capes for both women and men. The wool comes from the mountain town of Béjar, near Salamanca. Celebrities who have been spotted donning Seseña capes include Picasso, Hemingway, and recently Hillary Rodham Clinton and daughter Chelsea. Open Monday to Friday 10am to 2pm and 4:30 to 8pm, Saturday 10am to 2pm.

CARPETS

Ispahan. Serrano, 5. ☎ **91-575-20-12.** Metro: Retiro. Bus: 1, 2, 9, and 15.

In this 19th-century building, behind bronze handmade doors, are three floors devoted to carpets from around the world, notably Afghanistan, India, Nepal, Iran, Turkey, and the Caucasus. One section features silk carpets. It's open Monday to Saturday 10am to 2pm and 4:30 to 8:30pm (till 8pm on Saturday).

CERAMICS

✪ **Antigua Casa Talavera.** Isabel la Católica, 2. ☎ **91-547-34-17.** Metro: Santo Domingo. Bus: 1, 2, 46, 70, 75, or 148.

"The first house of Spanish ceramics" has wares that include a sampling of regional styles from every major area of Spain, including Talavera, Toledo, Manises, Valencia, Puente del Arzobispo, Alcora, Granada, and Seville. Sangría pitchers, dinnerware, tea sets, and vases are all handmade. Inside one of the showrooms is an interesting selection of tiles painted with reproductions of scenes from bullfights, dances, and folklore. There's also a series of tiles depicting famous paintings in the Prado. At its present location since 1904, the shop is only a short walk from Plaza de Santo Domingo. This shop does not take credit cards but there are two ATMs within a block's walk. Open Monday to Friday 10am to 1:30pm and 5 to 8pm, Saturday 10am to 1:30pm.

CRAFTS

El Arco de los Cuchilleros Artesania de Hoy. Plaza Mayor, 9 (basement level). ☎ **91-365-26-80.** Metro: Puerta del Sol or Opera.

Set within one of the 17th-century vaulted cellars of Plaza Mayor, this shop is entirely devoted to unusual craft items from throughout Spain. The merchandise is one of a kind and in most cases contemporary; it includes a changing array of pottery, leather, textiles, wood carvings, glassware, wickerwork, papier mâché, and silver jewelry. The hardworking owners deal directly with the artisans who produce each item, ensuring a wide inventory of handcrafts. The staff is familiar with the rituals of applying for tax-free status of purchases here and speaks several different languages. It's open Monday to Saturday 11am to 9pm and Sunday 1am to 8pm.

DEPARTMENT STORES

El Corte Inglés. Preciados, 3. ☎ **91-379-80-00.** Metro: Puerta del Sol.

This flagship of the largest department-store chain in Madrid sells hundreds of souvenirs and Spanish handcrafts—damascene steelwork from Toledo, flamenco dolls, and embroidered shawls. Some astute buyers report that it also sells glamorous fashion articles, such as Pierre Balmain designs, for about a third less than equivalent items in most European capitals. Services include interpreters, currency-exchange windows, and parcel delivery either to a local hotel or overseas. Open Monday to Saturday 10am to 9:30pm.

EMBROIDERIES

Casa Bonet. Núñez de Balboa, 76. ☎ **91-575-09-12.** Metro: Núñez de Balboa.

The intricately detailed embroideries produced in Spain's Balearic Islands (especially Majorca) are avidly sought for bridal chests and elegant dinner settings. A few examples of the store's extensive inventory are displayed on the walls. Open Monday to Friday 10:45am to 2pm and 5 to 8pm, Saturday 10:15am to 2pm.

ESPADRILLES

Casa Hernanz. Toledo, 18. ☎ **91-366-54-50.** Metro: Puerta del Sol, Opera, or La Latina.

A brisk walk south of Plaza Mayor delivers you to this store, in business since 1875. In addition to espadrilles, they sell shoes in other styles as well as hats. Open Monday to Friday 9am to 1:30pm and 4:30 to 8pm, Saturday 10am to 2pm.

FANS & UMBRELLAS

Casa de Diego. Puerta del Sol, 12. ☎ **91-522-66-43.** Metro: Puerta del Sol.

Here you'll find a wide inventory of fans, ranging from plain to fancy, from plastic to exotic hardwood, from cost-conscious to lavish. Some fans tend to be a bit overpriced; shopping around may increase your chances of finding a real bargain. Now open year-round Monday to Saturday 9:30am to 8pm.

FASHION

For the man on a budget who wants to dress reasonably well, the best outlet for off-the-rack men's clothing is one of the branches of El Corte Inglés department store chain (see above). Most men's boutiques in Madrid are very expensive and may not be worth the investment.

Herrero. Preciados, 7. ☎ **91-521-29-90.** Metro: Puerta del Sol or Callao.

The sheer size and buying power of this popular retail outlet for women's clothing make it a reasonably priced emporium for all kinds of feminine garb as well as various articles for gentlemen. It is open Monday to Saturday 10:30am to 8:15pm; some Sundays noon to 8:15pm. An additional outlet is on the same street at no. 16 (☎ **91-521-15-24**), with the same hours.

Modas Gonzalo. Gran Vía, 43. ☎ **91-547-12-39.** Metro: Callao or Puerta del Sol.

This boutique's baroque, gilded atmosphere evokes the 1940s, but its fashions are strictly up to date, well made, and intended for stylish adult women. No children's garments are sold. Open Monday to Saturday 10am to 1:30pm and 4:30 to 8:30pm.

FLEA MARKETS

✪ **El Rastro.** Plaza Cascorro and Ribera de Curtidores. Metro: La Latina. Bus: 3 or 17.

Foremost among markets is El Rastro (translated as either "flea market" or "thieves' market"), occupying a roughly triangular district of streets and plazas a few minutes' walk south of Plaza Mayor. Its center is Plaza Cascorro and Ribera de Curtidores. This market will delight anyone attracted to a mishmash of fascinating junk interspersed with antiques, bric-a-brac, and paintings. *Note:* Thieves are rampant here (hustling more than just antiques), so secure your wallet carefully and be alert. Insofar as scheduling your visit to El Rastro, bear in mind that this is a flea market involving hundreds of merchants who basically pull up their display tables and depart whenever their goods are sold or they get fed up with the crowds. In theory, vendors are in place, hawking their wares every day 9:30am to 1:30pm, and after a leisurely lunch, again from 5 to 8pm. But the absolutely best day for scheduling a visit here is Sunday morning, when the neighborhood has a higher percentage of merchants and salespersons than any other time of the week.

FOOD & WINE

Mallorca. Velázquez, 59. ☎ **91-431-99-09.** Metro: Velásquez.

Madrid's best-established gourmet shop opened in 1931 as an outlet selling a pastry called *ensaimada,* and this is still one of the store's most famous products. Tempting arrays of cheeses, canapés, roasted and marinated meats, sausages, and about a dozen kinds of pâté accompany a spread of tiny pastries, tarts, and chocolates. Don't overlook the displays of Spanish wines and brandies. A stand-up tapas bar is always clogged with clients three deep, sampling the wares before they buy larger portions to take home. Tapas cost 150 to 400 ptas. ($2.70) per *ración* (portion). Open daily 9:30am to 9pm.

LEATHER

✪ **Loewe.** Gran Vía, 8. ☎ **91-522-68-15.** Metro: Banco de España or Gran Vía.

Since 1846 this has been the most elegant leather store in Spain. Its gold-medal-winning designers have always kept abreast of changing tastes and styles, but the inventory still retains a timeless chic. The store sells luggage, handbags, and jackets for men and women (in leather or suede). Open Monday to Saturday 9:30am to 8pm. There is another branch with the same hours, and much the same merchandise, at Serrano, 26 (☎ **91-577-6056**).

PERFUMES

Oriental Perfumeries. Mayor, 1. ☎ **91-521-59-05.** Metro: Puerta del Sol.

Located at the western edge of the Puerta del Sol, this shop carries one of the most complete stocks of perfume in Madrid—both national and international brands. It also sells gifts, souvenirs, and costume jewelry. Open Monday to Saturday 10am to 8:30pm.

Perfumería Padilla. Preciados, 17. ☎ **91-522-86-29.** Metro: Puerta del Sol.

This store sells a large and competitively priced assortment of Spanish and international scents for women. It maintains a branch at calle del Carmen, 8 (☎ **91-522-66-83**). Both branches are open Monday to Saturday 10am to 8:30pm.

PORCELAIN

Lasarte. Gran Vía, 44. ☎ **91-521-49-22.** Metro: Callao.

This imposing outlet is devoted almost exclusively to Lladró porcelain, and the staff can usually tell you about new designs and releases the Lladró company is planning for the near future. Open Monday to Friday 9:30am to 8pm, Saturday 10am to 8pm.

SHOPPING MALLS

ABC Serrano. Serrano, 61 or Castellana, 34. Metro: Serrano.

Set within what used to function as the working premises of a well-known Madrileño newspaper (*ABC*), this is a complex of about 85 upscale boutiques that emphasize fashion, housewares, cosmetics, and art objects. Although each of the outfitters inside is independently owned and managed, most of them maintain hours of Monday to Saturday 10am to midnight. On the premises, you'll find cafes and restaurants to keep you fed between bouts of shopping, lots of potted and flowering shrubbery, and acres and acres of Spanish marble and tile.

Galería del Prado. Plaza de las Cortes, 7. Metro: Banco de España or Atocha.

Spain's top designers are represented in this marble-sheathed concourse below the Palace Hotel. It opened in 1989 with 47 different shops, many featuring *moda joven* (fashions for the young). Merchandise changes with the season, but you will always find a good assortment of fashions, Spanish leather goods, cosmetics, perfumes, and jewelry. You can eat and drink in the complex. The entrance to the gallery is in front of the hotel, facing the broad tree-lined Paseo del Prado across from the Prado itself. Open Monday to Saturday 10am to 9pm.

7 Madrid After Dark

Madrid abounds with dance halls, *tascas,* cafes, theaters, movie houses, music halls, and nightclubs. Because dinner is served late in Spain, nightlife doesn't really get under way until after 11pm, and it generally lasts until at least 3am—Madrileños are so fond of prowling around at night that they are known around Spain as *gatos* (cats). If you arrive at 9:30pm at a club, you'll have the place all to yourself, if it's even open.

In most clubs a one-drink minimum is the rule: Feel free to nurse one drink through the entire evening's entertainment.

In summer Madrid becomes a virtual free festival because the city sponsors a series of plays, concerts, and films. Pick up a copy of the *Guía del Ocio* (available at most newsstands) for listings of these events. This guide provides information about occasional discounts for commercial events, such as the concerts that are given in Madrid's parks. Also check the program of **Fundación Juan March,** calle Castello, 77 (☎ 91-435-42-40; metro: Núñez de Balboa). Tapping into funds bequeathed to it by a generous financier (Sr. Juan March), it stages free concerts of Spanish and international classical music within a concert hall at its headquarters at calle Castello, 77. In most cases, they are 90-minute events that are presented every Monday and Saturday at noon and every Wednesday at 7:30pm.

Flamenco in Madrid is geared mainly to prosperous tourists with fat wallets, and nightclubs are expensive. But since Madrid is preeminently a city of song and dance, you can often be entertained at very little cost—in fact, for the price of a glass of wine or beer if you sit at a bar with live entertainment.

Like flamenco clubs, discos tend to be expensive, but they often open for what is erroneously called afternoon sessions (7 to 10pm). Although discos charge entry fees, at an afternoon session the cost might be as low as 500 ptas. ($3), rising to 2,000 ptas. ($12) and beyond for a night session—that is, beginning at 11:30pm and lasting until the early morning hours. Therefore, go early, dance until 10pm, then proceed to dinner (you'll be eating at the fashionable hour).

Nightlife is so plentiful in Madrid that the city can be roughly divided into the following "night zones."

PLAZA MAYOR/PUERTA DEL SOL The most popular areas from the standpoint of both tradition and tourist interest, they can also be dangerous, so explore them with caution, especially late at night. They are filled with tapas bars and *cuevas* (drinking caves). Here it is customary to begin a *tasca* crawl, going to tavern after tavern, sampling the wine in each, along with a selection of tapas. The major streets for such a crawl are Cava de San Miguel, Cava Alta, and Cava Baja. You can order *pinchos y raciones* (tasty snacks and tidbits).

GRAN VÍA This area contains mainly cinemas and theaters. Most of the after-dark action takes place on little streets branching off the Gran Vía.

PLAZA DE ISABEL II/PLAZA DE ORIENTE   This is another area much frequented by tourists. Many restaurants and cafes flourish here, including the famous Café de Oriente.

CHUECA   Along such streets as Hortaleza, Infantas, Barquillo, and San Lucas, this is the gay nightlife district, with dozens of clubs. Cheap restaurants, along with a few female striptease joints, are also found here. This area can be dangerous at night, so watch for pickpockets and muggers. As of late, there has been greater police presence at night.

ARGÜELLES/MONCLOA   For university students, this part of town sees most of the action. Many dance clubs are found here, along with alehouses and fast-food joints. The area is bounded by Pintor Rosales, Cea Bermúdez, Bravo Murillo, San Bernardo, and Conde Duque.

The Sultry Sound of Flamenco

The lights dim and the flamenco stars clatter rhythmically across the dance floor. Their lean bodies and hips shake and sway to the music. The word *flamenco* has various translations, meaning everything from "gypsified Andalusian" to "knife," and from "blowhard" to "tough guy."

Accompanied by stylized guitar music, castanets, and the fervent clapping of the crowd, dancers are filled with tension and emotion. Flamenco dancing, with its flash, color, and ritual, is evocative of Spanish culture although its origins remain mysterious.

Experts disagree as to where it came from, but most claim Andalusia as its seat of origin. It was the gypsy artist who perfected both the song and the dance. Gypsies took to flamenco like "rice to paella," in the words of the historian Fernando Quiñones.

The deep song of flamenco represents a fatalistic attitude to life. Marxists used to say it was a deeply felt protest of the lower classes against their oppressors, but this seems unfounded. Protest or not, over the centuries rich patrons, often brash young men, liked the sound of flamenco and booked artists to stage *juergas,* or fiestas, where dancer-prostitutes became the erotic extras. By the early 17th century flamenco was linked with pimping, prostitution, and lots and lots of drinking, both in the audience and by the artists.

By the mid–19th century flamenco had gone legitimate and was heard in theaters and *café cantantes.* By the 1920s even the pre-Franco Spanish dictator, Primo de Rivera, was singing the flamenco tunes of his native Cádiz. The poet Federico García Lorca and the composer Manuel de Falla preferred a purer form, attacking what they viewed as the degenerate and "ridiculous" burlesque of *flamenquismo,* the jazzed-up, audience-pleasing form of flamenco. The two artists launched a Flamenco Festival in Grenada in 1922. Of course, in the decades since, their voices have been drowned out, and flamenco is more *flamenquismo* than ever.

In his 1995 book *Flamenco Deep Song,* Thomas Mitchell draws a parallel to flamenco's "lowlife roots" and the "orgiastic origins" of jazz. He notes that early jazz, like flamenco, was "associated with despised ethnic groups, gangsters, brothels, free-spending blue bloods, and whoopee hedonism." By disguising their origins, Mitchell notes, both jazz and flamenco have entered the musical mainstream.

THE PERFORMING ARTS

Madrid has a number of theaters, opera companies, and dance companies. To discover where and when specific cultural events are being performed, pick up a copy of *Guía del Ocio* at any city newsstand. The sheer volume of cultural offerings might stagger you; for a concise summary of the highlights, see below.

Tickets to dramatic and musical events usually range in price from 700 to 3,000 ptas. ($4.20 to $18), with discounts of up to 50% granted on certain days of the week (usually Wednesday and matinees on Sunday).

The concierges at most major hotels can usually get you tickets to specific concerts, if you are clear about your wishes and needs. They of course charge a considerable markup, part of which is passed along to whichever agency originally booked the tickets.

You'll save money if you go directly to the box office. In the event your choice is sold out, you may be able to get tickets (with a reasonable markup) at **Localidades Galicia** at Plaza del Carmen, 1 (☎ **91-531-27-32;** metro: Puerta del Sol). This agency also markets tickets to bullfights and sporting events. It is open Tuesday to Saturday 9:30am to 1:30pm and 4:30 to 7:30pm, Sunday 9:30am to 1:30pm, and daily 9:30am to 8pm in May.

Here follows a grab bag of nighttime diversions that might amuse and entertain you. First, the cultural offerings:

Major Performing Arts Companies

For those who speak Spanish, the **Compañía Nacional de Nuevas Tendencias Escénicas** is an avant-garde troupe that performs new and often controversial works by undiscovered writers. On the other hand, the **Compañía Nacional de Teatro Clásico,** as its name suggests, is devoted to the Spanish classics, including works by the ever-popular Lope de Vega and Tirso de Molina.

Among dance companies, the national ballet of Spain—devoted exclusively to Spanish dance—is the **Ballet Nacional de España.** Their performances are always well attended. The national lyrical ballet company of the country is the **Ballet Lírico Nacional.**

World-renowned flamenco sensation Antonio Canales and his troupe, **Ballet Flamenco Antonio Canales,** offer spirited high-energy performances. Productions are centered on Canales's impassioned *Torero,* his interpretation of a bull-fighter and the physical and emotional struggles within the man. For tickets and information, you can call Madrid's comprehensive ticket agency, the previously recommended **Localidades Galicia,** Plaza del Carmen, 1 (☎ 91-531-27-32), for tickets to cultural events and virtually any other event in Castille. Other agencies include **Casa de Catalunya** (☎ **91-538-33-33**) or **Corte Inglés** (☎ **91-432-93-00**). Both Casa de Catalunya and Cortes Inglés have satellite offices located throughout Madrid.

Madrid's opera company is the **Teatro de la Opera,** and its symphony orchestra is the outstanding **Orquesta Sinfónica de Madrid.** The national orchestra of Spain, widely acclaimed on the continent, is the **Orquesta Nacional de España,** which pays particular homage to Spanish composers.

Classical Music

Auditorio del Parque de Atracciones. Casa de Campo. Metro: Lago or Batán.

The schedule of this 3,500-seat facility might include everything from punk-rock musical groups to the more highbrow warm-weather performances of visiting symphony orchestras. Check with Localidades Galicia to see what's on at the time of your visit (see "The Performing Arts," above).

Auditorio Nacional de Música. Príncipe de Vergara, 146. ☎ **91-337-01-39** or 91-337-01-40. Box office 91-337-03-07. Tickets 1,000–1,200 ptas. ($6–$7.20). Metro: Cruz del Rayo.

Sheathed in slabs of Spanish granite, marble, and limestone and capped with Iberian tiles, this hall is the ultramodern home of both the National Orchestra of Spain and the National Chorus of Spain.

Standing just north of Madrid's Salamanca district, it ranks as a major addition to classical music in Europe. Inaugurated in 1988, it is devoted exclusively to performances of symphonic, choral, and chamber music. In addition to the Auditorio Principal (Hall A), whose capacity is almost 2,300, there's a hall for chamber music (Hall B), as well as a small auditorium (seating 250) for intimate concerts.

Fundación Juan March. Castelló, 77. ☎ **91-435-42-40.** Metro: Núñez de Balboa.

This foundation sometimes holds free concerts at lunchtime. The advance schedule is difficult to predict, so call for information.

La Fidula. Calle Huerta, 57. ☎ **91-429-29-47.** Cover 500–700 ptas. ($3–$4.20). Metro: Antón Martín.

Serving as a bastion of civility in a sea of rock and roll and disco chaos, this club is a converted 1800s grocer. Today, it presents chamber music concerts nightly at 11:30pm with an additional show at 1am on weekends. The club offers the prospect of a tranquil, cultural evening on the town, at a moderate price. They take performances here seriously—late arrivals may not be seated for concerts. It is open Monday to Thursday and Sunday 7pm to 3am and Friday and Saturday 7pm to 4am.

Teatro Cultural de la Villa. Plaza de Colón. ☎ **91-575-60-80.** Tickets, depending on event, 1,300–4,500 ptas. ($7.80–$27). Metro: Serrano or Colón.

Spanish-style ballet along with *zarzuelas* (operettas), orchestral works, and theater pieces are presented at this cultural center. Tickets go on sale 5 days before the event of your choice, and performances are usually presented at two evening shows (8 and 10:30pm).

✪ **Teatro Real.** Plaza Isabel II. ☎ **91-516-06-60.** Tickets 4,000–32,000 ptas. ($24–$192). Metro: Opera.

Reopened in 1997 after a massive $157 million renovation, this theater is one of the world's finest acoustic settings for opera. Its extensive state-of-the-art equipment affords elaborate stage designs and special effects. Luis Antonio García Navarro, the internationally heralded maestro from Valencia, is the musical and artistic director of the Royal Opera House, at least until 2002, and he works with leading Spanish lyric talents, including Plácido Domingo. Today the building is the home of the Compañía del Teatro Real, a company specializing in opera, and is a major venue for classical music. On November 19, 1850, under the reign of Queen Isabel II, the Royal Opera House opened its doors with Donizetti's *La Favorita.*

THEATER

Madrid offers many different theater performances, useful to you only if your Spanish is very fluent. If it isn't, check the *Guía del Ocio* for performances by English-speaking companies on tour from Britain or select a concert or subtitled movie instead.

In addition to the major ones listed below, there are at least 30 other theaters, including one devoted almost entirely to children's plays, the **Sala la Bicicleta** (☎ **91-463-29-00**), in the Ciudad de los Niños at Casa de Campo. Nonprofessional groups stage dozens of other plays in such places as churches.

Teatro Calderón. Atocha, 18. ☎ **91-429-5238.** Tickets 3,000–8,000 ptas. ($18–$48). Metro: Tirso de Molina.

This is the largest theater in Madrid, with a seating capacity of 2,000. In the past this venue included everything from dramatic theater to flamenco, but in recent years it has taken a more serious turn by presenting mostly opera, with performances beginning most evenings at 8pm. At press time, a long-running favorite was Bizet's *Carmen,* whose setting within Spain partly justifies its enduring popularity among Madrileños.

Teatro de la Comedia. Príncipe, 14. ☎ **91-521-49-31.** Tickets 1,300–2,600 ptas. ($7.80–$15.60); 50% discount on Thurs. Metro: Sevilla. Bus: 15, 20, or 150.

This is the home of the Compañía Nacional de Teatro Clásico. Here, more than anywhere else in Madrid, you're likely to see performances from the classic repertoire of such great Spanish dramatists as Lope de Vega and Calderón de la Barca. There are no performances on Wednesday, and the theater is completely shut down during July and August. The box office is open daily 11:30am to 1:30pm and 5 to 6pm, and for about an hour before the performances.

Teatro Español. Príncipe, 25. ☎ **91-429-62-97.** Tickets 2,300–4,000 ptas. ($13.80–$24); 50% discount on Wed. Metro: Sevilla.

This company is funded by Madrid's municipal government, its repertoire a time-tested assortment of great and/or favorite Spanish plays. The box office is open daily 11:30am to 1:30pm and 5pm to the opening of the show.

Teatro Lírico Nacional de la Zarzuela. Jovellanos, 4. ☎ **91-524-54-00.** Tickets 1,200–4,500 ptas. ($7.20–$27). Metro: Sevilla.

Near Plaza de la Cibeles, this theater of potent nostalgia produces ballet and an occasional opera in addition to *zarzuela.* Show times vary. The box office is open daily from noon to show time.

Teatro María Guerrero. Tamayo y Baus, 4. ☎ **91-310-29-49.** Tickets 1,650–3,600 ptas. ($9.90–$21.60); 50% discount on Wed. Metro: Banco de España or Colón.

Funded by the government, the María Guerrero (named after a much-loved Spanish actress) works in cooperation with the Teatro Español (see above) for performances of works by such classic Spanish playwrights as Lope de Vega and García Lorca. The box office is open daily 11:30am to 1:30pm and 5 to 6pm.

Teatro Nuevo Apolo. Plaza de Tirso de Molina, 1. ☎ **91-369-0637.** Cover usually 2,800 ptas. ($16.80). Metro: Tirso de Molina.

Nuevo Apolo is the permanent home of the renowned Antología de la Zarzuela company. It is on the restored site of the old Teatro Apolo, where these musical variety shows have been performed since the 1930s. Prices and times depend on the show. The box office is open daily 11:30am to 1:30pm and 5 to 6pm; show times vary.

JAZZ & CABARET

✪ **Café Central.** Plaza del Angel, 10. ☎ **91-369-41-43.** Cover charge 1,300 ptas. ($7.80); prices can vary depending on show. Metro: Antón Martín.

Off the Plaza de Santa Ana beside the famed Gran Hotel Victoria, the Café Central has a vaguely turn-of-the-century art deco interior, with an unusual series of stained-glass windows. Many of the customers read newspapers and talk at the marble-top tables during the day, but the ambience is far more animated during the nightly jazz sessions, which are ranked among the best in Spain, often drawing top artists. Open Sunday to Thursday 1:30pm to 2:30am, Friday and Saturday 1:30pm to 3:30am; live jazz is offered daily 10pm to midnight. Beer costs 400 ptas. ($2.40).

Café del Foro. Calle San Andres, 38. ☎ **91-445-37-52.** No cover (but may be imposed for a specially booked act). Metro: Bilboa. Bus: 40, 147, 149, or N19.

This old-time favorite in the Malasaña district has suddenly become hip again. You never know exactly what the show for the evening will be, although live music of some sort generally starts at 11:30pm. Cabaret is often featured, along with live merengue, bolero, and salsa. There's a faux starry sky above the stage area, plus Roman colonnades that justify the name Café del Foro. Open daily 7pm to 3am.

Café Jazz Populart. Calle Huertas, 22. ☎ **91-429-84-07.** Cover 250–1,000 ptas. ($1.50–$6). Metro: Antón Martín or Sevilla. Bus: 6 or 60.

This club is known for its exciting jazz groups, which encourage the audience to dance. It specializes in Brazilian, Afro-bass, reggae, and new wave African music. When the music starts, usually around 11pm, the prices of drinks are nearly doubled. Open daily 6pm to 3 or 4am. Beer costs 350 ptas. ($2.10), whisky with soda 600 ptas. ($3.60), when live music isn't playing. After the music begins, beer costs 600 ptas. ($3.60), whisky with soda 950 ptas. ($5.70).

Clamores. Albuquerque, 14. ☎ **91-445-79-38.** Cover Tues–Sat usually 600–1,200 ptas. ($3.60–$7.20), but varies with act; no cover Sun–Mon. Metro: Bilbao.

With dozens of small tables and a huge bar in its dark and smoky interior, Clamores, which means noises in Spain, is the largest and one of the most popular jazz clubs in Madrid. Established in the early 1980s, it has thrived because of the diverse roster of American and Spanish jazz bands who have appeared here. The place is open daily 7pm to around 3am, but jazz is presented only Tuesday to Saturday. Tuesday to Thursday, performances are at 11pm and again at 1am; Saturday, performances begin at 11:30pm, with an additional show at 1:30am. There are jam sessions on Sunday night, and no live performances on Monday night, when the format is recorded disco music. Regardless of the night of the week you consume them, drinks begin at around 700 ptas. ($4.20) each.

FLAMENCO

Café de Chinitas. Torija, 7. ☎ **91-559-51-35.** Dinner and show 9,800 ptas. ($58.80); cover charge for show without dinner (but with 1 drink included) 4,450 ptas. ($26.70). Metro: Santo Domingo. Bus: 1 or 2.

One of the best flamenco clubs in town, Café de Chinitas is set one floor above street level in a 19th-century building midway between the Opera and Gran Vía. It features an array of (usually) gypsy flamenco artists from Madrid, Barcelona, and Andalusia, with acts and performers changing about once a month. You can arrange for dinner before the show, although many Madrileños opt for dinner somewhere else and then arrive just for drinks and the flamenco. Open Monday to Saturday, with dinner served 9 to midnight and the show lasting 10:30pm to 2am. Reservations are recommended.

Casa Patas. Calle Cañizares, 10. ☎ **91-369-04-96.** Admission 3,000 ptas. ($18). Metro: Tirso de Molina.

This club is now one of the best places to see "true" flamenco as opposed to the more touristy version presented at Corral de la Morería (see below). It is also a bar and restaurant, with space reserved in the rear for flamenco. Shows are presented midnight on Thursday, Friday, and Saturday and more often during Madrid's major fiesta month of May. The best flamenco in Madrid is found here. Proof of the pudding is that flamenco singers and dancers often hang out here after hours. Tapas—priced at 450 to 2,500 ptas. ($2.70 to $15)—are available at the bar. The club is open daily 8pm to 2:30am.

Corral de la Morería. Morería, 17. ☎ **91-365-84-46.** Cover 1-drink minimum 4,300 ptas. ($25.80); 11,000 ptas. ($66) with dinner. Metro: La Latina or Puerta del Sol.

In the old town, the Morería ("where the Moors reside") sizzles with flamenco, but it's definitely a tourist crowd. Colorfully costumed strolling performers warm up the audience around 11pm; a flamenco show follows, with at least 10 dancers. It's much cheaper to eat somewhere else first, paying only the one-drink minimum. Open daily 9:15pm to 2am.

DANCE CLUBS

The Spanish dance club takes its inspiration from those of other Western capitals. In Madrid, most clubs are open from around 6pm to 9pm, later reopening around 11pm. They generally start rocking at midnight or thereabouts.

Joy Eslava. Arenal, 11. ☎ **91-366-37-33.** Admission 2,000 ptas. ($12), including first drink. Metro: Puerta del Sol.

Set near the Puerta del Sol, this place has survived the passing fashions of Madrileño nightlife with more style than many of its (now-defunct) competitors. Virtually everyone in Madrid is likely to show up here, ranging from traveling sales reps in town from Düsseldorf to the youthful members of the Madrileño *movida.* Open nightly 10pm to 6:30am. Drinks are 1,500 ptas. ($9) each.

Kapital. Atocha, 125. ☎ **91-420-29-06.** Admission 2,000 ptas. ($12), including first drink. Metro: Atocha.

This is the most sprawling, labyrinthine, and multicultural disco in Madrid at the moment. Set within what was originally a theater, it contains seven different levels, each sporting at least one bar and an ambience that's often radically different from the one you just left on a previous floor. Voyeurs of any age, take heart—there's a lot to see at the Kapital, with a mixed crowd that pursues whatever form of sexuality seems appropriate at the moment. Open Thursday to Sunday 11:30pm to 5:30am. Second drinks from 1,000 ptas. ($6) each.

Pachá. Calle Barcelo, 11. ☎ **91-446-01-37.** Admission 2,000 ptas. ($12), including first drink. Metro: Tribunal.

The carefully contrived setting is pseudo-opulent, and the drinks sometimes hard to get because of the milling crowds. Despite that, Pachá thrives as one of the late-night staples in Madrid for the mid-20s to late-40s clientele (a crowd that often segregates itself by age into distinctly different areas of the place). More than other nightclubs in Madrid, this has been the subject of complaints from neighbors about late-night noise. It's open Monday to Saturday 11pm to 6:30am.

PUBS & BARS

Balmoral. Hermosilia, 10. ☎ **91-431-41-33.** Metro: Serrano.

Exposed wood and comfortable chairs here evoke a London club. The clientele tends toward journalists, politicians, army brass, owners of large estates, bankers, diplomats, and the occasional literary star. *Newsweek* magazine dubbed it one of the "best bars in the world." No food other than tapas is served. Open Monday to Saturday 12:30pm to 2:30 or 3am. Beer is 500 ptas. ($3); drinks are from 900 ptas. ($5.40).

Balneario. Juan Ramón Jiménez, 37. ☎ **91-350-87-76.** Metro: Cuzco.

Clients enjoy potent drinks in a setting with fresh flowers, white marble, and a stone bathtub that might have been used by Josephine Bonaparte. Near Chamartín Station on the northern edge of Madrid, Balneario is one of the most stylish and upscale bars

Make
Learning
Fun & Easy

With IDG Books Worldwide

Available at your local bookstores

in the city. It is adjacent to and managed by one of Madrid's most elegant and prestigious restaurants, El Cabo Mayor, and often attracts that dining room's clients for aperitifs or after-dinner drinks. Tapas include endive with smoked salmon, asparagus mousse, and anchovies with avocado. Open Monday to Saturday noon to 2:30am. Drinks are 650 to 1,000 ptas. ($3.90 to $6); tapas cost 500 to 1,800 ptas. ($3 to $10.80).

Bar Cock. De la Reina, 16. ☎ **91-532-28-26.** Metro: Gran Vía.

This bar on two floors attracts some of the most visible artists, actors, models, and filmmakers in Madrid. The name comes from the word *cocktail*, or so they say. The decoration is elaborate and unique, in contrast to the hip clientele, and the martinis are Madrid's best. Open daily 7pm to 3am; closed December 24 to 31. Drinks are 1,000 ptas. ($6).

Bar Taurino. In the Hotel Reina Victoria, Plaza Santa Ana. ☎ **91-531-45-00.** Metro: Antón Martín.

This bar remains the top gathering spot for bullfight aficionados. A multitiered place, it is still a shrine to Manolete, the greatest matador of the 1950s who was praised by Hemingway. This is no rough-and-tumble bar, but a cultured space often attracting Madrid society. It reaches the peak of its excitement during the San Isidro bullfighting festival, when Spain's top bullfighters often make appearances here in their full death-in-the-afternoon suits of light. Hours are daily 11:30am to 11:30pm.

✪ Chicote. Gran Vía, 12. ☎ **91-532-67-37.** Metro: Gran Vía.

This is Madrid's most famous cocktail bar. It's classic retro chic, with the same 1930s interior design it had when the foreign press came to sit out the Civil War, although the sound of artillery shells along the Gran Vía could be heard at the time. Long a favorite of artists and writers, the bar became a haven for prostitutes in the late Franco era. No more. It's back in the limelight again, a sophisticated and much-frequented rendezvous. Open Monday to Saturday 8am to 3am (until 4am on Friday and Saturday). Drinks cost from 1,000 ptas. ($6) Monday to Saturday, but the waiters serve them with such grace you don't mind.

Hispano Bar/Buffet. Paseo de la Castellana, 78. ☎ **91-411-48-76.** Metro: Nuevos Ministerios.

This establishment does a respectable lunch trade every day for members of the local business community who crowd in to enjoy the amply portioned *platos del día.* They might include a platter of roast duck with figs or orange sauce, or a supreme of hake. After around 5pm, however, the ambience becomes that of a busy after-office bar, patronized by stylishly dressed women and many local entrepreneurs. The hubbub continues on into the night. Open daily 1:30pm to 2am. Full meals at lunchtime cost around 4,500 to 5,000 ptas. ($27 to $30), while beer, depending on the time of day you order it, costs about 300 ptas. ($1.80).

La Venencia. Calle Echegary, 7. ☎ **91-429-73-13.** Metro: Sevilla.

On one of the traditional *tasca* streets in Old Madrid, this tavern has a distinct personality. It is dedicated to the art of serving Spain's finest sherry—and that's it. Don't come in here asking for an extra dry martini. Our favorite remains Manzanilla, a delicate fino with just a little chill on it. If Luis Buñuel were to need extras in a film, surely the patrons here would be an ideal backdrop. To go with all that sherry, the waiters (a little rough around the edges) will serve tapas, especially those garlicky marinated olives, *majoama* (cured tuna), and blue-cheese canapés. Barrels form the decor, along with antique posters long turned tobacco-gold from the cigarette smoke. Open daily 7:30pm to 1:30am (until 2am on Friday and Saturday).

Los Gabrieles. Echegaray, 17. ☎ **91-429-62-61.** Metro: Puerta de Sol, Sevilla.

Located in the heart of one of Madrid's most visible warrens of narrow streets, in a district that pulsates with after-dark nightlife options, this historic bar served throughout most of the 19th century as the sales outlet for a Spanish wine merchant. Its cellar was once a fabled Gypsy bordello. In the 1980s its two rooms were transformed into a bar and cafe, where you can admire lavishly tiled walls with detailed scenes of courtiers, dancers, and Andalusian maidens peering from behind mantillas and fans. Open daily noon to 3:30am. Beer costs 300 to 400 ptas. ($1.80 to $2.40).

Palacio Gaviria. Calle del Arenal, 9. ☎ **91-526-6069.** Cover 2,000 ptas. ($12), including first drink. Metro: Puerta del Sol or Opera.

Its construction in 1847 was heralded as the architectural triumph of one of the era's most flamboyant aristocrats, the marqués de Gaviria. Famous as one of the paramours of Queen Isabella II, he outfitted his palace with the ornate jumble of neoclassical and baroque styles that later became known as *Isabelino.* In 1993, after extensive renovations, the building was opened to the public as a concert hall for the occasional presentation of classical music and as a late-night cocktail bar. Ten high-ceilinged rooms now function as richly decorated, multipurpose areas for guests to wander in, drinks in hand, reacting to whatever, or whomever, happens to be there at the time. (One room is discreetly referred to as having been the bedroom-away-from-home of the queen herself.) No food is served, but the libations include a stylish list of cocktails and wines. The often-dull music doesn't match the elegance of the decor. Thursdays to Saturdays are usually dance nights, everything from the tango to the waltz. Cabaret is usually featured on most other nights. Open Monday to Friday 9pm to 3am, Saturday and Sunday 9pm to 5am. Second drinks start at 1,200 ptas. ($7.20).

Teatriz. Hermosilla, 15. ☎ **91-577-53-79.** Metro: Serrano.

Part of its function is as a restaurant where soft lighting and a decor by world-class decorator Philippe Starck create one of the most stylish-looking and avant-garde environments in Madrid. A meal averages around 3,000 ptas. ($18) at lunch and 4,000 ptas. ($24) in the evening, but if it's just a drink you're looking for, consider an extended session at any of the site's three bars. Here, in a setting not quite like a disco but with a sound system almost as good, you'll find a music bar environment where stylish folk of all persuasions enjoy drinks and the gossip that seems to both originate and be magnified at a place like this. The restaurant is open daily 9am to 1pm and 1:30 to 4pm. The bars are best appreciated every night from 9pm to 3am.

✪ **Viva Madrid.** Manuel Fernández y González, 7. ☎ **91-429-3640.** Metro: Sevilla.

A congenial and sudsy mix of students, artists, and tourists cram into this place, where antique tile murals and blatant belle époque nostalgia contribute to an undeniable charm. Crowded and noisy, it's a place where lots of beer is swilled and spilled. It's set in a neighborhood of antique houses and narrow streets near the Plaza de Santa Ana. Open Friday noon to 1am, Saturday noon to 2am. Beer costs 500 ptas. ($3); whisky begins at 875 ptas. ($5.25).

GAY & LESBIAN BARS

Black and White. Gravina (at corner of Libertad). ☎ **91-531-11-41.** Metro: Chueca.

This is the major gay bar of Madrid, located in the center of the Chueca district. A guard will open the door to a large room—painted, as you might expect, black and white. There's a disco in the basement, but the street-level bar is the premier gathering spot, featuring drag shows beginning at 3am Thursday to Sunday, male striptease,

Summer Terrazas

At the first blush of spring weather, Madrileños rush outdoors to drink, talk, and sit at a string of open-air cafes, called *terrazas,* throughout the city. The best and most expensive ones are along Paseo de la Castellana between the Plaza de la Cibeles and the Plaza Emilio Castelar, but there are dozens more throughout the city.

You can wander up and down the boulevard, selecting one that appeals to you; if you get bored, you can go on later to another one. Sometimes these terrazas are called *chiringuitos.* You'll find them along other paseos, the Recoletos and the Prado, both fashionable areas but not as hip as the Castellana. For old traditional atmosphere, the terraces at the Plaza Mayor win out. The Plaza Santa Ana has several atmospheric choices within the old city. Friday and Saturday are the most popular nights for drinking; many locals sit here all night.

---

and videos. Old movies are shown against one wall. *Warning:* This bar is frequented by young, potentially dangerous hustlers. Open Monday to Friday 8pm to 5am, Saturday and Sunday 8pm to 6am. Beer is 500 ptas. ($3); whisky costs 850 ptas. ($5.10).

Café Figueroa. Augusto Figueroa, 17 (at corner of Hortaleza). ☎ **91-521-16-73.** Metro: Chueca.

This turn-of-the-century cafe attracts a diverse clientele, including a large number of gay men and lesbians. It's one of the city's most popular gathering spots for drinks and conversations. Open daily 12:30pm to 1am. Beer from 400 ptas. ($2.40); whisky costs from 700 ptas. ($4.20).

Cruising. Perez Galdos, 5. ☎ **91-521-51-43.** Metro: Chueca.

One of the landmark gay bars of Madrid, a center for gay consciousness-raising and gay cruising, this place has probably been visited at least once by every gay male in Castile. There are virtually no women inside, but always a hustler looking for a tourist john. It doesn't get crowded or lively until late at night. Open daily 7pm to 3:30am. Beer costs from 400 to 500 ptas. ($2.40 to $3).

Leather Bar. Calle Pelayo, 42. ☎ **91-308-14-62.** No cover, but a minimum charge of 400 ptas. ($2.40). Metro: Chueca.

This is another of the premier bars for gay men in Madrid, but despite its supposed emphasis on leather and uniforms, only about 25% of the men who show up actually wear them. You'll find two bars on the establishment's street level and a disco in the basement where same-sex couples can dance. The place can be fun, especially since, in the words of one of the more gregarious bartenders, "I think everybody's gay." Beer costs 450 ptas. ($2.70). It's open Sunday to Thursday 9pm to 3am, Friday and Saturday 9pm to 3:30am.

Refugio. Calle Doctor Cortezo, 1. ☎ **91-369-40-38.** Cover 1,000 ptas. ($6); 500 ptas. ($3) before 2. Metro: Tirso de Molina.

This is one of the best-established, most deeply entrenched clubs for gay men in Madrid, with a strong emphasis on dancing, drinking, and dialogue, or simply standing and cruising whenever it feels appropriate. The interior is like a grotto with nude gladiator statues, equaled only by the caged dancing boys stirring up libidos. Larger than many of its gay competitors in Madrid, it sometimes hosts theme nights (golden oldies nights, merengue nights, and so on) that regrettably don't really get going until very, very late. It's open nightly midnight to 6am.

Rick's. Calle Clavel, 8. No phone. Metro: Chueca.

Rick's takes its name from *Everybody Comes to Rick's,* the original title of the Bogie classic, *Casablanca.* Many gay bars in the Chueca barrio are sleazy, but this is a classy joint, just like the fictional Rick's in Morocco. It's decorated with Bogie paraphernalia, including marble floors and gilt columns. The only thing missing is a piano player singing "As Time Goes By," and Bergman, of course. Gay men patronize the place, with the occasional woman showing up, too. Incongruously, it has a foosball table in the bar, but lavender walls. It's open daily 11:30am "until some time in the morning."

CAVE CRAWLING

To capture a peculiar Madrid joie de vivre of the 18th century, visit some *mesones* and *cuevas* (taverns). From Plaza Mayor, walk down the Arco de Cuchilleros until you find a gypsylike cave that fits your fancy. Young people love to meet in the taverns of Old Madrid for communal drinking and songfests. The sangría flows freely, the atmosphere is charged, and the room is usually packed with the sounds of guitars wafting into the night air. Sometimes you'll see a strolling band of singing students going from bar to bar, colorfully attired, with ribbons fluttering from their outfits.

Mesón de la Guitarra. Cava de San Miguel, 13. ☎ **91-559-95-31.** Metro: Puerta del Sol or Opera.

Our favorite *cueva* in the area, Mesón de la Guitarra is loud and exciting on any night of the week, and it's as warmly earthy as anything you'll find in Madrid. The decor combines terra-cotta floors, antique brick walls, hundreds of sangría pitchers clustered above the bar, murals of gluttons, old rifles, and faded bullfighting posters. Like most things in Madrid, the place doesn't get rolling until around 10:30pm, although you can stop in for a drink and tapas earlier. Don't be afraid to start singing an American song if it has a fast rhythm—60 people will join in, even if they don't know the words. Open daily 7pm to 2am. Beer is 250 ptas. ($1.50); wine is from 125 ptas. (75¢); tapas are 800 to 1,000 ptas. ($4.80 to $6).

Mesón del Champiñón. Cava de San Miguel, 17. No phone. Metro: Puerta del Sol or Opera.

The bartenders keep a brimming bucket of sangría behind the long stand-up bar as a thirst quencher for the crowd. The name of the establishment in English is Mushroom, and that is exactly what you'll see depicted in various sizes along sections of the vaulted ceilings. A more appetizing way to experience a *champiñón* is to order a *ración* of grilled, stuffed, and salted mushrooms, served with toothpicks. Two tiny, slightly dark rooms in the back are where Spanish families go to hear organ music performed. Unless you want to be exiled to the very back, don't expect to get a seat. Practically everybody prefers to stand. Open daily 6pm to 2am.

Sesamo. Príncipe, 7. ☎ **91-429-65-24.** Metro: Sevilla or Puerta del Sol.

In a class by itself, this *cueva* dating from the early 1950s draws a clientele of young painters and writers with its bohemian ambience. Hemingway was one of those early visitors (a plaque commemorates him). At first you'll think you're walking into a tiny snack bar—and you are. But proceed down the flight of steps to the cellar. Here, the walls are covered with contemporary paintings and quotations. At squatty stools and tables, an international assortment of young people listens to piano music and sometimes piano or guitar playing. Open daily 6pm to 2:30am. A pitcher of sangría (for four) is 1,200 ptas. ($7.20); beer costs 300 ptas. ($1.80).

A CASINO

The **Casino Gran Madrid** is at km29 along the Carretera La Coruña (the A6 highway running between Madrid and La Coruña), Apartado, 62 (☎ **91-856-11-00**). The largest casino in Madrid, it appeals to non-gamblers with a roster of dining and entertainment facilities, including two restaurants, four bars, and a nightclub. And if you happen to enjoy gambling, there are facilities for French and American roulette, blackjack, punto y banco, baccarat, and chemin de fer. Presentation of a passport at the door is essential—without it, you won't be admitted. Entrance costs 500 ptas. ($3.35), although that fee is often waived for residents of some of Madrid's larger hotels who arrive with a ticket that's sometimes provided gratis by the hotel's management. The casino and all of its facilities are open daily 4pm to 5am.

An à la carte restaurant in the French Gaming Room offers international cuisine, with dinners costing from 7,000 ptas. ($42). A buffet in the American Gaming Room will cost around 3,000 ptas. ($18). The restaurants are open 9:15pm to 2am. The casino is about 18 miles (29km) northwest of Madrid, along the Madrid–La Coruña N-VI highway. If you don't feel like driving, the casino has buses that depart from Plaza de España, 6, every afternoon and evening at 4:30, 6, 7:30, and 9pm. Note that between October and June, men must wear jackets and ties; T-shirts and tennis shoes are forbidden in any season. To enter, European visitors must present an identity card and non-European visitors must present a passport.

4 Side Trips from Madrid

Madrid makes an ideal base for excursions because it's surrounded by some of Spain's major attractions. The day trips listed below to both New Castile and Old Castile range from 9 miles to 100 miles (14km to 161km) outside Madrid, allowing you to leave in the morning and be back by nightfall. In case you choose to stay overnight, however, we've included a selection of hotels in each town.

The satellite cities and towns around Madrid include Toledo, with its El Greco masterpieces; the wondrous El Escorial monastery; Segovia's castles that seem to float in the clouds; and the Bourbon palaces at La Granja. Cuenca, which is actually in La Mancha, is the longest excursion; so unless you want to spend a good part of the day getting there and back, you should consider it an overnight trip. For a selection of other cities in Old Castile—each of which is better visited on an overnight stopover rather than a day trip from Madrid—see chapter 5, "Old Castile & León."

1 Toledo

42 miles (68km) SW of Madrid, 85 miles (137km) SE of Ávila

If you have only 1 day for an excursion outside Madrid, go to Toledo—a place made special by its Arab, Jewish, Christian, and even Roman and Visigothic elements. A national landmark, the city that so inspired El Greco in the 16th century has remained relatively unchanged. You can still stroll through streets barely wide enough for a man and his donkey—much less for an automobile.

Surrounded on three sides by a bend in the Tagus River, Toledo stands atop a hill overlooking the arid plains of New Castile—a natural fortress in the center of the Iberian Peninsula. It was a logical choice for the capital of Spain, but it lost its political status to Madrid in the 1500s. Toledo has remained the country's religious center, as the seat of the Primate of Spain.

If you're driving, the much-painted skyline of Toledo will come into view about 3½ miles (6km) from the city. When you cross the Tagus River on the 14th-century Puente San Martín, the scene is reminiscent of El Greco's moody, storm-threatened *View of Toledo,* which hangs in New York's Metropolitan Museum of Art. The artist reputedly painted that view from a hillside that is now the site of Parador Nacional de Conde Orgaz. If you arrive at the right time, you can enjoy an apéritif

Madrid Environs

0 ———— 30 mi
0 ———— 30 km

✈ Airport

N110

SIERRA DE GUADARRAMA

Segovia

San Ildefonso
la Granja
604

SIERRA DE GREDOS

To
← Ávila
600

607

Colmenar
Viejo

E5

NI   M103

N320   Guadalajara

E90

VALLE DE LOS CAÍDOS

San Lorenzo
de El Escorial

El Pardo

NVI

Galapagar

Aravaca

✈ Barajas Airport

Alcalá de
Henares

Las Rozas

MADRID   NII

404

602

Mejorada
del Campo

Alcorcón

600   Leganés

Arganda

San Martín
de la Vega

Chinchón

NV

E90

Ciempozuelos

E901

Illescas

N401

Aranjuez

To
Cuenca →

N400

Ocaña

N400

N301

N403

Toledo

NIV

502

E5

401   N401

La Guardia

Toledo

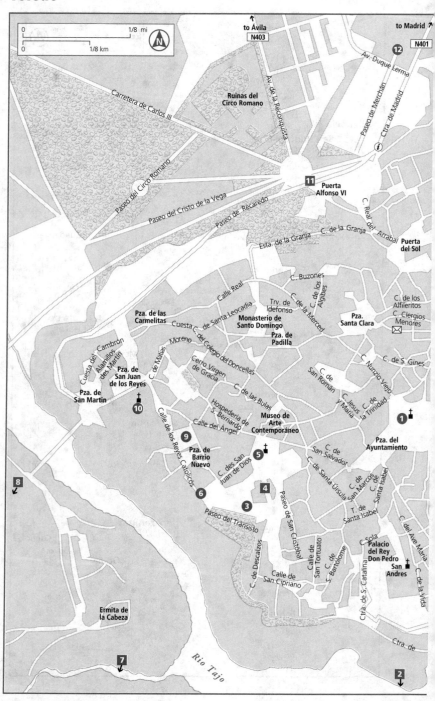

to Ávila
N403

to Madrid
N401

12

Av. Duque Lerma

Paseo de Merchán

Ctra. de Madrid

Carretera de Carlos III

Ruinas del
Circo Romano

Av. de la Reconquista

Paseo del Circo Romano

Paseo del Cristo de la Vega

Paseo de Recaredo

11 Puerta
Alfonso VI

C. Real del Arrabal
Puerta
del Sol

Esta. de la Granja

C. de la Granja

C. Buzones

Calle Real

C. de los Algibes

C. de la Merced

Pza.
Santa Clara

C. de los
Alfileritos
C. Clergios
Menores

Pza. de las
Carmelitas

Trv. de
Idefonso

Monasterio de
Santo Domingo

Cuesta C. de Santa Leocadia

C. del Colegio del Doncellas

Pza. de
Padilla

C. de S. Gines

Cuesta del Cambrón

Alamillos del Martín

Moreno

C. de Matías

Cerro Virgen
de Gracia

C. de las Bulas

C. de
San Román

C. de Jesus
y María

C. de
la Trinidad

C. Nunzio Viejo

Pza. de
San Juan
de los Reyes

Pza. de
San Martín

10

Calle de los Reyes Católicos

Hospedería de
S. Bernardo

Calle del Ángel

Museo de
Arte
Contemporáneo

1

9

Pza. de
Barrio
Nuevo

C. des San
Juan de Dios

5

C. de
San Salvador

Pza. del
Ayuntamiento

6

3

4

Paseo del Tránsito

Paseo de San Cristóbal

C. de Santa Úrsula

C. de
San Marcos

T. de
Santa Isabel

C. de
Santa Isabel

8

C. de Descalzos

Calle de
San Cipriano

Calle de
San Tortuato

C. de
S. Bartolomé

Sola

Palacio
del Rey
Don Pedro

San
Andres

C. del Ave María

C. de la Vida

Ermita de
la Cabeza

Ctra. de S. Catalina

Ctra. de

Rio Tajo

7

2

0   1/8 mi
0   1/8 km

N

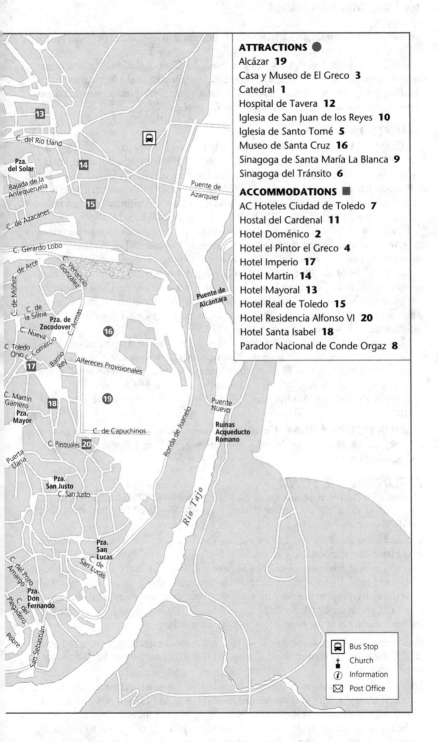

on the parador's terrace and watch one of the famous violet sunsets of Toledo (see "Where to Stay," below).

Another Toledan highlight is the **Carretera de Circunvalación,** the route that threads through the city and runs along the Tagus. Clinging to the hillsides are rustic dwellings, the *cigarrales* of the Imperial City immortalized by 17th-century dramatist Tirso de Molina, who named his trilogy *Los Cigarrales de Toledo.*

ESSENTIALS

GETTING THERE **RENFE** trains run here frequently every day. Those departing Madrid's Atocha Railway Station for Toledo run daily 7am to 9:50pm; those leaving Toledo for Madrid run daily 7am to 9pm. Traveling time is approximately 2 hours, and a one-way fare costs 640 ptas. ($3.85). RENFE also runs two express trains a day to and from Toledo, taking only 1 hour and making a stop at Aranjuez. For train information in Madrid, call ☎ **91-328-90-20;** in Toledo call ☎ **925-22-30-99.**

It's actually easier to take the bus from Madrid than the train. Buses are maintained by several companies, the largest of which include **Continental or Galiano.** They depart from Madrid's Estación Sur de Autobuses (South Bus Station), calle Méndez Alvaro (☎ **91-468-42-00** for information), every day between 6:30am and 10pm at 30-minute intervals. The fastest leave Monday to Friday on the hour. Those that depart weekdays on the half hour, and those that run on weekends, take a bit longer. Travel time, depending on whether the bus stops en route, is between 1 hour and 1 hour 20 minutes. One-way transit costs 590 ptas. ($3.55).

Once you reach Toledo, you'll be deposited at the Estación de Autobuses, which lies beside the river, about ¾ mile from the historic center. Although many visitors opt to walk, be ready to climb a hill. Bus numbers 5 and 6 run from the station uphill to the center, charging 115 ptas. (70¢) for the brief ride. Pay the driver directly.

If you're driving, exit Madrid via Cibeles (Paseo del Prado) and take the N-401 south.

VISITOR INFORMATION The **tourist information office** is at Puerta de Bisagra (☎ **925-22-08-43**). It's open Monday to Friday 9am to 6pm, Saturday 9am to 7pm, and Sunday 9am to 3pm.

EXPLORING THE TOWN

Alcázar. Calle General Moscardó, 4, near the Plaza de Zocodover. ☎ **925-22-30-38.** Admission 200 ptas. ($1.20) adults, free for children under 10. Tues–Sun 10am–2pm and 4–6pm (6:30pm July–Sept). Bus: 5 or 6.

The Alcázar, at the eastern edge of the old city, dominates the Toledo skyline. It became world famous at the beginning of the Spanish Civil War when it underwent a 70-day siege that almost destroyed it (see "The Siege of the Alcázar," below). Today it has been rebuilt and turned into an army museum housing such exhibits as a plastic model of what the fortress looked like after the Civil War, electronic equipment used during the siege, and photographs taken during the height of the battle. A walking tour gives a realistic simulation of the siege. Allow an hour for a visit.

Casa y Museo de El Greco. Calle Samuel Leví, 3. ☎ **925-22-40-46.** Admission 200 ptas. ($1.20) adults, free for children under 10. Tues–Sat 10am–2pm and 4–6pm; Sun 10am–2pm. Bus: 5 or 6.

Located in Toledo's *antiguo barrio judío* (the old Jewish quarter, a labyrinth of narrow streets on the old town's southwestern edge), the House of El Greco honors the great master painter, although he didn't actually live here. In 1585 the artist moved into one of the run-down palace apartments belonging to the marqués de Villena. Although he was to live at other Toledan addresses, he returned to the Villena palace in 1604 and remained there until his death. Only a small part of the original residence was saved from decay. In time, this and a neighboring house became the El Greco museum; today it's furnished with authentic period pieces.

You can visit El Greco's so-called studio, where one of his paintings hangs. The museum contains several more works, including a copy of *A View of Toledo* and three portraits, plus many pictures by various 16th- and 17th-century Spanish artists. The garden and especially the kitchen also merit attention, as does a sitting room decorated in the Moorish style.

✪ **Cathedral de Toledo.** Arco de Palacio. ☎ **925-22-22-41.** Free admission to cathedral; Treasure Room 500 ptas. ($3). Daily 10:30am–1:30pm and 3:30–6pm. Bus: 5 or 6.

Ranked among the greatest Gothic structures, the cathedral actually reflects several styles, since more than 2½ centuries elapsed during its construction (1226–1493). Many historic events transpired here, including the proclamation of Joanna the Mad and her husband, Philip the Handsome, as heirs to the throne of Spain.

Among its art treasures, the *transparente* stands out—a wall of marble and florid baroque alabaster sculpture overlooked for years because the cathedral was too poorly lit. Sculptor Narciso Tomé cut a hole in the ceiling, much to the consternation of Toledans, and now light touches the high-rising angels, a *Last Supper* in alabaster, and a Virgin in ascension.

The 16th-century *Capilla Mozárabe*, containing works by Juan de Borgona, is another curiosity of the cathedral. Mass is still held here using Mozarabic liturgy.

The Treasure Room has a 500-pound, 15th-century gilded monstrance—allegedly made with gold brought back from the New World by Columbus—that is still carried through the streets of Toledo during the feast of Corpus Christi.

Other highlights of the cathedral include El Greco's *Twelve Apostles* and *Spoliation of Christ* and Goya's *Arrest of Christ on the Mount of Olives.*

The cathedral shop, where you buy tickets to enter, is well organized and stocks a variety of quality souvenirs, including ceramics and damascene.

Hospital de Tavera. Hospital de Tavera, 2. ☎ **925-22-04-51.** Admission 500 ptas. ($3). Daily 10:30am–1:30pm and 3:30–6pm.

This 16th-century Greco-Roman palace north of the medieval ramparts of Toledo was originally built by Cardinal Tavera; it now houses a private art collection. Titian's portrait of Charles V hangs in the banqueting hall. The museum owns five paintings by El Greco: *The Holy Family, The Baptism of Christ,* and portraits of St. Francis, St. Peter, and Cardinal Tavera. Ribera's *The Bearded Woman* also attracts many viewers. The collection of books in the library is priceless. In the nearby church is the mausoleum of Cardinal Tavera, designed by Alonso Berruguete.

✪ **Iglesia de Santo Tomé.** Plaza del Conde, 4, Vía Santo Tomé. ☎ **925-25-60-98.** Admission 150 ptas. (90¢). Daily 10am–6:45pm (closes at 5pm in winter). Closed Dec 25 and Jan 1.

This modest little 14th-century chapel, situated on a narrow street in the old Jewish quarter, might have been overlooked had it not possessed El Greco's masterpiece *The Burial of the Count of Orgaz,* created in 1586. To avoid the hordes, go when the chapel first opens.

Monasterio de San Juan de los Reyes. Calle Reyes Católicos, 17. ☎ **925-22-38-02.** Admission 150 ptas. (90¢) adults, free for children 8 and under. Winter, daily 10am–1:45pm and 3:30–6pm; summer, daily 10am–1:45pm and 3:30–7pm. Bus: 2.

Founded by King Ferdinand and Queen Isabella to commemorate their triumph over the Portuguese at Toro in 1476, the church was started in 1477 according to the plans of architect Juan Guas. It was finished, together with the splendid cloisters, in 1504, dedicated to St. John the Evangelist, and used from the beginning by the Franciscan friars. An example of Gothic-Spanish-Flemish style, San Juan de los Reyes was restored after the damage caused during Napoléon's invasion and after its abandonment in 1835; since 1954 it has been entrusted again to the Franciscans. The church is located at the extreme western edge of the old town, midway between the Puente (bridge) of San Martín and the Puerta (gate) of Cambrón.

۞ Museo de Santa Cruz. Calle Miguel de Cervantes, 3. ☎ **925-22-14-02.** Free admission. Mon–Sat 10am–6pm; Sun 10am–2pm. Bus: 5 or 6. Pass beneath the granite archway on the eastern edge of the Plaza de Zocodover and walk about 1 block.

Today a museum of art and sculpture, this was originally a 16th-century Spanish Renaissance hospice, founded by Cardinal Mendoza, "the third King of Spain," who helped Ferdinand and Isabella gain the throne. The facade is almost more spectacular than any of the exhibits inside. It's a stunning architectural achievement in the classical plateresque style. The major artistic treasure inside is El Greco's *The Assumption of the Virgin,* his last known work. Paintings by Goya and Ribera are also on display along with gold items, opulent antique furnishings, Flemish tapestries, and even Visigoth artifacts. In the patio of the museum you'll stumble across fragments of carved stone and sarcophagi lids. One of the major exhibits is of a large Astrolablio tapestry of the zodiac from the 1400s. In the basement you can see artifacts, including elephant tusks, from archaeological digs throughout the province.

Sínagoga del Tránsito. Calle Samuel Leví, s/n. ☎ **925-22-36-65.** Admission 400 ptas. ($2.40). Tues–Sat 10am–1:45pm and 4–5:45pm; Sun 10am–1:45pm. Closed Jan 1, May 1, Dec 24–25, and Dec 31. Bus: 2.

One block west of the El Greco home and museum stands this once-important house of worship for Toledo's large Jewish population. A 14th-century building, it is noted for its superb stucco Hebrew inscriptions, including psalms inscribed along the top of the walls and a poetic description of the Temple on the east wall. The synagogue is the most important part of the **Museo Sefardí (Sephardic Museum),** which opened in 1971 and contains art objects as well as tombstones with Hebrew epigraphy, some of which are dated before 1492.

Sínagoga de Santa María La Blanca. Calle Reyes Católicos, 2. ☎ **925-22-72-57.** Admission 150 ptas. (90¢). Apr–Sept, daily 10am–2pm and 3:30–7pm; Oct–Mar, daily 10am–2pm and 3:30–6pm. Bus: 2.

In the late 12th century, the Jews of Toledo erected an important synagogue in the Almohada style, which employs graceful horseshoe arches and ornamental horizontal moldings. Although by the early 15th century it had been converted into a Christian church, much of the original remains, including the five naves and elaborate Mudéjar decorations, mosquelike in their effect. The synagogue lies on the western edge of the city, midway between the El Greco museum and San Juan de los Reyes.

ENJOYING THE OUTDOORS

Anglers wanting to try their luck in the Tagus River often head for Toledo, since the river forms a natural moat around the city. The Spanish government has introduced black bass at Finisterra Dam, which lies some 28 miles (45km) southeast of the city. In various reservoirs you can catch large pike and carp. To fish these waters, you must obtain a permit in Madrid at either **ICONA,** calle Veincesa, 4 (☎ **91-580-39-09**), or from the **Federación Española de Pesca,** Navas de Tolosa, 3 (☎ **91-532-83-53**).

The best place for swimming is the Parador Nacional de Conde Orgaz (see "Where to Stay," below), but its pool is available only to guests. The best outdoor pool—and a welcome relief in July and August—is at the **Camping Circo Romano,** calle III, 19 (☎ **925-22-04-42**), a campground just north of the old city walls. It's open June to September daily 10am to 8pm. Admission Monday to Friday is 700 ptas. ($4.20); Saturday and Sunday it's 800 ptas. ($4.80).

SHOPPING

In swashbuckling days, the swordsmiths of Toledo were renowned. They're still around and still turning out swords today. Toledo is equally renowned for its *damasquinado,* or damascene work, the Moorish art of inlaying gold, even copper or silver threads, against a matte black steel backdrop. Today Toledo is filled with souvenir shops hawking damascene. The price depends on whether the item is handcrafted or machine made. Sometimes machine-made damascene is passed off as the more expensive handcrafted item, so you have to shop carefully. Bargaining is perfectly acceptable in Toledo, but if you get the price down, you can't pay with a credit card—only cash.

Marzipan (called *mazapán* locally) is often prepared by nuns and is a local specialty. Many shops in town specialize in this treat made of sweet almond paste.

The province of Toledo is also renowned for its pottery, which is sold in so many shops at competitive prices that it's almost unnecessary to recommend specific branches hawking these wares. However, over the years we've found that the large roadside emporiums on the outskirts of town on the main road to Madrid often are better bargains than the shops within the city walls, where rents are higher.

Better yet, for the best deals, and if you're interested in buying a number of items, consider a trip to **Talavera la Reina,** 47 miles (76km) west of Toledo, where most of the pottery is made. Since Talavera is the largest city in the province, it is hardly a picture-postcard little potter's village. Most of the shops lie along the main street of town, where you'll find store after store selling this distinctive pottery in multicolored designs.

Pottery hunters also flock to **Puente del Arzobispo,** another ceramic center, known for its green-hued pottery. From Talavera drive west on the N-V to Oropesa, then south for 9 miles (14km) to a fortified bridge across the Tagus. In general, ceramics here are cheaper than those sold in Toledo.

Just past Oropesa at the turnoff to Lagartera is the village where the highly renowned and sought-after embroidery of La Mancha originates. Virtually every cottage displays samples of this freeform floral stitching, shaped into everything from skirts to tablecloths. Of course, shops in Toledo are also filled with samples of this unique embroidery.

Established in 1910, **Casa Bermejo,** calle Airosas, 5 (☎ **925-28-53-67**), is a factory and store that employs almost 50 artisans, and you can watch them at work. The outlet carries a wide array of damascene objects fashioned into Toledo's traditional Mudéjar designs—swords, platters, pitchers, and other gift items. But not all the items follow the inspiration of the medieval Arabs. This outfit engraves many of the ornamental swords awarded to graduates of West Point in the United States, as well as the decorative, full-dress military accessories used by the armies of various countries of Europe, including France. Open Monday to Friday 9am to 1pm and 3 to 6pm, Saturday 9am to 1pm. Closing times are later in July and August, determined solely by business traffic.

Around since the 1920s, **Felipe Suarez,** Paseo de los Canónigos, 19 (☎ **925-22-56-15**), has manufactured damascene work in various forms, ranging from unpretentious souvenir items to art objects of rare museum-quality beauty that sell for as much as 2,000,000 ptas. ($12,000). You'll find swords, straight-edged razors, pendants, fans, and an array of pearls. The shop is open daily 10am to 7pm throughout the year.

The Siege of the Alcázar

Although the Alcázar of Toledo has suffered many a siege, one particularly dramatic encounter in 1936 made world headlines. The Republicans were fighting to gain control of conservative, staunchly Catholic Toledo. Franco's rebel troops were commanded by one tough officer, Col. José Moscardó. Not only were his troops inside the Alcázar, but women and children were holed up here as well. The Alcázar, although under heavy attack, withstood 70 days of bombardment.

On July 23, a Republican officer reached Moscardó by telephone within the Alcázar. The colonel was informed that Nationalist forces had kidnapped Luis, his 16-year-old son. Moscardó was told that unless he immediately surrendered the fortress, Luis would be executed.

To show that they did indeed have the child, they put Luis on the phone to his father. "Papá!" he shouted, "They say they are going to shoot me if you don't surrender."

Without hesitation, Moscardó told his son: "Then commend your soul to God, shout 'Viva España!' and die like a hero."

The Republicans were good to their word. Luis was shot in the head. The fortress was surrendered in September of that year. In the Alcázar today the wall phone on which the colonel spoke to his son for the last time still hangs.

You'll also find superb craftsmanship in damascene work at **Santiago Sanchez Martín,** calle Rio Llano, 15 (☎ 925-22-77-57), which specializes in the elaborately detailed arabesques whose techniques are as old as the Arab conquest of Iberia. Look for everything from decorative tableware (platters, pitchers, etc.) to mirror frames, jewelry, letter openers, and ornamental swords. It's open Monday to Friday 9am to 2pm and 5 to 7pm.

Many long-time residents of Toledo remember **Casa Telesforo,** Plaza de Zocodover, 13 (☎ 925-22-33-79), as the outfit that supplied the marzipan consumed at their childhood birthday parties and celebrations. A specialist in this almond-and-sugar confection, it sells the best marzipan in town, made into such whimsical shapes as hearts, diamonds, flowers, and fish. It's open daily 9am to 10pm, later in summer, depending on the crowds.

WHERE TO STAY
EXPENSIVE

✪ **AC Hoteles Ciudad de Toledo.** Carretera De Circumvalación, 15, 41005 Toledo. ☎ **925/28-51-25.** Fax 925/28-47-00. www.ac-hoteles.com. E-mail:ciud.resep@ac-hoteles.com. 49 units. A/C MINIBAR TV TEL. 20,000 ptas. ($120) double; 25,000 ptas. ($150) suite. AE, MC, V. Free parking. Bus: 5.

Opened in 1998, this is the first hotel in years to offer a choice superior to the government-run parador. On a beltway south of the city—follow the directions to the parador—this deluxe property is a member of a chain that also includes the swanky Santo Mauro in Madrid. The epitome of luxury living, this hotel across the river from the city is entered at the third floor. You move down through the spiraling architectural design to reach the rest of the hotel. Bedrooms are spacious and luxuriously furnished, all in contemporary styling, with tiled bathrooms. The suites have oversize bathtubs and hydromassage.

Dining: The food is excellent, with both regional and international specialties featured. In addition to the main restaurant, a 24-hour cafeteria is also open.

Amenities: Laundry, dry cleaning, concierge, room service, baby-sitting.

✪ **Parador Nacional de Conde Orgaz.** Cerro del Emperador, 45002 Toledo. ☎ 925-22-18-50. Fax 925-22-51-66. E-mail: toledo@parador.es. 76 units. A/C MINIBAR TV TEL. 21,000 ptas. ($126) double; 26,000 ptas. ($156) suite. AE, DC, MC, V. Free parking. Drive across Puente San Martín and head south for 2½ miles (4km).

You'll have to make reservations well in advance to stay at this parador, which is built on the ridge of a rugged hill where El Greco is said to have painted his *View of Toledo*. That view is still here, and it is without a doubt one of the grandest in the world. The main living room/lounge has fine furniture—old chests, leather chairs, and heavy tables—and leads to a sunny terrace overlooking the city. On chilly nights you can sit by the fireplace. The guest rooms are the most luxurious in all of Toledo, far superior to those at Maria Cristina. They are spacious and beautifully furnished with repro-ductions of regional antique pieces. Most of the rooms come with roomy modern bathrooms clad in marble (others are tiled) and equipped with hair dryers and robes.

Dining: The hotel's restaurant serves fine Castilian cuisine.

Amenities: Room service, laundry/valet, outdoor pool.

MODERATE

✪ **Hostal del Cardenal.** Paseo de Recaredo, 24, 45003 Toledo. ☎ **925-22-49-00.** Fax 925-22-29-91. www.cardenal.macom.es. E-mail: cardenal@macom.es. 27 units. A/C TV TEL. 12,600 ptas. ($75.60) double; 17,150 ptas. ($102.90) suite. AE, DC, MC, V. Parking 1,900 ptas. ($11.40). Bus: 2 from rail station.

This place has long been acclaimed as the best restaurant in Toledo (see below), but we'll let you in on a secret: You can rent rooms here, too. They're not as grand as those at the Parador, but they're wonderful nevertheless, especially if you want an old Toledan atmosphere. The entrance to this unusual hotel is set into the stone of the ancient city walls, a few steps from the Bisagra Gate. To enter the hotel you must climb a series of terraces to the top of the crenellated walls of the ancient fortress. Here, grandly symmetrical and very imposing, is the hostal, the former residence of the 18th-century cardinal of Toledo, Señor Lorenzana. Just beyond the entrance, still atop the city wall, you'll find flagstone walkways, Moorish fountains, rose gardens, and cascading vines. The building has tiled walls; long, narrow salons; dignified Spanish furniture; and a smattering of antiques. Bedrooms are small to medium, each one well appointed with a firm mattress and quality linen, plus a tidily organized bathroom with a stall shower. The only parking is what's available free on the street. A member of the hotel staff will call you a taxi if you don't want to walk the steep ascent (on nar-row to nonexistent sidewalks) into the historic district.

Hotel Doménico. Cerro del Emperador, 45002 Toledo. ☎ **925-28-01-01.** Fax 925-28-02-03. 50 units. A/C MINIBAR TV TEL. 16,380–18,075 ptas. ($98.30–$108.45) double; 26,075 ptas. ($156.45) suite. AE, MC, V. Free parking. Bus: 7

One of the finest four-star hotels in Toledo, Doménico is located among Los Cigar-rales, the typical country houses lying south of the city and offering panoramic views. The building, although modern, is constructed in a traditional style. Launched in 1993, the hotel is only a 5-minute drive to the historic core of Toledo. Bedrooms are medium in size and comfortably furnished. Some of the rooms have windows in the roof for greater light. The beds have excellent mattresses, and amenities include safes, plus bathrooms with showers and hair dryers. The second- and third-floor units have terraces opening onto the swimming pool or views of the city. A terrace restaurant offers a fine national and international cuisine, and there is also a cafeteria bar. Room service is available until 10:30pm, and other services include a concierge and laundry.

✪ Hotel el Pintor El Greco. Alamillos del Tránsito, 13, 45002 Toledo. ☎ **925-28-51-91.** Fax 925-21-58-19. E-mail: elgreco@estanciases.es. 33 units. A/C TV TEL. 14,700–18,000 ptas. ($88.20–$108) double. AE, DC, MC, V. Parking 700 ptas. ($4.20).

In the old Jewish quarter, one of the most traditional and historic districts of Toledo, this hotel was converted from a typical *casa Toledana,* which had once been used as a bakery. With careful restoration, especially of its ancient facade, it was transformed into one of Toledo's best and most atmospheric small hotels—the only one to match the antique charm of Hostal del Cardenal, although it remains relatively unknown. Decoration in both the public rooms and bedrooms is in a traditional Castilian style. Phones, piped-in music, air-conditioning, satellite TV, and individual security boxes have been added to the immaculately kept bedrooms. Bedrooms come in a variety of shapes and sizes, as befits a building of this age, but all are equipped with firm mattresses and small bathrooms with stall showers and adequate shelf space. At the doorstep of the hotel are such landmarks as the Monasterio de San Juan de los Reyes, Sínagoga de Santa María la Blanca, Sínagoga del Tránsito, Casa y Museo de El Greco, and Iglesia de Santo Tomé. Public parking is available for 800 ptas. ($4.80) per day.

Hotel María Cristina. Marqués de Mendigorría, 1, 45003 Toledo. ☎ **925-21-32-02.** Fax 925-21-26-50. 63 units. A/C MINIBAR TV TEL. 12,200 ptas. ($73.20) double; 22,150 ptas. ($132.90) suite. AE, DC, MC, V. Parking 1,000 ptas. ($6).

Adjacent to the historic Hospital de Tavera and near the northern perimeter of the old town, this stone-sided, awning-fronted hotel resembles a palatial country home. If you're willing to forgo the view from the parador and the charm of Hostal del Cardenal, this hotel is a good backup. Originally built as a convent in 1560 and later used as a hospital, it was turned into this comfortable hotel in the late 1980s. Sprawling and historic, it contains clean, attractively furnished bedrooms, each with a comfortable bed and an immaculate bathroom, often with a tub and shower combo.

On site is the very large and well-recommended restaurant, El Abside, where fixed-price lunches and dinners are served, ranging in price from 1,875 to 2,500 ptas. ($11.25 to $15). There's also a bar. The food is much better, however, at Hostal del Cardenal.

Amenities include 24-hour room service, laundry, concierge, and baby-sitting.

Hotel Residencia Alfonso VI. Calle General Moscardó, 2, 45001 Toledo. ☎ **925-22-26-00.** Fax 925-21-44-58. www.alfonsovi.macom.es. E-mail: alfonsovi@macom.es. 83 units. A/C TV TEL. 13,500–15,000 ptas. ($81–$90) double; 28,000 ptas. ($168) suite. AE, MC, V. Bus: 5 or 6.

Built in the early 1970s, this hotel has been kept up to date with frequent renovations. Run by the same management as the Carlos V, it is a superior hotel with better appointments and comfort, although a few of the public rooms appear so faux Castilian they look like movie sets. It sits near a dense concentration of souvenir shops in the center of the old city, at the southern perimeter of the Alcázar. Inside you'll discover a high-ceilinged, marble-trimmed decor with a scattering of Iberian artifacts, copies of Spanish provincial furniture, and dozens of leather armchairs. Rooms, for the most part, are medium in size, each well appointed with cushiony furnishings, including comfortable mattresses on the Spanish beds. Bathrooms are tiled and a bit small. There's also a stone-floored dining room, where well-prepared, fixed-price meals range from 1,300 to 3,000 ptas. ($7.80 to $18) each.

INEXPENSIVE

Hotel Imperio. Cadena, 5, 45001 Toledo. ☎ **925-22-76-50.** Fax 925-25-3183. www.
teleline.es/personal/himperio/. E-mail: himperio@teleline.es. 21 units. A/C TV TEL. 6,200 ptas.
($37.20) double. AE, DC, MC, V.

Long a budget favorite, this modest hotel lies a few yards from the Alcázar and
Cathedral. Built in the 1980s, the hotel was recently renovated (and just in time),
adding more comfort to the small rooms. The furnishings are rather severe, but the
beds are comfortable and renewed. However, for the price this is one of the city's best
choices. Rooms on the second floor have balconies overlooking the street. A snack bar
is on site, but some fine restaurants lie just outside the door. The only parking available is on the street, and room service is offered until 10pm. Other amenities include
laundry and a concierge.

Hotel Martin. Calle Covachuela, 12, 45003 Toledo. ☎/fax **925-22-17-33.** E-mail:
hotelmartin@pyme.com. 17 units. A/C MINIBAR TV TEL. 6,750 ptas. ($40.50) double. MC, V.
Parking 1,000 ptas. ($6).

A good, serviceable choice, the two-story Martin opened in 1992 near the Bisagra
Gate, the main medieval doorway to the city of Toledo. It lies only a 10-minute walk
from the historic center. The hotel has a homey atmosphere, with a red-brick facade,
old streetlights out front, and vertical windows. The interior is decorated in wood and
pastel colors. The rooms are medium in size and furnished comfortably. Bathrooms
are impeccably maintained, with showers and hair dryers. Amenities include room service until 11pm, plus a laundry. A continental breakfast is served in the coffee bar.

Hotel Mayoral. Avenida de Castilla–La Mancha, 3, 45003 Toledo. ☎ **925-21-60-00.**
Fax. 925-21-69-54. 110 units. A/C MINIBAR TV TEL. 12,500 ptas. ($75) double. AE, DC,
MC, V. Parking 1,000 ptas. ($6). Bus: 5 or 6.

In front of the walls of Toledo next to the bus station, this hotel was inaugurated in
1989 and met with instant approval. A rather formal entrance followed by a severe
hallway leads to comfortable, well-furnished, medium-size bedrooms with good beds
and well-maintained bathrooms equipped with hair dryers. Most of the guest rooms
have balconies with views of interior patios, although a few have a panoramic view of
Toledo. Mayoral maintains an excellent restaurant serving both Spanish and international cuisine, plus a cozy bar. A buffet breakfast is served daily, and other amenities
include room service, laundry, and a concierge.

Hotel Real de Toledo. Calle Real del Arrabal, 4, 45003 Toledo. ☎ **925-22-93-00.**
Fax 925-22-87-67. www.socranet.com/hotelreal. 54 units. A/C TV TEL. 11,000 ptas. ($66)
double. AE, DC, MC, V. Parking 1,000 ptas. ($6). Bus: 5 or 6.

This 19th-century building is within the ancient city walls between the Bisagra and
Sun Gates and has been a hotel since 1991. The facade, made from Castillian brick,
is dotted with large-framed windows. Despite the age of the building, the interior is
modern and comfortable. Many of the rooms open onto a view, but although each is
comfortable and well equipped, some don't get enough light. Bathrooms are small and
well maintained. Amenities include laundry, a concierge, and a small on-site cafeteria.

Hotel Santa Isabel. Calle Santa Isabel, 24, 45002 Toledo. ☎ **925-25-31-20.** Fax. 925-
25-31-36. www.santa-isabel.com. E-mail: santa-isabel@arrakis.ed. 24 units. A/C TV TEL.
6,500 ptas. ($39) double. AE, DC, MC, V. Parking 900 ptas. ($5.40). Bus: Centro.

In a building dating from the 15th century, Santa Isabel lies in the heart of Toledo,
close to the cathedral and most sights of historic interest. Opposite the Convent of
Santa Isabel from which it takes its name, the hotel still has much of its original

character. The interior, however, has been austerely modernized. Bedrooms are small and spartan, but immaculately kept with comfortable beds. Some units have fine views of the interior patio; others open onto the street. Amenities include a cafeteria serving breakfast.

WHERE TO DINE
MODERATE

✪ **Asador Adolfo.** La Granada, 6. ☎ **925-22-73-21.** Reservations recommended. Main courses 2,800–3,600 ptas. ($16.80–$21.60); fixed-price menu 5,500–6,500 ptas. ($33–$39). AE, DC, MC, V. Daily 1–4pm; Mon–Sat 8pm–midnight. Bus: 5 or 6. SPANISH.

Located less than a minute's walk north of the cathedral, at the corner of calle Hombre de Palo behind an understated sign, Asador Adolfo is one of the finest restaurants in town (although we still prefer the Hostal del Cardenal). Sections of the building were first constructed during the 1400s, but the thoroughly modern kitchen has recently been renovated. Massive beams support the dining room ceiling, and here and there the rooms contain faded frescoes dating from the original building.

Game dishes are a house specialty; with partridge with white beans and venison consistently rating among the best anywhere. Non-game offerings include hake flavored with local saffron as well as a wide array of beef, veal, or lamb dishes. To start, try the *pimientos rellenos* (red peppers stuffed with pulverized shellfish). The house dessert is marzipan, prepared in a wood-fired oven and noted for its lightness.

✪ **Hostal del Cardenal.** Paseo de Recaredo, 24. ☎ **925-22-08-62.** Reservations required. Main courses 1,200–2,800 ptas. ($7.20–$16.80); fixed-price menu 2,080 ptas. ($12.50). AE, DC, MC, V. Daily 1–4pm and 8:30–11:30pm. Bus: 2 from rail station. SPANISH.

Treat yourself to Toledo's best-known restaurant, owned by the same people who run Madrid's Sobrino de Botín (see chapter 3, "Madrid"). The chef prepares regional dishes with flair and originality. Choosing from a menu very similar to that of the fabled Madrid eatery, begin with "quarter of an hour" (fish) soup or white asparagus, then move on to curried prawns, baked hake, filet mignon, or smoked salmon. Roast suckling pig is a specialty, as is partridge in casserole. Arrive early to enjoy a sherry in the bar or in the courtyard.

La Abadia. Plaza de San Nicolás, 3. ☎ **925-25-07-46.** Reservations recommended. Main courses 1,500–2,500 ptas. ($9–$15); set menu 3,475 ptas. ($20.85). DC, MC, V. Fri–Sat noon–3pm; daily 8pm–midnight. CASTILIAN.

The "Abbey" (its English name) started life as a *cerveceria*, or alehouse, before it was turned into a convivial restaurant and tapas bar. Next to San Nicolás church, it stands at the intersection of Núnez de Arce and calle de Alfileteros. It is ideal for a huge Castilian meal or for wine drinking and tapas eating. The decor is a tasteful combination of modern and rustic styles, and the interior is separated into two sections—with separate restaurant and bar areas. In honor of its old function as a *cerveceria*, a wide variety of international beers is offered. One of the best dishes—and one beloved by many Toledanos—is a partridge casserole with white wine, bay leaves, and onions. Fillet of venison in a mushroom sauce is another worthy choice, as is *ensalada de verdura a la parilla,* or a salad of freshly grilled vegetables. Some of the most delightful tapas include croquettes, roasted red peppers, and such meats as venison and Serrano ham. The most unusual dessert is an ice cream made of Manchego cheese.

Venta de Aires. Circo Romano, 35. ☎ **925-22-05-45.** Reservations recommended. Main courses 1,800–2,600 ptas. ($10.80–$15.60); fixed-price menu 2,500–3,500 ptas. ($15–$21). AE, DC, MC, V. Daily 1–4pm and 8–11pm. SPANISH.

Just outside the city gates southwest of the *Circo Romano* (Roman Circus), Venta de Aires has served Toledo's pièce de résistance, *perdiz* (partridge), since 1891 when the place was just a tiny roadside inn. This dish is best eaten with the red wine of Méntrida. For dessert, try the marzipan. On your way out, take note of former President Richard Nixon's entry in the guest book (he dined here in 1963)—believe it or not, they're still talking about the visit.

INEXPENSIVE

El Catavinos. Av. Reconquista, 10. ☎ **925-22-22-56.** Reservations recommended. Main courses 900–2,000 ptas. ($5.40–$12); set menu 1,275 ptas. ($7.65); *menu de degustación* 3,500 ptas. ($21). AE, DC, MC, V. Tues–Sat noon–midnight; Sun 8pm–midnight. SPANISH/CASTILIAN.

El Catavinos means "wine taster" in Spanish, and indeed this charming restaurant started its life as a wine cellar. On the periphery of the center, a 10-minute walk from the Puerta de Bisagra, the restaurant has a convivial bar downstairs and a restaurant upstairs decorated with old photographs of Peru. In fair weather, guests often eat out on the terrace. The menu is filled with exciting dishes, including such delicacies as partridge salad, bell peppers with a stuffing of hare, and grilled venison and veal meatballs in a savory tomato sauce. The *menu de degustación* is a cornucopia of seven different plates, each accompanied by a different wine. The desserts offered include a cheesecake made from goat milk with a sweet white wine.

La Perdiz. Calle Reyes Católicos, 7. ☎ **925-21-46-58.** Reservations recommended. Main courses 1,500–2,000 ptas. ($9–$12); set menu 2,500 ptas. ($15). AE, MC, V. Tues–Sat noon–11pm; Sun noon–4pm. CASTILIAN.

La Perdiz is named from the favorite dish of Toledans, partridge. That bird is best showcased here in a dish called *perdiz estofada a la toledano* (partridge stew with white wine, bay leaf, and onions). Another excellent choice is venison in a mushroom sauce. The menu has some imaginative offerings, such as a fresh fried cheese tossed in an orange dressing.

The best dessert and a local favorite is a marzipan tart with almond biscuits. On occasion a roast suckling pig is featured. The location is in the center of the old Jewish ghetto, about midpoint between two synagogues, Santa Maria la Blanca and Tránsito. The restaurant has two floors with views of the historic district. Locals, and with good reason, cite the place for its good-quality cuisine at an affordable price. The same people who run La Perdiz also operate **Asador Adolfo** (see above), Toledo's premier restaurant, but prices at La Perdiz are far more reasonable.

La Tarasca. Calle Hombre de Palo, 6. ☎ **925-22-43-42.** Reservations not required. Main courses 1,500–2,600 ptas. ($9–$15.60); set menu 2,200 ptas. ($13.20). MC, V. Daily 7:30am–11pm. CASTILIAN.

This restaurant, the domain of the Martin brothers, serves good food but is mainly recommended for its convenience, as it lies only a couple of blocks north of the cathedral. With two dining rooms and a cafeteria, it is also open throughout the day, even serving breakfast. The decor, although plain, still evokes the 19th century. Walls are painted green with wood paneling resting under beams, and the rooms are joined by archways. The cuisine consists of the hearty, robust fare that Toledans feast on, including the traditional opener, *sopa castella,* a hearty soup made with various meats and beans. You can opt for such standard dishes as grilled steak and potatoes, but braised game hen would be more traditional, or perhaps local trout. One of our favorite dishes is *pimientos rellenos* (stuffed peppers), or *cordoniz a la toledana* (roast quail with savory brown sauce). All desserts, including the puddings, are homemade.

TOLEDO AFTER DARK

Begin your nighttime crawl through Toledo with a stop at **Bar Ludeña,** Plaza de la Madelena, 13, Corral de Don Diego, 10 (☎ **925-22-33-84**), where a loyal clientele comes for delectable tapas. Fixed-price menus range from 1,200 to 2,500 ptas. ($8.05 to $16.75). Glasses of wine are sometimes passed through a small window to clients standing outside enjoying the view of the square. The bar is little more than a narrow corridor, serving *raciónes* of tapas that are so generous they make little meals, especially when served with bread. The roasted red peppers in olive oil are quite tasty, along with the stuffed crabs and *calamares* (squid). Huge dishes of pickled cucumbers, onions, and olives are available. They also have a tiny dining room behind a curtain at the end of the bar serving inexpensive fare.

Despite the many tourists that throng its streets during the day, Toledo is quiet at night, with fewer dance clubs than you'd expect from a town of its size. If you want to hear some recorded music, head for **Bar La Abadia,** calle Nuñez de Arce, 5 (☎ **925-25-11-40**), where crowds of local residents, many of them involved in the tourism industry, crowd elbow to elbow for pints of beer, glasses of wine, and access to the music of New York, Los Angeles, or wherever. A roughly equivalent competitor is **Bar Camelot,** calle Cristo de la Luz, s/n (no phone), which occupies an old, stone-sided building within the historic core of Toledo. Both are open nightly from 8:30pm to around 4am.

2 Aranjuez

29 miles (47km) S of Madrid, 30 miles (48km) NE of Toledo

This Castilian town at a confluence of the Tagus and Jarama Rivers was once home to Bourbon kings in the spring and fall. With the manicured shrubbery, stately elms, fountains, and statues of the Palacio Real and surrounding compounds, Aranjuez remains a regal garden oasis in what is otherwise an unimpressive agricultural flatland known primarily for its strawberries and asparagus.

ESSENTIALS

GETTING THERE Trains depart about every 20 minutes from Madrid's Atocha Railway Station to make the 50-minute trip to Aranjuez, a one-way fare costing 480 ptas. ($2.90). Twice a day you can take an express train from Madrid to Toledo, which makes a brief stopover at Aranjuez. This trip takes only 30 minutes. Trains run less often along the east-west route to and from Toledo (a 40-minute ride). The Aranjuez station lies about a mile outside town. For information and schedules, call ☎ **91-891-02-02.** You can walk it in about 15 minutes, but taxis and buses line up on calle Stuart (2 blocks from the city tourist office). The bus that makes the run from the center of Aranjuez to the railway station is marked N–Z.

Buses for Aranjuez depart every 30 minutes from 7:30am to 10pm from Madrid's Estación Sur de Autobuses, calle Méndez Alvaro. In Madrid, call ☎ **91-468-42-00** for information. Buses arrive in Aranjuez at the City Bus Terminal, calle Infantas, 8 (☎ **91-891-01-83**).

Driving is easy and takes about 30 minutes once you reach the southern city limits of Madrid. To reach Aranjuez, follow the signs to Aranjuez and Granada, taking highway N-IV.

VISITOR INFORMATION The **tourist information office** is at Plaza de San Antonio, 9 (☎ **91-891-04-27**), open Monday to Friday 10am to 2pm and 4 to 6pm.

EXPLORING ARANJUEZ

✪ **Palacio Real.** Plaza Palacio. ☎ **91-891-13-44.** Admission 650 ptas. ($3.90) adults, 250 ptas. ($1.50) students and children. Apr–Sept, Wed–Mon 10am–6:15pm; Oct–Mar, Wed–Mon 10am–5:15pm. Bus: Routes from the rail station converge at the square and gardens at the westernmost edge of the palace.

As you enter a cobblestoned courtyard, you can tell just by the size of the palace that it's going to be spectacular. Ferdinand and Isabella, Philip II, Philip V, and Charles III all made their way through here. The structure you see today dates from 1778 (the previous buildings were destroyed by fire). Its salons show the opulence of a bygone era, with room after room of royal extravagance. Many styles are blended: Spanish, Italian, Moorish, and French. And, of course, no royal palace would be complete without a room reflecting the rage for chinoiserie that once swept over Europe. The Porcelain Salon is also of special interest. A guide conducts you through the huge complex (a tip is expected).

Jardín de la Isla. Directly northwest of the Palacio Real. No phone. Free admission. Apr–Sept, daily 8am–8:30pm; Oct–Mar, daily 8am–6:30pm.

After the tour of the Royal Palace, wander through the Garden of the Island. Spanish impressionist Santiago Ruisiñol captured its evasive quality on canvas, and one Spanish writer said that you walk here "as if softly lulled by a sweet 18th-century sonata." A number of fountains are remarkable: the "Ne Plus Ultra" fountain, the black-jasper fountain of Bacchus, the fountain of Apollo, and the ones honoring Neptune (god of the sea) and Cybele (goddess of agriculture).

You may also stroll through the Jardín del Parterre, located in front of the palace. It's much better kept than the Garden of the Island but not as romantic.

Casita del Labrador. Calle Reina, Jardín del Príncipe. ☎ **91-891-03-05.** Admission 550 ptas. ($3.30) adults, 225 ptas. ($1.35) students and children. May–Sept, Tues–Sun 10am–6:30pm; Oct–Apr, Tues–Sun 10am–5:30pm.

"The Little House of the Worker," modeled after the Petit Trianon at Versailles, was built in 1803 by Charles IV, who later abdicated in Aranjuez. The queen came here with her youthful lover, Godoy (whom she had elevated to the position of prime minister), and the feeble-minded Charles didn't seem to mind a bit. Surrounded by beautiful gardens, the "bedless" palace is lavishly furnished in the grand style of the 18th and 19th centuries. The marble floors represent some of the finest workmanship of that day; the brocaded walls emphasize the luxurious lifestyle and the royal toilet is a sight to behold (in those days, royalty preferred an audience). The clock here is one of the treasures of the house. The casita lies half a mile east of the Royal Palace; those with a car can drive directly to it through the tranquil Jardín del Príncipe.

WHERE TO STAY

Hostal Castilla. Carretera Andalucia, 98, 28300 Aranjuez. ☎ **91-891-26-27.** 17 units. TV TEL. 7,500 ptas. ($45) double. AE, DC, MC, V.

On one of the town's main streets north of the Royal Palace and gardens, the Castilla consists of the ground floor and part of the first floor of a well-preserved early 18th-century house. Most of the accommodations overlook a courtyard with a fountain and flowers. Owner Martin Soria speaks English. There are excellent restaurants nearby, and the hostal has an arrangement with a neighboring bar to provide guests with an inexpensive lunch. This is a good location from which to explore either Madrid or Toledo on a day trip. Parking is available along the street.

WHERE TO DINE

✪ **Casa José.** Calle Abastos, 32. ☎ **91-891-14-88.** Reservations recommended. Main courses 1,800–3,000 ptas. ($10.80–$18). AE, DC, MC, V. Tues–Sun 1–4pm; Tues–Sat 9pm–midnight. SPANISH/INTERNATIONAL.

Set near Town Hall and the Church of Antonio, this well-managed restaurant occupies two ground-floor rooms of a 300-year-old house in the heart of town. It is the premier restaurant of the entire area, and local gastronomes drive for miles around to dine here. The regional food is prepared with intelligence, and any of the daily offerings is well worth ordering. Look for a menu of fresh local ingredients that changes at least four times a year, with an emphasis on pork, veal, fish, chicken, and shellfish. Of special note are braised lamb chops in a fresh tomato and cilantro sauce, Jabugo ham with broad beans, shrimp in garlic sauce, hake with green sauce, and thick juicy steaks.

Casa Pablo. Almibar, 42. ☎ **91-891-14-51.** Reservations recommended. Main courses 2,000–2,600 ptas. ($12–$15.60); 4-course fixed-price menu 3,000 ptas. ($18). AE, MC, V. Daily 1–4:30pm and 8pm–midnight. Closed Aug. SPANISH.

An unpretentious restaurant near the bus station in the town center, Casa Pablo was established in 1941. At tables set outside under a canopy, you can enjoy red and pink geraniums along the tree-lined street; in cooler weather you eat either upstairs or in the cozy and clean rear dining room. The fixed-price menu includes four courses, a carafe of wine, bread, and gratuity. If it's hot and you don't want a heavy dinner, try a shrimp omelete or half a roast chicken; once we ordered just a plate of asparagus in season, accompanied by white wine. If you want a superb dish, try a fish called *mero* (Mediterranean pollack of delicate flavor), grilled over an open fire.

La Rana Verde. Reina, 1. ☎ **91-891-32-38.** Reservations recommended. Main courses 1,200–2,500 ptas. ($7.20–$15); fixed-price menu 1,500–3,900 ptas. ($9–$23.40). MC, V. Daily 9pm–midnight. SPANISH.

"The Green Frog," just east of the Royal Palace next to a small bridge spanning the Tagus, is still the traditional choice for many. Opened in 1905 by Tomas Diaz Heredero, it is owned and run by a third-generation member of his family, who has decorated it in 1920s style. The restaurant looks like a summerhouse, with its high-beamed ceiling and soft drooping ferns. The best tables overlook the river. As in all the restaurants of Aranjuez, asparagus is a special feature. Game, particularly partridge, quail, and pigeon, can be recommended in season; fish, too, including fried hake and fried sole, makes a good choice. Strawberries are served with sugar, orange juice, or ice cream.

3 San Lorenzo de El Escorial

30 miles (48km) W of Madrid, 32 miles (52km) SE of Segovia

Aside from Toledo, the most important excursion from Madrid is to the austere royal monastery of San Lorenzo de El Escorial. Philip II ordered the construction of this granite-and-slate behemoth in 1563, 2 years after he moved his capital to Madrid. Once the haunt of aristocratic Spaniards, El Escorial is now a resort where hotels and restaurants flourish in the summer as hordes come to escape the heat of the capital. Aside from the appeal of its climate, the town of San Lorenzo itself is not very noteworthy. But because of the monastery's size, you might decide to spend a night or two at San Lorenzo—more if you have the time.

San Lorenzo makes a good base for visiting nearby Segovia and Ávila, the royal palace at La Granja, the Valley of the Fallen—and the even more distant university city of Salamanca.

ESSENTIALS

GETTING THERE   More than two dozen trains depart daily from Madrid's Atocha, Nuevos Ministerios, and Chamartín train stations. During the summer extra coaches are added. For schedules and information, call ☎ **91-328-90-20.** A one-way fare costs 790 ptas. ($4.75), and trip time is a little more than 1 hour.

The railway station is about a mile outside town along Carretera Estación (☎ **91-890-07-14**). The Herranz bus company meets all arriving trains with a shuttle bus that ferries arriving passengers to and from the Plaza Virgen de Gracia, about a block east of the entrance to the monastery.

Empresa Herranz, calle Reina Victoria, 3, in El Escorial (☎ **91-890-41-22** or 91-890-41-25), runs some 40 buses per day back and forth between Madrid and El Escorial. On Sunday service is curtailed to 10 buses. Trip time is an hour, and a round-trip fare costs 750 ptas. ($4.50). The same company also runs one bus a day to **El Valle de los Caídos (The Valley of the Fallen).** It leaves El Escorial at 3:15pm with a return at 5:30pm. The ride takes only 15 minutes, and a round-trip fare is 870 ptas. ($5.20), El Valle only.

If you're driving, follow the N-VI highway (marked on some maps as A-6) from the northwest perimeter of Madrid toward Lugo, La Coruña, and San Lorenzo de El Escorial. After about a half hour, fork left onto the C-505 toward San Lorenzo de El Escorial. Driving time from Madrid is about an hour.

VISITOR INFORMATION   The **tourist information office** is at Floridablanca, 10 (☎ **91-890-15-54**). It is open Monday to Friday 10am to 2pm and 3 to 5pm, Saturday 10am to 2pm.

SEEING THE SIGHTS

✪ **Real Monasterio de San Lorenzo de El Escorial.** Calle San Lorenzo de El Escorial, 1. ☎ **91-890-59-03.** Comprehensive ticket 850 ptas. ($5.10) adults, 350 ptas. ($2.10) children, guided tour 950 ptas. ($5.70). Apr–Sept, Tues–Sun 10am–7pm; Oct–Mar, Tues–Sun 10am–6pm.

This huge granite fortress houses a wealth of paintings and tapestries and serves as the burial place for Spanish kings. Foreboding both inside and out because of its sheer size and institutional look, El Escorial took 21 years to complete, a remarkably short time considering the bulk of the building and the primitive construction methods of the day. After his death, the original architect Juan Bautista de Toledo was replaced by Juan de Herrera, the greatest architect of Renaissance Spain, who completed the structure.

Philip II, who collected many of the paintings exhibited here in the New Museums, did not care for El Greco but favored Titian instead. Still, you'll find El Greco's *The Martyrdom of St. Maurice,* rescued from storage, and also his St. Peter. Other superb works include Titian's *Last Supper* and Velázquez's *The Tunic of Joseph.*

The Royal Library houses a priceless collection of 60,000 volumes—one of the most significant in the world. The displays range from the handwriting of St. Teresa to medieval instructions on playing chess. See, in particular, the Muslim codices and a Gothic *Cantigas* from the 13th-century reign of Alfonso X ("The Wise").

You can also visit the Philip II Apartments; they are strictly monastic, and Philip called them the "cell for my humble self" in this "palace for God." Philip became a religious fanatic and requested that his bedroom be erected overlooking the altar of the 300-foot-high basilica, which has four organs and a dome based on Michelangelo's drawings for St. Peter's. The choir contains a crucifix by Cellini. By comparison the Throne Room is simple. On the walls are many ancient maps. The Apartments of the Bourbon Kings are lavishly decorated, in contrast to Philip's preference for the ascetic.

Under the altar of the church you'll find one of the most regal mausoleums in the world, the Royal Pantheon, where most of Spain's monarchs from Charles I to Alfonso XII, including Philip II, are buried. In 1993 Don Juan de Borbón, the count of Barcelona and the father of King Juan Carlos (Franco passed over the count and never allowed him to ascend to the throne) was interred nearby. On a lower floor is the "Wedding Cake" tomb for children.

Allow at least 3 hours for a visit. The guided tour doesn't take you to all the sites, but you are free to explore on your own afterward.

Casa de Príncipe (Prince's Cottage). Calle Reina, s/n. ☎ **91-891-03-05.** Admission included in comprehensive ticket to El Escorial, see above. Apr–July and Sept, Sat–Sun and holidays 10am–5:45pm; Aug, Tues–Sun 10am–5:45pm; Oct–Mar, Sat–Sun and holidays 10am–6:45pm.

This small but elaborately decorated 18th-century palace near the railway station was originally a hunting lodge built for Charles III by Juan de Villanueva. Most visitors stay in El Escorial for lunch, visiting the cottage in the afternoon.

El Valle de los Caídos (Valley of the Fallen). ☎ **91-890-56-11.** Admission 650 ptas. ($3.90) adults, 250 ptas. ($1.50) students and children. Apr–Sept, Tues–Sun 9:30am–7pm; Oct–Mar, Tues–Sun 10am–6pm. Bus: Tour buses from Madrid usually include an excursion to the Valley of the Fallen on their 1-day trips to El Escorial (see "Getting There," above). Car: Drive to the valley entrance, about 5 miles (8km) north of El Escorial in the heart of the Guadarrama Mountains. Once here, drive 3½ miles (6km) west along a wooded road to the underground basilica.

This is Franco's El Escorial, an architectural marvel that took 2 decades to complete, dedicated to those who died in the Spanish Civil War. Its detractors say it represents the worst of neofascist design; its admirers say they have found renewed inspiration by coming here.

A gargantuan cross nearly 500 feet high dominates the Rock of Nava, a peak of the Guadarrama Mountains. Directly under the cross is a basilica with a mosaic vault, completed in 1959. When José Antonio Primo de Rivera, the founder of the Falange party and a Nationalist hero, was buried at El Escorial, many, especially influential monarchists, protested that he was not a royal. Infuriated, Franco decided to erect another monument—this one. Originally it was slated to honor the dead on the Nationalist side only, but the intervention of several parties led to a decision to include all the *caídos* (fallen). In time the mausoleum claimed Franco as well; his body was interred behind the high altar.

A funicular extends from near the basilica entrance to the base of the gigantic cross on the mountaintop above (where there's a superb view). The fare is 350 ptas. ($2.10), and the funicular runs daily 10:30am to 1:15pm and 4 to 6pm.

On the other side of the mountain is a Benedictine monastery that has sometimes been dubbed "the Hilton of monasteries" because of its seeming luxury.

WHERE TO STAY
MODERATE

Hotel Botánico. Calle Timoteo Padros, 16, 28200 San Lorenzo de El Escorial. ☎ **91-890-78-79.** Fax 91-890-81-58. 20 units. A/C TV TEL. 15,000 ptas. ($90) double; 19,300–30,000 ptas. ($115.80–$180) suite. AE, MC, V. Free parking.

True to its name, the hotel stands in a lovely manicured garden of both indigenous and exotic shrubbery. Although the building is traditionally Castilian, the decor seems vaguely alpine, with wood paneling and beams in the reception rooms. The clean, well-lit rooms are large and comfortable, with especially good beds. There is a restaurant inside the hotel specializing in rice and fish dishes. Main courses range from 1,500 to 2,500 ptas. ($9 to $15) and there is a fixed-price menu at 5,000 ptas. ($30).

Hotel Victoria Palace. Calle Juan de Toledo, 4, 28200 San Lorenzo de El Escorial. ☎ **91-896-98-90.** Fax 91-896-98-96. E-mail: victoria@iies.es. 96 units. TV TEL. 12,500–18,600 ptas. ($75–$112) double. AE, MC, V. Parking 1,800 ptas. ($10.80).

The Victoria Palace, with its view of El Escorial, is the finest hotel in town, a traditional establishment that has been modernized without losing its special aura of style and comfort. It is surrounded by beautiful gardens and has an outdoor swimming pool. The good-sized rooms (some with private terraces) are well furnished and maintained, each with a quality mattress plus a small, tiled, and immaculately kept bathroom, often with a tub and shower combo. The rates are reasonable enough, and a bargain for a four-star hotel. The dining room serves some of the best food in town.

INEXPENSIVE

✪ **Hostal Cristina.** Juan de Toledo, 6, 28200 San Lorenzo de El Escorial. ☎ **91-890-19-61.** Fax 91-890-12-04. www.jazzviajeros.com. E-mail: hcristina@jazzviajeros.com. 16 units. TV TEL. 6,500 ptas. ($39) double. MC, V.

An excellent budget choice, this hotel is run by the Delgado family, which opened it in the mid-1980s. It doesn't pretend to compete with comfort and amenities of the Victoria Palace or even the Miranda & Suizo (see below), but it has its devotees nonetheless. About 50 yards from the monastery, it stands in the center of town, offering clean and comfortable but simply furnished rooms. The beds have firm mattresses, and accommodations range from small to medium, each equipped with a small tiled bathroom with a shower stall. The helpful staff will direct you to the small garden. Since the food served in the restaurant is both good and plentiful, many Spanish visitors prefer to book here for a summer holiday. Parking is available along the street.

Miranda & Suizo. Calle Floridablanca, 20, 28200 San Lorenzo de El Escorial. ☎ **91-890-47-11.** Fax 91-890-43-58. 52 units. TEL. 12,000 ptas. ($72) double; 16,000–20,000 ptas. ($96–$120) suite. AE, DC, MC, V.

On a tree-lined street in the heart of town within easy walking distance of the monastery, this excellent middle-bracket establishment ranks as a leading two-star hotel. It's the second choice in town, with rooms not quite as comfortable as those at the Victoria Palace. The Victorian-style building has good guest rooms nevertheless, some with terraces; 10 have TVs. Many of the rooms are rather spacious and each comes with a firm mattress and a well-maintained private bathroom with shower. The furnishings are comfortable, the beds often made of brass; sometimes you'll find fresh flowers on the tables. In summer, there is outside dining. Parking is available nearby for 1,000 ptas. ($6) per day.

WHERE TO DINE
MODERATE

Charolés. Calle Floridablanca, 24. ☎ **91-890-59-75.** Reservations required. Main courses 2,800–3,800 ptas. ($16.80–$22.80). AE, DC, MC, V. Daily 1–4pm and 9pm–midnight. SPANISH/INTERNATIONAL.

The thick, solid walls of this establishment date, according to its managers, "from the monastic age"—and probably predate the town's larger and better-known monastery of El Escorial. The restaurant within was established around 1980 and has been known ever since as the best dining room in town. It has a flower-ringed outdoor terrace for use during nice weather. The cuisine doesn't quite rate a star, but chances are you'll be satisfied. The wide choice of menu items based entirely on fresh fish and meats includes grilled hake with green or hollandaise sauce, shellfish soup, pepper steak, a *pastel* (pie) of fresh vegetables with crayfish, and herb-flavored baby lamb chops. A strawberry or kiwi tart is a good dessert choice.

EL ESCORIAL AFTER DARK

No longer the dead place it was during the long Franco era, the town now comes alive at night, fueled by the throngs of young people who pack into the bars and taverns, especially those along calle Rey and calle Floridablanca. Some of our favorite bars, offering vats of wine or kegs of beer, include the **Piano Bar Regina,** Floridablanca (☎ **91-890-68-43**), **Gurriato,** Leindro Rubio, 3 (☎ **91-890-47-10**), and **Don Felipe II,** Floridablanca (☎ **91-896-07-65**). The hottest disco is **Move it,** Plaza de Santiago, 11 (☎ **91-890-54-91**), which rarely imposes a cover unless some special group is featured.

4 Segovia

54 miles (87km) NW of Madrid, 42 miles (68km) NE of Ávila

Less commercial than Toledo, Segovia more than anywhere else typifies the glory of Old Castile. Wherever you look, you'll see reminders of a golden era, whether it's the most spectacular Alcázar on the Iberian Peninsula or the well-preserved, still-functioning Roman aqueduct.

Segovia lies on the slope of the Guadarrama Mountains, where the Eresma and Clamores rivers converge. This ancient city stands in the center of the most castle-rich part of Castile. Isabella herself was proclaimed queen of Castile here in 1474.

The narrow, winding streets of this hill city must be covered on foot to fully view the Romanesque churches and 15th-century palaces along the way.

ESSENTIALS

GETTING THERE   Nine trains leave Madrid's Chamartín Railway Station every day, arriving 2 hours later in Segovia, where you can board bus no. 3, departing every quarter hour for the Plaza Mayor. The trains that leave from Chamartín first travel through Atocha station, making it closer to some travelers' hotels. A one-way rail fare costs 775 ptas. ($4.65). The station at Segovia is on the Paseo Obispo Quesada, s/n (☎ **921-42-07-74**), a 20-minute walk southeast of the town center.

Buses arrive and depart from the Estacionamiento Municipal de Autobuses, Paseo de Ezequile González, 10 (☎ **921-42-77-25**), near the corner of the Avenida Fernández Ladreda and the steeply sloping Paseo Conde de Sepúlveda. There are 10 to 15 buses a day to and from Madrid (which depart from Paseo de la Florida, 11; metro: Norte), and about four a day traveling between Ávila, Segovia, and Valladolid. One-way tickets from Madrid cost around 765 ptas. ($4.60).

If you're driving, take the N-VI (on some maps it's known as the A-6) or the Autopista del Nordeste northwest from Madrid, toward León and Lugo. At the junction with Route 110 (signposted SEGOVIA), turn northeast.

VISITOR INFORMATION   The **tourist information office** is at Plaza Mayor, 10 (☎ **921-46-03-34**). It is open daily 10am to 2pm and 5 to 8pm.

EXPLORING SEGOVIA

You'll find the best **shopping** between the Roman aqueduct, the cathedral, and the Alcázar. Head especially for calle de Juan Bravo, calle Daoiz, and calle Marqués del Arco. Although their merchandise is mirrored by other shops nearby, two of the most appealing shops for ceramic pottery, woodcarvings, wrought-iron, and art objects include **Salvador Lucio,** calle Marqués del Arco, s/n (☎ **921-46-05-52**), and **Kokul Artesania,** calle Marqués del Arco, 20 (☎ **921-46-04-50**).

✪ Cabildo Catedral de Segovia. Plaza Catedral, Marqués del Arco. ☎ **921-43-53-25.** Free admission to cathedral; cloisters, museum, and chapel room 300 ptas. ($1.80) adults, 50 ptas. (30¢) children. Spring and summer, daily 9am–7pm; off-season, daily 9:30am–6pm.

Constructed between 1515 and 1558, this is the last Gothic cathedral built in Spain. Fronting the historic Plaza Mayor, it stands on the spot where Isabella I was proclaimed queen of Castile. Affectionately called *la dama de las catedrales,* it contains numerous treasures, such as the Blessed Sacrament Chapel (created by the flamboyant Churriguera), stained-glass windows, elaborately carved choir stalls, and 16th- and 17th-century paintings, including a reredos portraying the deposition of Christ from the cross by Juan de Juni. The cloisters are older than the cathedral, dating from an earlier church that was destroyed in the so-called War of the Communeros. Inside the cathedral museum you'll find jewelry, paintings, and a collection of rare antique manuscripts.

✪ El Alcázar. Plaza de La Reina Victoria Eugenia. ☎ **921-46-07-59.** Admission 400 ptas. ($2.40) adults, 250 ptas. ($1.50) children 8–14, free for children 7 and under. Apr–Sept, daily 10am–7pm; Oct–Mar, daily 10am–6pm. Bus: 3. Take either calle Vallejo, calle de Velarde, calle de Daoiz, or Paseo de Ronda.

View the Alcázar first from below, at the junction of the Clamores and Eresma Rivers. It is on the west side of Segovia, so you may not spot it when you first enter the city. But that's part of the surprise.

The castle dates from the 12th century, but a large segment containing its Moorish ceilings was destroyed by fire in 1862. Restoration has continued over the years.

Royal romance is associated with the Alcázar. Isabella first met Ferdinand here, and today you can see a facsimile of her dank bedroom. Once married, she wasn't foolish enough to surrender her royal rights, as replicas of the thrones attest—both are equally proportioned. Philip II married his fourth wife, Anne of Austria, here as well.

Walk the battlements of this once-impregnable castle, from which its occupants hurled boiling oil onto the enemy below. Ascend the hazardous stairs of the tower, originally built by Isabella's father as a prison, for a panoramic view of Segovia.

Esteban Vicente Contemporary Art Museum. Plazuela de las Bellas. ☎ **921-46-20-10.** Admission 400 ptas. ($2.40) adults, 200 ptas. ($1.20) seniors and students, free for children under 12. Mon–Sat 11am–2pm and 4–7pm; Sun 11am–2pm.

In the heart of the city in a newly renovated 15th-century palace, a permanent collection of some 142 works by the abstract-expressionist artist Esteban Vicente has opened. The Spanish-born artist, now in his late 90s, has described himself as "an American painter, with very deep and loving Spanish roots." Born in a small town outside Segovia in 1903, he remained in Spain until 1927, eventually (since 1936) residing in New York where he played a pivotal role in the development of American abstract art. Today he is one of the last surviving members of the New York school, whose members included Rothko, de Kooning, and Pollock. Vicente's paintings and collages convey his sense of structure and feelings of luminous serenity with colors of astonishing vibrancy, brilliance, and range. His paintings are shown at the Metropolitan Museum of Art, the Museum of Modern Art, and the Whitney, all in New York— and now Segovia.

Iglesia de la Vera Cruz. Carretera de Zamarramala. ☎ **921-43-14-75.** Admission 200 ptas. ($1.20). Apr–Sept, Tues–Sun 10:30am–1:30pm and 3:30–7pm; Oct–Mar, Tues–Sun 10:30am–1:30pm and 3:30–6pm.

Built in either the 11th or the 12th century by the Knights Templar, this is the most fascinating Romanesque church in Segovia. It stands in isolation outside the walls of the old town overlooking the Alcázar. Its unusual 12-sided design is believed to have been copied from the Church of the Holy Sepulchre in Jerusalem. Inside you'll find an inner temple, rising two floors, where the knights conducted night-long vigils as part of their initiation rites.

Monasterio del Parral. Calle del Marqués de Villena (across the Eresma River). ☎ 921-43-12-98. Free admission. Mon–Sat 10am–2:30pm and 4–6:30pm; Sun 10–11:30am and 4–6:30pm. Take Ronda de Sant Lucía, cross the Eresma River, and head down calle del Marqués de Villena.

The restored "Monastery of the Grape" was established for the Hieronymites by Henry IV, a Castilian king (1425–74) known as "The Impotent." The monastery lies across the Eresma River about a half mile north of the city. The church is a medley of styles and decoration—mainly Gothic, Renaissance, and plateresque. The facade was never completed, and the monastery itself was abandoned when religious orders were suppressed in 1835. Today it's been restored and is once again the domain of the *jerónimos*, Hieronymus priests and brothers. Inside, a robed monk will show you the various treasures of the order, including a polychrome altarpiece and the alabaster tombs of the Marquis of Villena and his wife—all the work of Juan Rodríguez.

✪ **Roman Aqueduct (Acueducto Romano).** Plaza del Azoguejo.

This architectural marvel was built by the Romans nearly 2,000 years ago. Constructed of mortarless granite, it consists of 118 arches, and in one two-tiered section it soars 95 feet to its highest point. The Spanish call it El Puente. It spans the Plaza del Azoguejo, the old market square, stretching nearly 800 yards. When the Moors took Segovia in 1072, they destroyed 36 arches, which were later rebuilt under Ferdinand and Isabella in 1484.

WHERE TO STAY
EXPENSIVE

✪ **Parador de Segovia.** Carretera Valladolid, s/n (N-601), 40003 Segovia. ☎ 921-44-37-37. Fax 921-43-73-62. www.parador.es. E-mail: segovia@parador.es. 120 units. A/C MINIBAR TV TEL. 21,000 ptas. ($126) double; from 32,000 ptas. ($192) suite. AE, DC, MC, V. Covered parking 1,000 ptas. ($6); free outside.

This 20th-century tile-roofed parador sits on a hill 2 miles (3km) northeast of Segovia (take the N-601). It stands on an estate called El Terminillo, which used to be famous for its vines and almond trees, a few of which still survive. If you have a car and can get a reservation, book in here; you'll pay more, but it's much more comfortable here than at either Los Arcos or Los Linajes (see below). The good-sized rooms are deluxe, containing such extras as safes and tiled bathrooms with shower/tub combos. Furnishings are tasteful, and large windows open onto panoramic views of the countryside. Some of the older rooms here are a bit dated, however, with lackluster decor.

Dining/Diversions: The parador has one of the better restaurants in Segovia; its windows open onto a panoramic view of the mountains of Sierra de Guadarrama. A complete meal here, of either regional specialties or international dishes, costs around 3,700 ptas. ($22.20). The hotel also offers a bar.

Amenities: Two outdoor pools, indoor pool, sauna, tennis courts.

MODERATE

Hotel Infanta Isabel. Plaza Mayor, 40001 Segovia. ☎ 921-46-13-00. Fax 921-46-22-17. 27 units. A/C MINIBAR TV TEL. 12,700–15,000 ptas. ($76–$90) double. AC, DC, MC, V. Parking 1,000 ptas. ($6).

Named after Queen Isabel, the great-grandmother of the present king, the hotel stands overlooking the charming central square and is within a stone's throw of the majestic cathedral. This is where the queen would stay when on her way to the nearby summer palace of La Granja. The present owners have modernized the interior considerably but a good deal of the building's 19th-century grandeur, such as the staircase, remains. Each room is decorated in its own style with an eye to comfort. The hotel has every convenience; satellite TV and modern bathrooms strike a reassuring 20th-century note.

Hotel Los Linajes. Dr. Velasco, 9, 40003 Segovia. ☎ **921-46-04-75.** Fax 921-46-04-79. 53 units. A/C TV TEL. 11,000–13,000 ptas. ($66–$78) double; from 14,900–16,900 ptas. ($89–$102) suite. AE, DC, V. Parking 1,100 ptas. ($6.60). Bus: 1.

In the historical district of St. Stephen at the northern edge of the old town stands this hotel, the former home of a Segovian noble family. While the facade dates from the 11th century, the interior is modern, except for some Castilian decorations. Following a 1996 renovation, the hotel looks a bit brighter and fresher than Los Arcos. Bedrooms, in a range of sizes and shapes, are comfortable with fine beds and tidily kept tiled bathrooms. One of the best hotels in town, Los Linajes has gardens and patios where guests can enjoy a panoramic view over the city. The hotel also has a bar/lounge, coffee shop, disco, and garage.

Los Arcos. Paseo de Ezequiel González, 26, 40002 Segovia. ☎ **800-528-1234** in the U.S., or 921-43-74-62. Fax 921-42-81-61. 59 units. A/C MINIBAR TV TEL. 15,500 ptas. ($93) double. AE, DC, MC, V. Parking 1,000 ptas. ($6).

This concrete-and-glass five-story structure opened in 1987 and is generally cited as the best in town, although you may prefer Los Linajes instead (see above). Well run and modern, it attracts the business traveler, but tourists frequent the place in droves as well. Rooms are generally spacious but furnished in a standard international bland way, except for the beautiful rug-dotted parquet floors. There are built-in furnishings and tiny combination bathrooms with hair dryers, along with private safes. Rooms are well kept, with good beds, although some furnishings look worn.

Even if you don't stay here, consider dining at the hotel's La Cocina de Segovia, which is the only hotel dining room that competes successfully with Mesón de Cándido (see "Where to Dine," below). As at the nearby competitors, roast suckling pig and roast Segovia lamb—perfectly cooked in specially made ovens—are the specialties. There's also a tavernlike cafe and a bar. In all, it's a smart, efficiently run, and pleasant choice, if not a terribly exciting one.

INEXPENSIVE

Las Sirenas. Juan Bravo, 30, 40001 Segovia. ☎ **921-46-26-63.** Fax 921-46-26-57. 39 units. A/C TV TEL. 8,500 ptas. ($51) double. AE, DC, MC, V.

Standing on the most charming old plaza in Segovia opposite the Church of St. Martín, this hotel was built around 1950 and has been renovated several times. However, it has long since lost its Franco-era supremacy to Los Arcos (see above). Modest and well maintained, it is decorated in a conservative style. Each room is filled with functional, simple furniture, with good beds. However, rooms are somewhat small. Breakfast is the only meal served, but the staff at the reception desk can direct clients to cafes and *tascas* nearby.

WHERE TO DINE

El Bernardino. Cervantes, 2. ☎ **921-46-24-74.** Reservations recommended. Main courses 1,400–2,500 ptas. ($8.40–$15); fixed-price menu 2,800 ptas. ($16.80). AE, DC, MC, V. Daily 1–4pm and 8:30–11pm. CASTILIAN.

El Bernardino, a 3-minute walk west of the Roman aqueduct, is built like an old tavern. Lanterns hang from beamed ceilings, and the view over the red-tile rooftops of the city is delightful. There is also a summer terrace. The *menú del día* might include paella, roast veal with potatoes, flan or ice cream, plus bread and wine. You might begin your meal with *sopa castellana* (soup made with ham, sausage, bread, egg, and garlic). The roast dishes are exceptional here, including roast suckling pig from a special oven and roast baby lamb. You can also order grilled rib steak or stewed partridge.

José María. Cronista Lecea, 11. ☎ **921-46-60-17.** Reservations recommended. Main courses 1,500–2,500 ptas. ($9–$15); fixed-price menu 4,000–6,000 ptas. ($24–$36). AE, DC, V. Daily 1–4pm and 8–11:30pm. SEGOVIAN.

This centrally located bar and restaurant 1 block east of the Plaza Mayor serves quality regional cuisine in a rustic stucco-and-brick dining room. Before dinner, locals crowd in for tapas at the bar, then move into the dining room for such Castilian specialties as roast suckling pig, rural-style conger eel, and freshly caught sea bream. Try the cream of crabmeat soup, roasted peppers, salmon with scrambled eggs, house-style hake, or grilled veal steak. For dessert, a specialty is the ice cream tart with a whisky sauce.

✪ **Mesón de Cándido.** Plaza del Azoguejo, 5. ☎ **921-42-59-11.** Reservations recommended. Main courses 2,000–4,000 ptas. ($12–$24); fixed-price menu 3,500 ptas. ($21). AE, DC, MC, V. Daily 12:30–4:30pm and 8–midnight. CASTILIAN.

For years this beautiful old Spanish inn, standing on the eastern edge of the old town, has maintained a monopoly on the tourist trade. Apart from the hotel restaurants—specifically La Cocina de Segovia at the Los Arcos—it is the town's finest dining choice. The Candido family took it over in 1905, and fourth- and fifth-generation family members still run the place, having fed, over the years, everybody from Hemingway to Nixon. The oldest part of the restaurant dates from 1822, and the restaurant has gradually been enlarged since then. The proprietor of the House of Candido is known as *mesonero mayor de Castilla* (the major innkeeper of Castile). He's been decorated with more medals and honors than paella has grains of rice. The restaurant's popularity can be judged by the crowds of hungry diners who fill every seat in the six dining rooms. The à la carte menu includes those two regional staples: *cordero asado* (roast baby lamb) and *cochinillo asado* (roast suckling pig). Some of the seating areas are cramped and confining. Opt for a table on the second floor, facing the Aqueduct, or one of the outdoor cafe tables in front.

Mesón Duque. Calle Cervantes, 12. ☎ **921-46-24-87.** Reservations recommended. Main courses 850–2,500 ptas. ($5.10–$15). AE, DC, MC, V. Daily 12:30–5pm and 8–11:30pm. CASTILIAN.

Set on the street that links Segovia's ancient Roman aqueduct with the city's medieval core, this restaurant was established in 1895 and has fed many successive generations of local residents ever since. The severely dignified interior looks as though it hasn't changed since it was built. The decor includes heavy ceiling beams, exposed stone, rough-textured plaster, and battered 19th-century farming artifacts. Come here for the kind of cuisine that was in vogue when the restaurant was built, with very few concessions to modern tastes. There's an excellent cream of crabmeat soup; roasted suckling pig slow-cooked on a spit; savory roasted lamb with aromatic rosemary, thyme, and garlic; and different preparations of grilled chicken, veal, beef, and pork. An excellent accompaniment for any of these would be kidney beans cooked with chunks of salted cod, fresh spinach, and mounds of mashed potatoes or rice.

A SIDE TRIP TO LA GRANJA

To reach La Granja, 7 miles (11km) southeast of Segovia, you can take a 20-minute bus ride from the center of the city. Six to 10 buses a day leave from Paseo Conde de

Sepulveda at Avenida Fernández Ladreda. A one-way fare costs 105 ptas. (65¢). For information, call ☎ **921-42-77-25.**

✪ **Palacio Real de La Granja.** Plaza de España, 17, San Ildefonso (Segovia). ☎ **921-47-00-19.** Admission 650 ptas. ($3.90) adults, 250 ptas. ($1.50) children 5–14, free for children 4 and under. Apr–May, Mon–Fri 10am–1:30pm and 3–5pm, Sat–Sun 10am–6pm; June–Sept, daily 10am–6pm; Oct–Mar, Mon–Sat 10am–1:30pm and 3–5pm, Sun 10am–2pm.

San Ildefonso de la Granja was the summer palace of the Bourbon kings of Spain who replicated the grandeur of Versailles in the province of Segovia. Set against the snow-capped Sierra de Guadarrama, the slate-roofed palace dominates the village that grew up around it (a summer resort these days).

The builder of La Granja was Philip V, grandson of Louis XIV and the first Bourbon king of Spain (his body, along with that of his second queen, Isabel de Fernesio, is interred in a mausoleum in the Collegiate Church). Philip V was born at Versailles on December 19, 1683, which may explain why he wanted to re-create that atmosphere at Segovia.

At one time a farm stood on the grounds of what is now the palace—hence its totally incongruous name, *la granja,* meaning "the farm." The palace was built in the first part of the 18th century. Inside you'll find valuable antiques (many in the Empire style), paintings, and a remarkable collection of Flemish tapestries, as well as those based on Goya cartoons from the Royal Factory in Madrid.

Most visitors seem to find a stroll through the gardens more pleasing, so allow adequate time for that. The fountain statuary is a riot of cavorting gods and nymphs hiding indiscretions behind jets of water. The gardens are studded with chestnuts and elms. A spectacular display takes place when the water jets are turned on.

SEGOVIA AFTER DARK

Just head for the Plaza Mayor, Plaza Azoguejo, and the busy calle del Carmen that runs into the Plaza Azagejo. You're sure to find some fun in the scattering of simple bars and cafes that grow more crowded at night as the days grow hotter. If you want to go dancing, two of the most popular discos include **Mansion,** calle de Juan Bravo (no phone), which is open nightly 11pm till dawn for dancing, drinking, and flirting with the 20- to 30-year-old crowd, and the somewhat more stylish competitor, **Bar Ginasio,** Paseo del Salón (no phone), which is open nightly 8pm till dawn, a bit more atmospheric and frequented by people from age 25 to around 50.

5 Alcalá de Henares

18 miles (29km) E of Madrid

History hasn't been kind to this ancient town, which once flourished with colleges, monasteries, and palaces. When a university was founded here in the 15th century, Alcalá became a cultural and intellectual center. Europe's first polyglot Bible (supposedly with footnotes in the original Greek and Hebrew) was published here in 1517, but the town declined during the 1800s when the university moved to Madrid. Today Alcalá is one of the main centers of North American academics in Spain, cooperating with the Fulbright Commission, Michigan State University, and Madrid's Washington Irving Center. Overall, the city has taken on new life. Commuters have turned it into a virtual suburb, dubbing it "the bedroom of Madrid."

ESSENTIALS

GETTING THERE   Trains travel between Madrid's Atocha or Chamartín station and Alcalá de Henares every day and evening. Service is every 15 minutes (trip time:

30 minutes) and round-trip fare from Madrid costs 610 ptas. ($3.65). The train station
(☎ **91-328-90-20**) in Alcalá is at Paseo Estación.

Buses from Madrid depart from Avenida América, 18 (Metro: América), every 15
minutes. A one-way fare is 260 ptas. ($1.55). Bus service is provided by Continental-
Auto, and the Alcalá bus station is on Avenida Guadalajara, 36 (☎ **91-888- 16-22**),
2 blocks past calle Libreros.

Alcalá lies adjacent to the main national highway (N-11), connecting Madrid with
eastern Spain. As you leave central Madrid, follow signs for Barajas Airport and
Barcelona.

VISITOR INFORMATION   The **tourist information office** is at Callejón de
Santa María, 1 (☎ **364-18-76**). It will provide a map showing all the local attractions. Open daily 10am to 2pm and 4 to 6:30pm (until 7:30pm July to September).

EXPLORING ALCALÁ DE HENARES

Capilla de San Ildefonso. Pedro Gumíelz. ☎ **91-882-13-54.** Admission included in tour
of Colegio (see below). Hours same as Colegio (see below).

Next door to the Colegio is the Capilla de San Ildefonso, the 15th-century chapel of
the old university. It also houses the Italian marble tomb of Cardinal Cisneros, the
founder of the original university. This chapel also has an *artesonado* (artisan's) ceiling
and intricately stuccoed walls.

Colegio Mayor de San Ildefonso. Plaza San Diego. ☎ **91-882-13-54.** Admission
300 ptas. ($1.80). Tours (mandatory) Mon–Fri 11:30am, 12:30, 1:30, 5, and 6pm; Sat–Sun
11 and 11:45am, 12:30, 1:15, 2, 4:30, 5:15, 6, 6:45, and 7:30pm.

Adjacent to the main square, Plaza de Cervantes, is the Colegio Mayor de San Ildefonso, where Lope de Vega and other famous Spaniards studied. You can see some of
their names engraved on plaques in the examination room. The old university's
plateresque facade dates from 1543. From here you can walk across the Patio of Saint
Thomas (from 1662) and the Patio of the Philosophers to reach the Patio of the Three
Languages (from 1557), where Greek, Latin, and Hebrew were once taught. Here is
the *Paraninfo* (great hall or old examination room), now used for special events. The
hall has a Mudéjar carved-panel ceiling. The Paraninfo is entered through a restaurant,
Hostería del Estudiante (see "Where to Dine," below).

Museo Casa Natal de Cervantes. Calle Imagen 2, 48. ☎ **91-889-96-54.** Free admission.
Tues–Sun 10:15am–1:30pm and 4:15–6:30pm.

Visitors come to see the birthplace of Spain's literary giant Miguel de Cervantes, the
creator of *Don Quixote*, who may have been born here in 1547. This 16th-century
Castilian house was reconstructed in 1956 around a beautiful little courtyard, which
has a wooden gallery supported by pillars with Renaissance-style capitals, plus an old
well. The house contains many Cervantes manuscripts and, of course, copies of *Don
Quixote*, one of the world's most widely published books (available here in many
languages).

WHERE TO DINE

Hostería del Estudiante. Calle Colegios, 3. ☎ **91-888-03-30.** Reservations recommended. Main courses 3,500–5,000 ptas. ($21–$30); fixed-price menus 3,500 ptas. ($21).
AE, DC, MC, V. Daily 1–4pm; Mon–Sat 9–11:30pm; Sun 9–10:30pm. Closed July (dinner only)
and Aug. CASTILIAN.

Located within the university complex, this remarkable 1510 building is an attraction
in its own right. It opened as a restaurant in 1929, and its typically Castilian recipes
haven't been altered since. In the cooler months, if you arrive early you can lounge in

front of a 15-foot open fireplace. Oil lamps hang from the ceiling, pigskins are filled with local wine, and rope-covered chairs and high-backed carved settees capture the spirit of the past. Run by the Spanish parador system, the restaurant offers a tasty (and huge) three-course set-price lunch or dinner featuring such regional specialties as roast suckling lamb, *huevos comigos* (three eggs fried with mushrooms), and trout Navarre style. For dessert, try the cheese of La Mancha.

6 El Pardo

8 miles (13km) N of Madrid

After visiting Alcalá de Henares, spend an afternoon in El Pardo, the place Franco called home. During the Civil War many Spaniards died here, and much of the town was destroyed during the famous advance toward University City. But there's no trace of destruction today, and the countryside, irrigated by the Manzanares River, is lush and peaceful. If possible, go to the top of the hill and take in the view.

ESSENTIALS

GETTING THERE   Local city buses depart every 15 minutes from Madrid's Paseo de Moret (metro: Moncloa). A one-way fare costs 145 ptas. (85¢). Call ☎ 91-376-01-04 for more information.

Driving can be confusing on the minor roads. Head north from the city limits, following signs to La Coruña, then branch off to the west in the direction of "El Monte de El Pardo."

VISITOR INFORMATION   Spring and fall can be chilly, so dress accordingly. The Manzanares River flows nearby, but there are no convenient rail lines and no tourist office.

EXPLORING EL PARDO

Palacio de El Pardo. Manuel Alonso. ☎ **91-376-15-00.** Admission 650 ptas. ($3.90) adults, 250 ptas. ($1.50) students and children under 12. Mon–Sat 10:30am–6pm; Sun 9:30am–4pm. Closed during official state visits, or whenever it's being used as a guesthouse for top-priority foreign dignitaries.

During the regime of Franco, this was the Spanish equivalent of England's Sandringham Palace or France's Rambouillet—a presidential or royal retreat for the head of state, replete with memories of an Imperial past and the trappings of monarchy. Occupied by Castilian powerbrokers since medieval times, it was Franco's main residence until his death, when his body lay in state surrounded by all the honors and pageantry his political regime could muster.

When El Pardo was opened to the public in 1976, it quickly became one of the most popular sights around Madrid, replete with lore, legends, and gossip about the quirks, peccadilloes, and marital conflicts of Europe's most durable fascist.

You can visit only as part of a guided tour that's conducted mostly in Spanish with occasional English insertions. Tours depart at 15-minute intervals throughout the opening hours listed above and last 45 minutes. Your tour will lead you past lavishly furnished rooms once used for state receptions. Franco's ornate gilt throne reveals some of his royal pretensions. Amid noteworthy collections of Empire furniture are family mementos that include extensive wardrobes of the once-mighty Generalissimo. A collection of wax effigies, at least 10 of them, model some of Franco's state uniforms. Highlights of the tour include a visit to the Tapestry Room, with many masterpieces created in the 18th and early 19th century based on cartoons by Goya, Bayeu, Aguirre, and González Ruiz. The Salon de Consejos features a 19th-century coved ceiling and one of Franco's most prized possessions: a 15th-century sideboard that belonged to Queen Isabella.

On the grounds of the palace, and closed for an indefinite period at this writing because of restorations, stands the 18th-century **Casita del Príncipe (Prince's Cottage).** Compact and charming, it was built during the reign of Charles III, probably by his son, and frequented by his wife, often as a site for discreet romantic trysts. Also on the grounds, and also closed at this writing for restorations, is the **Palacio de la Quinta,** a satellite palace annexed by the crown in 1745 from the duke of Arcos.

WHERE TO DINE

Pedro's. Avenida de la Guardia, s/n. ☎ **91-376-08-83.** Reservations recommended. Main courses 2,000–3,200 ptas. ($12–$19.20); fixed-price menus 2,000 ptas. ($12). AE, DC, MC, V. Daily 1–5pm and 8pm–2 or 3am. INTERNATIONAL.

Set to the side of El Pardo's monumental facade, this is a low-key, likable restaurant that has been owned and operated since the 1960s by several generations of the Peres family. The three generations of family members who now run it contain three individuals named Pedro, and they all insist that the name of their jointly owned restaurant be spelled with an apostrophe. You can dine within the well-scrubbed red interior or move to a flower-ringed terrace in back, where there's a view over a verdant garden. Menu items are influenced by one of the Pedro's culinary sojourns in Switzerland. Thanks to that time abroad, the fricassee of rabbit or the filet mignon in brandy sauce is likely to be as flavorful as the four kinds of paella featured on the menu. They include versions with shellfish, tinted black from squid ink, and workaday concoctions layered with chicken, vegetables, and a less dense collection of shellfish. Also look for grilled fillet of veal and roasted lamb and/or pork, and when it's available, roasted wild boar.

7 Chinchón

32 miles (52km) SE of Madrid, 16 miles (26km) NE of Aranjuez

The main attraction of Chinchón is the *cuevas* **(caves),** where Anis de Chinchón, an aniseed liqueur, is manufactured. You can buy bottles of the liqueur in Plaza Mayor, at the center of town.

Wander along the town's steep and narrow streets, past houses with large bays and spacious carriageways. Although closed to the public, the 15th-century **Chinchón Castle,** seat of the Condes of Chinchón, can be viewed from outside. The most interesting church, **Nuestra Señora de la Asunción,** dating from the 16th and 17th centuries, contains a painting by Goya.

GETTING THERE Chinchón is most often visited from Aranjuez (see above), which is only a 15-minute ride away. Buses run twice a day from Aranjuez but only Monday to Friday, leaving from calle Almibar next to the Plaza de Toros in Aranjuez. Schedules tend to be erratic, so call for information (☎ **91-891-39-37**). A one-way fare is 185 ptas. ($1.10).

You can drive from Alcalá to Toledo, bypassing Madrid by taking the C-300 in a southwesterly arc around the capital. About halfway here, follow signs to CUEVAS DE CHINCHÓN. Another option is to take the E-901 southeast of Madrid toward Valencia, turning southwest at the turnoff for Chinchón.

WHERE TO STAY

Hotel Nuevo Chichon. Urbanización Nuevo Chinchón, Carretera a Titulcia, km 1.5, 28370 Chinchón. ☎ **91-894-05-44.** Fax 91-893-51-28. E-mail: nuevochinchon@teleline.es. 18 units. A/C TV TEL. 9,200 ptas. ($57.95) double. AE, MC, V. Free parking.

This is a relatively new hotel, built in 1994, whose owners have invested lots of time and money in making it appear older and more nostalgic than it is. Low slung and modern from the outside, it contains small bedrooms whose headboards are painted in old-fashioned folkloric patterns. The overall effect is cozy, with a sense of low-key charm. There's a restaurant and bar on the premises.

Parador de Chinchón. Avenida Generalísimo, 1, 28370 Chinchón. ☎ **91-894-08-36.** Fax 91-894-09-08. 38 units. A/C MINIBAR TV TEL. 18,000 ptas. ($108) double; 25,000 ptas. ($150) suite. AE, DC, MC, V. Parking 1,250 ptas. ($7.50).

Set near the town center, this hotel lies within the carefully restored 17th-century walls of what was originally an Augustinian convent. After a stint as both a civic jail and a courthouse, it was transformed in 1972 into a government-run parador and is the best place to stay in town. A team of architects and designers converted it handsomely, with glass-walled hallways opening onto a stone-sided courtyard. The hotel has two bars and two dining halls. Severely dignified rooms still manage to convey their ecclesiastical origins. Rooms range from small to medium, each with a quality mattress and fine linen along with well-maintained tiled bathrooms. Facilities include an outdoor swimming pool open in summer.

WHERE TO DINE

Mesón Cuevas del Vino. Benito Horteliano, 13. ☎ **91-894-02-85.** Reservations recommended on holidays. Main courses 2,000–3,600 ptas. ($12–$21.60); fixed-price menu 3,800 ptas. ($22.80). No credit cards. Wed–Mon 1:30–4pm and 8–11:30pm. Closed Aug 1–20. SPANISH.

This establishment is famous for its wine cellars, and you can sample the stock at lunch or dinner. Hanging from the rafters are hams cured by the owners, along with flavorful homemade spiced sausages. Chunks of ham and sausage cooked in oil, plus olives and crunchy bread, are served. Your meal might begin with sliced *chorizo* (Spanish sausage); blood pudding; slices of La Mancha cheese; *sopa castellana* made with garlic, ham, and eggs; and thin-sliced cured ham. Main courses place heavy emphasis on roast suckling lamb and pig that emerge crackling from a wood-burning oven. Desserts include flan, biscuits coated in cinnamon and sugar, and liquefied and sweetened almonds presented in a soupy mixture in a bowl.

8 Ávila

68 miles (109km) NW of Madrid, 41½ miles (67km) SW of Segovia

The ancient city of Ávila is completely encircled by well-preserved 11th-century walls, which are among the most important medieval relics in Europe. The city has been declared a national landmark, and there is little wonder why. The walls aren't the only attraction, however. Ávila has several Romanesque churches, Gothic palaces, and a fortified cathedral. It is among some 80 cities designated by UNESCO as World Heritage Sites. (Six of these cities are in Spain; the other five are Santiago de Compostela, Segovia, Toledo, Cáceres, and Salamanca.)

Ávila's spirit and legend are most linked to St. Teresa, born here in 1515. This Carmelite nun who helped defeat the Reformation and founded a number of convents experienced visions of the Devil and angels piercing her heart with burning hot lances. She was eventually imprisoned in Toledo. Many legends sprang up after her death, including the belief that a hand severed from her body could perform miracles. Finally, in 1622, she was declared a saint.

Note: Bring warm clothes if you're visiting in the early spring.

ESSENTIALS

GETTING THERE　There are more than two dozen trains leaving daily from Madrid for Ávila, about a 1½- to 2-hour trip each way. Depending on the schedule, trains depart from Chamartín, Atocha, and Príncipe (Norte) railway stations. The 8am train from Atocha, arriving in Ávila at 9:26am, is a good choice, considering all there is to see. Tickets cost 835 to 1,800 ptas. ($5 to $10.80). The Ávila station is at Avenida José Antonio (☎ **920-25-02-02**), about a mile east of the Old City. You'll find taxis lined up in front of Ávila's railway station and at the more central Plaza Santa Teresa. For information, call ☎ **920-21-19-59** or 920-22-01-49.

Buses leave Madrid daily from Paseo Florida, 11 (metro: Norte), in front of the Norte railway station. In Ávila the bus terminal (☎ **920-22-01-54**) is at the corner of Avenida Madrid and Avenida Portugal, northeast of the center of town. A one-way ticket from Madrid costs 915 ptas. ($5.50).

To drive there, exit Madrid from its northwest perimeter and head northwest on highway N-VI (A-6), toward La Coruña, eventually forking southwest to Ávila. Driving time is around 1½ hours.

VISITOR INFORMATION　The **tourist information office** is at Plaza Catedral, 4 (☎ **920-21-13-87**). It is open April to October Monday to Friday 10am to 2pm and 4 to 7pm, Saturday 9:30am to 2pm and 4 to 7pm, and Sunday 9:30am to 2pm and 4:30 to 8:30pm. Off-season hours are Monday to Friday 10am to 2pm and 5 to 8pm and Saturday 9:30am to 2pm.

EXPLORING THE TOWN

Begun on orders of Alfonso VI as part of the general reconquest of Spain from the Moors, the 11th-century ✪ **Walls of Ávila,** built over Roman fortifications, took 9 years to complete. They average 33 feet in height and have 88 semicircular towers and more than 2,300 battlements. Of the nine gateways, the two most famous are the St. Vincent and the Alcázar, both on the eastern side. In many respects the walls are best viewed from the west. Whatever your preferred point of view, you can drive along their entire length: 1½ miles (2km).

Basilica de San Vicente. Plaza de San Vicente. ☎ **920-25-52-30.** Admission 200 ptas. ($1.20). Daily 10am–2pm and 4–8pm.

Outside the city walls at the northeast corner of the medieval ramparts, this Romanesque-Gothic church in faded sandstone encompasses styles from the 12th to the 14th centuries. It consists of a huge nave and a trio of apses. The eternal struggle between good and evil is depicted on a cornice on the southern portal. The western portal, dating from the 13th century, contains Romanesque carvings. Inside is the tomb of St. Vincent, martyred on this site in the 4th century. The tomb's medieval carvings, which depict his torture and subsequent martyrdom, are fascinating.

Carmelitas Descalzas de San José. Las Madres, 4. ☎ **920-22-21-27.** Admission to museum, 100 ptas. (60¢). Apr–Oct, daily 10am–1:30pm and 4–7pm; off-season, daily 10am–1:30pm and 3–6pm. From Plaza de Santa Teresa and its nearby Church of San Pedro, follow calle del Duque de Alba for about 2 blocks.

Also known as the *Convento de las Madres* (Convent of the Mothers), this is the first convent founded by St. Teresa, who started the Reform of Carmel in 1562. Two churches are here—the primitive one, where the first Carmelite nuns took the habit, and one built by Francisco de Mora, architect of Philip III, after the saint's death. The museum displays many relics, including, of all things, St. Teresa's left clavicle.

A Saint & Her City

The walled city of Ávila is forever linked with the legend of St. Teresa, one of the most famous of all Catholic saints. She is most often cited as a mystic but was an adventurer, pioneer, poet, and reformer. She was born in 1515 into a large Jewish family and named Teresa de Cepeda y Ahumada. Her birth was 12 years before the reign of Philip II, who ruled from 1527 to 1598, presiding over Spain's "Golden Century."

Taking the Carmelite veil at 18, she is reported to have had her first vision at the age of 40. She toured Castile, seeking reforms and hoping to return the Carmelite order to its original vows of poverty and piety. For example, she advocated that the nuns discard shoes and wear sandals, which led to the misnomer "the Barefoot Carmelites." She founded her first Carmelite convent in 1562 and in time opened 16 other convents. It is said that her unfailing sense of humor and her abundant gift for friendship saved her from the dreaded Inquisition, which imprisoned her friend, mentor, and fellow Ávilan, St. John of the Cross. Many of her reforms were abandoned upon her death in 1582. The church canonized her although she remained a controversial figure, and many church leaders opposed making her a saint.

Ávila abounds with Teresian memorabilia. She was fond of playing drums and bells and was always proclaiming, "God deliver me from sullen saints." If you'd like to pay homage to St. Teresa, you can order her favorite dish, partridge. It's a local specialty served in many of Ávila's restaurants. A servant was once perplexed at her obvious enjoyment of a large helping of partridge. He felt she was demonstrating too much pleasure in eating it. "My child," she said to him, "there is a time for penitence, but there is also a time for partridge."

But we doubt if the saint herself could have tolerated one highly touted local specialty: a sticky-sweet candy called *yemas de Santa Teresa.* We recommend that you avoid this glob as surely St. Teresa herself would have. She'd probably push it away from the table and order more partridge.

✪ **Catedral de Ávila.** Plaza Catedral. ☎ **920-21-16-41.** Admission 300 ptas. ($1.80) adults, free for children under 8. May–Sept, daily 10am–1:30pm and 3:30–5pm; Oct–Apr, daily 10am–1:30pm and 3:30–5:30pm.

Built into the old ramparts of Ávila, this cold, austere cathedral and fortress (begun in 1099) bridges the gap between the Romanesque and the Gothic, and, as such, enjoys a certain distinction in Spanish architecture. One local writer compared it to a granite mountain. The interior is unusual, built with a mottled red-and-white stone.

Like most European cathedrals, Ávila lost its purity of design through the years as new chapels and wings—one completely in the Renaissance mode—were added. A Dutch artist, Cornelius, designed the seats of the choir stalls, also in Renaissance style, and the principal chapel holds a reredos showing the life of Christ by Pedro Berruguete, Juan de Borgoña, and Santa Cruz. Behind the chapel the tomb of Bishop Alonso de Madrigal—nicknamed "El Tostado" ("The Parched One") because of its brownish color—is Vasco de Zarza's masterpiece. The Cathedral Museum contains a laminated gold ceiling, a 15th-century triptych, a copy of an El Greco painting, as well as vestmentsand 15th-century songbooks.

Convento de Santa Teresa. Plaza de la Santa. ☎ **920-21-10-30.** Free admission. Convent May–Sept, daily 9:30am–1:30pm and 3:30–9pm; Oct–Apr, daily 9:30am–1:30pm and 3:30–8:30pm. Sala de Reliquias daily 9:30am–1:30pm and 3:30–7:30pm. Bus: 1, 3, or 4.

This 17th-century convent and baroque church, 2 blocks southwest of the Plaza de la Victoria, is at the site of St. Teresa's birth. To the right of the convent is the tiny Sala de Reliquias exhibiting some of her relics, including a finger from her right hand, the sole of one of her sandals, and a cord she used to flagellate herself.

Monasterio de Santo Tomás. Plaza Granada, 1. ☎ **920-22-04-00.** Admission to museum 200 ptas. ($1.20); cloisters 100 ptas. (60¢). Museum daily 11am–12:45pm and 4–6pm; cloisters Mon–Sun 10am–1pm and 4–8pm. Bus: 1, 2, or 3.

This 15th-century Gothic monastery was once the headquarters of the Inquisition in Ávila. For 3 centuries it housed the tomb of Torquemada, the first general inquisitor, whose zeal in organizing the Inquisition made him a notorious figure in Spanish history. Legend has it that after the friars were expelled from the monastery in 1836, a mob of Torquemada-haters ransacked the tomb and burned the remains somewhere outside the city walls. His final burial site is unknown.

Prince John, the only son of Ferdinand and Isabella, was also buried here, in a sumptuous sepulcher in the church transept. The tomb was desecrated during a French invasion; now, only an empty crypt remains.

Visit the Royal Cloisters, in some respects the most interesting architectural feature of the place. In the upper part of the third cloister, you'll find the Museum of Far Eastern Art, which exhibits Vietnamese, Chinese, and Japanese art and handcrafts.

WHERE TO STAY

Ávila is a summer resort—a refuge from Castilian heat—but the hotels are few in number, and the Spanish book nearly all the hotel space in July and August. Make sure to have a reservation in advance. Mesón El Sol y Residencia Santa Teresa (see "Where to Dine," below) also rents rooms.

MODERATE

Gran Hotel Palacio de Valderrábanos. Plaza Catedral, 9, 05001 Ávila. ☎ **800-528-1234** in the U.S. and Canada, or 920-25-51-00. Fax 920-25-16-91. 73 units. A/C MINIBAR TV TEL. 15,000 ptas. ($90) double; 25,000 ptas. ($150) suite. AE, DC, MC, V. Parking 1,000 ptas. ($6) per day. Bus: 1, 2, or 3.

Set immediately adjacent to the front entrance of the cathedral behind an entryway that is a marvel of medieval stonework, this is one of the most elegant and historic hotels of Castile. Originally built in the 1300s as a private home by an early bishop of Ávila (and a member of the Valderrábanos family), it contains a once-fortified lookout tower (whose circumference encloses one of the suites), high-beamed ceilings, and intricately chiseled stonework. The public rooms have a somber elegance, with slightly faded baronial furniture that adds to the old-fashioned feeling. If possible, ask for a bedroom overlooking the cathedral. Rooms come in a variety of shapes, but each is usually medium in size, well furnished with comfortable beds and firm mattresses. Bathrooms are well organized, with a hair dryer and plush towels. The restaurant **El Fogón de Santa Teresa** is a high-ceilinged bastion of formality serving traditional Castilian meals, with fixed-price menus at 3,700 ptas. ($24.80) each. Hotel amenities include a concierge, laundry/valet, and baby-sitting.

Hotel Reina Isabel. Avenida José Antonio, 17, 05001 Avila. ☎ **920-25-10-10-22.** Fax 920-25-11-73. www.reinaisabel.com. E-mail:hotel@reinaisabel.com. 60 units. A/C MINIBAR TV TEL 16,500 ptas. ($99) double; 25,000 ptas. ($150) suite. AE, DC, MC, V. Parking 900 ptas. ($5.40).

Cited for its elegant decoration, this hotel has a severe facade but warms considerably once you're inside. Rated four stars, it lies about a 6-minute walk outside the walls of the old city. The interior is classically designed, with separate areas depicting various epochs in Spanish history, complete with furnishings and objets d'art from the 14th to the 18th centuries, including a magnificent altarpiece from the 15th century. The spacious bedrooms are similarly decorated and furnished with classical motifs, with marble floors and comfortable beds. All have state-of-the-art bathrooms, and each suite has a whirlpool tub. On site is a cafeteria offering a set menu. The hotel also operates an excellent restaurant, nearby **Copacabana,** San Millán, 9 (☎ **920-21-11-10**).

✪ **Meliá Palacio de Los Velada.** Plaza de la Catedral, 10, 05001 Ávila. ☎ **800-336-3542** in the U.S. and Canada, or 920-25-51-00. Fax 920-25-49-00. 85 units. A/C MINIBAR TV TEL. 18,500 ptas. ($111) double. AE, MC, V. Parking 1,000 ptas. ($6).

When the Spanish chain Meliá opened this splendid gem to guests in 1995, it quickly became the most sought-after accommodation in the province, surpassing even the government-run paradors. Four centuries ago, this palace sheltered the likes of Charles V and Philip II. Arrayed around a central courtyard, today's hotel offers a luxury that was unimaginable when those kings spent the night.

The styling in the public rooms and the luxuriously furnished guest rooms make even the paradors look like they need a face-lift. Enjoying the best location in town—right in the center near the cathedral—the hotel receives guests in the setting of a medieval palace, with massive stones and antiques throughout. All the modern conveniences, including wide, comfortable beds have been installed, along with state-of-the-art plumbing. Each of the tiled bathrooms is equipped with a hair dryer. The elegant dining room serves some of the town's finest meals, including game (on occasion), succulent lamb, and excellent steaks. Service in the dining room is courtly and supremely efficient. Hotel amenities include a concierge, room service, laundry service, conference rooms, bicycle rentals. A shopping arcade is nearby.

✪ **Parador de Ávila.** Marqués de Canales de Chozas, 2, 05001 Ávila. ☎ **920-21-13-40.** Fax 920-22-61-66. 61 units. MINIBAR TV TEL. 16,000 ptas. ($96) double; 30,000 ptas. ($180) suite. AE, DC, MC, V. Free outside parking; garage 1,200 ptas. ($7.20).

Two blocks northwest of Plaza de la Victoria, this parador stands on a ridge overlooking the banks of the Adaja River. Once it was known as the Palace of Benavides, from the 15th century; its facade forms part of the square. The palace has a dignified entranceway with most of its public lounges opening onto a central courtyard with an inner gallery of columns. The recently refurbished rooms contain tasteful furnishings: stone fireplaces, highly polished tile floors, old chests, leather armchairs, paintings, and sculptures. The rooms, generally medium size, come with all the modern comforts, including good mattresses and tiled bathrooms equipped with a hair dryer. The dining room, with its leaded-glass windows opening onto a terraced garden, serves passable Castilian dishes. Hotel amenities include a concierge, laundry service, conference rooms, baby-sitting, and currency exchange service.

INEXPENSIVE

El Rastro. Plaza del Rastro, 1, 05001 Ávila. ☎ **920-21-12-18.** Fax 920-25-16-26. 10 units. 6,350 ptas. ($38.10) double. No credit cards.

Situated near the junction of calle Caballeros and calle Cepadas is the best choice for the bargain hunter. Few visitors know that they can spend the night at this old Castilian inn built into the city walls. The small guest rooms are basic and clean. We recommend the restaurant here, too (see below).

Gran Hostal San Segundo. San Segundo, 28, 05001 Ávila. ☎ **920-25-25-90.** Fax 920-25-27-90. 14 units. TV TEL. 8,000 ptas. ($48) double. AE, DC, MC, V. Free parking on the street.

This small hotel and restaurant is just outside the immense walls surrounding the historic center of Ávila. The elegant 19th-century building itself has just been renovated with a mind to both maintaining its historical charm and incorporating modern comfort. The soft salmon-hued reception rooms have high ceilings, and the medium-size guest rooms are spotlessly clean, simple, and unpretentious. The hotel has an Italian restaurant, which also prepares typically regional dishes such as *Carne Avilena,* a T-bone steak, roast lamb, and the rich and tasty *cochinillo* (roasted piglet), cooked in its own juice and served with nothing more than bread. The restaurant is open daily noon to 4pm and 8pm to midnight.

✪ **Hosteria de Bracamonte.** Bracamonte, 6, 05001 Ávila. ☎ **920-25-38-38.** 18 units. MINIBAR TV TEL. 12,000 ptas. ($72) double. MC, V. Parking available along the street.

The most tranquil spot in town is this little gem decorated in a classic Castilian style. It lies 1 block north of Plaza de Victoria, the main square within the city walls. A restful and quiet oasis, it has a number of charming features, including a lovely patio and a dark-wood Castilian motif throughout. Converted to a small inn in 1989, the *hosteria* retains some of its aristocratic origins as the town house of Gov. Don Juan Teherán y Monjaraz. Rooms are spacious and have whitewashed walls; some have fireplaces and four-poster beds. Mattresses and linens are of fine quality.

WHERE TO DINE

El Rastro. Plaza del Rastro, 1. ☎ **920-21-12-19.** Reservations required on weekends only. Main courses 1,800–2,500 ptas. ($10.80–$15); fixed-price menu 1,800 ptas. ($10.80). AE, DC, MC, V. Daily 1–4pm and 9–11pm. CASTILIAN.

An old inn built into the 11th-century town walls, El Rastro serves typical Castilian dishes, with more attention given to freshness and preparation than to culinary flamboyance. Specialties include roast baby lamb and tender white veal, raised in the region and known for its succulence. It is prepared at least four different ways. Dessert recipes have been passed down from Ávila's nuns. Try, if you dare, the highly touted *yemas de Santa Teresa* (St. Teresa's candied egg yolk), although when we dined here with travel expert Arthur Frommer, he found it a particularly horrible dessert—and we agree. Yet Ávila residents keep praising it as a specialty. To our taste, there are far better selections on the menu. They also maintain a small hotel with 10 comfortable rooms, each with TV and bathroom and no phone (see "Where to Stay," above).

Hosteria de Bracamonte. Bracamonte, 6. ☎ **920-25-12-80.** Reservations recommended. Main courses 1,200–2,200 ptas. ($7.20–$13.20). MC, V. Wed–Mon 12:30–4pm and 7–11pm. SPANISH/CASTILIAN.

Parts of the building that contain this place are 400 years old, but even in recent remodelings, every effort was made to duplicate the original ceiling beams, rough-textured plaster, and artfully chiseled stone of the original design. The kitchen focuses on grills and old-fashioned roasts, many of which are remembered fondly from the childhood of the regular guests. Examples include roasted tender baby lamb with herbs and garlic, grilled pork or veal chops, roasted chicken, and all manner of steaks, cutlets, ribs, and, to a lesser degree, seafood. The largest of the restaurant's four dining rooms is usually devoted to the care and feeding of busloads of groups traveling together, so you might find a bit more intimacy in one of the three smaller dining areas.

Mesón El Sol y Residencia Santa Teresa. Avenida 18 de Julio, 25, 05003 Ávila. ☎ **920-22-02-11.** Fax 920-22-41-13. Reservations recommended. Main courses 1,000–2,500 ptas. ($6–$15); fixed-price menu 1,800 ptas. ($10.80). AE, DC, MC, V. Daily 1–4pm and 9–11pm. Bus: 2. CASTILIAN.

Just a short walk from the historic center of town, you may be distracted by the aromas emanating from the kitchen of the lowest-priced inn in Ávila—a place known for its good food, moderate prices, and efficient service. Full meals may include seafood soup, fried hake, veal with garlic, and house-style flan. The inn also rents 18 simply furnished rooms, a double going for 6,500 to 8,500 ptas. ($39 to $51).

9 Cuenca

100 miles (161km) E of Madrid, 202 miles (325km) SW of Zaragoza

This medieval town once dominated by the Arabs is a spectacular sight with its *casas colgadas,* the cliff-hanging houses set on multiple terraces that climb up the impossibly steep sides of a ravine. The Júcar and Huécar Rivers meet at the bottom.

ESSENTIALS

GETTING THERE   Trains leave Madrid's Atocha Railway Station about eight times throughout the day. Trains arrive in Cuenca at Paseo del Ferrocarril in the new city (☎ **969-22-07-20**), after a journey lasting anywhere from 2½ to 3 hours. A one-way ticket from Madrid costs 1,355 to 1,600 ptas. ($8.15 to $9.60).

There are also about eight buses from Madrid every day. Buses arrive at calle Fermín Caballero, s/n (☎ **969-22-70-87** for information and schedules). A one-way fare costs 1,305 to 1,600 ptas. ($7.85 to $9.60).

Cuenca is the junction for several highways and about a dozen lesser roads that connect it to towns within its region. From Madrid, take the N-III to Tarancon, then the N-400, which leads directly into Cuenca.

VISITOR INFORMATION   The **tourist information office** is at calle San Pedro, 6 (☎ **969-23-21-19**), next to the cathedral off Plaza Mayor. Hours are daily 9am to 2pm and 4 to 7pm.

EXPLORING THE AREA

The chief sight of Cuenca is the town itself. Isolated from the rest of Spain, it requires a northern detour from the heavily traveled Valencia–Madrid road. Deep gorges give it an unreal quality, and eight old bridges spanning two rivers connect the ancient parts of town with the growing new sections. One of the bridges is suspended over a 200-foot drop.

Cuenca's streets are narrow and steep, often cobbled, and even the most athletic tourist will tire quickly. But you shouldn't miss it, even if you have to stop and rest periodically. At night you're in for a special treat when the *casas colgadas* are illuminated. Also, try to drive almost to the top of the castle-dominated hill. The road gets rough as you approach the end, but the view makes the effort worthwhile.

If you have the time, you can easily make a side trip to the ✪ **Ciudad Encantada (Enchanted City),** Carretera de la Sierra, about 25 miles (40km) to the northeast of Cuenca. Storms and underground waters have created a city here out of large rocks and boulders, shaping them into bizarre designs: a seal, an elephant, a Roman bridge. Take CU-912, turning northeast onto CU-913. Ciudad Encantada is signposted.

Catedral de Cuenca Plaza. Pío XII. Free admission. Daily 8:45am–2pm and 4–7pm (closes at 6pm in winter). Bus: 1 or 2.

Begun in the 12th century, this Gothic cathedral was influenced by England's Norman style, becoming the only Anglo-Norman cathedral in Spain. Part of it collapsed in the 20th century but has been restored. A national monument filled with religious art treasures, the cathedral is a 10-minute walk from the Plaza Mayor, up calle Palafox. The cathedral's *museo diocesano* exhibits two canvases by El Greco, a collection of Flemish tapestries (some beautifully designed), and a statue of the Virgin del Sagrario from the 1100s.

✪ **Museo de Arte Abstracto Español.** Calle los Canónigos, s/n. ☎ 969-21-29-83. Admission 500 ptas. ($3) adults, 250 ptas. ($1.50) students. Tues–Fri 11am–2pm and 4–6pm; Sat 11am–2pm and 4–8pm; Sun 11am–2:30pm. Bus: 1 or 2.

North of Plaza Mayor housed in a cliff-hanging dwelling, this ranks as one of the finest museums of its kind in Spain. It was conceived by painter Fernando Zóbel, who donated it in 1980 to the Juan March Foundation. The most outstanding abstract Spanish painters are represented, including Rafael Canogar (especially his *Toledo*), Luís Feito, Zóbel himself, Tápies, Eduardo Chillida, Gustavo Torner, Gerardo Rueda, Millares, Sempere, Cuixart, and Antonio Saura (see his grotesque Geraldine Chaplin and his study of Brigitte Bardot, a vision of horror, making the French actress look like an escapee from Picasso's *Guernica*).

WHERE TO STAY

Hotel NH Ciudad de Cuenca. Ronda de San José, 1, 16004 Cuenca. ☎ 969-23-05-02. Fax 969-23-05-03. www.nh-hoteles.es. E-mail: nhc-cuenca@nh-hoteles.es. 72 units. A/C MINI-BAR TV TEL. 15,100 ptas. ($90.60) double; 19,500 ptas. ($117) suite. AE, DC, MC, V. Parking 1,000 ptas. ($6). Bus: 2.

Since you can't always get into the parador, consider this stellar selection the second-best choice in town. In operation since the mid-1990s, it lies in a rapidly developing residential area close to the old town. Its exterior design is severe and clinical, but its interior is filled with comfort and grace notes—and it's also loaded with amenities. The wooden floored rooms are comfortable and well appointed, with well-selected upholstery, comfortable beds, and fully equipped bathrooms with hair dryers. The sole suite has a hydro-massage. The hotel operates a spacious restaurant and bar/cafe and prides itself on its buffet breakfasts. Other facilities include room service, laundry, a concierge, baby-sitting, a gym, and a sauna.

Leonor de Aquitania. Calle San Pedro, 60, 16001 Cuenca. ☎ 969-23-10-00. Fax 969-23-10-04. www.hotelleonordeaquitania.com. 49 units. A/C MINIBAR TV TEL. 10,900 ptas. ($65.40) double; 21,000 ptas. ($126) suite. AE, DC, MC, V. Free parking.

Perched high up on the hillside above an almost sheer drop, the hotel enjoys spectacular views of both the old city of Cuenca from one angle and the narrow valley rising from the harsh though beautiful precipice opposite. The reception rooms have been maintained in extremely good, conservative taste, and the hotel evokes an elegantly restrained and comfortable charm. The medium-size rooms are exceedingly well cared for, and each comes with a firm mattress and an immaculate tile bathroom. The Hebrea Hermosa (the beautiful Jewish maiden) suite is one of the most charming in this quiet medieval city, which lies precariously between two deep gorges. There is a restaurant inside the hotel that operates in the day and serves, among other things, a fixed-price menu for 2,300 ptas. ($13.80).

✪ **Parador de Turismo de Cuenca.** Convento de San Pablo, Paseo de la Hoz del Huécar, 16001 Cuenca. ☎ **969-23-23-20.** Fax 969-23-25-34. 63 units. A/C MINIBAR TV TEL. 18,500 ptas. ($111) double; 30,000 ptas. ($180) suite. AE, DC, MC, V. Parking 1,100 ptas. ($6.60).

This government-sponsored hotel occupies the dignified premises of what was originally built in 1523 as a Dominican monastery. A noteworthy example of late Gothic architecture, it lies on a hillside above Cuenca, about a half mile northwest of the town's historic center. It is clearly the town's prestige address. Opened for business after extensive renovations in 1992, its timeless three stories contain masses of intricately chiseled 16th-century stonework (some enhanced with glass panels overlooking the river), a church, a severely beautiful cloister, and a swimming pool. There's a bar, a high-ceilinged restaurant, and two floors of medium-size rooms, which, despite comfortably traditional furniture and modern bathrooms, richly convey their ecclesiastical origins.

✪ **Posada de San José.** Julián Romero, 4, 16001 Cuenca. ☎ **969-21-13-00.** Fax 969-23-03-65. www.arrakis.es/~psanjose. E-mail: psanjose@arrakis.es. 30 units (22 with bathroom). 4,700 ptas. ($28.20) double without bathroom, 7,500–9,500 ptas. ($45–$57) double with bathroom. AE, DC, MC, V. Bus: 1 or 2.

Posada de San José stands in the oldest part of Cuenca, a short walk north of the cathedral. The 17th-century cells that used to shelter the sisters of this former convent now house overnight guests who consider its views of the old city the best in town. It sits atop a cliff overlooking the forbidding depths of a gorge. Accommodations are small but are still quite comfortable, with very good beds with firm mattresses. Bathrooms are also small, with shower stalls. Owners Antonio and Jennifer Cortinas renovated this place into one of the best bargain hotels of the region, with the bar perhaps the most charming of its well-decorated public rooms. Parking is available along the street.

WHERE TO DINE
El Figón de Pedro. Cervantes, 13. ☎ **969-22-68-21.** Reservations recommended. Main courses 950–2,000 ptas. ($5.70–$12); menú del día 3,000 ptas. ($18). AE, DC, MC, V. Daily 1:30–4pm; Mon–Sat 9–11pm. Closed Feb. CASTILIAN.

Set in the business section of the new town at the foot of the hills that lead you to the wonders of medieval Cuenca, this restaurant belongs to one of Spain's most celebrated restaurateurs, Pedro Torres Pacheco. Given this, and by turning a quick blind eye to the abundance of late '60s concrete, the location is well worth a visit. The airconditioned restaurant is relatively intimate, with 13 tables and the traditional Castillian decor of plates on walls and folkloric memorabilia. The cuisine, however, is not half as predictable. The *mortuelo* (local pâté made from partridge, pork, ham, and hare) should definitely be sampled, as should the gazpacho and *bacalao ajo arriero* (a puree of cod, garlic, eggs, and olive oil). The desserts here are interesting, unlike those in many Spanish restaurants, especially the original Moorish *alaju* (almonds, bread crumbs, honey, and orange water) and the Miguelito, a flat almond cake. When sated, you can then toast the meal with a glass of resoli, the strong local liquor.

✪ **Mesón Casa Colgadas.** Canónigos, 3. ☎ **969-22-35-09.** Reservations recommended. Main courses 1,850–2,800 ptas. ($11.10–$16.80); fixed-price menus 3,300–3,800 ptas. ($19.80–$22.80). AE, DC, MC, V. Daily 1:30–4pm; Wed–Mon 9–11pm. SPANISH/ INTERNATIONAL.

One of the most spectacular dining rooms in Spain stands on one of the most precarious precipices in Cuenca. Established in the late 1960s, it occupies a five-story 19th-century house with sturdy supporting walls and beams. Pine balconies and windows overlook the ravine below and the hills beyond. In fact, it's the most pho-tographed "suspended house" in town, and dinner here is worth every peseta. The menu includes regional dishes and a wide variety of well-prepared international favorites. Drinks are served in the tavern room on the street level, so even if you're not dining here, you may want to drop in for a drink and the view. You'll find the Mesón Casa Colgadas just south of the cathedral and near the Museum of Spanish Abstract Art.

Togar. Avenida República Argentina, 3. ☎ **969-22-01-62.** Reservations required. Main courses 900–2,200 ptas. ($5.40–$13.20); fixed-price menu 2,500–3,000 ptas. ($15–$18). AE, DC, MC, V. Daily 1–4pm; Mon–Sat 8–11pm. Closed 1 week in July (dates vary). Bus: 1 or 6. SPANISH.

Rich with local flavor and aggressively cost-conscious, this is a simple but likable *tasca* on the southwestern periphery of town. Established in 1955, and set within an angu-lar building erected the same year, it offers homemade cookery whose inspiration derives from the various regions of Spain. One of the specialties is *revuelto Togar*, an egg, ham, and shrimp dish served with herbs and crusty bread. Also available are well-peppered versions of pork, several kinds of rich soups, and various beef and fish dishes.

Old Castile & León 5

Spain owes much to Castile, Aragón, and León, since these three kingdoms helped unify the various regions of the country. Modern Spain was conceived when Isabella of Castile married Ferdinand of Aragón on October 19, 1469. Five years later she was proclaimed queen of Castile and León. The Moors were eventually driven out of Granada, the rest of Spain was conquered, and Columbus sailed to America—all during the reign of these two Catholic monarchs.

This proud but controversial queen and her unscrupulous husband fashioned an empire whose influence extended throughout Spain, Europe, and the New World. The power once held by Old Castile shifted long ago to Madrid, but there remain many reminders of its storied past.

The ancient kingdom of León, which was eventually annexed to Castile, is made up of three cities: Salamanca, Zamora, and the provincial capital of León. Today the district is known for its many castles.

In Old Castile we'll cover the inland provincial capital of Valladolid, where Isabella married Ferdinand and where a brokenhearted Columbus died on May 19, 1506. From here we'll move on to Burgos, once the capital of Old Castile. Vivar, a small town near here, produced Spain's greatest national hero El Cid, who conquered the Moorish kingdom of Valencia.

For other destinations in the region, refer to chapter 4, "Side Trips from Madrid."

1 Ciudad Rodrigo

54 miles (87km) SW of Salamanca, 177 miles (285km) W of Madrid

A walled town dating from Roman days, Ciudad Rodrigo is known for its 16th- and 17th-century townhouses, built by the conquistadors. It was founded in the 12th century by Count Rodriguez González and is today a national monument. Located near the Portuguese frontier, it stands high on a hilltop and is known for the familiar silhouette of the square tower of its Alcázar. This walled part of the city is referred to as the Casco Viejo.

The ramparts were built in the 12th century along Roman foundations. Several stairways lead up to a mile-long sentry path. You can wander these ramparts at leisure and then walk through the streets with their many churches and mansions. It is not one chief monument that is the allure, but rather the city as a whole.

The town's major attraction is its cathedral, **Santa María,** which combines Romanesque and Gothic styles with a neoclassical tower.

The cathedral, known locally as Casco Viejo, was mostly built between 1170 and 1230, although subsequent centuries have seen more additions. It can be reached going east of Plaza Mayor through Plaza de San Salvador. The Renaissance altar on the north aisle is an acclaimed work of ecclesiastical art; look also for the Virgin Portal at the west door, which dates from the 1200s. For 200 ptas. ($1.20) you'll be admitted to the cloisters, which are in a variety of architectural styles, including a plateresque door. Hours are daily 10am to 1pm and 4 to 6:30pm.

The **Plaza Mayor** is a showpiece of 17th-century architecture, with two Renaissance palaces. This is the main square of the city.

Your transportation in Ciudad Rodrigo will be your trusty feet, as walking is the only way to explore the city. Pick up a map at the tourist office (see below).

ESSENTIALS

GETTING THERE   The only real way to get here is from Salamanca. Because train service is infrequent and the train station is a long way from the walls of the old city, it's easier to take the bus from Salamanca; you'll get off at the Ciudad Rodrigo station at calle Campo de Toledo (☎ **923-46-12-17**). Monday through Friday, 11 buses arrive from Salamanca; on Saturday and Sunday, five buses. The trip takes 1 hour and costs 730 ptas. ($4.40) one-way.

The N-620 is the main road from both Salamanca and Portugal. Driving time from Salamanca is about 1¼ hours.

VISITOR INFORMATION   The **tourist information office** is at Plaza Amayuelas, 5 (☎ **923-46-05-61**). It is open Monday to Friday 10am to 2pm and 5 to 8pm, and Saturday 10am to 2pm and 4 to 7pm.

SPECIAL EVENTS   Carnival festivities in February in Ciudad Rodrigo feature a running of the bulls, traditional dances, and costumes.

WHERE TO STAY

Conde Rodrigo I. Plaza de San Salvador, 9, 37500 Ciudad Rodrigo. ☎ **923-46-14-04.** Fax 923-46-14-08. 34 units. A/C MINIBAR TV TEL. 6,500–7,000 ptas. ($39–$42) double. DC, MC, V. Parking 1,000 ptas. ($6).

Its central location next to the cathedral is a big plus for this two-star hotel; try for a room opening onto the square. The recently renovated rooms are small and totally devoid of style, but they're comfortable. The building itself has some medieval flavor, with its thick walls of chiseled stone. The hotel restaurant is a good buy, offering well-prepared Castilian food such as roast meats, spicy sausages, and fresh fish. Public parking is available off the street.

WHERE TO DINE

Estoril. Traversia Talavera, 1. ☎ **923-46-05-50.** Reservations recommended. Main courses 1,500–1,800 ptas. ($9–$10.80); *menú del día* 1,500 ptas. ($9). DC, MC, V. Daily noon–4pm and 8:30pm–midnight; Fri–Sat until 3 or 4am. CASTILIAN/BASQUE.

A short walk from Plaza Mayor, this popular restaurant was built and founded in 1967. The air-conditioned interior is decorated in typical regional style with bullfight photographs. Specialties of the house include roasted meats, such as roast suckling pig, with a special emphasis on roasted goat. Seafood, such as sole and hake, is presented in the Basque style. The seafood soup is particularly good. Everything is accompanied by a variety of regional wines, including Cosechero Rioja.

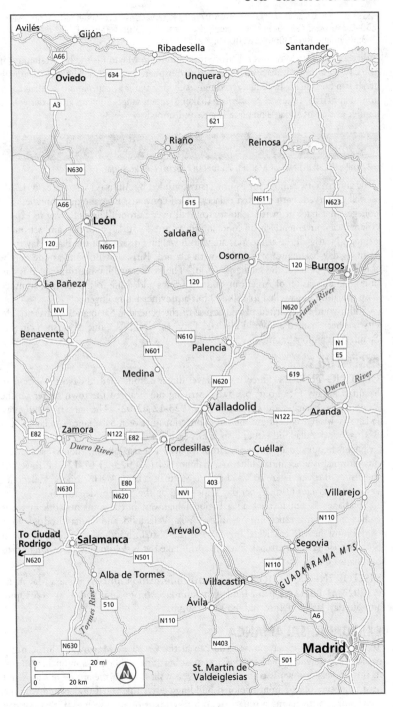

Mayton. La Colada, 9. ☎ **923-46-07-20.** Reservations recommended. Main courses 850–2,250 ptas. ($5.10–$13.50); fixed-price menu 1,500 ptas. ($9). AE, DC, MC, V. Daily 1–3:30pm and 8–11:30pm. CASTILIAN.

Adjacent to Plaza Mayor in a 17th-century building, Mayton is the best restaurant in the city. Its antique walls reverberate with atmosphere and legend. The menu is mostly fresh fish and shellfish, done exceedingly well. Try the *sopa castellana* (Castilian soup) for an appetizer, followed by *merluza* (hake) in green sauce. You can also order veal, as tender as that of Ávila. The place is air-conditioned.

2 Salamanca

127 miles (204km) NW of Madrid, 73 miles (118km) E of Portugal

This ancient city, famous for its university founded by Alfonso IX in the early 1200s, is well preserved, with turreted palaces, faded convents, Romanesque churches, and colleges that have attracted scholars from all over Europe. The only way to explore Salamanca conveniently is on foot, so arm yourself with a good map and set out to explore. Nearly all the attractions are within walking distance of the Plaza Mayor.

In its day Salamanca was ranked with Oxford, Paris, and Bologna as one of "the four leading lights of the medieval world." The intellectual life continues to this day, and a large invasion of American students brings added life to the town in summer. Its population has swelled to 180,000 but a provincial aura lingers.

Still a youthful, spirited place because of the venerable Salamanca University, the city has been named a "World Heritage City" by UNESCO, one of six such cities in Spain. No country has more.

ESSENTIALS

GETTING THERE   Three trains travel directly from Madrid's North Station to Salamanca daily (3½ hours one-way), arriving northeast of the town center on the Paseo de la Estación de Ferrocarril (☎ **923-12-02-02**). The fare is 2,090 ptas. ($12.55). More frequent are the rail connections between Salamanca, Ávila, Ciudad Rodrigo, and Valladolid (around six trains each per day).

There's frequent daily bus service from Madrid. The trip takes 2½ hours. Salamanca's bus terminal is at avenida Filiberto Villalobos, 71 (☎ **923-23-67-17**), northwest of the center of town. There are also buses to Salamanca from Ávila, Zamora, Valladolid, León, and Caceres (2 to 13 per day, depending on the point of departure).

Salamanca is not located on a national highway, but a good network of roads converge there from such nearby cities as Ávila, Valladolid, and Ciudad Rodrigo. One of the most heavily trafficked highways is the N-620, leading into Salamanca from both Barcelona and Portugal. From Madrid, take the N-VI northwest, forking off to Salamanca on the N-501.

VISITOR INFORMATION   The **tourist information office** is at Plaza Mayor, 13 (☎ **923-21-83-42**). Open Monday to Saturday 9am to 2pm and 4:30 to 6:30pm, and Sunday 10am to 2pm and 4:30 to 6:30pm.

EXPLORING SALAMANCA

To start, spend as much time as you can at the ✪ **Plaza Mayor,** an 18th-century baroque square widely acclaimed as the most beautiful public plaza in Spain. No trip to this university town is complete unless you walk through the arcade of shops and feast your eyes on the honey-colored buildings. After this you'll understand why the *plaza mayor,* a town's main square, is an integral part of Spanish life. If it's a hot day

ATTRACTIONS ●
Casa de las Conchas **8**
Casa Museo Unamuno **20**
Catedral Nueva **18**
Catedral Vieja **17**
Convento de las Dueñas **9**
Convento de San Estéban **11**
Museo de Salamanca **21**
Plaza Mayor **5**
Universidad de Salamanca **19**

ACCOMMODATIONS ■
Gran Hotel **12**
Hostal Laguna **10**
Hostal Plaza Mayor **6**
Hotel Don Juan **7**
Hotel Lasa **1**
Hotel las Torres **2**
Hotel Monterrey **3**
Hotel Rector **15**
Hotel Roma **4**

Hotel San Polo **14**
NH Palacio de
Castellanos **13**
Parador Nacional de
Salamanca **16**

and you want what everybody else in the Plaza Mayor is drinking, stop in a cafe and order *leche helado*, an icy vanilla and almond milkshake that's very refreshing and not too filling.

Even before reaching the Plaza Mayor, you may want to stop and admire the facade of the landmark **Casa de las Conchas (House of Shells),** which appears as you walk north from the Patio de las Escuelas (site of the Universidad de Salamanca; see below) on calles de Libreros and San Isidro. This much-photographed building is at the corner of Rua Mayor and calle de la Compañía, 2 (☎ **923-26-93-17**). The restored 1483 house is noted for its facade of 400 simulated scallop shells. A professor of medicine at the university and a doctor at the court of Isabella created the house as a monument to Santiago de Compostela, the renowned pilgrimage site. The shell is the symbol of the Order of Santiago. You can visit the courtyard Monday to Friday 9am to 9pm, Saturday 9am to 2pm and 4 to 7pm, and Sunday 10am to 2pm. Admission is free.

Casa Museo Unamuno. Calle de Libreros, 25. ☎ **923-29-44-00.** Free admission. Mon–Fri 9am–1:30pm and 4–6pm; Sat–Sun 10am–1:30pm. July 7–Sept 30, open only mornings. Last tours leave 30 minutes before closing time. Bus: 1.

The poet and philosopher Miguel de Unamuno—one of the world's most renowned scholars—lived from 1900 to 1914 in this 18th-century home beside the university. Here he wrote many of the works that made him famous. You can see some of his notebooks and his library, along with many personal mementos.

Catedral Nueva (New Cathedral). Plaza Juan XXII. ☎ **923-21-74-76.** Admission 300 ptas. ($1.80). Daily 9am–2pm and 4–8pm. Bus: 1.

The "new" cathedral dates from 1513. It took more than 200 years to complete it, so the edifice represents many styles: It's classified as late Gothic, but you'll see baroque and plateresque features as well. José Churriguera contributed some rococo elements, too. The building has a grand gold-on-beige sandstone facade, elegant chapels, the best-decorated dome in Spain, and bas-relief columns that look like a palm-tree cluster. Unfortunately, its stained glass is severely damaged. The cathedral lies in the southern section of the old town, about 5 blocks south of the Plaza Mayor at the edge of the Plaza de Anaya.

Catedral Vieja (Old Cathedral). Plaza Juan XXII. ☎ **923-21-74-76.** Admission 300 ptas. ($1.80). Apr–Sept, daily 10am–1:30pm and 4–7:30pm; Oct–Mar, daily 9am–1pm and 4–6pm. Bus: 1.

Adjoining the New Cathedral is this older Spanish Romanesque version, begun in 1140. Its simplicity provides a dramatic contrast to the ornamentation of its younger but bigger counterpart. After viewing the interior, stroll through the enclosed cloisters with their Gothic tombs of long-forgotten bishops. The chapels are of special architectural interest. In the Capilla de San Martín the frescoes date from 1242, and in the Capilla de Santa Bárbara, final exams for Salamanca University students were given. The Capilla de Santa Catalina is noted for its gargoyles.

Museo Art Nouveau–Art Deco. Calle Gilbraltar, 14. ☎ **923-12-14-25.** Admission 300 ptas. ($1.80) adults, 200 ptas. ($1.20) students and children. Tues–Fri 11am–2pm and 4–8pm; Sat–Sun 11am–9pm.

The Art Nouveau–Art Deco Museum contains more than 1,500 pieces, all part of the collection of the Manuel Ramos Andrade Foundation. Spanning the late 19th century to the 1930s, the collection includes bronze and marble figurines, jewelry, furniture, paintings, and a collection of some 300 porcelain dolls. Numerous works by Emile Gallé and René Lalique are also on display.

Museo de Salamanca (Casa de los Doctores de la Reina). Patio de las Escuelas, 2. ☎ **923-21-22-35.** Admission 200 ptas. ($1.20). Tues–Fri 10am–2pm and 4:30–7:30pm; Sat 10am–2pm. Bus: 1.

Built in the late 15th century by Queen Isabella's physician, this structure located near the university is a fine example of the Spanish plateresque style. The Fine Arts Museum is here, boasting a collection of paintings and sculptures dating from the 15th to the 20th centuries.

Convento de las Dueñas. Plaza del Concillo de Trento. ☎ **923-21-54-42.** Admission 200 ptas. ($1.20). June–Sept, daily 10am–1pm and 4–7pm; Oct–May, daily 10:30am–1pm and 4:30–5:30pm.

Across calle Buenaventura from Convento de San Esteban (see below) is one of the most popular sights of Salamanca, a former Mudéjar palace of a court official. The cloisters date from the 16th century, and are, in the opinion of some architectural critics, the most beautiful in Salamanca. Climb to the upper gallery for a close inspection of the carved capitals covered with demons and dragons, saints and sinners, and animals of every description—some from the pages of *The Divine Comedy.* There's also a portrait of Dante.

Convento de San Esteban. Plaza del Concilio de Trento. ☎ **923-21-50-00.** Admission 200 ptas. ($1.20). Daily 9:30am–1pm and 4–8pm.

Of all the old religious sites of Salamanca, St. Stephen's Convent is one of the most dramatic. The golden-brown plateresque facade of this late Gothic church competes with the cathedral in magnificence. Inside, José Churriguera in 1693 created a high altar that is one of Salamanca's greatest art treasures. The *Claustro de los Reyes* (Cloister of the Kings) is both plateresque and Gothic in style. The convent lies 2 blocks east of the New Cathedral on the opposite side of busy calle San Pablo at the southern terminus of calle de España (Gran Vía).

Universidad de Salamanca. Patio de las Escuelas, 1. ☎ **923-29-44-00.** Admission 300 ptas. ($1.80). Mon–Fri 9:30am–1pm and 4–7pm; Sat 9:30am–1:30pm and 4–6pm; Sun 10am–1pm. Enter from Patio de las Escuelas, a widening of calle de Libreros.

The oldest university in Spain was once the greatest in Europe. In front of the plateresque facade of the building, a statue honors Hebrew scholar Fray Luís de León. Arrested for heresy, Fray Luís was detained for 5 years before being cleared. When he returned, he began his first lecture: "As I was saying yesterday . . ." Fray Luís's remains are kept in the chapel, which is worth a look. You can also visit a dim 16th-century classroom, cluttered with crude wooden benches, but the library upstairs is closed to the public. The university is 2 blocks from the cathedral in the southern section of the old town.

SHOPPING

The town's two main shopping neighborhoods extend around the calle Melendez and the historic borders of the Plaza Mayor. Both areas are good bets for fashion and housewares. You may also want to head for the town's largest department store, **Corte Fiel,** Plaza Mayor (☎ **923-21-92-40**), or the menswear branch at calle Doro, 24 (☎ **923-215290**). And if you're looking for handcrafts, head for **Artesanía Hernandez,** calle Conde de Cadarrus, 21 (☎ **923-12-07-98**), whose inventories represent most of the trades that used to proliferate in the region around Salamanca.

WHERE TO STAY
EXPENSIVE

Gran Hotel. Plaza Poeta Iglesias, 5, 37001 Salamanca. ☎ **923-21-35-00.** Fax 923-21-35-00. 136 units. A/C MINIBAR TV TEL. 16,000 ptas. ($96) double; 25,000 ptas. ($150) suite. AE, DC, MC, V. Parking 1,000 ptas. ($6).

Because of its location and the legends that surround it, this hotel has been a favorite since it was built in 1930. Set on the southeast corner of the Plaza Mayor, it became the traditional favorite of bull breeders and matadors, as well as of the literati of this ancient university town. Because its owners have kept it up-to-date, the hotel is still going strong, although accommodations at the Parador Nacional de Salamanca (see below) are better appointed. In 1994 the hotel was completely renovated, with modern plumbing added, but with much of the old-fashioned charm left intact. Each bedroom is well maintained, with quality mattresses and handsomely equipped bathrooms with hair dryers and plush towels.

   Dining: Castilian-style meals are served à la carte in the hotel's **Restaurante Feudal.** Service in both the hotel and the restaurant could stand some improvement.

Amenities: Concierge, room service, laundry service, baby-sitting, conference rooms.

Hotel Monterrey. Azafranal, 21, 37001 Salamanca. ☎ **923-21-44-01.** Fax 923-21-44-01. 144 units. A/C TV TEL. 15,000–17,500 ptas. ($90–$105) double; 20,000–30,000 ptas. ($120–$180) suite. AE, DC, MC, V. Parking 2,250 ptas. ($13.50).

Run by the same company that operates the Gran Hotel (see above), this hotel isn't as good as its sibling, but it's an okay backup choice. Its location near the Plaza Mayor is ideal and its wood and velvet lobby is inviting. The conservatively and simply furnished midsize guest rooms, although not as well appointed as those of the Gran, are still quite comfortable, each with a firm mattress. The price, especially of the cheaper rooms, is a good value for Salamanca.

Dining: Castilian specialties are served in the fine restaurant, **El Fogón;** there's also an inviting cafe.

✪ **Hotel Rector.** Rector Esperabé, 10, 37008 Salamanca. ☎ **923-21-84-82.** Fax 923-21-40-08. www.teleline.terra.es/personal/hrector. E-mail: hotelrector@telelines.es. 13 units. A/C MINIBAR TV TEL. 17,000–19,000 ptas. ($102–$114) double; 22,000 ptas. ($132) suite. AE, DC, MC, V. Parking 1,000 ptas. ($6).

Far better than either the parador or the Gran Hotel, this little inn has become the best place to stay in Salamanca; nothing matches it in either atmosphere or tranquillity. Located just beyond the Roman bridge, it was a private mansion until the owners, who live on the upper floors, converted it into a hotel in 1990. The rooms are not really hotel quarters, but resemble the elegantly furnished and spacious bedrooms you'd find in the home of a grand Spanish don. Rooms are elegantly appointed with luxury mattresses and beautifully tiled and kept bathrooms complete with hair dryers. Don't expect all the amenities found in a full-service hotel (no restaurant, for example), but the staff here is extremely professional and polite. Since this place is such a gem, you have to reserve well in advance.

Amenities: Laundry and dry-cleaning service, baby-sitting, concierge.

✪ **NH Palacio de Castellanos.** San Pablo, 58–64, 37008 Salamanca. ☎ **923-26-18-18.** Fax 923-26-18-19. www.nh-hoteles.es. 62 units. A/C MINIBAR TV TEL. 20,000 ptas. ($120) double; from 25,000 ptas. ($150) suite. AE, DC, MC, V. Parking 1,900 ptas. ($11.40).

The grandest palace in Salamanca, this deluxe hotel was built on the site of the original 15th-century Palacio de Castellanos and lies in old Salamanca near the Plaza Mayor with good views in most directions. We like it much better than the parador. The elegant marble-floored lobby, supported by towering pillars, sets the posh tone, along with Oriental carpeting. The good-size rooms are state of the art, with sleek modern furnishings and deluxe bedding, bedside controls, and safes. The tiled bathrooms have tub/shower combos and hair dryers, toiletries, scales, and robes.

Dining/Diversions: Locals head here to impress a business client or celebrate a special occasion at the Trento Restaurant, which features specialties from the Basque and Navarre regions. There is also Salamanca's poshest cocktail bar on site.

Amenities: Room service, concierge, laundry/dry cleaning.

Parador Nacional de Salamanca. Teso de la Feria, 2, 37008 Salamanca. ☎ **923-19-20-82.** Fax 923-19-20-87. 108 units. A/C MINIBAR TV TEL. 17,500 ptas. ($105.00) double; 25,000 ptas. ($150) suite. AE, DC, MC, V. Free parking outside; 1,000 ptas. ($6) garage.

Situated just across the Tormes River, this multilevel parador with a modern facade opened in the early 1980s. It sits less than a mile south of the historic center of town. It's a fine choice, but isn't as special as some of Spain's other paradors (the public areas are looking a bit worn, for example). Each of the well-furnished and comfortable midsize bedrooms has two or three framed lithographs, a mirador-style balcony, and a hair dryer.

Dining: A formal restaurant serves respectable regional and international cuisine.

Amenities: On site are a garden, a parking garage, and an outdoor swimming pool. Room service, concierge, dry cleaning/laundry.

MODERATE

Hotel Lasa. Acerca de Recoletos, 21, 47004 Valladolid. ☎ **983-39-02-55.** Fax 983-30-25-61. E-mail: hotellasa@cempresarial.com. 62 units. AC TV TEL. 12,900 ptas. ($77.40) double. AE, DC, MC, V. Parking 1,000 ptas. ($6).

Only 5 minutes from the center of town, this is a welcoming and friendly hotel in a classical Spanish design with balconies. A comfortable lobby with polished floors leads to an array of well-appointed bedrooms. There isn't a clue that this was a women's prison in the 19th century. Fortunately, today's visitors live better than the inmates of yesterday in bright, airy bedrooms with dark wood furnishings, comfortable beds, and well-maintained bathrooms. Units are homey, with throw rugs, traditional pieces, and prints and mirrors on the walls. The on-site restaurant has an international menu, and there is a cozy bar plus an outdoor terrace. The hotel also offers limited room service.

Hotel las Torres. Plaza Mayor, 26 (at the intersection of calle Concejo), 37002 Salamanca. ☎ **923-21-21-00.** Fax 923-21-21-01. 44 units. A/C MINIBAR TV TEL. 14,000 ptas. ($84) double; 19,000 ptas. ($114) suite. AE, DC, MC, V. Parking 1,300 ptas. ($7.80).

Dignified and well maintained, and with a congenial staff, this hotel occupies an good spot near the northwest corner of Plaza Mayor. A recent restoration of a historic monument, the hotel may look a little seedy, but it's not. It has a narrow reception area sheathed with polished marble. The modern, comfortable rooms, although not overly large, are well upholstered and contain excellent beds. Each has a well-designed marble and tile bathroom, a safe, and in many cases a view of the plaza. There's an unpretentious restaurant on the premises. Additional seating spills over beneath the arcades of the plaza, allowing indoor-outdoor dining and lots of opportunities for people-watching.

Hotel San Polo. Calle Arroyo de Santodomingo, 1–3, 37008 Salamanca. ☎ **923-21-11-77.** 38 units. 14,500 ptas. ($87) double; 27,500 ptas. ($165) suite. AE, MC, V. Parking 1,300 ptas. ($7.80).

In the historic center, this hotel was built upon the ruins of an 11th-century church in the mid-1990s. Some of the Romanesque architectural elements have been incorporated into the contemporary building, which makes it more atmospheric. In spite of that, the small rooms are a bit sterile, but comfortable. Many open onto views of the cathedral of Salamanca, and they are grabbed first, of course. An on-site restaurant serves Castilian cuisine, and amenities include room service, laundry, and a concierge. The hotel lies at the intersection of Paseo del Rector Esperabé and avenida Reyes de España.

INEXPENSIVE

Hostal Laguna. Consuelo, 19, 37001 Salamanca. ☎/fax **923-21-87-06.** 13 units (6 with bathroom). 4,280 ptas. ($25.70) double without bathroom, 5,350 ptas. ($32.10) double with bathroom. MC, V.

This unpretentious hotel lies in the center of the historic core of Salamanca, close to both cathedrals and next to the Torre del Clavero. It is also near Plaza Mayor and the university. Its facade is traditional, with distinctive balustrades, and the interior has been recently renovated with spartan but large, comfortable, and clean bedrooms.

Each comes with a simple but good bed, either a twin or double. A few units have cramped bathrooms with shower stalls.

Hostal Plaza Mayor. Plaza del Corrillo, 20, 37002 Salamanca. ☎ **923-26-20-20.** Fax 923-21-75-48. 19 units. A/C TV TEL. 8,500 ptas. ($51) double. MC, V. Parking 1,500 ptas. ($9).

If you're in town mainly to sightsee and dine out, and don't want to spend much on a room, make this hostal your number one choice. A modest establishment, it offers great value for clean, comfortable, small rooms. Each has an immaculately maintained private bathroom with a shower. The location is one of the finest in the city, right at the Plaza Mayor opposite the church of St. Martin. The four-story building has been a hotel only since 1996, and it's quickly being discovered by bargain hunters. There is limited room service, plus a restaurant on the second floor. However, we've never dined there as we're always lured away by the tapas bars in the vicinity of the Plaza Mayor.

✪ **Hotel Don Juan.** Calle Quintana, 6, 37001 Salamanca. ☎ **923-26-14-73.** Fax 23-262-475. E-mail: hoteldonjuan@wanadoo.es. 16 units. A/C TV TEL. 9,000 ptas. ($54) double. MC, V. Parking 1,000 ptas. ($6) nearby.

For the serious budget traveler, this little family hotel right off the landmark Plaza Mayor is a gem. In the center of Salamanca's Zona Monumental, it's in a restored 200-year-old landmark building with a granite facade of colorful balconies. The decade-old hotel has a completely modernized interior that is light and airy. You're given a warm welcome by the owners, the Berrocal family. The rooms are small but clean and comfortable with tasteful decor. All the bathrooms are well maintained. If available, opt for a room with a balcony overlooking the cathedral. At the 24-hour cafeteria you can order breakfast in the morning or snacks throughout the day; there is also limited room service, laundry, and a concierge.

WHERE TO DINE

✪ **Chez Victor.** Espoz y Mina, 26. ☎ **923-21-31-23.** Reservations required. Main courses 2,000–3,500 ptas. ($12–$21); fixed-price menu 6,000 ptas. ($36). AE, DC, MC, V. Tues–Sun 2–3:30pm; Tues–Sat 9–11:30pm. Closed Aug. FRENCH BASQUE.

Set within the historic center of town, this is the most glamorous restaurant around. Its food is easily the best in town, as the owner-chef Victoriano Salvador spent some 15 years in France learning and perfecting his innovative cuisine. He returned home to open this restaurant, which won the only star Michelin has ever granted to a Salamanca restaurant. Amid monochromatic and deliberately understated modern decor, you'll enjoy dishes prepared with market-fresh ingredients.

Specialties include freshly prepared fish—perhaps sea wolf in black squid sauce, broiled turbot in a hot vinaigrette sauce, or, even better, bluefin tuna steak in sesame seeds. Try the veal médaillons in lemon sauce or, if it's offered, ribs of pork stuffed with prunes and served with a honey-mustard sauce. Despite the modernity of the cuisine, the portions are ample and well suited to Spanish tastes.

Restaurant Chapeau. Gran Via, 20. ☎ **923-26-57-95.** Reservations recommended. Main courses 2,100–3,000 ptas. ($12.60–$18); fixed-price menu 3,200 ptas. ($19.20). AE, DC, MC, V. Daily 1–4pm and 8:30pm–midnight. INTERNATIONAL.

Set on the main street of Salamanca in a stone-sided building erected around 1900, this is a well-managed, socially prominent restaurant that has hosted most of the political and business dignitaries of town at one time or another. A tactful uniformed staff works hard presenting dishes that cater to conservative Castilian tastes as well as to more international kinds of palates. In the high-ceilinged dining room you're likely to find fish imported from the coast of Cantabria, including hake, sole, and mullet, either baked, fried, roasted, or added as the main components of a savory roster of stews and soups. Meat dishes include grilled, roasted, and stewed versions of veal, pork, beef, and chicken, any of which might be preceded with salads, pastas, soups, or an Iberian version of *carpaccio* (raw, thin-sliced beef) drizzled with olive oil and fresh herbs.

Río de la Plata. Plaza del Peso, 1. ☎ **923-21-90-05.** Reservations recommended. Main courses 1,200–5,000 ptas. ($7.20–$30); *menú del día* 2,500 ptas. ($15). MC, V. Tues–Sun 1:30–3:30pm and 8pm–12:30am. Closed July. CASTILIAN.

This tiny basement restaurant, 2 blocks south of Plaza Mayor on a small side square formed by the junction of Plaza Poeta Iglesia and calle San Justo, has thrived since 1958. The kitchen uses fresh ingredients, preparing a traditional but simple *cocida castellana* (Castilian stew), house-style sole, roast baby goat, many varieties of fish, and pungently flavored sausages. Although modest, the place serves good-quality dishes. The linen is crisply ironed and the service usually impeccable. On a wintry night in Salamanca, this is one of the most inviting places in the city, with its cozy dark wood and fireplace. Locals fill up the place every night, which is endorsement enough.

Trento. San Pablo, 58–64. ☎ **923-26-18-18.** Reservations recommended. Main courses 2,000–2,500 ptas. ($12–$15); set menu 2,500 ptas. ($15). AE, DC, MC, V. Daily 1:30–4pm and 8:30–11:30pm. CASTILIAN/BASQUE/NAVARRESE.

The town's grandest palace, the Palacio de Castellanos (see above), also contains Salamanca's most stylish restaurant, operating since 1993. The decor was inspired by 19th-century France, with old rugs and paintings of Parisian street scenes. Each table is illuminated by its own lamp. Fortunately, the chefs don't rely only on an elegant setting. You can savor the subtle balance of imaginative flavors in dishes like a heart of lettuce served with fillet of whitefish and fresh vegetables. That Spanish reliable, sweet peppers stuffed with salt cod, is especially good here, served with salmon sauce. Also of note is fillet of veal with a Périgord sauce. For dessert, try *tocillinos de cielo con frambuesa,* hearty pudding made with fresh raspberries.

SALAMANCA AFTER DARK

Don't expect a huge variety of nightlife options; this is a small-scale university town with an emphasis on undergraduate shenanigans. Your best bet is a stroll around the Plaza Mayor, where you'll pass cafes and bars that lend themselves to lingering or loitering, depending on your point of view. You might also wander onto such neighboring medieval streets as the calle de Bordedores, calle San Vicente, calle Rua Mayor, and calle Varillas, any of which offer tucked away spots for a quick caffeine or alcohol fix. Two Salamanca discos of particular note are **Disco Morgana,** calle Iscar Peira (no phone), and its better-established, more historic competitor, **Camelot,** calle Bordadores (☎ **923-21-21-82**). The latter occupies a stone monastery whose occupants 400 years ago would undoubtedly have been horrified at the goings-on within these premises that long ago echoed only with prayer and plainsong. And for a more modern spin on Salamanca's nightlife, head for the **Pub Rojo y Negro,** calle Espoz y Mina, 22 (no phone), where bouts of karaoke are interspersed with chatter, wine, whisky, and foaming mugs of Spanish beer.

AN EASY SIDE TRIP TO ALBA DE TORMES

Admirers of St. Teresa may want to make the 11-mile (18km) pilgrimage southeast of Salamanca to visit the medieval village of Alba de Tormes. Follow highway C-510, and cross a bridge with 22 arches spanning the Tormes River. Head between the Iglesia de

San Pedro and the Basilica de Santa Teresa to Plaza de Santa Teresa, where you will come upon the **Convento de las Carmelitas,** Plazuela de Santa Teresa (☎ 923-30-00-43), and the **Iglesia de Santa Teresa,** Plaza de Santa Teresa, 4. The church is a combination of Gothic, Renaissance, and baroque styles. The marble vault over the altar contains the ashes of Spain's most beloved saint, St. Teresa of Ávila, who died here in 1582. One of the two reliquaries flanking the altar is said to contain her arm; the other is said to hold the remains of her heart. Opposite the entrance door in the rear of the church is a grating through which you can look at the cell in which she died. Pope John Paul II visited Alba de Tormes in 1982 on the occasion of the 400th anniversary of St. Teresa's death. Admission is free. The complex is open Monday to Saturday 10am to 1:30pm and 4 to 7:30pm, Sunday 10am to 2pm; donations requested.

3　Zamora

40 miles (64km) N of Salamanca, 148 miles (238km) NW of Madrid

Little known to North American visitors, Zamora (pronounced Tha-*mor*-a) is the quintessential city of Old Castile, blending ancient and modern, but noted mainly for its Romanesque architecture. In fact, Zamora is often called a "Romanesque museum." A medieval frontier city, it rises up starkly from the Castilian flatlands, a reminder of the era of conquering monarchs and forgotten kingdoms.

You can explore Zamora's highlights in about 4 hours. Stroll along the main square, dusty Plaza Canovas; cross the arched Romanesque bridge from the 1300s; and take in at least some of the Romanesque churches for which the town is known, many of which date from the 12th century. The cathedral is the best example, but others include **Iglesia de la Magdalena,** rua de los Francos, and **Iglesia de San Ildefonso,** calle Ramos Carrión. You might also want to look at **Iglesia de Santa María la Nueva,** Plaza de Santa María, and **Iglesia de Santiago el Burgo,** calle Santa Clara.

The crowning achievement, however, at the far west end of Zamora, is the **Cathedral San Salvador,** Plaza Castillo o Pio XII. It is topped by a gold-and-white Eastern-looking dome. Inside, you'll find rich hangings, interesting chapels, two 15th-century Mudéjar pulpits, and intricately carved choir stalls. Later architectural styles, including Gothic, have been added to the original Romanesque features, but this indiscriminate mixing of periods is typical of Spanish cathedrals. Inside the cloister, the Museo de la Catedral features ecclesiastical art, historical documents, church documents, and an unusual collection of "Black Tapestries" dating from the 1400s. The cathedral is free but admission to the museum costs 300 ptas. ($1.80) for adults. The cathedral can generally be visited throughout the day. The museum is open April through September, Tuesday to Saturday 11am to 2pm and 5 to 8pm, Sunday 11am to 2pm, and Monday 5 to 8pm. Off-season hours are Tuesday to Saturday 9am to 2pm and 4 to 6pm, and Sunday 11am to 2pm.

ESSENTIALS

GETTING THERE　There are four trains to and from Madrid every day and two to and from La Coruña (the trips take 3 and 6 hours, respectively). The railway station is at calle Alfonso Peña (☎ 980-52-11-10), about a 15-minute walk from the edge of the old town. Follow avenida de las Tres Cruces northeast of the center of town. One-way fare from Madrid to Zamora is 3,200 ptas. ($19.20).

Thirteen to twenty-one bus connections a day from Salamanca make this the easiest way to get in and out of town. Travel time between the cities is an hour. There are seven buses a day from Madrid; the trip takes 3½ hours and costs 2,135 ptas. ($12.80) one-way. The town's bus station lies a few paces from the railway station, at calle Alfonso Peña, 3 (☎ 980-52-12-81).

Zamora is at the junction of eight different roads and highways. Most of the traffic from northern Portugal into Spain comes through Zamora. Highways headed north to León, south to Salamanca, and east to Valladolid are especially convenient. From Madrid, take the A-6 superhighway northwest toward Valladolid, cutting west on the N-VI and west again at the turnoff onto 122.

VISITOR INFORMATION   The **tourist information office** is at calle Santa Clara, 20 (☎ 980-53-18-45). It's open Monday to Friday 9am to 2pm and 5 to 7pm, Saturday and Sunday 10am to 2pm and 5 to 8pm.

SPECIAL EVENTS   Holy Week in Zamora, the week before Easter, is a celebration known throughout the country. Street processions, called *pasos,* are among the most spectacular in Spain. If you plan to visit at this time, make your hotel reservations well in advance.

WHERE TO STAY

Hostal Chiqui. Benavente, 2, 49002 Zamora. ☎ **980-53-14-80.** 14 units. TV. 4,500–5,300 ptas. ($27–$31.80) double. No credit cards.

If you're looking for a bargain and don't mind a few minor inconveniences, try this simple second-floor pension. The guest rooms are spartan but clean. No breakfast is served, but cafes are within walking distance. Chiqui is behind the post office in the northwest section of the old town, near a corner of busy calle Santa Clara.

✪ **Hostería Real de Zamora.** Cuesta de Pizarro, 7, 49027 Zamora. ☎/fax **980-53-45-45.** E-mail: hostzamora@wanadoo.es. 19 units. MINIBAR TV TEL. 10,500 ptas. ($63) double. Rates include breakfast. AE, DC, MC, V.

This most charming small hotel in town, sporting walls that date from the 1400s, occupies the long-ago headquarters of Zamora's dreaded Inquisition. (Before that, ironically, this was the site of a Jewish-owned building reputed to have been the home of the explorer Pizarro.) Today, the outstanding historical features of the building include a medieval reservoir, a patio perfect for enjoying a cup of tea or coffee, and a verdant garden along the city's medieval fortifications. An excellent example of a taste-fully modernized aristocratic villa, it stands a few steps to the west of the northern embankment of the city's most photographed bridge, the Stone Bridge. The midsize rooms contain simple but solid furnishings, including good beds, and offer safety-deposit boxes. The well-maintained bathrooms are equipped with hair dryers. If you drive to the hotel, you'll have to rely on street parking.

   Dining/Diversions: The restaurant **Pizarro,** with the air of a baronial private dining room, offers three-course fixed-price meals. Adjacent to it is the **Restaurante Hostería Real,** offering basically the same menu and a bar.

   Amenities: 24-hour room service, laundry, baby-sitting.

✪ **Parador Turístico de Zamora.** Plaza de Viriato, 5, 49001 Zamora. ☎ **980-51-44-97.** Fax 980-53-00-63. 52 units. A/C MINIBAR TV TEL. 15,000–17,000 ptas. ($90–$102) double; 17,500–20,000 ptas. ($105–$120) suite. AE, DC, MC, V. Parking 1,000 ptas. ($6).

The site of this parador has always held a legendary role in Zamora. Originally forti-fied as an *Alcazaba* by the Moors during their occupation of Zamora, it was later expanded into a palace during the late Middle Ages. Most of that original monument was demolished and rebuilt upon its ancient foundations in 1459 by the Count of Alva y Aliste, and today the structure retains the severe, high-ceilinged dignity of its

15th-century Gothic form. Renovated by the Spanish government in the late 1960s, it is today one of the most beautiful paradors in Spain, and obviously the best and most tranquil place to stay in town.

Set 2 blocks south of Plaza Mayor, near the junction of Plaza de Viriato and calle Ramos Carrión, the parador is richly decorated with medieval armor, antique furniture, tapestries, and potted plants. In winter, glass partitions close off a large inner patio centered on an antique well; baronial fireplaces provide much-appreciated warmth. Midsize bedrooms are white walled, well maintained, and tastefully decorated with conservative furniture, including beds with firm mattresses. The tidy bathrooms are equipped with hair dryers.

Dining/Diversions: A sumptuous but rustic dining room has a view of the swimming pool and surrounding countryside. There's also a cozy bar.

Amenities: Room service, laundry/valet, baby-sitting, pool, and a gym with sauna.

WHERE TO DINE

París. Avenida de Portugal, 14. ☎ **980-51-43-25.** Reservations recommended. Main dishes 1,600–2,600 ptas. ($9.60–$15.60); *menú del día* 1,800 ptas. ($10.80). AE, DC, MC, V. Mon–Sat 1–6pm and 8pm–midnight. SPANISH/INTERNATIONAL.

This elegantly decorated, air-conditioned restaurant is known for its fish, often made with a regionally inspired twist. Specialties include vegetable flan, braised oxtail, Zamora-style clams, and a delectable hake. Dishes, of course, change with the seasons. Most critics rate this restaurant number one in town. It is on the main traffic artery (avenida de Portugal) that funnels traffic south to Salamanca.

Serafín. Plaza Maestro Haedo, 10. ☎ **980-53-14-22.** Main courses 1,200–2,800 ptas. ($7.20–$16.80); fixed-price menus 1,850–3,000 ptas. ($11.10–$18). AE, DC, MC, V. Daily 1–4:30pm and 8:30pm–midnight. SPANISH.

At the northeast edge of the old town, about a block south of the busy traffic hub of Plaza Alemania and Avenida de Alfonso IX, this air-conditioned haven with an attractive bar makes a relaxing retreat from the sun. The specialties change with the season but might include seafood soup Serafín, paella, fried hake, Iberian ham, and a savory *cocido* (stew).

ZAMORA AFTER DARK

Calle Los Herreros, also called calle de Vinos, contains more bars per square foot than any street in Zamora—about 16 of them in all. Each is willing to accommodate a stranger with a leisurely glass of wine or beer and a selection of tapas. Calle Los Herreros is a narrow street at the southern end of the old town, about 2 blocks north of the Duero River, within the shadow of the *Ayuntamiento Viejo* (Old Town Hall), 1 block south of Plaza Mayor.

4 León

203 miles (327km) NW of Madrid, 122 miles (196km) N of Salamanca

Once the leading city of Christian Spain, this old cathedral town was the capital of a centuries-old empire that declined after uniting with Castile. León today is the gateway from Old Castile to the northwestern routes of Galicia. It is a sprawling city, but nearly everything of interest to visitors—monuments, restaurants, and hotels—can be covered on foot once you arm yourself with a good map.

Once the heartbeat of a great kingdom, today León is a sleepy provincial city off the beaten track. But its wealth of old monuments, its top-notch accommodations, and a certain regal quality in the air still make the town feel like a capital.

Outlying mountain villages offer their own architectural gems, fine ski runs, and tasty concoctions of local trout and meat. Also, the region is particularly renowned for its soft-spoken, pristine Castilian accent. In sum, León is an excellent place to experience the tranquillity of the Spanish heartland, as well as an obligatory stop for students of medieval architecture.

ESSENTIALS

GETTING THERE   León has good rail connections to the rest of Spain—11 trains daily from Madrid. The station, Estación del Norte, Avenida de Astorga, 2 (☎ 987-27-02-02), is on the western bank of the Bernesga River. Cross the bridge near Plaza de Guzmán el Bueno. The *rápido* train from Madrid takes 5 hours; the TALGO, 4 hours. A one-way ticket from Madrid ranges from 3,200 to 4,400 ptas. ($19.20 to $26.40), but travelers should be aware there are many different types of tickets, which change regularly.

Most of León's buses arrive and depart from the Estación de Autobuses, Paseo Ingeniero Saenz de Miera (☎ 987-21-10-00). Three to five buses per day link León with Zamora and Salamanca, and there are 11 per day from Madrid (trip time: 4½ hours). A one-way ticket on a direct regular bus from Madrid is 2,610 ptas. ($15.65), rising to 4,200 ptas. ($25.20) for the *supra* (comfortable) service.

León lies at the junction of five major highways coming from five different regions of Spain. From Madrid's periphery, head northwest on the N-VI superhighway toward La Coruña. At Benavente, bear right onto the N-630.

VISITOR INFORMATION   The **tourist information office** is at Plaza de Regla, 4 (☎ 987-23-70-82). It's open Monday to Friday 9am to 1:30pm and 5 to 7pm, Saturday and Sunday 10am to 2pm and 4 to 8pm.

EXPLORING THE TOWN

✪ **Catedral de León (Santa Maria de Regla).** Plaza de Regla. ☎ **987-87-57-70.** Admission to cathedral free; cloisters and museum 500 ptas. ($3). Cathedral, daily 8:30am–1:30pm and 4–7pm; cloisters and museum, Mon–Sat 9:30am–1:30pm and 4–7pm. Bus: 4.

The usual cathedral elements are virtually eclipsed here by the awesome **stained-glass windows**—some 125 in all (plus 57 oculi), dating from the 13th century. They are so heavy they have strained the walls of the cathedral. Look for a 15th-century altarpiece

---

Luminous in León

In the church-building sweepstakes of the Middle Ages, every Gothic cathedral vied to distinguish itself with some superlative trait. Milan Cathedral was the biggest, Chartres had the most inspiring stained-glass windows, Palma de Majorca had the largest rose window, and so on.

Structurally speaking, the boldest cathedral was at León. This edifice set the record for the highest proportion of window space, with stained-glass windows soaring 110 feet to the vaulted ceiling, framed by the slenderest of columns, occupying 18,000 square feet, or almost all the space where you'd expect the walls to be.

The roof is held up not by walls, but by flying buttresses on the exterior. Inside, the profusion of light and the illusion of weightlessness astonish even medievalists. The architects Juan Pérez and Maestro Enrique, who designed the cathedral in the 13th century, were, in effect, precursors of Mies van der Rohe, 7 centuries before the age of steel girders draped with plate-glass curtain walls.

depicting the Entombment in the Capilla Mayor, as well as a Renaissance trascoro by Juan de Badajoz. The nave dates from the 13th and 14th centuries; the Renaissance vaulting is much later. Almost as interesting as the stained-glass windows are the cloisters, dating in part from the 13th and 14th centuries and containing faded frescoes and Romanesque and Gothic tombs; some capitals are carved with starkly lifelike scenes. Visitors can also tour a museum containing valuable art and artifacts, including a Bible from the 10th century, notable sculptures, and a collection of romantic images of the Virgin Mary. The cathedral is on the edge of the old city, 7 blocks east of the town's most central square, Plaza de Santo Domingo.

Panteón y Museos de San Isidoro. Plaza San Isidoro, 4. ☎ **987-22-96-08.** Admission 400 ptas. ($2.40). Sept–June, Mon–Sat 10am–1:30pm and 4–6:30pm, Sun 10am–1:30pm; July–Aug, Mon–Sat 9am–2pm and 3–8pm, Sun 9am–2pm. Bus: 4 or 9.

This church, a short walk northwest of the cathedral, was dedicated to San Isidoro de Sevilla in 1063 and contains 23 tombs of Leónese kings. One of the first Romanesque buildings in León and Castile, it was embellished by Ferdinand I's artists. The columns are magnificent, the capitals splendidly decorated, and the vaults covered with murals from the 12th century. Unique in Spain, the Treasury holds rare finds—a 10th-century Scandinavian ivory, an 11th-century chalice, and an important collection of 10th- to 12th-century cloths from Asia. The library contains many ancient manuscripts and rare books, including a Book of Job from 951, a Visigothic Bible, an 1162 Bible, plus dozens of miniatures.

SHOPPING

Something about the city's antique architecture seems to encourage the acquisition of old-time handcrafts made from time-honored material like terra-cotta, stone, copper, wrought-iron, and leather. Plaza de la Catedral and the streets that radiate out from it are particularly rich in battered, overcrowded kiosks with this type of artifact, and part of the fun of a trip within the city's historic core involves acquiring several pieces of it. For a more up-to-date roster of shopping options, consider a quick march through the vast stacks within Léon's biggest department store, **Corte Inglés,** Fray Luis de Leon, 21 (☎ **987-26-31-00**). Inside, look for men's and women's clothing, books and gift items, and hints of the high-fashion priorities of cities as far away as Barcelona and Madrid.

WHERE TO STAY

Guzmán El Bueno. López Castrillón, 6, 24003 León. ☎ **987-23-64-12.** 26 units. 5,500 ptas. ($33) double. No credit cards. Walk up calle Generalísimo from Plaza de Santo Domingo, turn left onto calle de Cid; López Castrillón is a pedestrian-only street, branching off to the right.

The most inexpensive accommodation we recommend in León is the no-frills Guzmán El Bueno, on the second floor of a centrally located boardinghouse. In all, it's a safe destination, widely known among international student travelers drawn to its low prices. Some rooms have phones; all are clean with decent beds. Be warned in advance that the staff speaks only Spanish. Parking is available along the streets within walking distance of the hotel.

Hotel Alfonso V. Padre Isla, 1, 24002 León. ☎ **987-22-09-00.** Fax 987-22-12-44. www. lesein.es/alfonsov. E-mail: alfonov@lesein.es. 57 units. A/C MINIBAR TV TEL. 17,900 ptas. ($107.40) double; 29,000 ptas. ($174) suite. AE, DC, MC, V. Parking 1,300 ptas. ($7.80).

Although we infinitely prefer the parador, this hotel in the heart of the city is less expensive and is famed for its classic contemporary decor. The pre-Franco hotel has been dramatically modernized with a stunning sculpture-filled lobby that rises seven wavy floors to a glass roof. The rooms, mostly medium in size, are a study in post-modernism, fitted with French windows, excellent soundproofing, and firm beds with luxury mattresses, plus tiled bathrooms with plush towels and hair dryers.

Dining/Diversions: The restaurant, which attracts the business leaders of the community, is known for its natural dishes using the finest local produce. Tables are spaced far enough apart so you don't hear others' conversations. The bar is an international rendezvous point.

Amenities: Room service, concierge, laundry/dry cleaning.

Hotel Paris. Calle Ancha, 18, 24003 Leon. ☎ **987-23-86-00.** Fax 987-27-15-72. E-mail: hparis@lesein.es. 56 units. MINIBAR TV TEL. 11,050 ptas. ($66.30) double; 13,000 ptas. ($78) suite. AE, DC, MC, V.

Lying between the old and new towns, this hotel east of plaza Santo Domingo has belle époque touches and a warm, inviting atmosphere. Consider it a cozy nest for your León sightseeing. A restored 19th-century building, the hotel has a marble-floored lobby leading to comfortable surroundings. Bedrooms are more intimate than spacious, but comfortable with fine bed linens and good bathroom facilities with showers. Floral bedspreads and the occasional antique add grace notes. Those old photographs in the public rooms are not just of Paris—the hotel's namesake—but other European cities as well, including León. Limited room service is available, as well as laundry service.

Hotel Quindós. Gran Vía de San Marcos, 38, 24002 León. ☎ **987-23-62-00.** Fax 987-24-22-01. www.hotelquindos.com. E-mail: hotelquindos@hotelquindos.com. 96 units. TV TEL. 11,900 ptas. ($71.40) double. AE, DC, MC, V. Bus: 4 or 9.

This functional hotel has been tastefully decorated with modern paintings to spruce it up considerably. The snug, comfortable, well-maintained rooms are a good value, each fitted with a firm mattress and a small but efficient tiled bathroom. The hotel has two restaurants, one with menus typical of Old Castile, another more elegant dining room serving international cuisine. You can enjoy baked fish of the day, sirloin with onion jelly, or marinated pigeon. The Quindós is 3 blocks south of Plaza de San Marcos, in the central commercial district in the northwest quadrant of the old town.

✪ Parador San Marcos. Plaza de San Marcos, 7, 24001 León. ☎ **987-23-73-00.** Fax 987-23-34-58. E-mail: leonparadorsanmarcos@es. 260 units. MINIBAR TV TEL. 23,000 ptas. ($138) double; 55,000 ptas. ($330) suite. AE, DC, MC, V. Free parking.

This 16th-century former monastery with its celebrated plateresque facade is one of the most spectacular hotels in Spain. The government has remodeled it at great expense, installing extravagant authentic antiques and quality reproductions as well as improving the facade. Before its monastery days, the old *hostal* used to put up pilgrims bound for Santiago de Compostela in the 12th century. The parador also contains a church with a scallop-shell facade and an archaeological museum. The good-size guest rooms are sumptuous, each with luxury mattresses and a bathroom equipped with a hair dryer. The parador is northwest of the cathedral on the outskirts of the old town, on the east bank of the Bernesga River.

Dining: The hotel restaurant serves adequate Spanish and regional cuisine, including breakfast, and lunch and dinner 12:30 to 2pm and 9:30pm to 12:30am.

Amenities: Room service, concierge, baby-sitting, laundry and dry-cleaning service, conference rooms.

WHERE TO DINE

Alborada. Condesa de Sagasta, 24. ☎ **987-22-19-12.** Reservations recommended. Main courses 1,500–2,200 ptas. ($9–$13.20); *menú del día* 1,800 ptas. ($10.80). AE, MC, V. Tues–Sun 1–4pm and 8:30pm–midnight. Bus: 4 or 9. SPANISH.

This contemporary restaurant much favored by local residents is outside the city center, a 15-minute walk northwest of the cathedral adjacent to the Parador San Marcos. Within a modern interior the owner supervises the preparation of fresh fish and meat dishes loosely based on French and Spanish models. Signature dishes include *lubina al horno* (oven baked whitefish), fillet steak with pepper, hake casserole, and roast duck in orange sauce. A long wine list is available, and the room is air-conditioned.

Bodega Regia. General Mola, 9. ☎ **987-21-31-73.** Reservations not needed. Main courses 2,000–2,500 ptas. ($12–$15); set menu 2,200 ptas. ($13.20). AE, DC, MC, V. Mon–Sat 1:30–4pm and 9pm–midnight. Closed Jan 6–17 and 15 days in Sept. CASTILIAN.

Our favorite *bodega* in León lies within an easy walk of the cathedral in a restored 14th-century building. There is a central garden patio, with a rustic stone and clay floor emphasized by stone arches. A variety of tropical plants makes for a warm, inviting atmosphere where architectural touches of the medieval period have been retained. We salute the chef's attempt to keep his prices in line while offering an array of good fresh food. The menu includes *embutidos de León,* a local sausage that is extremely tasty, as well as *pimientos de Bierzo con vinagre de Jerez,* red peppers grilled in a sherry-vinegar dressing. Another popular sausage is *morcilla de León y picadillo,* an exceptional treat. *Bacalao a la leonesa* is salt cod cooked with herbs and proper seasonings, and *alubias con espinaca* is an exceptional vegetable dish of white beans and spinach.

Casa Pozo. Plaza San Marcelo, 15. ☎ **987-22-30-39.** Reservations recommended. Main courses 3,000–3,500 ptas. ($18–$21); fixed-price menus 1,500 ptas. ($9). AE, DC, MC, V. Daily 1–4pm; Mon–Sat 8–11:30pm. Closed Christmas. Bus: 4 or 9. SPANISH.

Two blocks south of the busy traffic hub of Plaza Santo Domingo and across from city hall, this restaurant is a longtime favorite with locals who appreciate its unassuming style and flavorful cuisine. Regulars call owner Gabriel del Pozo Alvarez "Pin," and he's the reason behind the success of the place. Specialties, all made from fresh ingredients, include peas with salty ham, shrimp with asparagus, *estofados* (stews), roast pork or lamb with herbs and spices, and a delicate smothered sole. Twelve varieties of fresh fish are available and the restaurant offers an excellent selection of Rioja wines.

Formela. Grand Via San Marcos, 36. ☎ **987-22-45-34.** Reservations recommended. Main courses 2,000–2,500 ptas. ($12–$15); set menu 2,200 ptas. ($13.20). AE, DC, MC, V. Mon–Sat 1:30–3:30pm and 9–11:30pm. CASTILIAN.

Five minutes from the historical district and next to the Parador San Marcos, La Formela serves the finest cuisine in León, and has the best service too. It is the smaller of two restaurants in Hotel Quindós. Located on the second floor, this restaurant is warm and inviting. The owner, Jaime Quindós, is a well-known art collector and former gallery owner. Walls are hung with contemporary paintings and a collection of antique Italian ornaments. There is an extensive collection of wines from throughout Spain but it is the cuisine that keeps diners happy. We have been consistently delighted by Señor Quindós's oft-renewed repertoire of dishes. The menu includes *cesina de León,* one of the most delectable of local sausages, along with *revuelto de León con patatas* or sautéed fresh vegetables with potatoes. The *ciervo estofado,* or venison casserole, is an alluring choice, as is *lubina a la espalda,* or fillet of grilled whitefish. For dessert, the chefs will prepare you a crêpe suzette or serve you *natillas caseras,* a Castilian-style pudding.

Mesón Leonés del Racimo de Oro. Caño Badillo, 2. ☎ **987-25-75-75.** Reservations required. Main courses 2,000–2,600 ptas. ($12–$15.60). AE, DC, MC, V. Wed–Sat 1:45–4pm and 9pm–midnight; Sun 1:45–4pm. CASTILIAN.

Behind Plaza Mayor and beside the cathedral, this bodega is housed in a structure from the early 1700s, and even it was built on older foundations. As such, it is one of the two or three oldest inns in León, and a lot of food and wine have been consumed on this site over the centuries. The building is what the Spanish call a *mesón típico* (house built in the regional style), and its tables overlook a patio. The food is consistently good, specializing in a regional cuisine—*mollejas con rabo de toro* (sweet meats with oxtail), for example, or *merluza* (hake) house style. You might begin with an appetizer of Serrano ham or clams, then follow with one of the roast meats, such as roast suckling lamb cooked in a wood-fired clay oven. The service is attentive.

LEÓN AFTER DARK

Few other cities in Spain evoke the mystery of the Middle Ages like León. To best appreciate the old-fashioned eloquence of the city, after dark wander around the Plaza Mayor, the edges of which are peppered with simple cafes and bars. None is particularly different from its neighbor, but overall the effect is rich, evocative, and wonderfully conducive to conversation and romance. Our favorite of the lot is the **Bar Universale,** Plaza Mayor (no phone), which serves tapas, sherries, wines, and beers in a setting that's particularly evocative and mellow. If your taste involves going out dancing, consider everybody's favorite León disco, **Tropicana,** calle José Maria Fernandez, 56 (☎ **987-25-70-35**). It's open nightly except Monday as a bar and cranks up the recorded music beginning at 10pm to a huge crowd of dance-a-holics.

5 Valladolid

125 miles (201km) NW of Madrid, 83 miles (134km) SE of León

From the 13th century until its eventual decay in the early 17th century, Valladolid was a royal city and an intellectual center attracting saints and philosophers. Isabella and Ferdinand were married here, Philip II was born here, and Columbus died here on May 19, 1506, broken in spirit and body after Isabella had died and Ferdinand refused to reinstate him as a governor of the Indies.

Valladolid is bitterly cold in winter, sweltering in summer. Today, after years of decline, the city is reviving economically and producing, among other things, flour, ironware, and cars. Consequently, it's polluted and noisy, and many of the older buildings have been replaced by more modern, utilitarian ones, although there are still many attractions remaining.

From the tourist office (see below), you can pick up a map that marks all the major monuments of Valladolid. These attractions can be covered on foot, although you may want to take a taxi to the two most distant points recommended: the Museo Nacional de Escultura and the Museo Oriental.

ESSENTIALS

GETTING THERE   Flights to Valladolid land at Vallanubla Airport, Highway N-601 (☎ **983-41-54-00**), a 15-minute taxi ride from the center of town. Aviaco routes daily flights to and from Barcelona and Madrid.

Valladolid is well serviced by 14 daily trains to and from Madrid (trip time: 3 to 4½ hours). A one-way fare is 1,900 to 3,200 ptas. ($11.40 to $19.20). Other cities with train links to Valladolid include Salamanca (10 trains per day) and Burgos (16 trains per day). The train station (Estación del Norte), calle Recondo, s/n, by the

Plaza Colon (☎ **983-20-02-02**), is about 1 mile south of the historic center of town, 1 block southwest of Campo Grande park.

The bus station is an 8-minute walk from the railway station, at Puente Colgante (☎ **983-23-63-08**), at the southern edge of town. There are more than a dozen buses every day to and from Madrid, 2¼ hours away. Eight buses per day arrive from Zamora (trip time: 1¼ hours), and three buses per day from Burgos (trip time: 1½ hours).

Valladolid lies at the center of the rectangle created by Burgos, León, Segovia, and Salamanca and is connected to each with good highways. From Madrid, driving time is about 2¼ hours. Take superhighway A-6 northwest from Madrid, turning north on 403.

VISITOR INFORMATION   The **tourist information office** is at calle de Santiago, 19 (☎ **983-34-40-13**). Hours are Monday to Friday 9am to 2pm and 5 to 9pm, Saturday and Sunday 10am to 2pm and 3 to 8pm.

SEEING THE SIGHTS

✪ **Museo Nacional de Escultura (National Museum of Sculpture).** Colegio de San Gregorio, calle Cadenas de San Gregorio, 1. ☎ **983-26-79-77.** Admission 400 ptas. ($2.40) adults, 200 ptas. ($1.20) students, free for children under 18 and adults over 65. Tues–Sat 10am–2pm and 4–6pm; Sun 10am–2pm.

Located near Plaza de San Pablo, this museum displays a magnificent collection of gilded polychrome sculpture, an art form that reached its pinnacle in Valladolid. The figures were first carved from wood, then painted with consummate skill and grace to assume lifelike dimensions. See especially the works by Alonso Berruguete (1480–1561), son of Pedro, one of Spain's great painters. From 1527 to 1532 the younger Berruguete labored over the altar of the Convent of San Benito—a masterpiece now housed here. In particular, see his *Crucifix with the Virgin and St. John* in Room II and his *St. Sebastian and the Sacrifice of Isaac* in Room III. Works by Juan de Juni and Gregorio Fernández are also displayed.

After visiting the galleries, explore the two-story cloisters. The upper level is florid, with jutting gargoyles and fleurs-de-lis. See the chapel where the confessor to Isabella I (Fray Alonso de Burgos) was buried—and be horrified by the gruesome sculpture *Death.*

Cathedral. Calle Arrive, 1. ☎ **983-30-43-62.** Free admission to Cathedral; museum, 350 ptas. ($2.10). Cathedral and museum, Tues–Fri 10am–1:30pm and 4:30–7pm; Sat–Sun 10am–2pm.

In 1580 Philip II commissioned Juan de Herrera, architect of El Escorial, to construct this monument in the city where he was born. When Philip died in 1598, work came to a stop for 18 years. Alberto Churriguera resumed construction, drawing up more flamboyant plans, especially for the exterior, in an unharmonious contrast to the severe lines of his predecessor. The classical, even sober, interior conforms more with Herrera's designs. A highlight is the 1551 altarpiece in the main apsidal chapel, the work of Juan de Juni. Art critics have commented that his polychrome figures seem "truly alive." The cathedral is in the heart of the city, east of Plaza Mayor and north of Plaza de Santa Cruz.

Iglesia de San Pablo. Plaza San Pablo, 4. ☎ **983-35-17-48.** Free admission. Daily 7:30–9:30am, 12:30–2pm, and 7–9:30pm.

Once a 17th-century Dominican monastery, San Pablo is very impressive with its Isabelline-Gothic facade. Flanked by two towers, the main entrance supports levels of lacy stone sculpture. The church lies 6 blocks north of the cathedral, 1 block south of busy avenida Santa Teresa. Mass is held daily, with eight masses on Sunday.

Museo Oriental. Paseo de Filipinos, 7. ☎ **983-30-68-00.** Admission 400 ptas. ($2.40), free for children 9 and under. Mon–Sat 4–7pm; Sun and holidays 10am–2pm.

Located in the Royal College of the Augustinian Fathers, near Campo Grande park, the museum has 14 rooms: 10 Chinese and 4 Filipino. It has the best collection of Asian art in Spain, with bronzes from the 7th century B.C. to the 18th century A.D., wooden carvings, 100 fine porcelain pieces, paintings on paper and silk from the 12th century to the 19th, and ancient Chinese coins, furniture, jade, and ivory. In the Filipino section, ethnological and primitive art is represented by shields and arms. Eighteenth-century religious art can be admired in extraordinary ivories, embroideries, paintings, and silversmiths' work. Popular art of the 19th century includes bronzes, musical instruments, and statuary.

Casa de Cervantes. Calle del Rastro, s/n. ☎ **983-30-88-10.** Admission 400 ptas. ($2.40); free on Sun. Tues–Sat 9:30am–3:30pm; Sun 10am–3pm.

Now a museum, this house was once occupied by Miguel de Cervantes, author of *Don Quixote,* who did much of his writing in Valladolid and remained here for the last years of his life. Behind its white walls the house is simply furnished, as it was in the author's day. It's half a block south of the cathedral, 2 blocks north of the city park, Campo Grande.

WHERE TO STAY

Enara. Plaza de España, 5, 47001 Valladolid. ☎ **983-30-02-11.** Fax 983-30-03-11. 24 units. TV TEL. 6,800 ptas. ($40.80) double. AE, MC, V. Closed Dec 24–25.

Located about a quarter mile south of the cathedral, near the junction of avenida 2 de Mayo and Paseo Miguel Iscar, Enara is arguably the best inexpensive accommodation in Valladolid. Its central location is backed up by contemporary, pleasantly furnished guest rooms, which are small but offer good comfort because of the fine beds and the immaculately kept bathrooms. The decoration is in the typical Castilian style with some antiques. There is no restaurant, but a continental breakfast is offered, and you'll be near many low-cost dining rooms and cafes. Originally built in the 19th century as a private house, it was converted into a hotel in the mid-1970s. Two of its three stories are devoted to simple but well-maintained rooms, and the ground floor contains the breakfast area. Parking is available along the Plaza de España.

Felipe IV. Calle de Gamazo, 16, 47004 Valladolid. ☎ **983-30-70-00.** Fax 983-30-86-87. 131 units. A/C MINIBAR TV TEL. 15,500 ptas. ($93) double; 28,000 ptas. ($168) suite. AE, DC, MC, V. Parking 1,600 ptas. ($9.60).

When it was built the Felipe IV was one of the grandest hotels in the city, although the Meliá (see below) has since usurped that position. Each of its midsized bedrooms is modernized, guaranteeing its ranking as a solidly acceptable establishment. A garage provides parking for motorists. The hotel is south of the busy traffic hub of Plaza de Madrid, a few blocks north of the rail station, near the eastern edge of the city park, Campo Grande. It attracts many business travelers, as a visit to the hotel dining room at night will reveal. A standard Spanish cuisine is served—nothing special.

Hotel Meliá Parque. Joaquin Garcia Morato, 17, 47007 Valladolid. ☎ **800/336-3542** in the U.S., or 983-22-00-00. Fax 983-47-50-29. 178 units. A/C TV TEL. 15,500 ptas. ($93) double; 24,500 ptas. ($147) suite. AE, DC, MC, V. Parking 1,700 ptas. ($10.20).

Completed in 1982, this modern chain hotel is 2 blocks west of the rail station on the city outskirts. It's popular with business travelers unwilling to negotiate the labyrinth of Valladolid's central streets. Although an acceptable choice in every way, it is not as luxuriously appointed or as comfortable as the Olid Meliá (see below). The good-size guest rooms are comfortable and functionally furnished with no surprises and few disappointments. It also offers special rooms and facilities for people with disabilities. The hotel has a restaurant featuring average Castilian meals.

Hotel Olid Meliá. Plaza San Miguel, 10, 47003 Valladolid. ☎ **800/336-3542** in the U.S., or 983-35-72-00. Fax 983-33-68-28. 221 units. A/C MINIBAR TV TEL. 15,000–18,300 ptas. ($90–$109.80) double; from 29,000 ptas. ($174) suite. AE, DC, MC, V. Parking 2,200 ptas. ($13.20).

Set in the heart of the historic zone about 5 blocks northwest of the cathedral, this is a modern hotel whose original construction in the early 1970s has been upgraded throughout the public rooms with a postmodern gloss. The good-size rooms are the most comfortable in town, filled with heavy Iberian furniture that seems to suit the hotel's neighborhood. Each unit comes with a firm mattress on a comfortable bed, plus an immaculately tiled bathroom with a hair dryer.

There's an in-house restaurant floored with cool slabs of polished stone, as well as a bar. Amenities include 24-hour room service, laundry, and baby-sitting. There is also a hairdresser/ barber on the premises, as well as a gym.

Hotel Roma. Heroes del Alcázar de Toledo, 6, 47001 Valladolid. ☎ **983-35-46-66.** Fax 983-35-54-61. 38 units. 9,000 ptas. ($54) double. MC, V. Parking 1,000 ptas. ($6).

A decent value hostelery, this two-star hotel stands close to the landmark Plaza Mayor in the center of Valladolid, and is one of the most convenient locations of any hotel in the city. Its white facade leads into a narrow reception where guests are escorted to one of the clean, comfortable, but small bedrooms. The units are well appointed and have mostly traditional pieces, graced with prints on the walls, curtains, and throw rugs, adding a more homelike touch. Bathrooms are well maintained and equipped, and a continental breakfast is served.

WHERE TO DINE

✪ **La Fragua.** Paseo de Zorrilla, 10. ☎ **983-33-87-85.** Reservations recommended. Main courses 2,000–3,500 ptas. ($12–$21). AE, DC, MC, V. Daily 1:30–4pm; Mon–Sat 9pm– midnight. Closed Aug. CASTILIAN.

You'll enjoy beautifully prepared Castilian dishes, the best in town, amid rustic decor at this restaurant just north of the rail station across busy Paseo de Zorrilla. You might begin with spicy sausage, followed by beef, chicken, or lamb, each carefully seasoned and served in generous portions. A wide variety of fish is imported daily, and the huge wine list offers many regional vintages, one of which the steward will choose for you if you request it. Dessert could include a cheese tart or a melt-in-your-mouth chocolate truffle. Owner Antonio Garrote proudly displays his culinary diplomas.

Mesón Cervantes. Rastro, 6. ☎ **983-30-61-38.** Reservations recommended. Main courses 2,000–3,000 ptas. ($12–$18). AE, DC, MC, V. Daily 9pm–midnight; Mon–Sat 1:30–4pm. Closed Aug. SPANISH/INTERNATIONAL.

Opened in 1973, this restaurant is regarded by some as the finest in the city. The owner, Alejandro, works the dining room and is capably complemented in the kitchen by his wife, Julia. Neighborhood residents favor this place for its lack of pretension and its delectable cuisine. Two particular favorites are sole with pine nuts and seasonal river crabs. Many other fish dishes, including hake and monkfish, are available. Roast suckling pig and roast lamb are also popular. Other specialties include peppers stuffed with crabmeat; tender veal scaloppini "Don Quixote," served with a piquant sauce; and *arroz con liebre* (herb-laden rice studded with chunks of roasted wild rabbit, in season). The restaurant stands beside the Casa de Cervantes, half a mile south of the cathedral.

Mesón Panero. Marina Escobar, 1. ☎ **983-30-70-19.** Reservations required. Main courses 1,800–2,600 ptas. ($10.80–$15.60); fixed-price menu 4,500 ptas. ($27). AE, DC, MC, V. Daily 1:30–4pm and 9pm–midnight. Closed Sun July–Aug. CASTILIAN/FRENCH.

The chef of this imaginative restaurant, Angel Cuadrado, can turn even the most austere traditional Castilian recipes into sensual experiences. Set near the water, this 1960s establishment lures diners with fresh fish, including a succulent brochette of sole and hake with fresh asparagus. One weekly favorite is *cocido castellano,* the famous regional stew. Roast lamb and suckling pig are also available, plus a selection of well-chosen wines. The Mesón Panero is near the Casa de Cervantes, a short walk from the tourist office.

VALLADOLID AFTER DARK

There are no great clubs to recommend in Valladolid, but that doesn't mean that the city isn't a lively, bustling place when darkness falls. Instead of grand clubs, it becomes a town of bars and pubs. **Calle del Paraíso** is in itself a virtual street of bars, with action overflowing later on to the pubby **Plaza del San Miguel.** Just enter the pub or bar that looks the most amusing with the most convivial crowd, and chances are you won't go wrong. Most of these pubs and bars cater to a younger crowd, often from the university. If you're 30 or older, you might want to patronize one of the cafes along **calle de Vincente Meliner,** especially those near Plaza Dorado.

6 Burgos

150 miles (242km) N of Madrid, 75 miles (121km) NE of Valladolid

Founded in the 9th century, this Gothic city in the Arlanzón River valley lives up to its reputation as the "cradle of Castile." Just as the Tuscans are credited with speaking the most perfect Italian, so the citizens of Burgos, with their distinctive lisp ("El Theed" for "El Cid"), supposedly speak the most eloquent Castilian.

El Cid Campeador, Spain's greatest national hero immortalized in the epic *El Cantar de Mío Cid,* is forever linked to Burgos. He was born near here and his remains lie in the city's grand cathedral.

Like all the great cities of Old Castile, Burgos declined seriously in the 16th century, only to be revived later. In 1936 during the Civil War, the right-wing city was Franco's Nationalist army headquarters.

Today, Burgos no longer enjoys its historical glory, but is a provincial city along the *meseta,* or plateau, of Spain. Dry as a desert and burning hot during the summer days, it comes alive at night and is filled with smoky cafes and dance clubs. Most of the bars, frequented by students, are in the area around the cathedral. Many of them don't start to party seriously until after 10pm, so it's a late-night town.

ESSENTIALS

GETTING THERE   Burgos is well connected to Madrid (eight trains daily make the 3½-hour trip), Barcelona (12 trains daily, 8- to 9-hour trip), the French border (nine trains daily), and Valladolid (16 trains daily). Depending on the train, one-way fares from Madrid range from 3,400 ptas. ($20.40); from Barcelona, 5,000 ptas. ($30); and from Valladolid, 1,700 ptas. ($10.20). The Burgos railway station is at the terminus of avenida de Conde Guadalhorce, half a mile southwest of the center. To get here, head for the major traffic hub in Plaza Castilla, then walk due south across the Arlazón River. For train information or a ticket, call ☎ **947-20-91-31.**

Between 12 and 17 buses a day make the 3-hour trip up from Madrid, and two or three buses per day make the 7½-hour trip from Barcelona. A one-way fare from

Madrid costs 1,955 ptas. ($11.75); 4,960 ptas. ($29.75) from Barcelona. The bus depot in Burgos is at calle Miranda (☎ **947-28-88-55**). Calle Miranda intersects the large Plaza de Vega, due south of (and across the river from) the cathedral.

Burgos is well connected to its neighbors by a network of highways, but its routes to and from Barcelona (6 hours away) are especially wide and modern. The road from Barcelona changes its name several times, from the A-2 to the A-68 to the E-4, but it is a superhighway all the way. From Madrid, follow the N-I north for about 3 hours; the highway is fast but less modern than the road from Barcelona.

VISITOR INFORMATION   The **tourist information office** is at Plaza Alonso Martínez, 7 (☎ **947-20-18-46**). It's open Monday to Friday 9am to 2pm and 5 to 7pm, Saturday and Sunday 10am to 2pm and 5 to 8pm.

EXPLORING THE TOWN

✪ **Catedral de Santa María.** Plaza de Santa María. ☎ **947-20-47-12.** Admission to chapels, cloisters, and treasury 400 ptas. ($2.40) adults; 250 ptas. ($1.50) students and seniors; 100 ptas. (60¢) children under 14. Daily 9:30am–1pm and 4–7pm.

Begun in 1221, this cathedral was one of the most celebrated in Europe. Built in diverse styles, predominantly flamboyant Gothic, it took 300 years to complete. Ornamented 15th-century bell towers flank the three main doorways by John of Cologne. The 16th-century Chapel of Condestable, behind the main altar, is one of the best examples of Isabelline-Gothic architecture, richly decorated with heraldic emblems, a sculptured filigree doorway, figures of apostles and saints, balconies, and an eight-sided star stained-glass window.

Equally elegant are the two-story 14th-century cloisters, filled with fine Spanish Gothic sculpture. The cathedral's tapestries, including one well-known Gobelin, are rich in detail. In one of the chapels you'll see an old chest linked to the legend of El Cid—it was filled with gravel and used as collateral by the warrior to trick money-lenders. The remains of El Cid himself, together with those of his wife, Doña Ximena, lie under Santa María's octagonal lanternlike dome. Finally, you might want to see the elaborate 16th-century Stairway of Gold in the north transept, the work of Diego de Siloé.

The cathedral is across the Arlazón River from the railway station, midway between the river and the Citadel.

Monasterio de las Huelgas. Calle Compás de Adentro. ☎ **947-20-16-30.** Admission 650 ptas. ($3.90) adults, 250 ptas. ($1.50) students and children. Oct–Mar, Tues–Sun 1am–1:15pm and 3:30–5:15pm; Apr–Sept, Tues–Sat 10:30am–1:15pm and 3:30–5:45pm, Sun 10:30am–2:15pm.

This cloister outside Burgos has seen a lot of action. Built in the 12th century in a richly ornamented style, it was once a summer place for Castilian royalty, as well as a retreat for nuns of royal blood. Inside, the Gothic church is built in the shape of a Latin cross. Despite some unfortunate mixing of Gothic and baroque, it contains much of interest—notably some 14th- and 17th-century French tapestries. The tomb of the founder Alfonso VIII and his queen, the daughter of England's Henry II, lie in the Choir Room.

Thirteenth-century doors lead to the cloisters, dating from that century and blending Gothic and Mudéjar styles. Despite severe damage to the ceiling, the remains of Persian peacock designs are visible. The beautiful Chapter Room contains the standard of the 12th-century Las Navas de Tolora (war booty taken from the Moors), and the Museo de Ricas Telas is devoted to 13th-century costumes removed from tombs. These remarkably preserved textiles give a rare peek at medieval dress.

The monastery is a mile off the Valladolid Road (the turnoff is clearly marked). From Plaza Primo de Rivera in Burgos, buses for Las Huelgas leave every 20 minutes.

SHOPPING

A city as old and historic as Burgos is chock-a-block with emporia selling almost infinite volumes of ceramics, wood carvings, and artifacts that include fireplace bellows crafted from leather, wood, and brass or copper. Many of these shops line the edges of the city's most central square, Plaza Mayor, and the streets radiating out from it. Two in particular are especially worthwhile, with an appealing mixture of old and new artifacts inside. Consider **Antiguedades Javor,** Plaza Santiago s/n (☎ **947-23-51-60**), and its most visible competitor, **Antiguedades La Flora,** calle Huerto del Rey, 6 (☎ **947-26-71-36**).

WHERE TO STAY
EXPENSIVE

✪ **Landa Palace.** Carretera Madrid-Irun (at km 236), 09001 Burgos. ☎ **947-20-63-43.** Fax 947-12-46-76. 39 units. A/C TV TEL. 23,000–30,000 ptas. ($138–$180) double; 33,000–35,000 ptas. ($198–$210) suite. MC, V. Free parking.

One of the greatest hotels of Castile, a member of Relais & Châteaux, this hotel is some 2 miles (3km) south of Burgos on N-I. A romantic getaway, it is in a handsomely restored castle from the 1300s with later additions. Pilgrims once stopped here en route to Santiago de Compostela in Galicia, but they wouldn't recognize the grandeur of the place today. Decorated with tasteful antiques, the lobby sets the tone with its white marble and ornate coffered ceiling. Bedrooms are spacious and cozily inviting with antique decorations and tile floors. Marble bathrooms are state of the art with all the extras, including plush towels and hair dryers. Although parts of the hotel look a little worn, the graciousness of the staff compensates.

Dining: A pool with dining terrace is in the back of the hotel, serving some of the finest food in the area.

Amenities: Laundry and dry-cleaning service, room service, concierge, babysitting, currency exchange desk.

MODERATE

Hotel Almirante Bonifaz. Vitoria, 22–24, 09004 Burgos. ☎ **947-20-69-43.** Fax 947-25-64-04. www.infonegocio.com/hotelalmirante. E-mail: hotelalmirantebonifaz@infonegocio.com. 79 units. MINIBAR TV TEL. 17,700 ptas. ($106.20) double; 22,500 ptas. ($135) triple. AE, DC, MC, V. Parking 1,250 ptas. ($7.50).

Solidly comfortable, modern, and decorated with a contemporary kind of efficiency, this hotel attracts many of the city's visiting businesspeople, who appreciate its low-key charm and central location. The hotel is near the river in the commercial heart of town. All but a few of the midsize rooms are air-conditioned, and all have private bathrooms with hair dryers.

À la carte Spanish meals are served in each of the hotel's three restaurants, the most glamorous of which is **Los Sauces.** There's also a bar. The hotel offers room service (available 7am to 10pm), laundry service, baby-sitting, car rentals, and a business center.

Hotel del Cid. Plaza de Santa María, 8, 09003 Burgos. ☎ **947-20-87-15.** Fax 947-26-94-60. 50 units. TV TEL. 16,500 ptas. ($99) double; 20,000 ptas. ($120) suite. AE, DC, MC, V. Parking 1,000 ptas. ($6).

Built in 1983 by the Alzaga family, who still own and operate it, this establishment stands in front of the cathedral and beside their restaurant. The restaurant is better known than the hotel, which grew up on the site of one of the first printing presses in Spain. Decorated like a 15th-century house, it boasts 20th-century amenities, including extra-large beds and private bathrooms with hair dryers in all its guest rooms, which were refurbished in 1992.

A well-respected restaurant, **Mesón del Cid,** serves Spanish and regional cuisine, much to the delight of its frequently returning diners. Room service, a concierge, and laundry and dry-cleaning service are available.

Hotel Fernán González. Calera, 17, 09002 Burgos. ☎ **947-20-94-41.** Fax 947-27-41-21. 84 units. A/C MINIBAR TV TEL. 17,500 ptas. ($105) double; 20,000 ptas. ($120) triple. DC, MC, V. Parking 1,000 ptas. ($6).

Across the Arlanzón River from the soaring bulk of the cathedral, a half block west of Plaza de Vega, this appealing and unusual hotel incorporates a scattering of Iberian antiques and architectural oddities into its modernized decor. Built in the 1970s, it was last renovated in 1994. Several of the sitting rooms contain grandly vaulted ceilings and columns; others are efficiently tiled and filled with contemporary leather-covered armchairs and chrome-and-glass tables. The good-size guest rooms are cozy, conservative, and comfortable, with quality beds and tiled bathrooms.

The hotel's dining room serves traditional Spanish as well as international cuisine at lunch and dinner. Bar service is available throughout the several lounges and sitting areas of the street level. There's also a late-night disco.

✪ **Hotel Rice.** Avenida Reyes Católicos, 30, 09005 Burgos. ☎ **947-22-23-00.** Fax 947-22-35-50. E-mail: hotelrice@hotelrice.com. 50 units. A/C MINIBAR TV TEL. 15,300 ptas. ($91.80) double; 20,000 ptas. ($120) triple. AE, DC, MC, V.

This hotel half a mile north of the center is the town's leading boutique hotel. On the first 5 floors of a pink 11-floor structure, it is imbued with charm, grace, and character, almost like a London town house. Once you enter the British-style lobby, you'll feel snug, cozy, and comfortable, taking in the Queen Anne chairs, the marble surfaces, the antique cabinets, and the elegant fabrics. The bedrooms have elegant touches, with luxury mattresses and the best bathrooms in Burgos, all in marble with large tubs, plush towels, pedestal sinks, and hair dryers. The restaurant serves international cuisine, and the bar is one of our favorite meeting points in the city. With its grand piano, it often provides entertainment.

INEXPENSIVE

Hotel España. Paseo del Espolón, 32, 09003 Burgos. ☎ **947-20-63-40.** Fax 947-20-13-30. 69 units. TV TEL. 9,000 ptas. ($54) double; 11,500 ptas. ($69) triple. MC, V. Closed Dec 20–Jan 20.

The best budget choice in town is a 5-minute walk southeast of the cathedral and a block south of Plaza Mayor on a leafy promenade filled with sidewalk cafes and Castilians taking early evening strolls. The small guest rooms lack style and imagination but are completely comfortable nonetheless, with good beds and tidy bathrooms. The management is helpful to visitors. When the España is full, they have been known to call around to other hostelries for stranded tourists.

Hotel Norte y Londres. Plaza de Alonso Martínez, 10, 09003 Burgos. ☎ **947-26-41-25.** Fax 947-27-73-75. 48 units. TV TEL. 10,500 ptas. ($63) double. AE, MC, V. Parking 1,000 ptas. ($6).

On a pleasant square a short walk northeast of the cathedral, this hotel has traces of faded grandeur, with its leaded stained-glass windows and crystal chandeliers. The building dates from the early 20th century; it was converted into a hotel in the 1950s and has flourished ever since. Rooms are good-sized, with basic furnishings, good beds, and large bathrooms equipped with yesteryear's finest plumbing. Breakfast is the only meal served.

WHERE TO DINE

The restaurants in the heart of Burgos, surrounding the cathedral, usually feature prices that soar as high as a Gothic spire. Every menu contains the roast lamb and suckling pig known throughout the area, or you might order *entremeses variados,* an appetizer sampler of many regional specialties.

Casa Ojeda. Vitoria, 5. ☎ **947-20-90-52.** Reservations required. Main courses 1,900–3,000 ptas. ($11.40–$18). AE, DC, MC, V. Daily 1:15–4:30pm; Mon–Sat 9–11:30pm. BURGALESE.

This top-notch restaurant combines excellent Burgos fare, cozy decor, attentive service, and moderate prices. Moorish tiles and low ceilings create an inviting ambience enhanced by intimate nooks, old lanterns, and intricate trelliswork. Upstairs the restaurant is divided into two sections: one overlooking the street and the other, the Casa del Cordón, where Ferdinand and Isabella received Columbus after his second trip to America (1497). The cookery is the best in town. À la carte dishes include roast lamb, Basque-style hake, sole Harlequin, and chicken in garlic. A house specialty is *alubias con chorizo y mirocilla* (small white beans with spicy sausages).

Mesón de los Infantes. Calle Corral de los Infantes. ☎ **947-20-59-82.** Reservations recommended. Main courses 1,000–2,800 ptas. ($6–$16.80); fixed-price menu 2,000 ptas. ($12). AE, DC, MC, V. Daily noon–4:30pm and 8pm–midnight. CASTILIAN/BASQUE.

Just below the gate leading into the Plaza de Santa María, this restaurant serves good food amid elegant Castilian decor. Many of the chef's specialties are based on recipes in use in Castile for centuries. The roast suckling pig is everybody's favorite, and you can also order *cocido madrileño,* assorted shellfish, river crabs Burgalese style, and beef tail with potatoes. Kidneys are sautéed in sherry, and a wide list of game is often featured, including hare, partridge, rabbit, and pigeon. Grills and roasts are also crowd-pleasers.

Rincón de España. Nuño Rasura, 11. ☎ **947-20-59-55.** Reservations recommended. Main courses 1,400–3,000 ptas. ($8.40–$18); fixed-price menus 1,500–3,000 ptas. ($9–$18). AE, DC, MC, V. Daily 1–4pm and 8pm–midnight; closed Tues night in winter. SPANISH.

This restaurant, about 1 block southwest of the cathedral, draws many discerning visitors. You can eat in a rustic dining room or outdoors under a large awning closed off by glass when the weather threatens. The restaurant offers *platos combinados,* as well as a more extensive à la carte menu. Some special dishes include black pudding sausage with peppers, barbecued lamb cutlets with potatoes, and roast chicken with sweet peppers. The food here is good, the portions are large, and the vegetables are fresh.

A SIDE TRIP TO SANTO DOMINGO DE LA CALZADA

Some 42 miles (68km) east of Burgos, and easily visited on a day trip, lies Santo Domingo de la Calzada. The crowning achievement of the town, which grew as a stopover for pilgrims en route to Santiago de Compostela, is the 13th-century **cathedral** (☎ **941-34-00-33**), a national landmark. For the most part Gothic in style, it nevertheless contains a hodgepodge of architectural elements—Romanesque chapels, a Renaissance choir, and a freestanding baroque tower. St. Dominic, for whom the city is named, is buried in the crypt. A centuries-old legend is attached to the cathedral: Supposedly a rooster stood up and crowed after it had been cooked to protest the innocence of a pilgrim who had been accused of theft and sentenced to hang. To this day, a live cock and hen are kept in a cage up on the church wall, and you can often hear the rooster crowing at mass. The cathedral is open Monday to Saturday 10am to 6pm and 4 to 7pm on Sunday to avoid the masses. It costs 250 ptas. ($1.50) for adults, 100 ptas. (60¢) for children. Sunday is free for everyone. Motorists can reach Santo Domingo de la Calzada by following either of the traffic arteries paralleling the river, heading east from Burgos Cathedral until signs indicate N-120.

Extremadura 6

This remote westernmost region of Spain has always been known simply as "the land beyond the River Douro." It extends from the Gredos and Gata mountain ranges all the way to Andalusia, and from Castile to the Portuguese frontier. Extremadura has a varied landscape of plains and mountains, meadows with holm and cork oaks, and fields of stone and lime. Spanish Extremadura (not to be confused with the Portuguese province of Estremadura) includes the provinces of Badajoz and Cáceres.

The world knows Extremadura best as the land of the conquistadors. Famous sons included Cortés, Pizarro, Balboa, and many others less well known but also important, such as Francisco de Orellana and Hernando de Soto. These men were mostly driven by economic necessity, finding it hard to make a living in this dry, sun-parched province. The money they sent back to their native land financed mansions and public structures that stand today as monuments to their long-ago American adventures.

Many of Extremadura's older civilizations have monuments too, like the Roman ruins in Mérida, Arab ruins found in Badajoz, and medieval palaces in Cáceres.

Extremadura is a popular destination for outdoor fun. Spaniards come here to hunt, to enjoy the fishing and watersports popular in the many reservoirs, and to ride horses along ancient trails. Because summer is intensely hot here, spring and fall are the best times to visit.

1 Guadalupe

117 miles (188km) W of Toledo, 140 miles (225km) SW of Madrid

Guadalupe lies in the province of Cáceres, 1,500 feet above sea level. The village has a certain beauty and a lot of local color. Everything of interest lies within a 3-minute walk from the bus drop-off point at avenida Don Blas Perez, also known as Carretera de Cáceres.

Around the corner and a few paces downhill is the Plaza Mayor, which contains the Town Hall (where many visitors go to ask questions in lieu of a tourist office).

The village is best visited in spring, when the balconies of its white-washed houses burst into bloom with flowers. Wander at your leisure through the twisting, narrow streets, some no more than alleyways. The buildings are so close together that in summer you can walk in the shade of the steeply pitched sienna-colored tile roofs. Celebrated for its shrine to the Virgin, Guadalupe is packed with vendors and is a major outlet of the religious-souvenir industry.

GETTING THERE

There is one bus every day to and from Madrid's Estación Sur, a 3-hour ride away. The road is poor, but the route through the surrounding regions is full of savage beauty. In Guadalupe the buses park a few paces uphill from the Town Hall. Call **Empresa La Sepulvedana,** Madrid (☎ **927-530-48-00**), for schedules.

One narrow highway goes through Guadalupe. Most maps don't give it a number; look on a map in the direction of the town of Navalmoral de la Mata. From Madrid, take the narrow, winding C-401 southwest from Toledo, turning north in the direction of Navalmoral de la Mata after seeing signs for Navalmoral de la Mata and Guadalupe. Driving time from Madrid is between 3½ and 4½ hours, depending on how well you fare with the bad roads.

WHAT TO SEE & DO

Except for a handful of your basic souvenir shops around the Plaza Mayor, don't expect a lot of particularly interesting shopping in Guadalupe. Two exceptions to this rule are the small but personalized **Cacharro Tienda,** Plaza Mayor, 12 (no phone), with an unusual collection of brass, copper, and iron, and the gift shop within the Hotel Lujuan, calle Gregorio Lopez, 19 (☎ **927-36-71-70**), which sells local hand crafted items, often in brass and copper.

Real Monasterio de Santa María de Guadalupe. Plaza de Juan Carlos, 1. ☎ **927-36-70-00.** Admission to museum and sacristy 300 ptas. ($1.80) adults, 100 ptas. (60¢) children 7–14, free for children 6 and under. Apr–Oct, daily 9:30am–1pm and 3:30–7pm; off-season, daily 9:30am–1pm and 3:30–6:30pm.

In 1325 a farmer searching for a stray cow reportedly spotted a statue of the Virgin in the soil. In time, this statue became venerated throughout the world, honored in Spain by Queen Isabella, Columbus, and Cervantes. Known as the Dark Virgin of Guadalupe, it is said to have been carved by St. Luke. A shrine was built to commemorate the statue and tributes poured in from all over the world, making Guadalupe one of the wealthiest foundations in Christendom. You can see the Virgin in a small alcove above the altar.

The church is noted for the wrought-iron railings in its naves and a magnificently decorated sacristy with eight richly imaginative 17th-century masterpieces by Zurbarán. Be sure to see the museum devoted to ecclesiastical vestments and to the choir books produced by 16th-century miniaturists. The 16th-century Gothic cloister is also flamboyant, with two galleries. The pièce de résistance is the stunning Mudéjar cloister, with its brick-and-tile Gothic-Mudéjar shrine dating from 1405 and a Moorish fountain from the 14th century.

WHERE TO STAY

Hospedería Real Monasterio. Plaza Juan Carlos, 1, 10140 Guadalupe. ☎ **927-36-70-00.** Fax 927-36-71-77. 47 units. A/C TEL. 8,000 ptas. ($48) double; 22,000 ptas. ($132) suite. MC, V. Closed Jan 12–Feb 12.

Once a waystation for pilgrims visiting the shrine, the Hospedería used to provide lodging for a small donation. Times have changed, but the prices remain moderate at this two-star hotel in the center of town, which is the second-best place to stay in town after the parador, and a whole lot cheaper. Since the place is installed in an antique monastery, the accommodations come in various shapes and sizes, but each is

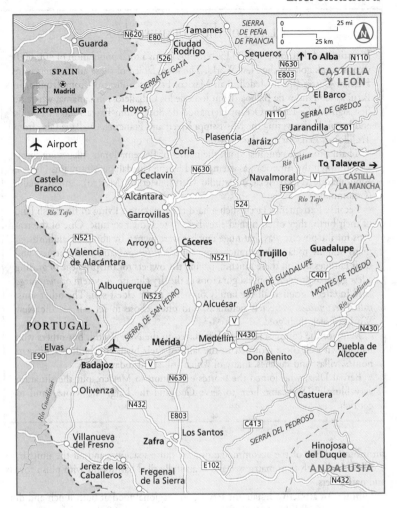

tastefully furnished and fitted with firm mattresses and well-maintained bathrooms with stall showers. There is a bar and the regional meals served in the restaurant are generally good. Top off a meal with a home-brewed *licor de Guadalupe*.

Parador Nacional Zurbarán. Marqués de la Romana, 12, 10140 Guadalupe. ☎ **927-36-70-75.** Fax 927-36-70-76. 41 units. A/C MINIBAR TV TEL. 16,000 ptas. ($96) double; 17,500 ptas. ($105) suite. AE, DC, MC, V. Parking 900 ptas. ($5.40).

Located in a scenic spot in the center of the village, the area's most luxurious accommodation is housed in a 16th-century building with a beautiful garden. Queen Isabella once stayed here, and the place often saw meetings between royal representatives and explorers, who signed their contracts here before setting out for the New World. The house is named after Francisco de Zurbarán, the great 17th-century painter who was born in the nearby town of Fuente de Cantos. There is a Zurbarán painting in one of the salons, along with ancient maps and engravings—many of them valuable works of art. Bedrooms are comfortable and partially decorated with reproduction medieval

Land of the Conquistadors

It's estimated that some 15,000 Extremeños (from a total population of 400,000) went to seek gold in the New World. The most fabled of these adventurers were Hernán Cortés (from Medellín) in Mexico; Francisco Pizarro (from Trujillo) in Peru; Vasco Núñez de Balboa (from Jerez de los Caballeros) in Panama, where he first sighted the Pacific Ocean; Hernando de Soto (from Barcarrota) in Florida and beyond, discovering the Mississippi River; and Francisco Orellana (also from Trujillo) in Ecuador and the Amazon.

Thanks to these conquistadors, the names of Extremaduran villages are sprinkled through the Americas, as exemplified by the Guadalupe Mountains (Texas), Albuquerque (New Mexico), Trujillo (Peru), Mérida (Mexico), and Medellín (Colombia).

Because Extremeños faced such a hard time making a living in the harsh land of their birth, they often turned elsewhere to seek their fortune. One of the reasons for the poverty was that huge ranches were owned by absentee landlords, as many still are today. These ranches are called *latifundios,* and often farmers and their families live on these ranches, paying the owners for the privilege of grazing a few goats or growing some slight crops in the dry climate. A system of *mayorazgo* (still in effect) granted all the family property to the eldest son. The other sons, called *secundinos,* were left penniless, and often chose to set sail for the New World to seek their gold.

Many of the conquistadors died or stayed in the New World, but others who had grown rich there returned to the land of their birth and built magnificent homes, villas, and ranches, many of which still stand today.

Bernal Díaz, who joined the Cortés expedition to Mexico, put the situation very bluntly. "We came here to serve God and the king," he wrote, "and to get rich."

furnishings. Most of the accommodations are quite spacious, and all the units have excellent beds with firm mattresses and beautifully tiled bathrooms with plush towels and hair dryers.

Dining: An attractive restaurant serves good regional food at both lunch and dinner. Try such local dishes as herb-flavored roast kid or pork Mudéjar style.

Amenities: Swimming pool, concierge, bar, garage, tennis court.

WHERE TO DINE

Both of the hotels recommended above also have good restaurants.

Mesón el Cordero. Alfonso Onceno, 27. ☎ **927-36-71-31.** Reservations recommended. Main courses 1,800–2,300 ptas. ($10.80–$13.80); fixed-price menu 1,600 ptas. ($9.60). AE, DC, MC, V. Tues–Sun 1–4pm and 7–11pm. Closed Feb 1–15. SPANISH.

Miguel and Angelita run Guadalupe's best independent restaurant, named for their specialty, *asado de cordero* (roast lamb flavored with garlic and thyme). The couple has operated this restaurant for more than 20 years and enjoys a devoted local following, which is recommendation enough. You might begin with another of their specialties, *sopa guadalupanas,* then follow with partridge "from the countryside" if you have a taste for game. The house dessert is a creamy custard, *flan casero.*

2 Trujillo

152 miles (245km) SW of Madrid, 28 miles (45km) E of Cáceres

Dating from the 13th century, the walled town of Trujillo is celebrated for the colonizers and conquerors born here. Among its illustrious natives were Francisco Pizarro, the conqueror of Peru, whose family palace on Plaza Mayor was built with gold from the New World, and Francisco de Orellana, the founder of Guayaquil, Equador, and the first European to explore the Amazon. Other Trujillano history-makers were Francisco de las Casas, who accompanied Hernán Cortés in his conquest of Mexico and founded the city of Trujillo in Honduras; Diego García de Paredes, who founded Trujillo in Venezuela; Nuño de Chaves, founder of Santa Cruz de la Sierra in Bolivia; and several hundred others whose names are found throughout maps of North, Central, and South America. There is a saying that 20 American countries were born here.

Celts, Romans, Moors, and Christians have inhabited Trujillo over the centuries. The original town, lying above today's modern one, was built on a granite ledge on the hillside. It is centered on the Plaza Mayor, one of the artistic landmarks of Spain. A Moorish castle and a variety of 16th- and 17th-century palaces, manor houses, towers, churches, and arcades encircle the plaza and overlook a bronze equestrian statue of Pizarro by American artists Mary Harriman and Charles Runse. Steep, narrow streets and shadowy little corners evoke the bygone times when explorers set out from here on their history-making adventures.

ESSENTIALS

GETTING THERE   There are nine buses per day to and from Madrid (trip time: 3½ or 4½ hours, depending on whether it's local or *expreso*). There are also six buses running daily from Cáceres, 45 minutes away, and six from Badajoz. A one-way ticket from Madrid to Trujillo costs 1,980 ptas. ($11.90); from Cárceres, 410 ptas. ($2.45); and from Badajoz, 1,250 ptas. ($7.50). Trujillo's bus station, calle Marqués Albayda (☎ 927-32-12-02), is on the south side of town on a side street that intersects with calle de la Encarnación.

Trujillo lies at a network of large and small roads connecting it to Cáceres via the N-521 and to Lisbon and Madrid via the N-V superhighway. Driving time from Madrid is around 4 hours.

VISITOR INFORMATION   The **tourist information office,** Plaza Mayor (☎ 927-32-06-56), is open April to October, daily 9am to 2pm and 5 to 7pm; off-season, daily 9am to 2pm and 4 to 6pm.

EXPLORING THE PLAZA & BEYOND

In the heart of Trujillo, the ✪ **Plaza Mayor** is one of the outstanding architectural sights in Extremadura. A statue honoring Francisco Pizarro, who almost single-handedly destroyed the Inca civilization of Peru, dominates it. The statue is an exact double of one standing in Lima. Many of the buildings on this square were financed with wealth brought back from the New World.

The most prominent structure on the square is the **Ayuntamiento Viejo (Old Town Hall),** with three tiers of arches, each tier squatter than the one below.

Iglesia de San Martín stands behind the statue dedicated to Pizarro. This granite church, originally from the 15th century, was reconstructed in the 16th century in Renaissance style. Inside are an impressive nave, several tombs, and a rare 18th-century organ still in working condition.

While you are on the square, observe the unusual facade of the **Casa de las Cadenas,** a 12th-century house draped with a heavy chain, a symbol that Philip II had granted the Orellana family immunity from heavy taxes.

You can then visit the **Palacio de los Duques de San Carlos,** a 16th-century ducal residence turned into a convent. Ring the bell to gain entry any time daily 9am to 1pm and 3 to 7pm. A donation of at least 100 ptas. (60¢) is appreciated, and a resident will show you around; appropriate dress (no shorts or bare shoulders) is required. The facade has Renaissance sculptured figures, and the two-level courtyard inside is even more impressive.

Palacio de la Conquista, also on the square, is one of the most grandiose mansions in Trujillo. Originally constructed by Hernán Pizarro, the present structure was built by his son-in-law to commemorate the exploits of this explorer, who accompanied his half-brother, Francisco, to Peru.

The stores that ring the Plaza Mayor have the town's best shopping; they stock stonework, leather, brass, copper, and ironwork. The best is **Bazar Sant'Olaria,** Plaza Mayor, 37 (☎ **927-32-01-70**), which has a selection of the best of virtually everything produced in the region. Handcrafted wood carvings are available from a small-scale artisan, **Domingo Pablos Barquillo,** Plazuela de San Judas, 3 (☎ **927-32-10-66**), whose intensely detailed effigies of saints and characters from Spanish literature are nothing short of charming.

Iglesia de Santa María. Calle de Ballesteros. No phone. Admission 100 ptas. (60¢). Daily 10am–2pm and 4:30–7:30pm.

This Gothic building with an outstanding Renaissance choir is the largest church in Trujillo, having been built over the ruins of a Moorish mosque. Ferdinand and Isabella once attended mass here. The proudest treasure is an altar retablo with 2 dozen panels painted by Fernando Gallego. Also here is the tomb of Diego García de Paredes, the "Samson of Extremadura," who is said to have single-handedly defended a bridge against an attacking French army with only a gigantic sword. To reach the church, go through the gate of the Plaza Mayor at Puerta de San Andrés and take calle de las Palomas through the old town.

Castillo. Crowning the hilltop. Free admission. Dawn to dusk; many visitors find it most dramatic at sunset.

Constructed by the Arabs on the site of a Roman fortress, this castle stands at the summit of the granite hill on which Trujillo was founded. Once at the castle, you can climb its battlements and walk along the ramparts enjoying a panoramic view of the austere countryside of Extremadura. Later, you can go below and see the dungeons. It is said that the Virgin Mary appeared here in 1232, giving the Christians renewed courage to free the city from Arab domination.

WHERE TO STAY

Hotel Victoria. Plaza del Campillo, 22, 10200 Trujillo. ☎ **927-32-18-19.** Fax 927-32-30-84. 28 units. A/C TV TEL. 10,165 ptas. ($61) double; 16,050 ptas. ($96.30) suite. AE, DC, V. Free parking.

This small, delightful hotel lies a 5-minute walk from the Plaza Mayor in an ornate 19th-century colonial mansion. The interior is light and airy, and the bedrooms surround what was once the interior patio of the house. Each level is adorned with a filigree design of pillars and ornate wrought-iron balustrades and capitals. The accommodations are spacious, with wooden ceilings, tiled marble floors, and comfortable beds, along with modern conveniences such as private well-equipped bathrooms with hair dryers. The hotel's restaurant serves regional and traditional Spanish fare, and there is an on-site cafeteria. Outside in the large garden is a swimming pool.

Las Cigueñas. Avenida de Madrid, s/n, Carretera N-V, 10200 Trujillo. ☎ **927-32-12-50.** Fax 927-32-13-00. 78 units. A/C MINIBAR TV TEL. 11,000 ptas. ($66) double; 15,000 ptas. ($90) suite. AE, DC, MC, V. Free parking.

Located east of the town center and convenient if you're driving, this is the second-best place to stay in Trujillo. It doesn't have the charm of the parador (see below), but it's cheaper. The hotel was built in two different three-story sections in 1971, with a major enlargement in 1983. A roadside hotel with a garden, it offers functional but clean and comfortable rooms, which, though small, are equipped with firm mattresses and private tiled bathrooms equipped with shower stalls. Its restaurant specializes in regional cuisine, and there is also a bar. You'll find Las Cigueñas on the main highway from Madrid, about a mile before Trujillo.

✪ **Parador Nacional de Trujillo.** Calle de Santa Beatriz de Silva, 10200 Trujillo. ☎ **927-32-13-50.** Fax 927-32-13-66. E-mail: trujillo@parador.es. 45 units. A/C MINIBAR TV TEL. 16,000 ptas. ($96) double; 18,000 ptas. ($108) suite. AE, DC, MC, V. Parking in garage 950 ptas. ($5.70).

Housed in the 1533 Convent of Santa Clara, this centrally located parador, about a block south of avenida de la Coronación, is a gem of Trujillo-style medieval and Renaissance architecture that's been faithfully restored since being converted into a parador in 1984. The beautifully decorated guest rooms, once nuns' cells, have canopied beds and spacious marble bathrooms with hair dryers and plush towels. The gardens and fruit trees of the Renaissance cloister are inviting, and there is a swimming pool in the courtyard of a new section that blends with the original convent architecture. You can have breakfast in the old refectory and dinner in what was once a long, vaulted chapel. Try the *caldereta extremena*, a stew made with lamb or baby goat.

WHERE TO DINE

The hotels recommended above also have good restaurants serving regional cuisine.

Mesón la Troya. Plaza Mayor, 10. ☎ **927-32-13-64.** Reservations recommended. Fixed-price menu 2,200 ptas. ($13.20). MC, V. Daily 1–4:30pm and 8:45pm–midnight. EXTREMADURAN.

Locals and visitors alike are drawn to this centrally located restaurant featuring regional cuisine and doing the province proud. Have a dry sherry in the bar that resembles the facade of a Spanish house. This cozy provincial theme also flows into the dining rooms, with their white walls decorated with ceramic plates, potted plants, and red tiles. Few people leave hungry after devouring the set menu, with its more than ample portions; food items change daily. Local dishes include *prueba de cerdo* (garlic-flavored pork casserole) and *carne con tomate* (beef cooked in tomato sauce). A table is always reserved for the village priest, who comes here for breakfast, lunch, and dinner and has done so for more than 27 years.

Pizarro. Plaza Mayor, 13. ☎ **927-32-02-55.** Reservations recommended. Main courses 1,000–2,000 ptas. ($6–$12); *menú del día* 1,500 ptas. ($9). AE, DC, MC, V. Wed–Sun 1:30–4pm and 8:30–10:30pm. EXTREMADURAN.

Locals cite this central hostal as the best place to go for regional Extremaduran cookery. Built in 1864, the inn is set on the town's main square and named for its famous son. The same family has owned and operated the place since 1919. Regional wines accompany meals that invariably include ham from acorn-fed pigs. You might begin with asparagus with mayonnaise sauce, then follow with *asado de cordero* (roast lamb flavored with herbs and garlic) or Roman-style fried *merluza* (hake). The kitchen's game specialty is *estofado de perdices* (partridge casserole).

3 Cáceres

185 miles (298km) SW of Madrid, 159 miles (256km) N of Seville

A national landmark and the capital of Extremadura, Cáceres is encircled by old city walls and has several palaces and towers, many financed by gold sent from the Americas by the conquistadors.

One of six cities in Spain designated World Heritage Sites by UNESCO, Cáceres was founded in the 1st century B.C. by the Romans as Norba Caesarina, but its present-day name is derived from *Alcazares,* meaning fortified citadel. After the Romans, it was settled by all the cultures that have made the south of Spain the unique cultural melting pot of influences it is today. The contemporary city offers a unique blend of the traces these successive invaders left behind.

ESSENTIALS

GETTING THERE Cáceres has the best rail connections in the province, with five trains per day from Madrid. Trip time ranges from 4 to 5 hours, and a one-way ticket costs from 3,400 to 4,000 ptas. ($20.40 to $24). There is also one train per day from Lisbon; the trip time is 4½ hours and a one-way fare is 4,475 ptas. ($26.85). One train per day also runs from Seville, taking 4 hours and costing 2,300 ptas. ($13.80).

The station in Cáceres is on avenida Alemania (☎ **927-23-37-61**) near the main highway heading south (Carretera de Sevilla). A green-and-white bus shuttles passengers about once an hour from the railway and bus stations (across the street from one another; board the shuttle outside the bus station) to the busiest traffic junction in the new city, Plaza de América. From there it's just a 10-minute walk to the edge of the old town.

Bus connections to Cáceres are more frequent than railway connections. From the city bus station (☎ **927-23-25-50**) on the busy Carretera de Sevilla, about a half mile south of the city center, buses arrive and depart for Madrid and Seville (one every 2 to 3 hours); transit by bus to Madrid takes 5 hours; transit by bus to Seville takes 4½ hours. There's also bus transport to Guadelupe (one per day); Trujillo (six or seven a day); Mérida (two a day); Valladolid (three a day); and Córdoba (two a day). Many travelers opt to walk the short distance from the Cáceres bus station to the city center.

Driving time from Madrid is about 5 hours. Most people approach Cáceres from eastern Spain via the N-V superhighway until they reach Trujillo. Here they exit onto the N-521, driving another 28 miles (45km) west to Cáceres.

VISITOR INFORMATION The **tourist information office,** Plaza Mayor, 20 (☎ **927-24-63-47**), is open Monday to Friday 9am to 2pm and 4 to 6:15pm, Saturday and Sunday 9:30am to 2pm.

EXPLORING THE OLD CITY

The modern city lies southwest of the *barrio antiguo,* **Cáceres Viejo,** which is enclosed by massive **ramparts.** The heart of the old city lies between Plaza Santa María and, a few blocks to the south, Plaza San Mateo. **Plaza Santa María** is an irregularly shaped, rather elongated square. On each of its sides are the honey-brown facades of buildings once inhabited by the nobility. On a casual stroll through the city's cobblestone streets, your attention will surely be drawn at first to the walls that enclose the old upper town. These are a mixture of Roman and Arab engineering, and their state of preservation is excellent. About 30 towers remain from the city's medieval walls, all of them heavily restored. Originally much taller, the towers reflected the pride and independence of their builders; when Queen Isabella took over, however, she ordered them cut down to size. The largest tower is at Plaza del General Mola. Beside it stands the Estrella Arco (Star Arch), constructed by Manuel Churriguera in the 18th century. To its right you'll see the Torre del Horno, a mud-brick adobe structure left from the Moorish occupation.

On the far side of Plaza Santa Maria rises the **Catedral de Santa María,** which is basically Gothic in style, although many Renaissance embellishments have been added. Completed sometime in the 1500s, this is the cathedral of Cáceres and it contains the remains of many conquistadors. It has three Gothic aisles of almost equal height and a carved retablo at the high altar dating from the 16th century. (Insert coins to light it up.)

La Casa de los Toledo-Montezuma was built by Juan Cano de Saavedra with money from the dowry of his wife, the daughter of Montezuma. The house is set into the northern corner of the medieval ramparts, about a block to the north of Plaza de Santa María. It is now a public records office.

Plaza Mayor is remarkably free from most of the blemishes and scarring effects that city planning and overregulation have made so common in other historically important sites. Passing through **El Arco de la Estrella (Arch of the Star),** you will then catch the most advantageous angle of Santa María Cathedral.

Some of the most appealing shops in Cáceres are on the streets radiating outward from the Plaza Mayor, with a particularly good selection of artifacts along either side of the **calle Pintores.**

Cuesta de la Compañía leads to Plaza San Mateo and the 14th-century **Iglesia de San Mateo,** which has a plateresque portal and a rather plain nave—except for the plateresque tombs, which add a decorative touch.

Two adjoining plazuelas near here embody the flavor of old Cáceres. The first of them, the **Plaza de las Veletas,** on the site of the old Alcázar, is the **Casa de las Veletas (Weather Vane House; ☎ 927-24-72-34),** which houses a provincial archaeological museum with priceless prehistoric and Roman pieces, along with a famous *alijibe* (Arab well). Its baroque facade, ancient Moorish cistern, five naves with horseshoe arches, and patio and paneling from the 17th century have been preserved. The museum displays Celtic and Visigothic remains, Roman and Gothic artifacts, and a numismatic collection. Admission is 200 ptas. ($1.20), and the museum is open Tuesday to Saturday 9:30am to 2:30pm, and Sunday 10am to 2:30pm. At the second plazuela, **San Pablo,** sits the **Casa de las Cigueñas (House of the Storks),** the only palace whose tower remains intact despite the order by Queen Isabella at the turn of the 15th century to reduce the height of all such strategic locations for military reasons. The building now serves as a military headquarters and is not open to the public.

You'll probably notice lots of storks nesting on most of the rooftops and bell towers in the town. This is a revealing sign of how Cáceres has managed to preserve not only its landmarks but also an environmentally sound balance between people and nature.

Church of Santiago was begun in the 12th century and restored in the 16th century. It has a reredos carved in 1557 by Alonso de Berruguete and a 15th-century figure of Christ. The church is outside the ramparts, about a block to the north of Arco de Socorro. To reach it, exit the gate, enter Plaza Socorro, then walk down calle Godoy. It is on your right.

If you want to see a more modern face of the region, and shop for housewares and fashion while you're at it, drive 15 minutes west of the town center to the **Centro Comercial Ruta de la Plata,** Carretera Portugal, where you'll find a scattering of boutiques, plus a number of simple snack bars and cafes.

WHERE TO STAY

Hotel Extremadura. Avenida Virgen de Guadalupe, 5, 10001 Cáceres. ☎ **927-22-16-00.** Fax 927-21-10-95. 67 units. A/C TV TEL. 12,000 ptas. ($72) double. AE, DC, MC, V. Parking 900 ptas. ($5.40).

This 1960s hotel offers straightforward rooms. They're a bit boxy and functionally furnished but are well maintained and reasonably comfortable, with good beds and immaculate tiled bathrooms with stall showers. Located about half a mile southwest of the historic center in a bustling commercial district, it offers air-conditioned relief from the heat, as well as a much-appreciated swimming pool. Prices are fair for what you get. The hotel's restaurant, Alazán, serves Spanish and international food, and there is also a bar. Their number of amenities is surprising, and include room service (available 7am to midnight), laundry, concierge, an in-house tour operator/travel agent, and car rentals.

✪ **Meliá Cáceres.** Plaza San Juan, 11, 10003 Cáceres. ☎ **927-21-58-00.** Fax 927-21-40-70. 86 units. A/C MINIBAR TV TEL. 20,500 ptas. ($123) double. AE, DC, MC, V.

The Meliá hotel chain continues to show up the government parador system by opening superior lodgings in towns long dominated by a parador. Although the Parador de Cáceres is fine in every way, the Meliá is superior in both service and amenities. This converted Renaissance palace is just south of the Plaza del Général Mola beside the entrance to the old town. Its bedrooms are better appointed, sunnier, and more spacious than those at the parador. Bathrooms are roomy and have hair dryers. Everything is tastefully converted, and there's lots of exposed stone, along with indirect lighting and sleek modern furnishings.

Dining: The cuisine is also superior to that at the parador; with international dishes and some of the better regional specialties of Extremadura.

Amenities: Concierge, laundry/dry cleaning, room service.

✪ **Parador de Cáceres.** Calle Ancha, 6, 10001 Cáceres. ☎ **927-21-17-59.** Fax 927-21-17-29. 31 units. A/C MINIBAR TV TEL. 17,500 ptas. ($105) double; 25,000 ptas. ($150) suite. AE, DC, MC, V. Free parking on street; garage parking 1,300 ptas. ($7.80).

This state-operated parador is set within what was originally a 15th century palace. Built in a severe style, it enjoys a tranquil location and a well-scrubbed, durable format of exposed stone, white plaster, and tile or stone floors. Pristine white corridors lead to dignified bedrooms outfitted in a starkly appealing combination of white walls and dark-grained, somewhat bulky furniture inspired by the austere decorative traditions of Extremadura. All the modern amenities have been installed here, including luxury mattresses and excellent bathrooms with toiletries and hair dryers. Suits of armor adorn some of the public areas, giving the place a vaguely feudal feel, but the patios that open onto masses of potted plants and flowers are quite welcoming.

Dining: The restaurant serves good regional cuisine. There's also a bar and cafeteria catering to general sightseers; it's open daily 11:30am to 11:30pm and is the most convenient place in town to stop in for snacks at odd hours.

Amenities: Room service, laundry/dry cleaning, concierge.

WHERE TO DINE

The cuisine offered at the parador and at many other places in Cáceres affords a novel experience to even seasoned travelers. You might try the famous *cuchifrito,* a suckling pig stewed in pepper, orange, and vinegar sauce, or the *caldereta de cordero,* lamb with pepper and almonds. A more daring choice would be *jabalí la carcereña,* a wild boar dish marinated in red wine and herbs. The most characteristic dessert in all of

Extremadura is *técula mécula,* an ancient example of the region's marzipan confectionery, which like most things in Cáceres has been passed down from one generation to the next for centuries.

✪ **Atrio.** Avenida de España, 30. ☎ **927-24-29-28.** Reservations recommended. Main courses 5,500–7,000 ptas. ($33–$42). DC, MC, V. Daily 1:30–4pm; Mon–Sat 9pm–midnight. SPANISH/CONTINENTAL.

Atrio serves the finest cuisine in the entire province. Even hard-to-please Michelin grants this place a star. Situated in a shopping mall cul-de-sac, the inside decor is elegant and somewhat unusual for this part of Spain—streamlined and sleek in white and sunflower yellow. The chef steers a skillful course between rich, regional flavors and more continental fare. The menu changes frequently to take advantage of the best of the various seasons. Prices can go much higher than those indicated above if truffles are added to your dish. Service is the finest in the area—in all, it's a professional and deluxe operation that comes as a surprise in such a provincial city.

El Figón de Eustaquio. Plaza San Juan, 12. ☎ **927-24-81-94.** Reservations recommended. Main courses 2,500–3,500 ptas. ($15–$21); fixed-price menus 1,800–2,800 ptas. ($10.80–$16.80). AE, DC, MC, V. Daily 1:30–4pm and 8pm–12:30am. EXTREMADURAN.

El Figón is a pleasant place serving regional cuisine that has been satisfying locals since 1948. You'll notice the four Blanco brothers who run the place doing practically everything. This includes preparing the amazingly varied dishes—for example, honey soup, *solomillo* (fillet of beef), and trout Extremaduran style (covered in ham), as well as typical Spanish specialties. The air-conditioned interior has a rustic decor. El Figón is west of the western ramparts of the old city near the intersection of avenida Virgen de Guadalupe and Plaza San Juan.

Torre de Sande. Calle de los Condes, 3. ☎ **927-21-11-47.** Reservations recommended. Main courses 2,000–2,250 ptas. ($12–$13.50); set menu 4,700 ptas. ($28.20). AE, DC, MC, V. Daily 2–5pm; Mon–Sat 9pm–1am. NOUVELLE SPANISH.

A 15th-century palace at the highest point in the city at the Plaza de San Mateo, this restaurant features a trio of separate dining rooms and a beautiful terraced garden in use as weather permits. The chef and owner, Cesar Raez, has been here since 1996. He has retained and restored the original furnishings and decorated the walls with copper etchings interspersed between granite archways looking out onto an ancient fountain. The view of the city from the garden is panoramic, and wonderful at night. The chefs combine regional flavors with the best of modern recipes, with palate-pleasing and marvelously succulent results. Try such delights as *boletus con foie* (mushrooms with duck liver), *ensalada de mango y salmon* (mango and salmon salad), *solomillo de retinto* (a prized local beefsteak), or *perdiz a la cantara con salsa* (partridge stuffed with liver and truffles in a port wine sauce). Desserts include *tapita de tres chocolates* (layer cake of three types of chocolate) and a sheep's milk pudding.

4 Mérida

44 miles (71km) S of Cáceres, 35 miles (56km) E of Badajoz

Founded in 25 B.C., Mérida is at the crossroads of the Roman roads linking Toledo and Lisbon and Salamanca and Seville. At one time the capital of Lusitania (the Latin name for the combined kingdoms of Spain and Portugal), Mérida was one of the most splendid cities in Iberia, ranking as a town of major importance in the Roman Empire; in fact, it was once called a miniature Rome. Its monuments, temples, and public works make it the site of some of the finest Roman ruins in Spain, and as such it is the tourist capital of Extremadura. Old Mérida can be covered on foot—in fact, that is the only way to see it. Pay scant attention to the dull modern suburb across the Guadiana River, which skirts the town with its sluggish waters.

ESSENTIALS

GETTING THERE   Trains depart and arrive from the **RENFE** station on the calle Cardero (☎ **924-31-81-09**), about half a mile north of the Plaza de España. Each day there are four trains to and from Cáceres (trip time: 1 hour), five trains to and from Madrid (4 hours), one to and from Seville (3 hours), and seven to and from Badajoz (1 hour). On a regular train a one-way ticket from Madrid costs 2,840 ptas. ($17.05); on the faster **TALGO** train, the one-way fare is 4,000 ptas. ($24).

The bus station is on avenida de la Libertad (☎ **924-37-14-04**) near the train station. Every day, there are three buses to and from Madrid (5½ hours), six to eight buses to and from Seville (3 hours), two buses to and from Cáceres (2 hours), and five to ten buses to Badajoz (1 hour). From Mérida to Madrid, the fare is 2,720 ptas. ($16.30); Mérida to Seville, 1,695 ptas. ($10.15); Mérida to Cáceres, 675 ptas. ($4.05); and Mérida to Badajoz, 610 ptas. ($3.65).

To drive, take the N-V superhighway from Madrid or Lisbon. Driving time from Madrid is approximately 5 hours; from Lisbon, about 4½ hours. Park in front of the Roman theater and explore the town on foot.

VISITOR INFORMATION   The **tourist information office,** at Pedro María Plano (☎ **924-31-53-53**), is open April through October, Monday to Friday 9am to 1:45pm and 5 to 7pm, Saturday 9:15am to 1:45pm. Off-season hours are Monday to Friday 9am to 2pm and 4 to 6pm, Saturday and Sunday 9:15am to 1:45pm. Those are the official hours, but don't expect the staff to interpret them too literally.

EXPLORING MÉRIDA

The **Roman bridge** over the Guadiana was the longest in Roman Spain—about half a mile—and consisted of 64 arches. It was constructed of granite under either Trajan or Augustus, then restored by the Visigoths in 686. Philip II ordered further refurbishment in 1610; work was also done in the 19th century. The bridge crosses the river south of the center of Old Mérida, its length increased because of the way it spans two forks of the river, including an island in midstream. In 1993, it was restored and turned into a pedestrian walkway. A semicircular suspension bridge for cars was constructed to carry the heavy traffic and save the bridge for future generations. Before the restoration and change, this bridge served as a main access road into Mérida, witnessing transportation evolve from hooves and feet to trucks and automobiles.

Another sight of interest is the old hippodrome, or **Circus Maximus,** which could seat about 30,000 spectators for chariot races. The original Roman masonry was carted off for use in other buildings, and today the site looks more like a parking lot. Excavations have uncovered rooms that may have housed gladiators. The former circus is at the end of avenida Extremadura on the northeastern outskirts of the old town, about half a mile north of the Roman bridge and a 10-minute walk east of the railway station.

Arco Trajano (Trajan's Arch) lies near the heart of the Old Town beside calle Trajano, about a block south of the Parador Vía de la Plata. An unadorned triumphal arch, it measures 16 yards high and 10 yards across.

Acueducto de los Milagros is the most intact of the town's two remaining Roman aqueducts; this one brought water from Proserpina, 3 miles (5km) away. From the aqueducts, water was fed into two artificially created lakes, Cornalvo and Proserpina.

The aqueduct is northwest of the old town, lying to the right of the road to Cáceres, just beyond the railway tracks. Ten arches still stand.

The latest monument to be excavated is the **Temple of Diana** (dedicated to Caesar Augustus). Squeezed between houses on a narrow residential street, it was converted in the 17th century into the private residence of a nobleman, who used four of the original Corinthian columns in his architectural plans. The temple lies at the junction of calle Sagasta and calle Romero Léal in the center of town.

While in the area, you can also explore the 13th-century **Iglesia de Santa María la Mayor,** Plaza de España. It has a 16th-century chapel graced with Romanesque and plateresque features. It stands on the west side of the square.

Teatro Romano. José Ramón Melida, s/n. ☎ **924-31-25-30.** Admission 600 ptas. ($3.60) adults (includes admission to Anfiteatro Romano), free for children. Daily 9am–1:45pm and 5–6:45pm.

This Roman theater, one of the best-preserved Roman ruins in the world, was built by Agrippa (Augustus's son-in-law) in 18 B.C. to house an audience of 6,000 people. Modeled after the great theaters of Rome, it was constructed by dry-stone methods, a remarkable achievement. During the reign of Hadrian (2nd century A.D.), a tall stage wall was adorned with statues and colonnades. Behind the stage, visitors today can explore excavations of various rooms. From the end of June to early July, they can also enjoy a season of classical plays.

Anfiteatro Romano. Calle José Ramón Melida, s/n. ☎ **924-31-25-30.** Admission included in Teatro Romano ticket (see above). Daily 9am–1:45pm and 5–6:45pm.

At the height of its glory, in the 1st century B.C., the amphitheater could seat 14,000 to 15,000 spectators. Chariot races were held here, along with gladiator combats and mock sea battles, for which the arena would be flooded. Many of the seats were placed dangerously close to the bloodshed. You can visit some of the rooms that housed the wild animals and gladiators waiting to go into combat.

✪ **Museo Nacional de Arte Romano.** Calle José Ramón Melida, 2. ☎ **924-31-16-90.** Admission 500 ptas. ($3) adults, 400 ptas. ($2.40) students, free for children. Tues–Sat 10am–1:45pm and 5–7pm; Sun 10am–2pm.

Located in a modern building adjacent to the ancient Roman amphitheater, to which it is connected by an underground tunnel, this museum is acclaimed as the greatest repository of Roman artifacts in Spain. Not only does it contain more than 30,000 artifacts from Augusta Emerita, capital of the Roman province of Lusitania, but it also incorporates part of a Roman road discovered in the early 1980s during the construction of the building. Many of the museum's sculptures came from the excavations of the Roman theater and amphitheater. You'll see displays of mosaics, figures, pottery, glassware, coins, and bronze objects. The museum is built of red brick in the form of a Roman basilica.

Alcazaba. Plaza de España. ☎ **924-31-73-09.** Admission 600 ptas. ($3.60). Apr–Sept, Mon–Sat 9am–2pm and 5–7:15pm, Sun 9am–2pm; Oct–Mar, Mon 9am–1pm, Tues–Sat 9am–1pm and 3–6pm.

On the northern bank of the Guadiana River beside the northern end of the Roman bridge (which it was meant to protect) stands the Alcázar, also known as the Conventual or the Alcazaba. Built in the 9th century by the Moors, who used fragments left over from Roman and Visigothic occupations, the square structure was later granted to the Order of Santiago.

Museo Arqueológico de Arte Visigodo. Plaza de España. ☎ **924-30-01-06.** Free admission. July–Sept, Tues–Sat 10am–2pm and 5–7pm, Sun 10am–2pm; Oct–June, Tues–Sat 10am–2pm and 4–6pm, Sun 10am–2pm.

In front of Trajan's Arch is this archaeological museum housing a treasure trove of artifacts left by the conquering Visigoths. Look especially for the two statues of Wild Men in one of the alcoves.

WHERE TO STAY

Hotel Emperatriz. Plaza de España, 19, 06800 Mérida. ☎ **924-31-31-11.** Fax 924-31-33-05. 43 units. A/C TV TEL. 13,500 ptas. ($81) double. AE, DC, MC, V. Free parking nearby.

A former 16th-century palace, the Emperatriz housed a long line of celebrated guests in its day, from Kings Philip II and III of Spain to Queen Isabella of Portugal and Charles V, the Holy Roman Emperor. Its intricate tiled gallery foyer is in the Moorish style. All the guest rooms are functionally furnished and comfortable, but try to get one facing the plaza for an unusual view of the storks' nests built on the eaves and cornices of the surrounding buildings. Many of the rooms have grown seedy over the years, but others have been renovated (request one of the restored rooms). Late-night noise can be a problem.

The restaurant serves many intriguing Extremaduran specialties, including soothing gazpacho made with white garlic and *tencas fritas* (fried tench, a typical fish of the region). Later you can visit the Emperatriz's nightclub and bar. A garden stands in the center of this good-value three-star hotel, located in the center of town just north of the ruins of the Alcazaba. Parking is available along the street.

Nova Roma. Súarez Somonte, 42, 06800 Mérida. ☎ **924-31-12-61.** Fax 924-30-01-60. 55 units. A/C TV TEL. 13,000 ptas. ($78) double. AE, DC, MC, V. Parking 1,500 ptas. ($9).

Lacking the charm of the Parador Vía de la Plata (see below), the 1991 Nova Roma wins hands-down for those with more modern taste. Clean, comfortable, and functionally furnished, it's a good value for this heavily frequented tourist town. Bedrooms range from small to medium, and each comes with firm mattresses and a compact tiled bathroom with shower stall. The hotel also runs a reasonably priced restaurant offering a *menú del día* for 1,400 ptas. ($8.40) with many regional dishes. The Nova Roma is west of the Teatro Romano and north of Plaza de Toros (bullring).

✪ **Parador Vía de la Plata.** Plaza de la Constitución, 3, 06800 Mérida. ☎ **924-31-38-00.** Fax 924-31-92-08. E-mail: merida@parador.es. 82 units. A/C MINIBAR TV TEL. 17,000 ptas. ($102) double; 28,000 ptas. ($168) suite. AE, DC, MC, V. Parking 1,100 ptas. ($6.60).

This parador is in the heart of town on the Plaza de la Constitución, in the former Convento de los Frailes de Jesus (dating from the 16th century). Although it has had a long and turbulent history and was once a prison, a salon has been installed in the cloister, and a central garden is studded with shrubbery and flowers. Old stone stairs lead to the bedrooms, which come in various shapes and sizes, each beautifully kept and furnished. Mattresses and bathrooms are luxurious, the best in town. Each unit comes with a hair dryer and plush towels. In the 1960s two dictators met here: Franco of Spain and Salazar of Portugal.

Dining: The parador has a cafeteria, an excellent restaurant serving regional and national dishes, and a bar.

Amenities: In addition to its garage, the parador has a pool, sauna, and gym.

Tryp Medea. Avenida de Portugal, s/n, 00800 Mérida. ☎ **924-37-24-00.** Fax 924-37-30-20. 126 units. A/C MINIBAR TV TEL. 17,000 ptas. ($102) double; 20,000 ptas. ($120) triple. AE, DC, MC, V. Garage parking 900 ptas. ($5.40); free parking on street. Bus: 4 or 6.

A 15-minute walk west of the town's historic center on the opposite bank of the Guadiana River, this hotel opened in 1993 and immediately ranked among the finest in the area. A member of the nationwide Tryp chain, the Medea uses large amounts of white marble in its lobby and bedrooms. Lots of mirrors, stylish postmodern furniture crafted from locally made wrought iron, and numerous modern accessories decorate the rooms, many of which offer views over the historic core of Mérida. Ranging from small to medium, each unit is well appointed, with firm mattresses and tidily arranged private bathrooms.

Dining/Diversions: There's a bar and a formal restaurant, **El Encenar** (named after a type of tree indigenous to Extremadura), serving international and regional specialties.

Amenities: An outdoor swimming pool, a health club/gymnasium, squash courts, a sauna, a helpful multilingual staff.

WHERE TO DINE

In addition to the listings below, all the hotels recommended above have good restaurants.

Briz. Félix Valverde Lillo, 5. ☎ **924-31-93-07.** Main courses 1,200–2,000 ptas. ($7.20–$12); fixed-price menu 1,500 ptas. ($9). MC, V. Mon–Sat 1–4pm and 9pm–midnight. EXTREMADURAN.

There is almost universal agreement, even among the locals, that the set menu at Briz represents the best value in town—not only reasonable in price but also very filling. Briz has been known for its Extremaduran regional dishes since 1949. Main dishes include heavily flavored lamb stew and *perdiz* in salsa (a gamy partridge casserole), which might be preceded by an appetizer of peppery sausage mixed into a medley of artichokes. Peppery veal steak and fried fillet of goat are other specialties. Strong, hearty wines accompany the dishes. You'll find Briz across from the post office.

Restaurante Nicolás. Félix Valverde Lillo, 13. ☎ **924-31-96-10.** Reservations recommended. Main courses 1,400–2,000 ptas. ($8.40–$12); fixed-price menu 2,000 ptas. ($12). AE, DC, MC, V. Daily noon–5pm; Mon–Sat 8:30pm–midnight. SPANISH.

Transformed from an old, run-down house in 1985, Nicolas is the most charming restaurant in town. If the lower dining room isn't to your liking, you'll find seating upstairs, as well as a pleasant garden for outdoor meals. You might enjoy roast baby goat, carefully seasoned roast lamb, and flavorful concoctions of sole, salmon, or monkfish. Roast partridge is the game specialty. Nicolás is located opposite the post office.

5 Badajoz

57 miles (92km) SW of Cáceres, 39 miles (63km) E of Mérida, 254 miles (409km) SW of Madrid

The capital of Spain's largest province, Badajoz stands on the banks of the Guadiana River near the once turbulent Portuguese border. A Moorish fortress and an old Roman bridge are but two reminders of the past. Sightseeing here is lackluster, but Badajoz does have some local color, provided mainly by its huge ramparts and its narrow medieval streets. This fortified site is best appreciated if you drive to Badajoz from the north. Park outside and walk into town; along the way you'll pass the 13th-century Gothic cathedral.

ESSENTIALS

GETTING THERE   Four trains daily arrive from Madrid (trip time: 5 to 8 hours). Eight trains per day arrive from Mérida (1½ hours), and three from Cáceres

(2½ hours). The railway station is at the terminus of Carolina Coronado in Badajoz (☎ **924-27-11-70**), a 15-minute walk northwest of the center of town.

From Madrid, 10 buses daily make the 4-hour trip; from Seville, there are five daily buses (4½ hours). From Mérida, there are eight buses daily (45 minutes). The bus station (☎ **924-25-86-61**) is at Carretera de Valverde about a half mile south of town. Take bus no. 3 from the bus station to the Plaza de España, in the center of town.

Badajoz straddles the superhighway N-V, which connects Madrid with Lisbon. The E-803 links it with Seville. Driving time from Madrid is around 4 hours; from Seville the time is about 3½ hours.

VISITOR INFORMATION   The **tourist information office,** Plaza de la Libertad, 3 (☎ **924-22-27-63**), is open Monday to Friday 9am to 2pm and 4 to 6pm, Saturday and Sunday 9am to 2pm.

WHERE TO STAY

Gran Hotel Zurbarán. Paseo Castelar, s/n, 06001 Badajoz. ☎ **924-22-37-41.** Fax 924-22-01-42. 213 units. A/C MINIBAR TV TEL. 19,000 ptas. ($114) double; 30,000 ptas. ($180) suite. AE, DC, MC, V. Parking 1,000 ptas. ($6).

Set above the heavy ramparts that flank the southern bank of the River Guadiana, this modern but slightly dated four-star hotel enjoys one of the most scenic positions in town, overlooking the welcome and verdant Parque de Castelar. The public rooms are decorated with lots of metal trim and a kind of 1970s-era pizzazz, but the guest rooms are comfortably equipped and have been recently remodeled. The medium accommodations come with comfortable beds fitted with fine linen and quality mattresses. Bathrooms are small but neatly organized tub and shower combos. The service is attentive.

Dining/Diversions: An in-house restaurant serves à la carte meals. There are also a bar and a disco.

Amenities: Concierge, laundry, room service, baby-sitting, outdoor pool, tennis courts, large garden with stately trees and flowers, in-house news kiosk and bookstore, shopping arcade.

Hotel Lisboa. Diaz Ambrono, 13, 06006 Badajoz. ☎ **924-27-29-00.** Fax 924-27-22-50. 176 units. A/C TV TEL. 8,000 ptas. ($48) double. MC, V. Parking 900 ptas. ($5.40).

One of Badajoz's major hotels, this eight-floor establishment is about a half mile west of the town center near the access roads of traffic coming in from Lisbon. Built in 1978, and appealing to many business travelers en route between Madrid and Lisbon, it offers uncomplicated modern rooms with conservative furnishings and an efficient staff. Even though rooms are cramped, the hotel is a great value considering the low prices. Beds are comfortable, and bathrooms, just barely big enough for the job, have shower stalls and adequate towels. The hotel contains a bar, a garage, and an economical restaurant.

Hotel Río. Adolfo Diaz Ambrona, 13, 06006 Badajoz. ☎ **924-27-29-00.** Fax 924-27-38-74. 80 units. A/C MINIBAR TV TEL. 12,500 ptas. ($75) double; 15,500 ptas. ($93) suite. AE, DC, MC, V. Free parking. Bus: Urbano no. 2 or 8.

Located near a bridge on the highway connecting Lisbon and Madrid, the Hotel Río offers views of a eucalyptus grove and the river. Amenities include an outdoor pool, a parking garage, bingo, a disco pub/restaurant, and a garden. The small and functional guest rooms are comfortably furnished and well maintained. The hotel attracts many of the Portuguese who come over for the night for a taste of Spain.

WHERE TO DINE

✪ **Aldeberán.** Avenida de Elvas, s/n, Urbanización Guadiana. ☎ **924-27-42-61.** Reservations recommended. Main courses 2,200–2,850 ptas. ($13.20–$17.10); fixed-price menu 4,800 ptas. ($28.80). AE, DC, V. Mon–Sat 1:30–3:45pm and 9–11:45pm. SPANISH/EXTREMADURAN.

Established in 1990 in a modern building overlooking the river, on the highway about a mile west of Badajoz's center, Aldeberán is the best restaurant in the entire area. It prides itself on its Extremaduran origins, having adopted the name of a race of local bulls. Although a range of fish and meat dishes are offered, the menu features succulent pork dishes prepared from *pata negra* (black-footed) pigs, a regional specialty. Offerings include *solomillo ibérico*, a tender pork fillet carefully seasoned and usually served with spinach; portions of wafer-thin cured ham, served au naturel or flavorfully mixed into salads of very fresh greens; hake in green sauce; and several different preparations of sole and monkfish. A signature dessert is ripe peaches flambéed in honey sauce and served with mint-flavored crème frâiche.

Mesón el Tronco. Calle Muñoz Torrero, 16. ☎ **924-22-20-76.** Reservations recommended. Main courses 1,250–2,800 ptas. ($7.50–$16.80); fixed-price menu 2,500 ptas. ($15). DC, MC, V. Tues–Sat 9am–4pm and 7pm–midnight. EXTREMADURAN.

You might not suspect an attractive restaurant exists here when you encounter the popular bar near the front door, but the excellent tapas hint at the delicacies available in the back room. The owner offers traditional Extremaduran dishes with a changing repertoire of daily specials. Menu items include gazpacho, *cocido* (stew) of the region, and lamb cutlets, all at affordable prices and served in air-conditioned comfort. Mesón el Tronco is in the center of town, 2 blocks west of the cathedral.

SIDE TRIPS FROM MÉRIDA & BADAJOZ

Jerez de los Caballeros makes an interesting journey from either Badajoz (46½ miles [75km] south on the N-432) or Mérida (61½ miles [99km] southwest on the N-360). It's a small town of white houses clustered on a hillside, with the cathedral on the summit. The birthplace of Balboa, the first European to discover the Pacific, is nearby—a modest whitewashed house at Capitán Cortés, 10. A statue honors the explorer in one of the town's small squares. Jerez de los Caballeros, with many belfries and towers, including the **Torre Sagrienta (Bloody Tower),** takes its name, traditions, and ambience from the *Caballeros del Templo* (Knights Templars), who were given the town after it was taken from the Moors in 1230.

Medellín, 25 miles (40km) east of Mérida and 62 miles (100km) east of Badajoz, is the little town where Hernán Cortés, conqueror of Mexico, was born. From the approach you'll see the old whitewashed buildings on the opposite side of the Guadiana River, with the ruins of medieval Medellín Castle dominating the skyline. A 17th-century stone bridge crosses the river into the town where you'll find a monument to Cortés in the main cobblestoned plaza. From either Mérida or Badajoz, take the N-V superhighway heading to Madrid; exit at the C-520, the road into Medellín.

6 Zafra

38 miles (61km) S of Mérida, 107 miles (172km) N of Seville

One of the most interesting stopovers in lower Extremadura, the white-walled town of Zafra is filled with old Moorish streets and squares. The 1457 **castle** of the dukes of Feria, the most important in the province, boasts both a sumptuous 16th-century Herreran patio and the Sala Dorada with its richly paneled ceiling. The place is now a government parador (see below). You'll want to spend time on the central square, the arcaded 18th-century **Plaza Mayor,** and its satellite, the 16th-century **Plaza Vieja (Old Square).** These are the two most important sights in Zafra, along with **Nuestra Señora de la Candelaria,** a church with nine panels by Zurbarán, displayed on the retablo in a chapel designed by Churriguera. The church, constructed in the Gothic-Renaissance style, has a redbrick belfry. Admission is free, and it's open Monday to Friday 10:30am to 1pm and 7 to 8:30pm, and Sunday 11am to 12:30pm.

ESSENTIALS

GETTING THERE   Five buses a day arrive from Mérida; a one-way ticket costs 600 ptas. ($3.60). For schedules, call ☎ **924-55-39-07.**

Zafra lies at the point where the highway from Seville (E-803) splits, heading east to Mérida and Cáceres and west to Badajoz. Driving there is easy. From Mérida to Zafra, allow an hour; from Seville, about 2½ hours. There's also a direct road from Córdoba.

VISITOR INFORMATION   The **tourist information office** is at Plaza de España, 30 (☎ **924-55-10-36**), open Monday to Friday 11am to 2pm and 6 to 8pm, Saturday 11am to 1:30pm.

WHERE TO STAY

Huerta Honda. López Asme, 32, 06300 Zafra. ☎ **924-55-41-00.** Fax 924-55-25-04. 40 units. A/C MINIBAR TV TEL. 9,500 ptas. ($57) double; 13,500 ptas. ($81) apt; 20,000 ptas. ($120) suite. AE, MC, V.

From the modern, recently renovated bedrooms of this hotel in front of the Plaza del Alcázar, you'll get views of the citadel and the old town. Living space here is a bit tight, but the beds are good and the bathrooms immaculately kept. There's a disco, as well as a garden and a pretty patio for midafternoon drinks. Under the same management, at no. 36 on the same street, is the restaurant Barbacana, a well-recommended dining room offering French and Basque cuisine. Meals cost from 3,800 to 4,000 ptas. ($22.80 to $24).

Parador Hernán Cortés. Plaza Corazón de María, 7, 06300 Zafra. ☎ **924-55-45-40.** Fax 924-55-10-18. 45 units. A/C MINIBAR TV TEL. 15,000 ptas. ($90) double; 25,000 ptas. ($150) suite. AE, DC, MC, V. Free parking along the Plaza Corazón de María.

This government-run parador in a restored castle near the Plaza de España is named after Cortés, who stayed here with the dukes of Feria before his departure for the New World. The castle was originally built in 1457 on a square plan with four round towers. The interior, beautiful but restrained, contains the chapel of the Alcázar, with an octagonal Gothic dome. In addition to being decorated in splendid taste, the Hernán Cortés is quite comfortable, boasting a patio, a garden, and a swimming pool. Although not the finest parador in Extremadura, the bedrooms here are medium in size or even spacious, and all the furnishings are sturdy and comfortable, especially the firm mattresses. Bathrooms are fairly roomy and equipped with hair dryers and plush towels. The magnificent-looking dining room offers regional meals from 3,500 ptas. ($21). A bar and a large lounge are also on the premises.

WHERE TO DINE

Barbacana. Avenida López Asme, 30. ☎ **924-55-41-00.** Reservations not required. Main courses 2,400–2,800 ptas. ($14.40–$16.80); set menu 4,500 ptas. ($27). MC, V. Tues–Sat 1:30–4pm and 9–11:30pm. CASTILIAN.

Next to the previously recommended Huerta Honda in the center of town, this is the city's most elegantly decorated restaurant. It just happens to serve the finest cuisine as an added bonus. The restaurant is housed on two floors, each with 10 tables, and the atmosphere is chic and sophisticated. Visitors will find the second-floor dining room more relaxed and salubrious. This restaurant has operated here for more than a decade, earning an enviable reputation throughout the region. The owner is an aficionado of the bullfight and has adorned the walls with many paintings depicting scenes from this sport. The cuisine is firmly rooted in the region, and you'll stuff yourself with well-prepared specialty after specialty. Such delicacies appear on the menu as *revuelto de trigeros* (sautéed green asparagus) or *trugas revueltas en ajo* (truffles sautéed in garlic). From there, you can proceed to such main courses as *merluza con almejas* (hake in clam sauce) or *cochinillo* (suckling pig).

7 | Andalusia

This once-great stronghold of Muslim Spain is rich in history and tradition, containing some of the country's most celebrated sightseeing treasures: the world-famous Mezquita (mosque) in Córdoba, the Alhambra in Granada, and the great Gothic cathedral in Seville. It also has many smaller towns just waiting to be discovered—Úbeda, Jaén, gorge-split Ronda, Jerez de la Frontera, and the gleaming white port city of Cádiz. Give Andalusia at least a week and you'll still have only skimmed the surface.

This dry, mountainous region embraces the Costa del Sol (Málaga, Marbella, and Torremolinos), a popular coastal strip covered separately in the following chapter. Go to the Costa del Sol for beach resorts, nightlife, and relaxation; visit Andalusia for its architectural wonders and beauty.

Crime alert: Anyone driving south into Andalusia and the Costa del Sol should be wary of thieves. Daylight robberies are commonplace, especially in Seville, Córdoba, and Granada. It is not unusual for a car to be broken into while tourists are enjoying lunch in a restaurant. Some establishments have hired guards (a service for which you should tip, of course). Under no circumstances should you ever leave passports and traveler's checks unguarded in a car.

1 Jaén, Baeza & Úbeda

International tourists discovered the province of Jaén, with three principal cities—Jaén, the capital; Baeza; and Úbeda—in the 1960s. For years, visitors whizzed through Jaén on the way south to Granada or bypassed it altogether on the southwest route to Córdoba and Seville. But the government improved the province's hotel outlook with excellent paradors, which now provide some of the finest accommodations in Andalusia.

JAÉN

60 miles (97km) E of Córdoba, 60 miles (97km) N of Granada, 210 miles (338km) S of Madrid

In the center of Spain's major olive-growing district, Jaén is sandwiched between Córdoba and Granada and has always been a gateway between Castile and Andalusia. Christian forces gathered here in 1492 before marching on Granada to oust the Moors.

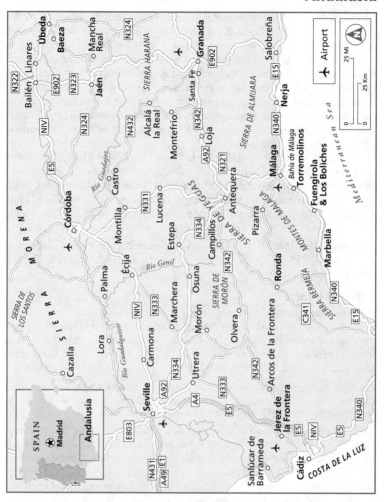

Jaén's bustling modern section is of little interest to visitors, but the **Moorish old town,** where narrow cobblestoned streets hug the mountainside, is reason enough to visit. A hilltop castle, now converted into a first-rate parador, dominates the city. On a clear day you can see the snow-covered peaks of the Sierra Nevada.

The city of Jaén is the center of a large province of 5,189 square miles (13,491 sq. km.) framed by mountains: the Sierra Morena to the north, the Segura and Cazorla ranges to the east, and those of Huelma, Noalejo, and Valdepeñas to the south. To the west, plains widen into the fertile Guadalquivir Valley and the landscape is rugged and irregular. Jaén province comprises three well-defined districts: the Sierra de Cazorla, a land of wild scenery; the plains of Bailén, Ajona, and Arjonilla, filled with wheat fields, vineyards, and old olive trees; and the valleys of the tributaries of the Guadalquivir.

ESSENTIALS

GETTING THERE It's easier to leave Jaén than it is to get here. Trains to Jaén run only from south to north. Northbound trains—including four daily to Madrid's

Atocha Railway Station—arrive and depart from Jaén's **RENFE** station on the Paseo de la Estación (☎ **953-27-02-02**) north of the center of town. The trip to Madrid takes 4 to 5 hours depending on the type of train. If you're traveling from north to south, however, it isn't quite so easy. Most southbound trains from Madrid, and all trains heading south to Seville and the rest of Andalusia, stop only at a larger railway junction that is inconveniently in the hamlet of Espeluy, 22 miles (35km) to the north. From Espeluy, trains are sometimes funneled a short ride to the east to the railway junction midway between Linares (31 miles [50km] from Jaén) and Baeza (the Estación de Linares-Baeza). Consult the Jaén tourist office or the railway station for advice on your particular routing.

The bus terminal is at Plaza Coca de la Piñera (☎ **953-25-01-06**), 1 block south of the central Parque de la Victoria. Either directly or after a transfer at Baeza, 30 miles (48km) to the north, buses travel 13 times a day to Granada (1½ hours away), 10 times to Úbeda (30 minutes), four times to Málaga (3 hours), and 10 times to Baeza (1 hour).

Four important highways, plus several provincial roads, converge on Jaén from four directions. From Madrid, follow the N-IV (E-5) to N-323 (E-902).

VISITOR INFORMATION   The **tourist information office** is at calle Arquitecto Bergés, 1 (☎ **953-22-27-37**). It's open Monday to Friday 8:30am to 2:30pm, and Saturday 10:30am to 1pm.

EXPLORING JAÉN

Jaén produces some of the most appealing pottery in the south of Spain, as well as some of the most intricately crafted baskets. You'll find outlets for the stuff all over the city's historic core, but two stores whose inventories are particularly well chosen include **Peñalver,** calle Bernabe Soriano, 17 (☎ **953-24-34-15**), and **Antanyo,** calle Virgen de la Capilla, 7 (☎ **953-24-37-35**).

Catedral de Santa María. Plaza de la Catedral. ☎ **953-23-42-33.** Free admission to cathedral; museum 100 ptas. (60¢). Cathedral, daily 8:30am–1pm and 4:30–8pm (closes at 7pm in winter); museum, Sat–Sun 11am–1pm. Bus: 8, 10, or 16.

The formality and grandeur of Jaén's cathedral stand witness to the city's past importance. Begun in 1555 and completed in 1802, it is a honey-colored blend of Gothic, baroque, and Renaissance styles, but mainly Renaissance. A huge dome dominates the interior with its richly carved choir stalls. The cathedral museum contains an important collection of historical objects in two underground chambers, including paintings by Ribera. The cathedral stands southwest of the Plaza de la Constitución.

Iglesia de la Magdalena. Calle de la Magdalena. ☎ **953-19-03-31.** Free admission. Daily 6am–8pm.

Of the many churches worth visiting in Jaén, La Magdalena is the oldest and most interesting. This Gothic church was once an Arab mosque.

Museo Provincial. Paseo de la Estación, 29. ☎ **953-25-06-00.** Admission 400 ptas. ($2.40). Tues 3–8pm; Wed–Sat 9am–8pm; Sun 9am–3pm.

The Provincial Museum's collection includes Roman mosaics, a Mudéjar arch, and many ceramics from the early Iberian, Greek, and Roman periods. On the upper floor is an exhibition of Pedro Berruguete paintings, including *Christ at the Column.* Look for a Paleo-Christian sarcophagus from Martos. The museum is between the bus and train stations.

Centro Cultural Palacio de Villardompardo. Plaza de Santa Luisa de Marillac, s/n. ☎ **953-23-62-92.** Free admission. Tues–Fri 9am–8pm (closes at 7pm in winter); Sat–Sun

9:30am–2:30pm. You must go on foot: In the old quarter of Jaén, follow signs indicating either Baños Arabes or Barrio de la Magdalena.

This is a three-in-one attraction, including some former Arab baths (known as *hamman*), a Museo de Artes y Costumbres Populares (folk art and crafts), and a Museo Internacional de Arte Naif (with works by self-taught artists from all over the world). The hours (see above) are the same for all three attractions, and none charge admission.

Underneath the palace, near calle San Juan and the Chapel of St. Andrew (San Andrés), are the former Arab baths. They represent some of the most important Moorish architecture from the 11th century ever discovered in Spain—in fact, they are the most significant ruins of Arab baths in the country. You can visit a warm room, a hot room, and a cold room—the last with a barrel vault and 12 star-shaped chandeliers. Later you can go upstairs to see the folk art and the Naif collection that opened in 1990.

WHERE TO STAY

Hotel Condesable Iranzo. Paseo de la Estacion, 32, 23008 Jaén. ☎ **953-22-28-00.** Fax 953-26-38-07. 165 units. A/C MINIBAR TV TEL. 8,500–10,500 ptas. ($51–$63) double; 14,000 ptas. ($84) suite. AE, DC, MC, V. Parking 1,100 ptas. ($6.60).

No hidden old-fashioned Andalusian charm here—what you see is what you get in this large 12-floor hotel occupying an entire corner of the main square. The building is no beauty, but it is well located, has a good view of the castle and the mountains, and has a wide range of facilities. In the public areas the decor is a shiny combination of marble, glass, and wood. The midsized rooms are functional and comfortable—a good deal for the low price. Apart from various convention rooms, the hotel has four reception areas, two coffee bars, a disco that stays open until 4am, and two restaurants, which serve very reasonably priced meals with a *menú del día* at 2,300 ptas. ($13.80).

Hotel Europa. Plaza de Belén, 1, 23003 Jaén. ☎ **953-22-27-00.** Fax 953-22-26-92. www. husa.es. E-mail: pemana@ofijaen.com. 37 units. A/C TV TEL. 9,700 ptas. ($58) double; 11,560 ptas. ($70) triple. Rates include continental breakfast. AE, DC, MC, V. Parking 860 ptas. ($5.15).

In the commercial and historical center of Jaén, this little hotel is a winner following a massive renovation, which brought everything up to date. Although the avant-garde decor is a little severe, it manages to be cozy and contemporary at the same time. The medium-size rooms have been spruced up, with firm new mattresses and sparkling clean bathrooms. The hotel has a coffee bar but no restaurant.

✪ Parador Castillo de Santa Catalina. Castillo de Santa Catalina, 23000 Jaén. ☎ **953-23-00-00.** Fax 953-23-09-30. 45 units. A/C MINIBAR TV TEL. 18,500 ptas. ($111) double. AE, DC, MC, V. Free parking. Follow Carretera al Castillo y Neveraol.

Three miles (5km) to the east on the hill overlooking the city, this castle is one of the government's showplace paradors, and staying here is reason enough to visit Jaén. In the 10th century the castle was a Muslim fortress surrounded by high protective walls and approached only by a steep, winding road. The castle is still reached by the same road; visitors enter through a three-story-high baronial hallway, and a polite staff shows them to their balconied and midsized rooms (doubles only), tastefully furnished and comfortable, with spick-and-span tile bathrooms equipped with hair dryers.

Dining: Dining at the castle is quite dramatic—the high-vaulted restaurant looks like a small cathedral with its wrought-iron chandeliers and stone arches, plus a raised hearth and a collection of copper kettles and ceramics. On either side of the lofty room, arched windows open onto either a terrace or a fabulous view of town. Lunch or dinner here includes typical Jaén dishes—usually made with the olives for which the area is famous—and regional wine.

Amenities: Room service, concierge, baby-sitting, dry cleaning/laundry.

Xauen. Plaza Deán Mazas, 3, 23001 Jaén. ☎ **953-24-07-89.** Fax 953-24-07-89. 35 units. A/C TV TEL. 8,000 ptas. ($48) double. MC, V. Parking 500 ptas. ($3).

This family-run hotel stands a block west of Plaza de la Constitución. The handcrafted detailing of the building and its central location make it an attractive choice, but it's certainly modest. The small guest rooms are simply furnished but comfortable, with good beds and immaculate bathrooms. Breakfast is served daily. If you're driving, you might have to park far away from the entrance.

WHERE TO DINE

Consider a meal in the luxurious hilltop parador commanding a view of Jaén (see above). It's one of the loveliest spots in the area.

Casa Vicente. Francisco Martín Mora, 1. ☎ **953-23-22-22.** Reservations recommended. Main courses 2,000–3,000 ptas. ($12–$18); set menu 3,000 ptas. ($18). AE, DC, MC, V. Mon–Sat noon–5pm and 8pm–midnight; Sun noon–5pm. Closed Aug. ANDALUSIAN.

Near the cathedral in the historic district, this restaurant is part of a palace dating from the 16th century, complete with granite columns and a central patio ringed by the dining areas. A bullfighting motif dominates. The "casa" is praised locally for the quality of its tapas and its good wine. The area surrounding the town is known for its vegetables, which are showcased here in such dishes as *espinaca esparragada* (spinach with a vegetable sauce) or *alcachofa natural* (artichokes in garlic). For a main dish, we recommend either the *lomo de orsa Mozárabe* (lamb in a sweet and sour sauce, based on an old Moorish recipe) or *bacalao encebollado* (salt cod sauteed with onions and sweet peppers). Two local desserts are rice pudding and *manjarblanco Mozárabe* (fudge, Moorish style).

Mesón Rio Chico. Calle Nueva, 14. ☎ **953-24-08-02.** Reservations recommended. Main courses 1,600–2,600 ptas. ($9.60–$15.60). AE, DC, MC, V. Tues–Sun noon–3:30pm and 9–11:30pm. ANDALUSIAN.

Charming, intimate, and serving authentic regional cuisine, this restaurant has been around since 1962 in a simple modern building in the heart of Jaén. Menu items include strongly flavored versions of hake, beefsteak, roasted pork, and chicken. Because there's room for only 45 diners at a time, it's important to reserve in advance. In spite of its informality and simplicity, many locals claim this is their favorite dining room in town, even though many recipes and dishes haven't been changed since the 1960s.

BAEZA

28 miles (45km) NE of Jaén, 191 miles (307.5km) S of Madrid

Historic Baeza (known to the Romans as Vilvatia), with its Gothic and plateresque buildings and cobblestoned streets, is one of the best-preserved old towns in Spain. At twilight, lanterns hang on walls of plastered stone, flickering against the darkening sky and lighting the narrow streets. The town had its heyday in the 16th and 17th centuries, and in the Visigothic period was the seat of a bishop.

ESSENTIALS

GETTING THERE   The nearest important railway junction, receiving trains from Madrid and most of Andalusia, is the Estación Linares-Baeza (☎ **953-65-02-02**),

8½ miles (14km) west of Baeza's center. For information about which trains arrive there, refer to the section on Jaén, above.

There are 10 buses a day to Úbeda; the ride is 15 minutes long, costing 100 ptas. (60¢) one way. From Jaén, there are seven buses per day (trip time: 1 hour), costing 445 ptas. ($2.65) one way. For more information, call ☎ **953-74-01-68.**

Baeza lies east of the N-V, the superhighway linking Madrid with Granada. Highway 321/322, which runs through Baeza, links Córdoba with Valencia.

VISITOR INFORMATION   The **tourist information office** is at Plaza del Pópulo (☎ **953-74-04-44**). It's open Monday to Friday 9am to 2:30pm, and Saturday 10am to 12:30pm.

EXPLORING BAEZA

Entering Baeza from Jaén you'll approach the main square, **Plaza del Pópulo,** a two-story open colonnade, and a good point to begin exploring. The buildings here date in part from the 16th century and one of the most interesting houses the tourist office (see above), where you can get a map to help guide you through the town. Look for the fountain containing four half-effaced lions, the Fuente de los Leones, which may have been brought here from the Roman town of Cantulo.

Head south along the Cuesta de San Gil to reach the Gothic and Renaissance **cathedral,** Plaza de la Fuente de Santa María (no phone), constructed in the 16th century on the foundations of an earlier mosque. Look for the *Puerta de la Luna* (Moon Door), in Arab-Gothic style, and in the interior, remodeled by Andrés de Vandelvira and his pupils, the carved wood and the brilliant painted *rejas* (iron screens). The Gold Chapel is especially outstanding. The cathedral is open daily 10:30am to 1pm and 4 to 7pm; admission is free.

After leaving the cathedral, continue up the Cuesta de San Felipe to the **Palacio de Jabalquinto,** a beautiful example of civil architecture in the flamboyant Gothic style, built by Juan Alfonso de Benavides, a relative of King Ferdinand. Its facade is filled with interesting decorative elements, and there is a simple Renaissance-style courtyard with marble columns. Inside, two lions guard the heavily decorated baroque stairway.

WHERE TO DINE

Casa Juanito. In the Hotel Juanito, Plaza del Arca del Agua, s/n. ☎ **953-74-00-40.** Reservations required Fri–Sat. Main courses 3,500–4,500 ptas. ($21–$27). MC, V. Daily 1–4pm; Tues–Sat 8–11pm. Closed Nov 1–15. ANDALUSIAN.

Owners Juan Antonio and Luisa Salcedo serve regional specialties from Andalusia and La Mancha. Devotees of the lost art of Jaén cookery, they revive ancient recipes in their frequently changing suggestions for the day. The hotel owners run a small olive oil outlet and use only their own produce when cooking. Game is served in season, and many vegetable dishes are made with ham. Among the savory and well-prepared menu items are *habas* (beans), fillet of beef with tomatoes and peppers, partridge in pastry crust, and codfish house style.

El Sali. Pasaje Cardenal Benavides, 9. ☎ **953-74-13-65.** Reservations not required. Main courses 1,000–2,600 ptas. ($6–$15.60); fixed-price menu 1,800 ptas. ($10.80). AE, DC, MC, V. Daily 1–4pm; Thurs–Tues 8:30–11:30pm. Closed Sept 20–Oct 15. SPANISH/ANDALUSIAN.

This restaurant is set in a modern building erected in the 1980s in the town center, adjacent to Plaza del Pópulo. In air-conditioned comfort diners enjoy what many locals regard as the most reasonable set menu in town, and in the summer diners can sit on a terrace that overlooks the city's Renaissance monuments. The owners serve not only the cuisine of Andalusia but also certain dishes from around Spain. They are known for their fresh vegetables, as exemplified by *la pipirana,* a cold medley of vegetables with tuna, accented with boiled eggs, fresh tomatoes, onions, and spices (only in summer). The atmosphere is relaxed, the service cordial, and the portions generous. You won't leave feeling hungry or overcharged.

ÚBEDA

6 miles (10km) NE of Jaén, 194 miles (312km) S of Madrid

A former stronghold of the Arabs often called the "Florence of Andalusia," Úbeda is a Spanish National Landmark filled with golden-brown Renaissance palaces and tile-roofed whitewashed houses. The best way to discover Úbeda's charm is to wander its narrow cobblestoned streets.

The government long ago created a parador here in a renovated ducal palace—you might stop for lunch if you're not pressed for time. Allow time for a stroll through Úbeda's shops, which specialize in leather craft goods and esparto grass carpets.

The palaces and churches of the city are almost endless. You might begin your tour at the centrally located **Plaza de Vázquez de Molina,** which is flanked by several mansions, including the Casa de las Cadenas, now the Town Hall. The mansions have been decaying for centuries, but many are now finally being restored.

ESSENTIALS

GETTING THERE   The nearest train station is the Linares-Baeza station (☎ **953-65-02-02**). For information on trains to and from the station, refer to the Jaén section (see above).

There are 15 buses daily to Baeza, less than 6 miles (10km) away, and to Jaén. Seven buses per day go to the busy railway station at Linares-Baeza, where a train can take you virtually anywhere in Spain. Bus service to and from Córdoba, Seville, and Granada is also available. Úbeda's bus station is in the heart of the modern town, on calle San José (☎ **953-75-21-57**), where signs will point you on a downhill walk to the *zona monumental.*

To drive here, turn off the Madrid–Córdoba road and head east for Linares, then on to Úbeda, a detour of 26 miles (42km). The turnoff is at the junction with Route 322.

VISITOR INFORMATION   The **tourist information office** is at avenida Cristo Rey, 2 (☎ **953-75-08-97**). It's open Monday to Friday 9am to 2:30pm, Saturday 11am to 2pm.

EXPLORING ÚBEDA

Iglesia El Salvador. Plaza de Vázquez de Molina. No phone. Free admission. Daily 9am–1pm and 5–7pm.

One of the grandest examples of Spanish Renaissance architecture, this church was designed in 1536 by Diego de Siloé. The richly embellished portal is mere window dressing for the wealth of decoration inside the church, including a sacristy designed by Andréas de Vandelvira and a single nave with gold-and-blue vaulting. The many sculptures and altarpieces and the spectacular rose windows are of special interest.

Iglesia de San Pablo. Plaza 1 de Mayo. No phone. Free admission. Daily 9am–1pm and 7–9pm.

This church in the center of the old town is almost as fascinating as the Iglesia El Salvador. The Gothic San Pablo is famous for its 16th-century south portal in the Isabelline style and for its chapels.

Hospital de Santiago. Calle Cristo Rey. ☎ **953-75-08-42.** Admission 225 ptas. ($1.35). Mon–Fri 8am–3pm and 3:30–10pm; Sat 8am–3pm.

On the western edge of town off the calle del Obispo Coros stands the Hospital of Santiago, completed in 1575 and still in use today. Built by Andrés de Vandelvira, "the Christopher Wren of Úbeda," over the years it has earned a reputation as the "Escorial of Andalusia." Today the hospital is a cultural venue, hosting concerts and containing a minor modern art museum.

Iglesia de Santa María de Los Reales Alcázares. Arroyo de Santa María. ☎ **953-75-07-77.** Free admission. Daily 9am–1pm and 5–7pm.

Another intriguing Úbeda church is Santa María de los Reales Alcázares, on the site of a former Arab mosque. The cloisters, with their fan vaulting, are Gothic; the interior, with its tiled and painted ceiling, blends the Gothic and Mudéjar styles. Also inside the church you'll find a gruesome statue of a mutilated Christ. Santa María is in the center of town, opposite the *Ayuntamiento* (Town Hall).

WHERE TO STAY

Hotel la Paz. Calle Andalucía, 1, 23400 Úbeda. ☎ **953-75-21-46.** Fax 953-75-08-48. 50 units. A/C TV TEL. 7,500–8,000 ptas. ($45–$48) double. AE, DC, MC, V. Parking 1,000 ptas. ($6).

Set on a sharply angled street corner in the heart of the commercial district opposite a statue to a military hero, this seven-story hotel contains comfortably unpretentious rooms. Each is decorated in simple Iberian style with dignified wood furniture and either pure white or papered walls. The hotel was built in 1971 and renovated in 1994 with new mattresses and rejuvenated plumbing. The street-level El Olivo restaurant opens directly onto the sidewalk and does a thriving business with the local community. There's a simple snack restaurant for coffee and drinks, plus a bar. Services include laundry and baby-sitting.

✪ **Palacio de la Rambla.** Plaza del Marqués, 1, 23400 Úbeda. ☎ **953-75-01-96.** Fax 953-75-02-67. 8 units. MINIBAR TV TEL. 14,000 ptas. ($84) double; 16,000 ptas. ($96) suite. Rates include buffet breakfast. AE, MC, V. Closed July 15–Aug 15. Parking 600 ptas. ($3.60).

When the Marquesa de la Rambla arrives in town, she stays here at her ancestral home dating from the 16th century. It's been in her family since it was constructed. Eight of its bedrooms are open to paying guests, who prefer the Renaissance *palacio* style. The spacious manorial bedrooms have many of their original furnishings, but everything has been supplemented with modern conveniences. Each has a private, fully equipped bathroom and is individually furnished, often with tapestries, objets d'art, and other remnants of aristocratic life in old Spain. The cloistered courtyard, an ideal retreat on a hot day, is surrounded by granite columns. An Andalusian breakfast is served each day.

✪ **Parador Nacional del Condestabe Dávalos.** Plaza de Vázquez de Molina, 1, 23400 Úbeda. ☎ **953-75-03-45.** Fax 953-75-12-59. 32 units. A/C MINIBAR TV TEL. 19,000–22,000 ptas. ($114–$132) double; 25,000 ptas. ($150) suite. AE, DC, MC, V.

In the heart of town on the most central square, near the Town Hall, stands this 16th-century palace turned parador, which shares an old paved plaza with the Iglesia El Salvador and its dazzling facade. The formal entrance to the Renaissance palace leads to an enclosed patio, encircled by two levels of Moorish arches, where palms and potted plants stand on the tile floors. The guest rooms, doubles only, are nearly two stories high, with beamed ceilings and tall windows. Antiques and reproductions adorn the rooms, and the beds are comfortable, the bathrooms immaculate.

Dining: Before lunch or dinner, stop in at the low-beamed wine cellar, with its stone arches, provincial stools and tables, and giant kegs of wine. Dinner is served in a tastefully decorated ground-floor room, where a costumed staff serves traditional Spanish dishes.

Amenities: Concierge, laundry and dry cleaning, massages, newspaper delivery, room service.

WHERE TO DINE

Parador Restaurante Nacional del Condestabe Dávalos. Plaza de Vázques de Molina. ☎ **953-75-03-45.** Reservations recommended. Main courses 2,000–2,800 ptas. ($12–$16.80); *menú del parador* 3,500 ptas. ($21); tasting menu 6,500 ptas. ($39) for 2 people. AE, DC, MC, V. Daily 1:30–4pm and 8:30–11pm. SPANISH/ANDALUSIAN.

This parador is the best place to dine for miles around. Although the cuisine here isn't the most creative, it's made with market-fresh ingredients prepared from recipes handed down through decades. The menu is wide ranging, with varied choices in all categories. Fish is the most limited offering, which is natural given that Jaén is so far inland. Start with a really typical dish of the area, such as cold soup with almonds, most delightful on a hot day. Partridge is a local favorite; appetizers might include stuffed green peppers with partridge, an unusual combination of stewed partridge with plums, or a refreshing salad with marinated partridge. The best fish dish, in our view, is grilled monkfish in a saffron sauce, but the grilled sole with garlic and an apple vinegar sauce is enticing. Meat eaters might be tempted by the regional dishes, such as oxtail in red wine sauce or stewed kid with pinenuts. The *menú del parador* is a good bet, including an appetizer plus fish or meat for a main course and dessert. For the adventurous palate, the tasting menu for two showcases four typical regional dishes nightly.

2 Córdoba

65 miles (105km) W of Jaén, 260 miles (419km) SW of Madrid

Ten centuries ago Córdoba was one of the greatest cities in the world, with a population of 900,000. The capital of Muslim Spain, it was Europe's largest city and a cultural and intellectual center. This seat of the Western Caliphate flourished with public baths, mosques, a great library, and palaces. Later, greedy hordes passed through sacking the city, tearing down ancient buildings, and carting off many art treasures. Despite these assaults, Córdoba still retains traces of its former glory—enough to challenge Seville and Granada as the most fascinating city in Andalusia.

Today this provincial capital is known chiefly for its mosque, but it abounds with other artistic and architectural riches, especially its lovely homes. The old Arab and Jewish quarters are famous for their narrow streets lined with whitewashed houses boasting flower-filled patios and balconies, and it's perfectly acceptable to walk along gazing into the courtyards. This isn't an invasion of privacy: The citizens of Córdoba take pride in showing off their patios as part of the city's tradition. And don't forget to bring along a good pair of walking shoes, as the only way to explore the monumental heart of the city is on foot.

Córdoba has recently joined the ranks of UNESCO's World Heritage sites, so you'll want to spend at least a couple of days here.

ESSENTIALS

GETTING THERE   Córdoba is a railway junction for routes to the rest of both Andalusia and Spain. There are about 22 **TALGO** and **AVE** trains daily between Córdoba and Madrid (1½ to 2 hours). Other, slower trains (*tranvías*) take 5 to 8 hours

JARDINES DIEGO DE RIVAS

JARDINES DE LA VICTORIA

JARDINES DEL ALCÁZAR

Guadalquivir

ATTRACTIONS ●
Alcázar de los Reyes
   Cristianos **2**
Conjunto Arqueológico
   Madinat Al-Zahra **15**
Mezquita-Catedral de
   Córdoba **6**
Museo Arqueológico
   Provincial **12**
Museo de Bellas Artes
   de Córdoba **19**
Museo de Julio Romero
   de Torres **19**
Museo Municipal de Arte
   Táurino **3**
Palacio Museo de Viana **21**
Sinagoga **6**
Torre de la Calhorra **1**

ACCOMMODATIONS ■
Armistad Córdoba **5**
El Conquistador Hotel **9**
Hotel Averroes **20**
Hotel Las Adelfa **17**
Hotel Macia Alfaros **18**
Hotel Maimónides **7**
Hotel Marisa **8**

Hotel Mezquita **10**
Hotel Residencia
   El Califia **13**
Hotel Selu **14**
Los Omeyas **11**
Parador Nacional
   de la Arruzafa **17**
Sol Inn Gallos **16**

0   1/8 mi
0   1/8 km

for the same transit. There are also 25 trains from Seville every day (1½ hours). The main railway station is on the town's northern periphery, at avenida de América, 130, near the corner of avenida de Cervantes. For information, call ☎ **957-49-02-02.** To reach the heart of the old town from the station, head south on avenida de Cervantes or avenida del Gran Capitán. While you're staying in Córdoba, if you want to buy a ticket or to get departure times and prices, you can go to the RENFE office at Ronda de los Tejares, 10 (☎ **957-47-58-54**).

There are several different bus companies serving Córdoba, each of which maintains a separate terminal. The town's most important bus terminal is at calle Diego Serrano, 14, a block south of avenida Medina Azahara, 29 (☎ **957-23-64-74**), on the western outskirts of town (just west of the gardens beside Paseo de la Victoria). The bus company there is called Alsina Graells Sur.

From the bus terminal operated by Empresa Bacoma, avenida de Cervantes, 22 (☎ **957-45-65-14**), a short walk south of the railway station, there are three buses per day to and from Seville (a 2-hour and 3-hour trip, respectively) and five daily buses to Jaén (3 hours). Buses arrive here from Madrid (5½ hours).

Córdoba lies astride the N-IV (E-5) connecting Madrid with Seville. Don't think of entering the complicated maze of streets in the old town with a car, though. You'll inevitably get lost and find no place to park. There are two small public parking lots outside the old town, one on calle Robledo, the other on calle Aeropeurto. Both are well positioned, well marked, and easy to find.

VISITOR INFORMATION The **tourist information office** is at calle Torrijos, 10 (☎ **957-47-12-35**). It's open Monday to Saturday 9:30am to 8pm and Sunday 9am to 2pm.

EXPLORING THE CITY

Among the many sights of Córdoba is the **Roman bridge (Puente Romano),** believed to date from the time of Augustus. It's hardly Roman anymore because not one of its 16 supporting arches is original. The sculptor Bernabé Gómez del Río erected a statue of St. Raphael in the middle of the bridge in 1651. The Roman bridge crosses the Guadalquivir River about 1 block south of the Mezquita.

Plaza de Toros on Grand Vía del Parque stages its major bullfights in May, although fights are presented at other times of the year. Watch for local announcements. Most hotels will arrange tickets for you, ranging in price (in general) from 1,000 to 2,000 ptas. ($6 to $12). Call ☎ **957-41-49-99** for information.

✪ **Mezquita-Catedral de Córdoba.** Torrijos and calle Cardenal Herrero, s/n. ☎ **957-47-05-12.** Admission 750 ptas. ($4.50) adults, 375 ptas. ($2.25) children under 13. May–Sept, daily 10am–7pm; Oct–Apr, daily 10am–6pm.

Dating from the 8th century, the Mezquita was the crowning Muslim architectural achievement in the West, rivaled only by the mosque at Mecca. It is a fantastic labyrinth of red-and-white peppermint-striped pillars. To the astonishment of visitors, a cathedral now sits awkwardly in the middle of the mosque, disturbing the purity of the lines. The 16th-century cathedral, a blend of many styles, is impressive in its own right, with an intricately carved ceiling and baroque choir stalls. Additional ill-conceived annexes later turned the Mezquita into an architectural oddity. Its most interesting feature is the mihrab, a domed shrine of Byzantine mosaics that once housed the Koran.

After exploring the interior, stroll through the Courtyard of the Orange Trees, which has a beautiful fountain. The hardy can climb a 16th-century tower built here on the base of a Moorish minaret to catch a panoramic view of Córdoba and its environs.

The Mezquita is south of the train station, just north of the Roman bridge.

✪ **Alcázar de los Reyes Cristianos.** Plaza Santo de los Mártires. ☎ **957-42-01-51.** Admission 425 ptas. ($2.55) adults, 150 ptas. (90¢) children. May–Sept, Tues–Sat 10am–2pm and 6–8pm, Sun 10am–2pm; Oct–Apr, Tues–Sat 9:30am–3pm and 4:30–6:30pm, Sun 9:30am–3pm. Gardens illuminated, May–Sept 10pm–1am. Bus: 3 or 12.

Commissioned in 1328 by Alfonso XI (the "Just"), the Alcázar of the Christian Kings is a fine example of military architecture. Ferdinand and Isabella governed Castile from this fortress on the river as they prepared to reconquer Granada, the last Moorish stronghold in Spain. Columbus journeyed here to fill Isabella's ears with his plans for discovery.

Located 2 blocks southwest of the Mezquita, this quadrangular building is notable for powerful walls and a trio of towers—the Tower of the Lions, the Tower of Allegiance, and the Tower of the River. The Tower of the Lions contains intricately decorated ogival ceilings that are the most notable example of Gothic architecture in Andalusia.

The beautiful gardens, illuminated at night, and the Moorish baths are celebrated attractions. The Patio Morisco is another lovely spot, its pavement decorated with the arms of León and Castile. A Roman sarcophagus is representative of 2nd- and 3rd-century funeral art and the Roman mosaics are outstanding—especially a unique piece dedicated to Polyphemus and Galatea.

Sinagoga. Calle de los Judíos. ☎ **957-20-29-28.** Admission 75 ptas. (45¢). Tues–Sat 10am–2pm and 3:30–5:30pm; Sun 10am–1:30pm. Bus: 3 or 12.

In Córdoba you'll find one of Spain's few remaining pre-Inquisition synagogues, built in 1350 in the *Barrio de la Judería* (Jewish Quarter), 2 blocks west of the northern wall of the Mezquita. The synagogue is noted particularly for its stucco work; the east wall contains a large orifice where the Tabernacle was once placed (inside, the scrolls of the Pentateuch were kept). After the Jews were expelled from Spain, the synagogue was turned into a hospital, until it became a Catholic chapel in 1588.

Museo de Bellas Artes de Córdoba. Plaza del Potro, 1. ☎ **957-47-33-45.** Admission 250 ptas. ($1.50) adults, free for children 11 and under. Tues 3–8pm; Wed–Sat 9am–8pm; Sun and public holidays 9am–3pm. Bus: 3, 4, 7, or 12.

As you cross the Plaza del Potro to reach the Fine Arts Museum, notice the fountain at one end of the square. Built in 1557, it shows a young stallion with forelegs raised, holding the shield of Córdoba.

Housed in an old hospital on the plaza, the Fine Arts Museum contains medieval Andalusian paintings, examples of Spanish baroque art, and works by many of Spain's important 19th- and 20th-century painters, including Goya. The museum is east of the Mezquita, about a block south of the Church of St. Francis (San Francisco).

Museo de Julio Romero de Torres. Plaza del Potro. ☎ **957-49-19-09.** Admission 425 ptas. ($2.55) adults, 210 ptas. ($1.25) children under 18, free for adults over 75. Free on Tues. Oct–Apr, Tues–Sat 10am–2pm and 5–7pm; May–Sept, Tues–Sat 10am–2pm and 6–8pm, Sun 9:30am–3pm.

Across the patio from the Fine Arts Museum, this museum honors Julio Romero de Torres, a Córdoba-born artist who died in 1930. It contains his celebrated *Oranges and Lemons,* and other notable works such as *The Little Girl Who Sells Fuel, Sin,* and *A Dedication to the Art of the Bullfight.* A corner of Romero's Madrid studio has been reproduced in one of the rooms, displaying the paintings left unfinished at his death.

Museo Municipal de Arte Táurino. Plaza de las Bulas (also called Plaza Maimónides). ☎ **957-20-10-56.** Admission 425 ptas. ($2.55), free for children under 18. May–Sept, Tues–Sat 10:30am–2pm and 6–8pm, Sun 9:30am–3pm; Oct–Apr, Mon–Sat 10am–2pm and 5–7pm, Sun 9:30am–3pm. Bus: 3 or 12.

Memorabilia of great bullfights are housed here in the Jewish Quarter in a 16th-century building, inaugurated in 1983 as an appendage to the Museo Municipal de Arte Cordobesas. Its ample galleries recall Córdoba's great bullfighters with suits of lights, pictures, trophies, posters, even stuffed bulls' heads. You'll see a wax likeness of Manolete in repose and the blood-smeared uniform of El Cordobés—both of these famous matadors came from Córdoba. The museum is about a block northwest of the Mezquita, midway between the mosque and the synagogue.

Torre de la Calahorra. Avenida de la Confederación, Puente Romano. ☎ **957-29-39-29.** Admission to museum, 500 ptas. ($3) adults, 400 ptas. ($2.40) children; multimedia presentation, 650 ptas. ($3.90) adults, 550 ptas. ($3.30) children. May–Sept, daily 10am–2pm and 4:30–8:30pm; Oct–Apr, daily 10am–6pm; *multivisión,* 11am, noon, 3pm, 4pm. Last tour 1 hour before closing time. Bus: 16.

The Tower of Calahorra stands across the river at the southern end of the Roman bridge. Commissioned by Henry II of Trastamara in 1369 to protect him from his brother, Peter I, it now houses a town museum where visitors can take a self-guided tour with headsets. One room houses wax figures of Córdoba's famous philosophers, including Averro and Maimónides. Other rooms exhibit a miniature model of the Alhambra, at Granada, complete with water fountains; a miniature Mezquita; and a display of Arab musical instruments. Finally, you can climb to the top of the tower for some panoramic views of the Roman bridge, the river, and the cathedral/mosque.

✪ **Museo Arqueológico Provincial.** Plaza Jerónimo Paz, 7. ☎ **957-47-40-11.** Admission 250 ptas. ($1.50). Tues 3–8pm; Wed–Sat 9am–8pm; Sun and public holidays 9am–3pm.

Córdoba's Archaeological Museum, 2 blocks northeast of the Mezquita, is one of the most important in Spain. Housed in a palace dating from 1505, it displays artifacts left behind by the various peoples and conquerors who have swept through the province. There are Paleolithic and Neolithic items, Iberian hand weapons and ceramics, and Roman sculptures, bronzes, ceramics, inscriptions, and mosaics. Especially interesting are the Visigothic artifacts. The most outstanding collection, however, is devoted to Arabic art and spans the entire Muslim occupation. Take a few minutes to relax in one of the patios, with its fountains and ponds.

Palacio Museo de Viana. Plaza de Don Gome, 2. ☎ **957-48-01-34.** Palace admission 400 ptas. ($2.40); patios 200 ptas. ($1.20). June–Sept, Thurs–Tues 9am–2pm; Oct–May, Thurs–Sat and Mon–Tues 10am–1pm and 4–6pm, Sun 10am–2pm. Closed June 1–15.

The public has seldom had access to Córdoba's palaces, but that's changed with the opening of this museum. Visitors are shown into a carriage house, where the elegant vehicles of another era are displayed. Note the intricate leather decoration on the carriages and the leather wall hangings, some of which date from the period of the Reconquest; there's also a collection of leather paintings. You can wander at leisure through the garden and patios. The palace is 4 blocks southeast of Plaza de Colón on the northeastern edge of the old quarter.

A NEARBY ATTRACTION

Conjunto Arqueológico Madinat Al-Zahra. Carretera Palma de Río, km 8. ☎ **957-32-91-30.** Admission 400 ptas. ($2.40). June 16–Sept 15, Tues–Sat 10am–1:30pm and 6–8:30pm, Sun 10am–1:30pm; Sept 16–Sept 30 and May 1–June 15, Tues–Sat 10am–2pm and 6–8:30pm, Sun 10am–2pm; Oct 1–Apr 30, Tues–Sat 10am–2pm and 4–6:30pm, Sun 10am–2pm. Bus: A bus leaves from the station on calle de la Bodega, but it lets you off about 2 miles (3km) from the site.

This palace, a kind of Moorish Versailles just outside Córdoba, was constructed in the 10th century by the first caliph of Andalus, Abd ar-Rahman III. He named it after the favorite of his harem, nicknamed "the brilliant." Thousands of workers and animals slaved to build this mammoth pleasure palace, said to have contained 300 baths and 400 houses. Over the years the site was plundered for building materials; in fact, it might have been viewed as a quarry for the entire region. Some of its materials, so it is claimed, went to build the Alcázar in Seville. The Royal House, rendezvous point for the ministers, has been reconstructed. The principal salon remains in fragments, though, so you have to imagine it in its majesty. Just beyond the Royal House are the ruins of a mosque constructed to face Mecca. The Berbers sacked the place in 1013.

SHOPPING

In Moorish times Córdoba was famous for its leather workers, known as "cordwainers." Highly valued in 15th-century Europe, their leather was studded with gold and silver ornaments, then painted with embossed designs (*guadamaci*). Large panels of it often served in lieu of tapestries. Today the industry has fallen into decline, and the market is filled mostly with cheap imitations. You might want to seek out the following shop, especially if you're interested in Córdoban handcrafts: **Artesanía Andaluza,** Tomás Conde, 3 (no phone), near the bullfight museum, features a vast array of Córdoban handcrafts, especially filigree silver from the mines of Sierra

Morena and some excellently crafted embossed leather, a holdover from the Muslim heyday. Lots of junk is mixed in with the good stuff, though, so beware.

Arte Zoco, calle de los Judios, s/n (no phone), is the largest association of crafts-people in Córdoba. Established in the Jewish Quarter as a business cooperative in the mid-1980s, it assembles on one site the creative output of about a dozen artisans whose mediums include leather, wood, silver, crystal, terra-cotta, and iron. About a half dozen of the artisans maintain their studios on the premises, so you can visit and check out the techniques and tools they use to pursue their crafts. You'll find everything from new, iconoclastic, and avant-garde designs to pieces that honor centuries-old traditions. Of special interest is the revival of the *Califar* pottery first introduced to Córdoba during the regimes of the Muslim caliphs. The shop is open Monday to Friday 9:30am to 8pm, Saturday and Sunday 9:30am to 2pm. The workshops and studios of the various artisans open and close according to the whims of their occupants, but are usually maintained Monday to Friday 10am to 2pm and 5:30 to 8pm.

Libreria Seferad, calle Romero, 4 (☎ **957-29-88-95**), set across from Córdoba's only synagogue, is a cubbyhole-sized place selling articles that hark back to the Sephardic culture of medieval Europe. You'll find tapes of Sephardic music and chants, pottery fashioned in traditional Sephardic designs, filigreed silver ornaments, and reference works to Ladino, the medieval Iberian dialect spoken by Jews throughout the Diaspora. Inventory is limited, and hours are erratic, usually Monday to Friday 10:30am to 8:30pm.

Angel López-Obrero and his two sons run **Meryan,** calleja de Las Flores, 2 (☎ **957-47-59-02**), on one of the most colorful streets in the city. In this 250-year-old building you can see artisans plying their crafts; although most items must be custom-ordered, some ready-made pieces are for sale, including cigarette boxes, jewel cases, attaché cases, book and folio covers, and ottoman covers. Open Monday to Friday 9am to 8pm and Saturday 9am to 2pm.

Córdoba has a branch of Spain's major department store, **El Corte Inglés,** at Ronda de los Tejares, 32 (☎ **957-47-02-67**). At least some of the staff speaks English. It's open Monday to Saturday 10am to 10:30pm.

WHERE TO STAY

At the peak of its summer season, Córdoba has too few hotels to meet the demand, so reserve as far in advance as possible.

EXPENSIVE

✪ **Armistad Córdoba.** Plaza de Maimónides, 3, 14004 Córdoba. ☎ **957-42-03-35.** Fax 957-42-03-65. www.nh-hoteles.es. 85 units. A/C MINIBAR TV TEL. 19,000 ptas. ($114) double. Parking 1,500 ptas. ($9).

In the heart of the Judería, or old Jewish quarter, this four-star hotel is the most desirable in town. Only a 4-minute walk from the mosque, this three-story structure opened in 1992 after renovations combined two existing 18th-century mansions. The houses face each other and are linked through a small patio of beautiful Andalusian arches and colorful Spanish tiles. The spacious bedrooms are equipped with modern comforts such as excellent beds, and designs are a tasteful combination of wood and fabric. Walls are painted in terra-cotta. In 1998 a newer and more modern wing opened with bedrooms that evoke Scandinavia with their Norwegian wood and sea blues and grays.

Dining/Diversions: The hotel restaurant serves excellent dishes, both regional and national, and there is a cafeteria on site. The hotel bar is a cozy rendezvous point.

Amenities: Concierge, room service, baby-sitting, laundry and dry cleaning.

El Conquistador Hotel. Magistral González Francés, 15, 14003 Córdoba. ☎ **957-48-11-02.** Fax 957-47-46-77. 102 units. A/C MINIBAR TV TEL. 20,000 ptas. ($120) double; from 25,000 ptas. ($150) suite. AE, DC, MC, V. Parking 1,950 ptas. ($11.70). Bus: 12.

Built centuries ago as a private villa, this first-class three-story hotel was tastefully renovated in 1986 into one of the most attractive in town, with triple rows of stone-trimmed windows and ornate iron balustrades. It sits opposite an unused rear entrance to the Mezquita. The marble-and-granite lobby opens into an interior courtyard filled with seasonal flowers, a pair of splashing fountains, and a symmetrical stone arcade. The quality, size, and comfort of the rooms—each with a black-and-white marble floor and a private bathroom—earn the hotel four government-granted stars. Bathrooms are well maintained and equipped with toiletries and a hair dryer.

Amenities: There is no restaurant, but a coffee shop and a bar serve snacks and drinks. Baby-sitting, room service, laundry and valet, garage, sauna, solarium, car-rental facilities. The lack of bellboys may be an annoyance in an otherwise quality operation.

Hotel Las Adelfas. Avenida de la Arruzafa, s/n, 14012 Córdoba. ☎ **957-27-7420.** Fax 957-27-2794. E-mail: adelfas@arrakis.es. 96 units. A/C MINIBAR TV TEL. 17,000 ptas. ($102) double; 25,000 ptas. ($150) suite. AE, DC, MC, V. Parking 750 ptas. ($4.50). Bus: 10 or 11.

This attractive, modern hotel is in the salubrious residential area El Brillante, a 10-minute drive from the center of Córdoba. The decade-old hotel stands on its own grounds, known as the Balcón de Córdoba, or balcony of Córdoba. The views of the city at night are panoramic. The spacious, tastefully decorated accommodations are large and furnished in luxurious contemporary fashion. Guests always find a bowl of seasonal fruit in their rooms as well as oversized beds with firm and comfortable mattresses. Bathrooms are good-sized, immaculately kept, and well equipped, each with a hair dryer.

Dining/Diversions: The hotel offers a good restaurant with an international menu, plus a cafeteria and cozy bar. In summer it serves barbecue meals outside on the terrace.

Amenities: Swimming pool with vista, laundry, access to a fully equipped gym nearby, beautiful gardens, tennis courts.

Hotel Macia Alfaros. Calle Alfaros, 18, 14001 Córdoba. ☎ **957-49-1920.** Fax 957-49-2210. www.maciahoteles.com. E-mail: alfaros@maciahoteles.com. 133 units. A/C MINIBAR TV TEL. 19,000 ptas. ($114) double; 21,500 ptas. ($129) minisuite. AE, DC, MC, V. Parking 1,400 ptas. ($8.40).

This four-star hotel is located between the city center and many of Córdoba's historic sites and places of interest. The look is vaguely Moorish, but it's merely the mock. Entered through a garage area, not a very attractive opening, the hotel improves remarkably once inside. It is spacious and bright, with large public areas and floors of stone and marble set off against Mudéjar motifs. Dating from 1992, the building has medium-sized bedrooms, each with a safe and fax/computer hookup. Bathrooms are clean and spacious, well equipped with a tub, shower, and hair dryer.

Dining: The hotel restaurant, **Los Alarifes,** serves an international menu but also offers Andalusian specialties. There is a coffee bar as well.

Amenities: Spectacular heated outdoor swimming pool, patios, 24-hour room service, concierge, currency exchange.

Hotel Maimónides. Calle Torrijos, 4, 14003 Córdoba. ☎ **957-47-1500.** Fax 957-48-3803. 82 units. A/C TV TEL. 19,000 ptas. ($114) double; 25,000 ptas. ($150) suite. AE, DC, MC, V. Parking 1,750 ptas. ($10.50).

This hotel in the heart of the historic district has its devotees, although it ranks down the list in charm from the Amistad Córdoba. Its location is ideal, right next to the

Mezquita. The brick facade conceals a recently renovated two-story hotel. Constructed in the mid-1970s, the Maimónides lost some of its Andalusian charm in its update. Today, except for a few tiles in the reception and restaurant area, you get functional bedrooms short on style but long on comfort with new beds and mattresses. Some rooms have a minibar, and all come with safety boxes. The bathrooms, although cramped, contain marble floors, good showers, and hair dryers.

Dining: Only breakfast is served.

Amenities: Laundry, concierge.

✪ **Parador Nacional de la Arruzafa.** Avenida de la Arruzafa, 33, 14012 Córdoba. ☎ **957-27-59-00.** Fax 957-28-04-09. www.parador.es. E-mail: Cordoba@parador.es. 94 units. A/C MINIBAR TV TEL. 18,500–22,000 ptas. ($111–$132) double; 23,000 ptas. ($138) suite. AE, DC, MC, V. Free parking.

Found 2½ miles (4km) outside town in a suburb called El Brillante, this parador, named after an Arab word meaning "palm grove," offers the conveniences and facilities of a luxurious resort hotel at reasonable rates. Occupying the site of a former caliphate palace, it's one of the finest paradors in Spain, with both a view and a swimming pool. The spacious guest rooms have been furnished with fine dark-wood pieces, and some have balconies for eating breakfast or relaxing over a drink. All have private bathrooms equipped with hair dryers.

Dining: A restaurant serves regional specialties, including *salmorejo* (a chilled vegetable variation of gazpacho), stewed oxtail, and a local cake called *pastel cordobés*.

Amenities: The government staff is a bit sleepy, but the hotel offers room service, laundry and valet, baby-sitting, a swimming pool, and a tennis court.

MODERATE

Hotel Residencia El Califa. Lope de Hoces, 14, 14004 Córdoba. ☎ **800/528-1234** in the U.S. and Canada, or 957-29-94-00. Fax 957-29-57-16. www.bestwestern.com. 70 units. A/C TV TEL. 14,000 ptas. ($84) double; 18,000 ptas. ($108) suite. AE, MC, V. Bus: 12.

Attracting mainly Spanish clientele, this centrally located hotel is a short walk northwest of the Mezquita. Although rather impersonal and a bit austere, it is generally a good value. Built in 1974, it rises three floors serviced by two elevators. Inside, the hotel has russet-colored marble floors, velour wall coverings, a spacious lounge, and a TV that seems to broadcast nonstop soccer matches. Upstairs, midsized guest rooms are reasonably comfortable and furnished in a functional modern style. The mattresses are excellent, and the efficiently organized private bathrooms come with shower stalls. In lieu of a restaurant, the hotel has a snack bar and a bar. Parking is available along the street.

Sol Inn Gallos. Medina Azahara, 7, 14005 Córdoba. ☎ **800/336-3542** in the U.S., or 957-23-55-00. Fax 957-23-16-36. 115 units. A/C TV TEL. 11,200–15,000 ptas. ($67.20–$90) double; 15,700 ptas. ($94.20) triple. AE, DC, MC, V.

Half a block from a wide, tree-shaded boulevard on the western edge of town, this aging 1970s hotel stands eight floors high, crowned by an informal roof garden. The hotel is a favorite of both groups and commercial travelers. The comfortable but small guest rooms have many extra comforts, such as balconies, firm mattresses, and neatly organized private bathrooms with hair dryers. An outdoor swimming pool awaits you to jump in on a hot Andalusian day. The hotel offers a restaurant, a drinking lounge, and a spacious public lobby.

INEXPENSIVE

Hotel Averroes. Campo Madrew de Dios, 38, 14002 Córdoba. ☎ **957-43-5981.** Fax 957-43-5981. www.madeinspain.net/hotelescordoba/averroes. E-mail: averroes@yet.es. 72 units. A/C TV TEL. 10,900 ptas. ($65.40) double. AE, DC, MC, V. Bus: 3.

In 1999 this hotel expanded, adding 20 more accommodations after renovating the house next door. The result now is a total of 72 bedrooms, all modernized and distributed throughout two, two-story buildings linked by an impressive patio *córdobes*. With its characteristic tiled walls and classic arches, the patio is a social area with outside tables where guests relax after a day of sightseeing. The bus that stops in front will take you to the town center in just 5 minutes, or else count on a 15-minute stroll. The medium-sized accommodations are comfortable, with marble floors, pastel walls, a private safe, and good-sized beds with extra firm mattresses. All have private and well-equipped bathrooms, each with a hair dryer. On site is a restaurant serving Andalusian cuisine, plus an informal cafeteria where you can order breakfast. Amenities include a concierge and room service until midnight. In 2000 the hotel constructed a swimming pool.

Hotel Marisa. Cardenal Herrero, 6, 14003 Córdoba. ☎ **957-47-3142.** Fax 957-47-4144. 28 units. A/C TEL. 9,500 ptas ($57) double. AE, MC, V. Parking 1,300 ptas. ($7.80).

In front of the Mezquita, this modest hotel is not only one of the most centrally located in Córdoba, but one of the city's best values. Completed in the early '70s, this two-floor hotel has had continuing renovations to keep it in good shape. Most recent improvements have been to the bathrooms, where the plumbing was renewed. Bedrooms are small but cozily comfortable. It's possible to reserve one with a balcony overlooking either the statue of the Virgin of Rosales or the Patio de los Naranjos (oranges). TV is found only in the public area. The architecture and furnishings are in a vague Andalusian style. The hotel does not have a cafeteria but serves a continental breakfast.

Hotel Mezquita. Plaza Santa Catalina, 1, 14003 Córdoba. ☎ **957-47-5585.** Fax 957-47-6219. 22 units. A/C TV TEL. 5,900 ptas. ($35.40) double; 9,850 ptas. ($59.10) suite. AE, DC, MC, V. Parking 2,000 ptas. ($12).

This two-story hotel faces the east side of the mosque and is the closest lodgings you'll find to the Mezquita. In 1998 the hotel was constructed on the site of two old houses, which are now connected by a patio. The decor includes a display of antiques arranged tastefully throughout. The architecture is typically Andalusian—arches, interior patios, and hand-painted tiles, along with old mirrors and chandeliers. The small but comfortable rooms are painted pastels to contrast with the dark oak furnishings. Naturally, the rooms overlooking the Mosque are the first to be booked. Bathrooms are well maintained and equipped; there is an on-site cafeteria offering breakfast and light snacks. Amenities are limited to laundry and a concierge.

Los Omeyas. Calle Encarnacion, 17, 14003 Córdoba. ☎ **957-49-22-67.** Fax 957-49-16-59. 36 units. A/C TV TEL. 8,000–9,000 ptas. ($48–$54) double; 10,000–11,000 ptas. ($60–$66) triple; 11,500–12,500 ptas. ($69–$75) quadruple. AE, DC, MC, V. Parking 1,600 ptas. ($9.60).

If you want to stay in the very heart of Córdoba, you couldn't be better located than this hotel, lying nestled in a tangle of streets in what was the Jewish quarter. The name comes from the Umayyad dynasty who ruled the Muslim empire of al-Andalus. Although recently refurbished, the Arab tradition is still clearly visible in white marble and lattice work. The hotel is naturally lit by a central colonnaded patio furnished with tables, and there is a salon and Arab-style bar. Although in no way grand, the rooms are extremely comfortable and tastefully decorated, and have complete bathrooms; those on the top floor offer a panoramic view of the ancient tower of the Mosque, which is literally around the corner.

WHERE TO DINE

By all means, shake free of your hotel for at least one meal a day in Córdoba. The restaurants are not just places at which to have a quick bite but may combine food with flamenco—so make an evening of it.

EXPENSIVE

Campos de Córdoba. Calle de los Lineros, 32. ☎ **957-49-7643.** Reservations recommended. Main courses 1,800–2,600 ptas. ($10.80–$15.60); set menu 5,000 ptas. ($30). AE, DC, MC, V. Daily noon–5pm; Mon–Sat 8pm–midnight. SPANISH/ANDALUSIAN.

This attractive restaurant, with its welcoming rustic atmosphere and decor, is a 10-minute walk from the mosque and situated at the Plaza del Potro. Since 1908 it has been both a wine cellar (*bodega*) and an Andalusian tavern. Since the early '80s Javier Campo has owned and run this inviting oasis of good food and wine. The walls are adorned with old fiesta posters, and there's an intriguing tapas bar at the entrance. Or you can retreat to the cozy Sacristy, a bar in back, past a wall of wine vats autographed by celebrity visitors. In honor of its former role as a *bodega,* the restaurant has one of the best selections of wine in town. Try the house wine, *montilla viejo.* The well-chosen menu prepared from fresh ingredients consists of local fare, such as a salt cod salad with an orange dressing or *frituritas de la casa con salmorejo* (tiny fried fish that are eaten whole and served with a thick Andalusian gazpacho). Locals gravitate here to sample *escabeche de perdiz,* pickled pieces of partridge, but you may find the *lubina al horno* (baked whitefish) more to your liking. Other specialties include *merluza rellena con verduritas* (hake stuffed with julienne vegetables) and *rabo de toro en salsa* (oxtail in a savory tomato sauce). For a tiny selection of a variety of sweets from the dessert trolley, ask for a *surtido de la casa.*

✪ **La Almudaina.** Plaza de los Santos Mártires, 1. ☎ **957-47-43-42.** Reservations required. Main courses 3,200–5,000 ptas. ($19.20–$30); fixed-price menus 3,500 ptas. ($21). AE, DC, MC, V. Daily noon–5pm; Mon–Sat 8:30pm–midnight. Closed Sun July–Aug. Bus: 12. SPANISH/FRENCH.

The owners of this historic restaurant near the Alcázar deserve as much credit for their renovations of a decrepit 15th-century palace as they do for the excellent cuisine produced in their bustling kitchen. Fronting the river in the old Jewish Quarter, La Almudaina is one of the most attractive eateries in Andalusia, where you can dine in one of the lace-curtained salons or on a glass-roofed central courtyard. Specialties include salmon crêpes; a wide array of fish, such as hake with shrimp sauce; and meats, such as pork loin in wine sauce. For dessert, try the not-too-sweet chocolate crêpe. The cuisine's success is in its use of very fresh ingredients that are deftly handled by the kitchen and not overcooked or overspiced.

Mesón el Purladero. Calle de la Hoguera, 5. ☎ **957-47-4342.** Reservations recommended. Main courses 1,800–2,500 ptas. ($10.80–$15); set menus 3,000–5,000 ptas. ($18–$30). AE, DC, MC, V. Mon–Sat noon–4pm and 8:30pm–midnight. Closed June 15–Sept 1. SPANISH/ANDALUSIAN.

In a 16th-century house that belonged to the first bishops of Córdoba, this restaurant in the Jewish quarter is right in the center of the tourist area. The owner, Edelmiro Jimenez, has been serving good food at this location since the early '80s. With its two floors, the *méson* offers seven dining areas, along with balconies and a central patio adorned with antique style murals. The whole place has been lovingly restored and tastefully decorated. The most lavish way to dine here is to order the *menu gastronómico de degustación,* which is a selection of various house specialties. From the à la carte menu you can begin with *salmorejo,* the thick Andalusian gazpacho, and then follow with such fare as *rabo de toro en salsa* (oxtail stew covered with a savory tomato sauce) or *dorada a la sal,* a meal of John Dory that has been salted to retain its juices and then baked. On a hot day, the best dessert might be the cold soufflé with vanilla ice cream.

MODERATE

Ciro's. Paseo de la Victoria, 19. ☎ **957-29-04-64.** Reservations recommended. Main courses 1,900–2,600 ptas. ($11.40–$15.60); fixed-price menu 2,600 ptas. ($15.60). AE, DC, MC, V. Daily 1–5pm and 8pm–midnight. Closed Sun in summer. ANDALUSIAN.

Once a simple cafeteria, Ciro's has been transformed into an accommodating, comfortably air-conditioned restaurant. The proprietors mix good service with modern Andalusian-style cuisine. The menu includes dishes such as a salmon-and-anchovy pudding, stuffed sweet peppers, hake in shrimp sauce, veal in red wine, and an array of dessert sorbets. Ciro's is directly south of the rail station, about a quarter of a mile northwest of the Mezquita.

El Blasón. José Zorrilla, 11. ☎ **957-48-06-25.** Reservations recommended. Main courses 2,200–2,600 ptas. ($13.20–$15.60). AE, DC, MC, V. Daily noon–4:30pm and 8pm–midnight. ANDALUSIAN.

Established in the late 1980s in a relatively modern building near the Gran Teatro that's been accessorized to commemorate old Andalusia, this is a well-recommended restaurant where the tab, without wine, rarely exceeds 5,000 ptas. ($30). You'll dine in any of four separate rooms, each evoking the mid–19th century, thanks to formal crystal chandeliers and a scattering of antiques. Especially appealing is an enclosed patio where ivy creeps up walls and the noises from the city outside are muffled. Cuisine is well prepared and in some cases described in terms that verge on the poetic. Examples include "salmon with oranges from the mosque," and "goose thigh in fruited wine." Braised oxtail is always a good bet here, as well as any of the roasted lamb dishes that emerge from ovens redolent with the scent of olive oil and herbs.

✪ **El Caballo Rojo.** Cardinal Herrero, 28, Plaza de la Hoguera. ☎ **957-47-53-75.** Reservations required. Main courses 1,800–3,200 ptas. ($10.80–$19.20). AE, DC, MC, V. Daily 1–4:30pm and 8pm–midnight. Bus: 12. SPANISH.

This restaurant is the most popular in Andalusia, and except for La Almudaina (see above), it remains the best in Córdoba, although often overrun by tourists. The place has a noise level no other restaurant here matches, but the skilled waiters seem to cope with all demands. Within walking distance of the Mezquita in the old town, it is found down a long open-air passageway flanked by potted geraniums and vines. Stop in the restaurant's popular bar for a pre-dinner drink, then take the iron-railed stairs to the upper dining room, where a typical meal might include gazpacho, a main dish of chicken, then ice cream and sangría. (The ice cream, incidentally, is likely to be homemade pistachio.) Try a variation on the usual gazpacho—almond-flavored broth with apple pieces. In addition to Andalusian dishes, the chef offers both Sephardic and Mozarabic specialties, an example of the latter being monkfish prepared with pinenuts, currants, carrots, and cream. Real aficionados come here for the *rabo de toro* (stew made with the tail of an ox or a bull). The cookery is robust and flavorsome.

INEXPENSIVE

El Churrasco. Romero, 16. ☎ **957-29-08-19.** Reservations required. Main courses 1,400–2,800 ptas. ($8.40–$16.80). AE, DC, MC, V. Daily 2–5:30pm and 7:45pm–midnight. Closed Aug. Bus: 12. SPANISH.

Housed in an ancient stone-fronted building in the Jewish Quarter northwest of the Mezquita, El Churrasco serves elegant meals in five dining rooms on two floors. You'll pass a bar and an open grill before reaching a ground-floor dining room that resembles a Moorish courtyard with rounded arches and a splashing fountain. Upstairs, more formal rooms display the owner's riveting collection of paintings. You can enjoy such specialties as grilled fillet of beef with whiskey sauce, succulent roast lamb, grilled salmon, and monkfish in a pinenut sauce—all accompanied by good service—but the signature dish here is the charcoal-grilled pork loin.

Restaurante Da Vinci. Plaza de Los Chirinos, 6. ☎ **957-47-75-17.** Reservations required. Main courses 1,300–1,900 ptas. ($7.80–$11.40); *menú del día* 1,600 ptas. ($9.60). V. Daily 1:30–4:30pm and 8pm–midnight. ANDALUSIAN.

Situated in a quiet neighborhood a block off the city's main boulevard, calle Cruz Conde, this is a good-value restaurant. Before heading into the dining room, stop for a drink in the comfortable bar near the entrance, where many guests order from a selection of tempting tapas. Both the cuisine and the decor are a blend of Andalusian, international, and Italian influences, arranged in a curious but pleasing mishmash. Menu items include roast meats (veal, pork, beefsteak, and lamb), a variety of pastas and salads, and many kinds of fish and seafood, especially hake, monkfish, squid, and salmon. This is standard Andalusian fare, with no innovation and little flair, but it's still good.

CÓRDOBA AFTER DARK

Nighttime fun in the oldest part of Córdoba usually means visiting several tapas bars surrounding the Mezquita. Foremost among them is **Casa Pepe,** calle Romero 1 (☎ **957-20-07-44**), an atmospheric old hideaway in an antique building where many generations have lifted a glass before you. It's open daily 1 to 4pm, and like most of the other places, reopens 8pm to 1am. Nearby is **Casa Salinas,** Puerto de Almodovar, s/n (no phone), offering glasses of sherry and plates of tapas. **Bar El Juramento,** calle Juramento, 6 (no phone), is old-fashioned enough to be cozy and crowded enough to be convivial. The oldest *bodega* in Córdoba (established around 1812) is the **Casa Miguel,** Plaza San Miguel, 7 (no phone). And for a bar where discussions about the relative merits of Andalusian bullfighters always seem more passionate than anywhere else in town, head for **Bar Circulo Taurino,** calle Manuel Maria Arcona, 1 (☎ **957-48-18-62**). Small, cramped, and loaded with memorabilia from bullfights past, it's near Plaza Colón. Looking for a particularly flavorful platter of thin-sliced Serrano ham? Head for a historic cellar near the Plaza del Potro: the **Bodega Campos,** calle Lineros, 32 (no phone), where you'll be joined by locals.

   La Canoa, Pasaje Ronda Los Tejares, 18–20 (☎ **957-47-17-61**), has a rustic interior decorated with wine-barrel tables and Carthusian cellar decor. A glass of wine or beer here will be more of a rapid pick-me-up than something to linger over for hours. You can order a ration of Serrano ham or a hefty platter of cheese if you're hungry. La Canoa, between the Plaza de Colón and the Paseo de la Victoria, is open Monday to Saturday noon to 4pm and 8pm to midnight. It's closed 2 weeks in August.

   Push back a thick curtain to enter the dimly lit **Casa Rubio,** Puerta de Almodóvar, 5 (☎ **957-29-00-64**), where you'll find a gruff but accommodating welcome at the rectangular bar or in one of a pair of rooms partially covered with Andalusian tiles. We like the leafy inner courtyard where iron tables and a handful of chairs wobble only slightly on the uneven flooring. Casa Rubio is open Thursday to Tuesday 8am to 3pm and 8pm to midnight.

   The city's most popular flamenco club is **El Cardenal,** calle Torijos, 12 (☎ **957-48-31-12**). Shows are presented at 10:30pm every Tuesday to Saturday, with a cover charge of 2,800 ptas. ($16.80), which includes the first drink. For more formal entertainment, check out the listings at the city's theatrical grande dame, the turn-of-the-century **Gran Teatro de Córdoba,** avenida Gran Capitán, 3 (☎ **957-48-02-37**), site of most of the ballet, opera, chamber-music, and symphony performances in town.

If you want to shake your booty, head for Córdoba's most popular disco, **Disco Plato,** calle Gongera, 10 (☎ **957-48-52-46**). Nothing old-fashioned here—it's a modern setting with lots of space devoted to a bar and a dance floor. This place attracts a broad age group and won't make a visitor in his or her mid-40s feel out of place. It's open Wednesday to Saturday 10:30pm to dawn, charging 700 ptas. ($4.20) entrance for men (women usually enter free). The price includes the first drink, and after that beers cost around 250 ptas. ($1.50) each. A younger crowd hits the dance floor to the sounds of salsa, merengue, Spanish pop, and U.S. disco classics from the 1980s at **Disco Cahira,** calle Conde de Roblado, s/n (no phone), which holds court nightly after 11pm within a busy commercial neighborhood of modern Córdoba.

3 Seville

341 miles (549km) SW of Madrid, 135 miles (217km) NW of Málaga

Sometimes a city becomes famous simply for its beauty and romance. Seville (Sevilla in Spanish), the capital of Andalusia, is such a place. In spite of its sultry summer heat and its many problems, such as high unemployment and street crime, it remains one of the most charming Spanish cities.

Don Juan and Carmen—aided by Mozart and Bizet—have given Seville a romantic reputation. Because of the acclaim of *Don Giovanni* and *Carmen,* not to mention *The Barber of Seville,* debunkers have risen to challenge this reputation. But if a visitor can see only two Spanish cities in a lifetime, they should be Seville and Toledo.

All the images associated with Andalusia—orange trees, mantillas, lovesick toreros, flower-filled patios, and castanet-rattling gypsies—come to life in Seville. But it's not just a tourist city; it's a substantial river port, and it contains some of the most important artistic works and architectural monuments in Spain.

Unlike other Spanish cities, Seville has fared rather well under most of its conquerors—the Romans, Arabs, and Christians. Rulers from Pedro the Cruel to Ferdinand and Isabella held court here. When Spain entered its 16th-century golden age, Seville funneled gold from the New World into the rest of the country, and Columbus docked here after his journey to America.

Be warned, however, that driving here is a nightmare: Seville was planned for the horse and buggy rather than for the car, and nearly all the streets run one way toward the Guadalquivir River. Locating a hard-to-find restaurant or a hidden little square will require patience and luck.

ESSENTIALS

GETTING THERE   Seville's Aeropuerto San Pablo, calle Almirante Lobo (☎ 95-44-90-23), is served by **Iberia** (☎ **902/400-500** toll-free within Spain), which flies several times a day to and from Madrid (and elsewhere via Madrid). It also flies several times a week to and from Alicante, Grand Canary Island, Lisbon, Barcelona, Palma de Majorca, Tenerife, Santiago de Compostela, and (once a week) Zaragoza. The airport is about 6 miles (10km) from the center of the city along the highway leading to Carmona.

Train service into Seville is now centralized into the Estación Santa Justa, avenida Kansas City, s/n (☎ 95-454-02-02 for information and reservations, or 95-454-03-03 for information). Buses C1 and C2 take you from this train station to the

Seville

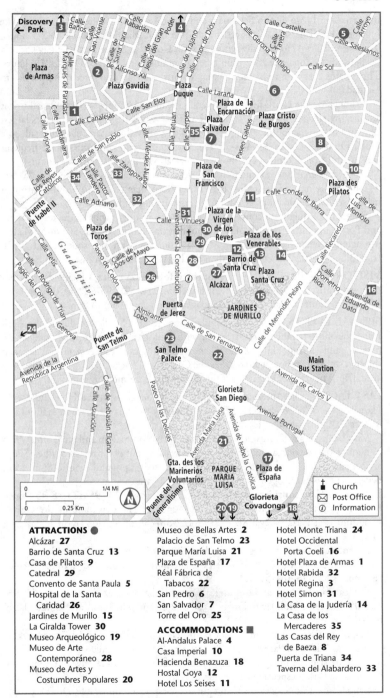

ATTRACTIONS ●

Alcázar **27**
Barrio de Santa Cruz **13**
Casa de Pilatos **9**
Catedral **29**
Convento de Santa Paula **5**
Hospital de la Santa
 Caridad **26**
Jardines de Murillo **15**
La Giralda Tower **30**
Museo Arqueológico **19**
Museo de Arte
 Contemporáneo **28**
Museo de Artes y
 Costumbres Populares **20**

Museo de Bellas Artes **2**
Palacio de San Telmo **23**
Parque María Luisa **21**
Plaza de España **17**
Réal Fábrica de
 Tabacos **22**
San Pedro **6**
San Salvador **7**
Torre del Oro **25**

ACCOMMODATIONS ■

Al-Andalus Palace **4**
Casa Imperial **10**
Hacienda Benazuza **18**
Hostal Goya **12**
Hotel Los Seises **11**

Hotel Monte Triana **24**
Hotel Occidental
 Porta Coeli **16**
Hotel Plaza de Armas **1**
Hotel Rabida **32**
Hotel Regina **3**
Hotel Simon **31**
La Casa de la Judería **14**
La Casa de los
 Mercaderes **35**
Las Casas del Rey
 de Baeza **8**
Puerta de Triana **34**
Taverna del Alabardero **33**

bus station at Prado de San Sebastián, and bus EA runs to and from the airport. The high-speed AVE train has reduced travel time from Madrid to Seville to 2½ hours. The train makes 17 trips daily with a stop in Córdoba. Sixteen trains a day connect Seville and Córdoba; the AVE train takes 45 minutes and a TALGO takes 1½ hours. Three trains a day run to Málaga, taking 3 hours; there are also three trains per day to Granada (4 hours).

Although Seville confusingly has several satellite bus stations servicing small towns and nearby villages of Andalusia, most buses arrive and depart from the city's largest bus terminal on the southeast edge of the old city, at Prado de San Sebastián, calle José María Osborne, 11 (☎ 95-441-71-11). Several different companies make frequent runs to and from Córdoba (2½ hours), Málaga (3½ hours), Granada (4 hours), and Madrid (8 hours). For information and ticket prices, call Alsina Graells at ☎ 95-441-88-11. A newer bus station is at **Plaza de Armas** (☎ 95-490-80-40), but it usually services destinations beyond Andalusia, including Portugal.

Several major highways converge on Seville, connecting it with all the rest of Spain and Portugal. During periods of heavy holiday traffic, the N-V (E-90) from Madrid through Extremadura—which, at Mérida, connects with the southbound N630 (E-803)—is usually less congested than the N-IV (E-5) through eastern Andalusia.

VISITOR INFORMATION   The **tourist information office,** Oficina de Información del Turismo, avenida de la Constitución, 21B (☎ 95-422-14-04), is open Monday to Saturday 9am to 7pm, Sunday and holidays 10am to 2pm.

SPECIAL EVENTS   The most popular times to visit Seville are during the April Fair—the most famous *feria* in Spain, with bullfights, flamenco, and folklore on parade—and during Holy Week when wooden figures called *pasos* are paraded through streets by robed penitents. See the Calendar of Events in chapter 2, "Planning Your Trip: The Basics," and contact the tourist office for more information.

FAST FACTS   The **American Express** office in Seville is in the Hotel Inglaterra, Plaza Nueva, 7 (☎ 95-421-16-17), open Monday to Friday 9:30am to 1:30pm and 4:30 to 7:30pm, Saturday 10am to 1pm.

Most banks in Seville are open Monday to Friday 9am to 2pm and on Saturday 9am to noon. (Always conceal your money before walking out of a bank in Seville.) Shops are generally open Monday to Saturday 9:30am to 1:30pm and 4:30 to 8pm. Most department stores are open Monday to Saturday 10am to 8pm.

There's a **U.S. consulate** at Paseo de las Delicias, 7 (☎ 95-423-18-85), open Monday to Friday 10am to 1pm and 2 to 4:30pm. The **consulate of the United Kingdom** is at Plaza Nueva, 8B (☎ 95-422-88-75), open Monday to Friday 8am to 3pm.

For medical emergencies, go to the **Hospital Universitario y Provincial,** avenida Doctor Fedriani, s/n (☎ 95-455-74-00). The **police station** is on avenida Paseo de las Delicias (☎ 95-461-54-50).

You can do laundry at **Lavandería Roma,** calle Sánchez Bedoya, 18 (☎ 95-421-05-35), open Monday to Friday 10am to 2pm and 5 to 8pm, and Saturday 10am to 2pm.

The **post office** is at avenida de la Constitución, 32 (☎ 95-421-64-76). Hours are Monday to Friday 8:30am to 8:30pm, Saturday 9:30am to 2pm.

With massive unemployment, the city has been hit by a crime wave in recent years. María Luisa Park is especially dangerous, as is the highway leading to Jerez de la Frontera and Cádiz. Dangling cameras and purses are especially vulnerable. Don't leave cars unguarded with your luggage inside. Regrettably, some daring attacks are made when passengers stop for traffic signals—as happens in some U.S. cities.

If you need a cab, call **Tele Taxi** at ☎ **95-462-22-22** or **Radio Taxi** at ☎ **95-458-00-00.** Cabs are metered and charge 52 ptas. (30¢) per kilometer.

SEEING THE SIGHTS

The only way to explore Seville is on foot, with a good map in hand—but remember to be alert to muggers.

THE TOP ATTRACTIONS

✪ **Catedral de Sevilla.** Plaza del Triunfo, avenida de la Constitución. ☎ **95-421-49-71.** Admission (including visit to Giralda Tower) 700 ptas. ($4.20) adults, 200 ptas. ($1.20) children and students. Daily 11am–5pm.

The largest Gothic building in the world, and the third-largest church in Europe after St. Peter's in Rome and St. Paul's in London, this church was designed by builders with a stated goal—that "those who come after us will take us for madmen." Construction began in the late 1400s and took centuries to complete.

Built on the site of an ancient mosque, the cathedral claims to contain the remains of Columbus, with his tomb mounted on four statues. Works of art abound, many of them architectural, such as the 15th-century stained-glass windows, the iron screens (*rejas*) closing off the chapels, the elaborate 15th-century choir stalls, and the Gothic reredos above the main altar. During Corpus Christi and Immaculate Conception observances, altar boys with castanets dance in front of the high altar. In the Treasury are works by Goya, Murillo, and Zurbarán as well as a touch of the macabre in a display of skulls.

After touring the dark interior, emerge into the sunlight of the Patio of Orange Trees, with its fresh citrus scents and chirping birds.

Giralda Tower. Plaza del Triunfo. Admission included in admission to cathedral (above). Same hours as cathedral (above).

Just as Big Ben symbolizes London, La Giralda conjures up Seville. This Moorish tower next to the cathedral is the city's most famous monument. Erected as a minaret in the 12th century, it has seen later additions, such as 16th-century bells. To climb it is to take the walk of a lifetime. There are no steps—you ascend an endless ramp. If you can make it to the top you'll have a dazzling view of Seville. Entrance is through the cathedral.

✪ **Alcázar.** Plaza del Triunfo, s/n. ☎ **95-50-23-23.** Admission 600 ptas. ($4.20). Oct–Mar, Tues–Sat 9:30am–6pm, Sun 9:30am–2:30pm; Apr–Sept, Tues–Sat 9:30am–8pm, Sun 9:30am–6pm.

Pedro the Cruel built this magnificent 14th-century Mudéjar palace north of the cathedral. It is the oldest royal residence in Europe still in use today: On visits to Seville, King Juan Carlos stays here. From the Dolls' Court to the Maidens' Court through the domed Ambassadors' Room, it contains some of the finest work of Sevillian artisans. In many ways it evokes the Alhambra at Granada. Ferdinand and Isabella, who at one time lived in the Alcázar and influenced its architectural evolution, welcomed Columbus here on his return from America. On the top floor, the Oratory of the Catholic Monarchs has a fine altar in polychrome tiles made by Pisano

Sightseeing Tip

Shorts and T-shirts are not allowed in the cathedral. Remember to dress appropriately before you set out so you're not turned away.

in 1504. The well-kept gardens, filled with beautiful flowers, shrubbery, and fruit trees, are alone worth the visit.

Hospital de la Santa Caridad. Calle Temprado, 3. ☎ **95-422-32-32.** Admission 400 ptas. ($2.40). Mon–Sat 9:30am–1:30pm and 3:30–6pm; Sun 9am–1pm.

This 17th-century hospital is intricately linked to the legend of Miguel Manara, portrayed by Dumas and Mérimée as the scandalous Don Juan. It was once thought that he built this institution to atone for his sins, but this has been disproved. The death of Manara's beautiful young wife in 1661 caused such grief that he retired from society and entered the "Charity Brotherhood," burying corpses of the sick and diseased as well as condemned and executed criminals. Today, the members of this brotherhood continue to look after the poor, the old, and invalids who have no one else to help them.

Nuns will show you through the festive orange-and-sienna courtyard. The baroque chapel contains works by the 17th-century Spanish painters Murillo and Valdés-Leál. As you're leaving the chapel, look over the exit door for the macabre picture of an archbishop being devoured by maggots.

Torre del Oro. Paseo de Cristóbal Colón. ☎ **95-422-24-19.** Admission 100 ptas. (60¢). Free on Tues. Tues–Fri 10am–2pm; Sat–Sun 11am–2pm.

The 12-sided Tower of Gold, dating from the 13th century, overlooks the Guadalquivir River. Originally it was covered with gold tiles, but someone long ago made off with them. Recently restored, the tower has been turned into a maritime museum, Museo Náutico, displaying drawings and engravings of the port of Seville in its golden heyday.

Casa de Pilatos. Plaza Pilatos, 1. ☎ **95-422-52-98.** Admission, museum 1,000 ptas. ($6); patio and gardens 500 ptas. ($3). Museum, daily 10am–2pm and 4–6pm; patio and gardens, daily 9am–7pm.

This 16th-century Andalusian palace of the dukes of Medinaceli recaptures the splendor of the past, combining Gothic, Mudéjar, and plateresque styles in its courtyards, fountains, and salons. According to tradition this is a reproduction of Pilate's House in Jerusalem. Don't miss the two old carriages or the rooms filled with Greek and Roman statues. The collection of paintings includes works by Carreño, Pantoja de la Cruz, Sebastiano del Piombo, Lucas Jordán, Batalloli, Pacheco, and Goya. The museum's first floor is seen by guided tour only, but the ground floor, patios, and gardens are self-guided. The palace is about a 7-minute walk northeast of the cathedral on the northern edge of Barrio de Santa Cruz, in a warren of labyrinthine streets whose traffic is funneled through the nearby calle de Aguilas.

Archivo General de Indias. Avenida de la Constitución, s/n. ☎ **95-421-12-34.** Free admission. Mon–Fri 10am–1pm.

The great architect of Philip II's El Escorial, Juan de Herrera, was also the architect of this building next to the cathedral, originally the Lonja (Stock Exchange). Construction on the Archivo General de Indias lasted from 1584 to 1646. In the 17th century it was headquarters for the Academy of Seville, which was founded in part by the great Spanish artist Murillo.

In 1785 during the reign of Charles III, the building was turned over for use as a general records office for the Indies. That led to today's Archivo General de Indias, said to contain some four million antique documents, even letters exchanged between patron Queen Isabella and explorer Columbus (he detailing his discoveries and impressions). These very rare documents are locked in air-conditioned storage to keep them from disintegrating. Special permission has to be acquired before examining some of them. Many treasure-hunters come here hoping to learn where Spanish galleons laden with gold went down off the coasts of the Americas. On display in glass cases are fascinating documents in which the dreams of the early explorers come alive.

✪ **Museo Provincial de Bellas Artes de Sevilla.** Plaza del Museo, 9. ☎ **95-422-07-90.** Admission 250 ptas. ($1.50), free for students. Tues 3–8pm; Wed–Sat 9am–8pm; Sun 9am–3pm. Bus: 21, 24, 30, or 31.

This lovely old convent off calle de Alfonso XII houses one of the most important Spanish art collections. A whole gallery is devoted to two paintings by El Greco, and works by Zurbarán are on exhibit; however, the devoutly religious paintings of the Seville-born Murillo are the highlight. An entire wing is given over to macabre paintings by the 17th-century artist Valdés-Leál. His painting of John the Baptist's head on a platter includes the knife—in case you don't get the point. The top floor, which displays modern paintings, is less interesting.

MORE ATTRACTIONS

✪ **BARRIO DE SANTA CRUZ**   What was once a ghetto for Spanish Jews, who were forced out of Spain in the late 15th century in the wake of the Inquisition, is today the most colorful district of Seville. Near the old walls of the Alcázar, winding medieval streets with names like *Vida* (Life) and *Muerte* (Death) open onto pocket-sized plazas. Flower-filled balconies with draping bougainvillea and potted geraniums jut out over this labyrinth, shading you from the hot Andalusian summer sun. Feel free to look through numerous wrought-iron gates into patios filled with fountains and plants. In the evening it's common to see Sevillians sitting outside drinking icy sangría under the glow of lanterns.

Although the district as a whole is recommended for sightseeing, seek out in particular the **Casa de Murillo (Murillo's House),** Santa Teresa, 8 (☎ **95-421-75-35**). Bartolomé Esteban Murillo, the great Spanish painter known for his religious works, was born in Seville in 1617. He spent his last years in this house in Santa Cruz, dying in 1682. Five minor paintings of the artist are on display. The furnishings, although not owned by the artist, are period pieces. Admission is 250 ptas. ($1.50), and the house is open Tuesday to Saturday 10am to 2pm and 6 to 8pm. The house is currently closed for renovations; check its status with the tourist office before heading here.

To enter the Barrio Santa Cruz, turn right after leaving the Patio de Banderas exit of the Alcázar. Turn right again at Plaza de la Alianza, going down calle Rodrigo Caro to Plaza de Doña Elvira. Use caution when strolling through the area, particularly at night; many robberies have occurred here.

PARQUE MARÍA LUISA   This park, dedicated to María Luisa, sister of Isabella II, was once the grounds of the Palacio de San Telmo. The palace, whose baroque facade is visible behind the deluxe Alfonso XIII Hotel, today houses a seminary. The former private royal park is now open to the public.

Running south along the Guadalquivir River, the park attracts those who want to take boat rides, walk along flower bordered paths, jog, or go bicycling. The most romantic way to traverse it is by rented horse and carriage, but this can be expensive, depending on negotiation with the driver.

In 1929 Seville was to host the Spanish American Exhibition, and many pavilions from around the world were erected here. The worldwide depression put a damper on the exhibition, but the pavilions still stand.

Exercise caution while walking through this park, as many muggings have been reported.

PLAZA DE AMÉRICA   Another landmark Sevillian square, Plaza de América represents city planning at its best: Here you can walk through gardens planted with roses, enjoying the lily ponds and the fountains and feeling the protective shade of the palms. And here you'll find a trio of elaborate buildings left over from the world exhibition that never materialized—in the center, the home of the government headquarters of Andalusia; on either side, two minor museums worth visiting only if you have time to spare.

Museo Arqueológico Provincial, Plaza de América, s/n (☎ 95-423-24-01), contains many artifacts from prehistoric times and the days of the Romans, Visigoths, and Moors. It's open Tuesday to Sunday 10am to 2:30pm. Admission is 250 ptas. ($1.50) for adults and free for students and children. Buses 30, 31, and 34 go there. Nearby is the **Museo de Artes y Costumbres Populares,** Plaza de América, s/n (☎ 95-423-25-76), displaying folkloric costumes, musical instruments, Córdoban saddles, weaponry, and farm implements that document the life of the Andalusian people. It's open Tuesday to Saturday 9am to 2:30pm, but closed on holidays. Admission is 250 ptas. ($1.50) for adults and free for children and students.

PLAZA DE ESPAÑA   The major building left from the exhibition at the Parque María Luisa (see above) is the half-moon-shaped Renaissance-style structure set on this landmark square. The architect, Anibal González, not only designed but also supervised the building of this immense structure; today it is a government office building. At a canal here you can rent rowboats for excursions into the park, or you can walk across bridges spanning the canal. Set into a curved wall are alcoves focusing on the characteristics of Spain's 50 provinces, as depicted in tile murals.

REAL FÁBRICA DE TABACOS   When Carmen waltzed out of the tobacco factory in the first act of Bizet's opera, she made its 18th-century original in Seville world-famous. This old tobacco factory was constructed between 1750 and 1766, and 100 years later it employed 10,000 *cigarreras,* of which Carmen was one in the opera. (She rolled cigars on her thighs.) In the 19th century, these tobacco women made up the largest female workforce in Spain. Many visitors arriving today, in fact, ask guides to take them to "Carmen's tobacco factory." The building, located on calle San Fernando near the city's landmark luxury hotel, the Alfonso XIII, is the second largest in Spain and is still here. But the Real Fábrica de Tabacos is now part of the Universidad de Sevilla. Look for signs of its former role, however, in the bas reliefs of tobacco plants and Indians over the main entrances. You'll also see bas-reliefs of Columbus and Cortés. Then you can wander through the grounds for a look at student life, Sevillian style. The factory is directly south of the Alcázar gardens.

BULLFIGHTS

From Easter until late October, some of the best bullfighters in Spain appear at the **Maestranza** bullring, on the Paseo de Colón (☎ 95-422-35-06). One of the leading bullrings in Spain, the stadium attracts matadors whose fights often get television and newspaper coverage throughout Iberia. Unless there's a special festival going on, bullfights (*corridas*) occur on Sunday. The best bullfights are staged during April Fair celebrations. Tickets tend to be pricey, and should be purchased in advance at the ticket office (*despacho de entradas*) on calle Adriano, beside the Maestranza bullfight stadium. You'll find many unofficial kiosks selling tickets placed strategically along the main shopping street, calle Sierpes. However, they charge a 20% commission for their tickets—a lot more if they think they can get it.

SHOPPING

ART   One of the most respected galleries in Seville, **Rafael Ortíz,** Marmolles, 12 (☎ **95-421-48-74**), specializes in contemporary paintings, usually from Iberian artists. Exhibitions change frequently, and because of the canniness of this emporium's judgments, inventories sell out quickly. It's open Monday to Saturday 10am to 1:30pm and 4:30 to 8pm.

BOOKS   The **English Bookshop,** Eduardo Dato, 36 (☎ **95-465-57-54**), is the kind of place where you can find tomes on gardening, political discourse, philosophy, and pop fiction, all gathered into one cozy place. Open Monday to Saturday 10am to 1:45pm and 4:30 to 9pm.

Set conveniently close to Seville's university, **Libreria Vértice,** San Fernando, 33 (☎ **95-421-16-54**), stocks books in a variety of languages. The polyglot inventory ranges from the professorial to Spanish romances of the soap-opera genre. Open Monday to Saturday 10am to 1:30pm and 4:30 to 8:30pm.

CERAMICS   In the town center, near the cathedral, **El Postigo,** Arfe, s/n (☎ **95-456-00-13**), has a wide selection of Andalusian ceramics. Some of the pieces are much, much too big to fit into your suitcase; others—especially the hand-painted tiles—make charming souvenirs that can easily be transported. Open Monday to Saturday 10am to 2pm, Monday to Friday 5 to 8:30pm.

Near the town hall, **Martian,** calle Sierpes, 74 (☎ **95-421-34-13**), sells a wide array of painted tiles and ceramics: vases, plates, cups, serving dishes, and statues, all made in or near Seville. Many of the pieces use ancient geometric patterns of Andalusia. Other floral motifs are rooted in Spanish traditions of the 18th century. Open Monday to Saturday 10am to 1:30pm and 4:30 to 8:30pm.

DEPARTMENT STORES   **El Corte Inglés,** Plaza Duque, 10 (☎ **95-422-09-31**), is the best of the several department stores clustered in Seville's commercial center. It features multilingual translators and rack after rack of every conceivable kind of merchandise for the well-stocked home, kitchen, and closet. If you're in the market for the brightly colored *feria* costumes worn by young girls during Seville's holidays, there's an impressive selection of the traditional regional fashion, along with all the latest designer fashions for everyday. Open Monday to Saturday 10am to 9pm.

Marks & Spencer, Plaza Duque, 6 (☎ **95-456-36-56**), is the Seville branch of a gigantic chain of middle-of-the-road department stores based in England. It caters to British expatriates and retirees based in the hills around Seville, so expect conservative, well-made clothes. Open Monday to Saturday 10am to 9pm.

FANS   Carmen fluttered her fan and broke hearts. You can, too, if you pick up a traditional Andalusian fan at **Casa Rubio,** Sierpes, 56 (☎ **95-422-68-72**). It stocks one of the city's largest selections, from the austere and dramatic to the florid and fanciful. Open Monday to Saturday 9:30am to 1:30pm and 4 to 8:30pm.

FASHION   See also "Department Stores," above. **Iconos,** avenida de la Constitución (☎ **95-422-14-08**), is a small, idiosyncratic boutique loaded with fashion accessories that can be used by everyone from teenage girls to mature women. Silk scarves, costume jewelry, and an assortment of T-shirts with logos lettered in varying degrees of taste—it's all here. Open Monday to Saturday 10am to 2pm, Monday to Friday 5 to 8pm.

Head for **Nicole Miller,** Albareda, 16 (☎ **95-456-36-14**), for chic outfits from this internationally successful designer. Open Monday to Saturday 10am to 2pm, Monday to Friday 5 to 8pm. More sleek, upscale fashions are available from **Victorio**

Impressions

Seville doesn't have an ambiance. It is ambiance.

—James A. Michener

Seville is a pleasant city, famous for oranges and women.

—Lord Byron

& Lucchino, Sierpes, 87 (☎ **95-422-79-51**). Open Monday to Saturday 10am to 2pm, Monday to Friday 5 to 8pm.

For traditional regional costumes, try **Perdales,** Cuna, 23 (☎ **95-421-37-09**), which outfits many of the region's professional flamenco performers. Much of its merchandise is akin to couture; other items are less expensive and sold off the rack. Open Monday to Saturday 10am to 2pm, Monday to Friday 5 to 8pm.

GIFTS   Artesania Textil, Sierpes, 70 (☎ **95-456-28-40**), specializes in the nubby and rough textiles that reflect the earthiness of contemporary Spanish art. Weavings—some using linen, others the rough fibers of Spanish sheep—are the specialty here. Examples include place mats, tablecloths, blankets, shawls, and wall hangings. Open Monday to Saturday 10am to 2pm, Monday to Friday 5 to 8pm.

Souvenirs of the city, T-shirts, hammered wrought-iron whatnots, and ceramics are available at **Matador,** avenida de la Constitución, 28 (☎ **95-422-62-47**). Open Monday to Saturday 10am to 2pm, Monday to Friday 5 to 8:30pm.

More upscale gifts, such as crystal and art objects, can be found at **Venecia,** Cuna, 51 (☎ **95-422-99-94**). Open Monday to Saturday 10am to 2pm, Monday to Friday 5 to 8:30pm.

MUSIC   There's a **Virgin Megastore** at Sierpes, 81 (☎ **95-421-21-11**), offering the latest sounds from across Europe and North America while also stocking some traditional regional music. It also sells computer games (having brought Nintendo to Andalusia) and a limited roster of books. Open Monday to Friday 10am to 2pm, Saturday 10am to 9pm.

RIDING GEAR   If you're passionately interested in horses (or know someone who is), **Arcab,** Paseo Cristobal Colon, 8 (☎ **95-456-14-21**), can provide an array of Andalusian-style riding costumes, harnesses, saddles, bridles, and buckles that will make you and your mount feel like direct descendants of the conquistadors. Open Monday to Friday 10am to 2pm, Saturday 10am to 9pm.

WHERE TO STAY

During Holy Week and the Seville Fair, hotels often double, even triple, their rates. Price increases are often not announced until the last minute. If you're going to be in Seville at these times, arrive with an ironclad reservation and an agreement about the price before checking in.

VERY EXPENSIVE

✪ **Hotel Alfonso XIII.** San Fernando, 2, 41004 Sevilla. ☎ **800/221-2340** in the U.S. and Canada, or 95-422-28-50. Fax 95-421-60-33. www.ittsheraton.com. 146 units. A/C MINIBAR TV TEL. 48,000–64,000 ptas. ($288–$384) double; 90,000–115,000 ptas. ($540–$690) suite. AE, DC, MC, V. Parking 2,750 ptas. ($16.50).

Set at the southwestern corner of the gardens that front Seville's famous Alcázar, in the historic heart of town, this five-story rococo building is one of the three or four most legendary hotels in Spain and is the premier address in Seville. Built as an aristocratic shelter for patrons of the Ibero-American Exposition of 1929 and named after the then-king of Spain, it reigns as a super-ornate and super-expensive bastion of glamour. Built in the Mudéjar/Andalusian revival style, its rooms and hallways glitter with hand-painted tiles, acres of marble and mahogany, antique furniture embellished with intricately embossed leather, and a spaciousness nothing short of majestic.

Dining/Diversions: San Fernando restaurant offers Italian and continental cuisine. A lobby bar features midday coffee amid potted palms and memorials to another age, its blue, white, and yellow tiles reflecting the colors of Seville.

Amenities: 24-hour room service, laundry and valet, concierge, car rentals with or without drivers, baby-sitting, a spectacular garden, outdoor pool, tennis courts, shops, arcade-enclosed courtyard with potted flowers and splashing fountain.

EXPENSIVE

Al-Andalus Palace. Avenida Palmera, s/n, 43012 Sevilla. ☎ **95-423-66-15.** Fax 95-423-02-00. 328 units. A/C MINIBAR TV TEL. 35,375 ptas. ($212.25) double; 45,000 ptas. ($270) suite. AE, DC, MC, V. Parking 1,200 ptas. ($7.20). Bus: 34.

No hotel in Seville has a more avant-garde modern design than this four-star choice just 5 minutes from the center in the Heliopolis district, an upmarket residential area. Front public rooms are suspended by cable, and the glass facade reflects both the blue skies of Seville and the marble floors. Bedrooms are large, elegantly appointed, and brightly lit with large windows. They are well equipped with excellent mattresses, and some have balconies overlooking the hotel swimming pool. Decor and furnishings are minimalist—functional but modern with neutral, muted color schemes. Many accommodations have small living rooms and suites with their own breakfast bars. Bathrooms are finished in marble and have large tubs and mirrors; the suites contain a hydro-massage.

Dining/Diversions: The top rated **El Patio** has an international à la carte menu. A buffet restaurant called **Guadalquivir** is on site, as is a chic cocktail bar, **Pigalle.**

Amenities: Swimming pool, garden, gym, sauna, massage, steam baths, tennis courts, 24-hour room service, laundry, facilities for persons with disabilities, golf course nearby.

✪ **Casa Imperial.** Calle Imperial, 29, 41003 Sevilla. ☎ **954-50-03-00.** Fax 954-50-03-30. www.casaimperial.com. E-mail: info@casaimperial.com. 24 units. A/C MINIBAR TV TEL. 30,781 ptas. ($184.70) double; 36,650 ptas. ($219.90) suite. Rates include breakfast buffet. Free parking.

In the historic center of Seville, this hotel is one of charm and grace. Launched in the mid-1990s, the *casa* stands near Casa Pilatos and dates from the 15th century when it was the home of the butler to the Marquis of Tarifa. The interior is refined and elegant, and there are four Andalusian patios adorned with exotic plants. The beamed ceilings are original, and sparkling chandeliers hang from the ceilings. The bedrooms are large—many have small kitchens, plus ample terraces and private bathrooms. The bathrooms are tastefully decorated with luxurious tubs, some of which are antiques.

Dining/Diversions: There's a passable restaurant serving international food, plus a cozy bar.

Amenities: 24-hour room service, laundry, concierge, free access to a nearby health club with a swimming pool.

Hotel Occidental Porta Coeli. Eduardo Dato, 49, 41018 Sevilla. ☎ **954-53-35-00.** Fax 954-53-2342. E-mail: reservas-portacoeli@occidental-hoteles.com. 244 units. A/C MINIBAR TV TEL. 25,000 ptas. ($150) double; 45,000 ptas. ($270) suite. AE, DC, MC, V. Parking 1,500 ptas. ($9). Bus: 2 or 3.

Don't come here to recapture the romance and legend of old Seville. You won't find it. In fact, the facade of this modern hotel a 10-minute walk from the city center is so impersonal and bland you might think you've landed in Iran. But once inside there is grand comfort and even style. In business since the mid-'80s, the hotel was last renovated in 1999. A courteous and efficient staff welcomes you to an interior both inviting and avant-garde. The spacious rooms are furnished in a medley of classical and contemporary styles, and most open onto balconies. Bathrooms are state of the art, with such conveniences as hair dryers.

Dining/Diversions: Florencia Restaurant, the hotel's most formal choice, hires top chefs and offers an international menu but emphasizes regional specialties. There's an English-style pub, **Farnecio,** plus a cafeteria.

Amenities: Indoor swimming pool, patio garden for sunbathing, 24-hour room service, laundry, concierge, guided tours arranged.

Las Casas del Rey de Baeza. Calle Santiago, Plaza Jesus de la Redencion, 2, 41003 Seville. ☎ **95-456-14-96.** Fax 95-456-14-41. http://lascasas.zoom.es. E-mail: baeza@zoom.es. 44 units. A/C MINIBAR TV TEL. 20,000 ptas. ($120) double; 23,000 ptas. ($138) suite. AE, DC, MC, V. Parking 2,000 ptas. ($12).

Less luxurious than its sibling, La Casa de la Judería (see below), this antique hotel close to the Casa de Pilatos is still a winning choice with its stone floors and 19th-century Andalusian architecture. A hotel since 1998, it has an interior patio surrounded by a cozy coterie of rooms and a long Andalusian balcony. Some of the beautifully furnished bedrooms have living rooms, and the decor is finely honed in marble and wood with comfortable furnishings. Bathrooms contain the usual amenities, such as excellent plumbing along with such features as a hair dryer.

Dining: Breakfast is the only meal served.

Amenities: Concierge, room service, laundry.

✪ **Taverna del Alabardero.** Zaragoza, 20, 41001 Sevilla. ☎ **95-456-06-37.** Fax 95-456-36-66. www.esh.es. E-mail: hotelalabardero@esh.es. 7 units. A/C MINIBAR TV TEL. 19,800 ptas. ($118.80) double; 28,000 ptas. ($168) suite. Rates include continental breakfast. AE, DC, MC, V. Parking 2,000 ptas. ($12).

This tavern not only houses one of the two best restaurants in Seville, but is perhaps the single most charming place to stay in the city. Close to the bullring and a 5-minute walk from the cathedral, this is a restored 19th-century mansion. There is a spectacular central patio, and a romantic atmosphere. The units on the third floor have balconies overlooking street scenes as well as whirlpool tubs. All the bedrooms are spacious and comfortable, each individually decorated in a specific regional style. Bathrooms are well appointed and contain hair dryers.

Dining: The second-floor restaurant is reviewed in "Where to Dine," below. On warm days, guests can relax on the patio or terrace, ordering drinks or desserts.

Amenities: 24-hour room service, laundry, concierge.

MODERATE

Bécquer. Calle Reyes Católicos, 4, 41001 Sevilla. ☎ **95-422-89-00.** Fax 95-421-44-00. www.hotelbecquer.com. E-mail: becquer@hotelbecquer.com. 118 units. A/C TV TEL. 13,900 ptas. ($83.40) double. AE, DC, MC, V. Parking 1,500 ptas. ($9). Bus: 21, 24, 30, or 31.

A short walk from the action of the Seville bullring and only 2 blocks from the river, Bécquer is on a street full of cafes where you can order tapas and drink Andalusian wine. The Museo Provincial de Bellas Artes is also nearby. Built in the 1970s, the hotel was enlarged and much renovated in the late 1980s. It occupies the site of a former mansion and retains many objets d'art rescued before that building was demolished. Guests register in a wood-paneled lobby before being shown to one of the functionally furnished bedrooms, which are well kept and reasonably comfortable—in all, a good value in a pricey city. All have private bathrooms. Only breakfast is served, but you'll find a bar and lounge, as well as a garage.

○ **Hotel Doña María.** Don Remondo, 19, 41004 Sevilla. ☎ **95-422-49-90.** Fax 95-421-95-46. 69 units. A/C TV TEL. Jan–Feb and July–Aug 14,000 ptas. ($84) double; Mar–June and Sept–Dec 20,000–28,000 ptas. ($120–$168) double. AE, DC, MC, V. Parking 2,000 ptas. ($12).

Staying at this four-star, four-story hotel is a worthwhile investment, partly because of the tasteful Iberian antiques in the stone lobby and upper hallways. Also, the location a few steps from the cathedral creates a dramatic view from the Doña María's rooftop terrace. An ornate neoclassical entryway is offset with a pure white facade and iron balconies, which hint at the building's origin in the 1840s as a private villa. Amid the flowering plants on the upper floor you'll find a swimming pool ringed with garden-style lattices and antique wrought-iron railings. Each of the one-of-a-kind rooms has a private bathroom and is well furnished and comfortable, although some are rather small. A few have four-poster beds, others a handful of antique reproductions. Light sleepers might find the noise of the church bells jarring. Breakfast is the only meal served.

Hotel Los Seises. Calle Segovias, 6, 41004 Sevilla. ☎ **954-22-94-95.** Fax 954-22-43-34. www.sol.com/hotel-los-seises. E-mail: seises@jet.es. 42 units. A/C MINIBAR TV TEL. 18,000 ptas. ($108) double. AE, DC, MC, V. Parking 2,200 ptas. ($13.20).

This three-story hotel opened in 1992 immediately behind the cathedral in the old Jewish quarter of Santa Cruz. It was once the 16th-century palace of the archbishop of Seville. Renovations have added modern amenities but many of the old Andalusian touches have been retained. In this category of antique hotels, we still prefer the Casa Imperial, but what you get here isn't bad. At least it was the Pope's choice when he visited Seville. Traditional stucco walls are adorned with modern paintings in contrast to the antique tiles. Rooms range from small to spacious, and each is equipped with good beds and restored bathrooms containing a hair dryer. The restaurant serves standard Andalusian meals. One of the most stunning aspects of this hotel is the panoramic vista of La Giralda, which you can enjoy while sunbathing next to the rooftop pool. Amenities include limited room service, laundry, and a concierge.

Hotel Monte Triana. Clara de Jesús Montero, 24, 41010 Sevilla. ☎ **954-34-1832.** Fax 954-34-3328. E-mail: hmtventas@cli.ccs.es. 116 units. A/C MINIBAR TV TEL. 15,000 ptas. ($90) double. AE, DC, MC, V. Parking 1,000 ptas. ($6). Bus: 43.

In the Triana district, this three-star hotel is a 15-minute walk from the commercial center and the historic monuments. A hotel since 1991, the building rises four floors behind a dull facade with large windows. Business travelers are more attracted to the hotel than tourists, although it is perfectly acceptable for both. Most of the rooms are on the interior away from street noises, and connected to a pleasant patio. The decor is not inspired but functional, although there is comfort here. The housekeeping is first-rate and the bathrooms are well equipped, including hair dryers and complimentary toiletries. A cafeteria serves breakfast and assorted dishes throughout the day, and amenities include room service until 11pm, laundry, and private safes in the bedrooms.

Hotel Plaza de Armas. Avenida Marqués de Paradas, s/n, 41001 Sevilla. ☎ **954-490-1992.** Fax 954-90-1832. www.nh-hoteles.es. 262 units. A/C MINIBAR TV TEL. 15,500 ptas. ($93) double; 19,500 ptas. ($117) suite. AE, DC, MC, V.

This three-star hotel of glass and steel is in direct contrast to the antique *casas* of Seville converted into hotels. It was purpose-built in 1992 and is the city's most modern-looking structure, lying in the center close to the Plaza de Armas, La Giralda, and the cathedral. The interior design consists of architectural lines of almost Japanese simplicity intermixed with steel and wood. The rooms are airy and colorful in severe contemporary style, with oversized beds and comfortable mattresses, plus roomy bathrooms fully equipped with such features as hair dryers. There's a bar and formal restaurant serving Mediterranean cuisine. Amenities include a swimming pool, solarium, room service until 11pm, laundry, and facilities for persons with disabilities.

Hotel Regina. Calle San Vicente, 97, 41002 Sevilla. ☎ **854-490-7562.** Fax 954-90-7562. 72 units. A/C MINIBAR TV TEL. 19,000 ptas. ($114) double; 21,500 ptas. ($129) duplex. AE, DC, MC, V. Parking 1,200 ptas. ($7.20).

Right in the historic center, facing the Parque de la Cartuga and close to the Museo de Bellas Artes, this inviting hotel was constructed in 1992 in anticipation of the Seville Exposition. Its spacious pastel rooms are filled with light woods. The bedrooms are comfortable and firm, the bathrooms immaculate and filled with amenities, including a hair dryer. The hotel staff can arrange guided tours of the city. On site is a cafeteria offering breakfasts and light meals daily until 11pm. Amenities include laundry and private safes in the rooms.

✪ **Hotel Simon.** Calle Garcia de Vinuesa, 190, 41001 Sevilla. ☎ **954-22-66-60.** Fax 954-22-66-15. 31 units. A/C TV TEL. www.sol.com/hotel-simon. E-mail: hotel-simon@jet.es. 12,000 ptas. ($72) double. AE, DC, MC, V.

This two-story, former 18th-century mansion next to the cathedral in the Arenal district is a bargain hunter's delight. For a hotel rated only one star by the government, it's a cozy nest of charm and comfort. Within is a beautifully ornate staircase and a patio of tropical plants. The social areas are chic and comfortable, and the TV lounge displays bric-a-brac belonging to the original mansion. Reservations are recommended as far in advance as possible because the word is out that this is a stylish establishment charging low prices. The rooms are medium to large, and each is individually decorated in keeping with the history of this place. Many antiques grace the rooms. Walls are adorned with paintings. On site is a cafeteria serving informal fare, and other amenities include a laundry and concierge.

✪ **La Casa de la Judería.** Plaza Santa Maria la Blanca, callejon de Dos Hermanas, 7, 41004 Sevilla. ☎ **95-442-2170.** Fax 95-442-2170. www.zoom.es. E-mail: juderia@zoom.es. 104 units. A/C MINIBAR TV TEL. 18,000 ptas. ($108) double; 29,000 ptas. ($174) suite. AE, DC, MC, V. Parking 2,000 ptas. ($12).

In the Santa Cruz district, the old Jewish barrio of Seville, this hotel was installed in a palace from the 1600s once owned by the Duke of Beja, a great character in the history of Spain's aristocracy and known as the patron of Cervantes. Within easy walking distance of the cathedral and other sights of historic interest, the building has been a hotel since 1991. It's now one of the best places to stay in Seville, offering an excellent bang for your peseta. All the bedrooms, medium in size, are individually decorated and furnished in an antique style, sometimes with four-poster beds with top-quality mattresses. All the accommodations have balconies, some facing street scenes and others opening onto one of the four interior patios in the classic Andalusian style. Many units have living rooms, and all the suites contain a whirlpool tub. Bathrooms are beautifully maintained, with complimentary toiletries and hair dryers. Amenities include 24-hour room service, laundry, gym, and a concierge, plus guided tours to the historical center. The hotel has a cafeteria and a cozy piano bar at night.

✪ **Las Casas de los Mercaderes.** Calle Alvarez Quintero, 9–13, 41004 Sevilla. ☎ **95-422-56858.** Fax 95-422-9884. http://lascasas.zoom.es. E-mail: mercaderes@zoom.es. 47 units. A/C MINIBAR TV TEL. 17,500 ptas. ($105) double. AE, DC, MC, V. Parking 1,000 ptas. ($6).

In the business center of Seville, this restored mansion lies close to the cathedral between the squares of San Francisco and Salvador. Its name reflects the history of the area, which was once home to many immigrant merchants. The 19th-century original has been fully renovated—at the time, an 18th-century patio was discovered. Much of the original style and grace notes were retained, and it is one of the leading choices in the city. Most of the medium-sized rooms have balconies and classic Spanish furnishings. Bathrooms are modern and well equipped, with all the expected facilities such as a hair dryer. Amenities include limited room service, laundry, and concierge, plus a coffee bar where breakfast is served.

Puerta de Triana. Reyes Católicos, 5, 41001 Sevilla. ☎ **954-21-54-04.** Fax 954-21-54-01. 62 units. A/C TV TEL. 18,000 ptas. ($108) double. AE, DC, MC, V.

This five-story budgeteer's dream is only a 5-minute walk from the cathedral in the Paseo Colón district. Last renovated in 1992, it was constructed in the early '70s in neoclassic style. The interior is surprisingly elegant and tasteful for an establishment charging such low prices. Antique styles are mixed with modern features. Given two stars by the government, the hotel offers simply but comfortably furnished bedrooms, each immaculately maintained. The bedrooms have none of the ornate nature of the public rooms but are quite welcoming. If you're driving to this location near the Plaza de Toros, you can ask the staff to direct you to one of the nearby garages where discounts for hotel guests are available.

INEXPENSIVE

Hostal Goya. Mateus Gago, 31, 41004 Sevilla. ☎ **95-421-11-70.** Fax 95-456-29-88. 20 units (10 with bathroom). Jan–Mar and May–Dec 6,500 ptas. ($39) double without bathroom, 7,000 ptas. ($42) double with bathroom; Apr 8,000 ptas. ($48) double without bathroom, 9,000 ptas. ($54) double with bathroom. No credit cards.

Its location in a narrow-fronted townhouse in the oldest part of the barrio is one of the Goya's strongest virtues. The building's gold-and-white facade, ornate iron railings, and picture-postcard demeanor are all noteworthy. Rooms are cozy and simple, without phones or TVs. Guests congregate in the marble-floored ground-level salon, where a skylight floods the couches and comfortable chairs with sunlight. No meals are served. Reserve well in advance. Parking is often available along the street.

Hotel La Rabida. Calle Castelar, 24, 41001 Sevilla. ☎ **94-422-0960.** Fax 95-422-7345. www.sol.com/hotel-rabida. E-mail: hotel-rabida@sol.com. 105 units. A/C MINIBAR TV TEL. 9,300 ptas. ($55.80) double. AE, MC, V.

This former 19th-century mansion once belonged to one of Seville's most aristocratic families. The four-story building, a hotel for half a century, is in the Arenal district, a 5-minute walk from the cathedral. Modestly renovated in 1998, the hotel offers small but clean and modernized bedrooms with renewed plumbing. The hotel's most attractive feature is a lobby patio crowned by a stained-glass skylight. Amenities are limited to laundry and an on-site cafeteria.

Residencia Murillo. Calle Lope de Rueda, 7–9, 41004 Sevilla. ☎ **95-421-60-95.** Fax 95-421-96-16. www.sol.com/hotel-murillo. E-mail: murillo@nexo.com. 57 units. TEL. 7,100–8,900 ptas. ($42.60–$53.40) double; 8,800–11,200 ptas. ($52.80–$67.80) triple. AE, DC, MC, V. Parking 2,000 ptas. ($12) nearby.

Tucked away on a narrow street in the heart of Santa Cruz, the old quarter, the Residencia Murillo (named after the artist who used to live in this district) is almost next to the gardens of the Alcázar. Inside, the lounges harbor some fine architectural characteristics and antique reproductions; behind a grilled screen is a retreat for drinks. Many of the rooms we inspected were cheerless and gloomy, so have a look before checking in. Like all of Seville's hotels, the Murillo is in a noisy area.

You can reach this *residencia* from the Menéndez y Pelayo, a wide avenue west of the Parque María Luisa, where a sign leads you through the Murillo Gardens on the left. Motorists should try to park in Plaza de Santa Cruz. Then walk 2 blocks to the hotel, which will send a bellhop back to the car to pick up your suitcases. If there are two in your party, station a guard at the car, and if you're going out at night, call for an inexpensive taxi to take you instead of strolling through the streets of the old quarter—it's less romantic but a lot safer.

ACCOMMODATIONS NEARBY

✪ **Hacienda Benazuza.** Calle Virgen de las Nieves, s/n, 41800 Sanlúcar la Major, Seville. ☎ **95-570-33-44.** Fax 95-570-3410. 44 units. A/C MINIBAR TV TEL. 35,000–42,000 ptas. ($210–$252) double; 45,000–124,000 ptas. ($270–$744) suite. AE, DC, MC, V. Free parking. Closed July 15–Aug 31. From Seville, follow the signs for Huelva and head south on the A-49 highway, taking exit no. 6.

Set on a hillside above the agrarian hamlet of Sanlúcar la Mayor, 12 miles (19km) south of Seville, this legendary manor house is surrounded by 40 acres of olive groves and its own farmland. Its ownership has been a cross section of every major cultural influence that has swept through Andalusia since the Moors laid its foundations in the 10th century. After the Catholic conquest of southern Spain, the site became a much-feared stronghold of the fanatically religious *Caballeros de Santiago.*

In 1992 Basque-born entrepreneur Rafael Elejabeitia bought the property and spent millions of pesetas to transform it into one of Andalusia's most charming hotels. Careful attention was paid to preserving the ancient Moorish irrigation system, whose many reflecting pools nourish the gardens. All but a few of the bedrooms are in the estate's main building, and each is individually furnished with Andalusian antiques and Moorish trappings, representative of the original construction.

Dining: The most formal of the hotel's three restaurants is **La Alquería,** with first-class service and Andalusian/international cuisine. **El Patio** is an indoor-outdoor restaurant overlooking the estate's red-brick patio and palm trees. (Both of the above serve lunch and dinner daily, and are open to non-residents who reserve in advance.) A lunch buffet beside the swimming pool, where everyone seems to show up in bathing suits and jewelry, is offered in **La Alberca.**

Amenities: Laundry, 24-hour room service, concierge, tennis courts with a resident pro, paddle tennis courts, golf range, billiard room, outdoor pool. There is a mini-museum of Andalusian agriculture in an antique building originally designed as an olive press. Many other sporting options are within driving distance and can be arranged by the concierge staff.

WHERE TO DINE
VERY EXPENSIVE

✪ **Egaña Oriza.** San Fernando, 41. ☎ **95-422-72-11.** Reservations required. Main courses 2,800–5,900 ptas. ($16.80–$35.40); fixed-price menus 5,200–9,600 ptas. ($31.20–$57.60). AE, DC, MC, V. Restaurant, Mon–Fri 1:30–3:30pm, Mon–Sat 9–11:30pm; bar, daily 9am–midnight. Closed Aug. BASQUE/INTERNATIONAL.

Seville's most stylish and best restaurant is set within the conservatory of a restored mansion adjacent to the Murillo Gardens. Much of its reputation stems from its role as one of the few game specialists in Andalusia—a province otherwise devoted to seafood. The restaurant was established by Basque-born owner and chef José Mari Egaña, who manages to combine his passion for hunting with his flair for cooking. Many of the ingredients used here have been trapped or shot within Andalusia, a region whose potential for sports shooting is underutilized, according to Sr. Egaña.

The view from the dining room encompasses a garden and a wall that formed part of the fortifications of Muslim Seville.

Specialties depend on the season, but might include ostrich carpaccio, gazpacho with prawns, steak with foie gras in grape sauce, casserole of wild boar with cherries and raisins, *quenelles* of duck in a potato nest with apple puree, stewed mountain sheep cooked with figs, rice with stewed thrush, and woodcock flamed in Spanish brandy. The wine list provides an ample supply of hearty Spanish reds to accompany these dishes. Dessert might feature a chocolate tart slathered with freshly whipped cream. Sr. Egaña's wife Mercedes runs the establishment's two-story dining room.

La Isla. Arfe, 25. ☎ **95-421-26-31.** Reservations recommended. Main courses 4,500–6,500 ptas. ($27–$39). AE, DC, MC, V. Daily 1–5pm and 8pm–midnight. Closed Aug. SPANISH/ANDALUSIAN.

Set in two large Andalusian dining rooms (thick plaster walls, tile floors, and taurine memorabilia), this air-conditioned restaurant began shortly after World War II and has thrived ever since. Its seafood is trucked or flown in from either Galicia or Huelva, one of Andalusia's major ports, and is always fresh. Menu items include *merluza a la primavera* (hake with young vegetables), *solomillo a la Castellana* (grilled beefsteak with strips of Serrano ham), chicken croquettes, and shellfish soup. The restaurant is a short walk from the cathedral within a very old building erected, the owners say, on foundations laid by the ancient Romans.

EXPENSIVE

El Burladero. In the Hotel Tryp Colón, Canalejas, 1. ☎ **95-422-29-00.** Reservations recommended. Main courses 2,000–4,000 ptas. ($12–$24); fixed-price menus 4,100–4,500 ptas. ($24.60–$27). AE, DC, MC, V. Daily 1:30–4:30pm and 9pm–midnight. Closed Aug. CONTINENTAL.

This restaurant in one of Seville's most prominent hotels is awash with the memorabilia and paraphernalia of the bullfighting trade. The interior wall tiles were removed from one of the pavilions at the 1929 Seville World's Fair, and the photographs adorning the walls are a veritable history of bullfighting. (The restaurant is named after the wooden barricade—*el burladero*—behind which bullfighters in an arena can escape from the charge of an enraged bull.) It boasts a popular bar, where a wide assortment of Sevillanos meet and mingle before their meals.

Menu specialties include upscale interpretations of local country dishes, with an attractive mix of items from other regions of Spain as well. Examples include *bacalao al horno con patatas* (baked salt cod with potatoes and saffron sauce); roasted shoulder of lamb stuffed with a deboned bull's tail and served in a richly aromatic sauce; clams with white kidney beans; a local version of *cocido*, a boiled amalgam of sausages, meats, chickpeas, and vegetables; and a stew of eel meat heavily laced with garlic and spices. Dishes from other parts of Europe include duck liver, truffled fillet steak in puff pastry, and salmon cooked in lemon-flavored dill sauce.

Florencia. In the Hotel Occidental Porta Coeli, Eduardo Dato, 49. ☎ **954-53-23-42.** Reservations recommended. Main courses 2,000–3,500 ptas. ($12–$21); set menu 7,000 ptas. ($42). AE, DC, MC, V. Daily 1:30–3:30pm and 9pm–midnight. Closed Aug. Bus: 2 or 3. MEDITERRANEAN.

With one of Seville's most elegant and sophisticated decors, this is the finest hotel dining in the city. Consider a visit here even if you're not a guest. Florencia has 15 beautifully laid tables set against a backdrop of tapestry-hung walls. The chef, Juan Martin, has a big reputation throughout Spain and presides over the Chefs' Association of Seville. The flavor combinations are contemporary, and you'll relish dish after dish prepared with the freshest ingredients. The menu boasts a wide variety of dishes featuring duck, including a delectable duck with fried white beans laced with ham. Another savory offering is *ensalada de bacalao con tomate* (salt cod salad with tomatoes) and *arroz marinero con Bogavante* (rice with crayfish). The locals rave about *corazon de solomillo al foie con zetas al vino* (beef heart with liver and mushroom in a red wine sauce) although this might be an acquired taste. For dessert nothing is more luscious than the napoleon with fresh fruit.

La Dehesa. Calle Luis de Morales, 2. ☎ **954-57-62-04.** Reservations required. Main courses 2,500–3,000 ptas. ($15–$18); set menu 5,500 ptas. ($33). AE, DC, MC, V. Daily 1:30–4pm and 8:30pm–midnight. ANDALUSIAN.

One of the leading restaurants of Seville, in the center of town 5 minutes from the train station and a 20-minute walk from the cathedral, La Dehesa is known for its regional decor. The restaurant has been serving gastronomes in Seville since the early '90s and is owned by the Melia hotel chain. It is decorated like an elegant *bodega* with stucco walls and windows containing potted plants. Each corner is a shrine to a particular bullfighter, all of whom have donated memorabilia. The menu specializes in grilled meats but does all dishes exceedingly well. Try the flavor-filled *ensaladita de la Dehesa* (shrimp, avocado, and a green leaf salad), tender grilled lamb cutlets, or fresh hake, perfectly grilled. You might begin in the classic local style with an Andalusian gazpacho. Desserts are all homemade, including tarts and an especially delightful platter of crêpes stuffed with nuts and banana ice cream.

MODERATE

Casa Robles. Calle Álvarez Quintero, 58. ☎ **95-421-31-50.** Reservations recommended. Main courses 1,500–2,500 ptas. ($9–$15); fixed-price menus 4,800–10,500 ptas. ($28.80–$63). AE, DC, MC, V. Daily 1–4:30pm and 8pm–1am. ANDALUSIAN.

Praised by local residents and visitors alike, this restaurant began life as an unpretentious bar and *bodega* in 1954. Over the years, thanks to a staff directed by owner-chef Juan Robles and his children, it developed into a courteous and bustling restaurant scattered over two floors of a building a short walk from the cathedral. Amid an all-Andalusian decor, you can enjoy such dishes as fish soup in the Andalusian style, *lubina con naranjas* (whitefish with Sevillana oranges), hake baked with strips of Serrano ham, and many kinds of fresh fish. The dessert list is long, diverse, and very tempting.

Enrique Becerra. Gamazo, 2. ☎ **95-421-30-49.** Reservations recommended. Main courses 2,200–2,600 ptas. ($13.20–$15.60). AE, DC, MC, V. Mon–Sat 1–5pm and 8pm–midnight. ANDALUSIAN.

This is a cozy, snug retreat in a whitewashed house with wrought-iron window grilles near the cathedral, and its home-cooked dishes are prepared with flavor and flair. The restaurant takes its name from its smart, helpful owner, who installed it in a late 19th-century building. This popular tapas bar and dining spot has an intimate setting that welcomes you with the feeling that your business is really appreciated. While perusing the menu, you can sip dry Tío Pepe and nibble herb-cured olives with lemon peel. The gazpacho here is among the city's best, and the sangría is served ice cold. Specialties include hake *real,* sea bream Bilbao style, and a wide range of meat, fish, and vegetarian dishes. The wine list is one of the best in Seville.

La Albahaca. Plaza de Santa Cruz, 12. ☎ **95-422-07-14.** Reservations recommended. Main courses 2,600–3,000 ptas. ($15.60–$18); fixed-price menus 4,500–5,500 ptas. ($27–$33). AE, DC, MC, V. Mon–Sat noon–4pm and 8pm–midnight. BASQUE/FRENCH.

Located on a prominent square in the Barrio de Santa Cruz, this restaurant with an open-air terrace offers a limited but savory menu that has become a favorite of locals. Specialties include a salad of carpaccio of codfish with fresh asparagus and herbs, seafood soup, shellfish bisque, grilled lamb chops, partridge braised in sherry, salmon wrapped in parchment, and chocolate pudding for dessert. The restaurant is in a manor home built in 1929.

Rincón de la Casana. Santo Domingo de la Calzada, 13. ☎ **954-53-17-10.** Reservations required. Main courses 1,900–2,900 ptas. ($11.40–$17.40); set menu 1,950 ptas. ($11.70). AE, DC, MC, V. Daily 1–4:30pm; Mon–Sat 8pm–12:30am. ARGENTINEAN/ANDALUSIAN.

Close to the old town, this landmark restaurant has been winning new converts since the mid-'80s. Converted from an old building, it has a main door of intricate carving and craftsmanship, and its roof is red tiled in the traditional style. The two-story interior has one of the most interesting decors in the city, with antique tiles and typical Andalusian artifacts. At the entrance is the mounted head of the last bull killed by the famous matador José Luís Vasquez. The chefs know their ingredients right down to the last olive. On our last visit we savored such creations as *chuleton de buey* (ox steak) and *carne con chimichuri* (steak with chopped parsley and garlic dressing in virgin olive oil). Desserts are freshly made every day, including traditional puddings and tasty tarts, most often with fresh fruit.

✪ **Taverna del Alabardero.** Calle Zaragoza, 20, 41001 Seville. ☎ **95-456-06-37.** Fax 95-456-36-66. Reservations recommended. Main courses 1,600–2,800 ptas. ($9.60–$16.80). AE, DC, MC, V. Daily 1–3:30pm and 8pm–midnight. Closed Aug. Bus: 13, 25,or 26. ANDALUSIAN.

One of Seville's most prestigious and well-recommended restaurants occupies a 19th-century townhouse near Plaza Nueva, 3 blocks from the cathedral. Famous as the dining choice of nearly every politician and diplomat who visits Seville, it has recently hosted the king and queen of Spain, the king's mother, the Spanish president and members of his cabinet, and dozens of well-connected but merely affluent visitors. Amid a collection of European antiques and oil paintings, you'll dine in any of two main rooms or three private ones, and perhaps precede your meal with a drink or tapas in the building's flowering patio. There's a garden in back with additional tables. Menu items include spicy peppers stuffed with pulverized thigh of bull, an Andalusian fish (*urta*) on a compote of aromatic tomatoes with coriander, a fillet of codfish with essence of red peppers, and Iberian beefsteak with foie gras and green peppers.

INEXPENSIVE

Hostería del Laurel. Plaza de los Venerables, 5. ☎ **95-422-02-95.** Reservations recommended. Main courses 950–2,500 ptas. ($5.70–$15). AE, DC, MC, V. Daily noon–4pm and 7:30pm–midnight. ANDALUSIAN.

In one of the most charming buildings on tiny, difficult-to-find Plaza de los Venerables in the labyrinthine Barrio de Santa Cruz, this hideaway restaurant has iron-barred windows stuffed with plants. Inside, amid Andalusian tiles, beamed ceilings, and more plants, you'll enjoy good regional cooking. Many diners stop for a drink and tapas at the ground-floor bar before going into one of the dining rooms. The *hostería* is attached to a three-star hotel.

La Raza. Isabel la Católica, 2. ☎ **95-423-38-30.** Reservations recommended. Main courses 1,300–2,300 ptas. ($7.80–$13.80). AE, DC, MC, V. Daily noon–5pm and 8pm–midnight. ANDALUSIAN.

A terrace restaurant in Parque María Luisa, La Raza is known for its setting and its tapas. It has seen better days, but the staff is attentive and the food is very good. Begin with gazpacho, then go on to one of the meat dishes or perhaps an order of the savory paella. On Friday and Saturday there is often music to entertain guests, many of them American and Japanese tourists.

Pizzeria San Marco. Calle Mesón de Moro, 6. ☎ **95-421-43-90.** Reservations recommended. Main courses 750–1,500 ptas. ($4.50–$9). MC, V. Tues–Sun 1:30–4:30pm and 8:30pm–12:30am. ITALIAN.

Although the name may make it sound like a fast-food joint, this is actually a well-managed restaurant with sit-down service and bilingual waiters. Pizza is only one of the many items featured on the menu; most people opt for pasta, salmon salad, duck in orange sauce, osso bucco, chicken Parmesan, and several forms of scallopini. There's a congenial corner for drinking, named Harry's Bar in honor of grander role models in Venice and elsewhere.

Despite the allure of the food, the real interest of the place is its setting. It is within what was originally, more than 1,000 years ago, an Arab bathhouse. Its interior reminds some visitors of a secularized mosque, despite the presence of a modern wing added around 1991 in anticipation of increased business from Seville's Expo celebration. The establishment is within the Barrio de Santa Cruz, on an obscure side street running into calle Mateus Gago.

Río Grande. Calle Betis, s/n. ☎ **95-427-39-56.** Reservations required. Main courses 1,600–5,000 ptas. ($9.60–$30); fixed-price menu 2,750 ptas. ($16.50). AE, DC, MC, V. Daily 1–5pm and 8pm–1am. Bus: 41 or 42. ANDALUSIAN.

This classic Sevillian restaurant is named for the Guadalquivir River, which its panoramic windows overlook. It sits against the bank of the river near Plaza de Cuba in front of the Torre del Oro. Some diners come here just for a view of the city monuments. Most dishes are priced at the lower end of the scale. A meal might include stuffed sweet pepper *flamenca*, fish-and-seafood soup seaman's style, the chef's fresh salmon, chicken-and-shellfish paella, bull tail Andalusian-style, or garlic chicken. A selection of fresh shellfish is brought in daily. Large terraces contain a snack bar, the Río Grande Pub, and a bingo room. You can often watch sports events on the river in this pleasant (and English-speaking) spot.

SEVILLE AFTER DARK

When the sun goes down, think sherry, wine, and tapas. After a couple of drinks have got you going, you might venture to a flamenco club, or possibly even try to learn the intricate steps of one of southern Spain's most addictive dances, La Sevillana.

DRINKS & TAPAS

Tapas are said to have originated in Andalusia, and the old-fashioned **Casa Román,** Plaza des los Venerables (☎ **95-421-64-08**), looks as if it has been dishing them up since day one, but it's actually been around only since 1934. Definitely include this place on your *tasca* hopping through the old quarter. At the deli counter in front you can make your selection; you might even pick up the fixings for a picnic in the Parque María Luisa. Casa Román is in the Barrio de Santa Cruz. It's open Monday to Friday 9am to 3pm and 5:30pm to 12:30am, Saturday and Sunday 10am to 3pm and 6:30pm to 12:30am. Tapas are priced from 550 ptas. ($3.85).

El Rinconcillo, Gerona, 40 (☎ **95-422-31-83**), has a 1930s ambience, partly because of its real age and partly because of its owners' refusal to change one iota of the decor—this has always been one of the most famous bars in Seville. It may actually be the oldest bar in Seville, with a history going back to 1670. Amid dim lighting, heavy ceiling beams, and iron-based, marble-topped tables, you can enjoy a beer or a full meal along with the rest of the easygoing clientele. The bartender will mark your tab in chalk on a well-worn wooden countertop. El Rinconcillo is especially known for its salads, omelets, hams, and selection of cheeses. Look for the art nouveau tile murals. El Rinconcillo is at the northern edge of the Barrio de Santa Cruz, near the Santa Catalina Church. It's open Thursday to Tuesday 1pm to 2am. A complete meal costs around 3,000 ptas. ($18).

The best seafood tapas in town are served at **La Alicantina,** Plaza del Salvador, 2 (☎ **95-422-61-22**), amid the glazed-tile decor typical of Seville. Both the bar and the sidewalk tables are always filled to overflowing. The owner serves generous portions of clams marinara, fried squid, grilled shrimp, fried codfish, and clams in béchamel sauce. La Alicantina, about 5 blocks north of the cathedral, is open daily 11:30am to 3:30pm and 7:30 to 11:30pm. Tapas range upward from 300 ptas. ($1.80).

At the northern end of Murillo Gardens, opening onto a quiet square with flower boxes and an ornate iron railing, **Modesto,** Cano y Cueto, 5 (☎ **95-441-68-11**), also serves fabulous seafood tapas. The bar is air-conditioned, and you can choose your appetizers just by pointing. Upstairs there's a good-value restaurant offering a meal for 2,000 ptas. ($12), including such dishes as fried squid, baby sole, grilled sea bass, and shrimp in garlic sauce. Modesto is open daily 8pm to 2am. Tapas are priced from 500 ptas. ($3).

Our favorite bar in town is undoubtedly ✪ **Abades,** calle Abades, 1 (☎ **95-422-56-22**), where a converted mansion in the Barrio de Santa Cruz has been turned into something resembling the living room on a luxurious movie set. In the heart of the Jewish ghetto, it evokes the style of the Spanish Romantic era. The house dates from the 19th century when it was constructed around a central courtyard with a fountain; it became notorious as a love den in Franco's era. Drinks and low-key conversations are the style here, and although you might spot the occasional celeb, you'll see lots of folks in jeans enjoying the comfort of the sofas and wicker armchairs. The ingredients of the special house drink called *aqua de Sevilla* are a secret, but we suspect sparkling white wine, pineapple juice, and eggs (the whites and yolks mixed in separately, of course). Classical music is played in the background. Take a taxi to get here at night, as it might not be safe to wander late along the narrow streets of the barrio. In summer, it's open daily 9pm to 4am; in winter, hours are daily 8pm to 2:30am.

FLAMENCO

When the moon is high in Seville and the scent of orange blossoms is in the air, it's time to wander the alleyways of Santa Cruz in search of the sound of castanets. Or take a taxi to be on the safe side.

Consider a visit to **Club Los Gallos,** Plaza de Santa Cruz, 11 (☎ **95-421-69-81**), a well-managed and reputable nightclub where male and female performers stamp, clap, and exude rigidly controlled Iberian passion on a small stage in front of appreciative observers. A cover charge of 3,500 ptas. ($21) includes the first drink, after which beer costs around 300 ptas. ($1.80) each. No meals are served, and advance reservations are a good idea.

Its leading competitor, charging roughly the same prices with more or less the same program, is **El Arenal,** calle Rodo, 7 (☎ **95-421-64-92**), where you'll sit at tiny, cramped tables with barely enough room to clap—but you will, because of the smoldering emotions conveyed in the performances here.

In central Seville on the riverbank between two historic bridges, **El Patio Sevillano,** Paseo de Cristóbal Colón, 11 (☎ **95-421-41-20**), is a showcase for Spanish folk song and dance performed by exotically costumed dancers. The presentation includes a wide variety of Andalusian flamenco and songs, as well as classical pieces by composers such as Falla, Albéniz, Granados, and Chueca. From March to October there are three shows nightly, beginning at 7:30pm, 10pm, and 11:45pm. There are only two shows November to February, beginning nightly at 7:30 and 10pm. Drinks cost from 500 to 1,000 ptas. ($3 to $6). Admission, including one drink, is 3,800 ptas. ($22.80).

DANCING THE SEVILLANA

Flamenco is danced in solitary grandeur, but everyone joins in with the communal but complicated dance steps of the *sevillana*. The best place to check it out is **El Simpecao,** calle Bertis, s/n (no phone). Beginning at 11pm every night of the year, recorded music presents four distinctly different facets of the complicated and old-fashioned dance steps in which dozens of everyday folk strut their Andalusian style in a way you rarely see outside Spain. The setting is modern and just a wee bit battered. Entrance is free; bottled beer costs from around 300 ptas. ($1.80) each.

DANCE CLUBS

If you're interested in the latest dance tunes, Seville's most popular club is **Disco Antigüedades,** calle Argote de Molina (no phone). About 2 blocks north of the cathedral in a much-renovated antique building, it opens nightly at 11pm, charging around 650 ptas. ($3.90) entrance, which includes the price of the first drink. Expect lots of salsa and merengue in addition to more international fare from across Europe and the United States.

GAY BARS

Seville has a large gay and lesbian population, much of it composed of foreigners, including Americans, Germans, and British, and of Andalusians who fled here for a better life, escaping smaller, less tolerant towns and villages. Gay life thrives in such bars as **Isbiliyya Café-Bar,** Paseo de Colón (☎ 95-421-04-60), which is usually open in summer daily 7pm to 3am. The bar is found across the street from the Puente Isabel II bridge, near Bar Capote. Outdoor tables are a magnet in summer. Another option on the gay scene is **Poseidon,** calle Marqués de Parades, 30 (☎ 95-421-31-92). This bar and dance club—mercifully air-conditioned in summer—draws not only a mixed crowd but an assortment of ages, although most patrons tend to be under 30. It jumps Thursday to Saturday 10:30pm to 5am.

THE PERFORMING ARTS

To keep abreast of what's happening in the arts and after dark in Seville, pick up a copy of the free monthly leaflet *El Giraldillo,* or consult the listings in the local press, *Correo de Andalucía, Sudoeste, Nueva Andalucía,* or *ABC Sevilla.* Everything is listed here, from jazz to classical music concerts and from art exhibits to dance events. You can also call a cultural hot line at ☎ 010 to find out what's happening. Most of the staff at the other end speaks English.

Keep an eye out for classical concerts that are sometimes presented in the cathedral of Seville, the church of San Salvador, and the Conservatorio Superior de Música at Jesús del Gran Poder. Variety productions, including some plays for the kids, are presented at **Teatro Alameda,** Crédito (☎ 95-438-83-12). The venerable **Teatro Lope de Vega,** avenida María Luisa (☎ 95-423-45-46), is the setting for ballet performances and classical concerts, among other events. Near Parque María Luisa, this is the leading stage of Seville, but knowledge of Spanish is necessary.

It wasn't until the 1990s that Seville got its own opera house, but **Teatro de la Maestranza,** Paseo de Colón, 22 (☎ 95-422-65-73), quickly became one of the world's premier venues for operatic performances. Naturally, the focus is on works inspired by Seville itself, including Verdi's *La Forza del destino* or Mozart's *Marriage of*

The Legacy of al-Andalus

The Moors who once occupied Andalusia—notably Seville, Granada, and Córdoba—left more than such architectural treasures as the Giralda Tower in Seville, the great mosque in Córdoba, and the Alhambra in Granada. Their intellectual and cultural legacy still influence modern life throughout the Western world.

The celebrated Arab princesses and sultans with their harems are long gone, encountered today only in the tales of Washington Irving and others. Yet from the year 711 A.D., the Moors (Muslims who were an ethnic mixture of Berbers, Hispano-Romans, and Arabs) occupied southern Spain for nearly 8 centuries and turned it into a seat of learning. It was a time of soaring achievements in philosophy, medicine, and music.

Moorish rule brought the importation of the eggplant and the almond, as well as the Arabian steed—not to mention such breakthroughs in academia as astronomy (including charting the positions of the planets) and a new and different view of Aristotle. Arab numerals replaced the more awkward Roman system, and from the Arabs came the gift of algebra. Ibn Muadh of Jaén wrote the first European treatise on trigonometry.

Intellectual giants emerged, like the Córdoba-born Jewish philosopher Maimónides. It is said that Columbus evolved his theories about a new route to the East after hours and hours of studying the charts of Idrisi, an Arabian geographer who drew up a world map as early as 1154. Arabs relied upon the compass as a navigational aid long before its use among Portuguese explorers.

Córdoba desired to shine brighter than Baghdad as a center of science and the arts. In time it attracted Abd ar-Rahman II, who introduced the fifth string to the Arab lute, leading to the development of the six-string guitar. He also ordained the way food should be eaten at mealtimes, a legacy that lives to this day. Before, everybody just helped himself randomly to whatever had been prepared; but he devised a method where courses were served in a regimented order, ending with dessert, fruit, and nuts. Today, Andalusian chefs are reviving many of the old recipes from the Arab cupboard, such as lamb cooked with honey.

Arab poetry may have inspired the first ballads sung by European troubadours, who had an enormous impact on later Western literature. Also, many Spanish words today have their origins in the Arabic language, including *alcázar* for fortress, *arroz* for rice, *naranja* for orange, and *limón* for lemon.

The Moors brought an irrigation system to Andalusia, increasing crop production; many of today's systems follow those 1,000-year-old channels. And paper first arrived in Europe through Córdoba.

Although the fanatical Isabella la Católica may have thrown a fit at the heretical idea, it was really a trio of peoples who shaped modern Spain as a nation: the Jews, the Christians, and most definitely the Arabs. The Arabs and the Jews were ousted by Isabella and Ferdinand at the close of the 15th century, but their influence still lingers.

Figaro, although jazz, classical music, and even the quintessentially Spanish *zarzuelas* (operettas) are also performed here. The opera house may be visited only during performances. Tickets (which vary in price, depending on the event staged) can be purchased daily 10am to 2pm and 5 to 8pm at the box office in front of the theater.

SIDE TRIPS FROM SEVILLE
CARMONA

An easy hour-long bus trip from the main terminal in Seville, Carmona is an ancient city dating from Neolithic times. Twenty-one miles (34km) east of Seville, it grew in power and prestige under the Moors, establishing ties with Castile in 1252.

Surrounded by fortified walls, Carmona has three Moorish fortresses—one a parador, and the other two, the **Alcázar de la Puerta de Córdoba** and **Alcázar de la Puerta de Sevilla.** The top attraction is **Seville Gate,** with its double Moorish arch opposite St. Peter's Church. Note too **Córdoba Gate** on calle Santa María de Gracia, which was attached to the ancient Roman walls in the 17th century.

The town itself is a virtual national landmark, filled with narrow streets, white-washed walls, and Renaissance mansions. **Plaza San Fernando** is the most important square, with many elegant 17th-century houses. The most important church is dedicated to **Santa María** and stands on the calle Martín López. You enter a Moorish patio before exploring the interior with its 15th-century white vaulting.

In the area known as Jorge Bonsor (named for the original discoverer of the ruins) there's a **Roman amphitheater** as well as a **Roman necropolis** containing the remains of 1,000 families who lived in and around Carmona 2,000 years ago. Of the two important tombs, the Elephant Vault consists of three dining rooms and a kitchen. The other, the Servilia Tomb, was the size of a nobleman's villa. On site is a **Museo Arqueológico** (☎ 95-414-08-11) displaying artifacts found at the site. April to October hours are Tuesday to Saturday 9am to 2pm and 4 to 6pm; off-season, Tuesday to Friday 10am to 2pm, Saturday and Sunday 10am to 2pm. Admission is 250 ptas. ($1.50).

If you're driving to Carmona, exit from Seville's eastern periphery onto the N-V superhighway, following the signs to the airport, then to Carmona on the road to Madrid. The Carmona turnoff is clearly marked.

Where to Stay & Dine

✪ **Casa de Carmona.** Plaza de Lasso, 1, 41410 Carmona (Sevilla). ☎ **95-419-10-00,** or 212/686-9213 for reservations within North America. Fax 95-419-01-89. www.casadecarmona. com. E-mail: reservations@casadecarmona.com. 30 units. A/C MINIBAR TV TEL. 23,000–27,000 ptas. ($138–$162) double; 90,000 ptas. ($540) suite. Add about 30% for Feria de Sevilla and Easter (Semana Santa). AE, DC, MC, V. Free parking.

One of the most elegant and intimate hotels in Andalusia, this plushly furnished hideaway was originally built as the home of the Lasso family during the 1500s. Several years ago, a team of entrepreneurs added the many features required for a luxury hotel, all the while retaining the marble columns, massive masonry, and graceful proportions of the building's original construction. The most visible public room still maintains vestiges of its original function as a library. Each good-sized bedroom is a cozy enclave of opulent furnishings, with a distinct decor theme inspired by ancient Rome, medieval Andalusia, or Renaissance Spain. All the immaculately kept tiled bathrooms are equipped with hair dryers.

Dining: On the premises is an outdoor restaurant serving modern interpretations of Andalusian and international cuisine, with meals served daily 1 to 4pm and 9 to 11:30pm and priced from around 4,000 ptas. ($24) each.

Amenities: Set at the edge of the village, the hotel has an outdoor swimming pool with a flowery terrace, an inner courtyard covered against the midsummer heat with canvas awning, and a small exercise room. Concierge, room service, laundry and dry cleaning, newspaper delivery, baby-sitting, currency exchange.

ITÁLICA

Lovers of Roman history will flock to **Itálica** (☎ **95-599-73-76**), the ruins of an ancient city 5½ miles (9km) northwest of Seville on the major road to Lisbon, near the small town of Santiponce.

After the battle of Ilipa, Publius Cornelius Scipio Africanus founded Itálica in 206 B.C. Two of the most famous of Roman emperors, Trajan and Hadrian, were born here. Indeed, master builder Hadrian was to have a major influence on his hometown. In his reign the **amphitheater,** the ruins of which can be seen today, was among the largest in the Roman Empire. Lead pipes that carried water from the Guadalquivir River still remain. A small museum displays some of the Roman statuary found here, although the finest pieces have been shipped to Seville. Many mosaics are on exhibit, depicting beasts, gods, and birds, and others are constantly being discovered. The ruins, including a Roman theater, can be explored for 250 ptas. ($1.50). The site is open April to September, Tuesday to Saturday 9am to 6:30pm and on Sunday 9am to 3pm. October to March, it's open Tuesday to Saturday 9am to 5:30pm and on Sunday 10am to 4pm.

If you're driving, exit from the northwest periphery of Seville following the signs for highway E-803 in the direction of Zafra and Lisbon. But if you don't have a car, take the bus marked CALLE DE SANTIPONCE leaving from calle Marqués de Parada near the railway station in Seville. Buses depart every hour for the 30-minute trip.

4 Jerez de la Frontera

54 miles (87km) S of Seville, 368 miles (592.5km) SW of Madrid, 21 miles (34km) NE of Cádiz

The charming little Andalusian town of Jerez made a name for itself in England for the thousands of casks of golden sherry it has shipped there over the centuries. Nearly 3,000 years old, Jerez is nonetheless a modern, progressive town with wide boulevards, although it does have an interesting old quarter. Busloads of visitors pour in every year to get free drinks at one of the *bodegas* where wine is aged and bottled.

The name of the town is pronounced Her-*ez* or Her-*eth,* in Andalusian or Castilian, respectively. The French and the Moors called it various names, including Heres and Scheris, which the English corrupted to Sherry.

ESSENTIALS

GETTING THERE   **Iberia** and **Avianco** offer flights to Jerez Monday to Friday from Barcelona and Zaragoza; daily flights from Madrid; and several flights a week to and from Valencia, Tenerife, Palma de Majorca, and Grand Canary Island. No international flights land at Jerez. The airport at Carretera Jerez-Sevilla is about 7 miles (11km) northeast of the city center (follow the signs to Seville). Call ☎ **956-15-00-00** for information.

Trains from Madrid arrive daily. A ticket from Madrid to Jerez on the TALGO costs 7,600 to 8,800 ptas. ($45.60 to $52.80), and the trip takes 4½ hours. The railway station in Jerez is at Plaza de la Estación (☎ **956-34-23-19**) at the eastern end of calle Medina.

Bus connections are more frequent than train connections, and the location of the bus terminal is more convenient. You'll find it on calle Cartuja at the corner of calle Madre de Díos, a 12-minute walk east of the Alcázar. About 17 buses arrive daily from Cádiz (1 hour away) and 3 per day travel from Ronda (2¾ hours). Seven buses a day arrive from Seville (1½ hours). Phone ☎ **956-34-52-07** for more information.

Jerez lies on the highway connecting Seville with Cádiz, Algeciras, Gibraltar, and the ferryboat landing for Tangier, Morocco. There's also an overland road connecting Jerez with Granada and Málaga.

VISITOR INFORMATION   The **tourist information office** is at calle Larga, 39 (☎ 956-33-11-50). To reach it from the bus terminal, take calle Medina to calle Honda, and continue along as the road turns to the right. The English-speaking staff can provide directions, transportation suggestions, open hours, and so on for any *bodega* you might want to visit. You will also be given a map pinpointing the location of various *bodegas*. It's open April to October, Monday to Friday 9am to 2pm and 5 to 8pm, Saturday 9am to 2pm; off-season, Monday to Saturday 8am to 3pm and 5 to 7pm.

EXPLORING THE AREA
✪ TOURING THE *BODEGAS*

Jerez is not surrounded by vineyards as you might expect. Instead, the vineyards lie to the north and west of Jerez, within the "Sherry Triangle" marked by Jerez, Sanlúcar de Barrameda, and El Puerto de Santa María (the latter two towns on the coast). This is where top-quality *albariza* soil is found, the highest quality containing an average of 60% chalk, which is ideal for the cultivation of grapes used in sherry production, principally the white *Palomino de Jerez*. The ideal time to visit is September. However, visitors can count on the finest in hospitality year-round since Jerez is widely known for the warm welcome it bestows.

There must be more than 100 *bodegas* in and around Jerez where you can not only see how sherries are made, bottled, and aged, but also get free samples. Among the most famous producers are Sandeman, Pedro Domecq, and González Byass, the maker of Tío Pepe.

On a typical visit to a *bodega*, you'll be shown through several buildings in which sherry and brandy are manufactured. In one building, you'll see grapes being pressed and sorted; in another, the bottling process; in a third, thousands of large oak casks. Then it's on to an attractive bar where various sherries—amber, dark gold, cream, red, sweet, and velvety—can be sampled. If either is offered, try the very dry La Ina sherry or the Fundador brandy, one of the most popular in the world.

Warning: These drinks are more potent than you might expect!

Most *bodegas* are open Monday to Friday only, 10:30am to 1:30pm. Regrettably, many of them are closed in August, but many do reopen by the third week of August to prepare for the wine festival in early September.

Of the dozens of *bodegas* you can visit, the most popular are listed below. Some of them charge an admission fee and require a reservation.

A favorite among British visitors is **Harveys of Bristol,** calle Arcos, 57 (☎ 956-15-10-02), which doesn't require a reservation. An English-speaking guide leads a 2-hour tour year-round, except for the first 3 weeks of August. Visit Monday to Friday for tours at noon, costing 300 ptas. ($1.80).

You'll definitely want to visit **Williams & Humbert Limited,** Nuño de Cañas, 1 (☎ 956-34-45-39), which offers tours at noon and 1:30pm Monday to Friday, charging 300 ptas. ($1.80). Their premium brands include the world-famous Dry Sack Medium Sherry, Canasta Cream, Fino Pando, and Manzanilla Alegría, in addition to Gran Duque de Alba Gran Reserva Brandy. It is wise to reserve in advance.

Another famous name is **González Byass,** Manuel María González, 12 (☎ 956-34-00-00); admission is 500 ptas. ($3.35), and reservations are required. Tours depart at 10am, 11am, noon, and 1pm Monday to Friday. Equally famous is **Domecq,** calle

San Ildefonso, 3 (☎ 956-35-70-00), requiring a reservation but charging no admission. Tours depart at 10am, 11am, and noon Monday to Friday.

Since many people go to Jerez specifically to visit a *bodega,* August or weekend closings can be very disappointing. If this happens to you, make a trip to the nearby village of **Lebrija,** about halfway between Jerez and Seville, 8½ miles (14km) west of the main highway. Lebrija, a good spot to get a glimpse of rural Spain, is a local winemaking center where some very fine sherries originate. At one small *bodega,* that of Juan García, you are courteously escorted around by the owner. There are several other *bodegas* in Lebrija, and the local citizens will gladly point them out to you. It's all very casual, and much more informal than the *bodegas* of Jerez.

THE DANCING HORSES OF JEREZ

A rival of sorts to Vienna's famous Spanish Riding School is the **Escuela Andaluza del Arte Ecuestre (Andalusian School of Equestrian Art),** avenida Duque de Abrantes, 11 (☎ 956-30-77-98). In fact, the long, hard schooling that brings horse and rider into perfect harmony originated in this province. The Viennese school was started with Hispano-Arab horses sent from this region, the same breeds you can see today. Every Thursday at noon, crowds come to admire the Dancing Horses of Jerez as they perform in a show that includes local folklore. Numbered seats sell for 2,400 ptas. ($14.40), with unnumbered seats going for 1,500 ptas. ($9). When performances aren't scheduled, you can visit the stables and tack room, observing as the elegant horses are being trained. Hours are Monday to Wednesday and Friday 11am to 1pm, costing 450 ptas. ($2.70). Bus 18 goes here.

WHERE TO STAY
EXPENSIVE

Guadalete. Avenida Duque de Abrantes, 50, 11407 Jerez de la Frontera. ☎ **956-18-2288.** Fax 956-18-2293. www.hotel-guadalete.com. E-mail: guadalete@hotel-guadalete.com. 125 units. A/C MINIBAR TV TEL. 20,800 ptas. ($124.80) double; 43,000 ptas. ($258) suite. AE, MC, V. Free parking.

In a tranquil and exclusive area north of Jerez, and a 15-minute walk to the historic core, this four-star hotel opened in 1992. It occupies a modern brick structure of three floors and, although not as good as the Royal Sherry Park, is one of the town's leading hotels, often hosting business travelers in town to deal with the sherry industry. A marble-floored lobby, spacious and contemporary public rooms, palm tree gardens, and two tempting and large swimming pools give this place somewhat of a resort aura. Rooms are medium in size to spacious and have large beds fitted with quality mattresses and elegant linen. The state-of-the-art bathrooms contain complimentary toiletries and have hair dryers. The hotel is decorated with original watercolors and lithographs painted by local artists in the '70s.

Dining/Diversions: The **Cartuja** restaurant serves traditional dishes from the Andalusian kitchen in a charming, English-style atmosphere. There is a snack bar for *platos combinados* and a bar with a good selection of sherries.

Amenities: Room service 7am to midnight, laundry, concierge, swimming pools, nearby golf courses. The hotel organizes visits to the *bodegas.*

Hotel Avenida Jerez. Avenida Alcalde Álvaro Domecq, 10, 11405 Jerez de la Frontera. ☎ **956-34-74-11.** Fax 956-33-72-96. www.nh-hoteles.es. E-mail: nh@nh-hoteles.es. 95 units. A/C MINIBAR TV TEL. 18,900 ptas. ($113.40) double; 26,000 ptas. ($156) suite. AE, DC, MC, V. Parking 1,500 ptas. ($9).

Very close to the commercial heart of Jerez, this hotel occupies a modern balconied structure of seven stories and is the best hotel within Jerez itself, although Montecastillo (see below) on the outskirts is a serious challenger. Inside, cool polished stone floors, leather armchairs, and a variety of potted plants create a restful haven. The good-sized rooms are discreetly contemporary and decorated in neutral colors, with big windows, comfortable beds, and private bathrooms equipped with hair dryers.

Dining/Diversions: The hotel maintains a pleasant and unpretentious cafeteria providing coffee-shop–style snacks and platters of Spanish food. There's also a bar.

Amenities: Room service (available daily 7am to 11pm), baby-sitting, concierge, laundry and valet, car-rental desk.

Hotel Royal Sherry Park. Avenida Alcalde Álvaro Domecq, 11 Bis, 11405 Jerez de la Frontera. ☎ **956-31-76-14.** Fax 956-31-13-00. www.travelcom.es/sherry. E-mail: reservas@ sherryparkhotel.com. 170 units. A/C MINIBAR TV TEL. 18,250 ptas. ($109.50) double; 28,000–32,000 ptas. ($168–$192) suite. AE, DC, MC, V. Free parking.

Especially noted for its setting within a palm-fringed garden and for a large swimming pool whose tiled edges attract many sun-loving residents, this is one of the best modern hotels in Jerez. Located on a wide and verdant boulevard north of the historic center of town, it contains a marble-floored lobby, efficiently modern public rooms, and fairly standard but comfortable bedrooms, each with a private tiled bathroom. The uniformed staff lays out a copious breakfast buffet and serves drinks at several hideaways, both indoors and within the garden.

Dining/Diversions: El Abaco Restaurant, which spills over onto an outdoor terrace, serves flavorful international cuisine. A bar with a good selection of sherries and whiskeys is nearby.

Amenities: Room service (available daily 8am to midnight), laundry and valet, concierge, baby-sitting, outdoor swimming pool, car rentals, shopping boutiques.

Montecastillo. Carrertera N-342, 11406 Jerez de la Frontera. ☎ **956-15-12-00.** Fax 956-15-12-09. 120 units. A/C MINIBAR TV TEL. 19,000–26,000 ptas. ($114–$156) double; 62,500–125,000 ptas. ($375–$750) suite. AE, DC, MC, V. Free parking.

Giving Hotel Avenida Jerez serious competition is this deluxe country club in the rolling hills of the sherry *campiña,* or wine country. The most tranquil retreat in the area, it has bedrooms with scenic-view balconies overlooking a Jack Nicklaus–designed 18-hole golf course. Just a 10-minute ride from the center of Jerez, the hotel is elegantly furnished and professionally run. The spacious guest rooms are decorated in a provincial French style with elegant fabrics, beautiful linens, and large beds fitted with quality mattresses. The marble bathrooms are elegant with plush towels, toiletries, and hair dryers.

Dining: At **Montecastillo,** favorite regional meals are combined with traditional Spanish and international dishes for some of the best cuisine in the area.

Amenities: Room service, laundry and dry cleaning, baby-sitting. In addition to the golf course, there are swimming pools and a sauna. Horseback riding and tennis are available nearby, and there are paddle tennis facilities at the adjacent and exclusive Montecastillo Country Club.

MODERATE

La Cueva Park. Carretera de Arcos, km 6.5, Apartado, 536, 11406 Jerez de la Frontera. ☎ **956-18-9120.** Fax 956-18-9121. www.madeinspain.net/hotelcadiz/lacuevapark. 58 units. A/C MINIBAR TV TEL. 18,000 ptas. ($108) double; 40,000 ptas. ($240) suite. AE, DC, MC, V. Parking 1,000 ptas. ($6).

This charming hotel in a century-old building 4 miles from the center of town attracts motorists, although it is just half a mile from the bus station. The architecture is typical of Andalusia with a tiled roof overhanging thick brick walls. Gardens surround the hotel. All the medium-size units are comfortably furnished. There are nine white-walled bungalow-style apartments classified as suites, each with its own cooking area, living room, and terrace. The hotel restaurant, Mesón la Cueva, serves high quality Andalusian and international dishes. There is an on-site cafeteria, an outdoor swimming pool, and laundry service.

INEXPENSIVE

El Coloso. Pedro Alonso, 13, 11402 Jerez de la Frontera. ☎/fax **956-34-90-08.** E-mail: martaorden@hotmail.com. 25 units. A/C TV TEL. 7,500 ptas. ($45) double; 22,000 ptas. ($132) suite. Rates include breakfast buffet. MC, V. Parking 800 ptas. ($4.80).

A few steps from the Plaza de la Angustias in the historic center, this is one of the best bargains in town, modest but recommendable in its unpretentious way. The decor is in the conventional local style with whitewashed walls and a trio of Andalusian-style patios with balconies opening onto street scenes of Jerez. The hotel opened in 1969, and was last renovated in 1998. Bedrooms are a bit cramped but beautifully maintained with good beds. Breakfast is the only meal served. Even though low budget, it doesn't sacrifice comfort or cleanliness.

Hotel Ávila. Calle Ávila, 3, 11140 Jerez de la Frontera. ☎ **956-33-48-08.** Fax 956-33-68-07. 32 units. A/C TV TEL. 7,000–7,800 ptas. ($42–$46.80) double. AE, DC, MC, V. Parking 1,200 ptas. ($7.20) nearby.

One of the better bargains in Jerez, the Ávila is a modern three-story building erected in 1968 and renovated in 1987. It is near the post office and Plaza del Arenal in the commercial center of town. Inside, its rooms are clean, comfortable, and well maintained, although not special in any way. The beds, however, are quite comfortable, and the bathrooms well maintained and equipped with shower stalls.

Hotel Serit. Higueras, 7, 11402 Jerez de la Frontera. ☎ **956-34-07-00.** Fax 956-34-07-16. E-mail: hotelserit@redicom.es. 35 units. A/C TV TEL. 8,000–10,000 ptas. ($48–$60) double. AE, DC, MC, V. Parking 1,000 ptas. ($6).

The modern three-star Hotel Serit near Plaza de la Angustias offers good priced rooms that are comfortable and functionally furnished. Ranging from small to medium, rooms are equipped with firm mattresses and small but well-maintained private bathrooms, each with a shower stall and a hair dryer. There's a pleasant bar downstairs, plus a modern breakfast lounge. Laundry and room service are provided.

WHERE TO DINE

El Bosque. Alcalde Álvaro Domecq, 26. ☎ **956-18-08-80.** Reservations required. Main courses 2,500–4,500 ptas. ($15–$27). AE, DC, MC, V. Mon–Sat 1:30–5pm and 8:30pm–2am. SPANISH/INTERNATIONAL.

Less than a mile northeast of the city center, El Bosque is the city's most elegant restaurant and was established just after World War II. A favorite of the sherry-producing aristocracy, it retains a strong emphasis on bullfighting memorabilia, which makes up most of the decoration.

Order the excellent *rabo de toro* (bull's-tail stew) if you want to dine like a native. You might begin with a soothing gazpacho, then try one of the fried fish dishes, such as hake Seville style. Rice with king prawns and baby shrimp omelets are popular dishes. Occasionally, Laguna duck in honey with chestnuts and pears is a feature. Desserts are usually good, especially the pistachio ice cream.

Gaitán. Calle Gaitán, 3. ☎ **956-34-58-59.** Reservations recommended. Main courses 1,000–2,500 ptas. ($6–$15); fixed-price menu 2,200 ptas. ($13.20). AE, DC, MC, V. Daily 1–4:30pm; Mon–Sat 1–4:30pm and 8:30–11:30pm. ANDALUSIAN.

Owner Juan Hurtado has won acclaim for the food served here at his small restaurant near Puerta Santa María. Surrounded by celebrity photographs, you can enjoy such

Andalusian dishes as garlic soup, various stews, duck à la Sevillana, and fried seafood. One special dish is lamb cooked with honey, based on a recipe so ancient it dates from the Muslim occupation of Spain. For dessert, the almond tart is a favorite.

✪ **Mesa Redonda.** Manuel de la Quintana, 3. ☎ **956-34-00-69.** Reservations required. Main courses 1,800–2,000 ptas. ($10.80–$12); set menu 4,500 ptas. ($27). AE, DC, MC, V. Mon–Sat 1:30–4pm and 9–11pm. Closed last week in July and first 3 weeks in Aug. TRADITIONAL SPANISH.

This restaurant is a rare treat. The owner and chef, José Antonio Romero, and his wife, Margarita, for the past 15 or so years have sought out the traditional recipes once served in the private homes of the aristocratic sherry dons of Jerez. They present them to you in winning and tasty combinations in a setting that is like visiting someone's private residence, complete with library filled with old recipe books and literature about food and wine. Only 10 tables are available and are easily filled. The menu is ever changing, as is the culinary repertoire of this couple. The cookery is simple and superb. Try *albondiguillas marineras* (fish balls in a shellfish sauce) and most definitely *hojaldre de rape y gambas* (a pastry filled with monkfish and prawns). Most recommendable are the *filetes de lenguado con zetas* (fillet of sole with mushrooms) and *cordero asado* (grilled lamb). For dessert, there is nothing finer than the lemon-and-almond cake.

Restaurante Tendido 6. Calle Circo, 10. ☎ **956-34-48-35.** Reservations required. Main courses 550–2,000 ptas. ($3.30–$12). AE, DC, MC, V. Mon–Sat 1–4pm and 8pm–midnight. SPANISH.

This combination restaurant and tapas bar has loyal clients who come from many walks of life. The chef creates a dignified regional cuisine that includes grilled rump steak, fish soup, and a wide array of Spanish dishes, including Basque and Castilian cuisine. There's nothing really exciting here, but the long-tested recipes are flavorful and the place is a good value. The Tendido is on the south side of Plaza de Toros.

SIDE TRIPS FROM JEREZ DE LA FRONTERA
MEDINA SIDONIA

This survivor of the Middle Ages is one of the most unspoiled hillside villages of Spain, about 29 miles (46.5km) east of Cádiz and 22 miles (35.5km) southeast of Jerez de la Frontera. Motorists from Jerez should follow the 440 southeast.

A village that time forgot, Medina Sidonia has cobblestoned streets, tile-roofed white buildings dotting the hillside, a Gothic church, a Moorish gate, and steep alleyways traveled by locals on donkeys. The Arab influence is everywhere, and the surrounding countryside is wild and seldom visited. The pockets of fog that sometimes settle over the land will make you think you're on the Yorkshire moors.

From Medina Sidonia, it's a 2½-hour drive to the port city of Algeciras, or you can take the Jerez road back to Seville.

✪ ARCOS DE LA FRONTERA

Twenty miles (32km) east of Jerez de la Frontera, this old Arab town, now a National Historic Monument, was built in the form of an amphitheater. Sitting on a rock and surrounded by the Guadalete River on three sides, it contains many houses that have been hollowed out of this formation. From the old city, there's a high-in-the-clouds view that some visitors consider without rival on the Iberian Peninsula.

The city is filled with whitewashed walls and narrow winding streets that disappear into steps. It holds a lot of historical interest and has a beautiful lake complete with paddleboats and a Mississippi riverboat.

The most exciting attraction is the **view from the principal square,** the Plaza del Cabildo, a rectangular esplanade overhanging a deep river cleft. You can see a Moorish castle, but it is privately owned and cannot be visited by the public. You can, however, visit a church on the main square, the **Iglesia de Santa María,** constructed in 1732 in a blend of Gothic, Renaissance, and baroque styles. Its western front, and its most outstanding architectural achievement, is in plateresque style. The second major church of the town, **Iglesia de San Pedro,** stands on the northern edge of the old *barrio* (quarter) at the far end of the cliff and is known for its 16th- and 18th-century tower. This church, which grew up on the site of a Moorish fortress, owns artworks by Zurbarán and Murillo, among others. Check with the tourist office (see below) about gaining admission to these churches, as they are often closed for security reasons. Several art thefts have occurred in the area.

Even if you don't succeed in gaining entrance to the churches, it is reason enough to visit Arcos merely to wander its alleys and view its ruins from the Middle Ages. If you have to return to wherever you're going for the night, stay at least long enough to have a drink in the patio of the parador (recommended below) and take in the monumental view.

There is no train service to this little bit of paradise, but you can take a bus from Jerez de la Frontera, Seville, or Cádiz. Motorists from Jerez should follow the 342 east until they see the turnoff for Arcos.

The **tourist information office** is at Plaza del Cabildo (☎ **956-70-22-64**), open Monday to Friday 9am to 2pm and 5 to 7pm, Saturday 9am to 2pm, and Sunday 11am to 2pm.

Where to Stay

El Convento Hotel. Maldonado, 2, 11630 Arcos de la Frontera. ☎ **956-70-23-33.** Fax 956-70-41-28. 11 units. A/C MINIBAR TV TEL. 12,800 ptas. ($76.80) double. AE, DC, MC, V. Parking 500 ptas. ($3).

In the historic center behind the parador, this intriguing two-story hotel is built into the old convent of Las Mercedarias—from which it takes its name of "El Convento." Word has spread about the low prices, charm, and comfort of this little inn, so reservations are important. The decor is rustic with white walls and wooden beams in the typical Andalusian style. Rated only one star by the government (what do they know?), the graceful inn opens onto views of the old city and the surrounding countryside. Accommodations are medium in size and comfortably furnished with renovated bathrooms, each equipped with a hair dryer. The hotel's restaurant (actually 5 minutes away) is well known for the quality of its cuisine (see "Where to Dine," below).

Hotel los Olivos. Paseo de Boliches, 30, 11630 Arcos de la Frontera. ☎ **956-70-08-11.** Fax 956-70-20-18. E-mail: h.olivos@teleline.es. 19 units. A/C MINIBAR TV TEL. 9,630 ptas. ($57.80) double. AE, DC, MC, V. Parking 700 ptas. ($4.20).

Just a 5-minute walk from the *zona monumental,* or historic core of the town, and parallel to the main street, this hotel opened in the late 1980s and was last renovated in 1998. This charming old Andalusian building is on a corner, with a patio at its core. The social areas of the inn are tastefully laid out and overlook olive groves, as do several of the rooms. Accommodations are decorated in a regional style with white walls and ceilings, along with wood trim and paintings of rural Andalusian scenes. Bedrooms are small but comfortably furnished and well maintained. At an on-site cafeteria guests can order breakfast or light snacks. Los Olivos has room service until 8pm, plus laundry and a concierge.

Parador de Arcos de la Frontera. Plaza del Cabildo, 11630 Arcos de la Frontera. ☎ **956-70-05-00.** Fax 956-70-11-16. 24 units. A/C MINIBAR TV TEL. 18,500 ptas. ($111) double. AE, DC, DISC, MC, V. Free parking.

The best place to stay is this government-run parador in a restored palace in the heart of the old quarter. Built in the 1700s, it was the palace and government seat of the king's magistrate (*corregidor*) in Arcos. From the balconies are views of the valley of the Guadalete with its river, plains, and farms. In good weather you can take your meals (try the pork with garlic) on one of these balconies; lunch or dinner costs 3,500 ptas. ($21). The decor consists of tiles and antiques. The good-sized rooms are handsomely furnished and beautifully maintained; perhaps you'll be assigned the one where Charles de Gaulle once stayed. Bathrooms are tiled and efficiently organized, each one equipped with a hair dryer.

Where to Dine

El Convento Restaurant. Maldonado, 2. ☎ **956-70-23-33.** Reservations recommended. Main courses 1,800–2,500 ptas. ($10.80–$15). AE, DC, MC, V. Daily 1:30–3:30pm and 7:30–10pm. ANDALUSIAN.

Connected to the previously recommended hotel, this is the finest dining room in Arcos. It is run by a husband-and-wife team who have won accolades nationally for their cuisine. The chefs are proud of their local heritage in food and like to share it with you, beginning with their soups. They not only serve gazpacho from the freshest tomatoes of summer but also prepare tasty concoctions from whatever vegetable is in season, including asparagus in spring. In autumn they have good game dishes, perhaps partridge in a velvety smooth almond sauce. Lamb is cooked with the aromatic fresh herbs of the countryside, and all their desserts are homemade.

5 Cádiz

76 miles (122km) S of Seville, 388 miles (625km) SW of Madrid

The oldest inhabited city in the Western world, founded in 1100 B.C., this modern, bustling Atlantic port is a kind of Spanish Marseilles, a melting pot of Americans, Africans, and Europeans who are docking or passing through. The old quarter teems with local characters, little dives, and seaport alleyways. But despite its thriving life, the city does not hold major interest for tourists, except for the diverse cultures that have shaped it. Phoenicians, Arabs, Visigoths, Romans, and Carthaginians all passed through Cádiz and left their imprints. Throughout the ages this ancient port city has enjoyed varying states of prosperity, especially after the discovery of the New World.

At the end of a peninsula, Cádiz separates the Bay of Cádiz from the Atlantic, and from numerous sea walls around the town you have views of the ocean. It was here that Columbus set out on his second voyage.

ESSENTIALS

GETTING THERE   Trains arrive from Seville (taking 2 hours), Jerez de la Frontera (40 minutes), and Córdoba (5 hours). The train station is located on avenida del Puerto (☎ **956-25-43-01**), on the southeast border of the main port.

If you're taking a bus from Madrid, you'll probably have to transfer in Seville. Buses arrive in Cádiz at two separate terminals. From Seville (12 per day; 2 hours), Jerez de la Frontera (six per day; 1 hour), Málaga, Córdoba, and Granada, buses arrive at the **Estación de Comes terminal,** Plaza de la Hispanidad, 1 (☎ **956-21-17-63**), on the north side of town, a few blocks west of the main port. Far less prominent is the terminal run by the **Transportes Los Amarillos,** avenida Ramón de Carranza, 31

(☎ **956-28-58-52**), several blocks to the south, which runs frequent buses to several nearby towns and villages, most of which are of interest only for local residents and workers.

Driving from Seville, the A-4 (also called E-5), a toll road, or N-IV, a toll-free road running beside it, will bring you into Cádiz.

VISITOR INFORMATION   The **tourist information office** is at Calderón de la Barca, 1 (☎ **956-21-13-13**). It's open Monday to Friday 9am to 7pm, Saturday 10am to 2pm.

EXPLORING CÁDIZ

Despite being one of the oldest towns in Europe, Cádiz has few remnants of antiquity. It is still worth visiting, however, especially to wander through the old quarter, which retains a special charm.

Plaza de San Juan de Dios is the ideal place to sit at a sidewalk cafe and people-watch in the shadow of the neoclassical **Isabellino Ayuntamiento (Town Hall),** with its outstanding chapter house. The **Oratorio de San Felipe Neri,** Santa Inés (☎ **956-21-16-12**), where the Cortés (Parliament) met in 1812 to proclaim its constitution, has an important Murillo (*Conception*) and a history museum. Admission is free, and it's open August to June daily 8:30 to 10am and 7:30 to 9:45pm. The **Hospital de Mujeres (Women's Hospital)** has a patio courtyard dating from 1740 and a chapel with El Greco's *Ecstasy of St. Francis.*

Museo de Cádiz. Plaza de Mina, s/n. ☎ **956-21-22-81.** Admission 250 ptas. ($1.50), free Sun. Tues 2:30–8pm; Wed–Sat 9am–8pm; Sun 9:30am–2:30pm.

This fully restored museum contains one of Spain's most important Zurbarán collections, as well as paintings by Rubens and Murillo (including the latter's acclaimed picture of Christ). The archaeology section displays Roman, Carthaginian, and Phoenician finds, and ethnology exhibits include pottery, baskets, textiles, and leather works.

Catedral de Cádiz. Plaza Catedral. ☎ **956-28-61-54.** Free admission to Cathedral; museum 500 ptas. ($3) adults, 200 ptas. ($1.20) children. Tues–Sat 10am–12:30pm.

This magnificent 18th-century baroque building by architect Vicente Acero has a neoclassical interior dominated by an outstanding apse. The tomb of Cádiz-born composer Manuel de Falla lies in its splendid crypt; music lovers from all over the world come here to pay their respects. Haydn composed *The Seven Last Words of Our Savior on the Cross* for this cathedral. The treasury/museum contains a priceless collection of Spanish silver and embroidery, and paintings by Spanish, Italian, and Flemish artists.

WHERE TO STAY

Cádiz has a number of inexpensive accommodations, some of which are quite poor. However, for a moderate price you can afford some of the finest lodgings in the city. Note that rooms are scarce during the February carnival season.

Parador Hotel Atlántico. Duque de Nájera, 9, 11002 Cádiz. ☎ **956-22-69-05.** Fax 956-21-45-82. E-mail: cadiz@parador.es. 149 units. A/C MINIBAR TV TEL. 15,000 ptas. ($90) double; 18,500–33,000 ptas. ($111–$198) suite. AE, DC, MC, V. Parking 1,500 ptas. ($9) for garage.

Actually a modern resort hotel, this national parador is built on one of the loveliest beaches of the Bay of Cádiz at the western edge of the old town. It is clearly the outstanding choice of accommodation here, dwarfing the competition. The white six-story building has a marble patio, a salon decked in rattan and cane, and spacious rooms that feature balconies with tables and chairs for relaxed ocean viewing. More than half of the rooms were renovated in 1995, when all the mattresses were renewed and the plumbing restored. Palm trees surround the Atlántico's swimming pool. The hotel boasts a bar and a dining room known for its superb Andalusian cuisine, particularly the seafood.

Regio 1. Ana de Viya, 11, 11009 Cádiz. ☎ **956-27-93-31.** Fax 956-27-91-13. 44 units. A/C TV TEL. 10,500 ptas. ($63) double. AE, DC, MC, V. Parking in garage 500 ptas. ($3).

Built in 1978, this aging hotel rises six stories and is about a block inland from the harbor and Paseo Marítimo. The small rooms are simple but airy and comfortable—nowhere near the equal of the Atlántico (see above), but then its prices are much more reasonable. Breakfast is the only meal served. The overflow from this hotel is sometimes directed to the hotel's twin, the superior Regio 2 (see below).

Regio 2. Avenida Andalucía, 79, 11008 Cádiz. ☎ **956-25-30-08.** Fax 956-25-30-09. 45 units. A/C TV TEL. 10,500 ptas. ($63) double. AE, DC, MC, V. Parking 500 ptas. ($3).

Business was successful enough in the late 1970s to justify the construction of this five-story twin of an already existing hotel, the Regio 1 (see above). Run by the same management and sharing some of their staff and amenities in common, it was built in 1981 about 200 yards from its twin. It offers air-conditioning in each of its simple but pleasant rooms, which are more comfortable and in better shape than those of Regio 1. Both hotels are a very short walk from the ocean. The Regio 2 operates a cafeteria serving *platos combinados* (combination plates) daily.

WHERE TO DINE

Achuri. Calle Plocia, 15. ☎ **956-25-36-13.** Reservations recommended. Main courses 1,500–2,500 ptas. ($9–$15); set menu 3,500 ptas. ($21). AE, MC, V. Sun–Wed 1–4:30pm; Thurs–Sat 1–4:30pm and 9pm–midnight. Closed Dec 24–Jan 7. BASQUE/ANDALUSIAN.

Since 1947, Achuri, 1 block behind the Palace of Congress in the historic district, has been one of the best loved restaurants in this old port city. It's been in the same family for half a century earning a fine reputation for its good food. The interior is in a typical Mediterranean port style with white stucco walls adorned with paintings interspersed with windows letting in plenty of sunshine. The menu includes fresh anchovies in virgin olive oil with a green leaf salad. Try also the *merluza al achuri* (hake casserole with a green asparagus sauce) or *pardo al brandy* (red snapper in a brandy sauce). Another excellent dish is *bacalao en rosa verde* (salt cod in a tomato and vegetable sauce). Desserts include a lemon mousse or *tocinillo de cielo* (a hearty regional pudding).

El Faro. Calle San Félix, 15. ☎ **956-21-10-68.** Reservations recommended. Main courses 1,500–2,500 ptas. ($9–$15); fixed-price menu 3,500 ptas. ($21). AE, DC, MC, V. Daily 1–4:30pm and 8:30pm–midnight. SEAFOOD.

Unless you're a devotee of seafood, this might not be your preferred restaurant in Cádiz. There's only a limited selection of meat with the main emphasis on the array of fresh fish and shellfish available in its large dining room. (There's an additional, much smaller room to the side, usually reserved for groups of locals.) Established in 1964, and the favorite restaurant of many visitors, El Faro occupies the white-walled premises of one of the simple houses near the harbor front in Cádiz's oldest neighborhood. Menu items include fried lamb chops and beefsteak and a long list of seafood, such as seafood soup, roulades of sole with spinach, hake with green sauce, monkfish with strips of Serrano ham, and lobster.

El Ventorillo del Chato. Carretera de Cádiz a San Fernando, km 2. ☎ **956-25-00-25.** Reservations recommended. Main courses 1,900–2,500 ptas. ($11.40–$15); set menu 5,500 ptas. ($33). AE, DC, MC, V. Mon–Sat 1–4pm and 9pm–midnight. ANDALUSIAN.

El Chato, which means "pug nose" in English, was the nickname of the original founder of this inn launched in 1780. It stands on the isthmus linking the port city to the mainland. Once a hostelry for wayfarers, it still has its old wooden floors, ceramic tiles, and a large collection of keys and muskets from the Napoleonic era. There are two floors, including the basement where flamenco shows are sometimes performed on the original *tablao* (special flamenco dance floor). The food is excellent, the ingredients well chosen, and the chefs skilled at their time-tested recipes. Try the *arroz del señorito,* a paella of shellfish that has been taken from the shells and cleaned before cooking, or the *arroz negro con chocos* (squid with rice colored by its own ink). Other specialties include *dorada en berenjena confitada al vino tinto* (John Dory with eggplant cooked with a red wine sauce). Desserts are tempting, especially ice cream with three types of chocolate or homemade cake with orange sauce.

CÁDIZ AFTER DARK

Most dance clubs around Cádiz come and go with the seasons, but **La Boîte,** Edificio Isecotel, Paseo Marítimo, s/n (☎ **956-26-13-16**), has stayed alive longer than many of its competitors, attracting a large crowd of Andalusian youth and other revelers with recorded music and air-conditioning. In the old town on an avenue running alongside Playa de la Victoria, it's open nightly 10:30pm to 6am. There is a one-drink minimum but no cover; a beer costs 500 ptas. ($3).

6 Costa de la Luz

Isla Cristina, one of the coast's westernmost cities, is 34 miles (55km) west of Huelva, 403 miles (649km) southwest of Madrid; Tarifa, at the opposite end of the coast, lies 59 miles (95km) southeast of Cádiz, 429 miles (691km) southwest of Madrid.

West of Cádiz, near Huelva and the Portuguese frontier, is the rapidly developing *Costa de la Luz* (Coast of Light), which hopes to pick up the overflow from Costa del Sol. The Luz coast stretches from the mouth of the Guadiana River, forming the boundary with Portugal, to Tarifa Point on the Straits of Gibraltar. Dotting the coast are long stretches of sand, pine trees, fishing cottages, and lazy whitewashed villages. The Huelva district forms the northwestern half of Costa de la Luz. The southern half stretches from Tarifa to **Sanlúcar de Barrameda,** the spot from which Magellan embarked in 1519 on his voyage around the globe. Columbus also made this the home port for his third journey to the New World. Sanlúcar today is widely known in Andalusia for its local sherry, Manzanilla, which you can order at any of the city's wine cellars (*bodegas*). If you make it to Sanlúcar, you'll find the **tourist information office** at Calzada de Ejército (☎ **956-36-61-10**), just 1 block inland from the beach. It's open Monday to Friday 10 to 11am and 6 to 8pm, Saturday and Sunday 11am to 1pm. Do not count on a great deal of guidance, however. To travel between the northern and southern portions of Costa de la Luz, you must go inland to Seville, since no roads go across the Coto Doñana and the marshland near the mouth of the Guadalquivir.

ESSENTIALS

GETTING THERE   Huelva, the coast's most prominent city, is serviced by trains from Seville 2 hours away. If you're going on to Portugal from here, you can take a bus to Ayamonte where you can board a ferry to the gateway of Vila Real de Santa Antonio, the beginning of Portugal's Algarve coast.

Buses run several times a day from Seville, where connections can be made to all parts of Spain. From Huelva, about eight buses a day depart for Ayamonte and the Portuguese frontier.

Huelva is easily reached by car in about an hour from Seville, 55 miles (88.5km) to the east, via a broad and modern highway, the E-01.

VISITOR INFORMATION The **tourist information office** is in Huelva at avenida de Alemania, 12 (☎ **959-25-74-67**), open Monday to Friday 8:30am to 7:30pm, Saturday 9am to 2pm.

EXPLORING THE AREA

At Huelva, a large statue on the west bank of the river commemorates the departure of Christopher Columbus on his third voyage of discovery. About 4½ miles (7km) up on the east bank of the Tinto River, a monument marks the exact spot where his ships were anchored while they were being loaded with supplies before departure.

South of Huelva is the **Monasterio de la Rábida,** Palos de la Frontera (☎ **959-35-04-11**), in whose little white chapel Columbus prayed for success on the eve of his voyage. Even without its connections to Columbus, the monastery would be worth a visit for its paintings and frescoes. A guide will show you around the Mudéjar chapel and a large portion of the old monastery, which is open Tuesday to Sunday 10am to 1pm and 4 to 6:15pm. Admission is free, but donations are accepted. The monastery is on the east bank of the Tinto. Take bus number 1 from Huelva.

WHERE TO STAY & DINE

Accommodations are severely limited along Costa de la Luz in summer, so it's crucial to arrive with a reservation. You can stay at a government-run parador east of Huelva in Mazagón (see below) or in Ayamonte, near the Portuguese frontier. Where you are unlikely to want to stay overnight is the dreary industrial port of Huelva itself.

Ayamonte was built on the slopes of a hill on which a castle stood. It is full of beach high-rises, which, for the most part, contain vacation apartments for Spaniards in July and August. Judging by their license plates, most of these visitors come from Huelva, Seville, and Madrid, so the Costa de la Luz is more Spanish in flavor than the overrun and more international Costa del Sol.

Ayamonte has clean, wide, sandy beaches and mostly calm waves. Portions of the beaches are even calmer because of sandbars 55 to 110 yards from the shore, which become virtual islands at low tide. The nearest beaches to Ayamonte are miles away at Isla Canela and Moral.

Parador Nacional Costa de la Luz. El Castillito, 21400 Ayamonte. ☎ **959-32-07-00.** Fax 959-32-07-00. 53 units. A/C MINIBAR TV TEL. 12,500–16,000 ptas. ($75–$96) double; 18,000–25,000 ptas. ($108–$150) suite. AE, DC, MC, V. Free parking. From the center of Ayamonte, signs for the parador lead you up a winding road to the hilltop, about ½ mile (1km) southeast of the center.

The leading accommodation in Ayamonte, this parador opened in 1966 and was completely renovated in 1991. Commanding a sweeping view of the river and the surrounding towns along its banks—sunsets are memorable here—the parador stands about 100 feet above sea level on the site of the old castle of Ayamonte. Built in a severe modern style with Nordic-inspired furnishings, it numbers among its facilities a swimming pool, a garden, central heating, a dining room, and a bar. Most rooms are medium in size, and each is comfortably appointed, with good beds and tidy bathrooms, each equipped with a hair dryer. Good regional meals cost from 3,200 ptas. ($21.45). If it's featured, try *raya en pimiento* (stingray with red pepper); *calamar relleno* (stuffed squid) is another specialty.

Parador Nacional Cristóbal Colón. Carretera de Matalascañas, s/n, 21130 Mazagón. ☎ **959-53-63-00.** Fax 959-53-62-28. 44 units. A/C MINIBAR TV TEL. 17,500–21,000 ptas. ($105–$126) double; 24,000–26,000 ptas. ($144–$156) suite. AE, DC, MC, V. Free parking. Exit from Magazón's eastern sector, following the signs to the town of Matalascañas. Take the coast road (Hwy. 442) to the parador.

One of the best accommodations in the area is 14 miles (22.5km) from Huelva and 3½ miles (6km) from the center of Mazagón. A rambling 1960s structure, the parador has comfortable, spacious guest rooms with balconies and terraces overlooking a tranquil, expansive garden and pine groves that slope down to the white-sand beach of Mazagón. Swimmers and sunbathers can also enjoy the large pool, and there are tennis courts. The dining room features two *menús del día* at 3,700 ptas. ($24.80), and a children's menu at 1,500 ptas. ($10.05).

7 Ronda

63 miles (101.5km) NE of Algeciras, 60 miles (97km) W of Málaga, 91 miles (146.5km) SE of Seville, 367 miles (591km) S of Madrid

This little town high in the Serranía de Ronda Mountains (2,300 feet [698m] above sea level) is one of the oldest and most aristocratic places in Spain. The main tourist attraction is a 500-foot gorge, spanned by a Roman stone bridge, Puente San Miguel, over the Guadelevín River. On both sides of this hole in the earth are cliff-hanging houses, which look as though they would plunge into the chasm with the slightest push.

Ronda is an incredible sight. The once difficult road here is now a wide highway with guardrails. The town and the surrounding mountains were legendary hideouts for bandits and smugglers, but today the Guardia Civil has just about put an end to that occupation.

The gorge divides the town into an older part, the Moorish and aristocratic quarter, and the newer section south of the gorge, built principally after the Reconquest. The old quarter is by far the more fascinating; it contains narrow, rough streets and buildings with a marked Moorish influence (watch for the minaret). After the lazy resort living of Costa del Sol, make a side excursion to Ronda; its unique beauty and refreshing mountain air are a tonic.

Ronda is great for the explorer. Local children may attach themselves to you as guides. For a few pesetas it might be worth it to hire one, since it's difficult to weave your way in and out of the narrow streets.

ESSENTIALS

GETTING THERE   There are three trains daily from Málaga (2 hours), three per day from Seville (3½ hours), and three per day from Granada (3 hours). Most rail routes into Ronda require a change of train in the railway junction of Bobadilla several miles to the northeast. Ronda's railway station is in the western edge of the new city, on the avenida Andalucía (☎ **95-287-16-73**).

The main bus company in Ronda is **Los Amarillos,** which runs daily bus service from both Málaga and Seville. Buses arrive and depart from the bus station on the western edge of the new town, at Plaza Concepcion Garcia Redonda, 2 (☎ **95-218-7061**). To Málaga there are six buses a day Monday to Friday and four on weekends. To Seville, there are five buses a day Monday to Friday, three on Saturday, and four on Sunday.

Five highways converge on Ronda from all parts of Andalusia. All five head through mountainous scenery, but the road south to Marbella through the Sierra Palmitera is one of the most winding and dangerous.

VISITOR INFORMATION   The **tourist information office** is at Plaza de España, 9 (☎ **95-287-12-72**), open Monday to Friday 9am to 2pm and 4 to 7pm, Saturday and Sunday 10am to 2pm.

EXPLORING RONDA

The still-functioning **Baños Árabes** are reached from the turnoff to Puente San Miguel. Dating from the 13th century, the baths have glass roof-windows and hump-shaped cupolas. They are generally open Tuesday to Sunday 9am to 2pm and 4 to 6pm. Admission is free, but you should tip the caretaker who shows you around.

   Palacio de Mondragón, El Campillo (☎ **95-287-84-50**), was once the private home of one of the ministers to Charles III. Flanked by two Mudéjar towers, it now has a baroque facade. Inside are Moorish mosaics. It's open Monday to Friday 10am to 7pm and Saturday and Sunday 10am to 3pm; admission is 250 ptas. ($1.50), but free for children under 14.

   Casa del Rey Moro, Marqués de Parada, 17, is misnamed, as this House of the Moorish King was actually built in the early 1700s. However, it is believed to have been constructed over Moorish foundations. The interior is closed, but from the garden you can take an underground stairway, called La Mina, which leads you to the river, a distance of 365 steps. Christian slaves cut these steps in the 14th century to guarantee a steady water supply in case Ronda came under siege.

   Ronda has the oldest bullring in Spain. Built in the 1700s, **Plaza de Toros** is the setting for the yearly Goyesque Corrida in honor of Ronda native son Pedro Romero, one of the greatest bullfighters of all time. If you want to know more about Ronda bullfighting, head for the **Museo Taurino** (☎ **95-287-41-32**), reached through the ring. It is open June to September daily 10am to 8pm, October to May daily 10am to 6pm. Admission is 300 ptas. ($1.80).

   Exhibits at the museum document the exploits of the noted Romero family. Francesco invented the killing sword and the muleta, and his grandson, Pedro (1754–1839), killed 5,600 bulls during his 30-year career. Pedro was the inspiration for Goya's famous Tauromaquia series. There are also exhibits devoted to Cayetano Ordóñez, the matador immortalized by Hemingway in *The Sun Also Rises.*

A NEARBY ATTRACTION: PREHISTORIC CAVE PAINTINGS

Near Benaoján, **Cueva de la Pileta** (☎ **95-216-73-43**), 15½ miles (25km) southwest of Ronda, plus a 1¼-mile (2km) hard climb, has been compared to the Caves of Altamira in northern Spain where prehistoric paintings were discovered toward the end of the 19th century. In a wild, beautiful area known as the Serranía de Ronda, José Bullón Lobato, grandfather of the present owners, discovered this cave in 1905. More than a mile in length and filled with oddly and beautifully shaped stalagmites and stalactites, the cave was found to contain five fossilized human skeletons and two animal skeletons.

   In the mysterious darkness, prehistoric paintings have been discovered depicting animals in yellow, red, black, and ocher, as well as mysterious symbols. One of the highlights of the tour is a trip to the chamber of the fish, containing a wall painting of a great black seal-like creature about 3 feet long. This chamber, the innermost heart of the cave, ends in a precipice that drops vertically nearly 250 feet.

   In the valley just below the cave lives a guide who will conduct you around the chambers, carrying artificial light to illuminate the paintings. Plan to spend at least an hour here. Tours are given daily 10am to 1pm and 4 to 5pm. Admission, including the 1-hour tour, is 800 ptas. ($4.80) adults, 500 ptas. ($3) children.

   You can reach the cave most easily by car from Ronda, but those without private transport can take the train to Benaoján. The cave, whose entrance is at least 4 miles

(6.5km) uphill, is in the rocky foothills of the Sierra de Libar midway between two tiny villages: Jimera de Libar and Benaoján. The valley that contains the cave is parallel to the valley holding Ronda, so the town of Ronda and the cave are separated by a steep range of hills requiring a rather complicated detour to either the south or the north of Ronda, then doubling back.

WHERE TO STAY
EXPENSIVE
✪ **Parador de Ronda.** Plaza de España, 29400 Ronda. ☎ **95-287-75-00.** Fax 95-287-81-88. www.parador.es. E-mail: ronda@parador.es. 78 units. A/C MINIBAR TV TEL. 16,000–20,000 ptas. ($96–$120) double; 22,000–28,000 ptas. ($132–$168) suite. AE, DC, MC, V. Parking 1,200 ptas. ($7.20).

When this parador opened in 1994, it surpassed the Reina Victoria (see below) to become the finest accommodation in the area. It sits on a high cliff overlooking the fantastic gorge that cuts a swath more than 500 feet deep and 300 feet wide through the center of this mountain town. Stretching along the edge of the gorge to a bridge, Puente Nuevo, built over the Tajo in 1761, the parador is surrounded by a footpath with scenic overlooks offering views of the gorge and the torrents of the Guadalevín River below. The parador fronts the old food market and the original Town Hall on the town's most historic square. The good-sized guest rooms are beautifully furnished, often opening onto views of the rugged peaks surrounding Ronda. Each accommodation comes with an immaculately kept and tiled bathroom, equipped with a hair dryer.

Dining/Diversions: Overlooking the gorge, the parador dining room (open to the pubic) features a typically regional cuisine of almond soup, gazpacho, wild game dishes—whatever's good and fresh in any season. There is also a bar-cafeteria.

Amenities: Room service, laundry, baby-sitting; the grounds include a swimming pool.

MODERATE
✪ **Hotel Reina Victoria.** Paseo Dr. Fleming, 25, 29400 Ronda. ☎ **95-287-12-40.** Fax 95-287-10-75. 89 units. A/C TV TEL. 15,000–17,000 ptas. ($90–$102) double; 23,000 ptas. ($138) suite. AE, DC, MC, V. Free parking.

On the eastern periphery of town a short walk from the center, this country-style hotel was built in 1906 by an Englishman in honor of his recently departed monarch, Queen Victoria. It's near the bullring, with terraces that hang right over a 490-foot precipice. Hemingway frequently visited the hotel, but the Reina Victoria is known best as the place where poet Rainer Maria Rilke wrote *The Spanish Trilogy*. His third-floor room has been set aside as a museum with first editions, manuscripts, photographs, and even a framed copy of his hotel bill. A life-size bronze statue of the poet stands in a corner of the hotel garden.

Rooms are big, airy, and comfortable, some with complete living rooms containing sofas, chairs, and tables. Many have private terraces with garden furniture. The beds are sumptuous, and the bathrooms boast all the latest improvements.

Dining here can be recommended, as the food is well prepared. The hotel has an outdoor pool and a well-stocked bar.

INEXPENSIVE
Hotel Don Miguel. Villanueva, 8, 29400 Ronda. ☎ **95-287-77-22.** Fax 95-287-83-77. 19 units. A/C TV TEL. 10,500 ptas. ($63) double. AE, DC, MC, V. ($4.50). Closed Jan 10–24. Parking 750 ptas.

From the narrow street leading to it, this hotel presents a severely dignified white-fronted facade very similar to that of its neighbors. From the back, however, the hotel looks out over the river gorge of a steep ravine, adding drama to those rooms over-looking it. Set a few steps east of Plaza de España, and composed of several inter-connected houses, it offers a vine-strewn patio above the river, a warmly modernized interior accented with exposed brick and varnished pine, and small, simple but comfortable rooms, each with a firm mattress. The restaurant, Don Miguel, is recom-mended separately (see "Where to Dine," below).

Hotel la Española. Calle José Aparicio, 3, 29400 Ronda. ☎ 952-87-10-51. Fax 952-87-80-01. www.ronda.net/usuar/laespanola. E-mail: laespanola@ronda.net. 16 units. A/C TV TEL. 13,000 ptas. ($78) double; 14,000 ptas. ($84) suite. Rates include buffet breakfast. AE, DC, MC, V. Parking 1,500 ptas. ($9).

Near the bullring and Puente Nuevo, this hotel began life as a down-market hostel but, since its renovation in 1998, it has gained a favorable reputation as a hotel offer-ing good value in clean, decent, and comfortable surroundings. The hotel's two floors have a rustic style with stone walls and wood furnishings. The rooms are compact but inviting and well kept. Four of the bedrooms open onto views of the distant mountains, with the rest facing the street. There is a restaurant complete with terrace opening onto a panorama of Ronda and a mountain range far beyond. Limited room service is offered, as are laundry and a concierge.

Hotel Residencia Polo. Mariano Soubirón, 8, 29400 Ronda. ☎ 95-287-24-47. Fax 95-287-24-49. 33 units. A/C TV TEL. 7,500–10,500 ptas. ($45–$63) double. AE, DC, MC, V. Parking 1,400 ptas. ($8.40).

The Polo is a professionally run hotel in the commercial, modern heart of Ronda near a large shopping arcade. Its accommodations are pleasantly, though not elegantly, decorated and maintained. Rooms are spacious, with even the closets and private bath-rooms large enough for your needs. The hotel has a bar and restaurant and offers room service.

Hotel San Gabriel. José Maria Holgado, 19, 29200 Ronda. ☎ 952-19-03-92. Fax 952-19-01-17. www.ronda.net/usuar/hotelsgabriel. E-mail: sangabriel@ronda.net. 16 units. A/C MINIBAR TV TEL. 11,000 ptas. ($66) double; 13,000 ptas. ($78) suite. AE, DC, MC, V.

This charming 1736 mansion stands in the historic core of Ronda a short walk from the gorge. A family-run hotel, the building was painstakingly renovated by the owner and his sons and daughter, who give you Ronda's warmest welcome. Inside, all is styl-ish, tasteful, and homelike, filled with antiques, even an old library. Stained-glass windows, a Spanish-style billiard table, and a *cine* salon—complete with seats taken from the city's old theater—create a museum feel, but a comfortable one. Each bed-room is spacious and well appointed, all with exterior views, individual decoration, and well-equipped bathrooms. There's a patio where guests can relax and take in the beauty of the place. Try for room 15, a cozy top floor nest on two levels. Breakfasts and snacks can be purchased in the cafeteria, and there is limited room service. Just off calle Armiñán, the hotel is close to plaza del Gigante.

WHERE TO DINE

Casa Santa Pola. Calle Santo Domingo, 3. ☎ 952-87-92-08. Reservations not needed. Main courses 1,200–1,500 ptas. ($7.20–$9); set menu 1,500 ptas. ($9). AE, DC, MC, V. Daily noon–4pm and 7–11pm. INTERNATIONAL/ANDALUSIAN.

Constructed in the 19th century but altered and rebuilt over the years, this building on the outskirts of the city opens onto views of the gorge. A relative newcomer to the Ronda dining scene, it is composed of three levels built onto the mountainside; access is through the third floor. The interior is a mix of Moorish, rococo, and contempo-rary, with a decor of antique ornaments, wooden floors, archways between rooms, terra-cotta walls, and red bistro-style tablecloths. Many of the good-tasting meals are cooked in a traditional brick oven, especially the succulent *cochinillo* (roast suckling pig). Another excellent dish is *lomo asado*, or grilled fillet beef steak. There is a savory *rabo de toro* (roast oxtail). Desserts are homemade and traditional to the area. On certain nights diners are treated to shows organized by the owner, Tomás Mayo.

Don Miguel Restaurant. Plaza de España, 3. ☎ **95-287-10-90.** Reservations not required. Main courses 1,200–6,600 ptas. ($7.20–$39.60); *menú del día* 2,500 ptas. ($15). AE, DC, MC, V. Daily 12:30–4pm and 8–11pm. Closed Jan 10–24. ANDALUSIAN.

At the end of the bridge facing the river, this restaurant offers diners views of the upper gorge. It has enough tables set outside on two levels to seat 300 people, and in summer this is a bustling place. The food is good, and the waiters are polite and speak enough English to get by. There is a pleasant bar for drinks and tapas. Try one of the seafood selections or the house specialty, stewed bull's tail. The also-recommended Hotel Don Miguel (see "Where to Stay," above) runs the restaurant.

Mesón Santiago. Marina, 3. ☎ **95-287-15-59.** Reservations required. Main courses 1,500–2,000 ptas. ($9–$12); fixed-price menus 1,500–2,000 ptas. ($9–$12). MC, V. Daily 10am–5pm. SPANISH.

Santiago Ruíz Gil operates one of the best inexpensive restaurants in Ronda, serving lunch only. A three-course *menú del día,* with bread and wine, is a good deal. If you order from the *especialidades de la casa,* count on spending more. Try the *caldo de cocido,* a savory stew with large pieces of meat cooked with such vegetables as garbanzos and white beans, almost a meal in itself. You might like the tongue cooked in wine and served with potato salad. All the servings are generous. The more expensive à la carte menu is likely to include partridge, lamb, mountain trout, and regional meats. Fresh asparagus and succulent strawberries are available in season. Mesón Santiago is located near Plaza del Socorro.

Pedro Romero. Virgen de la Paz, 18. ☎ **95-287-11-10.** Reservations required on day of *corrida.* Main courses 1,200–2,200 ptas. ($7.20–$13.20). AE, DC, MC, V. Daily 12:30–4pm and 8–11pm. SPANISH/ANDALUSIAN.

Named after famed bullfighter Pedro Romero, this restaurant attracts aficionados of that sport. In fact, it stands opposite the bullring and gets extremely busy on bullfighting days, when it's almost impossible to get a table. While seated under a stuffed bull's head, surrounded by photographs of young matadors, you might begin your meal with the classic garlic soup, then follow with a well-prepared array of meat or poultry dishes.

✪ **Tragabuches.** Calle José Aparicio, 1. ☎ **952-19-02-19.** Reservations recommended on weekends. Main courses 2,000–2,600 ptas. ($12–$15.60); set menu 6,500 ptas. ($39). AE, DC, MC, V. Daily 1–4pm; Mon–Sat 7:30pm–midnight. MODERN SPANISH.

In 1999 chef-owner Sergio López was hailed by Spanish gastronomes as the most talented young chef in Spain. If anything, he's even better today and has clearly staked out his role as the provider of the finest and most creative cuisine in Ronda. There are two dining rooms here, each with a stylish and contemporary decor. There is a cozier dining room in back, although if tables are full you might have to sit up front. Against a typical backdrop of white walls, tables are decked out with pastel cloths and seat covers. The inventive menu is likely to feature well-crafted dishes like *cochinillo asado* (grilled suckling pig) or *rape en salsa de vinagreta, pulpo y verdura* (monkfish in a vinaigrette sauce with octopus and fresh vegetables). Begin perhaps with a cheese taco or the tasty liver pâté. The excellent desserts include a range of homemade cakes and ice cream. It's located between the Plaza de España and Plaza de Toros.

8 Granada

258 miles (415km) S of Madrid, 76 miles (122km) NE of Málaga

This former stronghold of Moorish Spain in the foothills of the snowcapped Sierra Nevada is full of romance and folklore. Washington Irving (*Tales of the Alhambra*) used the symbol of this city, the pomegranate (*granada*), to conjure up a spirit of romance. In fact, the name probably derives from the Moorish word *Karnattah.* Some historians have suggested that it comes from Garnatha Alyehud, the name of an old Jewish ghetto.

Washington Irving may have helped publicize the glories of Granada to the English-speaking world, but in Spain the city is known for its ties to another writer: Federico García Lorca. Born in 1898, this Spanish poet and dramatist, whose masterpiece was *The House of Bernarda Alba,* was shot by soldiers in 1936 in the first months of the Spanish Civil War. During Franco's rule García Lorca's works were banned in Spain, but that situation has changed and he is once again honored in Granada where he grew up.

About 2,200 feet above sea level, Grenada sprawls over two main hills, the Alhambra and the Albaicín, and is crossed by two rivers, the Genil and the Darro.

Cuesta de Gomérez is one of the most important streets in Granada. It climbs uphill from Plaza Nueva, the center of the modern city, to the Alhambra. At Plaza Nueva the east-west artery, calle de los Reyes Católicos, goes to the heart of the 19th-century city and the towers of the cathedral. The main street of Granada is the Gran Vía de Colón, the principal north-south artery.

Calle de los Reyes Católicos and the Gran Vía de Colón meet at the circular Plaza de Isabel la Católica, graced by a bronze statue of the queen offering Columbus the Santa Fé agreement, which granted the rights to the epochal voyage to the New World. Going west, calle de los Reyes Católicos passes near the cathedral and other major sights in the downtown section of Granada. The street runs to Puerta Real, the commercial hub of Granada with many stores, hotels, cafes, and restaurants.

ESSENTIALS

GETTING THERE   Iberia flies to Granada once or twice daily from Barcelona and Madrid, several times a week from Palma de Majorca, three times a week from Valencia, and every Thursday from Tenerife in the Canary Islands. Granada's airport is 10 miles (16km) west of the center of town; call ☎ **958-24-52-00** for information. A convenient Iberia ticketing office is 2 blocks east of the cathedral at Plaza Isabel la Católica, 2 (☎ **958-22-75-92**). A shuttle bus departs several times daily connecting this office with the airport, costing 425 ptas. ($2.55) one way.

Two trains connect Granada with Madrid's Atocha Railway Station daily (taking 6 hours). Overnight trains from Madrid generally take 8 hours. Many connections to the rest of Spain are funneled through the railway junction at Bobadilla, a 2-hour ride to the west. The train station is at avenida Andaluces (☎ **958-27-12-72**).

Most buses pull into a station on the fringe of Granada at Carretera de Madrid. **Alsina Graells** (☎ **958-18-54-80**) is the most useful company here, offering 6 buses per day from Córdoba (3 hours), 12 per day from Jaén (1½ hours), 9 per day from Madrid (5 hours), 15 from Málaga (2 hours), and 6 from Sevilla (3 hours).

Granada is connected by superhighway to Madrid, Málaga, and Seville. Many sightseers prefer to make the drive from Madrid to Granada in 2 days, rather than one. If that is your plan, Jaén makes a perfect stopover.

Granada & the Alhambra

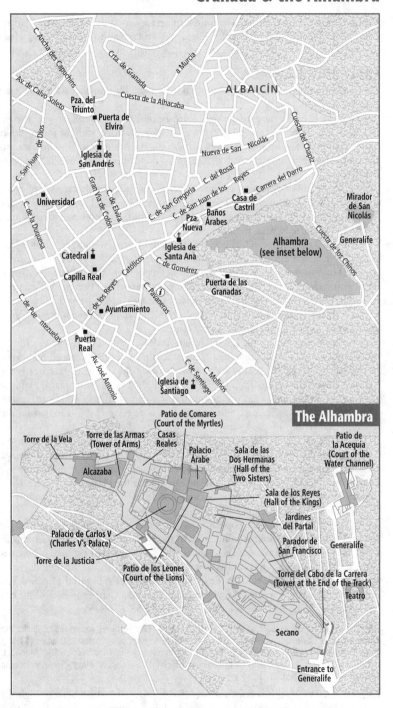

ALBAICÍN

C. Ancha des Capuchins
Crta. de Granada
a Murcia
Av. de Calvo Soleto
Cuesta de la Alhacaba
Pza. del Triunto
Puerta de Elvira
C. San Juan de Dios
Nueva de San Nicolás
Cuesta del Chapiz
Iglesia de San Andrés
C. del Rosal
C. de Elvira
Gran Vía de Colón
Universidad
C. de San Gregoria
C. de San Juan de los Reyes
Carrera del Darro
Casa de Castril
Mirador de San Nicolás
C. de la Duquesa
Pza. Nueva
Baños Árabes
Alhambra (see inset below)
Generalife
Cuesta de los Chinos
Catedral
Iglesia de Santa Ana
C. de Gomérez
Capilla Real
Católicos
C. de los Reyes
Puerta de las Granadas
C. Pavaneras
Ayuntamiento
C. de Puentezuelas
Puerta Real
Av. José Antonio
C. de Santiago
C. Mollins
Iglesia de Santiago

The Alhambra

Torre de la Vela
Torre de las Armas (Tower of Arms)
Casas Reales
Patio de Comares (Court of the Myrtles)
Palacio Árabe
Sala de las Dos Hermanas (Hall of the Two Sisters)
Patio de la Acequia (Court of the Water Channel)
Alcazaba
Sala de los Reyes (Hall of the Kings)
Jardines del Partal
Palacio de Carlos V (Charles V's Palace)
Torre de la Justicia
Patio de los Leones (Court of the Lions)
Parador de San Francisco
Generalife
Torre del Cabo de la Carrera (Tower at the End of the Track)
Teatro
Secano
Entrance to Generalife

VISITOR INFORMATION   The **tourist information office** is at Plaza de Mariana Pineda, 10 (☎ **958-22-59-90**), open Monday to Friday 9am to 7pm, Saturday 10am to 2pm. There is also a small tourist office in the Alhambra next to the Puerto Vino.

EXPLORING GRANADA

Try to spend some time walking around Old Granada. Plan on about 3 hours to see the most interesting sights.

Puerta de Elvira is the gate through which Ferdinand and Isabella made their triumphant entry into Granada in 1492. It was once a grisly place, with the rotting heads of executed criminals hanging from its portals. The quarter surrounding the gate was the Arab section (*morería*) until all the Arabs were driven out of the city after the Reconquest.

One of the most fascinating streets in Granada is **calle de Elvira;** west of it the Albaicín, or old Arab quarter, rises on a hill. In the 17th and 18th centuries, many artisans occupied the shops and ateliers along this street and those radiating from it. Come here if you're looking for antiques.

The most-walked street in Granada is **Carrera del Darro,** running north along the Darro River. It was discovered by the Romantic artists of the 19th century; many of their etchings (subsequently engraved) of scenes along this street were widely circulated, doing much to spread the fame of Granada throughout Europe. You can still find some of these old engravings in the musty antiques shops. Carrera del Darro ends at **Paseo de los Tristes (Avenue of the Sad Ones),** so named for the funeral corteges that used to go by here on the way to the cemetery.

On calle de Elvira stands the **Iglesia de San Andrés,** begun in 1528, with its Mudéjar bell tower. Much of the church was destroyed in the early 19th century, but several interesting paintings and sculptures remain. Another old church in this area is the **Iglesia de Santiago,** constructed in 1501 and dedicated to St. James, patron saint of Spain. Built on the site of an Arab mosque, it was damaged in an 1884 earthquake. The church contains the tomb of architect Diego de Siloé (1495–1563), who did much to change the face of the city.

Despite its name, the oldest square in Granada is **Plaza Nueva,** which, under the Muslims, was the site of the bridge of the woodcutters. The Darro River was covered over here, but its waters still flow underneath the square (which in Franco's time was named Plaza del General Franco). On the east side of the Plaza Nueva is the 16th-century **Iglesia de Santa Ana,** built by Siloé. Inside its five-nave interior you can see a Churrigueresque reredos and coffered ceiling.

The *corrida* isn't really very popular here, but if you want to check out a bullfight anyway, they're usually limited to the week of the Fiesta de Corpus Christi from May 29 to June 6 or the *Día de la Cruz* (Day of the Cross) observed on May 3. There is also a fight on the last Sunday in September. The **Plaza de Toros,** the bullring, is on avenida de Doctor Olóriz, close to the soccer stadium. On the day of the fight, tickets can be purchased in the center of town on calle Escudo del Carmen in back of the city hall from 5 to 9pm. For more information, call ☎ **958-77-24-51.**

✪ **Alhambra.** Palacio de Carlos V. ☎ **958-22-09-12.** Comprehensive ticket, including Alhambra and Generalife (below), 1,000 ptas. ($6); Museo Bellas Artes 250 ptas. ($1.50); Museo Hispano-Musulman 250 ptas. ($1.50); illuminated visits 1,000 ptas. ($6). Mar–Oct, daily 9am–7:45pm, floodlit visits daily 10pm–midnight; Nov–Feb, daily 9am–5:45pm, floodlit visits daily 8–10pm. Bus: 2.

Later enriched by Moorish occupants into a lavish palace, the Alhambra was originally constructed for defensive purposes on a rocky hilltop outcropping above the Darro

River. The modern city of Granada was built across the river from the Alhambra, about half a mile from its western foundations.

When you first see the Alhambra, you may be surprised by its somewhat somber exterior. You have to walk across the threshold to discover the true delights of this Moorish palace. Tickets are sold in the office at the Entrada del Generalife y de la Alhambra. Enter through the incongruous 14th-century Gateway of Justice. Most visitors do not need an expensive guide but will be content to stroll through the richly ornamented open-air rooms, with their lacelike walls and their courtyards with fountains. Many of the Arabic inscriptions translate as "Only Allah is conqueror."

The most-photographed part of the palace is the Court of Lions, named after its highly stylized fountain. This was the heart of the palace, the most private section where the sultan enjoyed his harem. Opening onto the court are the Hall of the Two Sisters, where the favorite of the moment was kept, and the Gossip Room, a factory of intrigue. In the dancing room in the Hall of Kings, entertainment was provided nightly to amuse the sultan's party. Eunuchs guarded the harem but apparently not very well—according to legend one sultan beheaded 36 Moorish princes here because one of them was suspected of having been intimate with his favorite.

You can see the room where Washington Irving lived (in the chambers of Charles V) while he was compiling his *Tales of the Alhambra*. The best-known tale is the legend of Zayda, Zorayada, and Zorahayda, the three beautiful princesses who fell in love with three captured Spanish soldiers outside "La Torre de las Infantas."

Irving credits the French with saving the Alhambra for posterity, but in fact they were responsible for blowing up seven of the towers in 1812, and it was a Spanish soldier who cut the fuse before more damage could be done. When the duke of Wellington arrived a few years later, he chased out the chickens, the gypsies, and the transient beggars who were using the Alhambra as a tenement and set up housekeeping here himself.

Charles V may have been horrified when he saw the cathedral in the middle of the great mosque at Córdoba, but he is responsible for architectural meddling here, building a Renaissance palace at the Alhambra—which, although quite beautiful, is terribly out of place. Today it houses the **Museo Bellas Artes en la Alhambra** (☎ **958-22-48-43**), open Tuesday to Saturday 9am to 2pm. Of minor interest, it displays mostly religious paintings and sculpture dating from the 1500s to the present. It also shelters the **Museo Hispano-Musulman en la Alhambra** (☎ **958-22-62-79**) devoted to Hispanic-Muslim art and open Tuesday to Saturday 9am to 2:30pm.

Note: Because of the overwhelming crowds, there is a chance you may not be admitted to the Alhambra, as the government is forced to limit the number of people who can enter. Your best bet is to go as early as possible, but, even then, some people arriving at 10am may not be admitted until 1:30pm. If you arrive after 4pm, it is unlikely you'll get in at all.

Many visitors opt for a taxi or the bus to the Alhambra, but some hardy souls enjoy the uphill climb from the cathedral at Plaza de la Lonja (signs indicate the winding roads and the steps that lead to the Alhambra). If you decide to walk, enter the Alhambra via the Cuesta de Gomérez, which, although steep, is the quickest and shortest pedestrian route. It begins at Plaza Nueva, about 4 blocks east of the cathedral, and goes steeply uphill to Puerta de las Granadas, the first of two gates to the Alhambra. The second, another 200 yards uphill, is Puerta de la Justicia, which accepts 90% of the touristic visits to the Alhambra. Beware of self-styled guides milling around the parking lot; they may just be interested in picking your pocket.

⚙ **Generalife.** Alhambra, Cerro de Sol. ☎ **958-22-09-12.** Comprehensive ticket, including Alhambra and Generalife, 750 ptas. ($4.50); see Alhambra, above. For open hours, see Alhambra, above. Exit from the Alhambra via Puerta de la Justicia, then circumnavigate the Alhambra's southern foundations until you reach the gardens of the summer palace, where Paseo de los Cipreses quickly leads you to the main building of the Generalife.

The sultans used to spend their summers in this palace (pronounced Hay-nay-rahl-*ee*-fay), safely locked away with their harems. Built in the 13th century to overlook the Alhambra, the Generalife's glory is its gardens and courtyards. Don't expect an Alhambra in miniature: The Generalife was always meant to be a retreat, even from the splendors of the Alhambra. This palace was the setting for Irving's story of the prince locked away from love.

⚙ **Catedral and Capilla Real.** Plaza de la Lonja, Gran Vía de Colón, 5. ☎ **958-22-29-59.** Admission to cathedral 300 ptas. ($1.80); chapel 300 ptas. ($1.80). Cathedral and chapel daily 10:30am–1:30pm and 3:30–6:30pm (4–7pm in winter).

This richly ornate Renaissance cathedral with its spectacular altar is one of the country's architectural highlights, acclaimed for its beautiful facade and gold-and-white interior. It was begun in 1521 and completed in 1714. Behind the cathedral (entered separately) is the flamboyant Gothic Royal Chapel, where the remains of Queen Isabella and her husband Ferdinand lie. It was their wish to be buried in recaptured Granada, not Castile or Aragón. The coffins are remarkably tiny—a reminder of how short they must have been. Accenting the tombs is a wrought-iron grill, itself a masterpiece. Occupying much larger tombs are the remains of their daughter, Joanna the Mad, and her husband, Philip the Handsome. The cathedral is in the center of Granada off two prominent streets, the Gran Vía de Colón and the calle de San Jerónimo. The Capilla Real abuts the cathedral's eastern edge.

Albaycín. Bus: 7 to calle de Pagés.

This old Arab quarter on one of the two main hills of Granada doesn't belong to the city of 19th-century buildings and wide boulevards. It, and the surrounding gypsy caves of Sacromonte, are holdovers from an older past. The Albaycín once flourished as the residential section of the Moors, even after the city's reconquest, but it fell into decline when the Christians drove them out. This narrow labyrinth of crooked streets escaped the fate of much of Granada, which was torn down in the name of progress. Fortunately it has been preserved, as have its cisterns, fountains, plazas, whitewashed houses, villas, and the decaying remnants of the old city gate. Here and there you can catch a glimpse of a private patio filled with fountains and plants, a traditional elegant way of life that continues.

Monasterio Cartuja. Camino de Alfacar, s/n. ☎ **958-16-19-32.** Admission 350 ptas. ($2.10). Daily 10am–1pm and 4–7pm (closes at 6pm in winter). Bus: 8 from cathedral.

This 16th-century monastery, off the Albaicín on the outskirts of Granada, is sometimes called the "Christian answer to the Alhambra" because of its ornate stucco and marble and the baroque Churrigueresque fantasy in the sacristy. Its most notable paintings are by Bocanegra, its outstanding sculpture by Mora. The church of this Carthusian monastery was decorated with baroque stucco in the 17th century, and its 18th-century sacristy is an excellent example of latter-day baroque style. Napoléon's armies killed St. Bruno here, and La Cartuja is said to be the only monument of its kind in the world. Sometimes, one of the Carthusian monks will take you on a guided tour.

Casa-Museo Federico García Lorca. Virgen Blanca, 6, Fuentevaqueros. ☎ **958-51-64-53.** Admission 200 ptas. ($1.20). Oct 7–Mar 31, 10am–7pm and 4–6pm; Apr 1–June 30, 10am–1pm and 5–7pm; July 1–Sept 30, 10am–1pm and 6–8pm.

Impressions

One should remember Granada as one should remember a sweetheart who has died.
—Federico García Lorca

Poet and dramatist Federico García Lorca spent many happy summers with his family here at their vacation home. He moved to Granada in 1909, a dreamy-eyed schoolboy, and he was endlessly fascinated with its life, including the Alhambra and the gypsies, whom he was later to describe compassionately in his *Gypsy Ballads*. The house is decorated with green trim and grillwork and filled with family memorabilia, including furniture and portraits. You can look out at the Alhambra from one of its balconies. Visitors may inspect the poet's upstairs bedroom and see his oak desk stained with ink. Look for the white stool that he carried to the terrace to watch the sun set over Granada. The house is in the Fuentevaqueros section of Granada, near the airport.

Casa-Museo de Manuel de Falla. Antequeruela Alta, 11. ☎ **958-22-94-21.** Admission 250 ptas. ($1.50). Apr–Sept, daily 9am–3pm; Oct–Mar, daily 10am–4pm.

The famous Spanish composer Manuel de Falla, known for his strongly individualized works, came to live in Granada in 1919 hoping to find a retreat and inspiration. He moved into a *carmen* (local dialect for a small white house) just below the Alhambra, and in time befriended García Lorca. In 1922, on the grounds of the Alhambra, they staged the Cante Jondo Festival, the purest expression of flamenco. Today visitors can walk through the gardens of the man who wrote such works as *Nights in the Gardens of Spain* and see his collection of handcrafts and ceramics, along with other personal memorabilia. In spite of the posted hours, a caretaker is not always present to guide you about. It's better to call in advance to see if someone is actually here. The location is about a block from the Alhambra Palace Hotel.

Baños Arabes. Carrera del Darro, 31. ☎ **958-22-23-39.** Free admission. Tues–Sat 10am–2pm.

The Moors called them the "baths of the walnut tree." Among the oldest buildings still standing in Granada, and among the best-preserved Muslim baths in Spain, they predate the Alhambra. Visigothic and Roman building materials are supposed to have gone into their construction, and it is remarkable that they escaped destruction during the reign of the Reyes Católicos (Ferdinand and Isabella).

Casa de Castril. Museo Arqueológico, Carrera del Darro, 41. ☎ **958-22-56-40.** Admission 250 ptas. ($1.70). Tues–Sat 10am–2pm. Bus: Neptuno-Albaicín.

This building has always been one of the most handsome Renaissance palaces in Granada. The plateresque facade of 1539 has been attributed to Diego de Siloé. In 1869 it was converted into a museum with a collection of minor artifacts found in the area.

SHOPPING

Alcaicería, once the Moorish silk market, is next to the cathedral in the lower city. The narrow streets of this rebuilt village of shops are filled with vendors selling the arts and crafts of Granada province. For the souvenir hunter, the Alcaicería offers one of the most splendid assortments in Spain of tiles, castanets, and wire figures of Don Quixote chasing windmills. Lots of Spanish jewelry can be found here, comparing favorably with the finest Toledan work. For the window-shopper in particular, it makes a pleasant stroll.

Artesanía Albaycín (Tienda Eduardo Ferrer Lucena), calle del Agua, 19 (☎ 958-27-90-56), is a standout in the Arab Quarter for intricately tooled Andalusian leather. The inventory includes useful items (purses, wallets, briefcases, coasters for those glasses of sherry you'll be consuming after your return home) as well as some truly odd items. The shop is open daily noon to 2pm and 5:30 to 8:30pm.

Casa Ferrer (Tienda Eduardo Ferrer Castillo), Cuesta de Gomérez, 30 (☎ 958-22-18-32), is the granddaddy of music stores in Andalusia. Founded in 1875 by an ancestor of the present owner, it stocks an assortment of Spanish guitars, each a hand-crafted work of aesthetic and musical art. Depending on its resonance and degree of ornamentation, guitars range in price from 40,000 to 400,000 ptas. ($240 to $2,400). Open Monday to Saturday 8:45am to 1:30pm, Monday to Friday 4:30 to 8:30pm.

At Tejidos Artisticos Fortuny, Plaza Fortuny, 1 (☎ 958-22-43-27), you can buy curtains, knotted carpets, nubby-textured draperies, tablecloths, placemats, and fabrics. Much of the merchandise is handwoven. Open Monday to Friday 10am to 2pm and 5 to 8:30pm.

WHERE TO STAY
EXPENSIVE

Hotel Alhambra Palace. Peña Partida, 2, 18009 Granada. ☎ 958-22-14-68. Fax 958-22-64-04. www.h-alhambrapalace.es. E-mail: h-alhambrapalace.es. 130 units. A/C MINIBAR TV TEL. 25,000 ptas. ($150) double; 35,000 ptas. ($210) suite. AE, DC, MC, V. Free parking. Bus: Destination Alhambra.

Evoking a Moorish fortress complete with a crenellated roofline, a crowning dome, geometric tile work, and the suggestion of a minaret, this legendary hotel is a good choice. The best known of Granada's hotels, it was built in 1910 in a sort of Mudéjar Revival style in a shady, secluded spot midway up the slope toward the Alhambra, a 10-minute walk from that attraction. The private rooms don't live up to the drama of the public areas. Try for a room with a balcony opening onto a view of the city of Granada The court rooms are less desirable because they lack double glazing and are subject to noise at night. Many are spacious and quite comfortable, with a few small ones in need of restoration. Frankly, whether you love or hate this hotel will depend on your room assignment—some are excellent, some a bit seedy. But there's nothing like this Moorish palace in all of Granada.

Dining/Diversions: The dining room, decorated Arabian Nights style, serves standard international and Andalusian cuisine, with a glassed-in dining terrace. Have a drink in the bar with its panorama of Granada.

Amenities: Concierge, room service, dry cleaning/valet, twice-daily maid service, baby-sitting, secretarial service, valet parking. As a special service to guests, the hotel can reserve tickets for early entrances into the Alhambra so you don't have to wait in miles and miles of lines. The service costs only 250 ptas. ($1.50).

✪ Parador Nacional de San Francisco. Alhambra, 18009 Granada. ☎ 800/343-0020 in the U.S., or 958-22-14-40. Fax 958-22-22-64. 36 units. A/C MINIBAR TV TEL. 35,000–42,000 ptas. ($210–$252) double. AE, DC, MC, V. Free parking. Bus: 3.

This most famous parador in Spain—and the hardest to get into—is set within the grounds of the Alhambra. It's housed in an old brick building with a new annex. The decor is tasteful and the place evokes a lot of history with its rich Andalusian ambience. The parador itself is within a former convent founded by the Catholic monarchs immediately after they conquered the city in 1492. Before that the building was part of the Muslim complex that included the Alhambra Palace and a mosque built in the middle of the 1300s by Caliph Yusuf I. The bodies of Ferdinand and Isabella were once placed here until their tombs could be readied in the cathedral. One side of the parador opens onto its own lovely gardens and the other fronts the Alhambra itself. From its terrace you have views of the Generalife gardens and the Sacromonte caves. Accommodations are generally roomy and comfortable, receiving their last renovation in 1992. Tile bathrooms with such extras as hair dryers add to the allure, and house-keeping is excellent. Try for a room in the older section, which is furnished with antiques; rooms in the more modern wing are less inspired.

Dining: See "Where to Dine," below, for the parador's restaurant recommendation.

Amenities: Concierge, currency exchange, room service, laundry service.

MODERATE

✪ **Hotel América.** Real de la Alhambra, 53, 18009 Granada. ☎ **958-22-74-71.** Fax 958-22-74-70. 14 units. TEL. 16,000 ptas. ($96) double; 19,000 ptas. ($114) suite. AE, DC, MC, V. Closed Dec–Feb. Parking nearby 1,500 ptas. ($9). Bus: 2.

This small hotel is located within the Alhambra's walls. Walk through the covered entryway of this former villa into the shady patio that's lively yet intimate, with large trees, potted plants, and ferns. Other plants cascade down white plaster walls entwined with ornate grillwork. The living room of this homey little retreat has a collection of regional decorative objects; some of the rooms have Andalusian reproductions. Although small, rooms are comfortably furnished and well maintained with compact bathrooms with shower stalls. Garden chairs and tables are set out for home-cooked Andalusian meals. The menu changes every day depending on what is fresh at the market that day. If a guest would like to dine in, dinner costs 2,200 ptas. ($14.75) per person. No meals are served on Sunday.

Hotel Anacapri. Calle Joaquin Costa, 7, 18010 Granada. ☎ **958-22-74-77.** Fax 958-22-89-09. E-mail: anacapri@batch-ps.es. 49 units. A/C TV TEL. 14,000 ptas. ($84) double. AE, DC, MC, V. Parking 1,800 ptas. ($10.80).

In the center of Granada next to the cathedral and a 10-minute walk from the Alhambra, this unpretentious four-floor hotel was renovated in the early '90s to become a bastion of comfort and tranquillity. It offers good service and clean, decent accommodations at an attractive price. The rooms are a bit small, but there is comfort here in the medley of old furniture with modern touches. The best rooms have antique windows, jutting beams, and terraces overlooking street scenes. A few of them feature a minibar. The bedrooms have firm mattresses, and the bathrooms are equipped with showers, adequate shelf space, and hair dryers. The Salon Social is a public area with tiled walls where you can relax as you contemplate an 18th-century *patio granadino* with a fountain at its center. A cafeteria serves a breakfast buffet, and 24-hour room service is offered, as is a laundry.

Hotel Inglaterra. Cettie Meriem, 4, 18010 Granada. ☎ **858-22-15-59.** Fax 958-22-71-00. www.nh-hoteles.es. E-mail: nh@nh-hoteles.com. 36 units. A/C MINIBAR TV TEL. 15,500 ptas. ($93) double. AE, DC, MC, V. Parking 1,600 ptas. ($9.60).

The NH chain purchased this old hotel 2 blocks northeast of the cathedral and 5 minutes from the Alhambra in 1992 and completely refurbished the run-down place, turning it into a hotel of comfort and a bit of style. Its five floors stand back from the thundering traffic of the main drag, Gran Vía de Colón. There is a large central patio encircled by rooms in the typical Andalusian style. Decor is classical but there are plenty of modern touches adding to the overall comfort of the place. Although the elevator goes only four floors, the rooms on the fifth landing open onto panoramic views of the Alhambra. Bedrooms are moderately spacious, well-maintained, and comfortably furnished with good beds and brightly colored decorations. The bathrooms are well cared for and equipped with hair dryers. A cafeteria serves breakfast, and amenities include a laundry and concierge but no room service.

✪ **Hotel Palacio Santa Inés.** Cuesta de Santa Inés, 18010 Granada. ☎ **958-22-23-63.** Fax 958-22-24-65. www.eee.es/Granada/hotels.sinces/. 13 units. A/C MINIBAR TV TEL. 15,000 ptas. ($90) double; 35,000 ptas. ($210) suite. AE, DC, MC, V. Parking 1,800 ptas. ($10.80).

This *antigua casa* is one of the most enchanting places to stay in Granada. A three-floor establishment, it is in the colorful Albaycín district, about a 5-minute walk from the Alhambra. The painstakingly restored little palace was in complete ruins until the mid-'90s when work began on it. Before that it was known in the 1500s as the Casa del Padre Eterno, or "House of the Eternal Father." Today it's a lovely, tranquil, and graceful inn, even a bit luxe. A two-floor 16th-century courtyard, time-aged wooden beamed ceilings, and silver chandeliers take you back to yesterday, as do the restored frescoes on the walls of the patio (said to have been painted by a student of Raphael). The rooms are medium sized and some have a small adjacent sitting room. Furnishings are comfortable and tasteful, and several accommodations open onto views of Granada. Much of the furniture is antique, and the modern bathrooms are well equipped, each with a hair dryer. Amenities are limited but there is room service 8am to 10pm, plus a laundry. The hotel is 1 block northwest of Carrera del Darro and Iglesia de Santa Ana.

Hotel Princesa Ana. Constitución, 37, 18014 Granada. ☎ **958-28-74-47.** Fax 958-27-39-54. 59 units. A/C MINIBAR TV TEL. 18,500 ptas. ($111) double; 35,000 ptas. ($210) suite. AE, DC, MC, V. Parking 1,300 ptas. ($7.80).

Set midway between the railway station and the Plaza de Toros, about 1½ miles (2.5km) northwest of the Alhambra, this balconied five-story hotel welcomes guests into a marble-sheathed interior decorated in tones of soft pink and white. Although it has been surpassed by newer four-star hotels since its construction in 1989, it retains an allure for foreign visitors and business travelers. The good-sized rooms have a British aura, with dark wood furnishings; the tile bathrooms with dual sinks are well maintained. Each comes with a hair dryer. On the premises is an intimate bar, plus a restaurant, La Princesa Ana, and a simple cafeteria. Amenities include room service, concierge, currency exchange.

✪ **Hotel Reina Cristina.** Calle Tablas, 4, 18002. ☎ **958-25-32-11.** Fax 958-25-57-28. www.hotelreinacristina.com. E-mail: clientes@hotelreinacristina.com. 43 units. A/C MINIBAR TV TEL. 15,000 ptas. ($90) double. Rates include breakfast buffet. AE, DC, MC, V. Parking 1,500 ptas. ($9).

Part of the lore and tragic legend of the city of Granada, this hotel shared a moment in Spanish history. One of the nation's greatest writers and Granada's favorite son, the poet and playwright Federico García Lorca, was arrested here by the right-wing forces of Generalísimo Franco and abducted. He was taken 2 miles away and executed. There's not a trace of that history today. The family-operated hotel now exudes grace, charm, and tranquillity, with helpful service. It's in the center of the city a 3-minute walk from the cathedral, in a renovated 19th-century mansion called a *casa granadina*. All the small bedrooms have undergone extensive renovation, and much of the original furnishings have been retained. Mattresses and bathrooms have been renewed. A restaurant and bar offers tapas and light snacks in addition to an à la carte menu, and amenities include room service 8am to midnight, laundry, and a concierge.

Hotel Triunfo Granada. Plaza del Triunfo, 19, 18010 Granada. ☎ **958-20-74-44.** Fax 958-27-90-17. 40 units. A/C MINIBAR TV TEL. 17,000 ptas. ($102) double. AE, MC, V. Parking 1,500 ptas. ($9).

A short walk from the cathedral in the historic core, this hotel dates from 1992 when it opened its doors to visitors seeking style at a moderate price. At the end of the Gran

Vía de Colón, it lies behind a classic facade revealing a modern interior with a marble-floored lobby and collection of regional decorative objects. Some of the public rooms are decorated with reproductions of Moorish and Roman art and artifacts. The mid-sized rooms include some antique furnishings, and some have balconies opening onto the street. Bathrooms are small but well-maintained, with marble walls and Moorish-inspired tiles. Hair dryers are included. Regional cookery and international fare are offered at the hotel's restaurant, Puerta Elvira. Amenities include room service 8am to midnight, laundry, concierge, and organized tours to the major attractions.

INEXPENSIVE

Casa del Aljarife. Placeta de la Cruz Verde, 2, 18010 Granada. ☎/fax **958-22-24-25.** www.lingolex.com/most. E-mail: most@redestb.com. 4 units. A/C TEL. 10,000 ptas. ($60) double; 20,000 ptas. ($120) suite. MC, V.

In the Albaycí district 4 blocks from Plaza Santa Ana, this is a little nugget known only to a few discerning travelers. Because of its small size, it might qualify as the local B&B. In a recently renovated 17th-century structure, it has a large patio with trees and a Moorish fountain with views of the Alhambra. A family concern, the *casa* is well cared for and has a welcoming atmosphere. Each room has its own unique style, and each of the three floors is decorated in a tasteful and typical Andalusian style. Rooms are medium sized or spacious and have new bathrooms. The owner, Christian Most, is gracious, apologizing for the lack of amenities by pointing out that "everything you need" is virtually outside the door.

Hotel Guadalupe. Avenida de los Alixares, s/n, 18009 Granada. ☎ **958-22-34-23.** Fax 958-22-37-98. www.eel.es/guadalupe. E-mail: guadalupeh@popnegocio.com. 58 units. A/C MINIBAR TV TEL. 8,900–14,800 ptas. ($53.40–$88.80) double. AE, DC, MC, V. Parking 1,500 ptas. ($9). Bus: 2.

This four-story building beside an inclined road leading up to the Alhambra stands just above the older and more famous Washington Irving Hotel. It was built in 1969 but seems older, with thick stucco walls, rounded arches, and jutting beams. The last renovation was in 1993 and the comfortably furnished but rather small rooms overlook the Alhambra. The compact tiled bathrooms have adequate shelf space and are equipped with a hair dryer. There's a fifth-floor à la carte restaurant, plus a pleasant bar in the lobby.

Hotel Reino de Granada. Recogidas, 53, 18005 Granada. ☎ **958-26-58-78.** Fax 958-26-36-42-37. 37 units. A/C TV TEL. 11,800 ptas. ($70.80) double. AE, DC, MC, V. Parking 1,200 ptas. ($7.20).

A 5-minute walk from the cathedral, this late '80s hotel presents a severe, four-story white facade to the street but is graced with Andalusian balconies that add some charm. In the commercial zone, it has midsized bedrooms last renovated in the mid-1990s. Not the city's finest choice, but it is a winner in value and does have a bit of atmosphere with its colorful orange and blue walls. The closets are good-sized, the mattresses firm, and the well-maintained bathrooms come with hair dryers. There is a 24-hour cafeteria with breakfast buffet, and amenities include 24-hour room service, concierge, and laundry.

Macía Plaza. Plaza Nueva, 4, 18010 Granada. ☎ **958-22-75-36.** Fax 958-22-75-33. 44 units. TV TEL. 9,000 ptas ($54) double. AE, DC, MC, V. Parking 1,300 ptas. ($7.80).

An attractive 1970s hotel at the bottom of the hill leading to the Alhambra, the Macía is a real bargain for what should be a three-star hotel. All the small guest rooms are functionally but comfortably furnished with good beds and tidy tiny bathrooms with shower stalls. About half have air-conditioning. Breakfast is the only meal served. Parking is available along the street.

WHERE TO DINE
EXPENSIVE

Las Tinajas. Martínez Campos, 17. ☎ **958-25-43-93.** Reservations recommended. Main courses 2,500–3,500 ptas. ($15–$21); set menu 3,775–4,275 ptas. ($22.65–$25.65). AE, DC, MC, V. Daily noon–5pm and 8pm–midnight. Closed July 15–Aug 15. ANDALUSIAN.

A large, typical *méson*, this restaurant a short walk from the cathedral is named for the huge amphorae depicted on the facade of the building. For more than 3 decades it has been the culinary showcase of José Alvarez. His decor is classical Andalusian with wood walls adorned with ceramic tiles and pictures of old Granada. Diners are surrounded by antique ornaments interspersed with modern elements and fixtures. There is a convivial but crowded bar where locals and visitors alike order Andalusian wines and a wide variety of delicious tapas. Señor Alvarez is proud of his Mediterranean culinary traditions and uses only the freshest ingredients. Begin with such delights as the cold zucchini and almond cream soup, or a white beet stuffed with ham and cheese. Follow with a delectable monkfish cooked with local herbs or the peppered sirloin steak. Desserts include Moorish cake with almonds and raspberries, made from a recipe left over from the days of the sultan, or else a hearty regional pudding with coffee-flavored cream. The location is immediately south of Puerta Real.

MODERATE

Alhabaca. Calle Verela, 17. ☎ **958-22-49-23.** Reservations recommended on weekends. Main courses 2,000–2,500 ptas. ($12–$15); set menu 1,750 ptas. ($10.50). AE, MC. Tues–Sun 1–4pm; Tues–Sat 8–11pm. Closed in Aug. ANDALUSIAN/SPANISH.

You'd have to live in Granada for quite a while to learn of this little bistro. It's known to locals and they don't exactly share the secret. In a century-old building, it has been owned by Javier Jimenez for the past 5 years. He seats 30 diners at 10 tables in this small, old-fashioned restaurant decorated in a rustic style with bare white walls. The traditional dishes he serves are unpretentious and tasty, especially the *salmorejo* (creamy tomato gazpacho) and *ensalada de dos salsas*, a green salad with two different dressings. Stuffed salmon is marvelous, as is *pastel de berenjena con salmon marinado* (layered pastry with eggplant and marinated salmon). For dessert, we recommend the velvety yogurt mousse.

Carmen de San Miguel. Plaza de Torres Bermejas, 3. ☎ **958-22-67-23.** Reservations recommended. Main courses 2,200–3,300 ptas. ($13.20–$19.80); 3-course *menú del día* 3,725–6,025 ptas. ($22.35–$36.15). AE, DC, DISC, MC, V. Mon–Sat 1:30–4pm and 8:30–11:30pm. INTERNATIONAL.

Set on the sloping incline leading up to the Alhambra, this likable restaurant offers spectacular views over the city center. The restaurant is proud of its glassed-in dining room and patio-style terrace whose banks of flowers are changed seasonally. Specialties include *rabo de toro* (stewed oxtail), an array of such fish dishes as grilled hake and well-seasoned *zarzuela* (seafood stew), and shoulder of lamb stuffed with pinenuts and herbs. The food, although good, doesn't quite match the view. The wines are from throughout the country, with a strong selection of Riojas.

Parador Nacional San Francisco. Real de la Alhambra. ☎ **958-22-14-40.** Reservations not accepted. Main courses 3,000–4,000 ptas. ($18–$24); fixed-price menu 3,800 ptas. ($22.80). AE, DC, MC, V. Daily 1–4pm and 8:30–11pm. Bus: 2. SPANISH.

Even if you can't afford to stay at this luxurious parador (see "Where to Stay," above), the most famous in Spain, consider heading here for a tranquil retreat after you've battled the tourist hordes in the Alhambra itself. The dining room is spacious, the service is polite, and you gaze upon the rose gardens and a distant view of the Generalife. The set menu at lunch, which changes daily, is repeated in the evening, although you can always order à la carte. At this 16th-century convent built by the Reyes Católicos, you get not only atmosphere, but also a cuisine that features regional dishes of Andalusia and Spanish national specialties. Lunch is the preferred time to dine here, because the terrace overlooking the palace is open then. A light outdoor lunch menu of sandwiches and salads can be ordered on the à la carte menu if you don't want to partake of the heavy major Spanish repast in the heat of the day. The cuisine is competent in every way, although at no point rising to any culinary achievement. Ingredients are fresh and deftly handled by a kitchen staff who prefer to stick to tried-and-true Spanish recipes perfected over the years. When in doubt, order the Andalusian specialties instead of the Spanish national dishes, as most of the chefs are Andalusian and seem more familiar with and better at this style of regional cookery.

Restaurante Cunini. Plaza de la Pescadería, 14. ☎ **958-25-07-77.** Reservations recommended. Main courses 1,500–3,000 ptas. ($9–$18); fixed-price menu 2,500 ptas. ($15). AE, DC, MC, V. Tues–Sun noon–4pm and 8pm–midnight. SEAFOOD.

The array of seafood specialties served at Cunini, perhaps 100 selections, extends even to the tapas served at the long stand-up bar. Many guests move on after a drink or two to the paneled ground-floor restaurant, where the cuisine reflects the whole of Spain. Meals often begin with soup—perhaps *sopa sevillana* (with ham, shrimp, and whitefish). Also popular is a deep fry of small fish called a *fritura Cunini*, with other specialties including rice with seafood, *zarzuela* (seafood stew), smoked salmon, and grilled shrimp. Plaza de la Pescadería is adjacent to the Gran Vía de Colón just below the cathedral.

۞ Ruta del Valleta. Carretera Vieja de la Sierra Nevada, km 5.5, Cenés de la Vega. ☎ **958-48-61-34.** Reservations recommended. Main courses 1,200–5,900 ptas. ($7.20–$35.40); fixed-price menus 5,500 ptas. ($33) without wine. AE, DC, MC, V. Daily 1–4pm; Mon–Sat 8pm–midnight. ANDALUSIAN.

Despite its origins in 1976 as an unpretentious roadhouse restaurant, this place rapidly evolved into what is usually acclaimed as the best restaurant in or around Granada. It is within the hamlet of Cenés de la Vega, about 3½ miles (6km) northwest of Granada's center, and has six dining rooms of various sizes, each decorated with a mixture of English and Andalusian furniture and accessories. (They include a worthy collection of hand-painted ceramics from the region, many of which hang from the ceilings.)

Its owners are a pair of Granada-born brothers, Miguel and José Pedraza, who direct the impeccable service rituals. Menu items change with the season, but are likely to include roast suckling pig; roasted game birds such as pheasant and partridge, often served with Rioja wine sauce; preparations of fish and shellfish, including monkfish with Andalusian herbs and strips of Serrano ham; fillet steak in a morel-studded cream sauce; and a dessert specialty of frozen rice pudding on a bed of warm chocolate sauce. The wine list is said to be the most comprehensive in the region.

INEXPENSIVE

Antigua Bodega Castanede. Calle Elvira, 5. ☎ **958-22-63-62.** Reservations not required. Main courses 500–1,500 ptas. ($3–$9); set menu 1,700 ptas. ($10.20). MC, V. Mon–Sat 12:30–5pm and 7:30pm–1:30am. ANDALUSIAN.

More and more discerning visitors are going to Andalusia wanting to dine in *típico* joints that rarely see a foreign visitor. Our nomination for the most rustic local *bodega* (wine cellar) in Granada is the Castanede. It's been here for more than a century and is the oldest of its type in the colorful Albaycín *barrio*. Only a 10-minute walk from the Alhambra, it is just off Plaza Nueva. A convivial, friendly spot, it is crowded with locals who know they can get tasty but unpretentious food here at low, low prices. On clay floors resting under wooden beams, there are only 11 tables for a proper sit-down meal, but many patrons crowd in at the bar placing their order. The antiquity of the place is represented in the furnishings and original wine barrels often used as tables. The place is praised locally for its wide ranges of tapas—there are 18 different stuffed versions of the humble potato alone. Other meals include a variety of thick stews served in traditional clay bowls, ideal if you're visiting on a cold day. You can order a *tabla iberica*, a selection of small dishes featuring cheese, ham, crab meat, shrimp, and venison. For the sweet tooth, go for the chocolate mousse or one of the homemade tarts.

Chikito. Plaza del Campilio, 9. ☎ **958-22-33-64.** Reservations recommended. Main courses 1,200–2,700 ptas. ($7.20–$16.20); fixed-price menu 2,100 ptas. ($12.60). AE, DC, MC, V. Thurs–Tues 1–4pm and 8–11:30pm. Bus: 1, 2, or 7. SPANISH.

Chikito sits across the street from the famous tree-shaded square where García Lorca met with other members of El Rinconcillo (The Little Corner), a dozen young men considered the best and the brightest in the 1920s, when they brought a brief but dazzling cultural renaissance to their hometown. The cafe where they met has now changed its name, but it's the same building. The present-day Chikito is both a bar and a restaurant. In fair weather, guests enjoy drinks and snacks on tables placed in the square; in winter they retreat inside to the tapas bars. There is also a complete restaurant facility, offering *sopa sevillana,* shrimp cocktail, Basque hake, baked tuna, oxtail, *zarzuela* (seafood stew), grilled swordfish, and Argentine-style veal steak. Regrettably, this literary shrine has barely civil waiters, who obviously lack patience with newcomers. You may want to skip dinner here and settle for tapas and a glass of sherry at the bar.

Mesón Antonio. Ecce Homo, 6. ☎ **958-22-95-99.** Reservations recommended. Main courses 1,000–2,000 ptas. ($6–$12). AE, MC, V. Mon–Sat 2–3:30pm and 9–10:30pm. Closed June–Sept. SPANISH.

This appealing and unpretentious restaurant, established in 1980, is one floor above street level in an unassuming 1740s house whose address is a bit hard to find. (The narrow street it's on is a few steps from the landmark Campo del Príncipe.) You traverse a communal patio before climbing a flight of stairs to reach a simply decorated dining room. All the specialties served here are prepared in wood-burning ovens. They might include roasted lamb in local herbs, *zarzuela* (seafood stew), several different steaks, and such vegetables as fresh asparagus and roasted leeks au gratin.

Polinario. Real de la Alhambra, 3. ☎ **958-22-29-91.** Reservations recommended. Luncheon buffet 1,500 ptas. ($9). MC, V. Daily 9am–4pm; bar daily 9am–7pm. Bus: 2. SPANISH.

Although its food is usually ordinary, this simple restaurant is one of only three within the walled confines of the Alhambra. (Another is the dining room of the local parador, which, while preferable, is more expensive.) The Polinario enjoys an enviable position in a very old building across from the Palace of Carlos V and does a thriving business every afternoon with organized tours. By the end of a hot day, the luncheon buffet might be a bit fatigued, but the Spanish cooking is adequate, and usually includes a selection of salads, soups, meats, and desserts.

Restaurant Mirador de Moraima. Calle Pianista Garcia Carillo, 2. ☎ **958-22-82-90.** Reservations recommended. Main courses 1,300–2,300 ptas. ($7.80–$13.80). AE, MC, V. Mon–Sat 1:30–3:30pm and 8:30–11:30pm. ANDALUSIAN/SPANISH.

Facing the Alhambra in a solidly built antique house that has witnessed thousands of dinners since it was established in 1988, this is a large, rambling, and well-recommended restaurant with a half-dozen dining rooms and three separate outdoor terraces. The hardworking staff prepares large quantities of such dishes as gazpacho, roasted goat in wine sauce, slabs of beefsteak with a sauce of aromatic herbs, several different preparations of codfish, grilled Spanish sausages, and roasted lamb. Don't expect subtlety or big-city sophistication here—what you'll get is generous portions of good cooking and a deeply entrenched pride in the region's rural traditions.

Restaurant O Caña. Plaza de Realejo, 7. ☎ **958-25-64-70.** Reservations not necessary. Main courses 900–2,000 ptas. ($5.40–$12); fixed-price menu 1,000 ptas. ($6). AE, DC, MC, V. Daily 1–4pm and 7:45–11:45pm. SPANISH.

Set behind a mosaic-sheathed facade in an antique building in Granada's Jewish Quarter, this recommended site has a long and appealing bar near its entrance, a salon where you might be tempted to sit down before a meal with a glass of sherry, and a well-managed dining room. Here portions are generous, well flavored, and authentic to the old-time traditions of Andalusia. Since it was established in 1905, the site has turned out endless versions of its specialties (bull's tail, grilled *solomillo* of beefsteak, Spanish sausages, grilled breast of duck, and endless amounts of suckling pig and roasted lamb). It has earned the loyalty of generations of local families, many of whom arrive en masse to dine together, especially on Sundays.

Restaurante Sevilla. Calle Oficios, 12. ☎ **958-22-12-23.** Reservations recommended. Main courses 1,500–4,500 ptas. ($9–$27); fixed-price menu 2,500 ptas. ($15). AE, DC, MC, V. Daily 1–4pm; Mon–Sat 8–11pm. SPANISH/ANDALUSIAN.

Attracting a mixed crowd of all ages, the Sevilla is definitely *típico,* but with an upbeat elegance. In the past you might have seen El Cordobés (when he was Spain's leading bullfighter), Brigitte Bardot, or even Andrés Segovia dining here. Even before them, the place was discovered by García Lorca, a patron in the 1930s, and Manuel de Falla. Most dishes are at the lower end of the price scale. Our most recent meal here included gazpacho, Andalusian veal, and caramel custard, plus bread and the wine of Valdepeñas. To break the gazpacho monotony, try *sopa virule,* made with pinenuts and chicken breasts. For a main course, we recommend the *cordero a la pastoril* (lamb with herbs and paprika). The best dessert is bananas flambé. You can dine inside, where it is pleasantly decorated, or have a meal on the terrace. There is also a bar. You'll find the place in the center of town opposite the Royal Chapel, near Plaza Isabel la Católica.

GRANADA AFTER DARK
DRINKS & TAPAS

A good place to begin your night is along the **Campo del Principe,** where at least seven old-fashioned tapas bars do a rollicking business during the cool of the evening. Our favorite among them is **La Esquinita,** Campo del Principe, s/n (☎ **958-22-71-06**). Small, atmospheric, and sometimes claustrophobic, it serves a clientele that mostly eats standing up, sometimes spilling into the street, rather than sitting at any of the trio of small tables. A specialty tapas here is a *ración* of fried fish that tastes absolutely sublime when accompanied by wine or cold beer.

Another good spot on the same street, bathed in an atmospheric and antique-looking patina of its own, is **Casa Paco,** Campo del Principe, s/n (no phone). Each of the tapas bars in this section opens around noon every day but becomes really appealing between 9pm and around 3am.

A perennial favorite set directly in front of the cathedral is **El Bodegas Castañera,** Elvira, 5 (☎ **958-22-97-06**). Inside, rows of antique wine barrels and exposed masonry bring to mind many generations of wine connoisseurs, whose ranks you'll be tempted to join, thanks to the fact that virtually nothing has been changed in this place in years.

Another contender for your bar business is **Casa Henrique,** calle Acero de Darro, s/n (no phone), an old-fashioned masonry-sided hole-in-the-wall lined with antique barrels of wine and sherries. Its specialty tapas consist of thin-sliced Serrano ham and heaping platters of steamed mussels with herbs and white wine.

One of the most popular tapas bars in Granada (at least with us) is **Casa Vino del Agua,** calle Algibe de Trillo (☎ **958-22-43-56**), a small, well-maintained bar with an adjoining restaurant in a small garden in the heart of the Albaicín. Everyone agrees that the cooling nighttime breezes show this convivial spot off to best advantage. Don't expect full-fledged platters; its strength is small-scale portions of cheeses, pâtés, and salads, which go especially well with glasses of wine and beer.

An equally historic spot with a verdant patio loaded with plants and shrubs is **Bar Pilar del Toro,** calle Hospital de Santa Ana, 12 (☎ **958-22-38-47**), near the cathedral and the Plaza Nueva. A more modern, larger bar is **Bar Torcuato,** calle Pages, 31 (no phone). An even larger competitor, **La Gran Taverna,** Plaza Nueva, 12 (☎ **958-22-88-46**), is a modern, bustling, and irreverent site that attracts coffee- and wine-tasters as well as lovers of sliced Serrano ham, fondues, and liqueurs. **Bar La Mancha,** calle Joaquin Costa, 10 (☎ **958-22-89-68**), is a roughly equivalent nearby site.

THE GYPSY CAVES OF SACROMONTE

These inhabited gypsy caves are the subject of much controversy. Admittedly, they are a tourist trap, one of the most obviously commercial and shadowy rackets in Spain. Still, the caves are a potent enough attraction if you follow some rules.

Once thousands of gypsies lived on the "Holy Mountain," so named because of several Christians martyred here. However, many of the caves were heavily damaged by rain in 1962, forcing hundreds of the occupants to seek shelter elsewhere. Nearly all the gypsies remaining are in one way or another involved with tourism. (Some don't even live here—they commute from modern apartments in the city.)

When evening settles over Granada, loads of visitors descend on these caves near the Albaicín, the old Arab section. In every cave you'll hear the rattle of castanets and the strumming of guitars, while everybody in the gypsy family struts his or her stuff. Popularly known as the *zambra,* this is intriguing entertainment only if you have an appreciation for the grotesque. Whenever a gypsy boy or girl comes along with genuine talent, he or she is often grabbed up and hustled off to the more expensive clubs. Those left at home can be rather pathetic in their attempts to entertain.

One of the main reasons for going is to see the caves themselves. If you're expecting primitive living, you may be in for a surprise—many are quite comfortable, with conveniences like telephones and electricity. Often they are decorated with copper and ceramic items—and the inhabitants need no encouragement to sell them to you.

If you want to see the caves, you can walk up the hill by yourself. Your approach will already be advertised before you get here. Attempts will be made to lure you inside one or another of the caves—and to get money from you. Alternatively, you can book an organized tour arranged by one of the travel agencies in Granada. Even at the end of one of these group outings—with all expenses theoretically paid in advance—there is likely to be an attempt by the cave dwellers to extract more money from you. As soon as the *zambra* ends, hurry out of the cave as quickly as possible. Many readers have been critical of these tours.

During the *zambra,* refuse to accept a pair of castanets, even if offered under the friendly guise of having you join in the fun. If you accept them, chances are you'll later be asked to pay for them. Buying anything in these caves is not recommended. Leave your jewelry at your hotel, and don't take more money than you're prepared to lose.

A visit to the caves is almost always included as part of the morning and (more frequently) afternoon city tours offered every day by such companies as **Grana Vision** (☎ **958-13-58-04**). Night tours of the caves (when the caves are at their most eerie, most evocative, and, unfortunately, most larcenous) are usually offered only to those who can assemble 10 or more people into a group. This might have changed by the time of your visit, so phone a reputable tour operator such as Grana Vision to learn if any newly developed options are available.

FLAMENCO

The best flamenco show in Granada is staged at **Jardines Neptuno,** calle Arabial, s/n (☎ **958-25-11-12**), nightly at 10:15pm. The acts are a bit racy, even though they have been toned down considerably for today's audiences. In addition to flamenco, performers attired in regional garb do folk dances and give guitar concerts. The show takes place in a garden setting. There's a high cover charge of 3,800 ptas. ($22.80), which includes a drink that you can nurse all evening. It's best to take a taxi here.

DANCE CLUBS

If you eventually tire of *bodega*-crawling, you might be tempted as the night progresses to go dancing in the town's most popular disco. It is **Granada 10,** calle Carcel Baja, 10 (☎ **958-22-40-01**). Open 12:30pm until 5am nightly, it charges 700 ptas. ($4.20) entrance, a price that includes the first drink. Beer costs 250 ptas. ($1.50).

GAY BARS

Granada has a number of bars that are not exclusively gay, but draw a mixed crowd of homosexual and straight locals and foreigners. Two of the best bets include **Al Pie de la Vela,** calle del Darro, 35 (☎ **958-22-85-39**), which is a cruisy bar attracting a mostly male clientele of mixed ages, although the 18-to-28 set seems to predominate. The club is open nightly 9:30pm to 4am. Another local favorite is **Versus,** Carrera del Darro, 25 (☎ **958-22-69-03**), with a gorgeous interior. It's beside the old Arab baths. In addition to its beautiful bar, Versus serves Spanish cuisine and attracts both gays and straights of mixed ages. It's open nightly 9pm to 4am.

8 The Costa del Sol

The mild winter climate and almost-guaranteed summer sunshine have made this razzle-dazzle stretch of Mediterranean shoreline a year-round attraction. From the harbor city of Algeciras it stretches east to the port city of Almería. Sandwiched in between is a steep, rugged coastline set against the Sierra Nevada. You'll find poor to fair beaches, sandy coves, whitewashed houses, olive trees, lots of new apartment houses, fishing boats, golf courses, souvenir stands, fast-food outlets, and widely varied populations—both human and vegetable.

This coastal strip, quite frankly, no longer enjoys the chic reputation it had in Franco's day. It is overbuilt and spoiled, although you can still find pockets of posh (including Puerto Banús, with its yacht-clogged harbor). One advantage of the area is that, thanks to European Community money, it is easier to get around than ever before. The infamous N-340 highway from Málaga to Estepona has become a fast, safe six-lane road. In days of yore it was the most dangerous highway in Spain.

The coast is probably even better for **golf** than for beaches. The best resorts are **Los Monteros** (☎ 95-277-17-00), in Marbella, which is the leading course; **Parador de Golf** (☎ 95-238-12-55), between Málaga and Torremolinos; **Hotel Atalaya Park** in Estepona (☎ 95-288-90-00); and **Golf Hotel Guadalmina,** in Marbella (☎ 95-288-22-11). To learn more, pick up a copy of the monthly magazine *Costa Golf* at any newsstand. Many golfers prefer to play a different course at every hotel. Usually, if you notify your hotel reception desk a day in advance, a staff member will arrange a playing time.

Water-skiing and windsurfing are available in every resort, and all types of boats can be rented from various kiosks at all the main beaches. You don't have to search hard for these outfitters—chances are they'll find you.

From June to October the coast is mobbed, so make sure you have a reservation in advance. And keep in mind that October 12 is a national holiday—visitors should make doubly sure of their reservations. At other times, innkeepers are likely to roll out the red carpet.

Many restaurants close around October 15 for a much-needed vacation. Remember, too, that many supermarkets and other facilities are closed on Sunday.

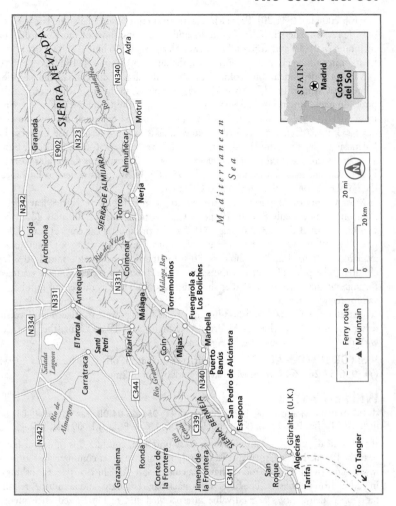

1 Algeciras

422 miles (679km) S of Madrid, 82 miles (132km) W of Málaga

Not really a destination in and of itself, Algeciras is the jumping-off point for Africa—it's only 3 hours to Tangier, Morocco. If you're planning an excursion, there's an inexpensive baggage storage depot at the ferry terminal. Algeciras is also a base for day trips to **Gibraltar.** For information, check with the Gibraltar Tourist Office, 158 Main St., Gibraltar (☎ **956-77-49-82**). It's open Monday to Friday 10am to 6pm, Saturday 10am to 2pm. If you don't have time to visit "the Rock," you can at least see it from Algeciras—it's only 6 miles (10km) away.

ESSENTIALS

GETTING THERE & DEPARTING   The local **RENFE** office is at calle Juan de la Cierva (☎ **956-63-02-02**). From Madrid, three trains daily make the 6-hour trip; the fare is 5,200 ptas. ($31.20). From Málaga, there are three trains daily; the fare is 2,115 ptas. ($12.70). The trip takes 5½ hours and runs along most of the Costa del Sol, including Marbella and Torremolinos. Trains leave Seville (6 hours) and Granada (5½ hours) three times a day. From either city, the fare is 3,150 ptas. ($18.90).

Various independent bus companies serve Algeciras. Empresa Portillo, avenida Virgen de Carmen, 15 (☎ **956-65-10-55**), 1½ blocks to the right when you exit the port complex, runs nearly a dozen buses a day along the Costa del Sol to Algeciras from Málaga. It also sends two buses a day to Córdoba (6 hours) and two buses a day to Granada (5 hours). To make connections to or from Seville, use Empresa La Valenciana, Viajes Koudubia, calle Juan de la Cierva, 5 (☎ **956-60-34-00**). Six buses a day go to Jerez de la Frontera, and eleven to Seville. **Transporres Generales Comes,** Hotel Octavio, calle San Bernardo, 1 (☎ **956-65-34-56**), sells tickets to **La Línea,** the border station for the approach to Gibraltar.

Most visitors in Algeciras plan to cross to Tangier, Morocco. Ferries leave every hour on the hour daily 8am to 10pm. A Class A ticket costs 4,500 ptas. ($27) per person, a Class B ticket 3,200 ptas. ($19.20). To transport a car costs at least 9,900 ptas. ($59.40) per vehicle, and cars aren't transported in stormy weather. Discounts are available: 20% for EurailPass holders, 30% for InterRail pass holders, and 50% for children. The price of tickets is the same at the dozens of travel agencies scattered throughout the town; don't bother shopping around. There is no central number to call for ferry information.

Carretera de Cádiz (E-15/N-340) runs from Málaga west to Algeciras. If you're driving south from Seville (or Madrid), take highway N-IV to Cádiz, then connect with the N-340/E-5 southwest to Algeciras.

VISITOR INFORMATION The **tourist information office,** at Juan de la Cierva (☎ **956-57-26-36**), is open Monday to Friday 9am to 2pm.

WHERE TO STAY

Hotel Alarde. Alfonso XI, 4, 11201 Algeciras. ☎ **956-66-04-08.** Fax 956-65-49-01. 68 units. A/C TV TEL. 9,000 ptas. ($54) double. AE, DC, MC, V. Parking 1,000 ptas. ($6).

If you want to get away from the tacky, noisy port area, consider this three-star hotel near the Parque María Cristina. It's a central location in a quiet commercial section of town. The small double rooms have balconies and Andalusian-style furnishings, including firm mattresses. The hotel has a snack bar, restaurant, and laundry. A restaurant, open daily, serves a good-value international and regional fixed-price menu. During our most recent stay we were impressed with both the staff and the inviting atmosphere.

Hotel Al-Mar. Avenida de la Marina, 2, 11201 Algeciras. ☎ **956-65-46-61.** Fax 956-65-45-01. www.eh.etursa.es/almar. E-mail: al-mar@eh.etursa.es. 193 units. A/C TV TEL. 10,000 ptas. ($60) double; from 12,000 ptas. ($72) suite. Rates include breakfast. AE, DC, MC, V. Parking 800 ptas. ($4.80).

The three-star Al-Mar is one of the best choices in town, with better rooms than the Alarde. It's near the port, where the ferries embark for Ceuta and Tangier. This large hotel boasts blue-and-white Sevillian and Moorish decor, as well as three restaurants, a handful of bars, and lots of verdant hideaways. The midsized guest rooms are well maintained, furnished in a Andalusian style, with good beds and tiled baths. A fourth-floor drawing room provides a panoramic view of the Rock.

Hotel Octavio. San Bernardo, 1, 11207 Algeciras. ☎ **956-65-27-00.** Fax 956-65-28-02. 77 units. A/C MINIBAR TV TEL. 16,000–40,000 ptas. ($96–$240) double. AE, DC, MC, V. Parking 1,400 ptas. ($8.40).

Beaches: The Good, the Bad & the Ugly

We'd like to report that the Costa del Sol is a paradise for swimmers. Surprisingly, it isn't, although it was the allure of beaches that originally put the "sol" in the Costa del Sol beginning in the 1950s.

The worst beaches—mainly pebbles and shingles—are at Nerja, Málaga, and Almuñécar. Moving westward, you encounter the gritty, grayish sands of Torremolinos. The best beaches here are at El Bajondillo and La Carihuela (which borders an old fishing village). Another good stretch of beach is along the meandering strip between Carvajal, Los Boliches, and Fuengirola. In addition, two good beaches—El Fuerte and La Fontanilla—lie on either side of Marbella. However, all these beaches tend to be overcrowded, especially in July and August when mama and papa from the hinterlands take the kids to the beach. Crowding is worst on Sundays from May to October when beaches are overrun with family picnickers as well as sunbathers.

All public beaches in Spain are free, and you shouldn't expect changing facilities. There might be a cold shower on the major beaches, but that's it.

Although it's not sanctioned or technically allowed by the government, many women, especially those from France, go topless on the beaches. Nudity is common on some of the less frequented beaches, although it is against the law; if you indulge, you will be subject to arrest by the civil guard. Many bathers flout the law and go nude anyway, but it's not advised. If you want to bare it all, head for the Costa Natura, about 2 miles (3km) west of Estepona. This is the site of the only official nudist colony along the Costa del Sol.

Conveniently located in the center of town near the railway station, the Octavio is our second choice after the Reina Cristina (and is more affordable). It's decorated with reproductions of English antiques, which contrast sharply with the building's angular modern exterior. The good-sized guest rooms are nicely furnished and well maintained, with excellent beds and tiled bathrooms. An American-style bar serves international drinks, and room service is available daily 8am to 11pm.

Hotel Reina Cristina. Paseo de la Conferencia, 11207 Algeciras. ☎ **956-60-26-22.** Fax 956-60-33-23. 160 units. AC TV TEL. 23,000 ptas. ($138) double; from 45,000 ptas. ($270) suite. AE, DC, MC, V. Free parking.

In its own park on the southern outskirts of the city (a 10-minute walk south of the rail and bus stations), this is the town's leading hotel. A Victorian building accented with turrets, ornate railings, and a facade appropriately painted with pastels, the Reina Cristina offers a view of the faraway Rock of Gibraltar. On the premises are a small English-language library and a semitropical garden held in place with sturdy retaining walls. The comfortable, high-ceilinged guest rooms have excellent furnishings, including comfortable beds and tiled baths.

There is a formal restaurant, La Parilla, a cafeteria-style dining room, and a bar. Room service is available 7am to midnight; amenities include laundry/valet service, concierge, baby-sitting, sauna, indoor and outdoor swimming pools, and tennis courts.

WHERE TO DINE

Because Algeciras is not distinguished for its restaurants, many visitors dine at their hotels instead of taking a chance at the dreary little spots along the waterfront.

Asador Iruna. Alfonso XI, 11. ☎ **956-63-28-18.** Reservations not needed. Main courses 1,600–2,300 ptas. ($9.60–$13.80). AE, DC, MC, V. Mon–Sat 1:30–4pm and 8:30–11pm. SPANISH.

Your most reliable meal will be at the Reina Cristina (see recommendation above), but if you'd like to chance an independent eatery, this is the best of the lot. It provides a soothing respite from the industrial port's dust, noise, and heat with a menu that incorporates some of Spain's most popular dishes. Dishes are hearty and filling, but not a lot more. Expect hearty soups, grilled beefsteak, roast chicken, Spanish sausages, and veal. Fish is fresh and flavor filled, and local fish includes hake, swordfish, squid, octopus, red snapper, mullet, and cod.

2 Tarifa

14 miles (22.5km) W of Algeciras, 443 miles (713km) S of Madrid, 61 miles (98km) SE of Cádiz

Instead of heading east from Algeciras along the Costa del Sol, we'd suggest a visit west to Tarifa. This old Moorish town is the southernmost point in Europe. After leaving Algeciras, the roads climb steeply and the drive to Tarifa is along one of Europe's most splendid coastal routes. In the distance you'll see Gibraltar, the straits, and the green hills of Africa—in fact, you can sometimes get a glimpse of houses in Ceuta and Tangier on the Moroccan coastline.

Named for the Moorish military hero Tarik, Tarifa has retained more of its Arab character than any other town in Andalusia. Narrow cobblestoned streets lead to charming patios filled with flowers. The main square is the Plaza San Mateo.

Two factors have inhibited the development of Tarifa's beautiful 3-mile (5km) white beach, the Playa de Lances: It's still a Spanish military zone, and the wind blows almost half the time. For windsurfers, though, the strong western breezes are unbeatable. Tarifa is filled with shops that rent windsurfing equipment and give advice about the best locales.

Many visitors also come to see Tarifa's historical artifacts and wander the crumbling city ramparts. The **Castle of Tarifa,** site of a famous struggle in 1292 between Moors and Christians, dominates the town. The castle was held by Guzmán el Bueno ("the Good"). When Christians captured his 9-year-old son and demanded surrender of the garrison, Guzmán tossed the Spanish a dagger, saying he preferred "honor without a son, to a son with dishonor." The execution was carried out. Sadly, the castle is not open to the public.

From Algeciras, **Transporres Generales Comes,** calle San Bernardo, 1 (☎ **956-65-34-56**), under the Hotel Octavio, runs several buses daily to Tarifa. The trip takes 30 minutes and costs 220 ptas. ($1.30). To drive, take the Cádiz highway, N-340/E-5, west from Algeciras.

3 Estepona

53 miles (85km) W of Málaga, 397 miles (639km) S of Madrid, 28½ miles (46km) E of Algeciras

A town of Roman origin, Estepona is a budding beach resort, less developed than Marbella or Torremolinos and more likable for that reason. Estepona contains an interesting 15th-century parish church, with the ruins of an old aqueduct nearby (at Salduba). Its recreational port is an attraction, as are its **beaches:** Costa Natura, km 257 on the N-340, the first legal nude beach of its kind along the Costa del Sol; La Rada, 2 miles (3km) long; and El Cristo, only 600 yards long. After the sun goes down, stroll along the Paseo Marítimo, a broad avenue with gardens on one side, beach on the other.

In summer, the cheapest places to eat in Estepona are the *merenderos,* little dining areas set up by local fishers and their families right on the beach. Naturally they feature seafood, including sole and sardine kebabs grilled over an open fire. You can usually order a fresh salad and fried potatoes; desserts are simple.

After your siesta, head for the tapas bars. You'll find most of them—called *freidurías* (fried-fish bars)—at the corner of the calle de los Reyes and La Terraza. Tables spill onto the sidewalks in summer, and *gambas a la plancha* (shrimp) are the favorite (but not the cheapest) tapas to order.

ESSENTIALS

GETTING THERE   The nearest rail links are in Algeciras. However, Estepona is on the bus route from Algeciras to Málaga. If you're driving, head east from Algeciras along the E-5/N-340.

VISITOR INFORMATION   The **tourist information office** is at avenida San Lorenzo, 1 (☎ **95-280-20-02**). It's open Monday to Friday 9:30am to 6pm.

WHERE TO STAY

Atalaya Park Golf Hotel & Resort. Carretera de Cádiz, km 168.5, 29688 Estepona. ☎ **95-288-90-00.** Fax 95-288-90-02. www.atalaya-park.es. E-mail: hotel@atalaya-park.es. 469 units. A/C MINIBAR TV TEL. 25,000–33,000 ptas. ($150–$198) double; 35,000–45,000 ptas. ($210–$270) suite. Rates include breakfast. AE, DC, MC, V. Free parking.

Located midway between Estepona and Marbella, this modern resort complex attracts sports and nature lovers. Its tranquil beachside location sits amid 20 acres of subtropical gardens. The hotel is among the largest, most opulent, and most expensive in and around Estepona. Spacious rooms furnished in elegant modern style are well maintained and inviting. Guests have complementary use of the hotel's extensive sports facilities. Many guests from northern Europe check in and almost never leave the grounds.

Dining/Diversions: The hotel's three restaurants serve Spanish and international food. Several bars are scattered throughout the property, and there is a dance club.

Amenities: Baby-sitting, concierge, laundry and valet, room service (breakfast only), sauna, health club, solarium, indoor and outdoor swimming pools, car-rental facilities, boutiques, tennis, watersports center. Two 18-hole golf courses are nearby.

Buenavista. Avenida de España, 180, 29680 Estepona. ☎ **95-280-01-37.** Fax 95-280-55-93. 40 units. A/C TV. 4,800–7,200 ptas. ($28.80–$43.20) double. AE, MC, V.

This comfortable if modest little five-story *residencia* beside the coastal road opened in the 1970s. The tiny guest rooms are likely to be noisy in summer because of heavy traffic nearby. Beds are comfortable, and the little tiled bathrooms have shower stalls. Buses from Marbella stop nearby.

✪ **Las Dunas.** Urbani La Boladilla Baja–Noreste, Carretera de Cádiz, km 163.5, 29689 Estepona. ☎ **95-279-43-45.** Fax 95-279-48-25. www.las-dunas.com. E-mail: lasdunas@las-dunas.com. 73 units. A/C MINIBAR TV TEL. 26,000–42,000 ptas. ($156–$252) double; 40,000–65,000 ptas. ($240–$390) 2-bedroom suite. Free parking.

One of the great hotels of the Costa del Sol and a member of the "Leading Hotels of the World," Las Dunas attracts fashionable Europeans pursuing the pampered life. Site of a world-class spa and one of the area's newest resorts, the five-star three-story hotel is constructed in a U-shape, evocative of a gigantic hacienda. It stands in the midst of gardens and fountains; regrettably, the beach nearby is mediocre. Suites outnumber standard doubles, and most units have furnished balconies overlooking the Mediterranean. All are sumptuously comfortable, with luxury mattresses, fine furnishings, and elegant fabrics. The roomy bathrooms have plush towels, hair dryers, and deluxe toiletries.

Dining/Diversions: The **Lido** restaurant is among the most elegant on the coast. Heinz Winkler, a Michelin-starred German chef, supervises the superb cuisine. A bistro, **East Meets West,** serves European and Asian food, and there's a piano bar with nightly entertainment.

Amenities: Spa treatments (specialties include thalassotherapy and ionized oxygen treatments), beauty treatments, room service, concierge, library, game room, pool, whirlpool, sauna. The staff makes arrangements for golf.

WHERE TO DINE

Costa del Sol. Calle San Roque, 23. ☎ **95-280-11-01.** Reservations Recommended. Main courses 850–2,200 ptas. ($5.10–$13.20); fixed-price menu 950–2,500 ptas. ($5.70–$15); *menú especial* 2,000 ptas. ($12). AE, MC, V. Tues–Sun 8am–3pm and 8–10:30pm. TRADITIONAL ENGLISH.

Recently renovated by its new owners, the Bowens, the Costa del Sol has undergone a complete identity change. The menu caters to a large community of expatriate and traveling Brits homesick for such dishes as fish-and-chips, steak-and-ale pie, and peppered Ulster pork. The traditional Sunday roast is always a winner. For dessert, try the apple pie or the treacle tart.

La Alcaria de Ramos. Urbanización El Paraiso Vista al Mar, 1, km 167, Carretera N340. ☎ **952-88-61-78.** Reservations recommended. Main courses 1,400–2,500 ptas. ($8.40–$15); set menu 3,500 ptas. ($21). MC, V. Mon–Sat 7:30pm–midnight. CREATIVE SPANISH.

Your best meal in Estepona is awaiting you at this restaurant on the outskirts of the resort en route to San Pedro. This country retreat has been decorated inside and out in pastel fuchsia, ocher, and white in the style of an old summer house along the Spanish coast. The windows are original and, in addition, there's a beautiful terrace garden where customers may dine as weather permits. The chef and owner, José Ramos, has won many national gastronomic competitions, and has been creating intriguing variations on traditional recipes since the early '90s. He will regale you with such dishes as *tortas de patatas* (potato cakes—yes, potato cakes, and how good they are!). Try also his *crêpes de aguacate con gambas* (avocado crêpes with shrimp) and his *pato asado con pure de manzana y col roja* (grilled duck with apple purée and red cabbage). Also worth ordering is the *parillada de pescado y mariscos* (assorted grilled fish and shellfish). For dessert, try his clever concoction *helado frito con frambuesa* (fried ice cream with raspberry sauce).

4 San Pedro de Alcántara

43 miles (69km) W of Málaga, 42½ miles (68.5km) E of Algeciras

Between Marbella and Estepona, this interesting village contains **Roman ruins** that have been officially classified as a national monument. The ruins are a fenced-off site in the center of the village with no formal entrance, but can be viewed in passing from the street. In recent years the village has been extensively developed as a resort suburb of Marbella. It now offers some good hotel selections, the best of which is listed below.

To get here, you can take a bus (they leave from Marbella every 30 minutes) or drive on the E-15 west from Marbella.

WHERE TO STAY

Golf Hotel Guadalmina. Hacienda Guadalmina, Carretera de Cádiz, 29680 San Pedro de Alcántara. ☎ **95-288-22-11.** Fax 95-288-22-91. www.spa.es/hotel-guadalmina. E-mail: info@hotel-guadalmina.com. 177 units. A/C MINIBAR TV TEL. 22,600–35,800 ptas. ($135.60–$214.80) double. AE, MC, V. Free parking.

At this large, country club–type resort, the first tee and the 18th green are next to the hotel. The golf course is open to both guests and non-guests. This is an informal place, like a private world on the shores of the Mediterranean. The resort is 50 yards (45.5m) from the beach, 8 miles (13km) east of Marbella, and 1¼ miles (2km) from the center of San Pedro de Alcántara. You reach it by a long driveway from the coastal road. The spacious guest rooms, which open onto the pool/recreation area and the sea, are attractively decorated in traditional Spanish style.

Dining: The hotel offers two excellent dining choices. One is a lunch-only, reed-covered poolside terrace overlooking the golf course and the sea, the other an interior room in the main building, with a sedate clubhouse aura. Informality and good food reign.

Amenities: In addition to the golf course, two seawater swimming pools attract those seeking the lazy life, while the tennis courts appeal to the more energetic.

5 Puerto Banús

5 miles (8km) E of Marbella, 486 miles (782km) S of Madrid

A favorite resort for international celebrities, this coastal village was created almost overnight in the traditional Mediterranean style. It's a dreamy place, the very image of what a Costa del Sol fishing village should look like, but rarely does. Yachts can be moored nearly at your doorstep. Along the harbor front you'll find an array of expensive bars and restaurants. Wandering through the quiet backstreets, you'll pass archways and patios with grilles.

To reach the town, you can take one of 15 buses that run daily from Marbella, or drive east from Marbella along the E-15.

WHERE TO STAY

Hotel Marbella-Dinamar. Urbanización Nueva Andalucía, Carretera de Cádiz, km 175, 29660 Puerto Banús. ☎ **95-281-05-00.** Fax 95-281-23-46. 116 units. A/C MINIBAR TV TEL. 17,500–28,000 ptas. ($105–$168) double. AE, DC, MC, V. Free parking.

Distinctly Moorish in feel, this striking, exotic resort celebrates the Arab domination of what is today Spanish Andalusia. Just 400 yards from both the beach and the borders of Puerto Banús's congested center, it was built around 1980. It has stark white walls, soaring arches, and a central courtyard with a large, abstractly shaped swimming pool. The midsized guest rooms each have simple furniture and two large beds; they look out on either the palm trees beside the pool or the sea. The resort offers two tennis courts (which are floodlit at night) and an indoor swimming pool. Guests have easy access to the casino at the neighboring Plaza Andalucía hotel and to one of the best all-around golf courses along the Costa del Sol. Perhaps best of all, the diversions of Puerto Banús are within a 3-minute walk.

WHERE TO DINE

Dalli's Pizza Factory. Muelle de Rivera. ☎ **95-281-86-23.** Reservations not accepted. Pastas 850–1,550 ptas. ($5.10–$9.30); meat platters 1,600–2,500 ptas. ($9.60–$15). AE, MC, V. Daily 1–3:30pm and 7pm–1am. PASTA.

The California-inspired philosophy at Dalli's offers a new way to save pesetas in high-priced Puerto Banús. Its specialty is pasta, pasta, and more pasta—served with a portion of garlic bread and a carafe of house wine, it's a great bargain. In a setting that's a cross between high-tech and art deco, you can order nutmeg-flavored ravioli with spinach filling, *penne all'arrabbiata,* lasagna, and several kinds of spaghetti. More filling are chicken cacciatore and scallopini of chicken and veal. They are served with—guess what?—pasta as a side dish. The owners, incidentally, are a trio of Roman-born brothers who were reared in England and educated in California.

Don Leone. Muelle Ribera, 44. ☎ **95-281-17-16.** Reservations recommended. Main courses 1,800–3,400 ptas. ($10.80–$20.40). AE, MC, V. Year-round, daily 8pm–2am; late Sept–late June, also daily 1–4pm. Closed Nov 21–Dec 21. INTERNATIONAL.

Many residents in villas around Marbella drive to this luxuriously decorated dockside restaurant for dinner, and it gets crowded at times. Begin with the house minestrone, then follow with pasta in clam sauce; lasagna is also a regular treat. Meat specialties include veal parmigiana and roast baby lamb, and the fish dishes are also worth a try, especially the *frita mista del pescados* (mixed fish fry). The food is competently prepared with fresh ingredients, although at times it fails to capture authentic Spanish flavor. The wine list is one of the best along the coast.

La Taberna del Alabardero. Muelle Benabola, A2. ☎ **95-281-27-94.** Reservations required. Main courses 2,200–3,500 ptas. ($13.20–$21). AE, DC, MC, V. Daily 1–4pm and 8pm–midnight. INTERNATIONAL.

This restaurant, the best in the port, is directly on the harbor in full view of the hundreds of strolling pedestrians. You can dine inside, but you might have more fun at one of the dozens of outdoor tables. The only hints of upper-crust status are immaculate napery, well-disciplined waiters, and discreet twinkle of expensive jewelry among the blue jeans or formal attire of the fashionable clientele. An armada of private yachts bobs at anchor a few feet away. The cuisine, although good, seems secondary to the see-and-be-seen set that hangs out here. Meals might include crêpes stuffed with chunks of lobster and crayfish, hake and small clams served in a Basque-inspired green sauce, fillet of duck's breast with green peppercorns or orange sauce, and a wide assortment of desserts.

6 Marbella

37 miles (59.5km) W of Málaga, 28 miles (45km) W of Torremolinos, 50 miles (80.5km) E of Gibraltar, 47 miles (76km) E of Algeciras, 373 miles (600.5km) S of Madrid

Although it's packed with tourists and only slightly less popular than Torremolinos, Marbella is still the nicest resort along the Costa del Sol, with some of the region's best upscale resorts coexisting with budget hotels. Despite the hordes, Marbella remains what it has always been, a pleasant Andalusian town at the foot of the Sierra Blanca. Traces of its past survive in its palatial town hall, medieval ruins, and ancient Moorish walls. Marbella's most charming area is the **old quarter,** with narrow cobblestoned streets and Arab houses, centered on the Plaza de los Naranjos.

The biggest attractions in Marbella, however, are **El Fuerte** and **La Fontanilla,** the two main beaches. There are other, more secluded beaches, but you need your own transportation to get there.

A long-ago visitor, Queen Isabella, was said to have exclaimed *"¡Que mar tan bello!"* ("What a beautiful sea!"), and the name stuck.

ESSENTIALS

GETTING THERE   Twenty buses run between Málaga and Marbella daily. Three buses each come from Madrid and Barcelona. The bus station is located on the outskirts of Marbella on avenida Trapiche, a 5-minute ride from the center of town.

If you're driving, Marbella is the first major resort as you head east on the N-340/E-15 from **Algeciras.**

Marbella

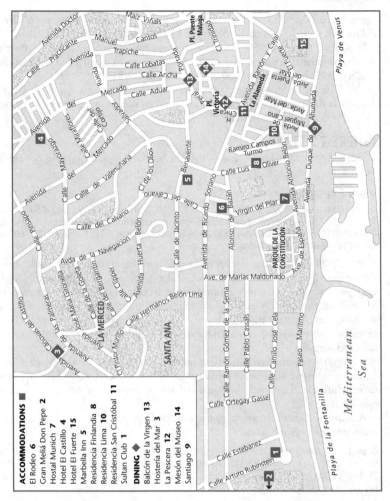

ACCOMMODATIONS ■
El Rodeo **6**
Gran Meliá Don Pepe **2**
Hostal Munich **7**
Hotel El Castillo **4**
Hotel El Fuerte **15**
Marbella Inn **5**
Residencia Finlandia **8**
Residencia Lima **10**
Residencia San Cristóbal **11**
Sultan Club **1**

DINING ◆
Balcón de la Virgen **13**
Hostería del Mar **3**
La Pescera **12**
Mesón del Museo **14**
Santiago **9**

VISITOR INFORMATION The **tourist information office** at Glorieta de la Fontanilla, s/n (☎ **95-277-14-42**), is open Monday to Friday 9:30am to 8pm, Saturday 9:30am to 2pm. Another tourist office with the same hours is on Plaza de los Naranjos (☎ **95-282-35-50**).

SHOPPING

Some other Andalusian village may inspire you to buy handcrafts (particularly pottery, wood carvings, or wrought iron), but Marbella's international glamour might just incite so much insecurity about your wardrobe that you'll want to rush out to accessorize. Should you suddenly feel underdressed, head for the old town. The cornucopia of fashion outlets includes, among many top European designers, every Hollywood starlet's favorite emporium, **Versace,** in the Centro Commercial Benabola, 8, Puerto Banús (☎ **95-281-02-96**).

If art is your passion, tour the art galleries that pepper the town. You'll spot high-rolling investors picking up contemporary treasures as part of a holiday shopping spree. Two of Marbella's most appealing art galleries lie in the old town: the **Galleria d'Arte Van Gestel,** Plaza de los Naranjos, 11 (☎ **95-277-48-19**), and **Galleria H,** calle 3D (☎ **95-281-12-60**). And if your search for fine art carries over to **Puerto Banús,** consider an overview of the contemporary artwork displayed at the **Sammer Gallery,** Jardines del Puerto, Local 3-A (☎ **95-281-29-95**).

On Saturday morning, forget the shops and head with the locals to **Nueva Andalucía flea market.** Everything is likely to be on sale, from Spanish leather goods to local pottery and embroideries.

WHERE TO STAY

Because the setting is ideal, some of the best hotels along the Costa del Sol are in Marbella.

VERY EXPENSIVE

Coral Beach. Carretera Cádiz, km 176, 29600 Marbella. ☎ **952-82-45-00.** Fax 952-82-62-57. www.hotelcoralbeach.com. E-mail: reservas@hotelcoralbeach.com. 170 units. A/C MINIBAR TV TEL. 32,000 ptas. ($192) double; 62,000 ptas. ($372) suite. AE, DC, MC, V. Closed Nov–Mar 15. Free parking.

Built in 1990, this four-star hotel is half a mile from Puerto Banús and 2 miles from the center of Marbella. A member of the Occidental Hotel chain, it represents a modern style of Mediterranean architecture, with a subtropical interior evoking the days of Moorish occupation with its fountains, patios, and plants. Strikingly contemporary, the hotel complex leads down to a sandy beach. The rooms are spacious and both tastefully and comfortably furnished, often with Moorish elements. They open onto balconies with views of the sea or gardens.

Dining/Diversions: For lunch right on the seashore, head for the **Beach Club.** Dinner is more formal, served in a gracious room with wicker chairs and potted palms called **Florencia.** The hotel also has a bar area where live entertainment is often presented.

Amenities: Two pools, gym, sauna, whirlpool, massage, beauty salon, 24-hour room service, concierge, laundry.

Gran Meliá Don Pepe. José Melia, 29600 Marbella. ☎ **800/336-3542** in the U.S., or 95-277-03-00. Fax 95-277-99-54. www.solmelia.es. 185 units. A/C MINIBAR TV TEL. 28,000–45,000 ptas. ($168–$270) double; 95,000–110,000 ptas. ($570–$660) suite. AE, MC, V. Free parking.

The Gran Meliá Don Pepe occupies 6 acres of prize-winning tropical gardens and lawns between the coastal road and the sea. It sits on a broad artificial beach set back from the road. The good-sized, well-furnished guest rooms, with tiled bathrooms and wall-to-wall carpeting, face either the sea or the Sierra Blanca range. The latter rooms can be noisy. The facilities are so vast that you could spend a week here and not use them all.

Dining/Diversions: The hotel has lounges, bars, and a restaurant, **La Farola,** serving international cuisine.

Amenities: 24-hour room service, laundry and valet, baby-sitting, three swimming pools, tennis courts, health club, Swedish sauna, Turkish baths, boutiques, yacht harbor, golf course.

✪ **Marbella Club.** Bulevar Príncipe Alfonso von Hohenlohe, s/n, 29600 Marbella. ☎ **800/ 448-8355** in the U.S., or 95-282-22-11. Fax 95-282-98-84. www.marbellaclub.com. E-mail: hotel@marbellaclub.com. 130 units. A/C MINIBAR TV TEL. 28,000–55,500 ptas. ($168–$333) double; 42,000–80,000 ptas. ($252–$480) suite; 120,000–250,000 ptas. ($720–$1,500) bungalow. AE, DC, MC, V. Free parking.

Until a few equally chic hotels were built along the Costa del Sol, the snobbish Marbella Club reigned almost without equal as the exclusive hangout of aristocrats and tycoons. Established in 1954, the resort sprawls over a landscaped property that slopes from its roadside reception area down to the beach. Composed of small, ecologically conscious clusters of garden pavilions, bungalows, and small-scale annexes (none higher than two stories), the Marbella Club has some of the loveliest gardens along the coast.

Hotel rooms along the Costa del Sol don't come much better than these varied and spacious choices, often with canopy beds and always with luxurious mattresses. Most of the bathrooms are roomy and clad in marble, with dual basins, plush towels, and hair dryers. Rooms have private balconies or terraces. The clientele is discreet, international, elegant, and appreciative of the resort's small scale and superb service.

Dining/Diversions: The Marbella Club Restaurant moves from indoor shelter to an outdoor terrace according to the season (see "Where to Dine," below). There's a bar in the garden nearby.

Amenities: 24-hour room service, baby-sitting, laundry and valet, massage, concierge, two swimming pools, beach with a lunch restaurant. Golf can be arranged nearby. Tennis courts at the Marbella Club's twin resort, Puente Romano, 2 minutes away.

✪ **Puente Romano.** Carretera de Cádiz, km 177, 29600 Marbella. ☎ **800/448-8355** in the U.S., or 95-282-09-00. Fax 95-277-57-66. www.puenteromano.com. E-mail: hotel@puenteromano.com. 226 units. A/C MINIBAR TV TEL. 29,000–55,000 ptas. ($174–$330) double; 35,000–300,000 ptas. ($210–$1,800) suite. AE, DC, MC, V. Free parking. By car, take the E-15 2½ miles (4km) west of Marbella.

This hotel was originally built as a cluster of vacation apartments, which influenced the attention to detail and the landscaping that surrounds it. In the early 1970s, a group of entrepreneurs transformed it into one of the most unusual hotels in the south of Spain. Although it sits close to the frenetic coastal highway midway between Marbella and Puerto Banús, and some critics have dismissed it as "more flash than class," it still enjoys a loyal following.

Inside the complex, arbor-covered walkways pass cascading water, masses of vines, and a subtropical garden. Each of the spacious Andalusian-Mediterranean–style accommodations is a showcase of fabrics, accessories, and furniture. Units have marble bathrooms, electronic safes, and semi-sheltered balconies with flowers.

Dining/Diversions: Three of the indoor/outdoor bars and restaurants overlook a terra-cotta patio bordered at one end by the stones of a reconstructed Roman bridge, the only one of its kind in southern Spain. There is also a nightclub.

Amenities: 24-hour room service, laundry and valet, baby-sitting, freeform swimming pool with edges bordered by trees, vines, and a waterfall. Sandy beach with watersports, tennis courts, boutiques, gym, sauna, solarium.

Sultan Club. Avenida Arturo Rubenstein, 29600 Marbella. ☎ **952-66-15-62.** Fax 952-66-55-58. www.entrebares.com. 76 units. A/C MINIBAR TV TEL. 34,000 ptas. ($204) double; 41,000 ptas. ($246) suite. AE, DC, MC, V. Parking: 850 ptas. ($5.10).

On the outskirts of Marbella a 10-minute drive from the center, this hotel is in the residential district of Milla de Oro, just a short walk to the beach. This five-story apartment hotel opened in 1997 and is meant to evoke luxury living like the sultans of old enjoyed. The Mediterranean architecture includes large balconies and white-painted walls. Moorish elements show up in a lobby decorated with colorful tiles and ceilings, and in wooden panels with Arabian carvings. The interior brims with tropical plants and fountains. You're not quite in Granada's Alhambra but at least you can enjoy the mock. The apartments contain one or two bedrooms, each with balconies, a small dining room, and a fully equipped kitchen, along with such extras as spacious bathrooms and a private safe.

Dining/Diversions: There are two restaurants, one with a menu of Andalusian and international dishes, and the other offering buffet meals. The hotel also has a bar.

Amenities: Two outdoor swimming pools (one with a bar), a heated indoor pool, concierge, room service until midnight, a gym, whirlpool, sauna, children's playroom, massage salon.

EXPENSIVE

Andalucía Plaza. Urbanización Nueva Andalucía, 29660 Apartado, 21, Nueva Andalucía Marbella. ☎ **95-281-20-00.** Fax 95-281-09-96. 410 units. A/C MINIBAR TV TEL. 22,500–30,000 ptas. ($135–$180) double; from 32,000 ptas. ($192) suite. Rates include American breakfast. AE, DC, MC, V.

Built in 1972, the six-story Andalucía Plaza resort complex is showing its age, but it offers more of a Spanish atmosphere than some other pricey choices. On the mountain side of the coastal road between Marbella and Torremolinos, it consists of twin buildings linked by a reception lounge and formal gardens. On the sea side is the hotel's beach club. The public rooms are spacious and decorated in bold, brassy style. The equally luxurious guest rooms have spacious bathrooms and reproduction Castilian furnishings, including twin beds with firm mattresses. The beach is on a 300-plus-foot strip of sand, 4 miles (6.5km) west of the center of Marbella and a 10-minute walk from Puerto Banús.

Dining/Diversions: The **Córdoba** restaurant serves upscale international meals. **Bar Toledo,** primarily a watering hole, offers light snacks and suppers. There's also a casino (see "Marbella After Dark," below).

Amenities: Limited room service, concierge, baby-sitting, laundry. Beach club with adjacent sunbathing terraces, tennis courts, two saunas, indoor and outdoor swimming pools, golf course. At the 1,000-berth marina ½ mile away, the hotel can arrange charters for deep-sea fishing.

Don Carlos. Jardines de las Goldondrinas, Carretera de Cádiz, km 192, 29600 Marbella. ☎ **95-283-11-40.** Fax 95-283-34-29. www.hotel-doncarlos.com. E-mail: resa@hotel-doncarlos.com. 240 units. A/C MINIBAR TV TEL. 20,000–44,500 ptas. ($120–$267) double; 35,000–129,000 ptas. ($210–$774) suite. AE, DC, MC, V. Free parking.

One of the most dramatic hotels on the coast, the Don Carlos rises on a set of angled stilts above a pine forest. Between the hotel and its manicured beach, the best in Marbella, are 130 acres of award-winning gardens. With cascades of water and thousands of subtropical plants, they require a full-time staff of 22 gardeners. There's far more to this hotel than the modern tower that rises above the eastern edge of Marbella. Its low-lying terraces and elegant eating and drinking facilities attract high-powered conferences from throughout Europe, as well as diners from along the Mediterranean coast. Each of the roomy accommodations has lacquered furniture, and bathrooms boast honey-colored marble and hair dryers. The hotel also has the finest tennis in the area.

Dining/Diversions: You can dine beside an oversized swimming pool or in **La Pergola,** where ficus and potted palms decorate hundreds of lattices. A hideaway, **Los Naranjos,** has a sun-flooded atrium and live piano music. Meals, including elaborate buffets, are served here and in the beachfront cabana. The most popular bar has English-inspired decor, a panoramic sea view, plenty of sofas, a dance floor, and a musical trio.

Amenities: 24-hour room service, laundry, baby-sitting, three swimming pools, use of five golf courses nearby, saunas, gym, 11 tennis courts, watersports (extra charge).

Le Méridien Los Monteros. Carretera de Cádiz, km 187, 29600 Marbella. ☎ **95-277-17-00.** Fax 95-282-58-46. www.monteros.com. E-mail: hotel@monteros.com. 168 units. A/C MINIBAR TV TEL. 31,500–47,100 ptas. ($189–$282.60) double; 39,000–59,100 ptas. ($234–$354.60) suite. Rates include breakfast. AE, DC, MC, V. Free parking.

Los Monteros, 400 yards from a beach and 4 miles (6.5km) east of Marbella, is one of the most tasteful resort complexes along the Costa del Sol. Situated between the coastal road and its private beach, it attracts those seeking intimacy and luxury. Its many small public rooms are Andalusian and Japanese in style. There are salons with open fireplaces, a library, and terraces. The midsized guest rooms are brightly decorated, with light-colored lacquered furniture, large marble bathrooms, and terraces.

Dining/Diversions: The hotel has a bar and four restaurants that open onto flower-filled patios, gardens, and fountains. **Grill El Corzo** is one of the finest grill rooms along the coast. There's soft, romantic music nightly, and the cuisine is a pleasing combination of French and Spanish.

Amenities: 24-hour room service, baby-sitting, laundry and valet. Guests have free use of the nearby 18-hole golf course, Río Real. Several pools, beach club with heated indoor pool, 10 tennis courts, five squash courts, riding club and school, fully equipped gymnasium with sauna, massage, and whirlpool.

MODERATE

Hotel Artola Golf. Carretera de Cádiz, km 194, 29600 Marbella. ☎ **952-83-13-90.** Fax 952-83-04-50. 29 units. TV TEL. 14,800 ptas. ($88.80) double; 18,000 ptas. ($108) suite. AE, DC, MC, V. Free parking.

Between Fuengirola and Marbella, half a mile from the beach, this charming two-story structure was originally an old staging post for travelers en route to Gibraltar. In the 1970s it was converted into an inn with a 9-hole golf course. The architecture is typically Andalusian, with a stucco and wood facade under a terra-cotta roof. A garden and patio surround the building. The interior decoration has retained some of its historical aura with colorful tiles plus decorative wooden wall panels and beams. The midsized bedrooms are comfortably furnished and tastefully decorated, often with Moorish details. All the units have balconies and fully equipped bathrooms. There is no restaurant, but the hotel does have a cafeteria and tapas bar with red brick arches, an ideal place to relax. Other amenities include a pool in the tropical garden.

Hotel El Fuerte. Avenida del Fuerte, s/n, 29600 Marbella. ☎ **800/448-8355** in the U.S., or 95-286-15-00. Fax 95-282-44-11. www.fuertehotels.com. E-mail: elfuerte@fuertehotels.com. 263 units. A/C MINIBAR TV TEL. 18,500–25,000 ptas. ($111–$150) double; from 35,000 ptas. ($210) suite. Rates include breakfast. AE, DC, MC, V. Parking 800 ptas. ($4.80).

This is the largest and most recommendable hotel in the center of Marbella. Directly on the waterfront, El Fuerte has a balconied angular facade and consists of two six-story towers. Originally built in 1957, it was last renovated in 1994. Catering to a sedate clientele of northern Europeans, it offers a palm-fringed swimming pool across the street from a sheltered lagoon and a wide-open beach. The hotel also has a handful of terraces, some shaded by flowering arbors, which are perfect hideaways for a quiet drink. The midsized guest rooms are contemporary, with piped-in music, terraces, and twin beds with firm mattresses.

The hotel has a coffee shop and a restaurant. The facilities for leisure activities include the pool, a floodlit tennis court, a health club, and a squash court.

Hotel Rincón Andaluz. Carretera Cádiz km. 173, 29660 Nueva Andalucia, Marbella. ☎ **952-81-15-17.** Fax 952-81-41-80. 227 units. A/C MINIBAR TV TEL. 18,000–26,500 ptas. ($108–$159) double; 24,000–30,000 ptas. ($144–$180) suite. Rates include breakfast. AE, DC, MC, V. Free parking.

In a stylish area of Marbella close to Puerto Banús, this four-star hotel is built to evoke a *pueblo andaluz* or little Andalusian village. Lying in a park, the low-level rustic-style buildings form an ideal retreat. The large bedrooms are tastefully decorated and fully equipped, and all the units have at least a small living room (larger in the suites). The ground-floor bedrooms have direct access to the gardens; the others open onto balconies. There are two swimming pools, a beauty center, a children's club, a hair dresser, boutiques, laundry service, and a desk for organizing activities. There are two restaurants (one specializing in seafood, one an informal cafeteria), plus two bars, one a part of the hotel's beach club.

Marbella Inn. Calle Jacinto Benavente, Bloque, 6, 29600 Marbella. ☎ **952-82-54-87.** Fax 952-82-54-87. 56 units. A/C TV TEL. 13,500 ptas. ($81) studio; 17,000 ptas. ($102) suite. AE, DC, MC, V. Parking 1,000 ptas. ($6).

The name of this hotel suggests a cozy inn. It is anything but. In operation since 1989, in the center of the old town 2 minutes from the beach, it is actually an eight-story apartment hotel. The severe modern facade is riddled with balconies, and the pristine interior has marble floors and lots of almost clinical white. The cheaper guest rooms are a bit small, although comfortably furnished; the larger ones have kitchens. Extras include a private safe. Everything is immaculately kept. The hotel's swimming pool overlooks the sea, and there is a small bar and cafeteria along with a sun terrace.

INEXPENSIVE

El Rodeo. Victor de la Serna, s/n, 29600 Marbella. ☎ **95-277-51-00.** Fax 95-282-33-20. 99 units. A/C TV TEL. 9,000–15,000 ptas. ($54–$90) double. AE, DC, MC, V.

Even though this modern hotel stands just off the main coastal road of Marbella, within walking distance of the bus station, the beach, and the old quarter, it is quiet and secluded. The facilities in the seven-story structure include a swimming pool, terrace, sunbathing area, solarium, and a newly renovated piano bar where many guests and locals gather. Elevators whisk you to the sunny, spacious second-floor lounges with country furnishings; there's also a bar with tropical bamboo chairs and tables. Continental breakfast is served in the cheerful breakfast room. The midsized guest rooms are functional, with several shuttered closets, lounge chairs, and white desks. The hotel is year-round; peak season and rates run June to October.

Hostal El Castillo. Plaza San Bernabé, 2, 29600 Marbella. ☎ **95-277-17-39.** 25 units. 5,000–5,500 ptas. ($30–$33) double. MC, V. Free parking.

At the foot of the castle in the narrow streets of the old town, this small hotel opens onto a minuscule triangular area used by the adjoining convent and school as a playground. There's a small, covered courtyard, and the simple second-floor guest rooms have only inner windows. The spartan rooms are scrubbed clean and have white-tile bathrooms. No morning meal is served, and only a little English is spoken.

Hostal Munich. Calle Virgen del Pilar, 5, 29600 Marbella. ☎ **95-277-24-61.** 18 units. TEL. 4,800 ptas. ($28.80) double. No credit cards.

Set back from the street and shielded by banana and palm trees, this unassuming three-story lodging is a short walk from the water and the bus station. Some guest rooms have balconies; all are simply furnished but well kept, with good beds. The homey lounge is warm and inviting.

Residencia Finlandia. Finlandia, 12, 29600 Marbella. ☎/fax **95-277-07-00.** 11 units. TEL. 6,200–7,500 ptas. ($37.20–$45) double. AE, DC, MC, V.

The slightly tattered 1970s Finlandia is only a 5-minute walk from the center of the old quarter and 200 yards (182m) from the beach. In the Huerta Grande, a peaceful residential section, it's clean and well run. Guest rooms are spacious but rather plain, with contemporary furnishings. Your bed will be turned down at night.

Residencia Lima. Antonio Belón, 2, 29600 Marbella. ☎ **95-277-05-00.** Fax 95-286-30-91. 64 units. TEL. 13,000 ptas. ($78) double. AE, DC, MC, V.

Tucked away in a residential area right off the N-340/E-15 and near the sea, the Lima is more secluded than other hotels nearby. The modern eight-story structure features plain guest rooms with Spanish provincial furnishings and private balconies.

Residencia San Cristóbal. Ramón y Cajal, 3, 29600 Marbella. ☎ **95-277-12-50.** Fax 95-286-20-44. 97 units. A/C TV TEL. 10,000–12,000 ptas. ($60–$72) double. MC, V.

In the heart of Marbella 200 yards from the beach, this 1960s five-story hotel has long, wide terraces and flower-filled window boxes. The small, somewhat tattered guest rooms have walnut headboards, individual overhead reading lamps, and room dividers separating the comfortable beds from the small living areas. Each room has a private terrace—a perfect spot to enjoy breakfast.

A NEARBY PLACE TO STAY

✪ **El Castillo de Monda.** Monda 29110, Málaga. ☎ **095-245-71-42.** Fax 095-245-73-36. www.costadelsol.spa.es/hotel/monda. E-mail: monda@spa.es. 28 units. A/C TV TEL. 16,000–30,000 ptas. ($96–$180) double. AE, MC, V. Free parking.

In 1996 a group of entrepreneurs transformed the crumbling ruins of an 8th-century Moorish fortress into the showplace of a sleepy village 7½ miles (12km) north of Marbella. El Castillo de Monda adds a soothing note of calm and quiet to a region that grows glitzier by the year. The ceiling beams came from a demolished convent in Barcelona, and the thousands of glazed tiles from the outfit that's been manufacturing the historically accurate accessories for the restoration of the Alhambra. Guest rooms are beautifully maintained, generous in size, and traditionally furnished. The restaurant occupies a cool, high-ceilinged dining room.

WHERE TO DINE
EXPENSIVE

✪ **El Portalón.** Carretera de Cádiz, km 178. ☎ **95-282-78-80.** Reservations recommended. Main courses 2,200–3,200 ptas. ($13.20–$19.20). AE, DC, MC, V. Daily 1pm–12:30am. SPANISH/INTERNATIONAL.

This is one of Marbella's most stylish, sophisticated dining enclaves. Its staff is one of the most urbane and international in town, serving clients from throughout Europe with aplomb and obvious pride. Menu selections include some time-honored Iberian dishes, such as suckling lamb and pig slowly roasted in a wood-burning oven, grilled meats, and impeccably fresh fish imported daily. Calorie-conscious, low-fat dishes are like those you might expect to find at a California spa—lobster salad, grilled sea bass with a julienne of fresh vegetables, and entrecôte of beef with fresh vegetables and red wine sauce (served on the side if you request). A recent addition is an art deco style pavilion called the "vinoteca," which serves an excellent selection of wines from all over Spain.

The restaurant is about a mile west of town beside the road leading to Puerto Banús, across from the beach and adjacent to the entrance to the Marbella Club.

✪ **La Hacienda.** Urbanización Hacienda Las Chapas, Carretera de Cádiz, km 193. ☎ **95-283-12-67.** Reservations recommended. Main courses 2,200–3,500 ptas. ($13.20–$21); fixed-price menu 7,000 ptas. ($42). AE, DC, MC, V. Summer, daily 8:30–midnight; winter, Wed–Sun 1–3:30pm and 8:30–11:30pm. Closed Nov 15–Dec 20. INTERNATIONAL.

La Hacienda, a tranquil choice 8 miles (13km) east of Marbella, serves some of the best food along the Costa del Sol. In cooler months you can dine in the rustic tavern before an open fireplace. In fair weather, meals are served on a patio partially encircled by open Romanesque arches. The chef is likely to offer foie gras with lentils, lobster croquettes (as an appetizer), and roast guinea hen with cream, minced raisins, and port. The flavorful food is prepared with the freshest ingredients and presented with style. An iced soufflé finishes the meal nicely.

✪ **Marbella Club Restaurant.** In the Marbella Club, Bulevar Príncipe Alfonso von Hohenlohe, s/n. ☎ **95-282-22-11.** Reservations recommended. Lunch buffet 8,000 ptas. ($48); dinner main courses 3,500–8,500 ptas. ($21–$51). AE, DC, MC, V. Open year-round 1:30–4pm; summer daily 9pm–12:30am; winter daily 8:30–11:30pm. INTERNATIONAL.

Our favorite meals here have been whenever the staff moves the action onto the terrace in good weather. Lunch is traditionally an overflowing buffet served in the beach club. Dinners are served amid blooming flowers, flickering candles, and the strains of live music—perhaps a Spanish classical guitarist, a small chamber orchestra playing 19th-century classics, or a South American vocalist. Menu items, inspired by European cuisines, change with the season. You might begin with beef carpaccio or lobster salad delicately flavored with olive oil. Specialties include one of the coast's most savory paellas, and tender veal cutlets from Ávila.

Villa Tiberio. Carretera de Cádiz, km 178.5. ☎ **95-277-17-99.** Reservations recommended. Main courses 1,800–3,200 ptas. ($10.80–$19.20). AE, DC, V. Mon–Sat 7:30pm–12:30am. ITALIAN.

Villa Tiberio's proximity to the upscale Marbella Club (a 5-minute walk away) ensures a flow of visitors from that elite hotel. In what was originally built as a private villa during the 1960s, it serves the most innovative Italian food in the region, and attracts the many north European expatriates living nearby. Appetizers include thinly sliced smoked beef with fresh avocados and oil-and-lemon dressing, and *fungi fantasia* (a large wild mushroom stuffed with seafood and lobster sauce). Especially tempting is the *pappardelle alla Sandro*—large flat noodles studded with chunks of lobster, tomato, and garlic. Other versions come with cream, caviar, and smoked salmon. Main dishes include sea bass with cherry tomatoes, basil, and black truffle oil; duck baked with orange and Curaçao liqueur; and *osso bucco* (braised veal shanks).

MODERATE

Balcón de la Virgen. Remedios, 2. ☎ **95-277-60-62.** Reservations recommended. Main courses 975–2,500 ptas. ($5.85–$15). AE, DC, MC, V. Daily 7pm–midnight. Closed Tues Nov–May. SPANISH.

In an antique house in the historic core of old Marbella, this restaurant is named after a 200-year-old statue of the Virgin that adorns a wall niche surrounded by flowers and vines. A short walk from the Plaza de los Naranjos, it's popular because of its good food, attentive service, and reasonable prices. The menu—derived mostly from Andalusia and, to a lesser degree, the rest of Spain—features Málaga-style meat stew, baked hake with olive oil and herbs, marinated swordfish, roasted pork, and grilled fillets of beef.

Hostería del Mar. Cánovas del Castillo, 1. ☎ **95-277-02-18.** Reservations recommended. Main courses 1,600–2,200 ptas. ($9.60–$13.20). AE, MC, V. Mon–Sat 1–4pm and 7:30pm–midnight. MEDITERRANEAN.

Consistently good, the Hostería del Mar's cuisine is known throughout the region for being both delicious and unusual. In the dining room you'll sit beneath decorative ceiling beams and eat off hand-painted porcelain. In summer there are tables on a tree-shaded patio. Delectable meals might include calves' sweetbreads in mustard sauce, clams stuffed with ratatouille, roast duck with roasted-fig-and-cassis sauce, Catalán-style shrimp with chicken, and a casserole of monkfish with white wine sauce, clams, and fresh asparagus. The sumptuous desserts include a selection of cold soufflés. The restaurant is at the beginning of the bypass road that runs beside the Hotel Meliá Don Pepe.

Mesón del Museo. Plaza de los Naranjos, 11. ☎ **95-282-56-23.** Reservations recommended. Main courses 2,250–5,000 ptas. ($13.50–$30). AE, DC, MC, V. Mon–Sat 7:30–11pm. Closed Sun Dec 23–May 1, July–Aug. FRENCH.

Mesón del Museo is on the upper floor of an 18th-century building that contains one of the oldest art and antique galleries in Marbella. The dining room is decorated with Iberian accessories and Andalusian antiques. A new chef has recently shifted the menu's focus to French dishes. Try delicious fried Camembert, followed by fillet of sole stuffed with langostines in a champagne sauce. A selection of French and Spanish wines complements the menu.

Santiago. Duque de Ahumada, 5. ☎ **952-77-00-78.** Reservations required. Main courses 900–12,000 ptas. ($5.40–$72). AE, DC, MC, V. Daily 1–5pm and 7pm–1am. SEAFOOD/INTERNATIONAL.

As soon as you enter Santiago, the bubbling lobster tanks give you an idea of what's in store. The decor, the tapas bar near the entrance, and the summertime patio together with fresh fish dishes make this one of the most popular eating places in town. On our most recent visit, we arrived early for lunch and found that the mussels for our mussels marinara were just being delivered. Savory fish soup is well prepared and well spiced. Follow with a generous serving of sole in champagne or grilled or sautéed turbot. On a hot day, the seafood salad, garnished with lobster, shrimp, and crabmeat and served with a sharp sauce, is especially recommended. In addition to seafood, the menu offers many meat dishes. For dessert, we suggest a serving of Manchego cheese.

INEXPENSIVE

La Pescera. Plaza de la Victoria, s/n. ☎ **952-77-80-54.** Reservations recommended Thurs–Sat night. Main courses 900–3,360 ptas. ($5.40–$20.15). AE, DC, MC, V. Daily 1–3:30pm and 7:30–11pm. ANDALUSIAN.

Beside a historic square in the heart of old Marbella, this is a bustling, well-managed restaurant. It has twin dining rooms, a loyal local clientele, and a reputation for serving well-prepared fish and seafood. There's a worthwhile roster of meat dishes, such as grilled steaks and pork fillets, but most diners opt for fish. Specialties range from working-class dishes such as *bacalao frito* (fried codfish) to more esoteric versions of shellfish and crayfish—kept alive and healthy until the last moment in big on-site holding tanks.

A NEARBY PLACE TO DINE

El Refugio. Carretera de Ojén, C-337. ☎ **95-288-10-00.** Main courses 750–2,250 ptas. ($4.50–$13.50); fixed-price menu 3,750 ptas. ($22.50). AE, DC, MC, V. Daily 1–4pm and 8–10:30pm. SPANISH.

If the summer heat has you down, retreat to the Sierra Blanca just outside Ojén. Motorists come here to enjoy both the mountain scenery and the cuisine at

A Marbella *Tasca* Crawl

To really rub shoulders with the locals and experience a taste of Spain, take your meals in the tapas bars. You can eat well in most places, and Marbella boasts more hole-in-the-wall tapas bars than virtually any other resort town in southern Spain. Even if you set out with a specific place in mind, you'll likely be waylaid en route by a newer, older, bigger, smaller, brighter, or more mysterious joint you want to try. That's half the fun.

Prices and hours are remarkably consistent: The coffeehouse that opens at 7am will switch to wine and tapas when the first patron asks for it (sometimes shortly after breakfast), then continue through the day dispensing wine, sherry, and, more recently, bottles of beer to accompany the food. On average, tapas cost 250 to 1,000 ptas. ($1.50 to $6) per *ración,* but some foreign visitors configure them into *platos combinados.*

Tapas served along the Costa del Sol are principally Andalusian in origin, with an emphasis on seafood. The most famous plate, *fritura malagueña,* consists of fried fish based on the catch of the day. Sometimes *ajo blanco,* a garlicky local version of gazpacho, is served, especially in summer. Fried squid or octopus is another favorite, as are little Spanish-style herb-flavored meatballs. *Tortilla* (an omelet, often with potatoes) is the most popular egg dish. Other well-known tapas selections include pungent tuna, grilled shrimp, *piquillos rellenos* (red peppers stuffed with fish), *bacalao* (salt cod), and mushrooms sautéed in olive oil and garlic.

Tapas bars line many of the narrow streets of Marbella's historic core, with rich pickings around La calle del Perral and, to a somewhat lesser extent, calle Miguel Cana. In August especially, when you want to escape wall-to-wall people and the heat and noise of the old town, head for one of the shoreline restaurants and tapas bars called *chiringuitos.* All serve local specialties, and you can order a full meal, a snack, tapas, or a drink. Our favorites include **Los Sardinales,** Playa de los Alicates (☎ **952-83-70-12**), which serves some of the best sangría in the area. You might return later for a succulent seafood dinner. Another favorite hangout is **Chiringuito La Pesquera,** Marbellamar Playa (☎ **952-77-03-38**), where you can order a plate of fresh grilled sardines.

El Refugio, up in the hills 9 miles (14.5km) north of Marbella. Meals are served in a rustic dining room, with an open terrace for drinks. Specialties include spicy regional sausages, roast pork, roast chicken, grilled steaks, and local pheasant in season. The lounge has an open fireplace and comfortable armchairs.

MARBELLA AFTER DARK

There's more international wealth hanging out in the watering holes of Marbella, and a wider choice of glam (or pseudoglam) discos, than you'll find virtually anywhere else in the south of Spain. Foremost among these is the chic **Oliva Valer,** in the Hotel Puente Romano, C.N. 340, km 177 (☎ **95-282-88-61**). A worthwhile, very stylish alternative, is **O! Marbella,** C.N. 340, km 192 (☎ **95-283-54-77**), adjacent to the Hotel Don Carlos. For a nightclub with a bit of Italian flair, consider **La Notte,** "Las Lomas" de Marbella Club (☎ **95-282-60-24**), where people often come for an after-dinner drink from the upscale restaurant La Méridiana, nearby.

If you're in the heart of historic Marbella, enjoy a night in the *bodegas* and taverns of the old town. One that's conveniently located adjacent to one of the town's widest thoroughfares is **Bodega La Venensia,** Pasoa del Duca Ahumada (no phone). Its wide choice of sherries, wines, and tapas welcomes lots of chattering patrons. In the old town, you might check out **Bar El Estrecha,** calle San Lazaro, s/n (no phone), or its nearby competitor, **Bar Mattutte,** in the calle Arte, s/n (no phone). One with a particularly large assortment of wines is **Vinacoteca,** in the calle Peral, s/n (no phone). Dedicated to the inventory of as many Spanish wines as possible, it provides the opportunity to compare the vintages produced in the surrounding region.

The best flamenco club in town is **Ana María,** Plaza del Santo Cristo, 4–5 (☎ **95-277-56-46**). We think it's simultaneously the most authentic place and the safest for foreign visitors with a limited knowledge of Spanish. The long, often-crowded bar area sells tapas, wine, sherry, and a selection of more international libations. On the stage, singers, dancers, and musicians perform flamenco and popular songs. This is late-night entertainment—the doors don't open till 11pm, and the crowd really gets going between midnight and 4am. It's closed November to March. Drink prices start at 1,500 ptas. ($9); the cover charge is 2,800 ptas. ($16.80).

Six miles (10km) west of Marbella, near Puerto Banús, **Casino Marbella,** Andalucía Plaza, Urbanización Nueva Andalucía (☎ **95-281-40-00**), is on the lobby level of the Andalucía Plaza resort complex (see "Where to Stay," above). Unlike the region's competing casino, at the Hotel Torrequebrada, the Marbella does not offer cabaret or nightclub shows. The focus is on gambling, and mobs of visitors from northern Europe engage with abandon. Individual games include French and American roulette, blackjack, punto y banco, craps, and chemin de fer.

You can dine before or after gambling in the Casino Restaurant, a few steps above the gaming floor. Meals go for about 3,800 ptas. ($22.80) per person, including wine. Jackets are not required for men, but shorts and T-shirts will be frowned on. The casino is open daily 8pm to 4 or 5am. There's a cover charge of 600 ptas. ($3.60); a passport is required for admission.

7 Fuengirola & Los Boliches

20 miles (32km) W of Málaga, 64½ miles (104km) E of Algeciras, 356½ miles (574km) S of Madrid

The fishing towns of Fuengirola and Los Boliches lie halfway between the more famous resorts of Marbella and Torremolinos. A promenade along the water stretches some 2½ miles (4km). Less developed Los Boliches is just half a mile from Fuengirola.

These towns don't have the facilities or drama of Torremolinos and Marbella. Except for two major luxury hotels, however, Fuengirola and Los Boliches are cheaper, and that has attracted hordes of budget-conscious European tourists.

The ruins of **San Isidro Castle** can be seen from a promontory overlooking the sea. The **Santa Amalja, Carvajal,** and **Las Gaviotas beaches** are broad, clean, and sandy. Everybody goes to the big **flea market** at Fuengirola on Tuesdays.

ESSENTIALS

GETTING THERE   From Torremolinos, take the Metro at La Nogalera station (under the RENFE sign). Trains depart every 30 minutes. The fare is 250 ptas. ($1.50).

Fuengirola is on the main Costa del Sol bus route from either Algeciras in the west or Málaga in the east.

If you're driving from Marbella, take the N-340/E-15 east from Marbella.

VISITOR INFORMATION   The **tourist information office,** avenida Jesús Santos Rein, 6 ☎ **95-246-74-57**), is open Monday to Friday 9:30am to 2pm and 5 to 8pm, Saturday 10am to 1pm.

WHERE TO STAY

✪ **Byblos Andaluz.** Urbanización Mijas Golf, 29640 Fuengirola. ☎ **95-247-30-50.** Fax 95-247-67-83. 144 units. A/C MINIBAR TV TEL. 30,000–42,000 ptas. ($180–$252) double; from 45,000 ptas. ($270) suite. AE, DC, MC, V. Free parking.

This luxurious resort with excellent recreational facilities is in a golf club setting 3 miles (5km) from Fuengirola and 6 miles (10km) from the beach. The grounds contain a white minaret, Moorish arches, tile-adorned walls, and an orange-tree patio inspired by the Alhambra grounds. The large rooms and suites are elegantly and individually designed and furnished in Roman, Arabic, Andalusian, and rustic styles. Private sun terraces and lavish bathrooms add to the comfort.

Dining: Choices include **Le Nailhac,** serving French food, and **El Andaluz,** with regional and Spanish specialties.

Amenities: The resort's two 18-hole Robert Trent Jones golf courses, tennis courts, spa facilities, gymnasium, and two outdoor swimming pools bask in the Andalusian sunshine. The health spa is in a handsome classic structure, Mijas Thalasso Palace. Laundry and valet, baby-sitting, room service, sauna, solarium, three indoor pools.

Florida. Paseo Marítimo, s/n, 29640 Fuengirola. ☎ **95-247-61-00.** Fax 95-258-15-29. 116 units. TV TEL. 10,000–12,500 ptas. ($60–$75) double. AE, DC, MC, V.

In the semitropical garden in front of the Florida, guests can enjoy refreshments under a wide, vine-covered pergola. During the summer there is live music and flamenco shows. Most of the small guest rooms have balconies overlooking the sea or mountains, although furnishings and decor are a bit bleak and severe. The floors are tile, and plastic furniture abounds, particularly in the lounge. It's a 10-minute walk from the train station.

Las Pirámides. Miguel Marquez, 29640 Fuengirola. ☎ **95-247-06-00.** Fax 95-258-32-97. www.costadelsol.spa.es/hotel/piramide/index.htm. E-mail: piramides@vnet.es. 316 units. A/C MINIBAR TV TEL. 15,000–22,500 ptas. ($90–$135) double; 20,000–25,000 ptas. ($120–$150) suite. Rates include breakfast. AE, MC, V. Parking 1,000 ptas. ($6).

This resort, a favorite of northern Europeans and tour groups, consists of two 10-story towers capped with pyramidal roofs. It's a citylike compound about 50 yards (45.5m) from the beach, with just about every kind of diversion: flamenco shows on the large patio, a cozy bar and lounge, traditionally furnished sitting rooms, a coffee shop, a poolside bar, and a gallery of boutiques and tourist facilities, such as car-rental agencies. All the good-sized guest rooms have slick modern styling, as well as terraces. There is room service, laundry/valet services, and baby-sitting.

WHERE TO DINE

Casa Vieja. Avenida de Los Boliches, 27, Fuengirola. ☎ **95-258-38-30.** Reservations recommended. Fixed-price 4-course menu 3,000 ptas. ($18). MC, V. Tues–Sat 7:30–10:45pm (last orders). FRENCH.

Inside the thick stone walls of a cottage built in the 1870s for a local fisherman, this restaurant is on the main street of Los Boliches, a short walk east of the center of Fuengirola. It recently underwent extensive renovations, gaining a covered garden for year-round outside dining as well as a blues and jazz bar. New owners David (who can help you select a wine) and Bernard have gone to great lengths to create a soft, romantic ambience. The extensive menu contains one sumptuous option after another. For starters, try warm goat cheese salad with honey vinaigrette or sea bass and salmon terrine. Follow with beef *carbonnades falmandes*, fish duo with white butter sauce, or pork fillet with caramelized mustard sauce. For desserts, don't pass up the signature chocolate fondant.

Don Pé. De la Cruz, 17 (off the avenida Ramón y Cajal), Fuengirola. ☎ **95-247-83-51.** Reservations recommended. Main courses 1,500–3,000 ptas. ($9–$18). V. Mon–Sat 7pm–midnight. CONTINENTAL.

In hot weather, Don Pé patrons dine in a courtyard where the roof can be adjusted to allow in light and air. In cold weather, a fire on the hearth illuminates the heavy ceiling beams and rustic accessories. The menu features a selection of game dishes, including médaillons of venison, roast fillet of wild boar, and duck with orange sauce. The ingredients are imported from the forests and plains of Andalusia.

El Paso. Calle Francisco Cano, 39, Los Boliches. ☎ **95-247-92-95.** Reservations recommended. Main courses 1,500–2,500 ptas. ($9–$15). MC, V. Daily 7pm–midnight (12:30am in summer). MEXICAN.

This 150-year-old building was originally the hamlet's largest plant for the canning of the local fleet's catch of sardines. Today, the stonework has been reconfigured with splashing fountains and decorative tiles into the resort's premier Mexican restaurant. You can order from a wide selection of Mexican beers and tequilas at the long and convivial bar area, or head into either of two dining rooms for such New World specialties as *chimichangas, tortillas, burritos, frijoles, fajitas,* and *guacamole.* Any of the barbecued meats make a savory main course.

La Cazuela. Calle Miguel Márquez, 8, Fuengirola. ☎ **95-247-46-34.** Reservations recommended. Main courses 1,200–2,200 ptas. ($7.20–$13.20). MC, V. Daily 6:30–11:30pm. SPANISH/INTERNATIONAL.

South of the center of Fuengirola at the edge of the road leading off to Marbella, this cozy restaurant has flourished since the 1970s. Its longtime owner, Francisco Calle, outfits his dining rooms with hand-painted, Spanish-style porcelain. The house specialty is a tender chicken Kiev, which fans cite as even better than the tasty fillets of grilled beef, grilled prawns with garlic, homemade pâtés, and crayfish. A worthy beginning for any meal is the cheese crêpes.

La Langosta. Calle Francisco Cano, 1, Los Boliches. ☎ **95-247-50-49.** Main courses 1,500–3,500 ptas. ($9–$21); fixed-price menus 1,500–2,200 ptas. ($9–$13.20). AE, DC, MC, V. Mon–Sat 7pm–midnight. Closed Dec–Jan. SPANISH/SEAFOOD.

Just a stone's throw from Fuengirola, La Langosta is one of the most-recommended restaurants in the area. The stylish two-story art deco dining room is a welcome relief from the ever-present Iberian rustic style of so many other restaurants in the region. The menu features a variety of seafood (it is just 2 blocks from the beach), as well as Spanish dishes that include *gazpacho Andaluz* and prawns *al ajillo* (in olive oil and garlic). Lobster is prepared thermidor style or virtually any way you want; among the beef offerings is an especially succulent version of chateaubriand. The staff seems particularly well trained and helpful.

8 Mijas

18½ miles (30km) W of Málaga, 363 miles (584.5km) S of Madrid

Just 5 miles (8km) north of coastal road N-340/E-15, this village is known as "White Mijas" because of its marble-white Andalusian-style houses. Mijas is at the foot of a mountain range near the turnoff to Fuengirola, and from its lofty height—1,476 feet (450m) above sea level—you get a panoramic view of the Mediterranean.

Celts, Phoenicians, and Moors preceded today's intrepid tourists to Mijas. The town itself, rather than a specific monument, is the attraction. The easiest way to get around its cobblestoned streets is to rent a burro taxi. If you consider Mijas overrun with souvenir shops, head for the park at the top of Cuesta de la Villa, where you'll see the ruins of a **Moorish fortress** dating from 833. If you're in town for a fiesta, you'll be attending events in the country's only square bullring (a bullsquare?).

There's frequent bus service to Mijas from the terminal at Fuengirola, 30 minutes away. To drive from Fuengirola, take the Mijas road north.

WHERE TO STAY

✪ **Hotel Mijas.** Urbanización Tamisa, 2, 29650 Mijas. ☎ **95-248-58-00.** Fax 95-248-58-25. 103 units. TV TEL. 13,500–15,500 ptas. ($81–$93) double; 28,000–30,000 ptas. ($168–$180) suite. AE, DC, MC, V. Free parking.

One of the most charming hotels on the Costa del Sol was built in the 1970s on steeply sloping land in the center of town. This four-story, Andalusian-inspired block of white walls, wrought-iron accents, and flowering terraces is sun flooded and comfortable throughout. There are sweeping views over the Mediterranean from most of the public areas and the tiny but still comfortable guest rooms. The staff is tactful and hardworking. There's a tavern and a lounge that has live music on some evenings. The hotel has tennis courts, a swimming pool, sauna, gymnasium, boutique, facilities for lawn bowling, a hairdresser, and a barber. There is no elevator.

WHERE TO DINE

Club El Padrastro. Paseo del Compás, 22. ☎ **95-248-50-00.** Reservations recommended. Main courses 1,500–3,200 ptas. ($9–$19.20); fixed-price menus 1,800–8,000 ptas. ($10.80–$48). AE, DC, MC, V. Daily 11am–11pm. INTERNATIONAL.

Part of the fun of dining at the town's best restaurant is getting there. You go to the cliff side of town and, if you're athletic, walk up 77 steps; if you're not, take the elevator to the highest point. El Padrastro serves international cuisine on its covered terraces with panoramic views of the coast. You can choose whether to eat inexpensively (stick with the regional dishes) or elaborately (break the bank and go for the chateaubriand with a bottle of the best Spanish champagne).

9 Torremolinos

9 miles (14.5km) W of Málaga, 76 miles (122km) E of Algeciras, 353 miles (568km) S of Madrid

This Mediterranean beach resort is the most famous in Spain. It's known as a melting pot for international visitors, mostly Europeans and Americans. Many relax here after a whirlwind tour of Europe—the living is easy, the people are fun, and there are no historical monuments to visit. Once a sleepy fishing village, Torremolinos has been engulfed in a cluster of cement-walled resort hotels. Prices are on the rise, but it remains one of Europe's vacation bargains.

ESSENTIALS

GETTING THERE   The nearby **Málaga** airport serves Torremolinos, and frequent trains also run from the terminal at Málaga. For train information, call ☎ **95-238-57-64.** Buses run frequently between Málaga and Torremolinos; call ☎ **95-238-24-19** for schedules.

If you're driving, take the N-340/E-15 west from Málaga or the N-340/E-15 east from Marbella.

VISITOR INFORMATION   The **tourist information office** is at Plaza de las Comunidades Autónomas (☎ **95-237-19-09**). It's open daily 8am to 3pm.

WHERE TO STAY
EXPENSIVE

Hotel Tropicana. Calle Tropico, 29620 Torremolinos.   ☎ **952-38-66-00.** Fax 952-38-05-68. www.costadelsol.spa.es/hotel/tropicana. 84 units. A/C MINIBAR TV TEL. 22,000 ptas. ($132) double. Rates include buffet breakfast. AE, DC, MC, V. Free parking.

Half a mile from Torremolinos on the beach, this hotel has operated successfully for 4 decades. In an architectural style typical of the Costa del Sol, it presents a balconied facade to the world with bamboo and palm trees. Management prides itself on the friendly atmosphere and service offered, and the interior decor reflects the bright, breezy atmosphere of the place. The reception area is graced with tropical plants, wicker chairs, and a marble floor; the midsized to spacious bedrooms are well furnished with sea views.

Dining: The hotel restaurant, **Mango,** is known for its barbecues.

Amenities: A pool, laundry, and games room, plus limited room service until 5pm. The portion of the beach running across the hotel's length is reserved for guests and has a beach bar.

Meliá Costa del Sol. Paseo Marítimo, 11, 29620 Torremolinos. ☎ **800/336-3542** in the U.S., or 95-238-66-77. Fax 95-238-64-17. www.solmelia.es. E-mail: melia.costa.sol@solmelia.com. 540 units. A/C TV TEL. 12,840–22,470 ptas. ($77.05–$134.80) double; 21,830–47,615 ptas. ($131–$285.70) suite. AE, DC, MC, V. Free parking.

There are two Meliá hotels in Torremolinos, both operated by the popular Spanish hotel chain. This one is more centrally located; the other Meliá is more luxurious. The midsized guest rooms here are modern and well maintained, and each has a firm mattress, safe, and tiled bathroom. However, the hotel is popular with package-tour groups, so you may not feel a part of things if you're here alone.

Dining/Diversions: The hotel food, although competently prepared, is not the reason to stay here. It includes the usual array of Spanish and regional dishes, plus dinner buffets and a health food menu. Once a week there's a free flamenco show for guests, and on the other 6 nights a pianist entertains dancing couples.

Amenities: Swimming pool, thalassotherapy center (for medicinal seawater treatments), shopping arcade, hairdresser.

Meliá Torremolinos. Carlota Alessandri, 109, 29620 Torremolinos. ☎ **800/336-3542** in the U.S., or 95-238-05-00. Fax 95-238-05-38. E-mail: melia.torremolinos@solmelia.es. 281 units. A/C TV TEL. 16,100–21,275 ptas. ($96.60–$127.65) double; from 27,600 ptas. ($165.60) suite. AE, DC, MC, V. Closed Nov–Mar. Free parking.

This is the more luxurious of the two Meliá hotels at the resort, but farther removed from the center. This hotel has deliberately lowered its official rank from five stars to four, which means you can enjoy the better amenities and service at lower prices. The six-story hotel, which stands in its own gardens, is on the western outskirts of town on the road to Cádiz. Guest rooms range from small to spacious. Many contain minibars; all have marble bathrooms and are well furnished and maintained.

Dining/Diversions: The hotel serves standard cuisine and has a number of bars. Flamenco shows are occasionally presented.

Amenities: Swimming pool, tennis courts, room service (breakfast only).

Sol Elite Don Pablo. Paseo Marítimo, s/n, 29620 Torremolinos. ☎ **95-238-38-88.** Fax 95-238-37-83. 443 units. A/C MINIBAR TV TEL. 15,500–23,000 ptas. ($93–$138) double. Rates include buffet breakfast. AE, DC, MC, V.

One of the most desirable hotels in Torremolinos, Don Pablo is in a modern building a minute from the beach, surrounded by its own garden and playground areas. The surprise is the glamorous interior, which borrows heavily from Moorish palaces and medieval castle themes. Arched-tile arcades have splashing fountains, and the grand staircase features niches with life-size stone statues of nude figures. The comfortably furnished guest rooms have sea-view terraces, and bathrooms have hair dryers and tub-and-shower combos.

Dining/Diversions: The buffet-only restaurant offers some of the most generous spreads along the coast. They include both Andalusian specialties and international dishes. Several places serve drinks. The full day and night entertainment program includes dancing at night to a live band and a disco.

Amenities: Fitness classes.

MODERATE

Hotel Cervantes. Calle las Mercedes, s/n, 29620 Torremolinos. ☎ **95-238-40-33.** Fax 95-238-48-57. E-mail: hotel-cervantes@spa.es. 410 units. A/C TV TEL. 12,700–18,700 ptas. ($76–$112) double. Rates include breakfast. Full board 5,600 ptas. ($33.60) per person. AE, DC, MC, V.

The four-star Cervantes is a 7-minute walk from the beach. It has a garden and is adjacent to a maze of patios and narrow streets of boutiques and open-air cafes. The self-contained facilities include a sun terrace, a sauna, massage, two pools (one covered and heated), hairdressers, a gift shop, a TV and video lounge, a card room, and games, such as billiards, table tennis, and darts. The guest rooms have modern furniture, piped-in music, safes, TVs, and spacious terraces; many have balconies with views of the sea.

Also on the premises are a restaurant, a bar with live music and entertainment, and a coffee shop. In midsummer this hotel is likely to be booked with tour groups from northern Europe.

Hotel Isabel. Paseo Marítimo, 97, Playa del Lido, 29620 Torremolinos. ☎ **952-38-17-44.** Fax 952-38-11-98. E-mail: hotelisabel@arrakis.es. 40 units. A/C TV TEL. 12,000 ptas. ($72) double. Rates include breakfast buffet. AE, DC, MC, V. Closed Dec–Feb. Parking 750 ptas. ($4.50).

In the tourist zone of the city overlooking the beach, this modern hotel lacks character or charm, but offers much comfort and is a mecca for sun-worshippers and party animals. Once an apartment hotel, it has spacious bedrooms with a modest white wall decor, oak furnishings, and fully equipped bathrooms. All units open onto balconies with sea view. In addition to a bar and cafeteria, there is an outdoor swimming pool, a small garden, a billiard room, laundry, and limited room service offered until 11pm.

Hotel Las Palomas. Carmen Montes, 1, 29620 Torremolinos. ☎ **95-238-50-00.** Fax 95-238-64-66. 300 units. TEL. 8,500–12,500 ptas. ($51–$75) double. AE, DC, MC, V.

Built at the height of Torremolinos's construction boom (1968), this well-managed hotel is one of the town's most attractive, surrounded by carefully tended gardens. Located near the coastal road, it's a 1-minute walk from the beach and a 10-minute walk south of the center of town. It has Andalusian decor in the public and guest rooms, and a clientele of repeat visitors who hail mostly from France, Belgium, and Holland. Each of the midsized rooms has a private balcony, a tiled bathroom, and furniture inspired by southern Spain. There's no air-conditioning, but many guests compensate by opening windows and balcony doors to catch the sea breezes. The hotel boasts a sauna, three swimming pools (one reserved for children), entertainment throughout the day and early evening, a handful of shops, a hairdresser, and an unending series of lunch and dinner buffets.

Sidi Lago Rojo. Miami, 1, 29620 Torremolinos. ☎ **95-238-76-66.** Fax 95-238-08-91. 144 units. A/C TV TEL. 12,500–15,000 ptas. ($75–$90) double. AE, DC, MC, V.

In the heart of the fishing village of La Carihuela, Sidi Lago Rojo is its finest place to stay. It stands only 150 feet from the beach and has its own gardens, swimming pool, sunbathing terraces, and refreshment bar. Built in the 1970s and renovated at least once since then, it offers studio-style guest rooms (doubles only), tastefully decorated with contemporary Spanish furnishings and tile bathrooms. All rooms have terraces with views; some have minibars. In the late evening there is disco dancing. The hotel has a good restaurant.

Sol Don Pedro. Avenida del Lido, 29620 Torremolinos. ☎ **952-38-69-00.** Fax 952-38-69-35. www.solmelia.es. E-mail: sol.don.pedro@solmelia.es. 295 units. A/C TV TEL. 8,800–14,000 ptas. ($52.80–$84) double. Rates include buffet breakfast. AE, DC, MC, V. Free parking.

Less than a mile from the center on the resort on the Paseo Maritimo, this modern four-story hotel opens onto Bajondillo Beach. In operation since the early '80s, it is a virtual hotel factory with a huge room count. When it's booked (which is the case in summer), the hotel is like a massive beehive of sun-worshippers from all over Europe and America. Constructed with arches in a style both classic and modern, it has a plain, functional, and not unpleasant interior. Bedrooms are midsized to spacious, have wooden fittings and small balconies, and come with well-maintained bathrooms. The hotel restaurant offers buffet meals three times a day, and there is a poolside snack bar plus a lounge bar. In addition, there are two outdoor swimming pools, a children's play area, a garden, a games room, two tennis courts, room service, laundry, and a concierge.

INEXPENSIVE

Hostal Los Jazmines. Avenida de Lido, 6, 29620 Torremolinos. ☎ **95-238-50-33.** Fax 95-237-27-02. 85 units. TV TEL. 5,800–7,000 ptas. ($34.80–$42) double. AE, DC, MC, V.

Located on one of the best beaches in Torremolinos, Hostal Los Jazmines faces a plaza at the foot of the shady avenida del Lido. Sun-seekers will find it replete with terraces, lawns, and an irregularly shaped swimming pool. The small guest rooms (all doubles) seem a bit impersonal, but they have their own little balconies and compact bathrooms. From here it's a good hike up the hill to the town center. Meals are served alfresco or inside an appealing dining room.

Hotel El Pozo. Casablanca, 2, 29620 Torremolinos. ☎ **95-238-06-22.** Fax 95-238-71-17. 28 units. TV TEL. 6,800–9,000 ptas. ($40.80–$54) double. DC, MC, V.

This hotel isn't for light sleepers—it's in one of the liveliest sections of town, a short walk from the train station. It's usually filled with budget travelers, including many students from northern Europe. The lobby-level bar has professional French billiards, heavy Spanish furniture, and a view of a small courtyard. From your window or terrace you can view the promenades below. The small guest rooms are furnished in a simple, functional style—nothing special, but the price is right.

✪ **Miami.** Aladino, 14, 29620 Torremolinos. ☎ **95-238-52-55.** 27 units. TEL. 5,000–8,500 ptas. ($30–$51) double. No credit cards. Free parking.

The Miami, near the Carihuela section, might remind you of a 1920s Hollywood movie star's home. High walls and private gardens surround the swimming pool. Fuchsia and bougainvillea climb over the rear patio's arches and a tile terrace is used for sunbathing and refreshments. The country-style living room contains a walk-in fireplace, and the compact guest rooms are furnished in traditional and comfortable style. Each has a balcony. Breakfast is the only meal served.

NEARBY PLACES TO STAY

Where Torremolinos ends and Benalmádena-Costa to the west begins is hard to say. Benalmádena-Costa is packed with hotels, restaurants, and tourist facilities.

✪ **Hotel Torrequebrada.** Carretera de Cádiz, km 220, 29630 Benalmádena. ☎ **95-244-60-00.** Fax 95-244-27-46. www.torrequebrada.com. E-mail: reservas@torrequebrada.com. 340 units. A/C MINIBAR TV TEL. 38,000–42,000 ptas. ($228–$252) double; from 45,000 ptas. ($270) suite. Rates include breakfast. Discounts for stays of 5 or more days. AE, DC, MC, V. Free parking.

In the late 1980s this became one of the largest five-star luxury hotels along the Costa del Sol. Three miles (5km) west of Torremolinos, it opens onto its own beach and offers a wide range of facilities and attractions. You'll find one of the largest casinos in Europe and a world-class golf course. The hotel is furnished in muted Mediterranean colors, with both antique and modern furniture. The spacious, handsomely furnished rooms occupy two 11-story towers. All accommodations have large terraces with sea views, plus private safes and tiled bathrooms with plush towels.

Dining/Diversions: A restaurant, **Café Royal,** overlooks the gardens and the sea; it enjoys a five-fork rating for its international cuisine. Adjacent to the garden, and overlooking the sea, the **Pavillion** has buffet and cafeteria service throughout the day. A flamenco show is presented at 10:30pm Tuesday to Saturday. Guests gather in a piano bar at night or roll the dice in the huge casino.

Amenities: Outstanding golf course, pools, health club, tennis courts, nine levels of underground parking, room service, laundry and dry cleaning, baby-sitting.

Tritón. Avenida António Machado, 29, 29491 Benalmádena-Costa. ☎ **95-244-32-40.** Fax 95-244-26-49. E-mail: hotel_triton@spa.es. 373 units. A/C MINIBAR TV TEL. 18,500–26,000 ptas. ($111–$156) double; from 42,000 ptas. ($252) suite. Rates include breakfast. AE, DC, MC, V. Free parking.

Less than 2 miles (3km) north of Torremolinos, the Tritón is a Miami Beach–style resort colony in front of the Benalmádena-Costa marina. The high-rise stack of midsized guest rooms includes an impressive pool and garden area. Surrounding the swimming pool are subtropical trees and vegetation, plus thatched sunshade umbrellas. All the rooms have well-maintained tile bathrooms and wide windows opening onto balconies. Among the public rooms are multilevel lounges and two wood-paneled bars.

Dining/Diversions: There is a main restaurant, with a three-tiered display of hors d'oeuvres, fruits, and desserts; a barbecue grill; and a luncheon terrace. A bar features a live orchestra in July and August.

Amenities: Swimming pool, Swedish sauna, tennis courts, room service, dry cleaning and laundry, concierge.

WHERE TO DINE

The cuisine in Torremolinos is more American and continental European than Andalusian. The hotels often serve elaborate four-course meals, but you might want to sample more casual local offerings. A good spot to try is the food court **La Nogalera,** the major gathering place between the coast road and the beach. Head down the calle del Cauce to this compound of modern whitewashed Andalusian buildings. Open to pedestrian traffic only, it's a maze of passageways, courtyards, and patios for eating and drinking. You can find anything from sandwiches to Belgian waffles to scrambled eggs to pizza.

AT LA NOGALERA

El Gato Viudo. La Nogalera, 11. ☎ **95-238-51-29.** Main courses 900–2,200 ptas. ($5.40–$13.20). AE, DC, MC, V. May–Oct, daily 1–4pm and 6–11:30pm; Nov–Apr, Thurs–Tues 1–4pm and 6–11:30pm. SPANISH.

El Gato Viudo has been a tradition with local diners for almost 40 years. Simple and amiable, this old-fashioned tavern occupies the street level and cellar of a building off calle San Miguel and offers sidewalk seating. The menu includes such good dishes as grilled fish; marinated hake; roasted pork, steak, and veal; calamari with spicy tomato sauce; grilled shrimp; and shellfish or fish soup. The atmosphere is informal, and the staff is accustomed to coping with diners from virtually everywhere.

Golden Curry. Calle Casablanca, 6, La Nogalera, Bloque 6. ☎ **95-237-48-55.** Main courses 750–1,200 ptas. ($4.50–$7.20). AE, DC, MC, V. Sat–Thurs 1–4pm; daily 7pm–midnight. INDIAN.

One floor above street level, in the commercial heart of Torremolinos, this restaurant specializes in traditional Mogul dishes of India, adapted and altered to suit British tastes. The two chefs and the Calcutta-born owner all worked in Indian restaurants in London before emigrating to Spain, and many patrons are Brits on holiday. Menu items include chicken Madras, chicken in onion sauce, lamb slow-cooked in spices and served with lentils, and succulent prawns. The best of the vegetarian offerings arrive as an array of small dishes.

AT LA CARIHUELA

If you want to get away from the high-rises and honky-tonks, head to nearby La Carihuela. In the old fishing village on the western outskirts of Torremolinos you'll find some of the best bargain restaurants. Walk down a hill toward the sea to reach the village.

Casa Juan. Calle Mar, 14, La Carihuela. ☎ **95-238-41-06.** Reservations recommended. Main courses 900–2,800 ptas. ($5.40–$16.80). AE, DC, MC, V. Tues–Sun 12:30–4:30pm and 8pm–midnight. Closed Dec. SEAFOOD.

In a modern-looking building in old-timey La Carihuela, this seafood restaurant is about a mile west of Torremolinos's center. Menu items include selections from a lavish display of fish and shellfish prominently positioned near the entrance. You might try *mariscada de mariscos* (shellfish), a fried platter of mixed fish, codfish, kebabs of meat or fish, or paella. Of special note is *lubina a la sal*—sea bass packed in layers of roughly textured salt, broken open at your table and deboned in front of you. When the restaurant gets busy, as it often does, the staff is likely to rush around hysterically—something many local fans think adds to its charm.

El Roqueo. Calle del Carmen, 35, La Carihuela. ☎ **95-238-49-46.** Reservations recommended. Main courses 1,500–2,500 ptas. ($9–$15); fixed-price menu 1,500 ptas. ($9). AE, DC, MC, V. Wed–Mon noon–4pm and 8pm–midnight. Closed Nov 1–Dec 8. SEAFOOD.

Established in 1975 in the heart of the village, El Roqueo is the perfect place for a seafood dinner near the sea. Begin with savory *sopa de mariscos* (shellfish soup). Then try a specialty of the chef, a delectable fish baked in rock salt; you can also order grilled sea bass or shrimp. Top everything off with soothing caramel custard. Some of the more expensive fish courses are priced by the gram, so order carefully.

AT PLAYAMAR

El Vietnam del Sur. Playamar, Bloque, 9. ☎ **95-238-67-37.** Reservations required. Main courses 850–1,500 ptas. ($5.10–$9). AE, DC, MC, V. Sat–Sun and holidays 1–4pm; daily 7pm–1am. Closed Jan. VIETNAMESE.

The inexpensive food here is good for sharing. Begin with spring rolls, served with mint and a spicy dipping sauce. The chef's specials include fried stuffed chicken wings and beef with rice noodles. The wine list is short and moderately priced. The restaurant has an outdoor dining terrace.

At Los Alamos

Frutos. Carretera de Cádiz, km 228, Urbanización Los Alamos. ☎ **95-238-14-50.** Reservations recommended. Main courses 900–2,500 ptas. ($5.40–$15); fixed-price menu 2,200 ptas. ($13.20). AE, DC, MC, V. Daily 1–4pm; Mon–Sat 8pm–midnight. SPANISH/INTERNATIONAL.

Malagueños frequent this place in droves, drawn by good old-style cooking. The cuisine is Spanish with a vengeance, portions are large, and service is hectic. Diners enjoy the day's catch, perhaps *rape* (monkfish), angler fish, or the increasingly rare *mero* (grouper). Also available are garlic-studded leg of lamb and oxtail prepared in a savory ragout. Frutos is next to the Los Alamos service station, 1¼ miles (2km) from the town center.

At Benalmádena-Costa

✪ **Mar de Alborán.** Alay, 5. ☎ **95-244-64-27.** Reservations recommended. Main courses 1,500–3,300 ptas. ($9–$19.80); *menú del día* 4,500 ptas. ($27). AE, DC, MC, V. Sun and Tues–Fri 1:30–4pm; Tues–Sat 8:30–midnight. Closed Dec 22–Jan 22. BASQUE/ANDALUSIAN.

This restaurant's elegantly airy decor seems appropriate for its location near the sea, just a short walk from the resort's Puerto Marina. It serves the specialties of both Andalusia and the Basque region of northern Spain. Menu items change with the season. They might include cold terrine of leeks; Basque *piperadda* in puff pastry; *piquillos rellenos* (red peppers stuffed with pulverized fish in a sweet pepper sauce), or *bacalao* (salt cod) "Club Ranero," served with garlic and red-pepper cream sauce. You can also try *kokotxas,* the Basque national dish of hake cheeks in green sauce with clams; anglerfish with prawns; or foie gras served with sweet Málaga wine and raisins. The restaurant's game dishes (available in season) are renowned. Dessert might be a frothy version of peach mousse with puree of fruit and dark-chocolate sauce.

TORREMOLINOS AFTER DARK

Torremolinos has more nightlife than any other spot along the Costa del Sol. The earliest action is always at the bars, which are lively most of the night, serving drinks and tapas. Sometimes it seems that in Torremolinos there are more bars than people, so you shouldn't have trouble finding one you like. Note that some bars are open during the day as well.

We like the **Bar Central,** Plaza Andalucía, Bloque, 1 (☎ **95-238-27-60**), for coffee, brandy, beer, cocktails, limited sandwiches, and pastries, served indoors or on a large, French-style covered terrace. It's a good spot to meet people. Prices begin at 175 ptas. ($1.05) for a beer, 450 ptas. ($2.70) for a hard drink. Open Monday to Saturday 8am to 11:30pm (later in summer).

In the very center of town, **Joyeria Kohinoor,** San Miguel, 30 (☎ **95-238-32-40**), is for bullfight aficionados. Kegs of beer, stools, and the terrace in the main shopping street make it a perfect spot for a before-dinner sherry or an after-dinner beer. Prices for table service begin at 350 ptas. ($2.10) for a pitcher of beer or sangría. Open daily 10am to 10pm in winter, 10am to 2am in summer.

La Bodega, San Miguel, 40 (☎ **95-238-73-37**), relies on its colorful clientele and the quality of its tapas to draw customers, who seem to rank this place above the dozens of other *tascas* in this popular tourist zone. You'll be fortunate to find space at one of the small tables because many consider the bar food plentiful enough for a satisfying lunch or dinner. Once you begin to order—platters of fried squid, pungent tuna, grilled shrimp, tiny brochettes of sole—you might not be able to stop. Most tapas cost 250 to 1,000 ptas. ($1.50 to $6). A beer costs 195 ptas. ($1.15), a hard drink at least 450 ptas. ($2.70). Open daily 12:30pm to midnight.

Ready to dance off all those tapas? **El Palladium,** Palma de Mallorca (☎ 95-238-42-89), a well-designed nightclub in the town center, is one of the most convivial in Torremolinos. Strobes, spotlights, and a sound system (described as loud and distortion-free) set the scene. There's even a swimming pool. Expect to pay 350 ptas. ($2.10) or more for a drink; cover is 1,000 ptas. ($6), including one drink after 11pm. Open 11pm to 6am.

Gay men and women from throughout northern Europe are almost always in residence in Torremolinos; if you want to meet some of them, consider a drink or two at **Abadia,** La Nogalera, 9 (no phone). Other options, all around La Nogalera, include **Contactos,** La Nogalera, 204 (no phone), which does not get busy till well after 10pm, and **Morbos,** La Nogalera, 113 (no phone), which is open till 5am. The most popular gay disco in town is the **Tension,** La Nogalera, 524 (no phone), which plays popular dance music for a very cruisy crowd.

One of the Costa del Sol's major casinos, **Casino Torrequebrada,** Carretera de Cádiz, Benalmádena-Costa (☎ 95-244-25-45), is on the lobby level of the Hotel Torrequebrada (see "Where to Stay," above). It has tables devoted to blackjack, chemin de fer, punto y banco, and two kinds of roulette. The casino is open daily 8am to 4am.The nightclub offers a flamenco show year-round, at 11pm on Thursday, Friday, and Saturday nights; in midsummer, there might be more glitz and more frequent shows (ask when you get there or call). Nightclub acts begin at 10:30pm (Spanish revue) and 11:30pm (Las Vegas revue). The restaurant is open nightly 8:30pm to 11pm. Casino admission is 600 ptas. ($3.60); with one drink, both shows, casino and cabaret/nightclub admission, it's 4,500 ptas. ($27); with dinner, it's 8,800 ptas. ($52.80). Bring your passport to be admitted.

10 Málaga

340 miles (547.5km) S of Madrid, 82 miles (132km) E of Algeciras

Málaga is a bustling commercial and residential center whose economy does not depend exclusively on tourism. Its chief attraction is the mild off-season climate. Summer can be sticky.

Málaga's most famous citizen was Pablo Picasso, born in 1881 at Plaza de la Merced, in the center of the city. The artist unfortunately left little of his spirit—and only a small selection of his work—in his birthplace.

ESSENTIALS

GETTING THERE   Travelers from North America must transfer for Málaga in Madrid or Barcelona. From within Europe, some airlines (including British Airways from London) offer nonstop flights to Málaga. **Iberia** has frequent service, and even more flights offered through its affiliate airlines, which include **Binter, Viva,** and **Aviaco.** Flights can be booked through Iberia's reservations line (☎ 800/772-4642 in the U.S. or 902-40-05-00 in Spain).

At least five trains a day serve Málaga from Madrid. The trip takes around 4 hours. Three trains a day connect the Andalusian city of Seville with Málaga, a 3-hour run. For ticket prices and rail information in Málaga, call RENFE (☎ 95-36-02-02).

Buses from all over Spain arrive at the terminal on the Paseo de los Tilos, behind the RENFE offices. Buses run to all the major Spanish cities, including Madrid (8 buses per day), Córdoba (5 per day), and Seville (10 per day). From Madrid, the trip is 7 hours; from Barcelona, 17 hours; from Valencia, 12 hours. Call ☎ 95-235-00-61 in Málaga for bus information.

From the resorts in the west (such as Torremolinos and Marbella), you can drive east along the N-340/E-15 to Málaga. If you're in the east at the end of the Costa del Sol (Almería), take the N-340/E-15 west to Málaga, with a stopover at Nerja.

VISITOR INFORMATION   The **tourist information office** is at Pasaje de Chinitas, 4 (☎ **95-221-34-45**). It's open Monday to Friday 9am to 1pm.

SPECIAL EVENTS   The most festive time in Málaga is the first week in August, when the city celebrates its reconquest by Ferdinand and Isabella in 1487. The big *feria* (fair) is an occasion for parades and bullfights. A major tree-shaded boulevard, **Paseo del Parque,** is transformed into a fairground featuring amusements and restaurants.

EXPLORING MÁLAGA

Unlike the rest of the Costa del Sol, Málaga has several historical sites of interest to the average visitor.

Alcazaba. Plaza de la Aduana, Alcazabilla. ☎ 95-221-60-05. Admission to museum 35 ptas. (20¢). Museum Tues–Fri 9:30am–1:30pm and 5–8pm; Sat 10am–1pm; Sun 10am–2pm. Bus: 4, 18, 19, or 24.

The remains of this ancient Moorish palace are within easy walking distance of the city center, off Paseo del Parque. Plenty of signs point the way up the hill. The fortress was erected in the 9th or 10th century, although there have been later additions and reconstructions. Ferdinand and Isabella stayed here when they reconquered the city. The Alcazaba now houses an archaeological museum, with exhibits of cultures ranging from Greek to Phoenician to Carthaginian. With government-planted orange trees and purple bougainvillea making the grounds even more beautiful, the view overlooking the city and the bay is among the most panoramic on the Costa del Sol.

Málaga Cathedral. Plaza Obispo. ☎ 95-221-59-17. Admission 200 ptas. ($1.20). Mon–Sat 10am–12:45pm and 4–6:30pm. Closed holidays. Bus: 14, 18, 19, or 24.

This 16th-century Renaissance cathedral in Málaga's center, built on the site of a great mosque, suffered damage during the Spanish Civil War. However, it remains vast and impressive, reflecting changing styles of interior architecture. Its most notable attributes are the richly ornamented choir stalls by Ortiz, Mena, and Michael. The cathedral has been declared a national monument.

Castillo de Gibralfaro. Cerro de Gibralfaro. Free admission. Daylight hours. Microbus: H, leaving hourly from cathedral.

On a hill overlooking Málaga and the Mediterranean are the ruins of an ancient Moorish castle-fortress of unknown origin. It is near the government-run parador, and might easily be tied in with a luncheon visit.

Warning: Do not walk to Gibralfaro Castle from town. Readers have reported muggings along the way, and the area around the castle is dangerous. Take the bus from the cathedral.

Museo de Bellas Artes. Calle San Agustín, 8. ☎ 95-221-83-82. Admission 200 ptas. ($1.20). Mon–Fri 10am–1:30pm and 4–7pm; Sat 10am–1:30pm. Bus: 4, 18, 19, or 24.

Behind the cathedral, this former Moorish palace houses a modest collection of paintings, including a gallery devoted to native son Pablo Picasso. It also displays works by Murillo, Ribera, and Morales, along with Andalusian antiques, mosaics, and sculptures.

Picasso House-Museum. Plaza de la Merced. ☎ 95-221-50-05. Free admission. Mon–Sat 10am–2pm and 5–8pm; Sun 11am–2pm.

A well-told tale concerns the birth of Picasso: In October 1891, when the artist was born, he was unable to draw breath until his uncle blew cigar smoke into his lungs.

Don't Be a Victim

Málaga has one of the highest crime rates in Spain. The most common complaint is purse snatching, with an estimated 75% of the crimes committed by juveniles. Stolen passports are also a problem. Keep your wits about you.

Whether this rather harsh entry into the world had any effect on his work is mere speculation. What cannot be denied is the effect he was to have on the world. He was born in a five-story building in the heart of Málaga's historic quarter; this is where he spent the first 17 months of his life. The house is now more of a museum, with about 200 works on display. The museum mounts monthly exhibitions featuring avant-garde movements from Picasso's time.

SHOPPING

The region around Málaga produces artfully rustic pottery, which makes a worthwhile souvenir. A handful of highly appealing outlets are scattered throughout the city's historic core. The best include **Almazul,** calle Beatas, 53 (☎ **95-221-28-43**); **Fina,** calle Coronel, 4 (no phone), on a small street near the calle San Juan; and **Los Artesanos,** Cister, 13 (☎ **95-260-45-44**). Outside the town limits, the most comprehensive collection of ceramics and pottery can be found at **La Vistillas,** Carretera Mijas, km 2 (☎ **95-45-13-63**), about 1¼ miles (2km) from Málaga's center.

WHERE TO STAY

For such a large city in a resort area, Málaga has a surprising lack of hotels. Book well in advance, especially if you want to stay in a parador.

EXPENSIVE

Hotel Larios. Calle Marqués de Larios, 2, 29005 Málaga. ☎ **952-22-22-00.** Fax 952-22-24-07. www.hotel-larios.com. E-mail: info@hotel-larios.com. 40 units. A/C MINIBAR TV TEL. 21,000 ptas. ($126) double; 28,000 ptas. ($168) suite. AE, DC, MC, V. Free parking.

On the main street of the old town, this four-star three-story hotel was constructed in an impressive art deco architectural style. It ranks just under the parador as the most desirable place to stay. The interior is contemporary and stylish, with a terrace opening onto a panoramic view of the city. The midsized bedrooms are decorated in a minimalist but stylish way. All have comfortable furnishings, including excellent mattresses, and the suites come with a whirlpool tub. Because of the popularity of the hotel, it is advised to book well in advance.

Dining/Diversions: The hotel restaurant is known for its formal service and good food, offering an array of both international and Andalusian specialties. Other drinking and dining facilities include a bar and a cafeteria for breakfast and light snacks.

Amenities: Room service until midnight, laundry, concierge.

Málaga Palacio. Cortina del Muelle, 1, 29015 Málaga. ☎ **95-222-51-00.** Fax 95-221-51-85. 230 units. A/C MINIBAR TV TEL. 17,500–22,000 ptas. ($105–$132) double; 29,000 ptas. ($174) suite. AE, DC, MC, V. Parking 1,000 ptas. ($6) nearby. Bus: 4, 18, 19, or 24.

The leading hotel in the town center, the Palacio opens onto a tree-lined esplanade near the cathedral and the harbor. The 1960s building was constructed flatiron style; it rises 15 stories and is crowned by an open-air swimming pool and refreshment bar. Most of the balconies offer views of the port, and down below you can see horses pulling turn-of-the-century carriages. The midsized guest rooms are traditionally furnished and have firm beds and tiled bathrooms. The street-floor lounges mix antiques with more modern furnishings.

Dining: There's no restaurant on-site, but many dining options lie within walking distance. A cafeteria serves breakfast.

Amenities: Room service (breakfast only), concierge, baby-sitting, hairdresser for women and men, boutiques, laundry and dry cleaning. Facilities for sports, including golf and tennis, are nearby.

Parador de Málaga-Gibralfaro. Monte Gibralfaro, 29016 Málaga. ☎ **95-222-19-02.** Fax 95-222-19-04. www.paradores.es. E-mail: gibralfaro@parador.es. 38 units. A/C MINIBAR TV TEL. 18,500–22,000 ptas. ($111–$132) double. AE, DC, MC, V. Free parking. Take the coastal road, Paseo de Reding, which becomes avenida de Pries and then Paseo de Sancha. Turn left onto Camino Nuevo and follow the small signs.

Restored in 1994, this is one of Spain's oldest, most tradition-laden paradors. It enjoys a scenic location high on a plateau near an old fortified castle. Overlooking the city and the Mediterranean, it has views of the bullring, mountains, and beaches. Originally a famous restaurant, the parador has been converted into a fine hotel with two dining rooms. The guest rooms have private entrances, living-room areas, and wide glass doors opening onto private sun terraces. The medium-size rooms are tastefully decorated with modern furnishings and reproductions of Spanish antiques.

Dining: A hotel restaurant serves adequate Spanish fare.

Amenities: Room service, concierge, currency exchange, swimming pool, laundry and dry cleaning.

Tryp Guadalmar. Urbanización Guadalmar, Carretera de Cádiz, km 238, 29080 Málaga. ☎ **95-223-17-03.** Fax 95-224-0385. www.tryp.es. E-mail: guadalmar@trypnet.com. 200 units. A/C MINIBAR TV TEL. 16,650–22,200 ptas. ($99.90–$133.20) double; 40,000 ptas. ($240) suite. Children under 12 half price in parents' room. AE, DC, MC, V. Free parking.

Drenched in sunlight, this nine-story modern hotel sits across from a private beach 2 miles (3km) west of the center of Málaga. It benefited from a radical renovation in 1996 and a takeover by the well-respected Tryp chain. Accommodations are spacious, airy, and simply furnished, and each room has a private sea-view balcony. You're likely to get heavy doses of families with children at this hotel. An air of anonymity prevails as the staff struggles with constant exposure to the comings and goings of large numbers of vacationers.

Dining/Diversions: A restaurant, **La Bodega,** has a view of the sea. For dancing, head for **La Corrida,** the hotel's bar, which features live music.

Amenities: Baby-sitting, laundry and dry cleaning, children's playground, indoor and outdoor pools.

MODERATE

Hotel Don Curro. Calle Sancha de Lara, 7, 29015 Málaga. ☎ **952-22-72-00.** Fax 952-21-59-46. 118 units. A/C MINIBAR TV TEL. 12,950 ptas. ($77.70) double; 16,625 ptas. ($99.75) suite. AE, DC, MC, V. Parking 1,350 ptas. ($8.10).

In central Málaga 10 minutes from the beach, this three-star hotel is one of the most traditional in town. In 1933 the Casa Curro opened here and received guests until 1965 when it was rebuilt and greatly expanded, although still operated by the same family. The hotel was renamed but its classic decor retained. The eight-story building has contrasting architectural styles, with an older lobby from 1933 and an added modern annex. The lobby is a cozy retreat with dark woods and a marble floor. The midsized bedrooms are more spartan, but still have grand comfort in the decor and furnishings. Amenities are restricted to a small buffet restaurant and limited room service until 11pm.

Hotel Los Naranjos. Paseo de Sancha, 35, 29016 Málaga. ☎ **95-222-43-19.** Fax 95-222-59-75. 41 units. A/C MINIBAR TV TEL. 16,500 ptas. ($99) double; 22,000 ptas. ($132) suite. AE, DC, MC, V. Parking 1,500 ptas. ($9). Bus: 11.

The well-run, well-maintained Los Naranjos is one of the more reasonably priced choices in the city. It's 1 mile from the heart of town on the eastern side of Málaga, past the Plaza de Toros (bullring), near the best beach in Málaga, the Baños del Carmen. The hotel offers midsized guest rooms in contemporary style. Some bathrooms have only showers, not tubs. The public rooms are decorated in typical Andalusian style, with colorful tiles and ornate wood carving. Breakfast (which costs extra) is the only meal served.

Parador Nacional del Golf. Carretera de Málaga, Apartado, 324, 29080 Torremolinos, Málaga. ☎ **95-238-12-55.** Fax 95-238-89-63. www.paradores.es. 60 units. A/C MINIBAR TV TEL. 18,000 ptas. ($108) double. AE, DC, MC, V. Free parking.

A tasteful resort hotel created by the Spanish government, this hacienda-style parador is flanked by a golf course on one side and the Mediterranean on another. It's less than 2 miles (3km) from the airport, 6½ miles (10.5km) from Málaga, and 2½ miles (4km) from Torremolinos. Each guest room has a private balcony with a view of the golfing greens, the circular swimming pool, or the water. Some units have whirlpool tubs. The furnishings are attractive, and the beds excellent. Long tile corridors lead to the air-conditioned public rooms: graciously furnished lounges, a bar, and a restaurant.

INEXPENSIVE

El Cenachero. Barroso, 5, 29001 Málaga. ☎ **95-222-40-88.** 14 units. TV. 5,800–6,500 ptas. ($34.80–$39) double. No credit cards. Bus: 15.

Opened in 1969, this modest little hotel is 5 blocks from the park near the harbor. The nicely carpeted guest rooms are simply and functionally furnished; half have showers, the rest have full bathrooms. No meals are served.

Hostal Residencia Carlos V. Cister, 10, 29015 Málaga. ☎ **95-221-51-20.** Fax 95-221-51-29. 50 units. TV TEL. 7,200–8,500 ptas. ($43.20–$51) double. AE, DC, MC, V. Parking 1,400 ptas. ($8.40). Bus: 15 from the rail station.

This hotel is in a central location near the cathedral, with an interesting facade decorated with wrought-iron balconies and *miradores* (viewing stations). The lobby is fairly dark, but this remains a reliable, conservative choice. An elevator will take you to your small room, furnished in a no-frills style, but well maintained.

Hostal Residencia Derby. San Juan de Díos, 1, 29015 Málaga. ☎ **95-222-13-01.** 17 units, 12 with bathroom. TEL. 4,200 ptas. ($25.20) double with sink; 4,800 ptas. ($28.80) double with bathroom. No credit cards. Bus: 7, 9, 12, 14, 15, 16, or 17.

The Derby is a real find. A fourth-floor boarding house, it's in the heart of town, on a main square directly north of the train station. Some of the rather basic, cramped rooms have excellent views of the Mediterranean and the port of Málaga. Most units have a shower, not a tub. No breakfast is served.

A LUXURIOUS PLACE TO STAY NEARBY

✪ **La Bobadilla.** Finca La Bobadilla, Apartado, 144, 18300 Loja (Granada). ☎ **958/ 32-18-61.** Fax 958/32-18-10. www.la-bobadilla.com. E-mail: info@la-bobadilla.com. 62 units. A/C MINIBAR TV TEL. 36,900–54,400 ptas. ($221.40–$326.40) double; from 62,600 ptas. ($375.60) suite. AE, DC, MC, V. Free parking. From the Málaga airport, follow signs toward Granada, but at km 175 continue through the village of Salinas. Take road marked SALINAS/RUTE; after 2 miles (3km), follow signposts for hotel to the entrance.

An hour's drive northeast of Málaga, La Bobadilla is the most luxurious retreat in southern Spain. It is a secluded oasis in the foothills of the Sierra Nevada near the town of Loja, which is 44 miles (71km) north of Málaga. La Bobadilla is a 13-mile (21km) drive from Loja.

The hotel complex is built like an Andalusian village, a cluster of whitewashed *casas* constructed around a tower and a white church. Every *casa* has a roof terrace and a balcony overlooking the olive-grove-studded district. Each sumptuous accommodation is individually designed, from the least expensive doubles to the most expensive King's Suite (which has plenty of room for bodyguards). The hotel caters to a pampered coterie of international guests, and the service is perhaps the finest in Spain.

The hotel village stands on a hillside, on 1,750 acres of private, unspoiled grounds. If you get bored in this lap of luxury, you can always drive to Granada, an hour away. Should you decide to marry your companion at the resort, the chapel has a 30-foot-high organ with 1,595 pipes.

Dining/Diversions: Even the king of Spain has dined at **La Finca,** which serves Spanish and international cuisine. **El Cortijo** specializes in regional cuisine. Concerts, featuring flamenco, are presented on Friday and Saturday nights.

Amenities: Laundry and valet, 24-hour room service, massage, baby-sitting; two tennis courts, horseback riding, archery, outdoor swimming pool, heated indoor swimming pool, whirlpools, Finnish sauna, Turkish steam bath, fitness club, bicycles, beauty salon.

WHERE TO DINE
EXPENSIVE

Café de Paris. Vélez Málaga, 8. ☎ **95-222-50-43.** Reservations required. Main courses 1,500–3,200 ptas. ($9–$19.20); *menú del día* 3,500 ptas. ($21). AE, DC, MC, V. Mon–Sat 1–4pm and 8pm–midnight. Closed July 1–15. Bus: 13. FRENCH/SPANISH.

Café de Paris, Málaga's best restaurant, is in La Malagueta, the district surrounding the Plaza de Toros (bullring). Proprietor and chef de cuisine José García Cortés worked at many important dining rooms before carving out his own niche. Some critics have suggested that the chef's cuisine is beyond the average Malagueño's taste, or at least pocketbook—particularly the caviar, game (including partridge), and foie gras.

Much of Cortés's cuisine has been adapted from classic French dishes to please the Andalusian palate. Menus change frequently, reflecting both the chef's imagination and the availability of produce. You might be served crêpes gratinée filled with baby eels or local whitefish baked in salt (it doesn't sound good but is excellent). Stroganoff is made not with the usual beef but with ox meat. Save room for the creative desserts, such as citrus-flavored sorbet made with champagne or custard-apple mousse.

MODERATE

El Chinitas. Moreno Monroy, 4. ☎ **95-221-09-72.** Reservations recommended. Main courses 1,200–2,800 ptas. ($7.20–$16.80). AE, DC, MC, V. Daily 1–4pm and 8pm–midnight. SPANISH.

In the heart of Málaga a short walk from the tourist office, this is one of the most established restaurants in town. Many regular patrons follow a ritual: They consume a round of tapas and drinks at the associated Bar Orellana next door (which maintains the same hours, minus the mid–afternoon closing), then head to Chinitas for a meal. The place is often filled with local residents, which is a good sign. The menu changes but might include a mixed fish fry, grilled red mullet, shrimp cocktail, grilled sirloin, or shellfish soup. The service is both fast and attentive.

Las Trevedes. In El Corte Inglés Department Store, Andalucía, 4. ☎ **95-230-00-00.** Main courses 1,600–3,200 ptas. ($9.60–$19.20); buffet 4,000 ptas. ($24). AE, DC, MC, V. Mon–Sat 1–4:30pm. Bus: 15. SPANISH.

Although it originated to lure shoppers into Málaga's best department store, this restaurant quickly developed a clientele of its own. On the sixth floor of El Corte Inglés, the local branch of the national chain, it offers a buffet table of salads and hot and cold meats and fish, as well as à la carte service. The setting is dignified and comfortable, with a well-trained staff. You might try green peppers stuffed with shellfish, fillet of pork in pepper-cream sauce, or several kinds of brochettes, and order from a long list of wines.

Parador de Málaga-Gibralfaro. Monte Gibralfaro. ☎ **95-222-19-02.** Main courses 2,000–2,600 ptas. ($12–$15.60); fixed-price menu 3,800 ptas. ($22.80). AE, DC, MC, V. Daily 1–4pm and 8:30–11pm. Microbus: H, by the cathedral. SPANISH.

This government-owned restaurant, on a mountainside high above the city, is especially notable for its view. You can look down into the heart of the Málaga bullring, among other sights. Meals are served in the attractive dining room or under the arches of two wide terraces, which provide views of the coast. Featured dishes include *hors d'oeuvres parador*—your entire table covered with tiny dishes of tasty tidbits. Two other specialties are an omelet of *chanquetes*, tiny whitefish popular in this part of the country, and chicken Villaroi.

Parador Nacional del Golf. Carretta de Málaga, Apartado, 324, Málaga. ☎ **95-238-12-55.** Main courses 1,800–2,500 ptas. ($10.80–$15); fixed-price menu 3,800 ptas. ($22.80). AE, DC, MC, V. Daily 1:30–4pm and 8:30–11pm. SPANISH.

This government-owned restaurant has an indoor/outdoor dining room that opens onto a circular swimming pool, golf course, and private beach. The interior room, furnished with reproductions of antiques, has a refined country-club atmosphere. Before-lunch drinks at the sleek modern bar tempt golfers, among others, who then proceed to the covered terrace for their Spanish meals.

Refectorium. Calle Cervantes, 8. ☎ **95-221-89-90.** Reservations recommended on weekends and at bullfights. Main courses 900–2,000 ptas. ($5.40–$12). AE, DC, MC, V. Daily 1–5pm and 9pm–12:30am. SPANISH.

Located behind the Málaga bullring, this place becomes hectic during any bullfight. It fills with aficionados and often, after the fight, with the matadors too. But you can dine here anytime, especially when the pace is less frantic. The cuisine has an old-fashioned flair, and the servings are generous. The typical soup of the Málaga area is *ajo blanco con uvas* (cold almond soup flavored with garlic and garnished with big muscatel grapes). For a classic opener, try a plate of garlic-flavored mushrooms seasoned with bits of ham. The fresh seafood is a delight, including *rape* (monkfish) and angler fish; lamb might be served with a saffron-flavored tomato sauce. Desserts are like Mama made, including rice pudding.

INEXPENSIVE

La Manchega. Marín García, 4. ☎ **95-222-21-80.** Main courses 750–1,500 ptas. ($4.50–$9); fixed-price menu 1,500 ptas. ($9). No credit cards. Daily 11am–midnight. Bus: 7 or 9. SPANISH.

This crowded, popular tavern and restaurant has thrived since 1954. The 1920s building sits on a popular pedestrian-only street in Málaga's downtown commercial zone. La Manchega has sidewalk tables, a ground-floor bar with tile walls, and a decorator's attempt to create an indoor Andalusian courtyard. A *salon comedor* offers additional space on an upper floor. Menu items include peppery fish soup, shrimp omelets, Málaga-style soup, beans with Serrano ham, snails, eels, and a full selection of seafood, including grilled shrimp, hake, monkfish, clams, and mussels.

Mesón Danes (Faarup). Barroso, 7. ☎ **95-222-74-42.** Main courses 875–2,100 ptas. ($5.25–$12.60); *menú del día* 1,200 ptas. ($7.20). AE, DC, MC, V. Mon–Sat 11am–4:30pm and 7pm–midnight. Closed Aug. Bus: 15. DANISH/SPANISH.

Here you can enjoy low-cost Danish and Spanish snacks, including soup, fish, and meat. The cheapest *menú del día* represents one of the best food values in Málaga. Mesón Danes is near the harbor and city center.

MÁLAGA AFTER DARK

The fun of nightlife in Málaga is wandering (although a few destinations do stand out). More than just about any other city in the region, Málaga offers night owls the chance to stroll a labyrinth of inner-city streets, drinking wine at any convenient *tasca*, and talking with friends and new acquaintances.

We suggest that you start out along the town's main thoroughfare, **calle Larios,** which runs adjacent to the city's port. Off calle Larios, you can gravitate to any of the *tascas*, discos, and pubs lining the edges of the **calle Granada.** Of particular interest, in terms of the fun and atmosphere you're likely to find inside, are **Bar Pimpil,** calle Granada, s/n (no phone), and **La Posada,** calle Granada, s/n (no phone).

We'll let you in on a secret. If you want to eat well and cheaply, do as the locals do and head for either or both of the taverns below. Although nothing is refined, the food is some of the finest in Málaga, and some of the least expensive. You can easily fill up on two or three orders of tapas because portions are extremely generous.

The entrance to **Bar Loqüeno,** Marín García, 9 (☎ **95-222-30-48**), is behind a wrought-iron-and-glass door. It leads into a stucco-lined room decorated in a local tavern style with a vengeance. There are enough hams, bouquets of garlic, beer kegs, fishnets, and sausages to feed an entire village for a week. However, there's hardly enough room to stand, and you'll invariably be jostled by a busy waiter shouting "Calamari!" to cooks in the back kitchens.

La Tasca, Marín García, 1–6 (between calle Larios and calle Nueva; ☎ **95-222-24-75**), is not the place to go if you're looking for a quiet, mellow spot where no one ever raises a voice. The most famous bar in Málaga, this is a hole-in-the-wall; but it has style, conviviality, and a large staff crowded behind the bar to serve the sometimes-strident demands of practically everyone in Málaga, many of whom bring their children. Try the *croquetas* (croquettes) and the pungent shish kebabs laced with garlic and cumin. If you see an empty seat, try to commandeer it politely. Otherwise you'll stand in what might be awestruck observation of the social scene around you. Tapas and beer are very cheap. Open daily noon to 4pm and 8pm to midnight.

Nearby, an all-pedestrian street, **calle Compagnía,** and a square, **Plaza Uncibaj,** are home to simpler *tascas*. Completely unpretentious (and in some cases without any discernable name), they serve glasses of wine and tapas similar to those available from their neighbors.

Looking for art history? As part of your *tasca* crawl, head for the **Plaza de la Merced,** where at least one simple bar accents the square that contains the birthplace of Pablo Picasso. (At press time the site was closed for renovation; it almost certainly will not reopen during the lifetime of this edition.) Two popular dance bars are **Saloma,** calle Luis de Valazquez, s/n, and **Cosa Nuestra,** calle Las Lazcano, 5. Don't even think of heading to either before 11pm, but once you're there, the music will probably continue till at least 4am.

11 Nerja

32 miles (51.5km) E of Málaga, 104 miles (167.5km) W of Almería, 340 miles (547.5km) S of Madrid

Nerja is known for its good beaches and small coves, its seclusion, its narrow streets and courtyards, and its whitewashed flat-roofed houses. Nearby is one of Spain's greatest attractions, the Cave of Nerja (see below).

At the mouth of the Chillar River, Nerja gets its name from the Arabic word *narixa,* meaning "bountiful spring." Its most dramatic spot is the **Balcón de Europa,** a palm-shaded promenade that juts out into the Mediterranean. The walkway was built in 1885 in honor of a visit from the Spanish king Alfonso XIII in the wake of an earthquake that had shattered part of nearby Málaga. The phrase "Balcón de Europa" (Balcony of Europe) is said to have been coined by the king during one of the speeches he made in Nerja praising the beauty of the panoramas around him. To reach the best beaches, head west from the Balcón and follow the shoreline.

ESSENTIALS

GETTING THERE   At least 10 buses per day make the 1½ hour trip from Málaga. From Almería, four buses a day make the 3-hour trip. Call the bus station, calle San Miguel, 3 (☎ **95-252-15-04**), for information and schedules.

If you're driving, head along the N-340/E-15 east from Málaga or take the N-340/E-15 west from Almería.

VISITOR INFORMATION   The **tourist information office** is at Puerta del Mar, 2 (☎ **95-252-15-31**). It's open Monday to Friday 10am to 2pm and 5:30 to 8:30pm, Saturday 10am to 1pm.

SPECIAL EVENTS   A **cultural festival** takes place here in July. In the past it has drawn leading artists, musicians, and dancers from around the world, including Yehudi Menuhin, Maya Plisetskaya, and the Bolshoi Ballet.

EXPLORING THE CUEVA DE NERJA

The most popular outing from Málaga and Nerja is to the ✪ **Cueva de Nerja (Cave of Nerja),** Carretera de Maro, s/n (☎ **95-252-96-35**). Scientists believe this prehistoric stalactite and stalagmite cave was inhabited from 25,000 to 2000 B.C. It was undiscovered until 1959, when a handful of boys found it by chance. When fully opened, it revealed a wealth of treasures left from the days of the cave dwellers, including Paleolithic paintings. They depict horses and deer, but as of this writing the room with cave paintings is not open to the public. The archaeological museum in the cave contains a number of prehistoric artifacts. You can walk through stupendous galleries where ceilings soar to a height of 200 feet.

The cave is in the hills near Nerja. From here you get panoramic views of the countryside and sea. The cave is open daily 10am to 2pm and 4pm to 6:30pm. Admission is 650 ptas. ($3.90) for adults, 350 ptas. ($2.10) for children 6 to 12, free for children under 6. Buses to the cave leave from Muelle de Heredia in Málaga hourly 7am until 8:15pm. Return buses are also hourly until 8:15pm. The journey takes about 1 hour.

WHERE TO STAY
EXPENSIVE

Hotel Mónica. Playa de la Torrecilla, s/n, 29780 Nerja. ☎ **95-252-11-00.** Fax 95-252-11-62. 235 units. A/C MINIBAR TV TEL. 18,000–24,000 ptas. ($108–$144) double. AE, DC, MC, V. Free parking.

Viewed from the air, Hotel Mónica looks something like a three-pronged propeller. At ground level, it has North African arches and green-and-white panels. The four-star hotel opened in 1986 in an isolated beachfront location about a 10-minute walk from the Balcón de Europa.

Glistening white marble in the lobby is highlighted with elaborately detailed cast-iron balustrades, curved marble staircases, and bas-reliefs, paintings, and sculptures. Some of the stairwells even contain oversize copies, set in tiles, of Claude Monet's beach scenes. The comfortable, good-sized guest rooms have private balconies and tiled bathrooms.

Dining: Two restaurants have outdoor terraces or patios and serve standard international and Andalusian cuisine.

Amenities: A curved swimming pool is built into a terrace a few feet above the beach. Room service, baby-sitting, concierge, laundry and dry cleaning.

✪ **Parador Nacional de Nerja.** Calle Almuñecar, 8, Playa de Burriana-Tablazo, 29780 Nerja. ☎ **95-252-00-50.** Fax 95-252-19-97. www.parador.es. E-mail: hotel-nerja@parador.es. 73 units. A/C MINIBAR TV TEL. 16,000–22,000 ptas. ($96–$132) double. AE, DC, MC, V. Free parking.

This government-owned hotel is on the outskirts of town a 5-minute walk from the center. The modern design incorporates beamed ceilings, tile floors, and hand-loomed draperies. On the edge of a cliff, the hotel centers on a flower-filled courtyard with splashing fountain. The spacious guest rooms are furnished in understated but tasteful style, and bathrooms are equipped with hair dryers.

Dining: A restaurant serves international and Spanish meals.

Amenities: Large swimming pool, tennis courts, an elevator running to the sandy beach below.

MODERATE

Hotel Balcón de Europa. Paseo Balcón de Europa, 2, 29780 Nerja. ☎ **95-252-08-00.** Fax 95-252-44-90. 111 units. A/C MINIBAR TV TEL. 12,600–24,640 ptas. ($76–$147) double; 23,100–30,800 ptas. ($139–$185) suite. AE, DC, MC, V. Parking 1,100 ptas. ($6.60).

Occupying the best position in town, at the edge of the Balcón de Europa, this 1970s hotel offers guest rooms with private balconies overlooking the water and the rocks. At a private beach nearby, parasol-shielded tables offer a place for a peaceful vista. The comfortable, midsized guest rooms have modern furniture, including firm beds, and marble floors. There's a private garage a few steps away.

Guests can dine at the fourth-floor restaurant Azul, which offers a panoramic view, or at the beach restaurant, Nautico, both serving international food. The Nautico serves lunch and dinner in summer, lunch only in winter. The facilities include a sauna, health club, and solarium; the services include baby-sitting, laundry, and room service.

Plaza Cavana. Plaza Cavana, 10, 29180 Nerja. ☎ **952-52-40-00.** Fax 952-52-40-08. 35 units. A/C MINIBAR TV TEL. 15,500 ptas. ($93) double. Rates include breakfast buffet. DC, MC, V. Parking: 1,000 ptas. ($6).

In the center of town, just behind El Balcón de Europa and a short walk from the beach, this two-story hotel has an old-fashioned Andalusian charm. It lies behind a typical white facade with wooden balconies. The lobby has a classic decor with marble floors, and there is a garden patio where guests can relax. Rooms are elegant, spacious, and comfortable, and all of them open onto balconies with either sea or mountain views. A restaurant specializes in traditional Spanish cuisine. For breakfast and light meals, there is a cafeteria and snack bar. Amenities include a heated swimming pool, whirlpool tub, sauna, and laundry.

INEXPENSIVE

Hostal Mena. El Barrio, 15, 29780 Nerja. ☎ **95-252-05-41.** 12 units. TV. 3,800–6,000 ptas. ($22.80–$36) double. No credit cards.

This century-old little *residencía* is near the Balcón de Europa. It's a charming place, with hundreds of blue-and-white Andalusian tiles lining the back walls of the central hallway. The small guest rooms are plain and functional, with good beds. The family that runs the hostal is very helpful. No meals are served.

Hostal Miguel. Almirante Ferrándiz, 31, 29780 Nerja. ☎ **95-252-15-23.** Fax 95-252-65-35. www.algonet.se/~jaenhag. E-mail: hostalmiguel@hotmail.com. 9 units. 4,500–6,500 ptas. ($27–$39) double. MC, V.

The family-run Miguel is a pleasant, unpretentious inn whose simply furnished, somewhat small rooms have been renovated to add more Andalusian flavor. They're in a 19th-century building with iron-rimmed balconies, on a quiet back street about a 3-minute walk from the Balcón de Europa, across from the well-known Pepe Rico Restaurant. Breakfast is the only meal served, usually on a lovely roof terrace with a view of the mountains and sea.

WHERE TO DINE

Casa Luque. Plaza Cavana, 2. ☎ **95-252-10-04.** Reservations required. Main courses 1,600–2,800 ptas. ($9.60–$16.80); tasting menu 3,200 ptas. ($19.20). AE, DC, MC, V. Daily 11am–4pm and 7–11:30pm. ANDALUSIAN.

With its impressive canopied and balconied facade near the heart of town, Casa Luque looks like a dignified private villa. The interior has an Andalusian courtyard, and in summer there's a sea-view terrace. Dishes are tasty and helpings quite filling—you'll find good value here. Meals change according to the season and might include Andalusian gazpacho, shoulder of ham, *osso bucco* (braised veal shank), pork fillet, hot-pepper chicken Casanova, or grilled meats. The limited selection of fish includes grilled Mediterranean grouper.

El Colono. Granada, 6. ☎ **95-252-18-26.** Reservations required. Wed and Fri, flamenco shows with fixed-price menus 3,200–4,500 ptas. ($19.20–$27); other nights, fixed-price lunch and dinner 1,800 ptas. ($10.80). No credit cards. Tues–Sun 8pm–midnight. Closed Nov 15–Dec 20. ANDALUSIAN/FRENCH.

A family place for a night of Spanish fun—that's El Colono, near the Balcón de Europa a 3-minute walk from the main bus stop in Nerja. Guitar music and flamenco dancing are the entertainment highlights, and you can dine here in a tavern atmosphere, enjoying set menus of local specialties. If you just want a glass of wine, you can still enjoy the shows (three per evening, from 8pm until "the wee hours").

Pepe Rico Restaurant. Almirante Ferrándiz, 28. ☎ **95-252-02-47.** Reservations recommended. Main courses 1,800–2,500 ptas. ($10.80–$15); fixed-price menu 1,800 ptas. ($10.80) at lunch, 3,800 ptas. ($22.80) at dinner. DC, MC, V. Wed–Mon 12:30–3pm and 7–11pm. Closed Dec 10–20 and Jan 10–Feb 17. INTERNATIONAL.

Established in 1966, Pepe Rico is one of Nerja's finest restaurants. It's in a white building with grille windows and little balconies on the front; a large rear balcony overlooks a flower-filled courtyard. Dining is either in a tavern room with plaster walls and ivy vines that creep in from the patio, or on the patio itself, where you can order meals alfresco.

The specialty of the day, which might be a Spanish, German, Swedish, or French dish, ranges from almond-and-garlic soup to duck in wine. The impressive list of hors d'oeuvres includes smoked swordfish, salmon mousse, and prawns *pil-pil* (with hot chile peppers). Main dishes include fillet of sole, roast leg of lamb, prawns Café de Paris, and steak dishes. Considering the quality of the food, the prices are reasonable.

Restaurante de Miguel. Pintada, 2. ☎ **95-252-29-96.** Reservations recommended. Main courses 1,500–2,500 ptas. ($9–$15); fixed-price menu 2,800 ptas. ($16.80). MC, V. Daily 8pm–midnight. Closed Feb and 2 Mondays each month. INTERNATIONAL.

This restaurant is the best in town. Established in 1986 by a Nerja resident, at first it drew only local families hoping for their friend to succeed. Since then, mostly because of the excellent food, the place has attracted a devoted crowd of foreign visitors and expatriate residents of the Costa del Sol. It is in the center of town near the busiest traffic intersection, behind a plate-glass tank loaded with fresh lobsters, fish, and shellfish. Its small air-conditioned interior is one of the most upscale places in Nerja, with white marble floors, elegant crystal and porcelain, and crisp white napery. The well-prepared menu includes cream of shrimp soup flavored with cognac, tournedos with goat-cheese sauce, and sea bass with Pernod and fennel. There's a wide selection of beef and steak dishes and, of course, fresh fish from the tank.

Restaurante Rey Alfonso. Paseo Balcón de Europa, s/n. ☎ **95-252-09-58.** Reservations recommended. Main courses 800–2,200 ptas. ($4.80–$13.20). MC, V. Thurs–Tues 11am–4pm and 7–11pm. Closed Nov. SPANISH/INTERNATIONAL.

Few visitors to the Balcón de Europa realize that they're standing directly above one of the most unusual restaurants in town. The restaurant's menu and decor don't hold many surprises, but the close-up view of the crashing waves makes dining here worthwhile. Have a drink at the bar if you don't want a full meal. Specialties include a well-prepared *paella valenciana,* Cuban-style rice, five preparations of sole (from grilled to meunière), several versions of tournedos and entrecôte, beef Stroganoff, crayfish in whisky sauce, and crêpes suzette for dessert. You enter from the bottom of a flight of stairs that skirts the rocky base of a late-19th-century *miradora* (viewing station), which juts seaward as an extension of the town's main square.

Valencia & the Costa Blanca 9

Spain's third-largest city, Valencia—celebrated for oranges and paella—lies in the midst of a *huerta,* a fertile crescent of alluvial plain that's irrigated by a centuries-old system. The area is a breadbasket of Spain, a place where "the soil never sleeps."

For such a major city, Valencia is relatively unexplored by tourists, even though it has some rewarding treasures, including a wealth of baroque architecture, fine museums, good cuisine, and a proud if troubled history.

The Costa Blanca (White Coast) begins rather unappealingly at Valencia but improves considerably as it winds its way south toward Alicante. The overbuilt route south is dotted with fishing ports and resorts known chiefly to Spanish and other European vacationers. The success of **Benidorm** began in the 1960s, when this fishing village was transformed into an international resort. **Alicante,** the official capital of the Costa Blanca, enjoys a reputation as a winter resort because of its mild climate. **Murcia** is inland but on the main road to the Costa del Sol, so hordes of motorists pass through it.

1 Valencia

218 miles (351km) SE of Madrid, 224 miles (361km) SW of Barcelona, 404 miles (650km) NE of Málaga

Valencia's charms—or lack thereof—are much debated. Some claim that the city where El Cid faced the Moors is one of the most beautiful on the Mediterranean. Others write it off as drab, provincial, and industrial. The truth lies somewhere in between.

Set amid orange trees and rice paddies, Valencia's reputation as a romantic city seems more justified by its past than by its present. Hidden between modern office buildings and monotonous apartment houses, remnants of an illustrious past do remain. However, floods and war have been cruel to Valencia, forcing Valencianos to tear down buildings that today would be architectural treasures.

Valencia has a strong cultural tradition. Its most famous son was writer Vicente Blasco Ibáñez, best known for his novel about bullfighting, *Blood and Sand,* and for his World War I novel, *The Four Horsemen of the Apocalypse.* Both were filmed twice in Hollywood, with Rudolph Valentino starring in the first version of each. Joaquín Sorolla, the famous Spanish impressionist, was another native of Valencia. You can see his works at a museum dedicated to him in Madrid.

ESSENTIALS

GETTING THERE   Iberia flies to Valencia from Barcelona, Madrid, Málaga, and many other cities. There are also flights between Palma de Majorca and Valencia. You'll land 9 miles (14.5km) southwest of the city; bus no. 15, which leaves hourly, will take you into the city for 150 ptas. (90¢). For flight information, contact the Iberia Airlines office, calle Paz, 14 (☎ 96-352-75-52).

Trains run to Valencia from all parts of Spain. The Estación del Norte (North Station), calle Xàtiva, 24, is close to the heart of the city, making it a convenient arrival point. Its information office, calle Renfe (☎ 90-24-40-202), is open daily 7am to 9pm. From Barcelona, 11 trains—both the **TALGO** (which takes 4 hours and is more expensive) and the *rápido* (6 hours)—arrive daily. Eleven trains daily connect Madrid to Valencia—the **TER** (5 hours and more expensive) and the *rápido* (7½ hours). From Málaga, on the Costa del Sol, the trip takes 9 hours.

Buses arrive at Valencia's Estació Terminal d'Autobuses, avenida de Menéndez Pidal, 15 (☎ 96-349-72-22), about a 30-minute walk northwest of the city's center. Take bus no. 8 from the Plaza del Ayuntamiento. Thirteen buses a day, at least one every hour, run from Madrid (5 hours away), 10 buses from Barcelona (5 hours), and five buses from Málaga (11 hours).

You can take a **ferry** to and from the Balearic Islands (see chapter 18). Ferries to Palma de Majorca take 6 hours. Ferries leave Valencia for Ibiza at midnight Thursday to Tuesday from June 15 to September 15. Travel agents in Valencia sell tickets, or you can buy them from the Transmediterránea office at the port, Estació Marítima (☎ 96-393-95-00), on the day of your departure. To reach the port, take bus no. 4 or 19 from the Plaza del Ayuntamiento.

The easiest route if you're driving is the express highway (E-15) south from Barcelona. You can also use a national highway, E-901, from Madrid northwest of Valencia. From Alicante, take the E-15 express highway north. If you're coming from Andalusia, the roads are longer, more difficult, and not connected by express highways. You can drive from Málaga north to Granada and cut across southeastern Spain on the 342, which links with the 340 into Murcia. From there, take the road to Alicante for an easy drive into Valencia. The Barcelona–Valencia toll is 3,000 ptas. ($18).

VISITOR INFORMATION   The **tourist information office** is at Plaza del Ayuntamiento, 1 (☎ 96-351-04-17). It's open Monday to Friday 8:30am to 2:15pm and 4:15 to 6pm, Saturday 9am to 12:45pm.

GETTING AROUND   Most local buses leave from Playa del Ayuntamiento, 22. You can buy tickets at any newsstand. The one-way fare is 110 ptas. (65¢), and a 10-ride booklet sells for 695 ptas. ($4.15). Bus no. 8 runs from Playa del Ayuntamiento to the bus station at avenida Menéndez Pidal. A bus map is available at the EMT office, calle En Sanz, 4. It's open Monday to Friday 8am to 3:30pm. For bus information, call ☎ 96-352-83-99.

If you need a taxi, call ☎ 96-370-33-33 or 96-357-13-13.

SPECIAL EVENTS   The **Fallas de San José,** honoring the arrival of spring, is held in March (dates vary). It is a time for parades, street dancing, fireworks, and bullfights. Neighborhoods compete to see who can erect the most intricate and satirical papier-mâché effigy, or *ninot.* Some 300 *ninots* then appear in the street parades. The festival ends with *la nit del foc,* or "fire night," when effigies are burned. Historically, this inferno was to exorcise social problems and bring luck to farmers in the coming summer.

The Costa Blanca

Sagunto

234

Requena

Valencia

To
Majorca →

NIII E901

N322

La
Albufera

To
Ibiza →

Casas Ibáñez

N332

N330

N340

E15
A7

Játiva

N430

N430

N340

Almansa

Alcoy

Seco River

N332

N330

N344

A7 E15

Benidorm

N301

Alicante

E15

Elche

A7

Mula

Murcia

N332

E15

N340

N301

Totana

N332

Cartagena

SPAIN

★ Madrid

Costa
Blanca

0   100 mi
0   100 km

FAST FACTS   The local **American Express** representative is **Duna Viajes,** calle Cirilo Amorós, 88 (☎ **96-374-15-62**). It's open Monday to Friday 10am to 2pm and 5 to 8pm, Saturday 9am to 2pm.

The **U.S. Consular Agency** is at calle Paz, 6 (☎ **96-351-69-73**); it's open Monday to Friday 10am to 1pm.

In a medical emergency, call ☎ **091** or 092, or go to the **Hospital Clínico Universitario,** avenida Blasco Ibáñez, 17 (☎ **96-386-26-00**).

Don't be surprised if you see signs in a language that's not Spanish or Catalán. It is *valenciano,* a dialect of Catalán. Often you'll be handed a "bilingual" menu in Castilian Spanish and in *valenciano.* Many citizens of Valencia are not caught up in this cultural resurgence, and view the promotion of the dialect as possibly damaging to the city's economic goals. Most street names appear in *valenciano.*

The self-service laundry **Lavandería El Mercat,** Plaza del Mercado, 12 (☎ **96-391-20-10**), is open Monday to Friday 10am to 2pm and 4:30 to 8:30pm, Saturday 10am to 2pm.

The local **telephone office** at Plaza del Ayuntamiento, 24 (☎ **96-003**), is open Monday to Saturday 9am to 11pm. Making a long-distance call here is much cheaper than making one from your hotel room.

EXPLORING VALENCIA

Corridas (bullfights) are staged for a week during the *fallas* observances in the summer (see "Spain Calendar of Events" in chapter 2). Today locals seem more interested in soccer than in bullfighting. Nevertheless, one of the largest rings in Spain is adjacent to the rail station at calle de Xátiva, 28 (☎ **96-351-93-15**).

Catedral (Seu). Plaza de la Reina. ☎ **96-391-81-27.** Admission to cathedral free; to Miguelete 200 ptas. ($1.20); to Museo de la Catedral 200 ptas. ($1.20). Cathedral, daily 7:30am–1pm and 4:30–8:30pm; Miguelete, Mon–Sat 10am–12:30pm and 4:30–7:30pm, Sun 10am–1pm and 5–7:30pm; Museo de la Catedral, Mon–Sat 10am–1pm and 4–6pm. Bus: 9, 27, 70, or 71.

For 500 years, this cathedral has claimed to possess the Holy Grail, the chalice Jesus used at the Last Supper; it's on display in a side chapel. The subject of countless legends, the Grail was said to have been used by Joseph of Arimathea to collect Jesus' blood as it fell from the cross. It looms large in Sir Thomas Malory's *Morte d'Arthur,* Tennyson's *Idylls of the King,* and Wagner's *Parsifal.*

Although this 1262 cathedral represents a number of styles, including Romanesque and baroque, Gothic predominates. Its huge arches have been restored, and in back is a handsome domed basilica. It was built on the site of a mosque torn down by the Catholic monarchs.

After seeing the cathedral, you can scale an incomplete 155-foot-high Gothic tower—known as **Miguelete** (or Micalet in local dialect). It affords a panoramic view of the city and the fertile *huerta* beyond. Or visit the **Museo de la Catedral,** where works by Goya and Zurbarán are on exhibit.

Palau de la Generalitat. Caballeros, 2. ☎ **96-386-34-61.** Free admission. Mon–Fri 9am–2pm. Bus: 5.

In the old aristocratic quarter of Valencia, this Gothic palace built in the 15th and 16th centuries is one of the most fascinating edifices in Spain. It has two square towers (one constructed as recently as 1952), carved wooden ceilings and galleries, and frescoes. It now serves as the headquarters of the regional government (Generalitat).

Valencia

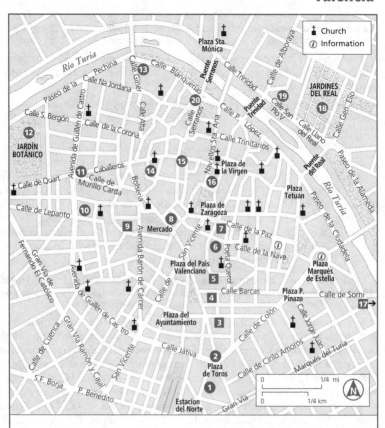

‡ Church
ⓘ Information

Río Turia

Plaza Sta.
Mónica

JARDINES
DEL REAL

JARDÍN
BOTÁNICO

Calle S. Bergón

Paseo de la

Pechina

Calle Na Jordana

Calle Giner

Calle Blanquerías

13

Calle Trinidad

Calle de Alboraya

Calle Gen Elío

Avenida de Guillén de Castro

Calle de la Corona

Calle Alta

20

Calle Serranos

Puente Serranos

Calle P. López

Puente Trinidad

19

Calle San Pío V

Calle Llano del Real

18

Paseo de la Alameda

Calle de Quart

Caballeros

Calle de Murillo Carda

11

14

Bolsería

15

Navellos Sta. Ana

Calle Serranos

Calle Trinitarios

16

Plaza de la Virgen

Puente del Real

Río Turia

Plaza Tetuán

Calle de Lepanto

10

9

Mercado

8

Avenida Barón de Cárcer

San Vicente

Plaza de Zaragoza

7

Calle de la Paz

6

Calle de la Nave

Paseo de la Ciudadela

Gran Vía de Fernando El Católico

Avenida de Guillén de Castro

Plaza del País Valenciano

5

Poeta Querol

Calle Barcas

4

Plaza P. Pinazo

Plaza Marqués de Estella

Calle de Sorni

17→

Calle de Cuenca

Gran Vía Ramón y Cajal

San Vicente

Plaza del Ayuntamiento

3

Calle de Colón

Calle Jorge Juan

Calle de Cirilo Amorós

Marqués del Turia

S.F. Borja

P. Benedito

Calle Játiva

2
Plaza de Toros

1

Gran Vía

Estación del Norte

0   1/4 mi
0   1/4 km

N

ATTRACTIONS ●

Casa Museo José Benliure **13**
Catedral **16**
Instituto Valencia
  de Arte Moderno **10**
Jardín Botánico **12**
Jardines del Real **18**
La Lonja de la Seda **8**
Museo San Pío **19**
Museo Nacional de Cerámica **6**
Museo Taurino **1**
Palau de la Generalitat **15**
Plaza de Toros **2**
San Nicolás **14**
Torres de Quart **11**
Torres de Serranos **20**

ACCOMMODATIONS ■

Hostal Residencia Bisbal **9**
Hotel Astoria Palace **5**
Hotel Consul del Mar **17**
Hotel Inglés **7**
Hotel Reina Victoria **4**
Hotel Villacarlos **17**
Melía Rey Don Jaime **17**
Sorolla **3**

SPAIN

Madrid ✪

Valencia

La Lonja de la Seda. Plaza del Mercado. ☎ **96-391-36-08.** Free admission. Tues–Fri 9am–1:30pm and 5–7pm; Sat–Sun 9am–1:30pm. Closed holidays. Bus: 4, 7, 27, 60, or 81.

This former silk exchange, completed in 1498, is the most splendid example of secular Gothic architecture in Spain. A beautiful building, La Lonja has twisted spiral columns inside and stained-glass windows.

Museu San Pío (Museu Sant Píus V). San Pío V, 9. ☎ **96-393-20-46.** Free admission. Tues–Sat 10am–2:15pm and 4–7:30pm; Sun 10am–2:15pm. Bus: 1, 5, 6, 8, 11, 18, 26, 29, 36, or 79. Metro: Alameda.

This treasure house of paintings and sculptures, which stands on the north bank of the Turia River, contains a strong collection of Flemish and native Valencian art. Of particular note are those by the 14th- and 15th-century Valencian "primitives." The most celebrated painting is a 1640 self-portrait by Velázquez, and a whole room is devoted to Goya. Other artists exhibited include Bosch, Morales, El Greco (*St. John the Baptist*), Ribera, Murillo, Pinturicchio, and Sorolla. Of special interest is a salon displaying the works of contemporary Valencian painters and an important sculpture by Mariano Benlliure. The ground-floor archaeological collection encompasses early Iberian, Roman (including an altar to a pagan emperor), and early Christian finds.

✪ **Instituto Valencia de Arte Moderno (IVAM).** Calle Guillém Castro, 118. ☎ **96-386-30-00.** Admission 350 ptas. ($2.10) adults, free for children. Julio González Center, Tues–Sun 10am–7pm; Center del Carmen, Tues–Sun 11am–2:30pm and 4:30–7pm. Bus: 5.

This giant complex consists of two sites: an ultramodern building and a 13th-century former convent. Its opening gained Valencia prime status among the world's art capitals.

The **Julio González Center** is named for the avant-garde Spanish artist whose paintings, sculptures, and drawings form the nucleus of the permanent collection. Much influenced by Picasso, González was a pioneer in iron sculpture. His work in turn exerted a profound influence on the American sculptor David Smith, among others.

The other site is the nearby **Center del Carmen,** the old convent, with cloisters from the 14th and the 16th centuries. It devotes three halls to changing exhibits of contemporary art. Permanent displays include works of Ignacio Pinazo, whose paintings and drawings mark the beginning of modernism in Valencia.

The institute is on the western edge of the old quarter, near the Torres de Quart.

Ciudad de las Artes y de las Ciencias (City of the Arts and Sciences). Monte Olivete. ☎ **902-10-00-31.** Admission to L'Hemisferic, Tues–Fri 1,000 ptas. ($6) adults; 700 ptas. ($4.20) children, students, seniors; Sat–Sun and holidays 1,000 ptas. ($6). Prices for other sections not available at press time. L'Hemisferic, Tues–Fri 11am–8:30pm; Sat 11am–3pm and 5–11pm; Sun 11am–3pm and 5–8:30pm. Other venues, Sun and Tues–Thurs 11am–9:30pm; Fri–Sat 11am–11pm. Bus: 13, 14, or 15 to Centro Comercio de Saler.

In a bid to rival Seville's Expo and Barcelona's redeveloped port, Valencia recently unveiled what has been billed as "the largest urban complex in Europe for cultural, educational, and leisure expansion." It's in the southern part of the city, on a 90-acre site in a carefully landscaped park of lush greenery and peaceful lagoons. Started 10 years ago, it should be complete by 2001. The point of the complex is to make learning fun. The state-of-the-art educational center consists of four main buildings:

L'Hemisferic: Designed by award-winning architect Santiago Calatrava, this building offers documentaries and an exploration of the universe. A laser show (with changing programs) runs on a 900-square-foot concave IMAX screen, with the sound-track in four languages, and six-channel stereo.

L'Oceanografic: Twenty acres of the complex are dedicated to an amazing arrangement of lagoons and leisure pavilions. They re-create marine habitats from every ocean. There is a dolphinarium for aquatic shows and a miniport for playing with remote-controlled boats. Submarine glass walkways connect the areas, and there is an underwater restaurant.

Palacio de las Artes: A seemingly weightless 150-foot-high glass and metal construction contains one outdoor and two indoor auditoriums. All three have the latest technology for the performance of plays, opera, and music.

Museo de las Ciencias: This enormous building houses an interactive museum where visitors are encouraged to look and touch. It has an information center networked to educational resources and an exhibition center for high-technology companies.

BEACHES & MORE

BEACHES   The beaches to the north and south of the port, Playa de la Punta and Playa de Levante, are too polluted for swimming. To go to the beach, head south in the direction of **El Saler,** where you'll find cleaner waters.

BOATING   **Club Náutico Valencia,** Camí del Canal, 91 (☎ **96-367-90-11**), has a sailing school that rents boats for scuba diving, fishing, and snorkeling. It maintains a full yacht service facility.

GOLF   There are four major golf courses in the area. One of the best is **Golf El Saler** at the Parador Luis Vives (☎ **96-161-03-84**), 11 miles (18km) south of Valencia in a setting of pine dunes. Another good course is the **Club de Campo del Bosque,** Carretera Godelleta, km 4.1, Chiva (☎ **96-180-41-42**), 2½ miles (4km) from Valencia. Or try the **Club de Golf Escorpión at Bétera** (☎ **96-160-12-11**), 12 miles (19km) northwest en route to Liria. All three are 18-hole courses. There's a 9-hole course, the **Manises Golf Club** (☎ **96-152-18-71**), on the Carretera Riba Roja, km 4 at Manises, 7½ miles (12km) west of Valencia.

SHOPPING

There are fewer souvenir shops and tourist facilities in workaday Valencia than in any other Spanish city its size. Instead, you're likely to find everyday reality in the form of middle-brow department stores and food and wine emporiums. The best shopping streets include the **Plaza Ayuntamiento, calle Don Juan de Austria, calle Colon,** and the streets thereabouts. For a peek at what aging Valencian *duennas* are storing in their cellars and attics, head for the *rastro* (flea market) in the avenida de Suecia near the soccer stadium, beginning around 8:30am every Sunday. The city's largest department store, **El Corte Inglés,** calle Pintor Sorolla (☎ **96-351-24-44**), sells a wide array of anything you might need, including local handcrafts, crystal and porcelain, and other luxury items.

Valencia is home to some of Spain's best pottery. The region produces Lladró porcelain, Manises stoneware, and glassware. Local craftspeople take pride in their *azuelejos*—brightly colored ceramic tiles, first developed during the Muslim occupation of Andalusia.

One worthy detour is to **Manises,** 5½ miles (9km) west of Valencia. It's known as a center for ceramics and for its *azulejos.* As a pottery center, Manises dates from the Middle Ages. Representatives from all the major kingdoms of Europe came here to purchase the wares, which are characterized by their distinctive blue-and-white patterns. The town is packed with ceramics factories and retail outlets. From the center of Valencia, several buses run frequently to Manises. The tourist office will give you a bus schedule.

Another good stop for the serious shopper is nearby **Paterna,** about 4 miles (6.5km) northwest of Valencia off C-234 (it's signposted all the way). It has dozens of pottery stores with prices far below those in the center of Valencia.

Continuing farther north to the province of Castellón, you'll find the towns of **Alcora** and **Onda.** They're justly celebrated for their pottery, much of which is reasonably priced because the "middleperson" is often eliminated. In addition to pottery, several shops in Onda sell some of the best-crafted *azulejos* in this part of Spain. **Alcora** is 12 miles (19km) northwest of Castellón de la Plana along the C-232; **Onda,** 9 miles (15km) west along the C-223.

In the city of Valencia itself, head for **Lladró,** calle Poeta Querol, s/n (☎ **96-351-1625**), where prices are consistent with those at other retail outlets. Or seek out the shop adjacent to the factory, **Casa de Lladró,** Carretera de Alborraya, s/n, in the suburb of Tavernas Blanques (☎ **96-185-01-77**), 3 miles (5km) north of the city center. The factory retail outlet sells slightly damaged or irregular pieces, at lower prices. To visit the factory, call 1 month in advance.

WHERE TO STAY

In July and August, when Valencia can be uncomfortably hot and humid, some hoteliers lower prices significantly if business is slow. It never hurts to ask.

EXPENSIVE

Hotel Astoria Palace. Plaza Rodrigo Botet, 5, 46002 Valencia. ☎ **96-352-67-37.** Fax 96-398-10-00. www.hotel-astoria-palace.com. E-mail: info@hotel-astoria-palace.com. 203 units. A/C MINIBAR TV TEL. 19,500–29,700 ptas. ($117–$178.20) double; 26,000–38,800 ptas. ($156–$232.80) junior suite. AE, DC, MC, V. Parking 1,500 ptas. ($9) nearby. Bus: 9, 10, 27, 70, or 71.

On a small, charming square in the heart of town, this modern business hotel has some of the best-furnished public and private rooms in Valencia. A favorite of such Spanish stars as opera singer Montserrat Caballé, bullfighter Manuel Benítez ("El Cordobés"), and an impressive roster of writers and politicians, the Astoria is plush, well managed, and appealing. Many of the tastefully furnished guest rooms overlook a statue of Grecian maidens and swans in the square outside. The highest prices are for three premium floors, which have a private lounge and separate check-in. Each of the tiled bathrooms is equipped with a hair dryer. The hotel is 5 short blocks south of the cathedral.

Dining/Diversions: **Vinatea** serves regional and international three-course fixed-price lunches and dinners. There's also a bar.

Amenities: 24-hour room service, laundry and limousine service, concierge, baby-sitting; car rentals, boutiques, gym, whirlpool.

Hotel Reina Victoria. Barcas, 4, 46002 Valencia. ☎ **96-352-04-87.** Fax 96-352-27-21. www.husa.es. E-mail: hreinavictoriavalencia@husa.es. 100 units. A/C MINIBAR TV TEL. 15,000–22,000 ptas. ($90–$132) double. Weekend prices include breakfast. AE, DC, MC, V. Parking 1,600 ptas. ($9.60). Bus: 4, 7, or 27.

Although it has lost some of its charm and luster in recent years, the Reina Victoria has a reputation as the most architecturally glamorous hotel in Valencia. Built in 1913, the hotel has welcomed many distinguished guests, including Alfonso XIII and its namesake Queen Victoria herself, Dalí, Manolete, Picasso, Falla, García Lorca, and Miró. Bristling with neoclassical detailing and wrought-iron accents, it overlooks the flower gardens and fountains of Valencia's central square, the Plaza del País Valenciano. Rooms range from small to medium (only a few are really spacious) and have first-class mattresses and private safes. The tiny bathrooms contain both a tub and a shower. The hotel is in the heart of town, a 5-minute walk from the railway station.

Dining/Diversions: The **Bar Inglés** is a popular rendezvous, and the hotel's restaurant, **El Levant,** serves international food in a dignified setting. There's a cafeteria-style restaurant.

Amenities: Concierge, laundry and dry cleaning, room service, baby-sitting, business services, conference rooms, boutiques.

Meliá Rey Don Jaime. Avenida de Baleares, 2, 46023 Valencia. ☎ **800/336-3542** in the U.S., or 96-337-50-30. Fax 96-337-15-72. 319 units. A/C MINIBAR TV TEL. 15,000–28,000 ptas. ($90–$168) double; 55,000 ptas. ($330) suite. AE, DC, MC, V. Parking 1,350 ptas. ($8.10). Bus: 19, 41, 89, or 90.

A respected member of one of Spain's largest hotel chains, the Meliá towers over the urban landscape about half a mile southeast of the cathedral. Many guests appreciate the hotel's proximity to the convention and concert hall (Palau de la Música) midway between the Old Town and the port. The stylish public rooms are sheathed in marble, rough stone, and tile work, whereas the guest rooms are sunny, well-maintained enclaves of contemporary style. The best units—more spacious and better furnished— are on the third floor. However, all rooms come with fine mattresses, private safes, and hair dryers. Many of the accommodations on the upper floors open onto panoramic views of the port and the sea.

Dining/Diversions: The **Restaurante Christina** serves international cuisine. The richly paneled bar, with leather sofas and armchairs, evokes a private club in England.

Amenities: 24-hour room service, laundry and valet, concierge, baby-sitting, business center, car-rental kiosk, solarium, rooftop swimming pool.

MODERATE

✪ **Hotel Consul del Mar.** Avenida del Puerto, 39, 46021 Valencia. ☎ **96-362-54-32.** Fax 96-362-16-25. 40 units. A/C TV TEL. 13,000–18,000 ptas. ($78–$108) double. AE, DC, MC, V. Parking 1,200 ptas. ($7.20). Bus: 1, 2, or 4.

This hotel occupies a meticulously renovated 19th-century structure that retains much of the old architectural decoration. Guest rooms are good-sized and often furnished with antiques, including the beds. Each has a luxury mattress and a private safe; bathrooms have hair dryers, hydromassage baths, and deluxe toiletries. The hotel, whose facade is beautifully lit at night, has a good restaurant, room service, laundry, and dry cleaning.

Hotel Inglés. Marqués de Dos Aguas, 6, 46002 Valencia. ☎ **96-351-64-26.** Fax 96-394-02-51. 63 units. A/C MINIBAR TV TEL. 21,000 ptas. ($126) double. AE, DC, MC, V. Parking 2,000 ptas. ($12). Bus: 6, 9, 11, 31, or 32.

This turn-of-the-century hotel, the former palace of the Duke and Duchess of Cardona, has aged well. In the heart of old Valencia, it stands opposite another Churrigueresque palace. Guest rooms vary in size, with most overlooking the tree-lined street. They offer comforts such as sofa beds with fine linens and immaculately kept bathrooms equipped with plush towels and hair dryers. Ask for a room with a view of one of the city's many palaces. The lounge and dining room have chandeliers, gilt mirrors, provincial armchairs, and murals. The service is discreet and polite.

Hotel Villacarlos. Avenida del Puerto, 60, 46023 Valencia. ☎ **96-337-50-25.** Fax 96-337-50-74. 51 units. A/C MINIBAR TV TEL. Mon–Thurs 15,500 ptas. ($93) double; Fri–Sun 9,500 ptas. ($57) double. AE, DC, MC, V. Parking 1,600 ptas. ($9.60). Bus: 19.

Located close to the river, the hotel is within easy walking distance of most of the city's monuments. Following Barcelona's lead, Valencia has been keen to adopt the new, and the Hotel Villacarlos is a prime example. The hotel has a simple postmodern facade that makes the reception area's bright orange decor all the more surprising. Abstract paintings in orange and blue (the hotel's color scheme) adorn the walls—remember your sunglasses if you have a headache. In the guest rooms, blue and orange are kept to a minimum. There's cable TV and good air-conditioning. The furniture is functional and new, including comfortable beds and full-length mirrors. Bathrooms are well stocked.

The restaurant offers *menús del día* for 2,500 to 3,000 ptas. ($16.75 to $20.10) at lunch and a buffet in the evening.

INEXPENSIVE

Hostal Residencia Bisbal. Pie de la Cruz, 9, 46001 Valencia. ☎ **96-391-70-84.** Fax 96-392-37-37. 15 units. 4,500–5,500 ptas. ($27–$33) double. No credit cards. Parking 1,900 ptas. ($12.75). Bus: 8, 27, 29, or 81.

Conveniently located in the old city, this husband-and-wife operation has simply furnished rooms. They're a bit small, but tidy and comfortable, with good beds. No meals are served, but you'll find many bars and restaurants nearby. The English-speaking staff is very helpful.

Sorolla. Convento de Santa Clara, 5, 46002 Valencia. ☎ **96-352-33-92.** Fax 96-352-14-65. 50 units. A/C TV TEL. 12,000 ptas. ($72) double. AE, DC, MC, V. Parking nearby 1,700 ptas. ($10.20). Bus: Any route from the rail station.

In the city center, this six-story hotel built in the 1960s is named after Valencia's most famous artist. The guest rooms have narrow balconies and compact, utilitarian furnishings, including good beds. Comfort, not style, is the key. No meals are served.

WHERE TO DINE
EXPENSIVE

Civera. Calle Lerida, 11. ☎ **96-347-59-17.** Reservations recommended. Main courses 2,500–3,500 ptas. ($15–$21); set menu 8,000 ptas. ($48). AE, DC, MC, V. Tues–Sun 1–4pm; Tues–Sat 8–11pm. Closed Aug. SPANISH/MEDITERRANEAN/SEAFOOD.

In the stylish Torres de Serrano district, a modern part of town near the Bellas Artes Museum, this traditional restaurant is the domain of the Civera brothers. Since the '70s they have offered high-quality, good-tasting seafood here. You have a choice of six dining sections, evoking the atmosphere of a ship with blue-and-white-painted walls, high-beamed ceilings, and sailing artifacts such as navigators, ropes, nets, and knots. The menu includes such dishes as *salpicon de mariscos,* a seafood combination, or oysters flavored with garlic or fresh calamari with vegetables. Lobster can be ordered broiled or boiled. Meat courses worthy of note are a variety of different Levante sausages or round top sirloin steak. The desserts range from fresh fruit to homemade cakes.

El Timonel. Felix Pizcueta, 13. ☎ **96-352-63-00.** Reservations recommended. Main courses 2,000–3,000 ptas. ($12–$18); set menu 4,500 ptas. ($27). AE, DC, MC, V. Tues–Sun 1:30–4pm and 8:30pm–midnight. Metro: Corte Ingles. MEDITERRANEAN/SEAFOOD.

Only 2 blocks from the building, Jaime Sauz established this restaurant in 1993 and has left a string of satisfied diners since. A comfortable and cozy interior is decorated in style of a yacht, evocative of the chef's use of fresh fish and seafood. Expect bass, flounder, red mullet, and a delectable local white fish called *lliva.* The fish is usually grilled. Señor Sauz believes if the product is fresh enough, it doesn't have to be mucked up with a lot of sauces. One of the best dishes is *dorada a la sal,* John Dory baked in a coating of salt to seal in its juices. Rice dishes blended with seafood (similar to paella) have always been one of the mainstays of the local diet, and excellent ones are served here—none better than *arroz de bogavante,* or rice with prawns and lobster. For meat eaters, we recommend the *chuleton de buey* (breaded oxtail steaks) or the *chuleticas de cordero lechal* (small spring lamb cutlets).

Eladio. Calle Chiva, 40. ☎ **96-384-22-44.** Reservations recommended. Main courses 1,800–3,500 ptas. ($10.80–$21). AE, DC, MC, V. Mon–Sat 1–4pm and 8–11:30pm. Closed Aug. SPANISH/INTERNATIONAL.

Borrowing from culinary teaching he learned during his apprenticeship in Switzerland, Eladio Rodríguez prepares flavorful cuisine based on seasonal ingredients. The menu changes daily depending on what is fresh and available. Some diners particularly praise his shellfish and fish from his native Galicia, which might include hake, monkfish, or sea wolf, prepared as simply or as elaborately as you want. Many order fish grilled simply over charcoal and served with garlic butter sauce. Noteworthy dishes include octopus and ragout of shellfish, anglerfish, and salmon. Pastries, prepared by Eladio's wife Violette, make a suitable finish. The setting is calm and pleasant.

✪ **Oscar Torrijos.** Calle Dr Sumsi, 4. ☎ **96-373-29-49.** Reservations required. Main courses 1,800–3,500 ptas. ($10.80–$21); *menú de gourmet* 2,000 ptas. ($12); tasting menu 5,000 ptas. ($30). AE, DC, MC, V. Mon–Sat 1–4pm and 9–11:30pm. Closed Aug 15–Sept 15. Metro: Calle Colon. MEDITERRANEAN/INTERNATIONAL.

This stellar restaurant serves the best cuisine in Valencia. The menu, described by owner and chef Oscar Torrijos as Mediterranean, displays the knowledge of French and German cooking he acquired while working in Switzerland. Specialties include rice dishes (for which Valencia is famous)—in particular, paella. Rice with rape and artichokes is excellent, as is rice with king prawns. Fish from the Mediterranean and the Atlantic features heavily on the menu. Señor Torrijos also makes delicious foie gras. Wine buffs should note that there are some 25,000 quality bottles in his cellar. The restaurant is centrally located in the Barrio Carmen.

MODERATE

El Gourmet. Calle Taquígrafo Martí, 3. ☎ **96-395-25-09.** Reservations recommended. Main courses 2,000–3,800 ptas. ($12–$22.80); fixed-priced menu 2,550 ptas. ($15.30). AE, DC, MC, V. Mon–Sat 1–4pm and 9–11:30pm. Closed 1 week at Easter and Sat–Sun in Aug. SPANISH/INTERNATIONAL.

This restaurant has long been known as an honest establishment where well-trained waiters serve good-quality, reasonably priced food. Set in the center of Valencia, it serves up such dishes as hake with clams, partridge with herbs in puff pastry, oxtail stew, fried fillets of veal or pork, scrambled eggs with eggplant and shrimp, and seasonal vegetables.

Palace Fesol. Hernán Cortés, 7. ☎ **96-352-93-23.** Reservations recommended. Main courses 1,800–3,000 ptas. ($10.80–$18). AE, DC, MC, V. Mon–Sun 1–4pm; Tues–Sat 9–11:30pm. Closed Sat–Sun June 15–Sept 15. Bus: 5. Metro: Colon. MEDITERRANEAN.

In the years after World War I, the Palace Fesol became famous for its namesake specialty, lima beans. Today many more excellent dishes grace the menu at the "bean palace," with typical Valencian paella high on the list at lunch. You can also order several chicken dishes served with rice (included under the general name *paella* because they are cooked in paella pans). Dinner selections include *zarzuela de mariscos* (shellfish medley), grilled red mullet and baby hake, baby lamb cutlets, and chateaubriand. Photos of film stars, bullfighters, and other celebrities line the walls. The restaurant is cooled by old-fashioned ceiling fans and decorated with beamed ceilings, lanterns, and a hand-painted tile mosaic.

INEXPENSIVE

✪ **El Plat.** Ciscar, 3. ☎ **96-374-12-54.** Reservations recommended. Main courses 1,800–4,000 ptas. ($10.80–$24). AE, MC, V. Tues–Sun 1–3:30pm; Tues–Sat 9–11pm. Closed Easter week. SPANISH/INTERNATIONAL.

If you want a taste of the dish that brought Valencia its culinary fame, El Plat will deliver. The local media hail it as "El Rey del Arroz" (Rice King) because it features a variation of the city's most famous dish, paella, every day. Other choices include typical Spanish fare of meat and fish dishes. The decor reflects the location—whitewashed walls and displays of local art create a bright environment that serves as a constant reminder you are on the "white coast." The service is helpful and friendly, and the atmosphere festive.

Patos. Calle del Mar, 28. ☎ **96-392-1522.** Reservations recommended. Main courses 1,000–1,800 ptas. ($6–$10.80); fixed-price lunch 1,500 ptas. ($9); fixed-price dinner 1,800 ptas. ($10.80). MC, V. Daily 1–4pm and 8:30–midnight. Bus: El Carte Inglés. SPANISH.

In a slightly battered turn-of-the-century townhouse, this restaurant in the town center has thrived since the early 1980s. At least part of its reputation derives from its daily preparations of *patos* (duck), which is better here than anywhere else in town. Expect pressed and grilled versions with orange, cherry, or herb sauce, usually accompanied by fresh vegetables and potatoes. There are two dining rooms plus an outdoor terrace overlooking a garden. Other choices include pizza, pasta, steak, grilled pork loin, and such desserts as flan and freshly baked pastries.

VALENCIA AFTER DARK

Where you go at night in Valencia depends on when you visit. The best area in the cooler months is in the center, in the historic **Barrio Carmen.** Valencia is famous for its *marcha* (nightlife) and for its bohemian bars. The **calle Alta** is a good street to start your bar hopping *tasca* crawl.

An evening out in Valencia might also involve a series of *tasca* crawls that focus on the historic core around the **Plaza de Ayuntamiento.** Some of the most evocative *tascas* don't even have clear signs—your best bet involves jumping in and out of whichever appeals to you. Among our favorites, a short walk from Town Hall and Valencia's tourism office, are the **Bar Canovas,** Plaza de Canovas del Castillo, s/n (no phone), and the **Bar Zaena,** calle Antiguo Reino de Valencia, s/n (no phone).

Another longtime local favorite is **Barcas,** Barcas, 7 (☎ **96-352-12-33**), among banks and office buildings in the heart of town directly north of the Estación del Norte. It serves drinks and tapas (including small servings of paella) at the stand-up bar. You could conceivably stop here for your first cup of coffee at 7am and for your final nightcap at 1am. In the evening there is often live music. The establishment is more popular as a bar than as a restaurant. It's open daily 7am to 1am. Drink prices start at 450 ptas. ($2.70), and tapas cost 300 to 1,500 ptas. ($1.80 to $9).

In summer the emphasis switches to the beach, Playa de Malvarrosa. Valencia is hot and steamy, and the cooling night breezes blowing in from the sea are especially welcome. From teens to 40-somethings, people congregate around open-air bars. They play music, often have dance floors, and are open from late May through September. Drinks usually cost 500 to 800 ptas. ($3 to $4.80). There are also discos in this part of town, one of which is the **Disco Caballito de Mar,** calle Eugenia Vines, 22 (☎ **96-371-07-64**). They are more expensive, and drinks are several hundred pesetas more than in the open-air bars.

Valencia is Spain's third-biggest city and, after Madrid and Barcelona, the country's biggest gay center. Most of the action is in the historic center in the **Barrio Carmen,** particularly along calle Quart. Valencia is a progressive, liberal city, and visitors need have no fear about being "out" on the street. For more information, interested parties can stop in at or call the **Lambda organization.** It has a **coffee shop,** calle Salvador Giner, 9 (☎ **96-391-20-84**), where the staff is very helpful. There are many clubs, bars, coffee shops, saunas, hotels, and restaurants from which to choose. The best publication for what's happening when is Madrid-based *Shangay,* distributed free in gay establishments.

The Disappearing *Barracas*

The orchard lands around Valencia once held hundreds of *barracas,* shedlike farm buildings where workers lived. These symbols of life in the area are now disappearing. *Barracas* are built of mud mixed with rice husks and strengthened with reeds to form whitewashed walls. The ground plan is rectangular, and a cross tops the front wall. The steep, saddle-back roof provides easy drainage of scarce (though torrential) rainwater and shelter from the summer heat.

The lower rooms of the structure are laid out in rows, and the top room (*andana*) is used for storage or for raising silkworms. A smaller *barraca,* used as a kitchen or for stables, is often attached. *Barracas* can still be seen in and around Valencia at El Saler, at El Palma, and in the areas of Fuente San Luis and La Punta. The tourist office in Valencia can locate these areas on a map for you.

Other interesting but disappearing forms of architecture are found in the area around Alicante known as La Marina Alta. You can see two very typical house types: the *riu-rau* and the *naia.* Both have porticos of semicircular, usually whitewashed arches and very low springers. The *riu-rau's* arched porticoes are used as drying places for raisins, whereas those of the *naia* are the setting for family life.

The latest offering on the club scene is **Le Goulou,** calle Quart, 30 (no phone), open nightly 10pm to 3am. The long-established **Venial,** calle Quart, 26 (☎ 96-391-73-56), is a few doors down. It opens at 11pm and closes at 2:30am Sunday to Thursday, and 6:30am on Friday and Saturday, when there is a charge of 1,200 ptas. ($7.20) with a drink included.

If you want to forget dancing and concentrate on late-night naughtiness, head to **La Guerra,** calle Quart, 47 (☎ 96-391-36-75). It has five action-packed floors, a labyrinth, and the latest Californian "movies" nightly 8pm to 3am.

As in many cities, gay men have to some degree elbowed lesbian interests out of the way, but Valencianas are fighting back. Women wanting a boy-free zone can try **Donna Donna,** calle Portal Valldigna, 2 (no phone), open Thursday to Sunday 6pm to 2am. The lesbian disco **Mogambo,** Sangre, 2 (no phone), is more mixed and attracts a youngish crowd. Entry is 1,200 ptas. ($7.20), which covers one drink. Mogambo is open Thursday to Sunday 11pm to 4am. As in the rest of Spain, the night starts late, and 10pm is considered quite early. At this time, one of the best places to go is the **Café de la Seu,** calle Santo Caliz, 7 (☎ 96-391-57-15). All shades of pinkdom can have a relaxing drink for 300 to 600 ptas. ($1.80 to $3.60) 8pm to 2am, Tuesday to Sunday.

On the cultural front, **Palau de la Música,** Paseo de la Alameda, 30 (☎ 96-337-50-20), is a contemporary concert hall in a dried-out bed of the Turia River, between the Aragón and Angel Custudio bridges. Opened in 1987, it occupies a sort of Hispano-Muslim venue, with palm trees, "temples," and reflecting pools. Call to find out the day's program or ask at the tourist office (see "Essentials," above). Details of major concerts are also published in the newspapers. Ticket prices vary.

For additional ideas, consult a recent copy of *Que y Donde,* a magazine available at any news kiosk for around 200 ptas. ($1.20).

SIDE TRIPS FROM VALENCIA
LA ALBUFERA

Eleven miles (18km) south of Valencia lies La Albufera, a land of rice paddies and reed beds. The largest wetland along Spain's Mediterranean coast, it was called "an agreeable lagoon" in the writings of Pliny the Elder. Sand dunes separate the fresh-water from the saltwater.

La Albufera is a national park. Its lake is home to some 250 species of waterfowl, including a European version of the endangered flamingo. It abounds with such fish as mullet, tench, and eel, still caught by ancient traps. You can rent an *albuferenc* (flat-bottomed boat) from local fishers, but make sure to negotiate prices beforehand. As you go about the lake, you can see *barracas,* whitewashed houses with thatched and steeply pitched roofs (see the box "The Disappearing *Barracas*"). Some of these structures, on stilts, can be reached only by boat.

La Albufera is famed for giving the world paella, and nearly all the restaurants in the area serve the classic dish. Try **Raco de l'Olla,** Carretera de El Palma, s/n (☎ **96-162-01-72**), 8 miles (13km) south of Valencia on the El Saler road near the turnoff to El Palma. The restaurant opened in the 1960s and has served paella to thousands of visitors from around the world. Most of the year it is open only for lunch, Tuesday to Sunday 11am to 6pm. In July and August it is open 9pm to midnight Monday to Saturday. Meals cost 3,500 to 4,000 ptas. ($21 to $24); American Express and Visa are accepted. It's also customary to stop in the town of **El Palma** to order a plate of *alli al pebre* (garlic-flavored eels) before heading north to Valencia or south to Alicante.

SAGUNTO

Another popular excursion is to Sagunto, 15½ miles (25km) north of Valencia. It's accessible by bus or rail. Sagunto is known for holding out against Hannibal's conquering Carthaginian soldiers for 9 months in 219 B.C. The Iberians set themselves on fire rather than surrender. In time, the Romans discovered the town, and later the Visigoths and the Muslims overran it.

Its **Roman ruins** today are just that: ruins. But it makes an interesting stopover. In the 2nd century A.D. Sagunto had an amphitheater seating 8,000. (Theatrical performances are still staged in the remains.) It also has an old **Acrópolis/** *castillo* **(castle);** the remains of its Moorish walls and ramparts stretch for about ½ mile.

The best place for food is near the castle: **L'Armeler,** calle Subida del Castillo, 44 (☎ **96-266-43-82**). Meals cost 3,800 to 5,000 ptas. ($22.80 to $30) with wine. The restaurant is open Tuesday to Saturday 1:30 to 4pm and 8:30 to 11pm. It serves French and Spanish food in the ambience of a *vieja mansión* (old mansion). Try one of the splendid pâtés, salmon casserole, or beef fillet with truffle sauce. The terrace provides a fine view.

2 Benidorm

27 miles (43km) NE of Alicante, 84 miles (135km) S of Valencia

Before tourists discovered its 3½ miles (6km) of beaches, Benidorm was a tiny fishing village. But now summer vacationers pour in, and a new concrete hotel seems to be built every day. With its heavy northern European influence, Benidorm has become the most overrun beach town east of Torremolinos. It has both ardent fans and determined detractors.

According to an 1890s guidebook, Benidorm was a "very tranquil place where drunkenness was unknown." What a change had come over the resort by the 1970s and 1980s, when it attracted a rowdy, beer-drinking crowd. Today some 180,000 people a day visit the long beach strip.

After the bad press of the past, city officials are trying to clean up Benidorm and make it more of an upmarket (rather than package-tour) destination. The Aiguera

Park and its amphitheater exemplify the change. It offers such free cultural activities as dancing, jazz, soul music, and even a Russian choir.

Despite efforts to upgrade its image, Benidorm still has high-rises and economical package tourists. In winter, pensioners from all over Europe, even Russia, fill the villas and small hotels. In summer, however, the place takes on a much more youthful aura. The resort has two fine white-sand beaches.

ESSENTIALS

GETTING THERE   From Alicante, there are hourly train departures for Benidorm. Buses from Valencia and Alicante leave almost hourly, too.

If you're driving, take the E-15 expressway south from Valencia or north from Alicante. The one-way toll from Alicante to Benidorm is 700 ptas. ($4.20); the one-way toll from Valencia to Benidorm is 1,500 ptas. ($9).

VISITOR INFORMATION   The **tourist information office** is at avenida Martínez Alejos, 16 (☎ **96-585-32-24**). It's open Monday to Saturday 10am to 2pm and 5 to 8pm.

WHERE TO STAY

Make sure you reserve in advance between mid-June and September. If you arrive without a reservation, you'll be out of luck. During this time hotel managers often slap the full-board requirement onto their rates. To beat this, book one of the rare *residencías,* which serve breakfast only.

Don Pancho. Avenida del Mediterráneo, 39, 03500 Benidorm. ☎ **96-585-29-50.** Fax 96-586-77-79. 252 units. A/C MINIBAR TV TEL. 15,000–22,000 ptas. ($90–$132) double. AE, DC, MC, V.

One of the best hotels in Benidorm, Don Pancho is a high-rise a short distance from the beach. Each of the well-furnished, well-maintained guest rooms opens onto a small balcony. The midsized rooms are doubles and can be rented for single use. The tiled bathrooms have hair dryers. Facilities include a swimming pool and a lighted tennis court.

Gran Hotel Delfín. Playa de Poniente (La Cala), 03500 Benidorm. ☎ **96-585-34-00.** Fax 96-585-71-54. 90 units. A/C MINIBAR TV TEL. 16,800–22,000 ptas. ($100.80–$132) double. AE, DC, MC, V. Closed Nov–Mar. Free parking.

About 2 miles (3km) west of the center of town, away from the traffic-clogged mayhem that sometimes overwhelms the center of Benidorm, this 1960s hotel is beside the very popular Poniente Beach. It is the resort's finest hotel, catering to a sun-loving crowd of vacationers who appreciate its airy spaciousness and lack of formality. Guest rooms are sparsely decorated, with masonry floors and much-used furniture, some in a darkly stained Iberian style. Nonetheless, the accommodations are quite comfortable and the tiled bathrooms well maintained.

The in-house restaurant, El Delfín, serves a fixed-price *menú del día* for 2,800 ptas. ($16.80). There are two bars, one of which serves drinks near the pool. There is an outdoor swimming pool in a large garden and tennis courts.

Hotel Brisa. Avenida de Madrid, 31, Playa de Levante, 03500 Benidorm. ☎ /fax **96-585-54-00.** 75 units. A/C TV TEL. July 15–Sept, 18,000 ptas. ($108) double; Oct–June 15, 15,000 ptas. ($90) double. Summer rates include half board; off-season rates include breakfast. MC, V.

Just across from one of the town's most popular beaches, this hotel is a five-story modern building with a swimming pool and a small garden. The sunny guest rooms, simply furnished with sturdy furniture, have good beds and tile floors. This is very much a beach hotel, where many guests bring uncomplicated wardrobes, and in some cases their children, in anticipation of lazy days on the beach. There's a bar on the premises, and an airy, sun-flooded dining room. Many summer guests are from northern Europe.

Hotel Canfali. Plaza de San Jaime, 5, 03500 Benidorm. ☎ **96-585-08-18.** Fax 96-585-00-66. 39 units. TV TEL. 6,000–16,000 ptas. ($36–$96) double. Rates include full board. No credit cards.

A seaside villa between the Playa de Levante and the Playa de Poniente, the Canfali is one of the best small hotels in town. Originally built in 1950, it was enlarged in 1992. Its position is a scene-stealer—on a low cliff at the end of the esplanade, with a staircase winding down to the beach. The best rooms have balconies with sea views. Although the hotel is spacious and comfortable, its decor is undistinguished, its guest rooms functional. Terraces overlook the sea, a perfect spot for morning coffee.

Hotel Cimbel. Europa, 1, 03500 Benidorm. ☎ **96-585-21-00.** Fax 96-586-06-61. 140 units. A/C MINIBAR TV TEL. 15,000–22,000 ptas. ($90–$132) double. AE, DC, MC, V. Parking 1,325 ptas. ($8.90). Bus: 1, 2, 3, 4, or 5.

On one of the most popular beaches in town, this hotel especially appeals to sun worshipers, who step from the lobby practically onto the sand. There's also a swimming pool. The small guest rooms are functionally furnished but comfortable, with good beds and hair dryers. The hotel restaurant's *menú del día*, for 2,800 ptas. ($18.75), often features fresh catches. Bar Hall, a nighttime gathering spot, has a terrace. Also on the premises are a disco, a cafeteria, and safe-deposit boxes.

WHERE TO DINE

Pérgola. Acantillado-Edificio Coblanca, 10, calle Hamburgo, Rincón de Loix. ☎ **96-585-38-00.** Reservations recommended. Main courses 1,500–2,800 ptas. ($9–$16.80). MC, V. Tues–Sun 1–3:30pm and 8pm–midnight. SPANISH/INTERNATIONAL.

Of the many buildings along the sea at the Playa de Levante, this is the one nearest the center of Benidorm. Established in 1979, it offers a sweeping view over the bay, an airy, stylish interior, and a flower-strewn terrace for warm-weather lunches and dinners. Skillfully prepared choices include seafood crêpes with clams, a combination platter of hake and salmon drizzled with crabmeat sauce, stuffed crabs, stewed codfish with garlic confit, duck breast with pears, and rack of beef with mustard sauce.

Tiffany's. Avenida del Mediterráneo, 51. ☎ **96-585-44-68.** Reservations recommended. Main courses 2,200–2,800 ptas. ($13.20–$16.80). AE, DC, MC, V. Daily 7:30pm–midnight. Closed Jan 7–Feb 7. SPANISH/INTERNATIONAL.

One of the town's better restaurants, Tiffany's has attracted visitors since the 1970s, serving meals with well-rehearsed dignity. A live pianist plays occasionally. The food offerings change with the seasons and the availability of the ingredients, but might include a roulade of fillet of sole stuffed with caviar and shrimp, tournedos Tiffany (with foie gras and truffles), a fish or veal dish, and a dessert of homemade chocolate eclairs with warm chocolate sauce.

BENIDORM AFTER DARK

The best nightclub in the region is the **Benidorm Palace,** Carretera de Diputación, s/n, Rincón de Loix (☎ **96-585-16-60**). The cover (including one drink) is a steep 3,000 to 5,500 ptas. ($18 to $33), but the place features the latest music, a large dance floor, and the biggest stage in Europe (130 feet wide). The stage fills with 50 international artists, often entertaining an audience of 1,500. Shows have ranged from "Hurrah for Hollywood" to Russian dancers. Always count on glamorous dancing women as part of the show. There are expansive bars and ample seating. It's open Tuesday to Saturday 9pm to 2am; shows start at 10:30pm. Drinks cost 500 ptas. ($3.35).

Casino Royal Palm, Carretera Nacional, 332, km 114 (☎ **96-589-07-00**), offers gambling in a modern building surrounded by the rolling hills of the Costa Blanca. Most visitors come to try their hand at roulette (French and American), blackjack, and *boules.* An on-site restaurant, Costa Blanca, serves à la carte Spanish meals from 3,200 ptas. ($19.20) per person every evening from 9pm to 2am. The casino is open nightly 8pm to 4am. It's about 4½ miles (7km) from Benidorm, beside the highway to Alicante. Casino admission is 600 ptas. ($3.60); a passport is required for admission.

3 Alicante

50 miles (80.5km) N of Murcia, 25 miles (40km) S of Benidorm, 107 miles (172km) S of Valencia, 259 miles (417km) SE of Madrid

Alicante, capital of the Costa Blanca, is popular in both summer and winter. Many consider it the best all-around city in Spain. As you amble about its esplanades, you almost feel as if you were in Africa: Women in caftans and peddlers hawking carvings from Senegal or elsewhere often populate the waterfront.

San Juan, the largest beach in Alicante, is a short distance from the capital. It's lined with villas, hotels, and restaurants. The bay of Alicante has two capes, and on the bay is **Postiguet Beach.** The bay stretches all the way to the **Cape of Santa Pola,** a town with two good beaches, a 14th-century castle, and several seafood restaurants.

ESSENTIALS

GETTING THERE   Alicante's **Internacional El Altet Airport** (☎ **96-691-90-00**) is 12 miles (19km) from the city. There are as many as six daily flights from Madrid, about three flights per week from Seville, and three weekly from Barcelona. Three flights arrive weekly from Ibiza and Málaga (on the Costa del Sol). Thirteen buses daily connect the city to the airport; the fare is 125 ptas. (75¢). The Iberia Airlines ticket office (☎ **96-691-91-00**) is at the airport.

Five trains a day make the 3-hour trip from Valencia. Five trains a day come from Barcelona (11 hours), and six a day from Madrid (9 hours). The **RENFE** office is at the Estación Término, avenida Salamanca (☎ **96-902-24-02-02**).

Different bus lines from various parts of the coast converge at the terminus, calle Portugal, 17 (☎ **96-513-07-00**). There is almost hourly service from Benidorm (see above) and from Valencia (4 hours). Buses also run from Madrid, a 5- to 6-hour trip.

To drive here, take the E-15 expressway south along the coast from Valencia. The expressway and N-340 run northeast from Murcia.

Transmediterránea runs three **ferries** a day to and from Ibiza (3 hours). Call the office in Valencia (☎ **96-367-06-44**) for tickets and information. Flebasa, Estación Marítima, Puerto de Denia (☎ **96-578-40-11**), offers service to Ibiza (7 hours) daily, and to Formentera (10 hours) twice weekly.

VISITOR INFORMATION   The **tourist information office** is at Explanada d' Espanya, 2 (☎ **96-520-00-00**). It's open Monday to Friday 10am to 8pm, Saturday 10am to 2pm and 3 to 8pm.

FAST FACTS   For medical assistance, go to the **Hospital General,** calle Maestro Alonzo (☎ **96-593-89-99**). In an emergency, dial ☎ **091;** to reach the city police, call ☎ **96-514-88-88.**

EXPLORING ALICANTE

With its wide, palm-lined avenues, this town was made for walking—and that's just what you'll do! The magnificent **Explanada d'Espanya,** extending around part of the yacht harbor, includes a great promenade of mosaic sidewalks under the palms. All the boulevards are clean and lined with unlimited shopping options. At Alicante's leading department store, El Corte Inglès, you can find bargains without being trampled by mobs, as in Madrid. Alicante is known for its parks, gardens, and lines of palm trees, and it boasts several old plazas, some paved with marble.

High on a hill, the stately **Castell de Santa Bárbara** (☎ 96-526-31-31) towers over the bay and provincial capital. The Greeks called the fort Akra Leuka (White Peak). Its original defenses, erected by the Carthaginians in 400 B.C., were later used by the Romans and the Arabs. The fortress's grand scale is evident in its moats, drawbridges, tunneled entrances, guard rooms, bakery, cisterns, underground storerooms, hospitals, batteries, powder stores, barracks, high breastworks, deep dungeons, and the Matanza Tower and the Keep. From the top of the castle is a panoramic view over land and sea. The castle is accessible by road or elevator (board at the Explanda d'Espanya). Admission by elevator is 400 ptas. ($2.40). In summer it's open daily 10am to 7:30pm; in winter, daily 9am to 6:30pm.

It is also possible to drive to the top. A paved road off avenida Vasquez de Mella leads directly to a parking lot beside the castle. If you drive, admission is free.

On the slopes of the Castillo de Santa Bárbara behind the cathedral is the **Barrio de Santa Cruz.** Forming part of the **Villa Vieja (the old quarter),** it is a colorful section with wrought-iron window grilles, banks of flowers, and a view of the entire harbor.

Alicante isn't all ancient. Facing the Iglesia Santa Maria is the **Museu Colecció Art del Segle XX,** Plaza de Santa Maria, 3 (☎ 96-514-07-68). Housed in the city's oldest building, it contains modern art. Constructed as a granary in 1685, the restored building features works by Miró, Calder, Cocteau, Vasarély, Dalí, Picasso, and Tápies. Other notable artists include Braque, Chagall, Giacometti, Kandinsky, and Zadkine. You'll also see a musical score by Manuel de Falla. The museum was formed in 1977 with the donation of a private collection by the painter and sculptor Eusebio Sempere, whose works are on display. It is open May through September, Tuesday to Saturday 10:30am to 1:30pm and 6 to 9pm; October through April, Tuesday to Saturday 10am to 1pm and 5 to 8pm. Admission is free.

SHOPPING

Despite the hurly-burly of tourism that unfolds around you at almost every street corner, there are many worthwhile shopping opportunities. Some of the best involve handmade artifacts—ceramics, hand-tooled leather, wood carvings, ornamental boxes, candleholders, and small-scale mosaics. One of the best all-purpose shops is **Fran Holuba,** calle Jaime Segarra, 16 (☎ 96-524-45-95), which carries examples of each of the major artisanal forms described above. A shop specializing only in ceramics is **Albarado,** calle Moreno, 6 (☎ 96-526-47-62), a few paces from the beach. For modern (not religious) sculpture crafted from wood and such stones as marble, head for the studio of **Pedro Soriano,** Plaza San Antonio, 2 (☎ 96-520-78-54). Its leading competitor is **Ibáñez Bernabeu,** calle Sipreses, 56 (☎ 96-528-08-53). Ibáñez Bernabeu will sell you an unusual sculpture off its showroom floor or commission a replica of whatever you like (if you have the time and the power to articulate your artistic vision). Appointments must be made by telephone before visiting. For general merchandise, head for the town's largest department store, **El Corte Inglés,** avenida Maison Nave, 53 (☎ 96-592-50-01).

WHERE TO STAY
EXPENSIVE

Hotel Meliá Alicante. Playa de El Postiguet, 03001 Alicante. ☎ **800/336-3542** in the U.S., or 96-520-50-00. Fax 96-520-47-56. 545 units. A/C MINIBAR TV TEL. 23,000 ptas. ($138) double; 32,000 ptas. ($192) suite. Weekend room rates include breakfast. AE, DC, MC, V. Parking 1,800 ptas. ($10.80).

Built in 1973 on a spit of landfill jutting into the Mediterranean, this massive hotel almost dwarfs every other establishment in town. Midsize guest rooms are painted in sunny colors and have balconies, usually with sweeping panoramas of sailboats in the nearby marina or over the beach. The public rooms are contemporary, with lots of marble. The hotel is midway between the main harbor and the very popular El Postiguet beach.

Dining/Diversions: Two restaurants serve à la carte meals. There is a bar near the pool, an indoor piano bar, and a *sala de fiestas* for drinking, conversation, or dancing.

Amenities: Concierge, laundry, 24-hour room service, baby-sitting, outdoor swimming pools.

Hotel Tryp Gran Sol. Rambla Méndez Núñez, 3, 03002 Alicante. ☎ **800/272-8674** in the U.S., or 96-520-30-00. Fax 96-521-14-39. www.tryp.net. 123 units. A/C MINIBAR TV TEL. 21,000 ptas. ($126) double; 25,000 ptas. ($150) suite. AE, DC, MC, V. Parking 1,000 ptas. ($6).

In the heart of the tourist zone a block from the beachfront Paseo Marítimo, this 1970 hotel towers above most of the buildings in town. A member of the widely known Tryp chain, it offers simple guest rooms with unimaginative but comfortable furnishings. Bathrooms have tile or marble accents and hair dryers. One-third of the rooms were recently renovated.

Dining/Diversions: The **Ramblas Restaurant** and a popular bar are on the 26th floor, where big windows offer sweeping views of the town and coastline.

Amenities: Room service (until midnight), laundry, concierge, baby-sitting, car rentals, reading room, game room, TV room, meeting facilities.

MODERATE

Hotel Residencia Leuka. Calle Segura, 23, 03004 Alicante. ☎ **96-520-27-44.** Fax 96-514-12-22. 108 units. A/C MINIBAR TV TEL. Mon–Thurs 10,500 ptas. ($63) double; Fri–Sun 6,500 ptas. ($39) double. AE, DC, MC, V. Parking 1,000 ptas. ($6). Bus: 22.

The Leuka is best booked for the weekend, when it offers good value and is free of packs of businesspeople. Although it's about a 15-minute walk from the sea, it is close to the station and two of the city's main thoroughfares. Guests have easy access to almost all destinations by bus. The 10-story building has an anonymously ugly 1970s facade. However, all the rooms have good-size balconies, and units above the third floor offer wonderful views of the castle. Guest rooms are quite plain, but spacious and reasonably comfortable. The bar serves a three-course *menú del día* at lunch for 1,500 ptas. ($9); one-course *platos combinados* cost 1,200 to 1,500 ptas. ($7.20 to $9) at night.

Sol Inn Hotel. Calle Gravina, 9, 03002 Alicante. ☎ **96-521-07-00.** Fax 96-521-09-76. www.solmelia.es. E-mail: sol.alicante@solmelia.es. 66 units. A/C MINIBAR TV TEL. Mon–Thurs 12,000 ptas. ($72) double; Fri–Sun 9,500 ptas. ($57) double. Weekend rates include breakfast. AE, DC, MC, V. Parking 1,000 ptas. ($6). Bus: 21.

True to its name, this three-star hotel is decorated in sunny hues. Reasonable and no-frills, it's on a narrow street 30 yards from the Mediterranean and a short stroll from the historic castle. The comfortable rooms are basic but spacious enough, and all have hair dryers. There is a bar downstairs, and many restaurants and bars nearby.

INEXPENSIVE

Hotel Residencia San Remo. Navas, 30, 03001 Alicante. ☎ **96-520-95-00.** Fax 96-520-96-68. 27 units. A/C TV TEL. 7,000–8,000 ptas. ($42–$48) double. AE, DC, MC, V. Bus: B.

A white-plaster seven-floor building, the San Remo offers small, unpretentious rooms. Some have balconies, and all have good beds and tiny tiled bathrooms with shower stalls. Breakfast is the only meal served. The welcome is warm, and the price is right. Room service is provided 8am to 2pm and 7 to 9pm.

Portugal. Calle Portugal, 26, 03003 Alicante. ☎ **96-592-92-44.** 16 units (8 with bathroom). 3,800–4,200 ptas. ($22.80–$25.20) double with sink; 4,500–4,800 ptas. ($27–$28.80) double with bathroom. No credit cards. Parking 1,200 ptas. ($7.20).

The two-story Portugal is 1 block from the bus station, about 4 blocks from the railway station, and a 3-minute walk from the harbor. The small accommodations, furnished in tasteful modern style, are immaculate but basic. Guests in units with private bathrooms will find their rooms a bit cramped but serviceable. For those who share, the corridor bathrooms are adequate.

WHERE TO DINE

The characteristic dish of Alicante is rice, served many different ways. The most typical sauce is aïoli, a kind of mayonnaise made from oil and garlic. Dessert selections are the most varied on the Costa Blanca; *turrón de Alicante* (Spanish nougat) is the most popular.

Delfín. Explanada d'Espanya, 12. ☎ **96-521-49-11.** Reservations recommended. Main courses 2,500–3,200 ptas. ($15–$19.20); *menú del día* 5,000 ptas. ($30). AE, DC, MC, V. Daily 1–4pm and 8pm–midnight. MEDITERRANEAN.

On the town's most visible promenade, this restaurant has an upstairs dining room with views over the harbor and yacht basin. The service is discreet and attentive, the ingredients fresh, and the dishes flavorful. Specialties might include smoked salmon on toast with a gratin of shrimp, fillet of beef grilled with a goat-cheese topping, sauté of sweetbreads flavored with foie gras and strips of duck meat, crêpes stuffed with seafood, or paella. An array of tempting pastries rolls from table to table on a trolley.

La Dársena. Muelle del Puerto (Explanada d'Espanya). ☎ **96-520-75-89.** Reservations required at lunch. Main courses 1,300–2,000 ptas. ($7.80–$12); fixed-price menu 4,200 ptas. ($25.20). AE, DC, MC, V. Mon–Sun 1–4pm; Tues–Sat 8:30–11pm. SPANISH.

Paella is the best choice at this popular place overlooking the harbor. Some 20 other rice dishes are good, though—for example, *arroz con pieles de bacalao* (rice with dried codfish). Try crab soup flavored with Armagnac or a tart made with tuna and spinach.

Nou Manolín. Calle Villegas, 3. ☎ **96-520-0368.** Reservations recommended. Main courses 1,800–3,000 ptas. ($10.80–$18); *menú del día* 3,800 ptas. ($22.80). AE, DC, MC, V. Daily 1–4pm and 8:30pm–midnight. REGIONAL/SPANISH.

When he established it in 1972, the founder of this restaurant named it after an almost-forgotten neighborhood bar (El Manolín), which his grandfather had maintained before the Spanish Civil War. Nou Manolín's street level contains a busy bar area, but diners usually gravitate to the upstairs dining room, where tiled walls and uniformed waiters contribute to the ambience of an elegant *tasca*. Menu items include many kinds of fish cooked in a salt crust, as well as delectable paella, several kinds of stew, fresh shellfish, and a wide selection of Iberian wines.

Restaurante El Jumillano. César Elquezábel, 64. ☎ **96-521-17-64.** Reservations recommended. Main courses 1,800–2,800 ptas. ($10.80–$16.80). AE, DC, MC, V. Mon–Sat 1–4pm and 8pm–midnight; Sun noon–4pm. Closed Sun July–Sept. Bus: D or F. SPANISH.

This was a humble wine bar when it opened in 1936 near the old city. The original wine-and-tapas bar is still going strong, but the food has improved immeasurably. Today the original owner's sons (Juan José and Miguel Pérez Mejías) offer a cornucopia of succulent food, including fresh fish laid out in the dining room on the sun-bleached planks of an antique fishing boat. Many menu items derive from locally inspired recipes. The specialties include a "festival of canapés," slices of cured ham served with fresh melon, shellfish soup with mussels, Alicante stew, pigs' trotters, a savory fillet of beef seasoned with garlic, and a full gamut of grilled hake, sea bass, and shellfish.

ALICANTE AFTER DARK

A town devoted to the pursuit of hot times, Alicante never seems to lack for a bar. You can find alcohol and socializing at almost any time of the day or night. One of the town's densest concentrations of watering holes lies adjacent to the port. Night owls wander from one bar to the next along the length of the **Muelle del Puerto** (a stretch of pavement that's also known as the Explanada d'Espanya). There are at least 20 nightspots that rock through the night. Three of the most popular and visible are **Bar Potato; Casa Yum-Yum,** where tapas are consumed with something approaching vigor; and **Mesón del Puerto.** Their addresses are all Muelle del Puerto, s/n, and they have no phones. Also consider the bar at one of our favorite restaurants, **La Dársena** (see "Where to Dine," above), even if you don't wish to dine.

Alternatively, consider walking through the narrow streets of Alicante's **Casco Antiguo.** Streets particularly rich in *bodegas* and *tavernas* include **calle Laboradores, calle Cien Fuegos,** and the **Plaza Santa Face.** We usually prefer to wander aimlessly through this district, popping in and out wherever we feel most comfortable. If you want to plan ahead, consider **El Mesón,** in the calle Labradores, 23; **La Tapería,** Plaza Santa Face, s/n; and **El Pote Gallego,** Plaza Santa Face, s/n. Again, no phones.

Alicante has a well-established and relatively large gay scene for a city of its size. The numbers swell in July and August, with tourists from the rest of Spain and Madrid in particular. For information, contact the Lambda organization, calle Doctor Santa Oblaya, 7, in the San Blas area (☎ **96-513-26-10**). It's open Wednesday 7 to 9pm, Saturday 7 to 10pm.

The evening starts at one of several bars. A popular haunt is **Monecristo** (☎ **96-512-31-89**), calle Ab-El-Hamet, 1, which is open daily 8:15pm to 3am. Another, **Missing** (☎ **96-521-67-28**), calle Gravina, 4, is open daily 9pm to 3:30am. The bar and club **El Jardineto,** calle Baron de Finestat (no phone), operates 11pm to 3am Sunday to Thursday, until 5 or 6am on Friday and Saturday.

4 Elche

13 miles (21 km) SW of Alicante, 35 miles (56km) NE of Murcia, 252 miles (406km) SE of Madrid

Sandwiched between Alicante and Murcia, the little town of Elche is famous for its age-old mystery play, lush groves of date palms, and shoe- and sandal-making.

On August 14 and 15 for the past 6 centuries, the ✪ **Misteri d'Elx (Mystery of Elche)** has celebrated the Assumption of the Virgin. It is reputedly the oldest dramatic liturgy in Europe. Songs are performed in an ancient form of Catalán. Admission is free, but it's hard to get a seat unless you book in advance through the tourist office (see "Essentials," below). The play takes place at the Church of Santa María, which dates from the 17th century.

Unless you visit at the time of the mystery play, the town's date palms hold the most appeal. The 600,000-tree palm forest is unrivaled in Europe. It's said that Phoenician (or perhaps Greek) seafarers originally planted the trees. A thousand years ago, the Moors created the irrigation system that still maintains the palms. Stroll through the **Huerto del Cura (Priest's Grove),** open daily 9am to 6pm, to see the palm garden and collection of tropical flowers and cacti. In the garden, look for the **Palmera del Cura (Priest's Palm),** from the 1840s, with seven branches sprouting from its trunk. In the grove you will see one of the most famous ladies of Spain, *La Dama de Elche.* This is a replica—the original 500 B.C. limestone bust, discovered in 1897, is on display in the National Archaeological Museum in Madrid.

ESSENTIALS

GETTING THERE   The central train station is the Estación Parque, Plaza Alfonso XII. Trains arrive almost hourly from Alicante. Call ☎ **96-545-62-54** for schedules.

The bus station (☎ **96-545-58-58**) is at avenida de la Libertat. Buses travel between Alicante and Elche on the hour.

Take the N-340 highway from Alicante and proceed southwest if you're driving.

VISITOR INFORMATION   The **tourist information office** is at Passeig de l'Estació (☎ **96-545-38-31**). It's open Monday to Friday 10:30am to 2pm and 4 to 6pm, Saturday and Sunday 10:30am to 1:30pm.

WHERE TO STAY

✪ **Huerto del Cura.** Porta de La Morera, 14, 032003 Elche. ☎ **96-545-80-40.** Fax 96-542-19-10. 86 units. A/C MINIBAR TV TEL. Mon–Thurs 19,000 ptas. ($114) double, Fri–Sun 12,000 ptas. ($72) double; July 26–Sept 5, 14,000 ptas. ($84) double. AE, DC, MC, V. Parking 1,300 ptas. ($7.80).

Staying here is a unique experience. Huerto del Cura stands in the so-called Priest's Grove, and you'll have panoramic views of the palm trees from your room. The privately owned parador consists of a number of immaculately kept cabins in the grove. Each is well furnished and roomy, with comfortable mattresses and efficiently organized, tiled bathrooms. Service is impeccable. A swimming pool under the palms separates the cabins from the main hotel building. A tennis court, sauna, solarium, and cafeteria are on the grounds. There is an attractive bar and a high-quality dining room, Els Capellans.

WHERE TO DINE

Parque Municipal. Paseo Alfonso XIII, s/n. ☎ **96-545-34-15.** Reservations recommended. Main courses 1,800–2,200 ptas. ($10.80–$13.20); fixed-price menu 1,500 ptas. ($9). MC, V. Daily 1–4pm and 8–11pm. INTERNATIONAL.

A large open-air restaurant and cafe in the middle of a public park, the Parque Municipal is a good place to go for decent food and relaxed service. Many regional dishes appear on the menu; try one of the savory rice dishes as a main course, followed by "cake of Elche." Two specialties are paella and Mediterranean sea bass, sailor's style.

Restaurante La Finca. Partida de Perleta, 1–7. ☎ **96-545-60-07.** Reservations recommended. Main courses 2,200–3,200 ptas. ($13.20–$19.20); fixed-price menus 4,500–6,500 ptas. ($27–$39). AE, DC, MC, V. Daily 1–5pm; Tues–Sat 8:30pm–midnight. MEDITERRANEAN.

In the countryside near the Elche football stadium, 3 miles (5km) south of town along the Carretera de El Alted, La Finca opened in 1984. Its good food has attracted customers ever since. The menu changes frequently, based on the season and what's fresh. Both fish and meat are prepared in creative ways, although time-tested recipes are used as well. Try tuna-stuffed peppers or veal kidneys with potatoes. Chocolate mousse might be available for dessert.

5 Murcia

52 miles (84km) SW of Alicante, 245 miles (394km) SE of Madrid, 159 miles (256km) SW of Valencia

This ancient Moorish city of sienna-colored buildings is an inland provincial capital on the main road between Valencia and Granada. It is on the Segura River.

ESSENTIALS

GETTING THERE   From Alicante, 9 to 17 trains daily make the 1½-hour trip. From Barcelona (7 to 10 hours), there are three trains daily; from Madrid (4 to 5 hours), three or four trains daily. From the Estació del Carmen, calle Industria, s/n (☎ 968-25-21-54), take bus no. 11 to the heart of the city.

Buses arrive at calle San Andrés (☎ 968-29-22-11), behind the Museo Salzillo. The information window is open daily 7am to 10pm. There's frequent service from Granada (4 to 5 hours), Cádiz (12½ hours), Córdoba (9 hours), Valencia (3 ¾ hours), and Seville (7 to 9 hours).

If you're driving, take the N-340 southwest from Alicante.

VISITOR INFORMATION   The **tourist information office** is at calle San Cristobal (☎ 968-36-61-00). It's open Monday to Friday 9:30am to 2pm, Saturday 5 to 7:30pm.

SPECIAL EVENTS   Murcia's **Holy Week celebration,** from Palm Sunday to Easter Sunday, is an ideal time to visit. Its processions are spectacular, with about 3,000 people taking part, and some sculptures of Salzillo (see below) are carried through the streets. Musicians blow horns so big they have to be carried on wheels.

EXPLORING MURCIA

Although it suffered much from fire and bombardment during the Spanish Civil War, the city abounds in grand 18th-century houses.

The principal artistic treasure is the **cathedral,** Plaza Cardenal Belluga (☎ 968-21-63-44), a medley of Gothic, baroque, and Renaissance styles. Begun in the 1300s, its bell tower was built in four different periods by four different architects. You can climb the tower for a view of Murcia and the enveloping *huerta* (plain). Capilla de los Vélez, off the ambulatory, is the most interesting chapel. You can see works by the famous local sculptor, Francisco Salzillo (1707–83), as well as the golden crown of the Virgen de la Fuensanta, patron of Murcia. Off the north transept, the museum of the cathedral contains such relics as Salzillo's polychrome wood sculpture of the penitent St. Jerome. You can visit daily 10am to 1pm and 5 to 7pm. Admission is free, but it costs 250 ptas. ($1.50) to visit both the museum and the bell tower.

The other major sight is the **Museo de Salzillo,** San Andrés, 1 (☎ 968-29-18-93). The son of an Italian sculptor father and a Spanish mother, Francisco Salzillo won fame with his sculptures in polychrome wood. This museum displays his finest work, plus many terra-cotta figurines based on biblical scenes. It is open Tuesday to Saturday 9:30am to 1pm and 4 to 7pm, Sunday 11am to 1pm. Admission is 500 ptas. ($3).

Another attraction is the **Museo de Arqueología,** calle Gran Vía Alfonso X, El Sabio, 9 (☎ 968-23-46-02), one of the best in Spain. Through artifacts—mosaics, pottery fragments, Roman coins, ceramics, and other objects—it traces life in Murcia province from prehistoric times. The two most important collections are devoted to objects from the Hispano-Moorish period of the 12th to the 14th centuries and to Spanish ceramics of the 17th and 18th centuries. Hours in July and August are Monday to Friday 9am to 1:30pm; September through June, it's open Monday to Friday 9am to 2pm and 5 to 8pm, Saturday 11am to 2pm. Admission is 75 ptas. (45¢).

WHERE TO STAY

Hotel Conde de Floridablanca. Princesa, 18, 30002 Murcia. ☎ **968-21-46-26.** Fax 968-21-32-15. 97 units. A/C MINIBAR TV TEL. 9,500 ptas. ($57) double. AE, DC, MC, V. Parking 1,200 ptas. ($7.20). Bus: 2, 5, 6, or 11.

Rising from the center of the Barrio del Carmen near the cathedral, this hotel is ideally situated for exploring the old city. Originally built in 1972, it was thoroughly renovated and enlarged in 1992. The building is attractively decorated in conservative modern style, with comfortable and appealing midsized guest rooms. Guests have the use of a safe. The hotel serves breakfast, and a bar and restaurant offer dinner and drinks.

Hotel Hispano 1. Calle Trapería, 8, 30001 Murcia. ☎ **968-21-61-52.** Fax 968-21-68-59. 46 units. TEL. 5,500 ptas. ($33) double. AE, DC, MC, V. Bus: 2, 5, 6, or 11.

An older version of Hispano 2 (see below), run by the same people, this good-value hotel is still reliable after all these years. It stands right next to the cathedral. The well-kept guest rooms are functional and homey, but a bit small, although the beds are firm. The hotel restaurant serves regional cuisine.

Hotel Hispano 2. Calle Radio Murcia, 3, 30001 Murcia. ☎ **968-21-61-52.** Fax 968-21-68-59. 35 units. A/C MINIBAR TV TEL. 8,000–12,000 ptas. ($48–$72) double. AE, DC, MC, V. Parking 1,000 ptas. ($6). Bus: 2, 5, 6, or 11.

The older Hispano 1 (see above) proved so successful that the owners inaugurated this property in 1976. The comfortably furnished guest rooms are superior to those at the older sibling. The Hispano 1 offers well-prepared and reasonably priced regional food and tapas.

Hotel Meliá 7 Coronas. Paseo de Garay, 5, 30000 Murcia. ☎ **800/336-3542** in the U.S., or 968-21-77-72. Fax 968-22-12-94. 153 units. A/C MINIBAR TV TEL. 22,000 ptas. ($132) double. AE, DC, MC, V. Parking 1,500 ptas. ($9). Bus: 2, 5, 6, or 11.

A member of the well-recommended nationwide chain, this is the finest hotel in town. The angular 1971 building offers comfortable midsized guest rooms and a cool, refreshing terrace with bar service and a legion of flowering plants. The restaurant serves à la carte Spanish and French cuisine. There's also a bar. The hotel is within a 15-minute walk east of the cathedral, near the gardens abutting the northern edge of the Río Segura.

Residencia Rincón de Pepe. Calle de Apóstoles, 34, 30007 Murcia. ☎ **968-21-22-39.** Fax 968-22-17-44. 148 units. A/C MINIBAR TV TEL. 14,500–15,600 ptas. ($87–$93.60) double. AE, DC, MC, V. Parking 1,450 ptas. ($8.70).

This modern hotel hidden on a narrow street in the heart of the old quarter is attached to a well-known restaurant, Rincón de Pepe (see below). It has a good-size lounge and a new casino, as well as a bar. The small to medium guest rooms are up-to-date, with many built-in conveniences.

A NEARBY RESORT

✪ **Hyatt Regency La Manga.** Los Belones, 30385 Cartagena, Murcia. ☎ **800/223-1234** in the U.S., or 968-33-12-34. Fax 968-33-12-35. www.lamanga.hyatt.com. E-mail: enqueries@cesser.com. 249 units. A/C MINIBAR TV TEL. 36,000–55,000 ptas. ($216–$330) double; 69,300–176,000 ptas. ($416–$1,056) suite; 14,800–29,000 ptas. ($89–$174) studio apt.; 19,200–46,500 ptas. ($115–$279) 1- to 3-bedroom apt. AE, DC, MC, V. Free parking.

One of the best resorts in Spain is away from the coast near the eastern part of Andalusia. Nestled on 1,400 acres (the grounds are larger than the land controlled by the Principality of Monaco), it's the only resort in Europe with three championship golf courses. It features a comprehensive array of sports facilities. The decor is inspired by the aristocratic private villas of Andalusia. Families usually opt for one of the functional four-star apartments in the airy Los Lomos complex. Fifty apartments (as well as about 20 time-shared units not accessible to the public) make up a re-creation of an Andalusian pueblo. Couples and clients staying for a week or less tend to gravitate toward the luxurious doubles. The grand five-star accommodations occupy the resort's architectural showcase, the Príncipe Felipe, named for the son of King Juan Carlos.

Dining/Diversions: The **Ampola** restaurant has views over the golf courses. Other dining options include **La Cala,** a Mexican restaurant; **Luigi's,** an Italian pizza and pasta restaurant; and a jazz bar, **Andaie.** There's also a sandwich shop.

Amenities: Baby-sitting, 24-hour room service, hairdressing, laundry and valet, concierge, health and fitness club, children's camp with facilities for supervision and baby-sitting, four outdoor swimming pools and sundeck, tennis center with 18 courts (14 lighted), golf and tennis pro shops. A beach with water-sports facilities and kiosks is 10 minutes away by shuttle bus.

WHERE TO DINE

Acuario. Plaza Puxmaria, 1. ☎ **968-21-99-55.** Reservations recommended. Main courses 1,800–2,200 ptas. ($10.80–$13.20); fixed-price menu 3,000 ptas. ($18). AE, DC, MC, V. Mon–Sat 1–4pm and 8:30pm–midnight. Closed 2 weeks in Aug. Bus: 2, 5, 6, or 11. REGIONAL/INTERNATIONAL.

This restaurant near the cathedral allows you to dine in air-conditioned comfort. Since it opened in 1987, it has been known for excellent Murcian cuisine and its selection of international dishes. You might begin with pâté of salmon, following with *merluza* (hake) in sherry sauce, a tender tournedos, or the chef's specialty, eggplant cooked with Serrano ham and mushrooms. If it's available, the lemon soufflé is delectable.

✪ **Rincón de Pepe.** Plaza de Apóstoles, 34. ☎ **968-21-22-39.** Reservations recommended. Main courses 2,000–4,500 ptas. ($12–$27). AE, DC, MC, V. Daily noon–4pm; Mon–Sat 8pm–midnight. Closed Aug. Bus: 3, 4, or 8. SPANISH/INTERNATIONAL.

Many visitors won't leave town without going to this culinary landmark. Established in the mid-1920s, it's the best restaurant in town. You can spend a lot or a little, depending on what you order. Specialties change frequently, and the menu varies seasonally. You might enjoy pig's trotters and white beans, spring lamb kidneys in sherry, or white beans with partridge. Shellfish selections include Carril clams, a platter of assorted grilled seafood and fish, and grilled red prawns. Among the meat and poultry specialties are roast spring lamb Murcian style and duck in orange sauce.

10 Barcelona

Blessed with rich and fertile soil, an excellent harbor, and a hard-working population, Barcelona has always prospered. When Madrid was still a dusty Castilian backwater, Barcelona was a powerful, diverse capital, influenced more by the Mediterranean empires that conquered it than by the cultures of the arid Iberian plains to the west. Carthage, Rome, and Charlemagne-era France overran Catalonia, and each left an indelible mark on the region's identity.

The Catalán people have clung fiercely to their unique culture and language, both of which Franco systematically tried to eradicate. But Catalonia has endured, becoming a semiautonomous region of Spain (with Catalán its official language). And Barcelona, the region's lodestar, has truly come into its own. The city's most powerful monuments open a window onto its history: the intricately carved edifices of the medieval Gothic Quarter; the curvilinear *modernisme* (Catalán art nouveau) that inspired Gaudí's Sagrada Família; and the seminal surrealist works of Picasso and Miró, in museums that mark Barcelona as a crucial incubator for 20th-century art.

As if those attractions weren't enough, Barcelona is on the doorstep of some of Europe's great playgrounds and vacation retreats. The Balearic Islands lie to the east, the Costa Brava to the north, the Penedés wine country to the west, and to the south, the Roman city of Tarragona, the monastery at Montserrat, and such Costa Dorada resort towns as Sitges.

Despite its allure, Barcelona grapples with problems common to many major cities—the increasing polarization of rich and poor, rising drug abuse, and an escalating crime rate, mostly theft. But in reaction to a rash of negative publicity, city authorities have, with some degree of success, brought crime under control in the tourist zones.

A revitalized Barcelona eagerly prepared for and welcomed thousands of visitors as part of the 1992 Summer Olympic Games, but the action didn't end when the last medal was handed out. Barcelona turned its multimillion-dollar building projects into permanently expanded facilities for sports and tourism. Its modern $150 million terminal at El Prat de Llobregat Airport can accommodate 12 million passengers a year, and ever-pragmatic Barcelona raced to the 21st century with a restructuring program called "Post Olympic." The city is fast emerging as one of the hottest tourist cities in Europe.

Landmark buildings and world-class museums fill the historic city. They include Antoni Gaudí's famed Sagrada Família, the Museu

Picasso, the Gothic cathedral, and Les Rambles, the famous tree-lined promenade that cuts through the heart of the old quarter.

An array of nightlife (Barcelona is a *big* bar town) and shopping possibilities, plus nearby wineries, ensure that you'll be entertained round the clock. It makes for some serious sightseeing; you'll need plenty of time to take it all in—in fact, almost as much time as it takes to see Madrid.

1 Catalonian Culture

Barcelona (which was described in the Middle Ages as "the head and trunk of Catalonia") has always thrived on contact and commerce with countries beyond Spain's borders. From its earliest days, the city has been linked more closely to France and the rest of Europe than to Iberia. Each of the military and financial empires that swept through Catalonia left its cultural imprint.

LANGUAGE

Catalonia lies midway between France and Castilian Spain. The province is united by a common language, **Catalán.** The region's linguistic separation is arguably the single most important element in its people's streak of independence.

Modern linguists attribute the earliest division of Catalán from Castilian to two phenomena. The first was the cultural links and trade ties between ancient Barcina and the neighboring Roman colony of Provence, which shaped the Catalán tongue along Provençal and Languedocian models. The second major event was the invasion of the eastern Pyrenees by Charlemagne in the late 800s, and the designation of Catalonia as a Frankish march (buffer zone) between Christian Europe and Moorish-dominated Iberia.

Although Catalán is closely related to Castilian Spanish, even those travelers who are fluent in Spanish are occasionally confronted with unfamiliar words in Barcelona. Don't be surprised if maps or brochures have addresses in Castilian, but then you find signs in Catalán on the street.

Today Catalán is the most widely spoken non-national language in Europe.

ARCHITECTURE

Like many other cities in Spain, Barcelona claims its share of Neolithic dolmens and ruins from the Roman and Moorish periods. Monuments survive from the Middle Ages, when the Romanesque solidity of no-nonsense barrel vaults (sometimes with ribbing), narrow windows, and fortified design were widely used.

In the 11th and 12th centuries religious fervor swept through Europe, and pilgrims began to flock to Barcelona on their way west to Santiago de Compostela, bringing with them French building styles and the need for new and larger churches. The style that emerged, called Catalonian Gothic, had softer lines and more elaborate ornamentation than traditional Gothic. Appropriate for both civic and religious buildings, it used *ogival* (pointed) arches, intricate stone carvings, large interior columns, exterior buttresses, and vast rose windows set with colored glass. One of Barcelona's purest and most-loved examples of this style is the Church of **Santa María del Mar,** north of the city's harbor.

The Barcelona visitors best remember, however, is the Barcelona of *modernisme,* an art nouveau movement that, from about 1890 to 1910, put the city on the architectural map. A highly articulate school of Catalán architects blended pre-Raphaelite voluptuousness and Catalonian romanticism, heavily laced with a yearning for the curved lines and organic forms easily recognized in nature.

Although the great adventures that befell me there occasioned me no great pleasure, but rather much grief, I bore them the better for having seen the city [Barcelona].

—Don Quixote

The movement's most famous architect was Antoni Gaudí. The chimneys of his buildings look like half-melted mounds of chocolate twisted into erratic spirals; his horizontal lines flow over vertical supports. Some of Gaudí's most distinctive creations include Casa Milá, Casa Batlló, Parc Güell, and the landmark Temple Expiatori de la Sagrada Família (left incomplete at his death).

Other modernist architects of this era looked for inspiration to medieval models, particularly the fortified castles and sculpted gargoyles and dragons of 12th-century Barcelonan counts. Examples include Domènech i Montaner and Puig i Cadafalch, whose elegant mansions and concert halls seemed perfectly suited to the enlightened, sophisticated prosperity of the 19th-century Catalonian bourgeoisie. A 19th-century economic boom neatly coincided with the profusion of geniuses who suddenly emerged in the building business. Entrepreneurs who had made their fortunes in the fields and mines of the New World commissioned some of the beautiful and elaborate villas in Barcelona and nearby Sitges.

Initiated in 1858, the expansion of Barcelona into the northern **Eixample district** laid the groundwork for the *modernisme* architects' designs. The gridlike pattern of streets in the Eixample was intersected with broad diagonals. Although opposed by local landowners and never endowed with the detail of its original design, it provided a carefully planned, elegant path in which a growing city could showcase its finest buildings.

A city competition conducted in the late 1850s was to decide the final architect to draw up the plans for the Eixample. Antoni Rovira won the competition and produced a radical plan. The apartment buildings, which surrounded park areas, were to be democratically occupied—"by the people of Barcelona." The plan was never carried out. The Spanish Ministry of Works approved a rectangular grid plan devised by Ildefons Cerdà, and Catalán officials felt that Madrid centralism had quashed their grand new scheme. The gardens in Cerdà's more conservative plan were never built, and the property passed to greedy landlords who constructed more buildings. Ruthless property speculation came immediately after work on the Eixample began in 1860. This dramatic story of failed hopes and dreams is told in Eduardo Mendoza's novel *The City of Marvels* and Robert Hughes's *Barcelona*.

Consistent with the general artistic stagnation in Spain during the Franco era (1939–75), the 1950s saw a tremendous increase in the number of anonymous housing projects around the periphery of Barcelona. Since the death of Franco, a cultural renaissance has ensued: New and more creative designs for buildings are again being executed.

ART

From the cave paintings discovered at Lérida to several true giants of the 20th century—Picasso, Dalí, and Miró—Catalonia has had a long and significant artistic tradition. It is the Spanish center of the plastic arts.

The first art movement to attract attention in Barcelona was **Catalonian Gothic sculpture,** which held sway from the 13th to the 15th centuries and produced such renowned masters as Bartomeu and Pere Johan. Sculptors working with Italian masters brought the Renaissance to Barcelona, but few great Catalonian legacies remain from this period. The rise of baroque art in the 17th and 18th centuries saw Catalonia filled with several impressive examples, but nothing worth a special pilgrimage.

In the neoclassical period of the 18th century, Catalonia, and particularly Barcelona, arose from an artistic slumber. Art schools opened and foreign painters arrived, exerting considerable influence. The 19th century produced many Catalonian artists who followed the general European trends of the time without forging any major creative breakthroughs.

The 20th century brought renewed artistic ferment in Barcelona, as reflected by the arrival of Málaga-born Pablo **Picasso.** (The Catalán capital today is the site of a major Picasso museum.) The great surrealist painters of the Spanish school, Joan **Miró** (who also has an eponymous museum in Barcelona) and Salvador **Dalí** (whose fantastical museum is along the Costa Brava, north of Barcelona), also came to the Catalonian capital.

Many Catalán sculptors achieved acclaim in this century, including Casanovas, Llimon, and Blay. The Spanish Civil War brought cultural stagnation, yet against all odds many Catalán artists continued to make bold statements. Antoni Tàpies was one of the principal artists of this period (one of the newest museums in Barcelona is devoted to his work). Among the various schools formed in Spain at the time was the neofigurative band, which included such artists as Váquez Díaz and Pancho Cossio.

Today many Barcelona artists are making major names for themselves, and their works are sold in the most prestigious galleries of the Western world. Outstanding among these is **Susana Solano,** who ranks among the most renowned names in Spanish contemporary art. In her metal sculptures and installations, she creates what one critic called "spatial objects that combine rigorously geometrical structures with sensually flowing shapes and material qualities."

MUSIC & DANCE

The counts of Barcelona, we are told, were great music lovers, and the Catalán appreciation of music continues to this day. Richard Strauss dedicated the musical center, the Palau de la Música Catalána, in 1908.

In addition to importing the great talents of Europe, the people of Catalonia create music. Many of their own artists and composers, most prominently Pablo Casals, have earned international acclaim.

But few artistic traditions enjoy the renown of the *sardana,* the national dance. This is truly a street dance, accompanied by *coblas* (brass bands). You can perform a *sardana* almost anywhere and at any time, provided you get some like-minded people to join you. Age doesn't matter—everybody joins in the spontaneous outburst. The dance's roots are unknown. Some claim that it originated on a Greek island and was brought to Barcelona by seafarers; others say it came from the Italian island of Sardinia, which would at least account for its name.

To see this dance, go to the Plaça de Sant Jaume in the Barri Gòtic on Sunday at noon. It's a group dance with participants forming a ring. Any number can participate; the ring just gets bigger. Joining hands, the dancers raise their arms and dance in repetitive rhythms in complete silence. Cataláns view the dance as a statement of their national identity. It has also represented peaceful resistance to oppression—they danced it during the dreaded Franco era.

2 Orientation

ARRIVING

BY PLANE Most travelers to Barcelona fly to Madrid and change planes there, although there are direct flights to Barcelona on TWA and Delta. Iberia offers many daily shuttle flights between Barcelona and Madrid—at 15-minute intervals during peak hours on weekdays—plus service from Valencia, Granada, Seville, and Bilbao. Generally cheaper than Iberia, both **Air Europa** (☎ 93-298-33-28) and **Spanair** (☎ 93-298-33-62) run shuttles between Madrid and Barcelona. Shuttle schedules depend on demand, with more frequent service in the early morning and late afternoon. For more information on flying into Madrid, refer to "Getting There," in chapter 2.

The airport, **El Prat de Llobregat,** 08820 Prat de Llobregat (☎ 93-298-38-38), is 7½ miles (12km) southwest of the city. The route to the center of town is carefully signposted. A train runs between the airport and Barcelona's Estació Central de Barcelona-Sants every day from 6:14am (the first airport departure) to 10:13pm (from Sants) or 10:43pm (the last city departure). The 21-minute trip cost 305 ptas. ($1.85) Monday to Friday, 350 ptas. ($2.10) Saturday and Sunday. If your hotel is near Plaça de Catalunya, you might opt for an Aerobús. It runs daily every 15 minutes between 5:30am and midnight from the airport and 11:15pm from the Plaça de Catalunya. The fare is 475 ptas. ($2.85). A taxi from the airport into central Barcelona costs approximately 3,000 to 3,500 ptas. ($18 to $21).

BY TRAIN   A train called the **Barcelona-TALGO** provides rail service between Paris and Barcelona in 11½ hours. For many other routes from the rest of Europe, you change trains at Port Bou, on the French-Spanish border. Most trains issue seat and sleeper reservations.

Trains arrive at the **Estació de França,** avenida Marqués de L'Argentera (metro: Barceloneta, L3), from points throughout Spain as well as from international cities. From Madrid there are four TALGOS trains per day that make the trip in 7 hours, and two night trains that take 9½ hours; from Seville, there are two trains daily making the 12-hour trip; and from Valencia, there are 11 trains daily making the 3½-hour trip. There are express night trains to and from Paris, Zurich, Milan, and Geneva.

The modernized 1929 station has a huge screen with updated information on train departures and arrivals, personalized ticket dispatching, a passenger attention center, a tourism information center, showers, internal baggage control, a first-aid center, and centers for hotel reservations and car rentals. It is much more than a departure point: The station also has an elegant restaurant, a cafeteria, a book-and-record store, a jazz club, and even a disco. Estació de França is steps from Ciutadella Park, the zoo, and the port, and is near Vila Olímpica.

RENFE also has a terminal at **Estació Central de Barcelona-Sants,** Plaça de Països Catalánes (metro: Sants-Estació). For general RENFE information, call ☎ 902-24-01-02.

BY BUS   Bus travel to Barcelona is possible but not popular—it's pretty slow. Barcelona's Estació del Nord is the arrival and departure point for **Enatcar** (☎ 93-245-25-28) buses to and from southern France and Italy. Enatcar also operates 21 buses per day to and from Madrid (trip time: 7½ hours) and 9 buses per day to and from Valencia (4½ hours). A one-way ticket from Madrid costs 3,200 ptas. ($19.20); from Valencia, 2,900 ptas. ($17.40).

Linebús (☎ 93-265-07-00) offers six trips a week to and from Paris. **Julià Via,** carrer Viriato (☎ 93-490-40-00), operates four buses a week to and from Frankfurt and another four per week to and from Marseille.

For bus travel to the beach resorts along the Costa Brava (see chapter 12, "Girona & the Costa Brava"), go to **Sarfa,** Estació del Nord (☎ 93-265-11-58). Trip time is usually 1 hour, 20 minutes.

BY CAR   From **France** (the usual European road approach to Barcelona), the major access route is at the eastern end of the **Pyrenees.** You have a choice of the express highway (**E-15**) or the more scenic coastal road. But be warned: If you take the coastal road in July and August, you will often encounter bumper-to-bumper traffic. You can also approach Barcelona via **Toulouse.** Cross the border into Spain at **Puigcerdá** (where there are frontier stations), near the principality of Andorra. From there, take the N-152 to Barcelona.

From **Madrid,** take the N-2 to Zaragoza, then the **A-2** to El Vendrell, followed by the **A-7** motorway to Barcelona. From the **Costa Blanca** or **Costa del Sol,** follow the E-15 north from Valencia along the eastern Mediterranean coast.

BY FERRY   Transmediterránea, Moll Sant Bertran, s/n (☎ 93-295-91-00), operates daily trips to and from the Balearic islands of Majorca (trip time: 8 hours) and Minorca (9 hours). In summer, it's important to have a reservation as far in advance as possible.

VISITOR INFORMATION

Barcelona has two types of tourist offices. The local government office deals with Spain in general and Catalunya in particular, with basic information about Barcelona. This organization has an office at the airport, **El Prat de Llobregat** (☎ 93-478-47-04), which you'll pass as you clear customs. Summer hours are Monday to Saturday 9:30am to 8:30pm; off-season hours are Monday to Saturday 9:30am to 8pm; year-round, it's open Sunday 9:30am to 3pm. There is another large office in the center of Barcelona at the **Palau de Rubert,** Passeig de Gràcia, 107 (☎ 93-238-40-40), where there are often exhibitions. It's open daily 10am to 7pm.

The other organization, the **Oficina de Informació de Turisme de Barcelona,** Plaça de Catalunya, 17-S (☎ 93-304-34-21 or 906-30-12-82 from inside Spain), deals exclusively with the city of Barcelona. The staff can help you make hotel reservations in person and by telephone (☎ 93-304-34-34). This is also where you can get detailed information about the city and the Barcelona card for tourist discounts. The office is open daily 9am to 9pm. The same organization has an office at the **Estació Central de Barcelona-Sants** (Sants railway station), Plaça de Päisos Catalánes (no phone; metro: Sants-Estació). In summer it is open daily 8am to 8pm; off-season, Monday to Friday 8am to 8pm, Saturday and Sunday 8am to 2pm.

CITY LAYOUT

MAIN SQUARES, STREETS & ARTERIES   Plaça de Catalunya (Plaza de Cataluña in Spanish) is the city's heart; the world-famous **Rambles** (Ramblas) are its arteries. Les Rambles begins at the Plaça Portal de la Pau, with its 164-foot-high monument to Columbus and a panoramic view of the port, and stretches north to the Plaça de Catalunya. Along this wide promenade you'll find bookshops and newsstands, stalls selling birds and flowers, and benches or cafe tables and chairs, where you can sit and watch the passing parade.

At the end of the Rambles is the **Barri Xinés** (Barrio Chino, or Chinese Quarter). It has long enjoyed notoriety as a haven of prostitution and drugs, populated in Jean Genet's *The Thief's Journal* by "whores, thieves, pimps, and beggars." Still a dangerous district, it is best viewed during the day, if at all.

Off the Rambles lies **Plaça Reial** (Plaza Real), the most harmoniously proportioned square in Barcelona. Come here on Sunday morning to see the stamp and coin collectors peddle their wares.

The major wide boulevards of Barcelona are the **avinguda** (avenida) **Diagonal** and **Passeig** (Paseo) **de Colom,** and an elegant shopping street, the **Passeig de Gràcia.**

A short walk from the Rambles will take you to the **Passeig del Moll de la Fusta,** a waterfront promenade developed in the 1990s. It's home to some of the best (but

The Barcelona Card

An ideal way to appreciate Barcelona better and save money at the same time is with the Barcelona card. It's definitely a bargain if you stay in the city for more than an afternoon and do any sightseeing at all. For 24 hours it costs 2,500 ptas. ($15) for adults, 2,000 ptas. ($12) for children 6 to 15. For 48 hours it is 3,000 ptas. ($18) for adults, 2,500 ptas. ($15) for children; for 72 hours, 3,500 ptas. ($21) and 3,000 ptas. ($18).

The card offers visitors many advantages. The 24-hour card covers 10 free journeys on the metro or bus, and the 48- and 72-hour cards offer unlimited travel on all public transport. Cardholders get 25% discounts on the Tombbus (which runs along the best shopping route in central Barcelona) and the Tibibus (to the Fun Fair on Mount Tibidabo). On airport and tourist buses, fares are reduced by 15%.

Culture vultures who hold the card can get discounts of 30% to 50% in 28 museums. Eleven theaters and shows grant a 10% to 25% discount, which also applies at 16 leisure and night venues. Barcelona is famous for its designers, whose work ranges from clothes to ceramics. With this card you get a 12% discount at 23 leading stores. Finally, there is an 8% discount in 11 restaurants. The cards specify where they can be used. They're for sale at the tourist offices at the airport, at Sants station, and in the Plaça de Catalunya (see "Visitor Information," above).

not the cheapest) restaurants in Barcelona. If you can't afford the prices, come here at least for a drink in the open air and a view of the harbor.

To the east is the old port, **La Barceloneta,** which dates from the 18th century. This strip of land between the port and the sea has traditionally been a good place for seafood.

Barri Gòtic (Barrio Gótico, or Gothic Quarter) is east of the Rambles. This is the site of the city's oldest buildings, including the cathedral.

North of Plaça de Catalunya, the **Eixample** unfolds. An area of wide boulevards, in contrast to the labyrinthine Gothic Quarter, it contains two major roads that lead out of Barcelona: the avinguda Diagonal and Gran Vía de les Corts Catalánes. Another major neighborhood, working-class **Gràcia,** is north of the Eixample.

Montjuïc, one of the city's mountains, begins at Plaça d'Espanya, a traffic rotary, beyond which are Barcelona's famous fountains. Montjuïc was the setting for the principal events of the 1992 Summer Olympic Games. The other mountain is **Tibidabo,** in the northwest, which boasts great views of the city and the Mediterranean. It has an amusement park.

FINDING AN ADDRESS/MAPS   Finding a Barcelona address can be a problem. The city abounds with long boulevards and a complicated maze of narrow, twisting streets. Knowing the street number, if there is one, is essential. The designation s/n (*sin número*) means that the building has no number. It's crucial to learn the cross street if you're seeking a specific address.

The rule about street numbers is that there is no rule. On most streets, numbering begins on one side and runs up that side until the end, then runs in the opposite direction on the other side. Number 40 might be opposite 408. But there are many exceptions. Sometimes street numbers on buildings in the older quarters have been obscured by the patina of time.

Arm yourself with a good map before setting out. Free maps from tourist offices and hotels aren't adequate because they don't label the little streets. The best map for exploring Barcelona, published by **Falk,** is available at most bookstores and news-stands, such as those found along the Rambles. This pocket map includes all the streets, with an index of how to find them.

Neighborhoods in Brief

Barri Gòtic   This section rises to the north of Passeig de Colom, with its **Columbus Monument.** Its eastern border is a major artery, Via Laietana, which begins at La Barceloneta at Plaça d'Antoni López and runs north to Plaça d'Urquinaona. Les Rambles forms the western border of the Gothic Quarter, and on the northern edge is the Ronda de Sant Pere, which intersects with **Plaça de Catalunya** and the **Passeig de Gràcia.** The heart of this medieval quarter is the **Plaça de Sant Jaume,** which was a major crossroads in the old Roman city. Many of the structures in the old section are ancient, including the ruins of a Roman temple dedicated to Augustus. Antique stores, restaurants, cafes, museums, some hotels, and bookstores fill the area today. It is also the headquarters of the **Generalitat,** seat of the Catalán government.

Les Rambles   Also commonly known as **La Rambla.** The most famous promenade in Spain, ranking with Madrid's Paseo del Prado, it was once a drainage channel. These days, street entertainers, flower vendors, news vendors, cafe patrons, and strollers flow along its length. The gradual 1-mile descent toward the sea has often been called a metaphor for life because its bustling action combines cosmopolitanism and crude vitality.

Les Rambles actually consists of five sections, each a particular *rambla*—Rambla de Canaletes, Rambla dels Estudis, Rambla de Sant Josep, Rambla dels Caputxins, and Rambla de Santa Mònica. The shaded pedestrian esplanade runs from the Plaça de Catalunya to the port—all the way to the Columbus Monument. Along the way you'll pass the **Gran Teatre del Liceu,** on Rambla dels Caputxins, one of the most magnifi-cent opera houses in the world until it caught fire in 1994 and had to be rebuilt. Miró did a sidewalk mosaic at the Plaça de la Boquería. During the stagnation of the Franco era, this street grew seedier and seedier, but the opening of the Ramada Renaissance hotel and the restoration of many buildings have brought energy and hope for the street.

Barri Xinés   Despite the name ("Chinese Quarter"), this isn't Chinatown—histori-ans are unsure how the neighborhood got its name. For decades it's had an unsavory reputation. Franco outlawed prostitution in 1956, but apparently no one ever told the denizens of this district of narrow, often murky, old streets and dark corners. Petty thieves, drug dealers, and purse-snatchers are just some of the neighborhood characters. Nighttime is dangerous, so exercise caution; still, most visitors like to take a quick look to see what all the excitement is about. Just off Les Rambles, the area is primarily between the waterfront and carrer de l'Hospital. Although it has a long way to go, Barri Xinés is undergoing tremendous change that began before the '92 Olympics. An urban renewal program has led to the destruction of some of the seedier parts of the *barrio.* The opening of the **Museu d'Art Contemporani** at Plaça dels Angels has led to a revitalization of the area and the opening of a lot more art galleries. The official name Barcelona has given to this district is **El Raval.**

Barri de la Ribera   Another neighborhood that stagnated for years but is now well into a renaissance, the Barri de la Ribera is adjacent to the Barri Gòtic, going east to Passeig de Picasso, which borders the Parc de la Ciutadella. The centerpiece of this district is the **Museu Picasso,** housed in the 15th-century Palau Agüilar, Montcada, 15. Numerous art galleries have opened around the museum, and the old quarter is fashionable. Many mansions in this area were built during one of Barcelona's major maritime expansions, principally in the 1200s and 1300s. Most of these grand homes still stand along **carrer de Montcada** and other nearby streets.

La Barceloneta & the Harbor Front   Although Barcelona has a long seagoing tradition, its waterfront was in decay for years. Today, the waterfront promenade, **Passeig del Moll de la Fusta,** bursts with activity. The best way to get a bird's-eye view of the area is to take an elevator to the top of the Columbus Monument in Plaça Portal de la Pau.

Near the monument were the **Reials Drassanes,** or royal shipyards, a booming place during Barcelona's maritime heyday in the Middle Ages. Years before Columbus landed in the New World, ships sailed around the world from here, flying the traditional yellow-and-red flag of Catalonia.

To the east is a mainly artificial peninsula, **La Barceloneta** (Little Barcelona). Formerly a fishing district dating mainly from the 18th century, it's now filled with seafood restaurants. The blocks here are long and surprisingly narrow—architects planned them that way so that each room in every building fronted a street. Many bus lines terminate at the Passeig Nacional, site of the **Barcelona Aquarium.**

The Eixample   To the north of the Plaça de Catalunya is the Eixample, or Ensanche, the section of Barcelona that grew beyond the old medieval walls. This great period of enlargement (*eixample* in Catalán) came mainly in the 19th century. Avenues form a grid of perpendicular streets, cut across by a majestic boulevard—**Passeig de Gràcia,** a posh shopping street ideal for leisurely promenades. The area's main traffic artery is **avinguda Diagonal,** which links the expressway and the heart of the congested city.

The Eixample was the center of Barcelona's *modernisme* movement, and it possesses some of the most original buildings any architect ever designed. Gaudí's Sagrada Família is one of the major attractions.

Montjuïc & Tibidabo   Montjuïc, called Hill of the Jews after a Jewish necropolis there, gained prominence in 1929 as the site of the World's Fair and again in 1992 as the site of the Summer Olympic Games. Its major attractions are the Joan Miró museum, the Olympic installations, and the **Poble Espanyol** (Spanish Village), a 5-acre site constructed for the World's Fair. Examples of Spanish art and architecture are on display against the backdrop of a traditional Spanish village. Tibidabo (1,650 feet [503m]) is where you should go for your final look at Barcelona. On a clear day you can see the mountains of Majorca (the largest and most famous of the Balearic Islands), some 130 miles (209km) away. Reached by train, tram, and cable car, Tibidabo is the most popular Sunday excursion in Barcelona.

Pedralbes   Pedralbes is where wealthy Barcelonans live, some in stylish blocks of apartment houses, others in 19th-century villas behind ornamental fences, still others in stunning *modernisme* structures. Set in a park, the **Palau de Pedralbes** (avinguda Diagonal, 686) was constructed in the 1920s as a gift from the city to Alfonso XIII, the grandfather of King Juan Carlos. The king abdicated and fled in 1931, and never made much use of the palace. Today it has a new life, housing a museum of carriages and a group of European paintings called the **Colecció Cambó.**

Vila Olímpica   This seafront property contains the tallest buildings in the city. The revitalized site, in the post–Olympic Games era, is the setting for many imported-car showrooms, designer clothing stores, restaurants, and business offices. The "village" was where the athletes lived during the 1992 games. A miniature city is taking shape, complete with banks, art galleries, nightclubs, bars, and even pastry shops.

3 Getting Around

To save money on public transportation, buy a card that's good for 10 trips. **Tarjeta T-1,** for 795 ptas. ($4.75), is good for the metro and the bus. **Tarjeta T-2,** for 760 ptas. ($4.55), covers everything but the bus. Passes (*abonos temporales*) are available at **Transports Metropolita de Barcelona,** Plaça de la Universitat. It's open Monday to Friday 8am to 7pm, Saturday 8am to 1pm.

To save money on sightseeing tours during the summer, ride on **Bus Turistic,** which passes by 24 of the most popular sights. You can get on and off the bus as you please, and the price covers the Tibidabo funicular and the Montjuïc cable car and funicular. Tickets, which can be purchased on the bus or at the tourist office at Plaça de Catalunya, cost 1,800 ptas. ($10.80) for 1 day, 2,300 ptas. ($13.80) for 2 days.

BY SUBWAY

Barcelona's metro system consists of five main lines; it crisscrosses the city more frequently and with greater efficiency than the bus network. Two commuter trains run between the city and the suburbs. Service operates Monday to Friday 5am to 11pm, Saturday 5am to 1am, and Sunday and holidays 6am to 1am. The one-way fare is 145 ptas. (85¢). Each metro station entrance is marked with a red diamond. The major station for all subway lines is **Plaça de Catalunya.**

BY BUS

Some 50 bus lines traverse the city, and as always, you don't want to ride them at rush hour. The driver issues a ticket as you board at the front. Most buses operate daily 6:30am to 10pm; some night buses go along the principal arteries from 11pm to 4am. Buses are color-coded—red ones cut through the city center during the day, and yellow ones do the job at night. The one-way fare is 145 ptas. (85¢).

BY TAXI

Each yellow-and-black taxi bears the letters SP (*servicio público*) on its front and rear. A lit green light on the roof and a LIBRE sign in the window indicate the taxi is free to pick up passengers. The basic rate begins at 300 ptas. ($2). Check to make sure you're not paying the fare of a previously departed passenger; taxi drivers have been known to "forget" to turn back the meter. Each additional kilometer in slow-moving traffic costs 110 to 120 ptas. (75¢ to 80¢). Supplements might apply—150 ptas. ($1) for a large suitcase placed in the trunk, for instance. Rides to the airport sometimes carry a supplement of 300 ptas. ($2). For a taxi, call ☎ **93-330-08-04.**

BY CAR

Driving in congested Barcelona is frustrating and potentially dangerous. Besides, it's unlikely you'd ever find a place to park. Try other means of getting around. Save your car rentals for excursions and for when you're ready to move on.

All three of the major U.S.-based car-rental firms are represented in Barcelona, both at the airport and (except for Budget) downtown. The longest hours and some of the most favorable rates are at the airport office of **Budget** (☎ **93-298-35-00**), open daily 7am to midnight, without a midday break.

Avis, carrer de Casanova, 209 (☎ **93-209-95-33**), is open Monday to Friday 8am to 1pm and 4 to 7pm, Saturday 8am to 1pm. **Hertz** is at Tuset, 10 (☎ **93-217-80-76**); it's open Monday to Friday 8am to 2pm and 4 to 7pm, Saturday 9am to 1pm. Hertz and Avis are closed on Sunday except in the airport, where they are open 7am to midnight daily. This forces clients of those companies to trek out to the airport to pick up or return their cars; however, after-hours arrangements can be made.

Barcelona Metro

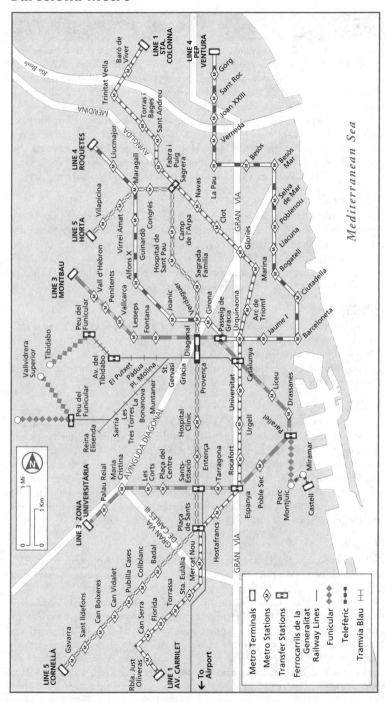

Remember that it's usually cheaper and easier to arrange your car rental before leaving the United States. For more information on car rentals in Spain, refer to "Getting Around," in chapter 2.

BY FUNICULAR & RAIL LINKS

At some point in your journey, you may want to visit Tibidabo or Montjuïc (or both). A train called **Tramvía Blau** (Blue Streetcar) goes from Plaça Kennedy to the bottom of the funicular to Tibidabo. It operates every 15 to 20 minutes 9:05am to 9:35pm on weekends only. The fare is 300 ptas. ($1.80) one-way, 450 ptas. ($2.70) round-trip. During the week, buses run from the Plaça Kennedy to the bottom of the funicular from approximately 7am to 9:30pm daily. The bus costs 145 ptas. (85¢) one-way.

At the end of the run, you can go the rest of the way by funicular to the top, at 1,650 feet (503m), for a stunning panoramic view of Barcelona. The funicular operates only when the Fun Fair at Tibidabo is open. Opening times vary according to the time of year and the weather conditions. As a rule, the funicular starts operating 20 minutes before the Fun Fair opens, then every half hour. During peak visiting hours, it runs every 15 minutes. The fare is 300 ptas. ($1.80) one-way, 400 ptas. ($2.40) round-trip.

The **Tibibus** (☎ 93-211-79-42) goes from the Plaça de Catalunya, in the center of the city, to Tibidabo from June 24 to September 15, Tuesday to Sunday, and on every weekend off-season. It runs every 30 minutes from 10:30am to 6:30pm and sometimes 8:30pm, depending on when the park closes. The one-way fare is 270 ptas. ($1.60). To reach Montjuïc, the site of the 1992 Olympics, take the **Montjuïc funicular** (☎ 93-318-70-74). It links with subway line 3 at Parallel. The funicular operates June 13 to September 30 daily, 11am to 10pm. In winter it operates daily 10:45am to 8pm. The round-trip fare is 600 ptas. ($3.60).

A **cable car** linking the upper part of the Montjuïc funicular with Castell de Montjuïc is in service in winter, daily 11:15am to 6:30pm (until 7:30pm on weekends). The one-way fare is 400 ptas. ($2.40); the round-trip fare is 600 ptas. ($3.60) for adults, 500 ptas. ($3) for children. From June 28 to September 15 and holidays, it operates Monday to Friday 11:15am to 8pm, until 9pm on weekends.

The **Montjuïc telèferic** (cable car) runs from Barceloneta to Montjuïc. Service June 20 to September 15 is daily 10:30am to 7pm, and noon to 5pm in winter. The fare is 1,000 ptas. ($6) one-way, 1,200 ptas. ($7.20) round-trip.

Fast Facts: Barcelona

American Express   The office is at Passeig de Gràcia, 101 (☎ 93-217-00-70; metro: Diagonal), near the corner of carrer del Rosselló. It's open Monday to Friday 9:30am to 6pm, Saturday 9am to noon.

Consulates   For information on embassies, refer to chapter 2, "Fast Facts: Spain." The **U.S. Consulate,** Reina Elisenda, 23 (☎ 93-280-22-27; train: Reina Elisenda), is open Monday to Friday 9am to 12:30pm and 3 to 5pm. The **Canadian Consulate,** Passeig de Gràcia, 77, 3rd floor (☎ 93-215-07-04; metro: Passeig de Gràcia), is open Monday to Friday 10am to noon. The **U.K. Consulate,** avinguda Diagonal, 477 (☎ 93-366-62-00; metro: Hospital Clinic), is open Monday to Friday 9:30am to 1:30pm and 4 to 5pm. The **Australian Consulate** is at Gran Vía Carlos III, 98, ninth floor (☎ 93-330-94-96; metro: María Cristina), and is open Monday to Friday 10am to noon.

Currency Exchange   Most banks exchange currency Monday to Friday 8:30am to 2pm and—in the downtown area, except in the summer—on Saturday 8:30am to 1pm. A major *oficina de cambio* (exchange office) is at the Estació Central de Barcelona-Sants, the principal rail station. It's open Monday to Saturday 8:30am to 10pm, Sunday 8:30am to 2pm and 4:30 to 10pm. Exchange offices at Barcelona's airport, El Prat de Llobregat, are open daily 6:30am to 11pm.

Dentist   Call the **Clínica Dental Beonadex,** Passeig Bonanova, 69, 3rd floor (☎ **93-418-44-33**), for an appointment. It's open Monday 3 to 9pm, Tuesday to Friday 8am to 3pm.

Doctors   See "Hospitals," below.

Drugstores   The most centrally located one is **Farmacia Manuel Nadal i Casas,** Rambla de Canaletes, 121 (☎ **93-317-49-42;** metro: Plaça de Catalunya). It's open daily 9am to 1:30pm and 4:30 to 10pm. Pharmacies take turns staying open late at night. Those that aren't open post the names and addresses of pharmacies in the area that are.

Emergencies   Fire, ☎ **080;** police, ☎ **092;** ambulance, ☎ **061.**

Hospitals   Barcelona has many hospitals and clinics, including **Hospital Clínic** and **Hospital de la Santa Creu i Sant Pau,** at the intersection of carrer Cartagena and carrer Sant Antoni Maria Claret (☎ **93-291-90-00;** metro: Hospital de Sant Pau).

Internet Access   **El Café de Internet,** avenida de las Corts Catalánes, 656 (☎ **34-93-412-1915;** e-mail: JordiCarcellaChoia@sevicom.es), is open daily 9am to midnight; the cost is 600 ptas. ($3.60) for 30 minutes.

Laundry   Ask at your hotel for the self-serve laundry nearest you, or try one of the following. **Lavandería Brasilia,** avinguda Meridiana, 322 (☎ **93-352-72-05;** metro: Plaça de Catalunya), is open Monday to Friday 9am to 1:30pm and 4 to 8pm, Saturday 10am to 7pm. Also centrally located is **Lavandería Yolanda,** carrer Carma, 114 (☎ **93-329-43-68;** metro: Liceu, at Les Rambles). It is open Monday to Friday 9am to 1:30pm and 4 to 8pm, Saturday 9am to 1:30pm.

Newspapers & Magazines   *The International Herald-Tribune* is sold at major hotels and nearly all the news kiosks along Les Rambles. Sometimes you can buy *USA Today* or one of the London newspapers, such as the *Times.* Barcelona's leading daily newspapers, which often list cultural events, are *El Periódico* and *La Vanguardia.*

Police   In an emergency, call ☎ **092.**

Post Office   The main post office is at Plaça d'Antoni López (☎ **93-318-38-31;** metro: Jaume I). It's open Monday to Saturday 8:30am to 9:30pm for sending letters and telegrams, and Sunday 9am to 2pm for letters and 8am to 10pm for telegrams.

Safety   Be particularly careful with cameras, purses, and wallets, all favorite targets of thieves and pickpockets in Barcelona, and particularly on the world-famous Rambles. The southern part of Les Rambles, near the waterfront, is the most dangerous section, especially at night. Proceed with caution.

Taxis   See "Getting Around," earlier in this chapter.

Telephone   Dial ☎ **1003** for information in Barcelona. For elsewhere in Spain, dial ☎ **1009.** Most local calls cost 25 ptas. (15¢). Hotels impose surcharges on phone calls, especially long distance, either in Spain or abroad.

There is no longer a central telephone office, but calls can be made in comfort and security from phone centers on Les Rambles.

Transit Information   For general RENFE (train) information, dial ☎ **93-490-02-02.** For airport information, call ☎ **902-24-02-02.**

4 Where to Stay

Barcelona's hotel options have never been better or more plentiful. It may be one of the most expensive cities in Spain, but prices at Barcelona's first-class and deluxe hotels are completely in line with those in other major European cities—and they even look reasonable when stacked up against the prices in Paris and London. A favorable U.S. dollar exchange rate makes prices more affordable.

Safety is an important factor when choosing a hotel. Some of the least expensive hotels are not in good locations. A popular area for budget-conscious travelers is the **Barri Gòtic** (Gothic Quarter), in the heart of town. You'll live and eat less expensively here than in any other part of Barcelona, but you should be careful when returning to your hotel late at night.

More modern, but more expensive, accommodations can be found north of the Barri Gòtic in the **Eixample district,** centered on the metro stops Plaça de Catalunya and Universitat. Many buildings are in the *modernisme* style, from the first 2 decades of this century—and sometimes the elevators and plumbing are of the same vintage. The Eixample is a desirable and safe neighborhood, especially along its wide boulevards. Noise is the only problem you might encounter.

Farther north, above the avinguda Diagonal, you'll enter the **Gràcia** area, where you can enjoy distinctively Catalán neighborhood life. The main attractions are a bit distant but reached easily by public transportation.

Many of Barcelona's hotels were built before the invention of the automobile, and even those that weren't rarely found space for a garage. When parking is available at the hotel, the price is indicated; otherwise, the hotel staff will direct you to a garage. Expect to pay upward of 2,000 ptas. ($13.40) for 24 hours, and if you do have a car, you might as well park it and leave it there, because we'd never recommend driving around the city.

CIUTAT VELLA

The Ciutat Vella (Old City) forms the monumental center of Barcelona, taking in Les Rambles, Plaça de Sant Jaume, Via Laietana, Passeig Nacional, and Passeig de Colom. Its older structures contain some of the city's best hotel bargains. Most of the glamorous, and more expensive, hotels are in Sur Diagonal (see below).

VERY EXPENSIVE

✪ **Le Meridien Barcelona.** Les Rambles, 111, 08002 Barcelona. ☎ **800/543-4300** in the U.S., or 93-318-62-00. Fax 93-301-77-76. www.meridienbarcelona.com. E-mail: lemeridien@ meridienbarcelona.com. 205 units. A/C MINIBAR TV TEL. 42,000–52,000 ptas. ($252–$312) double; from 65,000 ptas. ($390) suite. AE, DC, MC, V. Parking 2,000 ptas. ($12). Metro: Liceu or Plaça de Catalunya.

This is the finest hotel in the old town, as the roster of famous guests (such as Michael Jackson) can surely attest. It's superior in both amenities and comfort to its two closest rivals in the area, the Colón and the Rivoli Ramblas (note that it's also more expensive than either of these choices). Originally built in 1956, it's a medley of artful pastels and tasteful decorating. Guest rooms are spacious and comfortable, with extra-large beds, heated bathroom floors, on-command movies, hair dryers, and two

Barcelona Accommodations

Avenida Palace **13**
Claris **8**
Duques de Bergara **9**
Gran Hotel Havana **10**
Granvía **11**
Hotel Balmes **5**
Hotel Colón **18**
Hotel Condes
  de Barcelona **6**
Hotel Continental **21**
Hotel Cortés **19**
Hotel Derby/
  Hotel Gran Derby **2**
Hotel Espana **25**
Hotel Hespería **1**
Hotel Majestic **7**
Hotel Meliá
  Barcelona Sarriá **3**
Hotel Princess Sofía **3**
Hotel Regencia Colón **17**
Hotel Ritz **12**
Hotel San Agustín **24**
Hotel Wilson **4**
Meridien Barcelona **22**
Mesón Castilla **14**
Montecarlo **16**
Rey Juan Carlos **3**
Rivoli Ramblas **20**
Turín **14**

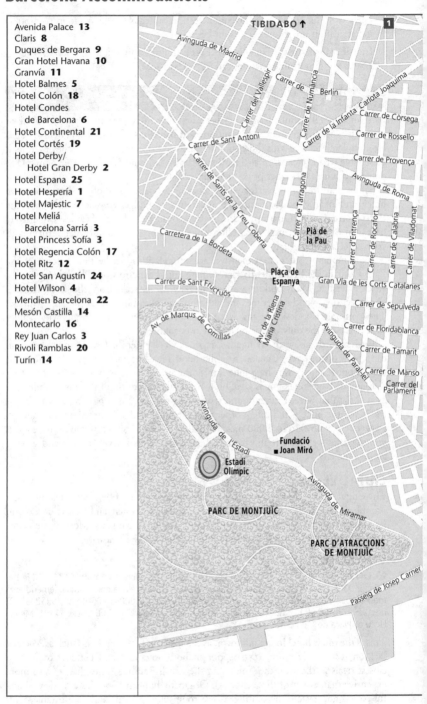

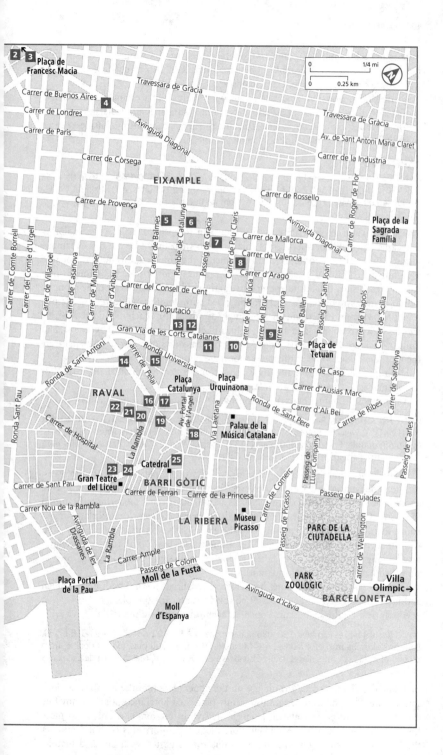

Plaça de Francesc Macià

Carrer de Buenos Aires

Carrer de Londres

Carrer de Paris

Travessara de Gràcia

Avinguda Diagonal

Carrer de Còrsega

Travessara de Gràcia

Av. de Sant Antoni Maria Claret

Carrer de la Industria

EIXAMPLE

Carrer de Rossello

Carrer de Provença

Carrer de Balmes

Rambla de Catalunya

Passeig de Gràcia

Carrer de Pau Claris

Avinguda Diagonal

Carrer de Roger de Flor

Plaça de la Sagrada Família

Carrer de Mallorca

Carrer de Valencia

Carrer d'Aragó

Carrer del Comte Borrell

Carrer del Comte d'Urgell

Carrer de Villarroel

Carrer de Casanova

Carrer de Muntaner

Carrer d'Aribau

Carrer del Consell de Cent

Carrer de la Diputació

Carrer de R. de Llúcia

Carrer del Bruc

Carrer de Girona

Carrer de Bailén

Passeig de Sant Joan

Carrer de Napols

Carrer de Sicilia

Gran Via de les Corts Catalanes

Plaça de Tetuan

Ronda de Sant Antoni

Carrer de Pelai

Ronda Universitat

Carrer de Casp

Carrer de Sardenya

Ronda Sant Pau

RAVAL

Plaça Catalunya

Plaça Urquinaona

Carrer d'Ausias Marc

Carrer d'Ali Bei

Carrer de Ribes

Passeig de Carles I

Carrer de Hospital

Av. Portal de l'Angel

Via Laietana

Ronda de Sant Pere

La Rambla

Palau de la Música Catalana

Passeig de Lluís Companys

Catedral

Carrer de Sant Pau

Gran Teatre del Liceu

BARRI GÒTIC

Carrer de Ferran

Carrer de la Princesa

Passeig de Comerç

Passeig de Picasso

Passeig de Pujades

PARC DE LA CIUTADELLA

Carrer de Wellington

Carrer Nou de la Rambla

LA RIBERA

Museu Picasso

Avinguda de les Drassanes

La Rambla

Carrer Ample

Passeig de Colom

Moll de la Fusta

PARK ZOOLOGIC

Villa Olímpic →

Plaça Portal de la Pau

Moll d'Espanya

Avinguda d'Icàvia

BARCELONETA

0   1/4 mi

0   0.25 km

phones in each room. All rooms have double-glazed windows, but that doesn't fully block out noise from Les Rambles. The Renaissance Club, an executive floor popular with businesspeople, provides extra amenities.

Dining/Diversions: A chic lobby bar, open daily 7pm to 2am, has live piano music. The main restaurant, **Le Patio,** serves fine continental and Catalán cuisine.

Amenities: 24-hour room service, laundry, concierge, baby-sitting, business center, rooms for travelers with disabilities. Small gym nearby.

EXPENSIVE

Hotel Colón. Avinguda de la Catedral, 7, 08002 Barcelona. ☎ **800/845-0636** in the U.S., or 93-301-14-04. Fax 93-317-29-15. E-mail: colon@nexus.es. 148 units. A/C MINIBAR TV TEL. 26,000–40,000 ptas. ($156–$240) double; from 46,000 ptas. ($276) suite. AE, DC, MC, V. Bus: 16, 17, 19, or 45.

The Colón is an appropriate choice if you plan to spend a lot of time exploring Barcelona's medieval neighborhoods. Blessed with what might be the most dramatic location in the city, opposite the main entrance to the cathedral, this hotel sits behind a dignified neoclassical facade with carved pilasters and ornamental wrought-iron balustrades. Inside, you'll find conservative and slightly old-fashioned public rooms, a helpful staff, and good-sized guest rooms filled with comfortable furniture. Despite recent renovations, they retain an appealingly dowdy charm. Each room comes with a hair dryer, a private safe, and a first-rate firm mattress. Not all rooms have views, and units in back are quieter. Sixth-floor rooms with balconies overlooking the square are the most desirable. Some of the lower rooms are rather dark.

Dining: The hotel maintains two well-recommended restaurants, the **Grill** (for continental specialties) and **Carabela.**

Amenities: 24-hour room service, laundry and valet, limousine, concierge, baby-sitting.

Hotel NH Calderón. Rambla de Catalunya, 26, 08007 Barcelona. ☎ **93-301-00-00**. Fax 93-412-41-93. www.nh-hoteles.es. 283 units. A/C MINIBAR TV TEL. Mon–Thurs 26,100 ptas. ($156.60) double; Fri–Sun 22,500 ptas. ($135) double. AE, DC, MC, V. Parking 2,000 ptas. ($12). Metro: Passeig de Gràcia or Plaça de Catalunya.

Efficient, well maintained, and well staffed with a multilingual corps of employees, this hotel delivers exactly what it promises: Safe and comfortable accommodations in a well-conceived, standardized format that's akin to many other modern hotels around the world. Originally built in the 1960s, this 10-story hotel wasn't particularly imaginative then, but was greatly improved in the early 1990s after its acquisition by NH, with frequent renovations ever since. Accommodations have comfortable, contemporary-looking furnishings with hints of high-tech design, good lighting, lots of varnished hardwood, and colorful fabrics.

Dining/Diversions: The hotel has a formal restaurant serving both a Catalonian and international cuisine, and a bar often filled with businesspeople.

Amenities: Health club, sauna, open-air swimming pool on the roof.

Rivoli Ramblas. Les Rambles, 128, 08002 Barcelona. ☎ **93-302-66-43**. Fax 93-318-87-60. E-mail: rivoli@alba.mssl.es. 87 units. A/C MINIBAR TV TEL. 33,000 ptas. ($198) double; from 85,000 ptas. ($510) suite. Rates include breakfast. AE, DC, MC, V. Metro: Plaça de Catalunya or Liceu.

Behind a dignified art deco townhouse on the upper section of the Rambles, a block south of the Plaça de Catalunya, this recently renovated hotel incorporates many fine examples of avant-garde Catalán design in its stylish interior. The Colón has more tradition and style, and the Meridien more modern comfort; this is choice number three in the old town. The minimalist public rooms glisten with polished marble.

Guest rooms are carpeted, soundproofed, and elegant, but rather cramped. Guest rooms have safe-deposit boxes, VCRs, radios, and TVs with satellite hookups.

Dining/Diversions: Le Brut Restaurant serves regional, Spanish, and international dishes. **Blue Moon** cocktail bar features piano music. A rooftop terrace, suitable for coffee or drinks, offers a view over the rooftops of one of Barcelona's most architecturally interesting neighborhoods.

Amenities: Room service, baby-sitting, concierge, laundry and valet, small health club and fitness center, sauna, solarium, car rentals, boutiques.

MODERATE

✪ **Duques de Bergara.** Bergara, 11, 08002 Barcelona. ☎ **93-301-51-51.** Fax 93-317-34-42. 149 units. A/C MINIBAR TV TEL. 26,000 ptas. ($156) double; 34,000 ptas. ($204) triple. AE, DC, MC, V. Public parking nearby 3,000 ptas. ($18). Metro: Plaça de Catalunya.

This upscale hotel occupies an 1899 townhouse built for the duke of Bergara. In 1998, the original five-story structure more than doubled in size with the addition of a new seven-story tower. Guest rooms throughout have the same conservative, traditional comforts. Each unit has large, comfortable beds with first-rate mattresses, elegant fabrics, and good lighting. The roomy marble bathrooms are equipped with plush towels and hair dryers. Public areas contain most of the paneling, stained glass, and decorative accessories originally installed by modernisme architect Emilio Salas i Cortes, a professor of the movement's greatest luminary, Gaudí. In the reception area, look for stained-glass panels displaying the heraldic coat of arms of the building's original occupant and namesake, the duke of Bergara.

On the premises are a restaurant, El Duc (see "Where to Dine," below), a bar and cafe one floor above the lobby, and an outdoor swimming pool that's generally a hopping social scene in the afternoon and early evening.

Hotel Regencia Colón. Sagristans, 13–17, 08002 Barcelona. ☎ **93-318-98-58.** Fax 93-317-28-22. 55 units. A/C MINIBAR TV TEL. 18,000 ptas. ($108) double; 20,500 ptas. ($123) triple. AE, DC, MC, V. Metro: Plaça de Catalunya or Urquinaona.

This stately stone six-story building stands directly behind the pricier Hotel Colón and in the shadow of the cathedral. The Regencia Colón attracts tour groups because it's a good value for Barcelona. The formal lobby seems a bit dour, but the well-maintained rooms are comfortable and often roomy, albeit worn. Rooms are insulated against sound, and 40 have full bathrooms with tubs (the remainder have showers only). All have comfortable beds and piped-in music. The hotel's location is a plus.

Montecarlo. Les Rambles, 124, 08002 Barcelona. ☎ **93-412-04-04.** Fax 93-318-73-23. E-mail: montecarlobcn@abaforum.es. 74 units. A/C MINIBAR TV TEL. 18,000–23,000 ptas. ($108–$138) double; 26,500 ptas. ($159) triple. AE, DC, MC, V. Parking 2,000 ptas. ($12). Metro: Plaça de Catalunya.

This hotel beside the Rambles was built around 200 years ago as an opulent private home. In the 1930s it was transformed into the comfortably unpretentious hotel you'll find today. It offers a level of comfort superior to that of most competitors. Each of the midsized guest rooms is efficiently decorated and comfortable. Double-glazed windows help keep out some of the noise. Public areas include some of the building's original accessories, with carved doors, a baronial fireplace, and crystal chandeliers.

INEXPENSIVE

Granvía. Gran Vía de les Corts Catalánes, 642, 08007 Barcelona. ☎ **93-318-19-00.** Fax 93-318-99-97. 50 units. A/C MINIBAR TV TEL. 13,500 ptas. ($81) double. AE, DC, MC, V. Parking 2,300 ptas. ($13.80). Metro: Plaça de Catalunya.

A grand hotel on one of the most fashionable boulevards in Barcelona, the Granvía has public rooms that reflect the opulence of the 1860s—chandeliers, gilt mirrors, and French provincial furniture—and a grand balustraded staircase. It's your best choice if you want to feel like royalty but not pay a king's ransom. Although the traditional guest rooms contain interesting antique reproductions, they are comfortable rather than luxurious. Expect fancifully shaped headboards and pastel-colored chenille bedspreads, along with upholstery that needs refreshing. Rooms vary in shape and size. The courtyard, graced with a fountain and palm trees, holds tables for alfresco drinks; in the garden room off the courtyard, continental breakfast for 1,300 ptas. ($7.80) is served. Centrally heated in the winter, the hotel has one drawback: street noise, which might disturb light sleepers.

Hotel Continental. Rambla de Canaletes, 138, 08002 Barcelona. ☎ **93-301-25-70.** Fax 93-302-73-60. www.hotelcontinental.com. E-mail: hotel_continental@seker.es. 35 units. MINIBAR TV TEL. 10,700–13,500 ptas. ($64.20–$81) double; 15,500 ptas. ($93) triple; 18,000 ptas. ($108) quad. Rates include buffet breakfast. AE, DC, MC, V. Metro: Plaça de Catalunya.

This hotel occupies the upper two floors of a commercial building in a safe section of the upper Rambles. The flowery, slightly faded reception area is accented with 19th-century statues. The small to midsized rooms are pleasant and modern; 10 have semicircular balconies overlooking the Rambles. Although the decor in some rooms seems to shout "Laura Ashley gone mad," everything is comfortable. Amenities include safe-deposit boxes and hair dryers. The buffet breakfast is served daily 6am to noon.

Hotel Cortés. Santa Ana, 25, 08002 Barcelona. ☎ **93-317-91-12.** Fax 93-302-78-70. 43 units. TV TEL. 10,500 ptas. ($63) double. Rates include breakfast. AE, DC, MC, V. Metro: Plaça de Catalunya.

A short walk from the cathedral, the Cortés was built around 1910 and, like many of its competitors, thoroughly renovated in time for the 1992 Olympics. It competes effectively with the Continental. Midsized to small guest rooms are scattered over five floors. About half overlook a quiet central courtyard, the other half open onto the street. On the ground floor, the unpretentious restaurant and bar serves breakfast.

Hotel España. Carrer Sant Pau, 11, 08002 Barcelona. ☎ **93-318-17-58.** Fax 93-317-11-34. 60 units. TEL. 10,800 ptas. ($64.80) double. AE, DC, MC, V. Metro: Liceu or Drassanes.

Although the rooms at this cost-conscious hotel have none of the architectural grandeur of Barcelona's modernist age, they're well-scrubbed, comfortably sized, functional, and outfitted with furniture and accessories derived from the hotel's most recent renovation in 1992. The building itself is a relic of the city's turn-of-the-century splendor, as it was constructed in 1902 by fabled architect Domenech I Montaner, designer and architect of the Palau de la Música. There's an elevator for the building's four floors, a facade that still evokes the past, and a hard-working staff that's comfortable with non-Spanish-speaking visitors. The lower Rambla, near where this hotel sits, evokes either cultural fascination or indignation, depending on how urbanized you are, but overall, it's an acceptable and well-managed choice at a relatively reasonable price. There's a restaurant on the premises, the España, open daily for lunch and dinner, that serves food and drink to locals and hotel residents alike.

Hotel San Agustín. Plaça de San Agustín, 3, 08001 Barcelona. ☎ **93-318-16-58.** Fax 93-317-29-28. 76 units. A/C TV TEL. 15,000 ptas. ($90) double; 18,500 ptas. ($111) triple; 22,000–25,000 ptas. ($132–$150) quad; 29,000 ptas. ($174) 2-room family unit. Rates include breakfast. AE, DC, MC, V. Metro: Liceu.

This tastefully renovated five-story hotel stands in the center of the old city, near the covered produce markets overlooking the brick walls of an unfinished Romanesque church. The small guest rooms are comfortable and modern, with such amenities as piped-in music, safe-deposit boxes, and tiled bathrooms with hair dryers. Some units are equipped for travelers with disabilities. The hotel runs a good restaurant that serves reasonably priced meals.

✪ **Mesón Castilla.** Valldoncella, 5, 08002 Barcelona. ☎ **93-318-21-82.** Fax 93-412-40-20. 56 units. A/C TEL. 15,000 ptas. ($90) double. V. Parking 2,000 ptas. ($12). Metro: Plaça de Catalunya or Universitat.

This two-star hotel, a former apartment building, has a Castilian facade with a wealth of art nouveau detailing. Owned and operated by the Spanish hotel chain HUSA, the Castilla is charming and well maintained, and it certainly has a fantastic location, right in the center of the city close to Les Rambles. Its nearest rival is the Regencia Colón, to which it is comparable in atmosphere and government ratings. It is far superior to the Cortés and the Continental. The midsized rooms are comfortable—beds have ornate Catalán-style headboards—and some open onto large terraces. The tiled bathrooms are equipped with hair dryers. Breakfast is the only meal served, but it is a fine buffet, with ham, cheese, and eggs.

Turín. Carrer Pintor Fortuny, 9–11, 08001 Barcelona. ☎ **93-302-48-12.** Fax 93-302-10-05. www.hotelturin@icab.es. 60 units. A/C TV TEL. 14,500 ptas. ($87) double; 17,500 ptas. ($105) triple. AE, DC, MC, V. Parking 2,000 ptas. ($12). Metro: Plaça de Catalunya.

This neat, well-run, three-star hotel is in a terra-cotta grillwork building in a shopping district. It offers small, streamlined accommodations with balconies and tiled bathrooms with hair dryers. The restaurant specializes in grilled meats and fresh fish. The Turín is a safe choice, but in its price range inferior in atmosphere to the Mesón Castilla.

SUR DIAGONAL
VERY EXPENSIVE

✪ **Claris.** Carrer de Pau Claris, 150, 08009 Barcelona. ☎ **800/888-4747** in the U.S., or 93-487-62-62. Fax 93-215-79-70. www.derbyhotels.es. E-mail: info@derbyhotels.es. 120 units. A/C MINIBAR TV TEL. Mon–Thurs 42,000 ptas. ($252) double, from 50,000 ptas. ($300) suite; Fri–Sun 28,000 ptas. ($168) double, from 35,000 ptas. ($210) suite. Fri–Sun rates include breakfast. AE, DC, MC, V. Parking 2,250 ptas. ($13.50). Metro: Passeig de Gràcia.

One of the most unusual hotels in Barcelona, this postmodern lodging is the only five-star deluxe property in the city center. It incorporates vast quantities of teak, marble, steel, and glass behind the historically important facade of a landmark 19th-century building (the Verdruna Palace). Although we prefer the Ritz (see below), many hail the Claris as the city's top choice. Opened in 1992 (in time for the Olympics), it's a seven-story structure with a swimming pool and garden on its roof. There's a small museum of Egyptian antiquities from the owner's collection on the second floor. The blue-violet guest rooms contain state-of-the-art electronic accessories as well as unusual art objects—Turkish kilims, English antiques, Hindu sculptures, Egyptian stone carvings, and engravings. The spacious rooms are among the most opulent in town, with wood marquetry and paneling, custom furnishings, safes, and some of the city's most sumptuous beds. Bathrooms are roomy and filled with thick towels, deluxe toiletries, and generous shelf space. If money is no object, book one of the 20 individually designed duplex units.

Dining: The **Restaurante Claris** serves Catalán meals in the Ampurdán style. A restaurant sponsored by the international emporium Caviar Caspa serves light but

---

ⓕ Family-Friendly Hotels

Hotel Colón *(see p. 400)* Opposite the cathedral in the Gothic Quarter, this hotel has been compared to a country home. Families ask for, and often get, spacious rooms.

Hotel Hesperia *(see p. 408)* At the northern edge of the city, this hotel has gardens and a safe neighborhood setting. Rooms are large enough to hold an extra bed.

Hotel Princesa Sofía *(see p. 404)* Although primarily a business hotel, the Princesa Sofía has an excellent baby-sitting service and two pools (one indoor, one outdoor). It's ideal for the business traveler and his or her family.

---

elegant lunches and suppers. Sturgeon eggs from many distributors accompany smoked meats, smoked fish, and bubbly wines.

Amenities: Laundry and valet, baby-sitting, room service, swimming pool, sauna, currency exchange.

Hotel Princesa Sofía. Plaça de Pius XII, 4, 08028 Barcelona. ☎ **93-330-71-11.** Fax 93-508-10-01. www.interconti.com. E-mail: barcelona@interconti.com. 500 units. A/C MINIBAR TV TEL. 38,000–48,000 ptas. ($228–$288) double; from 70,000 ptas. ($420) suite. AE, DC, MC, V. Parking 2,600 ptas. ($15.60). Metro: Palau Reial or María Cristina.

About 2 miles (3km) northwest of Barcelona's historic center, the bustling high-rise Princesa Sofía is the city's busiest, most business-oriented modern hotel. Although it opened as a five-star hotel, its new four-star government rating is more accurate. Built in 1975 and renovated in the early 1990s, it is much nicer than the Hilton. Packed with glamorous touches, the Princesa Sofía hosts dozens of daily conferences and social events. Guest rooms contain comfortable furniture, often with a vaguely British feel. Rooms, usually midsized, are well appointed, with safes, thick carpeting, and king-size beds with quality mattresses. The tiled bathrooms contain hair dryers and dual marble vanities.

Dining/Diversions: Le Gourmet restaurant serves lackluster continental and Catalán meals. **L'Empordá** is slightly less expensive, and the coffee shop, **El Snack 2002,** is open until midnight. There's a bar and a branch of Régine's disco.

Amenities: 24-hour room service, laundry and valet, concierge, baby-sitting, in-house Iberia Airlines branch, boutique, barber and hairdresser, car rentals, amply equipped gym and health club, sauna, indoor and outdoor swimming pools, extensive conference and meeting facilities, a well-managed business center offering translation (English and French) and secretarial services.

✪ **Hotel Ritz.** Gran Vía de les Corts Catalánes, 668, 08010 Barcelona. ☎ **93-318-52-00.** Fax 93-318-01-48. www.ritzbcn.com. E-mail: ritz@ritzbcn.com. 125 units. A/C MINIBAR TV TEL. 40,000–60,000 ptas. ($240–$360) double; 55,000–220,000 ptas. ($330–$1,320) suite. AE, DC, MC, V. Parking 3,500 ptas. ($21). Metro: Passeig de Gràcia.

Acknowledged by many as the finest, most prestigious, and most architecturally distinguished hotel in Barcelona, the art deco Ritz was built in 1919. Richly remodeled during the late 1980s, it has welcomed more millionaires, famous people, and aristocrats (and their official and unofficial consorts) than any other hotel in northeastern Spain. One of the finest features is a cream-and-gilt neoclassical lobby, where afternoon tea is served to the strains of a string quartet. The sumptuous guest rooms are as formal, high-ceilinged, and richly furnished as you'd expect. Some have Regency furniture, bathrooms accented with mosaics, and bathtubs inspired by those in ancient

Rome. You get all the luxuries here: elegant fabrics, deluxe mattresses, plush towels, hair dryers, and private safes.

Dining/Diversions: The elegant **Restaurante Diana** serves French and Catalán cuisine. In the paneled **Bar Parilla,** music from a grand piano will soothe your frazzled nerves.

Amenities: 24-hour room service, laundry, limousine service, concierge, babysitting, business center, car rentals, shopping kiosks and boutiques.

Rey Juan Carlos I. Avinguda Diagonal, 661, 08028 Barcelona. ☎ **800/448-8355** in the U.S., or 93-448-08-08. Fax 93-364-32-64. www.hilton.com. 432 units. A/C MINIBAR TV TEL. 46,000 ptas. ($276) double; 70,000 ptas. ($420) suite. Occasional weekend discounts. AE, DC, MC, V. Free parking. Metro: Zona Universitària.

Named for the Spanish king who attended its opening and has visited several times, this five-star hotel competes effectively with the Ritz, Claris, and Hotel Arts. Opened just before the Olympics, it rises 17 stories at the northern end of the Diagonal, in a wealthy neighborhood known for corporate headquarters, banks, and upscale stores. Note that it's a bit removed, however, from many of Barcelona's top attractions. The design includes a soaring inner atrium with glass-sided elevators. Midsized to spacious guest rooms contain many electronic extras, conservatively comfortable furnishings, and oversized beds. Many have views over Barcelona to the sea. Thoughtful touches include good lighting, adequate work space, spacious closets, and blackout draperies, plus marble bathrooms with hair dryers.

Dining/Diversions: The hotel's most elegant restaurant is **Chez Vous,** a glamorous and panoramic locale with impeccable service and French and Catalán meals. Saturday night a dinner dance offers a live orchestra accompanied by a set-price menu. The **Café Polo** serves an endless series of buffets at lunch and dinner.

Amenities: 24-hour room service, laundry, concierge staff, swimming pool, health club, jogging track, men's and women's hairdresser, car-rental facilities, business center.

EXPENSIVE

Avenida Palace. Gran Vía de les Corts Catalánes, 605 (at Passeig de Gràcia), 08007 Barcelona. ☎ **93-301-96-00.** Fax 93-318-12-34. 160 units. A/C MINIBAR TV TEL. 31,000 ptas. ($186) double; 50,000–72,000 ptas. ($300–$432) suite. AE, DC, MC, V. Metro: Plaça de Catalunya or Passeig de Gràcia.

In an enviable 19th-century neighborhood filled with elegant shops and apartment buildings, this hotel is behind a pair of mock-fortified towers. Despite its relative modernity (it dates to 1952), it evokes an old-world sense of charm, partly because of the attentive staff, scattering of flowers and antiques, and 1950s-era accessories that fill its public rooms. Guest rooms are solidly traditional and quiet, with some set aside for nonsmokers. The soundproofed rooms range from midsized to spacious, with safes, comfortable beds, and mostly wood furnishings. Bathrooms are well equipped, with dual basins, hair dryers, and heat lamps.

Dining/Diversions: El Restaurante Candelabro serves lunch and dinner Monday to Friday. The bar and lounge contains a scattering of interesting antiques.

Amenities: Concierge, translation and secretarial services, currency exchange, hairdresser and barber, room service, express checkout, baby-sitting.

Gran Hotel Havana. Gran Vía de les Corts Catalánes, 647, 08010 Barcelona. ☎ **93-412-11-15.** Fax 93-412-26-11. www.hoteles-silken.com. E-mail: silken@hoteles-silken.com. 145 units. A/C MINIBAR TV TEL. 25,000 ptas. ($150) double. AE, DC, MC, V. Parking 2,200 ptas. ($13.20). Metro: Diagonal.

Civic leaders and architects praise this hotel as an example of a sophisticated recycling of a historic monument. It was built in the 1870s as an almost obscenely large private home, then converted into a hotel (Havana) in the 1950s. In 1991, in anticipation of a flood of visitors for the Barcelona Olympic Games, its six-story interior was gutted and rebuilt in a minimalist, high-tech format whose blues and grays emulate the colors of the nearby sea. Its staff cites postmodern Milan as the source of its inspiration, shown by an absolute lack of decorative frippery in the comfortable rooms, a strong emphasis on geometric shapes, and an ample use of marble, especially in the bathrooms and the public areas. There's a hard-working, multilingual staff, and a strong sense of successful marketing by the Silken Group, a Barcelona-based chain whose other hotels are concentrated in the northern and central regions of Spain.

Dining/Diversions: The hotel has a very respectable restaurant, serving an international and regional cuisine, but you'll find far better food outside your door. There is a business-type bar.

Amenities: Room service, baby-sitting, laundry and dry cleaning, concierge.

✪ **Hotel Condes de Barcelona.** Passeig de Gràcia, 73–75, 08008 Barcelona. ☎ **93-488-22-00.** Fax 93-467-47-81. www.condesdebarcelona.com. E-mail: cbhotel@condesdebarcelona.com. 183 units. A/C MINIBAR TV TEL. 30,000 ptas. ($180) double; 56,000–65,000 ptas. ($336–$390) suite. AE, DC, MC, V. Parking 2,000 ptas. ($12). Metro: Passeig de Gràcia.

Off the architecturally splendid Passeig de Gràcia, this four-star hotel, originally a private villa (1895), is one of Barcelona's most glamorous. Business was so good it opened a 74-room extension across the street (Carrer Majorca), which regrettably lacks the flair of the original. It boasts a unique neo-medieval facade, influenced by Gaudí's *modernisme.* The curved lobby-level bar and restaurant add a touch of art deco. All the comfortable midsized guest rooms contain marble bathrooms, reproductions of Spanish paintings, and soundproofed windows. Some rooms are already beginning to show post-Olympic wear and tear.

Dining/Diversions: The restaurant serves lunch and dinner daily. A cafe features regional dishes. Guests enjoy the piano bar.

Amenities: Laundry, baby-sitting, room service, outdoor swimming pool.

Hotel Majestic. Passeig de Gràcia, 68, 08007 Barcelona. ☎ **93-488-17-17.** Fax 93-488-18-80. www.hotelmajestic.es. E-mail: recepcion@hotelmajestic.es. 322 units. A/C MINIBAR TV TEL. 36,000 ptas. ($216) double; 50,000–70,000 ptas. ($300–$420) suite. AE, DC, MC, V. Parking 2,200 ptas. ($13.20). Metro: Urquinaona.

The Majestic has functioned as one of Barcelona's most visible landmarks since the 1920s, when it was built in a sought-after location within a 10-minute walk from Plaça Catalunya. In the early 1990s it was radically renovated and upgraded into four-star status while retaining the dignified stateliness of the public areas, but with an added sense of color and contemporary drama in the bedrooms. Today, each is outfitted in a different, usually monochromatic, color scheme, with carpets, artwork, and upholsteries. Staff is hard-working and conscientious, albeit sometimes swamped with tour buses containing dozens of clients arriving all at once.

Dining/Diversions: The hotel has two restaurants, the most celebrated of which is the **Drolma,** attracting hip foodies from within the city. The **Salon Condado** is more ordinary, serving breakfasts and often dinners for groups traveling together. The hotel has a bar.

Amenities: Room service, laundry and dry cleaning, concierge, baby-sitting, swimming pool, gym, sauna.

Hotel Meliá Barcelona Sarrià. Avinguda Sarrià, 50, 08029 Barcelona. ☎ **800/336-3542** in the U.S., or 93-410-60-60. Fax 93-321-51-79. 314 units. A/C MINIBAR TV TEL. 32,000 ptas. ($192) double; from 42,000 ptas. ($252) suite. AE, DC, MC, V. Parking 2,450 ptas. ($14.70). Metro: Hospital Clínic.

One block from the junction of the avinguda Sarría and the avinguda Diagonal in the heart of the business district, this five-star hotel opened in 1976. Some rooms were renovated in the early to mid-1990s, but others look a bit worn. It offers comfortably upholstered, carpeted guest rooms done in neutral international modern. They have wide beds with firm mattresses. A member of the Meliá chain, the hotel caters to both the business traveler and the vacationer.

Dining/Diversions: A restaurant serves Catalán and international dishes, and a cocktail bar has piano music 6 nights a week.

Amenities: 24-hour room service, concierge, laundry and valet, executive floor, private parking, baby-sitting, business center, one of the best-equipped health clubs in Barcelona.

MODERATE

Hotel Balmes. Carrer Mallorca, 216, 08008 Barcelona. ☎ **93-451-19-14.** Fax 93-451-00-49. www.derbyhotels.es. E-mail: info@derbyhotels.es. 92 units. A/C MINIBAR TV TEL. 24,400 ptas. ($146.40) double. AE, DC, MC, V. Parking 2,000 ptas. ($12). Metro: Diagonal.

Set in a seven-story structure built in the late 1980s, this chain hotel successfully combines a conservative decor with modern accessories and a well-trained staff. Bedrooms are vaguely English in their inspiration, with a warm color scheme of yellows and browns, marble-trimmed bathrooms, and enough space to allow residents, many of whom are in town on business, to live and work comfortably. If you're looking for a maximum of peace and quiet, rooms overlooking the back of the hotel—site of an outdoor swimming pool and a small garden—are quieter and calmer than those facing the busy street. There's a bar on the premises, but the in-house restaurant follows a limited schedule, serving breakfast daily and lunch Monday to Friday only.

Hotel Derby/Hotel Gran Derby. Carrer Loreto, 21–25 and 28, 08029 Barcelona. ☎ **93-322-32-15.** Fax 93-410-08-62. www.derbyhotels.es. E-mail: info@derbyhotels.es. 151 units. A/C MINIBAR TV TEL. Hotel Derby 25,000 ptas. ($150) double; Grand Derby 28,000 ptas. ($168) junior suite. AE, DC, MC, V. Parking 2,250 ptas. ($13.50). Metro: Hospital Clínic.

These twin hotels are in a tranquil neighborhood 2 blocks south of the busy intersection of the avinguda Diagonal and avinguda Sarría. The Derby has 111 conventional hotel rooms; the Gran Derby, across the street, contains 40 junior suites, many with small balconies overlooking a flowered courtyard. The larger Derby contains the drinking, dining, and entertainment facilities. The British aesthetic includes well-oiled hardwood panels, soft lighting, and comfortably upholstered armchairs. Less British in feel than the public rooms, midsized guest rooms and suites are outfitted with simple furniture in a variety of decorative styles. All are comfortable and quiet.

Although the hotel does not have a restaurant, its unpretentious coffee shop serves Spanish, British, and international food. The Scotch Bar, an upscale watering hole, has won several awards for the diversity of its cocktails.

INEXPENSIVE

✪ **Hotel Astoria.** París, 203, 08036 Barcelona. ☎ **93-209-83-11.** Fax 93-202-30-08. www.derbyhotels.es. E-mail: info@derbyhotels.es. 117 units. A/C MINIBAR TV TEL. 22,000 ptas. ($132) double. AE, DC, MC, V. Parking nearby 1,800 ptas. ($10.80). Metro: Diagonal.

One of our favorite hotels, and an excellent value, the Astoria is near the upper part of the Rambles and the Diagonal. It has an art deco facade that makes it appear older than it is. The high ceilings, geometric designs, and brass-studded detail in the public rooms could be Moorish or Andalusian. The comfortable midsized guest rooms are soundproofed; half have been renovated, with slick louvered closets and glistening white paint. The more old-fashioned units have warm textures of exposed cedar and elegant, pristine modern accessories. For an American-style buffet breakfast (1,400 ptas./$8.40), the Astoria is one of the best bets in town. Its offers eggs, bacon, juice, fried potatoes, even pancakes, and a lot more.

NORTE DIAGONAL
MODERATE

Hotel Hespería. Los Vergós, 20, 08017 Barcelona. ☎ **93-204-55-51.** Fax 93-204-43-92. www.hoteles-hesperia.es. 134 units. A/C MINIBAR TV TEL. 22,000 ptas. ($132) double. AE, DC, MC, V. Parking 1,750 ptas. ($10.50). Metro: Tres Torres.

This hotel on the northern edge of the city a 10-minute taxi ride from the center sits amid the verdant gardens of one of Barcelona's most pleasant residential neighborhoods. Built in the late 1980s, the hotel was last renovated before the 1992 Olympics. You'll pass a Japanese rock garden to reach the stone-floored reception area with its adjacent bar. Sunlight floods the monochromatic guest rooms (all doubles—prices for singles are the same). Most rooms are medium-size, and all emphasize comfort and convenience. Beds have quality mattresses and fine linen; bathrooms have a generous assortment of good-sized towels. The uniformed staff offers fine service, and a restaurant serves regional cuisine.

INEXPENSIVE

Hotel Wilson. Avinguda Diagonal, 568, 08021 Barcelona. ☎ **93-209-25-11.** Fax 93-200-83-70. www.husa.es. E-mail: depcomcen@husa.es. 57 units. A/C MINIBAR TV TEL. 18,000 ptas. ($108) double; 25,000 ptas. ($150) suite. AE, DC, DISC, MC, V. Parking 2,000 ptas. ($12). Metro: Diagonal.

This comfortable hotel in an architecturally rich neighborhood is a member of the HUSA chain. The small lobby isn't indicative of the rest of the building. The second floor opens into a large, sunny coffee shop, bar, and TV lounge. The guest rooms are well kept, generally spacious, and furnished in traditional style. Amenities include private safes and hair dryers. Laundry service is available.

VILA OLÍMPICA
VERY EXPENSIVE

Hotel Arts. Carrer de la Marina, 19–21, 08005 Barcelona. ☎ **800/241-3333** in the U.S., or 93-221-10-00. Fax 93-221-10-70. www.ritzcarlton.com. 482 units. A/C MINIBAR TV TEL. 55,000–80,000 ptas. ($330–$480) double; 75,000 ptas. ($450) suite. AE, CB, DC, MC, V. Parking 3,200 ptas. ($19.20). Metro: Ciutadella-Vila Olímpica.

Managed by the Ritz-Carlton chain, this hotel occupies 33 floors of one of the tallest buildings in Spain, and one of Barcelona's only skyscrapers. (The upper floors of the 44-floor postmodern tower contain the private condominiums of some of the country's most gossiped-about aristocrats and financiers.) The hotel is about 1½ miles (2.5km) southwest of Barcelona's historic core, near the sea and the Olympic Village. Its decor is contemporary and elegant. The spacious, well-equipped guest rooms have built-in furnishings, generous desk space, safes, and large, sumptuous beds with deluxe mattresses and quality linen. Clad in pink marble, the deluxe bathrooms have fluffy robes, Belgian towels, hair dryers, dual basins, and phones. Views take in the skyline and the Mediterranean. The young staff is polite and hard-working, the product of months of Ritz-Carlton training. Japanese retailer Sogo operates an upscale cluster of luxury boutiques next door.

Dining: The **Newport Room** pays homage to new American and New England cuisine; **Café Veranda** is an airy indoor/outdoor restaurant; and **Goyesca** serves Spanish food and shellfish.

Amenities: 24-hour room service, laundry, excellent concierge staff, fitness center, outdoor pool, business center.

5 Where to Dine

If money is no object, you'll find some of the grandest culinary experiences in Europe here. Diverse Catalán cuisine reaches its pinnacle in Barcelona, and many of the finest dishes feature fresh seafood. But you don't get just Catalán fare—the city is rich in the cuisines of all the major regions of Spain, including Castile and Andalusia. Because of Barcelona's proximity to France, many of the finer restaurants serve French or French-inspired dishes.

On the other end of the spectrum, finding an affordable restaurant in Barcelona is easier than finding an inexpensive, safe hotel. There are sometimes as many as eight restaurants and tapas bars on a block. Reservations are seldom needed, except in the most expensive and popular places. The **Barri Gòtic** offers the cheapest meals. There are many budget restaurants in and around the **carrer de Montcada,** site of the Picasso museum. Dining rooms in the **Eixample** tend to be more formal and expensive, but less adventurous.

CIUTAT VELLA
EXPENSIVE

✪ **Agut d'Avignon.** Trinitat, 3 (at carrer d'Avinyó). ☎ **93-302-60-34.** Reservations required. Main courses 2,000–5,000 ptas. ($12–$30). AE, DC, MC, V. Daily 1–4:30pm and 9pm–12:30am. Metro: Jaume I or Liceu. CATALÁN.

One of our favorite restaurants in Barcelona is in a tiny alleyway near the Plaça Reial. The city's restaurant explosion has toppled Agut d'Avignon from its position as best in the city, but it's still going strong after 40 years and has a dedicated following. It attracts politicians, writers, journalists, financiers, industrialists, and artists—and even the king and cabinet ministers, along with visiting dignitaries. Since 1983 Mercedes Giralt Salinas and her son, Javier Falagán Giralt, have run the restaurant. A small 19th-century vestibule leads to the multilevel dining area, which has two balconies and a main hall evoking a hunting lodge. You might need help translating the Catalán menu. The traditional specialties are likely to include acorn-squash soup served in its shell; fisherman's soup with garlic toast; haddock stuffed with shellfish; sole with *nyoca* (a medley of nuts); large shrimp with aïoli; duck with figs; and fillet beef steak in sherry sauce.

Casa Leopoldo. Sant Rafael, 24. ☎ **93-441-30-14.** Reservations required. Main courses 1,800–5,500 ptas. ($10.80–$33); fixed-price menu 5,500 ptas. ($33). AE, DC, MC, V. Tues–Sun 1:30–4pm; Tues–Sat 9–11pm. Closed Aug and Easter week. Metro: Liceu. SEAFOOD.

An excursion through the somewhat seedy streets of the Barri Xinés is part of the Casa Leopoldo experience. At night it's safer to come by taxi. This colorful restaurant founded in 1939 serves some of the freshest seafood in town to a loyal clientele. There's a popular stand-up tapas bar in front, and two dining rooms. Specialties include eel with shrimp, barnacles, cuttlefish, seafood soup with shellfish, and deep-fried inch-long eels.

Quo Vadis. Carme, 7. ☎ **93-302-40-72.** Reservations recommended. Main courses 1,500–3,500 ptas. ($9–$21); *menú del día* 4,000 ptas. ($24). DC, MC, V. Mon–Sat 1:15–4pm and 8:30–11:30pm. Metro: Liceu. SPANISH/CONTINENTAL.

Elegant and impeccable, this is one of the finest restaurants in Barcelona. In a century-old building near the open stalls of the Boquería food market, it was established in

Barcelona Dining

Agua **32**
Agut **39**
Agut d'Avignon **46**
Alt Heidelberg **20**
Bar Turó **3**
Beltxenea **14**
Biocenter **25**
Bodega la Plata **41**
Bodegueta **11**
Botafumeiro **6**
Brasserie Flo **19**
Ca La María **22**
Café de L'Academia **47**
Can Costa **33**
Can Culleretes **50**
Can Isidre **23**
Can Majó **34**
Casa Alfonso **18**
Casa Calvet **17**
Casa Leopoldo **24**
Casa Tejada **4**
Egipte **26**
El Caballito Blanco **13**
El Duc **20**
El Túnel **44**
Els Quatre Gats **29**
Gaig **15**
Garduña **52**
Jaume de Provença **2**
L'Olive **8**
La Balsa **5**
La Buena Brasa **21**
La Cuineta **49**
La Dama **9**
La Dentellière **38**
La Jarra **40**
La Llauna **1**
La Rosca **28**
Las Campanas **42**
Los Caracoles **45**
Mercat de la Boquería **51**
Neichel **3**
Pitarra **43**
Pla de la Garasa **31**
Quo Vadis **27**
Ramonet **36**
Reno **7**
Restaurante Hofmann **30**
Rey de la Gamba **35**
Roig Robí **10**
Rosalert **16**
7 Portes **37**
Seynor Parellada **48**
Talaia Mar **32**
Tragaluz **12**
Via Veneto **3**

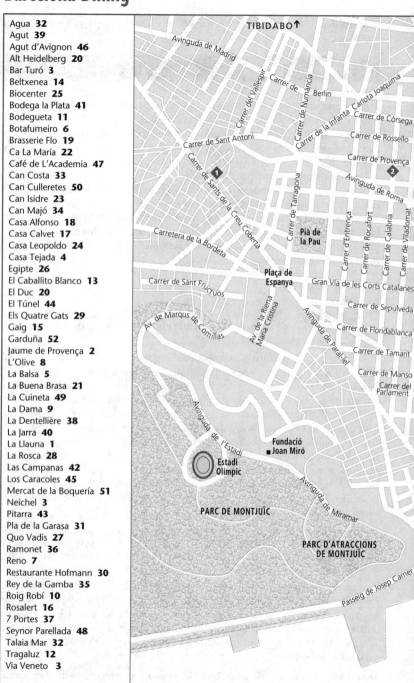

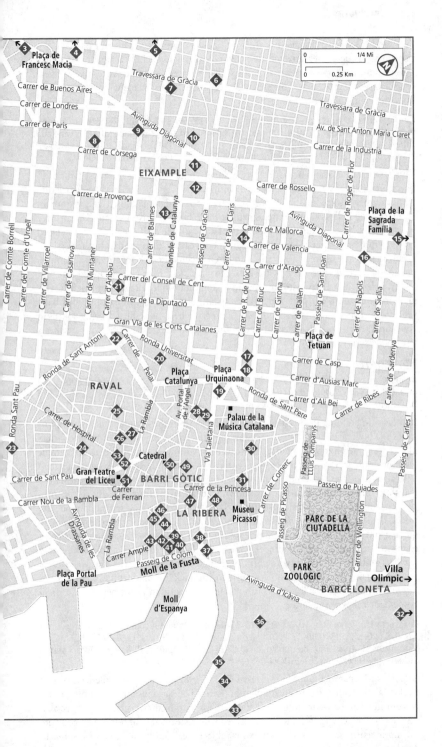

1967 and has done a discreet but thriving business ever since. The four paneled dining rooms exude conservative charm. Culinary creations include a ragout of seasonal mushrooms, fried goose liver with prunes, fillet of beef with wine sauce, and a variety of grilled or flambéed fish. There's a wide choice of desserts made with seasonal fruits imported from all over Spain.

✪ **Restaurant Hoffmann.** Argenteria, 74–78. ☎ **93-319-58-89.** Reservations recommended. Main courses 2,200–4,500 ptas. ($13.20–$27); fixed-price lunch (includes wine and coffee) 4,800 ptas. ($28.80); tasting menu 7,500 ptas. ($45). AE, DC, MC, V. Mon–Fri 1:30–3:30pm and 9–11:30pm. Metro: Jaume I. CATALÁN/FRENCH/INTERNATIONAL.

This restaurant in the Barri Gòtic has suddenly become one of the most famous in Barcelona, partly because of its creative cuisine, partly because of its close association with a respected school that trains employees for Catalonia's hotel and restaurant industry. The culinary and entrepreneurial force behind it is German/Catalán Mey Hoffmann, whose restaurant overlooks the facade of one of Barcelona's most beloved Gothic churches, Santa María del Mar. In good weather, three courtyards hold tables. Menu items change every 2 months and often include French ingredients. Examples include a superb *fine tarte* with deboned sardines, foie gras wrapped in puff pastry, baked John Dory with new potatoes and ratatouille, a ragout of crayfish with green risotto, succulent pigs' feet with eggplant, and rack of lamb with grilled baby vegetables. Especially flavorful, if you appreciate beef, is a fillet steak cooked in Rioja and served with shallot confit and potato gratin. Fondant of chocolate makes a worthy dessert.

MODERATE

Agut. Gignas, 16. ☎ **93-315-17-09.** Reservations required. Main courses 2,800–3,200 ptas. ($16.80–$19.20); fixed-price lunch 1,200–1,600 ptas. ($7.20–$9.60). MC, V. Tues–Sun 1:30–4pm; Tues–Sat 9pm–midnight. Closed Aug. Metro: Jaime 1. CATALÁN.

In a historic building in the Barri Xinés, 3 blocks from the harbor front, Agut epitomizes the bohemian atmosphere surrounding this fairly seedy area. For three quarters of a century, this has been a family-run business, with Maria Agut Garcia the current reigning empress. (Don't confuse Agut with the more famous Agut d'Avignon nearby.) The aura is of the '40s and '50s, with a cozy little bar to the right as you enter. Paintings on the walls are from well-known Catalán artists from the '40s to the '60s. The cuisine is solid and time-tested fare. It is vigorous cookery served at moderate prices. Begin with *mil hojas de butifarra amb zets* or layers of pastry filled with Catalán sausage and mushrooms, or the *terrine de albergines amb fortmage de cabra* (terrine of eggplant with goat's cheese gratinée). One of our favorite dishes is *soufle de rape amb gambes* (soufflé of monkfish with shrimp). For gastronomes only, try the *pie de cerdo relleno con foie amb truffles* (pork feet stuffed with duck liver and truffles). For dessert, if you order *sortido,* you'll get a combination plate with an assortment of the small homemade cakes of the house.

Brasserie Flo. Jonqueras, 10. ☎ **93-319-31-02.** Reservations recommended. Main courses 1,800–3,600 ptas. ($10.80–$21.60); fixed-price menu 3,000 ptas. ($18). AE, DC, MC, V. Mon–Thurs 1–4pm and 8:30pm–midnight; Fri–Sun 1–4pm and 8:30pm–1am. Metro: Urquinaona. FRENCH/INTERNATIONAL.

A group of Frenchmen opened this restaurant in 1982 in a former textile factory. It is as close as Barcelona gets to an Alsatian brasserie. The spacious art deco dining room is palm-filled and air-conditioned. Begin perhaps with fresh foie gras or the specialty, a large plate of *choucroute* (sauerkraut) served with a steamed ham hock. Also good are shrimp in garlic, salmon tartare with vodka, black rice, and stuffed sole with spinach. The familiar fare is solid, satisfying, and filling.

Can Culleretes. Quintana, 5. ☎ **93-317-64-85.** Reservations recommended. Main courses 1,200–2,200 ptas. ($7.20–$13.20); *menú del día* 2,300 ptas. ($13.80). MC, V. Tues–Sun 1:30–4pm; Tues–Sat 9–11pm. Closed 3 weeks in July. Metro: Liceu. Bus: 14 or 59. CATALÁN.

Founded in 1786 as a *pastelería* (pastry shop) in the Barri Gòtic, this oldest Barcelona restaurant retains many original architectural features. All three dining rooms are decorated with tile dadoes and wrought-iron chandeliers. The well-prepared food features authentic dishes of northeastern Spain, including sole Roman style, *zarzuela a la marinera* (shellfish medley), cannelloni, and paella. From October to January, special game dishes, including *perdiz* (partridge), are available. Signed photographs of celebrities, flamenco artists, and bullfighters who have visited decorate the walls.

Egipte. Les Rambles, 79. ☎ **93-317-74-80.** Reservations recommended. Main courses 1,400–2,500 ptas. ($8.40–$15); fixed-price menus 1,200–2,000 ptas. ($7.20–$12). AE, DC, MC, V. Daily 1–4pm and 8pm–midnight. Metro: Liceu. CATALÁN/SPANISH.

A neighborhood favorite, this tiny place behind the central marketplace jumps day and night. The excellent menu includes spinach *vol-au-vent* (traditionally served with an egg on top), *lengua de ternera* (tongue), and the signature *berengeras* (stuffed eggplant). The local specialty is codfish in cream sauce. The ingredients are fresh, and the price is right. Expect hearty market food and a total lack of pretension.

Els Quatre Gats. Montsió, 3. ☎ **93-302-41-40.** Reservations required Sat–Sun. Main courses 1,400–3,000 ptas. ($8.40–$18); fixed-price menu (Mon–Sat) 1,800 ptas. ($10.80). AE, MC, V. Daily 1–4pm; Mon–Sat 7:30pm–midnight. Cafe daily 8am–2am. Metro: Plaça de Catalunya. CATALÁN.

A Barcelona legend since 1897, the "Four Cats" (in Catalán slang, "just a few people") was a favorite of Picasso, Rusinyol, and other artists, who once hung their works on its walls. On a narrow cobblestoned street in the Barri Gòtic near the cathedral, the fin-de-siècle cafe has been the setting for poetry readings by Joan Maragall, piano concerts by Isaac Albéniz and Ernie Granados, and murals by Ramón Casas. It was a base for members of the *modernisme* movement and figured in the city's intellectual and bohemian life.

Today, the restored bar is a popular meeting place. The fixed-price meal is one of the better bargains in town, considering the locale. The unpretentious Catalán cooking here is called *cucina de mercat* (based on whatever looked fresh at the market). The constantly changing menu reflects the seasons. No hot food is served on Sunday.

La Cuineta. Paradis, 4. ☎ **93-315-01-11.** Reservations recommended. Main courses 2,000–3,200 ptas. ($12–$19.20); fixed-price menu 3,200 ptas. ($19.20). AE, DC, MC, V. Daily 1–4pm and 8pm–midnight. Metro: Jaume I. CATALÁN.

This restaurant near the Catalán government offices is a culinary highlight of the Barri Gòtic. Decorated in typical regional style, it favors local cuisine. The fixed-price menu is a good value, or you can order à la carte. The most expensive appetizer is *bellota* (acorn-fed ham), but we suggest a market-fresh Catalán dish, such as *favas* (broad beans) stewed with *butifarra*, a tasty, spicy local sausage.

✪ Los Caracoles. Escudellers, 14. ☎ **93-302-31-85.** Reservations required. Main courses 1,800–8,000 ptas. ($10.80–$48). AE, DC, MC, V. Daily 1pm–midnight. Metro: Drassanes. CATALÁN/SPANISH.

In a labyrinth of narrow cobblestoned streets, Los Caracoles is the port's most colorful and popular restaurant—and has been since 1835. It has won acclaim for its spit-roasted chicken and for its namesake snails. A long, angular bar is up front, with a two-level restaurant in back. You can watch the busy preparations in the kitchen, where dried herbs, smoked ham shanks, and garlic bouquets hang from the ceiling. In summer, tables spill outside. The excellent food features all sorts of Spanish and Catalán specialties. Everybody from Richard Nixon to John Wayne has stopped in, and Salvador Dalí was a devoted patron. Today's clientele may not be as legendary, but hordes keep coming. Tourists often make this their number-one restaurant stop in Barcelona, but it is no tourist trap—Los Caracoles delivers the same aromatic and robust food it always has. If you avoid the fresh shellfish dishes, you'll find most offerings are at the lower end of the price scale.

INEXPENSIVE

Biocenter. Pintor Fortuny, 25. ☎ **93-301-45-83.** Main courses 672–1,000 ptas. ($4.05–$6); fixed–price menu 1,200 ptas. ($7.20). No credit cards. Bar, Mon–Sat 9am–5pm; food, Mon–Sat 1–5pm. Metro: Plaça de Catalunya. VEGETARIAN.

This is the largest and best-known vegetarian restaurant in Barcelona, the creation of Catalonia-born entrepreneur Pep Cañameras, who is likely to be directing the service from behind the bar. Vegetarians or not, patrons congregate over drinks in the front room. Some stay for meals in one of two ground-floor dining rooms, amid paintings and artwork by the owner and his colleagues. There's a salad bar, an array of vegetarian casseroles, soups (such as gazpacho or lentil), and a changing selection of seasonal vegetables.

Café de L'Academia. Carrer Lledó, 1 (Barri Gòtic), Plaça Sant Just. ☎ **93-315-00-26.** Reservations required. Main courses 1,000–1,700 ptas. ($6–$10.20); fixed-price menu (lunch only) 1,275 ptas. ($7.65); set dinner 3,500 ptas. ($21). AE, MC, V. Mon–Fri 9am–noon, 1:15–4pm, and 9pm–midnight. Closed last 2 weeks Aug. Metro: Jaume 1. CATALÁN/ MEDITERRANEAN.

In the center of Barri Gòtic a short walk from Plaça Sant Jaume, this 28-table restaurant looks expensive but is really one of the best and most affordable in the medieval city. The building dates from the 15th century, but the restaurant was founded only in the mid-1980s. Owner Jordí Casteldi offers an elegant atmosphere in a setting of brown stone walls and ancient wooden columns. At a small bar you can peruse the varied menu and study the wines offered. Dishes of this quality usually cost three times as much in Barcelona. The chef is proud of his "kitchen of the market," suggesting that only the freshest ingredients from the day's shopping are featured. Try such delights as *lassanye de butifarra I ceps* (lasagna with Catalán sausage and flap mushrooms), *bacalla gratinado i musselina de carofes* (salt cod gratinée with an artichoke mousse), or *terrina d'berengeras amb fortmage de cabra* (terrine of eggplant with goat cheese). A delectable specialty is *codorniz rellena en cebollitas tiernas y foie de pato* (partridge stuffed with tender onions and duck liver).

✪ El Duc. In the Duques de Bergara, Bergara, 11. ☎ **93-301-51-51.** Reservations recommended. Main courses 1,200–2,200 ptas. ($7.20–$13.20); fixed-price menu (Mon–Fri only) 2,500 ptas. ($15). AE, DC, MC, V. Daily 1–4pm and 8–11pm. Metro: Plaça de Catalunya.

On the lobby level of the hotel (see above), this well-managed restaurant serves food a lot better than the fare at other hotel dining rooms. Adjacent to the Plaça de Catalunya, it offers a conservative roster of flavorful dishes. They include prawn cocktails, goose-liver pâté, maigret of duckling in fruit sauce, tenderloin of beef "Café de Paris," grilled entrecôte, fried fish, Asturian hake, and large prawns served with a gratin of scallops. For such an elegant enclave, prices are extremely reasonable.

Garduña. Morera, 17. ☎ **93-302-43-23.** Reservations recommended. Main courses 1,200–3,800 ptas. ($7.20–$22.80); fixed-price lunch 1,200–1,800 ptas. ($7.20–$10.80); fixed-price dinner 1,800 ptas. ($10.80). AE, DC, MC, V. Mon–Sat 1–4pm and 8pm–midnight. Metro: Liceu. CATALÁN.

Calling All Chocoholics!

Established in 1930, **Dulcinea,** Vía Petrixol, 2 (☎ **93-302-68-24**), is the most famous chocolate shop in Barcelona. The specialties are *melindros* (sugar-topped soft-sided biscuits), and the regulars who flock here love to dunk them into the very thick hot chocolate—so thick, in fact, that drinking it feels like eating a melted chocolate bar. A cup of hot chocolate with cream costs 400 ptas. ($2.40), and a *ración* of *churros* (a deep-fried pastry), which is dipped in the hot chocolate, goes for 150 ptas. (90¢); no credit cards. Dulcinea is open daily 9am to 1pm and 4:30 to 9pm; closed in August. Take the Metro to Liceu.

This is the most famous restaurant in Barcelona's covered food market, La Boquería. Originally conceived as a hotel, it has concentrated on food since the 1970s. Battered, somewhat ramshackle, and a bit claustrophobic, it's fashionable with an artistic set that might have been designated as bohemian in an earlier era. It's near the back of the market, so you'll pass endless rows of fresh produce, cheese, and meats before you reach it. You can dine downstairs, near a crowded bar, or a bit more formally upstairs. Food is ultrafresh—the chefs certainly don't have to travel far for the ingredients. You might try "hors d'oeuvres of the sea," cannelloni Rossini, grilled hake with herbs, *rape* (monkfish) *marinera,* paella, brochettes of veal, fillet steak with green peppercorns, seafood rice, or a *zarzuela* (stew) of fresh fish with spices.

La Dentellière. Carrer Ample, 26. ☎ **93-319-68-21.** Reservations recommended. Main courses 1,000–1,500 ptas. ($6–$9); set-price lunch 1,100 ptas. ($6.60); set-price dinner 2,500 ptas. ($15). MC, V. Tues–Sat 1:30–4pm and 8:30–11pm. Metro: Drassanes. FRENCH.

Charming, and steeped in the French aesthetic, this bistro occupies a 200-year-old historic building in the heart of the Barri Gòtic. Inside, you'll find a small corner of provincial France, thanks to the dedicated effort of Evelyne, the French writer who owns the place. Beneath the centuries-old ceiling beams, in a pair of antique-strewn dining rooms noted for their slightly cramped tables, you'll order from an imaginative menu that includes a lasagne made from strips of salted codfish, peppers, and tomato sauce, and a delectable carpaccio of fillet of beef with pistachios, lemon juice, vinaigrette, and Parmesan cheese. The wine list is particularly imaginative, with worthy vintages mostly from France and Spain.

La Rosca. Juliá Portet, 6. ☎ **93-302-51-73.** Reservations recommended. Main courses 2,500–2,800 ptas. ($15–$16.80); fixed-price menu 1,000 ptas. ($6). No credit cards. Sun–Fri 9am–4pm and 8pm–midnight. Closed Aug 20–30. Metro: Urquinaona and Catalunya. CATALÁN/SPANISH.

For more than half a century, owner Don Alberto Vellve has welcomed customers into this little Barri Gòtic eatery, close to Plaça de Catalunya. On a short street, the place is easy to miss, except to devotees who have been coming here for decades. Go here if you'd like to see the type of place where people dined inexpensively in the Franco era. A mixture of Catalán and modern Spanish cuisine is served in this house, which is small and in an old rustic style with high ceilings and white walls. The decor has nostalgic touches, such as old bullfighting posters and pictures of Barcelona in the mid-20th century. There are 60 unadorned tables, which diners fill quickly to take advantage of the cheap three-course luncheon menu. Dig into such hearty fare as veal stew or assorted fish and shellfish grilled. Baby squid is cooked in its own ink, and one of the best and most typical dishes is white beans sauteed with ham and Catalán sausage. For a true treat, ask for the *rape a la planate* (grilled monkfish).

Pitarra. Avinyó, 56. ☎ **93-301-16-47.** Reservations required. Main courses 1,200–2,000 ptas. ($7.20–$12); fixed-price lunch 1,500 ptas. ($9). AE, DC, MC, V. Mon–Sat 1–4pm and 8:30–11pm. Closed August 3–30. Metro: Liceu. CATALÁN.

Founded in 1890, this restaurant in the Barri Gòtic was named after the 19th-century Catalán playwright who lived and wrote in the back room. Try grilled fish chowder or a Catalán salad, followed by grilled salmon or squid Málaga style. Valencian paella is another specialty. The cuisine does not even pretend to be imaginative but adheres strictly to time-tested recipes—"the type of food we ate when growing up," in the words of one diner.

Pla de la Garsa. Assaonadors, 13. ☎ **93-315-24-13.** Reservations recommended for weekends. Main courses 900–2,000 ptas. ($5.40–$12); fixed-price menu (lunch) 1,200 ptas. ($7.20). AE, DC, MC, V. Mon–Sat 1:15–3:45pm and 8pm–midnight; Sun 1:30–4pm. Metro: Jaume 1. MEDITERRANEAN/CATALÁN.

In Barrio Ribera close to the cathedral, this historic building has been fully renovated but still retains some 19th-century fittings, such as a cast-iron spiral staircase used to reach another dining area upstairs. However, the ground floor is more interesting. Here you'll encounter the owner, Ignacio Sulle, an antiques collector who has filled his establishment with an intriguing collection of objets d'art. He boasts one of the city's best wine lists, and features a daily array of traditional Catalán and Mediterranean favorite dishes, and is also known for his variety of French cheese. Every dish has a special something that raises it to a gastronomic height. Begin with one of the pâtés, especially the goose, or a confit of duck thighs. You can also order meat and fish pâtés. One surprise is a terrine with black olives and anchovies. For a main course you can order a perfectly seasoned beef bourguignonne or *fabetes fregides amb menta i pernil* (beans with meat and diced Serrano ham). The cheese selection is one of the finest we've found in town, especially bountiful in Catalán goat cheese, including Serrat Gros from the Pyrenees.

Senyor Parellada. Carrer Argentaria, 37. ☎ **93-310-50-94.** Reservations recommended. Main courses 750–2,300 ptas. ($4.50–$13.80). AE, MC, V. Mon–Sat 1–3:30pm and 9–10:30pm. Metro: Jaume I. CATALÁN.

The glossy contemporary-looking interior of this place is in distinct contrast to a battered-looking facade of a building that's at least a century old. Inside, in a pair of lemon-yellow and blue dining rooms, you'll find menu items such as Italian-style cannelloni, stuffed cabbage, codfish "as it was prepared by the monks of the Poblet monastery," baked monkfish with mustard and garlic sauce, roasted duck served with figs, and roasted rack of lamb with red wine sauce. Patrons flock faithfully to this bistro, knowing they'll be served a traditional cuisine of northeast Spain with fine local produce. The chefs seem to know how to coax the most flavor out of the premium ingredients.

SUR DIAGONAL
VERY EXPENSIVE

Beltxenea. Majorca, 275. ☎ **93-215-30-24.** Reservations recommended. Main courses 2,600–5,500 ptas. ($15.60–$33); tasting menu 7,500 ptas. ($45). AE, DC, MC, V. Mon–Fri 1:30–4pm; Mon–Sat 8:30–11:30pm. Closed 2 weeks in Aug. Metro: Passeig de Gràcia. BASQUE/FRENCH.

In a building originally designed in the late 19th century as an apartment building, this restaurant celebrates Basque cuisine. The Basques are noted as the finest chefs in Spain, and this is indeed grand cuisine. It's served here in one of the most elegantly and comfortably furnished restaurants in the city. Schedule a meal for a special night—it's worth the money. The menu might include hake fried with garlic or garnished with clams and served with fish broth. Roast lamb, grilled rabbit, and pheasant are well prepared and succulent, as are the desserts. There's dining outside in the formal garden during the summer.

✪ Jaume de Provença. Provença, 88. ☎ **93-430-00-29.** Reservations recommended. Main courses 2,200–7,000 ptas. ($13.20–$42). AE, DC, MC, V. Tues–Sun 1–4pm; Tues–Sat 9–11:30pm. Closed Easter week and Aug. Metro: Entença. CATALÁN/FRENCH.

A few steps from the Estació Central de Barcelona-Sants railway station, at the western end of the Eixample, this is a small, cozy restaurant with rustic decor. It is the only restaurant along the Diagonal that can compare to La Dama. Named after its owner and chef, Jaume Bargués, it features modern interpretations of traditional Catalán and southern French cuisine. Examples include gratin of clams with spinach, a salad of two different species of lobster, foie gras and truffles, and pigs' trotters with plums and truffles. Or you might order crabmeat lasagna, cod with saffron sauce, sole with mushrooms in port-wine sauce, or an artistic dessert specialty of orange mousse.

✪ La Dama. Diagonal, 423. ☎ **93-202-06-86.** Reservations required. Main courses 3,000–4,000 ptas. ($18–$24); fixed-price menus 6,500–9,000 ptas. ($39–$54). AE, DC, MC, V. Daily 1:30–3:30pm and 8:30–11:30pm. Metro: Provença. CATALÁN/INTERNATIONAL.

This is one of the few restaurants in Barcelona that deserves, and gets, a Michelin star. In one of the grand 19th-century buildings for which Barcelona is famous, this stylish and well-managed restaurant serves a clientele of local residents and civic dignitaries. You take an art nouveau elevator (or the sinuous stairs) up one flight to reach the dining room. Specialties include salmon steak served with vinegar derived from *cava* (sparkling wine) and onions, cream of potato soup flavored with caviar, a salad of crayfish with orange-flavored vinegar, an abundant platter of autumn mushrooms, and succulent preparations of lamb, fish, shellfish, beef, goat, and veal. The building, designed by Manuel Sayrach, is 3 blocks west of the intersection of avinguda Diagonal and Passeig de Gràcia.

EXPENSIVE

Can Isidre. Les Flors, 12. ☎ **93-441-11-39.** Reservations required. Main courses 2,200–5,000 ptas. ($13.20–$30). AE, DC, MC, V. Mon–Sat 1:30–4pm and 8:30–11:30pm. Closed Sat–Sun June–Aug. Metro: Paral-lel. CATALÁN.

In spite of its seedy location (take a cab at night!), this is perhaps the most sophisticated Catalán bistro in Barcelona. Opened in 1970, it has served King Juan Carlos and Queen Sofía, Julio Iglesias, and the famous Catalán band leader, Xavier Cugat. Isidre Gironés, helped by his wife, Montserrat, is known for his fresh cuisine beautifully prepared and served. Try spider crabs and shrimp, a foie gras salad, sweetbreads with port and flap mushrooms, or carpaccio of veal Harry's Bar style. The selection of Spanish and Catalán wines is excellent.

✪ Casa Calvet. Carrer Casp, 48. ☎ **93-412-40-12.** Reservations recommended. Main courses 2,050–3,300 ptas. ($12.30–$19.80). AE, MC, V. Mon–Sat 1–4pm and 7–11:30pm. Metro: Castro. CATALÁN/CONTINENTAL.

This is one of the most visible and sought-after restaurants of the Eixample district, with a reputation and cachet that has attracted everyone from the Mayor of Barcelona to Queen Sofia and her daughter, the Infanta Cristina. It is on the ground floor of one of the great modernist apartment buildings of Barcelona, a stained-glass and wood-trimmed fantasy designed by Antoni Gaudí in 1899. Menu items are artful and sophisticated, reflecting influences from both Catalonia and France. Stellar examples include fresh pan-fried duck liver served in a bitter orange sauce; ravioli stuffed with oysters and clams and served in a sparkling *cava* sauce; and grilled fillet of pork with chestnuts and cider sauce.

MODERATE

La Buena Brasa. Aribau, 159. ☎ **93-410-47-83.** Reservations recommended. Main courses 1,500–2,000 ptas. ($9–$12). MC, V. Daily noon–5pm and 8pm–midnight. Metro: Diagonal. MEDITERRANEAN.

The name of this restaurant translates as "the good charcoal grill," which certainly provides a clue to what the house specialties will be. The owner, José Luis Iglesias, welcomes a host of discerning Barcelona professional people who come not for the glamorous surroundings, but for the fresh cuisine, called *cocina de mercado*. You might begin with a selection of tapas ranging from smoked salmon to pâtés, everything from *esqueixada* (shredded salt-dried cod in a vinaigrette of oil and vinegar given extra flavor by onions and tomatoes) or a *escalivada* mixing fresh eggplant, red peppers, and onions cooked on hot coals and served with anchovies. Other excellent dishes include *arroz y bacalao frito con pimientos y ajos tiernos* (rice with fried salt cod, peppers, and tender garlic), and *calcots a la Brasa* (a local variety of grilled spring onion). Most diners come here for the grilled meats, especially rabbit, goat, and lamb. The best dessert is an excellent *tarta al whisky,* or whisky cake.

L'Olive. Muntaner, 171 (corner of Corsega). ☎ **93-430-90-27.** Reservations recommended. Main courses 1,500–2,600 ptas. ($9–$15.60); *menú completo* 4,500 ptas. ($27). AE, DC, MC, V. Daily 1–4pm; Mon–Sat 8:30pm–midnight. Metro: Muntaner and Hospital Clinic. CATALÁN/SPANISH.

You assume that this two-floor restaurant is named for the olive that figures so prominently into its cuisine, but actually it's named for the owner, Josep Olive. You can be born with no more apt a name for a Mediterranean restaurateur. The building is designed in a modern Catalán style with walls adorned with reproductions of famous Spanish painters, such as Miró, Dalí, or Picasso. The tables are topped in marble, the floors impeccably polished. There are sections on both floors where it's possible to have some privacy, and overall the feeling is one of elegance with a touch of intimacy. You won't be disappointed by anything on the menu, especially *bacalla cache* (raw salt cod) or *filet de vedella al vi negre al forn* (veal fillets cooked in the oven in a red wine sauce), and especially the *salsa maigret* of duck with strawberry sauce. One specialty is *amanida de col llombarda amb seitons* (a salad of finely shredded red cabbage that has been parboiled in sherry vinegar and tossed with a purée of olive oil and a small fish similar to white anchovies). Monkfish flavored with roasted garlic is always a palate pleaser, and you can finish with a *crema Catalán* (a flan), or one of the delicious Catalán pastries.

✪ Rosalert. Avenida Diagonal, 301. ☎ **93-207-10-19.** Reservations recommended. Main courses 1,500–2,000 ptas. ($9–$12); *menú completo* 6,000 ptas. ($36). AE, DC, MC, V. Tues–Sun 9am–6pm and 8pm–2am. Closed Aug 10–30. Metro: Verdaguer/Sagrada Família. CATALÁN/SEAFOOD.

At the corner of Carrer Napols close to La Sagrada Família, this restaurant has been the domain of Jordí Alert for more than 4 decades. He specializes in *comida de mar a la plancha,* or grilled seafood, and does so in a typical setting of hardwood floors and tile-covered walls. His seafood or crustaceans are grilled on a heated iron plate without any additives. There is no more awesome glass tank of live shellfish in Barcelona. You choose your meal, and the poor victim is extracted with a net and thrown on the grill. Of course, you find all the typical offerings, such as tiny octopus, succulent mussels, fat shrimp, calamares, fresh oysters, and langoustines. If you're daring, you can order such unusual seafood as *dátils* ("dates" in English). This is a delicious shellfish whose shape resembles a date. Begin with one of the freshly made tapas, such as salt cod in vinaigrette or broad beans laced with garlic and virgin olive oil. Your best bet might be the *parrillada*, or assorted fish and shellfish from the grill. One of the best offerings is turbot cooked on the grill with potatoes and fresh mushrooms.

Talaia Mar. Marina, 16 (Port Maritim). ☎ **93-221-90-90.** Reservations recommended. Main courses 1,950–3,550 ptas. ($11.70–$21.30). AE, DC, MC, V. Daily 1:30–4pm and 8pm–midnight. Metro: Via Olimpica. SEAFOOD/INTERNATIONAL.

Some architects have compared the form of this avant-garde restaurant to a postmodern mirador (glassed-in bay window) whose panorama faces the port of Barcelona and the open sea. Established in 1992 with an interior shaped like a half-moon, it's more stylish and sleek than many of its nearby competitors, with a cuisine that's hip, well conceived, and mostly based on fresh ingredients. Look for a wide variety of grilled fish, many of them hauled in fresh from deep offshore waters that morning and served as simply as possible, sometimes with only lemon or butter sauce. Shellfish are prominently displayed in cases as part of a meal's theatricality, and roasted pork and lamb are always a worthwhile choice here.

INEXPENSIVE

Ca La María. Tallers, 76. ☎ **93-318-89-93.** Reservations recommended Sat–Sun. Main courses 1,200–1,600 ptas. ($7.20–$9.60). AE, DC, MC, V. Mon–Sun 1:30–4pm; Tues–Sat 8:30–11pm. Metro: Universitat. CATALÁN.

This small (18 tables) blue-and-green-tiled bistro is on a quiet square opposite a Byzantine-style church near the Plaça de la Universitat. Look for constantly changing daily specials. This is not a place for haute cuisine. A bit battered-looking, it serves endearingly homelike food—if you grew up in a family of Catalán cooks. The dishes are often surprisingly tasty—try baby squid with onions and tomatoes, anglerfish with burned garlic, or veal sirloin cooked to order.

El Caballito Blanco. Mallorca, 196. ☎ **93-453-10-33.** Main courses 1,000–3,900 ptas. ($6–$23.40). AE, MC, V. Tues–Sun 1–3:45pm; Tues–Sat 9–10:45pm. Closed Aug. Metro: Hospital Clínic. SEAFOOD/INTERNATIONAL.

This Barcelona standby famous for seafood has long been popular with the locals. The fluorescent-lit dining area does not offer much atmosphere, but the food is good, varied, and relatively inexpensive (unless you order lobster or other expensive shellfish). The "Little White Horse," in the Passeig de Gràcia area, features a huge selection, including monkfish, mussels marinara, and shrimp with garlic. If you don't want fish, try the grilled lamb cutlets. Several different pâtés and salads are offered. There's a bar to the left of the dining area.

⊕ Family-Friendly Restaurants

Dulcinea *(see p. 415)* This makes a great refueling stop any time of the day—guaranteed to satisfy any chocoholic.

Poble Espanyol *(see p. 434)* A good introduction to Spanish food. All the restaurants in the "Spanish Village" serve comparable food at comparable prices—let the kids choose what to eat.

Tragaluz. Pasaje Concepción, 5, Eixample. ☎ **93-487-01-96.** Reservations recommended. Main courses 1,500–3,500 ptas. ($9–$21). AE, MC, V. Daily 1:30–4pm and 8:30pm–midnight. Metro: Diagonal or Provença. MEDITERRANEAN.

Named after the turn-of-the-century modernist building that contains it, this well-respected restaurant offers three very contemporary-looking beige dining rooms on separate floors. Menu items are derived from fresh ingredients that vary with the season. Depending on the month of your visit, you might find terrine of duck liver, Santurce-style hake (with garlic and herbs), fillet of sole stuffed with red peppers, and beef tenderloin in a Rioja wine sauce. One of the best desserts is a semi-soft slice of deliberately underbaked chocolate cake. Diners seeking low-fat dishes will find solace here, as will vegetarians. The vegetables served are the best and freshest on the market that day. You'll find a sushi restaurant downstairs. The Tragaluz chefs are adept at taking local products and turning them into flavorful, carefully prepared dishes. Most dishes are at the lower end of the price scale.

NORTE DIAGONAL
VERY EXPENSIVE

✪ **Botafumeiro.** Gran de Gràcia, 81. ☎ **93-218-42-30.** Reservations recommended for dining rooms. Main courses 3,200–6,000 ptas. ($19.20–$36). AE, DC, MC, V. Daily 1pm–1am. Metro: Enrique Quiroga. SEAFOOD.

Although the competition is strong, this classic *marisquería* consistently puts Barcelona's finest seafood on the table. Much of the allure comes from the attention of the white-jacketed staff. If you like, you can eat at the bar. If you do venture to the rear, you'll find a series of attractive dining rooms noted for the ease with which business deals seem to be arranged during the lunch hour. International businesspeople often rendezvous here, and the king of Spain is sometimes a patron.

Menu items include fresh seafood prepared in a glistening modern kitchen visible from parts of the dining room. The establishment prides itself on its fresh and salt-water fish, clams, mussels, lobster, crayfish, scallops, and several varieties of crustaceans that you may never have seen before. Stored live in holding tanks or in enormous crates near the entrance, many of the creatures are flown in daily from Galicia, home of owner Moncho Neira. With the 100 or so fish dishes, the menu lists only four or five meat dishes, including three kinds of steak, veal, and a traditional version of pork with turnips. The wine list offers a wide array of *cavas* from Catalonia and highly drinkable choices from Galicia.

✪ **Gaig.** Passeig de Maragall, 402. ☎ **93-429-10-17.** Reservations recomended. Main courses 5,000–6,000 ptas. ($30–$36); *menú gastronómico* 8,850 ptas. ($53.10). AE, DC, MC, V. Tues–Sun 1:30–4:30pm; Tues–Sat 9–11pm; Sun 1:30–4pm. Closed 3 weeks in Aug. Metro: Horta. MODERN CATALÁN.

One of the shining culinary showcases of Barcelona, Gaig was founded some 130 years ago by the great-grandmother of present owner Carlos Gaig. Back then it was known as a *fonda,* or small inn for travelers. Despite the age of the building, the interior design is both modern and luxurious, having recently been restyled. The restaurant is celebrated locally for the quality and freshness of its food. If you order a meal with eggs, those eggs will have been contributed by chickens seen wandering about the patio where customers often dine alfresco in the summer months. The cuisine of Gaig centers on traditional Catalán recipes transformed and altered to suit lighter and more modern palates. Among the stellar dishes to order are *arroz del delta con pichon y zetas* (rice with partridge and mushrooms), *rape asado a la Catalána* (grilled monkfish with local herbs), and *els petits filet de vedella amb prunes i pinyons* (small veal fillets with prunes and pinenuts). One of the tastiest dishes is marinated roast pork thigh. Desserts include *crema de Sant Joseph* (a warm flan with wild strawberries on top), homemade chocolates, and a selection of tartes.

EXPENSIVE

✪ **Neichel.** Pedralbes, 16. ☎ **93-203-84-08.** Reservations required. Main courses 2,500–4,200 ptas. ($15–$25.20). AE, MC, V. Mon–Fri 1:30–3:30pm; Mon–Sat 8:30–11pm. Closed holidays and Aug. Metro: Palau Reial or María Cristina. FRENCH/MEDITERRANEAN.

Alsatian-born owner Jean Louis Neichel has been called "the most brilliant ambassador French cuisine has ever had within Spain." Neichel is almost obsessively concerned with gastronomy—the savory presentation of some of the most talked-about preparations of seafood, fowl, and sweets in Spain.

Your meal might include a "mosaic" of foie gras with vegetables, strips of salmon marinated in sesame and served with *escabeche* (vinaigrette) sauce, or slices of raw and smoked salmon stuffed with caviar. The prize-winning terrine of sea crab floats on a lavishly decorated bed of cold seafood sauce. Move on to *escalope* of turbot served with *coulis* (puree) of sea urchins, fricassee of Bresse chicken served with spiny lobsters, sea bass with a mousseline of truffles, Spanish milk-fed lamb served with the juice of Boletus mushrooms, or rack of lamb gratinéed in an herb-flavored pastry crust. The selection of European cheeses and the changing array of freshly made desserts are nothing short of spectacular.

Reno. Tuset, 27. ☎ **93-200-91-29.** Reservations required. Main courses 1,400–3,800 ptas. ($8.40–$22.80). AE, DC, MC, V. Sun–Fri 1–4pm; Sun–Sat 8:30–11:30pm. Metro: Diagonal. CATALÁN/FRENCH.

One of the finest and most enduring haute cuisine restaurants in Barcelona, Reno sits behind sidewalk-to-ceiling windows hung with fine-mesh lace to shelter diners from prying eyes on the octagonal plaza outside. The impeccably mannered staff is formal but not intimidating. Seasonal specialties might include partridge simmered in wine or port sauce, a platter of assorted fish smoked on the premises, hake with anchovy sauce, or fillet of sole stuffed with foie gras and truffles or grilled with anchovy sauce. An appetizing array of pastries wheels from table to table on a cart. Dessert might also be crêpes flambéed at your table.

Roig Robí. Séneca, 20. ☎ **93-218-92-22.** Reservations required. Main courses 2,200–4,500 ptas. ($13.20–$27); fixed-price menu 7,500 ptas. ($45). AE, DC, MC, V. Mon–Fri 1:30–4pm; Mon–Sat 9–11pm. Metro: Diagonal. CATALÁN.

This restaurant—the name means "ruby red" (the color of a perfectly aged Rioja) in Catalán—serves excellent food from an imaginative kitchen with a warm welcome. Although we're not as excited about this restaurant as we once were, it does remain one of the city's most dependable choices. Order an aperitif at the L-shaped oak bar, then head down a long corridor to a pair of flower-filled dining rooms. In warm weather, glass doors open onto a verdant walled courtyard. Menu items include fresh beans with pinenut sauce, *hake al Roig Robí*, fresh mushroom salad with green beans and fresh tomatoes, and shellfish from Costa Brava. Monkfish comes with clams and onion confit, ravioli stuffed with spring herbs, and chicken stuffed with foie gras. Cockscomb salad is available for those with adventuresome palates.

✪ **Via Veneto.** Ganduxer, 10. ☎ **93-200-72-44.** Reservations required. Main courses 2,500–4,500 ptas. ($15–$27). AE, DC, MC, V. Mon–Fri 1:15–4pm; Mon–Sat 8:45pm–midnight. Closed Aug 1–20. Metro: La Bonanova. INTERNATIONAL.

Consistently well-prepared cuisine attracts diners to this conservatively decorated restaurant a short walk from the Plaça de Francesc María. The kitchen is always inventing imaginative Catalán recipes based on fresh local ingredients, such as tartare of fresh fish with caviar, roasted salt cod with potatoes, and veal kidney with truffle sauce. Loin of roast suckling pig comes with seasonal baby vegetables, and fillet steak is served in a brandy, cream, and peppercorn sauce. There's a wide array of wines. Dessert might be a richly textured combination of melted chocolate, cherries, Armagnac, and vanilla ice cream.

MOLL DE LA FUSTA & BARCELONETA
EXPENSIVE

✪ **Can Costa.** Passeig Don Joan de Borbò, 70. ☎ **93-221-59-03.** Reservations recommended. Main courses 2,000–5,500 ptas. ($12–$33). AE, MC, V. Daily 12:30–4pm; Mon–Sat 8–11:30pm. Metro: Barceloneta. SEAFOOD.

One of the oldest seafood restaurants in this seafaring town is Can Costa, whose big windows overlook the water. Established in the late 1930s, it has two busy dining rooms, a practiced staff, and an outdoor terrace. Fresh seafood prepared according to traditional recipes rules the menu. It includes the best baby squid in town—sauteed in a flash so that it has a nearly grilled flavor, almost never overcooked or rubbery. A long-standing chef's specialty is *fideuá de peix,* a relative of the classic Valencian shellfish paella, with noodles instead of rice. Desserts are made fresh daily.

Can Majó. Almirante Aixada, 23. ☎ **93-221-54-55.** Reservations recommended. Main courses 2,000–3,800 ptas. ($12–$22.80); fixed-price menu 6,000 ptas. ($36). AE, MC, V. Tues–Sun 1:30–4:30pm and 9–11:30pm. Metro: Barceloneta. SEAFOOD.

In the old fishing quarter of Barceloneta, Can Majó attracts many people from fancier areas who come here for a great seafood dinner. The Suárez-Majó family operates the business where their grandmother first opened a bar. Start with *entremeses* (hors d'oeuvres), for which you can select barnacles, oysters, prawns, whelks, clams, and crab—whatever was caught that day. The clams with white beans are recommended. The classic vegetable gazpacho comes with fresh mussels and shrimp. Or try a house specialty, *pelada* (Catalán for "paella").

Ramonet. Carrer Maquinista, 17. ☎ **93-319-30-64.** Reservations recommended. Main courses 2,500–4,200 ptas. ($15–$25.20); fixed-price menus 4,800–7,000 ptas. ($28.80–$42). AE, DC, MC, V. Daily 10am–4pm and 8pm–midnight. Usually closed Aug 10–Sept 10. Metro: Barceloneta. SEAFOOD.

In a Catalán-style villa near the seaport, this rather expensive restaurant has served a large variety of fresh seafood since 1763. The front room, with stand-up tables for seafood tapas, beer, and regional wine, is often crowded. In the two dining rooms, you can choose from a variety of seafood—shrimp, hake, and monkfish are almost always available. Other specialties include pungent anchovies, grilled mushrooms, black rice, braised artichokes, tortilla with spinach and beans, and mussels "from the beach."

MODERATE

7 Portes. Passeig d'Isabel II, 14. ☎ **93-319-30-33.** Reservations required. Main courses 3,000–4,500 ptas. ($18–$27). AE, DC, MC, V. Daily 1pm–midnight. Metro: Barceloneta. SEAFOOD.

This is a lunchtime favorite for businesspeople (the Stock Exchange is across the way) and an evening favorite for many in-the-know diners who have made it their preferred restaurant in Catalonia. Festive and elegant, it's been going since 1836. Regional dishes include fresh herring with onions and potatoes, a different paella daily (sometimes with shellfish, for example, or with rabbit), and a wide array of fresh fish. You might order succulent oysters or an herb-laden stew of black beans with pork or white beans with sausage. Portions are enormous. The restaurant's name means "Seven Doors," and it really does have seven doors. Waiters wear the long white aprons of the belle époque era.

El Túnel. Ample, 33–35. ☎ **93-315-27-59.** Reservations recommended for lunch. Main courses 1,500–2,500 ptas. ($9–$15). MC, V. Tues–Thurs 6pm–midnight; Fri–Sat 6pm–1:30am. Closed Aug. Metro: San Jaume. SPANISH.

This long-established restaurant serves delectable fish soup, cannelloni with truffles, kidney beans with shrimp, roast kid, fish stew, and fillet of beef with peppers. The food is uncomplicated but delicious. The service is eager, the wine cellar extensive. El Túnel is close to the general post office.

INEXPENSIVE

Agua. Passeig Maritim de la Barceloneta, 30 (Port Marítim). ☎ **93-225-12-72.** Reservations recommended. Main courses 950–2,250 ptas. ($5.70–$13.50). AE, MC, V. Daily 1:30–4:30pm and 8:30pm–midnight (1am on Fri–Sat). Metro: Ciudadela. CATALÁN/SEAFOOD.

It bustles, it's hip, and it serves well-prepared fish and shellfish in a hyper-modern setting overlooking the beach. A terrace beckons anyone who wants an in-your-face view of the water, but if the wind is blowing with a bit too much chill, you can retreat into the big-windowed blue-and-yellow dining room. Here, amid display cases showing the catch of the day, you can order heaping portions of meats and fish to be grilled over an open fire. Excellent examples include grilled versions of chicken, fish, shrimp, crayfish, and an especially succulent version of stuffed squid. Most of them are served with as little culinary fanfare, and as few sauces, as possible, allowing the freshness and flavor of the raw ingredients to shine through the chargrilled coatings. Risottos, some of them studded with fresh clams and herbs, are usually winners, with many versions suitable for vegetarians.

NEAR ESTACIÓN DE SANTS
INEXPENSIVE

La Llauna. Plaça D'Osca, 2. ☎ **93-422-32-25.** Reservations recommended on weekends. Main courses 800–3,000 ptas. ($4.80–$18); *menú del día* (at lunch) 1,700 ptas. ($10.20). MC, V. Thur–Tues 1–4pm and 8pm–midnight. Metro: Plaça de Sants and Estación de Sants. CATALÁN.

The name of this restaurant is a reference to the pot in which *calcots* are cooked. Available only in the spring, this rare dish is similar to a spring onion but twice or more the size with an almost meaty taste. It isn't easy to find this delicacy in Barcelona, but this restaurant specializes in *calcots,* cooking them over an open charcoal grill. It has two floors for diners, each decorated in a Catalán rustic style with white walls and posters of local country life. Prices are very reasonable. The menu includes a selection of well-prepared regional dishes based on local products and fresh ingredients. Locals begin with *pa amb tomaquet* (toasted bread with tomatoes and olive oil), going on to sample such hearty fare as various grilled meats with fried potatoes or *gambas a la Llauna o con conejo* (shrimp or rabbit with *calcots* in wine sauce).

WEST OF TIBIDABO

La Balsa. Infanta Isabel, 4. ☎ **93-211-50-48.** Reservations required. Main courses 2,200–3,500 ptas. ($13.20–$21); fixed-price lunch 3,000 ptas. ($18); fixed-price dinner 6,500–7,000 ptas. ($39–$42). AE, MC, V. Tues–Sat 2–3:30pm; Mon–Sat 9–11:30pm. Closed Easter week. No buffet in Aug. INTERNATIONAL.

On the uppermost level of a circular tower built as a cistern, La Balsa offers a view over most of the surrounding cityscape. To reach it, you climb to the structure's original rooftop where you're likely to be greeted by owner and founder Mercedes López. Food emerges from a cramped but well-organized kitchen several floors below. (The waiters are reputedly the most athletic in Barcelona, because they must run up the stairs carrying steaming platters.) The restaurant serves such dishes as a *judías verdes* (salad of broad beans) with strips of salmon in lemon-flavored vinaigrette, stewed veal with wild mushrooms, a salad of warm lentils with anchovies, and pickled fresh salmon with chives. Undercooked maigret (breast) of duck is served with fresh, lightly poached foie gras, and baked hake (flown in from Galicia) is prepared in squid-ink sauce. The restaurant is 1¼ miles (2km) north of the city's heart—you'll need a taxi—in the Tibidabo district, close to the Science Museum (Museu de la Ciència). It's often booked several days in advance.

OUR FAVORITE *TASCAS*

The bars listed below are known for their tapas; for more recommendations, refer to the "Barcelona After Dark" section, below.

Alt Heidelberg. Ronda Universitat, 5. ☎ **93-318-10-32.** Tapas 250–750 ptas. ($1.50–$4.50); combination plates 1,000–1,450 ptas. ($6–$8.70). MC, V. Mon–Fri 8am–1:30am; Sat–Sun noon–2am. Metro: Universitat. GERMAN/TAPAS.

A Barcelona institution since the 1930s, Alt Heidelberg serves German beer on tap, a good selection of German sausages, and Spanish tapas. You can also order full meals—sauerkraut garni is a specialty.

Bar del Pi. Plaça Sant Josep Oriol, 1. ☎ **93-302-21-23.** Tapas 250–600 ptas. ($1.50–$3.60). No credit cards. Mon–Fri 9am–11pm; Sat 9:30am–10pm; Sun 10am–10pm. Metro: Liceu. TAPAS.

One of the most famous bars in the Barri Gòtic, this establishment is midway between two medieval squares opening onto the church of Pi. Tapas are limited; most visitors come to drink coffee, beer, or wine. You can sit inside at one of the cramped bentwood tables, or stand at the crowded bar. In warm weather, take a table beneath the single plane tree on the landmark square. The plaza usually draws an interesting group of young bohemian sorts and travelers.

Bar Turò. Tenor Viñas, 1. ☎ **93-200-69-53.** Tapas 300–1,500 ptas. ($1.80–$9). MC, V. Sun–Thurs 9am–1am; Fri–Sat 9am–3am. Metro: Maria Cristina. TAPAS.

In an affluent residential neighborhood north of the old town, Bar Turò serves some of the best tapas in town. In summer you can sit outside or retreat to the narrow confines of the bar. You select from about 20 kinds of tapas, including Russian salad, fried squid, and Serrano ham.

Bodega la Plata. Mercè, 28. ☎ **93-315-10-09.** Tapas 250–1,000 ptas. ($1.50–$6). No credit cards. Mon–Sat 10am–11pm. Metro: Barceloneta. TAPAS.

Established in the 1920s, La Plata is one of a trio of famous *bodegas* on this narrow medieval street. It occupies a corner building whose two open sides allow aromatic cooking odors to permeate the neighborhood. This *bodega* contains a marble-topped bar and overcrowded tables. The culinary specialty is *raciónes* (small plates) of deep-fried sardines—head and all. You can make a meal with two servings coupled with the house's tomato, onion, and fresh anchovy salad.

Bodegueta. Rambla de Catalunya, 100. ☎ **93-215-48-94.** Tapas from 250 ptas. ($1.50). No credit cards. Mon–Sat 8am–1:45am; Sun 7pm–1:30am. Metro: Diagonal. TAPAS.

Founded in 1940, this old wine tavern specializes in Catalán sausage. Wash it all down with inexpensive Spanish wines. Beer costs 150 to 300 ptas. (90¢ to $1.80); wine goes for 150 ptas. ($1).

Casa Alfonso. Roger de Lluria, 6. ☎ **93-301-97-83.** Tapas 1,200–2,500 ptas. ($7.20–$15). No credit cards. Mon–Tues 9am–10pm; Wed–Sat 9am–1am. Metro: Urquinaona. TAPAS.

Spaniards love their ham, which comes in a great many forms. The best of the best is *jamón Jabugo,* the only one sold at this traditional establishment. Entire hams hang from steel braces. They're taken down, carved, and trimmed before you into paper-thin slices. This particular form of cured ham, generically called *jamón Serrano,* comes from pigs fed acorns in Huelva, in deepest Andalusia. Devotees of all things porcine will ascend to piggy-flavored heaven.

Casa Tejada. Tenor Viñas, 3. ☎ **93-200-73-41.** Tapas 350–2,500 ptas. ($2.10–$15). MC, V. Daily 9am–2am. Metro: Muntaner. TAPAS.

Covered with rough stucco and decorated with hanging hams, Casa Tejada (established in 1964) offers some the best tapas. Arranged behind a glass display case, they include such dishes as marinated fresh tuna, German-style potato salad, ham salad, and five preparations of squid (including one that's stuffed). For variety, quantity, and quality, this place is hard to beat. There's outdoor dining in summer.

La Jarra. Mercè, 9. ☎ **93-315-17-59.** Tapas 350–600 ptas. ($2.10–$3.60). No credit cards. Thurs–Tues 11:30am–1am. Metro: Barceloneta. TAPAS.

Established in the 1950s, La Jarra occupies a tile-covered L-shaped room. It's somewhat bleak, but residents claim it is one of the most authentic tapas bars in the old town. You can order a *ración* (portion) of marinated mushrooms or well-seasoned artichokes Rioja style, but the culinary star is the ever-present haunch of *jamón Canario* (Canary Island ham). It's carved while you watch into lean, succulent morsels served with boiled potatoes, olive oil, and lots of salt. It resembles roast pork in flavor and appearance.

Las Campanas (Casa Marcos). Mercè, 21. ☎ **93-315-06-09.** Tapas 150–1,250 ptas. (90¢–$7.50). No credit cards. Thurs–Tues 12:30–4pm and 7pm–2am. Metro: Jaume I. TAPAS.

From the street (there's no sign), Las Campanas looks like a storehouse for cured hams and wine bottles. Patrons flock to the long, stand-up bar for *chorizo* pinioned between two pieces of bread. Sausages are usually eaten with beer or red wine. The place opened in 1952, and nothing has changed since. A tape recorder plays nostalgic favorites, from Edith Piaf to the Andrews Sisters.

Rey de la Gamba. Joan de Borbò, 48–53. ☎ **93-221-75-98.** Tapas 550–10,000 ptas. ($3.30–$60). MC, V. Daily 11am–1am. Metro: Barceloneta. SHELLFISH.

The "King of Prawns" could also be called the House of Mussels, since it sells more of that shellfish. In the 18th-century fishing village of Barceloneta, this place packs them in, especially on weekends. A wide array of seafood accompanies cured ham—the combination is a tradition.

6 Seeing the Sights

THE TOP ATTRACTIONS

One of Barcelona's greatest attractions is not a single sight but an entire neighborhood, the ✪ **Barri Gòtic (Gothic Quarter).** This is the old aristocratic quarter, parts of which have survived from the Middle Ages. Spend at least 2 or 3 hours exploring its narrow streets and squares, which continue to form a vibrant, lively neighborhood. Start by walking up the carrer del Carme, east of Les Rambles. A nighttime stroll takes on added drama, but exercise caution—safety is an issue here. The buildings are austere and sober for the most part, the cathedral being the crowning achievement.

Roman ruins and the vestiges of 3rd-century walls add further interest. This area is intricately detailed and filled with many attractions that are easy to miss (see map).

✪ **La Sagrada Família.** Majorca, 401. ☎ **93-207-30-31.** Admission (includes video) 800 ptas. ($4.80); elevator to the top (about 200 feet) 200 ptas. ($1.20). Daily, Nov–Feb 9am–6pm; Mar and Sept–Oct, 9am–7pm; Apr and Aug, 9am–8pm. Metro: Sagrada Família.

Gaudí's incomplete masterpiece is one of the country's more idiosyncratic creations— if you have time to see only one Catalán landmark, make it this one. Begun in 1882 and incomplete at the architect's death in 1926, this incredible cathedral—the Church of the Holy Family—is a bizarre wonder. The languid, amorphous structure embodies the essence of Gaudí's style, which some have described as art nouveau run wild. Admission includes a 12-minute video on Gaudí's religious and secular works. Work continues on the structure, but without any sure idea of what Gaudí intended. Some say that the cathedral will be completed by the mid-21st century.

✪ **Catedral de Barcelona.** Plaça de la Seu, s/n. ☎ **93-315-15-54.** Admission to cathedral free; to museum 100 ptas. (60¢). Cathedral, daily 8am–1:30pm and 4–7:30pm; cloister museum, daily 10am–1pm and 4–7pm. Metro: Jaume I.

Barcelona's cathedral is a celebrated example of Catalonian Gothic architecture. Construction began at the end of the 13th century and was nearly completed in the mid–15th century (although the west facade dates from the 19th century). The three naves, cleaned and illuminated, have splendid Gothic details. With its large bell towers, blending of medieval and Renaissance styles, beautiful cloister, high altar, side chapels, sculptured choir, and Gothic arches, it ranks as one of the most impressive cathedrals in Spain. Vaulted galleries in the cloister, enhanced by forged iron grilles, surround a garden of magnolias, medlars, and palm trees. The historian Cirici called this "the loveliest oasis in Barcelona." The cloister, illuminated on Saturdays and fiestas, also contains a museum of medieval art. Its most notable work is the 15th-century *La Pietat* of Bartolomé Bermejo. At noon on Sunday you can see the *sardana*, a Catalonian folk dance, performed in front of the cathedral.

✪ **Museu Picasso.** Montcada, 15–19. ☎ **93-319-63-10.** Admission 700 ptas. ($4.20) adults, 400 ptas. ($2.40) students and people under 25, free for children under 13. Tues–Sat 10am–8pm; Sun 10am–3pm. Metro: Jaume I.

Two old palaces on a medieval street contain this museum of the work of Pablo Picasso (1881–1973). He donated some 2,500 of his paintings, engravings, and drawings to the museum in 1970. Picasso was particularly fond of Barcelona, where he spent much of his youth. In fact, some of the paintings were done when he was only 9. One portrait dating from 1896 depicts his stern aunt, Tía Pepa. Another, completed when Picasso was 16, depicts *Science and Charity* (his father was the model for the doctor). Many works, especially the early paintings, show the artist's debt to van Gogh, El Greco, and Rembrandt; a famous series, *Las Meninas* (1957), is said to "impersonate" the work of Velázquez (if you've just been to the Prado in Madrid, or are about to go, this is a particularly interesting comparison). The *La Vie* drawings from the blue period are perhaps the most interesting. His notebooks contain many sketches of Barcelona scenes. Because the works are arranged in rough chronological order, you can get a wonderful sense of Picasso's development, and watch as he discovered a trend or had a new idea, mastered it, grew bored with it, and then was off to something new. You'll learn that Picasso was a master portraitist and did many traditional representational works before his flights of fancy took off.

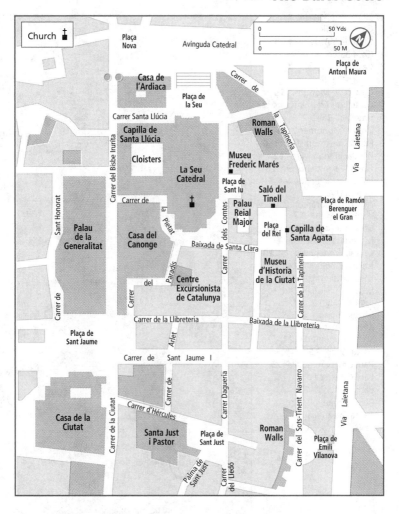

Church ✝

Plaça Nova

Avinguda Catedral

0 — 50 Yds
0 — 50 M

Plaça de Antoni Maura

Casa de l'Ardiaca

Plaça de la Seu

Carrer de

Carrer Santa Llúcia

Capilla de Santa Llúcia

Roman Walls

Via Tapineria

Via Laietana

Carrer del Bisbe Irurita

Cloisters

La Seu Catedral

Museu Frederic Marés

Plaça de Sant Iu

Saló del Tinell

Carrer de

la Pietat

Palau Reial Major

Plaça del Rei

Capilla de Santa Agata

Plaça de Ramón Berenguer el Gran

Sant Honorat

Palau de la Generalitat

Casa del Canonge

Carrer dels Comtes

Baixada de Santa Clara

Museu d'Historia de la Ciutat

Carrer de la Tapineria

Carrer de

Paradis

Carrer del

Centre Excursionista de Catalunya

Carrer de la Llibreteria

Baixada de la Llibreteria

Plaça de Sant Jaume

Arlet

Carrer de Sant Jaume I

Carrer de la Ciutat

Carrer d'Hércules

Carrer de

Carrer Dagueria

Carrer del Sots-Tinent Navarro

Via Laietana

Casa de la Ciutat

Santa Just i Pastor

Plaça de Sant Just

Roman Walls

Plaça de Emili Vilanova

Palma de Sant Just

Carrer del Lledó

Museu Nacional d'Art de Catalunya. Palau Nacional, Parc de Montjuïc. ☎ **93-622-03-60.** Admission 800 ptas. ($4.80) adults, 400 ptas. ($2.40) youths 7–20, free for children under 7. Tues–Wed and Fri–Sat 10am–7pm; Thurs 10am–9pm; Sun 10am–2:30pm. Metro: Espanya.

This museum, which recently underwent massive renovations, is the major depository of Catalán art. The National Art Museum of Catalonia is perhaps the most important center for Romanesque art in the world. More than 100 pieces, including sculptures, icons, and frescoes, are on display. The highlight is the collection of murals from various Romanesque churches. The frescoes and murals are displayed in apses much like those in the churches in which they were found. They're in sequential order, giving the viewer a tour of Romanesque art from its primitive beginnings to the more advanced, late Romanesque and early Gothic eras.

Barcelona Attractions

Casa Amatller **8**
Casa de L'Ardiaca **18**
Casa Batlló **7**
Casa Lleó Morera **9**
Casa Milà **3**
Castell de Montjuïc **13**
Castell de Tres Dragons **23**
Catedral **19**
Colom Monument **14**
Fundació Antoni Tàpies **6**
Fundació Joan Miró **12**
Gran Teatre del Liceu **16**
Monastir de Pedrables **1**
Museu d'Art
  Contemporáreo
  de Barcelona **17**
Museu d'Art Modern **26**
Museu de la Ciència **1**
Museu Frederic Marès **20**
Museu Geològie **24**
Museu Marítim **14**
Museu Nacional d'Art
  de Catalunya **11**
Museu Picasso **22**
Museu Tèxtil i
  d'Indumentària **21**
Palau Güell **15**
Parc de la Ciutadella **25**
Parc Güell **11**
Parc Zoologic **27**
Poble Espanyol **10**
Sagrada Família **4**

TIBIDABO ↑ ↑
①

Avinguda de Madrid

Carrer del Vallespir
Carrer de Numància
Carrer de Berlin
Carrer de la Infanta Carlota Joaquima
Carrer de Còrsega
Carrer de Rossello
Carrer de Sant Antoni
Carrer de Provença
Avinguda de Roma
Carrer de Sants de la Creu Coberta
Carrer de Tarragona
Carrer d'Entrença
Carrer de Rocafort
Carrer de Calàbria
Carrer de Viladomat
Carretera de la Bordeta
Pià de
la Pau
Carrer de Sant Fructuós
Plaça de
Espanya
Gran Vía de les Corts Catalanes
Av. de Marqus de Comillas
Carrer de Sepulveda
⑩
Av. de la Riena Maria Cristina
Avinguda de Paral·lel
Carrer de Floridablanca
Carrer de Tamarit
Carrer de Manso
Carrer del Parlament
⑪
Avinguda de l'Estadi
⑫
Estadi
Olímpic
Avinguda de Miramar
PARC DE MONTJUÏC
PARC D'ATRACCIONS
DE MONTJUÏC
⑬
Passeig de Josep Carner

Plaça de
Francesc Macia

Carrer de Buenos Aires

Carrer de Londres

Carrer de Paris

Travessara de Gràcia

Avinguda Diagonal

Carrer de Còrsega

Carrer de Provença

EIXAMPLE

Travessara de Gràcia

Av. de Sant Antoni Maria Claret

Carrer de la Industria

Carrer de Rossello

Carrer de Roger de Flor

Carrer de Mallorca

Plaça de la
Sagrada
Família **4**

Carrer de Comte Borrell
Carrer del Comte d'Urgell
Carrer de Villarroel
Carrer de Casanova
Carrer de Muntaner
Carrer d'Aribau
Carrer de Balmes
Rambla de Catalunya
Passeig de Gràcia
Carrer de Pau Claris

Carrer de Valencia

Carrer d'Aragó

Avinguda Diagonal

5 **6** **7**
        8
        9

Carrer del Consell de Cent

Carrer de la Diputació

Gran Via de les Corts Catalanes

Carrer de R. de Llúcia
Carrer del Bruc
Carrer de Girona
Carrer de Bailèn
Passeig de Sant Joan
Carrer de Napols
Carrer de Sicilia

Plaça de
Tetuan

Carrer de Casp

Ronda de Sant Antoni

Carrer de Pelai

Ronda Universitat

Plaça
Catalunya

Plaça
Urquinaona

Carrer d'Ausias Marc

Ronda de Sant Pere

Carrer d'Ali Bei

Carrer de Ribes

Carrer de Sardenya

Passeig de Carles I

Ronda Sant Pau

17
RAVAL

Carrer de Hospital

La Rambla

Av. Portal de l'Angel

Via Laietana

18
19 **20**

BARRI GÒTIC

Carrer de Sant Pau

16

Carrer de Ferran

Carrer de la Princesa

Passeig de Comerç

Passeig de Lluis Companys

Passeig de Picasso

Passeig de Pujades

23
24 **25**

PARC DE LA
CIUTADELLA

Carrer de Wellington

Carrer Nou de la Rambla

15

21 **22**

LA RIBERA

La Rambla

Carrer Ample

Avinguda de les Drassanes

Passeig de Colom

Plaça Portal
de la Pau **14**

Moll de la Fusta

Avinguda d'Icàvia

26

27

BARCELONETA

Villa
Olímpica →

Moll
d'Espanya

Aquarium

0   1/4 mi
0   0.25 km

⭐ **Frommer's Favorite Barcelona Experiences**

A Walk Through the Barri Gòtic. You'll pass through 15 centuries of history in one labyrinthine district.

Watching the *Sardana*. The national dance of Catalonia is performed at noon on Sunday at the Plaça de San Jaume in front of the cathedral.

A Trip to the Top of Montjuïc. Barcelona spreads out at your feet. This stop will provide enough amusement to fill 3 days.

Soaking Up Designer Bar Culture. Bars of all shapes and sizes are the chic places to go at night—Barcelona has more than any other city in Spain. Catalán design is paramount.

Drinking *Cava* in a Xampanyería. Enjoy a glass of bubbly, Barcelona style. The wines are excellent, and Cataláns swear that their *cavas* taste better than French champagne.

A Tour of Barcelona's Harbor. Stroll from the pier in front of the Columbus Monument to the breakwater.

Exploring the Museu Picasso. Examine the evolution of the world's greatest 20th-century artist from the age of 9.

Marveling at La Sagrada Família. Gaudí's "sand-castle cathedral" is a testimony to the architect's talent and religious belief.

A Visit to Poble Espanyol. Artificial village, to be sure, but it gives you a chance to see the architecture of all of Spain without leaving Barcelona.

Fundació Joan Miró. Plaça de Neptú, Parc de Montjuïc. ☎ **93-329-19-08.** Admission 800 ptas. ($4.80) adults, 450 ptas. ($2.70) students, free for children under 15. June–Sept, Tues–Wed and Fri–Sat 10am–8pm, Thurs 10am–9:30pm, Sun 10am–2:30pm; Nov–May, Tues–Wed and Fri–Sat 11am–7pm, Thurs 10am–9:30pm, Sun 10am–2:30pm. Bus: 50 at Plaça d'Espanya.

Born in 1893, Joan Miró was one of Spain's greatest artists, known for his whimsical abstract forms and brilliant colors. Some 10,000 works by the Catalán surrealist, including paintings, graphics, and sculptures, are collected here. The building has been greatly expanded in recent years, following the design of Catalán architect Josep Lluís Sert, a close friend of Miró's. An exhibition in a modern wing charts (in a variety of media) Miró's artistic evolution, from his first drawings at the age of 8 to his last works. The museum frequently mounts temporary exhibitions of contemporary art.

Parc Güell. At end of carrer de Llarrard. ☎ **93-424-38-09.** May–Sept, daily 10am–9pm; Oct–Apr, daily 10am–6pm. Bus 24, 25, 31, or 74.

Gaudí began this idiosyncratic park as a real-estate venture for a friend, the well-known Catalán industrialist Count Eusebi Güell, but it was never completed. Although only two houses were constructed, it makes for an interesting excursion. The city took over the property in 1926 and turned it into a public park. One of the houses, **Casa-Museu Gaudí,** carrer del Carmel, 28 (☎ **93-219-38-11**), contains models, furniture, drawings, and other memorabilia of the architect. (Ramón Berenguer, not Gaudí, designed the house.) Admission is 300 ptas. ($2.10). Open daily 10am to 8pm.

Gaudí completed several of the public areas, which today look like a surrealist Disneyland, complete with a mosaic pagoda and a lizard fountain spitting water.

Gaudí had planned to make this a model community of 60 dwellings, arranged somewhat like a Greek theater. A central grand plaza was built above a market, as well as an undulating bench decorated with ceramic fragments. The bizarre Doric columns of the would-be market are hollow, part of Gaudí's drainage system.

IF YOU HAVE MORE TIME

Museu Barbier-Mueller Art Precolombí. Carrer de Montcada, 12–14. ☎ **93-310-45-16.** Admission 500 ptas. ($3) adults, 250 ptas. ($1.50) students, free for children under 12. Free to all first Sat of every month. Tues–Sat 10am–8pm; Sun and holidays 10am–3pm. Metro: Jaume I. Bus: 14, 17, 19, 39, 40, 45, or 51.

Inaugurated by Queen Sofia in 1997, this is one of the most important collections of pre-Columbian art in the world. In the restored Palacio Nadal, which was built during the Middle Ages, the collection contains almost 6,000 pieces of tribal and ancient art. Josef Mueller (1887–1977) acquired the first pieces by 1908. Pre-Columbian cultures created religious, funerary, and ornamental objects of great stylistic variety with relatively simple means. Stone sculpture and ceramic objects are especially outstanding. For example, the Olmecs, who settled on the Gulf of Mexico at the beginning of the first millennium B.C., executed notable monumental sculpture in stone and magnificent figures in jade. Many exhibits focus on the Mayan culture, the most homogenous and widespread of its time, dating from 1000 B.C. Mayan artisans mastered painting, ceramics, and sculpture. Note the work by the pottery makers of the Lower Amazon, particularly those from the island of Marajó.

Museu Frederic Marès. Plaça de Sant Iú, 5–6. ☎ **93-310-58-00.** Admission 300 ptas. ($1.80) adults, free for children under 12. Tues and Thurs 10am–5pm; Wed, Fri, and Sat 10am–7pm; Sun 10am–2pm. Metro: Jaume I. Bus: 17, 19, or 45.

One of the biggest repositories of medieval sculpture in the region is the Frederic Marès Museum, just behind the cathedral. It's in an ancient palace with impressive interior courtyards, chiseled stone, and soaring ceilings, an ideal setting for the hundreds of polychrome sculptures. The sculpture section dates from pre-Roman times to the 20th century. In the same building is the Museu Sentimental, a collection of everyday items that help to illustrate life in Barcelona during the past 2 centuries. The ticket price includes admission to both museums.

Center of Contemporary Culture of Barcelona (CCCB). Montalegre, 5. ☎ **93-306-41-00.** Admission 600 ptas. ($3.60) adults, 400 ptas. ($2.40) students and adults over 65, free for children under 16. Tues and Thurs–Fri 11am–2pm and 6–8pm; Wed and Sat 11am–8pm; Sun 11am–7pm. Metro: Plaça de Catalunya or Universitat.

In the Ciutat Vella, the Center of Contemporary Culture of Barcelona focuses on the city. It explores Barcelona's culture, history, and present role as a modern European city.

L'Aquarium de Barcelona. Port Vell. ☎ **93-221-74-74.** Admission 1,400 ptas. ($8.40) adults, 950 ptas. ($5.70) children 4–12 and students, free for children under 4. June–Aug, daily 9:30am–11pm; Sept, daily 9:30am–9:30pm; Oct–May, daily 9:30am–9pm. Metro: Drassanes or Barceloneta.

One of the most impressive testimonials to sea life anywhere opened in 1996 in Barcelona's Port Vell, a 10-minute walk from the bottom of the Rambles. The largest aquarium in Europe, it contains 21 glass tanks positioned along either side of a wide curving corridor. Each tank depicts a different marine habitat, with emphasis on everything from multicolored fish and corals to seagoing worms to sharks. The highlight is a huge "oceanium" representative of the Mediterranean as a self-sustaining ecosystem. You view it from the inside of a glass-roofed, glass-sided tunnel that runs along its entire length, making fish, eels, and sharks appear to swim around you.

Museu Marítim. Avinguda de las Drassanes, s/n. ☎ **93-318-32-45.** Admission 800 ptas. ($4.80) adults, 400 ptas. ($2.40) children 7–17 and seniors, free for children under 7. Tues–Sat 10am–7pm. Closed holidays. Metro: Drassanes. Bus: 14, 18, 36, 38, 57, 59, 64, or 91.

In the former Royal Shipyards (Drassanes Reials), this 13th-century Gothic complex was used to construct ships for the Catalán-Aragonese rulers. The most outstanding exhibition is a reconstruction of *La Galería Real* of Don Juan of Austria, a lavish royal galley. Another special exhibit features a map by Gabriel de Vallseca that belonged to explorer Amerìgo Vespucci.

Museu de la Ciència (Science Museum). Teodor Roviralta, 55. ☎ **93-212-60-50.** Admission to museum and planetarium, 750 ptas. ($4.50) adults, 650 ptas. ($3.90) children under 17. Museum only 500 ptas. ($3) adults, 350 ptas. ($2.10) children. Planetarium only 250 ptas. ($1.50). Tues–Sun 10am–8pm. Bus: 17, 22, 58, or 73.

Museu de la Ciència of the La Caixa Foundation is one of the most popular in Barcelona, with more than 500,000 visitors annually. Its modern design and hands-on activities have made it the most important science museum in Spain and a major cultural attraction.

Visitors can touch, listen to, watch, and participate in a variety of exhibits. From the beauty of marine life to the magic of holograms, the museum introduces a world of science. Watch the earth turn beneath a Foucault Pendulum; ride on a human gyroscope; hear a friend whisper from 65 feet (19.5m) away; feel an earthquake; or use the tools of a scientist to examine intricate life forms with microscopes and video cameras.

More than 300 exhibits explore the wonders of science, from space travel to life sciences. In the "Optics and Perception" exhibits, visitors interact with prisms, lenses, and holograms, and walk inside a kaleidoscope. In the "Living Planet" area, baby sharks swim, a tornado swirls, and plants magically change their form when touched.

In the "Mechanics" exhibit, visitors can lift an 88-pound (40kg) weight with little effort. Lasers and musical instruments provide fun ways to learn about sound and light waves. Throughout the exhibits, there are computers to help you delve deeper into various topics. Visitors can walk inside a submarine and make weather measurements in a working weather station. For those who want to explore new worlds, there are planetarium shows where the beauty of the night sky surrounds the audience.

To reach the museum, ride the bus from Plaça de Catalunya all the way to avinguda del Tibidabo. Then follow the signs for 2 blocks, turning left onto carrer Teodor Roviralta, where you'll see the museum. The building is at the southern foothills of Tibidabo, reached by following avinguda del Tibidabo.

Fundació Antoni Tàpies. Aragó, 255. ☎ **93-487-03-15.** Admission 700 ptas. ($4.20) adults, 350 ptas. ($2.10) students, free for children under 11. Tues–Sun 11am–8pm. Metro: Passeig de Gràcia.

When it opened in 1990 this became the third Barcelona museum devoted to the work of a single artist. In 1984 the Catalán artist Antoni Tàpies set up a foundation bearing his name, and the city of Barcelona donated an ideal site: the old Montaner i Simon publishing house, near the Passeig de Gràcia in the Eixample district. One of the city's landmark buildings, the brick-and-iron structure was built between 1881 and 1884 by that exponent of Catalán art nouveau, architect Lluís Domènech i Montaner. The core of the museum is a collection of works by Tàpies (most contributed by the artist), covering stages of his career as it evolved into abstract expressionism. Here you can see the entire spectrum of media in which he worked: painting, assemblage, sculpture, drawing, and ceramics. His associations with Picasso and Miró are apparent. The largest of the works is on top of the building: a controversial gigantic sculpture, *Cloud and Chair*, made from 9,000 feet of metal wiring and tubing.

Museu d'Art Modern. Plaça d'Armes, Parc de la Ciutadella. ☎ **93-319-57-28.** Admission 500 ptas. ($3) adults, 250 ptas. ($1.50) youths 8–21, free for children under 8. Tues–Sat 10am–7pm; Sun 10am–2:30pm. Closed Jan 1, Dec 25. Metro: Arc de Triomf. Bus: 14, 16, 17, 39, 40, 41, 51, 57, 59, or 64.

This museum shares a wing of the Palau de la Ciutadella with the Catalán parliament. Constructed in the 1700s, it was once used as an arsenal. It later became a royal residence before being turned into a museum early in this century. Its collection of art focuses on the early 20th century and features the work of Catalán artists, including Martí Alsina, Vayreda, Casas, Fortuny, and Rusiñol. The collection encompasses some 19th-century Romantic and neoclassical works, as well as *modernisme* furniture (including designs by architect Puig i Cadafalch).

Monestir de Pedralbes. Baixada del Monestir, 9. ☎ **93-203-92-82.** Admission 400 ptas. ($2.40) adults, 250 ptas. ($1.50) students and seniors over 64, free for children under 13. Tues–Sun 10am–2pm. Metro: Reina Elisenda. Bus: 22, 63, 64, 75, or 114.

One of the oldest buildings in Pedralbes (the city's wealthiest residential area) is this monastery founded in 1326 by Elisenda de Montcada, queen of Jaume II. Still a convent, the establishment is the mausoleum of the queen, who is buried in its Gothic church. Walk through the cloisters, with nearly two dozen arches on each side, rising three stories high. A small chapel contains the chief treasure of the monastery, murals by Ferrer Bassa, who was the major artist of Catalonia in the 1300s.

This monastery was a minor attraction until 1993, when 72 paintings and eight sculptures from the famed Thyssen-Bornemisza collection went on permanent display. Among the outstanding works of art are Fra Angelico's *The Virgin of Humility* and 20 paintings from the early German Renaissance period. Italian Renaissance paintings range from the end of the 15th century to the middle of the 16th century. They include works by Dosso Dossi, Lorenzo Lotto, Tintoretto, Veronese, and Titian. Such old masters as Rubens, Zurbarán, and Velázquez represent the baroque era.

Museu Arqueològic. Passeig de Santa Madrona, 39–41, Parc de Montjuïc. ☎ **93-423-21-49.** Admission 400 ptas. ($2.40) adults, 300 ptas. ($1.80) students, free for children. Tues–Sat 9:30am–7pm; Sun 10am–2:30pm. Metro: Espanya. Bus: 55.

The Museu Arqueològic occupies the former Palace of Graphic Arts built for the 1929 World's Fair. It reflects the long history of this Mediterranean port city, beginning with prehistoric Iberian artifacts. The collection includes articles from the Greek, Roman (glass, ceramics, mosaics, bronzes), and Carthaginian periods. Some of the more interesting relics were excavated in the ancient Greco-Roman city of Empúries in Catalonia; other parts of the collection came from the Balearic Islands.

Museu d'Art Contemporani de Barcelona. Plaça dels Angels, 1. ☎ **93-412-08-10.** Admission 750 ptas. ($4.50) adults, 500 ptas. ($3) students, free for children. Tues–Sat 11am–7:30pm; Sun 10am–3pm. Metro: Plaça de Catalunya.

A soaring white edifice in the once-shabby but rebounding Raval district, the Museum of Contemporary Art is to Barcelona what the Pompidou Center is to Paris. Designed by the American architect Richard Meier, the building is a work of art itself, manipulating sunlight to offer brilliant, natural interior lighting. On display in the 74,000 square feet of exhibit space is the work of modern luminaries such as Tápies, Klee, Miró, and many others. The museum has a library, bookshop, and cafeteria.

Museu de les Arts Decoratives. Palau Reial de Pedralbes, avinguda Diagonal, 686. ☎ **93-280-50-24.** Admission 400 ptas. ($2.40). Free 1st Sun of every month. Tues–Sat 10am–7pm; Sun and holidays 10am–3pm. Metro: Palau Reial. Bus: 7, 63, 67, 68, or 75.

In a beautiful park, this palace was constructed as a municipal gift to King Alfonso XIII. He didn't make much use of it, however, as he was forced into exile in 1931.

Today it houses a collection of objets d'art, furniture, jewelry, and glassware from the 14th century to the present. More than 200 pieces, all of Spanish origin, are on display.

Museu Egipci de Barcelona. Calle València, 284. ☎ **93-488-01-88.** Admission 700 ptas. ($4.20) adults, 500 ptas. ($3) students and children. Mon–Sat 10am–2pm and 4–8pm; Sun 10am–2pm. Guided tours Sat. Closed holidays. Metro: Passeig de Gràcia.

Spain's only museum dedicated specifically to Egyptology contains more than 250 pieces from the personal collection of founder Jordi Clos (owner of the Hotel Claris). On display are sarcophagi, jewelry, hieroglyphics, sculptures, and artwork. Exhibits focus on ancient Egyptians' everyday life, including education, social customs, religion, and food. The museum has its own lab for restorations. A library with more than 3,000 works is open to the public.

Museu d'Història de la Ciutat. Plaça del Rei. ☎ **93-315-11-11.** Admission (includes multimedia show) 700 ptas. ($4.20) adults, 500 ptas. ($3) children and students. Tues–Sat 10am–2pm and 4–8pm; Sun 10am–2pm. Bus: 16, 17, 19, 22, or 45.

Connected to the Royal Palace (see below), this museum traces the history of the city from its early days as a Roman colony to its role in the 1992 Summer Olympics. The museum is in a 15th-century mansion, the Padellás House. Many exhibits date from Roman days, with much else from medieval times.

Palau Reial (Royal Palace). Plaça del Rei. ☎ **93-315-11-11.** Admission 700 ptas. ($4.20). Summer, Tues–Sat 10am–8pm; off-season, Tues–Sat 10am–2pm and 4–8pm; year-round, Sun 10am–2pm. Bus: 16, 17, 19, 22, or 45.

The former palace of the counts of Barcelona, this later became the residence of the kings of Aragón. It is believed that Isabella and Ferdinand received Columbus here when he returned from his first voyage to the New World. Here, some say, the monarchs got their first look at a Native American. The Saló del Tinell, a banquet hall with a wood-paneled ceiling held up by half a dozen arches, dates from the 14th century. Rising five stories above the hall is the Torre del Reí Martí, a series of porticoed galleries.

Poble Espanyol. Marqués de Comillas, Parc de Montjuïc. ☎ **93-325-78-66.** Admission 950 ptas. ($5.70) adults, 525 ptas. ($3.15) children 7–14, free for children under 7. Audiovisual hall free. Mon 9am–8pm; Tues–Thurs 9am–2am; Fri–Sat 9am–4am; Sun 9am–midnight. Metro: Espanya.

In this re-created Spanish village built for the 1929 World's Fair, various regional architectural styles are reproduced. From the Levant to Galicia, 115 life-size reproductions of buildings and monuments represent the 10th to the 20th centuries. At the entrance, for example, stands a facsimile of the gateway to the walled city of Ávila. The center of the village has an outdoor cafe where you can sit and have drinks. Numerous shops sell provincial crafts and souvenir items, and in some of them you can see artists at work, printing fabric and blowing glass. Since the 1992 Olympics, the village has included 14 restaurants, one disco, and eight musical bars. In addition, visitors can see an audiovisual presentation about Barcelona and Catalonia. Many families delight in the faux Spanish atmosphere, but the more discriminating find it a bit of a tourist trap—overly commercialized and somewhat cheesy. It's a matter of personal taste. You'll find lots of mediocre places to eat here.

Mirador de Colón. Portal de la Pau. ☎ **93-302-52-24.** Admission 250 ptas. ($1.50) adults, 150 ptas. (90¢) children 4–12, free for children under 4. Sept 25–March, Mon–Fri 10am–2pm and 3:30–6:30pm, Sat–Sun and holidays 10am–6:30pm; Apr–May, Mon–Fri 10am–2pm and 3:30–7:30pm, Sat–Sun 10am–7:30pm; June–Sept 24, daily 9am–8:30pm. Closed Jan 1, Jan 6, and Dec 25–26. Metro: Drassanes. Bus: 14, 18, 36, 57, 59, or 64.

This monument to Christopher Columbus was erected at the Barcelona harbor on the occasion of the Universal Exhibition of 1888. It consists of three parts, the first being a circular structure raised by four stairways (19½ feet [6m] wide) and eight iron heraldic lions. On the plinth are eight bronze bas-reliefs depicting Columbus's principal feats. (The originals were destroyed; these are copies.) The second part is the base of the column, consisting of an eight-sided polygon, four sides of which act as buttresses; each side contains sculptures. The third part is the 167-foot column, which is Corinthian in style. The capital boasts representations of Europe, Asia, Africa, and America—all linked together. Finally, over a princely crown and a hemisphere recalling the newly discovered part of the globe, is a 25-foot-high bronze statue of Columbus—pointing, ostensibly, to the New World—by Rafael Ataché. Inside the iron column, an elevator ascends to the *mirador*. From here, a panoramic view of Barcelona and its harbor unfolds.

MORE ARCHITECTURAL HIGHLIGHTS

Architecture enthusiasts will find a wealth of fascinating sights in Barcelona. Primary among them, of course, are the fantastical creations of Antoni Gaudí and his *modernisme* cohorts.

Casa Milà. Passeig de Gràcia, 92. ☎ **93-484-59-80.** Metro: Diagonal.

Commonly called La Pedrera, Casa Milà is the most famous apartment complex in Spain. Antoni Gaudí's imagination went wild when he planned its construction; he even included vegetable and fruit shapes in his sculptural designs. Controversial and much criticized upon its completion, today it stands as a classic example of *modernisme* architecture. The entire building was restored in 1996. The ironwork around the balconies forms an intricate maze, and the main gate has windowpanes shaped like turtle shells. Phantasmagorical chimneys known in Spanish as *espantabrujas* (witch-scarers) fill the rooftop. From the rooftop, you'll have a view of Gaudí's unfinished cathedral, La Sagrada Família. The Espai Gaudí (Gaudí Space) in the attic has an intriguing multimedia display of the controversial artist's work. Tours of the famous rooftops are available daily 10am to 8pm, with tours in English Monday to Friday at 6pm, Saturday and Sunday at 11am. Admission and a tour cost 600 ptas. ($3.60) for adults, 350 ptas. ($2.10) for students, free for children under 12.

Casa Amatller. Passeig de Gràcia, 41. ☎ **93-216-01-75.** Metro: Passeig de Gràcia.

Constructed in a cubical design with a Dutch gable, this building was created by Puig i Cadafalch in 1900. It stands in sharp contrast to its neighbor, the Gaudí-designed Casa Batlló (see below). The architecture of the Casa Amatller, imposed on an older structure, is a vision of ceramic, wrought iron, and sculptures. The structure combines grace notes of Flemish Gothic—especially on the finish of the facade—with elements of Catalán architecture. The gable outside is in the Flemish style. Inside, visitors may view the original Gothic revival interior, now the headquarters of the Institut Amatller d'Art Hispanic. Admission is free, but donations are welcome. You must phone ahead to schedule a visit. The interior is open on Thursday at 10am, 11am, and noon.

Casa Batlló. Passeig de Gràcia, 43. ☎ **93-488-06-66.** Mon–Fri 10am–4pm. Metro: Passeig de Gràcia.

Next door to the Casa Amatller, Casa Batlló was designed by Gaudí in 1905. Using sensuous curves in iron and stone, the architect gave the facade a lavish baroque exuberance. The balconies have been compared to "sculpted waves." The upper part of the facade evokes animal forms, and delicate tiles spread across the design. The downstairs building is the headquarters of an insurance company. Many tourists walk inside for a view of Gaudí's interior, which is basically as he designed it. This is a place of business, so be discreet.

Casa Lleó Morera. Passeig de Gràcia, 35. No phone. Metro: Passeig de Gràcia.

Between the carrer del Consell de Cent and the carrer d' Aragó stands one of the most famous buildings of the *modernisme* movement. It is one of the trio of structures called the Mançana de la Discòrdia (Block of Discord), an allusion to the mythical judgment of Paris. Three of Barcelona's most famous *modernisme* architects, including Gaudí, competed with their works along this block. Florid Casa Lleó, designed by Domènech i Montaner in 1905, was revolutionary in its day. That assessment still stands. The building is private, and the interior is closed to the public.

Casa de la Ciutat/Ayuntamiento. Plaça de Sant Jaume. ☎ **93-402-70-00.** Metro: Jaume I.

Constructed at the end of the 14th century, the building that houses the municipal government is one of the best examples of Gothic civil architecture in the Catalán Mediterranean style. Across the landmark square from the Palau de la Generalitat, it has been endlessly renovated and changed. Behind a neoclassical facade, the building has a splendid courtyard and staircase. Its major architectural highlights are the 15th-century Salón de Ciento (Room of the 100 Jurors) and the black marble Salón de las Crónicas (Room of the Chronicles). The Salón de Ciento, in particular, represents a medley of styles. You can enter the building on Sunday 10am to 2pm or by special arrangement.

Olympic Memories

Galería Olímpica. Passeig Olimpic, s/n, lower level. ☎ **93-426-06-60.** Admission 400 ptas. ($2.40). Apr–Sept, Tues–Sat 10am–1pm and 4–8pm, Sun 10am–2pm; Oct–Mar, Tues–Sat 10am–1pm and 4–6pm, Sun 10am–2pm. Metro: Espanya. Bus: 9 or 13.

An enthusiastic celebration of the 1992 Olympic Games in Barcelona, this is one of the few museums in Europe exclusively devoted to sports and statistics. Exhibits include photos, costumes, and memorabilia, with heavy emphasis on the events' pageantry, the number of visitors who attended, and the fame the events brought to Barcelona. Of interest to statisticians, civic planners, and sports buffs, the gallery contains audiovisual information about the building programs that prepared the city for the onslaught of visitors. There are conference facilities, an auditorium, video recordings of athletic events, and archives. In the cellar of the Olympic Stadium's southeastern perimeter, the museum is most easily reached by entering the stadium's southern gate (Porta Sud).

Bullfighting

Cataláns do not pursue this art form, or sport, with as much fervor as Castilians. Nevertheless, you may want to attend a *corrida* in Barcelona. Bullfights are held from April to September, usually on Sunday at 6:30pm at Plaça de Toros Monumental, Gran Vía de les Corts Cataláns (☎ **93-245-58-04**). Buy tickets in advance from the office at Muntaner, 24 (☎ **93-453-38-21**). Tickets cost 1,800 to 6,500 ptas. ($10.80 to $39).

Parks & Gardens

Barcelona isn't just museums; much of its life takes place outside, in its unique parks and gardens. See the entry on Parc Güell under "The Top Attractions," above.

Tibidabo Mountain, north of the port, offers the finest panoramic view of Barcelona. A funicular takes you up 1,600 feet to the summit. The ideal time to visit this summit (the culmination of the Sierra de Collserola) is at sunset, when the city lights are on. At the time of the Olympics, an 850-foot communications tower, Mirador Torre de Collserola, was built. Although attacked by traditionalists for destroying the natural beauty of the mountain, Torre de Collserola offers the most panoramic views in all of Catalonia. It costs 500 ptas. ($3) to go up the tower. From Plaça de Catalunya, take bus no. 58 to avinguda del Tibidabo, where you can board a special bus to the funicular. Hop aboard to scale the mountain. The funicular runs daily when the park is open, starting 20 minutes before the Fun Fair. The fare is 300 ptas. ($1.80) one-way, 400 ptas. ($2.40) round-trip.

In the southern part of the city, the mountain park of **Montjuïc** has splashing fountains, gardens, outdoor restaurants, and museums, making for quite an outing. A re-created Spanish village, the **Poble Espanyol,** and the **Joan Miró museum** are also in the park. (See individual listings, above, for information.) There are many walks and vantage points for viewing the Barcelona skyline.

The park was the site of several Olympic events. An illuminated fountain display, the **Fuentes Luminosas,** is on view at Plaça de la Font Magica, near the Plaça d' Espanya. It runs from 8 to 11pm every Saturday and Sunday October to May, 9pm to midnight on Thursday, Saturday, and Sunday from June to September.

To reach the top, take bus no. 61 from Plaça d'Espanya or the Montjuïc funicular. The funicular is open June 13 to September 30 daily 11am to 10pm. In winter it operates daily 10:45am to 8pm. The round-trip fare is 600 ptas. ($3.60).

Parc de la Ciutadella, avinguda Wellington, s/n (☎ 93-225-67-80), gets its name (Park of the Citadel) because it is the site of a former fortress. After Philip V won the War of the Spanish Succession (Barcelona was on the losing side), he got his revenge: He ordered that the "traitorous" residential suburb be leveled. In its place rose a citadel. In the mid–19th century it, too, was leveled, but some architectural evidence survives in a governor's palace and an arsenal. Today lakes, gardens, and promenades fill most of the park, which also holds a **zoo** (see "Especially for Kids," below) and the **Museu d'Art Modern** (see "More Attractions," above). Gaudí contributed to the monumental fountain in the park when he was a student; the lampposts are also his. The park is open daily 8am to 9pm. Admission is free. To reach the park, take the metro to Ciutadella.

Parc de Joan Miró, near the Plaça de Espanya, is dedicated to one of Catalonia's most famous artists. It dates to the 1990s and occupies an entire block. One of Barcelona's most popular parks, it is often called Parc de l'Escorxador (slaughter-house), a reference to its former occupant. Its main features are an esplanade and a pond from which a giant sculpture by Miró, *Woman and Bird,* rises. Palm, pine, and eucalyptus trees, as well as playgrounds and pergolas, complete the picture. To reach the park, take the metro to Espanya. It is open throughout the day.

ESPECIALLY FOR KIDS

The Catalán people have great affection for children, and although many of the attractions of Barcelona are for adults, an array of amusements is designed for the young—and the young at heart.

Children from 3 to 7 have their own place at the **Museu de la Ciència,** Teodor Roviralta, 55 (☎ 93-212-60-50). "Clik del Nens" is a science playground just for them where they can walk on a giant piano, make bubbles, lift a hippopotamus, and enter an air tunnel. They observe, experiment, and examine nature in an environment created just for them. Special 1-hour guided sessions take place daily. (See "More Attractions," above.)

At the **Poble Espanyol,** Marqués de Comillas, Parc de Montjuïc (☎ 93-325-78-66), kids find a Spanish version of Disneyland. Frequent fiestas enliven the place, and it's fun for everybody, young and old. (See "More Attractions," above.)

Parc Zoologic. Parc de la Ciutadella. ☎ **93-225-67-80.** Admission 1,500 ptas. ($9) adults, 950 ptas. ($5.70) students and children, free for children under 3. Summer, daily 9:30am–7:30pm; off-season, daily 10am–5pm. Metro: Ciutadella.

Modern, with barless enclosures, this ranks as Spain's top zoo. One of the most unusual attractions is the famous albino gorilla Snowflake (Copito de Nieve), the only one of its kind in captivity in the world. The main entrances to the Ciutadella Park are on the Passeig de Pujades and Passeig de Picasso.

Parc d'Atraccions (Tibidabo). Plaça Tibidabo, 3–4, Cumbre del Tibidabo. ☎ **93-211-79-42.** Ticket for all rides 2,400 ptas. ($14.40) adults, 600 ptas. ($3.60) adults over 64, free for children under 5. May to mid-June, Wed–Sun noon–8pm; mid-June to Sept, Tues–Sun noon–8pm; off-season, Sat–Sun and holidays 11am–8pm. Transit: Bus no. 58 to avinguda del Tibidabo to Tramvía Blau, then take funicular.

On top of Tibidabo, this park combines tradition with modernity—rides from the beginning of the century complete with 1990s novelties. In summer the place takes on a carnival-like atmosphere.

ORGANIZED TOURS

Pullmantur, Gran Vía de les Corts Catalánes, 635 (☎ 93-317-12-97; metro: Plaça de Catalunya), offers a number of tours and excursions with English-speaking guides. For a preview of the city, you can take a morning tour. They depart from the company's terminal at 9:30am, and take in the cathedral, the Gothic Quarter, Les Rambles, the monument to Columbus, and the Spanish Village and the Olympic Stadium. Tickets cost 4,800 ptas. ($28.80). An afternoon tour leaves at 3:30pm and visits some of the most outstanding architecture in the Eixample, including Gaudí's Sagrada Família, Parc Güell, and a stop at the Picasso Museum. This tour costs 5,000 ptas. ($30).

Pullmantur also offers several excursions outside Barcelona. The daily tour of the monastery of Montserrat includes a visit to the Royal Basilica to view the famous sculpture of the Black Virgin. This tour, which costs 6,000 ptas. ($40.20), departs at 9:30am and returns at 2:30pm to the company's terminal. A full-day Girona–Figueres tour includes a visit to Girona's cathedral and its Jewish quarter, plus a trip to the Dalí museum. This excursion, which costs 12,500 ptas. ($75), leaves Barcelona at 9am and returns at approximately 6pm. Call ahead—a minimum number of participants is required or the tour isn't conducted.

Another company that offers tours of Barcelona and the surrounding countryside is **Juliatours,** Ronda Universitat, 5 (☎ 93-317-64-54). Itineraries and prices are similar to Pullmantur's. One tour, the "Visita Ciudad Artística," focuses on the city's artistic significance. The tour also passes Casa Lleó Morera, designed in 1905 by Domènech i Montaner in a floral modernist mode, and takes in many of Gaudí's brilliant buildings, including the Casa Milá (La Pedrera) and La Sagrada Família. Also included is a visit to the Museu Picasso or Museu d'Art Modern, depending on the day of your tour. This tour, which leaves at 3:30pm and returns at 6:30pm, costs 5,000 ptas. ($30).

7 Active Pursuits

AN OUTSTANDING FITNESS CENTER

The city's main fitness center is adjacent to the Olympic Stadium in an indoor-outdoor complex whose main allure is its two beautifully designed swimming pools.

Built for the 1992 Summer Olympics, the facility contains a health club and gym. It's open to the public for 1,300 ptas. ($7.80) for a full day's pass. For the address and hours, see the Piscina Bernardo Picornell listing in "Swimming," below.

GOLF

One of the city's best courses, **Club de Golf Vallromanas,** Afueras, s/n, Vallromanas, Barcelona (☎ 93-572-90-64), is 20 minutes north of the center by car. Nonmembers who reserve tee times in advance are welcome to play. The greens fee is 8,000 ptas. ($48) on weekdays, 14,000 ptas. ($84) on weekends. The club is open Wednesday to Monday 9am to 9pm. Established in 1972, it is the site of Spain's most important golf tournament.

   Reial Club de Golf El Prat, El Prat de Llobregat (☎ 93-379-0278), is a prestigious club that allows nonmembers to play under two conditions: They must have a handicap issued by the governing golf body in their home country, and they must prove membership in a golf club at home. The club has two 18-hole par-72 courses. Greens fees are 12,800 ptas. ($76.80) on weekdays, 27,000 ptas. ($162) on weekends. From Barcelona, follow avinguda Once de Septiembre past the airport to Barrio de San Cosme. From there follow the signs along carrer Prat to the golf course.

SWIMMING

Most city residents head to the beaches near the Vila Olímpica or Sitges when they feel like swimming. If you're looking for an uncrowded pool, you'll find one at the **Esportiu Piscina DeStampa,** carrer Rosich, s/n, in the Hospitalet district (☎ 93-334-56-00). It's open Monday to Friday 8am to 10pm, Saturday 10am to 2pm and 4 to 8pm, and Sunday 10am to 2pm. Weekday admission is 375 ptas. ($2.25); Saturday and Sunday, it's 450 ptas. ($2.70).

   A much better choice, however, allows you to swim where some Olympic events took place, at **Piscina Bernardo Picornell,** avinguda de Estadi, 30–40, on Montjuïc (☎ 93-423-40-41). Adjacent to the Olympic Stadium, it incorporates two of the best swimming pools in Spain (one indoors, one outdoors). Custom-built for the Olympics, they're open to the public Monday to Friday 7am to midnight, Saturday 7am to 9pm, and Sunday 7am to 4pm. Admission costs 1,500 ptas. ($9) and allows full use throughout the day of whichever pool is open, plus the gymnasium, the sauna, and the whirlpools. Bus no. 61 makes frequent runs from the Plaça d'Espanya.

8 Shopping

For fashion and style, Barcelonans look more to Paris and their own sense of design than to Madrid. *Moda joven* (young fashion) is all the rage.

   If your time and budget are limited, you may want to patronize Barcelona's major department store, **El Corte Inglés,** for an overview of Catalán merchandise at reasonable prices. Barcelona is filled with boutiques, but clothing is expensive, even though the city has been a textile center for centuries.

   Markets (see below) are very popular and are suitable places to search for good buys.

THE SHOPPING SCENE

If you're a window shopper, stroll along the **Passeig de Gràcia** from the avinguda Diagonal to the Plaça de Catalunya. Along the way, you'll see some of the most elegant and expensive shops in Barcelona, plus an assortment of splendid turn-of-the-century buildings and cafes, many with outdoor tables. Another prime spot is the **Rambla de Catalunya** (upper Rambles).

Another shopping expedition is to the **Mercat de la Boquería,** Rambla, 91 (☎ **93-318-25-84**), near carrer del Carme. Here you'll see a wide array of straw bags and regional products, along with a handsome display of the food you're likely to eat later: fruits, vegetables (artfully displayed), breads, cheeses, meats, and fish. Vendors sell their wares Monday to Saturday 8am to 8pm.

In the **old quarter** not far from Plaça de Catalunya, the principal shopping streets are all five Rambles, plus carrer del Pi, carrer de la Palla, and avinguda Portal de l'Angel, to cite some major thoroughfares. Moving north in the **Eixample** are Passeig de Catalunya, Passeig de Gràcia, and Rambla de Catalunya. Even farther north, **avinguda Diagonal** is a major shopping boulevard. Other prominent shopping streets include Bori i Fontesta, via Augusta, carrer Muntaner, Travessera de Gràcia, and carrer de Balmes.

In general, shopping hours are Monday to Saturday 9am to 8pm. Smaller shops may close 1:30 to 4pm.

The **American Visitors Bureau,** Gran Vía, 591 (☎ **93-301-01-50**), between Rambla de Catalunya and carrer de Balmes, will pack and ship your purchases and gifts, and even handle excess luggage and personal effects. The company operates a travel agency that books flights and hotel accommodations. It's open Monday to Friday 9am to 1pm and 4 to 7pm, Saturday by appointment only.

Watch for sales (*rebajas* or *rebaixes* in Catalán) in mid-January, late July, and August. Stores getting rid of their winter or summer stock often offer heavy discounts.

SHOPPING A TO Z

Prices in Barcelona tend to be slightly lower than in London, Paris, and Rome.

You'll find stylish, attractively designed **clothing** and **shoes. Decorative objects** are often good buys. In the city of Miró, Tàpies, and Picasso, **art** is a major business and the reason gallery owners from around the world visit. You'll find dozens of galleries, especially in the Barri Gòtic and around the Picasso Museum. Barcelona is also noted for its **flea markets,** where good purchases are always available if you search hard enough.

Antiques abound, but rising prices have put many of them beyond the means of the average shopper. However, the list below includes some shops where you can at least look. Most shoppers from abroad settle happily for handcrafts, and the city is rich in offerings, ranging from pottery to handmade furniture. Barcelona has been in the business of creating and designing **jewelry** since the 17th century, and its offerings and prices are of the widest possible range.

What follows is only a limited selection of some of the hundreds of shops in Barcelona.

ANTIQUES

El Bulevard des Antiquaris. Passeig de Gràcia, 55. No central phone. Metro: Passeig de Gràcia.

This 70-unit complex just off one of the town's most aristocratic avenues has a huge collection of art and antiques assembled in a series of boutiques. There's a cafe-bar on the upper level. Summer hours are Monday to Friday 9:30am to 8:30pm; winter hours, Monday 4:30 to 8:30pm, Tuesday to Saturday 10:30am to 8:30pm. Some boutiques keep shorter hours.

Sala d'Art Artur Ramón. Palla, 23. ☎ **93-302-59-70.** Metro: Jaume I.

One of the finest antiques and art dealers in Barcelona can be found at this three-level emporium. Set on a narrow flagstone-covered street near Plaça del Pi (the center of the antiques district), it stands opposite a tiny square, the Placeta al Carrer de la Palla. The store, which has been operated by four generations of men named Artur Ramón, contains everything from Romanesque works to Picassos. Prices are high, as you'd expect, for items of quality and lasting value. Open Monday to Saturday 10am to 1:30pm and 5 to 8pm.

Urbana. Còrsega, 258. ☎ **93-218-70-36.** Metro: Hospital Sant Pau.

Urbana sells an array of architectural remnants (usually from torn-down mansions), antique furniture, and reproductions of brass hardware. There are antique and reproduction marble mantelpieces, wrought-iron gates and garden seats, even carved wood fireplaces with the *modernisme* look. It's an impressive, albeit costly, array of merchandise. Open Monday to Friday 10am to 2pm and 4:30 to 8pm.

BOOKS

LAIE. Pau Claris, 85. ☎ **93-318-17-39.** Metro: Plaça de Catalunya or Urquinaona.

The best selection of English-language books, including travel maps and guides, is at LAIE, a block from the Gran Vía de les Corts Catalánes. It's open Monday to Friday 10am to 9pm, Saturday 10:30am to 9pm. The bookshop has an upstairs cafe with international newspapers and a little terrace. It serves breakfast, lunch (salad bar), and dinner. The cafe is open Monday to Saturday 9am to 1am. The shop also schedules cultural events, including art exhibits and literary presentations.

DEPARTMENT STORES

El Corte Inglés. Plaça de Catalunya, 14. ☎ **93-302-12-12.** Metro: Plaça de Catalunya.

One of the local representatives of the largest and most glamorous department store chain in Spain, this branch sells a wide variety of merchandise. It ranges from Spanish handcrafts to high-fashion items, from Catalán records to food. The store has restaurants and cafes and offers consumer-related services, such as a travel agent. It has a department that will mail your purchases home. Open Monday to Saturday 10am to 9:30pm. El Corte Inglés has two other Barcelona locations: avinguda Diagonal, 617–619 (☎ **93-419-28-28;** metro: María Cristina), and avinguda Diagonal, 471 (☎ **93-419-20-20;** metro: María Cristina).

DESIGNER HOUSEWARES

Vinçón. Passeig de Gràcia, 96. ☎ **93-215-60-50.** Metro: Diagonal.

Fernando Amat's Vinçón is the best in the city, with 10,000 products—everything from household items to the best in Spanish contemporary furnishings. Its mission is to purvey good design, period. Housed in the former home of artist Ramón Casas— a contemporary of Picasso's during his Barcelona stint—the showroom is filled with the best Spain has. The always-creative window displays alone are worth the trek: Expect *anything*. Open Monday to Saturday 10am to 2pm and 4:30 to 8:30pm.

FABRICS & WEAVINGS

Coses de Casa. Plaça de Sant Josep Oriol, 5. ☎ **93-302-73-28.** Metro: Jaume I.

Appealing fabrics and weavings are displayed in this 19th-century store, called simply "Household Items." Many are handwoven in Majorca, their boldly geometric patterns inspired by Arab motifs of centuries ago. The fabric, for the most part, is 50% cotton, 50% linen; much of it would make excellent upholstery material. Open Monday to Friday 9:30am to 1:30pm and 4:30 to 8pm, Saturday 10am to 2pm and 5 to 8pm.

FASHION

Antonio Miró. Consejo de Ciento, 349. ☎ **93-487-06-70.** Metro: Passeig de Gràcia.

This shop is devoted exclusively to the clothing design of Miró, but without the Groc label (see below). It carries fashionable men's and women's clothing. Before buying anything at Groc, survey the wares at this store, which seems even more stylish.

Groc. Rambla de Catalunya, 100. ☎ **93-215-74-74.** Metro: Plaça de Catalunya.

One of the most stylish shops in Barcelona, Groc is expensive but filled with high-quality men's and women's apparel made from the finest natural fibers. The men's store is downstairs, the women's store one flight up. Open Monday to Saturday 10am to 2pm and 4 to 8:30pm (the men's department stays open all day). August hours are Monday to Friday 11am to 2pm and 5 to 8pm.

GALLERIES

Art Picasso. Tapinería, 10. ☎ **93-310-49-57.** Metro: Jaume I.

Here you can get good lithographic reproductions of works by Picasso, Miró, and Dalí, as well as T-shirts emblazoned with the masters' designs. Tiles often carry their provocatively painted scenes. Open Monday to Saturday 10am to 8pm, Sunday 10am to 3pm.

Sala Parés. Petritxol, 5. ☎ **93-318-70-20.** Metro: Plaça de Catalunya.

Established in 1840, this is a Barcelona institution. The Maragall family recognizes and promotes the work of Spanish and Catalán painters and sculptors, many of whom have gone on to acclaim. Paintings are displayed in a two-story amphitheater, with high-tech steel balconies supported by a quartet of steel columns evocative of Gaudí. Exhibitions of the most avant-garde art in Barcelona change about every 3 weeks. Open Monday to Saturday 10:30am to 2pm and 4:30 to 8:30pm.

GIFTS

Beardsley. Petritxol, 12. ☎ **93-301-05-76.** Metro: Plaça de Catalunya.

Named after the Victorian English illustrator, this store is on the same street where the works of Picasso and Dalí were exhibited before they became world famous. The wide array of gifts, perhaps the finest selection in Barcelona, includes a little bit of everything—dried flowers, writing supplies, silver dishes, unusual bags, and lots more. Open Monday to Friday 9:30am to 1:30pm and 4:30 to 8pm, Saturday 10am to 2pm and 5 to 8:30pm.

LEATHER

Loewe. Passeig de Gràcia, 35. ☎ **93-216-04-00.** Metro: Passeig de Gràcia.

Barcelona's biggest branch of this prestigious Spanish leather-goods chain is in one of the best-known *modernisme* buildings in the city. Everything is top-notch, from the elegant showroom to the expensive merchandise to the helpful salespeople. The company exports its goods to branches throughout Asia, Europe, and North America. Open Monday to Saturday 9:30am to 2pm and 4:30 to 8pm.

MARKETS

El Encants antiques market is held every Monday, Wednesday, Friday, and Saturday in Plaça de les Glóries Catalánes (metro: Glóries). Go any time during the day to survey the selection.

Coins and postage stamps are traded and sold in **Plaça Reial** on Sunday from 10am to 2pm. It's off the southern flank of Les Rambles (metro: Drassanes). A book and coin market is held at the Ronda Sant Antoni every Sunday 10am to 2pm (metro: Universitat).

MUSIC

Casa Beethoven. Les Rambles, 97. ☎ **93-301-48-26.** Metro: Liceu.

Established in 1920, this store carries the most complete collection of sheet music in town. The collection naturally focuses on the works of Spanish and Catalán composers. Music lovers might make some rare discoveries. Open Monday to Friday 9am to 8pm, Saturday 9am to 1:30pm and 5 to 8pm.

PORCELAIN

Kastoria 2. Avinguda Catedra, 6–8. ☎ **93-310-04-11.** Metro: Plaça de Catalunya.

This large store near the cathedral is an authorized Lladró dealer, and stocks a big selection of the famous porcelain. It also carries many kinds of leather goods, including purses, suitcases, coats, and jackets. Open Monday to Saturday 10am to 7pm, Sunday 10am to 2pm.

POTTERY

Artesana i Coses. Placeta de Montcada, 2. ☎ **93-319-54-13.** Metro: Jaume I.

Here you'll find pottery and porcelain from every major region of Spain. Most of the pieces are heavy and thick-sided—designs in use for centuries. Open Monday to Saturday 10am to 2pm and 4 to 8pm.

Itaca. Carrer Ferran, 26. ☎ **93-301-30-44.** Metro: Liceu.

Here you'll find a wide array of handmade pottery from Catalonia and other parts of Spain, plus Portugal, Mexico, and Morocco. The merchandise has been selected for its basic purity, integrity, and simplicity. Open Monday to Friday 10am to 2pm and 4:30 to 8pm, Saturday 10am to 8:30pm.

SHOPPING CENTERS & MALLS

The landscape has exploded since the mid-1980s with the construction of several American-style shopping malls. Some are too far from the city's historic core to be convenient for most foreign visitors, but here's a description of some of the city's best.

Centre Comercial Barcelona Glories. Avinguda Diagonal, 208. ☎ **93-486-04-04.** Metro: Glories.

Built in 1995, this is the largest shopping center in downtown Barcelona, a three-story emporium of the good life. It's based on the California model but is crammed into a distinctly urban neighborhood. It has more than 100 shops, some posh, others much less so. Although there's a typical shopping-mall anonymity to some aspects of this place, you'll still be able to find almost anything you might have forgotten while packing. Open Monday to Saturday 10am to 10pm.

Diagonal Center (Lilla Diagonal). Avinguda Diagonal, 557. ☎ **93-444-00-00.** Metro: María Cristina.

This two-story mall contains stores devoted to luxury products, as well as a scattering of bars, cafes, and simple but cheerful restaurants favored by office workers and shoppers. It has about half the number of shops the Centre Comercial Barcelona Glories (see above) offers. Built in the early 1990s, it even has an area devoted to video games where teenagers can make as much electronic noise as they want while their guardians shop. Open Monday to Saturday 10am to 9pm.

Maremagnum. Moll d'Espanya, s/n. ☎ **93-225-81-00.** Metro: Drassanes.

The best thing about this place is its position adjacent to the waterfront on Barcelona's historic seacoast; it's also well suited to outdoor promenades. Built in the early 1990s near the Columbus Monument, it contains a handful of shops selling touristy items, and lots of cafes, bars, and places to sit. You might get the idea that only a few of the people who come here are interested in shopping.

Poble Espanyol. Marqués de Comillas, Parc de Montjuïc. ☎ **93-325-78-66.** Metro: Espanya, then take free red double-decker bus to Montjuïc, or bus no. 13 (145 ptas./85¢).

Technically, this is not a shopping mall but a "village" (see "More Attractions," above). It has about 35 stores selling typical folk crafts from every part of Spain: glassware, leather goods, pottery, paintings, carvings, and so forth. Store hours vary, but you can visit any time during the day.

STRAW PRODUCTS

La Manual Alpargatera. Avinyó, 7. ☎ **93-301-01-72.** Metro: Jaume I or Liceu.

In addition to its large inventory of straw products, such as hats and bags, this shop is known mainly for its footwear. Espadrilles (*alpargatas* in Spanish), basic rope-soled shoes said to be 1,000 years old, are made on the premises. Some Cataláns wear espadrilles only when performing the *sardana,* their national dance. To find the shop, turn off Les Rambles at carrer Ferran, walk 2 blocks, and make a right. Open Monday to Saturday 9:30am to 1:30pm and 4:30 to 8pm.

UMBRELLAS

Julio Gómez. Rambla de Sant Josep, 102–104 (also called Rambla de las Flors). ☎ **93-301-33-26.** Metro: Liceu.

For more than a century Julio Gómez has rung up umbrella sales here. In a workshop out back, women labor over the unique umbrellas or lace-trimmed silk or cotton parasols. There are also Spanish fans, walking sticks capped with silver, and other memorabilia. It all adds up to an evocative piece of shopping nostalgia. Open Monday to Saturday 9:30am to 1:30pm and 4 to 8pm.

9 Barcelona After Dark

Barcelona comes alive at night, and the array of nighttime diversions is staggering. There is something to interest almost everyone and to fit most pocketbooks. The **funicular ride** to Tibidabo and the illuminated **fountains** of Montjuïc are especially popular, and fashionable **clubs** operate in nearly every major district of the city. For families, the **amusement parks** are the busiest venues.

Locals sometimes opt for an evening in the *tascas* (taverns), or perhaps settling in for a bottle of wine at a cafe, an easy and inexpensive way to spend an evening people-watching. Serious drinking in pubs and cafes begins by 10 or 11pm. But for the most fashionable bars and discos, Barcelonans delay their entrances until at least 1am.

Your best source of local information is a little magazine called *Guía del Ocio,* which previews "La Semana de Barcelona" (This Week in Barcelona). It's in Spanish, but most of its listings will probably be comprehensible. Almost every news kiosk along Les Rambles carries it.

Nightlife begins for many Barcelonans with a **promenade** (*paseo*) along Les Rambles in the early evening, usually from 5 to 7pm. Then things quiet down a bit until a second surge of energy brings out the crowds again, from 9 to 11pm. After that the esplanade clears out quite a bit, but it's always lively.

If you've been scared off by press reports about Les Rambles between the Plaça de Catalunya and the Columbus Monument, know that the area's really been cleaned up in the past decade. Still, you will feel safer along the Rambla de Catalunya, in the Eixample, north of the Plaça de Catalunya. This street and its offshoots are lively at night, with many cafes and bars. During the Franco era the center of club life was the cabaret-packed district near the south of Les Rambles, but the area is known for nighttime muggings—use caution if you go there.

Cultural events are also big in the Catalonian repertoire, and old-fashioned **dance halls** survive in some places. Although **disco** has waned in some parts of the world, it is still going strong in Barcelona. Decaying movie houses, abandoned garages, and long-closed vaudeville theaters have been taken over and restored as nightlife venues.

Flamenco isn't the rage here that it is in Seville and Madrid, but it still has its devotees. The city is also filled with **jazz** aficionados. Best of all, the old tradition of the **music hall** with vaudeville lives on.

In the summer, you'll see plenty of free entertainment—everything from opera to monkey acts—just by walking the streets. The Rambles is a particularly good place to watch.

THE PERFORMING ARTS

Culture is deeply ingrained in the Catalán soul, and the performing arts are strong. In fact, some take place on the street, especially along Les Rambles. Crowds often gather around a singer or a mime. A city square will suddenly come alive on Saturday night with a spontaneous festival; "tempestuous, surging, irrepressible life and brio," is how the writer Rose MacCauley described it.

Long a city of the arts, Barcelona experienced a cultural decline during the Franco years, but now it is filled once again with the best opera, symphonic, and choral music. At the venues listed here, unless otherwise specified, ticket prices depend on the event.

CLASSICAL MUSIC

Palau de la Música Catalána. Sant Francesc de Paula, 2. ☎ **93-295-72-00.** Box office Mon–Sat 10am–9pm.

In a city chock-full of architectural highlights, this one stands out. In 1908, Lluís Domènech i Montaner, a Catalán architect, designed this structure using stained glass, ceramics, statuary, and ornate lamps, among other elements. It stands today, restored, as a classic example of *modernisme.* Concerts and leading recitals take place here.

THEATER

Theater is presented in the Catalán language and therefore will not be of interest to most visitors. For those who do speak the language, or perhaps are fluent in Spanish (even then, though, you're unlikely to understand much), here are some recommendations.

✪ **Gran Teatre del Liceu.** Rambla dels Caputxins. ☎ **93-485-99-00.** Metro: Liceu.

This monument to belle époque extravagance, a 2,700-seat opera house, is one of the grandest theaters in the world. It was designed by the Catalán architect Josep Oriol Mestves. On January 31, 1994, fire gutted the opera house, shocking Catalonians, many of whom regarded this place as the very citadel of their culture. The government immediately vowed to rebuild, and the new Liceu was reopened in 1999, well before the millennium deadline set by the cultural czars.

Mercat de Los Flors. Lleida, 59. ☎ **93-426-18-75.** Tickets 1,500–3,000 ptas. ($9–$18). Metro: Espanya.

Housed in a building constructed for the 1929 International Exhibition at Montjuïc, this is the other major Catalán theater. Peter Brook first used it as a theater for a 1983 presentation of *Carmen.* The theater focuses on innovators in drama, dance, and music, as well as European modern dance companies. The 999-seat house has a restaurant overlooking the city rooftops.

Teatre Lliure. Montseny, 47. ☎ **93-218-92-51.** Tickets 2,000–2,500 ptas. ($12–$15) Tues–Thurs; 2,500–3,000 ptas. ($15–$18) Fri–Sun. Metro: Fontana.

This self-styled free theater is the city's leading Catalán-language playhouse. Once a workers' union, the building has been the headquarters of a theater cooperative since 1976. Its directors are famous in Barcelona for their bold presentations, including works by Bertolt Brecht, Luigi Pirandello, Jean Genêt (who wrote about Barcelona), and even Molière and Shakespeare. New dramas by Catalán playwrights are also presented. The house seats 200 to 350.

Teatre Nacional de Catalunya. Plaça de les Arts, 1. ☎ **93-306-57-00.** Tickets 3,200–3,700 ptas. ($19.20–$22.20). Closed Aug. Metro: Monumental.

Josep María Flotats heads this major company. The actor-director trained in the tradition of theater repertory, working in Paris at Théâtre de la Villa and the Comédie Française. His company presents both classic and contemporary plays.

FLAMENCO

El Tablao de Carmen. Poble Espanyol de Montjuïc. ☎ **93-325-68-95.** Dinner and show 7,800 ptas. ($46.80); drink and show 4,200 ptas. ($25.20).

This club presents a highly rated flamenco cabaret in the re-created village. You can go early and explore the village, and even have dinner. This place has long been a tourist favorite. The club is open Tuesday to Sunday 8pm to past midnight—around 1am on weeknights, often until 2 or 3am on weekends, depending on business. The first show is always at 9:30pm; the second show is at 11:30pm on Tuesday, Wednesday, Thursday, and Sunday, and midnight on Friday and Saturday. Reservations are recommended.

Los Tarantos. Plaça Reial, 17. ☎ **93-318-30-67.** Cover (includes 1 drink) 1,500 ptas. ($9). Metro: Liceu.

Established in 1963, this is the oldest flamenco club in Barcelona, with a rigid allegiance to the tenets of Andalusian flamenco. Its roster of artists changes regularly. They often come from Seville or Córdoba, stamping out their well-rehearsed passions in ways that make the audience appreciate the arcane nuances of Spain's most intensely controlled dance idiom. No food is served. The place resembles a cabaret theater, where up to 120 people at a time can drink, talk quietly, and savor the nuances of a dance that combines elements from medieval Christian and Muslim traditions. Each show lasts around 1¼ hours. Shows are Monday to Saturday at 10pm and midnight.

Tablao Flamenco Cordobés. Les Rambles, 35. ☎ **93-317-66-53.** Dinner and show 7,800 ptas. ($46.80); 1 drink and show 4,200 ptas. ($25.20). Closed Jan. Metro: Drassanes.

At the southern end of Les Rambles, a short walk from the harbor front, you'll hear the strum of the guitar, the sound of hands clapping rhythmically, and the haunting sound of the flamenco, a tradition here since 1968. Head upstairs to an Andalusian-style room where performances take place with the traditional *cuadro flamenco*—singers, dancers, and guitarist. Cordobés is said to be the city's best flamenco showcase. From November to March (except one week in December), the show with dinner begins at 8:30pm, the show without dinner at 10pm. April to October and December 25 to December 31, four shows are offered nightly with dinner, at 8pm and 9:45pm; without dinner at 9:30pm and 11:15pm. Reservations are required.

CABARET, JAZZ & MORE

Arnau. Avinguda del Parallel, 60. ☎ **93-329-21-04.** Cover (includes 1 drink) from 2,000 ptas. ($12). Metro: Parallel.

A veteran of the many changes that have affected the worlds of cabaret and entertainment since its heyday in the 1970s, this place has managed to keep up with the times and the demands of the marketplace. Shows mingle touches of Catalán folklore with glitz and glitter, hints of family nostalgia, and doses of melodrama. Two shows are presented Wednesday to Sunday, at 10:30pm. Drink prices start at 700 ptas. ($4.20).

Barcelona Pipa Club. Plaça Reial, 3. ☎ **93-302-47-32.** Cover (includes 1 soft drink or beer) 1,000 ptas. ($6). Metro: Liceu.

If you find the Harlem Jazz Club (below) small, wait until you get to the "Pipe Club." Long beloved by jazz aficionados, this is for true devotees. Ring the buzzer and you'll be admitted (at least we hope you will), then climb two flights up in a run-down building. This is hardly a trendy nightclub, with five rooms decorated with displays or photographs of pipes. Depending on the performer, music ranges from New Orleans jazz to Brazilian rhythms. The club and its comfortable bar are open daily 10pm to 5am; jazz is featured Thursday to Sunday.

Espai Barroc. Carrer Montcada, 20. ☎ **93-310-06-73.** Cover (includes 1 drink) 2,500 ptas. ($15). Metro: Jaime I.

One of Barcelona's most culture-conscious nightspots occupies some of the showplace rooms of the Palau Dalmases, a stately palace in the Barri Gòtic. In a room lined with grand art objects, you can listen to recorded opera arias and sip glasses of beer or wine. The most appealing night is Thursday—beginning at 11pm 10 singers perform a roster of arias from assorted operas, one of which is invariably *Carmen.* Since its establishment in 1996, the place has thrived. Almost everyone around the bar apparently has at least heard of the world's greatest operas, and some can even discuss them more or less brilliantly. Open Tuesday to Sunday, 8pm to 2am.

Harlem Jazz Club. Comtessa de Sobradiel, 8. ☎ **93-310-07-55.** 1-drink minimum. No cover. Closed Aug. Metro: Jaume.

On a nice street in the Ciutat Vella, this is one of Barcelona's oldest and finest jazz clubs. It's also one of the smallest, with just a handful of tables. No matter how many times you've heard "Black Orpheus" or "The Girl from Ipanema," they always sound new again here. Music is viewed with a certain reverence; no one talks when the performers are on. Live jazz, blues, tango, Brazilian music—the sounds are always fresh. Open Tuesday to Thursday and Sunday 8pm to 4am, until 5am Friday and Saturday. Live music begins at 10:30pm on Tuesday to Thursday and Sunday, and 11:30pm on Friday and Saturday. The second set is at midnight (1am on Friday and Saturday).

Jamboree. Plaça Reial, 17. ☎ **93-301-75-64.** Cover (includes 1 drink) 1,500–2,000 ptas. ($9–$12). Metro: Liceu.

In the heart of the Barri Gòtic, this has long been one of the city's premier locations for good blues and jazz, although it doesn't feature jazz every night. Sometimes a world-class performer will appear here, but most likely it'll be a younger group. The crowd knows its stuff and demands only the best talent. On our last visit, we were entertained by an evening of Chicago blues. Or you might find that a Latin dance band has been scheduled. Open daily 11pm to 5am; shows begin at midnight.

Luz de Gas. Carrer de Muntaner, 246. ☎ **93-209-77-11.** Cover (includes 1 drink) 2,000 ptas. ($12). Bus: 7, 15, 33, 58, or 64.

This theater and cabaret has the hottest Latino jazz on weekends. On weeknights there is cabaret. The place is an art nouveau delight, with colored glass lamps and enough voluptuous nudes to please Rubens himself. The club was once a theater, and its original seating has been turned into different areas each with its own bar. The lower two levels open onto the dance floor and stage. If you'd like to talk, head for the top tier, which has a glass enclosure. Call to see what the lineup is on any given night: jazz, pop, soul, rhythm and blues, salsa, bolero, whatever.

DANCE CLUBS & DISCOS

Bikini. Deu i Mata, 105. ☎ **93-322-00-05.** Cover 1,000–3,000 ptas. ($6–$18). Metro: Les Corts.

In the basement of a commercial-looking shopping center is this wide-ranging nightlife compound, with at least two dance floors for every conceivable genre (including funk, indie, rock-and-roll, and golden-oldie music). There's a separate room for Puerto Rican salsa (the owners refer to it as a "salsoteca"), and a large area devoted to emerging musical groups. Music changes every night of the week, and has even been known to include sophisticated adaptations of conventional tango music. Open Monday to Thursday 7pm to 4:30am, Friday and Saturday 7pm to 6am.

La Paloma. Tigre, 27. ☎ **93-301-68-97.** Cover 900 ptas. ($5.40). Metro: Universitat.

Those feeling nostalgic may want to drop in on Barcelona's most famous dance hall. Remember the fox-trot? The mambo? If not, learn about them here, along with the tango, the cha-cha, and the bolero. Live orchestras provide the music. The ornate old hall is open Wednesday to Sunday. Matinees are 6 to 9:30pm; night dances are 11:30pm to 5am. Drink prices start at 1,000 ptas. ($6).

Up and Down. Numancia, 179. ☎ **93-280-29-22.** Cover (includes 1 drink) 1,000–2,000 ptas. ($6–$12). Metro: María Cristina.

The chic atmosphere here attracts elite Barcelonans of all ages. The more mature patrons, specifically the black-tie, post-opera crowd, head upstairs, leaving the downstairs section to loud music and flaming youth. Up and Down is the most cosmopolitan disco in Barcelona, with impeccable service, sassy waiters, and a welcoming atmosphere. Technically, this is a private club—you can be turned away at the door. The restaurant is open Monday to Saturday 10pm to 2am, and prices for meals run 3,500 ptas. ($21) and up. The disco is open Tuesday to Saturday midnight to 6am. Drinks in the disco cost 1,400 ptas. ($8.40) for a beer and at least 1,900 ptas. ($11.40) for a hard drink.

BARS & PUBS

Café Bar Padam. Rauric, 9. ☎ **93-302-50-62.** Metro: Liceu.

The clientele and decor here are modern and hip. The bar, which attracts many gay patrons, is on a narrow street in the Ciutat Vella, about 3 blocks east of the Rambla dels Caputxins. The only color in the black-and-white rooms comes from fresh flowers and modern paintings. Jazz is sometimes featured. Open Monday to Saturday 7pm to 2am.

Coctelería Boadas. Carrer Taller, 1 (at Les Rambles). ☎ **93-318-95-92.** Metro: Plaça de Catalunya.

At least part of the fun at this bustling cocktail bar derives from trying to remember the parade of famous patrons who have come here since the place was established in 1933. The art deco setting might remind you of swinging old Havana—where the founder got his start before moving back to his family's home turf. Many patrons order Hemingway's favorite drink, a *mojito* (the Cuban rum equivalent of a mint julep). Open Monday to Saturday noon to 2am (till 3am on Friday and Saturday).

Cocktail Bar Boadas. Tallers, 1. ☎ **93-318-95-92.** Metro: Plaça de Catalunya.

This intimate, conservative bar is usually filled with regulars. Established in 1933, it is near the top of Les Rambles. Many visitors stop in for a pre-dinner drink and snack before wandering to one of the district's many restaurants. It stocks a wide array of Caribbean rums, Russian vodkas, and English gins, and the skilled bartenders know how to mix them all. The place is especially well known for its daiquiris. Open daily noon to 2am (till 3am on Friday and Saturday).

Dirty Dick's. Taberna Inglesa, Carrer Marc Aureli, 2. ☎ **93-200-89-52.** Metro: Muntaner.

An English-style pub in a residential part of town, Dirty Dick's has lots of dark paneling and exposed brick, with banquettes for quiet conversation. If you sit at the bar you'll be faced with a tempting array of tiny sandwiches that taste as good as they look. The pub is at the crossing of Vía Augusta, a main thoroughfare through the district. Open daily 6pm to 2:30am.

El Born. Passeig del Born, 26. ☎ **93-319-53-33.** Metro: Jaume I.

Facing a rustic-looking square, this former fish store has been cleverly converted. There are a few tables near the front, but our preferred spot is the inner room decorated with rattan furniture and modern paintings. The music might be anything from Louis Armstrong to classic rock and roll. The upstairs buffet serves dinner. The room is somewhat cramped, but you'll find a simple, tasty collection of fish, meat, and vegetable dishes, all carefully laid out. A full dinner without wine costs around 2,500 to 4,000 ptas. ($15 to $24). Beer and wine are quite cheap. Open Monday to Saturday 6pm to 3am.

Pub 240. Aribau, 240. ☎ **93-209-09-67.** Cover 2,500 ptas. ($15).

This elegant bar, which bears no resemblance to a traditional pub, consists of three sections: a bar, a small amphitheater, and a lounge for talking and listening to music. Rock and South American folk music play, and the place is jammed almost every night. Open daily 7pm to 5am.

Zig-Zag Bar. Platón, 13. ☎ **93-201-62-07.** Metro: Muntaner.

Favored by actors, models, cinematographers, and photographers, this bar claims to have inaugurated Barcelona's trend toward high-tech minimalism in its watering holes. Open Monday to Thursday 10pm to 2:30am, Friday and Saturday 10pm to 3am.

CHAMPAGNE BARS

The Cataláns call their own version of sparkling wine *cava*. In Catalán, champagne bars are called *xampanyerías.* The Spanish wines are often excellent, and some consider them better than their French counterparts. With more than 50 Spanish companies producing *cava,* and each bottling up to a dozen grades of wine, the best way to learn about Spanish champagne is to visit the vineyard or to sample the products at a *xampanyería.*

Champagne bars usually open at 7pm and stay open into the wee hours of the morning. They serve tapas, ranging from caviar to smoked fish to frozen chocolate truffles. Most establishments sell only a limited array of house *cavas* by the glass, and more esoteric varieties by the bottle. You'll be offered a choice of *brut* (slightly sweeter) or *brut nature.* The most acclaimed brands include Mont-Marçal, Gramona, Mestres, Parxet, Torello, and Recaredo.

Xampanyería Casablanca. Bonavista, 6. ☎ **93-237-63-99.** Metro: Passeig de Gràcia.

Someone had to fashion a champagne bar after the Bogart-Bergman film, and this is it. It serves four kinds of house *cava* by the glass, plus a good selection of tapas, especially pâtés. Open Sunday to Thursday 6:45pm to 2:30am, Friday and Saturday until 3am.

Xampú Xampany. Gran Vía de los Corts Catalánes, 702. ☎ **93-265-04-83.** Metro: Girona.

At the corner of the Plaça de Tetuan, this x*ampanyería* offers a variety of hors d'oeuvres in addition to wine. Abstract paintings, touches of high tech, and bouquets of flowers break up the pastel color scheme. Open daily 6pm to 3:30am.

A BIT OF NOSTALGIA

Bar Pastis. Carrer Santa Mònica, 4. ☎ **93-318-79-80.** Metro: Drassanes.

Valencianos Carme Pericás and Quime Ballester opened this tiny bar just off the southern end of Les Rambles in 1947. They made it a shrine to Edith Piaf, and her songs still play on an old phonograph in back of the bar. The decor consists mostly of paintings by Ballester, who had a dark, rather morbid vision of the world. You can order four kinds of pastis in this dimly lit "corner of Montmartre." Outside the window, check out the view—usually a parade of transvestite hookers. The crowd is likely to include almost anyone, especially people who used to be called bohemians. There's live music Sunday and Tuesday at 11:30pm. Open Monday to Thursday 7:30pm to 2:30am, Friday, Saturday, and Sunday until 3am.

Els Quatre Gats. Montsió, 3. ☎ **93-302-41-40.** Metro: Urquinaona.

In 1897, Pere Romeu and three of his friends, painters Ramón Casas, Santiago Rusiñol, and Miguel Utrillo, opened a cafe for artists and writers at the edge of the Barri Gòtic. Early on, they staged a one-man show for a young artist named Pablo Picasso. He didn't sell a single painting, but did stick around to design the art nouveau menu cover. The cafe folded in 1903, becoming a private club and art school and attracting Joan Miró.

   In 1978, two Cataláns reopened the cafe in the Casa Martí, a building designed by Josep Puig i Cadafalch, one of the leading architects of modernisme. The cafe displays works by major modern Catalán painters, including Tàpies. You can drink coffee, taste wine, eat a full meal (see "Where to Dine," above)—and even try, if you dare, potent *Marc de Champagne,* an eau-de-vie distilled from the local *cava.* Open Monday to Saturday 8am to midnight, Sunday 6pm to midnight.

GAY & LESBIAN BARS

Arena Classic. Diputació, 233. No phone. Cover Thurs–Fri 600 ptas. ($3.60), Sat and holidays 1,000 ptas. ($6). Metro: Universitat.

Attracting gay men and lesbians, this club successfully combines '70s and '80s dance music to keep you moving and grooving till the wee hours. Thursdays there's a special party organized by a local lesbian group. Open Thursday to Saturday 11pm to 4am.

El Convento. Carrer Bruniquer, 59 (Plaça Joanic). No phone. Cover (includes 1 drink) 1,000 ptas. ($6). Metro: Joanic.

This may be like no other disco you've ever seen. It's decorated like a church, with depictions of the Virgin Mary and even candles adding to the ecclesiastical atmosphere. But the clientele consists mainly of young gay males in a party mood. The club often presents shows and organized parties. A novelty, to say the least. Open daily midnight to 5am.

Metro. Sepúlveda, 185. No phone. Cover 1,000 ptas. ($6). Metro: Universitat.

One of the most popular gay discos in Barcelona, Metro attracts a diverse crowd—from young fashion victims to more rough-and-ready macho types. One dance floor plays contemporary house and dance music, and the other traditional Spanish music mixed with Spanish pop. This is a good opportunity to watch men of all ages dance the "Sevillanas" together in pairs with a surprising degree of grace. One interesting feature appears in the bathrooms, where videos have been installed in quite unexpected places. Open daily midnight to 5am.

New Chaps. Avinguda Diagonal, 365. ☎ **93-215-53-65.** Metro: Diagonal.

Gay Barcelonans refer to this saloon-style watering hole as Catalonia's premier leather bar. In fact, the dress code usually is leather of a different stripe: more boots and jeans than leather and chains. Behind a pair of swinging doors evocative of the old American West, Chaps contains two different bar areas. Open daily 9pm to 3am (until 3:30am on Friday and Saturday).

Punto BCN. Muntaner, 63–65. No phone. Metro: Eixample.

Barcelona's largest gay bar attracts a mixed crowd of young trendies and foreigners. Always crowded, it's a good base to start out your evening. With every drink you receive free entry to Arena, Arena Classic (see above), and Arena VIP. There is a very popular happy hour on Wednesday from 6 to 9pm. On Friday and Saturday there are lots of surprises and giveaways. Open daily 6pm to 2:30am.

Satanassa. Carrer Aribau, 27. No phone. Cover (includes 1 drink) 1,000 ptas. ($6) Fri–Sat; no cover Sun–Thurs. Metro: Universitat.

This is a staple on Barcelona's gay circuit. It has a dance floor, provocative art, and a clientele whose percentage of gay women has greatly increased in the past several years. Open daily 11pm to 3am.

A CASINO

Between the coastal resorts of Sitges and Villanueva, about 25 miles (40km) southwest of Barcelona and 2 miles (3km) north of Sitges, stands the **Gran Casino de Barcelona,** Sant Pere (San Pedro) de Ribes (☎ **93-893-36-66**). Catalonia's major casino, it is in a 19th-century villa and attracts restaurant clients as well as gamblers. A set menu in the restaurant (reservations recommended) costs 5,000 ptas. ($30), and drinks go for around 900 ptas. ($5.40). For admission to the casino, you'll pay 550 ptas. ($3.30) and must show your passport. The casino is open year-round Sunday to Thursday 5pm to 4am, Friday and Saturday until 5am.

10 Side Trips from Barcelona

The major day trips, such as those to the monastery of Montserrat and the resorts along the Costa Brava, are covered in chapters 11, "Catalonia," and 12, "Girona & the Costa Brava." If you have a day to spare, you might also want to consider the following.

PENEDÉS WINERIES: HOME OF *CAVA*

From the Penedés wineries comes the famous *cava,* Catalán champagne, which can be sampled in Barcelona's champagne bars. You can see where the wine originates by journeying 25 miles (40km) from Barcelona, on highway A-2, to Exit 27. There are also daily trains to Sant Sadurní d'Anoia, home to 66 *cava* firms. Trains depart from Barcelona Sants.

The firm best equipped to receive visitors is **Codorníu** (☎ **93-818-32-32**), the largest producer of *cava,* with some 40 million bottles a year. Public transportation is unreliable, so try to visit by car. It is sometimes possible to get a taxi from the station at Sant Sadurní d'Anoia.

Groups of at least four are welcome at Codorníu. It's not necessary to make an appointment before showing up. Tours are presented in English, among other languages, and take 1½ hours; they visit some of the 10 miles (16km) of underground cellars by electric cart. Take a sweater, even on a hot day. A former pressing section has been turned into a museum, with exhibits of winemaking instruments through the ages. The museum is in a building designed by the great modernisme architect Puig i Cadafalch—one reason King Juan Carlos has declared the plant a national historic and artistic monument.

The tour ends with a *cava* tasting. Tours are conducted Monday to Friday throughout the day. The ideal time for a visit is for the autumn grape harvest. Admission is free Monday to Friday; Saturday and Sunday 200 ptas. ($1.20).

CARDONA: A CATALÁN CASTLE VILLAGE

Another popular excursion from Barcelona is to Cardona, 60 miles (97km) northwest. Take the N-11 west, then go north on Route 150 to Manresa. Cardona is 20 miles (32km) northwest of Manresa along Route 1410.

The home of the dukes of Cardona, the town is known for its canonical church, **Sant Vicenç de Cardona,** inside the walls of the castle. The church was consecrated in 1040. The great Catalán architect Josep Puig i Cadafalch wrote, "There are few elements in Catalán architecture of the 12th century that cannot be found in Cardona, and nowhere better harmonized." The church reflects the Lombard style of architecture. The castle (now a parador; see below) was the most important fortress in Catalonia.

WHERE TO STAY & DINE

Parador Nacional Duques de Cardona. Castillo de Cardona, s/n, 08261 Cardona. ☎ **93-869-12-75.** Fax 93-869-16-36. www.parador.es. 54 units. A/C TV TEL. 16,000–18,500 ptas. ($96–$111) double; 20,000 ptas. ($120) suite. AE, DC, MC, V.

Sitting atop a cone-shaped mountain that towers 330 feet (100.5m) above Cardona, this restored castle opened as a four-star parador in 1976. Once the seat of Ludovici Pio (Louis the Pious) and a stronghold against the Moors, it was later expanded and strengthened by Guifré el Pilós (Wilfred the Hairy). In the 9th century it belonged to Charlemagne's nephew Don Ramón Folch. The massive fortress proved impregnable to all but the inroads of time, and several ancient buildings in this hilltop complex have been restored and made part of the parador.

The spacious accommodations, some with minibars, have canopy beds and woven bedspreads and curtains. The guest rooms command panoramic views. The public rooms are decorated with antique furniture, tapestries, and paintings of various periods. The bar is in a former dungeon, and meals are served in the stone-arched medieval dining room where the counts once ate. A complete meal of regional dishes costs 3,500 ptas. ($21). Try the Catalán bouillabaisse, accompanied by wines whose taste would be familiar to the Romans. Food is served daily 1 to 4pm and 8 to 10:30pm.

THE ABELLO MUSEUM

The recently opened **Abello Museum,** carrer Berenguer, 122, Mollet del Valls (☎ **93-593-80-70**), is 12 miles (19km) from Barcelona. Follow Autopista 17 and turn off at the Mollet exit. The trip takes about 20 minutes. By public transportation, the CA5 train to Mollet departs from the Sants railway station in Barcelona.

The Abello Museum's collection is one of the most important in Spain. It houses works by its namesake, the Catalán artist Joan Abello, and pieces dedicated to him by his friends Salvador Dalí, Pablo Picasso, and Joan Miró. The museum also contains 19th- and 20th-century paintings and sculptures, Catalán art, Romanesque and Baroque carvings, Asian art, bullfighting memorabilia, furniture, ceramics, and glass. Admission is 300 ptas. ($1.80) for adults, 150 ptas. (90¢) for students and children.

It is open Tuesday to Friday 11am to 2pm and 4 to 8pm, Saturday 11am to 8pm, and Sunday 11am to 3pm.

THE PABLO CASALS MUSEUM

The **Pablo Casals Museum,** calle Santa Anna, 2 (☎ **977-665-684**), is in the house where the famous cellist was born in 1878 and spent the first 11 years of his life. The museum is in El Vendrall, 50 miles (80.5km) south of Barcelona. By car, take the A7 to Carra-Ruga, then follow signs south.

The exhibits include general memorabilia of Casals' youth and home life. Of particular note is a photograph of the young musician wearing a sailor suit, as well as the piano where his father, a musician, gave lessons. Also interesting is the museum's re-creation of an authentic late 19th-century Catalán village home. Admission is free. It's open daily 11am to 1pm and Monday to Saturday 5 to 7pm.

11 Catalonia

You can take several noteworthy 1-day excursions from Barcelona. The most popular is to the Benedictine monastery of **Montserrat,** northwest of Barcelona. To the south, the Roman city of **Tarragona** has been neglected by visitors but is particularly interesting to those who appreciate ancient history. Beach lovers should head for the resort town of **Sitges.**

About six million people live in Catalonia, and twice that many visit every year. It is one of Europe's playgrounds, with its beaches along the **Costa Brava** (see chapter 12, "Girona & the Costa Brava") and the **Costa Dorada,** centered on Sitges. Tarragona is the capital of its own province, and Barcelona, of course, is the political, economic, and cultural center of Catalonia (see chapter 10, "Barcelona").

The province of Catalonia forms a triangle bordered by the French frontier to the north, the Mediterranean Sea to the east, and the province of Aragón to the west. The northern coastline is rugged, whereas the Costa Dorada is flatter, with miles of sandy beaches as well as a mild, sunny climate.

Pilgrims may go to Montserrat for its scenery and religious associations, and history buffs to Tarragona for its Roman ruins, but just plain folks head to the Costa Dorada for fun. Named for its strips of golden sand, this seashore extends along the coastlines of Barcelona and Tarragona provinces. Avid beachcombers sometimes traverse the entire coast.

One popular stretch is **La Maresme,** extending from Río Tordera to Barcelona, a distance of 40 miles (64km). Allow at least 2½ hours to cover it without stops. The Tarragonese coastline extends from Barcelona to the Ebro River, a distance of 120 miles (193km); a trip along it will take a whole day. Highlights along this coast include **Costa de Garraf,** a series of creeks skirted by the corniche road after Castelldefels, Sitges, and Tarragona. One of the most beautiful stretches of the coast is **Cape Salou,** south of Tarragona in a setting of pinewoods.

We'll begin our tour through this history-rich part of Catalonia by going not along the coast, but rather inland to the Sierra de Montserrat, which has more spectacular views than any location along the coast. Wagner used it as the setting for his opera *Parsifal.* The serrated outline made by the sierra's steep cliffs led the Catalonians to call it *montserrat* (sawtooth mountain). Today it remains the religious center of Catalonia. Thousands of pilgrims annually visit the town's monastery with its Black Virgin.

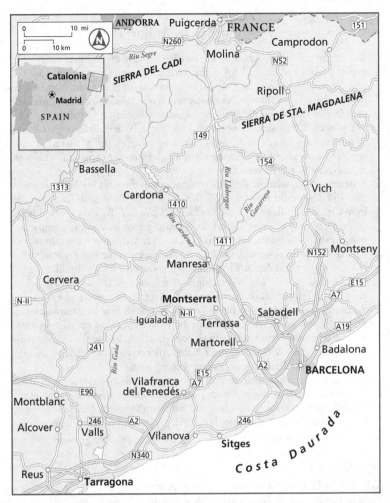

Catalonia

The **Monestir de Poblet** in Tarragona is the other major monastery of Catalonia. It, too, is a world-class attraction.

1 Montserrat

35 miles (56km) NW of Barcelona, 368 miles (592km) E of Madrid

The monastery at Montserrat, which sits atop a 4,000-foot mountain 7 miles (11km) long and 3½ miles (5.5km) wide, is one of the most important pilgrimage spots in Spain. It ranks alongside Zaragoza and Santiago de Compostela. Thousands travel here every year to see and touch the medieval statue of La Moreneta (The Black Virgin), the patron saint of Catalonia. Many newly married couples flock here for her blessing.

Avoid visiting on Sunday, if possible, as thousands of locals pour in, especially if the weather is nice. Remember that the winds blow cold up here even in summer, so visitors should take along warm sweaters, jackets, or coats. In winter, thermal underwear might not be a bad idea.

A Journey to Andorra

You might never have heard of the tiny principality of Andorra, sandwiched between Spain and France high in the eastern Pyrenees. Charlemagne gave this country its independence in 784, and with amused condescension, Napoléon let Andorra keep its autonomy. The principality is now ruled by two co-princes, the president of France and the Spanish archbishop of La Seu d'Urgell.

Less than 288 square miles (464 sq km) in size, Andorra is a storybook land of breathtaking scenery—cavernous valleys, snowcapped peaks, rugged pastureland, and deep gorges. It's long been popular for summer excursions and, more recently, as a winter ski resort.

Because of its isolation, Andorra retained one of the most insular peasant cultures in Europe until as late as 1945. But since the 1950s, tourists have increased from a trickle to a flood—12 million every year, in fact. This has wreaked havoc on Andorra's traditional way of life and turned a huge part of the country into one vast shopping center. Andorrans live almost entirely on monies earned from tax-free shopping, along with the thriving ski market in the winter months.

Some suggest that Andorra has ruined its mountain setting with urban sprawl because taxis, crowds, and advertising have transformed the once-rustic principality into a busy center of trading and commerce. At first glance, the route into the country from Spain looks like a used-car lot, and its mile-long traffic jams are legendary. New hotels and hundreds of shops have opened in the past decade to accommodate the French and Spanish pouring across the frontiers to buy duty-free merchandise. A magazine once called Andorra "Europe's feudal discount shopping center." In addition, gasoline is cheap here.

Most people make their base in the capital, Andorra-la-Vella (in Spanish, Andorra-la-Vieja), or the adjoining town, Les Escaldes, where there are plenty of shops, bars, and hotels. Shuttles run between the towns, but most shoppers prefer to walk. Most of the major hotels and restaurants are on the main street of

ESSENTIALS

GETTING THERE   The best and most exciting way to go is via the Catalán railway, **Ferrocarrils de la Generalitat de Catalunya** (Manresa line), with five trains a day leaving from the Plaça d'Espanya in Barcelona. The central office is at Plaça de Catalunya, 1 (☎ 93-205-15-15). The train connects with an aerial cable way (Aeri de Montserrat), which is included in the fare of 1,855 ptas. ($11.15) round-trip.

The train, with its funicular tie-in, has taken over as the preferred means of transport. However, a long-distance bus service is provided by **Autocars Julià** in Barcelona. Daily service from Barcelona to Montserrat is generally available, with departures near Estació Central de Barcelona-Sants, Plaça de Països Catalánes. One bus makes the trip at 9am, returning at 5pm; the round-trip ticket costs 1,500 ptas. ($9). Contact the Julià company at carrer Viriato (☎ 93-490-40-00).

To drive here, take the N-2 southwest of Barcelona toward Tarragona, turning west at the junction with the N-11. The signposts and exit to Montserrat will be on your right. From the main road, it's 9 miles (14.5km) up to the monastery through eerie rock formations and dramatic scenery.

VISITOR INFORMATION   The **tourist information office** is at Plaça de la Creu (☎ 93-877-77-77). It's open daily 10am to 1:45pm and 3 to 5:30pm.

Andorra-la-Vella (avinguda Meritxell) or on the main street of Les Escaldes (avinguda Carlemany). French francs and Spanish pesetas can be used interchangeably, and hotel, restaurant, and shop prices are quoted in both currencies.

But unless you've come just to shop, you will want to leave the capital for a look at this tiny principality. Two nearby villages, La Massana and Ordino, can be visited by car or by bus (leaving about every 30 minutes from the station in Andorra-la-Vella). Buses cross the country from south to north and vice versa. The drive to Andorra takes you through some of the finest mountain scenery in Europe, with a backdrop of peaks, vineyards, and rushing brooks. From Barcelona, drive via Puigcerda to La Seu d'Urgell. From here on the C-145, it's a quick 6 miles (10km) to the border of this autonomous principality, one of the world's smallest countries.

Although no one ever accused the Pyrenees of being more dramatic than the Alps, they are, in fact, far more rugged. The climate of dry air is brisk in winter, and some of Europe's best skiing can be found here. There is abundant snow from November lasting (usually) to April. Pas de la Casa-Grau Roig is the oldest resort, located just within the French border. Along with a slalom course, it has 18 trails for advanced skiers, plus some tame slopes for neophytes, and 25 lifts. The largest complex, however, is Soldeu-El Tarter, with 28 slopes (some designed for children) and a 7½-mile cross-country course. There are 22 ski lifts. The resort of Pals features 20 trails, 14 lifts, and a forest slalom course. Arinsal offers 25 slopes serving both the experienced skier and the beginner. But the most beautiful and dramatic resort of all is Ordino Arcalis, with 11 lifts and 16 slopes. Many British visitors flock here in winter, as Andorran ski packages are, in general, far more reasonable than those offered in Switzerland or Austria.

Warning: Border guards check very carefully for undeclared goods.

EXPLORING MONTSERRAT

One of the monastery's noted attractions is the 50-member ✪ **Escolanía,** one of the oldest and most renowned boys' choirs in Europe, dating from the 13th century. At 1pm daily you can hear them singing "Salve Regina" and the "Virolai" (hymn of Montserrat) in the basilica. The basilica is open daily 8 to 10:30am and noon to 6:30pm. Admission is free. To view the Black Virgin, a statue from the 12th or 13th century, enter the church through a side door to the right.

At the Plaça de Santa María you can also visit the **Museu de Montserrat** (☎ 93-877-77-77), known for its collection of ecclesiastical paintings, including works by Caravaggio and El Greco. Modern Spanish and Catalán artists are also represented (see Picasso's early *El Viejo Pescador,* dating from 1895). Works by Dalí and such French impressionists as Monet, Sisley, and Degas are shown. The collection of ancient artifacts is quite interesting, and make sure to look for the crocodile mummy, which is at least 2,000 years old. The museum is open Monday to Friday 10am to 6pm, Saturday and Sunday 9:30am to 6:30pm, charging 500 ptas. ($3) for adults and 300 ptas. ($1.80) for children and students.

The 9-minute **funicular ride** to the 4,119-foot-high peak, Sant Jeroni, makes for a panoramic trip. The funicular operates about every 20 minutes April to October, daily

10am to 6:40pm. The cost is 925 ptas. ($5.55) round-trip. From the top, you'll see not only the whole of Catalonia but also the Pyrenees and the islands of Majorca and Ibiza.

You can also make an excursion to **Santa Cova (Holy Grotto),** the alleged site of the discovery of the Black Virgin. The grotto dates from the 17th century and was built in the shape of a cross. You go halfway by funicular but must complete the trip on foot.

The chapel is open April to October daily 9am to 6:30pm; off-season hours are daily 10am to 5:30pm. The funicular operates April to October only, every 15 minutes daily 10am to 7pm, at a cost of 350 ptas. ($2.10) round-trip.

WHERE TO STAY & DINE

Few people spend the night here, but most visitors want at least one meal. If you don't want to spend a lot, buy a picnic in Barcelona or ask your hotel to pack a meal.

Abat Cisneros. Plaça de Monestir, 08199 Montserrat. ☎ **93-877-77-01.** Fax 93-877-77-24. 56 units. TV TEL. 5,800–10,500 ptas. ($34.80–$63) double. AE, DC, MC, V. Parking 450 ptas. ($2.70).

This well-maintained modern hotel on the main square of Montserrat has few pretensions and a history of family management dating from 1958. The small rooms are simple and clean, each equipped with a comfortable bed, and the tiled bathrooms come with hair dryers. The in-house restaurant offers fixed-price meals for around 2,500 ptas. ($15) per person. Many regional dishes of Catalonia are served. The hotel's name is derived from a title given to the head of any Benedictine monastery during the Middle Ages.

2 Tarragona

60 miles (97km) S of Barcelona, 344 miles (554km) E of Madrid

The ancient Roman port city of Tarragona, on a rocky bluff above the Mediterranean, is one of the grandest, but most neglected, sightseeing centers in Spain. Despite its Roman and medieval remains, it is merely the second oldest city of Catalonia.

The Romans captured Tarragona in 218 B.C., and during their rule the city sheltered one million people behind 40-mile-long (64km) city walls. One of the four capitals of Catalonia when it was an ancient principality, and once the home of Julius Caesar, Tarragona today consists of an old quarter filled with interesting buildings, particularly the houses with connecting balconies. The upper walled town is mainly medieval, the town below newer.

In the new town, walk along Ramble Nova, a wide and fashionable boulevard that is the main artery of life. Running parallel with Ramble Nova to the east is the Ramble Vella, which marks the beginning of the old town. The city has a bullring, good hotels, and even beaches. The Romans were the first to designate Tarragona a resort town.

After seeing the attractions listed below, cap off your day with a stroll along the Balcó del Mediterráni (the Balcony of the Mediterranean), where the vistas are especially beautiful at sunset.

ESSENTIALS

GETTING THERE   Daily, 30 to 40 trains make the 1½-hour trip to and from the Barcelona-Sants station. Five trains per day make the 8-hour trip from Madrid. In Tarragona, the **RENFE** office is in the train station, Plaza Pedrera, s/n (☎ **977-24-02-02**).

From Barcelona, there are 10 buses per day to Tarragona (1½ hours); from Valencia, 9 buses (3½ hours), and from Alicante, 6 buses (6½ hours). Call ☎ 977-22-20-72 in Tarragona for more information.

To drive, take the A-2 southwest from Barcelona to the A-7, then take the N-340. The route is well marked. This is a fast toll road. The one-way cost of the toll road from Barcelona to Tarragona is 1,200 ptas. ($7.20).

VISITOR INFORMATION The **tourist information office** is at Fortuny, 4 (☎ 977-23-34-15). It's open Monday to Friday 9am to 3pm and 4 to 7pm, Saturday 9am to 2pm.

EXPLORING THE TOWN

✪ **Amfiteatre Romà.** Parc del Milagro. ☎ 977-24-25-79. Admission 475 ptas. ($2.85). June–Sept, Tues–Sun 10am–1:30pm and 4–5pm Bus: 1.

At the foot of Miracle Park and dramatically carved from a cliff that rises from the beach, this Roman amphitheater recalls the days in the 2nd century when thousands gathered here for amusement.

Catedral. Plaça de la Seu. ☎ 977-23-86-85. Admission to cathedral and museum 300 ptas. ($1.80). Mar 16–June 30, daily 10am–12:30pm and 4–6:45pm; July 1–Oct 15, daily 10am–7pm; Oct 16–Nov 15, daily 10am–12:30pm and 3–6pm; Nov 16–Mar 15, daily 10am–1:45pm. Bus: 1.

Situated at the highest point of Tarragona is this 12th-century cathedral, whose architecture represents the transition from Romanesque to Gothic. It has an enormous vaulted entrance, fine stained-glass windows, Romanesque cloisters, and an open choir. In the main apse, observe the altarpiece of St. Thecla, patron of Tarragona, carved by Pere Joan in 1430. Two flamboyant doors open into the chevet. The east gallery is the Museu Diocesà, with a collection of Catalán art.

Museu Nacional Arqueològic. Plaça del Rei, 5. ☎ 977-23-62-09. Admission 400 ptas. ($2.40). June 1–Sept 30, Tues–Sat 10am–8pm, Sun 10am–2pm; off-season, Tues–Sat 10am–1:30pm and 4–7pm, Sun 10am–2pm. Bus: 8.

Overlooking the sea, the Archaeology Museum houses a collection of Roman relics—mosaics, ceramics, coins, silver, sculpture, and more. The outstanding attraction here is the *Head of Medusa*, with its penetrating stare.

✪ **Museu Necròpolis.** Paleocristians, avinguda de Ramón y Cajal, 80. ☎ 977-251515. Admission to Necròpolis plus museum 400 ptas. ($2.40). June 1–Sept 30, Tues–Sat 10am–8pm, Sun and holidays 10am–2pm; off-season, Tues–Sat 10am–1:30pm and 4–7pm, Sun and holidays 10am–2pm. Bus: 4.

This is one of the most important burial grounds in Spain, used by the Christians from the 3rd to the 5th centuries. It stands outside town next to a tobacco factory whose construction led to its discovery in 1923. While on the grounds, visit the Museu Paleocristià, which contains a number of sarcophagi and other objects discovered during the excavations.

Passeig Arqueològic. Plaça del Pallol. ☎ 977-24-57-96. Admission 420 ptas. ($2.50). Oct–May, Mon–Sat 10am–1pm and 3–7pm, Sun and holidays 10am–2pm; June–Sept, Mon–Sat 9am–8pm, Sun and holidays 10am–2pm. Bus: 1.

At the far end of Plaça del Pallol, an archway leads to this half-mile walkway along the ancient ramparts, built by the Romans on top of gigantic boulders. The ramparts have been much altered over the years, especially in medieval times and in the 1600s. There are scenic views from many points along the way.

SHOPPING

You'll find a scattering of handcraft shops throughout Tarragona's historic core, with a particularly dense concentration along the Ramble Nova. (Its central section is an all-pedestrian zone.) Any of them might provide a handcrafted souvenir of your visit. But for the densest concentration in town of shops and boutiques, head for the **Centro Commercial Parc Central,** on the avinguda Roma. Although the main focus here revolves around a supermarket, the site has at least 40 shops selling whatever you'd need in terms of clothing, sundries, and household goods.

NEARBY THEME PARK THRILLS

A 10-minute ride from the heart of Barcelona, **Port Aventura Amusement Park,** Port Aventura (☎ **902-20-22-20**), is the biggest theme park in Spain. Universal Studios has acquired a prime stake in it and has plans to make it even larger. On a vast 2,000 acres, it will be expanded to become the largest entertainment center in Europe. Since its inauguration in 1995, it has already become one of the Mediterranean's favorite family destinations.

The park is a microcosm of five distinct worlds, with full-scale re-creations of classic villages ranging from Polynesia to Mexico, from China to the old American West. It also offers a thrilling variety of rollercoaster and white-water rides, all centered on a lake you can travel via the deck of a Chinese junk.

Over the coming years Universal will expand the site, including, of course, a mammoth replica of a Hollywood studio lot. The park is open daily March 26 to June 19, 10am to 8pm; June 20 to September 13, 10am to midnight; September 14 to January 11, 10am to 8pm. Closed January 12 to March 25. Admission costs 4,100 ptas. ($24.60) for adults, 3,100 ptas. ($18.60) for children. Nighttime admission is 2,500 ptas. ($15) for adults or 1,900 ptas. ($11.40) for children. The fee includes all shows and rides.

Some 50% of the trains on the Barcelona-Sitges-Tarragona line stop at Port Aventura. From Barcelona, the trip takes 1½ hours, and a one-way fare costs 150 ptas. (90¢). A taxi from the center of Tarragona costs 1,900 ptas. ($11.40) one-way.

WHERE TO STAY
EXPENSIVE

Hotel Imperial Tarraco. Paseo de las Palmeras/Rambla Vella, 43003 Tarragona. ☎ **977-23-30-40.** Fax 977/21-65-66. E-mail: imperial@tinet.fut.es. 170 units. A/C MINIBAR TV TEL. 12,000–25,000 ptas. ($72–$150) double; 22,000–35,000 ptas. ($132–$210) suite. AE, DC, MC, V. Free parking. Bus: 1.

Located about ¼ mile south of the cathedral, atop an oceanfront cliff whose panoramas include a sweeping view of both the sea and the Roman ruins, this hotel is the finest in town. Designed in the form of a crescent, it has guest rooms that may angle out to sea and almost always include small balconies. The accommodations, all with private bathrooms, contain uncomplicated, plain modern furniture. However, all the beds are comfortable with fine linens and good mattresses. The public rooms display lots of polished white marble, Oriental carpets, and leather furniture. The staff responds well to the demands of both traveling businesspeople and art lovers on sight-seeing excursions.

The hotel has both a bar and a restaurant. Some Catalonian regional dishes are featured, and there is a *menú del día* for 4,000 ptas. ($24), although the food is rather standard. You'll find an outdoor pool, tennis courts, and a pleasant garden.

MODERATE TO INEXPENSIVE

Hotel Astari. Vía Augusta, 95, 43003 Tarragona. ☎ **977-23-69-00.** Fax 977-23-69-11. E-mail: astari@tinet.fut.es. 83 units. TV TEL. 9,500 ptas. ($57) double. AE, DC, MC, V. Parking 900 ptas. ($5.40). Bus: 9.

In-the-know travelers in search of peace and quiet on the Mediterranean come to the Astari, which opened its doors back in 1959 and was last renovated in 1992. This five-story resort hotel on the Barcelona road offers fresh and airy, although rather plain, accommodations. Most rooms are small but each comes with a good bed and a well-maintained private bathroom with a hair dryer. Other features of the hotel include a swimming pool and a solarium. The Astari has long balconies and terraces, one favorite spot being the outer flagstone terrace with its umbrella tables set among willows, orange trees, and geranium bushes. There is a cafeteria as well as a cocktail lounge. This is the only hotel in Tarragona with garage space for each guest's car.

Hotel Lauria. Rambla Nova, 20, 43004 Tarragona. ☎ **977-23-67-12.** Fax 977-23-67-00. 72 units. A/C TV TEL. 10,500–11,000 ptas. ($63–$66) double. AE, DC, MC, V. Parking 1,500 ptas. ($9). Bus: 1.

Set less than half a block north of the town's popular seaside promenade (Passeig de les Palmeres), beside the tree-lined Rambla, this straightforward three-star hotel offers unpretentious, functional, and clean rooms, each of which has been recently modernized. Rooms range from small to medium, and each tiled bathroom is equipped with a hair dryer. Long considered the leading hotel in town until the arrival of some newcomers, it still draws a loyal clientele of repeat visitors. The rooms in back open onto a view of the sea, a garden, and the hotel's swimming pool. Only the public rooms are air-conditioned. The ground floor contains an informal pizzeria.

Hotel Urbis. Carrer Reding, 20 bis, 43001 Tarragona. ☎ **800/528-1234** in the U.S. and Canada, or 977-24-01-16. Fax 977-24-36-54. E-mail: urbis@tinet.fut.es. 44 units. A/C MINIBAR TV TEL. 8,600–14,500 ptas. ($52–$87) double. Rates include buffet breakfast. AE, DC, DISC, MC, V. Parking 1,250 ptas. ($7.50). Bus: 3.

The rooms at this hotel off the Plaça de Corsini are three-star quality and much improved in recent years, with such added amenities as safes. Each is fitted with a double or twin bed with a comfortable mattress, and the tiled bathrooms have recently been renewed. The hotel offers a restaurant with an English menu. The nearby tourist office will give you a map for exploring Tarragona.

WHERE TO DINE

Barquet. Gasometro, 16. ☎ **977-24-00-23.** Reservations recommended. Main courses 2,800–5,000 ptas. ($16.80–$30); *menú del día* 1,500 ptas. ($9). AE, DC, MC, V. Mon–Sat 1–3:30pm and 8–11pm. Closed Aug. CATALÁN/SEAFOOD.

In the center of town, within a 5-minute walk of the cathedral, this restaurant specializes in seafood and shellfish prepared in the Catalán style. It was established in 1950 in the cellar of a relatively modern building and today is run by the third generation of its original owners. Within a pair of nautical-themed dining rooms you can enjoy such dishes as *sopa de pescados* Tarragona style, *romesco* (ragout) of sea bass with herbs, a local assemblage of fried finned creatures identified for many hundreds of years as *fideos rossejats,* and several different preparations of sole and hake. If you're not interested in seafood, a choice of grilled veal, chicken, or beef is offered. The list of Spanish and Catalán wines will complement any meal here. The staff is well trained, polite, and proud of their Catalán antecedents.

Cafetería Arimany. Rambla Nova, 43–45. ☎ **977-23-79-31.** Reservations not necessary. Main courses 1,200–2,200 ptas. ($7.20–$13.20); fixed-price menu 1,600 ptas. ($9.60). AE, DC, MC, V. Daily 8am–midnight winter; 8am–7pm summer. Bus: 1. CATALÁN/INTERNATIONAL.

When this central and popular cafeteria opens its doors at 8am, visitors and locals alike pour in for breakfast. Others come back for lunch, and some finish with a good-value dinner. You can eat here inexpensively or for more money, depending on your appetite. The shrimp in garlic oil is outstanding. Try the fresh fish of the day, based on the local catch, or perhaps squid cooked Roman style. The dessert specialty is "Pau Casals," named after a native Catalonian, the late, great cellist Pablo Casals. It is a chocolate cake served with a hot chocolate sauce. Another bakery specialty is *maginet* (a sugar cookie with nuts), the typical cookie of Tarragona.

Sol-Ric. Vía Augusta, 227. ☎ **977-23-20-32.** Reservations not necessary. Main courses 2,000–4,900 ptas. ($12–$29.40); fixed-price menu 1,800 ptas. ($10.80). AE, MC, V. Tues–Sat 1–4pm; Tues–Sun 8:30–11pm. Closed mid-Dec to mid-Jan. CATALÁN/INTERNATIONAL.

Many guests remember the service here long after memories of the good cuisine have faded. Dating from 1859, the place has a rustic ambience replete with antique farm implements hanging from the walls. There is an outdoor terrace as well as a central fireplace, usually blazing in winter. The chef prepares oven-baked hake with potatoes, tournedos with Roquefort, seafood stew, and several exotic fish dishes, among other specialties.

TARRAGONA AFTER DARK

Rambla Nova contains a handful of sleepy-looking bars, any of which might serve a cup of coffee or bottle of beer throughout the day and evening.

There's a little more action at the convivial **Club Nautico,** Passeig Marítimo, s/n (no phone), where tapas, wines, and drinks are served to an often crowded room overlooking the sea. Similar bars in the town's medieval core include **Bar Anticuario,** carrer Santa Ana, s/n (no phone).

You might also try **Cucudrulus,** carrer del Protectorado/Pau de Protectorat, s/n (no phone), which is a pub with heavy English overtones, an international crowd, and a knack for presenting emerging rock and roll bands of varying degrees of talent. At **Bar Poetes,** carrer Sant Llorenç, 15 (no phone), live bands sometimes perform in a cellar a very short walk from the cathedral.

Concerts and theatrical productions are staged in the city's cultural centerpiece, the **Teatro Metropol,** Rambla Nova, 46 (☎ **977-25-09-23**). Because of the language problem, you might skip theatrical events presented in Catalán in favor of some of the musical and dance presentations.

SIDE TRIPS FROM TARRAGONA

If you rent a car, you can visit two attractions within a 30- to 45-minute drive from Tarragona. The first stop is the **Monestir de Poblet,** Plaça Corona d'Aragó, 11, E-43448 Poblet (☎ **977-87-02-54**), 29 miles (47km) northwest of Tarragona, one of the most intriguing monasteries in Spain. Its most exciting features are the oddly designed tombs of the old kings of Aragón and Catalonia. Constructed in the 12th and 13th centuries and still in use, Poblet's cathedral-like church reflects both Romanesque and Gothic architectural styles. Cistercian monks still live here, passing their days writing, studying, working a printing press, farming, and helping to restore the building, which suffered heavy damage during the 1835 revolution. Admission to the monastery costs 500 ptas. ($3) for adults and 300 ptas. ($1.80) for children

The Beaches of the Costa Dorada

Running along the entire coastline of the province of Tarragona, for some 131 miles (211km) from Cunit as far as Les Cases d'Alcanar, is a series of excellent beaches and impressive cliffs, along with beautiful pine-covered headlands. In the city of Tarragona itself is El Milagre beach, and a little farther north are the beaches of L'Arrabassade, Savinosa, dels Capellans, and the Llarga. At the end of the latter stands La Punta de la Mora, which has a 16th-century watchtower. The small towns of Altafulla and Torredembarra, both complete with castles, stand next to these beaches and are the location of many hotels and urban developments.

Farther north again are the two magnificent beaches of Comarruga and Sant Salvador. The first is particularly cosmopolitan; the second is more secluded. Last comes the beaches of Calafell, Segur, and Cunit, all with modern tourist complexes. You'll also find the small towns of Creixell, Sant Vicenç de Calders, and Clarà, which have wooded hills in the background.

South of Tarragona, the coastline forms a wide arc that stretches for miles and includes La Piñeda beach. El Recó beach fronts the Cape of Salou where, in among its coves, hills, and hidden-away corners, many hotels and residential centers are located. The natural port of Salou is nowadays a center for international tourism.

Continuing south toward Valencia, you next come to Cambrils, a maritime town with an excellent beach and an important fishing port. In the background stand the impressive Colldejou and Llaberia Mountains. Farther south are the beaches of Montroig and L'Hospitalet, as well as the small town of L'Ametlla de Mar with its small fishing port.

After passing the Balaguer massif, the traveler eventually reaches the delta of the River Ebro, a wide lowland area covering more than 300 miles (483km), opening like a fan into the sea. This is an area of rice fields crisscrossed by branches of the River Ebro and by an enormous number of irrigation channels. There are also some lagoons that because of their immense size are ideal as hunting and fishing grounds. Moreover, there are some beaches over several miles in length and others in small, hidden-away estuaries. Two important towns in the region are Amposta, on the River Ebro itself, and Sant Carles de la Ràpita, a 19th-century port town favored by King Carlos III.

The Costa Dorada extends to its most southwesterly point at the plain of Alcanar, a large area given over to the cultivation of oranges and other similar crops. Its beaches, along with the small hamlet of Les Cases d'Alcanar, mark the end of the Tarragona section of the Costa Dorada.

13 and under and students. From March to October, it's open daily 10am to 12:30pm and 3 to 6pm. November to February it's open daily 10am to 12:30pm and 3 to 5:30pm. Except for Monday, when no guide service is available, visits to the monastery are usually set up as a part of tours, mostly in Spanish but with occasional English translations. They depart at 75-minute intervals throughout the monastery's open hours.

About 3 miles (4.8km) farther you can explore an unspoiled medieval Spanish town, **Montblanch.** At its entrance, a map pinpoints the principal artistic and architectural treasures—and there are many. Walk, don't drive, along the narrow, winding streets.

3 Sitges

25 miles (40km) S of Barcelona, 370 miles (596km) E of Madrid

Sitges is one of the most popular resorts of southern Europe, the brightest spot on the Costa Dorada. It's especially crowded in summer, mostly with affluent young northern Europeans, many of them gay. For years the resort largely drew prosperous middle-class industrialists from Barcelona, but those staid days have gone; Sitges is as swinging today as Benidorm and Torremolinos down the coast, but nowhere near as tacky.

Sitges has long been known as a city of culture, thanks in part to resident artist, playwright, and Bohemian mystic Santiago Rusiñol. The 19th-century *modernisme* movement began largely at Sitges, and the town remained the scene of artistic encounters and demonstrations long after the movement waned. Sitges continued as a resort of artists, attracting such giants as Salvador Dalí and poet Federico García Lorca. The Spanish Civil War (1936–39) erased what has come to be called the "golden age" of Sitges. Although other artists and writers arrived in the decades to follow, none had the name or the impact of those who had gone before.

ESSENTIALS

GETTING THERE   RENFE runs trains from Barcelona-Sants to Sitges, a 30-minute trip that costs 355 ptas. ($2.15). Call ☎ **93-490-02-02** in Barcelona for information about schedules. Four trains leave Barcelona per hour.

Sitges is a 45-minute drive from Barcelona along the C-246, a coastal road. An express highway, the A-7, opened in 1991. The coastal road is more scenic, but it can be extremely slow on weekends because of the heavy traffic, as all of Barcelona seemingly heads for the beaches.

VISITOR INFORMATION   The **tourist information office** is at carrer Sínis Morera, 1 (☎ **93-894-42-51**). It's open June to September 15, daily 9am to 9pm, and September 16 to May, Monday to Friday 9am to 2pm and 4 to 6:30pm, Saturday 10am to 1pm.

SPECIAL EVENTS   The **Carnaval** at Sitges is one of the outstanding events on the Catalán calendar. For more than a century, the town has celebrated the days before the beginning of Lent. Fancy dress, floats, feathered outfits, and sequins all make this an exciting event. The party begins on the Thursday before Lent with the arrival of the king of the Carnestoltes and ends with the Burial of a Sardine on Ash Wednesday. Activities reach their flamboyant best on Sant Bonaventura, where gay people hold their own celebrations.

FUN ON & OFF THE BEACH

The old part of Sitges used to be a fortified medieval enclosure. The castle is now the seat of the town government. The local parish church, called *La Punta* (The Point) and built next to the sea on top of a promontory, presides over an extensive maritime esplanade, where people parade in the early evening. Behind the side of the church are the Museu Cau Ferrat and the Museu Maricel (see "Museums," below).

Most people are here to hit the beach. The beaches have showers, bathing cabins, and stalls; kiosks rent motorboats and watersports equipment. Beaches on the eastern end and those inside the town center are the most peaceful—for example, **Aiguadoiç** and **Els Balomins. Playa San Sebastián, Fragata Beach,** and the **"Beach of the Boats"** (below the church and next to the yacht club) are the area's family beaches. A young, happening crowd heads for the **Playa de la Ribera** to the west.

We'll Have a Gay Old Time

Along with Ibiza, Key West, and Mikonos, Sitges has established itself firmly on the "A" list of gay resorts. It's a perfect destination for those who want a ready-made combination of beach and bars, all within a few minutes' walk of each other. It works well as a temporary, calmer alternative to Barcelona, which is about 30 minutes away by train, and so is great for a day trip or a few days out of the city. Off-season, it's pretty quiet on the gay front apart from the carnival in February, when hordes of gays and lesbians descend from Barcelona and the party really begins.

Summer, however, is pure hedonistic playtime, and the town draws the boys in from all over Europe. Sitges is never going to tax the intellect, but it might well exhaust the body. There is a gay beach crammed with the usual overload of muscles and summer accessories in the middle of the town in front of the Passeig Maritim. The other beach is nudist and farther out of town, between Sitges and Vilanova. The best directions are to go as far as the L'Atlántida disco and then follow the train track to the farther of the two beaches. The woods next to it are unsurprisingly packed with playful wildlife sporting short hair and deep tans.

All along the coast, women can and certainly do go topless. Farther west are the most solitary beaches, where the scene grows more racy, especially along the **Playas del Muerto,** where two tiny nude beaches lie between Sitges and Vilanova i la Geltrú. A shuttle bus runs between the cathedral and Golf Terramar. From Golf Terramar, go along the road to the club L'Atlántida, then walk along the railway. The first beach draws nudists of every sexual persuasion, and the second is almost solely gay. Be advised that lots of action takes place in the woods in back of these beaches.

MUSEUMS

Beaches aside, Sitges has some choice museums, which really shouldn't be missed.

Museu Cau Ferrat. Carrer del Fonollar. ☎ **93-894-03-64.** Admission 500 ptas. ($3) adults, 250 ptas. ($1.50) students, free for children under 16; combination ticket for the 3 museums listed in this section: 800 ptas. ($4.80) adults, 400 ptas. ($2.40) students and children. June 22–Sept 10, Tues–Sat 9:30am–2pm and 4–9pm, Sun 9:30am–2pm; Sept 11–June 21, Tues–Fri 9:30am–2pm and 4–6pm, Sat 9:30am–2pm and 4–8pm, Sun 9:30am–2pm.

The Catalán artist Santiago Rusiñol combined two 16th-century cottages to make this house, where he lived and worked; upon his death in 1931 he willed it to Sitges along with his art collection. More than anyone else, Rusiñol made Sitges a popular resort. The museum collection includes two paintings by El Greco and several small Picassos, including *The Bullfight.* A number of Rusiñol's works are on display. See the box on Rusiñol and his house/museum below.

Museu Maricel. Carrer del Fonallar. ☎ **93-894-03-64.** Admission 500 ptas. ($3) adults, 250 ptas. ($1.50) students, free for children under 16; admission included in combination ticket (see Museu Cau Ferrat, above). June 21–Sept 11, Tues–Sat 9:30am–2pm and 4–8pm, Sun 9:30am–2pm; Sept 12–June 20, Tues–Fri 9:30am–2pm and 4–6pm, Sat 9:30am–2pm and 4–8pm, Sun 9:30am–2pm.

Opened by the king and queen of Spain, Museu Maricel contains art donated by Dr. Jesús Pérez Rosales. The palace, owned by American Charles Deering when it was built right after World War I, is made up of two parts connected by a small bridge. The museum has a good collection of Gothic and Romantic paintings and sculptures, as well as many fine Catalán ceramics. There are three noteworthy works by Santiago Rebull and an allegorical painting of World War I by José María Sert.

Museu Romàntic ("Can Llopis"). Sant Gaudenci, 1. ☎ **93-894-29-69.** Admission 500 ptas. ($3) adults, 250 ptas. ($1.50) students, free for children under 16; admission included in combination ticket (see Museu Cau Ferrat, above). June 21–Sept 11, Tues–Sat 9:30am–2pm and 4–8pm, Sun 9:30am–2pm; Sept 12–June 20, Tues–Fri 9:30am–2pm and 4–6pm, Sat 9:30am–2pm and 4–8pm, Sun 9:30am–2pm.

This museum re-creates the daily life of a Sitges land-owning family in the 18th and 19th centuries. The family rooms, furniture, and household objects are most interesting. You'll find wine cellars and an important collection of antique dolls (upstairs).

WHERE TO STAY

In spite of a building spree, Sitges just can't handle the large numbers of tourists who flock here in July and August. By mid-October just about everything—including hotels, restaurants, and bars—slows down considerably or closes altogether.

EXPENSIVE

Hotel Calípolis. Avinguda Sofia, 2–4, 08870 Sitges. ☎ **93-894-15-00.** Fax 93-894-07-64. 170 units. A/C MINIBAR TV TEL. 18,500–23,000 ptas. ($111–$138) double; from 32,000 ptas. ($192) suite. AE, DC, MC, V. Parking 2,000 ptas. ($12).

This 11-story hotel fits in a gently undulating curve against the resort's beachfront and seaside promenade. The good-size rooms have expansive balconies, safes, satellite TV hookups, marble-sheathed bathrooms, and a comfortably conservative decor of contemporary furniture. Most offer sea views; the remainder offer views of the mountains.

Dining/Diversions: The hotel restaurant includes a flowering outdoor terrace and offers formal service with both international and Catalonian specialties. There's also a bar.

Amenities: Concierge, baby-sitting, car rentals, excursions to nearby tennis courts and golf courses; horseback riding, sailing, and trips to nearby historic monasteries can be arranged. The parking lot is available only during the congested summer months; the lot closes when street parking becomes available again in the fall.

Meliá Gran Sitges. El Puerto de Aiguadolç, 08870 Sitges. ☎ **800/336-3542** in the U.S., or 93-811-08-11. Fax 93-894-90-34. 307 units. A/C MINIBAR TV TEL. Mon–Thurs 25,000 ptas. ($150) double; Fri–Sun 18,000 ptas. ($108) double; 35,000 ptas. ($210) suite throughout week. Weekend rates include breakfast. AE, DC, MC, V. Parking 1,300 ptas. ($7.80).

Designed with steeply sloping sides reminiscent of a pair of interconnected Aztec pyramids, this hotel was built in 1992 as housing for spectators and participants in the Barcelona Olympics. Angled to curve around two sides of a large swimming pool and set a few yards from the beach, the hotel has a white-marble lobby with what feels like the largest window in Spain, overlooking a view of the mountains. Each midsize room is outfitted in shades of blue and comes with a large furnished veranda for sunbathing. Each of the immaculately kept tiled bathrooms has a hair dryer. Many guests at this hotel are here to participate in any of dozens of conferences and conventions held frequently in the establishment's battery of high-tech convention facilities. It's about a 15-minute walk east of the center of Sitges, near the access roads leading to Barcelona.

Dining/Diversions: The in-house restaurant, **Morai,** serves international and Catalonian cuisine with attentive service. The hotel has two bars.

Amenities: Concierge, baby-sitting, barber shop, room service, safety security boxes.

San Sebastián Playa. Port Alegre, 53, 08070 Sitges. ☎ **938-94-86-76.** Fax 938-94-04-30. www.tryp.es. E-mail:hotel@tryp.es. 51 units A/C MINIBAR TV TEL. 15,500–19,000 ptas. ($93–$114) double; 27,000 ptas. ($162) suite. AE, DC, MC, V. Parking: 1,500 ptas. ($9).

Rusiñol: The Enigmatic Figure of *Modernisme*

Cau Ferrat was the home and studio of artist and writer Santiago Rusiñol. Born in Barcelona in 1861, he was one of the most enigmatic figures of *modernisme,* or Catalán art nouveau, a literary and artistic trend that represented a spiritualist reaction to 19th-century positivism. He died in Aranjuez in 1931.

On return from a trip to Italy in 1892, he bought a couple of terraced fishers' cottages that had been built on the edge of a rocky coastline. Then he commissioned the architect Francesc Rogent to build a new house on the ground where the cottages stood.

Rusiñol described Cau Ferrat as a "refuge for those whose heart no longer feels the warmth it needs, a place to rest the spirit that has become weary from the toil of life, a hermitage near the sea for those injured by indifference and a hostel for the pilgrims of Holy Poetry."

Today, the collection at Cau Ferrat that arouses most interest is the painting and drawing collection. Works by the most outstanding artists of the modernisme period can be seen here—such artists as Ramón Casas, Aleix Clapés, Pere Ferran, Joan Llimona, Arcadi Mas i Fontdevila, Isidre Nonell, Dario de Regoyos, Miquel Utrillo, and Ignacio Zuloaga. There are also works by younger artists such as Herman Anglada i Camarasa and Picasso. Rusiñol's work is represented by a wide range of styles, from realism to symbolism.

Cau Ferrat is a treasure chest containing a large number of private objects that are inseparable from the private and social life of its creator. There are portraits of friends Casellas, Eleonora Duse, Casas, Utrillo, and Benito Pérez Galdós.

The Catalán writer Josep Pla defined Rusiñol as a "man who was horrified by industrial civilization, who postulated freedom in all domains, who tended to replace reality by literature and reason by sentiments, fascinated by nature and gardens, who searched for vagrancy and melancholy, sentimental expression, who valued the inaccessible, death and nihilism, dreams and indecision."

An outstanding painter and a renowned satirical writer, novelist, and dramatist, Rusiñol lived in Paris when impressionism made its appearance. In his own artwork he employed many elements of impressionism in technique, light, and color. However, he portrayed his own private and lyrical world. Rusiñol considered painting to be a spiritual language that transmitted his poetry rather than a medium that reflected the real world.

The best hotel in Sitges, opposite San Sebastián beach, this four-star hotel with its wedding cake facade has been in operation since 1990. The functional art deco interior is the most beautifully decorated of any hotel in Sitges. A lot of attention has gone into the guest rooms, which are spacious and comfortable with such modern conveniences as private safes and fully equipped bathrooms. Each has a balcony opening onto the sea.

Dining/Diversions: An attractive restaurant, **La Concha,** specializes in seafood and opens onto a terrace with access to and from the promenade. There is also a bar, plus a snack bar at the beach.

Amenities: Limited room service, laundry, concierge, outdoor pool, hydromassage, tropical garden.

Subur Maritim. Passseig Maritim, 08870 Sitges. ☎ **938-94-03-20.** Fax 939-94-95-91. www./hotelsuburmaritim.com. E-mail: info@hotelsuburmaritim.com. 42 units. A/C MINIBAR TV TEL. 22,450 ptas. ($134.70) double; 26,950 ptas. ($161.70) suite. Rates include breakfast buffet. AE, DC, MC, V.

In a residential area on the seafront facing a good beach, this four-star hotel is only a 5-minute walk from the center. It is a winning choice, made up of a traditional Catalán building and a more modern and functional structure. The interior is cozy, with traditional Catalán decor of wood fittings and cast-iron adornments on doors and windows, giving an overall aura of a typical coastal village hostelry. The amply sized guest rooms are comfortably furnished and tastefully decorated, each with a balcony.

Dining/Diversions: The hotel restaurant offers gourmet Mediterranean cuisine, specializing in seafood, and there is a poolside bar.

Amenities: Swimming pool, laundry, concierge, limited room service, kayaks and jet skis for rent.

Terramar. Paseo Marítimo, 80, 08870 Sitges. ☎ **938-94-00-50.** Fax 938-94-56-04. www.hotelterramar.com. E-mail: hotelterramar@hotelterramar.com. 209 units. A/C MINIBAR TV TEL. 21,000 ptas. ($126) double; 25,500 ptas. ($153) suite. Rates include breakfast buffet. AE, DC, MC, V. Closed Nov–Mar. Bus: 1.

Facing the beach in a residential area of Sitges, about half a mile from the center, this modern resort hotel with its balconied front evokes a many tiered yacht. The interior, however, is designed in a classical Mediterranean style with marble floors and white walls. Spacious guest rooms are comfortable with carpeted floors, colorful wall coverings, and well-maintained and fully equipped bathrooms.

Dining/Diversions: A large restaurant specializes in Mediterranean cuisine and seafood dishes. There is a bar plus a snack bar serving light meals throughout the day.

Amenities: Outdoor swimming pool, garden, two tennis courts, laundry, limited room service, 50% discount at nearby golf course.

MODERATE

El Galeón. Sant Francesc, 44, 08870 Sitges. ☎ **93-894-06-12.** Fax 93-894-63-35. 74 units. AC TV TEL. 7,500–12,500 ptas. ($45–$75) double. Rates include breakfast. MC, V. Closed Oct 20–Apr. Parking 1,500 ptas. ($9).

A leading three-star hotel only a short walk from both the beach and the Plaça d'Espanya, this well-styled hostelry blends a bit of the old Spain with the new. The small public rooms feel cozy; the good-size guest rooms, accented with wood grain, have a more streamlined aura. Each comes with a comfortable bed, plus a well-maintained bathroom with a shower stall. The hotel has a swimming pool and a patio in the rear.

Hotel Romàntic de Sitges. Carrer de Sant Isidre, 33, 08870 Sitges. ☎ **93-894-83-75.** Fax 93-894-81-67. 60 units. TEL. 9,800–12,500 ptas. ($58.80–$75) double. Rates include breakfast. AE, MC, V. Closed Nov–Mar 15.

Made up of three beautifully restored 19th-century villas, this hotel is only a short walk from both the beach and the train station. The hotel's romantic ground floor bar is an international rendezvous, and the public rooms are filled with artworks. You can have breakfast in the dining room or in a garden filled with mulberry trees. Rooms range from small to medium and are well maintained with good beds and tiled bathrooms. Overflow guests are housed in a nearby annex, the Hotel de la Renaixença.

Hotel Platjador. Passeig de la Ribera, 35, 08870 Sitges. ☎ **93-894-50-54.** Fax 93-811-03-84. 60 units. A/C TV TEL. 8,500–15,000 ptas. ($51–$90) double. Rates include breakfast. MC, V. Closed Nov–Apr.

One of the best hotels in town, the Platjador, on the esplanade fronting the beach, has comfortably furnished and recently restored guest rooms, all with private bathrooms and many with big French doors opening onto balconies and sea views. There is also a swimming pool. The dining room, facing the beach, is known for its good cuisine, including gazpacho, paella, fresh fish, and flan for dessert.

INEXPENSIVE

Hotel El Cid. San José, 39 bis, 08870 Sitges. ☎ **93-894-18-42.** Fax 93-894-6335. 77 units. 5,800–9,000 ptas. ($34.80–$54) double. Rates include continental breakfast. MC, V. Closed Nov–May.

El Cid's exterior suggests Castile and inside, appropriately enough, you'll find beamed ceilings, natural stone walls, heavy wrought-iron chandeliers, and leather chairs. The same theme is carried out in the rear dining room and in the pleasantly furnished rooms, which, though small, are still quite comfortable, with fine beds and linens. Breakfast is the only meal served. The hotel has a top-floor swimming pool and solarium. El Cid is off the Passeig de Vilanova in the center of town.

Hotel Subur. Passeig de la Ribera, s/n, 08870 Sitges. ☎ **93-894-00-66.** Fax 93-894-69-86. 96 units. A/C MINIBAR TV TEL. 12,500 ptas. ($75) double. Rates include breakfast. AE, DC, MC, V. Parking 1,200 ptas. ($7.20).

The first hotel built in Sitges (in 1916), the Subur was later torn down and reconstructed in 1960 and last renovated in 1992. Today, as always, it occupies a prominent position in the center of town on the seafront. Its small rooms are well furnished, with balconies opening onto the Mediterranean. The dining room, decorated with fine woods, offers a bountiful table of regional and international dishes, and there is a *menú del día* for guests for only 2,000 ptas. ($12). The hotel remains open year-round, even during the cooler months.

Sitges Park Hotel. Carrer Jesús, 16, 08870 Sitges. ☎ **93-894-02-50.** Fax 95-894-08-39. 85 units. A/C TV TEL. 7,800–12,000 ptas. ($46.80–$72) double. AE, DC, MC, V. Closed Dec–Feb.

Outside, the Sitges Park has an 1880s redbrick facade. Inside, past the desk, a beautiful garden with palm trees and a swimming pool awaits. This was once a private villa, owned by a family who made its fortune in Cuba. Rooms come in various shapes and sizes, but each is well furnished with good beds, plus a well-kept private bathroom clad in tiles. You'll find a good restaurant downstairs, and you can have your coffee or drinks indoors or outdoors at the cafe/bar, surveying the landmark Catalán tower on the premises. The hotel is about 50 yards from the bus station.

WHERE TO DINE
EXPENSIVE

El Velero. Passeig de la Ribera, 38. ☎ **93-894-20-51.** Reservations required. Main courses 1,800–5,000 ptas. ($10.80–$30); fixed-price menu 3,000 ptas. ($18). AE, DC, MC, V. Daily 1:30–4pm and 8:30–11:30pm. SEAFOOD.

This is one of the leading restaurants of Sitges, occupying a position along the beachfront promenade. The most desirable tables are found on the glass greenhouse terrace, opening onto the esplanade, although there is a more glamorous restaurant inside. Try a soup, such as clam and truffle or whitefish, followed by a main dish such as paella marinara (with seafood) or suprême of salmon in pinenut sauce.

MODERATE

Chez Jeanette. Sant Pau, 23. ☎ **93-894-00-48.** Reservations recommended. Main courses 1,200–2,650 ptas. ($7.20–$15.90); *menú del día* 1,850 ptas. ($11.10). AE, DC, V. Daily 7–11:30pm; Sat–Sun 1–4pm. Closed Dec 20–Jan 15. INTERNATIONAL.

A Frenchwoman named Jeanette established a Catalán-style restaurant here in 1975. She has since died, but her culinary tradition continues. Patrons flock to the rustic atmosphere created by textured stucco walls and a regional tavern decor. Set back on a restaurant-flanked street a short walk from the beach, it draws both straight and gay clients. From the standard menu, you can order such dishes as onion soup, *rape* (monkfish) with whisky, and entrecôte with Roquefort sauce. There are also several *platos del día.* The chef is proudest of his *parilla pescada,* a mixed grill of fresh fish from the Mediterranean.

✪ **Els Quatre Gats.** Sant Pau, 13. ☎ **93-894-19-15.** Reservations recommended. Main courses 3,000–4,500 ptas. ($18–$27); *menú del día* 2,500 ptas. ($15). AE, DC, MC, V. Thurs–Tues 1–4pm and 8–11pm. Closed Nov–Mar. CATALÁN.

When it was established in the early 1960s as a bar and cafe, it adopted the name of one of Catalonia's most historic cafes, Els 4 Gats, a Barcelona hangout that had been a favorite of Picasso. By 1968 the newcomer was firmly established as one of the leading restaurants in Sitges, serving a well-received *cocina del mercado,* based on whatever was fresh and available that day in the local markets. In a setting accented with paintings and varnished paneling, you can enjoy fresh grilled fish, garlic soup, lamb cutlets with local herbs, roast chicken in wine sauce, and veal kidneys in sherry sauce. Set on a side street near the sea, the restaurant is a few steps from the beachfront Passeig de la Ribera.

Fragata. Passeig de la Ribera, 1. ☎ **93-894-10-86.** Reservations recommended. Main dishes 2,500–3,500 ptas. ($15–$21). AE, DC, MC, V. Daily 1–4:30pm and 8:30–11:30pm. SEAFOOD.

Although its simple interior offers little more than well-scrubbed floors, tables with crisp napery, and air-conditioning, some of the most delectable seafood specialties in town are served here, and hundreds of loyal customers come to appreciate the fresh, authentic cuisine. Specialties include seafood soup, a mixed grill of fresh fish, codfish salad, mussels marinara, several preparations of squid and octopus, plus some flavorful meat dishes, such as grilled lamb cutlets.

La Masía. Passeig Vilanova, 164. ☎ **93-894-10-76.** Reservations required. Main courses 1,600–3,200 ptas. ($9.60–$19.20); *menú del día* 1,800 ptas. ($10.80). AE, DC, MC, V. Daily 1–4pm and 8:30–11:30pm. CATALÁN.

A provincial decor complements the imaginative regional specialties for which this place has been known since 1972. They include several preparations of codfish, roast suckling lamb well seasoned with herbs, *pollo ajillo* (garlic chicken, a regional dish), a wide array of fresh fish and shellfish, and monkfish with aïoli—the chef's pride. Every Catalonian's favorite dessert is *crema Catalána* (caramel pudding). If you prefer to dine outdoors, you can sit in the pleasant garden adjacent to the main dining room.

Mare Nostrum. Passeig de la Ribera, 60. ☎ **93-894-33-93.** Reservations required. Main courses 2,250–2,800 ptas. ($13.50–$16.80). AE, DC, MC, V. Thurs–Tues 1–4:30pm and 8–11pm. Closed Dec 15–Feb 1. SEAFOOD.

This landmark restaurant was established in 1950 in what had been a private home built in the 1890s. It has flourished ever since. The dining room has a waterfront view, and in warm weather tables are placed outside. The menu includes a full range of seafood dishes, among them grilled fish specialties and steamed hake with champagne. The fish soup is particularly delectable. Next door, the restaurant's cafe serves ice cream, milk shakes, sandwiches, a selection of tapas, and three varieties of sangría, including one with champagne and fruit.

Oliver's. Isla de Cuba, 39. ☎ **93-894-35-16.** Reservations required. Main courses 1,800–2,500 ptas. ($10.80–$15). MC, V. Sat–Sun 1–4pm; Tues–Sun 8:30–11:30pm. CATALÁN/ INTERNATIONAL.

On the northern fringe of the old town, directly south of the Plaça de Maristany, this angular bistro-style establishment is decorated like a regional tavern with local paintings. It is a good choice for dinner, unless you insist on being on the beachfront esplanade, 5 minutes away. The wines are reasonably priced, and the seafood is excellent—look for the chef's daily specials. Also try the grilled salmon, entrecôte flavored with herbs of Provence, grilled goat cutlets, or a daily soup prepared with fresh ingredients.

SITGES AFTER DARK

One of the best ways to pass an evening in Sitges is to walk the waterfront esplanade, have a leisurely dinner, then retire about 11pm to one of the open-air cafes for a nightcap and some serious people-watching. Few local dives can compete with the scene taking place on the streets.

If you're straight, you may have to hunt to find a bar that isn't predominantly gay. There are so many gay bars, in fact, that a map is distributed pinpointing their locales. Nine of them are concentrated on **Carrer Sant Bonaventura** in the center of town, a 5-minute walk from the beach (near the Museu Romàntic). If you grow bored with the action in one place, you just have to walk down the street to find another. Drink prices run about the same in all the clubs.

Mediterráneo, Sant Bonaventura, 6 (no phone), is the largest gay disco and bar. It sports a formal Iberian garden and sleek modern styling. And upstairs in this restored 1690s house just east of the Plaça d'Espanya are pool tables and a covered terrace. On summer nights, the place is filled to overflowing.

Other gay bars include **Bourbon's,** Sant Bonaventura, 13 (☎ **93-894-33-47**), which appeals to a predominately youngish crowd, and **El Candil,** carrer de la Carreta, 9 (no phone), with a wider age range and a darkroom and video shows. **El Horno,** Joan Tarrida, 6 (☎ **93-894-09-09**), with slight leather overtones that grow more prominent as the night progresses, opens earlier, at 5:30pm, and also features videos and a darkroom.

Another of the town's most popular and crowded nightspots, with DJs spinning the latest dance hits, is **Ricky's Disco,** Sant Pau, 25 (☎ **93-894-96-81**), which charges a cover of 1,200 ptas. ($7.20). This place caters to an international mix of gay and straight visitors. It's set back from the beach on a narrow street noted for its inexpensive restaurants and folkloric color.

Trailer, Angel Vidal, 36 (no phone), is a large, extremely popular club and the best place to end the night. It closes at 5:30am, and the entry cost of 1,500 ptas. ($9) includes the price of a drink.

12 Girona & the Costa Brava

The Costa Brava, the so-called wild coast, is a 95-mile (153km) stretch of coastline—the northernmost Mediterranean seafront in Spain—that begins north of Barcelona at Blanes and stretches toward the French border. Visit this area in May, June, September, or October and avoid July and August, when tour groups from northern Europe book virtually all the hotel rooms.

Undiscovered little fishing villages along the coast long ago bloomed into resort towns. **Tossa de Mar** is the most delightful of them. **Lloret de Mar** is immensely popular but too commercial and overdeveloped for many tastes. The most unspoiled spot is remote **Cadaqués.** Some of the smaller villages make excellent stops.

If you want to visit the Costa Brava but simply cannot secure a room in high season, consider taking a day trip by car from Barcelona or booking one of the daily organized tours that leave from that city. Allow plenty of time for driving. In summer the traffic jams can be fierce, and the roads between towns difficult and winding.

If you visit the coast in summer without a hotel reservation, you'll stand a fair chance of getting a room in Girona, the capital of the province and one of the most interesting medieval cities in Spain.

1 Girona

60 miles (97km) NE of Barcelona, 56 miles (90km) S of the French city of Perpignan

Founded by the Romans, Girona is one of the most important historical sites in Spain. Later, it became a Moorish stronghold. Later still, it reputedly withstood three invasions by Napoléon's troops (1809). For that and other past sieges, Girona is often called "The City of a Thousand Sieges."

Split by the Onyar River, this sleepy medieval city attracts crowds of tourists darting inland from the Costa Brava for the day. For orientation purposes, go to the ancient stone footbridge across the Onyar. From here, you'll have the finest view. Bring good walking shoes, as the only way to discover the particular charm of this medieval city is on foot. You can wander for hours through the **Call,** the labyrinthine old quarter, with its narrow, steep alleyways and lanes and its ancient stone houses, which form a rampart chain along the Onyar. Much of Girona can be appreciated from the outside, but it does contain some important attractions you'll want to see on the inside.

Girona & the Costa Brava

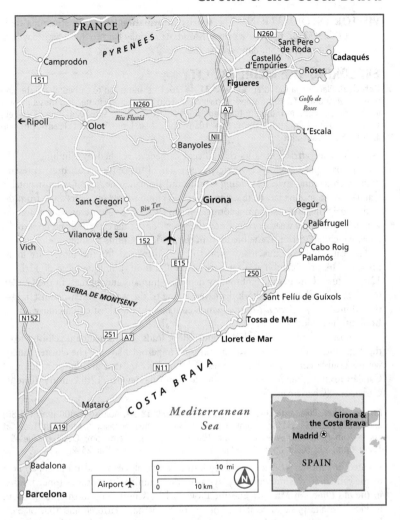

ESSENTIALS

GETTING THERE More than 26 trains per day run between Girona and Barcelona from 6:08am to 9:26pm, including two **TALGOS**. Trip time is 1 to 2 hours, depending on the train. Trains arrive in Girona at the Plaça Espanya (☎ 972-20-70-93 for information).

From the Costa Brava, you can take one of the **SARFA** buses (☎ 972-20-17-96 in Girona) to Girona. Three per day depart from Tossa de Mar (see the "Tossa de Mar" section later in this chapter). Barcelona Bus (☎ 972-20-24-32 in Girona) also operates express buses between Girona and Barcelona at the rate of 6 to 13 per day, depending on the season and demand.

From Barcelona or the French border, drivers connect with the main north-south route (A-7), taking the turnoff to Girona. From Barcelona, take the A-2 north to reach the A-7.

VISITOR INFORMATION   The **tourist information office** is at Rambla de la Libertat (☎ **972-22-65-75**). It's open Monday to Friday 8am to 8pm, Saturday 8am to 2pm and 4 to 8pm, Sunday 9am to 2pm.

EXPLORING THE MEDIEVAL CITY

Catedral. Plaça de la Catedral. ☎ **972-21-44-26.** Free admission to cathedral; cloister and museum 400 ptas. ($2.40). Cathedral: daily 9am–1pm and during cloister and museum visiting hours. Cloister and museum: July–Sept, Tues–Sat 10am–8pm, Sun 10am–2pm; Oct–Feb, Tues–Sat 10am–2pm and 4–6pm, Sun 10am–2pm; Mar–June, Tues–Sat 10am–2pm and 4–7pm, Sun 10am–2pm.

Girona's major attraction is its magnificent cathedral, reached by climbing a 17th-century baroque staircase of 90 steep steps. The 14th-century cathedral represents many architectural styles, including Gothic and Romanesque, but it is most notably Catalán baroque. The facade that you see as you climb those long stairs dates from the 17th and 18th centuries; from a cornice on top rises a bell tower crowned by a dome with a bronze angel weathervane. Enter the main door of the cathedral and go into the nave, which, at 75 feet, is the broadest in the world of Gothic architecture.

The cathedral contains many works of art, displayed for the most part in its museum. Its prize exhibit is a tapestry of the Creation, a unique piece of 11th- or 12th-century Romanesque embroidery depicting humans and animals in the Garden of Eden. The other major work displayed is one of the world's rarest manuscripts—the 10th-century *Códex del Beatus,* which contains an illustrated commentary on the Book of the Apocalypse.

From the cathedral's Chapel of Hope, a door leads to a Romanesque cloister from the 12th and 13th centuries, with an unusual trapezoidal layout. The cloister gallery, with a double colonnade, has a series of biblical scenes that are the prize jewel of Catalán Romanesque art. From the cloister you can view the 12th-century Torre de Carlemany (Charlemagne's Tower).

Museu d'Art. Pujada de la Catedral, 12. ☎ **972-20-38-34.** Admission 300 ptas. ($1.80) adults, 225 ptas. ($1.35) for students and adults over 65, free for children. Mar–Sept, Tues–Sat 10am–7pm (June–Aug, Wed hours are 10am–2pm), Sun 10am–2pm; Oct–Feb, Tues–Sat 10am–6pm, Sun 10am–2pm. Closed Jan 1, Jan 6, Easter Sun, and Dec 25–26.

Located in a former Romanesque and Gothic Episcopal palace (Palau Episcopal) next to the cathedral, this museum displays artworks spanning 10 centuries (once housed in the old Diocesan Museum and the Provincial Museum). Stop in the throne room to view the altarpiece of Sant Pere of Púbol by Bernat Martorell and that of Sant Miguel de Crüilles by Lluís Borrassa. Both of these works, from the 15th century, are exemplary pieces of Catalán Gothic painting. The museum is also proud of its altar stone of Sant Pere de Roda, which dates from the 10th and 11th centuries; this work in wood and stone, depicting figures and legends, was once covered in embossed silver. The 12th-century *Crüilles Timber* is a unique piece of Romanesque polychrome wood. *Our Lady of Besalù,* from the 15th century, is one of the best Virgins carved in alabaster.

Banys Arabs. Carrer Ferran el Catôlic. ☎ **972-21-32-62.** Admission 200 ptas. ($1.20). Apr–Sept, Mon–Sat 10am–7pm, Sun 10am–2pm; Oct–Mar, Tues–Sun 10am–2pm. Closed Jan 1, Jan 6, Easter Sun, and Dec 25–26.

These 12th-century Arab baths, an example of Romanesque civic architecture, are found in the old quarter of the city. Visit the *caldarium* (hot bath), with its paved floor, and the *frigidarium* (cold bath), with its central octagonal pool surrounded by pillars that support a prismlike structure in the overhead window. Although the Moorish baths were heavily restored in 1929, they give you an idea of what the ancient ones were like.

Museu Arqueològic. Sant Pere de Galligants, Santa Llúcia, 1. ☎ **972-20-26-32.** Admission 300 ptas. ($1.80) adults, 225 ptas. ($1.35) children and students. Tues–Sat 10am–1pm and 4:30–7pm; Sun 10am–1pm.

Housed in a Romanesque church and cloister from the 11th and 12th centuries, this museum illustrates the history of the country from the Paleolithic to the Visigothic periods, using artifacts discovered in nearby excavations. The monastery itself ranks as one of the best examples of Catalán Romanesque architecture. In the cloister, note some Hebrew inscriptions from gravestones of the old Jewish cemetery.

Museu d'Història de la Ciutat. Carrer de la Força. ☎ **972-22-22-29.** Free admission. Tues–Sat 10am–2pm and 5–7pm; Sun 10am–2pm.

Housed in the old 18th-century Capuchin Convent de Sant Antoni, this collection dates from the time of Puig d'en Roca (Catalonia's oldest prehistoric site) to the present. It includes Girona's (and Spain's) first electric streetlights. Additional displays of tools, technical materials, and the accoutrements of passing lifestyles make up a kind of municipal resume. From the original Capuchin convent, there remains the cemetery used for drying corpses before mummifying them (one of three of this type left in the world).

Església de Sant Feliu. Pujada de Sant Feliu. ☎ **972-20-14-07.** Free admission. Daily 9–10:30am, 11:30am–1pm, and 4–6:30pm; holidays 4–6:30pm.

This 14th-to 17th-century church was built over what may have been the tomb of Feliu of Africa, martyred during Diocletian's persecution at the beginning of the 4th century. Important in the architectural history of Catalonia, the church has pillars and arches in the Romanesque style and a Gothic central nave. The bell tower—one of the Girona skyline's most characteristic features—has eight pinnacles and one central tower, each supported on a solid octagonal base. The main facade of the church is baroque. The interior contains some exceptional works, including an altarpiece from the 16th century and an alabaster *Reclining Christo* from the 14th century. Notice the eight pagan and Christian sarcophagi set in the walls of the presbytery, the two oldest of which are from the 2nd century A.D. One shows Pluto carrying Persephone off to the depths of the earth.

SHOPPING

Consistent with its role as an international seaside resort, Girona has a network of shops catering to everything from sportswear to formal wear. The most appealing, and densely inventoried, shopping street is the **carrer Santa Clara,** one of whose most visible shops is **Adolfo Domínguez,** carrer Santa Clara, 36 (☎ 972-22-29-61), whose inventories of men's and women's clothing derives from Spain and the rest of Europe. For men's and women's sportswear, try **Tommy,** Rambla Llibertat, 28 (☎ 972-22-36-93), or its almost-adjacent neighbor specializing only in women's clothing, **Casual,** Rambla Llibertat, s/n (no phone). Finally, consider **Zara,** carrer Joán Maragall, s/n (☎ 972-22-13-05), as a stylish but very affordable emporium for both men and women.

If handcrafts appeal to you, consider a 20-mile (32km) eastward trek from Girona to the hamlet of **La Bispal,** which is set more or less midway between Girona and the town of Palamos. (From Girona, follow the signs pointing to Palamos.) Here, rows of simple shops display and sell the output of dozens of artisans who labor to produce sturdy, artfully rustic ceramics, some of which are too bulky to ship, others that can be packed and carried as part of your carry-on luggage.

WHERE TO STAY
MODERATE

Costabella. Avinguda de França, 61, 17007 Girona. ☎ **972-20-25-24.** Fax 972-20-22-03. 46 units. A/C MINIBAR TV TEL. 10,500–14,000 ptas. ($63–$84) double. AE, DC, MC, V. Free parking.

Built in the 1960s and renovated in 1989 and again in 1999, this hotel is about 2 miles (3km) north of Girona's center, beside the N-11 highway leading to Figueres, near the town's largest hospital. The midsize rooms are comfortable, outfitted in pastel colors, and conservatively modern, each fitted with good beds and tiled bathrooms. An in-house restaurant serves fixed-price meals, and breakfast is a generous buffet.

Hotel Carlemany. Plaça Miguel Santalo, 17002 Girona. ☎ **9072-21-12-12.** Fax 972-21-49-94. www.gm.es/carlemany. E-mail: carlemany@gm.es. 90 units. A/C TV TEL. 15,000 ptas. ($90) double; 21,000 ptas. ($126) suite. AE, MC, V. Parking 1,650 ptas. ($9.90).

In a commercial area only 10 minutes from the historic core, this 1995 four-star hotel is the city's best. A favorite of business travelers, it is sleek and contemporary with an ultramodern design and a cavernous interior of marble, polished wood, Oriental carpets, and tropical plants. The midsized to spacious bedrooms are soundproofed and are light, airy, and comfortable, with fully equipped bathrooms. El Pati Verd offers a tempting menu of Catalán and international dishes, and there is a 24-hour coffee shop. Guests relax at night in the Vienne Piano Bar. Amenities include room service, concierge, and laundry.

Hotel Ultonia. Avinguda Jaume I, 22, 17001 Girona. ☎ **972-20-38-50.** Fax 972-20-33-34. 45 units. A/C MINIBAR TV TEL. 10,500–12,500 ptas. ($63–$75) double. AE, DC, MC, V. Parking 800 ptas. ($4.80) nearby.

A three-star hotel just a short walk from the Plaça de la Independència, the Ultonia was restored in 1993 and is now better than ever. Since the late 1950s it has been a favorite with business travelers, but today it attracts more tourists, as it is close to the historical district. Rooms are compact and furnished in modern style with functional but comfortable beds. Double-glazed windows keep out the noise. Some of the rooms opening onto the avenue have tiny balconies. In just 8 to 12 minutes, you can cross the Onyar into the medieval quarter. Guests enjoy a breakfast buffet in the morning, but no other meals are served.

Meliá Confort Girona. Carretera Barcelona, 112, 17003 Girona. ☎ **972-40-05-00.** Fax 972-24-32-33. www.solmelia.com. E-mail: melia.confort.girona@solmelia.es. A/C MINIBAR TV TEL. 17,100 ptas. ($102.60) double; 24,000 ptas. ($144) suite. AE, DC, MC, V. Parking:1,300 ptas. ($7.80).

This is a runner-up to Carlemany. In a commercial district, this member of the large Spanish chain opened in 1990 and attracts mostly business travelers. About 20 minutes from the resorts of the Costa Brava, it is often used as an emergency accommodation in summer when the beach hotels are packed. Modern and functional, it lacks a personal touch in decorations, but rooms are spacious, well cared for, comfortable, and contain fully equipped bathrooms. The hotel restaurant serves Mediterranean and international dishes daily, and there is a bar open to midnight. Amenities include 24-hour service, laundry, and concierge.

INEXPENSIVE

Condal. Joan Maragall, 10, 17002 Girona. ☎ /fax **972-20-44-62.** 38 units. 5,800–7,200 ptas. ($34.80–$43.20) double. AE, MC, V.

Near the rail and bus stations west of the old town, this third-class 1960s hotel is, in the words of one frequent visitor, "aggressively simple." As such, it's recommended to bargain hunters only. The lounge and reception area are small; there is no elevator; and no meals (not even breakfast) are served—but these are minor concerns. The small rooms are clean and functional, and some of them open onto pleasant views. Each comes with a comfortable bed. The attendants speak only a little English, but they are more than willing to try.

Hotel Peninsular. Carrer Nou, 5, 17001 Girona. ☎ **972-20-38-00.** Fax 972-21-04-92. 45 units. TV TEL. 6,500 ptas. ($39) double. AE, DC, MC, V. Parking 850 ptas. ($5.10) nearby.

Devoid of any significant architectural character, this one-star hotel provides clean but uncontroversial accommodations in a location near the cathedral and the river. The small rooms, which benefited from a 1990 renovation, are scattered over five different floors. The hotel is better for short-term stopovers than for prolonged stays. Only breakfast is served, but 24-hour room service is available.

A NEARBY PLACE TO STAY

✪ **Hostal de la Gavina.** Plaça de la Rosaleda, 17248 S'Agaro (Girona). ☎ **972-32-11-00.** Fax 972-32-15-73. www.iponet.es/gavinaywwn.lhw.com. E-mail: gavina@iponet.es. 73 units. A/C MINIBAR TV TEL. 25,500–42,000 ptas. ($153–$252) double; from 38,000 ptas. ($228) suite. AE, DC, MC, V. Closed Nov–Apr. Parking 1,600 ptas. ($9.60) garage; free outside.

Since its establishment in the early 1980s, the Hostal de la Gavina has attracted some of the most glamorous people in the world, including King Juan Carlos, Elizabeth Taylor, and a host of celebrities from northern Europe. It is on a peninsula jutting seaward from the center of S'Agaro, within a thick-walled Iberian villa originally built as the private home of the Ansesa family (the owners of the hotel) in 1932. The public rooms, the main restaurant, and most of the accommodations are in the resort's main building, which has been enlarged and modified since its original construction. The spacious rooms are the most sumptuous in the area, with elegant appointments, deluxe fabrics, plush towels, toiletries, luxury mattresses, and hair dryers. Many of the paneled public rooms are enclaves of taste and style. A large and very modern swimming pool is a short walk away, above the town's public beach. Adjacent to the pool is a beach house, containing a whirlpool, a handful of boutiques, and a daytime restaurant.

Dining/Diversions: The daytime restaurant is **Las Conchas,** which serves fresh salads, brochettes, and light platters beside the pool. More formal evening meals are served in the main building, in the **Candlelight Restaurant,** which features well-prepared international specialties and an outdoor patio. There are also two bars.

Amenities: 24-hour room service, hairdresser, massage, laundry and valet, concierge, two tennis courts, paddle tennis courts, two bars, masses of well-tended gardens, whirlpool, swimming pool.

WHERE TO DINE

Bronsoms. Sant Francesc, 7. ☎ **972-21-24-93.** Reservations recommended. Main courses 1,200–2,200 ptas. ($7.20–$13.20); fixed-price menu 1,200 ptas. ($7.20). AE, MC, V. Tues–Sun 1–4pm and 8–11:30pm. CATALÁN.

Set in the heart of the old town, within an 1890s building that was originally a private home, this restaurant is one of the most consistently reliable in Girona. The subject of praise from newspapers as far away as Madrid, it has been under its present management since 1982, perfecting the art of serving a Catalán-based *cocina del mercado*—that is, cooking with whatever market-fresh ingredients are available each day. The frequently ordered house specialties include fish paella, *arroz negro* (black rice, tinted with squid ink and studded with shellfish), white beans, and several preparations of Iberian ham.

Cal Ros. Calle Cort Reial, 9. ☎ **972-21-73-79.** Reservations recommended. Main courses 950–2,500 ptas. ($6–$15.75). MC, V. Tues–Sun 1–4pm and Tues–Sat 8–11pm. CATALÁN.

Set in the oldest part of Girona, near the plaza de Cataluña, this restaurant has thrived as a culinary and municipal staple since the 1920s. It was named after a long-ago light-haired owner (Cal Ros translates from the Catalán as "the blond person"), although exactly who that was, no one today seems to remember. You'll be seated in any of four rustically outfitted dining rooms, each with heavy ceiling beams, exposed stone and plaster, and a sense of old Catalonia. Menu items include most of the staples of conservative Catalán cuisine, including a savory *sopa empordanesa,* made with veal, pork, and local herbs and vegetables; at least four kinds of local fish, usually braised with potatoes and tomatoes; tender fried fillets of veal with mushrooms; and flaky homemade pastries, some of them flavored with anise-flavored cream.

✪ **El Cellar de Can Roca.** Carret Taiala, 40. ☎ **972-22-21-57.** Reservations recommended. Main courses 1,800–3,800 ptas. ($10.80–$22.80); fixed-price menus 3,800–6,000 ptas. ($22.80–$36). AE, DC, MC, V. Tues–Sat 1–4pm and 9–11pm. CATALÁN.

Just 1¼ miles (2km) from the center of Girona, El Cellar de Can Roca is the best of the new spate of restaurants appearing in Girona, and represents the success of the campaign to transform Girona into one of the more fashionable and lively cities in Spain. Run by three young brothers, the restaurant is small and intimate, with only 12 tables. The interior is modern in appearance, with earthy tones. The cuisine is an interesting combination of traditional Catalán dishes creatively transformed into contemporary Mediterranean fare. Start with an avocado puree, and for dessert you can't pass up the mandarin orange sorbet with pumpkin compote.

Largada. Avinguda Ramon Folch, 7. ☎ **972-21-84-05.** Reservations recommended. Main courses 800–2,050 ptas. ($4.80–$12.30). AE, MC, V. Daily 1–4pm and 8pm–midnight. GRILLED MEATS/CATALÁN.

Popular and animated, this restaurant is in the heart of Girona's historic core, across the plaza from the post office, within a quartet of brick-trimmed dining rooms that resulted from the conversion of an antique house originally built in 1893. Its focal point is a wood-fired grill, from which tempting smells waft out onto the street, drawing customers in for succulent portions of grilled pork, beef, chicken, and seafood. Beer and wine taste wonderful with the food here; recognizing that, wines are relatively inexpensive, and the beer is always cold.

GIRONA AFTER DARK

Central Girona has a good number of tapas bars and cafes, some of which don't have easily distinguishable names. Many of them are scattered along **La Rambla,** around the edges of the keynote **Plaça de Independencia,** and within the antique boundaries of the **Plaça Ferrán el Católic.** Moving at a leisurely pace from one to another is considered something of an art form in the sultry heat of Girona's early evenings. Some animated tapas bars in the city center include **Bar de Tapes,** carrer Barcelona, 13, (☎ **972-41-01-64**), near the railway station, and **Tapa't,** Plaça de l'Oli (no phone), which is noteworthy for its old-timey, old-fashioned charm. Also appealing for its crowded conviviality and its impressive roster of shellfish and seafood tapas is **Bar Boira,** Plaça de Independencia, 17 (☎ **972-20-30-96**).

Beginning around 11pm, you might want to drop into one or another of the town's discos, the most popular of which includes **Disco/Sala de Fiestas Platea,** carrer Reial de Fontclara, s/n (☎ **972-22-72-88**). In the city's oldest core, it's open Wednesday to Sunday beginning at 11pm. (Be warned in advance that your greatest difficulty will be finding the place; the street it's on is a narrow alleyway just behind Girona's main post office.) Newer, with less of a track record but a rapidly evolving style that appeals to everyone between the ages of 23 and around 45 who likes to dance, is **Discoteca 7 Artes,** carrer Sant'Narcis, s/n (no phone), which is open Wednesday to Saturday from 11pm until at least 4am.

Despite the appeal of the above-mentioned sites, one of the most appealing things to do in Girona after dark, at least between June and September, is to cross to the opposite side of the river into the verdant precincts of the **Parque de la Devesa.** This park is an artfully landscaped terrain of stately trees, flowering shrubs, kiosk-style refreshment stands, and open-aired bars, which in some cases have disco music and patrons dancing on wooden decks. One of the most appealing is **Disco Glops,** Parque de la Devesa (no phone), which rocks and rolls in the open air every Wednesday evening from around 10:30pm till dawn. Entrance is free; beer costs around 250 ptas. ($1.50).

2 Lloret de Mar

62 miles (100km) S of the French border, 42 miles (68km) N of Barcelona

Although it has a good half-moon–shaped sandy beach, Lloret is neither chic nor sophisticated, and most of the people who come here are tourists on package tours and Europeans looking for an inexpensive vacation. The competition for cheap rooms is fierce.

Lloret de Mar has grown at a phenomenal rate from a small fishing village with just a few hotels to a bustling resort with more hotels than anyone can count. And more keep opening up, although there are never enough in July and August. The accommodations are typical of those in other Costa Brava towns, running the gamut from impersonal modern box-type structures to vintage whitewashed, flowerpot-adorned buildings on the narrow streets of the old town. There are even a few pockets of posh, including the Hotel Roger de Flor (see below). The area has rich vegetation, attractive scenery, and a mild climate.

ESSENTIALS

GETTING THERE   From Barcelona, take a train to Blanes, then take a bus 5 miles (8km) to Lloret.

If you drive, head north from Barcelona along the A-19.

VISITOR INFORMATION   The **tourist information office** is at Plaça de la Vila, 1 (☎ **972-36-47-35**). It's open daily 9am to 1pm and 4 to 8pm.

WHERE TO STAY

Many of the hotels—particularly the three-star establishments—are booked solidly by tour groups. Here are some possibilities if you reserve in advance.

EXPENSIVE

Gran Hotel Monterrey. Carretera de Tossa, 17310 Lloret de Mar. ☎ **972-36-40-50.** Fax 972-36-35-12. www.arrakis.es/ghmonter. E-mail: ghmonter@arrakis.es. 620 units. A/C MINIBAR TEL. 20,500 ptas. ($123) double; 27,000 ptas. ($162) suite. AE, DC, MC, V. Closed Oct–Mar. Free parking.

Ranked just under Roger de Flor, this four-star hotel is like a deluxe country club in a spacious park, a short walk from the casino, town center, and beaches. The hotel was founded in the '40s and has been partly renovated almost every year since its opened. It's well known as a retreat for those who want to recharge their batteries. The interior areas have big windows with expansive views. Rooms are spacious and luxuriously decorated with classic furnishings, and most of them have balconies or lounge areas, private safes, and well-maintained bathrooms with big tubs and robes.

Dining/Diversions: A hotel restaurant specializes in a French and Mediterranean cuisine. There are two bars, one devoted to karaoke.

Amenities: Two swimming pools (one indoor), limited room service, laundry and dry cleaning, concierge, three tennis courts, children's garden, sauna, hydromassage, beauty spa, whirlpool.

✪ **Hotel Roger de Flor.** Turó de l'Estelat, s/n, 17310 Lloret de Mar. ☎ **972-36-48-00.** Fax 972-37-16-37. E-mail: rogerdeflor@nexo.es. 95 units. TV. 18,000–24,000 ptas. ($108–$144) double; 32,000–38,000 ptas. ($192–$228) suite. AE, DC, MC, V. Free parking.

This much-enlarged older hotel, some of which is reminiscent of a dignified private villa, is a pleasant diversion from the aging and unimaginative slabs of concrete filling other sections of the resort. Set at the eastern edge of town, the hotel offers the most pleasant and panoramic views of any hotel. Potted geraniums, climbing masses of bougainvillea, and evenly spaced rows of palms add elegance to the combinations of new and old architecture. The midsized rooms are high-ceilinged, modern, and filled with excellent furnishings, including quality mattresses and fine linens. The public rooms contain plenty of exposed wood and spill out onto a partially covered terrace, which functions as a centerpiece for the dining and drinking facilities.

Dining/Diversions: The modern and panoramic **L'Estelat** restaurant, near an airy and comfortable bar, serves international food.

Amenities: Room service (offered 8am to 10:30pm), laundry, concierge, baby-sitting, car rentals, shopping boutique, outdoor swimming pool filled with pumped-in seawater set within the garden, tennis courts, billiard room, card lounge.

✪ **Hotel Santa Marta.** Playa de Santa Cristina, 17310 Lloret de Mar. ☎ **972-36-49-04.** Fax 972-36-92-80. 78 units. A/C MINIBAR TV TEL. 22,000–35,000 ptas. ($132–$210) double; 35,000–50,000 ptas. ($210–$300) suite. July–Sept full board is recommended for 12,000 ptas. ($72). AE, DC, MC, V. Closed Dec 23–Jan 31. Free parking.

This tranquil hotel, a short walk above a crescent-shaped bay favored by swimmers, is nestled amid a sun-flooded grove of pines. The spacious rooms offer private balconies overlooking the sea or a pleasant garden, and about two thirds contain minibars, TVs, and air-conditioning. Both the public rooms and the bedrooms are attractively paneled and filled with traditional furniture, including excellent beds. The hotel's seaside neighborhood is quiet but desirable, about 1½ miles (2km) west of the commercial center of town.

Dining/Diversions: Restaurante Santa Marta is recommended separately below. There is also an airy bar.

Amenities: Laundry and valet, concierge, baby-sitting, car-rental kiosk, solarium, limited room service.

MODERATE

Hotel Vila del Mar. Calle de la Vila, 55, 17310 Lloret de Mar. ☎ **972-36-50-08.** Fax 972-37-11-68. 36 units. A/C TV TEL. 15,600 ptas. ($93.60) double. AE, DC, MC, V. Parking 1,100 ptas. ($6.60).

This century-old hotel is a short walk from the beach, close to the heart of town near the bus station. Behind its exterior is a rather mundane but well-maintained interior with a nautical feel. The soundproof rooms are pleasantly decorated and well equipped, and bathrooms have hydromassage and a hair dryer. The on-site restaurant serves Mediterranean dishes, especially fish, and amenities include a swimming pool, a gym, a sauna, a nursery, 24-hour room service, laundry, and concierge.

INEXPENSIVE

Hotel Excelsior. Passseig Mossèn Jacinto Verdaguer, 16, 17310 Lloret de Mar. ☎ **972-36-61-76.** Fax 972-37-16-54. www.gna.es/lloret. E-mail: exc@mx2.redestb.es. 45 units. TV TEL. July–Sept (including obligatory half board), 8,800 ptas. ($52.80) per person double; Oct–June (including breakfast), 3.800–4,800 ptas. ($22.80–$28.80) per person double. AE, DC, V. Closed Oct 31–Apr 1. Parking 1,200 ptas. ($7).

This well-managed three-star hotel attracts a beach-oriented clientele from Spain and northern Europe, many of whom have returned every summer since the hotel opened in 1978. The Excelsior sits almost directly on the beach, rising six floors above the esplanade, and contains an elevator. All but a handful of the rooms offer either frontal or lateral views of the sea, and some have TVs. The furniture is modern but uninspiring. The hotel frequently renews its mattresses and its rooms. Mediterranean food in the restaurant, Les Petxinea, is well prepared, and clients seem generally content with the services provided. There is also a restaurant offering simple, buffet-style meals. During midsummer, half board is obligatory.

Hotel Marsol. Passeig Jacint Verdaguer, 7, 17310 Lloret de Mar. ☎ **972-36-57-54.** Fax 972-37-22-05. 115 units. A/C MINIBAR TV TEL. 8,500–13,500 ptas. ($51–$81) double. Rates include breakfast. AE, DC, MC, V.

Completely refurbished and vastly improved in 1992, this medium-size hotel opens directly onto beachfront action. Its chief drawing card is its rooftop swimming pool with sauna and solarium. Favored by an essentially European clientele, it offers sleekly modern small rooms, each with satellite TV, air-conditioning, radio, personal safe, good beds, soundproof windows, and minibar. Occupying the ground floor is a cafeteria serving drinks and snacks, plus a restaurant, Els Dofins, overlooking a palm-shaded plaza.

WHERE TO DINE

El Trull. Cala Canyelles, s/n. ☎ **972-36-49-28.** Reservations not necessary. Main courses 1,800–5,350 ptas. ($10.80–$32.10); fixed-price menus 1,800 ptas. ($10.80). AE, DC, MC, V. Daily 1–4pm and 8–11:30pm (till midnight on weekends). SEAFOOD.

Since its establishment in 1975, this restaurant has attracted hordes of Spanish clients who appreciate the beautiful scenery of the 2-mile (3km) trek north of Lloret into the nearby hills. Set in the modern suburb of Urbanización Playa Canyelles and known for its enduring popularity, El Trull positions its tables within view of a well-kept garden and a (sometimes crowded) swimming pool. The food is some of the best in the neighborhood. Menu items focus on seafood and include fish soup; a fish stew heavily laced with lobster; many variations of hake, monkfish, and clams; and an omelet "surprise." (The waiter will tell you the ingredients if you ask.)

Restaurante Santa Marta. In the Hotel Santa Marta, Playa de Santa Cristina. ☎ **972-36-49-04.** Reservations recommended. Main courses 3,200–3,800 ptas. ($19.20–$22.80); fixed-price menu 6,000 ptas. ($36). AE, DC, MC, V. Daily 1:30–3:30pm and 8:30–10:30pm. Closed Dec 23–Jan 31. INTERNATIONAL/CATALÁN.

Set in the previously recommended 40-year-old hotel about 1½ miles (2km) west of the commercial center of town (see "Where to Stay," above), this pleasantly sunny enclave offers well-prepared food and a sweeping view of the beaches and the sea. Menu specialties vary with the seasons but might include pâté of wild mushrooms in a special sauce, smoked salmon with hollandaise on toast, médaillons of monkfish served with a mousseline of garlic, a ragout of giant shrimp with broad beans, a fillet of beef Stroganoff, and a regionally inspired cassolet of chicken prepared with cloves.

LLORET DE MAR AFTER DARK

Casino Lloret de Mar. Carrer Esports, 1. ☎ **972-36-65-12.** Admission 550 ptas. ($3.30).

Games of chance include French and American roulette, blackjack, and chemin de fer, among others. There is a restaurant, buffet dining room, bar-boîte, and dance club, along with a swimming pool. The casino is southwest of Lloret de Mar, beside the coastal road leading to Blanes and Barcelona. Drive or take a taxi at night and bring your passport for entry. Hours are Monday to Friday 5pm to 4am and Saturday and Sunday 5pm to 4:30am. (The casino closes 30 minutes later in summer.)

Hollywood. Carrer Esports, 5. ☎ **972-36-74-63.**

This dance club at the edge of town is the place to be and be seen. Look for it on the corner of carrer Girona. It's open nightly 10pm to 5am, and drinks cost from 800 ptas. ($4.80).

3 Tossa de Mar

56 miles (90km) N of Barcelona, 7½ miles (12km) NE of Lloret de Mar

This gleaming white town, with its 12th-century walls, labyrinthine old quarter, fishing boats, and fairly good sands is perhaps the most attractive base for a Costa Brava vacation. It seems to have more joie de vivre than its competitors. The battlements and towers of Tossa were featured in the 1951 Ava Gardner and James Mason movie *Pandora and the Flying Dutchman,* still sometimes seen on late-night television.

In the 18th and 19th centuries Tossa survived as a port center, growing rich on the cork industry. But that declined in the 20th century, and many of its citizens emigrated to America. In the 1950s, thanks in part to the Ava Gardner movie, tourists began to discover the charms of Tossa and a new industry was born.

To experience these charms, walk through the 12th-century walled town, known as **Vila Vella,** built on the site of a Roman villa from the 1st century A.D. Enter through the Torre de les Hores.

Tossa was once a secret haunt for artists and writers—Marc Chagall called it a blue paradise. It has two main beaches, **Mar Gran** and **La Bauma.** The coast near Tossa, north and south, offers even more possibilities.

As one of few resorts to have withstood exploitation and retained most of its allure, Tossa enjoys a broad base of international visitors—so many, in fact, that it can no longer shelter them all. In spring and fall, finding a room may be a snap, but in summer it's next to impossible unless reservations are made far in advance.

ESSENTIALS

GETTING THERE   Direct bus service is offered from Blanes and Lloret. Tossa de Mar is also on the main Barcelona–Palafrugell route. Service from Barcelona is daily 7:40am to 7:10pm, taking 1½ hours. For information, call ☎ **972-30-42-36** or 972-34-09-03.

Drive north from Barcelona along the A-19.

VISITOR INFORMATION   The **tourist information office** is at Avinguda El Pelegrí, 25 (☎ **972-34-01-08**). It's open April to October, Monday to Saturday 9am to 9pm, Sunday 10am to 1pm; off-season, Monday to Friday 10am to 1pm and 4 to 7pm, Saturday 10am to 1pm.

WHERE TO STAY
VERY EXPENSIVE

Grand Hotel Reymar. Platja de Mar Menuda, 17320 Tossa de Mar. ☎ **972-34-03-12.** Fax 972-34-15-04. 166 units. A/C MINIBAR TV TEL. 18,000–29,500 ptas. ($108–$177) double; 25,000–49,000 ptas. ($150–$294) per person in suite. Rates include breakfast. AE, DC, MC, V. Closed Nov–Apr. Parking 1,200 ptas. ($7.20).

A triumph of engineering—the hotel occupies an unusual position on a jagged rock above the edge of the sea—this gracefully contoured building was constructed in the 1960s and renovated in the early 1990s. A 10-minute walk southeast of the historic walls of the old town, the Reymar has several levels of expansive terraces ideal for sun-bathing away from the crowds below, plus a wide variety of indoor/outdoor dining and drinking areas. Each has big windows, expansive views, and a clientele devoted to relaxing in the streaming sunlight. Each good-sized room has a balcony, a sea view, a safety-deposit box, a TV with satellite reception, a marble-covered bathroom, and a combination of modern wood-grained and painted furniture.

Dining/Diversions: The hotel has four restaurants (one open in midsummer only) and at least four bars scattered amid the terraces and beachfronts. There's also a dance club.

Amenities: Limited room service, laundry and valet, concierge, baby-sitting, out-door swimming pool, whirlpool, solarium, car rentals, children's playground, tennis courts.

MODERATE

Mar Menuda. Platja de Mar Menuda, 17320 Tossa de Mar. ☎ **800/528-1234** in the U.S., or 972-34-10-00. Fax 972-34-00-87. 50 units. 15,000 ptas. ($90) double with breakfast; 20,000 ptas. ($120) double including half board July 16–Aug 21. AE, DC, MC, V. Closed Nov–Dec. Parking 1,200 ptas. ($7.20) garage; free on street.

This rustically decorated Mediterranean-style hotel offers a pool, tennis courts, a gar-den, and a big parking lot. A restaurant serves competently prepared meals. The small rooms are pleasant and comfortably furnished, all with private bathrooms and 10 with air-conditioning, minibars, TVs, and phones (naturally, they are booked first).

INEXPENSIVE

Hotel Cap d'Or. Passeig de Vila Vella, 1, 17320 Tossa de Mar. ☎/fax **972-34-00-81.** 11 units. 9,000–10,000 ptas. ($54–$60) double. MC, V. Closed Nov–Mar.

Perched on the waterfront on a quiet edge of town, this 1790s building, originally a fish store, nestles against the stone walls and towers of the village castle. Built of rugged stone itself, the Cap d'Or is like an old country inn and seaside hotel combined. It is both neat and well run. Rooms come in different shapes and sizes, but are decently maintained, each with a good bed and a small tiled bathroom with a shower stall. The old-world dining room, with its ceiling beams and ladder-back chairs, has a pleasant sea view. Although the hotel is a bed-and-breakfast, it does have a terraza on the promenade offering tapas, salads, pizzas and ice cream.

Hotel Diana. Plaça de Espanya, 6, 17320 Tossa de Mar. ☎ **972-34-18-86.** Fax 972-34-18-86. 21 units. 9,500–13,000 ptas. ($57–$78) double. AE, DC, MC, V. Closed Nov–Apr.

Set back from the esplanade, this two-star hotel is a former villa designed in part by students of Gaudí. It boasts the most elegant fireplace on the Costa Brava. An inner patio—with towering palms, vines and flowers, and fountains—is almost as popular with guests as the sandy front yard beach. The spacious rooms contain fine traditional furnishings; many open onto private balconies.

Hotel Neptuno. La Guardia, 52, 17320 Tossa de Mar. ☎ **972-34-01-43.** Fax 972-34-19-33. 124 units. June–Sept 5,500 ptas. ($33) per person double; off-season (including breakfast), 3,500 ptas. ($21) per person double. Rates include breakfast. AE, DC, MC, V. Closed Nov–Mar. Free parking.

The popular Neptuno sits on a quiet residential hillside northwest of Vila Vella, somewhat removed from the seaside promenade and the bustle of Tossa de Mar's inner core. Built in the 1960s, the hotel was renovated and enlarged in the late 1980s. Inside, antiques are mixed with modern furniture, creating a personalized decor; the beamed-ceiling dining room is charming, and the bedrooms are tastefully lighthearted, modern, and sunny, each fitted with a good bed and a small tiled bathroom. A small pool with its own terraced garden has a view of the sloping forest next door. This place is a longtime favorite with northern Europeans, who often book it solid during July and August.

Hotel Tonet. Plaça de l'Església, 1, 17320 Tossa de Mar. ☎/fax **972-34-02-37.** 36 units. June–Sept 9,500 ptas. ($57) double; off-season 6,800 ptas. ($40.80) double. Rates include breakfast. AE, DC, MC, V. Parking 1,500 ptas. ($9) nearby.

Established in the early 1960s, in the earliest days of the region's tourist boom, this simple, family-run pension is one of the resort's oldest. Renovated since then, it is on a central plaza surrounded by narrow streets. It maintains the ambience of a country inn, with upper-floor terraces where guests can relax or have breakfast amid potted vines and other plants. There's a somewhat sleepy bar on the premises where tapas and snacks are served and a simple dining room for clients taking half board. The small rooms are rustically simple, with wooden headboards and furniture. Tonet maintains its own brand of well-entrenched Iberian charm.

Hotel Vora la Mar. Avinguda de La Palma, 14, 17320 Tossa de Mar. ☎ **972-34-03-54.** Fax 972-34-11-03. 60 units. TEL. 6,500–9,500 ptas. ($39–$57) double. AE, DC, MC, V. Closed Nov–Apr. Free parking 5 min. from hotel; 1,000 ptas. ($6) garage parking nearby.

On a quiet street a block away from the beach, this hotel was built in the 1950s and renovated in the 1970s. It has an outdoor cafe, a garden, and a dining room. The terrazzo-floored bedrooms are comfortable but rather small, many with balconies. The furnishings are a little tired, but the mattresses still have life and comfort in them.

WHERE TO DINE

Bahía. Passeig del Mar, 19. ☎ **972-34-03-22.** Reservations recommended. Main courses 1,500–3,975 ptas. ($9–$23.85); *menú del día* 1,000–3,500 ptas. ($6–$21). AE, DC, MC, V. Daily 1–4:30pm and 7:30–11:30pm. CATALÁN.

Adjacent to the sea, Bahía is well-known for a much-awarded chef and a history of feeding hungry vacationers since 1953. Menu favorites are for the most part based on time-honored Catalán traditions and include *simitomba* (a grilled platter of fish), brandade of codfish, baked monkfish, and an array of grilled fish—including *salmonete* (red mullet), *dorada* (John Dory), and *calamares* (squid)—depending on what's available from local fisherfolk. (Most fish served here are caught locally.)

✪ **Es Molí.** Carrer Tarull, 5. ☎ **972-34-14-14.** Reservations recommended. Main courses 1,500–3,800 ptas. ($9–$22.80); fixed-price menus 3,500–4,500 ptas. ($21–$27). AE, DC, MC, V. Daily 1–3:30pm and 7:30–11:30pm. Closed Dec 1–Apr 1. CATALÁN.

The best and most beautiful restaurant in Tossa is behind the church, in the courtyard of a stone-walled windmill built in 1856. You'll dine beneath one of three arcades, each facing a three-tiered fountain. There is a cluster of iron tables near the garden for those who prefer the sunlight. Among the specialties are an elaborately presented platter of local grilled fish, a delightful sole amandine, fisher's cream soup, salad Es Molí (garnished with seaweed), hazelnut cream soup, hake and shrimp in garlic sauce, crayfish flambéed with Calvados, and a long list of well-chosen wines. The impeccably dressed waiters serve with a flourish.

TOSSA DE MAR AFTER DARK

In Tossa de Mar's fast-changing nightlife, there is little stability or reliability. However, one club that's been in business for a while is the **Ely Club,** carrer Bernat, 2 (☎ 972-34-00-09). Fans from all over the Costa Brava come here to dance to up-to-date tunes. Daily hours are 10pm to 5am between March 15 and October 15 only. It is closed otherwise. In July and August there is a one-drink minimum. Beer starts at 500 ptas. ($3), and whisky drinks start at 1,000 ptas. ($6). The Ely Club is in the center of town between the two local cinemas.

4 Figueres

136 miles (219km) N of Barcelona, 23 miles (37km) E of Girona

In the heart of Catalonia, Figueres once played a role in Spanish history. Philip V wed Maria Luisa of Savoy here in 1701 in the church of San Pedro, thereby paving the way for the War of the Spanish Succession. But that historical fact is nearly forgotten today: The town is better known as the birthplace of surrealist artist Salvador Dalí in 1904.

There are two reasons for visiting Figueres: one of the best restaurants in Spain and the Dalí Museum.

ESSENTIALS

GETTING THERE   RENFE has hourly train service between Barcelona and Figueres. All trains between Barcelona and France stop here.

It's better and faster to take the train if you're coming from Barcelona. But if you're in Cadaqués (see the section later in this chapter), there are five daily SARFA buses making the 45-minute trip.

Figueres is a 40-minute drive from Cadaqués. Take the excellent north-south highway, the A-7, either south from the French border at La Jonquera or north from Barcelona, exiting at the major turnoff to Figueres.

VISITOR INFORMATION   The **tourist information office** is at the Plaça del Sol (☎ 972-50-31-55). The office is open June 21 to September, Monday to Saturday 8:30am to 8pm; October until Easter, Monday to Friday 8:30am to 3pm; and Easter to June 20, Monday to Friday 8:30am to 3pm and 4:30 to 8pm, Saturday 9am to 1pm.

VISITING THE DALÍ MUSEUM

✪ **Teatre Museu Dalí.** Plaça de Gala-Dalí, 5. ☎ **972-67-00.** Admission 1,000 ptas. ($6) adults, 800 ptas. ($4.80) students and adults over 65, free for children under 9. July to mid-Sept, daily 9am–7:45pm; mid-Sep to June, Tues–Sun 10:30am–5:45pm. Visits available various nights in July and Aug; call for information.

The internationally known Dalí was as famous for his surrealist and often erotic imagery as he was for his flamboyance and exhibitionism. At the Figueres museum, in the center of town beside the Rambla, you'll find his paintings, watercolors, gouaches, charcoals, and pastels, along with graphics and sculptures, many rendered with seductive and meticulously detailed imagery. His wide-ranging subject matter encompassed such repulsive issues as putrefaction and castration. You'll see, for instance, *The Happy Horse,* a grotesque and lurid purple beast the artist painted during one of his long exiles at Port Lligat. A tour of the museum is an experience. When a catalog was prepared, Dalí said with a perfectly straight face, "It is necessary that all of the people who come out of the museum have false information."

The Mad, Mad World of Salvador Dalí

Salvador Dalí (1904–89) became one of the leading exponents of surrealism, depicting irrational imagery of dreams and delirium in a unique, meticulously detailed style. Famous for his eccentricity, he was called "outrageous, talented, relentlessly self-promoting, and unfailingly quotable." At his death at age 84, he was the last survivor of the three famous *enfants terribles* of Spain (the poet García Lorca and the filmmaker Luís Buñuel were the other two).

For all his international renown, Dalí was born in Figueres and he died in Figueres. Most of his works are in the eponymous Theater-Museum there, built by the artist himself around the former theater where his first exhibition was held. Dalí was also buried in the Theater-Museum, next door to the church that witnessed both his christening and his funeral—the first and last acts of a perfectly planned scenario.

Salvador Felipe Jacinto Dalí i Domènech, the son of a highly respected notary, was born on May 11, 1904 in a house on carrer Monturiol in Figueres. In 1922 he registered at the School of Fine Arts in Madrid and went to live at the prestigious Residencia de Estudiantes. There, his friendship with García Lorca and Buñuel had a more enduring effect on his artistic future than his studies at the school. As a result of his undisciplined behavior and the attitude of his father, who clashed with the Primo de Rivera dictatorship over a matter related to elections, the young Dalí spent a month in prison.

In the summer of 1929, the artist René Magritte, along with the poet Paul Éluard and his wife, Gala, came to stay at Cadaqués, and their visit caused sweeping changes in Dalí's life. The young painter became enamored of Éluard's wife; Dalí left his family and fled with Gala to Paris, where he became an enthusiastic member of the surrealist movement. Some of his most famous paintings—*The Great Masturbator, Lugubrious Game,* and *Portrait of Paul Éluard*—date from

For additional insights into the often bizarre aesthetic sensibilities of Spain's most famous surrealist, consider a 25-mile (40km) trek from Figueres eastward along highway C-252, following the signs to Parlava. In the village of Púbol, whose permanent population almost never exceeds 200, you'll find the **Castell de Púbol,** carrer Gala Salvador Dalí, s/n (☎ **972-48-82-11**). Stately and severely dignified, dating from 1000, it was partially ruined when bought by Dalí as a residence for his estranged wife, Gala, in 1970, on the condition that he would come only when she invited him. (She almost never did.) After her death in 1982, Dalí moved in for 2 years, moving on to other residences in 1984 after his bedroom mysteriously caught fire one night. Quieter, more serious, and much less surrealistically flamboyant than the houses in Port Lligat and Figueres, the castle is noteworthy for its severe Gothic and Romanesque dignity and for furniture and decor that follow the tastes of the surrealist master. (Don't expect a lot of paintings—that's the specialty of the museum at Figueres.) Between June 15 and September 15, the castle is open daily 10:30am to 7:30pm. Between March 13 and June 14, and September 16 to November 1, it's open Tuesday to Sunday 10:30am to 5:30pm. It's closed in winter. Entrance costs 700 ptas. ($4.20) for adults, 500 ptas. ($3) for students, and free for children under 9.

his life at Port Lligat, the small Costa Brava town where he lived and worked off and on during the 1930s.

Following Dalí's break with the tenets of the surrealist movement, his work underwent a radical change, with a return to classicism and what he called his mystical and nuclear phase. He became one of the most fashionable painters in the United States and seemed so intent on self-promotion that the surrealist poet André Breton baptized him with the anagram "Avida Dollars." Dalí wrote a partly fictitious autobiography titled *The Secret Life of Salvador Dalí* and *Hidden Faces,* a novel containing autobiographical elements. These two short literary digressions earned him still greater prestige and wealth, as did his collaborations in the world of cinema (such as the dream set for Alfred Hitchcock's *Spellbound,* 1945) and in those of theater, opera, and ballet.

On August 8, 1958, Dalí and Gala were married according to the rites of the Catholic church in a ceremony performed in the strictest secrecy at the shrine of Els Àngels, just a few miles from Girona.

During the 1960s, Dalí painted some very large works, such as *The Battle of Tetuán.* Another important work painted at this period is *Perpignan Railway Station,* a veritable revelation of his paranoid-critical method that relates this center of Dalí's mythological universe to his obsession with painter Jean-François Millet's *The Angelus.*

In 1979 Dalí's health began to decline, and he retired to Port Lligat in a state of depression. When Gala died, he moved to Púbol, where, obsessed by the theory of catastrophes, he painted his last works, until he suffered severe burns in a fire that nearly cost him his life. Upon recovery he moved to the Torre Galatea, a building he had bought as an extension to the museum in Figueres. Here he lived for 5 more years, hardly ever leaving his room, until his death in 1989.

WHERE TO STAY

Empordá. Antigua Carretera de Francia, s/n (N-II), 17600 Figueres. ☎ **972-50-05-62.** Fax 972-50-93-58. www.hotelemporda.com. E-mail: hotelemporada@hotelemporada. com. 42 units. A/C TV TEL. 12,000–15,000 ptas. ($72–$90) double; 17,000–20,000 ptas. ($102–$120) suite. AE, DC, MC, V. Parking 1,200 ptas. ($7.20).

Although the restaurant here is a gastronomic landmark (see "Where to Dine," below), the hotel associated with it simply provides reasonably priced accommodations for those passing between France and Spain, usually on business. It does not lie near the beach, it does not have a pool, and although the midsized rooms are comfortable and distinguished, it is not designed as a place for long-term sojourns. It has three floors of rooms.

Hotel Pirineos. Ronda de Barcelona, 1, 17600 Figueres. ☎ **972-50-03-12.** Fax 972-50-07-66. 55 units. A/C TV TEL. 8,000 ptas. ($48) double. Rates include breakfast. AE, DC, MC, V. Parking 1,000 ptas. ($6).

This pleasant hotel near the main road leading to the center of town is a 5-minute walk from the Dalí Museum. The hotel's restaurant takes up most of the ground floor, and there's also a bar. Many of the comfortable but small rooms have balconies, but furnishings are rather plain, although the beds are good.

Hotel President. Ronad Ferial, 33, 17600 Figueres. ☎ **972-50-17-00.** Fax 972-50-19-97. 77 units. A/C MINIBAR TV TEL. 9,000 ptas. ($54) double. AE, DC, MC, V. Free parking.

Since 1970 this has been one of the most desirable accommodations in town, lying in the center of town a 5-minute walk to the Dali Museum. An austere exterior belies the welcoming comfort inside. Midsized rooms are neutrally decorated, with comfortable beds and new mattresses, and bathrooms have either a shower or combo tub/shower. The hotel restaurant serves standard fare, a medley of Mediterranean and French dishes. Amenities include limited room service, laundry, and concierge.

Hotel Ronda. Ronda Barcelona, 104, 17600 Figueres. ☎ **972-50-39-11.** Fax 972-50-16-82. 47 units. A/C TV TEL. 7,695 ptas. ($46.15) double. AE, MC, V. Free parking.

A 10-minute walk from the Dali Museum, this four-story hotel has welcomed travelers since the early '70s. They're housed in comfort at a very low price in a typically Catalán building with an unpretentious facade; the building has conventional Mediterranean-style white walls, ample balconies, and simple decorations. The small rooms are comfortable, clean, and unfrilly, each with a plain bathroom. The hotel is popular with budget-minded Europeans, so reservations in summer are important. It has a very good restaurant, El Raco, on site, and amenities include laundry and a concierge.

Hotel Travé. Carretera de Olot, 17600 Figueras. ☎ **972-50-05-91.** Fax 972-67-14-03. 70 units. A/C TV TEL. 8,500 ptas. ($51) double; 10,000–12,000 ptas. ($60–$72) suite. AE, DC, MC, V. Parking 700 ptas. ($4.20).

Built in the early '70s and last renovated in 1999, this budget hostelery has a rather austere exterior—really, a dull motel facade—but a warm and welcoming interior. Only a 5-minute walk from the center, its rooms are spacious, well maintained, and airy, albeit a bit dour in decor. The bathrooms are shiny and fully equipped. The management serves a good Mediterranean cuisine, and the amenities include a concierge, laundry, and a swimming pool.

WHERE TO DINE

Durán. Carrer Lasauca, 5, 17600 Figueres. ☎ **972-50-12-50.** Fax 972-50-26-09. Reservations required. Main courses 1,100–5,925 ptas. ($6.60–$35.55); fixed-price menus 2,500–4,000 ptas. ($15–$24). AE, DC, MC, V. Daily 12:45–4pm and 8:45–11:30pm. CATALÁN.

This popular place for a top-notch meal in the provinces had Dalí as a loyal patron. You might start with the Catalán salad, made with radishes, boiled egg, ham pâté, tuna fish, tomato, and fresh crisp salad greens. Other specialties include steak with Roquefort, *zarzuela* (fish stew), and *filetes de lenguado a la naranja* (sole in orange sauce). Like the Empordá (see below), the Durán specializes in game. Try, if it's available, the grilled rabbit on a plank, served with white wine. The French fries here, unlike those in most of Spain, are crisp and excellent. Finish off with a rich dessert or at least an espresso.

You can also stay at the Durán, in one of its 65 well-furnished rooms, each with private bathroom, air-conditioning, TV, and phone. A double goes for 9,800 ptas. ($58.80).

✪ **Empordá.** Antigua Carretera de Francia, s/n (N-II). ☎ **972-50-05-62.** Reservations required. Main courses 2,800–4,000 ptas. ($16.80–$24); fixed-price menu 5,500 ptas. ($33). AE, DC, MC, V. Daily 12:45–3:30pm and 8:30–10:30pm. CATALÁN.

A stop at this restaurant just might provide you with your finest meal in Catalonia. (See "Where to Stay," above, for its hotel recommendation.) Don't judge the place by its appearance, which is ordinary if not institutional-looking; there's nothing ordinary about the cuisine, as all the food-loving French who cross the border to dine here will tell you. This family-run restaurant, half a mile north of the center of town, gained a reputation early on among U.S. military personnel in the area for subtly prepared game and fish dishes. Salvador Dalí (who wrote his own cookbook) and Josep Pla, perhaps the country's greatest 20th-century writer, were fans. The appetizers are the finest along the Costa Brava, including such selections as duck foie gras with Armagnac, warm pâté of *rape* (monkfish) with garlic mousseline, and fish soup with fennel. The outstanding fish and seafood dishes include cuttlefish in Catalán sauce, suprême of sea bass with flan made with fennel and anchovy, and a brochette of grilled baby squids in vinaigrette. Among the meat selections are the chef's special *lieure à la royale* (hare), beef fillet in red-wine sauce with onion marmalade, and goose in a delectable mushroom sauce.

5 Cadaqués

122 miles (196km) N of Barcelona, 19 miles (30.5km) E of Figueres

This little village is still unspoiled and remote, despite the publicity it received when Salvador Dalí lived in the next-door village of Lligat in a split-level house surmounted by a giant egg. The last resort on the Costa Brava before the French border, Cadaqués is reached by a small winding road, twisting over the mountains from Rosas, the nearest major center. When you get to Cadaqués, you really feel you're off the beaten path. The village winds around half a dozen small coves, with a narrow street running along the water's edge. This street has no railing, so exercise caution.

Scenically, Cadaqués is a knockout: crystal-blue water, fishing boats on the sandy beaches, old whitewashed houses, narrow twisting streets, and a 16th-century parish up on a hill.

ESSENTIALS

GETTING THERE   Two to five buses per day run from Figueres to Cadaqués. Trip time is 1¼ hours. The service is operated by SARFA (☎ **972-25-87-13**).

VISITOR INFORMATION   The **tourist information office** is at Cotxe, 2 (☎ **972-25-83-15**). It's open Monday to Saturday 10:30am to 1pm and 4 to 7pm.

WHERE TO STAY

Hotel Playa Sol. Platja Planch, 3, 17488 Cadaqués. ☎ **972-25-81-00.** Fax 972-25-80-54. www.playasol.com. 50 units. A/C TV TEL. 13,000–22,000 ptas. ($78–$132) double. AE, DC, MC, V. Closed Jan–Feb. Parking 950–1,300 ptas. ($5.70–$7.80).

Located in a relatively quiet section of the port along the bay, this 1950s hotel has arguably the best view of the stone church at the distant edge of the harbor. The balconied building is constructed of brick and terra-cotta tiles. The small rooms are comfortably furnished; 25 are air-conditioned. The hotel doesn't have an official restaurant, but it does offer lunch over the summer from June 15 to September 15. There is a large verdant garden and an outside swimming pool.

Hotel Port Lligat. Salvador Dalí, 17488 Cadaqués. ☎ **972-25-81-62.** Fax 972-25-86-43. 30 units. TEL. 8,800–10,500 ptas. ($52.80–$63) double. Rates include breakfast. MC, V. Closed Nov; Dec–Feb open weekends only.

Many visitors find the relative isolation of this hotel—at the end of a winding gravel road a half mile outside Cadaqués—its most alluring feature. The terrace overlooks an idyllic harbor and an unusual house once occupied by Salvador Dalí. The gallery adjoining the reception lobby features a changing series of surrealist paintings. Also on the premises are a swimming pool with cabanas and a snack bar. The airy rooms, all doubles, have tile floors, exposed wood, good beds, tiled bathrooms, and balconies.

Hostal S'Aguarda. Carretera de Port Lligat, 28, 17488 Cadaqués. ☎ **972-25-80-82.** Fax 972-25-10-87. www.hotelsaguarda.es. 28 units. A/C TV TEL. 7,000–11,000 ptas. ($42–$66) double. AE, DC, MC, V. Closed Nov. Free parking.

Situated on the road winding above Cadaqués on the way to Port Lligat, this hostal has a panoramic view of the village's harbor and medieval church. Each of the modern, airy accommodations opens onto a flower-decked terrace. The rooms have tile floors and simple furniture, each with a comfortable bed. A swimming pool, solarium, and tennis courts are on the hotel grounds.

WHERE TO DINE

Don Quijote. Caridad Seriñana, 5. ☎ **972-25-81-41.** Reservations recommended. Main courses 950–2,500 ptas. ($5.70–$15); fixed-price menus 2,200–5,000 ptas. ($13.20–$30). MC, V. Daily noon–4pm and 7pm–midnight. Closed Nov–Mar. CATALÁN.

Located on the road leading into the village, this intimate bistro has a large vine-covered garden in front. You can dine either inside or alfresco. The well-prepared à la carte specialties include lamb chops, pepper steak, *zarzuela* (seafood stew), and gazpacho. The Don Quijote cup, a mixed dessert, is the best way to end a meal.

Es Trull. Port Ditxos, s/n. ☎ **972-25-81-96.** Reservations recommended. Main courses 1,800–3,500 ptas. ($10.80–$21); fixed-price menus 1,500–2,500 ptas. ($9–$15). AE, DC, MC, V. Daily 12:30–4pm and 7–11pm. Closed Nov–Easter. SEAFOOD.

On the harborside street in the center of town, this cedar-shingled cafeteria is named for the ancient olive press that dominates the interior. A filling fixed-price meal is served. According to the chef, if it comes from the sea and can be eaten, he will prepare it with that special Catalán flair. You might try mussels in a marinara sauce or grilled hake. Rice dishes are a specialty, not only paella, but also black rice colored with squid ink and rice with calamari and shrimp. Natural baby clams are yet another dining delight.

✪ **La Galiota.** Carrer Narciso Monturiol, 9. ☎ **972-25-81-87.** Reservations required. Main courses 2,000–3,000 ptas. ($12–$18); fixed-price menu 2,500–5,000 ptas. ($15–$30). AE, DC, MC, V. Daily 1:30–3:30pm and 8:30–10:30pm. Closed Nov–May. CATALÁN/FRENCH.

Dozens of surrealist paintings, including some by Dalí, adorn the walls of this award-winning restaurant, the finest in town. Located on a sloping street below the cathedral, the place has a downstairs sitting room and a dining room converted from what was a private house. The cuisine is not at all pretentious. The chef's secret is in selecting only the freshest of ingredients and preparing them in a way that enhances their natural flavors. The roast leg of lamb, flavored with garlic, is a specialty. The menu changes with the season but always features the best of French and Catalán fare. The marinated salmon is excellent, as are the sea bass and the sole with orange sauce.

CADAQUÉS AFTER DARK
L'Hostal. Paseo, 8A. ☎ **972-25-80-00.**

This distinctive place has attracted some of the most glamorous names of the art and music worlds. Some music critics have called it the second-best jazz club in Europe, and it certainly rates as the best club along the coast. It's a Dixieland bar par excellence, run by the most sophisticated entrepreneurial team in town. Habitués still remember when Salvador Dalí escorted Mick Jagger here, much to the delight of Colombian writer Gabriel García Márquez. In fact, the bar's logo was designed by Dalí himself. Heightening the ambience are the dripping candles, the high ceilings, and the heavy Spanish furniture. The best music is usually performed late at night. It's open daily 11am to 5am. Entrance is free. Beer costs from 500 to 800 ptas. ($3 to $4.80); whisky, 850 to 1,000 ptas. ($5.10 to $6).

Aragón 13

Landlocked Aragón, along with Navarre, forms the northeastern quadrant of Spain. It is an ancient land composed of three provinces: Zaragoza; remote Teruel, which is farther south; and Huesca, in the north as you move toward the Pyrenees. These are also the names of the provinces' three major cities.

Most of Aragón constitutes terra incognita for the average tourist— which is unfortunate, since it is one of the most history-rich regions of the country. You can visit it as an extension of your trip to Castile, to the west, or as a segment of your trek through Catalonia, to the east. Huesca, close to the mountains, is ideal for a summer visit—unlike most of Aragón, especially the fiercely hot southern section, which has Spain's worst climate. Winter is often bitterly cold, but spring and autumn are ideal.

Aragón is known best for two former residents: Catherine of Aragón, who foolishly married Henry VIII of England, and Ferdinand of Aragón, whose marriage to Isabella, queen of Castile and León in the 15th century, led to the unification of Spain.

Aragón also prides itself on its exceptional Mudéjar architecture and on its bullfighting tradition. In September many villages in the region have their own festivals, when bulls run through the streets. What they don't have is the good promotion that Hemingway gave the festival at Pamplona, in the neighboring province of Navarre. On the other hand, they aren't plagued with wine-drunk tourists—the curse of the Pamplona festival. In folklore, Aragón is known for the *jota,* a bounding, leaping dance performed by men and women since at least the 1700s.

Aragón's capital, Zaragoza, is the most-visited destination because it lies on the main route between Madrid and Barcelona. If you're driving from Madrid to Barcelona (or vice versa), make a detour to Zaragoza. If you get interested in Aragón while there, stick around to explore this ancient land.

1 Zaragoza

200 miles (322km) NE of Madrid, 190 miles (306km) W of Barcelona

Zaragoza (pronounced Tha-ra-*go*-tha) lies halfway between Madrid and Barcelona. This provincial capital, the seat of the ancient kingdom of Aragón, is a bustling, prosperous, commercial city of wide boulevards and arcades.

Zaragoza has not one, but two, cathedrals and, like Santiago de Compostela in Galicia, was a major pilgrimage center. According to legend, the Virgin Mary appeared to St. James, patron saint of Spain, on the banks of the Ebro River and ordered him to build a church there.

Zaragoza is at the center of a rich *huerta,* or plain. Its history dates from the Romans, who called it Caesar Augusta. Today, Zaragoza is a city of more than three quarters of a million people, just less than 75% of the entire population of Aragón.

The 40,000 students at the University of Zaragoza have livened up this once-staid city. Cafes, theaters, restaurants, music bars, and *tascas* have boomed in recent years, and more monuments have been restored and opened to the public.

ESSENTIALS

GETTING THERE **Aviaco** has direct flights to Zaragoza from Madrid and Barcelona. From the airport in Zaragoza, you can get a bus to the Plaza de San Francisco. The Iberia office in Zaragoza is at calle Bilbao, 11 (☎ **976-21-82-56**).

Eight trains arrive daily from Barcelona and eight from Madrid. The trip takes 4½ hours from Barcelona and 3½ to 5 hours from Madrid. The **RENFE** office in Zaragoza is at calle San Clemente, 13 (☎ **902-24-02-02**), just off Paseo de la Independencía.

There is one direct bus a day running between Zaragoza and Barcelona (7 hours away).

Zaragoza is easily reached on the E-90 (A-2) east from Madrid or west from Barcelona.

VISITOR INFORMATION The **tourist information office** is at Torreón de la Zuda-Glorieta Pio XII (☎ **976-39-35-37**), next to the Roman wall. It's open Monday to Friday 8:30am to 2:45pm and 3:30 to 8pm, Saturday and Sunday 10am to 1:30pm.

SPECIAL EVENTS One of the city's big festivities is the **Fiesta de la Virgen del Pilar,** held the week of October 12, with top-name bullfighters, religious processions, and general merriment.

SEEING THE SIGHTS

Basilica de Nuestra Señora del Pilar. Plaza de las Catedrales. ☎ **976-39-74-97.** Free admission to cathedral; museum 150 ptas. (90¢). Cathedral, daily 6am–9:30pm; museum, daily 9am–2pm and 4–6pm. Bus: 22 or 23.

This 16th- and 17th-century basilica on the bank of the Ebro River is in an almost Oriental style with its domes and towers. Thousands of the faithful travel here annually to pay homage to the tiny statue of the Virgin del Pilar in the Holy Chapel. The name of the cathedral, El Pilar, comes from the pillar upon which the Virgin is supposed to have stood when she asked Santiago (St. James) to build the church.

During the second week of October the church is a backdrop for an important festival devoted to Our Lady of the Pillar, with parades, bullfights, fireworks, flower offerings, and street dancing. Also of interest within the church are frescoes painted by Goya, who was born nearby.

You can also visit the Museo del Pilar, which houses the jewelry collection used to adorn the Pilar statue as well as sketches by Goya and other artists, including Bayeu. Much of the collection is ancient, such as an 18th-century ivory horn.

La Seo del Salvador. Plaza de la Seo. ☎ **976-29-12-38.** Museum admission 250 ptas. ($1.50). Museum, daily 10am–2pm and 4–8pm. Bus: 21, 22, 29, 32, 35, 36, 43, 44, or 45.

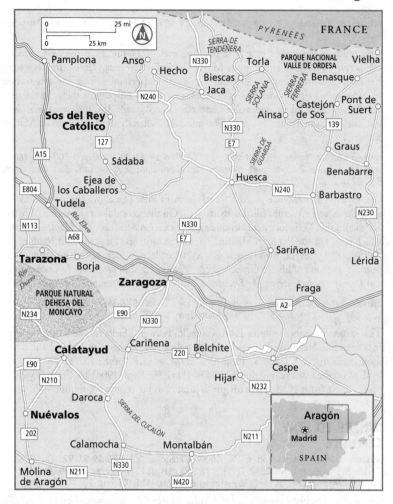

This Gothic-Mudéjar church, built between 1380 and 1550, is more impressive than El Pilar (see above). It has a rich baroque and plateresque facade and is a particularly fine example of Aragonese Gothic architecture. Among its more important features are the main altar and a fine collection of French and Flemish tapestries from the 15th to the 17th centuries, which are housed in the adjacent museum. The baroque cupolas in the Temple of Pilar were decorated by Goya and Bayeu.

Palacio de la Aljafería. Aljafería, calle Los Diputados. ☎ **976-28-95-28.** Admission 300 ptas. ($1.80) adults; 150 ptas. (90¢) students, free 11 and under. Tues–Sat 10am–2pm and 4–8pm; Sun 10am–2pm. Bus: 21 or 33.

This most unusual sight, a Moorish palace in Aragón, has been restored by the parliament and preserved as a national monument. Reminiscent of Córdoban architecture, it was built in the 11th century for Moorish kings but has seen considerable alterations and additions since then, particularly when Ferdinand and Isabella lived here.

Museo de Zaragoza. Plaza de los Sitios, 6. ☎ **976-22-21-81.** Free admission. Tues–Sun 9am–2pm. Bus: 30, 35, or 40.

This museum is installed in a 1908 building with 10 ground-floor rooms devoted to exhibits from the prehistoric to the Muslim period. The Roman legacy (rooms 4 to 8) has sculptures (the head of Augustus), mosaics, and ceramics. The fine arts section includes paintings by Goya (room 20); you can see his self-portrait there. In the next room you'll find his drawings *Los Caprichos* (*The Whims*). Also displayed is a Goya portrait of Carlos IV and his wife. The museum is directly north of Paseo de Marino Moreno.

Museo Camón Aznar. Espoz y Mina, 23. ☎ **976-39-73-28.** Admission 100 ptas. (60¢). Tues–Fri 9:15am–2:15pm and 6–9pm; Sat 10am–2pm and 6–9pm; Sun 8am–2pm. Bus: 22 or 23.

Occupying a Renaissance palace 1 block from El Pilar (see above), this museum has three floors and 23 rooms filled with artwork. On the second floor is a sketch of María Sarmiento that Velázquez made for his masterpiece *Las Meninas* (*The Maids of Honor*), which hangs in the Prado in Madrid. The Bayeu brothers (Francisco and Ramón) are represented by several works, as is Goya. His collection includes an important self-portrait, a version of his *Los Caprichos* (*The Whims*), *La Tauromaquia* (*The Tauromachy*), *Los Desastres de la Guerra* (*The Disasters of War*), and *Los Disparates* (*The Follies*).

Museo Pablo Gargallo. Plaza de San Felipe, 3. ☎ **976-39-20-58.** Free admission. Tues–Sat 10am–2pm and 5–9pm; Sun 10am–2pm. Bus: 22 or 23.

This museum honors sculptor Pablo Gargallo, born in Maella in 1881. It is installed in a beautiful Aragonese Renaissance-style palace (1659) that was declared a national monument in 1963. Gargallo, influential in the art world of the 1920s, is represented by 100 original works, ranging from *Dr. Petit's Fireplace* (1904) to *Great Prophet,* a bronze piece from 1933. The museum is located in the center, a 5-minute walk south of El Pilar.

WHERE TO STAY
EXPENSIVE

Boston. Camino de las Torres, 28, 50008 Zaragoza. ☎ **976-59-91-92.** Fax 976-59-74-10. 313 units. A/C MINIBAR TV TEL. 18,500 ptas. ($111) double; 25,000–29,000 ptas. ($150–$174) suite. AE, DC, MC, V. Parking 1,850 ptas. ($11.10). Bus: 29.

This eight-story hotel opened in 1992 in the heart of Zaragoza's modern business district, a 15-minute walk from the medieval neighborhoods that most visitors want to explore. Named in honor of Boston, Massachusetts, where the building's architect earned his degree, it's the city's best hotel and one of the tallest buildings in town. Many of its public areas are sheathed in layers of beige marble, occasionally accented with wood paneling. Throughout, the style is ultramodern, even futuristic, strongly infused with postmodern design and American ideas. Rooms are the town's finest—usually spacious, with all the modern comforts such as luxury mattresses and plush towels; each tiled bathroom is equipped with a hair dryer.

Dining: An in-house restaurant, **Niagara,** is one floor below the lobby level and serves filling fixed-price meals.

Amenities: Health club with sauna, 24-hour room service, concierge.

Hotel Palafox. Calle Casa Jiménez, s/n, 50004 Zaragoza. ☎ **976-23-77-00.** Fax 976-23-47-05. www.sendanet.es/soasa/hza/hoza26.htm. E-mail: palafox@sendanet.es. 184 units. A/C MINIBAR TV TEL. 20,500–25,000 ptas. ($123–$150) double; 28,000 ptas. ($168) suite. AE, MC, V. Parking 1,700 ptas. ($10.20). Bus: 22.

One of the top hotels in town, the Palafox looks somewhat like an apartment house. It was inaugurated in 1982 and rates five stars. A favorite of business travelers, it frequently hosts local events such as fashion shows. The midsized rooms have sleek traditional styling (often leather armchairs) and are well maintained and comfortable, with quality beds and neatly organized tiled bathrooms.

Dining: A hotel restaurant, **Puerto Sanco,** serves a traditional Aragonese cuisine.

Amenities: A rooftop swimming pool is the place to be during the long, hot summer. Sauna, massage, 24-hour room service.

MODERATE

Gran Hotel. Joaquín Costa, 5, 50001 Zaragoza. ☎ **976-22-19-01.** Fax 976-23-67-13. 134 units. A/C MINIBAR TV TEL. 15,900 ptas. ($95.40) double; from 19,500 ptas. ($117) suite. AE, DC, MC, V. Parking 1,800 ptas. ($10.80).

Located half a mile south of the cathedral, behind one of the most beautiful Hispano–art deco facades in town, this hotel is the most historic and most charming in Zaragoza and a good value. Established by King Alfonso XIII in 1929, the Gran has a domed rotunda for conversation and an array of formal public rooms and conference facilities with crystal chandeliers and classic furniture. Bedrooms have been restored into a neutral, traditional international style, yet they retain the high ceilings and spaciousness of their original design, as well as occasional touches of art deco. A favorite of the business community, the hotel offers excellent service. Hemingway and one of his biographers, A. E. Hotchner, stayed at the Gran when they were in Zaragoza.

The hotel has several restaurants, including the very elegant La Ontina where three-course fixed-price lunches and dinners are served daily. Current newspapers are available along with drinks in the bar. Other perks include 24-hour room service, laundry, and a concierge.

Hesperia. Conde de Aranda, 48, 50003 Zaragoza. ☎ **976-28-45-00.** Fax 976-28-27-17. www.hoteles-hesperia.es. E-mail: hhes@hoteles-hesperia.es. 85 units. A/C MINIBAR TV TEL. 15,000 ptas. ($90) double. AE, DC, MC, V. Parking 1,200 ptas. ($7.20).

In the historical center a 5-minute walk from the basilica of El Pilar, this five-story hotel has welcomed guests since 1994. A plain, modern exterior opens to reveal a marble-floored lobby where you'll encounter a friendly, efficient staff. There is no great stylishness here, but your comfort is ensured. Rooms are small but well furnished and inviting, each with a fully equipped bathroom. There is a hotel restaurant, El Borsao, specializing in Aragonese and Spanish cuisine, and a bar and cafeteria. Amenities include limited room service, concierge, and laundry.

Rey Alfonso I. Calle Coso, 17–19, 50003 Zaragoza. ☎ **976-39-48-50.** Fax 976-39-96-40. E-mail: reyalfonsol@husa.es. 117 units. A/C MINIBAR TV TEL. 12,000–17,500 ptas. ($72–$105) double. AE, DC, MC, V. Parking 1,4300 ptas. ($8.40). Bus: 22.

This clean, efficient hotel is a favorite with businesspeople, who prefer its location in the commercial heart of town. A prominent arcade marks the entrance. The hotel has a popular countertop-service snack bar and, in the basement, a comfortably modern restaurant. The small rooms are comfortable and modern, with especially good beds.

✪ **Vía Romana.** Calle de Don Jaime, 1, 50001 Zaragoza. ☎ **976-39-82-15.** Fax 976-29-05-11. 66 units. A/C MINIBAR TV TEL. 15,000 ptas. ($90) double. AE, DC, MC, V. Parking 1,300 ptas. ($7.80) nearby.

This is a real find in the old quarter, adjacent to Plaza del Pilar and behind a statue dedicated to Goya. A three-star hotel that is welcoming and comfortable, Vía Romana is in a superb location, especially if you want to cover the town on foot. The hotel has been beautifully restored, with a well-trained staff and inviting midsize rooms with good furnishings and comfortable beds, plus immaculately kept tiled bathrooms. For some reason, this hotel always seems fully booked in October, but you can make a reservation easily during other months. A snack bar/cafeteria is a convenient stopover if you're rushed, but the kitchen staff prepares tasty meals, both regional and international, in its more formal dining room as well. Room service, concierge, dry cleaning, and laundry are some extra features.

INEXPENSIVE

Don Yo. Juan Bruil, 4–6, 50001 Zaragoza. ☎ **976-22-67-41.** Fax 976-21-99-56. 181 units. A/C MINIBAR TV TEL. 8,800 ptas. ($52.80) double. AE, DC, MC, V.

Of course, we had to check this place out because of its intriguing name. Right in the center of town at the Plaza de Aragón and Plaza de la Independencía, it is a favorite among local journalists and draws a large repeat clientele among the business communities of Madrid and Barcelona. The hotel offers quiet, personal service, but it is not strong on atmosphere. The medium-sized rooms are well furnished, not particularly stylish, but well maintained and relaxing, with especially good beds. For comfort and good value, Don Yo is an appealing choice. The hotel's Doña Talverna is a fine choice for a meal; both regional specialties and international dishes are prepared with a certain flair. Room service, concierge, dry cleaning, and laundry are available.

Hotel Gran Via. Calle Gran Vía, 38, 50005 Zaragoza. ☎ **976-22-92-13.** Fax 976-22-07-07. 44 units. A/C MINIBAR TV TEL. 9,500 ptas. ($57) double; 10,000 ptas. ($60) suite. AE, DC, MC, V. Parking 1,500 ptas. ($9).

This two-story hotel on the Paseo Gran Vía, near the Church of Santa Engracia and close to the main shopping district, was constructed in 1980. Its architecture is modern and lacks character but is welcoming and comfortable, with rooms at a very reasonable price. You don't get a lot of frills here, as the rooms are small and functional but the white walls, carpeted floors, and excellent beds make for a restful overnight stopover. The hotel offers 24-hour room service, concierge, and laundry.

Ramiro I. Coso, 123, 50001 Zaragoza. ☎ **976-29-82-00.** Fax 976-39-89-52. www. pretur.es/. E-mail: hotels@pretur.es. 104 units. A/C MINIBAR TV TEL. 11,450–13,650 ptas. ($69–$82) double. AE, DC, MC, V. Parking 1,675 ptas. ($10). Take calle San Vincente de Paul south from the west end of the Cathedral. After 4 blocks, follow calle San Jorge west for 1 block to reach the hotel.

If you don't care about style and just want a comfortable place to sleep at a moderate price, head for the Ramiro I. It's an older establishment with much comfort although it seems to need more staff. A three-star hotel at the edge of the old town, it offers small rooms that are contemporary and functional, often booked by businesspeople, and, surprisingly, by very few tourists. There's an in-house restaurant as well as a bar.

WHERE TO DINE

Gurrea. San Ignacio de Loyola, 14. ☎ **976-23-31-61.** Reservations recommended. Main courses 2,500–3,000 ptas. ($15–$18); fixed-price menu 4,500–5,000 ptas. ($27–$30). AE, DC, MC, V. Daily 1–3:30pm; Mon–Sat 9–11:30pm. SPANISH/INTERNATIONAL.

This is a landmark in Zaragoza, committed to maintaining its reputation for good service, an attractive setting, and a time-honored cuisine. It's a favorite of the business crowd at lunchtime, and it's a good place to seal the deal. Quality ingredients are fashioned into beautifully presented delectable dishes. Menu items might include goose-meat terrine, duck with orange sauce, chateaubriand with foie gras, hake served with fruit sauce, venison meatballs (in season) with truffles, wild mushrooms with goose liver, and filet mignon in curry sauce—plus a killer array of desserts.

La Mar. Plaza Aragón, 12. ☎ **976-21-22-64.** Reservations recommended. Main courses 1,800–3,000 ptas. ($10.80–$18); fixed-price menu 5,000 ptas. ($30). AE, DC, MC, V. Mon–Sat 1:30–4pm and 9–11:30pm. SEAFOOD.

This is one of the top seafood restaurants in town. Service is leisurely, but if you're in the mood for a prolonged meal, the menu might include a full range of seasonal vegetables, peppers stuffed with seafood mousse, *dorada* cooked in a salt crust, baked sea bream, turbot with clams, grilled hake or monkfish, grilled squid, shellfish soup or shellfish rice. If you're not in the mood for fish, try the grilled beefsteak with several kinds of sauces.

La Rinconada de Lorenzo. Calle La Salle, 3. ☎ **976-55-51-08.** Reservations required. Main courses 3,000–4,000 ptas. ($18–$24); fixed-price menu 3,000 ptas. ($18). AE, DC, MC, V. Daily noon–4pm and 8–11:45pm. Bus: 40 or 45. ARAGONESE.

One of the best in town, this restaurant offers such unusual dishes as fried rabbit with snails. Oven-roasted lamb or lamb hock can be ordered in advance, but lamb skewers are always available. The chef prepares several versions of *migas* (fried bread crumbs) flavored with a number of different ingredients, including grapes and ham. Giant asparagus spears are often served. Even though Zaragoza is inland, fresh fish is always on the menu: hake, grilled sole, sea bream, and salmon, for example. Veal is featured on the menu with wild boar and veal ribs, as well as veal meatballs served in a bean stew. Desserts are all homemade, including rice pudding, chocolate mousse with cream, and fig ice cream with nuts. Regional red, white, and rosé wines make fine accompaniments.

Los Borrachos. Paseo de Sagasta, 64. ☎ **976-27-50-36.** Reservations recommended. Main courses 2,000–3,100 ptas. ($12–$18.60); tasting menu 4,500 ptas. ($27). AE, DC, MC, V. Daily 12:45–3:45pm and 8:45–11:45pm. SPANISH/FRENCH.

Solid, dignified, and committed to preserving an old-fashioned kind of service, this restaurant occupies a formal set of dining rooms near the heart of town. Menu items may include a combination platter of hake with lobster, wild boar with wine sauce, fillet of beef with a pepper-cognac sauce, roasted pheasant or rabbit, and an asparagus mousse accented with strips of Serrano ham. This restaurant's name, incidentally, translates as "The Drunkards," taken from the characters in a famous Velásquez painting.

ZARAGOZA AFTER DARK

Zaragoza seems sleepy and low-key until after around 11pm, when things perk up a bit. A good place to begin an evening's bar and pub crawl is the Plaza Santa Cruz, site of one of the city's most stylish bars, **Café Praga** (no phone) and its more relaxed and funky neighbor, **Embajada de Jamaica** (no phone), which will tempt you with party-colored drinks. A particularly animated bar belongs to a restaurant, the **Club Nautico,** Plaza Pilar (no phone), which overlooks the muddy waters of the Ebro River.

A popular hangout near the Plaza del Pilar is **Casa Amadico,** Jordán de Urriés, 3 (☎ **976-29-10-41**), where local government and business types congregate after work for tasty seafood tapas. Temptations include oysters, smoked salmon, lobster, and Serrano ham. It's open Tuesday to Sunday 1 to 4pm and 7pm to midnight, and closed in August. Another tapas bar worth a look is **Casa Luís,** Romea, 8 (☎ **976-29-11-67**), whose array of shellfish tapas includes oysters, shrimp, and razor clams in little bundles. It's open year-round, daily noon to 5pm and 8pm to midnight. A glass of wine costs 125 ptas. (75¢), and the selection of tapas ranges from 150 to 600 ptas. (90¢ to $3.60).

A disco that doesn't even begin to function until most of the others have closed is **Discoteca Kit,** calle Fernando el Católico, 70 (no phone), which begins to rock and roll around 6am. An outfit with more reasonable hours that begin around 11pm, and with the added benefit of an outdoor terrace where people dance under the moon and stars, is **Broadway,** calle Miguel Servet, 193 (☎ **976-41-67-40**). Another option is **Café Hispano,** Camino de las Torres, 42 (☎ **976-22-21-61**), a bar where singers (either professional or members of the crowd who've just gotta sing) croon danceable and drinkable songs.

If you just want to bar-hop and try different *tascas,* most of which aren't even identified with individual signs, consider a promenade along the calle Dr. Cerrada (near Plaza Pamplona), the nearby calle Dr. Casas, or calle La Paz, where neighborhood residents usually duck inside at regular intervals for a quick fix of wine or sherry.

SIDE TRIPS FROM ZARAGOZA

Goya aficionados (male ones only) can visit the **Cartuja de Aula Dei** (☎ **976-71-49-34**), a 16th-century Carthusian monastery 7 miles (11km) north of Zaragoza in Montañana. The young Goya, an Aragonese, completed one of his first important commissions here in 1774, a series of 11 murals depicting scenes from the lives of Christ and Mary. During the Napoleonic invasion, the murals suffered badly but have since been restored. Only men are admitted to this strictly run Carthusian community. The monastery is open the last Saturday of every month only from 9am to 3pm. Call ahead to arrange a time. From Zaragoza, bus number 28 departs about every half hour to the site (trip time: 20 minutes), with a one-way ticket costing 80 ptas. (50¢). Catch the bus at the stop near the Roman walls. You can also drive; take E-90 east out of town and follow the signs for Montañana.

Goya fans of both genders can go south from Zaragoza to the little village of **Fuendetodos,** where the artist was born in 1746. A small two-room cottage in the village (not his actual birthplace, however) was restored in 1985 and turned into a museum, **Casa de Goya,** Zuloaga, 3 (☎ **976-14-38-30**). You're shown transparencies of his most important works. It is open Tuesday to Sunday 11am to 2pm and 4 to 7pm. Admission is 300 ptas. ($1.80). Take the N-330 south to the town of Muel, then go 11 miles (18km) south to Villanueva del Huerve. Bear east on the A-220 and continue for 5 miles (8km) to Fuendetodos. From Zaragoza, Autobuses Samar Buil, calle Borao, 13 (☎ **976-43-43-04**) carries passengers to the village.

2 Tarazona

54½ miles (88km) W of Zaragoza, 182 miles (293km) NE of Madrid

To call this town the "Toledo of Aragón" may be a bit much, but it does deserve the name "Mudéjar City." Lying about halfway along the principal route connecting Zaragoza to the province of Soria, it is laid out in tiers above the quays of the Queiles River. Once the kings of Aragón lived here, and before that the city was known to the Romans. You can walk through the old barrio with its tall facades and narrow medieval streets.

ESSENTIALS

GETTING THERE   From Zaragoza, four buses leave daily for Tarazona (1½ hours away). If you're driving, head west from Zaragoza along the A-68, connecting with the N-122 to Tarazona.

VISITOR INFORMATION   The **tourist information office** is at calle Iglesias, 5 (☎ **976-64-00-74**). Hours are Monday to Friday 9am to 1:30pm and 4:30 to 7pm, Saturday and Sunday 10am to 1pm and 4 to 7pm.

EXPLORING TARAZONA

Tarazona's major attraction is its Gothic **cathedral,** begun in 1152 but essentially reconstructed in the 15th and 16th centuries. However, the Aragonese Mudéjar style is still much in evidence, especially as reflected in the lantern tower and belfry. The dome resembles that of the old cathedral in Zaragoza.

The town is also known for its 16th-century **Ayuntamiento (Town Hall),** which has reliefs across its facade depicting Ferdinand and Isabella retaking Granada. The monument stands on Plaza de España in the older upper town, on a hill overlooking the river. Take the Ruta Turística from here up to the church of Santa Magdalena, with a Mudéjar tower that forms the chief landmark of the town's skyline; its mirador opens onto a panoramic view. Continuing up the hill, you reach **La Concepción,** another church with a narrow brick tower.

WHERE TO STAY & DINE

Brujas de Bécquer. Teresa Cajal, 30, 50500 Tarazona. ☎ **976-64-04-00** or 976-64-04-04. Fax 976-64-01-98. 57 units. A/C TV TEL. 5,200–7,200 ptas. ($31.20–$43.20) double. AE, DC, MC, V. Parking garage 700 ptas. ($4.20).

Half a mile southeast of town beside the road leading to Zaragoza you'll find this unpretentious modern hotel, built in 1972 and renovated 20 years later. Rooms are modest but comfortable, and the beds are good with firm mattresses. The dining room serves fixed-price meals for 1,100 ptas. ($7.35) each, every day from 1 to 4pm and 8 to 10:30pm. Reservations are almost never needed. The hotel, incidentally, was named in honor of a 19th-century Seville-born patriot and poet (Gustavo Adolfo Bécquer) who praised the beauties of Aragón in some of his writing.

3 Calatayud

53 miles (85km) W of Zaragoza, 146 miles (235km) NE of Madrid

The Romans founded this town only to abandon it some time during the 2nd century, and it wasn't until the arrival of the Muslims in the 8th century that it was repopulated. The Moors were routed in 1120 by the conquering Catholic forces, who allowed some of the inhabitants to stay. But they were made virtual slaves and forced to live in a *morería* (Moorish ghetto). Some of the Moorish influence can still be seen in the town. Many 14th- and 15th-century church towers in Calatayud are reminiscent of minarets.

ESSENTIALS

GETTING THERE   Calatayud lies on the main rail line linking Madrid to Zaragoza. There are 12 trains a day from Madrid, 9 from Zaragoza, and 3 from Barcelona. There are 3 to 4 buses a day from Zaragoza (1½ hours away). Calatayud is on the E-90 linking Madrid with Zaragoza.

VISITOR INFORMATION   The **tourist information office,** at Plaza del Fuerte, s/n (☎ **976-88-63-22**), is open Monday to Friday 9am to 5pm.

EXPLORING CALATAYUD

The major attraction of Calatayud is **Santa María la Mayor,** calle de Opispo Arrué, a brick church built in Aragonese style with an ornate plateresque-Mudéjar facade and an exceptionally harmonious octagonal belfry. Nearby, on the calle Datao, **Iglesia de San Pedro de los Francos** is the leaning tower of Calatayud. It is a fine example of the Mudéjar style.

A walk along calle Unión leads to **La Parraguía de San Andrés,** with an elegant and graceful Mudéjar belfry.

Strike a path through the old Moorish quarter up the hill to the ruins of the castle that dominated Qal'at Ayyub (the old Arab name for the town). Once you're there, a panoramic view unfolds.

East of Calatayud, excavations continue to uncover the **Roman city of Bibilis,** on the Mérida–Zaragoza highway. It was the birthplace of Roman satirist Martial (ca. A.D. 40–104).

WHERE TO STAY & DINE

Hotel Calatayud. Autovia de Aragón Salida, km 237, 50300 Calatayud. ☎ **976-88-13-23.** Fax 976-88-54-38. 63 units. A/C TV TEL. 9,500 ptas. ($57) double. AE, DC, MC, V.

Of a lackluster lot, this low-slung, modern hotel is your best bet in town. About a mile (1.6km) east of Calatayud, on the N-II highway to Zaragoza, the hotel contains acceptable rooms with simple furnishings, plus good beds and well-maintained private bathrooms. It also offers a garden and a popular restaurant and bar, the only air-conditioned areas in the entire building.

4 Nuévalos/Piedra

73 miles (117.5km) W of Zaragoza, 143 miles (230km) E of Madrid

The town of Nuévalos, with its one paved road, isn't much of a lure, but thousands of visitors from all over the world flock to the **Monasterio de Piedra,** called the garden district of Aragón (see review below).

GETTING THERE

From Madrid, train connections reach Alhama de Aragón. Take a taxi from there to the monastery.

From Zaragoza, head southwest on the N-II through Calatayud. At the little town of Ateca, take the left turnoff, which is marked for Nuévalos and the Monasterio de Piedra, and drive for 14 miles (22.5km). If you're driving from Madrid, take the N-II and turn east at the spa town of Alhama de Aragón.

TOURING THE MONASTERY

In Nuévalos, the major attraction is the ✪ **Monasterio de Piedra** (☎ 976-84-90-11). *Piedra* means rock in Spanish, and after the badlands of Aragón, you expect bleak, rocky terrain. Instead, you have a virtual Garden of Eden, with a 197-foot waterfall. It was here in 1194 that Cistercian monks built a charter house on the banks of the Piedra River. The monks are long gone, having departed in 1835, and their former quarters have been reconstructed and turned into a hotel (see below).

Two pathways, marked in blue or red, meander through the grounds, and views are offered from any number of levels. Tunnels and stairways, dating from the 19th century, are the work of Juan Federico Mutadas, who created the park here. Slippery steps lead down to an iris grotto, just one of many quiet, secluded retreats. It is said the original monks inhabited the site because they wanted a "foretaste of paradise." To be honest, they were escaping the court intrigues at the powerful Monestir de Poblet in Tarragona province. The monastery at Piedra is only 2 miles (3km) from the hillside village of Nuévalos. You can wander through the monastery grounds daily 9am to 8pm in summer (closed at 5pm in winter) for an admission charge of 1,000 ptas. ($6) for adults, 550 ptas. ($3.30) for children.

WHERE TO STAY & DINE

Monasterio de Piedra. 50201 Nuévalos. ☎ **976-84-90-11.** Fax 976-84-90-54. TEL. 11,500–12,500 ptas. ($69–$75) double. AE, DC, MC, V.

This is one of the sshowplaces of Aragón. The grounds include a swimming pool, tennis courts, and, naturally, a garden, with little log bridges and masses of flowering plants and trees. The beautifully maintained rooms (all doubles), which you should reserve well in advance, have phones but no other amenities. Some open onto terraces.

Dining: A meal in the great hall is a medieval event. The room has been tastefully decorated and is a perfect backdrop for the fine Aragonese fare. Meals start at 2,500 ptas. ($15), and service is daily 8 to 11am, 1 to 4pm, and 9 to 11pm. On weekends the dining room can get crowded.

5 Sos del Rey Católico

262 miles (422km) N of Madrid, 37 miles (59.5km) SW of Pamplona

In northern Aragón, Sos del Rey Católico formed one of the Cinco Villas of Aragón, stretching along a 56-mile (90km) frontier with Navarre. These villages, in the far-distant part of northern Aragón, also included Tauste, Ejea, Uncastillo, and Sabada. Despite their small size, they were raised to the status of towns by Philip V, who was grateful for their assistance and loyalty in the War of Spanish Succession (1701–13).

The most visited town is Sos del Rey Católico, so named because it was the birth-place of Ferdinand, the Catholic king, in 1452. He entered the world's history books after his marriage to Isabella of Castile and León. Locals will point out the Palacio de Sada, where the future king is said to have been born. The town is more interesting than its minor monuments, and you can explore it at will, wandering its narrow cobbled streets and stopping at any place that attracts your fancy. The kings of Aragón fortified this village on the Navarre border with a thick wall. Much of that medieval character has been preserved—enough so that the village has been declared a national monument.

GETTING THERE

From Zaragoza to Sos, a 2½-hour ride away, there is a daily bus at 6:30pm, returning at 7am the next morning.

To drive from Zaragoza, take the N-330 to Huesca. Continue on N-330 to Jaca, then bear west on the N-240 toward Pamplona. Turn south at the cutoff to Sanguesa.

WHERE TO STAY & DINE

Parador Fernando de Aragón. Sianz de Vicuña, 1, 50680 Sos del Rey Católico. ☎ **948-88-80-11.** Fax 948-88-81-00. www.parador.es. 65 units. A/C MINIBAR TV TEL. 13,500–16,000 ptas. ($81–$96) double. AE, DC, MC, V. Closed Jan–Feb. Parking 1,000 ptas. ($6).

This member of the government-owned parador network is unusual because of the care that was taken to blend a six-story building into its medieval setting. Built in 1975 on much older foundations, it's composed mostly of stone and wood timbers, with lots of interior paneling and antique-looking accessories. Despite its location in the heart of the village, sweeping views open from some of the windows onto the nearby countryside. Coming in various shapes and sizes, each accommodation is well maintained and beautifully furnished, with quality beds and immaculately kept private bathrooms with plush towels. Hearty Aragonese food is served in the restaurant, where the *menú del día* costs 3,500 ptas. ($21). Service is daily 1 to 4pm and 8:30 to 10:30pm.

14 Navarre & La Rioja

The ancient land of Navarre (*Navarra* in Spanish, *Nafarroa* in Basque) shares an 81-mile (130km) frontier with France, with nine crossing points. This province with a strong Basque tradition is an important link between Iberia and the rest of the continent.

As a border region, Navarre has seen its share of conflict, and to this day the remains of lonely castles and fortified walled towns bear witness to that. But somehow this kingdom, one of the most ancient on the peninsula, has managed to preserve its own government and identity. Romans, Christians, Muslims, and Jews have all left their stamp on Navarre, and its architecture is as diverse as its landscape. It is also a province rich in folklore. Pagan rites were blended into Christian traditions to form a mythology that lives even today in Navarre's many festivals. Dancers and singers wear the famous red berets, the *jota* is the most celebrated folk dance, and the best-known sport is *pelota*—sometimes called *jai alai* in other parts of the world.

Navarre is also rich in natural attractions, but most foreign visitors miss them when they just visit for the **Fiesta de San Fermín** in July to see the running of the bulls through the streets of Pamplona, Navarre's capital and major city. Even if you do visit for the festival, try to explore some of the panoramic Pyrenean landscape.

Adjoining Navarre is La Rioja, the smallest region of mainland Spain—bordered not only by Navarre but also by Castile and Aragón. Extending along the Ebro River, this province has far greater influence than its tiny dimensions would suggest, because it is one of the most important wine-growing districts in Europe. The land is generally split into two sections: Rioja Alta, which gets a lot of rainfall and has a mild climate, and Rioja Baja, which is much hotter and more arid, more like Aragón. The capital of the province Logroño, a city of some 200,000, links the two regions.

The most visited towns are **Logroño** and **Haro,** the latter known for its wineries. **Santo Domingo de la Calzada** was a major stop on the ancient pilgrims' route on the way to Santiago de Compostela, while **Nájera** once served as capital for the kings of Navarre. Now little more than a village, it lies along the Najerilla River.

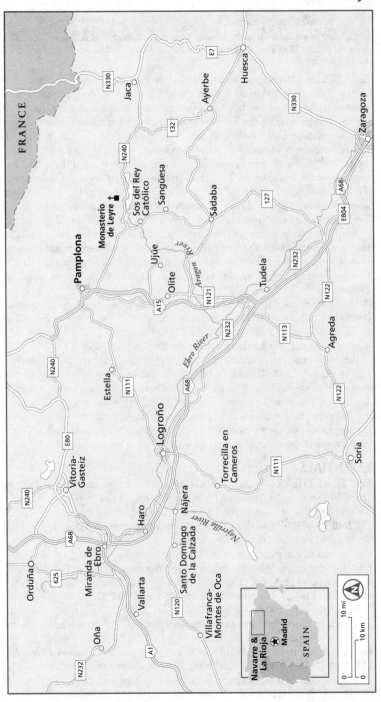

FRANCE

N330

Jaca

Ayerbe

E7

Huesca

N330

Zaragoza

132

N240

Sos del Rey
Católico

Sangüesa

Sádaba

127

A68

E804

Monasterio
de Leyre

Pamplona

Ujué

Olite

Aragón River

N121

N232

Tudela

N122

A15

N232

N113

Agreda

N240

Estella

N111

Logroño

A68

Ebro River

N122

E80

Torrecilla en
Cameros

N111

Soria

Vitoria-
Gasteiz

Haro

Nájera

Najerilla River

N240

A68

Miranda de
Ebro

Santo Domingo
de la Calzada

Orduña

625

Vallarta

N120

Villafranca-
Montes de Oca

Oña

N232

A1

Navarre &
La Rioja

Madrid

SPAIN

10 mi

10 km

0

0

1 Pamplona (Iruña)

56 miles (90km) SE of San Sebastián, 239 miles (385km) NE of Madrid, 104 miles (167.5km) NE of Zaragoza

In 1927, Ernest Hemingway wrote *The Sun Also Rises;* his descriptions of the running of the bulls made Pamplona known throughout the world. The book's glamour remains undiminished for the crowds who read it and then rush off to Pamplona to see the *encierros* during the Fiesta de San Fermín. Attempts to outlaw this world-famous ceremony have failed so far, and it remains a superstar attraction, particularly among bullfighting aficionados. The riotous festival usually begins on July 6 and lasts to the 14th. Fireworks and Basque flute concerts are only some of the spectacles giving added color to the fiesta. Wine flows and people party nonstop for the duration. Those who want to know they'll have a bed after watching the *encierro* should reserve a year in advance at one of the city's handful of hotels or boarding houses or stay in San Sebastián or some other neighboring town and visit Pamplona during the day.

But Pamplona is more than just a city where an annual festival takes place. Long the most significant town in Spain's Pyrenean region, it was also a major stopover for those traveling either of two frontier roads: the Roncesvalles Pass or the Velate Pass. Once a fortified city, it was for centuries the capital of the ancient kingdom of Navarre.

In its historic core, the Pamplona of legend lives on, but the city has been engulfed by modern real-estate development. The saving grace of new Pamplona is La Tacon-era, a spacious green swath of fountain-filled gardens and parkland west of the old quarter where you will see students from the University of Navarre.

Pamplona became the capital of Navarre in the 10th century. Its golden age was during the reign of Charles III (called "the Noble"), who gave it its cathedral, where he was eventually buried. Over the years the city has been the scene of many battles, with various factions struggling for control. Those who lived in the old quarter, the Navarrería, wanted to be allied with Castile, whereas those on the outskirts favored a French connection. Obviously, Castile eventually won out, although some citizens of Navarre today want Pamplona to be part of a newly created country of the Basque lands.

ESSENTIALS

GETTING THERE   Pamplona is the air hub of the Navarre region. The city is served by two weekday **Aviaco** flights from both Madrid and Barcelona; international connections can be made from either city. Arrivals are at Aeropuerto de Noaín (☎ **948-16-87-00**), 4 miles (6.5km) from the city center and accessible only by taxi, about 1,200 ptas. ($7.20).

Three trains a day arrive from Madrid (trip time: 5 to 6 hours) and two to three from Barcelona (7 to 9 hours). Pamplona also has three daily train connections from San Sebastián to the north (1¼ hours) and four to seven daily from Zaragoza to the south (2 to 3 hours). For information, call ☎ **948-13-02-02.**

Buses connect Pamplona with several major Spanish cities: four per day from Barcelona (6 hours), five to seven per day from Zaragoza (3½ hours), and nine per day from San Sebastián (1½ hours). Instead of being able to call for information, you'll have to consult the bulletin board's list of destinations at the **Estación de Autobuses** (☎ **948-22-38-54**) at calle Conde Oliveto (corner of calle Yanguas y Miranda). Nearly 20 privately owned bus companies converge here, and it's a mass of confusion.

The A-15 Navarra national highway begins on the outskirts of Pamplona and runs south to join A-68, midway between Zaragoza and Logroño. N-240 connects San Sebastián with Pamplona.

Pamplona

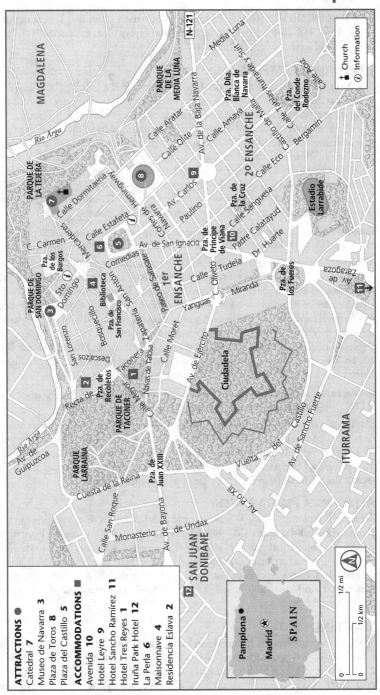

ATTRACTIONS ●
Catedral **7**
Museo de Navarra **3**
Plaza de Toros **8**
Plaza del Castillo **5**

ACCOMMODATIONS ■
Avenida **10**
Hotel Leyre **9**
Hotel Sancho Ramírez **11**
Hotel Tres Reyes **1**
Iruña Park Hotel **12**
La Perla **6**
Maisonnave **4**
Residencia Eslava **2**

✝ Church
ⓘ Information

SPAIN
Pamplona ●
Madrid ✳

1/2 mi
1/2 km

N-121

MAGDALENA

Río Arga

PARQUE DE LA TEJERA

PARQUE DE LA MEDIA LUNA

Media Luna

Media Luna

Calle Aoiz

Pza. del Conde Rodezno

Pza. Dña. Blanca de Navarra

Calle Aratar

Calle Olite

Av. de la Baja Navarra

Av. Calle Amaya

Calle Eco

Calle Ignacio de Maña

Castillo de Maya

Calle Tablas Iturralde y Suit

Bergamin

2º ENSANCHE

Estadio Larrabide

Calle Dormitaeria

Calle Estafeta

Mercaderes

Cortes de Navarra

Hemingway

Av. Carlos

Navarra

Paulino

Pza. de la Cruz

Calle Sanguesa

Padre Calatayud

Dr. Huarte

Pza. de los Fueros

Av. de Zaragoza

ITURRAMA

Av. de San Ignacio

Av. de San Ignacio

Pza. de Príncipe de Viana

Calle Oliveto

Tudela

Miranda

C. Carmen

Pza. de los Burgos

Sto. Domingo

PARQUE DE SAN DOMINGO

Biblioteca

Comedias

Pza. de San Francisco

Bosquecillo

Descalzos

San Lorenzo

San Antón

Zapatería

Taconera

Paseo de Sarasate

1er ENSANCHE

Calle Moret

Yanguas

C. Cristina

Recta de Recoletos

Pza. de Recoletos

PARQUE DE TACONER

Calle Mayor

Navas de Tolosa

Calle de Taloba

Av. de Ejército

Ciudadela

PARQUE LARRAINA

Río Arga

Av. de Guipuzcoa

Cuesta de la Reina

Calle San Roque

Pza. de Juan XXIII

Av. de Bayona

de Undax

Monasterio

Av. Pío XII

Vuelta del Castillo

Av. de Sancho Fuerte

SAN JUAN DONIBANE

VISITOR INFORMATION   The **tourist information office** is at Duque de Ahumada, 3 (☎ 948-20-65-40). It's open Monday to Friday 10am to 2pm and 4 to 7pm, Saturday and Sunday 10am to 2pm.

EXPLORING PAMPLONA

The heart of Pamplona is **Plaza del Castillo,** formerly the bullring, built in 1847. Today it is the seat of the autonomous provincial government. This elegant tree-lined paseo becomes a virtual communal bedroom during the Festival of San Fermín.

The narrow streets of the old quarter extend from three sides of the square. The present bullring, **Plaza de Toros,** is just east and south of this square alongside the Paseo Hemingway. Running parallel to the east of the square is **calle Estafeta,** a narrow street that is the site of the running of the bulls. With its bars and *tascas*, it attracts university students and is lively all year, even without a festival. During the festival it is the most frequented place in town next to the Plaza del Castillo. The bulls also run through the barricaded streets of Santo Domingo and Mercaderes.

Catedral. Curia. ☎ **948-22-56-79.** Free admission to cathedral; museum, 500 ptas. ($3). July 1–Sept 15, daily 10am–7pm; off-season, daily 8:30am–1:30pm and 4–7pm.

The most important sight in Pamplona is the cathedral, dating from the late 14th century on the site of a former Romanesque basilica. The present facade, a mix of neoclassical and baroque, was the work of Ventura Rodríguez, architect to Charles III. The interior is Gothic with lots of fan vaulting. In the center is the alabaster tomb of Charles III and his Castilian wife, Queen Leonor, done in 1416 by Flemish sculptor Janin de Lomme. The 14th- and 15th-century Gothic cloisters are a highlight of the cathedral. The Barbazán Chapel, off the east gallery, is noted for its vaulting. The Museo Diocesano, housed in the cathedral's refectory and kitchen, displays religious objects, spanning the era from the Middle Ages to the Renaissance.

Museo de Navarra. Cuesta de Santa Domingo, s/n. ☎ **948-42-64-92.** Admission 300 ptas. ($1.80). Tues–Sat 9:30am–2pm and 5–7pm; Sun 11am–2pm.

The major museum of Pamplona is housed in a 16th-century hospital, Nuestra Señora de la Misericordia, located close to the river. It has rich collections of Roman artifacts, including some 2nd-century mosaics, and Romanesque art, plus an important Goya portrait of the Marqués de San Adrián. Gothic and Renaissance paintings are on the second floor. Murals from the 13th century are another highlight.

ATTENDING A PELOTA MATCH

While in Pamplona, you might want to head about 3½ miles (6km) outside town to **Frontón Euskal–Jai Berri** (☎ 948-33-11-59), along the avenida de Francia, to check out a professional *pelota* (jai alai) match. Game times are Tuesday, Saturday, and Sunday at 4pm and on regional and national holidays. Four matches are usually played on game days, and tickets can be purchased any time during the sets. Admission to the bleachers is 1,600 to 1,800 ptas. ($9.60 to $10.80). We'd recommend leaving the betting to the experts.

SHOPPING

You'll find lots of Navarese handcrafts in kiosks scattered through the old city, but for a particularly well-inventoried outlet, head for **Echeve,** calle Estafeta, 47 (☎ 948-22-28-34); it sells such handcrafted items as vests, ceramics, hats, wood carvings, and *botas* (wine skins), which locals use to squirt wine, with great dexterity, into their open mouths. A roughly equivalent competitor is **Tienda Anel,** calle Comedias, 7 (☎ 948-22-44-38), which sells wine skins, neckerchiefs, and wide belts known as

The Running of the Bulls

Beginning at noon on July 6 and continuing nonstop to July 14, the ✪ **Fiesta de San Fermín** is one of the most popular events in Europe, drawing thousands of tourists who overtax the severely limited facilities of Pamplona.

Get up early (or don't go to bed in the first place), since the bulls run every day at 8am sharp. To watch, be in position behind the barricades along the calle Estafeta no later than 6am. Only the able-bodied and sober should plan to run. Women are officially not permitted to run, although many defy this ban each year.

There simply aren't enough beds or bullfight tickets to go around, and scalpers have a field day. Technically, tickets for a good seat in the ring go on sale at 8pm the night before the *corrida,* and tickets for standing room go on sale at 4pm on the day of the bullfight. But all the tickets are sold out, and since it is impossible to get them through a travel agent beforehand, tourists have to use scalpers.

The fiesta draws half a million visitors, many of whom camp in the city parks. Temporary facilities are set up, but there are never enough beds. Hotel reservations should be confirmed *at least* 6 months beforehand. If you look respectable, some *Pamplónicos* may rent you a room. Be aware, however, that they may gouge you for the highest price they think you're willing to pay, and your room might turn out to be a dirty floor shared with others in a slumlike part of the city. The tourist office will not make any recommendations during the festival—you're basically on your own. Many young visitors sleep on the grounds of the Ciudadela and Plaza Fueros traffic ring, but you could be mugged. Longtime visitors to Pamplona advise that it's better to sleep in a group, on top of your belongings, and during the day when it's safer than under cover of darkness. If you can't find a room, check your valuables at the bus station on the calle Conde Oliveto (where there are also showers—free, but cold).

As for bars and restaurants, ignore all the times given below. Most establishments operate around the clock at this time.

Warning: Some people go to the festival not to watch the bulls but to pick pockets. And don't take needless risks, such as leaping from a building in the hope friends below will catch you. Many people do this each year, and not all are caught.

gerrikos, favored by weight lifters and sports enthusiasts who feel a twinge in their backs whenever they're called upon to perform heavy-duty lifting.

If you're looking for fashion or accessories, head for a boutique called **Zara,** avenida Carlos III, 7 (☎ **948-22-75-04**), which is closed on Monday, or explore the aisles of Pamplona's biggest department store, **Unzu,** calle Mercaderes, 3 (☎ **948-20-91-00**).

WHERE TO STAY

During the Festival of San Fermín, prices are three to four times higher than those listed below. In some instances, a hotel commits itself to prices it will charge at *Fiesta* (the original name of *The Sun Also Rises* when it was first published in Britain). Other owners charge pretty much what they think they can get, and they can get a lot. Therefore, agree on the price when making a reservation, if you've been able to get a reservation in the first place. At other times of the year, Pamplona is a reasonably priced tourist destination.

EXPENSIVE

Avenida. Zaragoza, 5, 31003 Pamplona. ☎ **948-24-54-54.** Fax 948-23-23-23. E-mail: hotelavenida@ctv.es. 27 units. MINIBAR TV TEL. 15,500–28,500 ptas. ($93–$171) double. AE, DC, MC, V. Parking 1,200 ptas. ($7.20).

One of the best inns in town, this small, well-run place opened in 1989. The midsize guest rooms are well furnished and maintained; some are even better than the inn's three-star rating suggests. Furnishings tend toward the sleek and modern, and local watercolors add a warm touch. Sixteen units are air-conditioned.

Dining: Full lunches and dinners are served in the restaurant **Leyre,** known for its regional cuisine. Monday to Friday a *menú del día* is available at 1,500 ptas. ($9) and another on the weekend at 2,800 ptas. ($16.80). There's also a cafeteria on the premises, serving snacks and drinks daily 7am to 11pm.

Hotel Sancho Ramírez. Calle Sancho Ramírez, 11, 31008 Pamplona. ☎ **948-27-17-12.** Fax 948-17-11-43. 86 units. A/C MINIBAR TV TEL. 14,800–25,000 ptas. ($88.80–$150) double. AE, DC, MC, V. Parking 1,200 ptas. ($7.20). Bus: 7.

Half a mile south of the town center and built in 1981 (last renovated in 1990), the Sancho Ramírez has quickly stolen business away from its older competitors. Each of the reasonably priced units has a streamlined and contemporary decor; some contain minibars, and all the tiled bathrooms are equipped with hair dryers. Rooms are outfitted in a conservatively contemporary decor. It's not a particularly exciting hotel, rather bland and angular. A hotel restaurant serves regional cuisine.

Hotel Tres Reyes. Jardines de la Taconera, s/n, 31001 Pamplona. ☎ **800/448-8355** in the U.S., or 948-22-66-00. Fax 948-22-29-30. www.hotel3reyes.com. E-mail: hotel3reyes@abc. ibernet.com. 168 units. A/C MINIBAR TV TEL. 23,000 ptas. ($138) double; 45,000 ptas. ($270) suite. AE, DC, MC, V. Parking 2,200 ptas. ($13.20) indoors; free outside.

A short walk west of the old town, just 2 blocks north of the ancient citadel, this is one of the finest hotels in town, surpassed only by Iruña Park. Modern, with a cement-balconied 10-story facade that curves around a pleasant garden, it provides tasteful airy rooms with contemporary furnishings, lots of sunlight, and private bathrooms equipped with hair dryers. Many have balconies, and all are welcome refuges from the intensity of the local festivities.

Dining/Diversions: The **Grill Tres Reyes** serves well-prepared Basque and Navarre cuisine. There's also a bar and an inexpensive cafeteria.

Amenities: 24-hour room service, laundry, concierge, baby-sitting, daily exercise classes, car rentals, shopping boutiques, health club with sauna, gymnasium, squash courts, massage facilities, heated outdoor pool.

Iruña Park Hotel. Ronda Ermitagaña, s/n, 31008 Pamplona. ☎ **800/448-8335** in the U.S., or 948-17-32-00. Fax 948-17-23-87. 225 units. A/C MINIBAR TV TEL. 20,500 ptas. ($123) double; 35,000 ptas. ($210) suite. AE, DC, MC, V. Parking 1,650 ptas. ($9.90).

A short walk west of the Parque de la Ciudadela behind a facade of mirrored glass and white masonry, this is the largest and best hotel in town, often the site of conventions. A large staff maintains the blandly furnished but comfortable rooms, some suitable for people with disabilities. All the beds have quality mattresses, and amenities include private safes and hair dryers. The public rooms are modern and glossy, with deep armchairs and big windows.

Dining/Diversions: The **Royal Restaurant** serves regional and international cuisine. There's also a bar.

Amenities: Room service (daily 8am to 11pm), concierge, baby-sitting, laundry, car rentals, sauna, solarium, business center.

MODERATE

Hotel Leyre. Leyre, 7, 31002 Pamplona. ☎ **948-22-85-00.** Fax 948-22-83-18. www.webs.navarra.net/hleyre. E-mail: hleyre@cmn.navarra.net. 55 units. MINIBAR TV TEL. 15,500 ptas. ($93) double. AE, DC, MC, V. Parking 1,200 ptas. ($7.20). Bus: 11.

Conveniently located in the town center a few steps from the bus station, the Leyre was built around 1965 and renovated in 1996. It's been consistently popular with bull breeders and with matadors and their fans. The small rooms are comfortable but simple, with sturdy furniture, good beds, and high ceilings. A restaurant and a popular bar are on the premises.

La Perla. Plaza del Castillo, 1, 31001 Pamplona. ☎ **948-22-77-06.** Fax 948-22-15-19. 67 units. 10,000–15,000 ptas. ($60–$90) double; 22,000 ptas. ($132) suite. AE, DC, MC, V.

Opened in 1880 and last renovated long ago, this is not exactly the most outstanding hotel in town. But during the festival it becomes *the* place to stay, because it opens onto the main square of Pamplona and overlooks calle Estafeta, the straightaway of the *encierro* through which the bulls run. The small guest rooms are furnished with an old-fashioned flair, and in days of yore they sheltered everybody from Ernest Hemingway to U.S. Sen. Henry Cabot Lodge.

Maisonnave. Nueva, 20, 31001 Pamplona. ☎ **948-22-26-00.** Fax 948-22-01-66. www.hotelmaisonnave.es. E-mail: informacion@hotelmaisonnave.es. 138 units. A/C MINIBAR TV TEL. 12,500 ptas. ($75) double. AE, DC, MC, V. Parking 1,200 ptas. ($7.20). Bus: 5, 9, or 10.

Located in the historic old town of Pamplona, west of the Plaza del Castillo and within easy walking distance of the *tascas* and restaurants, this place is solidly booked for the fiesta. You must reserve at least 6 months in advance—and even then, say a prayer. The small rooms have been completely renovated, each well furnished, well maintained, and comfortably though blandly standardized. The hotel also offers a Navarrese restaurant serving regional and Spanish national cuisine on the first floor. On the sixth floor is another dining room, the Elmirador, with elaborate windows opening onto the scenery of Pamplona.

Residencia Eslava. Plaza Virgen de la O, 7, or calle Recoletas, 20, 31001 Pamplona. ☎ **948-22-22-70.** Fax 948-22-51-57. www.hotel-eslava.com. E-mail: correo@hotel-eslava. com. 28 units. TV TEL. 10,500 ptas. ($63) double. AE, DC, MC, V. Bus: 9.

Located right off Plaza de Recoletas, and a 10-minute walk from the bus station, this renovated hotel manages to combine the spirits of old and new Spain. Its small living room resembles the drawing room of a distinguished Spanish house. All the average-size guest rooms are tastefully decorated; some have balconies with views of the city walls and the vistas beyond. All come with comfortable beds and tiled bathrooms. A cellar lounge offers drinks.

WHERE TO DINE
EXPENSIVE

✪ **Europa.** Calle Espoz y Mina, 11. ☎ **948-22-18-00.** Reservations recommended. Main courses 3,000–6,000 ptas. ($18–$36); *menú del día* 3,250 ptas. ($19.50). AE, DC, MC, V. Mon–Sat 1–3:30pm and 9–11pm. SPANISH.

Located in the center of Pamplona near the Plaza del Castillo, this is, along with Josetxo (see below), the best restaurant in the entire region. Both have Michelin stars, which are rarely doled out in this part of Europe. Known for its creative interpreta-tions of regional recipes, the restaurant occupies several intimate, recently renovated dining rooms in what was originally built in the 1930s as a private house. The chef and culinary artist is Pamplona-born Pilar Idoate, who prepares a seasonal menu.

Examples include baked potatoes stuffed with truffles and minced crayfish, roulades of sole with mountain herbs, fillet steaks with Roquefort dressing, and such game dishes as venison and pheasant. Desserts include an orange mousse with a *marquesa de chocolate*.

Hartza. Juan de Labrit, 19. ☎ **948-22-45-68.** Reservations recommended. Main courses 3,200–4,000 ptas. ($19.20–$24). AE, DC, MC, V. Tues–Sun 1:30–3:30pm; Tues–Sat 9–11:30pm. Closed Aug and 10 days at Christmas. REGIONAL/INTERNATIONAL.

One of the oldest *bodegas* in town, a popular restaurant has flourished at this location near the bullring since the 1870s. Even though it doesn't have a Michelin star, it manages to give Josetxo and Europa (see above and below) serious competition. The chef's touch is delicate, and although Hartza doesn't attempt as many dishes as Josetxo, what it does create is sublime and inventive. There's a summer garden for outdoor dining, plus a street-level bar. The portions are generous (but expensive); specialties change with the seasons but might include well-seasoned vegetable soup, stuffed peppers, tournedos, hake and eel, and a selection of regional cheeses. The interior is air-conditioned during the hottest summer months.

✪ **Josetxo.** Plaza Príncipe de Viana, 1. ☎ **948-22-20-97.** Reservations recommended on weekends. Main courses 2,200–4,200 ptas. ($13.20–$25.20). AE, DC, V. Mon–Sat 1–3:30pm and 9–11pm. Closed Holy Week and Aug. BASQUE.

The finest and grandest restaurant in town, Josexto is run by a civic-minded local family with more than 30 years' experience in the restaurant trade. The chef has a magic combination: inventiveness and solid technique, backed up by the very freshest ingredients. Specialties vary with the seasons but might include cream-of-crabmeat soup, puff pastry stuffed with shellfish, lobster salad, a *panaché* (medley) of fresh vegetables with Serrano ham, sea bass cooked in white wine, variations of goose pâté, and several rabbit and trout dishes. Dessert might be a chocolate truffle tart layered with orange-flavored cream. The restaurant is beside a busy traffic circle, 4 blocks south of the Plaza del Castillo.

MODERATE

Alhambra. Calle Bergamín, 7. ☎ **948-24-50-07.** Reservations recommended. Main courses 2,500–3,000 ptas. ($15–$18). AE, DC, MC, V. Mon–Sat 1–3pm and 9–11:30pm. REGIONAL/SPANISH.

One of the best-known and most stable restaurants in Pamplona, and just a 15-minute walk from the cathedral, Alhambra was established shortly after World War II. Since 1985, it has been directed by a well-trained group of new owners, and in 1995 the restaurant was renovated and enlarged. Set within two paneled dining rooms, it features a complete selection of local wines and regional specialties, including carefully deboned sardines, grilled and served with truffles; grilled fillet of hake with local herbs; and selected cuts of fillet steak with sauces made from local mushrooms and garlic.

Casa Otano. Calle San Nicolás. ☎ **948-22-50-95.** Reservations recommended. Main courses 2,000–4,500 ptas. ($12–$27); set lunch 1,800 ptas. ($10.80). AE, MC, V. Mon–Sat 1–4pm and 9pm–midnight. NAVARRESE/SPANISH.

In the oldest part of town, on a narrow street that empties into the Plaza de Castillo, this is a busy and popular tavern-style restaurant with three dining rooms and a reputation for feeding generations of Pamplona residents. Established in the 1950s, the menu includes house-style hake (baked with garlic, green sauce, herbs, and clams), many different kinds of succulent grilled meats and fish, chicken roasted in sherry sauce, and thick cuts of delicious pork chops.

INEXPENSIVE

Erburu. Calle San Lorenzo, 19. ☎ **948-22-51-69.** Reservations recommended. Main courses 750–2,500 ptas. ($4.50–$15); fixed-price menu 1,500 ptas. ($9). AE, DC, V. Tues–Sun 10am to midnight. Closed 1 week in July. REGIONAL.

There's absolutely nothing fancy or artificial about this restaurant, which has been serving well-conceived, old-fashioned food for the past 30 years. It contains only 45 seats, staffed by a crew that seems to have been here since virtually the day the place opened. Many of the regular clients don't even ask for a menu, opting instead for platters of good-tasting food they've been served countless times in the past. Examples include snails in garlic sauce, braised oxtail, steaming bowls of kale and potato soup, hake in garlic-flavored green sauce, and several kinds of beef, pork, and chicken. Dessert might be an old-time portion of flan, accompanied, according to your wishes, with fresh fruit and/or ice cream.

PAMPLONA AFTER DARK

In a city famous for the way bulls run through its streets, there's something consistent about the local habit of wandering through the city's streets, particularly within the historic *casco antiguo.* Two streets in particular, **calle San Nicolas** and **calle de Jarauta,** are lined with *tascas,* bars, *bodegas,* and pubs. Lots of them don't even have signs, so just wander and drop in and out of whichever strikes your fancy.

One particularly atmospheric bar is **Mesón de la Navarrería,** calle el Navarrería, 15 (no phone). Amid a patina built up by years of cigarette smoke and spilled beer, it evokes old-time Navarre. A newer contender is Celtic import **O'Connor's Irish Pub,** Paseo Sarasate, s/n (no phone), where pints of Guinness and recorded Irish ballads enliven the old town.

Looking for a dance club to let off some late-night steam? Head for Pamplona's most popular disco, **Reverendos,** Monastero de Velate, 5 (☎ 948-26-15-93), where 20- and 30-somethings dance, flirt, and drink till all hours. The cover charge costs 1,000 ptas. ($6), which includes the price of a drink.

Dating from 1888, the art deco **Café Iruña,** Plaza del Castillo, 44 (☎ **948-22-20-64**), has an outdoor terrace that's popular in summer. The winter crowd is likely to congregate around the bar, ordering combination plates and snacks in addition to drinks. The place thrives as a cafe/bar daily 8am to 1am; however, it becomes more of a restaurant during the lunch hour. Platters of hot food are served to many of the local office workers and day laborers. The *menú del día* is 1,500 ptas. ($9), and a full lunch, served daily from 1 to 3:30pm, costs from 1,500 to 2,000 ptas. ($9 to $12). Beer goes for 180 ptas. ($1.10)at the bar, slightly more at a table.

Cafetería El Molino, Bayona, 13 (☎ **948-25-10-90**), centrally located in the commercial Barrio San Juan, doubles as a popular tapas bar. Late in the evening, the action really heats up. The huge assortment of tapas includes fried shrimp, squid, anchovies, fish croquettes, and Russian salad. Most tapas don't exceed 175 ptas. ($1.05), although some of the more expensive ones go for 350 ptas. ($2.10). Open Monday to Saturday 8am to 1am and Sunday 9am to 1am.

2 Olite

27 miles (43.5km) S of Pamplona, 229 miles (369km) N of Madrid

A historical city, Olite sits in a rich agricultural belt with a Mediterranean climate of short winters and long hot summers. Cornfields and vineyards, along with large villages, pepper the countryside. It is also the center of a winemaking industry carried on by cooperative cellars. These wine merchants hold a local festival each year September 14 to 18.

ESSENTIALS

GETTING THERE   Two to four trains per day from Pamplona run to Olite, taking 35 minutes one way. For rail information, call ☎ **948-70-06-28.**

Two bus companies, **Conda** (☎ **948-82-03-42**) and **La Tafallesa** (☎ **948-70-09-79**), run from Pamplona to Olite at the rate of 6 to 12 per day. The trip takes 45 minutes.

By car, take the A-15 expressway south from Pamplona.

VISITOR INFORMATION   The **tourist information office** is at Plaza Carlos II el Noble, s/n (☎ **948-71-24-34**). It's open Monday to Friday 10am to 2pm and 4 to 7pm, Saturday and Sunday 10am to 2pm.

EXPLORING OLITE

In the 15th century, this Gothic town was a favorite address of the kings of Navarre. Charles III put Olite on the map, ordering that the **Palacio Real,** Plaza Carlos III el Noble, be built in 1406. The towers and lookouts make visiting it an adventure. From April to September, hours are daily 10am to 2pm and 5 to 8pm; October to March, daily 10am to 6pm. Admission is 350 ptas. ($2.10) for adults, 200 ptas. ($1.20) for children.

Next to the castle stands a Gothic church, **Iglesia de Santa María la Real,** with a splendid 12th-century doorway decorated with flowers.

WHERE TO STAY & DINE

Parador Príncipe de Viana. Plaza de los Teobaldos, 2, 31390 Olite. ☎ **948-74-00-00.** Fax 948-74-02-01. www.parador.es. 43 units. A/C MINIBAR TV TEL. 18,500 ptas. ($111) double. AE, DC, MC, V.

This state-run parador in the center of town is in one of the wings of the Palacio Real (see above). Surrounded by watchtowers, thick walls, and massive buttresses, the building is one of the most impressive sights in town. Only 12 accommodations, however, are in the parador's medieval core, and they go for a premium over their comfortable counterparts, which are in a new wing added to the castle in 1963 when it became a parador. Regardless of their location in the compound, the rooms are dignified and quite comfortable, each with quality mattresses.

Rustic Lodgings in the Navarre Countryside

If you have some time to spend in the area, consider a rental at one of the government-sponsored rustic home stays, ranging from rooms in old farmhouses in the mountains to simple lodgings in homes in the region's small hamlets. Sometimes fully equipped apartments in the region are available. In nearly all cases, these lodgings are extremely reasonable in price and very affordable to families who'd like to experience the great outdoors in this often neglected part of Spain. Called *casas rurales,* the lodgings are documented in detail in a helpful guide called *Guía de Alojamientos de Turismo Rural.* These guides are distributed free at any of the tourist offices in Navarre, including the one at Pamplona. For reservations, call the office at ☎ **948-20-65-41,** where some members of the staff speak English.

Dining: Even if you're visiting just for the day, consider a meal here, which might include grilled ribs, rabbit with snails, or other regional offerings. Meals cost from 3,500 ptas. ($21). The restaurant is open daily 1 to 4pm and 8:30 to 11pm.

Amenities: Room service, baby-sitting, concierge.

SIDE TRIPS TO UJÚE & A HISTORIC MONASTERY

High up on a mountain of the same name, a short drive east along a secondary road from Olite, **Ujúe** seems plucked from the Middle Ages. Built as a defensive town, it has cobbled streets and stone houses clustered around its fortress **Church of Santa María,** dating from the 12th to the 14th century. The heart of King Charles II ("the Bad") was placed to rest here. The church towers open onto views of the countryside, extending to Olite in the west and the Pyrenees in the east.

On the Sunday after St. Mark's Day (April 25), Ujúe is an important pilgrimage center for the people of the area, many of whom, barefoot and wearing tunics, carry large crosses. They come to Ujúe to worship Santa María, depicted on a Romanesque statue dating from 1190. It was plated in silver in the second half of the 15th century.

If you have a car, you might also check out the **Monasterio de la Oliva,** 21 miles (34km) south of Olite. It was founded by King García Ramírez in 1164 and is an excellent example of Cistercian architecture. This monastery, one of the first to be constructed by French monks outside France, once had great influence; today the most notable feature is its 14th-century Gothic cloisters. The church, which dates from the late 12th century, is even more impressive than the cloisters. It has a distinguished portal and two rose windows. Pillars and pointed arches fill its interior. From April to September, it's open daily 9am to 8pm; October to March, daily 9am to 6pm.

3 Tudela

52 miles (84km) S of Pamplona, 196 miles (315.5km) N of Madrid

In the center of the food belt of the Ribera or Ebro Valley with a population of only 30,000, the ancient city of Tudela is the second largest in Navarre. Situated on the right bank of the Ebro, it had a long history as a city where Jews, Arabs, and Christians lived and worked together. The Muslims made it a dependency of the caliphate at Córdoba, a period of domination that lasted until 1119. The city had a large Moorish quarter, the *morería*, and many old brick houses are in the Mudéjar style. King Sancho VII ("the Strong"), who defeated the Saracens, chose Tudela as his favorite residence in 1251. It has been a bishopric since the 18th century.

ESSENTIALS

GETTING THERE   Tudela lies on the southern rail line south of Pamplona. Two **RENFE** trains pass through here, one connecting La Rioja to Zaragoza via Castejón de Ebro. Another train links Zaragoza to Vitoria-Gasteiz via Pamplona. For more information and schedules (subject to change), call ☎ **948-82-06-46.**

Conda buses (☎ **948-82-03-42**) go to Tudela from Pamplona at the rate of six to nine per day (trip time: 1 hour).

Take A-15 south from Pamplona, if you're driving.

VISITOR INFORMATION   The **tourist information office** at Plaza Viejal (☎ **948-82-15-39**) is open Monday to Friday 10am to 2pm and 4 to 7pm, Saturday and Sunday 10am to 2pm.

TOURING THE CATHEDRAL

Begin your exploration at the central Plaza de los Fueros, from where you can wander through a maze of narrow alleys laid out during the Moorish occupation.

At the square called Plaza Vieja, visit Tudela's most important monument, **Catedral de Santa Ana,** open Tuesday to Saturday 9am to 1pm and 4 to 7pm, Sunday 9am to 1pm. Constructed in the 12th and 13th centuries, it has an outstanding work of art on its facade, the Doorway of the Last Judgment, with about 120 groups of figures. Creation is depicted, but the artisans were truly inspired in showing the horrors of hell. The church contains many Gothic works of art, such as choir stalls from the 1500s. Several chapels are richly decorated, including one dedicated to Our Lady of Hope with masterpieces from the 15th century. The main altar contains an exceptional *retablo* painted by Pedro Díaz de Oviedo. The small but choice cloisters are the highlight of the tour, however, and cost 100 ptas. (60¢) to enter. Dating from the 12th and 13th centuries, they contain many Romanesque arches. Capitals on the columns include scenes from the New Testament.

WHERE TO STAY & DINE

Hotel Tudela. Avenida Zaragoza, 60, 31500 Tudela. ☎ **948-41-08-02.** Fax 948-41-09-72. 44 units. A/C MINIBAR TV TEL. 8,800 ptas. ($52.80) double. AE, DC, MC, V. Parking 1,275 ptas. ($7.65).

Directly in front of the bullring (Plaza de Toros), this hotel was built in the 1930s and tripled in size by 1992. Today, with five floors, it's the best hotel in town, modern and functional, with a polite and helpful staff. Rooms, although a bit boxy and standardized, are nevertheless comfortable, with firm mattresses and well-maintained private bathrooms.

An in-house restaurant is one of the best in the city. It draws a lively crowd, especially before and after bullfights, and serves well-prepared food. It offers typical fresh products of the Ribera region, along with some magnificent fish and grilled meat. Try the omelet with codfish or the baked monkfish. You can also order beefsteak, followed by homemade pastries and desserts. And sample such wines as Viña Magaña. You can dine in air-conditioned comfort and find parking on the premises. Reservations are recommended. Main courses range from 1,800 to 2,200 ptas. ($10.80 to $13.20); a bargain fixed-price menu can be had for 1,500 ptas. ($9). Lunch is served daily; dinner is served Monday to Saturday.

Morase. Paseo de Invierno, 2, 31500 Tudela. ☎ **948-82-17-00.** Fax 948-82-17-04. 7 units. A/C TV TEL. 8,500 ptas. ($51) double. AE, DC, MC, V. Closed Aug 1–7. Parking 600 ptas. ($3.60).

Not only is this one of the best places to stay in town, but it's also a leading restaurant. Built in 1963, it's small but very comfortable. The midsized guest rooms are modern and well maintained, each with a firm mattress.

With the finest dining room in town, the Morase is a special delight when the first of the asparagus comes in, praised by gastronomes all over Spain. The specialties sound conventional but are well prepared, including a *pastel* of vegetables and hake baked with garlic. The lamb from Navarre is delectable, as is roast pork with herbs or red peppers stuffed with puree of seafood. On the bank of the Ebro, the restaurant offers a garden, an air-conditioned dining room, and adequate parking. Reservations are recommended. You can opt for a *menú del día* for 2,500 to 3,500 ptas. ($15 to $21). Lunch is served daily, dinner Monday to Saturday.

4 Sangüesa

253 miles (407km) N of Madrid, 29 miles (47km) SE of Pamplona

Sangüesa is on the left bank of the Aragón River, at the Aragonese frontier. If after visiting the town you want to spend the night in the area, drive 9 miles (14.5km) across the border south to Sos del Rey Católico (see chapter 13, "Aragón"), one of the most charming towns of Aragón; it features an excellent parador. A monumental town in its own right, Sangüesa can also serve as a base for excursions in the area, including visits to some of Navarre's major attractions, such as the monastery at Leyre and Javier Castle.

Long known to the Romans, Sangüesa was later involved in the battle against Muslim domination in the 10th century. It has seen many wars, including occupation by supporters of Archduke Charles of Austria in 1710 and many a skirmish during the Carlist struggles of the 19th century. On several occasions it has been the seat of the parliament of Navarre. Pilgrims crossing northern Spain to Santiago de Compostela stopped at Sangüesa.

ESSENTIALS

GETTING THERE   Two to three buses bound for Sangüesa leave from Pamplona daily; the trip takes 45 minutes one way. For information, call ☎ **948-87-02-09.**

If you're driving from Pamplona, take the secondary road N-240 to Sangüesa.

VISITOR INFORMATION   The **tourist information office** is at calle Alfonso el Batallador, 20 (☎ **948-87-03-29**). It's open Monday to Friday 10am to 2pm and 4 to 7pm, Saturday and Sunday 10am to 2pm.

VISITING THE CHURCHES

The **Iglesia de Santa María** lies on Calle Mayor (☎ 948-43-04-97) and stands at the far end of town beside the river. Begun in the 12th century, it has a doorway from the 12th and 13th centuries that is an outstanding work of Romanesque art. The south portal, filled with remarkably carved sculptures, is Santa María's most outstanding feature. The vestry contains a 4½-foot-high processional monstrance from the 15th century.

The nearby **Iglesia de Santiago** (☎ 948-87-01-32) is a late traditional Romanesque structure from the 12th and 13th centuries. It has a battlement-type tower and contains an impressive array of Gothic sculpture, discovered under the church only in 1964. Look for the bizarre statue of St. James atop a big conch. Both churches are only open for masses.

WHERE TO STAY & DINE

Yamaguchy. Carretera de Javier, s/n, 31400 Sangüesa, ☎ **948-87-01-27.** Fax 948-87-07-00. www.interbook.net. E-mail: yamaguchy@interbook.net. 41 units. TV TEL. 7,600 ptas. ($45.60) double. AE, DC, MC, V. Free parking.

The best place to stay among extremely limited choices is this hotel ¼ mile (.4km) outside town on the road to Javier. In summer, its most attractive feature is its swimming pool. The small rooms are functional, modern, clean, and comfortable, each with a good bed.

Meals ranging from 3,000 ptas. ($18) are available daily from 1 to 3:30pm and 8 to 11pm and there is a *menú del día* for 1,800 ptas. ($10.80). The many Navarrese dishes served include lamb stew and steak. You can also sample award-winning red and rosé wines from local wine cellars.

SIDE TRIPS TO LEYRE & JAVIER CASTLE
LEYRE

The **Monasterio de San Salvador of Leyre** (☎ 948-88-40-11) is 10 miles (16km) east of Sangüesa, perched on the side of a mountain of the same name, overlooking the Yesa Dam. Of major historic and artistic interest, the main body of the monastery was constructed between the 11th and the 15th centuries on the site of a primitive pre-Romanesque church; in time, it became the spiritual center of Navarre. Many kings, including Sancho III, made it their pantheon. Its crypt, consecrated in 1057, ranks as one of the country's major works of Romanesque art.

When the church was reconstructed by the Cistercians in the 13th century, they kept the bays of the old Romanesque church. The outstanding and richly adorned 12th-century west portal is called the Porta Speciosa, and is covered with intricate carvings. In one section Jesus and his disciples are depicted atop mythical creatures. Some of the other artistic treasures of this once-great monastery are displayed at the Museo de Navarra in Pamplona.

When Navarre joined with Aragón, the power of Leyre declined. Finally, in the 19th century, the monastery was abandoned. It wasn't until 1954 that a Benedictine order came here and began the difficult restoration.

The monastery is 2½ miles (4km) from Yesa, which itself is on N-240, the major road linking Pamplona, Sangüesa, and Huesca. Take the N-240 into Yesa, then follow an uphill road marked LEYRE 2½ miles (4km) to the monastery. Visits are possible Monday to Friday 10:30am to 2pm and 4 to 7pm, Sunday 10:30 to 11:15am, 1 to 2pm, and 4 to 7pm. Admission is 225 ptas. ($1.35) for adults and 50 ptas. (30¢) for children.

At Leyre you'll also find one of the most unusual accommodations in Navarre, the **Hospedería,** Monasterio de Leyre, 31410 Leyre (☎ 948-88-41-00). This two-star inn with 32 rooms (all with private bathrooms and phones) was created from the annexes constructed by the Benedictines in the 1700s. Guest rooms open onto views of the Yesa Reservoir. The rate is 9,500 ptas. ($57) for a double room (MasterCard and Visa accepted), and parking is free. The hotel restaurant serves good Navarrese food in a rustic setting. Breakfast costs 850 ptas. ($5.10) and dinner averages 1,800 ptas. ($10.80). The restaurant is open daily 8:30 to 10am, 1 to 3:30pm, and 8 to 10:30pm. The Hospedería is closed December 10 to March 1.

JAVIER CASTLE

The second major excursion possible in the area is to **Castillo de Javier** (☎ 948-88-40-00), 5 miles (8km) from Sangüesa. The castle dates from the 11th century, but owes its present look to restoration work carried out in 1952. Francisco Javier (Xavier), patron of Navarre, was born here on April 7, 1506. Along with Ignatius Loyola, he founded the order of the Society of Jesus (the Jesuits) in the mid–16th century. The castle houses a magnificent 13th-century crucifix, and thousands of the faithful congregate at Javier on two consecutive Sundays in March. This is the most popular pilgrimage in Navarre. Known as the Javierada, it pays homage to Francisco Javier, who was canonized in 1622.

During your visit to the castle, visit the oratory, the guard chamber, the great hall, and the saint's bedroom. The castle is teeming with interesting art, including a 15th-century fresco called the *Dance of Death.* To get to the castle, take N-240 to Yesa, then follow an unmarked road that's signposted CASTILLO DE JAVIER. It's open daily 9am to 1pm and 4 to 7pm. Admission is free but donations are requested.

For food and lodging, go to the tranquil **Hotel El Mesón,** Explanada, 31411 Javier (☎ 948-88-40-35; fax 948-88-42-26), right in the center of the hamlet of Javier on the same unmarked road the castle is on. Management rents eight comfortably furnished rooms, but the hotel is closed December 15 to February. Doubles go for 6,400 ptas. ($38.40), and parking is free. The hotel's restaurant offers the best food in the area, with a fixed-price menu going for 1,950 ptas. ($11.70). American Express, MasterCard, and Visa are all accepted.

5 Logroño

205 miles (330km) N of Madrid, 57 miles (92km) W of Pamplona

The capital of the province of La Rioja, Logroño is also the major distribution center for the area's wines and agricultural products. Because La Rioja is so small, Logroño could serve as your base for touring all the major attractions of the province. Although much of Logroño is modern and dull, it does have an old quarter known to the pilgrims crossing this region to visit the tomb of St. James at Santiago de Compostela.

ESSENTIALS

GETTING THERE   There are four daily RENFE trains from Barcelona (trip time: 7 hours) and one per day from Madrid (5¼ hours). From Bilbao in the north, two to three trains arrive per day (3 hours). For information, call ☎ 941-24-02-02.

Five buses arrive daily from Pamplona (trip time: 2 hours) and four to five from Madrid (5 hours). For information, call ☎ 941-23-59-83.

Take N-111 southwest from Pamplona by car or A-68 northwest from Zaragoza.

VISITOR INFORMATION   The **tourist information office** is at Paseo del Principe de Vergara (☎ 941-26-06-65). It's open June to October, Monday to Saturday 10am to 2pm and 4:30 to 7:30pm, Sunday 10am to 2pm; November to May, Monday to Friday 9am to 2pm.

EXPLORING LOGROÑO

The **Catedral de Santa María de la Redonda,** Plaza del Mercado (☎ 941-25-76-11), has vaulting from the 1400s, although the baroque facade dates from 1742. Inside, you can visit its 1762 Chapel of Our Lady of the Angels, built in an octagonal shape with rococo adornments. Constructed on top of an earlier Romanesque church, today's cathedral is known for its broad naves and twin towers. It's open daily 8am to 1pm and 6 to 8:30pm.

From the square on which the cathedral sits, walk up calle de la Sagasta until you reach the 12th-century **Iglesia de Santa María de Palacio,** on Marqués de San Nicolás, once part of a royal palace. The palace part dates from 1130 when Alfonso VII offered his residence to the Order of the Holy Sepulchre. Most of what he left is long gone, of course, but there is still a pyramid-shaped spire from the 13th century.

Walk through the heart of Logroño, exploring the gardens of the broad **Paseo del Espolón.** In the late afternoon, all the residents turn out for their paseo.

A Special Event

About a third of all Rioja wine production comes from the Najerilla River's valleys. From September 15 to 30, the **Wine Harvest Festival** (☎ 941-26-06-65) takes place throughout the region of La Rioja. Barefoot locals stomp upon grapes spilling from oak casks, and area vineyards showcase their wares. Other activities include dances, parades, music, and bullfights.

While in Logroño, you can visit the **Bodegas Olarra,** Polígono Independencía de Cantabria, s/n (☎ **941-23-52-99**), open Monday to Friday 9am to 1pm and 3 to 7pm; closed August 3 to 31. Reserve in advance for a tour. It produces wines under the Otonal and Olarra labels.

WHERE TO STAY

Hotel Marquéz de Vallejo. Marquéz de Vallejo, 8, 26001 Logroño. ☎ **941-24-83-83.** Fax 941-24-02-88. 30 units. A/C TV TEL. 9,900 ptas. ($59.40) double. AE, MC, V.

In the center of town near the cathedral, close to the Plaza del Espolon, this little hotel is surrounded by restaurants and wine bars serving La Rioja vintages. Its balconied facade with wrought-iron railings is one of the most graceful in town, dating to 1911 (although the hotel was renovated in 1989). A warm traditional atmosphere awaits you, although the more basic interior doesn't match the elaborate facade. The style is modest but functional, well maintained, and welcoming. Rooms are midsized and furnished in neutral modern, but they are comfortable and have small bathrooms with shower stalls. Don't expect more in the way of amenities, except a cafeteria and a tapas bar.

Hotel Murrieta. Marqués de Murrieta, 1, 26005 Logroño. ☎ **941-22-41-50.** Fax 941-22-32-13. www.pretur.es. E-mail: hotels@pretur.es. 111 units. MINIBAR TV TEL. 11,500 ptas. ($69) double. AE, MC, V. Parking 1,450 ptas. ($8.70).

At the western border of the historic part of town, a block north of the Gran Vía, is this 1980s hotel offering midsized, comfortable, pristine rooms at a relatively good value. The public rooms, all modernized in the early '90s, are outfitted with colored marble, deep carpeting, and tasteful upholstery. Room service is available 7:30am to midnight; other extras include laundry, baby-sitting, and car rentals. Efficient and unpretentious, the Murrieta restaurant serves both regional and Spanish food, along with an appealing collection of Rioja wines. Uncomplicated à la carte lunches and dinners are served in the hotel's cafeteria.

La Numantina. Calle Sagasta, 4, 26001 Logroño. ☎/fax **941-25-14-11.** 29 units. TV TEL. 6,635 ptas. ($40) double. MC, V. Closed Dec 22–Jan 7.

This rather simple hotel, one of the best bargains in town, is on a street central to both the historic core and the commercial district. Its small and basic rooms are clean and reasonably comfortable, each with a good bed. No breakfast is served, but you can buy pastries at a shop across the street.

✪ **Meliá Confort Los Bracos.** Bretón de los Herreros, 29, 26001 Logroño. ☎ **941-22-66-08.** Fax 941-22-67-54. 72 units. A/C MINIBAR TV TEL. 16,500 ptas. ($99) double. AE, DC, MC, V. Parking 1,725 ptas. ($10.35).

This landmark four-star hotel is the finest in town, according to many wine merchants who journey here frequently on business. The town's toniest address offers an elegant reception hall and the most helpful staff in town. The street on which it sits is one of the best known in the city, and although it used to lie outside the walls, Logroño has now caught up with it. The midsized rooms are handsomely furnished, if rather monotonous in style. Room service, dry cleaning, laundry, and a concierge are among the creature comforts offered. The dining possibilities are limited to a somewhat dull cafeteria, but many good restaurants and cafes are within an easy walk.

WHERE TO DINE

Asador La Chata. Carnicerías, 3. ☎ **941-25-12-96.** Reservations required. Main courses 1,200–2,200 ptas. ($7.20–$13.20); fixed-price menu 3,000 ptas. ($18). AE, DC, MC, V. Daily 1:30–4pm; Wed–Sat 9–11pm. REGIONAL.

Founded in 1821 in a building close to the town's cathedral, this delightful choice exudes a sense of Old Navarre. Its tactful owners define it as an *asador*, which means it specializes in wood-roasted meat dishes, in this case in the style of the region. Lunch is an everyday event, and much patronized by workers in the local wine trade, but dinner is served only 4 evenings a week. Because of the establishment's small size (only 60 seats), advance reservations are essential. In a wood-paneled dining room ringed with artifacts of the wine trade, you can enjoy the two house specialties: fresh asparagus prepared with strips of locally cured ham, and *cabrito asado* (roast baby goat with herbs). Meats are succulently tender.

Casa Emilio. Pérez Galdós, 18. ☎ **941-25-88-44.** Reservations recommended. Main courses 1,800–2,500 ptas. ($10.80–$15); *menú del día* 3,000 ptas. ($18). AE, DC, MC, V. Mon–Sat 1:30–4pm and 9–11:30pm. Closed Aug. REGIONAL.

An ample bar greets you as you enter Casa Emilio, which serves primarily roasts, especially goat and beef. In air-conditioned comfort, you can also enjoy peppers stuffed with codfish or baked hake. From the well-stocked wine cellar come some of the finest Rioja wines. Casa Emilio is south of the old town, directly west of the major boulevard, Vara de Rey.

6 Haro

223 miles (359km) N of Madrid, 30 miles (48km) NE of Logroño

Center of the wine tours of the Rioja Alta district, the region around Haro has been compared to Tuscany. Come here to taste the wine at the *bodegas,* as international wine merchants do year-round (but especially after the autumn harvest).

ESSENTIALS

GETTING THERE   Four to five RENFE trains (☎ 941-31-15-97) run daily from Logroño (trip time: 1 hour one-way). There are also four to five connections per day from Zaragoza; the trip takes 3½ hours one-way.

Five to six buses per day run to Haro from Logroño. Trip time is 45 minutes to 1 hour one-way.

By car, follow the A-68 expressway (south of Logroño) northwest to the turnoff for Haro.

VISITOR INFORMATION   The **tourist information office** is at Plaza Monseñor Florentino Rodríguez, s/n (☎ 941-30-33-66). It is open Monday to Saturday 10am to 2pm and 4:30 to 7:30pm, Sunday 10am to 2pm.

SPECIAL EVENTS   Every June 29 the **Battle of Wine** erupts. It's an amusing, mock-medieval brawl in which opposing teams splatter each other with wineskins filled with the output from local vineyards.

EXPLORING HARO & VISITING THE BODEGAS

The town itself deserves a look before you head for the *bodegas.* Its old quarter is filled with mansions, some from the 16th century; the most interesting ones lie along **calle del Castillo.** At the center of the old quarter is the major architectural landmark of the town, the **Iglesia de San Tomás,** Plaza de la Iglesia. Distinguished by its wedding-cake tower and plateresque south portal, the 16th-century church has a Gothic interior.

You could spend up to 3 days touring the wineries in town, but chances are that a few visits will satisfy your curiosity. **Bodegas Muga,** Barrio de la Estación, s/n (☎ 941-31-04-98), near the rail station, offers tours (usually in Spanish) of its wine cellars. A tour in English is offered Monday to Friday at 11am.

Finally, pay a visit to **Rioja Alta,** avenida Vizcaya, s/n (☎ 941-31-03-46), not far from Muga. It's open Monday to Friday 9am to 2pm and 4 to 6pm (closed from mid-August to mid-September). Visits must be arranged in advance.

If you arrive in Haro in August or the first 2 weeks in September, when many of the *bodegas* are closed, settle instead for drinking wine in the *tascas* that line the streets between Parroquia and Plaza de la Paz. After a night spent there, you'll forget all about the *bodega* tours. Some of the finest wines in Spain are sold at these *tascas,* along with tapas—all at bargain prices.

WHERE TO STAY

Iturrimurri. Carretera N-124, km 41, s/n, 26200 Haro. ☎ **941-31-12-13.** Fax 941-31-17-21. E-mail: h.iturri@eniac.es. 52 units. A/C MINIBAR TV TEL. 11,800–15,800 ptas. ($71–$95) double. AE, DC, MC, V. Free parking.

Half a mile southeast of the city on the highway, this is the second choice hotel in Haro. The small but comfortable rooms are attractively furnished, many with impressive views. There is an animated cafeteria, as well as a large dining room serving regional meals accompanied by Rioja wines. Ample parking facilities are available. In summer, the garden and the swimming pool are compelling reasons to stay here.

Los Agustinos. Calle San Agustín, 2, 26200 Haro. ☎ **941-31-13-08.** Fax 941-30-31-48. 62 units. A/C TV TEL. 13,500 ptas. ($81) double; 26,000 ptas. ($156) suite. AE, DC, MC, V. Parking 900 ptas. ($5.40).

A former Augustinian convent has been turned into a four-star hotel in the center of Haro. Since its restoration and reopening in 1990, it has become the most desirable place to stay in a town that has always had too few accommodations. Owned by a Basque chain of hotels, it is in a "zone of tranquillity" (pedestrian zone). The rooms are well appointed and comfortable, each equipped with a good bed. The tidily arranged private bathrooms are equipped with hair dryers. A restaurant serves good-tasting regional meals, accompanied by selections from a well-stocked cellar of Rioja wines.

WHERE TO DINE

Beethoven I, II, y III. Santo Tomás, 3–5. ☎ **941-31-11-81.** Reservations required in summer. Main courses 1,800–2,200 ptas. ($10.80–$13.20); fixed-price menus 2,000–5,000 ptas. ($12–$30). MC, V. Daily 1:30–4pm and 9–11:30pm. REGIONAL/BASQUE.

This premier restaurant of Haro in the center of town is actually three restaurants, each standing beside one another. Each offers good food and value. One of them is a large old house where a bar has been installed. Have a drink here, then perhaps move next door to sample the more modern dining rooms at Beethoven II or III. They're justifiably famous for their platters of wild mushrooms, which chef Carlos Aquirre raises himself. Try the stuffed fillet of sole, vegetable stew, or wild pheasant, finishing off with an apple tart. The interiors are air-conditioned. The wine cellars are among the finest in the area.

Terete. Arana, 17. ☎ **941-31-00-23.** Reservations recommended. Main courses 3,000–4,000 ptas. ($18–$24); fixed-price menu 1,800 ptas. ($10.80). MC, V. Tues–Sun 1:15–4pm; Tues–Sat 8:30–11pm. Closed July 1–15 and Oct 15–31. REGIONAL.

This place has been an *horno asado* (restaurant specializing in roasts) since 1867 and is beloved by locals for its roast suckling pig. The service is discreet, the food savory and succulent—the kitchen has had a long time to learn the secrets of roasting meats. The dishes are all prepared according to traditional regional recipes. When the fresh asparagus comes in, that is reason enough to dine here. The local peaches in season make the best dessert. Naturally, the finest of Rioja wines are served. Terete is in the center of Haro.

The Basque Country

The Basque people are the oldest traceable ethnic group in Europe. Their language, called *Euskera* (also spelled "Euskara"), predates any of the commonly spoken Romance languages, its origins, like that of the Basque race itself, lost in obscurity. There are many competing theories. One commonly posited is that the Basques descended from the original Iberians, who lived in Spain before the arrival of the Celts some 3,500 years ago. Conqueror after conqueror, Roman to Visigoth to Moor, may have driven these people into the Pyrenees, where they stayed and carved out a life for themselves—filled with tradition and customs practiced to this day.

The region is called *Euskadi,* which in Basque means "collection of Basques." In a very narrow sense it refers to three provinces of Spain: Guipúzcoa (whose capital, **San Sebastián,** the number-one sightseeing destination in Euskadi, features La Concha, one of Spain's best-loved and most popular stretches of sand); Viscaya (whose capital is the industrial city **Bilbao**); and Alava (with its capital at **Vitoria**). But to Basque nationalists who dream of forging a new nation that will one day unite all the Basque lands, Euskadi also refers to the northern part of Navarre and three provinces in France, including the famed resort of Biarritz.

The three Spanish Basque provinces occupy the eastern part of the Cantabrian Mountains, between the Pyrenees and the valley of the Nervión. They maintained a large degree of independence until the 19th century, when they finally gave in to control from Castile, which continued to recognize their ancient rights and privileges until 1876.

Geographically, the Basque country straddles the western foothills of the Pyrenees, so the Basque people live in both France and Spain—but mostly in the latter. During the Spanish Civil War (1936–39), the Basques were on the Republican side defeated by Franco. Oppression during the Franco years has led to deep-seated resentment against the policies of Madrid.

The Basque separatist movement, ETA (Euskadi ta Askatasuna, or Basque Nation and Liberty), and the French organization Enbata (Ocean Wind) engaged, unsuccessfully, in guerrilla activity in 1968 to secure a united Basque state. On July 10, 1997, another event brought world attention (again) to the ETA. A 29-year-old Basque politician, Miguel Ángel Blanco, vanished from his home in the town of Ermua in the province of Viscaya. The kidnappers, all members of ETA, were

Basque Country

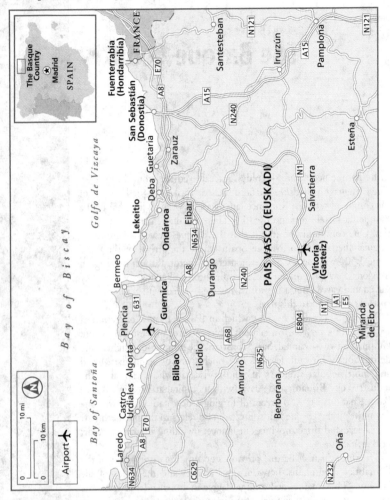

protesting against the jailing of Basque prisoners in the Canary Islands instead of in one of the Basque provinces. The central government has consistently refused to cave in to this demand, made on a number of occasions before. When ETA members learned that the government was once again refusing their demands, they killed Miguel Ángel. This led to an outpouring of protests among ordinary Basques who shouted *"Basta ya"* ("Enough already"). Thousands and thousands of people in the Basque provinces and throughout Spain took to the streets against the ETA. The consensus of the protesters seemed to be that violence and murder were not the way to achieve their long-desired autonomy. Still, many Basque nationalists fervently wish that the Basque people could be united into one autonomous state instead of being divided between France and Spain.

The riddle of the Basque language has puzzled linguists and ethnologists for years; its grammar, syntax, and vocabulary are unrelated to those of any other European language. Depending on the dialect spoken, the language is known as Euskera, Uskara, or Eskuara. Although on the wane since the beginning of this century, the Basque language is now enjoying a modest renaissance; it is taught in schools, and autonomous television stations in the Basque Country broadcast in the language.

Basques wear a *boina,* a beret of red, blue, or white woolen cloth as a badge of pride and a political statement. You may see nationalist graffiti as you travel, slogans such as *Euskadi Ta Askatasuna* ("Basques Nation & Liberty") painted everywhere. Although the separatist movement is still simmering, you'll find most of the people friendly, hospitable, and welcoming. Politics rarely intrudes on vacationers in this beautiful corner of Spain.

1 San Sebastián (Donostia)

13 miles (21km) W of the French border, 300 miles (483km) N of Madrid, 62 miles (100km) E of Bilbao

San Sebastián (*Donostia* in the Basque language) is the summer capital of Spain, and here the belle époque lives on. Ideally situated on a choice spot on the Bay of Biscay, it is surrounded by green mountains. From June to September the population swells as hundreds of Spanish bureaucrats escape the heat and head for this regional capital. A tasteful resort, it has few of the tawdry trappings associated with major beachfront cities. It is an ideal excursion center for trips to some of the Basque country's most fascinating towns.

Queen Isabella II put San Sebastián on the map as a tourist resort when she spent the summer of 1845 there. In time it became the summer residence of the royal court. On July 8, 1912, Queen María Cristina inaugurated the grand hotel named after her, and the resort became very fashionable. In what is now the city hall, built in 1887, a casino opened, and European aristocrats gambled in safety here during World War I.

San Sebastián is the capital of the province of Guipúzcoa, the smallest in Spain, tucked in the far northeastern corner bordering France. It is said that Guipúzcoa has preserved Basque customs better than any other province. Half of the *donostiarras*—residents of San Sebastián—speak Euskera. The city is a major seat of Basque nationalism, so be advised that protests, sometimes violent, are frequent.

San Sebastián contains an old quarter, **La Parte Vieja,** with narrow streets, hidden plazas, and medieval houses, but it is primarily a modern city of elegant shops, wide boulevards, sidewalk cafes, and restaurants.

La Concha is the city's most famous beach—especially in July and August when it seems as though half the population of Spain and France spends its days under striped canopies or dashing into the refreshingly cool waters of the bay. The shell-shaped La Concha is half-encircled by a promenade, where crowds mill during the evening. The adjoining beach is the **Playa de Ondarreta.** The climate here is decidedly more Atlantic than Mediterranean.

San Sebastián has a good, although insufficient, choice of hotels in summer, plus many excellent restaurants, most of which are expensive. Its chief drawback is overcrowding—it is overpopulated in July, and there are no beds to be had in August.

Bullfights, art and film festivals, sporting events, and cultural activities keep San Sebastián hopping during the summer season.

ESSENTIALS

GETTING THERE   From Madrid, **Iberia Airlines** (☎ 943-64-12-67 for flight information) offers two daily flights to San Sebastián, plus one daily flight from Barcelona. The domestic airport is at nearby Fuenterrabía. From Fuenterrabía buses run to the center of San Sebastián every 12 minutes, 7:48am to 10pm.

From Madrid, **RENFE** runs trains to the French border at Irún, many of which stop in San Sebastián (a 6- to 7-hour trip). An overnight train from Paris to Madrid stops in San Sebastián, just in time for breakfast (and San Sebastián's cafes serve the best croissants south of the Pyrenees). RENFE provides overnight train service from Barcelona to San Sebastián and on to Bilbao. For RENFE information, call ☎ **943-28-35-99.**

San Sebastián is well linked by a bus network to many of Spain's major cities, although if you're in Madrid, it's more convenient to take a train. Nine to 29 buses a day connect San Sebastián to Bilbao (trip time: 1¼ hours); three daily buses arrive from Barcelona (7 hours); and five buses run daily from Pamplona (1½ hours). These routes are covered by several private bus companies. The tourist office (see below) distributes an information pamphlet listing various routes, the companies that service these runs, and telephone numbers to call for schedules.

From Madrid, take the N-1 toll road north to Burgos, then follow A-1 to Miranda de Ebro. From here, continue on the A-68 north to Bilbao and then the A-8 east to San Sebastián. From Pamplona, take the A-15 north to the N-1 route, which leads right into San Sebastián.

VISITOR INFORMATION   The **tourist information office** is at calle Reina Regente, s/n (☎ **943-48-11-66**). It's open June to September, Monday to Saturday 8am to 8pm, Sunday 10am to 1pm; off-season, Monday to Friday 9am to 2pm and 3:30 to 7pm, Saturday 8am to 8pm.

SPECIAL EVENTS   Two weeklong events draw visitors from around the world. In mid-August, San Sebastián stages its annual carnival, **Aste Nagusia,** a joyous celebration of traditional Basque music and dance, along with fireworks, cooking competitions, and sports events. In mid-September, the San Sebastián **International Film Festival** draws luminaries from America and Europe. The actual dates of these festivals vary from year to year, so check with the tourist office (see above). In the second half of July, San Sebastián hosts a jazz festival, **Jazzaldia.**

EXPLORING & ENJOYING SAN SEBASTIÁN

San Sebastián means beach time, excellent Basque food, and strolling along the Paseo de la Concha. The monuments, such as they are, can easily be viewed before lunch.

Museo de San Telmo, Plaza Zuloaga, 1 (☎ **943-42-49-70**), housed in a 16th-century Dominican monastery, contains an impressive collection of Basque artifacts dating from prehistoric times. The museum includes works by Zuloaga (*Torreillos en Turégano,* for example), golden age artists such as El Greco and Ribera, and a large number of Basque painters. Standing in the old town at the base of Monte Urgull, the museum is open Tuesday to Saturday 10:30am to 1:30pm and 4 to 7pm, Sunday 10am to 2pm. Admission is 350 ptas. ($2.10) adults, 200 ptas. ($1.20) students and children.

The wide promenade **Paseo Nuevo** almost encircles Monte Urgull, one of the two mountains between which San Sebastián is nestled (**Monte Igueldo** is the other one). A ride along this promenade opens onto panoramic vistas of the Bay of Biscay. The paseo comes to an end at the **Palacio del Mar,** Muelle, 34 (☎ **943-44-00-99**), an oceanographic museum and aquarium. Like most cutting-edge aquariums, it boasts a mesmerizing collection of huge tanks containing myriad marine species. A transparent underwater walkway allows an entire 360-degree view of sharks, rays, and other fish as they swim around you. A maritime museum upstairs presents a fascinating synopsis of mankind's precarious relationship with the sea down through the ages through historical displays of fishing gear, naval artifacts, and marine fossils. Here you can also see the skeleton of the last whale caught in the Bay of Biscay, in 1878. The museum

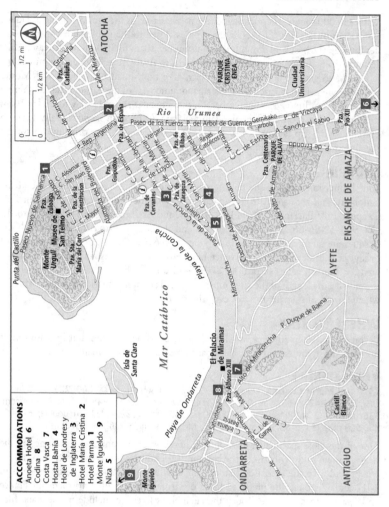

ACCOMMODATIONS
Anoeta Hotel 6
Codina 8
Costa Vasca 7
Hostal Bahía 4
Hotel de Londres y de Inglaterra 3
Hotel María Cristina 2
Hotel Parma 1
Monte Igueldo 9
Niza 5

is open July to May, daily 10am to 1:30pm and 3 to 7pm, and June, daily 10am to 10pm. Admission is 700 ptas. ($4.20) for adults, 350 ptas. ($2.10) for children ages 5 to 12, and free for children 4 and under.

Other sights include **El Palacio de Miramar,** which stands on its own hill opening onto La Concha. In the background is the residential district of Antiguo. Queen María Cristina, after whom the grandest hotel in the north of Spain is named, opened this palace in 1893, but by the turbulent 1930s it had fallen into disrepair. The city council took it over in 1971 and renovations continue. You can visit daily in summer 9am to 9:30pm and daily in winter 10am to 5pm. Because you can't go inside the palace, you must settle for a look at the lawns and gardens. The palace stands on land splitting the two major beaches of San Sebastián: Playa de la Concha and Playa de Ondarreta.

Another palace of interest is the **Palacio de Ayete,** which was constructed by the duke of Bailéen in 1878 and became the summer home of King Alfonso XIII and his queen, María Cristina, until their own Palacio Miramar (see above) was completed.

With 250,000 square feet of parkland, the palace served as the summer home of Franco from 1940 until 1975. The residence remains closed to the public, but you can wander through the beautiful grounds daily in summer 10am to 8:30pm or off-season daily 10am to 5pm. To reach it, take bus number 19 to Ayete from Plaza de Guipúzcoa.

Finally, to get the best view of the city, take the funicular to the top of **Monte Igueldo,** where from a gazebo you get a panoramic view of the bay and the Cantabrian coastline. From June 25 to September 25, the funicular runs Monday to Friday 10am to 9pm and Saturday and Sunday 10am to 10pm. Off-season service is daily 11am to 8pm. A round-trip fare costs 170 ptas. ($1). It's also possible to drive up. In spring, the air is rich with the scent of honeysuckle.

SHOPPING

Your immersion into Basque culture will probably prompt you to buy some of the handcrafts and accessories from the region. Two of the best outlets for them include **Txapela,** calle Puerto, 3 (☎ **943-42-02-43**), and **Arriluzea,** calle 31 de Augusto, 13 (☎ **943-42-56-66**). Both sell souvenirs and the rough cotton shirts for which the Basques are famous. And if you're looking for a *boina* (beret), or any other form of headgear, consider a visit to the venerable shelves of San Sebastián's oldest hat manufacturer, **Ponsol,** calle Narrica, 4 (☎ **943-42-08-76**). For virtually anything else in the city, try the length of the city's most congested shopping district, **Paseo de Muelle,** where dozens of merchants hawk everything from T-shirts to cameras and film.

WHERE TO STAY

If you book well in advance, you'll find many good hotel values, but in season most hoteliers insist you take at least half board (breakfast plus one main meal).

VERY EXPENSIVE

✪ **Hotel María Cristina.** Oquendo, 1, 20004 San Sebastián. ☎ **800/221-2340** in the U.S., or 943-42-49-00. Fax 943-42-39-14. www.westin.com. E-mail: hmc@westin.com. 136 units. A/C MINIBAR TV TEL. 38,200–75,250 ptas. ($229–$451.50) double; 61,600–430,900 ptas. ($370–$2,585) suite. AE, DC, MC, V. Parking 3,200 ptas. ($20).

One of the most spectacular belle époque hotels in Spain, enviably positioned in the heart of town midway between the bay and Río Urumea, this is the town's top choice. Set behind a facade of chiseled stone and ornate ironwork, the Cristina opened in 1912 and was once the preferred hotel of virtually every titled aristocrat in France and Spain who came here. Today the clientele is likely to include movie stars, film directors, and a crowd of newly moneyed moguls; this is where the glitterati stay during San Sebastián's film festival.

The hotel was richly remodeled in 1987. The public rooms are opulent with ormolu, Cuban mahogany, acres of onyx and exotic marbles, and rosewood marquetry. The spacious guest rooms are appropriately lavish, with luxury beds, bathrooms, and furnishings. Amenities include extra-plush towels and hair dryers.

Dining/Diversions: The main dining room, the restaurant **Easo,** serves Basque and international food in three-course, fixed-price lunches and dinners. The hotel contains one of the most beautiful bars in town, the **Gritti,** with occasional piano music.

Amenities: 24-hour room service, baby-sitting, laundry and valet, concierge, car rentals (with or without driver), business center.

EXPENSIVE

Costa Vasca. Avenida de Pio Baroja, 20008 San Sebastián. ☎ **943-21-10-11.** Fax 943-21-24-28. www.elebe.com. 203 units. A/C MINIBAR TV TEL. 21,000 ptas. ($126) double; 42,500 ptas. ($255) suite. AE, DC, MC, V. Free parking.

A large, red-brick hotel rated four stars by the government, the well-run Costa Vasca is 10 minutes from Ondarreta Beach and a 5-minute drive (or 10 minutes on foot) from the center of town. Next to El Palacio de Miramar, the interior of the hotel is modern and businesslike with plenty of space for conferences and banquets; however, it's ideal for the individual traveler too. The rooms are good-sized, airy, and comfortably furnished with fully equipped bathrooms, plus a small lounge area. Many of the accommodations have balconies. The decoration is tasteful but discreet.

Dining/Diversions: The hotel's formal restaurant serves excellent and traditional Basque dishes as well as international fare, and there is a cafeteria for breakfasts and light snacks, plus an international bar.

Amenities: Well-tended garden, limited room service, laundry, concierge, baby-sitting.

Hotel de Londres y de Inglaterra. Zubieta, 2, 20007 San Sebastián. ☎ **943-44-07-70.** Fax 943-44-04-91. www.paisvasco.com/hotel/londres. E-mail: h.londres@paisvasco.com. 145 units. A/C MINIBAR TV TEL. 21,000–23,000 ptas. ($126–$138) double; 25,000–30,000 ptas. ($150–$180) suite. AE, DC, MC, V. Parking 1,800 ptas. ($10.80) nearby.

Beside the northern edge of the town's most popular beach, Playa de la Concha, this venerable 19th-century hotel is one of the most stylish in town. It's not as plush as the María Cristina, but then again, it's significantly more affordable. Views from many of the balconies encompass the beach and a handful of rocky offshore islands. The traditional-style public rooms contain deep armchairs and big windows. Completely renovated in the past few years, the hotel has comfortably conservative, good-size guest rooms with a vaguely English decor, individual safes, and modern marble bathrooms with hair dryers.

Dining/Diversions: Serving both Basque and international cuisine is **La Brasserie Mari Galant.** A bar is adjacent to it, and there's also the street-level **Swing Bar.**

Amenities: Room service (1 to 4pm and 8:30 to 11pm), laundry and valet, concierge, baby-sitting, in-house tour operator/travel agent, car rentals, cafeteria, bingo parlor.

MODERATE

Anoeta Hotel. Paseo de Anoeta, 30, 20014 San Sebastián. ☎ **943-45-14-99.** Fax 943-45-20-36. www.hotellanoeta.com. E-mail: hotel@hotellanoeta.com. 26 units. A/C MINIBAR TV TEL. 13,500 ptas. ($81) double; 18,300 ptas. ($109.80) suite. AE, DC, MC, V. Parking: 1,000 ptas. ($6). Bus: 26 or 28.

Close to the sports arena and a 5-minute drive from the town center, this three-star hotel is named for the old village that once stood here but was long ago absorbed by the growing boundaries of San Sebastián. Anoeta features cherrywood, marble fittings, and a modern decor behind its brick facade. With a welcoming atmosphere, it is one of the better choices in the middle-bracket range. The rooms are generally small but are most inviting with comfortable beds, wooden furniture, carpeted floors, and fully equipped bathrooms. A restaurant specializes in Basque cuisine.

Monte Igueldo. Paseo del Faro, 134, Monte Igueldo, 20008 San Sebastián. ☎ **943-21-02-11.** Fax 943-21-50-28. 125 units. TV TEL. 18,500–21,000 ptas. ($111–$126) double; 23,000–25,000 ptas. ($138–$150) triple. AE, DC, MC, V. Free parking. Bus: Igueldo.

This first-class hotel is perched like a castle on the top of the mountain overlooking San Sebastián, a 10-minute drive from the center of town. The public rooms, guest rooms, and pool terrace all boast panoramic views of the coast. Each of the streamlined, modern rooms has a private balcony. Furnishings are standardized but reasonably comfortable; each room has a firm mattress and an immaculately kept tiled bathroom. A restaurant serves Spanish and international cuisine; there is a bar on the premises.

Niza. Zubieta, 56, 20007 San Sebastián. ☎ **943-42-66-63.** Fax 943-44-12-51. www.adegi.es/hotelniza. E-mail: niza@adegi.es. 41 units. TV TEL. 15,000–17,000 ptas. ($90–$102) double. AE, MC, V. Parking 1,700 ptas. ($10) nearby. Bus: 5 or 6.

This charming little hotel, which opens onto the Playa de la Concha, has real character and a great location. It has modern furnishings in the small rooms and antiques in the public lounges. The petit salon, for example, contains an Oriental rug, directoire chairs, a tall grandfather clock, and a rosewood breakfront. In direct contrast are the rather basic rooms, with wooden headboards, white walls, and wall-to-wall carpeting. There's a pizzeria in the cellar, plus a bar overlooking the sea.

INEXPENSIVE

Codina. Avenida Zumalacárregui, 21, 20008 San Sebastián. ☎ **943-21-22-00.** Fax 943-21-25-23. 77 units. TV TEL. July–Sept (including half board), 12,000 ptas. ($72) double; Oct–June, 10,000 ptas. ($60) double. AE, DC, MC, V. Parking 1,000 ptas. ($6). Bus: 5 or 25.

Set in an attractive upscale residential district, less than 250 yards (227.5m) from Playa Ondaretta, this six-story, modern-looking hotel was originally built in the mid-1960s. Each of the comfortably furnished, compact rooms has a view of the bay and simple, summery, virtually indestructible furniture, including good beds. On the side of the hotel that faces the busy avenida Zumalacárregui, you'll find a popular cafe and bar that serves traditional Basque cuisine.

Hostal Bahía. Calle San Martín, 54B, 20007 San Sebastián. ☎ **943-46-92-11.** Fax 943-46-39-14. 55 units. TV TEL. 8,900–13,900 ptas. ($53–$83) double. Rates include breakfast. DC, MC, V. Parking 1,750 ptas. ($10.50). Bus: 5, 6, 7, 8, or 9.

A good-value hotel just 1 block from the beach, the Bahía features guest rooms of varying sizes: Some are large enough to contain sofas and armchairs; others fall into the cubicle category. Each comes with a firm mattress and a tidy little bathroom with a shower stall. Many North Americans stay here and take public transportation to Pamplona for the running of the bulls.

Hotel Parma. Paseo de Salamanca, 10, 20003 San Sebastián. ☎ **943-42-88-93.** Fax 943-42-40-82. www.atenet.es/hagi/parma/index.htm. 27 units. TEL. 9,800–15,800 ptas. ($58.80–$94.80) double. AE, DC, MC, V. Parking 1,800 ptas. ($10.80). Bus: 5, 6, 8, 9, 21, or 28.

This clean, modern hotel in the center of town has beautiful views of the ocean. The Parma has small, up-to-date rooms cozily furnished in wood, with good, modern bathrooms with a shower stall. There is a downstairs snack bar as well as a pleasant TV lobby with armchairs and sofas. Breakfast is the only meal served.

WHERE TO DINE
EXPENSIVE

✪ **Akelare.** Paseo del Padre Orkolaga, 56. ☎ **943-21-20-52.** Reservations strongly recommended. Main courses 2,800–5,500 ptas. ($16.80–$33); tasting menu 9,500 ptas. ($57). AE, DC, MC, V. Tues–Sun 1–3:30pm; Tues–Sat 8:30–11pm. Closed Jan 2–Mar 7 and Sept 27–Oct 13. BASQUE.

A visit to Akelare is a must for serious foodies. Owner-chef Pedro Subijana won the 1983 National Prize for Gastronomy, awarded to the best chef in Spain. His preparations have influenced a generation of chefs and defined, perhaps more than any other, the entire philosophy of *la nueva cocina vasca* (modern Basque cuisine). Established in 1974, the restaurant is on the western edge of San Sebastián in a hexagonal villa originally built as a catering hall. Inside, a sweeping view through large windows encompasses the mists and raging currents of the Bay of Biscay far below. The plushly upholstered modern decor, with a hospitable fireplace, is an appropriate foil for dishes inspired by the Basque *caseríos* (farmsteads).

The perfect beginning to any meal here is puff pastry filled with fillets of anchovies, accompanied by a glass of chilled *fino* sherry. Traditional dishes might include fish cooked on a griddle with garlic and parsley; beans accompanied by bacon, chorizo, and pork ribs; baked rice with clams; or a special *marmitako* (fisherman's stew). More innovative are the snails with watercress sauce; boiled cabbage stuffed with duck meat and served with puree of celery; a warm salad of bonito fish served with a basil, lemon, chervil, and vinegar sauce; and fillet of duck with an assortment of exotic seasonal mushrooms. On occasion, Subijana may venture into the dining room to gauge the reaction to his inventions and to offer advice about the day's menu. The name of the restaurant, incidentally, translates from the Basque as "Witches' Sabbath."

✪ **Arzak.** Alto de Miracruz, 21. ☎ **943-28-55-93.** Reservations required. Main courses 3,000–5,500 ptas. ($18–$33); fixed-price menu 10,800 ptas. ($64.80) excluding drinks. AE, DC, MC, V. Tues–Sun 1–3:30pm; Tues–Sat 8:30–11:30pm. Closed June 15–July 3 and Nov 5–30. BASQUE.

One of the most famous restaurants in the Basque world (an honor it shares with Akelare; see above), this legendary establishment occupies the lavishly renovated childhood home of owner-chef Juan Mari Arzak. Well known in San Sebastián for his role in preparing a meal for Queen Elizabeth II of Britain (for which he later received an invitation to Buckingham Palace), Arzak combines staples of the Basque culinary legacy with many new creations of his own and is in the forefront of new Basque cuisine. Begin with a selection of fresh oysters or, even more elegant, natural foie gras. Crayfish is regularly featured as an appetizer, as is the chef's special *sopa de pescado* (fish soup). For a main course, consider *merluza* (hake) in a vinaigrette with onions and small squid. On the back of the menu is a list of classic dishes that have won the most praise among visitors since the restaurant's opening—everything from stuffed sweet peppers with a fish mousse to pheasant or partridge. For dessert, the orange flan with cream might just be the best you've ever had. The restaurant is on the main road leading from the center of town to the French border.

Casa Nicolasa. Calle Aldamar, 4. ☎ **943-42-07-55.** Reservations required. Main courses 2,800–4,800 ptas. ($16.80–$28.80); *menú del chef* 6,500 ptas. ($39). AE, DC, MC, V. Mon–Sat 1–3:30pm; Tues–Sat 8:30–11:30pm. Closed Jan 21–Feb 13. BASQUE.

Members of all-male eating clubs (a Basque tradition begun in the 19th century) have assured us that Casa Nicolasa serves the best cuisine at San Sebastián. That would be difficult to prove, especially in a city where international food critics have rated Arzak and Akelare even higher (see above).

In the heart of the resort, at the edge of the old town by the Mercado la Brecha, the restaurant features refined cuisine and impeccable service. Diners are made to feel like guests being served by a proper butler. Master chef José Juan Castillo, greatly aided by his gracious wife, Ana María, seems to believe that gastronomy should be elevated to a high art—and he does that convincingly here.

Many of the dishes served have stood the test of time; others reflect the culinary imagination of the 1990s. Foie gras is homemade and is the smoothest, albeit the most expensive, way to begin a meal here. *Rape* (monkfish) is prepared in various creative ways and, we have found, is one of the most satisfying main courses. Save room for dessert, as the pastry selections are one of the outstanding features of the kitchen. When business is at its peak in August and September, the restaurant is likely to open Monday night for dinner as well.

✪ **Martín Berasategui.** Loidi Kalea, 4, Lasarte. ☎ **943-00-31-62.** Reservations required. Main courses 2,200–4,000 ptas. ($13.20–$24); tasting menu 8,500 ptas. ($51). MC, V. Tues–Sat 8:30–11pm. Closed 2 weeks at Christmas. BASQUE.

Just when you thought the dining situation in San Sebastián couldn't stand any more starred chefs, along comes Martín Berasategui, whose cooking has excited food critics throughout Europe. Trained by his mother, who cooked for local fishers for a small fee, Berasategui opened his restaurant on the outskirts of town, and the world has literally flocked to his door ever since.

His cuisine is subtle and pure, and he uses butter and cream for desserts only. The hors d'oeuvres are among the best we've ever sampled in the region—from a curl of cider-marinated mackerel with fried anchovies in olive oil to morsels of rare tuna belly grilled over wooden charcoal. Starters include a rich-sounding lobster soup with barnacles. For a main dish, opt for such delectable choices as hake with baby clams or a refreshing gazpacho of *langostinos*. If you try one of the tasting menus, you'll get a summation of Berasategui's cuisine—perhaps pan-seared lambs' brains surrounded by baby salad greens and a fat and juicy slice of duck liver. The chef's attention to detail is terrific. For example, for a *porrusalda* (soup) made with, among other ingredients, fresh sea eel and ribbons of smoked eel, Berasategui collects the moisture the eels give off when smoked and mixes it back into the savory broth.

Panier Fleuri. Paseo de Salamanca, 1. ☎ **943-42-42-05.** Reservations required. Main courses 2,500–4,500 ptas. ($15–$27); fixed-price menu 5,000 ptas. ($30). AE, DC, MC, V. Thurs–Tues 1–3:30pm; Mon–Tues and Thurs–Sat 8:30–11pm. Closed June 1–24 and Dec 24–31. BASQUE/INTERNATIONAL.

Yet another celebrated restaurant in San Sebastián, this citadel of cuisine serves Basque dishes with a definite French flavor and flair, typical of the resort of Biarritz across the border in France. A third generation of the Fombedilla family of chefs has had a long time to perfect their cuisine. Service is discreet and elegant, and diners here have a chance to learn why Basque food preparation is regarded as among the finest in Europe. The setting alone is rewarding, in a formal dining room opening onto the pounding surf at the mouth of the Urumea River.

The chef, Tatus Fombellida, has won the National Prize for Gastronomy in Spain, and critics of San Sebastián cuisine claim she's better than ever. Her *faisan* (pheasant) and *becada asada* (roast woodcock) have been hailed as among the finest game dishes at the resort. Another delectable offering is sole baked with spinach and presented with a fresh hollandaise sauce, similar to what you might find in one of the better restaurants of Florence. Finish off this rich fare with a lemon sorbet with champagne.

Even better known than the cuisine here is the wine cellar, which contains many vintage bottles. The wine steward will guide you through an often perplexing selection, including mellow versions of such wines as Remelluri, Barón de Oña, and Viña Albina.

MODERATE

Bodegón Alejandro. Calle Fermín Calbetón, 4. ☎ **943-42-71-58.** Reservations recommended. Set-price menu 3,500 ptas. ($22.05). AE, MC, V. Tues–Sun 1–4pm; Tues–Sat 9–11pm. BASQUE.

In a pair of pale yellow, Basque-derived dining rooms accented with tiles and a sense of nostalgia for years gone by, this *bodega*-style restaurant focuses exclusively on a set-price menu whose composition changes virtually every day. Many of the ingredients come from the nearby marketplace, reflecting the seasonality and rich bounty of the Basque country. Menu items are based on recipes many diners remember from their childhoods, including red peppers stuffed with salt cod and herbs; seafood stews with rice; artichokes with clams; and roasted veal or braised pork in wine sauce. Any of a rotating series of pastries and cakes are high-caloric but eminently satisfying desserts.

Juanito Kojua. Puerto, 14. ☎ **943-42-01-80.** Reservations required. Main courses 1,850–5,500 ptas. ($11.10–$33); fixed-price menus 2,500–3,500 ptas. ($15–$21). AE, DC, MC, V. Daily 1–3:30pm; Mon–Sat 8:30–11:30pm. BASQUE/SEAFOOD.

This little seafood restaurant in the old town, off Plaza de la Constitución, has no decor to speak of, but it has become famous throughout Spain. There's always a wait, but it's worth it. There are two dining areas on the main floor, behind a narrow bar (perfect for an appetizer while you're waiting for your table), plus one downstairs—both air-conditioned in summer. Specialties may include paella, half a *besugo* (sea bream), *rape* (monkfish), and *lubina* (sea bass). The meats are good, too, but it's best to stick to the fresh fish dishes.

Urepel. Paseo de Salamanca, 3. ☎ **943-42-40-40.** Reservations required. Main courses 1,800–3,500 ptas. ($10.80–$21). AE, DC, MC, V. Mon and Wed–Sat 1–3:30pm and 8:30–11pm. Closed at Easter for Holy Week, July 1–23, and Dec 24–Jan 6. BASQUE/INTERNATIONAL.

Standing close to one of its major competitors, the equally rewarding Panier Fleuri (see above), Urepel is near the mouth of the Urumea River, at the edge of the old town. Its interior is not as elegant as the establishments reviewed above, but fans of this place aren't bothered by that at all. They're here for the food.

The restaurant is the domain of Tomás Almandoz, one of the outstanding chefs in the north of Spain. Seafood dominates the menu and is deftly handled, often served with delicate sauces. The main courses are made even better by an emphasis on fresh and perfectly prepared vegetables. *Rape, dorada,* and *cigalas* (crayfish) are likely to turn up on the menu. You can also order goose or duck, somewhat rare in San Sebastián. One specialty is *pato de caserío fileteado a la naranja* (regional-style duck flavored with oranges).

One local food critic got so carried away with the dessert cart and its presentation that she claimed, "It would take Velázquez to arrange a pastry so artfully"—an indication of how highly regarded this place is. We prefer it in the evening instead of at midday, when many of the tables are reserved by local businesspeople and government officials.

INEXPENSIVE

La Oka. San Martín, 46. ☎ **943-46-38-84.** Main courses 950–1,800 ptas. ($5.70–$10.80); fixed-price menu 1,800 ptas. ($10.80). AE, MC, V. Daily 1–3:30pm; Fri–Sat 8:30–11pm. BASQUE.

Don't come to La Oka, near the beach in the center of town, looking for glamour. Come for an inexpensive self-service cafeteria experience. Some critics, in fact, rate it the best self-service cafeteria in Spain. The diners represent a cross section of the city's office workers. The Basque cooking here is hearty and plentiful, and you can order a very good Valencia-style paella.

Rekondo. Paseo Igueldo, 57. ☎ **943-21-29-07.** Reservations recommended. Main courses 1,800–3,850 ptas. ($11.35–$24.25). AE, DC, MC, V. Thurs–Tues 1–3:30pm and 8:30–11:30pm. Closed 2 weeks in June and 3 weeks in Nov. BASQUE.

This is one of the most substantial restaurants in town, with a location near the beach and a clientele that often schedules meals here as part of wedding anniversaries and birthdays. The setting is a trio of formally decorated pale yellow dining rooms. Menu items include grilled chops and steaks, different preparations of hake and flounder, and spicy, garlic-laced versions of octopus and squids. Food is usually accompanied with any of a very large choice of vintages from throughout Europe. Chefs don't tax their imaginations but prepare solid, reliable fare based on time-tested recipes.

SAN SEBASTIÁN AFTER DARK

The best evening entertainment in San Sebastián is to go **tapas tasting** in the old quarter of town. Throughout the rest of Spain this is known as a *tapeo,* or tapas crawl. In San Sebastián it's called a ***poteo-ir-de-pinchos,*** or searching out morsels on toothpicks. Groups of young people often spend their evenings on some 20 streets in the old town, each leading toward Monte Urgull, the port, or La Brecha marketplace. Alameda del Bulevar is the most upscale of these streets; calle Fermín Calveton, one of the most popular. You'll find plenty of these places on your own, but here are some to get you going.

Bar Asador Ganbara, calle San Jerónimo, 21 (☎ 943-42-25-75), is decorated with a flair in light-colored wood and is a tapas lover's delight. The dishes are well prepared, using market-fresh ingredients. Try the house specialty and the chef's pride: small melt-in-your-mouth croissants filled with cheese, egg, bacon, and Serrano ham. Also sample the spider crab and prawns with mayonnaise. Tapas run 175 to 300 ptas. ($1.05 to $1.80), drinks from 200 to 500 ptas. ($1.20 to $3). In addition to its bar service, the establishment runs a restaurant in a separate section, offering a fixed-price menu at 3,200 ptas. ($19.20). The bar is open Tuesday to Sunday 11am to 3:15pm and Tuesday to Saturday 6 to 11:45pm. The restaurant is open Tuesday to Sunday from 1 to 3:30pm and Tuesday to Saturday 8 to 11:15pm. Calle San Jerónimo runs at right angles to calle Fermín Calveton.

The tasty tapas served at **Casa Alcalde,** Mayor, 19 (☎ 943-42-62-16), just a 5-minute walk from the Parque Alderdi Eder, are thinly sliced ham, cheese, and shellfish dishes. The different varieties are all neatly displayed, and priced from 200 to 300 ptas. ($1.20 to $1.80). You can also have full meals in a small restaurant at the back, for 3,000 to 4,500 ptas. ($18 to $27). It's open daily 10am to 11pm.

The variety of tapas and wines offered at **Casa Valles,** Reyes Católicos, 10 (☎ 943-45-22-10), seems endless. Go to hang out with the locals and feast on tidbits guaranteed to spoil your dinner. Most tapas cost 175 ptas. ($1.05), with a beer going for 225 ptas. ($1.35). Casa Valles is in the center of town behind the cathedral. Open daily 8:30 to 11:30pm (closed the last 2 weeks of June and the last 2 weeks of December).

Many locals say that **La Cepa,** 31 de Agosto, 7–9 (☎ 943-42-63-94), on the northern edge of the old town, serves perhaps the best tapas, and the Jabugo ham is one proof of this claim. Try the grilled squid or the salt cod–and–green pepper omelet. You can also order dinner here—a daily menu that costs 3,000 ptas. ($18). Tapas begin at 175 ptas. ($1.05), but could go up to 1,900 ptas. ($11.40) for a small portion of Jabugo ham. A glass of wine costs 125 ptas. (75¢). It's open daily 11am to midnight.

Delectable tapas can be found at **Aloña/Berri,** Berminghan, 24, Nuevo Gros (☎ 943-290-818), where you can feast on the delights of silky salt cod *brandade,* pigeon in pastry, and anchovies in red pepper cream from 175 ptas. ($1.05). At **Oñatz,** Urdaneta, 22 (☎ 943-455-547), they serve the city's most exquisite morsels, none better than a "haystack" of foie gras and apples. You can go on to the mussel and garlic flan or braised oxtail. At the family-run **Bar Juli,** Viteri, 27, Renteria (☎ 943-512-887), Igor, a graduate of Arzak (see "Where to Dine," above), lures and satisfies the most demanding palates of San Sebastián. Try his sushilike tuna salad and what have been called "the best seafood *croquetas* on the northern shore of Spain." Tapas cost from 175 to 350 ptas. ($1.05 to $2.10).

In most of the Basque country, the tapas-eating ritual is different from the rest of Spain. A platter of tapas, more correctly called *pinchos,* such as stuffed anchovies is placed out on the bar. Patrons spear the tasty morsels with toothpicks, and when they're done, servers tally up the toothpicks to determine how much is owed. A pale dry white wine, known as *xacoli,* is usually consumed chilled in a plain highball glass to accompany tapas such as eel with parsley, garlic, and virgin olive oil.

San Sebastián has other nightlife possibilities, but they dim when compared to a *tapeo.* Nevertheless, if disco isn't too retro for you, head for **Kabutzia,** Muelle (no phone), where a cover and one drink costs 2,000 ptas. ($12). The club opens at 8pm, with variable closing times, depending on business. The best live jazz is found at the jazz gallery, **Altxeri Galeria,** calle Reina Regente, 2 (☎ **943-42-29-31**), where a cover charge may or may not be imposed, depending on the group. It's open Sunday to Thursday 5pm to 1:30am and Friday and Saturday 5pm to 3:30am.

San Sebastián's only venue for gambling is the **Casino de San Sebastián,** Mayor, 1 (☎ **943-42-92-14**). The casino requires minimum bets of between 250 and 500 ptas. ($1.50 and $3) for the roulette tables and 250 ptas. ($1.50) for the blackjack tables. Entrance costs 650 ptas. ($3.90) per person, and requires the presentation of an identity card with a photograph or a passport. Jackets and neckties for men are not required. From September 16 to June 14, the casino is open daily 6:30pm to 3am (until 4am on Saturday and holidays), and between June 15 and September 15, it's open daily 6:30pm to 4am (till 5am on Saturday and on holidays).

SIDE TRIPS FROM SAN SEBASTIÁN

One of the reasons for coming to San Sebastián is to use it as a base for touring the surrounding area. Driving is best because bus connections are awkward or nonexistent.

PASAI DONIBANE

On the east bank of a natural harbor 6½ miles (10.5km) from San Sebastián, Pasai Donibane—formerly known by its Spanish name, Pasajes de San Juan—is one of the most typical of Basque fishing villages. Many visitors come here to dine. The village, with its codfish-packing factories, is on a sheltered harbor with fishing boats tied up at the wharf. The architecture is appealing: five- and six-story balconied tenementlike buildings in different colors.

Victor Hugo lived here in the summer of 1846 (it hasn't changed much since) at building number 63 on the narrow main street, San Juan.

In summer, don't take a car into the village. Parking is difficult, the medieval streets are one-way, and the wait at traffic signals is long because all southbound traffic has to clear the street before northbound motorists have the right of way.

A bus leaves every 15 minutes from the calle Aldamar in San Sebastián for **Pasajes de San Pedro,** Pasai Donibane's neighboring fishing village. From here, it's possible to walk to Pasai Donibane. Buses head back to San Sebastián from Pasajes de San Pedro at a quarter to the hour all day long.

Where to Dine

Txulotxo. San Juan, 82, Pasai Donibane. ☎ **943-52-39-52.** Reservations recommended. Main courses 1,500–2,000 ptas. ($9–$12); *menú del día* 2,000 ptas. ($12). AE, V. Wed–Mon 1:30–4:30pm; Wed–Sat and Mon 8:30–11:30pm. Closed Dec. BASQUE.

Right on the waterfront, this old stone building with a glass-enclosed dining room overlooking the harbor is one of the most authentic and typical of Basque restaurants. The house specialties are made from fish delivered daily. For openers, try the *sopa de pescado* (fish soup) or a mixture of *entremeses variados* (hors d'oeuvres). Although pasta dishes are featured, most diners opt for one of the good-tasting seafood selections, perhaps hake in green sauce or perfectly grilled shrimp. The grilled monkfish with clams and shrimp is done to perfection. There are new specialties worth trying, including brochettes and *crepes de txangurro.*

LOYOLA

Surrounded by mountain scenery, Loyola, 34 miles (55km) southwest of San Sebastián, is the birthplace of St. Ignatius, the founder of the Jesuits. He was born in 1491, died in 1556, and was canonized in 1622. The sanctuary at Loyola is the most visited attraction outside San Sebastián.

There are large pilgrimages to Loyola for the annual celebration on St. Ignatius Day, July 31. The activity is centered at the **Monasterio de San Ignacio de Loyola,** an immense structure built by the Jesuits in the 1700s around the Loyola family manor house near Azpeitia. An International Festival of Romantic Music is held here during the first week of August.

The **basilica** is the work of Italian architect Fontana. Surrounded by a 118-foot-high cupola by Churriguera, it is circular in design. From 12:30 to 3:30pm daily, visitors can enter the **Santa Casa,** with its 15th-century tower on the site of the former Loyola manor house. The rooms in which the saint was born and in which he convalesced have been converted into richly decorated chapels. At the entrance you can rent a tape detailing Loyola's life, and dioramas are shown at the end of the tour.

Six buses a day leave from Plaza Guipúzcoa, 2, San Sebastián, for Loyola (the first departing at 8:30am and the last at 8pm). Buses return about every 2 hours.

ONDÁRROA

Ondárroa, 30 miles (48km) west of San Sebastián, is described as a *pueblo típico,* a typical Basque fishing village. It's the area's largest fishing port. Lying on a spit of land, it stands between a hill and a loop of the Artibay River. Laundry hangs from the windows of the little plant-filled balconied houses, and most of the residents are engaged in canning and fish salting, if not fishing. The local church looks like a ship's prow at one end. Around the snug harbor you'll find many little places to drink and dine after taking a stroll through the village. From San Sebastián, Ondárroa is serviced by buses that run along the Costa Vasca. If you're driving, head west from San Sebastián along the coastal road.

LEKEITIO

The unspoiled but talked-about Basque fishing village of Lekeitio is 38 miles (61km) west of San Sebastián. There are those who consider it more authentic than Ondárroa. At the foot of Mount Calvario, Lekeitio opens onto a deeply indented bay. Queen Isabella II first gave the town prominence when she spent time here in the 19th century. Fishing may have diminished in recent years, but Lekeitio is still home to some of the Basque coast's trawlers. The island of San Nicolás converts the bay into a naturally protected harbor, a phenomenon that led to the village's growth. Note the 15th-century church guarding the harbor. Three tiers of flying buttresses characterize this monument, which has a baroque belfry. Go inside to the third south chapel, off the right nave, to see a remarkable altarpiece, *The Road to Calvary,* which was erected in a flamboyant Gothic style. A beach is across from the harbor, but the one at Carraspio, farther along the bay, is considered safer.

The town is noted for its festivals, including the **feast day of Saints Peter and Paul** on June 29, at which a *Kaxarranca,* a Basque folk dance, takes place. A dancer leaps about on top of a trunk carried through the streets by some hearty Basque fishers. Even better known is the controversial Jaiak San Antolín, or **goose festival,** September 1 to 8. A gruesome custom, it involves hanging live geese in the harbor. Youths leap from rowboats to grab the greased necks of the geese. Both youth and goose are dunked into the water, using a system of pulleys, until the youth cries uncle or the neck of the goose is wrenched off. Unless your tastes run to the macabre, you might want to skip this one. A candlelit march through the streets, with everyone dressed in white, does not mourn the unfortunate geese but signals the end of the festival.

Seven buses a day connect Lekeitio with Bilbao (45 minutes away), and four buses a day run from San Sebastián (1½ hours away). Driving from Ondárroa, take the coastal road northwest along the Costa Vasca.

Where to Dine

Restaurante Egaña. Santa Catalina, 4. ☎ **94-684-01-03.** Reservations not necessary. Main courses 1,000–1,600 ptas. ($6–$9.60); Tues–Fri *menús del día* 1,000–1,350 ptas. ($6–$8.10). AE, MC, V. Oct–June, Tues–Sun 1–4pm and 8–11pm; July–Sept, Tues–Sun 1–11pm. SEAFOOD.

Fans of Basque seafood can get their fill in this spacious, breezy dining room on the upper side of the village. The portions are large and generous, and the price is right. The place is unfussy and unpretentious: You are here to eat without frills. The menu depends on the catch of the day—try the Basque-style hake.

2 Fuenterrabía (Hondarribía)

14 miles (22.5km) E of San Sebastián, 317 miles (510km) N of Madrid, 11 miles (18km) W of St-Jean-de-Luz (France)

A big seaside resort and fishing port, Fuenterrabía (*Hondarribía* in Basque) is near the French frontier, and for that reason has been subject to frequent attacks over the centuries. In theory, it was supposed to guard access to Spain, but sometimes it hasn't performed that task too well.

ESSENTIALS

GETTING THERE   Fuenterrabía does not have a train station, but it is serviced by the station in nearby Irún (☎ **943-64-96-37** for information). Buses depart Irún's Plaza de San Juan for Fuentarrabía at 10- to 15-minute intervals. Irún is the end of the line for trains in northern Spain. East of Irún, you must board French trains.

Buses run every 15 minutes from Plaza Guipúzcoa in San Sebastián to Fuenterrabía, 1 hour away. Call ☎ **943-64-13-02** for information.

By car take A-8 east to the French border, turning toward the coast at the exit sign for Fuenterrabía.

VISITOR INFORMATION   The **office of tourism** at calle Javier Ugarte, 6 (☎ **943-64-54-58**), is open July and August, daily 10am to 8pm; off-season, Monday to Friday 9am to 1:30pm and 4 to 6:30pm, Saturday 10am to 2pm.

EXPLORING FUENTERRABÍA & ENVIRONS

The most interesting part of town is the **medieval quarter** in the upper market. Some of the villas here date from the early 17th century. The fishing district in the lower part of town is called **La Marina;** old homes, painted boats, and marine atmosphere there attract many visitors. Because restaurants in Fuenterrabía tend to be very expensive, you can fill up here on seafood tapas in the many taverns along the waterfront. The beach at Fuenterrabía is wide and sandy, and many prefer it to the more famous ones at San Sebastián.

Wander for an hour or two around the old quarter, taking in the calle Mayor, calle Tiendas y Pampinot, and calle Obispo. The **Castillo de Carlos V,** standing at the Plaza de las Armas, has been turned into one of the smallest and most desirable paradors in Spain (see "Where to Stay," below). It's hard to get a room here unless you reserve well in advance, but you can visit the well-stocked bar over the entrance hall.

Sancho Abarca, a king of Navarre in the 10th century, is supposed to have founded the original castle that stood on this spot, but the present look owes more to Charles V in the 16th century. You can still see the battle scars on the castle that date from the time of the Napoleonic invasion of Spain.

The most impressive church in the old quarter is the **Iglesia de Santa María,** a Gothic structure that was vastly restored in the 17th century and given a baroque tower. The proxy wedding of Louis XIV and the Infanta María Teresa took place here in June 1660.

If you have a car, you can take some interesting trips in the area, especially to **Cabo Higuer,** a promontory with panoramic views, reached by going 2½ miles (4km) north. Leave by the harbor and beach road. You can see the French coast and the town of Hendaye from this cape.

You can head west out of town along the **Jaizkibel Road,** which many motorists prefer at sunset. After going 3 miles (5km), you'll reach the shrine of the Virgin of Guadalupe, where another panoramic view unfolds. From here, you can see the French Basque coast. Even better views await if you continue along to the Hostal Jaizkibel. If you stay on this road, you will come to the little fishing village of Pasai Donibane (see "Side Trips from San Sebastián" above), 11 miles (18km) away.

WHERE TO STAY

✪ **Hotel Pampinot.** Kale Nagusia, 3, 20280 Fuenterrabía. ☎ **943-64-06-00.** Fax 943-64-51-28. 8 units. TV TEL. 15,000–17,500 ptas. ($90–$105) double; 18,000–22,000 ptas. ($108–$132) suite. AE, DC, MC, V. Closed Nov.

If the walls here could talk, they'd probably reveal more than those of any other hotel in the region. Built as an aristocratic mansion in 1587, it housed the Infanta María Teresa for a night as she headed toward France to marry Louis XIV. Today, it presents a richly textured stone facade with Renaissance detailing and heraldic symbols on one of the most historic streets of the old town. Inside, an antique sense of elegance is conveyed by beamed ceilings, exposed stonework, parquet flooring, and ornate ironwork. The midsized guest rooms are traditional and charming, with a mixture of antique and reproduction furniture, including good beds with firm mattresses. Each of the immaculately kept tiled bathrooms comes with a hair dryer. Parking is available along the street only.

Although breakfast is the only meal served, the staff can direct you to a choice of nearby eateries. Amenities include laundry, concierge, baby-sitting, and car rentals.

Jáuregui. Zuloaga, 5, 20280 Fuenterrabía. ☎ **943-64-14-00.** Fax 943-64-44-04. www.adegi.es/hjauregui. E-mail: jauregui@adegi.es. 53 units. MINIBAR TV TEL. 9,500–12,500 ptas. ($57–$75) double for single use; 12,500–15,500 ptas. ($75–$93) double; 15,500–28,000 ptas. ($93–$168) apt. AE, MC, V. Parking 1,000 ptas. ($6).

Opened in 1981 in the center of the old village, this is a good choice for moderately priced accommodations. The modern interior boasts comfortable accessories, and the hotel has a garage—a definite plus, since parking in Fuenterrabía is virtually impossible. Each of the small rooms is well furnished and maintained; thoughtful extras include a hair dryer in each bathroom, a safe in every room, and a shoeshine machine on each floor. Only breakfast is served.

Parador de Hondarribía. Plaza de Armas, 20280 Fuenterrabía. ☎ **943-64-55-00.** Fax 943-64-21-53. www.parador.es. E-mail: hondarribia@parador.es. 36 units. MINIBAR TV TEL. 16,000–20,000 ptas. ($96–$120) double. AE, DC, MC, V. Free parking.

This beautifully restored 10th-century castle, situated on a hill in the center of the old town, was once used by Emperor Charles V as a border fortification. The building itself is impressive, and so are the taste and imagination of the restoration. Antiques, old weapons, and standards hang from the high-vaulted ceilings and some of the comfortable provincial-style rooms open onto the Bay of Biscay. Units range from small to medium, and each is well equipped with firm mattresses plus hair dryers in the tiled bathrooms. Breakfast is the only meal served. It's best to reserve a room here well in advance.

Rio Bidasoa. Nafarroa Behera, 1, 20280 Fuenterrabia. ☎ **943-64-54-08.** Fax 943-64-51-70. www.adegi.es/hotelriobidasoa. E-mail: hotelriobidasoa@adegi.es. 37 units. A/C MINIBAR TV TEL. 16,500 ptas. ($99) double; 21,500 ptas. ($129) suite. AE, DC, MC, V. Free parking.

Five minutes from the center of town and only 3 miles west of the French border, this old mansion was completely renovated and remodeled to become the modern hotel you see today. It is surrounded by one of the most beautiful gardens in the area. The exterior is crisp and white, with balustrades trimmed in wood. The interior is inviting in the contemporary mode. Rooms are midsized to spacious and furnished in various contrasting styles and fashions, even in the same room, but they are comfortable and well appointed, with fully equipped bathrooms. A restaurant serves Basque and international dishes, and facilities include a cafeteria and a pool.

WHERE TO DINE

✪ **Ramón Roteta.** Villa Alnara. ☎ **943-64-16-93.** Reservations recommended. Main courses 2,200–3,500 ptas. ($13.20–$21). AE, MC, V. June–Sept, Tues–Sun 1:15–11pm; Oct–May, Tues–Sun 1:15–3:30pm, Tues–Sat 8:30–11pm. BASQUE.

Named after its owner and founder, this attractively furnished restaurant is one of Europe's most consistently respected purveyors of traditional Basque cuisine. Contained in what was originally a 1920s private villa, it is on the southern outskirts of town, near the local parador and the city limits of Irún. Menu specialties include a terrine of green vegetables and fish served with red-pepper-flavored vinaigrette, baked sea crabs with tiny potatoes and onions, fresh pasta with seafood, and the dessert specialty, a mandarin-orange tart flavored with rose petals. The villa is surrounded by a pleasantly unstructured garden that can be appreciated from a table on the terrace.

Sebastián. Mayor, 7. ☎ **943-64-01-67.** Reservations required. Main courses 1,500–3,200 ptas. ($9–$19.20); fixed-price menus 5,000–6,500 ptas. ($30–$39). AE, DC, DISC, MC, V. Tues–Sun 1–3:30pm and 8:30–11:30pm. Closed Nov. BASQUE.

In the oldest district of Fuenterrabía, close to the castle, this restaurant offers modern cuisine using top-notch ingredients appropriate to the season. The two floors of the restaurant feature thick masonry walls, among which are scattered an array of 18th-century paintings. Try one of the specialties: foie gras of duckling Basque style, terrine of fresh mushrooms, or médallions of sole and salmon with seafood sauce.

3 Guernica

266 miles (428km) N of Madrid, 52 miles (84km) W of San Sebastián

The subject of Picasso's most famous painting (returned to Spain from the Museum of Modern Art in New York and now displayed at the Reina Sofía Museum in Madrid), Guernica, the spiritual home of the Basques and the seat of Basque nationalism, was destroyed in a Nazi air raid on April 26, 1937, during the Spanish Civil War. It was the site of a revered oak tree, under whose branches Basques had elected their officials since medieval times. No one knows how many died during the

3½-hour attack—estimates range from 200 to 2,000. The bombers reduced the town to rubble, but a mighty symbol of independence was born. Although activists around the world attempted to rally support for the embattled Spanish Republicans, governments everywhere, including that of the United States, left the Spaniards to fend for themselves, refusing to supply them with arms.

The town has been attractively rebuilt close to its former style. The chimes of a church bell ring softly, and laughing children play in the street. In the midst of this peace, however, you'll suddenly come upon a sign: SOUVENIRS . . . REMEMBER.

The former Basque parliament, **Casa de Juntas (or Juntetxea),** is the principal attraction in town. It contains a historical display of Guernica and is open daily 10am to 2pm and 4 to 7pm in summer (to 6pm in winter). Admission is free. Outside are the remains of the ancient communal oak tree, symbol of Basque independence; it was not uprooted by Hitler's bombs. From the train station, head up the calle Urioste.

GETTING THERE

From Bilbao, trains run five times daily to Guernica. Trip time is 50 minutes. Call ☎ **94-625-11-82** for schedules.

Vascongados, at Estación de Amara in San Sebastián, runs buses to Bilbao, with connections to Guernica. Inquire at the station. From Bilbao, **CAV,** calle Hurtado de Amézaga (☎ **94-423-78-60**), operates 28 buses per day to Guernica Monday to Friday and five buses per day on the weekends. The trip time is 45 minutes.

From Bilbao, head east along the A-8 superhighway; cut north on the 6315 and follow the signs for Guernica. From San Sebastián, drive west along A-8, and cut north on the 6315. A more scenic, but slightly longer, route involves driving west from San Sebastián on the A-8, and branching off on the coastal road to Ondárroa. Continue on as the road turns south and follow the signs to Guernica.

A NEARBY PLACE TO DINE

Asador Zaldua. Sabino Arana, 10. ☎ **94-687-08-71.** Reservations required in summer. Main courses 1,600–2,500 ptas. ($9.60–$15); menú del día 3,500 ptas. ($21). AE, MC, V. June–Oct, Mon–Sat 1:30–3:30pm and 8:30–11pm; Nov–May, Fri–Sat 8:30–11pm only. Closed Dec 20–Jan 5. BASQUE.

Most of the specialties served here come from a blazing grill whose turning spits are visible from the dining room. A wide array of seafood and fish is available, some dishes baked to a flaky goodness in a layer of rock salt. The lobster salad alone is worth the trip here. The restaurant is 5½ miles (9km) north of the center of town on the road to Bermeo.

4 Bilbao

246 miles (396km) N of Madrid, 62 miles (100km) W of San Sebastián

Bilbao, Spain's sixth-largest city and biggest port, has been described as an "ugly, gray, decaying, smokestack city," and so it is—in part. But it has a number of interesting secrets to reveal, as well as good food, and as a rail hub it serves as a center for exploring some of the best attractions in the Basque country. Most of the city's sights can be viewed in a day or two. Many visitors flock here only to see the new and controversial $100 million Guggenheim Museum, designed by American architect Frank Gehry and called "the beast" by some locals because of its bizarre shape. From afar, it resembles a gargantuan sculpture, with a tumbling boxes profile and a 430-foot-long (131m) ship gallery.

Bilbao

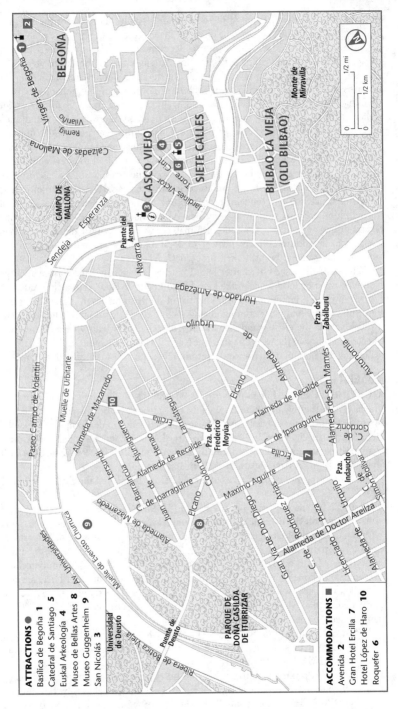

ATTRACTIONS ●
Basílica de Begoña **1**
Catedral de Santiago **5**
Euskal Arkeología **4**
Museo de Bellas Artes **8**
Museo Guggenheim **9**
San Nicolás **3**
Universidad de Deusto

ACCOMMODATIONS ■
Avenida **2**
Gran Hotel Ercilla **7**
Hotel López de Haro **10**
Roquefer **6**

BEGOÑA

CASCO VIEJO

SIETE CALLES

BILBAO LA VIEJA
(OLD BILBAO)

CAMPO DE MALLONA

Monte de Mirravilla

PARQUE DE DOÑA CASILDA DE ITURRIZAR

Virgen de Begoña
Remig
Vilariño
Calzadas de Mallona
Jardines Víctor
Torre Cint.
Esperanza
Sendeia
Navarra
Puente del Arenal
Paseo Campo de Volantín
Muelle de Uribitarte
Alameda de Mazarredo
Alameda de Mazarredo
Hurtado de Amézaga
Urquijo
Alameda de
Pza. de Zabálburu
Elcano
Alameda de Recalde
Alameda de San Mamés
Autonomía
Larreategui
Henao
Colón de
Ercilla
Pza. de Frederico Moyúa
C. de Iparraguirre
Ercilla
C. de Gordoniz
Pza. Indauchu
Alameda de
Juan de Barraianguarre
Alameda de Recalde
C. de Iparraguirre
Máximo Aguirre
Urquijo
C. de Bolívar
Simón Bolívar
Iturriburu
Lersundi
Chunuca
Gran Vía de Don Diego
C. de Rodríguez Arias
Alameda de Doctor Areilza
Alameda de
Licenciado Poza
Av. Universidades
Muelle de Everiso Churruca
Ribera de Botica Vieja
Puente de Deusto

0   1/2 mi
0   1/2 km

539

Bilbao is the industrial hub of the north and the political capital for the Basques. Shipping, shipbuilding, and steelmaking have made it prosperous, so there is no shortage of bankers or industrialists in Bilbao. Its commercial heart, bursting with skyscrapers and sky cranes, hums with activity. Among cities of the Basque region, it has the highest population (around 450,000); the metropolitan area, including the suburbs and many surrounding towns, is home to over one million inhabitants.

Bilbao has a wide-open feeling, extending more than 5 miles (8km) across the valley of the Nervión River, one of Spain's most polluted waterways. Many buildings wear a layer of grime. Some visitors compare Bilbao to the sooty postindustrial sprawl of an English port town. However, the extravagant Guggenheim museum is cast as a symbol of Basque economic revival, and locals hope it will lead to a revitalization of their city. Bilbao was badly hit by the 1970s economic crisis, leading to a closure of shipyards and steelworks. It has benefited greatly from a $1.5 billion reconversion grant, of which the Guggenheim project is one of the main beneficiaries. Signs of revitalization are also seen in a flashy new Metro system designed by Sir Norman Foster of England and a new airport terminal, the work of Spanish architect Santiago Calatrava. In addition, many owners of local buildings are removing layers of accumulated grime to beautify their properties.

Bilbao was established by charter June 15, 1300, which converted it from a village (*pueblo*), ruled by local feudal duke Don Diego López de Haro, into a city. Aided by water power and the transportation potential of the Nervión River, it grew and grew, most of its fame and glory coming during the industrial expansion of the 19th century. Many of the city's grand homes and villas for industrialists were constructed then, particularly in the wealthy suburb of Neguri. The most famous son of Bilbao was Miguel de Unamuno, the writer and educator more closely associated with Salamanca.

ESSENTIALS

GETTING THERE   Bilbao Airport (☎ 94-486-93-00) is 5 miles (8km) north of the city, near the town of Erandio. Flights arrive from Madrid, Barcelona, Alicante, Arrecife, Fuenteventura, Las Palmas, Málaga, Palma, Santiago de Compostela, Sevilla, Tenerife, Valencia, Vigo, Brussels, Frankfurt, Lisbon, London, Milan, Paris, and Zurich. Iberia's main booking office in Bilbao is at Ercilla, 20 (☎ 94-424-10-94); it's open Monday to Friday 8:30am to 1:30pm and 3 to 6pm.

From the airport into town, take red bus A3247 to the heart of the city for 150 ptas. (90¢).

The RENFE station, Estación de Abando (☎ 902-24-02-02), is on Hurtado de Amézaga, just off the Plaza de España. From here, you can catch short-distance trains within the metropolitan area of Bilbao and long-distance trains to most parts of Spain. Two trains per day run to and from Madrid (trip time: 6 hours on the afternoon train, 7 hours on the night train). Two trains per day run to and from Barcelona (11 hours), and one train per day goes to and from Galicia (12 hours). There are also two night trains per week to and from the Mediterranean Coast: one toward Alicante and Valencia (daily during the summer months) and the other toward Málaga (three times a week in the summer).

PESA, calle Hurtado de Amézaga (☎ 94-424-88-99), at the Estación Abando, operates more than a dozen buses per day to and from San Sebastián (trip time: 1¼ hours). **ANSA,** calle Autonomía, 17 (☎ 94-444-31-00), has nine buses per day from Madrid (trip time: 5 hours). It has four buses per day to and from Barcelona (7 hours). If you'd like to explore either Lekeitio or Guernica (see above) by bus, use the services of CAV, Plaza Encarnación, 7 (☎ 94-454-05-44). Seven buses per day go to Lekeitio Monday to Saturday and two on Sunday. Trip time is 45 minutes. Ten buses run each weekday to Guernica (trip time: 45 minutes). On weekends, only five buses per day go to Guernica.

Bilbao is beside the A-8, linking the cities of Spain's northern Atlantic seacoast to the western edge of France. It is connected by superhighway to both Barcelona and Madrid.

VISITOR INFORMATION   The **Bilbao Tourist Office** is at Plaza Arriaga, s/n (☎ **94-479-57-60**). It's open Monday to Friday 9am to 2pm and 4 to 7:30pm, Saturday 9am to 2pm, and Sunday 10am to 2pm. The Post Office is at Alameda de Urquijo, 19 (☎ **94-424-48-12**), and is open Monday to Friday 8:30am to 8:30pm, Saturday 9:30am to 2pm.

SPECIAL EVENTS   Festivals often fill the calendar, the biggest and most widely publicized being **La Semana Grande,** dedicated to the Virgin of Begoña and lasting from mid-August until early September. During the celebration, the Nervión River is the site of many flotillas and regattas. July 25 brings the festival of Bilbao's patron saint, **Santiago (St. James),** and July 31 is the holiday devoted to the region's patron saint, **St. Ignatius.**

EXPLORING BILBAO

The **Nervión River** meanders through Bilbao, whose historic core was built inside one of its loops, with water protecting it on three sides. Most of the important shops, banks, and tourist facilities lie within a short walk of the **Gran Vía,** running east-west through the heart of town. The old quarter is east of the modern commercial center, across the river.

THE TOP ATTRACTIONS

✪ **Guggenheim Museum.** Muella Evaristo Churruca, 1. ☎ **94-435-90-00.** Admission 800 ptas. ($4.80) adults, 400 ptas. ($2.40) seniors and students, free for children 12 and under. Tues–Sun 11am–8pm. Closed Jan 1 and Dec 25. Bus: 1, 10, 13, or 18.

The newest and biggest attraction in Bilbao is the Guggenheim Museum, at the intersection of the bridge called Puente de la Salve and the Nervión River. The 349,000-square-foot colossus is the focal point of a $1.5 billion redevelopment plan for the city. The internationally acclaimed Frank Gehry design features a 165-foot-high atrium—more than 1½ times the height of the rotunda of Frank Lloyd Wright's Guggenheim Museum in New York. Stretching under the aforementioned bridge and incorporating it in its design, the museum reanimates the promenade with a towering roof reminiscent of a blossoming metallic flower. The museum, which opened in fall 1997, is devoted to American and European art of the 20th century, featuring the works of such renowned artists as Kandinsky, Mondrian, Picasso, Ernst, Pollock, Lichtenstein, Oldenburg, Serra, and others.

The Guggenheim is not an encyclopedic museum like the Met in New York. It is conceived in 19 galleries to provide chapters of, but not the whole story of, modern art, from Braque to Picasso to Damien Hirst. Artwork lent by the Guggenheim in New York and Venice will rotate, and Bilbao will also host temporary exhibitions traveling here from New York.

Although some disgruntled Basque locals still call the museum "the colossal Californian cauliflower" or "a cheese factory," many architectural critics from around the world, including Paul Goldberger of the *New York Times,* have hailed Frank Gehry's unique structure as the first great building of the 21st century, even though conceived and constructed in the waning years of the 20th century. The structure is said to have been inspired by the Fritz Lang film classic *Metropolis,* and is viewed as a homage to Bilbao's industrial past and a commitment to its future. The massive museum is clad in shimmering titanium, which many observers find sexy and unmistakably elegant. The building takes up 24,000 square meters in the former dockyards beside the Nervión River, and about half of that space is devoted to the exhibition halls, connected by ramps and surrounding a central, glassed-in atrium that is impressive in size, the equivalent of a 17-story building. The museum has virtually abolished right angles and flat walls. As one critic put it, "it was as if Gehry were working in pastry rather than concrete or steel."

✪ **Museo de Bellas Artes.** Plaza del Museo, 2. ☎ **94-439-60-60.** Admission 400 ptas. ($2.40) adults, 200 ptas. ($1.20) seniors, students, and children. Free Wed. Tues–Sat 10am–1:30pm and 4–7:30pm; Sun 10am–2pm.

This is another one of Spain's important art museums, containing both medieval and modern works, including paintings by Velázquez, Goya, Zurbarán, and El Greco. Among the works of non-Spanish artists are *The Money Changers* by the Flemish painter Quentin Massys and *The Lamentation Over Christ* by Anthony Van Dyck. In its modern wing, the museum contains works by Gauguin, Picasso, Léger, Sorolla, and Mary Cassatt. The gallery is particularly strong in 19th- and 20th-century Basque artists, the foremost of which is the modern sculptor Eduardo Chillida, who created a massive piece titled *Monument to Iron.* If you tire of looking at the art, you can walk in the English-inspired gardens around the museum, 4 blocks south of the old quarter.

Museo a Euska/Museo Vasco. Cruz, 4. ☎ **94-415-54-23.** Admission 300 ptas. ($1.80) adults, 150 ptas. (90¢) children and students, free for children under 10. Tues–Sat 10:30am–1:30pm and 4–7pm; Sun 10:30am–1:30pm.

Devoted to Basque archaeology, ethnology, and history, this museum is in the center of the old quarter, south of calle Esperanza Ascao, housed in a centuries-old Jesuit cloister. Some of the exhibits showcase Basque commercial life during the 16th century. You see everything from ship models to shipbuilding tools, along with reconstructions of rooms illustrating political and social life. Basque gravestones are also on view. In addition, you'll see the equipment used to play the popular Basque game of *pelota.*

EXPLORING THE CASCO VIEJO (OLD QUARTER)

Despite the fact that Bilbao was established around 1300, it has curiously few medieval monuments. It does have an intriguing old quarter, however, on the east side of Nervión River and the site of its most interesting bars and restaurants. The custom is to go here at night and barhop, ordering small cups of beer or wine. A small glass of wine is called a *chiquiteo.*

The old quarter of Bilbao is connected to the much larger modern section on the opposite bank by four bridges. A few paces north of the old quarter's center are graceful arches, 64 in all, enclosing Plaza Nueva, also called Plaza de los Martires, completed in 1830.

The entire *barrio* has been declared a national landmark. It originally defined an area around seven streets, but it long ago spilled beyond that limitation. Its most important church is the **Iglesia de San Nicolás.** Behind this church you'll find an elevator on calle Esperanza Ascao, which, if working, carries sightseers to the upper town. You can also climb 64 steps from Plaza Unamuno. From here it's a short walk to the **Basílica de Begoña,** built largely in the early 1500s. Inside the dimly lit church, there is a brightly illuminated depiction of the Virgin, dressed in long, flowing robes. She is the patroness of the province. Also displayed are some enormous paintings by Luca Giordano.

While in the old town, you might visit the **Catedral de Santiago,** Plaza Santiago, which was originally built in the 14th century, then restored in the 16th century after a fire. The cathedral's facade was later rebuilt in the 19th century. These three churches are open daily 9am to 5pm. On Sundays you might take in the flea market, starting at 8am, on the streets of the old quarter.

To reach the old town on foot, the only way to explore it, take the Puente del Arenal from the Gran Vía, the main street of Bilbao.

WHERE TO STAY
EXPENSIVE

Gran Hotel Ercilla. Ercilla, 37–39, 48011 Bilbao. ☎ **94-470-57-00.** Fax 94-443-93-35. www.hotelercilla.es. E-mail: ercilla@hotelercilla.es. 345 units. A/C MINIBAR TV TEL. Mon–Thurs 23,000 ptas. ($138) double. Fri–Sun 15,000 ptas. ($90) double; 47,600 ptas. ($287) suite. AE, DC, MC, V. Parking 1,970 ptas. ($11.80).

Soaring high above the buildings surrounding it in the heart of Bilbao's business district, this is a tastefully decorated bastion of attentive service and good living. Midsized to spacious guest rooms are conservative and comfortably furnished, each with luxurious mattresses and roomy bathrooms with plush towels and hair dryers. Completely renovated in 1989 and 1990, the Ercilla is one of Bilbao's most desirable hotels, usually the preferred choice of Spanish politicians, movie stars, and journalists away from home.

Dining/Diversions: A Basque restaurant, **Bermeo,** is known as one of the best restaurants in Bilbao (see "Where to Dine," below). Adjacent to it is an American-inspired bar (with an English-inspired decor) providing a peaceful haven with richly grained hardwood paneling. There is an informal and stylishly modern snack bar, the **Ercilla** (open daily 7am to 2am), plus a high-tech, high-energy disco, **Bocaccio.**

Amenities: 24-hour room service, concierge, laundry and valet, baby-sitting, business center, car rental, safety-deposit boxes, boutiques.

✪ **Hotel López de Haro.** Obispo Orueta, 2–4, 48009 Bilbao. ☎ **94-423-55-00.** Fax 94-423-45-00. www.hotellopezdeharo.com. E-mail: lh@hotellopezdeharo.com. 53 units. A/C MINIBAR TV TEL. From 30,900 ptas. ($185) double; 37,900–48,400 ptas. ($227–$290) suite. AE, DC, MC, V. Parking 2,200 ptas. ($13.20).

Behind a discreet facade of chiseled gray stone, this elegant six-story 1990 hotel is filled with English touches and features marble flooring, hardwood paneling, and a uniformed staff. The comfortable midsize guest rooms contain flowered or striped upholstery, a modern bathroom with a hair dryer, and wall-to-wall carpeting or hardwood floors.

Dining: The hotel has two restaurants, one of which, **Club Náutico,** is recommended below in "Where to Dine."

Amenities: 24-hour room service, laundry and valet, limousines, concierge, baby-sitting, car rentals.

MODERATE

Avenida. Zumalacárregui, 40, 48007 Bilbao. ☎ **94-412-43-00.** Fax 94-411-46-17. 116 units. TV TEL. 13,500 ptas. ($81) double. Rates include breakfast. AE, MC, V. Free parking. Metro: Santutxu.

For those who want to be away from the center, and don't mind a bus or taxi ride or two, this is a welcoming choice. It is in the Barrio de Begoña, near one of the major religious monuments of Bilbao, the Basílica de Begoña. The five-story hotel was built in the late 1950s and its small rooms, furnished in a sober, functional modern style, are well kept and maintained. The hotel has a restaurant and snack bar and a helpful staff. During special fairs in Bilbao, rates increase by at least 10%.

INEXPENSIVE

Roquefer. Lotería, 2–4, 48005 Bilbao. ☎ **94-415-07-55.** Fax 94-423-18-16. E-mail: hotelripa@teleline.es. 18 units (6 with bathroom). 5,000 ptas. ($30) double without bathroom, 6,000 ptas. ($36) double with bathroom. No credit cards. Parking 1,000 ptas. ($6).

If you'd like to stay in the old quarter and avoid the high prices of business hotels, this is a very basic choice, suitable if your main concern is only a place to lay your head. The small rooms are simple and furnished in a functional style, each with a good bed. You'll be in the center of the *tasca* and restaurant district for nighttime prowls. To reach the hotel, take the bridge, Puente del Arenal, across the river to the old town.

WHERE TO DINE
EXPENSIVE

✪ **Bermeo.** In the Gran Hotel Ercilla, Ercilla, 37. ☎ **94-470-57-00.** Reservations required. Main courses 2,100–3,800 ptas. ($12.60–$22.80); fixed-price menu 5,800 ptas. ($34.80). AE, DC, MC, V. Sun–Fri 1–3:30pm; Mon–Sat 8:30–11:30pm. BASQUE.

One of the best hotel restaurants in all of Spain and one of the finest representatives of Basque cuisine anywhere in the world, Bermeo caters to the Basque world's most influential politicians, writers, and social luminaries. Within the modern walls of one of Bilbao's tallest hotels, the restaurant is decorated with richly conservative glowing wood panels, crisp linens, and copies of 19th-century antiques. Service from the uniformed and formal staff is impeccable. Menu items change with the seasons but might include a salad of lettuce hearts in saffron dressing with smoked salmon, homemade foie gras scented with essence of bay leaves, fresh thistles sautéed with ham, five preparations of codfish, stewed partridge with glazed shallots, and fillets of duckling with green peppercorns. For dessert, try the truffled figs or a slice of bilberry pie with cream.

✪ **Club Náutico.** In the Hotel López de Haro, Obispo Orueta, 2. ☎ **94-423-55-00.** Reservations recommended. Main courses 2,200–5,000 ptas. ($13.20–$30); fixed-price menus 5,000–10,500 ptas. ($30–$63). AE, DC, MC, V. Mon–Fri 1–3:30pm; Mon–Sat 8:30–11:30pm. BASQUE/FRENCH.

One of the top restaurants in the Basque world, the elegantly decorated Club Náutico is in the previously recommended Hotel López de Haro. Chef Alberto Velez is the former protégé of Alberto Zuluaga, who ran the kitchen here for years and was one of the most publicized culinary luminaries of northern Spain. The restaurant offers formal tables set with some of the finest china, crystal, and silverware available. Specialties include succulent local artichokes stuffed with foie gras, poached eggs with beluga caviar and oyster sauce, lobster sautéed with artichokes and balsamic vinegar, baked sea bass with béarnaise sauce, sautéed scallops with truffle sauce, and roast beef with a puree of radishes. A superb selection of Spanish and international wines is available by either the glass or the bottle.

Guría. Gran Vía de López de Haro, 66. ☎ **94-441-85-64.** Reservations required. Main courses 2,200–4,600 ptas. ($13.20–$27.60); fixed-price menus 5,800–9,000 ptas. ($34.80–$54). AE, DC, MC, V. Mon–Sat 1–4pm and 9pm–midnight. Closed last week of July and first week of Aug. BASQUE.

One of the most venerable restaurants of Bilbao, the air-conditioned Guría is expensive—and worth it, say its fans. The chef shows care and concern for his guests by serving only market-fresh ingredients. He is celebrated for his *bacalao* (codfish), which he prepares many ways. Try the sea bass with saffron or loin of beef cooked in sherry as an alternative. A slightly caloric but divine dessert is *espuma de chocolat*.

Guría is on the southern edge of one of the most monumental traffic arteries in town, 6 blocks west of Bilbao's most prominent square, Plaza de Federico Moyúa, 1 block south of the sprawling Parque de Dr. Casilda Ituriza. Inside you'll find a modern decor of exposed, dark-stained wood, two separate dining rooms, and a monochromatic color scheme.

✪ **Zortziko.** Alameda Marzaredo, 17. ☎ **94-423-97-43.** Reservations recommended. Main courses 1,850–3,900 ptas. ($11.10–$23.40); set-price tasting menu 7,900 ptas. ($47.40). AE, V. Mon–Sat 1–3:30pm; Tues–Sat 7–11:30pm. Metro: Abando. BASQUE/CONTINENTAL.

Of the city's many restaurants, this one is among the most convenient to the Guggenheim Museum, which is a few steps away. In a multi-roomed, vaguely French setting furnished in the late Victorian style, you'll find a formal and sophisticated environment that's comfortable dealing with a clientele from throughout Europe. Lunches tend to focus on business discussions among clients; dinners tend to be more leisurely and recreational. One of the most unusual dining areas is the wine cellar, where the only table is reserved, sometimes many days in advance, by diners who appreciate the cozy, sheltering sense of being surrounded by valuable vintages. It's more likely, however, that your table will be on the restaurant's street level, in a stylish setting increasingly in vogue among hipsters. In a city where the restaurant competition is fierce, this kitchen emerges at the very top. Menu items include most of the traditional Basque staples, including pigeon breast or sea bass marinated and roasted in red Rioja wine. The tasting menu presents a wide variety of Basque specialties, and as such, is sometimes presented as something of a Basque nationalist statement.

MODERATE

Matxinbenta. Ladesma, 26. ☎ **94-424-84-95.** Reservations required. Main courses 2,000–2,800 ptas. ($12–$16.80); *menú del día* 4,000 ptas. ($24). AE, DC, MC, V. Mon–Sat 1–4pm and 8–11:30pm. BASQUE.

Serving some of the finest Basque food in the city since the 1950s, this restaurant is popular for business lunches or dinners. Specialties include fresh tuna in piquant tomato sauce and a local version of ratatouille known as *piperada.* You can order veal cutlets cooked in port wine and finish with a mint-flavored fresh-fruit cocktail. The service is excellent. Matxinbenta contains three separate dining rooms, each modern, with contemporary furniture, potted plants, and lots of exposed wood. It's 1 block north of the Gran Vía, in the center of the city, adjacent to Bilbao's most visible department store, El Corte Inglés.

Restaurante Begoña. Virgen de Begoña, s/n. ☎ **94-412-72-57.** Reservations recommended. Main courses 1,800–3,200 ptas. ($10.80–$19.20). AE, MC, V. Mon–Sat 1:30–3:30pm and 8–11pm. Closed Aug. Bus: 48. BASQUE.

At this tranquil choice, near the Basílica de Begoña on the eastern bank of the river, the chef imaginatively combines classic dishes with modern ones. Specialties include stuffed onions, loin of pork, and sea bass with fine herbs. This restaurant offers good value, serving quality food at reasonable prices. A wine cellar offers prestigious vintages at competitive rates, and the service is attentive.

INEXPENSIVE

Aitxiar. Calle Maria Muñoz, 8. ☎ **94-415-09-17.** Reservations not necessary. Main courses 1,800–3,200 ptas. ($10.80–$19.20). V. Tues–Sun 9am–11pm. Metro: Plaza Unamuno. BASQUE.

Venerable and well respected for its good food, low prices, and utter lack of pretension, this restaurant in the Casco Viejo serves Basque cuisine in two dining rooms in a house built in the 1930s. Expect a decor that includes lots of exposed stone and wood, a hardworking waitstaff, strong flavors, and lots of regional and nationalistic pride. Menu items include potato soup with chunks of fresh tuna, and an array of very fresh fish hauled in that morning from nearby waters. Two of the most appealing are hake, which tastes marvelous in an herb-infused green sauce, and codfish, prepared in at least two different versions. Baby squid is a savory choice, as are the spicy sausages (*chuletas*), which taste best when consumed as an appetizer.

Victor Montes. Plaza Nueva, 8. ☎ **94-415-70-67.** Reservations recommended for full meals; not necessary for tapas bar. Tapas from 200 ptas. ($1.25); main courses 1,500–3000 ptas. ($9.45–$18.90). AE, MC, V. Daily 1–3:30pm; Mon–Sat 7:30–midnight. Metro: Casco Viejo. BASQUE/SPANISH.

Set in the heart of Bilbao's oldest neighborhood, this restaurant maintains a handful of battered, much-used dining rooms—some upstairs—where closely packed tables, racks of wine, and frantic waiters create a sense of good-natured hysteria, especially at lunchtime. If you opt for a meal here, expect copious portions of old-fashioned roasts, stews, soups, and salads, usually with an emphasis on fresh vegetables and seafood such as grilled squid, or fresh fava beans with nuggets of cod. Many locals, especially those in a hurry, tend to bypass a dining table altogether, opting for one or more *racións* of tapas. They are lined up atop the bar, served to clients on small plates, and taste wonderful when accompanied with sherry, wine, or beer.

BILBAO AFTER DARK

Basque cuisine is the finest in Spain, featuring *pintxos* (pronounced *peen*-chohz)—tapas. The best place for tapas bars is calle Licenciado Poza, between Alameda del Doctor Areilza and calle Iparraguirre. Favorites include **Atlanta,** calle Rodríguez Arias, 28 (☎ **94-427-64-72**), famous locally for its *jamon Serrano* (cured ham) sandwiches, and **Busterri,** calle Licenciado Poza, 43 (☎ **94-441-50-67**), well known locally for its grilled anchovies and *jamon jabugo.*

During your nights in Bilbao, you might be happiest wandering through the old town's narrow alleyways, two of which (calle Pozas and calle Barrencalle) are dotted with all manner of bars, *tascas,* and *bodegas.* After a drink or two, you might opt to go out dancing, or at least visit any of three popular discos to watch how it's done in the Basque country. Favorites include **Disco Rock Star,** Gran Vía, 89 (☎ **94-441-10-60**); **Disco-Pub Crystal,** calle Buenos Aires, 5 (no phone); and **El Palladium,** calle Iparraguirre, 11 (no phone). If you're looking for a gay bar, you'll find a scattering along the calle Barrencalle Barena, where the most popular of several nearby competitors includes the **Bar Consorcio** (no phone).

The major cultural venue in Bilbao is the **Teatro Arriaga,** Plaza Arriaga, s/n (☎ **94-416-35-33**), on the banks of the Nervión River. This is the setting for world-class opera, classical music concerts, ballet, and even *zarzuelas* (comic operas). Both *zarzuela* and opera are performed at **Teatro Coliso Alvia,** Alameda Urquijo, 13 (☎ **94-415-39-54**). Announcements of cultural events at the time of your visit are available at the tourist office (see "Visitor Information," earlier in this section).

5 Vitoria (Gasteiz)

41 miles (66km) S of Bilbao, 71 miles (114km) SW of San Sebastián, 218 miles (351km) N of Madrid

Quiet and sleepy until the early 1980s, Vitoria was chosen as headquarters of the Basque region's autonomous government. In honor of that occasion, it revived the name *Gasteiz,* by which it was known when founded in 1181 by King Sancho of

Navarre. Far more enduring, however, has been the name *Vitoria,* a battle site revered by the English. On June 21, 1813, Wellington won here against the occupying forces of Napoléon. A statue dedicated to the Iron Duke stands today on the neoclassical Plaza de la Virgen Blanca.

Shortly after its founding, the city became a rich center for the wool and iron trades, and this wealth paid for the fine churches and palaces in the medieval quarter. Many of the city's buildings are made of gray-gold stone. Local university students keep the taverns rowdy until the wee hours.

ESSENTIALS

GETTING THERE   Aeropuerto Vitoria-Foronda (☎ **945-16-35-00**) is 5 miles (8km) northwest of the town center and has direct air links to Madrid on Iberia Airlines. For flight information, call Iberia at ☎ **945-16-36-37** daily 7am to 11pm.

From San Sebastián, seven to nine trains daily make the 2-hour trip to Vitoria. For information, call ☎ **945-23-02-02.**

From San Sebastián, roughly four buses daily make the 1½-hour trip. Bus connections are also possible through Bilbao (8 to 12 buses daily make the 1-hour trip).

Take the E-5 north from Madrid to Burgos, cutting northwest until you see the turnoff for Vitoria. (Note that along its more northerly stretches this superhighway is identified as both E-5 and A-1.)

VISITOR INFORMATION   The **tourist information office** is at Parque de la Florida (☎ **945-13-13-21**). June to September, hours are Monday to Friday 9am to 7pm, Saturday 10am to 7pm, and Sunday 10am to 2pm. October to May, times are Monday to Thursday 9am to 1:30pm, and Friday 8am to 3pm.

SPECIAL EVENTS   One of the major jazz festivals in the north of Spain takes place here annually in mid-July. It's the weeklong **Festival de Jazz de Vitoria-Gasteiz.** For the big-name performers, tickets range from 500 to 2,000 ptas. ($3 to $12), but spontaneous entertainment takes place on the street for free, although donations are appreciated. The tourist office can supply complete details.

EXPLORING VITORIA

The most important sight in Vitoria is the **medieval district,** whose Gothic buildings were constructed on a series of steps and terraces. Most of the streets, arranged in concentric ovals, are named after medieval artisan guilds. The northern end is marked by the Catedral de Santa María, its southern flank by the Iglesia de San Miguel.

One of the most interesting streets in the *barrio* is **calle Cuchillaría,** which contains many medieval buildings. You can enter the courtyard at number 24, the Casa del Cordón, which was constructed in different stages from the 13th to the 16th century. Number 58, the Bendana Palace, built in the 15th century, has a fine ornate staircase set into its courtyard.

Catedral de Santa María (the "old" cathedral), calle Fray Zacaras (☎ **945-15-06-31**), was built in the 14th century in the Gothic style and is open Monday to Friday 11am to 2pm. It contains a good art collection, with paintings that imitate various schools, including those of Van Dyck, Caravaggio, and Rubens, as well as several tombs carved in a highly decorated plateresque style. Santa María is at the northern edge of the old town. This cathedral is not to be confused with the town's enormous neo-Gothic "new" cathedral on avenida Magdalena (just north of the Jardines la Florida).

The major historic square is **Plaza de la Virgen Blanca,** a short walk south of the medieval quarter. Its neoclassical balconies overlook the statue of Wellington. The square is named after the late-Gothic polychrome statue of the Virgen Blanca (the town's patron) that adorns the portico of the 13th-century **Church of San Miguel,** which stands on the square's upper edge. The 17th-century altarpiece inside was carved by Gregoria Hernández. The church is open Monday to Friday 11am to 3pm.

At **Plaza de España** (also known as Plaza Nueva), a satellite square a short walk away, the student population of Vitoria congregates to drink.

Vitoria has some minor museums, which are free. **Museo de Arqueología de Álava,** Correría, 116 (☎ 945-14-23-10), behind a half-timbered facade, exhibits artifacts such as pottery shards and statues unearthed from digs in the area. Some of these date from Celto-Iberian days; others are from the Roman era. The museum is open Tuesday to Friday 10am to 2pm and 4 to 6:30pm, Saturday 11am to 2pm.

Museo de Bellas Artes de Álava, Palacio de Agustín, Paseo de Fray Francisco, 8 (☎ 945-23-17-77), has a collection of several unusual weapons, a *Crucifixion* and portraits of Saints Peter and Paul by José Ribera, and a triptych by the Master of Ávila. It is open Tuesday to Friday 10am to 2pm and 4 to 6:30pm, Saturday 10am to 2pm, and Sunday 11am to 2pm.

WHERE TO STAY
EXPENSIVE

Hotel Residencia Gasteiz. Avenida Gasteiz, 45, 01009 Vitoria. ☎ **945-22-81-00.** Fax 945-22-62-58. E-mail: hoteldcgasteiz@barcelo.com. 150 units. A/C MINIBAR TV TEL. Mon–Thurs 20,000 ptas. ($120) double, Fri–Sun 12,000 ptas. ($72) double; Mon–Thurs 24,000 ptas. ($144) suite, Fri–Sun 15,500 ptas. ($93) suite. AE, DC, MC, V. Parking 1,500 ptas. ($9).

Located on the eastern flank of the broad, tree-lined boulevard that circumnavigates the old town, this is the most modern and solidly reliable hotel around. Built in 1982, it was completely renovated in 1994. Although not architecturally distinguished, it serves as the preferred meeting point for the city's business community, offering conservative and good-size rooms with uncomplicated furnishings and a series of comfortable (albeit not dramatic) public rooms. The tiled bathrooms are state of the art, and each is equipped with a hair dryer.

Dining/Diversions: Restaurante Artagnan, specializing in Basque and international cuisine, serves a set menu and à la carte dinners. The restaurant is closed every Sunday and from August 10 to September 10. There is a bar (which doubles as a cafeteria during the day).

Amenities: Room service (daily 7am to midnight), laundry, concierge, baby-sitting, car rentals.

MODERATE

Hotel General Álava. Gasteiz, 79, 01009 Vitoria. ☎ **945-21-50-00.** Fax 945-24-83-95. E-mail: hga@jet.es. 114 units. A/C TV TEL. Mon–Thurs 15,700 ptas. ($94) double. Fri–Sun 11,000 ptas. ($66) double, breakfast included; 16,800–24,000 ptas. ($101–$144) suite. AE, DC, MC, V. Parking 1,250 ptas. ($7.50).

Named after a local hero—a Spanish general who won an important battle against the French in 1815—this hotel is one of the best and most comfortably furnished in town. Rooms range from small to medium, each fitted with a firm mattress and a small tiled bathroom with a shower stall. Built in 1975, it attracts scores of business travelers from throughout Spain. It maintains an informal restaurant, a well-managed bistro (open only Monday to Friday) that offers a *menú del día* for 2,000 ptas. ($13.40), and a bar. The hotel is a 10-minute walk west of the town center, near the junction of calle Chile.

INEXPENSIVE

Achuri. Rioja, 11, 01005 Vitoria. ☎ **945-25-58-00.** Fax 945-26-40-74. 40 units. TV TEL. 6,800 ptas. ($40.80) double. AE, DC, MC, V.

This attractively priced modern hotel has a welcoming style. A short walk from the train station, it offers tidy and comfortably furnished but small rooms and laundry service. Breakfast is the only meal available, but you'll find several places serving food in the vicinity.

Hotel Dato. Eduardo Dato, 28, 01005 Vitoria. ☎ **945-14-72-30.** Fax 945-23-23-20. 14 units. TV TEL. 5,500 ptas. ($33) double. AE, DC, MC, V. Parking meters on street.

Three blocks south of the southern extremity of the old town in the pedestrian zone, this hotel has firmly established itself as the best budget accommodation in town. It has modern decor and amenities but only a few rooms, so reservations are wise. Rooms, ranging from small to medium, are well decorated, often with quite a bit of style, and each comes with a firm mattress and an immaculately kept tiled bathroom. No breakfast is served.

WHERE TO DINE

As in Bilbao, *tasca* hopping before dinner with the consumption of many small glasses (*chiquiteos*) of beer or wine at many different bars and taverns is very popular and fun for visitors to Vitoria. There are a number of places on the avenida de Gasteiz.

✪ **El Portalón.** Correría, 151. ☎ **945-14-27-55.** Reservations recommended. Main courses 1,800–3,500 ptas. ($10.80–$21); fixed-price menu 3,200 ptas. ($19.20). AE, DC, MC, V. Mon–Sat 1:15–3:30pm and 8:30–11:30pm. Closed Aug 10–Sept 1. BASQUE.

This is the finest and most interesting restaurant in town. It was originally built in the late 1400s as a tavern and post office near what was, at the time, one of the only bridges leading in and out of Vitoria. Rich with patina and a sense of history, the restaurant prides itself on serving extremely fresh fish from the nearby Gulf of Biscay, always prepared in traditional Basque style. Cream and butter are rarely used here. Menu items include a salad of endive with shellfish, vegetarian crêpes, a traditional hake dish known as *merluza koxkera*, ragout of fish and/or shellfish, and many variations of monkfish, turbot, and eel.

Mesa. Chile, 1. ☎ **945-22-84-94.** Reservations recommended. Main courses 1,200–2,200 ptas. ($7.20–$13.20); *menú de la casa* 1,200 ptas. ($7.20). AE, MC, V. Thurs–Tues 1–3:30pm and 9–11:30pm. Closed Aug 10–Sept 10. BASQUE.

For price and value, this ranks as one of the most competitive and worthwhile restaurants in town. In air-conditioned comfort you can partake of a number of Basque specialties, none better than the notable *merluza* (hake), the fish so beloved by Basque chefs. Fresh fish and a well-chosen selection of meats are presented nightly. The service is attentive. The setting is solid, sober, and severely dignified, with white walls and wood trim, and tables and chairs stained dark in the Iberian style.

16 | Cantabria & Asturias

The provinces of Cantabria and Asturias are historic lands that lay claim to attractions ranging from fishing villages along the coastlines to the Picos de Europa, a magnificent stretch of snowcapped mountains.

Cantabria was settled in prehistoric times and later colonized by the Romans. The Muslims were less successful in their invasion. Protected by the mountains, many Christians found refuge here during the long centuries of Moorish domination. Much religious architecture remains from this period, particularly Romanesque. Cantabria was once part of the Castilla y León district of Spain, but is now an autonomous region with its own government.

Most tourism is confined to the northern coastal strip; much of the inland mountainous area is poor and unpopulated. If you venture away from the coast, you usually need a rental car because public transport is inadequate at best. **Santander,** a rail terminus, makes the best center for touring the region; it also has the most tourist facilities. From Santander, you can get nearly anywhere in the province within a 3-hour drive.

The principality of Asturias lies between Cantabria in the east and Galicia in the west. It reaches its scenic (and topographical) summit in the **Picos de Europa,** where the first Spanish national park was inaugurated. With green valleys, fishing villages, and forests, Asturias is a land for all seasons.

The coastline of Asturias constitutes one of the major sightseeing attractions in northern Spain. Called the **Costa Verde,** it begins in the east at San Vicente de la Barquera and stretches almost 90 miles (145km) to Gijón. Allow about 6 hours to drive it without stops. The western coast, beginning at Gijón, goes all the way to Ribadeo, a border town with Galicia—a distance of 112 miles (180km). This rocky coastline, studded with fishing villages and containing narrow estuaries and small beaches, is one of the most spectacular stretches of scenery in Spain. It takes all day to explore.

Asturias is an ancient land, as prehistoric cave paintings in the area demonstrate. Iron Age Celtic tribes resisted the Romans, as Asturians proudly point out to this day. They also resisted the Moors, who subjugated the rest of Spain. The Battle of Covadonga in 722 represented the Moors' first major setback after their arrival in Iberia 11 years previously.

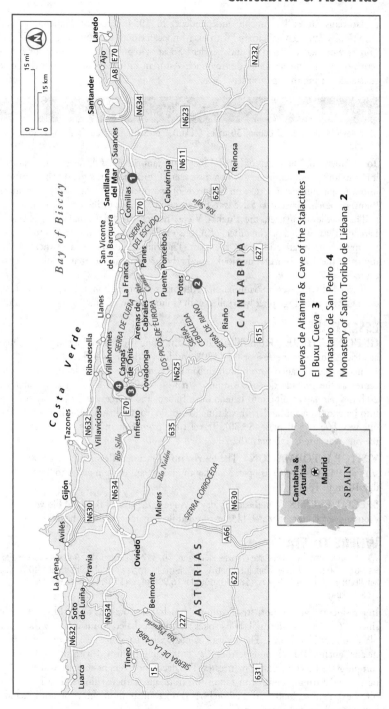

Cuevas de Altamira & Cave of the Stalactites **1**

El Buxu Cueva **3**

Monastario de San Pedro **4**

Monastery of Santo Toribio de Liébana **2**

Asturians are still staunchly independent. In 1934 Francisco Franco, then an ambitious young general, arrived with his Moroccan troops to suppress an uprising by miners who had declared an independent Socialist republic. His Nationalist forces returned again and again to destroy such Asturian cities as Gijón for their fierce resistance during the Spanish Civil War.

1 Laredo

37 miles (59.5km) W of Bilbao, 30 miles (48km) E of Santander, 265 miles (427km) N of Madrid

To an American, "the streets of Laredo" means the gun-slinging Old West. To a Spaniard it means an ancient maritime town on the eastern Cantabrian coast that has been turned into a major summer resort, with hundreds of apartments and villas along its 3 miles (5km) of beach. Playa de la Salvé is to the west and Playa de Oriñón to the east.

The medieval quarter, the **Puebla Vieja,** retains the traditional atmosphere of Laredo. It was walled on the orders of Alfonso VIII of Castile, who wanted to protect the town from pirate raids along the coast. The hillside **Iglesia de la Asunción,** dating from the 13th century, overlooks the harbor. It has five naves and rather bizarre capitals.

If you're driving west to Santoña, note the big monument honoring native son Juan de la Cosa, the cartographer who sailed with Columbus on his first voyage to America.

ESSENTIALS

GETTING THERE   From Bilbao, head west along the coastal highway (identified at various points as the A-8 or the E-70), and follow the signs to Laredo.

Bus service is available from both Bilbao and Santander. The station is in the town center at the avenida de José Antonio, s/n (☎ **94-260-49-67**). There are at least 20 buses per day coming into Laredo from Bilbao, and as many as 24 per day coming into Laredo from Santander. Travel time to Laredo from Bilbao is 40 minutes, and the one-way fare is 550 ptas. ($3.30). Travel time from Santander is 30 minutes, and the one-way fare is 450 ptas. ($2.70).

VISITOR INFORMATION   The **tourist information office,** Alameda de Miramar, s/n (☎ **942-61-10-96**), is open Monday to Friday 9am to 3pm and 4 to 8pm, Saturday 10am to 1pm.

SPECIAL EVENTS   On the last Friday of August, the annual **Battle of Flowers** draws thousands of visitors to watch bloom-adorned floats parade through the old town.

WHERE TO STAY

✪ **El Ancla del Laredo.** Calle Gonzalex Gallego, 10, 39770 Lardeo. ☎ **942-60-55-00.** Fax 942-61-16-02. www.cantabriainter.net/Ancla. E-mail: ancla@cantabriainter.net. 40 units. MINIBAR TV TEL. 14,900 ptas. ($89.40) double; 16,900 ptas. ($101.40) suite. AE, DC, MC, V. Free parking.

In a residential area a short stroll from the beach, this hotel has operated successfully since 1965. The architectural style evokes an English chalet, and it is clearly the finest place to stay in the area. The interior is cozy, with paraphernalia of the sea (*ancla* means "anchor"). Each midsize room is comfortably furnished with nautical motifs, soft pillows, and comfortable mattresses. The decoration is light and airy with wooden beams and fittings, along with rattan furniture and carpeted floors. The restaurant offers excellent seafood, and the hotel bar is open until midnight. Amenities include laundry and limited room service.

Risco. La Arenosa, 2, 39770 Laredo. ☎ **942-60-50-30.** Fax 942-60-50-55. 26 units. TV TEL. 11,500–15,000 ptas. ($69–$90) double. Rates include breakfast. AE, DC, MC, V. Free parking.

On a hillside overlooking Laredo, half a mile southeast of the center of town, this aging 1960s hotel opens onto impressive views of the old town and of one of the nearby beaches. It offers simple, functionally furnished rooms, each clean and comfortable with a firm mattress. In the garden are scattered tables for food service (see the restaurant recommendation below). Ample parking is provided.

WHERE TO DINE

Camarote. Vitoria, s/n. ☎ **942-60-67-07.** Reservations recommended. Main courses 2,000–2,800 ptas. ($12–$16.80); fixed-price menu 2,500 ptas. ($15). AE, DC, MC, V. Daily 1–4pm and 9pm–midnight. Closed Jan and Sun dinner in winter. SEAFOOD.

The owner of Camarote (in the center of town) is Felipe Manjarrés, and his chef de cuisine specializes in seafood, especially fresh fish. The decor is tasteful and attractive, and the outdoor terrace makes a pleasant alternative to the indoor dining room. The spinach with crayfish and the cheese tarts are truly excellent. Original recipes are used for salads with ham and shrimp as well as for those with tuna and fresh fruit. Try the grilled sea bream or a fillet steak Rossini.

Risco. La Arenosa, 2. ☎ **942-60-50-30.** Reservations recommended. Main courses 1,900–2,500 ptas. ($11.40–$15); *menús del día* 1,800–4,000 ptas. ($10.80–$24). AE, DC, MC, V. Daily 1–3:30pm and 8:30–11pm. SEAFOOD.

This is Laredo's most appealing restaurant, known for innovative seafood dishes. Assisted by a battery of helpers, the chef prepares such items as marinated salmon with pink peppercorns, scrambled eggs with lobster, and peppers stuffed with minced pigs' trotters or crabmeat. For dessert, try a fresh-fruit sorbet. Some tables are set up in the garden, or you can dine in a traditional room with views of the sea. The restaurant is on the ground floor of the Risco hotel (see "Where to Stay," above). During the busy months of July and August, it remains open on Monday.

2 Santander

244 miles (393km) N of Madrid, 72 miles (116km) NW of Bilbao

Santander has always been a rival of San Sebastián in the east, but it has never attained the premier status of that Basque resort. It did, however, become a royal residence from 1913 to 1930, after city officials presented an English-style Magdalena Palace to Alfonso XIII and his queen, Victoria Eugenia.

An ancient city, Santander was damaged by a 1941 fire, which destroyed the old quarter and most of its dwellings. It was rebuilt along original lines, with wide boulevards, a waterfront promenade, sidewalk cafes, shops, restaurants, and hotels.

Most visitors to Santander head for **El Sardinero,** a resort less than 1½ miles (2.5km) from the city. Buses and trolleys make the short run between the city center and El Sardinero both day and night. Besides hotels and restaurants, Santander has three **beaches,** Playa de Castaneda, Playa del Sardinero, and Playa de la Concha, where people stretch out under candy-striped umbrellas. If they become too crowded, take a 15-minute boat ride to **El Puntal,** a beautiful beach that is rarely crowded, even in August.

If you don't like crowds or beaches, go up to the lighthouse, a little more than 1¼ miles (2km) from El Sardinero, where the views are wide-ranging. A restaurant serves snacks both indoors and outdoors. Here, you can hike along the green cliffs or loll in the grass.

ESSENTIALS

GETTING THERE—Daily flights from Madrid and Barcelona land at Aeropuerto de Santander (☎ **942-25-10-07**), a little more than 4 miles (6.5km) from the town center, accessible by taxi only, costing 1,500 ptas. ($9). The local office of **Iberia** is at Paseo de Pereda, 18 (☎ **942-22-97-00**).

There are three trains daily from Madrid (trip time: 5 hours); a one-way fare costs 4,300 ptas. ($25.80). Four trains a day travel from Bilbao (3 hours). For rail information, call ☎ **942-28-02-02**.

Buses arrive at Plaza Estaciones (☎ **942-21-19-95**). There are 24 connections a day to and from Bilbao (trip time: 3 hours); a one-way ticket costs 925 to 1,500 ptas. ($5.55 to $9). Six to nine buses a day arrive from Madrid (6 hours), costing from 4,550 ptas. ($27.30).

N-634 continues west from Laredo to Santander, with an N-635 turnoff to reach the resort.

VISITOR INFORMATION   The **tourist information office** is at Jardines de Pereda (☎ **942-21-61-20**). It's open daily 9am to 1pm and 4 to 7pm.

SPECIAL EVENTS   The **Music and Dance Festival** in August is one of the most important artistic events in Spain (accommodations are very hard to come by during this time). Occasionally, this festival coincides with religious celebrations honoring Santiago (Saint James), the patron saint of Spain. Santander is an education center in summer as well. Courses are offered at the once-royal palace, now the Menéndez Pelayo International University. Students and teachers from North America and Europe come here to study and enjoy the area.

EXPLORING SANTANDER

Catedral. Somorrostro, s/n. ☎ **942-22-60-24**. Free admission. Daily 10am–1pm and 4–6pm.

Greatly damaged in the 1941 fire, this restored fortresslike 13th-century cathedral holds the tomb of historian/writer Marcelino Menéndez y Pelayo (1856–1912), Santander's most illustrious man of letters. The 12th-century crypt with a trio of low-slung aisles, untouched by fire, can be entered through the south portico. The Gothic cloister was restored after the fire. Roman ruins were discovered beneath the north aisle in 1983.

Museo Regional de Prehistoria y Arqueología de Cantabria. Calle Casimiro Sáinz, 4. ☎ **942-20-71-09**. Free admission. June 16–Sept 16, Tues–Sat 10am–1pm and 4–7pm, Sun 11am–2pm; Sept 17–June 15, Tues–Sat 9am–1pm and 4–7pm, Sun 11am–2pm.

This museum has some interesting artifacts discovered in the Cantabrian province—not only Roman but also some unusual prehistoric finds. Since it is unlikely you'll be allowed to visit the Cuevas de Altamira (see "Santillana del Mar & Cuevas de Altamira," later in this chapter), come here to see objects and photographs from these prehistoric caves with their remarkable paintings. Some of the items on display date from 15,000 years ago.

Museo Municipal de Bellas Artes. Calle Rubio, 6. ☎ **942-23-94-85**. Free admission. Mon–Fri 10am–1pm and 5–9pm; Sat 10am–1pm.

Located near the Ayuntamiento (Town Hall), the Municipal Museum of Fine Arts has some interesting Goya paintings, notably his portrait of Ferdinand VII, commissioned by the city, and his series of etchings called *Disasters of War*. You can see some of his continuing series of *Caprichos* (*Whims*). See also Zurbarán's *Mystic Scene* and an array of works by Flemish, Spanish, and Italian artists, many of them contemporary.

Biblioteca Menéndez y Pelayo. Calle Rubío, 4. ☎ **942-23-45-34.** Free admission. Mon 9am–1:30pm; Tues–Thurs 9am–2pm and 4–9:30pm.

Located in the same building as the Municipal Museum is this 45,000-volume library amassed by Menéndez y Pelayo and left to Santander upon his death in 1912. Guided tours are available. Opposite the building is the Casa Museo, which displays this great man's study and shows how modestly he lived.

SHOPPING

True aficionados of pottery and the nuances of ceramics usually drive from Santander to **Santillana del Mar,** 18 miles (29km) away, where handcrafted ceramics are in great abundance. But if you want to see a pared-down version of what's available in Santillana del Mar yet stay within Santander's city limits, head for any of the retailers on the calle Arrabal, in the city's commercial center. One of the most promising of them is **La Muralla,** 17 calle Arrabal (no phone).

An antiques gallery richly stocked with old furniture and paintings with rich veneers is **Fundación Marcellino Botín,** calle Pedrueca, 1 (☎ 942-22-60-72). Ironically, many of the boutiques and stores of Santander aren't in the city at all but within a 50-unit shopping center 2 miles from town, beside the road leading to the airport. Check out the **Centro Comercial Valle Real,** Carretera Bilbao, km 2.

And if you can't find whatever it is you need anywhere else in Santander, consider an excursion through the aisles of Santander's biggest department store, **Lainz,** calle Puente, 2 (☎ 942-21-42-00).

WHERE TO STAY

Santander is loaded with good-value hotels, from its year-round city hotels to its summer villas at El Sardinero. It gets crowded, so try to reserve well in advance.

IN TOWN

Hotel Central. General Mola, 5, 39004 Santander. ☎ **942-22-24-00.** Fax 942-36-38-29. 41 units. A/C TV TEL. 12,000–16,900 ptas. ($75.60–$106.45) double; 22,000–33,000 ptas. ($138.60–$207.90) suite. Discounts offered some weekends, depending on bookings. AE, MC, V.

The blue beaux-arts facade of this hotel, built around 1900, is one of the most attractive and ornate in its neighborhood. Inside is a much-modernized decor of stripped-down, rather angular modern accessories and a sense of 1980s-era modernity that's comfortable, even if it's not particularly cozy. The rooms are midsized and done in a comfortable modern style, with excellent mattresses and many cozy, homelike touches like bedside reading lamps and armchairs. On the premises is a bar and a restaurant serving simple meals. The location is about a block from the Plaza Forticada and the sea-fronting Jardines de Pereda.

Hotel Ciudad de Santander. Menéndez Pelayo, 13–15, 39006 Santander. ☎ **942-22-79-65.** Fax 942-21-73-03. www.nh-hoteles.es. E-mail: nh@nh-hoteles.es. 62 units. A/C MINI-BAR TV TEL. 15,000–20,000 ptas. ($90–$120) double; 20,000–25,000 ptas. ($120–$150) suite. AE, DC, MC, V. Parking 900 ptas. ($5.40) outdoors; 1,250 ptas. ($7.50) indoors. Bus: 5.

About 8 blocks north of Santander's busiest seaside promenade (Paseo de Pereda) in the center of the city's commercial heartland, this white-sided five-story rectangular hotel was built in 1989. Although it is the best address in the city itself, for true luxury check into Real at El Sardinero (see below). A big-windowed lobby here has marble floors, honey-colored wooden paneling, and modern accessories. The midsize rooms are monochromatic, similar to the lobby, with fully equipped bathrooms and convenient writing desks.

Dining: The hotel has an informal snack bar, plus a stone-and-glass-sheathed restaurant serving three-course fixed-price lunches and dinners.

Amenities: Room service (daily 7am to midnight), laundry and valet, concierge, car rentals.

Hotel México. Calderón de la Barca, 3, 39002 Santander. ☎ **942-21-24-50.** Fax 942-22-92-38. http://turismo.cantabria.org/sitesp/principal.htm. E-mail: mexico@ceoecant.es. 32 units. TV TEL. 11,500–16,700 ptas. ($69–$100.20) double. MC, V.

Only a block from the rail station, this is one of your best budget bets in the heart of the city, ideal for those without transportation who don't want to range far afield of the hotel, especially if they have luggage. The exterior may not be too enticing, but the atmosphere improves inside this family-operated inn. Even though it's in a congested area, street noises seem at a minimum, and the midsized rooms are well cared for and comfortably furnished, each with a firm mattress. Often they are in the old-fashioned architectural style of northern Spain, with glassed-in balconies and tall ceilings. Breakfast, the only meal served, is offered in a formal room with Queen Anne chairs and oak wainscoting.

AT EL SARDINERO

✪ **Hotel Real.** Paseo Pérez Galdós, 28, 39005 Santander. ☎ **942-27-25-50.** Fax 942-27-45-73. www.intermail.es/users/realsantander. E-mail: realsantander@husa.es. 123 units. A/C MINIBAR TV TEL. 25,000–42,000 ptas. ($150–$252) double; from 50,000 ptas. ($300) suite. AE, DC, MC, V. Free parking. Bus: 1, 2, 5, or 7.

Architecturally noteworthy—it was the first building in the entire region constructed of reinforced concrete—the Real was built in 1917 to house the entourage of courtiers who accompanied King Alfonso XIII on his midsummer vacations to Santander. Purchased and completely renovated by the prestigious HUSA chain in 1987, it is once again one of the most elegant hotels in northern Spain, filled with updated reminders of a more gracious age. Located about 2 miles (3km) east of the commercial center of town, near the site of the Royal Palace on a hillside above the Magdalena Beach, the Real contains richly conservative and spacious rooms, most with views of the sea and all with many comfort-inducing amenities, such as hair dryers, luxury mattresses, and plush towels.

Dining/Diversions: El Puntal restaurant serves regional and international three-course fixed-price lunches and dinners. Nearby is a cocktail lounge accented with potted palms and high ceilings and boasting a well-mannered staff.

Amenities: 24-hour room service, concierge, baby-sitting, laundry and valet, car rentals, golfing available nearby.

Hotel Rhin. Avenida Reina Victoria, 153, 39005 Santander. ☎ **942-27-43-00.** Fax 942-27-86-53. www.gruporhin.com. E-mail: rhin@gruporhin.com. 89 units. A/C MINIBAR TV TEL. 14,000–23,000 ptas. ($84–$138) double. AE, DC, DISC, MC, V. Parking 1,000 ptas. ($6). Bus: 1, 2, 5, or 7.

Built in the early 1970s and last renovated in 1995, this hotel has panoramic views of the city's beaches. It has improved considerably and earns a four-star rating from the government. The midsize rooms are handsome and very comfortable, and housekeeping is fastidious. A cafeteria and a restaurant both serve international cuisine, although food is not one of the reasons to stay here. Laundry service and room service are provided. Even though it is at the beach, the hotel is open year-round.

Palacio del Mar. Calle La Pareda, 5, El Sardinero, 39012 Santander. ☎ **942-39-24-00.** Fax 942-39-22-20. 67 units. A/C MINIBAR TV TEL. 20,900–32,800 ptas. ($131.65–$206.65) suite. Extra bed 6,000 ptas. ($37.80). AE, DC, MC, V. Parking 1,500 ptas. ($9).

One of the city's most modern hotels was built in the mid-1990s near the La Sardinero beaches, a short drive north of Santander's commercial core. The decor features a sinuous series of postmodern lines that might have been inspired by a Joan Miró painting, accented with winding staircases and walls made from glass blocks. Each of the spacious accommodations is a suite, with comfortable and contemporary-looking furniture, three phone extensions, and cheerful upholstery.

Dining/Diversions: The hotel has a formal restaurant decorated in an extreme modern style, its walls covered with art. Both international food and regional specialties are served here. There is a cozy bar whose dark shadows and pinspot lighting might evoke a fashionable disco.

Amenities: Room service, laundry and dry cleaning, concierge.

WHERE TO DINE

Most visitors to Santander dine at their hotels or boardinghouses, which sometimes offer better value for the money and more efficient service than city restaurants. For variety, however, here are a few suggestions.

IN TOWN

Bodega Cigaleña. Daoiz y Velarde, 19. ☎ **942-21-30-62.** Reservations not necessary. Main courses 1,200–2,800 ptas. ($7.20–$16.80); fixed-price menu 3,000 ptas. ($18). AE, DC, MC, V. Mon–Sat noon–4pm and 7:30pm–midnight. Closed June 20–July 1 and Oct 20–Nov 20. Bus: 5. REGIONAL.

Popular with the young set in Santander, this Castilian *bodega* in the city center serves typical regional cuisine in a rustic setting amid hanging hams, large wine kegs, and provincial tables. The set menu changes every day. A sample meal might be *sopa de pescado* (fish soup), shellfish paella, fruit of the season, bread, and wine. The Cigaleña offers a good choice of wines from an old Castilian town near Valladolid. Ask to see its Museo del Vino.

AT EL SARDINERO

La Sardina de Plata. Doctor Fleming, 3–4. ☎ **942-27-10-35.** Reservations required. Main courses 1,800–2,800 ptas. ($10.80–$16.80); tasting menu 5,500 ptas. ($33). AE, DC, MC, V. Wed–Mon 1:30–4pm; Wed–Sat and Mon 8:30pm–midnight. Bus: 1, 2, 5, or 7. SEAFOOD.

In a warren of small streets in the center of the old city, this nautically designed restaurant serves imaginative cuisine highlighted by delicate sauces. Selections might include such enticing dishes as cheese mousse, beef fillet with truffles and cognac, or a succulent fish salad. There is an extensive wine list. The service is courteous and efficient.

SANTANDER AFTER DARK

The most exciting thing to do in the evening is to head for the gaming tables of the **Gran Casino del Sardinero,** Plaza de Italia (☎ **942-27-60-54**), which has a cover charge of 500 ptas. ($3). It's open daily 8pm to 4am; be sure to bring your passport for entry. In the same complex is a bar/restaurant/cafe called **Lisboa** (☎ **942-27-10-20**), a good place to celebrate your winnings or try to forget what you've lost. It serves moderately priced meals, and some locals even drop in for breakfast. In summer it's especially crowded. It's open daily 9am to 2am.

3 Santillana del Mar & Cuevas de Altamira

18 miles (29km) SW of Santander, 244 miles (393km) N of Madrid

THE VILLAGE OF SANTILLANA

Among the most perfectly preserved medieval villages in Europe, ✪ **Santillana del Mar,** a Spanish national landmark, was once a famous place of pilgrimage. A monastery housed the relics of St. Juliana, a martyr in Asia Minor who refused to surrender her virginity to her husband. Pilgrims, especially the *grandees* of Castile, came to worship at this site. The name *Santillana* is a contraction of "Santa Juliana." The "del Mar" is misleading, as Santillana is not on the water but inland.

Jean-Paul Sartre called Santillana "the prettiest village in Spain," and we wouldn't want to dispute his esteemed judgment. In spite of all the tour buses, Santillana still retains its medieval atmosphere and is very much a village of dairy farmers to this day.

Wander on foot throughout the village, taking in its principal sites, including **Plaza de Ramón Pelayo** (sometimes called Plaza Mayor). Here the Parador de Santillana (see below) has been installed in the old Barreda Bracho residence.

A 15th-century tower, facing calle de Juan Infante, is known for its pointed arched doorway. A walk along calle de las Lindas (Street of Beautiful Women) may not live up to its promise, but it does include many of the oldest buildings in Santillana and two towers dating from the 14th and 15th centuries. Calle del Rio gets its name from a stream running through town to a central fountain.

ESSENTIALS

GETTING THERE   La Cantábrica (☎ 942-72-08-22) operates six buses a day from Santander but cuts back to four between September and June. Trip time is 45 minutes.

By car, take the N-611 out of Santander to reach the C-6316 cutoff to Santillana.

VISITOR INFORMATION   The **tourist information office** is at Plaza Mayor (☎ 942-81-82-51). Hours are daily 9:30am to 1pm and 4 to 7pm.

EXPLORING SANTILLANA

Visit the 800-year-old cathedral, the **Colegiata de Santillana,** calle Santo Domingo (☎ 942-81-80-04), which shelters the tomb of the village's patron saint, Juliana, and walk through its ivy-covered cloister. Other treasures displayed are 1,000-year-old documents and a 17th-century Mexican silver altarpiece. It's open April to October, daily 9:30am to 1pm and 4 to 7:30pm; off-season, daily 10am to 1pm and 4 to 6pm. Admission, including entrance to the Convent of the Poor Clares, is 300 ptas. ($1.80).

At the other end of the main street, the 400-year-old Covento de Regina Coelí, also called the **Convent of the Poor Clares (Museo Diocesano)** (☎ 942-81-80-04), houses a rich art collection inspired by a Madrid art professor who encouraged the nuns to collect and restore religious paintings and statues damaged or abandoned during the Spanish Civil War. The collection is constantly expanding. It's open daily 10am to 1pm and 4 to 8pm (closing at 6pm in winter). Admission is 150 ptas. (90¢).

WHERE TO STAY

Expensive

✪ **Parador de Santillana.** Plaza de Ramón Pelayo, 8, 39330 Santillana del Mar. ☎ 942-81-80-00. Fax 942-81-83-91. www.parador.es. 54 units. MINIBAR TV TEL. 17,000–19,500 ptas. ($102–$117) double. AE, DC, MC, V. Free parking.

A 400-year-old former palace filled with many beautiful antiques, this parador is one of the best and most popular in Spain. The public rooms are elegantly informal, with hand-hewn plank floors, old brass chandeliers, and refectory tables with bowls of fresh flowers to enhance the atmosphere. Large portraits of knights in armor hang in a gallery. Most of the guest rooms are unusually large, with antiques and windows on two sides; many have views of a small garden. The large bathrooms have all sorts of conveniences, including terrycloth robes. Note that the third-floor rooms are very small. Four-course evening meals and luncheons, offering rather standard fare, are served in the great dining hall.

Moderate

Hotel Altamira. Calle Cantón, 1, 39330 Santillana del Mar. ☎ **942-81-80-25.** Fax 942-84-01-36. 32 units. A/C TV TEL. 8,000–12,000 ptas. ($48–$72) double. AE, DC, MC, V.

This three-star hotel in the center of the village is a 400-year-old former palace; it's the best place to stay if you can't get into the government-run parador (see above). Although not as impressive as the parador, it often takes the overflow in its comfortable, well-maintained rooms, each fitted with a firm mattress on a twin or double bed. Dinner is available at two of the hotel's restaurants, El Cantón and El Racial. Both restaurants serve Castilian-inspired cuisine.

Los Infantes. Avenida L'Dorat, 1, 39339 Santillana del Mar. ☎ **942-81-81-00.** Fax 942-84-01-03. E-mail: linfantes@mundina.es. 48 units. TV TEL. 9,000–15,000 ptas. ($54–$90) double; 13,000–18,000 ptas. ($78–$108) suite. AE, DISC, MC, V. Parking 200 ptas. ($1.20).

This three-star hotel is a comfortable choice, although not as charming as the Altamira (see above). Located in an 18th-century building on the main road leading into the village, Infantes has successfully kept the old flavor of Santillana: beamed ceilings and lounges furnished with tapestries, antiques, clocks, and paintings. The small rooms are cozy and well kept, with wall-to-wall carpeting; two have small balconies. A restaurant serves Spanish and international cuisine.

Inexpensive

Hotel Siglo XVIII. Revolgo, 38, 39330 Santillana del Mar. ☎ **942-84-02-10.** Fax 942-84-02-11. 16 units. TV TEL. 8,500 ptas. ($51) double. AE, DC, MC, V. Closed Dec 12–Mar 1. Free parking.

Located a 5-minute walk from the old town, this small three-star hotel has operated since 1996 in an old building behind a stone facade. Inside, the decoration is cozy and homelike, with a lingering aura of the 18th century, dominated by carved wood, high-beamed ceilings, white walls, and tile floors. The rooms, some of which have balconies opening onto the surrounding landscape, are medium sized with plenty of comfort and light. An on-site cafeteria and bar is open daily, and amenities include a terraced garden, swimming pool, and 24-hour room service.

WHERE TO DINE

Dining isn't one of the compelling reasons to visit Santillana del Mar. Except for Los Blasones (see below), the only recommendable independent restaurant, your best bet is to dine at one of the previously recommended hotels. For atmosphere and quality of cuisine, the finest choice is Parador de Santillana (see above).

Los Blasones. Plaza de la Gándara, 8. ☎ **942-81-80-70.** Reservations recommended. Main courses 1,500–2,200 ptas. ($9–$13.20); fixed-price menu 2,800 ptas. ($16.80). AE, MC, V. Daily 1–4pm and 8–11:30pm. Closed Dec 10–Mar 10. REGIONAL.

Located in the center of town on the Plaza de la Gándara, this bar-restaurant, a local hangout, serves the best food in town among the independent restaurants. It's in a rustic building made of stone. Barbecue selections are featured, and the chef's specialty is *solomillo al queso de Treviso* (sirloin with cheese sauce). Try the perfectly grilled hake or the tasty stuffed peppers.

THE ALTAMIRA CAVES

About 1½ miles (2.5km) from Santillana del Mar are the ✪ **Cuevas de Altamira** (☎ **942-81-80-05**), famous for prehistoric paintings dating from the end of the Ice Age, paintings that have caused these caves to be called the "Sistine Chapel of prehistoric art." The cave paintings at Altamira are ranked among the finest prehistoric paintings ever discovered. They are rivaled but not matched by similar paintings discovered at Lascaux in the Dordogne Valley in France. These ancient depictions of bison and horses, painted vividly in reds and blacks on the caves' ceilings, were not discovered until the late 19th century. Once their authenticity was established, scholars and laypersons alike flocked to see these works of art, which provide a fragile link to our remote ancestors.

Severe damage was caused by the bacteria brought in by so many visitors, so now the Research Center and Museum of Altamira allows only 20 visitors per day June to September (no children under 13) and five visitors per day October to May. Admission is 400 ptas. ($2.40). If you don't have a car, you have to walk from Santillana del Mar, as there is no bus service. From the center of Santillana, signs point the way to the cave. You walk past the abandoned Iglesia de San Sebastián, then cut through the streets of the hamlet of Herrán. Signs there direct you right across a farmer's field until you reach the cave. If you wish to visit, write to this address 1 year in advance asking permission to see the main cave and specifying the number in your party and the desired date: **Centro de Investigación y Museo de Altamira,** 39330 Santillana del Mar, Cantabria, Spain (☎ **942-81-80-05**).

Reservations are not necessary for visits to the nearby **Cave of the Stalactites** and the little free museum at the site, open Monday to Saturday 10am to 1pm and 4 to 6pm, Sunday 10am to 1pm. Here you can see reproductions of the caves' artwork and buy color slides that show the subtleties of color. You'll also see pictures of what the bacteria did to these priceless paintings. To reach the area, you need to go by car or on foot because there is no bus service.

4 Los Picos de Europa

Potes: 71 miles (114km) W of Santander, 247 miles (398km) N of Madrid; Cangas de Onís: 91 miles (146.5km) W of Santander, 260 miles (419km) N of Madrid

These mountains are technically part of the Cordillera Cantábrica, which runs parallel to the northern coastline of Spain. In the narrow and vertiginous band known as Los Picos de Europa, they are by far at their most dramatic.

These "European Peaks" are the most famous and most legend-riddled mountains in Spain. Rising more than 8,500 feet (2,590m), they are not high by alpine standards, but their proximity to the sea makes their height especially awesome. During the Middle Ages, they were passable only with great difficulty. (Much earlier, the ancient Romans constructed a north-south road whose stones are still visible in some places.) An abundance of wildlife, the medieval battles that occurred here, and dramatically rocky heights have all contributed to the twice-told tales that are an essential part of the entire principality of Asturias.

The position of Los Picos defined the medieval borders between Asturias, Santander, and León. Covering a distance of only 24 miles (39km) at their longest point, they are geologically and botanically different from anything else in the region. Thousands of years ago, busy glaciers created massive and forbidding limestone cliffs, which today challenge the most dedicated and intrepid rock climbers in Europe.

As you're touring the majestic Picos de Europa, be on the lookout for some of the rarest wildlife remaining in Europe. On the beech-covered slopes of these mountains and in gorges laden with jasmine, you might spot the increasingly rare Asturcon, a shaggy, rather chubby wild horse so small it first looks like a toy pony. Another endangered species is the Iberian brown bear—but if you see one, keep your distance. The park is also home of the surefooted chamois goat and some rare butterflies. Many bird watchers flock here every year to see rare birds of prey, such as peregrine falcons, buzzards, and golden eagles. All wildlife is strictly protected by the government.

If you want to hike in this region, make sure you're well prepared. Many of the slopes are covered with loosely compacted shale, making good treads and hiking boots a must. Inexperienced hikers should definitely stick to well-established paths. In summer, temperatures can get hot and humid, and sudden downpours sweeping in from the frequently rainy coastline are common in any season. Hiking is not recommended between October and May, but you can drive or do the walk described below in Tour 3 in any season.

The Picos are divided by swiftly flowing rivers into three regions: From east to west, they are Andara, Urrieles, and Cornion.

By far the best way to see this region is by car. Most drivers arrive in the region on the N-621 highway, heading southwest from Santander, or on the same highway northeast from the cities of north-central Spain (especially León and Valladolid). This highway connects many of the region's best vistas in a straight line. It also defines the region's eastern boundary. If you're driving east from Oviedo, you'll take the N-6312, in which case the first town of any importance will be Cangas de Onís.

Travel by bus is much less convenient but possible if you have lots of time and have had your fill of the rich architecture of the Spanish heartland. The region's touristic hubs are the towns of Panes and Potes; both have bus service (two buses per day in summer, one per day in winter) from Santander and León. More frequent buses (five per day) come to Potes from the coastal town of Unquera (which is along the coastal train lines). From Oviedo, there are two buses daily to the district's easternmost town of Cangas; they continue a short distance farther southeast to Covadonga. Within the region, a small local bus runs once a day, according to an erratic schedule, along the northern rim of the Picos, connecting Cangas de Onís with Las Arenas. Frankly, bus service in this region is too time consuming for most visitors.

EXPLORING THE REGION

If you have a car, the number and variety of tours in this region are almost endless, but for the purposes of this guide, we have organized the region into three driving tours. Any of them, with their side excursions, could fill an entire day; if you're rushed and omit some of the side excursions, you'll spend half a day.

DRIVING TOUR 1—PANES TO POTES

18 miles (29km); 1 hour

Except for one optional detour, this drive extends entirely along one of the region's best roads, N-621, which links León and Valladolid to Santander. The drive is most noteworthy for its views of the ravine containing the Deva River, a ravine so steep that direct sunlight rarely penetrates it.

About two-thirds of the way to Potes, signs point you on a detour to the village of:

1. Lebana, half a mile off the main road. Here you'll find the church of **Nuestra Señora de Lebana,** built in the 10th century in the Mozarabic style, surrounded by a copse of trees at the base of tall cliffs. Some people consider it the best example of Arabized Christian architecture in Europe, with Islamic-inspired geometric motifs. If it isn't open, knock at the door of the first house you see as you enter the village—the home of the guardian, who will unlock the church if she's around. For this, she will expect a tip. If she's not around, content yourself with admiring the church from the outside, noting its spectacular natural setting.

Continuing for about another 5 miles (8km), you'll reach the village of:

2. Potes, a charming place with well-kept alpine houses against a backdrop of jagged mountains. Two miles (3km) southwest of Potes, near Turiano, stands the:

3. **Monastery of Santo Toribio de Liébana,** dating from the 17th century. Restored to the style it enjoyed at the peak of its vast power, a transitional Romanesque, it contains what is reputed to be a splinter from the True Cross, brought from Jerusalem in the 8th century by the Bishop of Astorga. The monastery is also famous as the former home of Beatus de Liébana, the 8th-century author of *Commentary on the Apocalypse,* one of medieval Spain's most famous ecclesiastical documents. Today the building remains a functioning monastery. Ring the bell during daylight hours, and one of the brothers will let you enter if you are properly attired.

At the end of a winding and breathtakingly beautiful road to the west of Potes is the:

4. **Parador del Río Deva,** where you can spend the night or just stop for lunch. The drive following the path of the Deva River for the most part will take you to:

5. **Fuente-Dé.** Once you're here, a *teleférico* carries you 2,000 feet up to an observation platform above a wind-scoured rock face. In summer this cable car operates daily in July and August 9am to 8pm; from September to June, hours are daily 10am to 6pm. Round-trip fare is 1,500 ptas. ($9). At the top you can walk 3 miles (5km) along a footpath to the rustic **Refugio de Aliva** (☎ **942-73-09-99**), open between June 15 and September 15. Doubles cost 8,000 to 9,500 ptas. ($48 to $57). If you opt for just a meal or a snack at the hostal's simple restaurant, remember to allow enough time to return to the *teleférico* before its last trip down. If you plan on taking the next driving tour (below), then head back to Potes.

DRIVING TOUR 2—POTES TO CANGAS DE ONÍS

93 miles (150km); 4 hours

This tour includes not only the Quiviesa Valley and some of the region's most vertiginous mountain passes, but also some of its most verdant fields and most elevated pastures. You might stop at an occasional village, but most of the time you will be going through deserted countryside. Your route will take you through several tunnels and high above mountain streams set deep into gorges. The occasional belvederes along the way always deliver on their promise of panoramic views.

1. **Potes** (see "Driving Tour 1" above) is your starting point. Take N-621 southwest to Riaño. At Riaño, turn north for a brief ride on N-625. Then take a winding route through the heart of the region by driving northwest on N-637. Although it's beautiful all along the way, the first really important place you'll reach is:

2. **Cangas de Onís,** the westernmost town in the region, where you can get a clean hotel room and a solid meal after a trek through the mountains. The biggest attraction in Cangas de Onís is an ivy-covered **Roman bridge,** lying west of the center, spanning the Sella River. Also of interest is the **Capilla de Santa Cruz,** immediately west of the center. One of the earliest Christian sites in Spain (and a holy spot many centuries before that), it was originally constructed in the 8th century over a Celtic dolmen and rebuilt in the 15th century.

A mile northwest of Cangas de Onís, beside the road leading to Arriondas, stands the:

3. **Monasterio de San Pedro,** a Benedictine monastery in the village of **Villanueva.** The church that you see was originally built in the 17th century, when it enclosed within its premises the ruins of a much older Romanesque church. Combining Baroque opulence and Romanesque simplicity, it has some unusual carved capitals showing the unhappy end of the medieval King Favila, supposedly devoured by a Cantabrian bear.

DRIVING TOUR 3—CANGAS DE ONÍS TO PANES

35 miles (56km); 1 hour

This tour travels along the relatively straight C-6312 from the western to the eastern entrance to the Picos de Europa region. A number of unusual excursions could easily stretch this into an all-day outing.

From Cangas de Onís, heading west about 1 mile (1.5km), you'll reach the turnoff to:

1. **El Buxu Cueva.** Inside the cave are a limited number of prehistoric rock engravings and charcoal drawings, somewhat disappointingly small. Only 25 people per day are allowed inside (respiration erodes the drawings), so unless you get there early, you won't get in. It's open Wednesday to Sunday 10am to 2pm and 4 to 6:30pm. Admission is 200 ptas. ($1.35).

Four miles (6.5km) east, signs point south in the direction of:

2. **Covadonga.** Revered as the birthplace of Christian Spain, it is about 6 miles (9.5km) off the main highway. A battle here in A.D. 718 pitted a ragged band of Christian Visigoths against a small band of Muslims. The resulting victory established the first niche of Christian Europe in Moorish Iberia. The town's most important monument is **La Santa Cueva,** a cave containing the sarcophagus of Pelayo (d. 737), king of the Visigothic Christians, and an enormous neo-Romanesque basilica, built between 1886 and 1901, commemorating the Christianization of Spain. At the end of the long boulevard that funnels into the base of the church stands a statue of Pelayo.

Return to the highway and continue east. You'll come to the village of Las Estazadas; then after another 7 miles (11km) you'll reach:

3. **Las Arenas de Cabrales** (some maps refer to it as Arenas). This is the headquarters of a cheese-producing region whose Cabrales, a blue-veined cheese made from ewes' milk, is avidly consumed throughout Spain.

Drive 3 miles (5km) south from Arenas, following signs to the village of:

4. **Puente de Poncebos** (shown on some maps as Poncebos). Here, the road ends abruptly (except perhaps for four-wheel-drive vehicles). This village is several miles downstream from the source of Spain's most famous salmon-fishing river, the Cares, which flows from its source near the more southerly village of Cain through deep ravines.

Beginning at Poncebos, a footpath has been cut into the ravine on either side of the Cares River. It is one of the engineering marvels of Spain, known for centuries as **"The Divine Gorge."** It crosses the ravine many times over footbridges and sometimes through tunnels chiseled into the rock face beside the water, making a hike along the banks of this river a memorable outing. You can climb up the riverbed from Poncebos, overland to the village of Cain, a total distance of 7 miles (11km). Allow between 3 and 4 hours. At Cain, you can take a taxi back to where you left your car in Poncebos if you don't want to retrace your steps.

After your trek up the riverbed, continue your drive on to the village of:

5. **Panes,** a distance of 14 miles (22.5km), to the eastern extremity of the Picos de Europa.

WHERE TO STAY & DINE IN THE AREA

Accommodations are extremely limited in these mountain towns. If you're planning an overnight stop, make sure you have a reservation. Most taverns will serve you food during regular opening hours without a reservation.

IN CANGAS DE ONÍS

Hotel Aultre Naray. Km 335, N-634, Peruyes, 33547 Asturias. ☎ **98-584-08-08.** Fax 98-584-08-48. www.aultrenaray.com. E-mail: aultre@aultrenaray.com. 10 units. TV TEL. 9,000–12,800 ptas. ($54–$77) double. AE, DC, MC, V. Free parking.

A small hotel with character, this establishment opened in 1995 in an Asturian country house dating from 1873. Its robust masonry work is typical of the last century, and it has a beautiful stone archway in the entrance. The decoration came from an interior design workshop in Madrid, resulting in a harmonious blend of traditional architecture with current design trends. The hotel has well-furnished mid-size bedrooms, each with a private tiled bathroom. Four rooms have sloping ceilings. There's a cozy sitting room with a fireplace for guests, a bar and dining room, and a garden. The hotel is in the foothills of the Escapa mountain range, enjoying a panoramic view of the mountains and an oak forest on the banks of the River Sella. The area is a perfect place for fishing; hiking in the mountains and canoeing are other popular diversions.

La Palmera. Soto de Cangas. ☎ **98-594-00-96.** Main courses 1,200–3,000 ptas. ($7.20–$18); *menú del día* 1,800 ptas. ($10.80). AE, DC, MC, V. Daily 1:30–4:30pm and 8:30–11:30pm. REGIONAL.

When the weather is right you can dine outside here, enjoying some mountain air with the food. Sometimes this place is overrun, but on other occasions you can have a meal in peace. The menu features game from the surrounding mountains, along with fillet of beef, lamb chops, and salmon in green sauce. Try the local mountain cheese. La Palmera is 2 miles (3km) east of Cangas de Onís on the road to Covadonga.

IN COSGAYA

Hotel del Oso. Carretera Espinama, s/n, 39539 Cosgaya. ☎ **942-73-30-18.** Fax 942-73-30-36. E-mail: hoteldeloso@mundina.es. 36 units. TV TEL. 8,500–9,500 ptas. ($51–$57) double. MC, V. Closed Jan 7–Feb 15. Free parking. From Potes, take the road signposted to Espinama 9 miles (14.5km) south.

This well-run little hotel is located in two buildings next to the Deva River, beside the road leading from Potes to the parador and cable car at Fuente-Dé. The place is ringed with natural beauty. Its small rooms are well furnished and maintained, and meals are taken at the Mesón del Oso (see below).

Mesón del Oso. Carretera Espinama, s/n. ☎ **942-73-30-18.** Main courses 1,500–2,800 ptas. ($9–$16.80). DC, MC, V. Daily 1–4pm and 9–11pm. Closed Jan 7–Feb 15. From Potes, take the route south toward Espinama 9 miles (14.5km). ASTURIAN.

Open to the public since 1981, this stone-built place is named after the bear that supposedly devoured Favilia, an 8th-century king of Asturias. Here, at the birthplace of the Christian warrior King Pelayo, you can enjoy Lebaniega cuisine, reflecting the bounty of mountain, stream, and sea. The portions are generous. Try trout from the Deva River, grilled tuna, roast suckling pig, or a mountain stew called *cocida lebaniego*, whose recipe derives from local lore and tradition. Dessert might be a fruit-based tart. There's an outdoor terrace.

IN COVADONGA

Hotel Pelayo. 33589 Covadonga. ☎ **98-584-60-61.** Fax 98-584-60-54. 45 units. TV TEL. 8,500–15,000 ptas. ($51–$90) double; 12,000–20,000 ptas. ($72–$120) suite. AE, DC, MC, V. Closed Dec 15–Feb 1. Free parking. Drive east and then south from Cangas de Onís, following the signs for Covadonga and the hotel.

There's no street address for this place, but it's in the shadow of the large 19th-century basilica that dominates the village. The view from its windows takes in a panoramic landscape. Guests come here to enjoy the mountain air, and many pilgrims check in while visiting religious shrines in the area. The place has a somewhat dated, but nevertheless appealing, family atmosphere. The small rooms are comfortable and well furnished, each with a good bed. The facilities include a parking lot, a garden, and a restaurant offering well-prepared lunch or dinner ranging from 1,800 to 2,000 ptas. ($10.80 to $12).

IN FUENTE-DÉ

Parador de Fuente-Dé. At 3.5km de Espinama, 39588 Espinama. ☎ **942-73-66-51.** Fax 942-73-66-54. www.parador.es. 78 units. MINIBAR TV TEL. 12,500–15,000 ptas. ($75–$90) double. AE, DC, MC, V. Closed Nov 15–Mar 1. Free parking. Drive 16 miles (26km) west of Potes.

The finest place to stay in the area, this government-run parador faces the Picos de Europa. Opened in 1975, it is at the end of the major road through the Liébana region. Hunters in autumn and mountain climbers in summer often fill its attractively decorated and comfortably furnished bedrooms, which are midsized to spacious. The place has a pleasant bar, and its restaurant serves good regional cuisine, with a *menú del día* costing 3,200 ptas. ($21.45).

IN POTES

Restaurant Martín. Roscabao, s/n. ☎ **942-73-02-33.** Main courses 850–1,800 ptas. ($5.10–$10.80); fixed-price menu 1,200 ptas. ($7.20). AE, V. Daily 1–4:30pm and 8–11pm. Closed Jan. REGIONAL.

This family-run establishment in the center of Potes is filled with regional charm and spirit. They prepare garbanzos (chickpeas) with bits of *chorizo* (sausage), other vegetables, and the rich produce of the region, depending on the season. They serve game from the Picos and fish from the Cantabrian coast. The dessert choices comprise more than a dozen tarts and pastries.

5 Gijón (Xixón)

294 miles (473km) N of Madrid, 119 miles (191.5km) W of Santander, 18 miles (29km) E of Oviedo

The major port of Asturias and its largest city is a summer resort and an industrial center rolled into one. As a port, Gijón (pronounced hee-*hon*) is said to predate the Romans. The Visigoths came through here, and in the 8th century the Moors wandered through the area, but none of those would-be conquerors made much of an impression.

The best part of the city to explore is the *barrio* of **Cimadevilla,** with its maze of alleys and leaning houses. This section, jutting into the ocean to the north of the new town, spills over an elevated piece of land known as Santa Catalina. Santa Catalina forms a headland at the west end of the **Playa San Lorenzo,** stretching for about 1½ miles (2.5km); this sandy beach has good facilities. After time at the beach, you can stroll through the **Parque Isabel la Católica** at its eastern end.

Gijón is short on major monuments. The city was the birthplace of Gaspar Melchor de Jovellanos (1744–1811), one of Spain's most prominent men of letters, as well as an agrarian reformer and liberal economist. Manuel de Godoy, the notorious minister, ordered that Jovellanos be held prisoner for 7 years in Bellver Castle on Majorca. In Gijón his birthplace has been restored and turned into the **Museo-Casa Natal de Jovellanos,** Plaza de Jovellanos, open Tuesday to Saturday 10am to 2pm and 4 to 8pm. Admission is free.

ESSENTIALS

GETTING THERE Gijón doesn't have an airport, but **Iberia** flies to the airport at Ranón, 26 miles (42km) away, a facility it shares with Oviedo-bound passengers.

Gijón has good rail links and makes a good gateway into Asturias. Three trains a day make the 6½- to 8½-hour trip from Madrid. León is a convenient rail hub for reaching Gijón because nine trains per day make the 2- to 3-hour trip between these cities. You can also take the narrow-gauge **FEVE** from Bilbao.

Six buses a day connect Gijón with Madrid (5½ hours away), and two buses per day run to and from Santander (4½ hours away). Four buses a day go to León (2 hours away).

From Santander in the east, drive west along the N-634. At Ribadesella, you can take the turnoff to the 632, which is the coastal road that will take you to Gijón. This is the scenic route. To save time, continue on N-634 until you reach the outskirts of Oviedo, then cut north on A-66, the express highway to Gijón.

VISITOR INFORMATION The **tourist information office** is at Marqués de San Estebán, 1 (☎ **98-534-60-46**). It's open Monday to Friday 9am to 2pm and 4 to 7pm, Saturday 9am to 2pm.

SPECIAL EVENTS The most exciting time to be in Gijón is on **Asturias Day,** the first Sunday in August. This fiesta is celebrated with parade floats, traditional folk dancing, and lots of music. But summers here tend to be festive even without a festival. Vacationers are fond of patronizing the cider taverns (*chigres*), eating grilled sardines, and joining in sing-alongs in the port-side *tascas*. Be aware that you can get as drunk on cider as you can on beer, maybe somewhat faster.

WHERE TO STAY
EXPENSIVE

Hernán Cortés. Fernández Vallín, 5, 33205 Gijón. ☎ **98-534-60-00.** Fax 98-535-56-45. 56 units. A/C MINIBAR TV TEL. 18,000–24,000 ptas. ($108–$144) double; 22,000–32,000 ptas. ($132–$192) suite. AE, DC, MC, V. Parking 1,250 ptas. ($7.50) nearby. Bus: 4 or 11.

About 1 block east of Plaza del 6 de Agosto, midway between Playa San Lorenzo and the harbor, this hotel named after the conquistador is one of the finest in town. Although it was recently renovated, its midsize guest rooms still retain a bit of the allure of yesteryear and provide such thoughtful extras as shoeshine equipment. The Cortés doesn't have a restaurant, but it does offer a nighttime cafeteria. The proprietors will serve lunch or dinner in your room from a neighboring restaurant.

✪ **Parador del Molino Viejo (Parador de Gijón).** Parque Isabel la Católica, s/n, 33203 Gijón. ☎ **800/223-1356** in the U.S., or 98-537-05-11. Fax 98-537-02-33. www.parador.es. 40 units. A/C MINIBAR TV TEL. 16,000–22,000 ptas. ($96–$132) double. AE, DC, MC, V. Free parking. Bus: 4 or 11.

Next to the verdant confines of Gijón's most visible park, about half a mile east of the town center and an easy walk from the popular beach Playa San Lorenzo, this is the premier place to stay. Awarded four stars by the government (which runs it), it was constructed around the core of an 18th-century cider mill. The parador is surrounded by a garden strewn with tables, beside a stream sheltering colonies of swans. It contains a marble-sheathed reception area, an unpretentious restaurant, and a cider bar that, on weekends, is quite popular with local residents. The guest rooms are somewhat cramped and surprisingly simple for a four-star hotel; however, they're tastefully restored with well-scrubbed wooden floors, thick shutters, traditional furniture, and larger-than-usual bathrooms.

MODERATE

Begoña. Carretera de la Costa, 44, 33205 Gijón. ☎ **98-514-72-11.** Fax 98-539-82-22. 250 units. TV TEL. 12,000–13,000 ptas. ($72–$78) double. AE, DC, MC, V. Parking 1,300 ptas. ($7.80). Bus: 4 or 11.

This functional modern hotel with much-appreciated parking has small rooms that are well furnished and comfortable, plus efficient chamber service to keep everything clean. Regional and national dishes, with many seafood concoctions, are served in the restaurant, where meals begin at 1,500 ptas. ($9). The hotel is on the southern outskirts of the new town, 1 block north of avenida Manuel Llaneza, the major traffic artery from the southwest.

La Casona de Jovellanos. Plaza de Jovellanos, 1, 33201 Gijón. ☎ **98-534-12-64.** Fax 98-535-61-51. 15 units. TV TEL. 7,500–13,600 ptas. ($45–$81.60) double; 7,500–22,000 ptas. ($45–$132) suite. AE, DC, MC, V. Parking nearby 1,300 ptas. ($7.80). Bus: 4 or 11.

This venerable hotel stands on the rocky peninsula that was the site of the oldest part of fortified Gijón, a short distance south of the Parque Santa Catalina. It contains only a few rooms, so reservations are imperative. The small rooms themselves are attractively furnished and well maintained, each with a comfortable bed. The hotel was built on foundations 3 centuries old. In 1794 the writer Jovellanos established the Asturian Royal Institute of Marine Life and Mineralogy here, and it was later transformed into this hotel within walking distance of the beach and yacht basin.

WHERE TO DINE

Casa Justo (Chigre Asturianu). Hermanos Feigueroso, 50. ☎ **98-538-63-57.** Reservations recommended. Main courses 1,800–3,000 ptas. ($10.80–$18); fixed-price menus 1,200–1,500 ptas. ($7.20–$9). AE, DC, MC, V. Fri–Wed 1pm–1am. Closed June 15–July 1. Bus: 4 or 11. REGIONAL.

Housed within a very old cider press, for years this place has been called Chigre Asturianu, but most locals still refer to it by its older designation. Renovations have added well-designed dining rooms and kitchens to what used to be a large and drafty building. The cuisine is based primarily on fish and shellfish but with plenty of Asturian regional dishes as well. Try octopus with potatoes, grilled fresh John Dory, or veal chops. There is a full array of wines. Here, too, you can sample that Roquefort-like cheese, Cabrales, made in the Picos de Europa. Casa Justo is south of the old town near Campo Sagrada on the road to Pola de Siero.

Casa Tino. Alfredo Truán, 9. ☎ **98-534-13-87.** Reservations recommended. Main courses 1,600–2,500 ptas. ($9.60–$15); *menú del día* 1,500 ptas. ($9). AE, DC, MC, V. Fri–Wed 1:15–3:30pm and 8:45–11:30pm. Bus: 4 or 11. REGIONAL.

Quality combined with quantity, at reasonable prices, is the hallmark of this restaurant near the police station, north of Manuel Llaneza and west of the Paseo de Begoña. Each day the chef prepares a different stew—sometimes fish and sometimes meat. The place is packed with chattering diners every evening, many of them regulars. Sample the white beans of the region cooked with pork, stewed hake, or marinated beefsteak, perhaps finishing with one of the fruit tarts.

Casa Victor. Carmen, 11. ☎ **98-534-83-10.** Reservations recommended. Main courses 2,500–3,000 ptas. ($15–$18); fixed-price menu 2,000 ptas. ($12). AE, DC, MC, V. Mon–Sat 1–3:30pm and 8:30–11:30pm. Closed mid-Dec to mid-Jan. Bus: 4 or 11. SEAFOOD.

Owner and sometime chef Victor Bango is a bit of a legend. He oversees the buying and preparation of the fresh fish for which this place is famous. The successful young people of Gijón enjoy the tavernlike atmosphere here, as well as the imaginative dishes—a mousse made from the roe of sea urchins, for example, is all the rage in Asturias these days. Well-chosen wines accompany such other menu items as octopus served with fresh vegetables and grilled steak. Casa Victor is located by the dockyards.

6 Oviedo (Uviéu)

126 miles (203km) W of Santander, 276 miles (444km) N of Madrid

Oviedo is the capital of Asturias. Despite its high concentration of industry and mining, the area has unspoiled scenery. Only 16 miles (26km) from the coast, Oviedo is very pleasant in summer, when much of Spain is unbearably hot. It makes an ideal base for excursions along the Costa Verde.

A peaceful city today, Oviedo has had a long and violent history. Razed in the 8th century during the Reconquest, it was rebuilt in an architectural style known as Asturian pre-Romanesque, which predated many of the greatest achievements under the Moors. Remarkably, this architectural movement was in flower when the rest of Europe lay under the black cloud of the Dark Ages.

As late as the 1930s Oviedo was suffering violent upheavals. An insurrection in the mining areas on October 5, 1934 led to a seizure of the town by miners, who set up a revolutionary government. The subsequent fighting led to the destruction of many historical monuments. The cathedral was also damaged, and the university was set on fire. Even more destruction came during the Spanish Civil War.

ESSENTIALS

GETTING THERE   Oviedo doesn't have an airport. The nearest one is at Ranón, 32 miles (51.5km) away, which it shares with Gijón-bound passengers. Call ☎ **98-555-18-33** for information.

From Madrid, there are six trains per day. Call **RENFE** at ☎ **98-525-02-02** for information.

One bus per day arrives from Santander (trip time: 1 hour). Seven buses pull in daily from Madrid (6 hours). For bus schedules, call ☎ **98-528-12-00.**

From the east or west, take N-634 across the coast of northern Spain. From the south, take N-630 or A-66 from León.

VISITOR INFORMATION   The **tourist information office** is at Plaza de Alfonso II el Casto (☎ **98-521-33-85**). Hours are Monday to Friday 9:30am to 1:30pm and 4:30 to 6:30pm, Saturday 9am to 2pm, and Sunday 11am to 2pm.

EXPLORING OVIEDO

Oviedo has been rebuilt into a modern city around the Parque de San Francisco. It still contains some historical and artistic monuments, however, the most important being the **cathedral** on the Plaza de Alfonso II el Casto (☎ **98-522-10-33**). The Gothic church was begun in 1348 and completed at the end of the 15th century (except for the spire, which dates from 1556). Inside is an altarpiece in the florid Gothic style, dating from the 14th and 15th centuries. The cathedral's 9th-century **Cámara Santa (Holy**

Chamber) is famous for the Cross of Don Pelayo, the Cross of the Victory, and the Cross of the Angels, the finest specimens of Asturian art in the world. Admission to the cathedral is free, but entrance to the Holy Chamber is 400 ptas. ($2.40) for adults and 300 ptas. ($1.80) for children 10 to 15; children under 10 are free. The cathedral is open May to October, Monday to Saturday 10am to 1pm and 4 to 7pm; November to April, Monday to Saturday 10am to 1pm and 4 to 6pm. Take bus number 1.

Behind the cathedral, the **Museo Arqueológico,** calle San Vicente, 5 (☎ 98-521-54-05), in a former convent dating from the 15th century, houses prehistoric relics discovered in Asturias, pre-Romanesque sculptures, a numismatic display, and old musical instruments. It's open Tuesday to Saturday 10am to 1:30pm and 4 to 6pm, Sunday 11am to 1pm. Admission is free.

Standing above Oviedo, on Monte Naranco, are two of the most famous examples of Asturian pre-Romanesque architecture. **Santa María del Naranco** (☎ 98-529-56-85), originally a 9th-century palace and hunting lodge of Ramiro I, offers views of Oviedo and the snowcapped Picos de Europa. Once containing baths and private apartments, it was converted into a church in the 12th century. Intricate stonework depicts hunting scenes, and barrel vaulting rests on a network of blind arches. The open porticoes at both ends were 200 years ahead of their time architecturally. The church is open April to September, daily 9:30am to 1pm and 3 to 7pm; October to March, daily 10am to 1pm and 3 to 5pm. Admission is 300 ptas. ($1.80).

About 100 yards away is **San Miguel de Lillo** (☎ 98-529-56-85). It, too, was built by Ramiro I, as a royal chapel, and was no doubt a magnificent specimen of Asturian pre-Romanesque architecture until 15th-century architects marred its grace. The stone carvings that remain, however, are exemplary. Most of the sculptures have been transferred to the archaeological museum in town.

The church is open daily 9:30am to 1pm, Monday to Saturday 3 to 7pm. Admission is 250 ptas. ($1.70) Tuesday to Sunday, free on Mondays. Ask at the tourist office for its 45-minute walking tour from the center of Oviedo to the churches. Check that the churches will be open at the time of your visit.

SHOPPING

Serious shoppers know that Oviedo offers some of the best outlets in Spain for handbags and shoes. For a number of the finest boutiques, head for the intersection of **Uria and Gil de Jaz.** In this district and on adjoining side streets you'll find some of the country's best-known designer boutiques, selling the same merchandise that goes at far higher prices in such cities as Madrid and Barcelona. Many artisans in this district make their own products—selling, for example, a variety of calfskin goods and hand-sewn leather. You'll also come across good sales on Asturian ceramic ware.

WHERE TO STAY
EXPENSIVE

✪ **Hotel de la Reconquista.** Gil de Jaz, 16, 33004 Oviedo. ☎ **98-524-11-00.** Fax 98-524-71-66. www.hoteldelareconquista.com. E-mail: direccion@hoteldelareconquista.com. 142 units. A/C MINIBAR TV TEL. 31,150 ptas. ($186.90) double; from 55,000 ptas. ($330) suite. AE, DC, MC, V. Parking 2,100 ptas. ($12.60). Bus: 1, 2, or 3.

Named after a subject dear to the hearts of the Catholic monarchs—the ejection of the Muslims from Iberia—this is one of the most prestigious hotels in Spain. Originally built between 1754 and 1777 as an orphanage and hospital, it received visits from Queen Isabella II in 1858 and a reworking of its baroque stonework during a restoration in 1958. The Reconquista was converted into a hotel in 1973 after the outlay of massive amounts of cash. Despite the growth of the city, it remains the second-largest building in Oviedo.

Today, the interior boasts a combination of modern and reproduction furniture, as well as a scattering of ecclesiastical paintings and antiques. The spacious guest rooms contain private bathrooms and are outfitted in antique styles, with views of the old town or of a series of elegantly antique interior courtyards. The hotel is 2 blocks north of the largest park in the town center, the Campo San Francisco.

Dining/Diversions: A cafeteria/restaurant, **Rey Casto,** offers both regional and national dishes. In addition there is a bar, plus a lounge bar with live piano music.

Amenities: 24-hour room service, concierge, currency exchange, safety-deposit boxes, doctor on call, baby-sitting upon request, sauna, hairdresser, shopping boutiques, business center.

MODERATE

Clarín. Caveda, 23, 33002 Oviedo. ☎ **98-522-72-72.** Fax 98-522-80-18. www.hotelclarin.es. E-mail: clarin@hotelclarin.es. 47 units. MINIBAR TV TEL. 15,500 ptas. ($93) double. AE, MC, V. Parking 1,300 ptas. ($7.80). Bus: 1, 2, or 3.

This recently built modern hotel in the old quarter is noted for its tasteful decor, with comfortable, inviting, and well-maintained but small rooms. On the premises, you'll find a cozy and well-managed cafeteria but no restaurant. The hotel stands right in the middle of the historic district within walking distance of many of the attractions.

El Magistral. Calle Jovellanos, 3, 33003 Oviedo. ☎ **985-21-51-16.** Fax 985-21-06-79. www.elmagistral.com. E-mail: hotel@elmagistral.com. 34 units. A/C MINIBAR TV TEL. 13,800 ptas. ($82.80) double. AE, DC, MC, V. Parking 1,200 ptas. ($7.20).

In the commercial district of Uria, this six-story hotel—rated three stars by the government—has welcomed guests since 1997. The modern design in public areas is dominated by glass and chrome with spot lighting and tiled floors. The midsize bedrooms are more traditional, with parquet floors, pastel walls, and fully equipped bathrooms. The hotel's restaurant is about 165 feet from the main building and has a fine reputation locally for its regional cuisine. Within the hotel itself is a cafeteria; amenities include limited room service and laundry.

Hotel La Gruta. Alto de Buenavista, s/n, 33006 Oviedo. ☎ **98-523-24-50.** Fax 98-525-31-41. 105 units. MINIBAR TV TEL. 12,500 ptas. ($75) double. AE, DC, MC, V. Free parking. Bus: 1, 2, or 3.

In this family-run hotel just outside the city limits, the small rooms are comfortably but simply furnished, many with views of the surrounding countryside. Amenities include safety-deposit boxes. Regional cuisine is served in the on-premises restaurant.

Hotel Principado. Calle San Francisco, 6, 33003 Oviedo. ☎ **98-521-77-92.** Fax 98-521-39-46. 70 units. MINIBAR TV TEL. 18,000 ptas. ($108) double; 18,500 ptas. ($111) suite. AE, DC, MC, V. Parking 1,500 ptas. ($9).

The well-managed Principado stands opposite the university. Guests have access to an underground public parking garage, easing the problem of parking in the center of town. The midsize rooms are comfortably furnished and well maintained. The dining room, featuring a regional menu, serves locals as well as guests. Although built in 1951, the hotel was completely renovated in 1991.

✪ **Hotel Vetusta.** Calle Covadonga, 2, 33002 Oviedo. ☎ **985-22-22-29.** Fax 985-22-22-09. E-mail: h-vetusta@catworld.com. 16 units. A/C TV TEL. 14,500 ptas. ($87) double. DC, MC, V. Parking 1,000 ptas. ($6).

In the center of the city a 5-minute walk from the cathedral, this four-story hotel takes its name from an imaginary fictional city invented by the author Clarin. It has been in operation since 1997, following the successful renovation of an old structure of wood and brick, split by wooden balconies. The interior has steel and wood fittings and is done in an ultracontemporary style. The small bedrooms are very compact but comfortably furnished, with fully equipped bathrooms. Some have balconies, and eight contain a hydromassage. On site is a 24-hour cafeteria, and room service operates 24 hours.

A NEARBY PLACE TO STAY

If you're driving to La Coruña and Santiago de Compostela, you may want to stop in the little town of Cornellana (Salas), 24 miles (39km) west of Oviedo on the route to Luarca.

Hotel La Fuente. Carretera N-634, 33876 Cornellana. ☎ **98-583-40-42.** 16 units. TV TEL. 6,500 ptas. ($39) double; 8,500 ptas. ($51) triple. MC, V. Free parking. Take the N-634 west to Cornellana.

This little inn on N-634 has a sitting room on each floor as well as a bathroom. The good-size bedrooms are simply furnished but comfortable. In the dining room overlooking the garden, you can order a three-course *menú del día*, which costs 1,200 ptas. ($7.20). The food is hearty and generous in portion, prepared according to old recipes and using regional products whenever possible.

WHERE TO DINE

Casa Conrado. Argüelles, 1. ☎ **98-522-39-19.** Reservations required. Main courses 2,250–3,250 ptas. ($13.50–$19.50); fixed-price menu 3,800 ptas. ($22.80). AE, DC, MC, V. Mon–Sat 1–4pm and 9pm–midnight. Closed Aug. Bus: 1. REGIONAL.

Almost as solidly established as the cathedral nearby, this restaurant offers good-tasting, hearty Asturian stews, seafood platters, seafood soups, several preparations of hake, including one cooked in cider, escalopes of veal with champagne, and a full range of desserts. It is a local favorite and a long-established culinary tradition. The service is attentive.

✪ **Casa Fermín.** Calle San Francisco, 8. ☎ **98-521-64-52.** Reservations recommended. Main courses 2,200–3,500 ptas. ($13.20–$21); *menú Asturiana* 3,200 ptas. ($19.20). AE, DC, MC, V. Mon–Sat 1:30–4pm and 8:30–11:30pm. Bus: 1 or 2. REGIONAL/INTERNATIONAL.

The chef here prepares the best regional cuisine in town in a building near the university and the cathedral. To order the most classic dish, ask for *fabada asturiana,* a bean dish with Asturian black pudding and Avilés ham. A tasty hake cooked in cider is another suggestion. Venison is a specialty in season (October to March). Try the traditional Cabrales cheese of the province. The restaurant decor is in pink and granite. Although it's been around for half a century, it has a contemporary air to it because it's filled with plants and covered with skylights. Casa Fermín is directly east of the Parque de San Francisco.

El Raitán. Trascorrales, 6. ☎ **98-521-42-18.** Reservations recommended. *Menú Asturiana* 4,000 ptas. ($24). AE, DC, MC, V. Mon–Sat 1:30–4pm and 9pm–midnight. Bus: 1. REGIONAL.

This restaurant south of the cathedral serves a set menu and bases all its dishes on regional ingredients, with meals accompanied by wines from La Rioja. A large array of well-prepared choices is available for each course. Each day the chef presents nine classic regional dishes that change with the season. The place has a tavern setting with overhead beams—atmospheric and intimate.

OVIEDO AFTER DARK

Very few of the many bars of Oviedo's old town stand out as particularly unique, so most night owls make it a point to wander from one joint to another as part of an evening's entertainment. Your best bet involves the old town neighborhoods around the Plaza del Paraguas, the Plaza da Fontán, and the Plaza Riego, each of which offers lots of unusual architecture in addition to hole-in-the-wall bars, many of which aren't identified with any discernible name. If you really want to go dancing as part of your nocturne in Oviedo, consider the town's most popular disco, **Estilo,** calle Pomarin, s/n (☎ **98-529-67-38**), where clients from the ages of 21 to around 30 rock and roll to recorded dance music, but never, ever, before midnight. It is open Thursday to Sunday.

Galicia 17

Extending above Portugal in the northwest corner of Spain, Galicia is a rainswept land of grass and granite, much of its coastline gouged by fjordlike inlets. It is a land steeped in Celtic tradition—in many areas its citizens, called *Gallegos,* speak their own language (not a dialect of Spanish but a separate language, *Gallego,* that sounds and looks like a combination of Portuguese and Spanish). Galicia consists of four provinces: La Coruña (including Santiago de Compostela), Pontevedra, Lugo, and Orense.

The Romans, who arrived after having conquered practically everything else in Europe, made quite an impression on the region. The Roman walls around the city of **Lugo** and the Tower of Hercules at **La Coruña** are part of that legacy. The Moors came this way, too, and did a lot of damage along the way. But finding the natives none too friendly and other battlefields more promising, they moved on.

Nothing did more to put Galicia on the tourist map than the **Camino de Santiago,** the Pilgrims' Route. It is the oldest, most traveled, and most famous route on the old continent. To guarantee a place in heaven, pilgrims journeyed to the supposed tomb of Santiago (St. James), patron saint of Spain. They trekked across the Pyrenees by the thousands, risking their lives in transit. The Camino de Santiago contributed to the development and spread of Romanesque art and architecture across Spain. Pilgrimages to the shrine lessened as medieval culture itself began its decline.

1 La Coruña

375 miles (604km) NW of Madrid, 96 miles (155km) N of Vigo

Despite the fact that La Coruña (*A Coruña* in Gallego) is an ancient city, it does not have a wealth of historical and architectural monuments. Celts, Phoenicians, and Romans all occupied the port, and it is another of the legendary cities that claim Hercules as its founder.

The greatest event in the history of La Coruña occurred in 1588, when Philip II's Invincible Armada sailed from here to England. Only half the ships made it back to Spain. The following year, Sir Francis Drake and his ships attacked the port in reprisal.

ESSENTIALS

GETTING THERE   There are five flights a week from Madrid to La Coruña. Serviced only by **Aviaco,** the Aeropuerto de Alvedro (☎ 981-18-72-00) is 6 miles (10km) from the heart of the city.

From Madrid (via Orense and Zamora), there is express train service two times a day (trip time: 8½ hours). Arrivals are at the La Coruña Station on calle Joaquín Planelles (☎ **902-24-02-02**). For the RENFE office, calle Fonseca, 3, call ☎ **981-15-02-02.**

From Santiago, there's frequent daily bus service leaving from the station on the calle Caballeros (☎ **981-23-96-44**). Four buses a day connect Madrid and La Coruña (trip time: 8½ hours). A one-way ticket from Madrid costs from 4,890 to 6,975 ptas. ($29.35 to $41.85)

La Coruña is reached from Madrid by the N-VI. You can also follow the coastal highway, the N-634, which runs all the way across the northern rim of Spain from San Sebastián to the east.

VISITOR INFORMATION   The **tourist information office** is at Dársena de la Marina, s/n (☎ **981-22-18-22**). The office is open Monday to Friday 9am to 2pm and 4:30 to 6:30pm, Saturday 10:30am to 1pm.

EXPLORING LA CORUÑA

La Coruña's old town is ideal for strolling around and stopping at any of the historic churches and mansions. **Plaza de María Pita**—named after the 16th-century Spanish Joan of Arc—divides the old town from the new. María Pita, a local housewife, was said to have spotted the approach of Drake's troops. Risking her own life, she fired a cannon shot to alert the citizens to an imminent invasion. For that act of heroism, she is revered to this day. Drake, on the other hand, is still a hated name in these parts.

You can take a stroll through the **Jardines de Méndez Núñez,** between the harbor and Los Cantones (Cantón Grande and Cantón Pequeño). Facing the police station and overlooking the port, the gardens are in the very center of town and make for a restful interlude during your sightseeing.

The cobbled **Plazuela de Santa Bárbara** also merits a visit—a tiny tree-shaded plaza, flanked by old houses and the high walls of the Santa Bárbara convent.

Jardín de San Carlos, along Paseo del Parrote, dates from 1843 and is near the Casa de la Cultura. This garden grew up on the site of an old fortress that once guarded the harbor. It contains the tomb of Gen. Sir John Moore, who fought unsuccessfully against the troops of Napoléon. He retreated with his British forces to La Coruña, where he was shot in a final battle. These gardens now make an ideal picnic spot.

Iglesia de Santa María del Campo, calle de Santa María, is a church with an elaborately carved west door from the 13th century, modeled in the traditional Romanesque-Gothic style. Beneath its rose window you'll see a Gothic portal from the 13th or 14th century. The tympanum is carved with a scene depicting the Adoration of the Magi.

Castillo de San Antón, a 16th-century fort, is now the **Museo Arqueológico e Histórico** (☎ **981-20-59-94**), standing out in the bay on the southeast side of the peninsula. It is open July to September, Tuesday to Saturday 11am to 9pm; October to June, Tuesday to Saturday 10am to 7pm. Admission is 400 ptas. ($2.40) for adults, but free for children ages 13 and under and adults 66 and over. In addition to having a panoramic location on its own islet, it displays many unusual artifacts from La Coruña province, including a collection of pre-Roman jewelry. Take bus number 3 or 3A.

The second-largest port in Spain, La Coruña is a popular vacation resort, so it gets very crowded in July and August. Riazor Beach, right in town, is a good, fairly wide beach, but the best one is Santa Cristina, about 3 miles (5km) outside town. There's regular round-trip bus service. The best way to go, however, is via the steamer that plies the bay.

Galicia

SHOPPING

Its relative isolation from the rest of Spain seems to contribute to the perception that ceramics and handcrafts in Galicia are somehow more rustic and charming than those in territories closer to Madrid and Barcelona. You can judge for yourself by taking a 30-mile (50km) westward detour from La Coruña to the Galician hamlet of Buño. (From La Coruña, follow the signs to Carballo along C-552, then detour when you see the signs to Buño.) Although Buño has lots of kiosks selling ceramics (virtually everyone in the hamlet is involved in some aspects of handcrafts), you can save yourself the drive by remaining in La Coruña and heading for a cooperative that markets Buño's products, **Alfares de Buño,** Plazuela de Los Angeles, 6 (no phone). A privately funded competitor, richly inventoried with pottery from Buño and other towns throughout Galicia, is **Obradoiro,** Plazuela de Los Angeles, 4 (no phone). The town's most visible and influential art gallery is the **Asociación de Artistas,** calle Riego de

Agua, 32 (☎ **981-22-52-77**). Host to dozens of exhibitions every year, it displays, solicits, markets, and publicizes the work of local artists throughout Spain and the rest of Europe.

Looking for antiques? Consider a stroll along calle Santiago, where such stores as **Antiguedades Encantes,** at no. 4 (no phone), and **Antiguedades Rosa Jordan,** at no. 7 (no phone), display the finery and ornaments of yesterday. Finally, if visits to the above-mentioned sites fail to produce the product you're looking for, consider a trek through the well-accessorized interior of La Coruña's largest department store, **El Corte Inglés,** calle Ramón y Cajal, 57–59 (☎ **981-29-00-11**).

WHERE TO STAY
EXPENSIVE

Hotel Finisterre. Paseo del Parrote, 20, 15001 La Coruña. ☎ **981-20-54-00.** Fax 981-20-84-62. www.hotelfinisterre.com. E-mail: info@hotelfinisterre.com. 127 units. MINIBAR TV TEL. 18,500–22,000 ptas. ($111–$132) double; 22,000–30,000 ptas. ($132–$180) suite. AE, DC, MC, V. Free parking. Bus: 1, 2, 3, or 5.

Immediately above the port, a short walk east of the tourist information office at the edge of the old town, this high-rise hotel is the finest and most panoramic in town. Bedrooms are small but comfortable, with wall-to-wall carpeting, lots of exposed wood, brightly contemporary upholstery, and private bathrooms with hair dryers and plush towels. The hotel is the preferred choice of business travelers. Although it was built in 1947, it has been remodeled many times since, the latest in 1991.

Dining/Diversions: A restaurant, **Ara Solis,** serves à la carte meals featuring fresh fish; there's also a bar.

Amenities: Room service, concierge, baby-sitting, laundry, tennis courts, four outdoor seawater swimming pools (two heated for year-round use, one reserved for children), garden, children's nursery, gym and health club, skating rink, sauna, ample opportunities for brisk and invigorating seafront walks, barber/hairdresser, nearby basketball court, gift shop.

María Pita. Avenida Pedro Barrie de la Maza, 1, 15003 La Coruña. ☎ **981-20-50-00.** Fax 981-20-55-65. www.tryp.es. E-mail: hotel@tryp.es. 180 units. A/C MINIBAR TV TEL. 23,125 ptas. ($138.75) double; 75,000 ptas. ($450) suite. AE, DC, MC, V. Parking 1,700 ptas. ($10.20).

On Orzan beach, close to the historic district, this graceful four-star hotel is one of the city's finest. It's in an elegant building with extensive glass windows. A member of the Tryp chain, it offers a well-lit, marble-floored interior and one of the most efficient staffs in the city. Bedrooms are generally large, and all the units are comfortable with wooden floors and tasteful decorations, including excellent mattresses. The most desirable accommodations come with private balconies overlooking the ocean.

Dining/Diversions: The hotel's Galician restaurant is known for its excellent seafood, especially shellfish. In addition, there is an on-site snack bar, and guests gather in the piano bar at night.

Amenities: Sauna, massage facilities, concierge, laundry and dry cleaning, 24-hour room service.

Meliá Confort. Ramón y Cajal, 53, 15006 La Coruña. ☎ **981-24-29-11.** Fax 981-23-67-28. www.solmelia.es. E-mail: melia.confort.coruna@solmelia.es. 181 units. A/C MINIBAR TV TEL. 16,000 ptas. ($96) double; 26,800 ptas. ($160.80) suite. AE, DC, MC, V. Free parking: Bus 23.

In the Centro Comercial Cuatro Caminos, a 20-minute walk from the center, this efficiently run five-story hotel is sleekly modern with a colorfully decorated interior.

The bedrooms are medium in size and furnished to be comfortable and functional, without any grand style. Business travelers especially like this one, although it's suitable for other visitors as well.

Dining/Diversions: The restaurant is reserved for groups, but the hotel cafeteria features a breakfast buffet. There's also a smart international bar.

Amenities: Sauna, whirlpool, gym, laundry and dry cleaning, concierge, 24-hour room service.

MODERATE

Ciudad de La Coruña. Ciudad Residencial La Torre, Paseo de Adormideras, s/n, 15002 La Coruña. ☎ **981-21-11-00.** Fax 981-22-46-10. 131 units. MINIBAR TV TEL. 12,000–15,000 ptas. ($72–$90) double; 17,000–19,000 ptas. ($102–$114) suite. AE, DC, MC, V. Free parking. Bus: 3, 3A, or 5.

On the northwestern tip of the peninsula, surrounded by sea grasses and dunes, this three-star establishment is cordoned off from the apartment-house complexes that surround it by a wide swath of green. Built in the early 1980s, the hotel features a swimming pool; a big-windowed bar; a gym with sauna, whirlpool, and solarium; and a ground-floor restaurant, which serves a *menú del día* for 1,850 ptas. ($11.10). Each attractively modern guest room has a kitchenette and a private bathroom. Accommodations are generally roomy and maintenance is excellent. There is a bar-style cafeteria serving coffee, drinks, and snacks.

Hotel Atlántico. Jardines de Méndez Nuñez, s/n, 15006 La Coruña. ☎ **981-22-65-00.** Fax 981-20-10-71. 199 units. A/C MINIBAR TV TEL. 15,500–18,500 ptas. ($93–$111) double; 20,000–25,000 ptas. ($120–$150) suite. AE, DC, MC, V. Parking 1,500 ptas. ($9). Bus: 1, 2, or 3.

This convenient, comfortable, and contemporary hotel contrasts with the lavishly ornate 19th-century park surrounding it, where crowds of Galicians promenade in fine weather. The Atlántico is in the building that houses the city's casino, a modern restaurant, and a disco, open Saturday and Sunday 10pm to 6am. Well-furnished guest rooms are among the most appealing in town, thanks to relatively spacious dimensions and comfortably contemporary furnishings a cut above less-expensive competitors. Each tiled bathroom is equipped with a hair dryer.

Hotel Avenida. Avenida Alfonso Molina, 30, 15008 La Coruña. ☎/fax **981-24-94-66.** www.hotelavenida.com. E-mail: avenida@hotelavenida.com. 88 units. MINIBAR TV TEL. 11,000 ptas. ($66) double; 20,000 ptas. ($120) suite. DC, MC, V. Parking 800 ptas. ($4.80).

A 15-minute walk from the historic core, this modern hotel is modest but inviting, lying half a mile from the beach. Doubles are small, usually with twin beds, but the suites are generous in size, often with brass beds and clusters of chairs. Bathrooms are sleekly modern and fully equipped. An informal, airy restaurant boasts a traditional Galician menu of seafood delicacies. An on-site cafeteria offers continental breakfast daily. Facilities include a private garden as well as such amenities as a concierge, laundry, and limited room service.

INEXPENSIVE

Almirante. Paseo de Ronda, 54, 15011 La Coruña. ☎ **981-25-96-00.** Fax 981-25-96-08. 20 units. TV TEL. 4,500–6,500 ptas. ($27–$39) double. AE, MC, V. Parking 700 ptas. ($4.20). Bus: 7, 14, or 14A.

There are few amenities here—just good, clean rooms, all doubles, at good prices. Both the room and bathroom dimensions are a bit skimpy, but the price is right. There is no restaurant, but a continental breakfast is served in the cafeteria. Room service is available. The location is a bonus: just 1 minute from the beach.

Hotel España. Juana de Vega, 7, 15004 La Coruña. ☎ **981-22-45-06.** Fax 981-20-02-79. 84 units. TV TEL. 6,500–9,500 ptas. ($39–$57) double. AE, DC, MC, V. Parking 1,200 ptas. ($7.20). Bus: 1, 2, or 23.

This pleasant but somewhat lackluster choice, just a few steps from the gazebos and roses of the Jardines de Méndez Núñez, has a narrow reception area, a comfortable series of long sitting rooms, and modern, simply furnished rooms. A cafeteria offers combination platters. The hotel has a bar and provides laundry service.

WHERE TO DINE

Two or so blocks from the waterfront, several restaurants specialize in Galician cuisine, all with competitive prices. It's customary to go window shopping for food here. The restaurants along two of the principal streets—calle de la Estrella and calle de los Olmos—all have display counters up front.

✪ **Casa Pardo.** Novoa Santos, 15. ☎ **981-28-71-78.** Reservations recommended. Main courses 1,850–3,200 ptas. ($11.10–$19.20); fixed-price menu 4,500–5,000 ptas. ($27–$30). AE, DC, MC, V. Mon–Sat 1:30–4pm and 9pm–midnight. GALICIAN.

Near the Palacio de Congresos south of the old town, this restaurant is justly acclaimed as the finest dining room in the city. Under the direction of Eduardo Pardo, it offers both a traditional cuisine and innovative seafood dishes. Fresh shellfish and fish dishes, everything from oysters to salmon, are prepared here with skill. The Galician turbot is delectable. Seafood items aren't the only selections on the menu— fresh meat and vegetable dishes are also well prepared. Patrons of this entrenched dining room prefer such wines as Terras Gauda and Viña Costeira. The restaurant is elegant but unstuffy. The fact that the first-rate staff is alert and informed about the graceful service rituals of old Spain makes this a subtle and relaxed, although undeniably formal, atmosphere.

✪ **El Coral.** Callejón de la Estacada, 9. ☎ **981-20-05-69.** Reservations recommended. Main courses 2,000–2,800 ptas. ($12–$16.80). AE, DC, MC, V. Daily 1–4pm and 9pm– midnight. Closed Sun except July 15–Sept 15. Bus: 1, 2, 5, or 17. GALICIAN/SEAFOOD/ INTERNATIONAL.

This is our favorite and one of the most popular dining spots at the port. In business since 1954, it offers polite service, cleanliness, and Galician cookery prepared with distinction. This restaurant specializes in shellfish, fish, meats, and Galician wines. The chef's specialty is *turbante de mariscos* (shellfish). You might also try the *calamares rellenos* (stuffed squid). A popular main course is *lubina* (sea bass) *al horno*. A pitcher (1 liter) of Ribero wine makes a good choice, and you can order Condados and Rioja wines. The front window forms an altar of shellfish in infinite varieties, a tapestry of crustaceans and mollusks. Inside, the atmosphere is intimate and elegant, with formally dressed waiters, crisp white linens, dark wood-paneled walls, and glittering crystal chandeliers.

Taverna Pil-Pil. Paralela a Orillamar, s/n. ☎ **981-21-27-12.** Reservations recommended. Main courses 1,000–2,000 ptas. ($6–$12). No credit cards. Tues–Sat 1–5pm and 8pm– 12:30am. Closed Sept 15–Oct 15. Bus: 3 or 3A. GALICIAN/SPANISH.

In spite of its size, this small tavern on the road leading to the Torre de Hércules has a fine culinary tradition and serves many elegant, moderately priced wines like the Albariño white. Host Luis Moya purchases fresh ingredients, often seafood, and handles them deftly in the kitchen. Try a mussel omelette as an appetizer, followed by one of the main courses, perhaps smoked salmon, and conclude with a velvety chocolate mousse.

LA CORUÑA AFTER DARK

Some of the most appealing bars in La Coruña are atmospheric holes-in-the-wall with a local clientele and a decor that has remained virtually unchanged since the end of the Spanish Civil War. A good example of this is **La Traida,** calle Torreiro, 1 (☎ **981-22-93-21**), whose *empanadas* and tapas are much sought after. The place's walls are lined with posters from past bullfights, political rallies, and art exhibitions. Don't look for a sign—there isn't one, at least not one marking the entrance. Equally appealing is **Bar La Bombilla,** Garera, 7 (☎ **981-22-46-91**), where flavorful tapas and strong red wines help a night go by faster. A roughly equivalent competitor is **Bar Yeboles,** calle Capitán Trancoso, 14 (☎ **981-20-62-20**), set close to Town Hall and the Plaza de María Pita, the town's main square. If you want to go dancing after your drinks and tapas, and if it's after around 11pm, consider a run into the town's most appealing and most popular disco, **Disco Playa Club,** avenida Pedro Barrie de la Massa, s/n (☎ **981-25-00-63**). Set on an oceanfront terrace, a few feet from the waves of Playa Riazor, it's open year-round and attracts dancers and drinkers even during the fogs of midwinter.

2 Santiago de Compostela

381 miles (613.5km) NW of Madrid, 46 miles (74km) S of La Coruña

All roads in Spain once led to this northwestern pilgrimage city. In addition to being the third-largest holy city of the Christian world, Santiago de Compostela is a university town and a marketplace for Galician farmers.

But it was the medieval pilgrims who made the city famous. A pilgrimage to the tomb of the beheaded apostle, St. James, was a high point for the faithful—peasant and prince alike—who journeyed here from all over Europe, often under difficult, sometimes life-threatening, conditions.

Santiago de Compostela's link with legend began in A.D. 813, when an urn was discovered containing what were believed to be the remains of St. James. A temple was erected over the spot, but the poor saint wasn't allowed to remain in peace. In the 16th century, church fathers hid the remains of the saint, fearing they might be destroyed in raids along the coast by Sir Francis Drake, who was ravaging this part of Galicia. Somewhat amazingly, the alleged remains—subject of millions of pilgrimages from across Europe—lay relatively forgotten.

For decades no one was exactly certain where they were. Then in 1879 a workman making repairs on the church discovered what were supposed to be the remains, hidden since the 1500s. Of course, skeptics seriously questioned the authenticity of these remains. To prove this was the actual corpse of St. James, church officials brought back a sliver of the skull of St. James from Italy. They claimed that it fit perfectly, like a puzzle piece, into the recently discovered skeleton.

Aside from its religious connections, Santiago de Compostela, with its flagstone streets, churches, and shrines, is one of the most romantic and historic of Spain's great cities. It has been declared a national landmark. Santiago has the dubious distinction of being the rainiest city in Spain, but the showers tend to arrive and end suddenly. Locals claim that the rain only makes their city more beautiful, and the rain-slick cobblestones might prompt you to agree.

ESSENTIALS

GETTING THERE   From Madrid, **Iberia** has daily flights to Santiago, and there are daily flights from Barcelona. The only international airport in Galicia is east of

Santiago de Compostela at Lavacolla (☎ **981-54-75-00** for flight information), 7 miles (11km) from the center on the road to Lugo.

From La Coruña, 16 trains make the 1-hour trip daily at a cost of 500 to 635 ptas. ($3 to $3.80). Two trains arrive daily from Madrid. The 8-hour trip costs 6,000 ptas. ($36). Call ☎ **981-52-02-02** for information.

Buses leave on the hour, connecting La Coruña with Santiago (1½ hours away), and cost 820 ptas. ($4.90). Three buses arrive in Santiago daily from Madrid (8 to 9 hours). The trip costs 5,440 ptas. ($32.65). Phone ☎ **981-58-77-00** for schedules.

If you're driving, take the express highway (A-9/E-50) south from La Coruña to reach Santiago. From Madrid, N-VI runs to Galicia. From Lugo, head south along N-640.

VISITOR INFORMATION   The **tourist information office** is at rúa del Villar, 43 (☎ **981-58-40-81**). Office hours are Monday to Friday 10am to 2pm and 4 to 7pm, Saturday 11am to 2pm.

STROLLING THROUGH SANTIAGO

Santiago de Compostela's highlight is undoubtedly its storied cathedral, and you should take at least 2 hours to see it. Afterward, take a stroll through this enchanting town, which has a number of other interesting monuments as well as many stately mansions along rúa del Villar and rúa Nueva.

The ✪ **Catedral,** Plaza del Obradoiro (☎ **981-56-15-27**), begun in the 11th century, is the crowning achievement of Spanish Romanesque architecture, and even though it actually reflects a number of styles, parts of it are spectacular. The Pórtico de la Gloria, carved by Mateo in the late 12th century, ranks among the finest produced in Europe at that time; the altar, with its blend of Gothic simplicity and baroque decor, is also extraordinary. The cathedral has three naves in cruciform shape and several chapels and cloisters. You can visit the crypt, where a silver urn contains what are believed to be the remains of the Apostle St. James. A cathedral museum displays tapestries and archaeological fragments. Next door, the **Palacio de Gelmírez** (☎ **981-57-23-00**), an archbishop's palace built during the 12th century, is another outstanding example of Romanesque architecture.

The Pórtico de la Gloria, carved by Maestro Mateo in 1188, was the original entrance to the cathedral. The three arches of the portico are carved with biblical figures from the Last Judgment. In the center, Christ is flanked by apostles and the 24 Elders of the Apocalypse. Below the Christ figure is a depiction of St. James himself. He crowns a carved column that includes a portrayal of Mateo at the bottom. If you observe this column, you will see that a series of five deep indentations has been made by pilgrims since the Middle Ages. They have placed their hands here and worn down the pillar in gratitude to Mateo for designing it. Even today pilgrims line up here to lean forward to place their hands on the pillar and touch foreheads with Mateo.

Admission to the cathedral is free; to the cloisters, 500 ptas. ($3); to the Palacio de Gelmírez, 200 ptas. ($1.20). Hours for the cathedral are daily 7am to 9pm; for the museum, July to October, Monday to Saturday 10am to 1:30pm and 4 to 7:30pm, Sunday 10am to 1:30pm and 4 to 7pm; November to June, Monday to Saturday 11am to 1pm and 4 to 6pm, Sunday 10am to 1:30pm and 4 to 7pm. For the Palacio de Gelmírez, the hours are July to September, daily 10:30am to 1:30pm and 4 to 7pm.

Most of the other impressive buildings are on Plaza del Obradoiro, also called Plaza de España. Next door to the cathedral is **Hostal de los Reyes Católicos,** now a parador (see "Where to Stay," below), formerly a royal hospice and, in the 15th century, a pilgrims' hospice. It was designed by Enrique de Egas, Isabella and

Santiago de Compostela

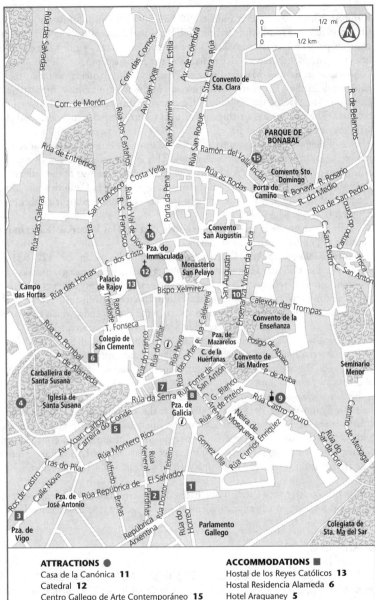

0   1/2 mi
0   1/2 km

ATTRACTIONS ●

Casa de la Canónica **11**
Catedral **12**
Centro Gallego de Arte Contemporáneo **15**
Monasterío de San Martín Pinario **14**
Palacio de Gelmírez **12**
Paseo de la Herradura **4**
Plaza de la Quintana **11**
Plaza de las Platerias **11**
Santa María del Sar **9**

ACCOMMODATIONS ■

Hostal de los Reyes Católicos **13**
Hostal Residencia Alameda **6**
Hotel Araguaney **5**
Hotel Area Central **2**
Hotel Compostela **8**
Hotel del Peregrino **3**
Hotel Gelmírez **1**
Hotel Maycar **7**
Hotel Universal **10**

Ferdinand's favorite architect. Tourists (☎ **981-58-22-00** for information) may visit the cloistered courtyard with its beautiful 16th- to 18th-century fountains and the main chapel with its beamed ceiling; however, you must have a guide from the cathedral in attendance. Hours are daily 10am to 1pm and 4 to 7pm.

Monasterío de San Martín Pinario, Plaza de la Immaculada, founded in 899 and rebuilt in the 17th century, remains one of the most important monasteries in Galicia. Its large facade was built in the Compostela baroque style, with massive Doric columns. The interior has a richly ornamented Churrigueresque high altar and choir stalls that are truly works of art.

One of the most important squares in the old town is **Plaza de la Quintana,** to the left of the cathedral's Goldsmith's Doorway. This is a favorite square with students, who often perch on the flight of broad steps that connect the rear of the cathedral to the walls of a convent. The square is dominated by **Casa de la Canónica,** the former residence of the canon, which has wrought-iron window bars, lending it a rather severe appearance.

South of the square is the Renaissance-style **Plaza de las Platerías (Silversmiths' Square),** which has an elaborate fountain.

Centro Gallego de Arte Contemporáneo, rúa Valle-Inclán, s/n (☎ **981-54-66-29**), is the Galician Center of Contemporary Art, highlighting artworks from regional, national, and international artists. The center's changing exhibits display the works of contemporary artists, and it hosts retrospectives. Until the opening of this center, contemporary art had virtually no place in the city's agenda, which emphasized the ancient or the antique. Inaugurated in 1993 by Portuguese architect Álvaro Siza, the building is a stark exterior study in slabs of granite. Among the several exhibition rooms is a terrace for open-air exhibits, affording a panoramic view of the old quarter of Santiago. The admission-free museum is open Tuesday to Saturday 11am to 8pm and Sunday 11am to 2pm.

Farther afield, visit the Romanesque **Santa María del Sar,** on calle Castron d'Ouro, half a mile down calle de Sar, which starts at the Patio de Madre. This collegiate church is one of the architectural gems of the Romanesque style in Galicia. Its walls and columns are on a 15-degree slant, thought to be attributable to either a fragile foundation or an architect's fancy. Visit the charming cloister with its slender columns. The church is open Monday to Saturday 10am to 1pm and 4 to 7pm. Admission is free.

Cap off your day with a walk along **Paseo de la Herradura,** the gardens southwest of the old town, from where you have an all-encompassing view of the cathedral and the old city.

SHOPPING

The artfully naive blue-and-white porcelain that's a trademark of the town is available for sale at **Sargadelos,** rúa Nueva, 16 (☎ **981-58-19-05**). A competitor that stocks similar ceramics, plus a wide range of other regional handcrafts, including textiles, metalwork, wood carvings, and a small amount of blown glass, is **Amboa,** rúa Nueva, 44 (☎ **981-58-33-59**). The best place in town to buy hammered silver, either in the form of jewelry or tableware, is **Fernando Mayer,** Plaza de las Platerías, 2 (☎ **981-58-25-36**). You can find meticulously crafted lace as well as textiles for the bathroom, dining room, and bedroom, at **Dosel,** rúa Nova, 26 (☎ **981-56-60-78**). And finally, to satisfy your hunger pangs between visits to pilgrimage sites, Santiago is home to some worthy pastry shops, including **Confitería La Mora,** rúa del Vilar, 60 (☎ **981-58-10-14**).

A favorite of most tourists is *tarta Santiago,* a tart sold at virtually every pastry shop in the city. Also very popular is a local cheese shaped like breasts. If you'd like to sample this regional produce, one of many places selling them is **Confitería Vilas,** Rosalía de Castro, 70 (☎ **981-596-858**).

Many of the local wines, including assorted bottles of Ribeiro, Condado, and most famous of all, Albariño, are sold without fanfare in grocery stores throughout Galicia. But for a specialist in the subtleties of Galician and other Spanish wines, head for **Vinoteca Manxares de Galicia,** rúa do Franco, 25 (☎ **981-57-72-27**).

WHERE TO STAY
VERY EXPENSIVE

✪ **Hostal de Los Reyes Católicos.** Plaza de Obradoido, 1, 15705 Santiago de Compostela. ☎ **981-58-22-00.** Fax 981-56-30-94. 136 units. A/C MINIBAR TV TEL. 28,000 ptas. ($168) double; from 55,000 ptas. ($330) suite. AE, DC, MC, V. Parking 2,200 ptas. ($13.20). Bus: 4, 21, 25, 26, 33, or 34.

This former 16th-century hospice, founded by Ferdinand and Isabella, has been turned into one of the most spectacular hotels in Europe. Next to the cathedral, it served as a resting place and hospital for pilgrims visiting the tomb of St. James. Even if you don't stay here, you should stop in and see it, but only on a guided tour (see the box "The World's Oldest Hotel").

The hotel has four huge open-air courtyards, each with its own covered walk, gardens, and fountains. In addition, there are great halls, French grillwork, and a large collection of antiques. A Gothic chapel is the setting for weekly concerts.

There's a full range of accommodations, everything from Franco's former bedchamber to small rooms. Many of the palatial rooms have ornate canopied beds draped in embroidered red velvet. Hand-carved chests, gilt mirrors, and oil paintings, along with private bathrooms, enhance the air of luxury. Bathrooms are quite sumptuous, with hair dryers, plush towels, and deluxe toiletries.

Dining/Diversions: The hotel's formal dining room, **Libredon,** serves both Galician and international cuisine. There is also an elegant bar.

Amenities: Room service, laundry, car rentals, hairdresser.

Hotel Araguaney. Calle Alfredo Brañas, 5, 15701 Santiago de Compostela. ☎ **981-59-59-00.** Fax 981-59-02-87. 80 units. A/C MINIBAR TV TEL. 28,000 ptas. ($168) double; from 35,000 ptas. ($210) suite. AE, DC, MC, V. Parking 1,680 ptas. ($10.10). Bus: 4, 21, 25, 26, 33, or 34.

Located in Santiago's commercial and residential zone, about 8 blocks southwest of the cathedral, this is a comfortably streamlined hotel, newly renovated and boasting some of the most up-to-date dining, drinking, and conference facilities in town. The stylish, modern rooms range from small to midsized, each comfortably furnished with firm mattresses. All the tiled bathrooms are equipped with hair dryers. Locals cite the hotel as their most well-run modern hotel. It has one of the best and most efficient staffs in town, and people in the area on business often prefer this up-to-date choice.

Dining/Diversions: The **Restaurante Luis XVI** and the **Restaurante Caney (O'Portón)** serve fixed-price lunches and dinners. A comfortable hotel bar offers an array of international drinks and Spanish brandies. The hotel has one of the most popular discos in Galicia.

Amenities: Room service (daily 7am to 4pm and 9pm to midnight), concierge, baby-sitting, in-house tour operator, laundry and valet, large and well-maintained swimming pool, sauna, shopping boutiques, business center, car rentals.

The World's Oldest Hotel

The oldest hotel in the world has been giving the weary bodies and souls of travelers a place of rest for nearly 5 centuries. In 1499 the Catholic kings founded the Hospital Real (Royal Hospice) in Santiago de Compostela to serve as a respite for the hundreds of thousands of pilgrims who came to pay homage to the shrine of Saint James. Known today as the **Hostal de Los Reyes Católicos,** the same structure proudly stands as the world's most ancient hotel, and certainly one of the most luxurious, offering its guests a truly unique hotel experience.

During the Middle Ages, Santiago prevailed, together with Jerusalem and Rome, as one of the three holy cities of Christendom. The cult of Santiago (Saint James), the son of Zebedee and the brother of John the Evangelist, drew hordes of pilgrims trekking across northern Spain in search of the tomb of the saint. The route to Santiago proved long, arduous, and dangerous; the pilgrims who did arrive came weary and fatigued. Having made the pilgrimage themselves, the Catholic monarchs experienced firsthand the dearth of accommodations along the way—hence the decision by Ferdinand and Isabella to construct monasteries and hospitals to house and protect visitors, the best effort culminating in this prominent structure.

Construction on the Hospital Real began in the 15th century and continued through the 18th century. Set on the magnificent Obradoiro Plaza, this grand edifice shares the square with the impressive cathedral of Santiago, with its blend of architectural styles. In addition to its luxury rooms, this five-star hotel boasts a concert and exhibition room surrounded by various cloisters in different styles. The hotel doorway reflects the plateresque style, and the windows display rich baroque detailing.

Architecturally, the old part of the city stopped developing in the baroque period and, as a result, its buildings exude an aura of impressive grandeur—in fact, a sense of mysticism permeates Santiago. It is fitting, then, that one of Spain's great monumental cities should be home to one of the country's most luxurious, historically significant hotels, let alone one of the world's oldest.

EXPENSIVE

Hotel Compostela. Hórreo, 1, 15702 Santiago de Compostela. ☎ **981-58-57-00.** Fax 981-55-52-81. 99 units. MINIBAR TV TEL. 16,500 ptas. ($99) double; 21,000 ptas. ($126) suite for 2. AE, DC, MC, V. Bus: 10.

This hotel is conveniently located just a few short blocks from the cathedral, but it is also, unfortunately, close to the heavily trafficked city center. It has a grand granite facade, which belies the modern interior, and bedrooms filled with clean, angular, machine-made furniture. Mattresses are firm, and the housekeeping is excellent. All the tiled bathrooms are equipped with hair dryers. Accommodations are generally roomy, although some units are quite small. A pleasant dining room and a cafe/bar are on the premises, offering a fixed-price lunch or dinner. The hotel was completely renovated in 1995.

Hotel del Peregrino. Rosalía de Castro, s/n, 15706 Santiago de Compostela. ☎ **981-52-18-50.** Fax 981-52-17-77. 149 units. A/C MINIBAR TV TEL. 20,000 ptas. ($120) double; 24,000 ptas. ($144) suite. AE, DC, MC, V. Free parking. Bus: 1 or 2.

This four-star hotel at the edge of town off the main road is conveniently located if you want to avoid traffic congestion in the town's center. The hotel is comfortable, unpretentious, and unfussy, drawing lots of business travelers. It has a good restaurant serving regional cuisine, a bar and snack bar, a rear garden with a swimming pool, and a disco. The decor is restrained and tasteful, the rooms modern and well furnished. Accommodations range from small to medium, and each tiled bathroom has a hair dryer.

MODERATE

Hotel Area Central. Calle Paris, 7C, 15707 Santiago de Compostela. ☎ **981-55-22-22.** Fax 981-55-22-23. 72 units. TV TEL 11,000 ptas. ($66) double; 16,000 ptas. ($96) suite. AE, DC, MC, V. Parking: 1,000 ptas ($6).

In the heart of the biggest shopping mall in Galicia, this seven-story hotel opened in 1997 and has done a thriving business offering comfortably modern accommodations at affordable prices. The historic core is within a 20-minute walk. Bedrooms are midsized, furnished with wooden pieces, and often open onto balconies. Bathrooms are lined in marble and fully equipped with tubs and a shower. An on-site cafeteria serves breakfast, and amenities include limited room service, concierge, and laundry.

Hotel Gelmírez. Hórreo, 92, 15702 Santiago de Compostela. ☎ **981-56-11-00.** Fax 981-55-52-81. 138 units. TV TEL. 13,000 ptas. ($78) double. AE, DC, MC, V. Bus: 6 or 10.

This soaring concrete structure near the train station is one of the largest hotels in the region. Built in the early 1970s, it has a comfortable and pleasant interior far more attractive than its plain facade suggests. The small guest rooms are furnished in a functional modern style—nothing special, but clean and comfortable. On the premises is a bistro/cafeteria/bar offering *platos combinados* (combination plates) from 1,200 ptas. ($8.05), along with a wide array of drinks.

INEXPENSIVE

Hostal Residencia Alameda. San Clemente, 32, 15705 Santiago de Compostela. ☎ **981-58-81-00.** Fax 981-58-86-89. 20 units, 13 with private bathroom. TV TEL. 5,500 ptas. ($33) double without bathroom, 7,500 ptas. ($45) double with bathroom. AE, DC, MC, V. Parking 800 ptas. ($4.80). Bus: 10.

Located on the second floor of a 1970s building in the cathedral district, the Alameda has comfortable, immaculate rooms in a very simple boardinghouse style; it was last renovated in 1997. Beds are good but the rooms are a bit cramped. The staff here is courteous and efficient. Ample adjacent parking is available. The Alameda serves breakfast only.

Hotel Maycar. Doctor Teijeiro, 15, 15701 Santiago de Compostela. ☎ **981-56-34-44.** Fax 981-58-96-53. 40 units. TV TEL. 6,500 ptas. ($39) double. No credit cards. Bus: 10 from train station.

This simple two-star hotel stands not far from the busy central Plaza de Galicia. The marble-trimmed lobby is unpretentious, and there is an elevator. The rooms are well maintained but very spartan. Nonetheless, each accommodation comes with a good bed, although you don't have a lot of room for your stuff. Breakfast is the only meal served.

Hotel Universal. Plaza de Galicia, 2, 15706 Santiago de Compostela. ☎ **981-58-58-00.** Fax 981-58-57-90. E-mail: hoteluniversal@verial.es. 54 units. TV TEL. 6,800–8,500 ptas. ($40.80–$51) double. AE, DC, MC, V. Parking 900 ptas. ($5.40).

Located south of the Fuente de San Antonio, just outside the center of the city, this is a pleasant and comfortable hotel despite its drab 1970s concrete facade. It has a modernized lobby, and there is a TV lounge on the premises. The aging guest rooms are furnished in a simple modern style, each with a good bed. Breakfast is the only meal served.

WHERE TO DINE

Alameda. Porta Faxeira, 15. ☎ **981-58-66-57.** Reservations recommended in summer. Main courses 2,500–4,500 ptas. ($15–$27); fixed-price menu 3,000 ptas. ($18). AE, DC, MC, V. Daily 1–4pm and 8pm–midnight. REGIONAL.

Since 1954 a constant stream of diners, both foreign and local, indicates the popularity of this government-rated "two-fork" restaurant, opposite the Parque de Alameda. There is a stylish cafeteria/snack bar on the ground floor, great for light meals and drinks; guests can sit at sidewalk tables in fair weather. The fare includes many Galician specialties, and the chef is noted for his paella. Start with the *caldo gallego* (Galician soup) and follow with another regional specialty, *lacón con grelos* (ham hock with greens). The *necoras* (spider crabs) are a real gourmet delight.

Casa Manolo. Rùa Traviesa, 27. ☎ **981-58-29-50.** Reservations not accepted. Set-price menu 750 ptas. ($4.70). No credit cards. Daily 1–4:30pm; Mon–Sat 8–11:30pm. GALICIAN.

Set in the large but cozy dining room of a brick-built house that's at least a century old, this family-run restaurant offers one of the best dining values in Santiago. There's only one option here: a two-course set-price menu whose components include different roasts and fillets. Veal cutlets, either breaded in the "Milanese" style, or with cheese in the "Parmigiana" style, are enduringly popular, as are the pastas (especially cannelloni stuffed with a form of ricotta cheese). Fillet steak served *a la plancha* (grilled) and pork chops are also good tasting. Don't expect glamour, as that's not what this place is selling. Instead, you'll get generous portions of rib-sticking food that's more reasonably priced than virtually anywhere else.

La Tacita d'Juan. Hórreo, 31. ☎ **981-56-32-55.** Reservations recommended. Main courses 1,500–2,800 ptas. ($9–$16.80). AE, MC, V. Mon–Sat 1:15–4pm and 8:30–midnight. Closed Aug 1–15. Bus: 10. REGIONAL.

A favorite place for business lunches, 5 minutes from the train station, this restaurant offers *caldo gallego* (Galician soup), fish soup, artichokes with ham, Basque-style eels, shellfish cocktail, and a wide array of fish platters. Two special meat courses are the ham hock with greens and *fabada asturiana*, the famous stew of Asturias. The portions are generous, and the service is attentive.

Moncho Vilas. Avenida de Villagarcía, 21. ☎ **981-59-83-87.** Reservations recommended. Main courses 2,300–3,800 ptas. ($13.80–$22.80); fixed-price menu 5,000 ptas. ($30). AE, DC, MC, V. Daily 1:30–4:30pm and 8:30pm–midnight. Bus: 4, 21, or 25. REGIONAL.

This restaurant is at the edge of the old quarter, on a drab street off avenida de Donallo Romero, but it's worth seeking out. It looks like a country tavern, and, in fact, the *tasca* in front is one of the most popular in the area, especially with locals. It's a family-run place with conscientious service. A few of the Galician dishes served here are based on meat (the fillet of beef with sherry sauce is especially good), but the real specialties are seafood creations, such as fish soup, hake, and grilled shrimp.

Restaurante Vilas. Rosalía de Castro, 88. ☎ **981-59-21-70.** Reservations required. Main courses 1,800–3,500 ptas. ($10.80–$21); fixed-price menu 4,000 ptas. ($24). AE, DC, MC, V. Mon–Sat 1–5pm and 8pm–midnight. SEAFOOD.

Located on the outskirts of the old town on the road to Pontevedra, this reliable Spanish tavern, housed in a three-story townhouse, has a devoted clientele, many from industry, politics, and the arts. Beyond the large bar near the entrance and display cases filled with fresh fish, you'll find the baronial stone-trimmed dining room. A wide variety of fish is available—fresh sardines, three different preparations of salmon, a *zarzuela* (seafood stew), and eels. Two kinds of paella are served, and non-fish dishes such as partridge and rabbit are also on the menu. The restaurant was founded in 1915 as a little eating house. Back then, it was on the outskirts of town, but the place was enveloped by the city long ago. It stands on a street named after the illustrious female poet of Galicia. Today, the restaurant is run by the grandsons of the original founders.

✪ **Toñi Vicente.** Calle Rosalía de Castro, 24. ☎ **981-59-41-00.** Reservations recommended. Main courses 2,800–3,500 ptas. ($16.80–$21); fixed-price menu 6,900 ptas. ($41.40). AE, DC, MC, V. Mon–Sat 1:30–4pm and 9pm–midnight. Closed first 2 weeks in Jan and Aug. GALICIAN/INTERNATIONAL.

Set in the heart of town, on two floors of a building erected around 1950, this is the finest and most flamboyantly international restaurant in Santiago or for miles around. Within dining rooms accented with a neoclassical overlay and a color scheme of blue and salmon, you can enjoy the celebrated cuisine of Toñi Vicente. Menu items change with the availability of the ingredients, but are likely to include such delectable dishes as a warm seafood salad with herbs, escalopes of veal with a confit of onions, turbot with chive sauce, unusual preparations of seasonal game dishes, and for dessert, a tart made with Galician pears.

SANTIAGO AFTER DARK

There's much more to do in the religious centerpiece of Galicia after dark than just pray. There are an estimated 200 bars and *cafeterías* on the rúa do Franco and its neighbor, rúa da Raiña. The pavement along those streets during crowded weekend evenings around 11pm is mobbed. You can have a lot of fun ducking into any of them, but two that are particularly convivial are **El 42,** rúa do Franco, 42 (no phone), and **Bar/Cafeteria Dakar,** rúa do Franco, 13 (☎ **981-57-81-92**). Two highly appealing competitors are **Pub Borriquita de Belén,** rúa San Pelayo, 22 (no phone), and its neighbor, **Bar Crechas,** rúa San Pelayo, 28 (no phone), both of which appeal to bar-hoppers thanks to occasional live music that packs clients in anytime after 10pm. Know in advance that the de rigueur method for pursuing after-dark diversion in Santiago involves hitting a roster of bars and tapas joints before midnight, and dancing the night away beginning anytime after midnight.

Two of the most likely dance options in town, both of which begin after midnight and continue until 4 or 5am, are **Disco Casting Araguaney,** rúa Montero Rios, 25 (☎ **981-59-59-00**), a rock-and-roll palace in the heart of the old city, and a counterpart that begins even later (around 5am), **Disco Black,** in the Hotel del Peregrino, Rosalía de Castro, s/n (☎ **981-52-18-50**).

3 Rías Altas

In Norway they're called fjords; in Brittany, abers; in Scotland, lochs; and in Galicia, *rías.* These inlets have been cut into the Galician coastline by the turbulent Atlantic pounding against its shores. Rías Altas is a relatively modern name applied to all the estuaries on the northern Galicia coast, from Ribadeo (the gateway to Galicia on the border with Asturias) to La Coruña (the big Atlantic seaport of northwest Spain). The part that begins at Ribadeo, part of Lugo province, is also called Marina Lucense. Four estuaries form the Artabro Gulf: La Coruña, Betanzoa, Ares, and Ferrol. All four converge on a single point, where the Marola crag rises.

ON THE ROAD FROM RIBADEO TO LA CORUÑA

From Ribadeo, take the corniche road west (N-634) until you reach the Ría de Foz. About 1½ miles (2.5km) south of the Foz–Barreiros highway, perched somewhat in isolation on a hill, stands the **Iglesia de San Martín de Mondoñeda,** part of a monastery that dates from 1112. Please keep in mind that while corniche roads are sinuous and panoramic, they are often located high above the road surface and have steep, usually rather dangerous, dropoffs on the other side.

The little town of **Foz** is a fishing village and a summer resort with beaches separated by a cliff. You might stop here for lunch.

From Foz, cut northwest along the coastal highway (C-642), going through **Burela,** another fishing village. You can make a slight detour south to **Sargadelos,** a ceramics center. You can purchase the famous Galician pottery here much more cheaply than elsewhere in Spain.

Back on the coastal road (C-642) at Burela, continue west approaching Ría de Vivero and the historic village of **Vivero.** Part of its medieval walls and an old gate, Puerta de Carlos V, have been preserved. The town has many old churches of interest, including the Gothic-style Iglesia San Francisco. Vivero is a summer resort, attracting vacationers to its beach, the Playa Covas, and makes a good lunch stop.

The road continues northwest to **Vicedo,** passing such beaches as Xillo and Aerealong. Excellent vistas of the estuary greet you, and oxen can be seen plowing the cornfields.

Driving on, you'll notice the coastline becoming more saw-toothed. Eventually you reach **Ortigueira,** a major fishing village at the head of the *ría* from which it takes its name. A Celtic folk festival is staged here at the end of August.

From here you can continue south along C-642 to **El Ferrol,** which used to be called El Caudillo, in honor of the late dictator Francisco Franco, who was born here and who used to spend part of his summers in this area. El Ferrol is one of the major shipbuilding centers of Spain, and since the 18th century it has been a center of the Spanish navy. It's a grimy town, but it lies on one of the region's most beautiful *rías*. In spite of its parador, few tourists will want to linger at El Ferrol (also spelled O Ferrol).

From El Ferrol, C-642 continues south, passing through the small town of **Puentedeume** (also spelled Pontedeume), on the Rías Ares. Historically, it was the center of the counts of Andrade. The last remains of their 14th-century palace can be seen, along with the ruins of a 13th-century castle, rising to the east.

Shortly below Betanzos, head west along N-VI until you reach La Coruña. The entire trip from Ribadeo is roughly 150 miles (241.5km) and takes at least 4 hours.

WHERE TO DINE ALONG THE COAST

Nito. Playa de Area, Vivero. ☎ **982-56-09-87.** Reservations recommended. Main courses 1,800–3,000 ptas. ($10.80–$18); fixed-price menu 2,000 ptas. ($12). AE, MC, V. Daily 1–4pm and 8pm–midnight. SEAFOOD.

Established in the early 1970s, this restaurant is in the center of Vivero, only 100 yards from the beach, with a sweeping view of the Atlantic. It starts serving dinner early for Spain (8pm) and maintains a nice balance between prices and quality of its ingredients, serving unpretentious but flavorful food. Shellfish, priced according to weight, is the specialty, but you can order grilled sea bream or perhaps a house-style beefsteak. Most diners begin their meal with a bowl of *caldo gallego* (Galician soup). A full range of wines is offered. Diners wanting to eat outside can sit on a garden-view terrace.

EXPLORING THE RÍAS ALTAS ON TWO WHEELS

Some of the best biking in Spain is found in the Rías Altas. Much of south and central Spain is too hot for biking, but here temperatures are generally cool, and an interesting vista unfolds at every turn. Depending on your time, stamina, and interest, the tourist office at Vivero, Plaza Mayor 27 (☎ **982-23-13-61**), can give you a map and some suggested routes.

Vivero is also the only town in Rías Altas that rents motorcycles or bikes. Go to **Viajes Arifran,** C. Rosalía de Castro, 54 (☎ **982-56-04-97**), open Monday to Friday 9:30am to 1pm and 4 to 7pm. In July and August, the rental shop is open on Saturday 9:30am to 1pm. Motorcycles rent for 9,000 ptas. ($54) a day, with bikes going for 1,000 ptas. ($6).

From Vivero the most scenic route is to the west, following along the C-642 to El Ferrol on the sea. A particularly dramatic stretch would be to head north along a secondary road when you come to the junction at the little town of Mera. Signs point north to another little town, Carino, opening onto views of Cabo Ortegal. To the east will be a sheltered body of water, Ría de Sta. Maria, and to the west the Atlantic Ocean. From Vivero you can also go inland heading south along Route 640, following the signs to the hamlet of Oral. You can also take the coastal road east from Vivero, signposted RIBADEO. Ribadeo is too built-up to interest most cyclists, but depending on your stamina, you can cycle to the little seaside villages of San Ciprian, Burella, and Foz.

FROM LA CORUÑA TO CAPE FISTERRA

This next section, the drive "to the end of the world," takes you from La Coruña to **Cape Fisterra** (called **Fisterra** or **Finisterre** on most maps). It's a 90-mile (145km) trip that takes at least 3 hours. For the ancients, Cape Fisterra was the end of the world as they knew it.

This route takes you along **A Costa da Morte (La Costa de la Muerte; The Coast of Death),** so called because of the numerous shipwrecks that have occurred here.

Leaving La Coruña, take the coastal road west (Highway 552), heading first to the road junction of **Carballo,** a distance of 22 miles (35.5km). From this little town, many of the small coastal harbors are within an easy drive. **Malpica,** to the northwest, is the most interesting, with its own beach. An offshore seabird sanctuary exists here, and Malpica itself was a former whaling port. From Malpica, continue to the tiny village of **Corme** at Punta Roncudo. This sheltered fishing village draws summer beach fans, as there are many isolated sand dunes.

From Corme, continue along the winding roads to the whitewashed village of **Camariñas,** which stands on the *ría* of the same name. A road here leads all the way to the lighthouse at Cabo Vilán. Camariñas is known as a village of expert lace makers, and you'll see the work for sale at many places.

The road now leads to **Mugia** (shown on some maps as "Muxia"), below which stands the lighthouse at Cabo Touriñan. Continue driving south along clearly marked coastal roads that are sometimes perched precariously on cliff tops overlooking the sea. They will lead you to **Corcubión,** a village with a Romanesque church. From here, follow signs that lead you along a lonely southbound secondary road to the end of the line, **Cabo Fisterra,** for a panoramic view. The sunsets from here are among the most spectacular in the world. The Roman poet Horace said it best: "The brilliant skylight of the sun drags behind it the black night over the fruitful breasts of earth."

4 Rías Bajas

After Cabo Fisterra, some of the most dramatic coastal scenery in Spain flanks coastal Highway 550, following the edge of one of the most tortuous shorelines in Europe. The four estuaries, collectively called the ✪ **Rías Bajas,** face the Atlantic from Cape Silleiro to Baiona to Point Louro in Muros. Two of these are in the province of

Pontevedra (Ría de Pontevedra and Ría de Vigo); one is in the province of La Coruña (Ría de Muros y Noya); and one (Ría de Arousa) divides its shores between the two provinces. The 20-mile (32km) Vigo estuary is the longest, stretching from Ponte Sampasio to Baiona.

DRIVING FROM MUROS TO SANTA UXEA DE RIBEIRA

The seaside town of **Muros** has many old houses and a harbor, but **Noya** (also spelled "Noia"), to the southeast, is more impressive. If you don't have a car but would like to see at least one or two *ría* fishing villages, you can do so at either Noya or Muros: Both are on a bus route connecting them with Santiago de Compostela. Eleven buses per day leave from Santiago heading for Noya, and nine run to Muros. Some of the tiny villages and beaches are connected by bus routes.

If you do drive, the entire trip is only 47 miles (76km); at a leisurely pace it should take you 2 hours. Noya is known for its braided straw hats with black bands. It has a number of interesting, handsome old churches, including the 14th-century **Igrexa de Santa María** (with tombstones dating from the 10th century) and the **Igrexa de San Francisco.** A lot of good beaches lie on the northern bank of the *ría* near Muros. Noya is your best bet for a lunch stop.

From Noya, the coast road (Highway 550) continues west to **Porto do Son.** You can take a detour to Cabo de Corrubedo, with its lighthouse, before continuing on to Santa Uxea de Ribeira at the southern tip. Ribeira is a fishing port and a canning center. At **Santa Uxea de Ribeira** you'll see Ría de Arousa, the largest and deepest of the inlets.

From Ribeira, continue east along the southern coastal road to **A Puebla de Caramiñal.** From here, take a marked route 6 miles (10km) inland into the mountains, to admire the most magnificent panorama in all of *rías* country—the **Mirador de la Curota,** at 1,634 feet (498m). The four inlets of the Rías Bajas can, under the right conditions, be seen from the belvedere. In clear weather you can view Cape Fisterra.

Back on C-550, drive as far as Padrón, where, it is claimed, the legendary sea vessel arrived bringing Santiago (St. James) to Spain. Padrón was also the home of romantic poet Rosalía de Castro (1837–85), sometimes called the Emily Dickinson of Spain. Her house, the **Casa Museo de Rosalía de Castro,** Carretera de Herbrón (☎ 981-81-12-04), is open to the public Tuesday to Sunday 9:30am to 1:30pm. Admission is 200 ptas. ($1.20). Padrón makes a good lunch stop.

From Padrón, follow the alleged trail of the body of St. James north along N-550 to Santiago de Compostela or take N-550 south to Pontevedra.

WHERE TO STAY & DINE

Ceboleiro II. Galicia, 15, Noya. ☎ **981-82-44-97.** Reservations not necessary. Main courses 1,600–2,200 ptas. ($9.60–$13.20); fixed-price menu 1,600–3,500 ptas. ($9.60–$21). AE, DC, MC, V. Daily 1–4pm and 9pm–midnight. SEAFOOD.

For about a century, this inn has provided food and accommodations to passersby. Set in the heart of Noya, it is owned and managed by three generations of the Fernández family. It offers hearty food from the sea, prepared in conservative but flavorful ways that usually correspond to the culinary traditions of Galicia and northern Portugal. The menu almost always includes several versions of hake, shellfish soup, several kinds of rice studded with fish or shellfish, pork and beef dishes, and, among other desserts, an apple tart. The establishment contains 13 simple but comfortable accommodations, each with private bathroom, TV, and telephone nearby. Doubles cost from 5,000 ptas. ($33.50).

Chef Rivera. Enlace Parque, 7, Padrón. ☎ **981-81-04-13.** Fax 981-81-14-54. Reservations recommended. Main courses 1,200–3,500 ptas. ($7.20–$21); fixed-price menu 2,500–3,500 ptas. ($15–$21). AE, DC, MC, V. Daily 1–4pm and 9pm–midnight. Closed Sun night in winter. GALICIAN/SPANISH.

The name of the owner, to everyone in town, is simply El Chef. His cuisine is innovative but based on traditional continental recipes. His wife, Pierrette, attends to service in the dining room, which resembles an English pub with its dark, warm colors and leather upholstery. Try the shellfish soup or stew or the house-style monkfish. The restaurant is known for its *pimientos de Padrón.* Tiny green peppers are sauteed with olive oil. There's nothing unusual about that; the trick is that about one in five of those peppers is hot, as in very spicy. You might finish your meal with lemon mousse. The couple rents 20 simply furnished guest rooms, at 6,000 to 6,800 ptas. ($36 to $40.80) for a double.

5 Pontevedra

36 miles (58km) S of Santiago de Compostela, 521 miles (839km) NW of Madrid

An aristocratic old Spanish town on the Lérez River and the capital of Pontevedra province, the city of Pontevedra still has vestiges of an ancient wall that once encircled the town. In medieval days, the town was called Pontis Veteris (Old Bridge).

Some of the best Gallego seamen lived in Pontevedra in the Middle Ages. Sheltered at the end of the Pontevedra Ría, the city was a bustling port, and foreign merchants mingled with local traders, seamen, and fishers. It was the home of Pedro Sarmiento de Gamboa, the 16th-century navigator and cosmographer who wrote *Voyage to the Magellan Straits.* In the 18th century the Lérez delta silted up and the busy commerce moved elsewhere, mainly to Vigo. Pontevedra entered a period of decline, which may account for its significant old section. Had it been a more prosperous town, the people might have torn down the ancient structures to rebuild.

The old *barrio,* a maze of colonnaded squares and cobbled alleyways, is between calle Michelena and calle del Arzobispo Malvar, stretching to calle Cobián and the river. The old mansions are called *pazos,* and they speak of former marine glory, since it was the sea that provided the money to build them. Seek out such charming squares as Plaza de la Leña, Plaza de Mugártegui, and Plaza de Teucro.

ESSENTIALS

GETTING THERE From Santiago de Compostela in the north, 16 trains per day make the 1-hour trip to Pontevedra at a cost of 635 ptas. ($3.80) one-way. **RENFE** has an office on calle Gondomar, 3 (☎ **986-85-13-13**), where you can get information. The actual rail and bus stations (☎ **986-85-13-13** for information about transportation in the area) are half a mile from the town center on Alféreces Provisionales.

Pontevedra has good links to major Galician cities. From Vigo in the south, the bus traveling time is only half an hour if you take one of the 12 inland expresses leaving from Vigo daily. From Santiago de Compostela in the north, a bus leaves every hour during the day for Pontevedra (1 hour away).

From Santiago de Compostela, head south along N-550 to reach Pontevedra.

VISITOR INFORMATION The **tourist information office** is at General Mola, 3 (☎ **986-85-08-14**). It's open Monday to Friday 9:30am to 2pm and 5 to 7pm, Saturday 10am to 12:30pm.

A SPECIAL EVENT ✪ *A Rapa das Bestas* **(The Capture of the Beasts)** is held every year in the beginning of July. In the hills of nearby San Lorenzo de Sabuceno, wild horses are rounded up and herded into a corral, in a ritual that evokes the Wild West. For information, contact the tourism office in Pontevedra (see above).

EXPLORING PONTEVEDRA

In the old quarter, the major attraction is the **Basílica de Santa María la Mayor,** calle del Arzobispo Malvar, with its avocado-green patina, dating from the 16th century. This plateresque church was constructed with funds provided by the mariners' guild. Its most remarkable feature is its west front, carved to resemble an altarpiece, with a depiction of the Crucifixion at top.

Museo Provincial, Pasantería, 10 (☎ **986-85-14-55**), with a hodgepodge of everything from the Pontevedra attic, contains displays ranging from prehistoric artifacts to a still life by Zurbarán. Many of the exhibits are maritime-oriented, and there is a valuable collection of jewelry. Hours are Tuesday to Saturday 10am to 1pm and 5 to 8:45pm. Admission is 200 ptas. ($1.20); free for European Union citizens. The museum opens onto a major square in the old town, the Plaza de Leña (Square of Wood).

Iglesia de San Francisco, Plaza de la Herrería, is another church of note. Its Gothic facade opens onto gardens. It was founded in the 14th century and contains a sculpture of Don Payo Gómez Charino, noted for his part in the 1248 Reconquest of Seville, when it was wrested from Muslim domination.

Directly south, the gardens lead to the 18th-century **Capilla de la Peregrina,** Plaza Peregrina, with a narrow half-moon facade connected to a rotunda and crowned by a pair of towers. It was constructed by followers of the cult of the Pilgrim Virgin, which was launched in Galicia sometime in the 17th century.

WHERE TO STAY
MODERATE

✪ **Parador Nacional Casa del Barón.** Baron 19, s/n, 36002 Pontevedra. ☎ **986-85-58-00.** Fax 986-85-21-95. www.parador.es. 47 units. MINIBAR TV TEL. 12,500–16,000 ptas. ($75–$96) double. AE, DC, MC, V.

The parador is in the old quarter of Pontevedra, in a well-preserved 16th-century palace near the Basílica de Santa María la Mayor. Built on either 13th- or 14th-century foundations, this hotel became one of Spain's first paradors when it opened in 1955. The interior has been maintained very much as the old *pazo* (manor house) looked. It includes a quaint old kitchen, or *lar* ("heart"), typical of Galician country houses and furnished with characteristic items. Off the vestibule is a courtyard dominated by a large old stone staircase. Many of the accommodations—all with private bathrooms, including hair dryers—are large enough to include sitting areas; the beds are comfortable, and the furnishings attractive. Many of the rooms overlook the walled-in formal garden.

Both lunch and dinner are served at the hotel restaurant. Specialty dishes, such as a casserole of shrimp with tomato sauce, are well prepared and served daily. It is a 4-mile (6.5km) drive to the beach.

INEXPENSIVE

Hotel Comercio. Augusto González Besada, 3, 36001 Pontevedra. ☎ **986-85-12-17.** Fax 986-85-99-91. 60 units. TV TEL. 5,500–7,500 ptas. ($33–$45) double. MC, V. Bus: 14 or 20 from train station.

This tall hotel with its modern facade and art deco–inspired cafe and bar, is an acceptable choice in its price category. Guest rooms are fairly comfortable, but only functional in style. Although small, the rooms contain comfortable beds with firm mattresses. A restaurant serves both lunch and dinner, with many regional specialties offered and a *menú del día* for 1,600 ptas. ($9.60).

Hotel Rías Bajas. Daniel de la Sota, 7, 36001 Pontevedra. ☎ **986-85-51-00.** Fax 986-85-51-00. 100 units. MINIBAR TV TEL. 9,500–14,000 ptas. ($57–$84) double; 12,500–16,000 ptas. ($75–$96) suite. AE, DC, MC, V. Parking 1,000 ptas. ($6).

On a busy street corner near Plaza de Galicia in the commercial center, this 1960s hotel is more comfortable than you might expect judging from the outside. The largest hotel in town, it is often used for community political meetings and press conferences. The lobby, in stone and wood paneling, has been designed to look like an English club. The midsize bedrooms are comfortable and well maintained, with private bathrooms.

The hotel doesn't have a restaurant but does offer a cafeteria. Amenities include laundry and dry-cleaning service, room service, in-room massage, baby-sitting, and access to a health club and 9-hole golf course.

Hotel Virgen del Camino. Virgen del Camino, 55, 36001 Pontevedra. ☎ **986-85-59-00.** Fax 986-85-09-00. 53 units. TV TEL. 9,000–12,500 ptas. ($54–$75) double. MC, V. Parking 1,000 ptas. ($6).

On a relatively quiet street off the highway C-531, at the edge of the suburbs, this balconied stucco hotel contains a comfortable English-style pub as well as spacious sitting rooms. The midsized bedrooms have wall-to-wall carpeting and private bathrooms, plus central heating in winter. The best doubles contain separate salons and sitting rooms. A cafeteria serves fixed-price meals. There is a laundry service on the premises and room service.

WHERE TO DINE

Casa Román. Augusto García Sánchez, 12. ☎ **986-84-35-60.** Main courses 1,600–4,000 ptas. ($9.60–$24); fixed-price menu 2,500 ptas. ($15). AE, DC, MC, V. Daily 1:30–4pm; Mon–Sat 9pm–midnight. Closed Sun night Sept–Jan. GALICIAN.

Known for the quality of its food, this long-established restaurant is on the street level of a brick apartment building in a leafy downtown development known as Campolongo, near Plaza de Galicia. To reach the dining room, you pass through a tavern. In addition to lobster (which you can see in the window), a wide array of well-prepared fish and shellfish dishes is served here, including sea bass, squid, sole, crab, and tuna.

✪ **Doña Antonia.** Soportales de la Herrería, 4 (2nd floor). ☎ **986-84-72-74.** Reservations required. Main courses 1,750–3,500 ptas. ($10.50–$21); tasting menu 4,500 ptas. ($27). AE, MC, V. Mon–Sat 1:30–4pm and 9–11:30pm. INTERNATIONAL.

Without question, Pontevedra's best restaurant is Doña Antonia, under a stone arcade on one of the town's oldest streets, east of the Jardines Vincenti. You climb one flight to reach the dining room. In such a provincial town, it is surprising to come across a restaurant of such sophistication and refinement. Although a few readers have sometimes reported a disappointing meal, most diners are filled with joy at this discovery. There's a pristine freshness to the dishes prepared with fish just caught off the coast. The reward for all this culinary vigilance is a loyal clientele of contented food lovers. Menu items include baked suckling lamb, scallopini with port, rolled fillet of salmon, and kiwi sorbet.

PONTEVEDRA AFTER DARK

The cool temperatures that descend over the hot, sultry plain surrounding Pontevedra seem to incite local residents into after-dark promenades through the old city. You'll find a random scattering of pubs and bars sprawling on either side of the streets that interconnect the Plaza Santa María la Mayor, in the northwestern quadrant of the town's historic core, with the very central Plaza de la Herrería. Part of the charm of the neighborhood involves stopping randomly at whatever pub or cafe appeals to you— each awakens from its slumber after around 8:30pm. By midnight on the weekends, rhythmic electronic music emanates from two of the town's most popular discos: **Equus,** calle Loreiro Crespo, 8 (☎ **986-86-40-15**), and **Disco Caravas,** calle Cobian Rafinac, 6 (no phone). Disco Caravas appeals to high-energy dance freaks in their early 20s; most folks in their 30s appreciate the slightly more mature venues at Equus. Don't even think of heading off to a Pontevedra disco before midnight, as it's likely to be locked until then (but the music keeps pumping until 4am). Expect entrance charges between 500 and 700 ptas. ($3.35 and $4.70) at both of these venues, depending on the night of the week.

6 Lugo

314 miles (505.5km) NW of Madrid, 60 miles (97km) SE of La Coruña

Lugo has known many conquerors. The former Celtic-Iberian settlement fell to the Romans, and centuries later the Moors used the land and its people to grow crops for them. Today, Lugo is one of the four provincial capitals of Galicia. It is generally bypassed by those taking the Pilgrims' Way to Santiago de Compostela. However, it makes a rewarding detour for a morning or afternoon of sightseeing.

ESSENTIALS

GETTING THERE   Lugo is on the rail link with Madrid. Two trains per day arrive from La Coruña.

Lugo has bus links with most of the major towns in the northwest, including Oviedo, with one per day making the 5-hour trip, and Orense, with five per day making the 2½-hour trip.

For those driving, N-VI connects Lugo with La Coruña as well as, at some distance, Madrid.

VISITOR INFORMATION   The **tourist information office** is at Praça Maior, 27 (☎ **982-23-13-61**). It is open Monday to Friday 9:30am to 1:30pm and 4:30 to 6pm, Saturday 10am to 1:30pm.

STROLLING AROUND ANCIENT LUGO

Lugo, split by the Miño River, is surrounded by a thick 1¼-mile (2km) ✪ **Roman wall,** the best preserved in all of Spain. The wall is about 33 feet (10m) high and has a total of 85 round towers; a sentry path can be approached by steps at the various town gates. Your best bet is to enter the old town at Puerto de Santiago, the most interesting of the ancient gates, and begin a most impressive promenade—what may well be one of the highlights of your tour of Galicia.

Along the way you'll come to the **cathedral,** built in 1129 and notable for its trio of landmark towers. Standing at the Plaza Santa María, it has many Romanesque architectural features, such as its nave, but it was subsequently given a Gothic overlay. Further remodeling took place in the 18th century, when many features were added, such as the Capilla de la Virgen de los Ojos Grandes (Chapel of the Wide-Eyed Virgin) at the east end, with a baroque rotunda. The highlight of the cathedral is a 13th-century porch at the north end, which provides shelter for a Romanesque sculpture *Jesus Christ in His Majesty.* The figure rises over a capital and seems to hang in space. At the far end of the transept rise huge wood-built altarpieces in the Renaissance style.

As you wander about—and that is far preferable to going inside the many monuments—you'll traverse the cobblestoned, colonnaded medieval streets and interesting squares of the old town, especially behind the cathedral. The 18th-century **Episcopal Palace,** called a *pazo* in Galician, faces the north side of the cathedral and opens onto Plaza Santa María. From the palace, old alleys behind it lead to a tiny nugget, **Plaza del Campo,** one of the most charming squares of Lugo, flanked with ancient houses and graced with a fountain at its core.

Or from the bishop's palace at the Plaza Santa María, you can take calle Cantones to Plaza de España, where you will see the **Ayuntamiento (Town Hall),** built in a flowery rococo style.

From the Town Hall, follow calle de la Reina north to the **Iglesia de San Francisco,** a church said to have been founded by St. Francis on his return from a pilgrimage west to the tomb of St. James. The cloister of the church, entered at Plaza de la Soledad, s/n, has been turned into the **Museo Provincial** (☎ 982-24-21-12). Many artifacts, such as sundials from Celtic and Roman days, are in this museum, along with folkloric displays. In July and August, it is open Monday to Friday 11am to 2pm and 5 to 8pm, Saturday 10:30am to 2pm. From September to June, it is open Monday to Saturday 10:30am to 2pm and 4:30 to 8:30pm, Sunday 11am to 2pm. Admission is free.

WHERE TO STAY
EXPENSIVE

Gran Hotel Lugo. Avenida Ramón Ferreiro, 21, 27002 Lugo. ☎ **982-22-41-52.** Fax 982-24-16-60. 168 units. A/C MINIBAR TV TEL. 16,000 ptas. ($96) double; 22,500 ptas. ($135) suite. AE, DC, MC, V. Parking 1,000 ptas. ($6). Bus: 1, 2, 3, or 4.

About half a mile west of the ancient city walls in a leafy residential neighborhood, this hotel is large, modern, and the best in town. Its guest rooms are conservative and comfortable, with marble and/or tile bathrooms (offering hair dryers) and restful monochromatic colors.

Dining/Diversions: The **Os Marisqueiros** restaurant serves regional and international three-course fixed-price lunches and dinners. Live music is sometimes performed in the **Atalaya Bar,** which is open Monday to Saturday 7pm to 4am. **Snack 2003** is a coffee shop/snack bar, and the adjoining **La Oca** is a combination pizzeria and pub.

Amenities: Room service (daily from 8am to midnight), laundry, concierge, babysitting, business center, car rentals, shopping boutiques, bingo hall, swimming pool.

MODERATE

Hotel Jorge Primeiro. La Campiña, 27192 Lugo. ☎ **982-30-32-55.** Fax 982-30-31-07. 23 units. TV TEL. 6,800–8,500 ptas. ($40.80–$51) double. AE, DC, MC, V. Bus: Destination La Campiña.

If you're driving, this little hotel about 2 miles (3km) north of town on Carretera N-640 is one of your best bets, particularly if you're arriving from neighboring Asturias. The old building has a bit of charm, and the well-maintained but small bedrooms are filled with modern comforts, such as firm mattresses. You can enjoy the scenery as you dine in the hotel restaurant, which serves regional fare and a *menú del día* for 1,200 ptas. ($8.05).

Méndez Núñez. Raiña, 1, 27001 Lugo. ☎ **982-23-07-11.** Fax 982-22-97-38. 84 units. TV TEL. 7,000–8,500 ptas. ($42–$51) double. AE, MC, V. Parking 160 ptas. (95¢) per hour in nearby garage. Bus: 1, 2, 3, or 4.

Just around the corner from Plaza Mayor, this hotel was built in 1888 and named in honor of a then-famous Spanish admiral who had just won an important battle against revolutionaries in Cuba. Rebuilt and modernized in 1970, the hotel is today one of the best managed in town, although not as highly rated as the Gran Hotel Lugo (see above). Midsize bedrooms are well maintained and comfortable, each equipped with an excellent bed. No meals other than breakfast are served, but many restaurants and cafes are in the neighborhood. The hotel is especially convenient for exploring the medieval streets of the town's old quarter.

WHERE TO DINE

Campos. Rúa Nova, 4. ☎ **982-22-97-43.** Reservations recommended. Main courses 1,600–3,000 ptas. ($9.60–$18); fixed-price menus 1,850–2,500 ptas. ($11.10–$15). AE, DC, MC, V. Daily noon–4:30pm and 7:30pm–midnight. Closed the last 2 weeks in Oct. Bus: 1, 2, 3, or 4. GALICIAN.

In the old quarter immediately adjacent to Plaza del Campo, this acclaimed restaurant is the creation of Amparo Yañez and his son, Manuel. Together, they offer imaginative combinations of fresh ingredients that are deftly prepared and much appreciated by their loyal clients. Winner of the 1995 *Gran Cocineros de Galicia* award, they feature seasonal game dishes, especially local pheasant, along with fresh fish, such as grouper with almonds. The best dessert is fresh local strawberries with honey and cream. Decor in the establishment's two dining rooms is restrained and elegant, and includes a monochromatic color scheme of soft beiges, with lots of visible hardwoods, in a building erected around 1900.

Ferreiros. Rua Nueva, 1. ☎ **982-22-97-28.** Reservations recommended. Main courses 850–2,500 ptas. ($5.10–$15); *menús del día* 1,800–2,000 ptas. ($10.80–$12). MC, V. Thurs–Tues 1–4pm and 8pm–midnight. Bus: 1, 2, 3, or 4. GALICIAN.

In business since the 1920s, this longtime favorite near the cathedral must be doing something right. In fact, it offers well-prepared and old-fashioned regional fare with a certain unpretentious flair. The portions are generous, and the food is fresh. The many shellfish dishes featured are the most expensive items on the menu. You can also order a big slab of rib of beef or monkfish prepared in different ways.

Mesón de Alberto. Calle de la Cruz, 4. ☎ **982-22-83-10.** Reservations recommended. Main courses 750–2,600 ptas. ($4.50–$15.60); fixed-price menu 2,500 ptas. ($15). AE, DC, MC, V. Mon–Sat 1–4pm and 8pm–midnight. Bus: 1, 2, 3, or 4. GALICIAN/SPANISH.

Alberto García is the culinary star of Lugo, and with good reason. Ably assisted by his wife, Flor, he offers a well-chosen menu of imaginative fish and meat dishes and the best wine cellar in town. In style the place resembles a rustic tavern, with a stand-up bar serving tapas, plus a handful of dining tables. The overflow is directed to a somewhat more formal dining room beside the tavern or to the second floor. Try Alberto's salad with eel and an exotic vinegar, monkfish served with a mountain cheese (Cabrales from Asturias), or beefsteak for two, prepared with his secret sauce. Mesón de Alberto is 1 block north of the cathedral in the old quarter.

7 El Grove & La Toja

395 miles (636km) NW of Madrid, 20 miles (32km) W of Pontevedra, 45 miles (72.5km) S of Santiago de Compostela

A summer resort and fishing village with some 5 miles (8km) of beaches of varying quality, **El Grove** is on a peninsula west of Pontevedra. It juts out into the Ría de Arousa, a large inlet at the mouth of Ulla River. The village, sheltered from Atlantic gales because of its eastern position, has become more commercial than many visitors would like, but it is still renowned for its fine cuisine. A shellfish festival is held here every October.

La Toja (*A Toxa* in Galician), an island linked to El Grove by a bridge, is a famous spa and the most fashionable resort in Galicia, known for its sports and leisure activities. The casino and the golf course are both very popular. The island is covered with pine trees and surrounded by some of the finest scenery in Spain.

La Toja first became known for health-giving properties when, according to legend, the owner of a sick donkey left it on the island to die. The donkey recovered, and its cure was attributed to the waters of an island spring.

GETTING THERE

The train from Santiago de Compostela goes as far as Vilagarcía de Arousa; take the bus from there. For train schedules, call the station in Santiago de Compostela (☎ **981-25-02-02**) for information.

From Pontevedra, buses heading for Ponte Vilagarcía de Arousa stop at La Toja. Call the transportation information number in Pontevedra (☎ **986-85-13-13**) for details.

From Pontevedra, drive east on the 550 coastal road via Sanxenxo. From Santiago de Compostela, expressway A-9 leads to Caldas de Reis, where you turn off onto the 550, heading west to the coast.

WHERE TO STAY & DINE IN EL GROVE

Hotel Amandi. Castelao, 94, 36980 El Grove. ☎ **986-73-19-42.** Fax 986-73-16-43. 30 units. TV TEL. 8,000–15,000 ptas. ($48–$90) double. Rates include breakfast. MC, V. Closed Jan.

This stylish and tasteful family-run hotel is a brisk 10-minute walk from the bridge that connects El Grove with La Toja. The midsize rooms are decorated with antique reproductions; most have tiny terraces with ornate cast-iron balustrades and sea views. Breakfast is the only meal served.

La Pousada del Mar. Castelao, 202. ☎ **986-73-01-06.** Reservations required July–Aug. Main courses 1,200–2,800 ptas. ($7.20–$16.80); fixed-price menu 3,000 ptas. ($18). AE, DC, MC, V. Daily 1–4pm; Mon–Sat 8:30pm–midnight. Closed Dec 10–Feb 1. SEAFOOD.

This warm, inviting place near the bridge leading to La Toja is the best dining spot outside those at the hotels. At times you can watch women digging for oysters in the river in front. The chef, naturally, specializes in fish, including a wide selection of shellfish. Among the specialties are a savory soup, outstanding shellfish paella, hake Galician style, and fresh grilled salmon. For dessert, try the *flan de la casa.*

WHERE TO STAY IN LA TOJA

Hotel Louxo. 36991 Isla de la A Toxa. ☎ **986-73-02-00.** Fax 986-73-27-91. 116 units. A/C MINIBAR TV TEL. 11,000–18,500 ptas. ($66–$111) double. AE, DC, MC, V. Free parking.

Set on flatlands a few paces from the town's ornate casino is this modern white building, sheltered from the Atlantic winds. It offers clean, stylish, and modern accommodations. Most rooms are midsized, and each is equipped with such amenities as a private safe and a hair dryer. The many ground-floor public rooms have rows of comfortable seating areas and sweeping views over the nearby tidal flats. The hotel serves an outstanding menu for 2,500 ptas. ($15), with an emphasis on fresh fish.

8 Túy (Túi)

18 miles (29km) S of Vigo, 30 miles (48km) S of Pontevedra

A frontier town first settled by the Romans, Túy is a short distance from Portugal, near the two-tiered road-and-rail bridge (over the Miño River) that links the two countries. The bridge was designed by Alexandre-Gustave Eiffel (he did a tower in Paris you may have heard of). If you're driving from Portugal's Valença do Minho, Túy is your introduction to Spain.

ESSENTIALS

GETTING THERE   Trains run daily for the 1½- to 2-hour trip from Vigo to Túy. From Vigo, buses run south to Túy hourly, taking 1 hour.

If you're driving from Vigo, head south along the A-9 expressway until you see the turnoff for Túy.

VISITOR INFORMATION   The **tourist information office** is at Puente Tripes, avenida de Portugal (☎ 986-60-17-89), open Monday to Friday 9am to 1pm and 4 to 6pm, Saturday 10am to 2:30pm.

EXPLORING TÚY

The winding streets of the old quarter lead to the **Catedral,** a national art treasure that dominates the *zona monumental.* The acropolislike cathedral-fortress, built in 1170, wasn't used for religious purposes until the early 13th century. Its principal ogival portal is exceptional. What is astounding about this cathedral is that later architects respected the original Romanesque and Gothic styles and didn't make changes in its design. If you have time, you may want to visit the Romanesque-style **Iglesia de San Bartolomé,** on the outskirts of town, and the **Iglesia de Santo Domingo,** a beautiful example of Gothic style (look for the bas-reliefs in the cloister). The latter church stands next to the Santo Domingo park. Walls built over Roman fortifications surround Túy.

WHERE TO STAY & DINE

Parador Nacional de San Telmo. Avenida de Portugal, s/n, 36700 Túy. ☎ **986-60-03-09.** Fax 986-60-21-63. 30 units. MINIBAR TV TEL. 12,500–16,000 ptas. ($75–$96) double; 17,000–22,000 ptas. ($102–$132) suite. AE, DC, MC, V. Free parking.

Advance reservations are essential if you want to stay in this elegant, fortress-style hacienda four streets north of the Miño River crossing. Built in 1968, the inn with its cantilevered roof was designed to blend in with the architectural spirit of the province, emphasizing local stone and natural woods. Brass chandeliers, paintings by well-known *gallegos,* and antiques combined with reproductions furnish the public rooms. In the main living room are a large inglenook fireplace, a tall banjo-shaped grandfather clock, hand-knotted rugs, 18th-century paintings, hand-hewn benches, and comfortable armchairs.

The midsize bedrooms are sober in style, but comfortable, and offer views across a colonnaded courtyard to the river and hills. They are furnished with Castilian-style pieces, and the tiled bathrooms are modern.

Dining: A dignified dining room has a high wooden ceiling and tall windows that offer a fine view of the surrounding hills. Even if you are not a hotel guest, it is worth dining on the regional cuisine served here. The hors d'oeuvres, served while you wait in the bar, consist of almost a dozen tapas. The fish dishes are excellent, especially (when available) lamprey, as well as salmon, shad, and trout. There is a *menú del día* for 3,500 ptas. ($21). Homemade cakes are offered for dessert.

Amenities: Pool, tennis courts.

The Balearic Islands 18

The Balearic Islands (*Los Baleares*), an archipelago composed of the major islands of Majorca, Minorca, and Ibiza, plus the diminutive Formentera, Cabrera, and the uninhabited Dragonera, lie off the coast of Spain, between France and the coast of northern Africa. Because they're located along the Mediterranean's major shipping lanes, the islands have known many rulers and occupying forces—Carthaginians, Greeks, Romans, Vandals, and Moors. But despite a trove of Bronze Age megaliths and some fine Punic artifacts, the invaders who have left the largest imprint on Balearic culture are the hordes of sun-seeking vacationers who descend every year.

After the expulsion of the Moors by Jaume I in 1229, the islands flourished as the kingdom of Majorca. When they were integrated into the kingdom of Castile in the mid–14th century, they experienced a massive decline. The early 19th century provided a renaissance for the islands; artists such as George Sand and her lover, Chopin, and later the poet Robert Graves established the islands, especially Majorca and Ibiza, as a haven for musicians, writers, and artists (read Sand's book *A Winter in Majorca*). Gradually the artist colony attracted tourists of all dispositions.

Today the Balearics are administered by an autonomous government, *Govern Balear.* **Majorca,** the largest island, is the most commercial and tourist oriented. It has both benefited and suffered from its huge tourism boom. Many of its scenic expanses have given way to sprawling hotels and fast-food joints, although parts remain beautiful indeed. Freewheeling **Ibiza,** world-renowned for its decadent ways, attracts the international party crowd, as well as visitors who come to the island for its tamer offerings, such as white-sand beaches and sky-blue waters. The smallest of the major islands, **Minorca,** the last to succumb to the tourist invasion, is the most serene. It is less touristy than Majorca and Ibiza, and for that reason, it is now experiencing an anti-tourist tourist boom.

The government of the islands has finally awakened to the damage caused by overdevelopment of Majorca and Ibiza from the 1960s to the 1980s. Under new guidelines, some 35% of this island group is now safeguarded from exploitation by builders.

Very few visitors have time to explore all three islands, so you'll have to decide early which one is for you. Many vacationers include one of the Balearic Islands as an add-on to a visit to Barcelona or the Costa Brava, while others view them as destinations unto themselves.

The Balearic Islands

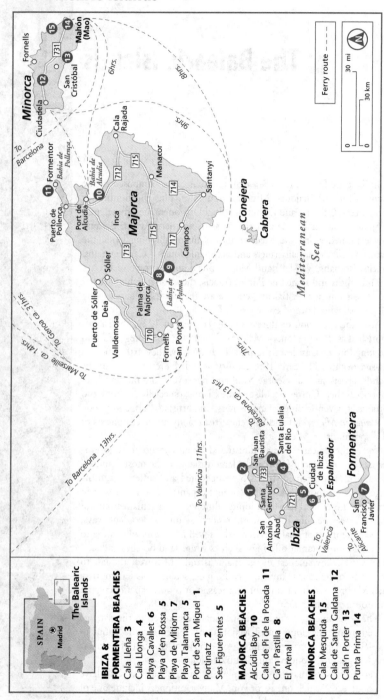

Ferry route - - - - -

N

30 mi
30 km

Minorca

Fornells

731

San Cristóbal

Mahón (Mao)

Ciudadela

To Barcelona

6hrs.

8hrs.

9hrs.

Formentor

Bahía de Pollença

Puerto de Pollença

Port de Alcúdia

Bahía de Alcudia

Cala Rajada

712

715

Manacor

714

Santanyí

Inca

Majorca

715

713

717

Campos

Puerto de Sóller

Sóller

Deiá

Valldemosa

Palma de Majorca

Bahía de Palma

710

Fornells

San Ponça

5hrs.

Conejera

Cabrera

Mediterranean Sea

7hrs.

To Barcelona Ca. 13 hrs.

To Barcelona 13hrs.

To Marseille ca. 14hrs.

To Genoa ca. 31hrs.

To Valencia 11hrs.

San Juan Bautista

733

Santa Eulalia del Rio

Santa Gertrudis

721

Ciudad de Ibiza

San Antonio Abad

Ibiza

Espalmador

Formentera

San Francisco Javier

To Valencia

To Alicante

IBIZA & FORMENTERA BEACHES

Cala Lleña **3**
Cala Llonga **4**
Playa Cavallet **6**
Playa d'en Bossa **5**
Playa de Mitjorn **7**
Playa Talamanca **5**
Port de San Miguel **1**
Portinatz **2**
Ses Figuerentes **5**

MAJORCA BEACHES

Alcúdia Bay **10**
Cala de Pi de la Posada **11**
Ca'n Pastilla **8**
El Arenal **9**

MINORCA BEACHES

Cala Mesquida **15**
Cala de Santa Galdana **12**
Cala'n Porter **13**
Punta Prima **14**

SPAIN

Madrid

The Balearic Islands

1 Majorca

The largest of the Balearic archipelago, Majorca (*Mallorca* in Spanish) is the most popular of Spain's Mediterranean islands, drawing millions of visitors each year. One prominent tourist is King Juan Carlos, who comes with his family to their summer residence, Marivent, in Cala Mayor.

About 130 miles (209km) from Barcelona and 90 miles (145km) from Valencia, Majorca has a coastline 310 miles (500km) long. The beautiful island is an explorer's paradise in its exterior, although horribly overbuilt along certain coastal regions. The north is mountainous; the fertile southern flatlands offer a landscape of olive and almond groves, occasionally interrupted by windmills.

The golden sands of Majorca are famous, with lovely beaches such as Ca'n Pastilla and El Arenal, but they tend to be overcrowded with sun worshippers on package tours. Tourist facilities line the shores of Cala Mayor and Sant Agustí; both have good beaches, including Playa Magaluf, the longest beach on the Calvià coast. Cala de San Vicente, 4 miles (6.5km) north of Pollença, is a beautiful beach bordered by a pine grove and towering cliffs. Sandy stretches of golden sand beaches lie between Cala Pi and Cala Murta in Formentor near the tip of the northern coast.

Majorca has much to offer—sun and surf, little harbors, hidden mountain villages, and historic sights. Brits, Americans, and Germans have all settled in, buying homes or apartments, but the "Chopin Heights Real Estate Development" (an actual development) is a bit much! (Chopin and his mistress, George Sand, were in the legendary vanguard of the tourists to Majorca. They spent a few months on the island in 1838.)

July and August are high season for Majorca; don't even think of coming then without a reservation. It's possible to swim comfortably from June to October; after that it's too cold (except for those hardy Scandinavians and Germans used to the chilly waters).

ISLAND ESSENTIALS

GETTING THERE   At certain times of the year the trip by boat or plane can be pleasant, but in August the routes to Palma must surely qualify as the major bottleneck in Europe. Don't travel without advance reservations, and be sure you have a return plane ticket if you come in August—otherwise you may not get off the island until September!

Iberia-Aviaco (☎ 971-75-67-54) flies to Palma's Aeroport Son San Joan (☎ 971-78-90-00) from Barcelona, Valencia, and Madrid. There are daily planes from Madrid and Valencia, and several daily flights from Barcelona in summer. **Spanair** (☎ 971-74-50-20) flies into Palma from Barcelona (up to three times a day during summer) and from Madrid, Bilbao, Minorca, Santiago de Compostela, Málaga, and Tenerife. **Air Europa** (☎ 971-17-81-00) flies to Palma from Barcelona a maximum of two times a day during peak season, and to a lesser extent, it flies to Palma from Madrid, Minorca, Ibiza, and Seville.

British and other European travelers should really consult a travel agent and look into the available package tours, which combine airfare and accommodations; they can save you a ton of money!

Countless charter flights also make the run. Bookings are very tight in August, and delays of at least 24 hours, sometimes more, are common. If you're flying—say, Iberia—on a transatlantic flight from New York to Madrid or Barcelona, you should have Majorca written into your ticket before your departure if you plan to visit the Balearics as part of your Spanish itinerary.

From the airport, bus number 17 takes you to the Plaça Espanya in the center of Palma 7am to 11:30pm daily; the cost is 325 ptas. ($1.95). A metered cab costs 2,580 ptas. ($15.50) for the 25-minute drive into the city center.

Transmediterránea, Estació Marítim in Palma (☎ **902-45-46-45** for schedules), operates two to five ferries a day from Barcelona, taking 8 hours and costing from 6,735 ptas. ($40.40) for one-way passage. There are six ferries per week from Valencia, Monday to Saturday, taking 8½ hours and costing 6,090 ptas. ($36.55) one-way. In Barcelona, tickets can be booked at the Transmediterránea office at Estació Marítim (☎ **93-295-91-37**), and in Valencia at the office at avinguda Manuel Soto Ingeniero, 15 (☎ **96-367-65-12**). Any travel agent in Spain can also book you a seat. Schedules and departure times (subject to change) should always be checked and double-checked.

A private ferry, operated by **Buquebus** (☎ **902-41-42-42** in Spain only), now makes the trip in just 3 hours, a full hour faster than the ferry run by the Spanish government. Buquebus is more expensive, however: 18,560 ptas. ($111.35) one-way, and 8,500 ptas. ($51) for tourist class.

GETTING AROUND At the tourist office in Palma, you can pick up a bus schedule that explains island routes. Or call **Emprese Municipal de Transportes** (☎ **971-43-10-24**). This company runs city buses from Estació Central D'Autobus, Plaça Espanya, the main terminal. The standard one-way fare is 175 ptas. ($1.05) within Palma; at the station you can buy a booklet good for 10 rides, costing 1,500 ptas. ($9).

The most popular destination routes on the island (Valldemossa, Deià, Sóller, and Port de Sóller) are offered by **Bus Nord Balear,** carrer Arxiduc Luís Salvador, 1 (☎ **971-42-71-87**) in Palma. **Autocares Mallorca,** Passeig La Victoria, 2 (☎ **971-54-56-96**), runs buses to the eastern coast, including Porto Cristo.

Ferrocarril de Sóller, carrer Eusebio Estada, 1 (☎ **971-75-20-51**), off Plaça Espanya, has train service, passing through majestic mountain scenery, to Sóller. Trains run 8am to 7:55pm, and a one-way ticket costs 770 ptas. ($4.60). A "tourist train" leaves daily at 10:40am and costs 1,115 ptas. ($6.70) before reaching Sóller. The only thing special about this route is a 10-minute stop at Mirador del Pujol d'en Banya—a privilege for which you pay dearly. The tourist train itself, however, is a worthy sightseeing trip. Privately owned, it was constructed by orange growers in the early 1900s and still uses the carriages of the belle époque days.

Another train runs to Inca; it's often called "the leather express" because most passengers are on board to buy inexpensive leather goods in the Inca shops. This line is the **Servicios Ferroviarios de Mallorca,** and it too leaves from Plaça Espanya (☎ **971-75-22-45** for more information and schedules). The train ride is only 40 minutes, with 40 departures per day Monday to Saturday and 32 per day on Sunday. A one-way fare costs 255 ptas. ($1.55).

For a radio taxi, call ☎ **971-75-54-40** or 971-40-14-14.

If you plan to stay in Palma, you don't need a car. The city is extremely traffic clogged. Scarcity of parking is another reason not to have a car. If you'd like to take our driving tour, you can rent cars at such companies as the Spanish-owned **Atesa** at Passeig Marítim (☎ **971-78-98-96**), where rentals range from 7,500 to 15,000 ptas. ($45 to $90) per day. **Avis** at Passeig Marítimo, 16 (☎ **971-73-07-20**) is well stocked with cars; its rates range from 9,000 to 28,000 ptas. ($54 to $168) per day. Both Atesa and Avis maintain offices at the airport. Reservations, however, should always be made in advance, especially in summer.

Majorca

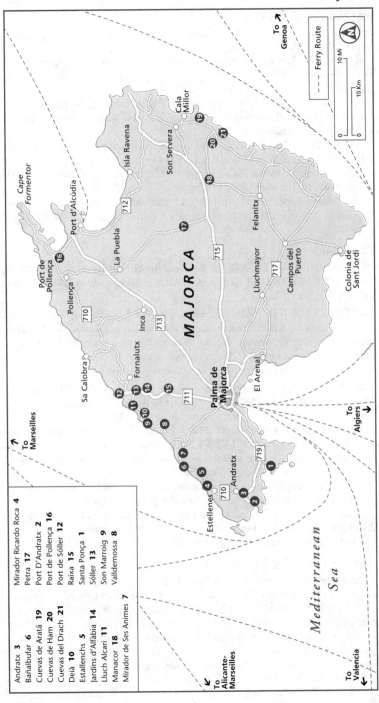

Andratx **3**
Bañalbufar **6**
Cuevas de Aratá **19**
Cuevas de Ham **20**
Cuevas del Drach **21**
Deià **10**
Estallenchs **5**
Jardins d'Alfàbia **14**
Lluch Alcari **11**
Manacor **18**
Mirador de Ses Ánimes **7**

Mirador Ricardo Roca **4**
Petra **17**
Port D'Andratx **2**
Port de Pollença **16**
Port de Sóller **12**
Raixa **15**
Santa Ponça **1**
Sóller **13**
Son Marroig **9**
Valldemossa **8**

PALMA DE MAJORCA

Palma, on the southern tip of the island, is the seat of the autonomous government of the Balearic Islands, as well as the center for most of Majorca's hotels, restaurants, and nightclubs. The Moors constructed Palma in the style of a casbah, or walled city. Its roots are still visible, although obscured by the high-rise hotels that have cropped up.

Old Palma is typified by the area immediately surrounding the cathedral. Mazes of narrow alleys and cobblestoned streets echo the era when Palma was one of the chief ports in the Mediterranean.

Today Palma is a bustling city whose massive tourist industry has more than made up for its decline as a major seaport. It's estimated that nearly half the population of the island lives in Palma. Majorca attracts the largest number of visitors of any place in the Balearics. The islanders call Palma simply *Ciutat* ("City"), and it is the largest of the Balearic ports, its bay often clogged with yachts. Arrival by sea is the most impressive, with the skyline characterized by Bellver Castle and the bulk of the cathedral.

ESSENTIALS

VISITOR INFORMATION   The **National Tourist Office** is in Palma at Plaça Reyna, 2 (☎ **971-71-22-16**). It's open Monday to Friday 9am to 7:30pm, Saturday 10am to 1:30pm.

GETTING AROUND   In Palma, you can get around on foot (the only way, really), especially if you plan to sightsee or shop in the Old Town. Likewise, you can explore the Paseo on foot. Otherwise, you can make limited use of taxis for getting around Palma or use one of the buses that cut across the city. Out on the island, you'll have to depend mainly on buses or rented cars for transportation.

FAST FACTS   The **U.S. Consulate,** avinguda Jaime III, 26 (☎ **971-72-26-60**), is open 10:30am to 1:30pm Monday to Friday. The **British Consulate,** Plaça Mayor, 3 (☎ **971-71-24-45**), is open 9am to 3pm Monday to Friday.

In case of an **emergency,** dial ☎ **112.** If you fall ill, head to the **Centro Médico,** avenida Juan March, 8 (☎ **971-75-14-14**), a private facility.

Majorca observes the same **holidays** as the rest of Spain but also celebrates June 29, the Feast of St. Peter, the patron saint of all fishers.

The central **post office** is at carrer Constitució, 6 (☎ **902-19-71-97**). Hours are Monday to Friday 8:30am to 8:30pm, Saturday 9:30am to 2pm.

Local newsstands and tobacco shops sell phone cards valued between 500 and 2,000 ptas. ($3 and $12). They can be used in any public telephone booth, and allow you to make both domestic and international calls.

FUN ON & OFF THE BEACH

There is a beach fairly close to the cathedral in Palma, but some readers have been discouraged from swimming here because of foul-smelling, albeit covered, sewers nearby. The closest public beach is **Playa Nova,** a 35-minute bus ride from downtown Palma. Some hotels, however, have private beaches. If you head east, you reach the excellent beaches of **Ca'n Pastilla.** The beaches at **El Arenal** are very well equipped with tourist facilities and have golden sands as well. Going to the southwest, you find good but often crowded beaches at **Cala Mayor** and **Sant Agustí.**

You can swim from late June to October; don't believe the promoters who try to sell you on mild Majorcan winters in January and February—it can get downright cold. Spring and fall can be heaven sent, and in summer the coastal areas are pleasantly cooled by sea breezes.

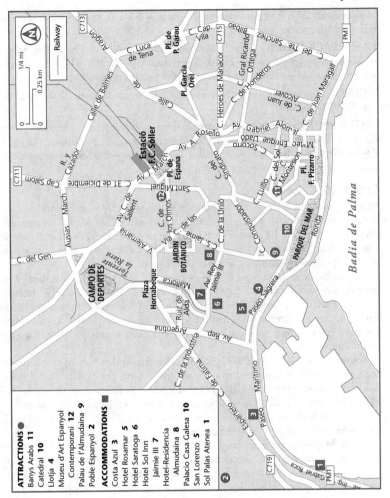

ATTRACTIONS ●
Banys Arabs **11**
Catedral **10**
Llotja **4**
Museu d'Art Espanyol
   Contemporani **12**
Palau de l'Almudaina **9**
Poble Espanyol **2**

ACCOMMODATIONS ■
Costa Azul **3**
Hotel Rosamar **5**
Hotel Saratoga **6**
Hotel Sol Inn
   Jaimie III **7**
Hotel-Residencia
   Almudaina **8**
Palacio Casa Galesa **10**
San Lorenzo **5**
Sol Palas Atenea **1**

BIKING   The best places for biking on the island are C'an Picafort, Alcúdia, and Port de Pollença, all along the north coast, because they are relatively flat. Most roads have special bike lanes on the island, as it's a popular sport here. For rentals, go to **Belori Bike,** Edificio Pilarki, calle Maravalla, 22, Arenal (☎ **971-49-03-58**). Depending on their model, and how many gears they have, pedal bikes rent for 800 to 2,500 ptas. ($4.80 to $15) per day.

GOLF   Majorca is a golfer's dream. The best course is the Son Vida Club de Golf, Urbanización son Vida, about 8 miles (13km) east of Palma along the Andrade highway. This 18-hole course is shared by the guests of the island's two best hotels, Arabella Golf Hotel and the Son Vida. However, the course is open to all players who call for reservations (☎ **971-79-12-10**). Greens fees are 9,000 ptas. ($54) for 18 holes.

HIKING   Because of the hilly terrain in Majorca, this sport is better pursued here than on Ibiza or Minorca. The mountains of the northwest, the Serra de Tramuntana, are best for exploring. The tourist office (see above) will provide you with a free booklet called *20 Hiking Excursions on the Island of Majorca,* which includes detailed maps and itineraries.

HORSEBACK RIDING The best stables on the island are at **The Riding School of Majorca,** at km 12 on the Palma–Sóller road. Call ☎ **971-61-31-57** to make arrangements and get directions from wherever you are on the island.

TENNIS If your hotel doesn't have a court, head for the **Club de Tenis,** carrer Sil, s/n (☎ **971-69-22-61**).

WATER SPORTS Most beaches have outfitters who will rent you windsurfers and dinghies. The best diving operation is **Planet Escuba,** Pont Adriano (☎ **971-23-43-06**). Divers here are highly skilled and will take you to the most intriguing sights underwater if you are a qualified diver.

SHOPPING

Shopping in Palma offers handcrafts, elegant leather goods, Majorcan pearls, and fine needlework. The best shopping is on the following streets: San Miguel, carrer Sindicato, Jaume II, Jaume III, carrer Platería, Vía Roman, and Passeig des Borne, plus the streets radiating from the Borne all the way to Plaça Cort, where the city hall stands. Most shops close on Saturday afternoon and Sunday.

Elegant boudoirs throughout Europe are furnished with finely textured needlework from the famous **Casa Bonet,** Plaça Federico Chopin, 2 (☎ **971-72-21-17**), founded in 1860. Each of the sheets, tablecloths, napkins, and pillowcases is made in Majorca from fine linen or cotton (also, for the less expensive items, from acrylic). Many are hand-embroidered, using ancient designs and floral motifs popularized by this establishment.

Loewe, Jaime III, 1 (☎ **971-71-52-75**), offers fine leather, elegant accessories for men and women, luggage, and chic apparel for women. For funkier leather items, head for **Pink,** avinguda Jaume III, 3 (☎ **971-72-23-33**). **Passy,** avinguda Jaume III, 6 (☎ **971-71-33-38**), offers high-quality, locally made shoes, handbags, and accessories for men and women. There's another branch at carrer Tous y Ferrer, 8 (☎ **971-71-73-38**), although it's not as well stocked.

Perlas Majorica, avinguda Jaume III, 11 (☎ **971-72-52-68**), is the authorized agency for the authentic Majorcan pearl. It's an elegant shop with fanciful wrought-iron gates. The pearl producers employ hundreds of artisans to make and design their stunning jewelry, and they offer a decade-long guarantee for their products. Pearls come in varied sizes and settings, of course.

SEEING THE SIGHTS

Most visitors don't spend much time exploring the historic sights in Palma, but there are a number of places to see if you've had too much sun.

Viajes Sidetours, Passeig Marítim, 16 (☎ **971-28-39-00**), offers numerous full- and half-day excursions throughout Palma and the surrounding countryside. The full-day excursion to Valldemossa and Sóller takes visitors through the monastery where former island residents Chopin and his lover, George Sand, spent their scandalous winter. After leaving the monastery, the tour explores the peaks of the Sierra Mallorquina, then makes its way to the seaside town of Sóller. A visit to the Arabian gardens of Raixa or Alfàbia is included in the 3,800 ptas. ($22.80) cost of the tour, on Wednesday only.

Another full-day tour of the mountainous western side of the island is conducted by train and boat, including a ride on one of Europe's oldest railways to the town of Sóller and the Monasterio de Lluch, as well as a boat ride between the port of Sóller and La Calobra. Daily tours cost 6,800 ptas. ($40.80). The eastern coast of Majorca is explored in the Caves of Drach and Hams tour. A concert on the world's largest underground lake (Lake Martel), tours through the caves, a stop at an olivewood works, and a visit to the Majorica Pearl Factory are all covered daily in the 5,800 ptas. ($34.80) cost. Times of departure may vary.

✪ **Catedral.** Carrer Palau Reial. ☎ **971-72-31-30.** Free admission to cathedral; museum and treasury 500 ptas. ($3). Mon–Fri 10am–6pm; Sat 10am–2pm. Bus: 15.

This graceful Catalonian Gothic cathedral, called La Seu, stands in the old town overlooking the seaside. It was begun during the reign of Jaume II (1276–1311) and completed in 1601. Its central vault is 144 feet high, and its columns rise 65 feet. There is a scalloped-edged, wrought-iron *baldachin* (canopy) by Gaudí over the main altar. The treasury contains supposed pieces of the True Cross and relics of St. Sebastián, patron saint of Palma. Museum and cathedral hours are often subject to change; call ahead to make sure they're accepting visitors before you go.

Castell de Bellver. Between Palma and Illetas. ☎ **971-73-06-57.** Admission 260 ptas. ($1.55) adults, 150 ptas. ($0.90) children, students, and seniors. Sun free. Daily 8am–8pm. Museum closed Sun. Bus: 3, 4, 21, or 22.

Erected in 1309, this hilltop round castle was once the summer palace of the kings of Majorca—during the short period when there were kings of Majorca. The castle, which was a fortress with a double moat, is well preserved and now houses the Museu Municipal, which is devoted to archaeological objects and old coins. It's really the view from here, however, that is the chief attraction. In fact, the name, Bellver, means exactly that: beautiful view.

Museu d'Art Espanyol Contemporani, Fundación Juan March. Carrer Sant Miquel, 11. ☎ **971-71-35-15.** Admission 500 ptas. ($3) adults, 250 ptas. ($1.50) seniors and children. Mon–Fri 10am–6:30pm; Sat 10am–1:30pm.

The Juan March Foundation's Museum of Spanish Contemporary Art reopened in 1997, with a series of newly acquired modern paintings. The works represent one of the most fertile periods of 20th-century art, with canvasses by Picasso, Miró, Dalí, and Juan Gris, as well as Antoni Tàpies, Carlos Saura, Miquel Barceló, Luis Gordillo, Susana Solano, and Jordi Teixidor. A room devoted to temporary exhibits was added to the restored museum. One series, for example, featured 100 Picasso engravings from the 1930s. The oldest and best-known work in the museum is Picasso's *Head of a Woman,* from his cycle of paintings known as Les Demoiselles d'Avignon. These works form part of the collection that the Juan March Foundation began to amass in 1973.

Llotja. Passeig Sagrera. ☎ **971-71-17-05.** Free admission. Tues–Sat 11am–2pm and 5–9pm; Sun 11am–2pm. Bus: 15.

This 15th-century Gothic structure is a leftover from the wealthy mercantile days of Majorca. La Lonja (its Spanish name) was, roughly, an exchange or guild. Exhibitions here are announced in local newspapers.

Banys Arabs. Carrer Serra, 7. ☎ **971-72-15-49.** Admission 175 ptas. ($1.05). Daily 9:30am–7pm. Bus: 15.

You can spend hours exploring the narrow streets of the medieval quarter (Barri Gòtic) east of the cathedral. Along the way, you may want to visit these Moorish baths that date from the 10th century. The baths are the only complete remaining Moorish-constructed buildings in Palma, evoking life in the heyday of the caliphate. One room contains a dome supported by 12 columns.

Palau de l'Almudaina. Carrer Palau Reial. ☎ **971-72-71-45.** Admission 400 ptas. ($2.40) adults, 225 ptas. ($1.35) children; free on Wed. Apr–Oct, Mon–Sat 10am–2pm and 4–6:30pm; off-season, Mon–Sat 10:30am–2pm and 4–6pm. Closed holidays. Bus: 15.

Long ago Muslim rulers erected this splendid fortress surrounded by Moorish-style gardens and fountains opposite the cathedral. During the short-lived reign of the kings of Majorca, it was converted into a royal residence that evokes the Alcázar at Málaga. Now it is one of the most popular attractions of Palma and houses a museum displaying antiques, arts, suits of armor, and Gobelin tapestries. Panoramic views of the harbor of Palma can be seen from here.

Poble Espanyol. Carrer Capitán Mesquida Veny, 39. ☎ **971-73-70-75.** Admission 800 ptas. ($4.80) adults, 700 ptas. ($4.20) children. Apr–Nov, daily 9am–8pm; Dec–Mar, daily 9am–6pm. Bus: 5.

This is a touristy collection of buildings evoking Spain in miniature and is similar to the Poble Espanyol in Barcelona. Bullfights are held in its *corrida* on summer Sundays. There are mock representations of such famous structures as the Alhambra in Granada, the Torre de Oro in Seville, and El Greco's House in Toledo.

Marineland. Costa d'en Blanes. ☎ **971-67-51-25.** Admission 1,900 ptas. ($11.40) adults, 1,025 ptas. ($6.15) children 3–12, free for children 2 and under. Mon–Fri 10:30am–1pm and 4–6pm; Sat–Sun 11:30am–2:30pm and 5–6:45pm. Closed 4 weeks Nov–Dec. Direct bus, marked MARINELAND, from Palma rail station.

Eleven miles (18km) west of Palma, just off the coast road en route to Palma Nova, this attraction offers a variety of amusements—dolphin, sea lion, and parrot shows. There's a Polynesian pearl-diving demonstration and a small zoo. You'll find a cafeteria, picnic area, and children's playground, as well as beach facilities.

WHERE TO STAY

Majorca has a staggering number of hotels, but it's still not enough to hold the crowds in August. If you go in high season, reserve well in advance.

Some of our hotel recommendations in Palma are in the El Terreno section, the heart of the local nightlife. Don't book into one of these hotels unless you like plenty of action, continuing until late at night. More conservative readers may find it unsavory. If you want peace and quiet, check our other suggestions.

Palma's suburbs, notably Cala Mayor, about 2½ miles (4km) from the center, and San Agustín, about 3 miles (5km) from town, continue to sprawl. In El Arenal, part of Playas de Palma, there is a huge concentration of hotels. The beaches at El Arenal are quite good but have a Coney Island atmosphere. We have a number of hotel recommendations in these suburbs for those who don't mind staying outside the city center.

Very Expensive

✪ **Arabella Sheraton Golf Hotel.** Carrer de la Vinagrella, 07013 Palma de Majorca. ☎ **971-79-99-99.** Fax 971-79-99-97. www.deg.com/arabella.htm. E-mail: arabella@arabella.es. 93 units. A/C MINIBAR TV TEL. 46,000–55,000 ptas. ($276–$330) double; from 62,000 ptas. ($372) suite. Rates include breakfast. AE, DC, MC, V. Parking free or 600 ptas. ($3.60) in garage. Bus: 7.

In 1992, the German-based Arabella chain bought this hotel, with its rolling grounds, as well as the Son Vida Hotel (which can be reached after a brisk 10-minute walk) and its 18-hole golf course. The ecology of the area surrounding the complex has been fiercely protected; it's about 3 miles (5km) northwest of the center of Palma. Don't come here expecting raucous good times on the beach; the resort is elegant and rather staid. Its focal point is a sprawling outdoor swimming pool, one of the most appealing on the island. There's no health club and no shuttle to the beach; many visitors drive to the several nearby beaches. But it does boast one of the only hotel bullrings in Spain!

The complex is low-rise, intensely landscaped, and offers views over the golf course (not of the sea) from many of its good-size rooms. Accommodations include white walls, dark-stained furnishings, wall-to-wall carpeting, and in all but the least expensive accommodations, a balcony or veranda.

Dining/Diversions: The **Plat d'Or** restaurant expects men to wear jackets and ties in the evening. A grill room, **Foravila,** is somewhat less formal yet very, very stylish. There are three bars.

Amenities: Room service, concierge, shuttle limousine to and from the airport, beauty salon/barbershop, plus complete sports facilities: golf, five tennis courts, minigolf, windsurfing, waterskiing, Turkish bath, sauna, whirlpool, horseback riding stables.

✪ **Palacio Casa Galesa.** Miramar, 8, 07001 Palma de Majorca. ☎ **971-71-54-00.** Fax 971-72-15-79. 12 units. A/C MINIBAR TV TEL. 30,250 ptas. ($181.50) double; 38,000–45,000 ptas. ($228–$270) suite. AE, MC, V. Closed 1 week at Christmas. Parking 1,700 ptas. ($10.20).

For generations this 15th-century townhouse languished as a decaying apartment building facing the side of the cathedral. Beginning in 1993, an entrepreneurial couple from Cardiff, Wales, restored the place, salvaging the original marble floors and stained-glass windows, sheathing the walls of the public areas with silk, and adding discreetly concealed modern amenities. Today, the setting is the most alluring in all of Palma, loaded with English and Spanish antiques and paintings, and accented throughout with bouquets of flowers. Most rooms overlook an enclosed courtyard draped with potted plants and climbing vines. The rooms come in various shapes and sizes and are quite opulent, with Persian rugs, antiques, plush towels, and luxury mattresses. There's no restaurant, but a hearty buffet is served each morning.

Amenities: Baby-sitting, concierge, currency exchange, laundry and dry-cleaning service, room service, in-room massage, health club with whirlpool and sauna.

Son Vida. Raixa 21, 07013 Palma de Majorca. ☎ **800/223-6800** in the U.S., or 971-79-00-00. Fax 971-79-00-17. www.hsonvida.balears.net. E-mail: hsonvida@balears.net. 170 units. A/C MINIBAR TV TEL. 37,000–45,000 ptas. ($222–$270) double; 71,600–134,000 ptas. ($429.60–$804) suite. Rates include breakfast. AE, DC, MC, V. Free parking. Bus: 7.

Set in a 13th-century castle in the Son Vida hills, on a secluded hilltop several miles from Palma, this hotel commands the most panoramic views on the island. Many rooms are in a modern wing, a pleasing reproduction of a Spanish hacienda. Inside, the public rooms are swathed in sumptuous fabrics, Oriental rugs, and chandeliers. Guest rooms in the new building are not quite as distinctive as those in the castle. Many rooms have private balconies or terraces. Expect spacious closets, bathrooms with touches of marble, hair dryers, deluxe toiletries, and plush towels. Most accommodations are spacious, with such amenities as two phones and private safes. All beds are wide and firm.

Dining/Diversions: Two restaurants, the **Bellver** and the **Jardín,** serve excellent international cuisine, enhanced by an extensive wine list. A piano bar, open from 10pm to 2am, is an ideal location for an after-dinner drink.

Amenities: 24-hour room service, shuttles to town and the beach, outdoor pool, tennis courts, golf course, fitness center, covered pool, solarium, Turkish bath, whirlpool, sauna, massage.

Expensive

Sol Palas Atenea. Passeig Ingeniero Gabriel Roca, 29, 07014 Palma de Majorca. ☎ **971-28-14-00.** Fax 971-45-19-89. www.solmelia.com. 370 units. A/C MINIBAR TV TEL. 25,000 ptas. ($150) double; 29,000 ptas. ($174) suite. Rates include breakfast. AE, DC, MC, V. Parking 1,650 ptas. ($9.90). Bus: 1.

A member of the Sol chain, this modern hotel offers extensive leisure facilities for vacationers, while still catering to business travelers. It overlooks the Bay of Palma, within walking distance of the town's major restaurants and shops. Spacious guest rooms have terraces, many overlooking the harbor or Bellver Castle. Furnishings are standardized, but the rooms are exceedingly comfortable, ranging from medium to spacious; all are fitted with excellently maintained tile bathrooms and wide, firm beds. An entire floor is designed for the special needs of the business traveler.

Dining/Diversions: A dining room and a cafe serve fine food. For evening entertainment you can choose from a piano bar, an outdoor terrace bar, or a nightclub.

Amenities: 24-hour room service, Club Elite floor for executives; outdoor and indoor pools, sauna, massage, whirlpool, solarium, beauty salon, shops.

Moderate

Hotel-Residencia Almudaina. Avinguda Jaume III, 9, 07012 Palma de Majorca. ☎ **971-72-73-40.** Fax 971-72-25-99. 78 units. A/C TV TEL. 11,875 ptas. ($71.25) double. AE, DC, MC, V. Free parking. Bus: 1 or 13.

Located on the main commercial street in Palma, this simple hotel offers comfortable, clean, basic rooms. Although small, each unit is well maintained and has a comfortable bed with a firm mattress. Because of its location, many of the rooms are quite loud; the quietest are in the rear. Some have terraces and glass doors letting in ample sunlight. The service is helpful, and the Almudaina has a cafeteria.

Hotel Saratoga. Passeig Majorca, 6, 07012 Palma de Majorca. ☎ **971-72-72-40.** Fax 971-72-73-12. 187 units. A/C MINIBAR TV TEL. 14,000–20,000 ptas. ($84–$120) double. Rates include breakfast. AE, MC, V. Parking 1,000 ptas. ($6). Bus: 50 from airport.

Under the arches of an arcade beside the old city's medieval moat stands the entrance to the Hotel Saratoga. Constructed in 1962 and renovated in 1992, the hotel features bright, well-furnished guest rooms, many with balconies or terraces with views of the bay and city of Palma. The mostly midsized rooms have fine linens and mattresses, and each of the tiled bathrooms is well maintained. The hotel has two pools—a small wading pool in the courtyard and a large rooftop pool. The Saratoga has a dining room and a seventh-floor bar, where live music and dances are presented.

✪ **San Lorenzo.** San Lorenzo, 14, 07012 Palma de Mallorca. ☎ **971-72-82-00.** Fax 971-71-19-01. www.fehm.es/pmi/sanlorenzo. E-mail: sanlorenzo@fehm.es. 6 units. A/C MINIBAR TV TEL. 20,000–25,000 ptas. ($120–$150) double; 32,500 ptas. ($195) suite. AE, DC, MC, V.

This small, attractive hotel is set in the middle of the maze of winding streets that form the old city of Palma. The building is 18th century and the decor is a pleasant mixture of traditional Majorcan and modern. The rooms are airy, painted white, and have good-sized, comfortable beds, satellite television, safes, and bathrooms that include hair dryers. All rooms have beamed ceilings and while some have only balconies, the more luxurious offer fireplaces and a private terrace. There is an indoor bar, but the real bonus is a pool, surrounded by lush foliage and a sun terrace—it's perfect for relaxing after a day of sightseeing or shopping.

Inexpensive

Costa Azul. Passeig Marítim, 7, 07014 Palma de Majorca. ☎ **971-73-19-40.** Fax 971-73-19-71. www.jehm.es/pmi/costa. E-mail: costa@arrakis.es. 126 units. A/C TV TEL. 13,500–18,000 ptas. ($81–$108) double. AE, MC, V. Bus: 3 or 21.

Head here for a bargain—despite the reasonable rates, you'll get views of the yachts in the harbor. This place isn't glamorous, but it does offer good value. A short taxi ride will deposit you at night on the Plaça Gomila in El Terreno with its after-dark diversions. Barren, well-worn rooms are clean, but furnished in very modest style, each with a good bed. On the ground floor is a bar and restaurant, very Iberian in decor, offering buffet meals three times a day. A tiny pool on the third floor is heated for winter visitors who are often booked in here on package tours from England.

Hotel Rosamar. Joan Miró, 74, 07015 Palma de Majorca. ☎ **971-73-27-23.** Fax 971-28-38-28. www.illes.balears.net/rosamar. 37 units. 7,500–8,500 ptas. ($45–$51) double. Rates include breakfast. MC, V. Bus: 3, 4, 21, or 22.

Hotel Rosamar, right on the main road in the boomtown El Terreno district, is popular with Germans and Scandinavians. Fresh, clean, but small rooms have balconies overlooking a front patio surrounded by tall palm trees—the focus of the social life of the young, lively crowd that frequents the Rosamar. There's a stand-up bar off the lobby.

Hotel Sol Inn Jaime III. Passeig Majorca, 14B, 07012 Palma de Majorca. ☎ **971-72-59-43.** Fax 971-72-59-46. 88 units. A/C MINIBAR TV TEL. 16,000 ptas. ($96) double. AE, DC, MC, V. Bus: 8.

This modern hotel has a pleasant contemporary lobby, a cafeteria, and a ground-floor cafe that usually spills out onto the sidewalk. All the small double rooms have sun terraces and basic contemporary furnishings, including good beds. The hotel is at the end of the major shopping street of Palma.

At Illetas

This suburb of Palma lies immediately west of the center.

Hotel Bon Sol. Paseo de Illetas, 30, 07015 Illetas. ☎ **971-40-21-11.** Fax 971-40-25-59. 88 units. A/C MINIBAR TV TEL. 18,700 ptas. ($112.20) double; 24,000–33,960 ptas. ($144–$203.75) suite. AE, DC, MC, V. Closed Oct. Free parking.

Set across from a beach, about 4 miles (6.5km) west of Palma, this four-star hotel was built in 1953 and renovated last in 1997. It charges less than hotels with similar amenities, and it's quite popular with vacationing families, who dine within the airy, somewhat spartan dining room. The core is a four-story, white-sided masonry tower, with some of the suites clustered into a simple collection of outlying villas. The hotel overlooks a garden, adjacent to the sea, with three swimming pools (two of them filled with seawater) and two tennis courts. The midsized rooms are larger than you might expect, efficient but comfortable and well suited to beachfront vacations.

Hotel Meliá de Mar. Paseo Illetas, 15, 07015 Calvia. ☎ **971-40-25-11.** Fax 971-40-58-52. 144 units. A/C MINIBAR TV TEL. 37,000–41,500 ptas. ($222–$249) double; from 85,000 ptas. ($510) suite. AE, DC, MC, V. Parking 1,500 ptas. ($9).

Originally built in 1964, and renovated most recently in 1998, the Meliá de Mar is one of the most comfortable (albeit expensive) hotels in Palma. This seven-story, four-star hotel is close to the beach and sports a large garden. The marble-floored lobby and light, summery furniture offer a cool refuge from the hot sun and a calm, deliberately uneventful setting that's evocative of some of the spa hotels of Central Europe. Rooms, mainly midsized, have many fine features, including private safes, original art, terra-cotta tiled balconies, marble or wrought-iron furnishings, excellent beds, and marble-clad bathrooms with plush towels, deluxe toiletries, hair dryers, and dual basins.

Dining/Diversions: A bar and a large, airy restaurant boast lots of space between tables and flavorful, but not particularly fussy, food.

Amenities: Swimming is available in an impressive pool, with the Mediterranean as a backdrop. The grounds have tennis and handball courts. Concierge, dry cleaning and laundry, massages, baby-sitting, currency exchange, valet parking.

At Portocolom

This hotel is on the eastern coast, reached by going east from Palma along C-717, then cutting north at the signposted directions.

✪ **Hotel Villa Hermosa/Restaurant Vista Hermosa.** Carretera Felanitx-Portocolom, km 6, 07670 Portocolom. ☎ **971-82-49-60.** Fax 971-82-45-92. 15 units. A/C MINIBAR TV TEL. 32,000 ptas. ($192) double; 42,000 ptas. ($252) suite. Rates include breakfast. AE, DC, MC, V. From Portocolom, follow signs to roads leading northeast to Felanitx.

This is one of the most creative five-star hotels on Majorca—a 1993 adaptation of a 19th-century farm. But it's not rustic; the building and outbuildings were recently reconstructed to profit from views that soar from the high-altitude hillside. Evocative of a severe, dignified monastery, set on elaborate terraces cut into the rocky hillside, the building (which has only 10 accommodations and a quite deliberate sense of privacy) wraps around a large, heated swimming pool. Rooms come in various shapes and sizes and each is exceedingly well furnished, with excellent beds and immaculately kept bathrooms with plush towels.

Dining: An in-house restaurant, **Vista Hermosa,** is the convivial center of social life here. Even if you aren't staying, you won't be alone if you opt for a meal—it's been booked solid virtually every night for at least a year. Meals are served daily 1 to 3:30pm and 7 to 10:30pm. There is an à la carte menu as well as a fixed-price menu for 6,000 ptas. ($36). Menu items are continental and sophisticated: maigret of duck flambéed in Calvados, loin of pork with basil and bacon, and fresh salmon with a confit of tomatoes.

Amenities: Swimming pool, on-site tennis courts, a small health club, room service, concierge.

At Santa Maria

✪ **Read's Hotel.** Ca'n Moragues, 07320 Santa Maria. ☎ **971-14-02-61.** Fax 971-14-07-62. www.readshotel.com. E-mail: readshotel@readshotel.com. 25 units. A/C TV TEL. 19,000–40,000 ptas. ($114–$240) double; 35,000–52,000 ptas. ($210–$312) suite. Rates include breakfast. AE, DC, MC, V. Free parking.

Peacefully located in beautiful countryside, this hotel is only 11 miles (18km) from Palma on the way to Inca Alcudia. The 16th-century Majorcan villa is now run by a British family and is a favorite spot for well-heeled northern Europeans. The building has been carefully renovated and furnished with a combination of good-quality reproduction furniture as well as genuine antiques. An unspoiled view of the Tramuntana Mountains forms the backdrop to the hotel, which is surrounded by gardens. Beamed ceilings and wooden shutters add an authentically traditional touch to the rooms, which have all been recently refurbished and painted in a variety of subtle Mediterranean colors. They are decorated with prints of classical architecture and Turkish rugs on traditional stone floors. There are various categories of rooms; the four deluxe doubles and 10 suites have French doors opening onto terraces with stunning views. The beds are all extremely comfortable and the bathrooms well stocked with hair dryers and plush towels. Four reception rooms include an extraordinary blue room with trompe l'oeil clouds painted on the walls and what was previously the olive pressing room, the *tafona,* in which the original fittings have been preserved.

Dining/Diversions: A hotel restaurant attracts foodies from Palma, and in summer diners can be served on an elevated terrace. Although a little pricey, the food is excellent and there is a special *menú del día,* without wine, of 7,000 ptas. ($42), which allows diners to choose any three dishes from the menu for the three courses. The tasting menu ranges from 9,000 to 12,000 ptas. ($54 to $72), depending on whether wine is included. There is also a bar.

Amenities: Indoor and outdoor swimming pool, sun terrace, whirlpool, tennis court, horseback riding, satellite television.

At Puigpunent

✪ **Gran Hotel Son Net.** Castillo Son Net, 07194 Puigpunent. ☎ **971-14-70-00.** Fax 971-14-70-01. www.sonnet.es. E-mail: son.net@jet.es. 24 units. A/C MINIBAR TV TEL. 35,000–42,250 ptas. ($210–$253.50) double; 95,000–110,000 ptas. ($570–$660) suite. AE, DC, MC, V. Free parking.

For those wanting a combination of total relaxation and luxury, this is the perfect destination. This 17th-century manor house is next to a nature reserve and nestles in a lush mountain valley 9 miles (14.5km) from Palma. It was converted from a private residence in 1998 by David Stein, a California tycoon and art collector. The result is one of Europe's best hotels. Apart from the glorious setting, the hotel boasts works by artists such as Hockney, Stella, and Christoph, and there's even a small Chagall on the walls. A classical Majorcan aristocratic sense of decoration has been followed faithfully, with white walls, stone floors, and dark wood beams and shutters. The rooms are spacious, the largest being 495 feet (151m) square, and all have satellite television. The bathrooms are fully equipped with necessities such as hair dryers and glamorous novelties such as antisteam mirrors. There are several reception rooms and an immense terrace with a seductive, curvaceous swimming pool of equally grandiose proportions. On Sunday, mass is said in the hotel's private chapel.

Dining: One of the very best features of the hotel is **Sa Tafona** restaurant, which is in the old olive pressing room and serves delicious food. Main courses range from 2,500 to 5,000 ptas. ($15 to $30), and there is a tasting menu for 7,000 ptas. ($42), wine extra.

Amenities: 24-hour room service, beauty salon, gym, sauna, whirlpool, tennis court, pool, access to the Internet.

At La Bonanova

This magnificently situated hotel is directly west of Palma and south of the sprawling grounds of Castell de Bellver, the round hilltop castle crowning Palma.

Valparaiso Palace. Calle Francisco Vidal Sureda, 23, 07015 Palma de Majorca. ☎ **971-40-03-00.** Fax 971-40-59-04. 174 units. A/C MINIBAR TV TEL. 36,000 ptas. ($216) double; from 55,000 ptas. ($330) suite. Rates include buffet breakfast. AE, DC, MC, V. Free parking.

Only minutes from the center of Palma and 1¼ miles from a good beach, this seven-story luxury property has operated since 1976 and was last renovated in 1996. The architecture is extremely modern and the entrance is set in the midst of landscaped gardens and an artificial lake. The lobby is impressive with its marble floors and pristine decor, and it's filled with an efficient and helpful staff. The rooms are spacious and handsomely furnished with comfortable mattresses and fully equipped bathrooms.

Dining/Diversions: Paraiso serves an eclectic range of cuisines and is one of the better hotel dining rooms on the island. There are two bistros for more informal dining, plus a lounge bar.

Amenities: Hairdresser, bridge room, two tennis courts, mini-golf, gym, sauna, massage, Turkish bath, three swimming pools (one indoor), limited room service, baby-sitting, laundry and dry cleaning, nearby golf courses.

At Palmanova

On the western coast, and west of Palma, this hotel enjoys a privileged position in the Urbanisation of Costa d'en Blanes, with two small beaches and an array of golf courses nearby. Count on a 10-minute drive from the center of Palma.

Hotel Punta Negra. Carretera Andaitz, km12, Costa d'en Blanes, 07181 Mallorca. ☎ **971-68-07-62.** Fax 917-68-39-19. E-mail: hpunta@teleline.es. 112 units. A/C MINIBAR TV TEL. 18,000 ptas. ($108) double; from 20,000 ptas. ($120) suite. Rates include continental breakfast. AE, DC, MC, V. Free parking.

In an exclusive area, this two-story hotel is surrounded by two Mediterranean beaches and an array of golf courses. Elegant and posh, it's constructed in a classical Majorcan style with white walls, antique furnishings, carpeted floors, and panoramic views of either the sea or pine forests. The hotel is only 1 mile from the yachting port of Puerto Portals. Spacious and beautifully furnished rooms are equipped with elegant bathrooms.

Dining/Diversions: In summer the **Garden Grill** prepares delicious locally caught broiled lobsters and fresh fish. There is a more formal restaurant serving international cuisine and opening onto beautiful views. Guests enjoy a music room and often listen to piano music, a violin, or a harp, perhaps a Spanish guitarist.

Amenities: Limited room service, concierge, laundry and dry cleaning, beauty salon, tennis club with clay courts, sauna, two swimming pools, three nearby golf courses.

WHERE TO DINE

The most typical main dish of Majorca is *lomo,* or pork loin, and it appears as the specialty in any restaurant offering Majorcan cuisine. *Lomo con col* is a method of preparation where the loin is enveloped in cabbage leaves and served with a sauce made with tomatoes, grapes, pinenuts, and bay leaf.

A local sausage, *sabrosada,* is made with pure pork and red peppers. Paprika gives it its characteristic bright red color. *Sopas mallorquínas* can mean almost anything, but basically it is mixed greens in a soup flavored with olive oil and thickened with bread. When *garbanzos* (chickpeas) and meat are added, it becomes a meal in itself.

The best known vegetable dish is *el tumbet,* a kind of cake with a layer of potato and another of lightly sauteed eggplant. Everything is covered with a tomato sauce and peppers, then boiled for a while. Eggplant, often served stuffed with meat or fish, is one of the island's vegetable mainstays. *Frito mallorquín* might include anything, but basically is a dish of fried onions and potatoes, mixed with red peppers, diced lamb liver, "lights" (lungs), and fennel. It's zesty, to say the least.

In the Balearic Islands, only Majorca produces wine, but this wine isn't exported. The red wine bottled around Felanitx and Binissalem adds Franja Roja and Viña Paumina to your wine list. Most of the wine, however, comes from Spain. *Café carajillo*—coffee with cognac—is a Spanish specialty particularly enjoyed by Majorcans.

Expensive

Diplomatic. Carrer Palau Reial, 5. ☎ **971-72-64-82.** Reservations recommended. Main courses 2,000–2,600 ptas. ($12–$15.60); fixed-price menu 1,500 ptas. ($9). AE, DC, MC, V. Mon–Fri 9am–10pm; Sat 9am–5pm. Bus: 1, 3, or 15. CONTINENTAL.

In the center of Palma, near the cathedral, this restaurant is an ideal spot for just about anything, from tapas to a full meal. Its fixed-price menu is a good value, but ordering à la carte is expensive. Set in a white stuccoed medieval building with exposed beams, it offers an intimate atmosphere. Start with pâté with green peppercorns. Next try sole with almonds, steak tartare, or the filet mignon in port wine. The owner and wine connoisseur Juan Contesti will be happy to help you select a vintage from his cellar to accompany your meal.

✪ **Koldo Royo.** Avinguda Gabriel Roca, 3. ☎ **971-73-24-35.** Reservations required. Main courses 1,800–2,800 ptas. ($10.80–$16.80); fixed-price menu (lunch only) 3,600 ptas.

($21.60); tasting menu 6,000 ptas. ($36). AE, MC, V. Mon–Fri 1:30–3:30pm; Mon–Sat 8:30–11:30pm. BASQUE.

This is the premier place to enjoy savory Basque cuisine; if you're baffled by the unusual dishes on the menu, a staff member will assist you. This big-windowed establishment lies about three-quarters of a mile south of Palma's cathedral, adjacent to a marina and one of the island's most popular beaches. Menu items run the gamut of Basque seafood dishes, including baked hake, tripe, lamprey eel, and roasted pork. Meal after meal, Koldo Royo serves the best food in Palma.

La Lubina. Muelle Viejo, s/n. ☎ **971-72-33-50.** Reservations recommended. Main courses 1,800–6,000 ptas. ($10.80–$36); fixed-price menu 2,500 ptas. ($15). AE, DC, MC, V. Daily 12:30–4pm and 8pm–midnight. Bus: 1, 4, or 21. SEAFOOD.

La Lubina's location on the old pier is responsible for the freshest seafood in Palma. Begin with an aperitif in the tiled bar and then dine in the formal dining room or the more casual enclosed terrace. The menu consists mainly of seafood, and La Lubina is known for its unique preparation and presentation. *Caldereta* (lobster served in an almond broth) is an excellent choice. Try the traditional Majorcan fish *en papillote* (baked in paper and encrusted with salt) or the grilled swordfish.

Lonja del Pescado (Casa Eduardo). Muelle Viejo, s/n. ☎ **971-72-11-82.** Reservations required. Main courses 1,400–2,000 ptas. ($8.40–$12). AE, MC, V. Tues–Sat 1–3:30pm and 8–11pm. Bus: 1 or 4. SEAFOOD.

Thriving since the 1930s, this no-frills restaurant serves the catch of the day, taken directly from the boat to the kitchen. Specialties include seafood paella and *zarzuela* (a fish stew). It's also possible to get fresh lobster. The rest of the menu consists of various types of fish, most prepared in the Majorcan style.

✪ **Mediterráneo 1930.** Passeig Marítimo, 33. ☎ **971-73-03-77.** Reservations recommended. Main courses 1,800–2,800 ptas. ($10.80–$16.80); fixed-price menu 2,500 ptas. ($15). AE, MC, V. Daily 1–4pm and 8–11:30pm. Bus: 1. MEDITERRANEAN.

Named after the art deco, 1930s-era styling that fills its interior, this is a well-managed, artfully hip restaurant adjacent to the Hotel Meliá Victoria. One of the top restaurants in Palma, with a sense of chic defined by its cosmopolitan owners Juan and Mary Martí, its beige and white decor is filled with verdant plants and art deco sculptures. The menu relies heavily on seafood, with special emphasis on fish slowly baked in a salt crust, a process that adds a light-textured flakiness to even the most aromatic fish. Another specialty is beefsteak cooked on a hot stone that's carried directly to your table and then served with such sauces as béarnaise, pepper, or port.

Porto Pí. Joan Miró, 174. ☎ **971-40-00-87.** Reservations required. Main courses 1,300–2,900 ptas. ($7.80–$17.40). DC, MC, V. Mon–Sat 1–3:30pm and 7:30–11:30pm. Bus: Palma-Illetas. MODERN MEDITERRANEAN.

This restaurant, a favorite of King Juan Carlos, occupies an elegant 19th-century mansion above the yacht harbor at the west end of Palma. Contemporary paintings

---

A Special Treat

Dating from 1700, **Can Juan de S'aigo,** carrer Sans, 10 (☎ **971-71-07-59**), is the oldest ice-cream parlor on the island. Correspondingly elegant and old world, it serves its homemade ice creams (try the almond), pastries, cakes, *ensaimadas* (light-textured and airy specialty cakes of Palma), fine coffee, and several kinds of hot chocolate amid marble-top tables, lots of wood, beautiful tile floors, and an indoor garden with a fountain.

---

complement the decor, and there is an outdoor terrace. The food has a creative Mediterranean influence. Specialties change with the season but might include house-style fish *en papillote,* angelfish with shellfish sauce, and quail stuffed with foie gras cooked in a wine sauce. Game is a specialty in winter.

✪ **Tristán.** Port Portals, Portals Nous. ☎ **971-67-55-47.** Reservations required. Main courses 1,800–4,200 ptas. ($10.80–$25.20). AE, DC, MC, V. Daily 1–3:30pm and 8:30–11pm. Closed mid-Nov to mid-Dec. Bus: 22. NOUVELLE CUISINE.

Several miles southwest of Palma, Tristán overlooks the marina of Port Portals. This is the finest restaurant in the Balearics, winning a coveted two stars from Michelin, a designation previously unheard of in the archipelago. The sophisticated menu varies, depending on what was best in the market that day. Selections may include pigeon in rice paper, a medley of Mediterranean vegetables, or the catch of the day, usually prepared in Majorcan style. But this is mere recitation. What it doesn't prepare you for is the exceptional burst of flavor when you sample the chef's creations.

Moderate

Arroseria Catranca. Passeig Marítim, 13. ☎ **971-73-74-47.** Reservations recommended. Main courses 1,200–3,000 ptas. ($7.20–$18). AE, DC, MC, V. Tues–Sun 1–4pm and Tues–Sat 8pm–midnight. Bus: 1. SEAFOOD.

This sophisticated, bilingual restaurant has a setting overlooking the port. Arroseria Catranca (whose name translates as "Rice Restaurant Catranca") specializes in seafood (in many cases, mixed with rice) served in 16 different variations. The best way to appreciate its somewhat offbeat charm is beginning a meal with grilled baby sardines or a well-seasoned version of *buñuelos de bacalau* (minced and herb-laden codfish formed into rounded patties). Either of these might be followed with a *parillada*—an array of grilled fish and shellfish—or any of the above-mentioned rice casseroles. Two of the best of them include black rice with squid and squid ink, or a particularly succulent version with spider crabs, clams, and mussels. Other variations include vegetables, roasted goat, or hake with tomatoes and garlic.

Caballito del Mar (Little Seahorse). Passeig de Sagrera, 5. ☎ **971-72-10-74.** Reservations recommended. Main courses 1,200–5,500 ptas. ($7.20–$33); *menú del día* 2,200 ptas. ($13.20). AE, DC, MC, V. Tues–Sun 1–4pm and 7pm–midnight. Bus: 5. SEAFOOD.

Although there are several outdoor tables, many guests prefer to dine inside because of the lively spirit of this popular place along the seafront. The decor is vaguely nautical, and the activity is sometimes frenzied, but that's part of its charm. The food is well prepared from fresh ingredients; specialties include a Majorcan version of bouillabaisse, *zarzuela* (fish stew), assorted grilled fish (our favorite), oysters in season, red bream baked in salt, or sea bass with fennel. If you want something other than seafood, try the duck in orange sauce.

Es Parlament. Carrer Conquistador, 11. ☎ **971-72-60-26.** Reservations recommended. Main courses 1,200–2,800 ptas. ($7.20–$16.80). No credit cards. Mon–Sat 1–4pm and 8–11pm. Closed Aug. Bus: 15. MAJORCAN.

Es Parlament is noted for the island's finest paella. The chef is proud of the half-dozen paella dishes, including "blind-man's paella," made without bones or shells, and "black paella," with the added ingredient of squid ink providing both coloring and extra flavoring. The restaurant, with its belle époque ambience, is housed in the Balearic Autonomous Parliament building.

Inexpensive

Ca'an Carlos. Carrer de s'Aigua, 5. ☎ **971-71-38-69.** Reservations recommended. Main courses 1,275–3,050 ptas. ($7.65–$18.30). AE, MC, V. Mon–Sat 1–4pm and 8–11pm. Closed 10 days in Aug. MAJORCAN.

Set in two dining rooms of a much-renovated stone-sided house that's at least a century old, this restaurant is the domain of an entrepreneur (named Carlos) who accentuates his native Majorcan roots in his cooking. Well-prepared menu items include *sabrosada,* a soft pork sausage flavored with pepper and paprika; chicken or fish croquettes; stuffed squid; eggplant stuffed with pulverized shellfish; and a version of the Majorcan national dish, *cocida Malorquina,* a succulent stew.

Cellar Pagés. Carrer Felipe Bauzá, 2. ☎ **971-72-60-36.** Reservations recommended. Main courses 850–1,600 ptas. ($5.10–$9.60); fixed-price menu 1,200 ptas. ($7.20). AE, DC, MC, V. Mon–Sat 1–4pm and 8:30–11pm. Bus: 15. MAJORCAN.

The set menu here can include soup, noodles, or gazpacho; steak or fish; and dessert, bread, and wine. From the à la carte menu you can select the fish of the day, which most guests prefer grilled. Other dishes include the classic kidneys in sherry or a roast chicken. Admittedly, this isn't the best cooking on the island, but the price is right. The rustic setting is cramped and intimate, with original paintings on the white stucco walls. The location is 75 yards west from the cathedral, a short walk from Plaça de la Reina.

La Bóveda. Calle Botería, 3. ☎ **971-71-48-63.** Reservations recommended for a table in the restaurant, not necessary for the tapas bar. Main courses 550–2,500 ptas. ($3.30–$15). AE, MC, V. Mon–Sat 1–4pm and 7–11:30pm. SPANISH.

Set in the oldest part of Palma, a few steps from the cathedral, this rustic-looking restaurant maintains a busy tapas bar near the entrance, and no more than 14 tables set near the bar or in the basement. Menu items include a predictable list of Spanish staples, each well prepared, including roasted or fried veal, pork, chicken, and fish, served with fresh greens, potatoes, or rice. Any of the roster of tapas from the bar (fava beans with strips of ham, spinach *tortillas,* grilled or deep-fried calamari, and shrimp with garlic sauce) can be served while you're at table, along with bottles of full-bodied red or more delicate white wines. A worthy and particularly refreshing dessert consists of freshly made sorbet, sometimes garnished with a shot of vodka or bourbon, depending on the flavor of the sorbet.

La Casita. Joan Miró, 68. ☎ **971-73-75-57.** Reservations recommended. Main courses 1,200–2,600 ptas. ($7.20–$15.60); fixed-price menu 1,200–1,800 ptas. ($7.20–$10.80). AE, DC, MC, V. Tues–Sun 1–4pm and 7pm–midnight. Closed Aug. Bus: 3. FRENCH/AMERICAN.

La Casita claims to serve French and American specialties, although the American influence is a bit hard to decipher. The ceiling fans, exposed wood, and paintings by John Winn-Morgan contribute to the ambience. À la carte dishes include French onion soup, tournedos with mushroom sauce, frogs' legs, pepper steak, and potato pancakes. For dessert, try the homemade apple pie.

Mesón Can Pedro. Carrer Rector Vives, 4. Génova. ☎ **971-40-24-79.** Reservations recommended. Main courses 750–2,000 ptas. ($4.50–$12). AE, DC, MC, V. Daily 1pm–1am. Bus: 4. MAJORCAN.

This restaurant has thrived since the early 1970s from a location in a hilltop suburb (Génova) overlooking Palma. A completely unpretentious local favorite, it's known for a bustling, animated atmosphere enhanced by odors wafting in from kitchens known for a succulent version of roasted baby lamb. Also worthwhile are T-bone steaks, roasted pork, spit-roasted chickens, spicy sausages, and different preparations of veal. One regional dish worth sampling is savory snails prepared with fennel and garlic and served with dollops of aïoli.

PALMA AFTER DARK

Palma is packed with bars and dance clubs. Sure, there are some fun hangouts along the island's northern tier, but for a rocking, laser- and strobe-lit club, you'll have to boogie in Palma.

Set directly on the beach, close to a dense concentration of hotels, **Tito's,** Passeig Marítimo (☎ **971-73-00-17**), charges a cover of 1,500 ptas. ($9), including the first drink. A truly international crowd gathers to mingle on a terrace overlooking the Mediterranean. This club is the most popular, panoramic, and appealing disco on Majorca. If you only visit one nightclub during your time on the island, this is it. Between June and September, it's open every night of the week from 11pm to at least 4am. The rest of the year, it's open only on Friday and Saturday, from 11pm to 4am.

Bar Barcelona, carrer Apuntadores, 5 (☎ **971-71-35-57**), a popular jazz club, evokes its namesake city with its spiral staircase and atmospheric, subdued lighting. Despite its location, in the heart of Palma's busiest nightlife area, it attracts a predominately local crowd who come to enjoy the live jazz on show every night 11pm to 3am. There is no cover charge, and drinks are reasonably priced, making this one of Palma's best values for a night out. It's open every night till 4am.

B.C.M., avinguda Olivera, s/n, Magaluf (☎ **971-13-15-46**), is the busiest, most lighthearted, and most cosmopolitan disco in Majorca. Boasting high-tech strobe lights and lasers, this sprawling, three-story venue offers a different sound system on each floor, giving you a wide variety of musical styles. If you're young, eager to mingle, and like to dance, this place is for you. The cover charge of 2,000 ptas. ($12) includes your first drink and entitles you to party till 4am.

Come and enjoy a Caribbean cocktail with one of Palma's more charismatic bar owners, Pasqual, who just might invite you to dance a bit of salsa at **Bodeguida del Medio,** Paseo el Mar, Cala Ratjada (no phone). The music is Latin inspired and the crowd is a mix of locals and visitors from almost everywhere. Try their delicious "mojito" cocktail, more potent than it tastes. Inside is rustic in tone, outside is more intimate and romantic with Chinese lanterns illuminating the garden, which overlooks the sea.

ABACO, carrer Sant Joan, 1 (☎ **971-71-59-11**), just might be the most opulently decorated nightclub in Spain—a cross between a harem and a czarist Russian church. The bar is decorated with a trove of European decorative arts. The place is always packed, with many customers congregating in a beautiful courtyard, which has exotic caged birds, fountains, more sculpture than the eye can absorb, extravagant bouquets, and hundreds of flickering candles. All this exoticism is enhanced by the lushly romantic music (Ravel's *Bolero,* at our last visit) piped in through the sound system. Whether you view this as a bar, a museum, or a sociological survey, be sure to go. The bar is open daily 9pm to 2:30am, February to December only. Wandering around is free; however, drinks cost a whopping 1,500 to 2,100 ptas. ($9 to $12.60).

At the end of the Andraitz motorway, adjacent to the Cala Figuera turnoff, the **Casino de Majorca,** Urbanización Sol de Mallarca, s/n, Costa del Calvía (☎ **971-13-00-00**), is the place to go in search of lady luck. The cover charge is 650 ptas. ($3.90); floor show with dinner but no drinks, 7,900 to 8,500 ptas. ($47.40 to $51); floor show without dinner but with two drinks, 5,900 ptas. ($35.40). Children under 12 get discounts of 50%. If you bring your passport, you can indulge in American or French roulette, blackjack, or dice, or simply pull the lever on one of the many slot machines. A glittery cabaret show, styled in Monte Carlo fashion, is accessible through a separate entrance from the section of the casino devoted to gambling. It's presented every Monday to Saturday at 10:30pm. You might want to precede it with dinner, which is served beginning at 8pm, although we usually prefer to dine elsewhere on the island, then arrive in time for the show at 10:30pm. The casino's gambling facilities are open Sunday to Thursday 8pm to 4am, and Friday and Saturday 8pm to 5am.

Although Majorca is generally a pretty permissive place, it doesn't have the gay scene that Ibiza does. Still, two of Palma's most noteworthy gay bars include **Sombrero,** avenida Joan Miró, 26 (☎ 971-73-16-00), a music pub attracting a predominately lesbian crowd, and **Baccus,** carrer Lluis Fábregas, 1 (☎ 971-45-77-89), catering to both gays and lesbians. Both of them are open nightly 9pm to at least 3am, and often later. Neither charges a cover, and beers in both sites begin at 400 ptas. ($2.40). If you feel like dancing, the largest and most popular disco in Palma is **Black Cat,** avenida Joan Miró, 75 (no phone), which attracts a mixed crowd of young locals as well as visitors from Spain and the rest of the world. There are nightly shows at 3:30am. It is open daily midnight to 6am but doesn't begin to get crowded until 2am. It is closed on Mondays over the winter. Admission is 1,000 ptas. ($6).

EXPLORING MAJORCA BY CAR: THE WEST COAST

Mountainous Majorca has the most dramatic scenery in the Balearics. It's best appreciated if you have your own car and can explore easily on your own. Below, we'll outline a good day-long outing of about 88 miles (142km) that begins and ends in Palma.

Leave Palma heading west on C-719, passing through some of the most beautiful scenery of Majorca. Just a short distance from the sea rises the Sierra de Tramontana. The road passes the heavy tourist development of Palma Nova before coming to **Santa Ponça,** a town with a fishing harbor divided by a promontory. A fortified Gothic tower and a watchtower are evidence of the days when this little harbor suffered repeated raids and attacks. It was in a cove here that Jaume I's troops landed on September 12, 1229, to begin the reconquest of the island from the Muslims.

From Santa Ponça, continue along the highway, passing Paguera, Cala Fornells, and Camp de Mar, all beautiful spots with sandy coves. Between Camp de Mar and Port D'Andratx are corniche roads, a twisting journey to **Port D'Andratx.** Summer vacationers mingle with fishers in this natural port, which is set against a backdrop of pines. Once the place was a haven for smugglers.

Leaving the port, continue northeast along C-719 to reach **Andratx,** 3 miles (5km) away. Because of frequent raids by Turkish pirates, this town moved inland. Lying 19 miles (30.5km) west of Palma, Andratx is one of the loveliest towns on the island, surrounded by fortifications and boasting a Gothic parish church and the mansion of Son Mas.

After leaving Andratx, take C-710 north, a winding road that runs parallel to the island's jagged northwestern coast. It's the highlight of the trip; most of the road is perched along the cliff edge. It's hard to drive and pay attention to the scenery at the same time. Pine trees often shade this corniche road. Stop at the **Mirador Ricardo Roca** for a panoramic view of a series of coves. These coves can be reached only from the sea.

The road continues to **Estallenchs,** a town of steep slopes surrounded by pine groves, olive and almond trees, and fruit orchards (especially apricot). Estallenchs sits at the foot of the Galatzo mountain peak. Stop and explore some of its steep, winding streets on foot. From the town, you can walk to the Cala de Estallenchs cove, where a spring cascades down the high cliffs.

The corniche road winds on to **Bañalbufar,** 5 miles (8km) from Estallenchs and about 16 miles (26km) west from Palma—one of the most scenic spots on the island. Set 110 yards (100m) above sea level, it seems to perch directly over the sea. ✪ **Mirador de Ses Animes,** a belvedere constructed in the 17th century, offers a panoramic view of the coastline.

Many small excursions are possible from here. You might want to venture over to **Port d'es Canonge,** reached by a road branching out from the C-710 to the north of Bañalbufar. It has a beach, a simple restaurant, and some old fishers' houses. The same road takes you inland to **San Granja,** a mansion that was originally constructed by the Cistercians as a monastery in the 13th century.

Back on C-710, continue to **Valldemossa,** the town where the composer Frédéric Chopin and the French writer George Sand spent their now-famous winter. After a visit to the **Cartuja** (Cathusian monastery), where they lived, you can wander at leisure through the steep streets of the old town. The cloister of **Ses Murteres** provides a romantic garden, and there is a pharmacy where Chopin, who was ill a lot during that winter, spent much time. The **Carthusian Church** is from the late 18th and early 19th centuries. Goya's father-in-law, Bayeu, painted the frescoes of the dome.

Beyond Valldemossa, the road runs along cliffs some 1,300 feet (395m) high until they reach **Son Marroig,** the former residence of Archduke Luis Salvador (see "Valldemossa & Deià (Deyá)," below), which is actually within the town limits of Deià. He erected a small neoclassical temple on a slope overlooking the sea to give visitors a panoramic vista. Son Marroig, his former mansion, has been turned into a museum. From an arcaded balcony, you can enjoy a view of the famous pierced rock, the Foradada, rising out of the water.

By now you have reached **Deià,** where a series of small tile altars in the streets reproduces scenes from the Calvary. This was the home for many years of the English writer Robert Graves. He is buried at the **Campo Santo,** the cemetery, which you may want to visit for its panoramic view, if nothing else. Many other foreign painters, writers, and musicians have found inspiration in Deià. For living and dining, this is the choice spot on Majorca, a virtual Garden of Eden.

Continue north along the highway. You come first to **Lluch Alcari,** which Archduke Salvador considered one of the most beautiful spots on earth. Picasso retreated here for a short period in the '50s. The settlement was once the victim of pirate raids, and you can see the ruins of several defense towers.

C-710 continues to **Sóller,** just 6 miles (10km) from Deià. The urban center has five 16th-century facades, an 18th-century convent, and a parish church of the 16th and 17th centuries. It lies on a broad basin where citrus and olive trees are abundant. Many painters, including Rusiñol, settled here and found inspiration.

Travel 3 miles (5km) north on C-711 to reach the coast and **Port de Sóller,** one of the best of the natural shelters along the island. It lies at the back of a bay that is almost round. A submarine base is here today, but it is also a harbor for pleasure craft. It has a lovely beach. The **Sanctuary of Santa Catalina** dominates one of the best views of the inlet.

Reached up a flight of stairs, **Restaurante Jaime,** carrer Archiduque Luis Salvador, 13 (☎ **971-63-90-29**), attracts both foreign visitors and the family trade. This unpretentious, family-run restaurant, in business since 1964, would make a good lunch stop in high-priced Deià. Grilled meats and fresh fish are a specialty. Even if you don't want a full meal, consider stopping here for dessert, such as the almond cake with almond ice cream, before finishing your drive. Hours are Tuesday to Sunday noon to 3pm and 7 to 11pm.

After leaving the Sóller area, you face a choice. If you've run out of time, you can cut the tour in half here and head back along C-711 to Palma with two stops along the way, or you can continue north, following the C-710 and local roads, to **Cape Formentor,** where even more spectacular scenery awaits you. Among the highlights of this coastal detour: **Fornalutx,** a lofty mountain village with steep cobbled streets, Moorish-tiled roofs, and groves of almond trees; the splendid, hair-raising road to the harbor village of **Sa Calobra,** plunging to the sea one minute, then climbing arduously past olive groves, oaks, and jagged boulders; and the 13th-century **Monasterio de Lluch,** some 28 miles (45km) north of Palma, which is home to the Black Virgin of Lluch, the island's patron saint. The well-known "boys' choir of white voices" sings there daily at noon and again at twilight.

Those ending the tour at this point can head south along C-711 with a stopover at **Jardins d'Alfàbia,** Carretera Palma–Sóller, km 17a, a former Muslim residence. This estate is in the foothills of the sierra and includes both a palace and romantic gardens. The gardens are richly planted, and you can wander among pergolas, a pavilion, and ponds. Inside the palace you can see a good collection of Majorcan furniture and an Arabic coffered ceiling. The gardens are open June to August, Monday to Friday 9:30am to 6:30pm, and Saturday 9:30am to 1pm; September to May, Monday to Friday 9:30am to 5:30pm, and Saturday 9:30am to 1pm. Admission is 400 ptas. ($2.40).

From Alfàbia, the highway becomes straight and Palma is just 11 miles (18km) away. But before reaching the capital, consider a final stop at **Raixa,** another charming place, built on the site of an old Muslim hamlet. It stands 1 mile (1.6km) outside the village of Buñola ("small vineyard"). The present building was once the estate of Cardinal Despuif and his family, who constructed it in the Italian style near the end of the 1700s. Ruins from Roman excavations are found on the grounds. Rusiñol came here, painting the place several times. It keeps the same hours as Jardins d'Alfàbia (see above).

After Raixa, the route leads directly to the northern outskirts of Palma.

VALLDEMOSSA & DEIÀ (DEYÁ)

Valldemossa is the site of the ✪ **Cartoixa Reial,** Plaça de las Cartujas, s/n (☎ **971-61-21-06**), where George Sand and the tubercular Frédéric Chopin wintered in 1838 and 1839. The monastery was founded in the 14th century, but the present buildings are from the 17th and 18th centuries. After monks abandoned the dwelling, the cells were rented to guests, which led to the appearance of Sand and Chopin, who managed to shock the conservative locals. They occupied cells 2 and 4. The only belongings left are a small painting and a French piano. The peasants burned most of it after the couple returned to the mainland, fearing they'd catch Chopin's tuberculosis. It may be visited Monday to Saturday 9:30am to 6pm for 1,200 ptas. ($7.20) adults, free for children under 10. Off-season it shuts down an hour earlier.

It's also possible to visit the **Palau del Rei Sancho,** next door to the monastery, on the same ticket. This is a Moorish retreat built by one of the island kings. You'll be given a guided tour of the palace by a woman in Majorcan dress.

From Valldemossa, continue through the mountains following the signposts for 6½ miles (10.5km) to Deià. But before your approach to the village, consider a stopover at **San Marroig** (☎ **971-63-91-58**), at the km 26 mark on the highway. Now a museum, this was once the estate of Archduke Luis Salvador. Born in 1847, the archduke fled court life and found refuge here with his young bride in 1870. A tower on the estate is from the 1500s. Many of his personal furnishings and mementos, such as photographs and his ceramic collection, are still here. The estate is surrounded by lovely gardens, and there are many panoramic views on the property. It is open April to October, Monday to Saturday 9:30am to 2pm and 3 to 8pm (closing at 6pm in winter). Admission is 350 ptas. ($2.10).

Set against a backdrop of olive-green mountains, **Deià (Deyá)** is peaceful and serene, with its stone houses and creeping bougainvillea. It has long had a special meaning for artists. Robert Graves, the English poet and novelist (*I, Claudius* and *Claudius the God*), lived in Deià, and died here in 1985. He is buried in the local cemetery.

After walking through the old streets, you can stand on a rock overlooking the sea and watch the sun set over a field of silvery olive trees and orange and lemon groves. Then you'll know why painters come here to live on the slopes of a 4,000-foot mountain.

Valldemossa lacks basic services, including a tourist office. It is connected to a bus service from Palma, however. **Bus Nord Balear** (☎ **971-26-24-75**) goes to Valldemossa five times daily for a one-way fare of 250 ptas. ($1.50). Buses leave from Palma at the bar at carrer Arxiduc Salvador, 1.

To reach Deià by public transportation from Palma, 17 miles (27km) away, just stay on the bus that stops in Valldemossa. If you're driving from Palma, take the Carretera Valldemossa–Deià to Valldemossa; from here, you can continue to Deià. Those with cars might want to consider one of the idyllic accommodations offered in this little Majorcan village, which has very few tourist facilities outside the hotels.

WHERE TO STAY

Deià offers some of the most tranquil and stunning retreats on Majorca—La Residencia and Es Molí—but it has a number of inexpensive little boarding houses as well.

Expensive

✪ **Hotel Es Molí.** Carretera de Valldemossa, s/n, 07179 Deià. ☎ **971-63-90-00.** Fax 971-63-93-33. www.fehm.es/hoteles/esmoli. E-mail: esmoli@fehm.es. 87 units. A/C MINIBAR TV TEL. 28,000–33,000 ptas. ($168–$198) double; 56,000–61,000 ptas. ($340–$366) suite. Supplement for a balcony 4,000 ptas. ($24) per room per day. $15 extra per person per day. Rates include breakfast; half-board 2,500 ptas. AE, DC, MC, V. Closed early Nov–late Apr. Free parking.

One of the best-recommended and most spectacular hotels on Majorca originated in the 1880s as a severely dignified manor house in the rocky highlands above Deià, home of the landowners who controlled access to the town's freshwater springs. In 1966 the manor house was augmented with two annexes, transforming into this luxurious four-star hotel. Rooms are beautifully furnished, monochromatic, and impeccably maintained, often with access to a private veranda overlooking the gardens or the faraway village. Some hardy souls make it a point to hike for 30 minutes to the public beach at Deià Bay; others wait for the shuttle bus to take them to the hotel's private beach, 4 miles (6 km) away.

Dining: An in-house restaurant, **Ca'n Quet,** has a stone-and-timber veranda with a view looking down the hillside (see recommendation under "Where to Dine," below).

Amenities: Room service, concierge, emphasis on multilingual, multicultural catering to clients and their needs, one of the most appealing swimming pools in Majorca (fed from the freshwater springs that used to sustain the village), private beach 4 miles (6 km) from hotel, tennis court on premises.

✪ **La Residencía.** Son Moragues, s/n, 07179 Deià. ☎ **971-63-90-11.** Fax 971-63-93-70. E-mail: laresidencia@atlas-iap.es. 63 units. A/C TEL. 25,000–40,000 ptas. ($150–$240) double; 45,000–107,000 ptas. ($270–$642) suite. Rates include breakfast. AE, DC, MC, V. Free parking.

This is the most stylish, hip, elegant hotel on Majorca, a renowned hostelry that became even more famous in the early 1990s when it was acquired by British businessman and founder of Virgin Airlines Richard Branson. The ambience is luxurious but unpretentious at these two tawny, stone, 16th-century manor houses, surrounded by 13 acres of rocky Mediterranean gardens. Guests have included everyone from Queen Sofia and the emperor of Japan to America's rock-and-roll elite. Spacious rooms are outfitted with rustic antiques, terra-cotta floors, romantic-looking four-poster beds, and in some cases, beamed ceilings, all with luxurious appointments, including plush towels and luxury mattresses. Open hearths, deep leather sofas, wrought-iron candelabra, and a supremely accommodating staff make this hotel internationally famous. Although it's technically defined as a four-star resort and a member of Relais & Châteaux, only the lack of such room amenities as minibars and TVs prevents it from reaching five-star status.

Dining: The more formal of the resort's two restaurants, **El Olivo,** lies within and around an antique olive press. A bar evokes the private salon of an arts-conscious landowner interested in abstract and surreal paintings. A less formal Mediterranean bistro, **Son Fony,** operates from beside the pool (at lunch in summer) and in a bistro-like Mediterranean area near the pool.

Amenities: Room service (8am to midnight), concierge, an elliptical 100-foot swimming pool lined with subtropical plants and bougainvillea, tennis court. Access to the beach, less than a mile away as the crow flies, requires a winding downhill minivan ride.

Inexpensive
Hotel Costa d'Or. Lluch Alcari, s/n, 07179 Deià. ☎ **971-63-90-25.** Fax 971-63-93-47. 43 units. A/C TV TEL. 10,500 ptas. ($63) double. Rates include breakfast. MC, V. Closed Nov–Apr 1.

This former villa, 1 mile (1.6km) north of Deià on the road to Sóller, has the best possible view of the vine-covered hills and the rugged coast beyond. Surrounded by private gardens filled with fig trees, date palms, and orange groves, this old-fashioned hotel is furnished with odds-and-ends furniture, but it's clean and comfortable. Most rooms have good views, and all come with good beds and tidy, small bathrooms. Good home-cooked meals are served in the restaurant.

WHERE TO DINE
✪ **Ca'n Costa.** Carretera Valldemossa–Deià, s/n. ☎ **971-61-22-63.** Reservations recommended. Main courses 1,200–2,200 ptas. ($7.20–$13.20). AE, DC, MC, V. Wed–Mon noon–4pm and 7:30–11pm. MAJORCAN/INTERNATIONAL.

This restaurant specializes in Majorcan cuisine but includes some international dishes to please the mostly foreign patronage. The owner has selected only the finest of wines from the island itself, which he has wisely combined with some good vintages from Rioja. The hearty regional fare includes roast pork loin with mushrooms from the fields and even thrush enveloped in cabbage. Try for a seat on the outdoor patio, with a panoramic vista of the coast.

Ca'n Quet. Carretera de Valldemossa–Sóller. ☎ **971-63-91-96.** Reservations required. Main courses 2,000–3,000 ptas. ($12–$18). AE, MC, V. Tues–Sun 1–4pm and 8–midnight. Closed Dec–Mar. INTERNATIONAL.

This restaurant, belonging to the Hotel Es Molí (see above), is one of the most sought-after dining spots on the island. Set on a series of terraces above a winding road leading out of town, the building is well scrubbed, modern, and stylish but with an undeniably romantic air. Cascades of pink geraniums ring its terraces, and if you wander along the sloping pathways you'll find groves of orange and lemon trees, roses, and a swimming pool ringed with neoclassical balustrades.

There is a spacious and sunny bar, an elegant indoor dining room with a blazing fire in winter and alfresco dining on the upper terrace under an arbor. The food is well prepared and the portions generous. Meals can include a salad of marinated fish, terrine of fresh vegetables, fish crêpes, shellfish stew, duck with sherry sauce, and an ever-changing selection of fresh fish.

El Olivo. In the La Residencia Hotel, San Canals. ☎ **971-63-93-92.** Reservations recommended. Main courses 2,600–4,500 ptas. ($15.60–$27); set-price menu 6,500–11,000 ptas. ($39–$66). AE, MC, V. Daily 1–3pm and 8–11pm. INTERNATIONAL/MEDITERRANEAN.

A 30- to 40-minute drive north of Palma, this is one of the island's most elegant and upscale restaurants, as shown by recent visits from Bruce Springsteen, the emperor of Japan, Sting, and the president, king, and queen of Spain. It's set within what was built several centuries ago as an olive press, a thick-walled outbuilding of La Residencía Hotel. Much of the illumination comes from theatrical-looking candelabra placed on every table, whose flickering light throws shadows against thick ceiling beams, antique accessories, and very formal table settings. The cuisine is modern and subtly flavored, and the chefs know how to take classic dishes and add inventive touches, making for an unexpected wake-up call for your tastebuds. Menu items include a salad of red mullet with julienne of vegetables and vinaigrette, roasted rack of lamb with tomato and herb sauce, baked hake with a seafood risotto, and a dessert specialty of almond soufflé.

Jaime. Carrer Arxiduc Luis Salvador, 13. ☎ **971-63-90-29.** Reservations recommended. Main courses 1,800–3,500 ptas. ($10.80–$21). AE, DC, MC, V. Mar–Oct, Tues–Sun 1–3pm and 7–10:30pm; Jan–Feb, Tues–Sun 1–3:30pm and Sat 7–10pm. Closed Nov–Dec. MAJORCAN.

Prices in Deià tend to be expensive, but this reasonably priced restaurant offers good-quality cuisine. Local families come here to dine, mingling with the foreign visitors. They usually begin with *sopa mallorquín* (Majorcan soup), perhaps followed with *arroz brut.* The specialties are always tenderloin of pork, several variations of codfish, a worthwhile roster of fresh fish based on market availability, and a dessert specialty of almond-flavored cake.

INCA

About 17 miles (27km) north of Palma is Inca, the island's second-largest city and Majorca's market and agricultural center.

Thursday is market day for farming equipment and livestock, but visitors will be more interested in the variety of low-priced leather goods—shoes, purses, jackets, and coats—sold here. In general, stores in Inca selling these leather goods are open Monday to Friday 9:30am to 7pm and on Saturday 9:30am to noon.

Modernization has deprived Inca of its original charm, but the parish church of Santa María la Mayor and the convent of San Jerónimo hold some interest, as does the original Son Fuster Inn, a reminder of an earlier, simpler era.

From Palma, trains (☎ **971-50-00-59**) run Monday to Saturday at the rate of 40 per day and 32 on Sunday. Trip time is only 40 minutes. A round-trip ticket costs 510 ptas. ($3.05).

Inca lies on C-713, the road leading to the Pollença–Formentor region.

WHERE TO DINE

Cellar Ca'n Amer. Carrer Paul, 39. ☎ **971-50-12-61.** Main courses 950–2,200 ptas. ($5.70–$13.20). AE, MC, V. June–Oct, Mon–Sat 1–5pm and 7pm–midnight; Nov–May, Sun 1–5pm. MAJORCAN.

If you can stay for lunch or dinner, we recommend this charming spot. In a building dating from 1850, you'll find the most authentic *cueva* (cave) dining on the island. A container of local wine, which everyone here seems to drink, is tapped from one of the dozens of casks that line the stone walls of the vaults. The interconnected dining rooms are furnished with wooden tables and rustic artifacts. A polite staff serves large portions of Majorcan specialties, including *lechona frit* (a mélange of minced pork offal fried and seasoned), bread and vegetable soup, Majorcan codfish, thrush wrapped in cabbage leaves, and the chef's version of roast suckling pig with a bitter but tasty sauce. There is an array of fresh seafood and fish.

PORT DE POLLENÇA/FORMENTOR

Beside a sheltered bay and between Cape Formentor to the north and Cape del Pinar to the south lies Port de Pollença, amid two hills: **Calvary** to the west and **Puig** to the east. From the town, the best views of the resort and the bay are from Calvary Chapel. The bay provides excellent waterskiing and sailing. The location is 40 miles (64.5km) north of Palma.

A series of low-rise hotels, private homes, restaurants, and snack bars lines the very attractive beach, which is somewhat narrow at its northwestern end but has some of the island's finest, whitest sand and warmest, clearest water. For several miles along the bay there is a pleasant pedestrian promenade. There is only one luxury hotel in the area, however, and that is out on the Formentor Peninsula.

Tons of fine white sand were imported to the beach at the southeastern end of Pollença Bay to create a broad ribbon of sunbathing space that stretches for several miles along the bay. Windsurfing, waterskiing, and scuba diving are among the water sports offered in the area.

Cabo de Formentor, "the devil's tail," can be reached from Port de Pollença via a spectacular road, twisting along to the lighthouse at the cape's end. Formentor is Majorca's fjord country—a dramatic landscape of mountains, pine trees, rock, and sea, plus some of the best beaches in Majorca. In Cape Formentor, you'll see *miradores,* or lookout windows, which provide panoramic views.

ESSENTIALS

GETTING THERE   Five buses a day leaving the Plaça Espanya in Palma pass through Inca and continue on to Port de Pollença.

You can continue on from Deià (see above) along C-710, or from Inca on C-713, all the way to Pollença.

VISITOR INFORMATION   The **tourist information office** (☎ **971-89-26-15**), on Carretera de Arta, is open May to October, Monday to Saturday 9am to 7pm. It's closed off-season. From November to March, another office can answer telephone queries (☎ **971-54-72-57**).

EXPLORING THE COAST

The plunging cliffs and rocky coves of Majorca's northwestern coast are a stunning prelude to Port de Pollença. The **Mirador de Colomer** provides an expansive view of the striking California-like coast that stretches from Punta de la Nau to Punta de la Troneta and includes El Colomer (Pigeon's Rock), named for the nests in its cave.

But it is the 12½-mile (20km) stretch of winding, at times vertiginous, road leading from Port de Pollença to the tip of the **Formentor Peninsula** that delivers the island's most intoxicating scenic views. Cliffs more than 650 feet (197m) high and spectacular rock-rimmed coves embrace intense turquoise waters. About halfway along this road is the **Cala de Pi de la Posada,** where you will find the Hotel Formentor (see "Where to Stay," below) and a lovely bathing beach. Continuing on to the end you'll come to the lighthouse at **Cabo de Formentor.**

Wednesday is **market day** in Port de Pollença, so head for the town square (there's only one) from 8am to 1pm and browse through the fresh produce, leather goods, embroidered tablecloths, ceramics, and more. Bargaining is part of the fun. Sunday is market day in the town of Pollença.

Alcúdia Bay is a long stretch of narrow, sandy beach with beautiful water backed by countless hotels, whose crowds rather overwhelm the area in peak season. The nightlife is more abundant and varied here than in Port de Pollença.

Between Port de Alcúdia and Ca'n Picafort is the **Parc Natural de S'Albufera,** Carretera Alcúdia–Artá, km 27, 07458 C'an Picafort (no phone). A wetlands area of lagoons, dunes, and canals covering some 1,975 acres (790 hectares), it attracts bird watchers and other nature enthusiasts. To date, more than 200 species of birds have been sighted here, among them herons, owls, ospreys, and warblers. The best times to visit are spring and fall, when migratory birds abound. Spring, too, offers a marvelous display of flora. The park is open daily, except Christmas, October 1 to March 30, 9am to 5pm, and April 1 to September 30, 9am to 7pm. Visits are free, but you must get a permit at the reception center, where all motorized vehicles must be left. Binoculars are available for rent. The reception center has further information.

In the town of Pollença, about 4 miles (6km) from Port Pollença, is an 18th-century stairway leading up to an *ermita* (hermitage). Consisting of 365 stairs, it is known as the **Monte Calvario (Calvary),** but you can also reach the top by car via carrer de las Cruces, which is lined with 10-foot-high concrete crosses.

Cala San Vicente, between Pollença and Port de Pollença, is a pleasant, small sandy cove with some notable surf. Several small hotels and restaurants provide the necessary amenities.

Various companies offer tours of Pollença Bay, and many provide glass-bottomed boats for viewing the varied aquatic creatures and plants. Many of these boats leave from Port de Pollença's Estació Marítim several times daily during the summer months, with less frequent departures in winter. Your hotel concierge or the marina can provide you with a schedule.

Part of the allure of a trip to the Balearics is boating in the Mediterranean; if you're in the market to rent either a small sailing craft or a glamorous yacht that comes with a full complement of staff and crew, Associación Provinciale d'Empresarios de Actividades Marítimas de Baleares, Muelle Viejo, 6, in Palma (☎ 971-72-79-86), can steer you in the right direction. Chances are they'll direct you to one of two well-respected maritime charter companies, both based in Palma. They are **Moorings Formentor,** Contramuelle, 12 (☎ 971-71-09-49), and **Alga Charter,** Plaza Jardines San Telmo, s/n (☎ 971-71-64-28). Both lease boats of different sizes by the day, week, or month.

If you want to go windsurfing, head for **Ski Costa Calvia,** carrer Estornell, 2, Sonferrer/Calvia (☎ 971-23-03-28), which is about 9 miles (14.5km) southeast of Palma.

WHERE TO STAY
In Puerto Pollença
Hotel Illa d'Or. Passeig Colón, 265, 07470 Port de Pollença. ☎ **971-86-51-00.** Fax 971-86-42-13. www.fehm.es. E-mail: illador@fehm.es. 120 units. A/C MINIBAR TV TEL.

18,150–30,000 ptas. ($109–$180) double; 37,000–60,000 ptas. ($222–$360) suite. Rates include breakfast. AE, DC, MC, V. Closed Nov 24–Feb 9. Free parking.

Originally built in 1929, and enlarged and improved several times since then, this four-story hotel sits at the relatively isolated northwestern edge of Pollença Bay—far from the heavily congested, touristed region around Palma. Decorated in a mixture of colonial Spanish and English reproductions, it offers a seafront terrace with a view of the mountains and airy, simply furnished rooms. Rooms are midsize to spacious, each with comfortable furnishings, including good beds. There are two swimming pools on the premises, and the beach is just a few steps away. A bar and two restaurants set the scene for socializing.

Hotel Miramar. Passeig Anglada Camarasa, 39, 07470 Port de Pollença. ☎ **971-86-64-00.** Fax 971-86-40-75. 84 units. A/C TEL. 16,000–17,500 ptas. ($96–$105) double. Rates include breakfast. AE, DC, MC, V. Closed Nov–Mar.

This centrally located hotel is one of the grandly old-fashioned hostelries in town, in a desirable position across the coastal road from the beach. It has ornate front columns supporting a formal balustrade, tiled eaves, and several jardinieres. The lobby is furnished with antiques, and the formal dining room has views of the sea. Some rooms have private verandas overlooking the flower-filled courtyard in back. All the small to midsized rooms are comfortably furnished and well maintained, each with a firm bed.

Hotel Pollentia. Passeig de Londres, s/n, 07470 Port de Pollença. ☎ **971-86-52-00.** Fax 971-86-60-34. 70 units. TEL. 12,200–13,800 ptas. ($73.20–$82.80) double. Rates include breakfast. AE, DC, MC, V. Closed Dec–Mar.

This hotel is half a mile from the commercial center of the resort, behind a screen of foliage. It's our favorite hotel in town because of its cool, airy spaciousness and the genial reception. The steps leading to the formal modern lobby are banked with dozens of terra-cotta pots overflowing with ivy and geraniums. The reception area has Majorcan glass chandeliers, and many of the well-furnished but small rooms have private terraces. Guests have access to a private terrace overlooking the Mediterranean, and the dining room offers a fine fixed-price meal of regional dishes.

In Cabo de Formentor

✪ **Hotel Formentor.** Platja de Formentor, 07470 Port de Pollença. ☎ **971-89-91-00.** Fax 971-86-51-55. www.fehm.es/pmi/formentor. E-mail: formentor@fehm.es. 127 units. A/C MINIBAR TV TEL. 38,000–55,000 ptas. ($228–$330) double; 62,000–75,000 ptas. ($372–$450) suite. $45 per person extra. Rates include breakfast; half-board 7,500 ptas. AE, DC, MC, V. Closed early Jan–early Mar.

Set on an isolated, sprawling, intensely manicured expanse of scrub-covered peninsula that once served as a private farm, Hotel Formentor is one of Europe's most spectacular and exclusive hotels. Far from the madding crowds of Palma, on the island's northern tip, it's elegant and unpretentious. Most of it is in a long, low-slung three-story building that's more modern-looking than its 1920s origins would imply. It has hosted an impressive roster of guests, including a 1995 summit meeting of the heads of state for all the countries in the European Union. Stage and film stars, and even the Dalai Lama, have stayed here. Accommodations are classically modern, spacious, and supremely comfortable, with some of the more expensive rooms containing reproductions of Iberian antiques that include elaborately carved beds.

Dining/Diversions: Most guests prefer to dine outdoors, enjoying regional and international cuisine on the tree-shaded terrace. There is a full formal restaurant inside, plus a beach restaurant, ideal for lunch if you don't want to change out of your bathing suit. The cuisine is among the area's finest. A piano bar is an amusing place for a drink.

Amenities: Terrace gardens descend gracefully to the resort's private beach, although there's a pool on site. Spacious sunbathing area, hairdresser, shops, tennis coach, riding instructor, business corner, health and beauty center, concierge, dry cleaning and laundry, massages, baby-sitting, currency exchange, valet parking, room service.

WHERE TO DINE

In Port de Pollença

Stay Restaurant. Muelle Nuevo, Estació Marítima, s/n. ☎ **971-86-40-13.** Reservations recommended July–Aug. Main courses 1,850–3,500 ptas. ($11.10–$21); fixed-price menu 4,200 ptas. ($25.20). AE, MC, V. Daily noon–4pm and 7:30–10:30pm. SPANISH/ INTERNATIONAL.

This restaurant offers a unique menu that changes about every 2 months, depending on what's available at the market. Main courses include fresh salmon fillets in a white wine sauce, roasted duck with a green peppercorn sauce, grilled fillet of beef with a sauce of foie gras de *canard* (duckling) and port wine, and our favorite, *parrillada de mariscos,* a platter of assorted grilled fish and seafood. Finish your meal with a strudel of fresh figs, almonds, and raisins smothered in a hot vanilla sauce.

In Pollença

Restaurant Clivia. Avinguda Pollentia, s/n. ☎ **971-53-46-16.** Reservations recommended. Main courses 2,200–3,000 ptas. ($13.20–$18). AE, DC, MC, V. Tues and Thurs–Sun 1–3pm; daily 7:30–11:30pm. Closed Nov 15–Dec 15. MALLORQUINA/SPANISH.

This is the best and most appealing restaurant in Pollença, even attracting a clientele from other districts of Majorca. The restaurant is composed of two dining rooms and an outdoor patio in a century-old house in the heart of town. It has a scattering of antique furniture and a tactful, well-organized staff that produces a limited list of meats (veal, chicken, pork, and beef) and a more appealing roster of seafood prepared with skill and finesse. Specialties depend on the availability of fish such as cod, monkfish, dorado, eel, squid, and whitefish, either baked in a salt crust or prepared as part of a succulent *parrillada* (platter) of shellfish that's among the freshest anywhere. Begin with a spicy fish soup and accompany it with fresh vegetables, such as asparagus or spinach. The restaurant's name derives from the variety of bright red flowers (*las clivias*) that are planted profusely beside the patio and that bloom throughout the summer.

MAJORCA'S EAST COAST: THE CAVA ROUTE

The east coast of Majorca is often called the *cava* route because of the caves that stud the coastline. Although there are scores, we'll include only the most important ones; other places mentioned are Manacor, where cultured Majorcan pearls are manufactured, and Petra, home of Fray Junípero Serra, founder of many California missions. In general, the east coast of Majorca does not have the dramatic scenery of the west coast but has worthy attractions in its own right.

Leave Palma on the freeway but turn onto Carretera C-715 in the direction of Manacor. About 35 miles (56km) east of Palma, you come to your first stop, Petra.

PETRA

Petra was founded by Jaume II over the ruins of a Roman settlement. This was the birthplace of Father Junípero Serra (1713–84), the Franciscan priest who founded the missions in California that eventually grew into San Diego, Monterey, and San Francisco. A statue commemorates him at the Capitol building in Washington, D.C., and you will also see a statue of Father Serra in this, his native village.

Museo Beato Junípero Serra, carrer Barracar (☎ 971-56-11-49), gives you an idea of how people lived on the island in the 18th century. The property was bought and fixed up by the San Francisco Rotary Club, which then presented it as a gift to the citizens of Petra in 1972. The museum, 500 yards from the center of the village, is open every day of the year but doesn't keep regular hours. Visits are by appointment only. Admission is free, but donations are encouraged.

MANACOR

The C-715 continues east to Manacor, the town where the famous artificial pearls of Majorca are manufactured. The trade name for the pearls is "Perlas Majorica," so avoid such knock-offs as "Majorca." You can visit the factories where the pearls are made, and purchase some if you wish. Jewelry here may be 5% to 10% cheaper than at most retail outlets in Barcelona.

The largest outlet is **Perlas Majorica,** Pedro Riche (☎ 971-55-09-00), which offers organized tours. On the road to Palma at the edge of town, it is open Monday to Friday 9am to 1pm and 2:30 to 7pm. On Saturday and Sunday, it is open 9:45am to 1pm. Admission is free. They'll explain how the pearls are made (from fish scales that simulate the sheen of a real pearl). Some 300 artisans work here, shaping and polishing the pearls, and they're used to being inspected by foreign visitors while at work. Perlas Majorica carry a 10-year guarantee.

CUEVAS DEL DRACH

From Manacor, take the road southeast to the sea—about 7½ miles (12km)—and the town of **Porto Cristo,** 38 miles (61km) east of Palma. Go a half mile south of town to **Cuevas del Drach (Caves of the Dragon)** (☎ 971-82-07-53), which contain an underground forest of stalactites and stalagmites as well as five subterranean lakes, where you can listen to a concert and later go boating à la Jules Verne. The roof appears to glitter with endless icicles. Martel Lake, 581 feet (176m) long, is the largest underground lake in the world. E. A. Martel, a French speleologist who charted the then mysterious caves in 1896, described it better than anyone: "As far as the eye can see, marble cascades, organ pipes, lace draperies, pendants or brilliants, hang suspended from the walls and roof." Tours depart daily, every hour from 10am to 5pm. Admission is 1,000 ptas. ($6).

If you don't have a car, you can take one of the four daily buses that leave from the railroad station in Palma (inquire at the tourist bureau in Palma for times of departure). The buses pass through Manacor on the way to Porto Cristo.

CUEVAS DEL HAM

Discovered in 1906, these caves, whose name means "fish hooks," are half a mile from Porto Cristo on the road to Manacor. **Cuevas del Ham** (☎ 971-82-09-88) are far less impressive than the Cuevas del Drach and can be skipped if you're rushed. Tours depart every 15 minutes daily year-round 10am to 6pm, charging 1,400 ptas. ($8.40) admission for adults, but nothing for children under 12. These caves contain white stalactites and follow the course of an underground river. There is a link to the sea, so the water level inside the cave's pools rises and falls according to the tides.

CUEVAS DE ARTÁ

Near Platja de Canyamel (Playa de Cañamel on some maps), ✪ **Cuevas de Artá** (☎ 971-84-12-93) lie on a stretch of land closing Canyamel Bay to the north. They are reached by a corniche road. These caves are said to be the inspiration for the Jules Verne tale *Journey to the Center of the Earth,* published in 1864. (Verne may have heard or read about the caves; it is not known if he ever actually visited them.) Formed by seawater erosion, the caves are about 35 yards (32m) above sea level, and some of the rooms rise about 150 feet (45.5m).

You enter an impressive vestibule and immediately see walls blackened by the torches used to light the caves for early tourists in the 1800s. There follows the *Reina de las Columnas* (Queen of the Columns), rising about 72 feet (22m) tall, then a lower room whose Dante-esque appearance has led to it being called "inferno." It is followed by a field of stalagmites and stalactites, the "purgatory rooms," which eventually lead to the "theater" and "paradise."

The caves were once used by pirates, and centuries ago provided a haven for Spanish Moors fleeing the persecution of Jaume I. The stairs in the cave were built for Isabella II for her 1860 visit. In time, such luminaries as Sarah Bernhardt, Alexandre Dumas, and Victor Hugo arrived for the tour. Tours depart daily, every half-hour 10am to 6pm. Admission is 1,000 ptas. ($6).

2 Ibiza

Ibiza (Ee-*bee*-tha) was once a virtually unknown and unvisited island; Majorca, its bigger neighbor, got all the business. But in the 1950s, Ibiza's art colony began to thrive, and in the 1960s it became the European resort most favored by the flower children. A New York art student once wrote, "Even those who come to Ibiza for the 'wrong' reason (to work!) eventually are seduced by the island's easy life. Little chores like picking up the mail from the post office stretch into day-long missions." Today, Ibiza is overrun by middle-class package-tour tourists, mainly from England, France, Germany, and Scandinavia, and it has become a major mecca for gay travelers, making it a wild combination of chic and middle-class.

At 225 square miles (585sq km), it is the third largest of the Balearic Islands. Physically, Ibiza has a jagged coastline, some fine beaches, whitewashed houses, secluded bays, cliffs, and a hilly terrain dotted with fig and olive trees. Warmer than Majorca, it's a better choice for a winter vacation, but it can be sweltering in July and August. Thousands of tourists descend on the island in summer, greatly taxing the island's limited water supply.

Ciudad de Ibiza boasts Playa Talamanca in the north and Ses Figueretes and Playa d'en Bossa in the south, two outstanding white sandy beaches. Las Salinas, in the south, near the old salt flats, offers excellent sands. Playa Cavallet and Aigües Blanques attract the nude sunbathers. Other good beaches include Cala Bassa, Port des Torrent, Cala Tarida, and Cala Conta—all within a short bus or boat ride from San Antonio de Portmany. The long sandy cove of Cala Llonga, south of Santa Eulalia del Rio, and the white sandy beach of El Cana to the north, are sacred to Ibiza's sun worshipers. In Formentera, Playa de Mitjorn stretches 3 miles (5km) and is relatively uncrowded. Set against a backdrop of pines and dunes, the pure white sand of Es Pujols is the most popular of Ibiza's beaches and deservedly so.

Many travelers still arrive dreaming of soft drugs and hard sex. Both exist in great abundance, but there are dangers. It's common to pick up the local paper and read the list of the latest group of people deported because of *irresponsibilidad económica* (no money) or *conducta antisocial* (drunk and disorderly conduct). Some young travelers, frankly, have forsaken Ibiza, taking a ferry 40 minutes away (and just 3 miles [5km] as the crow flies) to the tiny island of Formentera, where they find less harassment (although anyone looking suspicious will be noticed out here too). Formentera is the most southern of the Balearic Islands, and because of limited accommodations, restaurants, and nightlife, it is most often visited on a day trip from Ibiza.

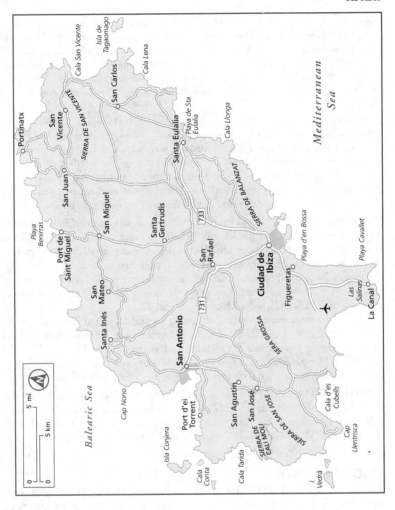

Eivissa is the local (Catalán) name for Ibiza. Catalán is the most common language of the island, but it is a dialectal variation—called *eivissenc* or *ibicenco*. The same language is spoken on Formentera.

ISLAND ESSENTIALS

GETTING THERE   Again, as with Palma, if you come in July and August, be sure you have a return ticket and a reservation. Stories of passengers who were stranded for days in Ibiza in midsummer are legend.

   Iberia (☎ 971-80-93-35) flies into **Es Codolar International Airport** (☎ 971-80-90-00), 3½ miles (5.5km) from Ciudad de Ibiza. Four daily flights connect Ibiza with Palma de Majorca, and five flights a day arrive from Barcelona. It's possible to take one of two daily flights from Valencia or one of three from Madrid. With the exception of charter flights winging in from virtually everywhere, Iberia is the main carrier servicing Ibiza. Its only other competitor on this route is Air Europa (☎ 971-80-91-91 in Ibiza), which offers flights to Ibiza from Barcelona (a maximum of two flights a day), as well as from Madrid and Palma, at intervals much less frequent than those offered aboard Iberia. The price of flights to Ibiza varies considerably because of season, promotion, and availability. Here's an indication of round-trip, coach-class fares on Iberia into Ibiza: from Barcelona, 15,000 to 33,000 ptas. ($90 to $198); from Palma, 11,000 to 18,000 ptas. ($66 to $108); from Madrid, 17,000 to 39,000 ptas. ($102 to $234). From Valencia via Palma, the fare is 15,000 to 27,000 ptas. ($90 to $162).

Transmediterránea, avinguda B.V. Ramón (☎ **971-31-50-50**), operates a ferry service to Barcelona at the rate of four per week on Monday, Wednesday, Friday, and Saturday, costing 6,050 ptas. ($36.30) for a one-way ticket. One boat per week departs from Valencia on Thursdays, with a one-way ticket going for 6,090 ptas. ($36.55). From Palma, there are three ferries per week, on Friday, Saturday, and Sunday; it costs 3,045 ptas. ($18.25) one-way. Check with travel agents in Barcelona, Valencia, or Palma regarding ferry schedules. You can book tickets through any agent.

GETTING AROUND   If you land at Es Cordola airport outside Ciudad de Ibiza, you will find bus service for the 3½-mile (5.5km) ride into town. Sometimes taxis are shared. In Ciudad de Ibiza, buses leave for the airport from avinguda Isidor Macabich, 24 (by the ticket kiosk), every hour on the hour, daily 7am to 10pm.

Once in Ibiza, you'll have to walk, but the city is compact and can be covered on foot. There are buses, however, leaving for the nearby beaches. The two main bus terminals are at avinguda Isidor Macabich, 20 and 42.

One of the most popular means of getting around the island, especially in the south, is by a moped or bicycle. Rental arrangements can be made through **Casa Valentín,** corner of avinguda B.V. Ramón and avinguda de la Paz, s/n (☎ **971-31-08-22**). Mopeds cost from 1,600 ptas. ($9.60) per day.

If you'd like to rent a car, both Hertz and Avis have offices at the airport.

VISITOR INFORMATION   The **tourist information office** is at Antonio Riquer, 2, in the port of Ciudad de Ibiza (☎ **971-30-19-00**). It is open Monday to Friday 9:30am to 1:30pm and 5 to 7pm, Saturday 10:30am to 1pm. There is another office at the airport (☎ **971-80-91-18**), which is open Monday to Saturday 9am to 2pm and 3 to 8pm, Sunday 9am to 2pm.

CIUDAD DE IBIZA

The island's capital, **Ciudad de Ibiza,** was founded by the Carthaginians 2,500 years ago. Today the town consists of a lively marina district around the harbor and an old town (D'Alt Vila) with narrow cobblestoned streets and flat-roofed, whitewashed houses. The yacht-clogged marina and the district's main street, Vara de Rey, are constant spectacles—from old fishermen to the local Ibizan women swathed in black to ubiquitous, scantily clad tourists. The marina district is fun to wander about with its art galleries, dance clubs, boutiques, bars, and restaurants.

Much of the medieval character of the old town has been preserved, in spite of massive development elsewhere. Many houses have Gothic styling and open onto spacious courtyards. These houses, some of which are 500 years old, are often festooned with geraniums and bougainvillea. The old quarter is entered through the Puerta de la Tablas, flanked by Roman statues.

Plaça Desamparadors, crowded with open-air restaurants and market stalls, lies at the top of the town. Traffic leaves town through the Portal Nou.

FUN ON & OFF THE BEACH

BEACHES   The most popular (and overcrowded) beaches are **Playa Talamanca** in the north and **Ses Figueretes** (also called Playa Figueretes) in the south. But you can find more remote, uncrowded spots, and don't be surprised to find a lot of nudity. The best beaches are connected by boats and buses. The remoter ones require a private car or private boat. Both Playa Talamanca and Ses Figueretes are near Ciudad de Ibiza, as is another popular beach, **Playa d'en Bossa** to the south.

To avoid the hordes here, keep going until you reach **Las Salinas,** near the old salt flats farther south. Here beaches include **Playa Cavallet,** one of the officially designated nudist strands (nudism doesn't always follow official designations laid down by Ibizan law).

The most horrendously overcrowded beach in Ibiza is **Playa San Antonio** at San Antonio de Portmany—if it got any worse, you'd have to stand up instead of lie down! However, a boat or bus will take you to several beaches southwest of the town, all far less congested. These include **Cala Bassa, Port des Torrent, Cala Tarida,** and **Cala Conta.**

Santa Eulalia de Rio, site of the third major tourist development in Ibiza, has a less crowded beach, but it's also less impressive. If you stay in this east coast town, you can find a better beach at Cala Llonga in the south or at one of the beaches along the north, including **Playa d'es Caná** and **Cala Lleña.** These beaches are among the finest on Ibiza.

If you venture to the north coast, you'll discover more good beaches at the tourist developments of **Portinatz,** which is at the very northern tip, and at **Puerto de San Miguel,** north of the small town of San Miguel. The quickest way to reach San Miguel from Ciudad de Ibiza is to go inland via Santa Gertrrudis, and then north. Along the way, you'll pass Rio de Santa Eulalia, the only river in the Balearics.

HORSEBACK RIDING   This is a scenic, memorable experience. Two outfitters are **C'an Mayans,** in Santa Gertrudis (☎ **608-63-68-84**), and **Es Buig,** also in Santa Gertrudis (☎ **971-18-73-88**). The price is 1,500 ptas. ($9) for a 1-hour ride, and an hour's class is 2,000 ptas. ($12).

SPORTS & FITNESS   **Ahmara Centro Deportivo,** Carretera Sant Josep, km 2.7, on the road to Sant Josep (☎ **971-39-55-06**), offers the best collection of health equipment on the island, along with a swimming pool, hot tub, sauna, and even a Turkish bath with massage. There are four squash courts. Badminton and indoor football are also played here. Tennis courts (and lessons) are available. The facility's steam room continually receives praise. Sheathed with marble and lavishly carved stone columns, it's been compared to the Roman baths of yore, within a thoroughly modern, thoroughly sybaritic context.

TENNIS   In addition to the better-maintained courts at Ahmara, recommended above, you'll find five public tennis courts at **Port San Miguel** (☎ **971-30-19-00**). Open during daylight hours, they're usually unsupervised. No appointments are necessary for access to these courts, but for information about their condition and whether there are players waiting to use them, contact the Hotel Hacienda directly.

SHOPPING

Fashion has been an important Ibiza industry since the late 1960s, when a nonconformist fashion philosophy took hold, combining elements of the traditional *pitiusa* (peasant dress) attire of the natives and the natural, free-flowing garments of the hippies who flocked here in the 1960s. In recent years Ibizan designs have become much more sophisticated and complex, but the individualistic spirit has not wavered.

At the corner of Conde Rosselón, master artisan Pedro Planells creates hand-sewn, original leather goods at **Pedro's,** carrer Aníbal, 8 (☎ **971-31-30-26**). Many items can be custom-made. Pedro creates stylish accessories and home furnishings in leather

Ciudad de Ibiza

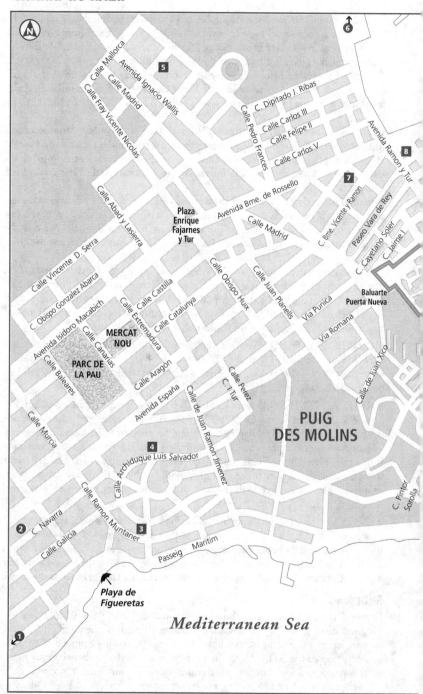

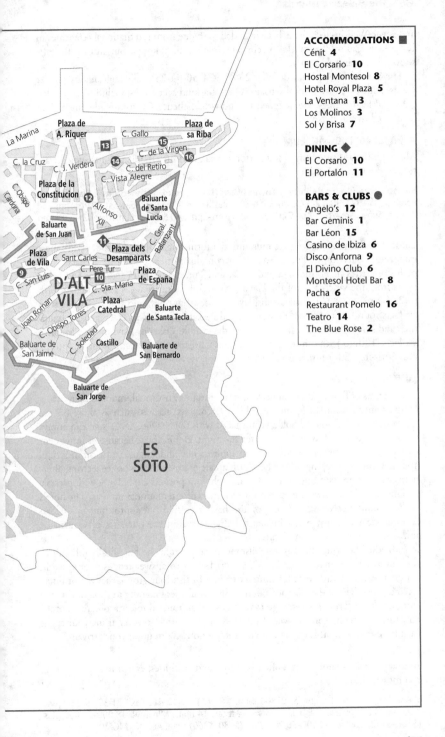

ACCOMMODATIONS ■
Cénit **4**
El Corsario **10**
Hostal Montesol **8**
Hotel Royal Plaza **5**
La Ventana **13**
Los Molinos **3**
Sol y Brisa **7**

DINING ◆
El Corsario **10**
El Portalón **11**

BARS & CLUBS ●
Angelo's **12**
Bar Geminis **1**
Bar Léon **15**
Casino de Ibiza **6**
Disco Anforna **9**
El Divino Club **6**
Montesol Hotel Bar **8**
Pacha **6**
Restaurant Pomelo **16**
Teatro **14**
The Blue Rose **2**

Plaza de A. Riquer
Plaza de sa Riba
La Marina
C. Gallo
C. la Cruz
C. de la Virgen
C. J. Verdera
C. del Retiro
C. Vista Alegre
Plaza de la Constitucion
C. Obispo Cardona
Alfonso XII
Baluarte de Santa Lucia
Baluarte de San Juan
C. Gral. Balanzant
Plaza de Vila
C. Sant Carles
Plaza dels Desamparats
C. San Luis
C. Pere Tur
Plaza de España
D'ALT VILA
C. Sta. Maria
Plaza Catedral
C. Joan Roman
Baluarte de Santa Tecla
C. Obispo Torres
C. Soledad
Castillo
Baluarte de San Jaime
Baluarte de San Bernardo
Baluarte de San Jorge

ES SOTO

and silver. Well-heeled clients have included everyone from international celebrities to King Juan Carlos. Pedro's keeps conventional Spanish hours, but during the off-season, hours and days vary.

The **Sandal Shop,** Plaça de Vila, 2 (☎ **971-30-54-75**), sells high-quality leather goods made by a cast of local artisans. One-of-a-kind accessories, including bejeweled belts and leather bags, are designed for individual clients. Custom-made sandals can be created to suit personal fashion tastes.

A FASCINATING MUSEUM

Although Ibiza is primarily a destination for sun and fun, there's a sightseeing attraction worth a special visit.

Museo Arqueològic de Ibiza y Formentera (Museum of Archaeology). Plaça de Catedral, 3. ☎ **971-30-12-31.** Admission 300 ptas. ($1.80). Winter, Tues–Sat 10am–1pm and 4–6pm, Sun 10am–2pm; Apr–Oct, Tues–Sat 10am–2pm and 5–8pm, Sun 10am–2pm. Closed holidays.

Located in Ibiza's old town, this museum in a former arsenal houses the world's most important collection of Punic remains. It contains pottery and other artifacts from prehistoric sites in Formentera and Ibiza, and Punic terra-cotta figurines and other items from the sanctuaries of Illa Plana (7th to 5th centuries B.C.) and Cuieram (4th to 2nd centuries B.C.). Also on display are vases, figurines, and other Carthaginian artifacts found in the island's burial grounds. Examples of Roman epigraphs, sculpture, and small glass bottles are included in the exhibit. Other displays include Moorish artifacts (10th to 13th centuries A.D.), various Christian wooden and stone sculptures, plus 14th- to 16th-century ceramics.

WHERE TO STAY

The chances of finding space in peak summer months are dismal, more so than in any Mediterranean resort in Spain. At other overcrowded resorts, such as those on the Costa Brava and Costa del Sol, a visitor faced with the NO VACANCY sign can always press on or go inland to find a room for the night. But in Ibiza, because of infrequent transportation, a visitor without a reservation in July and August can land in a trap. You may end up sleeping on the beach on an air mattress (if the police let you; alternatively, there are camping areas), even though your pockets are bulging with pesetas.

The island is not always prepared for its hordes of international tourists. The hotels can't be built fast enough. Many of the hastily erected ones sprouting up in San Antonio de Portmany, Santa Eulalia del Rio—even on the outskirts of Ciudad de Ibiza—are more frame than picture.

Individual bookings in most establishments range from the horrifically difficult to the impossible. In many cases hoteliers don't bother to answer requests for space in summer. Armed with a nice fat contract from a British tour group, they're not interested in the plight of the stranded pilgrim. So if you're set on going to Ibiza during the summer, ***book through a package tour*** to ensure an ironclad reservation. You'll probably find a better bargain, anyway. In the less-busy months, however, using your credit card to reserve a room is enough to guarantee a hotel room upon your arrival.

In Town

In town, hotels are limited and often lack style and amenities, except for the following recommendations.

El Corsario. Carrer Ponent, 5, 07800 Ibiza. ☎ **971-30-12-48.** Fax 971-39-19-53. www.ibiza-hotels.com/corsario. E-mail: elcorsario@ctv.es. 14 units. MINIBAR. 18,000–22,000 ptas. ($108–$132) double; 30,000–60,000 ptas. ($180–$360) suite. AE, DC, MC, V.

After your taxi deposits you near the church below, you'll have to walk the last 500 feet (152m) up a hill to reach this hotel, within a labyrinth of cobblestone pedestrian walkways. The house was built in 1570, and it is rumored that its terraces were built by corsairs. The modest rooms are pleasant and clean, often containing antiques. Each of the small, tiled bathrooms is equipped with a hair dryer. Some overlook an enclosed garden of trailing bougainvillea and cultivated flowers. The hotel's restaurant is one of the most romantic places to dine (see restaurant recommendations below). No parking is available.

Hostal Montesol. Vara de Rey, 2. ☎ **971-31-01-61.** Fax 971-31-06-02. 55 units. A/C TV TEL. 14,000 ptas. ($84) double. MC, V.

Completely renovated in 1997, this old favorite has given itself a new lease on life. Its proximity to the marina affords panoramic views of the sea and the small rooms are clean and comfortable, although rather sterile. Nonetheless, beds are good and have firm mattresses. This is a good bargain for Ibiza, especially if you plan to spend most of your time exploring the island and not in your room. There's an on-site cafeteria but no restaurant; however, many bistros are outside your door.

Hotel Royal Plaza. Carrer Pedro Francés, 27–29, 07800 Ibiza. ☎ **800/528-1234** in the U.S., or 971-31-00-00. Fax 971-31-40-95. www.xpress.es/ibizanet/royal. E-mail: royalpla@ xpress.es. 117 units. A/C MINIBAR TV TEL. 14,000–24,000 ptas. ($84–$144) double; 25,000–42,250 ptas. ($150–$253.50) suite. AE, DC, MC, V.

Located 3 blocks from the port, this six-story modern hotel offers in-town convenience plus a casual, resortlike atmosphere. For those who want to stay within Ciudad de Ibiza, this is the premier choice. The marble reception lobby exudes elegance. Well-appointed accommodations are midsized and carpeted; most have private terraces. Beds are firm and the bathrooms are tidily organized. The rooftop pool offers a sunbathing platform, with commanding views of the port and town of Ibiza.

During the summer months, a snack bar/restaurant serves good food; snacks are available daily 11:30am to midnight and meals 1:30 to 4pm and 8:30 to 11:30pm. A hotel bar is open daily 8am to 11pm.

✪ La Ventana. Sa Carrossa, 13, Dalt Vila, 07800 Ibiza. ☎ **971-39-08-57.** Fax 971-39-01-45. 14 units. A/C MINIBAR TV TEL. 15,000–26,000 ptas. ($90–$156) double; 35,000–40,000 ptas. ($210–$240) suite. AE, MC, V. Free parking.

This is a perfect name (the window) for what was once a castle and is now a hotel on the hillside of the old city, overlooking the Mediterranean. What is more, the hotel, peaceful as it is in itself, is one of the best places to get tickets for clubs featuring music. The present owners have succeeded in decorating the hotel simply but very stylishly with a mixture of clever lighting, beautiful fittings, and various Asian objets d'art. The rooms are painted in wonderful, almost Indian colors, and have great beds with floating canopies of white net. All include bathrooms or shower stalls, have satellite television, and some even offer French doors opening onto balconies. There is a chic bar downstairs and a fantastic terrace on the roof with wide Moroccan-style sofas and an amazing view of the old city and the sea beyond. The hotel incorporates a small, popular restaurant serving Mediterranean/international cuisine during the summer season, from May to October. It is open daily 7:30pm to 12:30am and main courses range from 1,200 to 3,800 ptas. ($7.20 to $22.80).

Sol y Brisa. Avinguda B.V. Ramón, 15, 07800 Ibiza. ☎ **971-31-08-18.** 18 units, with sink only. 3,500–5,000 ptas. ($21–$30) double. No credit cards.

This is an utterly basic hostelry, clean and well maintained by helpful owners. Young people on low budgets are especially fond of this place, which attracts a lot of

American students in summer (making it advisable to make a reservation as early as possible). Rooms are tiny, with tile floors that somehow make them seem cooler in July and August. Two courtyards are filled with plants in the old style of an *ibicenco* house.

In Playa de Ses Figueretes

On the edge of town, a number of modern beach hotels have been erected that are far superior to the ones in the city. With few exceptions, most are booked solidly in summer by tour groups.

Cénit. Arxiduc Lluís Salvador, 07800 Ibiza. ☎ **971-30-14-04.** Fax 971-30-07-54. 63 units. TEL. 8,500–9,000 ptas. ($51–$54) double. AE, DC, MC, V. Closed mid-Oct to Apr.

This is the bargain place to stay here. Circular in shape, the hotel looks like a quartered wedding cake. In the pueblo style, each floor has been staggered so as to provide a terrace for the rooms above. The small accommodations are routine but comfortable, although the beds are firm. The curved dining room, with its picture windows, is a pleasant place to enjoy a continental breakfast. The Cénit, which has a pool, is perched on a hillside a short walk from the beach.

Los Molinos. Ramón Muntaner, 60, 07800 Ibiza. ☎ **971-30-22-50.** Fax 971-30-25-04. 154 units. A/C MINIBAR TV TEL. 15,500–23,000 ptas. ($93–$138) double. AE, DC, MC, V. Free parking.

This modern resort is a favorite with snowbirds from the north of Europe. Situated less than a mile from Ibiza town, it's the finest hotel in Ses Figueretes. Nestled between the water and a medieval village, Los Molinos offers resort life combined with proximity to town. The midsized accommodations, most with private terraces facing the sea, are comfortably furnished, with safes, carpets, and twin beds pushed together European style. Public areas include a dining room with views of the Mediterranean, two bars, and a cafe providing snacks throughout the day. The hotel has two pools (one is heated).

WHERE TO DINE

It's hard to find authentic Ibizan cuisine. The clientele and often the chefs are mainly from continental Europe, and the menu choices cater almost exclusively to their tastes.

Because of the lack of agriculture in some parts of the island, fish has always been the mainstay of the local Mediterranean diet. But budget travelers may be put off by the price of some of this fare. Once the cheapest item you could order on a menu, fish is now one of the most expensive. The fish is sauteed, baked, or broiled and might be blended in a fisher's rice, *arros a la pescadora. Parrillada* and *zarzuela* are two stewlike dishes containing a wide assortment of fish.

As in Majorca, pork is important in the diet. Some islanders feed figs to these animals to sweeten their meat, which is turned into such pungent cooked sausages as *sobrasadas* or *longanizas.*

A local dish occasionally offered on some menus is a *sofrit pages,* a stew made with three kinds of meat and poultry—chicken, pork, and lamb—then cooked with pepper, cloves, cinnamon, and garlic. One of the best seafood plates is *borrida de rajada,* crayfish in an almond sauce.

The most famous dessert is *flaó,* a kind of cheesecake to which mint and anisette are added for flavoring. *Greixonera* is a spiced pudding, and *maccarrones de San Juan* is cinnamon- and lemon-flavored milk baked with cheese.

Wines are shipped over from the mainland; however, islanders make alcohol-based herbal concoctions. These include *rumaniseta,* made from rosemary, and *frigola,* golden in color and very sweet, with a strong aroma coming from wild thyme. A rather bitter aperitif known as *balo* comes from locally grown carob. For special occasions, islanders treasure *hierbas ibicencas*, made with numerous local herbs, including anise.

El Corsario. Carrer Ponent, 5. ☎ **971-30-12-48.** Reservations required. Main courses 2,500–4,000 ptas. ($15–$24); tasting menu 14,000 ptas. ($84). MC, V. Daily 8pm–midnight. Closed Nov–Apr. INTERNATIONAL.

Although we've reviewed its accommodations above, the dining room here, with its panoramic view, is so romantic it deserves special mention. This 400-year-old flower-draped villa is near the hilltop fortress. Your taxi deposits you about 500 feet (152m) down the hill in a square fronting an old church, and you must climb the slippery cobblestones to reach it. There's a stand-up bar, two pleasant dining rooms with a handful of neatly laid tables, and a view of the harbor. Menu specialties include various pastas, two different preparations of lamb, and especially fresh fish brought up from the harbor. The cookery is homestyle and well prepared, especially if you stick to the fish dishes.

El Portalón. Plaça dels Desamparats, 1–2. ☎ **971-30-39-01.** Reservations recommended. Main courses 950–3,950 ptas. ($5.70–$23.70). AE, DC, MC, V. Mon–Sat 12:30–3:30pm; daily 8pm–12:30am. Closed mid-Jan to mid-Feb. SPANISH/INTERNATIONAL.

Before you hit the bars (go very late, as is the fashion), dine here in the old town. Alfresco courtyard dining is a lure, as is the handsome crowd. El Portalón attracts gay as well as straight couples, usually European. The food is a combination of Spanish, Catalán, and continental. It's expensive, but worth the extra pesetas.

CIUDAD DE IBIZA AFTER DARK

In many ways, **El Divino Club,** Puerto Ibiza Nueva (☎ **971-19-01-76**), is the most physically beautiful disco on Ibiza. It prides itself on the supermodels, celebs, and trendies who have graced its premises with their presence. Wear the most hip outfit you packed. The club doesn't open its doors until 11:30am; it remains open nightly until 6am, but only June to September. The cover charge is 3,000 ptas. ($18) and up.

The crowd at the **Montesol** hotel bar, Vara de Rey, 2 (☎ **971-31-01-61**), a short walk from the harbor on the main street, is likely to include expatriates, newly arrived social climbers, and Spaniards along for the view. In many ways this is the greatest circus in town, made more pleasant by the well-prepared tapas and the generous drinks. If you enjoy people-watching, sit at one of the sidewalk tables. Montesol is open daily 8am to midnight.

Despite its age (it's one of the oldest discos on Ibiza, with a nightlife pedigree extending back to the 1960s), **Pacha,** avenida 8 de Agosto, s/n (☎ **971-31-36-12**), a spacious split-level disco near the casino, is still hip. Made up of three separate bar areas and dance floors, it continues to attract the young and the not-so-young, the bored, the restless, and the merely jaded. In summer, overheated dancers can cool off in a swimming pool. The music, primarily droning disco and rap, evokes a pounding cadence of jackhammers. Open May to October, daily midnight to 6am; November to April, Friday and Saturday midnight to 6am. The cover is a painful 5,000 to 7,000 ptas. ($30 to $42).

Disco Privelege, Urbanización San Rafael (☎ **971-19-81-60**), is a sprawling nightclub built to entertain 5,000, many of whom seem to rush the dance floor simultaneously. Wander from room to room, stopping wherever you feel the urge, as the interior contains more bars, semi-secluded patios, and romantic trysting spots than most hotels. Dance music, however, will conspire to keep you on the floor dancing, dancing, dancing. The club is open June to September, daily midnight to 7:30am. The cover is 4,000 to 5,000 ptas. ($24 to $30), but could be as high as 7,000 to 8,000 ptas. ($42 to $48) for special events, in particular English Monday nights, when DJs are imported from London.

Ibiza's newest, most controversial, and most appealing erotic club is **The Blue Rose,** carrer Navarra, 27, Figueretas (☎ **971-39-91-37**). There's a hefty cover of 5,000 ptas. ($30), including your first drink. It occupies what was originally established in the 1960s as the island's first disco. In 1998, amid the same black-and-white floor tiles where flower children used to tune in, turn on, and dance, California-born entrepreneur Joy Borne installed an intensely theatrical, high-class strip joint that's become one of the most popular places on an island obsessed with after-dark diversions. Defined as an American-style "Goddess Temple," where none of the exotic *artistes* object to getting an occasional bank note while they're on stage, the setting consists of a fireman's pole, equipment for some exhibitionistic acrobatics, and an area committed to exotic, tasteful nudity in a sexually provocative setting. Owned, operated, and for the most part staffed by women, drinks set you back from 1,200 ptas. ($7.20) after the first. It is open every night 11pm to 6am. Although most nights the club is filled with men watching women, Thursday nights feature male dancers performing for women 11pm to 3am, and male dancers performing for gay patrons 3am till closing. Most of the dancers come from northern Europe and, to a lesser extent, California.

There's gambling by the sea in the modern **Casino de Ibiza,** Passeig Juan Carlos I (Passeig Marítim; ☎ **971-31-33-12**). With the usual gaming tables and slot machines, it's open nightly 9:30pm to 4am. There's a separate room for slot machines that operate daily 6pm to 5am. The adjoining nightclub and dining hall offer live cabaret entertainment between May and October, with shows that feature a relatively tame assortment of magicians, comedians, and pretty women in feathers and spangles whose fancy stepping begins at 9:30pm. Casino entrance is 500 ptas. ($3); dinner and a show run you about 7,000 ptas. ($42). Passport required for admission.

With the possible exception of Mykonos, few other islands in the Mediterranean cater to gay travelers as much as Ibiza. A stroll through the Ciudad Ibiza's old town reveals dozens of gay bars catering to international visitors; most are open 9 or 10pm to 3am. Although many close and reopen with disconcerting frequency, some of the most deeply entrenched include **Disco Anfora,** carrer San Carlos, 7 (☎ **971-30-28-93**), an *haute-electronic* disco that blares away, to the dancing pleasure of a mostly gay clientele, between midnight and 6am every night in the summer. The cover charge of 1,500 ptas. ($9) includes the first drink. More geared toward drinking and talking than dancing is **Bar Léon,** calle de la Virgen, 3 (no phone), and its almost equivalent counterpart, **Bar Geminis,** Figueretas (no phone). Other gay sites include **Angelo's,** carrer Alfonso XII, 11 (no phone), which serves drinks beginning around 9pm every evening, and **Teatro,** calle de la Virgen, 57 (no phone), which has an outdoor bar. And if you're hungry, there's a restaurant in Ciudad Ibiza's inner core, **Restaurant Pomelo,** carrer de la Virgen (☎ **971-31-31-22**), catering to an international clientele with a huge percentage of gay patronage. The restaurant is open Easter to October, 8pm to between 1 and 2am.

SAN ANTONIO DE PORTMANY

Known to the Romans as Portus Magnus and before that a Bronze Age settlement, this thriving town was discovered in the 1950s by foreigners and has remained popular ever since. Tourism here is "megamass." The town today goes by two names—San Antonio de Portmany for Spanish speakers or Sant Antoni de Portmany for Catalán speakers.

In summer you have as much chance of finding a room here as you would booking a reservation on the last flight to the moon if the earth were on fire. Virtually all the hotels have a direct pipeline to tour-group agencies in northern Europe, and the individual traveler probably won't get the time of day. If you're determined to stay in the area during peak travel season, your best bet is trying to arrange a package tour.

The resort, with a 14th-century parish church, is built on an attractive bay. Avoid the impossibly overcrowded narrow strip of sand at San Antonio itself. Take a ferry or bus to one of the major beaches, including Cala Gració, 1 mile (1.6km) to the north, set against a backdrop of pines, or Port des Torrent, 3 miles (5km) southwest. Cala Bassa in the south is also popular. San Antonio overlooks the Isla Conejera, an uninhabited rock island. With its hordes of visitors, San Antonio has an easygoing lifestyle, plus lots of mildly entertaining nightlife. Even if you're staying in Ibiza or Santa Eulalia, you may want to hop over for the day or evening.

But San Antonio is not for the conservative. It's not unusual to see bottomless women on the beach—and topless women in dance clubs. Note, however, that even though marijuana is common here, buying and selling it is strictly against the law.

When visiting hooligans have had too much cheap booze, San Antonio can get dangerous. In the earlier part of the evening, however, you may want to patronize one of the bars or open-air terraces around avinguda Doctor Fleming.

ESSENTIALS

GETTING THERE   Buses leave from Ciudad de Ibiza every 30 minutes.

VISITOR INFORMATION   The **tourist information office** is at Passeig de Ses Fonts (☎ **971-34-33-63**). It's open Monday to Friday 9:30am to 8:30pm and Saturday and Sunday 9:30am to 1pm, May to October. Off-season hours are Monday to Saturday 9:30am to 1pm.

EXPLORING THE AREA

Throughout the day, boats leave from Passeig de Ses Fonts. They take you to **Cala Bassa,** a sandy beach on a thin strip, for 600 ptas. ($3.60) one-way, or to **Cala Conta,** a slightly rocky beach, for 550 ptas. ($3.30). If you negotiate, they will take you along the coastline northwest to the far point of Portinatx. This is virtually the only way to see the coastline, since there isn't a road running along it, and most visitors agree it's the most beautiful coastline of Ibiza.

North of the waterfront, the chief attraction is **Sa Cova de Santa Agnès,** a national monument and an object of eerie devotion. This has been a place of sacred worship ever since a sailor prayed to Santa Agnès during a rough storm and was saved. The sailor, to show his gratitude, placed a figure of the saint in this dark hole. It's become a place of pilgrimage ever since, and it's open free on Monday and again on Saturday 9am to noon.

If you have rented a car you can explore **Cueva de Ses Fontanelles,** north of Platja Calad Salada, where faintly colorful prehistoric paintings decorate the walls.

Offshore at the popular southern beach of Cala d'Hort is the intriguing **Es Vedrá rock,** where, in times of hardship and hunger, the Ibicencos would go, at great personal risk, to gather seagull eggs for survival. A Carmelite priest once recorded mystical revelations and meetings with "unearthly beings surrounded by light" while meditating on the island. Gigantic circles of light, up to 165 feet (50m) in diameter, have allegedly emerged from the sea here at times, discouraging fishers from working the area. It is said that a strong magnetic force emanating from Es Vedrá attracts such strange phenomena. Photographers and romantics, take note: After June 15 the sunrise here is especially dramatic, illuminating Es Vedrá while the surrounding hills remain in darkness.

WHERE TO STAY

The prospect of finding a room here in July and August is bleak—some Brits reserve a year in advance. British package tourists virtually occupy the crescent beach and busy harbor all during the warm months. You stand a better chance of finding lodgings in Ciudad de Ibiza.

Arenal Hotel. Avinguda Doctor Fleming, 16, 07820 San Antonio. ☎ **971-34-01-12.** Fax 971-34-25-65. 131 units. TEL. 7,500–15,500 ptas. ($45–$93) double. AE, DC, MC, V. Free parking.

This selection ranks among the top hotels in San Antonio de Portmany, offering value comparable to that of more expensively priced neighbors. During high season groups take over, but in October and from April to mid-May you can generally get a reservation if you write 2 weeks in advance. Off-season all you need to do is arrive.

Located at the edge of town on its own private beach, the Arenal is a four-story establishment with a swimming pool. The rooms are simple and attractive, furnished in contemporary style with comfortable beds and a balcony opening onto the sea or the little front garden lawn with palm trees.

Hotel Tropical. Cervantes, s/n, 07820 San Antonio. ☎ **971-34-00-50.** Fax 971-34-40-69. 142 units. TEL. 6,800–9,500 ptas. ($40.80–$57) double. Rates include breakfast. AE, DC, MC, V. Closed Nov–Mar.

Located away from the port area in a commercial section of town, this hotel's garden and swimming pool are across the street from its main building. The recreation area is like a small public park with dozens of reclining chairs and some billiard tables. The hotel was built in the early 1960s with a russet- and white-marbled lobby filled with armchairs. The Tropical is rated as one of the best hotels in the center, with comfortably furnished, modernized, but rather bland small to midsized rooms.

Hotel Village. Apartado, 27, Urbanización Caló den Real (along the road to Cala Vadella), 07830 Sant Josep, Ibiza. ☎ **971-80-80-01.** Fax 971-80-80-27. E-mail: village@ctv.es. 20 units. A/C MINIBAR TV TEL. 18,500–28,300 ptas. ($111–$170) double; 23,700–43,800 ptas. ($142–$263) suite. Rates include breakfast. MC, V. Free parking.

Located 15 miles west of Ibiza Town, this small, elegant hotel is one of our favorite refuges on the island. Just beyond the gleaming white marble lobby sits a cozy bar, ideal for aperitifs. The midsized guest rooms, also done in white marble, have terraces, most facing the sea, but several open onto the mountains. Each room is very comfortably furnished with adequate living space, plus tidy tiled bathrooms equipped with hair dryers. A walkway leads down the hill to a rocky beach, where guests can lounge in the sun and enjoy a drink at the beachside bar. There is an elegant dining room serving international cuisine with a Spanish influence, and the hotel offers tennis courts, a fitness center, and putting green.

Les Jardins de Palerm. Apartado, 62, 07080 San José, Ibiza. ☎ **971-80-03-18.** Fax 971-80-04-53. www.jardinsdepalerm.com. E-mail: palerm@ctv.es. 9 units. TV TEL. 18,000–26,000 ptas. ($108–$156) double; 22,000–42,000 ptas. ($132–$252) suite. Rates include breakfast. AE, MC, V. Closed Nov–Mar.

This intimate little hotel, outside the village of San José, is constructed in the style of a 17th-century hacienda. Patios and garden terraces scattered throughout the grounds are ideal locations for sunbathing, enjoying a lazy Ibiza afternoon, and getting away from the noise and bustle of the street. The small accommodations are rustic, with beamed ceilings, antiques, good beds, and ceiling fans. Each unit has its own terrace. Prices change every month—the lowest price quoted above is charged in the cool months of March, the highest tariff for the hot month of August.

Simple meals can be ordered and eaten on the terrace. A large outdoor pool is perfect for a dip in this sultry weather.

Pikes. Apartado, 104, 07820 San Antonio, Ibiza. ☎ **971-34-22-22.** Fax 971-34-23-12. 26 units. A/C MINIBAR TV TEL. 22,000–28,000 ptas. ($132–$168) double; 38,000–100,000 ptas. ($228–$600) suite. AE, DC, MC, V. Children under 12 must be accompanied by a parent.

Originally a *finca* (farm), this 600-year-old compound has been transformed into a luxurious playground for well-heeled travelers and celebrities from around the world. Touted for its "sophisticated informality," Pikes boasts spacious rooms with sensuous interiors, including king-size beds and oversized bathtubs. The hotel offers activities and entertainment for its guests, ranging from flamenco shows to costume balls. Pikes provides a VIP card that allows entrance to most of the area's clubs and casinos.

The hotel's restaurant serves an international cuisine in a series of intimate dining rooms. There is a poolside bar for sunbathers and a tennis court and fitness center as well. Management can arrange boating, golfing, and horseback riding.

WHERE TO DINE

Many of Ibiza's restaurants are tucked away in quiet coves or in the countryside, so you really need a car to sample the full range of the island's culinary savoir-faire.

✪ **Cana Juana.** Carretera Sant Josep, km 10, 6 miles (10km) from Ciudad Ibiza, on road to Sant Josep. ☎ **971-80-01-58.** Reservations recommended. Main courses 2,200–3,000 ptas. ($13.20–$18). AE, MC, V. Daily 8:30–11:30pm. Closed Nov–Dec. MEDITERRANEAN.

This 240-year-old villa has been converted into the finest restaurant on Ibiza, thanks to the dedicated efforts of owner and chef Juana Biarnes and her husband, co-owner and maître d'hôtel Michel. Before her present role, Juana was a pioneering female reporter in Spain, uncovering scandals and presenting new ideas to a Spanish readership before retreating to Ibiza to perfect her cooking skills. Examples of what's available include fillets of skate that are steamed and then grilled for added crispiness and served with strips of Jabugo ham and a confit of onions. Also appealing are such Catalán specialties as codfish with spinach, raisins, and pinenuts; and an earthy but flavorful dish every Catalán remembers from his or her childhood, *butifarra* sausage served with white beans. Other examples include a confit of *canard* (duckling) in the French style; baked potatoes served with truffles; and roasted *dorada* (John Dory) served with vinegar, olive oil, garlic, and baby lettuce. The restaurant's cellars contain a sophisticated roster of Spanish and European wines, with a vintage to complement virtually anything.

El Rincón de Pepe. Sant Mateu, 6. ☎ **971-34-06-97.** Reservations not necessary. Tapas 400–1,000 ptas. ($2.70–$6.70); main courses 1,200–2,200 ptas. ($7.20–$13.20). MC, V. Daily 11am–1:30am. Closed Nov–Easter. TAPAS.

Primarily a place for tapas and light snacks, this friendly cafe also serves a menu that includes Spanish dishes, as well as hamburgers, hot dogs, and a variety of fresh salads. The food is simple and good, the atmosphere convivial, and the bar an attractive arrangement in tile and wood.

Restaurante/Bar Rias Baixas. Carrer Ignacio Riguer, 4. ☎ **971-34-04-80.** Reservations required. Main courses 3,500–5,000 ptas. ($21–$30). AE, CB, DC, MC, V. Daily 1–4pm and 8pm–midnight. Closed Dec–Feb. GALICIAN.

This rustic air-conditioned Iberian dining room, with its stucco arches, beamed ceiling, and open fireplace, is an apt setting for the Galician specialties served here.

Seafood, flown in fresh every day from northern Spain, is the restaurant's specialty—mussels, Galician clams, crabmeat soup, *caldo gallego* (Galician broth), trout meunière, and Bilbao-style eels, each accompanied by a selection of Galician wine. Good-tasting beef, pork, and veal dishes are also available.

Sa Capella. Carretera de Santa Inés, 0.5km. ☎ **971-34-00-57.** Reservations recommended. Main courses 1,600–3,000 ptas. ($9.60–$18). MC, V. Daily 8pm–midnight. Closed Nov–Mar. MEDITERRANEAN.

This restaurant is set in a 600-year-old chapel with stone vaulting, rose windows, radiating alcoves, balconies, and chandeliers that can be lowered on pulleys from the overhead masonry. You pass beneath an arbor of magenta bougainvillea and are ushered to your table by a waiter dressed in red-and-white traditional Ibizan costume. Meals are flavorful and well versed in the culinary traditions of the Mediterranean. Examples include fresh broccoli as well as exotic mushrooms with strips of Serrano ham; John Dory cooked in a salt crust; roast suckling pig in the style of Segovia; shepherd's-style lamb chops served with potatoes and carrots; marinated mussels; roasted rabbit; and pepper steak. Dessert might consist of homemade cheesecake garnished with fresh raspberries. Partly because of its historic setting, partly because of its fine food, this dining choice has a deservedly devoted following.

THE NORTHERN COAST

The north remains largely untainted by the scourge of mass tourism, except for a handful of coves. Here you'll find some of the island's prettiest countryside, with fields of olive, almond, and carob trees and the occasional *finca* raising melons or grapes.

EXPLORING THE AREA

Off the road leading into Port de Sant Miquel (Puerto de San Miguel) is **Cova de Can Merca,** about 300 feet (91m) from the Hotel Galeón. There is a fine view of the bay from the hotel's snack bar. After a stunning descent down stairs clinging to the face of the cliff, you enter a cave that's more than 100,000 years old and forms its stalactites and stalagmites at the rate of about ¼ inch (.6cm) per 100 years. A favored hiding place for smugglers and their goods in former days, today it's a beautifully orchestrated surrealistic experience—including a sound-and-light display—not unlike walking through a Dalí painting. Many of the limestone formations are delicate miniatures. The half-hour tour is conducted in several languages for groups of up to 70. From Holy Week to the end of October, tours are offered daily every half hour 10:30am to 7:30pm. Admission is 800 ptas. ($4.80) for adults and 400 ptas. ($2.40) for children.

At the island's northern tip is **Portinatx,** a pretty series of beaches and bays now marred by a string of souvenir shops and haphazardly built hotels. For a taste of its original, rugged beauty, go past all the construction to the jagged coast along the open sea.

Every Saturday throughout the year there is a **flea market** just beyond Sant Carles (San Carlos) on the road to Santa Eulalia (you'll know where it is by all the cars parked along the road). Open from about 10am until 8 or 9pm, it offers all kinds of clothing (both antique and new), accessories, crafts, and the usual odds and ends.

If you want to escape to a lovely beach that remains a stranger to hotel construction, head for **Playa Benirras** just north of Port de Sant Miquel. An unpaved but passable road leads out to this small, calm, pretty cove, where lounge chairs are available and pedal boats are for rent. There are snack bars and restaurants here.

A beautiful drive leads from Sant Carles (San Carlos) along the coast to Cala Sant Vicent (San Vicente).

WHERE TO STAY

Hotel offerings are more limited in the north than in the traditional pockets of tourism in the south and west. Nevertheless, the island's finest hotel, the five-star Hacienda, is here, above Na Xamena Bay. Port de Sant Miquel, Cala Sant Vicent, and Portinatx—once tranquil, seaside havens—have become increasingly pockmarked with package-tour hotels.

Hotel Galeón. Puerto de San Miguel, 07815 Sant Joan de Labritja, Ibiza. ☎ **971-33-45-34.** Fax 971-33-45-35. 189 units. 9,500–14,500 ptas. ($57–$87) double. Rates include breakfast. AE, V. Closed Nov–Apr. Free parking.

One of two hotels overlooking the little bay, this basic hotel offers simple, clean, comfortable, but small guest rooms, each equipped with a good bed. Accommodations have terraces with views of the sea. Tennis courts and water sports are available. The hotel's restaurant serves a good but rather uninspired cuisine.

✪ **Hotel Hacienda.** Na Xamena, 07815 San Miguel, Ibiza. ☎ **971-33-45-00.** Fax 971-33-45-14. www.relaischateaux.fr/xamena. E-mail: htl.hacienda@vlc.servicom.es. 63 units. A/C MINIBAR TV TEL. 22,500–52,000 ptas. ($135–$312) double; 54,000–125,000 ptas. ($324–$750) suite. AE, DC, MC, V. Closed Nov to mid-Apr.

Located 14 miles (22.5km) northwest of Ciudad de Ibiza, this Moorish villa, set on a promontory overlooking Na Xamena Bay, is the top destination on Ibiza for well-heeled travelers and celebrities seeking leisure and sanctuary. Luxury, informality, privacy, and personal service—the Hacienda has it all. Public rooms are full of various cubbyholes, ideal for cozying up to a book or travel companion. Diners gather at tables beside the large outdoor pool during the warmer months. Spacious guest rooms are decorated with four-poster beds, sumptuous carpets, and balconies overlooking the Mediterranean. Many rooms have marble bathrooms and private whirlpools; all are equipped with hair dryers.

The hotel has an excellent terrace restaurant, **Las Cascadas,** providing panoramic vistas of the surrounding cliffs and sea. A bar offers snacks, and a pub/disco is available for evening entertainment. The Hacienda has three swimming pools (one for children), a tennis court, billiards room, bicycle rentals, horseback riding, and boat rentals; fishing excursions are arranged on request.

SANTA EULALIA DEL RÍO

Once patronized by expatriate artists from the capital, 9 miles (14.5km) to the south, Santa Eulalia del Río now attracts mostly middle-class northern Europeans.

Santa Eulalia is at the foot of the Puig de Missa, on the estuary of the only river in the Balearics. The principal monument in town is a fortress church standing on a hilltop, or *puig.* Dating from the 16th century, it has an ornate Gothic altar screen.

Santa Eulalia is relatively free of the sometimes plastic quality of San Antonio. Visitors often have a better chance of finding accommodations here than in the other two major towns.

ESSENTIALS

GETTING THERE   During the day, buses run between Ciudad de Ibiza and Santa Eulalia del Río every 30 minutes.

Seven boats a day run between Ciudad de Ibiza and Santa Eulalia del Río. The boats run on the hour, and the first leaves Ciudad de Ibiza at 10:30am and Santa Eulalia del Río at 9:30am. The boat ride takes 45 minutes and information can be obtained at ☎ **971-33-22-51.**

VISITOR INFORMATION   The **tourist information office** is at carrer Mariano Riquer Wallis (☎ **971-33-07-28**), open Monday to Friday, 9:30am to 1:30pm and 5 to 7:30pm, Saturday 9:30am to 1:30pm. In summer the office is open Monday to Friday, 9am to 1:30pm and 5 to 8pm, and Saturday 9am to 7:30pm.

EXPLORING THE AREA

You can reach the famous northern beaches from Santa Eulalia by bus or boat, departing from the harbor front near the boat basin. **Aigües Blanques** is one of the best beaches, just 6 miles (10km) north. (It's legal to go nude here.) It's reached by four buses a day. A long, sandy cove, **Cala Llonga,** is 3 miles (5km) south and is serviced by 10 buses a day. Cala Llonga fronts a bevy of package-tour hotels, so it's likely to be crowded. Boats depart Santa Eulalia for Cala Llonga every 30 minutes, 9am to 6pm. **Es Caná** is a white-sand beach, 3 miles (5km) north of town; boats and buses leave every 30 minutes, 8am to 9pm. Four buses a day depart for **Cala Llenya** and **Cala Nova.**

WHERE TO STAY

Hotel S'Argamassa Sol. Urbanización S'Argamassa, 07182 Santa Eulalia del Río. ☎ **971-33-00-51.** Fax 971-33-00-76. 230 units. A/C MINIBAR TV TEL. 15,000–20,000 ptas. ($90–$120) double. Rates include half board. AE, DC, MC, V. Closed Nov–Apr.

Two miles (3km) outside Santa Eulalia del Rio, near Roman ruins, the Hotel S'Argamassa is a well-run, family-oriented resort. The hotel is a short walk from the beach and maintains its own small pier. All the midsized guest rooms have terraces with sea views. Accommodations are comfortable; many have been recently renovated, and each comes with a firm bed. The hotel has no restaurant, but dining options are nearby.

There is an outdoor pool, bowling alley, playground, tennis courts, and a game room. For evening entertainment, music and dancing are offered in the lounge or cocktails at the poolside bar.

Hotel Ses Estaques. Ses Estaques, s/n, 07840 Santa Eulalia del Río. ☎ **971-33-02-00.** Fax 971-33-04-86. www.hotelestaques.com. E-mail: jmr@hotelestaques.com. 166 units. TEL. 12,000–16,000 ptas. ($72–$96) double. Rates include breakfast. AE, DC, MC, V. Closed Nov–Apr.

A much-favored hotel in this resort, close to the seashore at the edge of town, Ses Estaques is open only in the good weather months. On the walk to the private beach you will find a beautiful garden filled with roses, palms, and ivy, and the swimming pool is edged with pines and a poolside snack bar. Inside, the hotel is filled with extra touches and hideaway corners of charm. There's an aquarium in the spacious lobby, a pleasant tropical restaurant on the beach a short walk away, minigolf, and a tennis court. Each of the comfortable terrazzo-floored rooms has a balcony with a view of the garden or the sea. The hotel was last renovated in 1998, with new mattresses and plumbing added.

Hotel Tres Torres. Ses Estaques, s/n, 07840 Santa Eulalia del Río. ☎ **971-33-03-26.** Fax 971-33-20-85. 114 units. A/C TV TEL. 10,000–19,000 ptas. ($60–$114) double; 13,000–22,000 ptas. ($78–$132) suite. Rates include half-board. AE, DC, MC, V. Closed Nov–Apr.

A stylish modern hotel where many of the comfortable, midsized, and balconied rooms overlook the two swimming pools, Hotel Tres Torres has an art gallery, a jewelry shop, and a lobby filled with neo-Victorian wicker chairs. An airy and sunny dining room offers a view of the water.

San Marino. Apartado de Correos, 56, 07840 Santa Eulalia del Río. ☎ **971-33-03-16.** Fax 971-33-90-76. www.ibiza-hotel.com/sanmarino. E-mail: hotel-sanmarino@jet.es. A/C MINIBAR TV TEL. 9,500 ptas. ($57) double. AE, DC, MC, V. Parking 400 ptas. ($2.40).

The best hotel at the resort, this four-star selection opened its doors in 1989. The architecture is a mixture of classic and modern, constructed in a typically Spanish hotel style with balconies and white-painted walls. Inside, the tasteful decor is dominated by marble, wood, and glass, and decorated with leather furniture, plus walls hung with paintings and prints. Rooms are small to midsized but are most comfortable, with excellent mattresses and fully equipped bathrooms.

Dining/Diversions: A hotel restaurant, **La Granja,** specializes in Spanish cuisine, and does so very well. There is a pizzeria, plus a pastry shop. Entertainment is sometimes offered.

Amenities: Swimming pool, solarium, laundry, limited room service.

WHERE TO DINE

Doña Margarita. Puerto Deportiva. ☎ **971-33-22-00.** Reservations recommended. Main courses 2,200–4,500 ptas. ($13.20–$27). AE, DC, MC, V. Tues–Sun 1–3:30pm and 8–11:30pm. Closed Dec–Feb. SPANISH/INTERNATIONAL.

Although one of Santa Eulalia's most venerable restaurants moved into new premises in 1998, it managed to retain the loyalty of its local clientele and the managerial skill of its owner and resident matriarch, Margarita Ribas. A modern building with big windows that overlook the yachts bobbing at anchor in the nearby marina, it offers a solidly traditional menu that includes lots of very fresh fish that are painstakingly prepared. The fish is usually served with fresh salads, and finished off with succulent desserts that are fresh-made daily, including lemon mousse with raspberries. In between, you might enjoy mussels marinara, spicy fish soup, paella, salmon with green peppercorns, calves' kidneys with fried onions, a *parillada* of prawns or a *zarzuela* of shellfish, and a changing roster of fresh fish and shellfish whose ingredients vary according to their availability in the marketplace.

✪ **El Naranjo.** Carrer San José, 31. ☎ **971-33-03-24.** Reservations required. Main courses 1,400–2,500 ptas. ($8.40–$15). AE, MC, V. Tues–Sun 7:30–11:30pm. Closed Nov–Feb. CONTINENTAL.

This chic nighttime rendezvous has altogether the most beautiful courtyard in town. Many refer to this place as "The Orange Tree," its name in English. The orange tree patio, with its flowering bougainvillea vines, has such appeal that many diners don't mind its out-of-the-way location (in town, several blocks from the water). If your table isn't ready when you arrive, enjoy an aperitif in the cozy bar. The menu items are beautifully prepared and served. One newspaper called the chef "an artist." Dishes include fresh fish and duckling in red-currant-and-pepper sauce. Begin with *las tres mousses* (three mousses) as an appetizer, finishing with the lemon tart for dessert.

3 Formentera

For years, Formentera was known as the "forgotten Balearic." The smallest of the archipelago, it's a 30-square-mile (78sq km), flat limestone plain. In the east it is flanked by La Mola, a peak rising 615 feet (186.5m), and in the west it is protected by Berberia, at 315 feet (95.5m).

The Romans called it Frumentaria (meaning "wheat granary"), when they oversaw it as a booming little agricultural center. But that was then. A shortage of water coupled with strong winds has allowed only meager vegetation to grow, notably some fig trees and fields of wild rosemary (which seem to be home to thousands of green lizards).

A few hearty goats live on the island, and, like Ibiza, Formentera has a salt industry. Its year-round population of 5,000 swells in summer, mostly with day-trippers from Ibiza. Limited hotels have kept development in check, and most visitors come over for the day to enjoy the beaches, where they often swim without bathing suits and sun-bathe along the excellent stretches of sand. British and Germans form the majority of tourists that actually spend the night.

On the ferry ride over from Ibiza, you pass Isla Ahorcados (Hanged Men's Island), where criminals from Ibiza were once strung up, and the more reassuring Isla Espal-mador, with its sandy beaches. Carry some seasickness pills, as the ferry crossing can be turbulent.

ISLAND ESSENTIALS

GETTING THERE   Formentera is serviced by up to 29 ferryboats passages a day in summer and by about a dozen per day in winter. Boats depart from Ciudad de Ibiza, on Ibiza's southern coast, for La Savina (La Sabina), 2 miles (3km) north of the island's capital and largest settlement, Sant Francesc (San Francisco Javier). Depending on the design of the boat you select, passage across the 3-mile (5km) channel separating the islands takes between 35 minutes and 1 hour. For information on schedules, call ☎ **971-31-07-11,** although it's usually easier to ask employees at almost any hotel on the island, who are usually well versed in the hours of ferryboats to and from Ibiza.

GETTING AROUND   As ferryboats arrive at the quays of La Savina, taxis line up at the pier. One-way passage to such points as Es Pujols and Playa de Mitjorn costs 1,000 ptas. ($6) and 1,500 to 1,700 ptas. ($9 to $10.20), respectively, but it's always wise to negotiate or predetermine the fare before the journey begins. To call a taxi in Sant Francesc, dial ☎ **971-32-20-16;** in El Pujols, ☎ **971-32-80-16;** and in La Sabina, ☎ **971-32-20-02.** Regardless of when and where you call for a taxi, be prepared to wait.

Car rentals can be arranged through **Hertz** (☎ 971-32-22-42), whose kiosk is at La Sabina, close to where you disembark from the ferryboats.

If you want to enjoy seeing Formentera by a bicycle or a motor scooter, they can be rented from **Moto-Rent** in La Sabina (☎ 971-32-21-38) or in Pujols (☎ **971-32-24-88**). Motor scooters rent for 2,000 ptas. ($12) a day, bicycles for around 600 to 1,600 ptas. ($3.60 to $9.60) a day.

VISITOR INFORMATION   The **tourist information office** in Formentera is at Edificio de Servicios de Puerto, 1, in Port de la Sabina (☎ 971-32-20-57), open Monday to Friday 10am to 2pm and 5 to 7pm, Saturday 10am to 2pm.

HITTING THE BEACH

Beaches, beaches, and more beaches—that's why visitors come here. You can see the ocean from any point on the island. Some say the island has the best beaches in the Mediterranean—an opinion not without merit. Formentera has been declared a "World Treasure" by UNESCO, one of four places so honored because of its special character as an ecological and wildlife preserve. This implies an indirect control by UNESCO of activities that could jeopardize the island's ecological well being.

Meanwhile, day-trippers from Ibiza have fun sampling its long, sedate beaches and solitary coves before returning to Ibiza's ebullience in the evening.

The island is ringed with beaches, so selecting the one you think will appeal to you is about the only problem you'll face—that and whether you should wear a bathing suit.

Playa de Mitjorn, on the southern coast, is 3 miles (5km) long; it has many uncrowded sections. This is the principal area for nude sunbathing. A few bars and hotels occupy the relatively undeveloped stretch of sand. You can make **Es Copinyars,** the name of one of the beachfronts, your stop for lunch, as it has a number of restaurants and snack bars.

At **Es Calo,** along the northern coast, west of El Pilar, there are some small boarding houses, *hostales*. From this point, you can see the lighthouse of La Mola, which was featured in Jules Verne's *Journey Round the Solar System*, and, if weather conditions are right, Majorca.

Sant Ferran serves the beach of **Es Pujols,** darling of the package-tour operators. This is the most crowded beach on Formentera, and you may want to avoid it. The beaches, however, are pure white sand, with a backdrop of dunes and pine trees. It's a place to go windsurfing and is the site of several tourist amenities. The beach is protected by the Punta Prima headland.

Westward, **Cala Sahona** is another popular tourist spot, lying near the lighthouse on Cabo Berberia. Often pleasure vessels anchor here on what is the most beautiful cove in Formentera.

WHERE TO STAY

Accommodations are scarce, so you must arrive with an ironclad reservation should you want to spend the night or a longer time.

Club La Mola. Apartado, 23, 07871 Playa de Mitjorn, Formentera. ☎/fax **971-32-70-69.** 349 units. A/C MINIBAR TV TEL. 18,000–33,000 ptas. ($108–$198) double. Rates include half-board. AE, DC, MC, V. Closed Nov–Apr.

Located at Es Arenals, this is one of the best-equipped hotels on the island, and during the summer it is usually packed. Opening onto the longest beach on the island, La Mola is constructed in the style of a Spanish village. The good-size rooms are comfortable and well furnished, each with a firm bed and a tiled bathroom equipped with a hair dryer. Facilities include two swimming pools, tennis courts, much equipment for water sports, a gym, a garden, minigolf, and a disco. The restaurant serves Spanish and continental meals, but it's only standard fare.

Club Punta Prima. Punta Prima, 07871 Sant Ferran. ☎ **971-32-82-44.** Fax 971-32-81-28. 120 units. TV TEL. 16,500–18,500 ptas. ($99–$111) double; 18,000–20,000 ptas. ($108–$120) suite. Rates include half-board. MC, V. Closed Nov–Apr.

Built in 1987 in a low-slung, two-story format hugging the coastline a short walk from the beach, this is the best and best-accessorized hotel on Formentera, with a loyal clientele from northern Europe, which tends to return year after year. The good-sized rooms are comfortably furnished and well maintained, each with an excellent bed. Virtually everyone checks in here on the half-board plan, indulging in meals that are, more often than not, served as an ongoing series of buffets. Great attention has been paid to the enhancement and preservation of the site's isolated natural beauty.

Sa Volta. Apartado, 71, Sant Ferran, 07871 Es Pujols, Formentera. ☎ **971-32-81-25.** Fax 971-32-82-28. 27 units. TV TEL. 5,800–12,800 ptas. ($34.80–$76.80) double. AE, DC, MC, V.

This small hostal features good, clean, but very modest rooms, and charges reasonable prices. It was totally renovated in 2000, with new beds added. It has a cafeteria but no restaurant. However, you are in the midst of many cafes, restaurants, and nightlife possibilities because this is the tourist belt of Formentera. Reserve well in advance, as it's hard to get a room here.

WHERE TO DINE

Es Molí del Sal. Ses Illetes (al Noroeste). ☎ **608-13-67-73** (note different area code from rest of Balearics). Reservations required. Main courses 1,800–5,500 ptas. ($10.80–$33). AE, MC, V. Daily 9am–11pm. Closed Nov–Apr. SPANISH/CATALÁN.

This restaurant, the island's best, is in a restored windmill near the salt flats. It opens onto Platja de Ses Illetes, that slender northern tip of Formentera, the most desirable beachfront on the island. A small restaurant, it specializes in fresh fish and lobster and seems to please everybody. The cookery, although hardly spectacular, is good, simple fare prepared with fresh ingredients. The view of the sea and of Ibiza is panoramic.

4 Minorca

Minorca (also written "Menorca") is one of the most beautiful islands in the Mediterranean; miles of lovely beaches have made it a longtime favorite vacation spot for Europeans.

Barely 9 miles (14.5km) wide and less than 32 miles (51.5km) long, its principal city is Mahón (also called Maó; pop 25,000), set on a rocky bluff overlooking the great port, which was fought over for centuries by the British, French, and Spanish.

After Majorca, it is the second largest of the Spanish Balearic Islands, but it has more beaches than Majorca, Ibiza, and Formentera combined—they range from miles-long silver or golden crescents of sand to rocky bays, or *calas,* reminiscent of Norwegian fjords. Our favorite is Cala'n Porter, 7 miles (11km) west of Mahón. Towering promontories guard the slender estuary where this spectacular beach is found. Another of Minorca's treasures, Cala de Santa Galdana, is 14 miles (22.5km) south of Ciudadela. Its gentle bay and excellent sandy beach afford the most scenic spot on the island. Ila d'en Colom, an island in the Mahón bay, is bordered with great beaches, but can be reached only by boat.

The beaches along 135 miles (217km) of pine-fringed coastline are the island's greatest attraction, although many are not connected by roads. Nude bathing is commonplace, even though the practice is officially illegal. Golf, tennis, and sailing are available at reasonable fees, and windsurfing is offered at all major beaches.

With about 60,000 permanent inhabitants, Minorca plays host to about half a million visitors a year. But it is not overrun with tourist developments and has none of the junky excess that has plagued Ibiza and Majorca for years.

Unlike those islands, Minorca is not utterly dependent on tourism; it has some industry, including leatherwork, costume jewelry making, dairy farming, and even gin manufacturing. Life here is quieter and more relaxed; it is not a place to go for glittering nightlife. Some clubs in Ibiza don't even open until 4 in the morning, but on Minorca nearly everybody, local and visitor alike, is in bed well before then.

In addition to trips to the beach, there are some fascinating things to do for those interested in history, archaeology, music, and art. Many artists live in Minorca, and exhibitions of their work are listed regularly in the local paper. The Catedral de Santa María in Mahón has one of the great pipe organs of Europe, and world-famous organists have appeared here, giving free concerts.

In the south some 1,600 archaeological sites have been found, dating from prehistoric times. Of the mysterious monuments unearthed, the most spectacular are the *taulas,* Stonehenge-type structures made from two slabs of rock forming the letter *T.* Known only on Minorca, these megalithic structures are often more than 12 feet (4m) high.

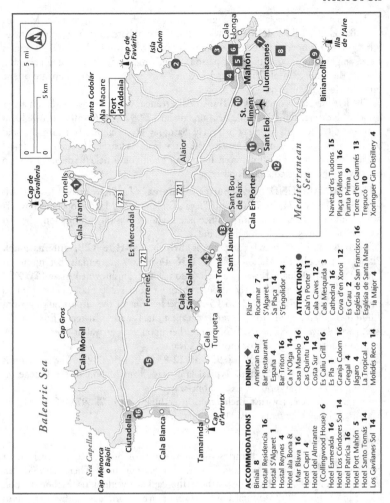

ACCOMMODATIONS ■
Biniali **8**
Hostal Residencia **16**
Hostal S'Algaret **1**
Hostal Reynes **4**
Hotel ala Bona & Mar Blava **16**
Hotel Capri **4**
Hotel del Almirante (Collingwood House) **6**
Hotel Esmeralda **16**
Hotel Los Cóndores Sol **14**
Hotel Patricia **16**
Hotel Port Mahón **5**
Hotel Santo Tomás **14**
Los Gavilanes Sol **14**

DINING ◆
American Bar **4**
Bar Restaurant España **4**
Bar Triton **16**
Ca N'Olga **14**
Casa Manolo **16**
Cas Quintu **16**
Costa Sur **14**
Es Caliu Grill **16**
Es Pla **1**
Granja Colom **16**
Gregal **4**
Jágaro **4**
La Tropical **4**
Molidés Reco **14**
Pilar **4**
Rocamar **7**
S'Algaret **1**
Sa Plaça **14**
S'Engolidor **14**

ATTRACTIONS ●
Cala'n Porter **11**
Cala Caves **12**
Cals Mesquida **3**
Cathedral **16**
Cova d'en Xoroi **12**
Es Grau **2**
Església de San Francisco **16**
Església de Santa Maria la Major **4**
Naveta d'es Tudons **15**
Plaça d'Alfons III **16**
Punta Prima **9**
Torre d'en Gaumés **13**
Trepucó **10**
Xoringuer Gin Distillery **4**

ISLAND ESSENTIALS

GETTING THERE   Minorca, lying off the eastern coast of Spain and northeast of Majorca, is reached by air or sea. The most popular method of reaching Minorca, certainly the quickest, is to fly, but you can take a ferry from mainland Spain or from the other two major Balearic Islands, Ibiza and Majorca.

It is always good to arrive with everything arranged in advance—hotel rooms, car rentals, ferry or airplane tickets. In July and August, reservations are vital, because of the limited hotel and transportation facilities.

Minorca International Airport (☎ **902-40-05-00** for information) is 2 miles (3km) outside the capital city of Mahón. It receives dozens of charter flights, mainly from Germany, Italy, the Scandinavian countries, and Britain. However, both **Iberia** and Aviaco (☎ **902-40-05-00** for information on both airlines) operate regularly scheduled domestic flights from Barcelona, Palma de Majorca, and even Madrid.

Regular **train service,** which operates frequently in the summer, connects Minorca with Barcelona, Palma de Majorca, and Ibiza. From Barcelona, the journey takes 9 hours aboard moderately luxurious lines. If you're on a real budget but still want a decent night's sleep, bunk in a four-person cabin, which is about the same price as a chair in the lounge. Meals can be purchased in a self-service restaurant onboard or else brought along if you're on a strict budget.

The ferry service is operated by **Transmediterránea,** whose offices in Mahón are at Estació Marítima, along Moll (Andén) de Ponent (☎ 971-36-60-50), open 8:30am to 1pm and 5 to 7pm Monday to Friday. Saturday hours are 8:30am to noon, and Sunday 3 to 5pm, but only to receive the ferry from Valencia. However, any travel agency in Barcelona or Palma, even Ibiza, can book you a ticket; you need not go directly to one of the company's offices.

GETTING AROUND Transportes Menorca (TMSA), carrer Joseph M. Quadrado, 7 (☎ 971-36-03-61), off Plaça s'Esplanada in Mahón, operates bus service around the island. The tourist office (see Mahón's "Visitor Information," below) has complete bus schedules for the island.

A good local car rental company is **British Car-Hire G.B. International,** Plaça s'Esplanada in Mahón (☎ 971-36-44-05), with rentals beginning at 15,000 ptas. ($90) for 3 days in the high season. The Spanish-owned **Atesa** (☎ 971-36-62-13) operates a desk at the airport, charging from 7,200 ptas. ($43.20) for its cheaper models. **Avis** (☎ 971-36-15-76) operates out of the airport, asking from 7,000 to 9,000 ptas. ($42 to $54) for its cheapest cars per day. Car-rental firms on the island will deliver a vehicle to the airport either upon your arrival or after you check into your hotel—but you must specify in advance.

To summon a local taxi, call ☎ 971-36-12-83 or 971-36-28-91. The taxi stop is at Plaça s'Esplanada in Mahón. Typical fare—say, from Mahón to the beaches at Cala'n Porter—is 1,800 ptas. ($10.80) one-way.

To rent a bicycle, try **Just Bicicletas,** carrer Infanta, 19 (☎ 971-36-47-51), in Mahón. A 1-day bike rental costs 1,000 ptas. ($6).

MAHÓN (MAÓ)

Mahón and neighboring Villacarlos still show traces of British occupation in their gorgeous Georgian architecture and Chippendale reproductions. There's also Golden Farm, the magnificent mansion north of the capital, overlooking Mahón harbor, where in October 1799 Admiral Lord Nelson enjoyed a brief rest and, according to local legend, hid out with his lady love, Emma Hamilton. In truth, Nelson was here alone working on *Sketches of My Life*.

The largest city on the island, Mahón is an east-coast port. In the Minorcan language, it is called Maó. Mahón has allegedly lent its name to one of the world's most popular sauces, mayonnaise.

Mahón was built on the site of an old castle standing on a cliff overlooking one of Europe's finest natural harbors, some 3½ miles (5.5km) long. The castle and the town wall erected to dissuade pirates are long gone, except for the archway of San Roque.

The first Christian king from the mainland, Alfonso II, established a base in the harbor in 1287. It became known as **Isla del Rey (Island of the King).** When the British constructed a hospital here to tend to wounded soldiers, it was called "Bloody Island."

Since 1722, when the seat of government was moved here from Ciudadela, Mahón has been the capital of Minorca.

ESSENTIALS

GETTING THERE   From the airport (see above), you must take a taxi into Mahón, as there is no bus link. The approximate cost is 1,400 ptas. ($8.40).

Mahón is the bus transport depot for the island, with departures from Plaça s'Esplanada in the heart of town. The most popular run—six buses per day—is to Ciudadela, but there are connections to other parts of the island. The tourist office (see "Visitor Information," below) distributes a list of schedules, and the list is published in the local newspaper, *Menorca Diario Insular.* Tickets are purchased once you're aboard. Make sure you carry some change.

VISITOR INFORMATION   The **tourist information office** is at Plaça s'Esplanada, 40 (☎ **971-36-37-90**), open May to October, Monday to Friday 8am to 8pm, Saturday 9am to 2pm; November to April, Monday to Friday 9am to 1pm and 5 to 7pm, Saturday 9am to 1pm.

CITY LAYOUT   The heart of Mahón is the Plaça de la Constitució, with its Town Hall from the 18th century, constructed in an English Palladian style.

Plaça s'Esplanada, seat of the tourist office and the bus departure point, is actually the main square. Here on Sundays locals gather to enjoy ice cream, the best in the Balearics. In summer, a market is held on Tuesday and Saturday 9am to 2pm. Island artisans from all over the island sell their wares at that time. The northern boundary of the city is formed by the **Puerto de Mahón,** which has many restaurants and shops along Muelle Comercial.

Mahón is not a beach town, but has some accommodations and is the center of the best shopping and nightclubs. The closest beaches for swimming are those at **Es Grau** and **Cala Mesquida.**

Villacarlos stretches east along the port, a virtual extension of the capital, and it doesn't have beaches either. Several good restaurants line the harbor leading toward Villacarlos. When the British founded this village, now a southeast suburb of Mahón, they called it Georgetown.

FUN ON & OFF THE BEACH

BEACHES   **Cala'n Porter,** 7 miles (11km) west of Mahón, is one of the most spectacular beaches on the island. It's a sandy beach at a narrow estuary inlet protected by high promontories. Thinly scattered houses perch upon a cliff. You can drop in on a bar here during the day. **La Cova d'en Xoroi,** ancient troglodyte habitations overlooking the sea from the upper part of the cliffs, can also be visited (see "Central & Southern Minorca," below).

Going around the cliff face you'll discover more caves at **Cala Caves.** People still live in some of these caves and there are boat trips to see them from Cala'n Porter.

North of Mahón on the road to Fornells you'll encounter many beachside settlements. Close to Mahón and already being exploited is **Cala Mesquida,** one of the best beaches. To reach it, turn off the road to Cala Llonga and follow the signs to PLAYA.

The next fork in the road takes you to **Es Grau,** another fine beach. Along the way you see the salt marshes of S'Albufera, abundant in migrant birds. Reached by bus from Mahón, Es Grau, 5 miles (8km) north of Mahón, opens onto a sandy bay and gets very crowded in July and August. From Es Grau you can take a boat to **Illa d'en Colom,** an island in the bay with some good beaches. There are several bars at Es Grau for refueling.

South of Mahón is the little town of San Lluís and the large sandy beach to the east, **Punta Prima.** Patronized heavily by occupants of the local *urbanizaciones,* this beach is serviced by buses from Mahón, with six departures daily. The same buses will take you to an attractive necklace of beaches, the **Platges de Son Bou,** on the southern shore. Many tourist facilities are found here (see "Central & Southern Minorca," below).

GOLF   The only course is **Urbanización Son Parc** (☎ 971-18-88-75), a traditional 9-hole course that recently added another nine holes.

HORSEBACK RIDING   For an equestrian tour of the island (subject to demand), call **Picadero Alaior** at ☎ 608-32-35-66 in Alaior, which is 7½ miles (12km) from Mahón on the road to Sanbu. The outfit is in front of the bridge by the beach. Both beginner and advanced riders are accommodated, and an hour costs 2,000 ptas. ($12).

WINDSURFING & SAILING   The best spots are at Fornells Bay, which is a mile wide and several miles long. **Windsurfing Fornells** (☎ 971-37-64-00) can supply you with gear.

SHOPPING

Es Portal, Sa Ravaleta, 23 (☎ 971-36-30-36), supplies Minorca's chic men and women with fashions from such high-priced and cutting-edge names as Moschino, Versace, Christian Lacroix, Dolce & Gabbana, and Armand Basi, as well as Spanish designers. Sophisticated accessories and shoes are available.

   Looky Boutique, carrer de Ses Moreres, 43 (☎ 971-36-06-48), is Minorca's outlet for chic, elegant leather accessories, which are produced in the company's factory in Ciudadela. The shop sells exquisite handbags, shoes, and leather clothing for men and women. Other locations include a shop in Ciudadela, at José María Quadrado, 14 (☎ 971-38-19-32), and in Fornells, at Passeig Marítim, 23 (☎ 971-37-65-45).

   Patricia, carrer de Ses Moreres, 31 (☎ 971-36-91-78), sells fine locally produced leather jackets, suits, skirts, and accessories. Other shops are at Camino Santandria/ Ronda Baleares (☎ 971-38-50-56).

SEEING THE SIGHTS

Most people don't take sightseeing too seriously in Mahón, as they are here mainly to enjoy the views of the port, to dine, or to shop. Even so, you may want to visit the **Església de Santa María la Major,** Plaça Constitució. The church was founded in 1287 by the Christian conqueror Alfonso III, who wanted to celebrate the Reconquest. Over the years, the original Gothic structure has been much altered, and it was rebuilt in 1772. It has a celebrated organ with four keyboards and more than 3,000 pipes, constructed in 1810 by Johan Kyburz, a Swiss artisan. Admiral Collingwood brought it to Mahón during the Napoleonic wars. A music festival in July and August showcases the organ, whose melodic sounds can be heard even as you sit drinking in a nearby cafe.

   The best way to see the changing aspect of Mahón's port involves taking an hour-long **catamaran tour.** Because part of the sailing craft's hull contains glass windows below the waterline, you'll get views of underwater life that would otherwise be possible only with a submarine. Tours begin year-round at 9:15am, then continue on the hour until 5:15pm. Departure time is not guaranteed, and the boat can leave up to 30 minutes later than scheduled. The cost is 950 ptas. ($5.70) for adults, 475 ptas. ($2.85) for children under 11. Tickets for this tour are available at **Xoringuer Gin Distillery,** Moll de Ponent, 93 (☎ 971-36-21-97).

   You can visit the **Xoriguer Gin Distillery** on the harbor front at Moll de Ponent, 93 (see above for phone number). Here giant copper vats simmer over wood-fed fires. Later, after watching the process by which the famed Minorcan gin is made, you can taste more than a dozen brews. The distillery and a store selling the products, including some potent liqueurs, is open Monday to Friday 8am to 7pm and Saturday 9am to 1pm.

SIDE TRIPS BACK IN TIME

From Mahón you can take excursions to some of the prehistoric relics in the area. One of these, marked off the Mahón–Villacarlos highway, is **Trepucó,** where you'll find both a 13-foot *taula* (huge T-shaped stone structure) and a *talayot* (circular stone tower). The megalithic monuments stand on the road to San Lluís, only about a mile from Mahón. Of all the prehistoric remains on the island, this is the easiest to visit. It was excavated by Margaret Murray and a team from Cambridge University in the 1930s.

Another legacy of prehistoric people can be visited at km 4 (a stone marker) off the Mahón–Ciudadela highway. The trail to **Talatí de Dalt** is marked. Your path will lead to this *taula* with subterranean caves.

Another impressive prehistoric monument is **Torre d'en Gaumés,** 9 miles (14.5km) from Mahón off the route to Son Bou (the path is signposted). You can take a bus from Mahón to Son Bou if you don't have a car. This megalithic settlement spreads over many acres, including both *taulas* and *talayots,* along with some ancient caves in which people once lived. The exact location is 2 miles (3km) south of Alayor off the road to Son Bou.

The restored **Naveta d'es Tudons** is accessible 3 miles (5km) east of Ciudadela, just to the south of the road to Mahón. This is the best-preserved and the most significant prehistoric collection of megalithic monuments on Minorca. Its *naveta* (a boat-shaped monument thought to be a dwelling or a burial chamber) is said to be among the oldest monuments constructed by humans in Europe. Archaeologists have found the remains of many bodies at this site, along with a collection of prehistoric artifacts, including pottery, decorative jewelry, and weapons—but they have now been removed to museums. The site is more easily visited if you're staying in Ciudadela.

WHERE TO STAY

Hostal Reynes. Carrer d'es Comerc, 26, 07700 Mahón. ☎ **971-36-40-59.** 28 units. 2,800–3,500 ptas. ($16.80–$21) double. No credit cards.

On a quiet, narrow street in the town center near the cathedral, this is a cozy, well-maintained, family-run, and very inexpensive hotel. Wide hallways lead to the simple but clean rooms on three floors of the building. Rooms are small but nicely maintained, each with a firm mattress. Meals are served in a well-scrubbed dining room with windows overlooking the street.

Hotel Capri. Carrer Sant Esteve, 8, 07703 Mahón. ☎ **971-36-14-00.** Fax 971-35-08-53. 75 units. A/C MINIBAR TV TEL. 10,500–17,000 ptas. ($63–$102) double. AE, DC, MC, V.

If you don't stay at the more expensive and superior Hotel Port Mahón (see below), this comfortable, modern hotel, conveniently situated in the heart of Mahón, is the next best choice. Each of the simple rooms is comfortably but blandly furnished with conservative furniture, and each has a private balcony. Well managed, with a sense of stewardship that derives from its long-term ownership and administration by a local family, the hotel has a bar and a restaurant that specializes in Balearic, Spanish, and international cuisine, with particularly good pizzas. A *menú del día* costs 1,600 ptas. ($9.60). Unlike many hotels on the island, this one is in the commercial core of Mahón and, as such, caters to business travelers from other parts of the Balearics and Europe and has more of a city-oriented outlook than hotels geared only to the resort trade. There's no pool, and the nearest beach is about 3 miles (5km) away, but there are such extras as turndown service, room service from early morning until midnight, a concierge, and baby-sitting if it's arranged a half day in advance.

Hotel del Almirante (Collingwood House). Carretera de Villacarlos, s/n, 07700 Mahón. ☎ **971-36-27-00.** Fax 971-36-27-04. www.menorca.net/almirante/hotel.html. E-mail: hotelalmirante@menorca.net. 40 units. TEL. 8,500–15,000 ptas. ($51–$90) double. Rates include breakfast. DC, MC, V. Closed Nov–Apr.

Originally built in the late 18th century for Admiral Collingwood, a close friend of Lord Nelson, this hotel later served as a convent, as the home of a German sculptor, and until the end of World War II, as the German embassy. Architecturally, it reflects a number of styles: Italianate, Georgian, and Minorcan.

In 1964 it was restored and enlarged into a hotel. The reception area, with its 18th-century staircase, is decorated with numerous oil paintings and, like the rest of the public rooms, successfully mixes antiques with British memorabilia. Facilities include a bar, a game room, a swimming pool, and a tennis court. Guests are housed in the main building or in one of the more modern bungalow accommodations. The rooms are a mixed bag—you don't really know what you get until the maid opens the door. But all are clean and well kept, and many rooms have terraces overlooking the Bay of Mahón. The British love it here.

Hotel Port Mahón. Avinguda Fort de L'Eau, 07701 Mahón. ☎ **971-36-26-00.** Fax 971-35-10-50. 80 units. A/C MINIBAR TV TEL. 10,500–25,000 ptas. ($63–$150) double; 20,000–38,000 ptas. ($120–$228) suite for 2. Rates include breakfast. AE, DC, MC, V.

Perched on a steep hillside above the harbor, this hotel looks like a large Georgian villa whose charms are largely of another era. It is, without question, the most traditional accommodation in Minorca, located in a residential neighborhood. It's one of the few large hotels staying open year-round, and half of its rooms are usually reserved for tour groups. Some guests have been coming here since the 1950s, which indicates the age level of many of the patrons.

There is a sense of calm and unhurried comfort in the airy stone-floored public areas. The rooms overlook the harbor, the bougainvillea-filled garden, or the quiet street outside. Each has an ornate balcony with louvered shutters and potted flowers. Elegant touches abound, like the stone cherub riding a carved snail that splashes water into a swimming pool.

A dining room, a popular spot for visitors, serves good-tasting regional and international meals daily 1 to 3pm and 8 to 10pm.

A Nearby Place to Stay in San Lluís

✪ **Biniali.** Carretera S'Uestrà, Binibeca, 50, 07710 Sant Lluís. ☎ **971-15-17-24.** Fax 971-15-03-52. 9 units. TEL. 15,000–18,000 ptas. ($90–$108) double. AE, DC, MC, V. Closed late Oct–Easter. Free parking.

Biniali is one of the most charming hotels and restaurants in Minorca, about a mile south of San Lluís on the island's southwestern coastal road to Binibeca. The house, surrounded by English-style gardens, was originally the home of a prosperous Minorcan farmer in the 18th century. The comfortable midsized rooms are decorated with a scattering of antiques, seven with terraces and two with separate salons. A few of the rooms are air-conditioned, and all of them come with firm beds. There is a small outdoor swimming pool.

Many nonresidents visit for meals. Tables are set out under an arcade overlooking the roses and geraniums in the garden or in one of the charmingly old-fashioned dining rooms. Specialties include fillet steak in port with truffle sauce, monkfish in a wild mushroom sauce, baked potato filled with lobster, *maigret* (breast) of duck in a sweet-and-sour currant sauce, and a selection of Minorcan cheeses. The restaurant is open daily 1:30 to 3pm and 8:30 to 11pm.

All in all, this is a retreat offering lots of peace, comfort, and quaintness within easy reach of Binibeca beach and the facilities and activities of Mahón.

WHERE TO DINE

Fish and seafood form most of the basis of the Minorcan diet. The sea harvest is abundant along the long coastline. The most elegant dish, *caldereta de langosta*, consists of pieces of lobster blended with onion, tomato, pepper, and garlic, and flavored with an herb liqueur. This is a favorite dish of King Juan Carlos when he visits Minorca.

Shellfish paella is also popular, as is *escupinas* ("warty Venus"), a local shellfish. *Tordos con col* (thrushes with cabbage) are served in autumn. A peasant dish, *pa amb oli*, often precedes a meal. This is bread flavored with salt and olive oil and rubbed with fresh tomato.

Wine is brought in from mainland Spain, but gin is made on the island, a legacy from the days of the British occupation. You can drink the gin by itself or mix it with lemon and ice. If the latter, ask the bartender for *palloza* (pronounced pa-*yoh*-tha). Mixed with soda or lemonade, the gin drink is called a *pomada*.

Expensive

Gregal. Moll de Llevant, 306. ☎ **971-36-66-06.** Reservations recommended. Main courses 1,200–5,500 ptas. ($7.20–$33). AE, DC, MC, V. Daily noon–3:30pm and 7:30–11:30pm. SEAFOOD/INTERNATIONAL.

Seafood is the specialty of this small, friendly restaurant. The decor is simple; checkered tablecloths and exposed beams lend a rustic air to the interior, and the catch of the day is often on display. Included on the menu are several meat and fowl dishes, most with Catalán or French influences. Along with traditional Spanish fare, a selection of international dishes appears as well. Greek specialties, including taramosalata, moussaka, and dolmades, are excellent choices.

Rocamar. Cala Fonduco, 32, 07720 Es Castell. ☎ **971-36-56-01.** Fax 971-36-52-99. Reservations recommended. Main courses 1,800–6,000 ptas. ($10.80–$36); fixed-price menu 2,000–4,000 ptas. ($12–$24). AE, DC, MC, V. Daily 1–3:30pm and 8–11pm. Closed Nov and Sun night Dec–Apr. MINORCAN/INTERNATIONAL.

This restaurant is famous on Minorca—the chef has a way of making simplicity sublime. You reach it by following a narrow rutted road parallel to the harbor. The beamed and paneled restaurant on the upper floor has views overlooking the harbor. Although some locals claim the cooking was more glorious in the past, it still shines today.

Dishes might include almond soup, marinated salmon with shellfish, *maigret* (breast) of duckling in port wine, or beef fillet with mustard sauce. Don't overlook the pleasant street-level snack bar (it's actually a restaurant in its own right). This establishment offers 32 simple rooms, most of which are booked by London-based tour groups. Each has a private bathroom and TV, and breakfast is included in the rate. Rooms rent for 5,000 ptas. ($33.50) for a double.

Moderate

✪ **Jàgaro.** Moll de Llevant. ☎ **971-36-23-90.** Reservations recommended. Main courses 950–6,600 ptas. ($5.70–$39.60); *menú del día* 2,000 ptas. ($12). AE, DC, MC, V. Daily noon–4pm and 7pm–midnight. Closed Sun night Nov–Apr. MEDITERRANEAN.

The seafood menu here is Minorca's most eclectic and interesting. Begin with *ensalada templada con cigalitos y setas,* a mix of warm prawns and wild mushrooms served on a bed of lettuce, or Jàgaro's interpretation of gazpacho, flavored with shrimp and melon. The *mosaico de verduras,* a plate of grilled fresh vegetables, is an excellent choice. Main courses may include *carpaccio de mero* (grouper) served with a tangy green-mustard sauce, *caldereta de langosta* (lobster stew), or *ortigas* (sea anemones). Seafood offerings are extensive, although meat dishes, including duck *maigret* (breast) in orange sauce and foie gras with sweet-and-sour sauce, are very appealing. An extensive wine list ensures a vintage to accompany any meal. For dessert, try one of the home-made ice creams or sorbets.

○ **Pilar.** Des Forn, 61. ☎ **971-36-68-17.** Reservations recommended. Main courses 1,800–2,600 ptas. ($10.80–$15.60); fixed-price lunch 2,500 ptas. ($15). MC, V. Tues–Sat 1:30–3:30pm; Sept–July, Mon–Sat 8:30–11:30pm. Aug, daily 8:30–11:30pm. Closed Dec–Jan. MINORCAN/MEDITERRANEAN.

At this small, stylish restaurant in the center of Mahón, you'll feel as though you're dining in somebody's home. Even the small kitchen where owner-chef Teodoro Beurrun works culinary wonders looks more like a domestic kitchen than a restaurant kitchen. There are about half a dozen tables indoors and another half a dozen spread around the rear patio in summer. A smattering of antique furnishings and impressionistic artworks contribute to the coziness.

The menu is understandably limited, but that does not apply to the quality and care taken in preparation. The market-fresh cuisine is largely *Menorquín* with innovative variations. Based on a rigid allegiance to seasonal, high-quality, and very fresh ingredients, menu items change at least four times a year. Examples include Catalán-style blood sausage in puff pastry, served with a marmalade of onions and tomatoes; a soufflé of squid with almonds, prepared with squid ink; and veal trotters stuffed with Balearic herbs and served with a thyme-flavored honey sauce. For dessert try the homemade *pastel de nueces con chocolate* (walnut cake with chocolate).

Inexpensive
American Bar. Plaça Reial, 8. ☎ **971-36-18-22.** Main courses 850–2,000 ptas. ($5.10–$12); *menú del día* 1,200 ptas. ($7.20). No credit cards. Mon–Sat 6:30am–10:30pm; Sun 6:30am–2pm. MINORCAN/INTERNATIONAL.

For years, this has been the traditional international meeting place in Mahón. Many come here for drinks on its pleasant terrace, but you can also order food, eating inside or alfresco. Menu items include traditional Catalán platters (soups, stews, grilled meats), as well as pastas, salads, and American-style burgers. Dessert might include locally made ice creams, many made with fresh fruit. No one will mind if you have a drink or two too many here; if you do, you certainly won't be alone.

Bar Restaurant España. Carrer Victori, 48–50. ☎ **971-36-32-99.** Reservations recommended. Main courses 950–3,000 ptas. ($5.70–$18); *menú del día* 1,000 ptas. ($6). MC, V. Daily 1–3:30pm and 7:30pm–1:30am. Closed Jan. SPANISH.

Originally established around 1938, this is one of the oldest continuously operating restaurants in Minorca, thanks to a solidly reliable clientele and well-prepared food served in generous portions at reasonable prices. Patrons include vacationing northern Europeans who tend to communicate with one another and the staff in English. Partly because of its cosmopolitan clientele, the menu is designed to appeal to a wide variety of palates. Examples include *cigales a la americana* (prawns in a spicy red sauce), shrimp with garlic, mussels marinara, baked fish (especially hake and cod), grilled veal and pork, and beefsteaks grilled and served with a decidedly Spanish flair.

La Tropical. Carrer Lluna, 36. ☎ **971-36-05-56.** Reservations not necessary. Main courses 950–2,600 ptas. ($5.70–$15.60); *menús del día* 1,200–3,200 ptas. ($7.20–$19.20). MC, V. Daily 8am–midnight. SPANISH/MINORCAN/INTERNATIONAL.

La Tropical is a three-in-one eatery. You can have snacks at the bar, and tapas as well as *bocadillos* (Spanish sandwiches) and *platos combinados* (combination plates) in the informal dining room, or full-fledged restaurant fare in the more formal dining area. The restaurant offers a good selection of Minorcan specialties, including a reasonably priced and savory fish-and-shellfish *caldereta* (stew). There is a daily market menu and an assorted selection of Spanish and international dishes.

CIUDADELA (CIUTADELLA DE MENORCA)

27 miles (43.5km) W of Mahón

At the western end of the island, the town of Ciudadela has a typically Mediterranean air about it. Lining the narrow streets of the old city are noble mansions of the 17th and 18th centuries as well as numerous churches. It was the capital until 1722, when the British chose Mahón instead, largely because its harbor channel is more navigable than the one at Ciudadela. Subsequently, the British built the main island road to link the two cities.

Like Mahón, Ciudadela perches high above its harbor, which is smaller than Mahón's. The seat of Minorca's bishopric, Ciudadela pontificates while Mahón administrates.

Known as Medina Minurka under the Muslims, Ciudadela retains some Moorish traces despite the 1558 Turkish invasion and destruction of the city. An obelisk in memory of the city's futile defense against that invasion stands in the pigeon-filled Plaça d'es Born (Plaza del Born), the city's main square overlooking the port.

ESSENTIALS

GETTING THERE   From the airport, you must take a taxi to Ciudadela, as there is no bus link. The cost is approximately 5,800 ptas. ($34.80) each way.

From Mahón six buses go back and forth every day. Departures are from Plaça s'Esplanada in Mahón.

VISITOR INFORMATION   The **tourist information office**, located at Plaça Catedral (☎ 971-38-26-93), is open April to October Monday to Friday 9am to 1:30pm and 5 to 7pm, Saturday 10am to 2pm.

EXPLORING CIUDADELA: THE BEACH & BEYOND

In Ciudadela, buses depart from Plaça d'Artrutx for most coastal destinations, including the best beaches. Of these, **Cala Santandria,** 2 miles (3km) to the south, is known for its white sands. This is a sheltered beach near a creek, and in the background are rock caves, which were inhabited in prehistoric times. The coves of **En Forcat, Blanes,** and **Brut** are near Ciudadela.

Cala de Santa Galdana, not reached by public transport, is the most stunning in the area, lying 14 miles (22.5km) south of Ciudadela. The bay here is tranquil and ringed with a beach of fine golden sand. Tall bare cliffs rise in the background, and the air is perfumed with the smell of pine trees. The road to this beach, unlike so many others on Minorca, is a good one.

The center of Ciudadela is **Plaça d'es Born,** site of tourist information. This was the center of life when the town was known to Jaume I. Back then Ciudadela was completely walled to protect itself from pirate incursions, which were a serious threat from the 13th century on. Much of the present look of this square, and of Ciudadela itself, is thanks to its demotion in 1722, when the capital was transferred to Mahón. For centuries that checked urban development in Ciudadela, and many buildings now stand that might have been torn down to make way for progress.

Plaça d'es Born looks over the port from the north. Once it was known as Plaza Generalíssimo, honoring the dictator Franco. The square was built around the obelisk that remembers the hopeless struggle of the town against the invading Turks who entered the city in 1558 and caused much destruction. On the west side of the square is the Ayuntamiento (Town Hall).

To the southwest of the square stands **Esglesia de San Francisco.** This is a 14th-century Gothic building, with some excellent carved wood altars. The town once had a magnificent opera house, Casa Salort, but that cultural note sounds no more, as it's been turned into a somewhat seedy movie theater. Another once-splendid palace, Palacio de Torre-Saura, also opens onto the square. Still owner occupied, it was constructed in the 1800s.

The **cathedral,** Plaça Pio XII, was ordered built by the conquering Alfonso III on the site of the former mosque. It is Gothic in style and fortresslike in appearance. The facade of the church, in the neoclassical style, was added in 1813. The church suffered heavy damage in 1936, during the Spanish Civil War, but has since been restored.

Ciudadela is at its liveliest at the **port,** where you'll find an array of little shops, bars, restaurants, sailboats, along with some impressive yachts in summer. **Carrer Quadrando** is another street worth walking, as it is lined with shops and arcades.

The Moorish influence still lingers in a block of whitewashed houses in the **Voltes,** off the Plaça s'Esplanada. In Ciudadela the local people still meet at **Plaça d'Alfons III,** the square honoring their long-ago liberator.

WHERE TO STAY
Expensive
Hotel Patricia. Passeig Sant Nicolau, 90, 07760 Ciudadela. ☎ **971-38-55-11.** Fax 971-48-11-20. 44 units. A/C MINIBAR TV TEL. 10,500–18,000 ptas. ($63–$108) double; 14,000–22,000 ptas. ($84–$132) junior suite. AE, DC, MC, V. Closed Nov–Feb. Free parking on street.

Built in 1988, this three-story building is in a centrally located position that business travelers find convenient and is Ciudadela's most respected, most luxurious hotel. Near the Plaça d'es Born, a half mile from the nearest beach (Playa de La Caleta), it has a polite hardworking staff well versed on the island's facilities and geography. The spacious rooms are comfortable, carpeted, outfitted pleasantly in pastels, and have large bathrooms, equipped with hair dryers.

Dining: There's no full-fledged restaurant in this hotel, but you can get simple platters of food, coffee, beer, and wine at the in-house cafeteria.

Amenities: Room service, concierge, baby-sitting, currency exchange, conference rooms.

Moderate
Hotel Almirante Farragut. Urbanización Los Delfines, Cala'n Forcat, 07760 Ciudadela. ☎ **971-38-80-00.** Fax 971-38-81-07. 489 units. A/C TV TEL. 6,800–23,000 ptas. ($40.80–$138) double. Rates include breakfast. AE, MC, V. Closed Nov–Apr.

Three miles (5km) outside Ciudadela, beside a small rock-lined inlet, this four-story building is one of the best hotels in the development of Los Delfines, a cluster of resort hotels initiated in the 1970s and 1980s. Public rooms are airy, large, sparsely furnished, and appropriate to the hotel's role as a warm-weather beach resort with an international clientele, often from England and Germany. Guest rooms are pleasant and standardized in both their amenities and their furnishings. Each has a balcony or terrace, usually overlooking either the rocky inlet or the open sea. Prices vary widely according to season, but lodgings that the hotel identifies as suites are nothing more than larger-than-usual double rooms.

Facilities include two saltwater pools for adults, one for children; two cafeterias; a disco; several TV and video rooms in Spanish, English, and German; two tennis courts; minigolf; shops; a salon; a supermarket; and an independently operated school for scuba divers. The hotel, incidentally, was named for U.S. Admiral Farragut, a 19th-century U.S. naval officer whose grandparents lived in one of the nearby villages.

Hotel Esmeralda. Pasaje de Sant Nicolau, 171, 07760 Ciudadela. ☎ **971-38-02-50.** Fax 971-38-02-58. 160 units. MINIBAR TEL. 12,000–23,000 ptas. ($72–$138) double. Rates include breakfast. Half-board 1,800 ptas. ($10.80) extra per person. AE, DC, MC, V. Closed Nov–Apr. Free parking.

This is a respectable three-star hotel, built in the 1960s and set near the entrance to the mouth of Ciudadela's harbor. It is within a 10-minute walk from the commercial heart of town, close to the better-accessorized Patricia Hotel, and rising three floors. The guest rooms are large but sparsely furnished, but bathrooms are big and bright and the beds are firm. In many cases, rooms have terraces and sea views. There's a pool on the premises, and the beach is within a 5-minute walk.

Inexpensive

Hostal Residencia Ciutadella. Carrer Sant Eloy, 10, 07760 Ciudadela. ☎/fax **971-38-34-62.** 17 units. TV TEL. 6,500–9,000 ptas. ($39–$54) double; 8,500–12,500 ptas. ($51–$75) triple. Rates include breakfast. AE, MC, V.

Near Plaça d'Alfons III, on a quiet street just off the main shopping artery, this small hotel offers comfortable, convenient, but small accommodations, each with a good bed. Tiled floors and floor-length windows provide an airy atmosphere. Furniture is covered in fresh, floral fabrics. *Beware:* This three-story hotel has no elevator.

Hotels Cala Bona & Mar Blava. Avinguda del Mar, 14–16, 07760 Ciudadela. ☎ **971-38-00-16.** Fax 971-48-20-70. 44 units. TV TEL. 6,500–8,500 ptas. ($39–$51) double. No credit cards. Closed Nov–Mar.

These two hotels stand just a short walk from the town center, with views overlooking the little bay. Stairs lead down to a small beach, with a larger beach just 5 minutes away. Guest rooms are clean and comfortable; almost all have views facing the water. The rooms at the Mar Blava are smaller than those at the Cala Bona. The hotels share an outdoor pool, a bar, and an outdoor terrace. A restaurant serves snacks and light meals.

A Nearby Place to Stay

Hotel Los Cóndores Sol. Playa Santo Tomás, s/n, 07749 San Cristóbal. ☎ **971-37-00-50.** Fax 971-37-03-48. 188 units. A/C TV TEL. 10,500–17,000 ptas. ($63–$102) double. Rates include half-board. AE, DC, MC, V. Closed late Oct–Apr 30.

This hotel gives the impression of a large, well-maintained hacienda, complete with lacy iron balconies and louvered shutters. Surrounded by lawns and flowering shrubs, it has a swimming pool, a private beach, and a sweeping view of rocky islets. Many guests make their balconies an extension of their midsize rooms, reading, sitting, and talking within sight of the sea. Beds are firm, the mattresses renewed as needed, and the tiled bathrooms come with hair dryers.

WHERE TO DINE

The port of Ciudadela offers a wide selection of restaurants for all palates and prices. Beyond that, there are some commendable choices in and around town.

Bar Triton. Muelle Ciutadela. ☎ **971-38-00-02.** Tapas and *platos combinados* 650–3,000 ptas. ($3.90–$18). MC, V. Daily noon–2am. TAPAS.

The best place for tapas in the port, Triton offers a wide range of snacks, including sausages, *tortillas* (Spanish omelets), meatballs, and a dozen or so seafood tapas, among them octopus, stuffed squid, and *escupiñas* (Minorcan clams). On the wall inside are photos and illustrations of the port before it was a haven for vacationers. As in those days, fishers still make up an important part of the clientele, and you'll often find the locals engaged in a friendly afternoon game of cards.

✪ **Casa Manolo.** Marina, 117. ☎ **971-38-00-03.** Reservations required in summer. Main courses 2,600–5,000 ptas. ($15.60–$30); off-season; fixed-price menu 3,500 ptas. ($21). AE, DC, MC, V. Daily 1–4:30pm and 7:30–11:30pm. Closed Sun mid-Nov to mid-Feb. SPANISH/MINORCAN.

Located at the port, across from the spot where the larger yachts anchor, Casa Manolo is a favorite of the yachting crowd. You can dine indoors in a room carved out of stone, or alfresco on the intimate terrace. King Juan Carlos has been seen here enjoying the elegant atmosphere and outstanding cuisine. The menu consists mainly of fresh seafood and lobster dishes. The specialty of the house is *arroz de pescado caldoso,* a dish resembling paella, but with more of a focus on fish. The *caldereta de langosta,* a lobster-based bouillabaisse, is one of our favorites. The hardworking and affable owner, María Postores, supervises all aspects of your dining experience.

Cas Quintu. Plaça d'Alfons III, 4. ☎ **971-38-10-02.** Reservations not necessary. Main courses 1,600–2,600 ptas. ($9.60–$15.60); fixed-price menu 1,600 ptas. ($9.60). AE, DC, MC, V. Daily 1–4:30pm and 8pm–midnight. SPANISH/MINORCAN.

Thriving since the early 1960s from a position on an ornate square in the most historic core of town, Cas Quintu offers both indoor and outdoor tables that afford vantage points for observations of the passing crowd. You can order drinks and light food in the cafe daily 9am to 2pm. This establishment's selection of tapas is among the best in town. Full meals are served outdoors or in one of a pair of rooms in back. Specialties include a zesty squid sauteed in butter, several different preparations of beefsteak, a perfect sole meunière, and a mixed grill of fish based on the catch of the day.

Es Caliu Grill. Carretera Cala Blanca. ☎ **971-38-01-65.** Reservations not necessary. Main courses 2,000–2,400 ptas. ($12–$14.40). MC, V. May–Oct, daily 1–4pm and 7pm–midnight; off-season, Fri–Sat 7pm–midnight, Sun 1–4pm and 7pm–midnight. SPANISH.

One and a half miles (2.5km) south of Ciudadela, along the main road between Cala Santandria and Cala Blanca, Es Caliu is the place to come when you've had your fill of seafood. Specializing in grilled meats of the freshest quality, it offers lamb, veal, pork, rabbit, quail, and spit-roasted suckling pig. But beyond fine food, you get a special ambience. Above the bar hang hams and garlic braids, and off to the side are stacked wine barrels. The family-style tables and benches are made of cut and polished logs. The outdoor terrace is roofed and smothered with cascading flowers; indoors are two rustic dining areas, one with a fireplace.

Granja Colom. Plaça de s'Esplanada (Plaça Colóm), 48. ☎ **971-48-23-45.** Tapas 375 ptas. ($2.25). No credit cards. Mon–Sat 10am–10pm (depending on crowd). TAPAS.

A gathering place for locals and tourists alike, this hangout offers a variety of fresh tapas and sandwiches; you can enjoy them in the rather raucous interior or at the calmer outdoor tables. A glass of Jerez (sherry), the perfect accompaniment to tapas, costs from 150 ptas. ($1).

CIUDADELA AFTER DARK

Café El Molino, Camino de Mao, 7 (☎ 971-38-00-00), is one of our favorite bars, a hangout near the avinguda de la Constitución. It has attracted virtually every drinker in town since it was established in 1905 within the circular premises of a windmill built in 1794. It provides a rustic but richly international contrast to the busy square it borders, and boasts the unusual distinction of having monumental walls and vaulted ceilings a lot older than those of the buildings surrounding it. The clientele includes visiting foreigners and local fishers, and the mood changes from that of an early morning cafe, whose opening is timed to coincide with the departure of fishing boats, to a late-night bar. This place is earthy, regional, and brusque, yet invaluable for an insight into old-time Minorca.

CENTRAL & SOUTHERN MINORCA

Topographically and climatically, this is the more tranquil part of the island. The beaches are more accessible, and the winds blow less—as a result, tourism has taken a firmer foothold here than in the north. Santo Tomás, Cala Galdana, Platges de Son Bou, Cala Bosch, and Punta Prima are some of the focal points for travelers.

Es Mercadal, a town of several thousand inhabitants at the foot of Monte Toro, is an ensemble of white houses with grace notes of color. Among its claims to local fame are two types of almond confectionery—*carquinyols* (small, hard cookies) and *amargos* (a kind of macaroon). The place to get both is **Pastelería Villalonga Ca's Sucrer,** Plaça Constitución, 11, Es Mercadal (no phone), open Tuesday to Saturday 9:30am to 1:30pm and 5 to 8:30pm, also open Sunday in winter, 11am to 2pm.

From Es Mercadal, you can take a road 2½ miles (4km) up to **Monte Toro,** the island's tallest mountain at 1,170 feet (355m), crowned with a sanctuary that is a place of pilgrimage for Minorcans. The winding road leads to a panoramic view of the island's rolling green countryside dotted with *fincas* (farm estates), trim fields, and stands of trees. From this vantage point you can clearly see the contrast between the flatter southern part of the island and the hilly northern region. The hilltop sanctuary includes a small, simple church with an ornate gilded altar displaying the image (reportedly found nearby in 1290) of the Virgin Mare de Déu d'el Toro, the island's patron saint. In 1936 the church was destroyed, but the statue was saved from the flames and a new church built. The church is open daily from early morning to sunset; admission is free. In the courtyard of the sanctuary is a bronze monument to those Minorcans who left in the 18th century, while the island was still a British colony, to colonize Spanish settlements in North America. The large statue of Christ commemorates the dead in the Spanish Civil War. There is a snack bar with a pleasant terrace here.

Platges de Son Bou is a stunning beach scarred by two outsized hotels. Although still enchanting, the mile-long, narrow beach and clear, turquoise waters are now often crowded, even in the off-season; in July and August they're best avoided. At the eastern end of the beach just beyond the two monster hotels are the ruins of a Paleo-Christian basilica, most probably dating from the 5th or 6th century. Visible in the cliffs beyond are cave dwellings, some of which appear quite prosperous, with painted facades and shades to keep out the noonday sun.

One-half mile to the east in Cala'n Porter is a unique nightspot. Embedded in a series of caves within a sheer cliff face rising from the sea, **La Cova d'en Xoroi** (☎ 971-37-72-36) is a conglomeration of bars, terraces, intimate nooks and crannies, and a disco floor. For sheer drama, the setting is without equal. As you walk down the entrance stairway, all magnificently unfolds before you. Then you come to the dance floor overlooking the sea at the cliff's edge—there's no window, just a railing. Prehistoric vessels were found inside these caves, which according to legend, were once the refuge of a Moor called Xoroi, who had abducted a local maid and made his home here with her and their family. You can visit this unusual spot during the day as well, 11am to 9pm. Admission is 1,500 ptas. ($9) and includes one drink. In the evening, from 11pm to 4am, La Cova d'en Xoroi transforms into a disco. Admission is 1,500 ptas. ($9), including your first drink. Drinks cost from 900 ptas. ($5.40).

WHERE TO STAY

Most of the hotels in this area cater almost exclusively to tour groups.

✪ **Hotel Santo Tomás.** Playa Santo Tomás, 07749 Es Migjorn Gran. ☎ **971-37-00-25.** Fax 971-37-02-04. 85 units. A/C MINIBAR TV TEL. 19,000–30,000 ptas. ($114–$180) double; 25,000–35,000 ptas. ($150–$210) suite. Rates include half-board. AE, DC, MC, V. Closed Nov–Apr.

One of our favorite hotels on Minorca, Santo Tomás offers the best quality and comfort on the island; it's the only four-star hotel on the beach. Public areas are airy and spacious and accommodations are comfortable, with amenities such as hair dryers and radios. Most rooms open onto a terrace that faces the sea. On the premises, guests will find a large swimming pool, surrounded by thatched umbrellas, providing shelter from the sun. A seaside bar offers refreshments, and guests may use a minigolf course. Various water sports can be arranged.

Los Gavilanes Sol. Urbanización Cala Galdana, s/n, 07750 Ferreries. ☎ **971-15-45-45.** Fax 971-15-45-46. 364 units. A/C MINIBAR TV TEL. 10,500–22,800 ptas. ($63–$136.80) double; 18,500–32,000 ptas. ($111–$192) suite. Rates include breakfast. MC, V. Closed Nov–Apr. Free parking.

A large resort hotel, Gavilanes Sol is fully equipped with swimming pools, discos, restaurants, and bars. It's atop a steep slope overlooking one of the most perfect beaches in the Mediterranean, surrounded by a grove of pines and palmettos. The original beauty of Cala Galdana has been substantially marred by construction, but you can enjoy the best end of its sandy, crescent-shaped beach and turquoise waters by staying here. Each of the sizable, functionally furnished rooms has a balcony, and all are equipped with a good bed. Other amenities include a hair dryer and a private safe.

Many of the guests here are on group tours from England, so the sweeping lobby-level terraces and the pub take on a British flavor. The hotel has a restaurant, a swimming pool, and a children's playground.

WHERE TO DINE

Some of the best dining in this area is offered in the inland villages rather than along the coast. **Es Mercadal,** in particular, has a few choice restaurants.

✪ **Ca N'Olga.** Pont Na Macarrana (near the carrer d'es Sol), Es Mercadal. ☎ **971-37-54-59.** Reservations recommended on weekends. Main courses 1,600–3,000 ptas. ($9.60–$18). AE, DC, MC, V. Mar–May and Oct–Dec, Wed–Sun 1–4pm and 8–11pm; June–Sept, daily 7:45–11:30pm. Closed Jan–Feb. MINORCAN/INTERNATIONAL.

A stylish, sophisticated spot that attracts a similar clientele, Ca N'Olga is warm, winsome, and intimate. Occupying a typical white-stucco Minorcan house some 150 years old, this restaurant offers dining on a pretty outdoor patio or at a handful of indoor tables.

The eclectic menu changes frequently with the market offerings. It is likely to include quail with onion-and-sherry vinegar and osso buco. Some standard dishes that tend to appear regularly are *cap roig* (scorpion fish), *cabrito* (baby goat), some kind of fish terrine, and mussels au gratin. Among the homemade desserts you'll often find a velvety smooth fig ice cream and chestnut pudding.

Costa Sur. Playa de Santo Tomás. ☎ **971-37-03-26.** Reservations not necessary. Main courses 1,050–2,500 ptas. ($6.30–$15). MC, V. Daily 7–11pm. Closed Nov–Apr. INTERNATIONAL.

The sophisticated aspirations of Costa Sur are hampered by its rather stark decor and well-meaning but untrained staff. The menu is equally divided between seafood and meat dishes, and the house rightly prides itself on its cheese soufflé, salmon crêpes, pepper steak, and *suquet de rape* (monkfish stew). It serves a smattering of succulent pasta dishes.

Molí d'es Reco. Es Mercadal. ☎ **971-37-53-92.** Reservations recommended in summer. Main courses 950–2,800 ptas. ($5.70–$16.80); *menú del día* 1,600 ptas. ($9.60). AE, MC, V. Daily 1–4pm and 7–11pm. MINORCAN.

Easily spotted by the 300-year-old windmill that inspired the name of this 1982 creation, Molí d'es Reco has a pleasant outdoor patio but a rather plain indoor dining area. Overall, the place is a bit touristy, but it offers hearty Minorcan fare including stuffed eggplant, *oliaigua amb tomatecs* (a soup with tomato, onion, parsley, green pepper, and garlic), snails with spider crab, partridge with cabbage, and *calamares a la menorquina* (stuffed squid with an almond-cream sauce).

Sa Plaça. Carrer d'Enmig (also avinguda de la Constitución), 2, Es Mercadal. ☎ **971-37-50-48.** Main courses 950–2,800 ptas. ($5.70–$16.80); fixed-price menu 1,200 ptas. ($7.20). MC, V. Daily 1–4pm and 8–10:30pm. MINORCAN.

Simple, unpretentious, and noted as a centerpiece of local gossip, this is a well-managed, family-run bistro and cafeteria rather than a full-fledged restaurant. In a simple and somewhat battered setting, you're free to order just coffee, a glass of wine, or any of 10 kinds of tapas and seek a refuge from the searing heat outside in a low-key environment that's thoroughly and completely Minorcan in its tastes, orientation, and self-definition.

S'Engolidor. 8 de Febrero, 58, Es Migjorn Gran. ☎ **971-37-01-93.** Reservations recommended on weekends. Main courses 1,400–1,900 ptas. ($8.40–$11.40). MC, V. May–Oct, daily 8–11pm. Closed Dec–Apr. MINORCAN.

In the village of Es Migjorn Gran (San Cristóbal), between Es Mercadal and Santo Tomás, is this cozy and relatively undiscovered restaurant. Except for a small sign on the door, it could be mistaken for any other house on this quiet side street. The building dates from 1740, with sections added throughout the years. The interior is simple: stark white walls accented with various works of art. The dining area consists of several small rooms, with only a few tables each. You can dine outdoors in one of the small patio areas; many overlook the owner's compact vegetable garden. The menu consists of various Minorcan specialties, including *olaigua*, eggplant stuffed with fish; rabbit and wild mushroom stew; and a particularly succulent version of roasted lamb. Owner José Luis maintains four simple rooms that, although clean and cozy, contain virtually no amenities other than a private bathroom and a sense of peace and quiet. A double room, with breakfast included, costs between 4,800 and 5,000 ptas. ($28.80 and $30) per night, and is available only between May and October.

FORNELLS & THE NORTHERN COAST

The road leading north from Es Mercadal to Fornells runs through some of the island's finer scenery. Mass-tourism hotels, so far, have not discovered this place, but there are several good dining choices. On the northern coast, the tiny town of Fornells snuggles around a bay filled with boats and windsurfers and lined with restaurants and a few shops. Built around four defense fortifications—the Talaia de la Mola (now destroyed), the Tower of Fornells at the harbor mouth, the fortress of the Island of Las Sargantanas (the Lizards) situated in the middle of the harbor, and the now-ruined Castle of San Jorge or San Antonion—Fornells today is a flourishing fishing village noted for its upscale restaurants featuring savory lobster *calderetas*.

West of Fornells is **Platja Binimella,** a beautiful beach (unofficially nudist) easily accessible by car. Its long, curving, sandy cove is peacefully set against undulating hills. A snack bar is the sole concession to civilization.

By far the most splendid panorama here is that from the promontory at **Cap de Cavalleria,** the northernmost tip of the island, marked by a lighthouse. Getting here requires some effort, however. At a bend in the road leading to Platja Binimella, a signpost indicates the turnoff to Cap de Cavalleria through a closed gate heading to a dirt road. The closed gate is typical of many of the roads leading to Minorca's undeveloped beaches. All the beaches in Spain, however, are public, so no one may impede access to them—although landowners might discourage visitors by making access difficult. The prevailing custom is simply to open the gate, go on through, and close it behind you. It is important that you close the gate because often they keep livestock confined to certain areas. As you follow the long dirt road (negotiable in a regular car or on a motorbike) out to Cap de Cavelleria, you come across several more sets of gates and travel through countryside that's somewhat reminiscent of the Scottish highlands, with cultivated fields and scattered grand *fincas,* or farmsteads. Shortly before the lighthouse is a parking area down to the left. You'll have to pick your way across the scrub and rocks for the views. The best one is from a circular tower in ruins up to the right of the lighthouse. Now brace yourself for a vista encompassing the whole of Minorca—a symphony of dramatic cliffs and jewel-blue water.

WHERE TO STAY

Hostal S'Algaret. Plaça S'Algaret, 7, 07748 Fornells. ☎ **971-37-65-52.** 21 units. A/C TEL. 8,500–12,500 ptas. ($51–$75) double. Rates include breakfast. AE, MC, V. Closed Nov–Mar.

This is for escapists only. It's really like an unpretentious inn. It's also a bit sleepy, so don't expect a lot in the way of hotel services. But adventurous do-it-yourself types often book the modest and very simply furnished guest rooms, which are clean and reasonably comfortable. Floors are tiled, the furnishings basic, but the spacious modern bathrooms are alluring. There are also sizable terraces opening onto views. If your expectations aren't high, you might go for this one. Few will complain, either, when the reasonable bill is presented.

WHERE TO DINE

Fornells is noted for its fine seafood restaurants specializing in the Minorcan *calderetas.* King Juan Carlos has been known to sail in here when he wants to savor the seafood stew, and in peak summer season people call their favorite Fornells restaurant days in advance with their orders.

✪ **Es Pla.** Pasage des Pla, Fornells. ☎ **971-37-66-55.** Reservations recommended July–Aug. Main courses 850–2,800 ptas. ($5.10–$16.80); *menú del día* 2,600–3,000 ptas. ($15.60–$18) from Sept 20–June 20. AE, MC, V. Daily 1–3:30pm and 7:30pm–midnight. MINORCAN/SEAFOOD.

If any restaurant in Minorca deserves a comparison to the grand Roman watering holes of *La Dolce Vita,* it would be this one, where King Juan Carlos and his family have come to dine several times. Stylish, airy, and elegant in a way that reflects the seagoing life of the island, Es Pla has thrived here since the 1960s, on a wood-floored porch that is only about 6 feet above the swell of the surf. Large and informal, it has a long, stainless steel bar area and an indoor-outdoor design. Menu items include a roster of perfectly prepared fish, meat, and shellfish, but the acknowledged culinary winner—and the most frequently ordered dish—is paella with crayfish.

S'Algaret. Plaça S'Algaret, 7, Fornells. ☎ **971-37-65-52.** Tapas 250–1,200 ptas. ($1.50–$7.20) per *ración* (serving); *menú del día* 1,800 ptas. ($10.80); platters 900–1,300 ptas. ($5.40–$7.80). AE, MC, V. Daily noon–4pm and 8–11pm. SPANISH.

Adjacent to the hostal of the same name (see above), S'Algaret is much frequented by locals and is one of the few economical alternatives for eating in Fornells (here you eat rather than dine). The restaurant is sleepy, quiet, small in scale, and unpretentious. You can nibble on good-tasting tapas, sandwiches, a varied selection of *tortillas* (Spanish omelets), and a smattering of *platos combinados* (combination plates), the ingredients of which change daily.

Appendix A: Spain in Depth

The once-accepted adage that "Europe ends at the Pyrenees" is no longer true. Today, the two countries forming the Iberian Peninsula at the southwestern end of the continent—Spain and Portugal—are totally integrated into Europe as members of the European Union (EU), with democratic governments and vibrant economies of their own. In fact, Spain has the second fastest-growing economy in the EU; new industries and an expanding infrastructure continue to alter its ancient landscape.

Political changes adopted after the 1975 death of Gen. Francisco Franco, Europe's remaining prewar dictator, contributed to a remarkable cultural renaissance. This rebirth has transformed Spain's two largest cities—Madrid, the capital, and Barcelona—into major artistic and intellectual centers. Amid some of the world's most innovative architecture and contemporary movements, art, literature, cinema, and fashion are constantly finding new and original expression; at night the cafes and bars hum with animated discussions on politics, the economy, and society. In every aspect of urban life, a visitor feels the Spanish people's reawakened self-confidence and pride in their newfound prosperity.

These developments contrast with Spain's unhappy experiences earlier this century, particularly during the devastating Civil War of 1936–39 and Franco's subsequent long iron-hand rule. During the Franco years, political and intellectual freedom was squelched, and Spain was snubbed by most of Europe.

Spain was previously, of course, a major world player. In the 16th century, it was the seat of a great empire; the Spanish monarchy dispatched fleets that conquered the New World, returning with its riches. Columbus sailed to America and Balboa to the Pacific Ocean; Cortés conquered Mexico for glory; and Pizarro brought Peru into the Spanish fold. The conquistadors too often revealed the dark side of the Spanish character, including brutality in the name of honor and glory, but they also represented a streak of boldness and daring.

It's difficult to visit this country without recalling its golden past: Those famous "castles in Spain" really do exist. Yet many Spaniards believe that Spain isn't merely a single country but a series of nations, united the way Yugoslavia used to be. Many groups, especially the Basques, the Cataláns, and the Gallegos in the northeast, are asserting their individuality in everything from culture to language. At least in the case of Basque separatists, that regional, "nationalistic" pride has taken violent turns. Castile and Andalusia, in the south, remain quintessentially Spanish. While linguistic and cultural differences are great, to the foreign visitor they are also subtle.

As the inheritors of a great and ancient civilization dating from before the Roman Empire, Spaniards inhabit a land that is not only culturally rich but geographically varied, with wooded sierra, arid plateaus, and sandy beaches. It is this exciting variety in landscape, as well as in art, architecture, music, and cuisine, that makes Spain one of the top countries in the world to visit.

1 Spain Today

As Spain begins its long journey into the millennium, tourism continues to boom and to dominate the economy—it remains a hot, hot industry with yearly arrivals in Spain bypassing the 45 million mark and closing in on 50 million.

The land is vibrant and fast-changing, an up-and coming destination that is expected to propel Spain into a tourism position that ranks alongside such front-runners as France, the United States, and Italy.

Increasingly, North Americans are becoming part of the changing landscape. While many European visitors head for the beach resorts, Americans occupy the number one position in visits to three top Spanish cities: Madrid, Barcelona, and Seville.

No longer interested in the "lager lout" image its coastal resorts earned in the 1970s and 1980s by hosting so many cheap package tours from Britain, Spain has reached out to a more upscale visitor. Bargain Spain of the $5-a-day variety is now a distant memory, as prices have skyrocketed. The government is trying to lure visitors away from the overcrowded coasts (especially Majorca, the Costa del Sol, and the Costa Brava) and steer them to the country's less-traveled, but more historic, destinations. Government paradors and other improved tourist facilities, better restaurants, and spruced-up attractions have sent the message.

In 1999, Spain joined other European countries in adopting the euro unit of money, but Spanish pesetas will continue to circulate in the year 2001. Actually citizens will not start using the new coins and bank notes until the beginning of 2002. The peseta, which has been the Spanish monetary unit since 1868, will disappear completely on July 1, 2002.

Backers of the euro, mainly the Spanish government, have presented the new currency as the solution to many problems, including unemployment and deficits. Many economists in Spain remain skeptical and are watching the country's entry into the euro market with great caution. Some economists are predicting a short-term property boom, as holders of undeclared "black market" pesetas rush to invest them before they are forced to convert them into euro dollars.

Although unemployment, which remains high, continues to plague the government, progress has been made. The country's debt is some 70% of the gross domestic product. Inflation is about 2.5%, an all-time low in the post-Franco era. Consumer spending remains cautious, however, since most of the new jobs being created are on short-term contracts.

Spain continues to change as it moves into the millennium. A drug culture and escalating crime—things virtually unheard of in Franco's day—are an unfortunate sign of Spain's entry into the modern world. The most remarkable advance has been in the legal status of women, who now have access to contraception, abortion, and divorce. Sights once unimaginable are now taking place: an annual lesbian "kiss-in" at Madrid's Puerto del Sol and women officiating as governors of men's prisons. Surprising in a Catholic country, the birth rate continues to remain one of the lowest in the developed world, and the population is aging.

Spain's monarchy seems to be working. In 1975, when the king assumed the throne after the death of Franco, he was called "Juan Carlos the Brief," implying that his reign would be short. But almost overnight he distanced himself from Franco's dark legacy and became a hardworking and serious sovereign. He staved off a coup attempt in 1981, and he and the other Spanish royals remain popular. Juan Carlos even makes do on a meager $7 million salary—less than one-tenth of what England's Queen Elizabeth is reputed to earn in a year.

The author John Hooper, in an updated version of his 1986 bestseller, *The New Spaniards*, remains optimistic about the future of Spain, in spite of its problems. He suggests Spaniards not forget that "to be true to themselves they may need to be different from others." Hooper believes the new Spain will have arrived at adulthood "not on the day it ceases to be different from the rest of Europe, but on the day that it acknowledges that it is." Hooper was referring to the exotic, romantic, and varied faces of Spain that set it apart from other nations of Europe, ranging from flamenco to its bullfighting and its Moorish architecture to its pagan ceremonies. Nowhere—not even in Italy—are the festival and traditional, flamboyant dress more a part of annual life than in Spain, where religious processions are full of intense passion.

2 History 101

Dateline

- 11th century B.C. Phoenicians settle Spain's coasts.
- 650 B.C. Greeks colonize the east.
- 600 B.C. Celts cross the Pyrenees and settle in Spain.
- 6th–3rd century B.C. Carthaginians make Cartagena their colonial capital, driving out the Greeks.
- 2nd century B.C.–2nd century A.D. Rome controls most of Iberia. Christianity spreads.
- 218–201 B.C. Second Punic War: Rome defeats Carthage.
- 5th century Vandals, then Visigoths, invade Spain.
- 8th century Moors conquer most of Spain.
- 1214 More than half of Iberia is regained by Catholics.
- 1469 Ferdinand of Aragón marries Isabella of Castile.
- 1492 Catholic monarchs seize Granada, the last Moorish stronghold. Columbus lands in the New World.

continues

BARBARIAN INVASIONS, THE MOORISH KINGDOM & THE RECONQUEST

Around 200 B.C., the Romans vanquished the Carthaginians and laid the foundations of the present Latin culture. Traces of Roman civilization can still be seen today. By the time of Julius Caesar, Spain (Hispania) was under Roman law and began a long period of peace and prosperity.

When Rome fell in the 5th century, Spain was overrun, first by the Vandals and then by the Visigoths from eastern Europe. The chaotic rule of the Visigothic kings lasted about 300 years, but the barbarian invaders did adopt the language of their new country and tolerated Christianity as well.

In A.D. 711, Moorish warriors led by Tarik crossed over into Spain and conquered the disunited country. By 714, they controlled most of it, except for a few mountain regions around Asturias. For 8 centuries, the Moors occupied their new land, which they called *al-Andalus*, or Andalusia, with Córdoba as the capital. A great intellectual center, Córdoba became the scientific capital of Europe; notable advances were made in agriculture, industry, literature, philosophy, and medicine. The Jews were welcomed by the Moors, often serving as administrators, ambassadors, and financial officers. But the Moors quarreled with one another, and soon the few Christian strongholds in the north began to advance south.

The Reconquest, the name given to the Christian efforts to rid the peninsula of the Moors, slowly reduced the size of the Muslim holdings, with Catholic monarchies forming in northern areas. The three powerful kingdoms of Aragón, Castile, and León were joined in 1469, when Ferdinand of Aragón married Isabella of Castile. Catholic kings, as they were called, launched the final attack on the Moors and completed the Reconquest in 1492 by capturing Granada.

That same year, Columbus, the Genoese sailor, landed on the West Indies, laying the foundations for a far-flung empire that brought wealth and power to Spain during the 16th and 17th centuries.

The Spanish Inquisition, begun under Ferdinand and Isabella, sought to eradicate all heresy and secure the primacy of Catholicism. Non-Catholics, Jews, and Moors were mercilessly persecuted, and many were driven out of the country.

THE GOLDEN AGE & LATER DECLINE

Columbus's voyage to America and the conquistadors' subsequent exploration of that land ushered Spain into its golden age.

In the first half of the 16th century, Balboa discovered the Pacific Ocean, Cortés seized Mexico for Spain, Pizarro took Peru, and a Spanish ship (initially commanded by the Portuguese Magellan, who was killed during the voyage) circumnavigated the globe. The conquistadors took Catholicism to the New World and shipped cargoes of gold back to Spain. The Spanish Empire extended all the way to the Philippines. Charles V, grandson of Ferdinand and Isabella, was the most powerful prince in Europe—King of Spain and Naples, Holy Roman Emperor and lord of Germany, duke of Burgundy and the Netherlands, and ruler of the New World territories.

But much of Spain's wealth and human resources were wasted in religious and secular conflicts. First Jews, then Muslims, and finally Catholicized Moors were driven out—and with them much of the country's prosperity. When Philip II ascended the throne in 1556, Spain could indeed boast vast possessions: the New World colonies; Naples, Milan, Genoa, Sicily, and other portions of Italy; the Spanish Netherlands (modern Belgium and the Netherlands);

- **1519** Cortés conquers Mexico. Charles I is crowned Holy Roman Emperor, as Charles V.
- **1556** Philip II inherits throne and launches the Counter-Reformation.
- **1588** England defeats Spanish Armada.
- **1700** Philip V becomes king. War of Spanish Succession follows.
- **1713** Treaty of Utrecht ends war. Spain's colonies reduced.
- **1759** Charles III ascends throne.
- **1808** Napoléon places brother Joseph on the Spanish throne.
- **1813** Wellington drives French out of Spain; the monarchy is restored.
- **1876** Spain becomes a constitutional monarchy.
- **1898** Spanish-American War leads to Spain's loss of Puerto Rico, Cuba, and the Philippines.
- **1923** Primo de Rivera forms military directorate.
- **1930** Right-wing dictatorship ends; Primo de Rivera exiled.
- **1931** King Alfonso XIII abdicates; Second Republic is born.
- **1933–35** Falange party formed.
- **1936–39** Civil War between the governing Popular Front and the Nationalists led by Gen. Francisco Franco.
- **1939** Franco establishes dictatorship, which will last 36 years.
- **1941** Spain technically stays neutral in World War II, but Franco favors Germany.
- **1955** Spain joins the United Nations.
- **1969** Franco names Juan Carlos as his successor.
- **1975** Juan Carlos becomes king. Franco dies.
- **1978** New, democratic constitution initiates reforms.

continues

- **1981** Coup attempt by right-wing officers fails.
- **1982** Socialists gain power after 43 years of right-wing rule.
- **1986** Spain joins the European Community (now the European Union).
- **1992** Barcelona hosts the Summer Olympics; Seville hosts EXPO '92.
- **1996** A conservative party defeats Socialist party, ending 13-year rule. José María Aznar chosen prime minister.
- **1998** Two cultural milestones for Spain: the inauguration of the controversial Guggenheim Museum at Bilbao and the reopening of Madrid's opera house, Teatro Real.
- **1999** Spain falls under the euro umbrella.
- **2000** Economy goes on an upswing. Complete euro unity looms.

and portions of Austria and Germany. But the seeds of decline had already been planted.

Philip, a fanatic Catholic, devoted his energies to subduing the Protestant revolt in the Netherlands and to becoming the standard-bearer for the Counter-Reformation. He tried to return England to Catholicism, first by marrying Mary I ("Bloody Mary") and later by wooing her half-sister, Elizabeth I, who rebuffed him. When, in 1588, he resorted to sending the Armada, it was ignominiously defeated; and that defeat symbolized the decline of Spanish power.

In 1700, a Bourbon prince, Philip V, became king, and the country fell under the influence of France. Philip V's right to the throne was challenged by a Hapsburg archduke of Austria, thus giving rise to the War of the Spanish Succession. When it ended, Spain had lost Flanders, its Italian possessions, and Gibraltar (still held by the British today).

During the 18th century, Spain's direction changed with each sovereign. Charles III (1759–88) developed the country economically and culturally. Charles IV became embroiled in wars with France, and the weakness of the Spanish monarchy allowed Napoléon to place his brother Joseph Bonaparte on the throne in 1808.

THE 19TH & 20TH CENTURIES Although Britain and France had joined forces to restore the Spanish monarchy, the European conflicts encouraged Spanish colonists to rebel. Ultimately, this led the United States to free the Philippines, Puerto Rico, and Cuba from Spain in 1898.

In 1876 Spain became a constitutional monarchy. But labor unrest, disputes with the Catholic Church, and war in Morocco combined to create political chaos. Conditions eventually became so bad that the Cortés, or parliament, was dissolved in 1923, and Gen. Miguel Primo de Rivera formed a military directorate. Early in 1930, Primo de Rivera resigned, but unrest continued.

On April 14, 1931, a revolution occurred, a republic was proclaimed, and King Alfonso XIII and his family were forced to flee. Initially the liberal constitutionalists ruled, but soon they were pushed aside by the socialists and anarchists, who adopted a constitution separating church and state, secularizing education, and containing several other radical provisions (for example, agrarian reform and the expulsion of the Jesuits).

The extreme nature of these reforms fostered the growth of the conservative Falange party (*Falange española,* or Spanish Phalanx), modeled after Italy and Germany's fascist parties. By the 1936 elections, the country was divided equally between left and right, and political violence was common. On July 18, 1936, the army, supported by Mussolini and Hitler, tried to seize power, igniting the Spanish Civil War. Gen. Francisco Franco, coming from Morocco to Spain, led the Nationalist (rightist) forces in the fighting that ravaged the country.

The popular front opposing Franco was forced to rely mainly on untrained volunteers, including a few heroic Americans called the "Lincoln brigade." For those who want an insight into the era, Ernest Hemingway's *For Whom the Bell Tolls* is a good read. It took time to turn untrained militias into an army fit to battle Franco's forces, and time was something to popular front didn't have.

It was a war to attract the attention of the world. By the summer of 1936 the USSR was sending rubles to aid the revolution by the republicans. Even Mexico sent war materiel to the popular front. Most—but not all—the volunteers were communists. Italy and Germany contributed war materiel to Franco's forces.

Madrid, controlled by the popular front, held out through a brutal siege that lasted for 28 months. Eventually, the government of the popular front moved to Valencia for greater safety in 1936.

But in the winter of 1936–37, Franco's forces slowly began to establish power, capturing the Basque capital of Bilbao and eventually Santander. The war shocked the world with its ruthlessness (World War II hadn't happened yet). Churches were burned, and mass executions occurred, especially memorable in the Basque town of Guernica, which became the subject of one of Picasso's most fabled paintings.

By October 1, 1936, Franco was clearly in charge of the leadership of nationalist Spain, abolishing popular suffrage and regional autonomy—in effect, launching a totalitarian rule for Spain.

The republicans were split by internal differences, and spy trials were commonplace. At the end of the first year of war, Franco held 35 of Spain's provincial capitals. In 1937 the republican forces were cut in two, and Madrid was left to fend for itself.

The last great offensive of the war began on December 28, 1938, with an attack by Franco's forces on Barcelona, which fell on January 26 after a campaign of 34 days. Republican forces fled toward France, as a succession of presidents occurred. On March 28 some 200,000 nationalist troops marched into Madrid, meeting no resistance. The war was over the next day when the rest of republican Spain surrendered. The war lasted 2 years and 254 days, costing some one million lives.

For memories and a sense of the Spanish Civil War, visitors can travel to El Valle de los Caídos (the Valley of the Fallen) outside El Escorial (see chapter 4, "Side Trips from Madrid").

Although Franco adopted a neutral position during World War II, his sympathies obviously lay with Germany and Italy, and Spain, although a nonbelligerent, assisted the Axis powers. This action intensified the diplomatic isolation into which the country was forced after the war's end—in fact, it was excluded from the United Nations until 1955.

Before his death, General Franco selected as his successor Juan Carlos de Borbón y Borbón, son of the pretender to the Spanish throne. After the 1977 elections, a new constitution was approved by the electorate and the king; it guaranteed human and civil rights, as well as free enterprise, and canceled the status of the Roman Catholic Church as the church of Spain. It also granted limited autonomy to several regions, including Catalonia and the Basque provinces, both of which, however, are still clamoring for complete autonomy.

In 1981, a group of right-wing military officers seized the Cortés and called upon Juan Carlos to establish a Francoist state. The king, however, refused, and the conspirators were arrested. The fledgling democracy overcame its first test. Its second major accomplishment—under the Socialist administration of

Prime Minister Felipe González, the country's first leftist government since 1939—was to gain Spain's entry into the European Community (now Union) in 1986.

The shocking news for 2000 was not political, but social. Spain came under increasing pressure to conform to short lunch breaks like those in the other EU countries. What? No 3-hour siesta? It was heresy. In spite of opposition, large companies began to cut lunch to 2 hours. Pro-siesta forces in Spain cited the American custom of "power naps" as reason to retain their beloved afternoon break.

So the siesta appears to be under serious attack, perhaps as a consequence of the Spanish economy's upswing, which created more new jobs than in any other country in the EU. More and more families are moving to the suburbs, and more women are joining the work force. A survey has revealed that only 25% of Spaniards still take the siesta.

In January 1999, Spain joined 10 other EU countries in adopting the euro as its new currency, although it will be going through a transitional period until January 1, 2002. Until that time, the peseta and the euro will continue to exist side by side.

3 Architecture Through the Ages

FROM THE ROMANS TO THE MOORS

Architectural roots in Spain date from the Romans, who built aqueducts and more than 12,000 miles of roads and bridges as a means of linking their assorted Iberian holdings. The greatest of them, **Via Augusta,** followed the Costa Brava, Costa Blanca, and Costa del Sol to transport armies and supplies between Cádiz and the Pyrenees.

This Hispano-Roman style involves prolific use of the vault and the arch, which you can see in such marvels as the **aqueduct at Segovia, the triumphal arch at Tarragona,** and the rectilinear, carefully planned community at **Mérida** (whose Roman monuments are among the best preserved in Europe).

Historians cite A.D. 409 as the end of the Roman age in Iberia, the beginning of political anarchy, and the migration into Spain of thousands of immigrants (Vandals, Alans, Suevians, and Visigothic tribespeople) from Central Europe. The newcomers, recent converts to some kind of Christianity, built crude chapels and fortresses based on a mishmash of aesthetic ideals from northern Europe and Byzantium, using engineering principles copied from the ancient Romans.

Spain's Romanesque style began to develop around A.D. 800, derived from the legacy of these crude Visigothic buildings (see "Pre-Romanesque & Romanesque Architecture," below). Meanwhile, a major new aesthetic was forcibly imposed upon Spain from the south.

HISPANO-MOORISH ARCHITECTURE

The Moors gained control of the Iberian Peninsula in the 8th century, and their 600-year rule left an architectural legacy that is among the most exotic and colorful in Europe. Regrettably, only a handful of *alcázares* (palaces), *alcazabas* (fortresses), and converted mosques remain intact today. Moorish buildings tended to be relatively flimsy and heavily accented with decorations. Many have collapsed (or were deliberately destroyed) in the Catholic zeal to "re-Christianize" Iberia.

The most visible traits of the Saracenic style included the use of forests of (sometimes mismatched) columns in mosques, each of which supported a network of horseshoe-shaped arches. They interconnected to support low, flat roofs. Some arches were scalloped, then decorated with geometric designs or calligraphic inscriptions from the Koran.

MOZARABIC ARCHITECTURE

Mozarabes were Christian Spaniards who retained their religion under the Muslim rule. They successfully blended Gothic and Moorish styles in their art and architecture. The few structures that remain intact from this period can be found in Toledo and include the **Monastery of El Cristo de la Luz,** originally built in the 900s as a mosque; a 12th-century synagogue, now the church of **Santa María de la Blanca;** and the **churches of Santiago del Arrabal and San Román.** A secular example of the style in Toledo is the **Puerto del Sol,** an ornate gate built into the walls that surround the old city. Constructed around 1200, about 150 years after Toledo's reconquest by Christian forces, it combines the distinctive Moorish horseshoe arch with feudal battlements and Christian iconography.

MUDÉJAR ARCHITECTURE

Equivalent in some ways to the above-mentioned Mozárabe style (with which it is frequently confused), Mudéjar refers to the architectural and decorative style developed by Spanish Muslims living in Christian territories after the Reconquista. A mix of Gothic and Moorish influences, it reached its peak between 1275 and 1350, made frequent use of brick instead of stone, and specialized in elaborate wood carvings that merged the Moorish emphasis on geometrics and symmetry with Christian themes. Regrettably, after the final Moorish stronghold fell to the Christians in 1492, Spanish monarchs did everything they could to purge any artistic legacy left by the Moors. Mudéjar influences, however, still cropped up in rural pockets of Spain until the middle of the 18th century, and, in some cases, even merged subtly with ornate features of the baroque.

PRE-ROMANESQUE & ROMANESQUE ARCHITECTURE

Ensconced in Asturias, feudal rulers of the Christian Visigothic tribes refined their architectural tastes. Stonework became better crafted than the crude models of the previous 2 centuries, and arches became more graceful. Under the rule of Alfonso the Chaste (791–842), dozens of pre-Romanesque churches were built in Oviedo, and a body believed to be that of Saint James was discovered, miraculously, in a field in Galicia. Thus was born **Santiago de Compostela (St. James of the Field),** the eventual site of a great cathedral and one of the most famous pilgrimage sites in the Christian world.

From these beginnings, and based on money and cultural influences from the floods of pilgrims pouring in from Italy, France, and other parts of Europe, a trail of Romanesque churches, shelters, monasteries, and convents sprang up across northern Spain, especially along the pilgrim route in Catalonia, Aragón, and northern Castile. The style is known for semicircular arches, small windows, crude but evocative carvings, and thick walls. It is best represented in the **church of San Gil in Zaragoza** and the **cloisters of San Pedro,** near Pamplona in the town of Estella.

SPANISH GOTHIC

This style surged across provinces adjacent to the French border (Catalonia and Navarre) beginning around 1250. By the late 1200s, churches that had been initiated in the Romanesque style (such as the **Burgos cathedral**) were

The Spectacle of Death

For obvious reasons, many people consider bullfighting cruel and shocking, but as Ernest Hemingway pointed out in *Death in the Afternoon:* "The bullfight is not a sport in the Anglo-Saxon sense of the word, that is, it is not an equal contest or an attempt at an equal contest between a bull and a man. Rather it is a tragedy: the death of the bull, which is played, more or less well, by the bull and the man involved and in which there is danger for the man but certain death for the bull."

When the symbolic drama of the bullfight is acted out, some believe it reaches a higher plane, the realm of art. Some people argue that it is not a public exhibition of cruelty at all, but rather a highly skilled art form that requires will to survive, courage, showmanship, and gallantry. Regardless of how you view it, the spectacle is an authentic Spanish experience and reveals much about the character of the land and its people.

The *corrida* (bullfight) season lasts from early spring until around mid-October. Fights are held in a *plaza de toros* (bullring), including the oldest ring in remote Ronda to the big-time Plaza de Toros in Madrid. Sunday is *corrida* day in most major Spanish cities, although Madrid and Barcelona may also have fights on Thursday.

Tickets fall into three classifications, and prices are based on your exposure to the famed Spanish sun: *sol* (sun), the cheapest; *sombra* (shade), the most expensive; and *sol y sombra* (a mixture of sun and shade), the medium-price range.

The *corrida* begins with a parade. For many viewers, this may be the high point of the afternoon's festivities, as all the bullfighters are clad in their *trajes de luce,* or luminous suits.

completed as sometimes flamboyant Gothic monuments. During the 1300s and 1400s, bishops in León, Toledo, and Burgos even imported architects and masons from Gothic strongholds in other parts of Europe to design their cathedrals. In Spain, the Gothic style included widespread use of ogive (high-pointed) arches and vaults and clustered pilasters, and an opening up of walls to incorporate large, usually stained-glass, windows.

THE RENAISSANCE

After the expulsion of the Moors from Iberia, and Columbus's first landings in the New World in 1492, Spain found itself caught up in a vivid, emphatic sense of its own manifest destiny. Searching for a national style of architecture, the Spanish monarchs adapted the aesthetic trends of Renaissance Italy into a "Hispanicized" style. Foremost among these was the 16th-century plateresque, which emulated in stone the finely worked forms that a silversmith might have hammered into silver plate. The style is best viewed on the exterior of the **University of Salamanca** and the **Chapel of the New Kings inside the cathedral at Toledo.**

CLASSICAL SPANISH ARCHITECTURE

The austere regime of Philip II not only welcomed but demanded a less ornate national style from the country's architects. Fervently religious and obsessively ambitious for the advancement of Spanish interests, he embraced the austere

Bullfights are divided into thirds. The first is the *tercio de capa* (cape), during which the matador tests the bull with various passes and gets acquainted with him. The second portion, the *tercio de varas* (sticks), begins with the lance-carrying *picadores* on horseback, who weaken, or "punish," the bull by jabbing him in the shoulder area. The horses are sometimes gored, even though they wear protective padding, or the horse and rider might be tossed into the air by the now-infuriated bull. The *picadores* are followed by the *banderilleros,* whose job it is to puncture the bull with pairs of boldly colored darts.

In the final *tercio de muleta,* the action narrows down to the lone fighter and the bull. Gone are the fancy capes. Instead, the matador uses a small red cloth known as a *muleta,* which, to be effective, requires a bull with lowered head. (The *picadores* and *banderilleros* have worked to achieve this.) Using the *muleta* as a lure, the matador wraps the bull around himself in various passes, the most dangerous of which is the natural; here, the matador holds the *muleta* in his left hand, the sword in his right. Right-hand passes pose less of a threat, since the sword can be used to spread out the *muleta,* making a larger target for the bull. After a number of passes, the time comes for the kill, the moment of truth.

After the bull dies, the highest official at the ring may award the matador an ear from the dead bull, or perhaps both ears, or ears and tail. For a truly extraordinary performance, the hoof is sometimes added. Spectators cheer a superlative performance by waving white handkerchiefs, imploring the judge to award a prize. The bullfighter may be carried away as a hero, or if he has displeased the crowd, he may be jeered and chased out of the ring by an angry mob. At a major fight, usually six bulls are killed by three matadors in one afternoon.

---

ancient Roman forms that had been revived during Italy's late Renaissance. The style's most megalomaniacal manifestation in Spain came with **Juan de Herrera's** gargantuan, brooding, military-looking monastery and palace at **El Escorial** (1563–84) on an isolated and windswept plateau outside Madrid. Philip II considered the style an appropriate manifestation of the stern principles of the Counter-Reformation and the new Inquisition that followed.

Later during the Renaissance, Herrera's rectilinear gridirons were replaced with the curved lines of the baroque. This style was avidly embraced by the Jesuits, one of the most powerful religious orders in Spain at the time, whose austere religious bent stood in marked contrast to their flamboyant architectural tastes. The baroque style appears at its most ornate in **Andalusia,** a region enjoying a building boom at the time thanks to the wealth that poured into its ports from the gold mines of Mexico and Peru.

Ironically, baroque was the style most enthusiastically embraced by the Spanish colonies in South America. Spain's interpretation of Italian baroque architecture is sometimes referred to as Churrigueresque, after **José Churriguera** (1665–1725), designer to the kings of Spain and architect of **Salamanca's New Cathedral.** The style is characterized by its dense concentrations of busy ornamentation that often completely disguised the basic form of the building itself. An example of baroque style in Spain is the wedding-cake facade of the **Murcia cathedral.**

FROM BAROQUE TOWARD MODERN

Under the Spanish Bourbon rulers of the 18th century, the favored style embraced the baroque and neoclassical influences of aristocratic France. **El Pardo, Riofrio,** and **Aranjuez** were all built as Europeanized hideaways. Even the design of the **Royal Palace in Madrid** was modeled after Versailles.

In the 19th century, the Romantic age encouraged a revolt against the ideals of balance and reason that had defined upscale European architecture during the late 1700s. Spanish architecture throughout the 19th century was torn between the value of the individual architect's eclectic, personalized, and sometimes flamboyant vision, and the inevitable reactions that swung the pendulum of public taste back toward greater restraint and symmetry. There developed a new respect for the Gothic, as many 500-year-old Gothic cathedrals were adapted or altered with neo-Gothic alterations that modern art historians sometimes view with horror.

Out of this tension emerged one of Spain's most widely recognized architectural giants, **Antoni Gaudí** (1852–1926). His idiosyncratic, organic style, called Catalán Art Nouveau, or *modernisme,* coincided neatly with the most intense building boom ever experienced in his hometown of **Barcelona.** Gaudí succeeded in fusing regional aesthetics and forms with a style that still challenges architectural thinking. He created curiously curved and sinuous, "organic-looking" buildings in protest against the rising anonymity of the industrial age and dull architecture without soul that would reach its most grotesque form in Nazi Germany long after Gaudí's death. One of the best examples of his ideas can be seen in Barcelona's **Casa Milá.**

ARCHITECTURE TODAY

Other than occasional models of genuine inspiration, such as the whimsical and surrealist buildings devised by **Salvador Dalí,** much of modern Spain's architecture is derived from the older, tried-and-true traditions. When it comes to recycling the feudal or Renaissance monuments of yesteryear, Spain has no equal, as evidenced by the country's network of historic paradors. Regrettably, some areas of modern Spain, including many neighborhoods of Madrid and long stretches of the Costa del Sol, have bristled with high-rise, concrete-and-glass apartment houses. Few boast any distinguishing features, provoking laments from traditionalists.

One example of genuine inspiration, however, is the work of **Rafael Moneo,** who lives in Madrid and has designed mainly in Spain, with such exceptions as the Davis Museum and Cultural Center at Wellesley, Massachusetts, in 1993. One of his most notable designs is the **Museo Nacional de Arte Roman in Mérida.** In 1996 he won the Pritzker Architecture Prize, viewed as the Oscar for architects. The Spanish architect **Santiago Calatrava** has been hailed as one of Europe's most innovative architects, although he trained as an engineer and sculptor. He seeks to build a bridge between architecture and art. In Barcelona, his **Bach de Roda-Felipe II Bridge** spans the rail tracks that run from north to south, linking the ocean and city itself. Other projects include the **Bilbao Airport Terminal** and the **"City of Sciences" in Valencia.**

Although Spain has a lot of homegrown talent, it also turns to foreign architects, especially for flashy signature projects. The most famous example of this is **Frank Gehry's Guggenheim Museum at Bilbao,** hailed as the first great building of the 21st century. One critic said that Gehry has "repudiated Modernist sanctity, symmetry, and right-angled geometrics in his own fearless way, taking them apart and putting them back together with a rollicking, cockeyed brilliance."

4 Spanish Art

ARTISTIC ROOTS

Spanish art has always been characterized by a mixture of passion and a usterity—a reflection of the country itself—that makes it one of the most unusual and riveting of national oeuvres anywhere.

Some of the best examples of prehistoric art were discovered in Spanish caves, including the hunting scenes in the **caves of Altamira and Puente Viesgo,** and the mysterious dolmens that stand like Celtic sentinels at **Antequera,** near Málaga. Equivalent dolmens (known locally as *talayots* and *navetas*) were erected on the Balearics between around 2500 and 1000 B.C.

By 1000 B.C., Spain became a crossroads of civilizations, a role it would play for the next 3,000 years. Many of the most prized artifacts in Spanish museums date from this era; the statue *The Lady of Elche,* the lions of Córdoba, and the bulls (*toros*) of Guisando all reflect the influence of **ancient Greeks and Phoenicians,** who used Spain's coast as a port of call on their trade routes. In such port cities as Cádiz, for example, rows of Phoenician sarcophagi have been unearthed.

HISPANO-MOORISH ART

Beginning in A.D. 711, when the first Moorish armies poured into Andalusia, the preconceptions of Spanish art changed forever. Forbidden by religious law to portray human or animal forms, Muslim artists restricted themselves to geometric patterns, ornate depictions of plant life, and calligraphic renderings of verses from the Koran. Their works influenced the Mozárabes, who brought these themes within a Christian context. The Moors also excelled at landscape architecture—the symmetrical placement of fountains, plants, and statues in some of the greatest gardens and pleasure pavilions ever built.

ROMANESQUE ART

Other than its architecture, the greatest artistic legacy of the Romanesque age, which began around A.D. 1000, was its sculpture. A vast number of churches and abbeys sprang up along the medieval world's most famous pilgrimage route (St. James's way across Asturias and Galicia), and each house of worship required sculpture to adorn the columns and altars. **San Juan de la Peña** was a master of the carved form, and his students branched out across the pilgrimage route, carving crude but symbolic references to apocryphal tales.

In Catalonia, aggressive merchants appropriated aesthetic ideals from Italy and France and had paintings executed on fresh plaster. Several of the most memorable of these Romanesque frescoes that remain today are credited to a mysterious painter, the **Master of Tahull,** who may have trained as far away as Byzantium. By 1300, Catalonia had been home to more than 1,000 artists, many of whom were inspired by this mysterious master.

GOTHIC ART

Beginning around 1250, as the Gothic aesthetic trickled from France into Spain, the production of painting and sculpture accelerated. Works followed religious themes, often rendered in the form of polychrome triptychs and altarpieces that stretched toward the soaring heights of a cathedral's ceiling. Many painters took their inspiration from such contemporary pre-Renaissance Italians as Giotto; others looked to France and Flanders, and the attention their painters paid to naturalistic, and sometimes stylized, detail. Eventually, the slumbering figures atop funerary sarcophagi came to resemble, in sometimes ghoulish detail, the living body of the person buried within, and decorative adornments became almost obsessive.

RENAISSANCE, BAROQUE & BEYOND

The defeat of the Muslims in 1492, and the colonialization the same year of the New World, marked the debut of the Renaissance in Spain. Choir stalls, altarpieces, funerary sarcophagi, and historical statues became commonplace throughout the newly united Spain. The popularity of gilding was a direct result of the precious metals flooding into the country from the mines of the New World. The **cathedrals of Burgos and Barcelona** and some of the chapels in the **cathedral at Granada** are fine examples of the heights to which Renaissance sculpture rose. A new technique, *estofado,* was introduced, whereby multiple colors were applied over a base of gold leaf, then rubbed or scratched to expose subtly gilded highlights in a way that prefigured the eventual rise of the baroque.

The greatest Spanish painter of the Renaissance was **El Greco** (Domenico Theotocopoulos, born in Crete in 1541; died 1614), whose interpretation of Iberian mysticism reached deeper into the Spanish soul than any painter before or since. He was well versed in classical references and trained in all the methods popular in both Italy (especially Venice) and Byzantium. His was an intensely personal vision—amplified emotion, elongated limbs, and characters lifted bodily, and ecstatically, toward heaven. His style, known today as mannerism, met with violent criticism and lawsuits from disgruntled patrons.

After El Greco, the leading Spanish painter was **Diego de Silva y Velázquez** (1599–1660). Appointed court painter to the vain and self-indulgent monarch Philip IV, he painted 40 portraits of Philip and dozens of other members of the royal family. (See his famous *Las Meninas* in the Prado.) Influenced by Rubens, who urged him to travel to Italy, his craftsmanship improved to the point where he has been hailed as the single greatest painter in the lexicon of Spanish art. Other important painters of this baroque period included **José Ribera** (1591–1652) and **Francisco de Zurbarán** (1598–1664). **Bartolomé Murillo** (1617–82) produced religious paintings that appealed, 200 years after his death, to the sentimentalism of the English Victorians.

The mantle of greatness was next passed to **Francisco de Goya y Lucientes** (1746–1828), an artist whose skill as a draftsman produced everything from tapestries to portraits of noble ladies. Rendered deaf in 1792 after a serious illness, Goya adopted a style of dark and brooding realism that many critics view as at least a century ahead of his contemporaries. In his work are vivid precursors of such future trends as romanticism and the psychological intricacies of expressionism. Victim of the political incompetencies of the Spanish regime, he was forced to flee in 1824 to Bordeaux, where he died, dejected, embittered, and broken.

MODERNISM & SURREALISM

Around the turn of the 20th century, artists of note were so frustrated by the official repression of the Spanish establishment that they emigrated, almost en masse, to Paris. Such outstanding innovators as **Joan Miró, Salvador Dalí,** and **Juan Gris** were among this group, whose names later became as closely associated with France as with Spain.

The most influential of these expatriates, of course, was **Pablo Picasso,** born in Málaga in 1881. Before the end of his extraordinary career, he would become the most famous artist of the 20th century, mastering a variety of styles and defining such major schools of art as cubism.

A divergent school, **surrealism,** was developed by Catalonia-born **Salvador Dalí.** His sometimes authentic, sometimes fraudulent commercial endeavors explored the subconscious levels of the human mind, using dream sequences whose content might have appealed to Jung and Freud.

Among the important Spanish abstract painters are **Antoni Tàpies,** a pioneer in the use of texture and geometric placement of shapes and forms, and **Juan José Tharrats.** Major sculptors include **Jorge Otieza, Eduardo Chillida** (whose abstract works bear almost no resemblance to the human form), and **Andréu Alfaro,** whose works hang in influential galleries in such cities as Barcelona and Madrid.

Born in Huesca in 1930, **Antonio Saura** began painting in 1947 and was first exhibited in 1950. He developed a technique of black-and-white outlines, always in the form of the female body. Among the younger generation, **Miguel Barceló,** born in 1957 in Majorca, has gone on to enjoy an international reputation. He spends a great amount of time in Africa, and his work has taken on many non-Western elements.

5 A Taste of Spain

Meals are an extremely important social activity in Spain, whether that means eating out late at night or having large family gatherings for lunch. Although Spain is faster paced than it once was, few Spaniards race through a meal on the way to an appointment.

The food in Spain is varied; the portions are immense, but the prices, by North American standards, are high. Whenever possible, try the regional specialties, particularly when you visit the Basque country or Galicia.

Many restaurants in Spain close on Sunday, so be sure to check ahead. Hotel dining rooms are generally open 7 days, and there's always something open in such big cities as Madrid and Barcelona or such well-touristed areas as the Costa del Sol. Generally, reservations are not necessary, except at popular, top-notch restaurants.

MEALS

BREAKFAST   In Spain, the day starts with a continental breakfast of coffee, hot chocolate, or tea, with assorted rolls, butter, and jam. Spanish breakfast might also consist of *churros* (fried fingerlike doughnuts) and hot chocolate that is very sweet and thick. However, most Spaniards simply have coffee, usually strong and black, served with hot milk: either a *café con leche* (half coffee, half milk) or *cortado* (a shot of espresso "cut" with a dash of milk). If you find it too strong and bitter for your taste, you might ask for a more diluted *café americano.*

LUNCH   The most important meal of the day in Spain, lunch is comparable to the farm-style noonday "dinner" in America. It usually includes three or four courses, beginning with a choice of soup or several dishes of hors d'oeuvres called *entremeses.* Often a fish or egg dish is served after this, then a meat course with vegetables. Wine is always part of the meal. Dessert is usually pastry, custard, or assorted fruit—followed by coffee. Lunch is served from 1 to 4pm, with "rush hour" at 2pm.

TAPAS   After the early evening stroll, many Spaniards head for their favorite *tascas,* bars where they drink wine and sample assorted tapas, or snacks, such as bits of fish, eggs in mayonnaise, or olives.

Because many Spaniards eat dinner very late, they often have an extremely light breakfast, certainly coffee and perhaps a pastry. However, by 11am they

Now you have two homes.

—Traditional Spanish farewell

are often hungry and lunch might not be until 2pm or later, so many Spaniards have a late-morning snack, often at a cafeteria. Favorite items to order are a *tortilla* (Spanish omelet with potatoes) and even a beer. Many request a large tapa served with bread.

DINNER   Another extravaganza: A typical meal starts with a bowl of soup, followed by a second course, often a fish dish, and by another main course, usually veal, beef, or pork, accompanied by vegetables. Again, desserts tend to be fruit, custard, or pastries.

Naturally, if you had a heavy and late lunch and stopped off at a tapas bar or two before dinner, supper might be much lighter, perhaps some cold cuts, sausage, a bowl of soup, or even a Spanish omelet made with potatoes. Wine is always part of the meal. Afterward, you might have a demitasse and a fragrant Spanish brandy. The chic dining hour, even in one-donkey towns, is 10 or 10:30pm. (In well-touristed regions and hardworking Catalonia, you can usually dine at 8pm, but you still might find yourself alone in the restaurant.) In most middle-class establishments, people dine around 9:30pm.

THE CUISINE

SOUPS & APPETIZERS   Soups are usually served in big bowls. Cream soups, such as asparagus and potato, can be fine; sadly, however, they are too often made from powdered envelope soups such as Knorr and Liebig. Served year-round, chilled gazpacho, on the other hand, is tasty and particularly refreshing during the hot months. The combination is pleasant: olive oil, garlic, ground cucumbers, and raw tomatoes with a sprinkling of croutons. Spain also offers several varieties of fish soup—*sopa de pescado*—in all its provinces, and many of these are superb.

In the paradors (government-run hostelries) and top restaurants, as many as 15 tempting hors d'oeuvres are served. In lesser-known places, avoid these *entremeses,* which often consist of last year's sardines and shards of sausage left over from the Moorish conquest.

EGGS   They are served in countless ways. A Spanish omelet, a *tortilla española,* is made with potatoes and usually onions. A simple omelet is called a *tortilla francesa. A tortilla portuguesa* is similar to the American Spanish omelet.

FISH   Spain's fish dishes tend to be outstanding and vary from province to province. One of the most common varieties is *merluza* (sweet white hake). *Langosta,* a variety of lobster, is seen everywhere—it's a treat but terribly expensive. The Portuguese in particular, but some Spaniards, too, go into raptures at the mention of *mejillones* (barnacles). Gourmets relish their seawater taste; others find them tasteless. *Rape* (pronounced *rah*-pay) is the Spanish name for monkfish, a sweet, wide-boned ocean fish with a scalloplike texture. Also try a few dozen half-inch baby eels. They rely heavily on olive oil and garlic for their flavor, but they taste great. Squid cooked in its own ink is suggested only to those who want to go native. Charcoal-broiled sardines, however, are a culinary delight—a particular treat in the Basque provinces. Trout Navarre is one of the most popular fish dishes, usually stuffed with bacon or ham.

PAELLA   You can't go to Spain without trying its celebrated paella. Flavored with saffron, paella is an aromatic rice dish usually topped with shellfish, chicken, sausage, peppers, and local spices. Served authentically, it comes steaming hot from the kitchen in a metal pan called a *paellera*. (Incidentally, what is known in America as Spanish rice isn't Spanish at all. If you ask an English-speaking waiter for Spanish rice, you'll be served paella.)

MEATS   Don't expect Kansas City steak, but do try the spit-roasted suckling pig, so sweet and tender it can often be cut with a fork. The veal is also good, and the Spanish *lomo de cerdo*, loin of pork, is unmatched anywhere. Tender chicken is most often served in the major cities and towns today, and the Spanish are adept at spit-roasting it until it turns a delectable golden brown. However, in more remote spots of Spain, "free-range" chicken is often stringy and tough.

VEGETABLES & SALADS   Through more sophisticated agricultural methods, Spain now grows more of its own vegetables, which are available year-round, unlike days of yore, when canned vegetables were used all too frequently. Both potatoes and rice are a staple of the Spanish diet, the latter a prime ingredient, of course, in the famous paella originating in Valencia. Salads don't usually get the attention they do in California, and are often made simply with just lettuce and tomatoes.

DESSERTS   The Spanish do not emphasize dessert, often opting for fresh fruit. Flan, a home-cooked egg custard, appears on all menus—sometimes with a burnt-caramel sauce. Ice cream appears on nearly all menus as well. But the best bet is to ask for a basket of fruit, which you can wash at your table. Homemade pastries are usually moist and not too sweet. As a dining oddity, many restaurants serve fresh orange juice for dessert—although it's not odd at all to Spaniards.

OLIVE OIL & GARLIC   Olive oil is used lavishly in Spain, the largest olive grower on the planet. You may not want it in all dishes. If you prefer your fish grilled in butter, the word is *mantequilla*. In some instances, you'll be charged extra for the butter. Garlic is also an integral part of the Spanish diet, and even if you love it, you may find Spaniards love it more than you do and use it in the oddest dishes.

WHAT TO DRINK

WATER   It is generally safe to drink water in all major cities and tourist resorts in Spain. If you're traveling in remote areas, play it safe and drink bottled water. One of the most popular non-carbonated bottled drinks in Spain is Solares. Nearly all restaurants and hotels have it. Bubbly water is *agua mineral con gas;* non-carbonated, *agua mineral sin gas*. Note that bottled water in some areas may cost as much as the regional wine.

SOFT DRINKS   In general, avoid the carbonated citrus drinks on sale everywhere. Most of them never saw an orange, much less a lemon. If you want a citrus drink, order old, reliable Schweppes. An excellent non-carbonated drink for the summer is called Tri-Naranjus, which comes in lemon and orange flavors. Your cheapest bet is a liter bottle of *gaseosa*, which comes in various flavors. In summer you should also try a drink that we've never had outside Spain, *horchata*—a nutty, sweet milklike beverage made of tubers called *chufas*.

COFFEE   Even if you are a dedicated coffee drinker, you may find the *café con leche* (coffee with milk) a little too strong. We suggest *leche manchada*, a little bit of strong, freshly brewed coffee in a glass that's filled with lots of frothy hot milk.

MILK   In the largest cities you get bottled milk, but it loses a great deal of its flavor in the process of pasteurization. In all cases, avoid untreated milk and milk products. About the best brand of fresh milk is Lauki.

BEER   Although not native to Spain, beer (*cerveza*) is now drunk everywhere. Domestic brands include San Miguel, Mahou, Águila, and Cruz Blanca.

WINE   Sherry (*vino de Jerez*) has been called "the wine with a hundred souls." Drink it before dinner (try the topaz-colored *finos,* a dry and very pale sherry) or whenever you drop into some old inn or *bodega* for refreshment; many of them have rows of kegs with spigots. *Manzanilla,* a golden-colored medium-dry sherry, is extremely popular. The sweet cream sherries (Harvey's Bristol Cream, for example) are favorite after-dinner wines (called *olorosos*). While the French may be disdainful of Spanish table wines, they can be truly noble, especially two leading varieties, Valdepeñas and Rioja, both from Castile. If you're not too exacting in your tastes, you can always ask for the *vino de la casa* (wine of the house) wherever you dine. The Ampurdán of Catalonia is heavy. From Andalusia comes the fruity Montilla. There are some good local champagnes (*cavas*) in Spain, such as Freixenet. One brand, Benjamín, comes in individual-sized bottles.

Beginning in the 1990s, based partly on subsidies and incentives from the European Union, Spanish vintners have scrapped most of the country's obsolete wine-making equipment, hired new talent, and poured time and money into the improvement and promotion of wines from even high-altitude or arid regions not previously suitable for wine production. Thanks to irrigation, improved grape varieties, technological developments, and the expenditure of billions of pesetas, *bodegas* and vineyards are sprouting up throughout the country, opening their doors to visitors interested in how the stuff is grown, fermented, and bottled. These wines are now earning awards at wine competitions around the world for their quality and bouquet.

Interested in impressing a newfound Spanish friend over a wine list? Consider bypassing the usual array of Riojas, sherries, and sparkling Catalonian *cavas* in favor of, say, a Galician white from Rias Baixas, which some connoisseurs consider the perfect accompaniment for seafood. Among reds, make a beeline for vintages from the fastest-developing wine region of Europe, the arid, high-altitude district of Ribera del Duero, near Burgos, whose alkaline soil, cold nights, and sunny days have earned unexpected praise from wine makers (and encouraged massive investments) in the past 5 years.

For more information about these and others of the 10 wine-producing regions of Spain (and the 39 officially recognized wine-producing *Denominaciones de Origen* scattered across those regions), contact **Wines from Spain,** c/o the Commercial Office of Spain, 405 Lexington Ave., 44th Floor, New York, NY 10174-0331 (☎ **212/661-4959**).

SANGRÍA   The all-time favorite refreshing drink in Spain, sangría is a red-wine punch that combines wine with oranges, lemons, seltzer, and sugar. Be careful, however; many joints that do a big tourist trade produce a sickly sweet Kool-Aid version of sangría for unsuspecting visitors.

WHISKY & BRANDY   Imported whiskeys are available at most Spanish bars but at a high price. If you're a drinker, switch to brandies and cognacs, where the Spanish reign supreme. Try Fundador, made by the Pedro Domecq family in Jerez de la Frontera. If you want a smooth cognac, ask for the "103" white label.

Appendix B:
Useful Terms & Phrases

1 Basic Vocabulary

Most Spaniards are very patient with foreigners who try to speak their language. Although you might encounter several regional languages and dialects in Spain, Castillian (Castellano, or simply Español) is understood everywhere. In Catalonia, they speak Catalán (the most widely spoken non-national language in Europe); in the Basque country, they speak Euskerra; in Galicia you'll hear Gallego. Still, a few words in Castellano will usually get your message across with no problem.

When traveling, it helps a lot to know a few basic phrases, so we've included a list of certain simple phrases in Castillian Spanish for expressing basic needs.

ENGLISH-CASTILLIAN SPANISH PHRASES

English	Spanish	Pronunciation
Good day	**Buenos días**	*bway*-nohss *dee*-ahss
How are you?	**¿Cómo está?**	*koh*-moh ess-*tah*?
Very well	**Muy bien**	mwee byen
Thank you	**Gracias**	*grah*-see-ahss
You're welcome	**De nada**	day *nah*-dah
Goodbye	**Adios**	ah-*dyohss*
Please	**Por favor**	pohr fah-*vohr*
Yes	**Sí**	see
No	**No**	noh
Excuse me	**Perdóneme**	pehr-*doh*-ney-may
Give me	**Déme**	*day*-may
Where is . . . ?	**¿Dónde está . . . ?**	*dohn*-day ess-*tah* . . . ?
the station	**la estación**	lah ess-tah-*seown*
a hotel	**un hotel**	oon oh-*tel*
a gas station	**una gasolinera**	*oon*-uh gah-so-lee-*nay*-rah
a restaurant	**un restaurante**	oon res-tow-*rahn*-tay
the toilet	**el baño**	el *bahn*-yoh
a good doctor	**un buen médico**	oon bwayn *may*-thee-co
the road to . . .	**el camino a/hacia . . .**	el cah-*mee*-noh ah/ *ah*-see-ah . . .
To the right	**A la derecha**	ah lah day-*reh*-chuh
To the left	**A la izquierda**	ah lah ees-ky-*ehr*-thah

English	Spanish	Pronunciation
Straight ahead	**Derecho**	day-*reh*-cho
I would like	**Quisiera**	key-see-*ehr*-ah
I want	**Quiero**	*kyehr*-oh
to eat.	**comer**	ko-*mayr*
a room.	**una habitación**	*oon*-nuh ha-bee-tah-*seown*
Do you have?	**¿Tiene usted?**	tyeh-nay oos-*ted*?
a book.	**un libro**	oon *lee*-bro
a dictionary.	**un diccionario**	oon deek-seown-*ar*-eo
How much is it?	**¿Cuánto cuesta?**	*kwahn*-to *kwess*-tah?
When?	**¿Cuándo?**	*kwahn*-doh?
What?	**¿Qué?**	kay?
There is (Is there . . . ?)	**¿Hay (. . . ?)**	eye . . . ?
What is there?	**¿Qué hay?**	kay eye?
Yesterday	**Ayer**	ah-*yer*
Today	**Hoy**	oy
Tomorrow	**Mañana**	mahn-*yahn*-ah
Good	**Bueno**	*bway*-no
Bad	**Malo**	*mah*-lo
Better (best)	**(Lo) Mejor**	(loh) meh-*hor*
More	**Más**	mahs
Less	**Menos**	*may*-noss
No smoking	**Se prohíbe fumar**	say pro-*hee*-bay foo-*mahr*
Postcard	**Tarjeta postal**	tar-*hay*-ta pohs-*tahl*
Insect repellent	**Rapelente contra insectos**	rah-pey-*yahn*-te *cohn*-trah een-*sehk*-tos

MORE USEFUL PHRASES

English	Spanish	Pronunciation
Do you speak English?	**¿Habla usted inglés?**	*ah*-blah oo-*sted* een-*glays*?
Is there anyone here who speaks English?	**¿Hay alguien aquí qué hable inglés?**	eye *ahl*-ghee-en ah-*key* kay *ah*-blay een-*glays*?
I speak a little Spanish.	**Hablo un poco de español.**	*ah*-blow oon *poh*-koh day ess-pah-*nyol*
I don't understand Spanish very well.	**No (lo) entiendo muy bien el español.**	noh (loh) ehn-tee-*ehn*-do moo-ee bee-ayn el ess-pah-nyol.
The meal is good.	**Me gusta la comida.**	may goo-sta lah koh-mee-dah
What time is it?	**¿Qué hora es?**	kay oar-ah ess?
May I see your menu?	**¿Puedo ver el menú (la carta)?**	puay-tho veyr el may-noo (lah car-tah)?
The check please.	**La cuenta por favor.**	lah quayn-tah pohr fa-vorh
What do I owe you?	**¿Cuánto lo debo?**	Kwahn-toh loh day-boh?
What did you say?	**¿Cómo?**	*Koh*-moh?
I want (to see) a room	**Quiero (ver) un cuarto** *or* **una habitación**	Key-*yehr*-oh vehr oon *kwar*-toh *oon*-nuh ha-bee-tah-*seown*
for two persons. with (without) bathroom.	**para dos personas con (sin) baño.**	*pahr*-ah doss pehr-*sohn*-as kohn (seen) *bah*-nyoh

English	Spanish	Pronunciation
We are staying here only . . .	Nos quedamos aquí solamente . . .	nohs kay-*dahm*-ohss ah-*key* sohl-ah-*mayn*-tay . . .
one night.	una noche.	oon-ah *noh*-chay
one week.	una semana.	oon-ah say-*mahn*-ah
We are leaving tomorrow.	Partimos (Salimos) mañana.	Pahr-*tee*-mohss (Sah-*lee*-mohss) mahn-*nyan*-ah
Do you accept traveler's checks?	¿Acepta usted cheques de viajero?	Ah-*sayp*-tah oo-*sted chay* kays day bee-ah-*hehr*-oh?
Is there a Laundromat near here?	¿Hay una lavandería cerca de aquí?	Eye oon-ah lah-*vahn*-day-ree-ah *sehr*-ka day ah-*key*?
Please send these clothes to the laundry.	Hágame el favor de mandar esta ropa a la lavandería.	*Ah*-ga-may el fah-*vhor* day mahn-*dahr* ays-tah rho-pah a lah lah-*vahn*-day-ree-ah.

NUMBERS

1	**uno** (*ooh*-noh)		17	**diecisiete** (de-*ess*-ee-*syeh*-tay)
2	**dos** (dohs)		18	**dieciocho** (dee-*ess*-ee-*oh*-choh)
3	**tres** (trayss)		19	**diecinueve** (dee-*ess*-ee-*nway*-bay)
4	**cuatro** (*kwah*-troh)		20	**veinte** (*bayn*-tay)
5	**cinco** (*seen*-koh)		30	**treinta** (*trayn*-tah)
6	**seis** (sayss)		40	**cuarenta** (kwah-*ren*-tah)
7	**siete** (*syeh*-tay)		50	**cincuenta** (seen-*kwen*-tah)
8	**ocho** (*oh*-choh)		60	**sesenta** (say-*sen*-tah)
9	**nueve** (*nway*-bay)		70	**setenta** (say-*ten*-tah)
10	**diez** (dee-ess)		80	**ochenta** (oh-*chen*-tah)
11	**once** (*ohn*-say)		90	**noventa** (noh-*ben*-tah)
12	**doce** (*doh*-say)		100	**cien** (see-*en*)
13	**trece** (*tray*-say)		200	**doscientos** (*dos*-se-en-tos)
14	**catorce** (kah-*tor*-say)		500	**quinientos** (keen-ee-*ehn*-tos)
15	**quince** (*keen*-say)		1,000	**mil** (meal)
16	**dieciseis** (de-*ess*-ee-sayss)			

TRANSPORTATION TERMS

English	Spanish	Pronunciation
Airport	**Aeropuerto**	Ah-ay-row-*por*-tow
Flight	**Vuelo**	Boo-*ay*-low
Rental car	**Alquila de Autos**	Al-key-lah day autos
Bus	**Autobús**	ow-toh-*boos*
Bus or truck	**Camión**	ka-mee-*ohn*
Lane	**Carril**	kah-*rreal*
Nonstop	**Directo**	dee-*reck*-toh
Luggage storage area	**Guarda equipaje**	gwar-daheh-key-*pah*-hay
Arrival gates	**Llegadas**	yay-*gah*-dahs
Originates at this station	**Local**	loh-*kahl*
Originates elsewhere; stops if seats available	**De Paso** **Para si hay lugares**	day *pah*-soh pah-rah *see* aye loo-gahr-*ays*
First class	**Primera**	pree-*mehr*-oh
Second class	**Segunda**	say-*goon*-dah

English	Spanish	Pronunciation
Nonstop	**Directo**	dee-*rek*-to
Baggage claim area	**Recibo de Equipajes**	ray-*see*-boh-day eh-key-*pah*-hays
Waiting room	**Sala de Espera**	*Saw*-lah day ess-*pehr*-ah
Toilets	**Aseos**	Ah-say-oos
Ticket window	**Taquilla**	tah-*key*-lah

Index

Abades, 281
Abat Cisneros, 458
ABC Serrano, 143
Abello Museum, 452
Abercrombie & Kent
  International, 35
AC Hoteles Ciudad de
  Toledo, 164
Accommodations, 1
  air travel packaged
    with, 49
  best bargains, 16
  best luxury, 14–15
  types of, 54–56
  using the Internet
    to book, 64
Achuri, 294, 549
Acuario, 383
Acueducto de los
  Milagros, 234
Acueducto Romano, 178
Agua, 423
Agut, 412
Agut d'Avignon, 409
Aiguadoiç, 464
Aigües Blanques, 646
Air Europa, 388
Air travel, 1
  basic information
    regarding, 42–43,
    50
  EuroPass for, 42
  getting the best
    airfare, 44–45
  in Alicante, 375
  in Barcelona, 387
  in Bilbao, 540
  in Granada, 302
  in Ibiza, 631
  in Jerez, 285
  in La Coruña, 573
  in Málaga, 347
  in Minorca, 651
  in Pamplona, 504

in San Sebastián, 523
in Santander, 554
in Santiago, 579
in Seville, 262
in the Balearic Islands,
  601
in Valencia, 360
in Valladolid, 213
in Vitoria, 547
packaged with
  accommodations, 49
using the Internet to
  book, 45, 61, 63–66
Aitxiar, 545
Akelare, 18, 528
Al Pie de la Vela, 317
Al-Andalus Palace, 271
Alameda, 586
Alba de Tormes, 205
Albaycín, 306
Alborada, 212
Alcaicería, 307
Alcalá de Henares,
  181–182
Alcazaba, 235, 348
Alcázar, 6, 160, 265
Alcázar de la Puerta de
  Córdoba, 284
Alcázar de la Puerta de
  Sevilla, 284
Alcázar de los Reyes
  Cristianos, 252
Alcázar of Toledo, 164
Alcora, 365
Alcúdia Bay, 626
Aldeberán, 239
Alfares de Buño, 575
Algeciras, 30, 319–321
Alhabaca, 312
Alhambra, 6, 302, 304,
  510
Alicante, 23, 375–379,
  381
Alkalde, 111

All Saints' Day, 34
Almirante, 577
Alonso Martínez, 117
Aloña/Berri, 532
Alt Heidelberg, 424
Altamira Caves, 559
Altxeri Galeria, 533
Amboa, 582
American Bar, 658
American Express, 29
American Institute for
  Foreign Study (AIFS),
  36
Amfiteatre Romà, 459
Anaco, 90
Andalucía Plaza, 330
Andalusia, 22, 29, 70,
  223, 242–243,
  245–317, 677
Andalusian School of
  Equestrian Art, 287
Andorra, 456–457
Andratx, 619
Anfiteatro Romano, 235
Anoeta Hotel, 527
Antanyo, 244
Antigua Bodega
  Castanede, 313
Antigua Casa Talavera,
  141
Antiguedades Encantes,
  576
Antiguedades Javor, 219
Antiguedades La Flora,
  219
Antiguedades Rosa
  Jordan, 576
Antiques, 140, 440–441,
  576
Antonio Barbadillo, 10
Arabella Sheraton Golf
  Hotel, 608
Aragón, 24, 491–501
Aranjuez, 170–172

Arcab, 270
Arce, 107
Arch of the Star, 231
Architecture, 247, 385, 674–676, 678
Archivo General de Indias, 266
ARCO, 30
Arco Trajano, 234
Arcos de la Frontera, 3, 290–292
Arenal Hotel, 642
Argüelles, 101, 145
Aristos, 100
Armistad Córdoba, 255
Army Museum, 132
Arquélles, 79
Arroseria Catranca, 616
Arte Zoco, 255
Artesania Textil, 270
Artesanía Albaycín, 308
Artesanía Andaluza, 254
Artesanía Hernandez, 201
Arturo Soria District, 122
Arzak, 529
Asador Adolfo, 168
Asador Iruna, 322
Asador La Chata, 518
Asador Zaldua, 538
Asociación de Artistas, 575
Aste Nagusia, 524
Asturias, 25, 550, 552
Asturias Day, 566
Atalaya Park Golf Hotel & Resort, 323
ATMs (Automatic teller machines), 28
Atocha Station, 93–94
Atrio, 233
Auditorio del Parque de Atracciones, 146
Auditorio Nacional de Música, 147
Autocars Julià, 456
Automobiles, 1
Autumn Festival, 12, 34
Avenida, 508, 543
Avenida Palace, 405
Avenue of the Sad Ones, 304
Ávila, 185–191
Ayuntamiento Viejo, 227

Backroads, 34
Badajoz, 237–239
Baeza, 3, 242, 246–247
Bahía, 484
Balcón de la Virgen, 334
Balearic Islands, The, 5, 25, 73, 360, 599–667
Ballet Flamenco Antonio Canales, 146
Ballet Lírico Nacional, 146
Ballet Nacional de España, 146
Balmoral, 150
Balneario, 150
Banys Arabs, 474, 607
Bañalbufar, 619
Baños Arabes, 307
Bar Asador Ganbara, 532
Bar Canovas, 370
Bar Circulo Taurino, 261
Bar Cock, 151
Bar del Pi, 424
Bar El Juramento, 261
Bar Ginasio, 181
Bar Juli, 532
Bar La Abadia, 170
Bar La Bombilla, 579
Bar La Mancha, 316
Bar Ludeña, 170
Bar Pilar del Toro, 316
Bar Potato, 379
Bar Restaurant España, 658
Bar Taurino, 151
Bar Triton, 661
Bar Turò, 424
Bar Universale, 213
Bar Yeboles, 579
Bar Zaena, 370
Barbacana, 240
Barcas, 370
Barcelona, 23, 29, 217, 384–385, 387, 673, 678
  accommodations, 397–409
  city layout, 389–392
  nightlife, 444
  restaurants, 409–425
  shopping, 439–444
  sightseeing, 425–439
  transportation services, 387–395
  visitor information, 389
  Web sites, 72
Barquet, 461
Barri de la Ribera, 391
Barri Gòtic, 391, 397, 409, 430
Barri Xinés, 391
Barrio Carmen, 370
Barrio de Santa Cruz, 267, 376
Bars, 1
  in Alicante, 379
  in Barcelona, 448–449
  in Bilbao, 546
  in Girona, 478
  in Granada, 315, 317
  in Ibiza, 639–640
  in La Coruña, 579
  in Madrid, 150–152, 154
  in Palma, 618–619
  in Pamplona, 511
  in Pontevedra, 594
  in San Lorenzo de El Escorial, 176
  in San Sebastián, 532–533
  in Santiago, 587
  in Toledo, 170
  in Valencia, 370–371
  in Valladolid, 217
  in Zamora, 208
  in Zaragoza, 497–498
Basilica de Nuestra Señora del Pilar, 492
Basilica de San Vicente, 186
Basílica de Begoña, 542
Basílica de Santa María la Mayor, 592
Basque country, 521–549
Battle of Flowers, 552
Battle of the Tomatoes, 33
Bay of Biscay, 19

Bazar Sant'Olaria, 228
Beaches, 4
Beethoven I, II, y III, 520
Begoña, 567
Beltxenea, 416
Benidorm, 23, 372–375
Benidorm Palace, 374
Bermeo, 544
Bécquer, 272
Biblioteca Menéndez y Pelayo, 555
Biking
    in Madrid, 82
    in the Balearic Islands, 605
Bilbao, 521, 538, 540–545
Biniali, 656
Biocenter, 414
Black and White, 152
Bloody Tower, 239
Boating, 365
Bocairente Festival of Christians and Moors, 31
Bodega Campos, 261
Bodega Cigaleña, 557
Bodega la Plata, 424
Bodega Morgadio, 11
Bodega Regia, 212
Bodegas, 286–287
Bodegas Muga, 11
Bodegas Riojanas, 11
Bodegas Señorío de Nava, 9
Bodegón Alejandro, 530
Bodegueta, 424
Boston Hotel, 494
Botafumeiro, 18, 420
Brasserie Flo, 412
Briz, 237
Bronsoms, 477
Brujas de Bécquer, 499
Buenavista, 323
Bullfighting Museum, 134
Bullfights, 1, 131, 268, 436, 507, 676–677
Burela, 588
Burgos, 22, 195
    accommodations, 219–221
    restaurants, 221

shopping, 219
sightseeing, 218–219
transportation services, 217–218
visitor information, 218
Byblos Andaluz, 338

Ca La María, 419
Ca N'Olga, 664
Ca'an Carlos, 616
Ca'n Costa, 623
Ca'n Pastilla, 604
Ca'n Quet, 623
Caballito del Mar, 616
Cabaret, 148, 446
Cabildo Catedral de Segovia, 177
Cabo de Formentor, 625–626
Cabo Fisterra, 589
Cabo Higuer, 536
Cacharro Tienda, 224
Cadaqués, 4, 472, 489–490
Cafetería Arimany, 462
Café Balear, 117
Café Central, 148
Café de Chinitas, 149
Café de L'Academia, 414
Café de la Seu, 371
Café de Paris, 352
Café del Foro, 149
Café Figueroa, 153
Café Jazz Populart, 149
Cal Ros, 478
Cala de Pi de la Posada, 626
Cala Mayor, 604
Calatayud, 24, 499–500
calle Cien Fuegos, 379
calle Colon, 365
calle de Elvira, 304
calle de Vincente Meliner, 217
calle del Paraíso, 217
calle Don Juan de Austria, 365
calle Laboradores, 379
calle Los Herreros, 208
Calvary, 625
Camariñas, 589
Camarote, 553
Cambrils, 463

Camelot, 205
Camino de Santiago, 573
Camino Tours, 35
Camping Circo Romano, 163
Campo del Principe, 315
Campo Santo, 620
Campos, 596
Campos de Córdoba, 259
Can Costa, 422
Can Culleretes, 413
Can Isidre, 417
Can Juan de S'aigo, 615
Can Majó, 422
Cana Juana, 643
Cangas de Onís, 562–564
Cantabria, 25, 550, 552
Cap de Cavalleria, 666
Capas Seseña, 141
Cape Fisterra, 589
Cape Formentor, 620
Cape Salou, 454
Cape of Santa Pola, 375
Capilla de la Peregrina, 592
Capilla de San Ildefonso, 182
Capture of the Beasts, 12, 32, 591
Car rentals
    in Barcelona, 393
    basic information regarding, 52–54
    using the Internet to book, 52
Carballo, 589
Cardona, 452
Caripén, 109
Carmelitas Descalzas de San José, 186
Carmen de San Miguel, 312
Carmona, 3, 284
Carnaval, 464
Carnavales de Cádiz, 31
Carrera del Darro, 304
Carretera de Cádiz, 320
Carretera de Circunvalación, 160
Carthusian Church, 620
Cartoixa Reial, 621

Cartuja, 620
Cas Quintu, 662
Casa Alberto, 110
Casa Alcalde, 532
Casa Alfonso, 425
Casa Amatller, 435
Casa Batlló, 435
Casa Benigna, 123
Casa Bermejo, 163
Casa Bonet, 142
Casa Calvet, 417
Casa Conrado, 571
Casa de Campo, 135
Casa de Carmona, 284
Casa de Castril, 307
Casa de Catalunya, 146
Casa de Cervantes, 215
Casa de Diego, 142
Casa de Goya, 498
Casa de Juntas, 538
Casa de la Canónica, 582
Casa de la Ciutat/ Ayuntamiento, 436
Casa de las Cadenas, 228
Casa de las Cigueñas, 231
Casa de las Conchas, 199
Casa de las Veletas, 231
Casa de Lladró, 366
Casa de Lope de Vega, 136
Casa de los Doctores de la Reina, 200
Casa de Murillo, 267
Casa de Pilatos, 266
Casa de Príncipe, 174
Casa del Aljarife, 311
Casa del Rey Moro, 298
Casa Eduardo, 615
Casa Emilio, 519
Casa Fermín, 571
Casa Ferrer, 308
Casa Henrique, 316
Casa Imperial, 271
Casa José, 172
Casa Juan, 345
Casa Justo, 567
Casa Leopoldo, 409
Casa Lleó Morera, 436
Casa Lucio, 120
Casa Luque, 357

Casa Manolo, 586, 662
Casa Miguel, 261
Casa Milà, 435
Casa Mingo, 125
Casa Museo de Rosalía de Castro, 590
Casa Museo Unamuno, 200
Casa Nicolasa, 529
Casa Ojeda, 221
Casa Otano, 510
Casa Pablo, 172
Casa Paco, 109, 315
Casa Pardo, 578
Casa Patas, 149
Casa Pepe, 261
Casa Pozo, 212
Casa Robles, 278
Casa Román, 280, 593
Casa Rubio, 261
Casa Salinas, 261
Casa Santa Pola, 300
Casa Tejada, 425
Casa Telesforo, 164
Casa Tino, 567
Casa Vallejo, 117
Casa Valles, 532
Casa Vicente, 246
Casa Vieja, 338
Casa Vino del Agua, 316
Casa y Museo de El Greco, 160
Casa Yum-Yum, 379
Casa-Museo de Manuel de Falla, 307
Casa-Museo Federico García Lorca, 306
Casa-Museu Gaudí, 430
Casco Antiguo, 379
Casco Viejo, 542
Casino de San Sebastián, 533
Casino Gran Madrid, 155
Casino Royal Palm, 375
Casinos, 155, 375, 451, 557
Casita del Labrador, 171
Casita del Príncipe, 184
Casón del Tormes, 89
Castell de Bellver, 607
Castell de Santa Bárbara, 376

Castellana, 79
Castellana Inter- Continental Hotel, 97
Castile, 22
Castillo, 228
Castillo de Carlos V, 535
Castillo de Gibralfaro, 348
Castillo de Javier, 516
Castle of Tarifa, 322
Catalonia, 23, 72, 384–386, 454–455, 45–461, 463, 465–471
Catedral (Compostela), 580
Catedral (Girona), 474
Catedral (Palma), 607
Catedral (Pamplona), 506
Catedral (Santander), 554
Catedral (Seu), 362
Catedral (Tarragona), 459
Catedral (Túy), 598
Catedral and Capilla Real, 306
Catedral de Ávila, 7, 187
Catedral de Barcelona, 8, 426
Catedral de Cádiz, 293
Catedral de Cuenca Plaza, 192
Catedral de León, 8, 209
Catedral de Santa Ana, 514
Catedral de Santa María, 8, 218, 231, 244, 547
Catedral de Santa María de la Redonda, 517
Catedral de Santiago, 542
Catedral de Santiago de Compostela, 9
Catedral de Sevilla, 8, 265
Catedral de Toledo, 8
Catedral Nueva, 200
Catedral Vieja, 200
Cathedral (Lugo), 594
Cathedral (Valladolid), 214

Cathedral de Toledo, 161
Cathedral San Salvador, 206
Cave of the Stalactites, 560
Caves of Altamira, 25
Caves of the Dragon, 629
Cáceres, 22, 223, 230–233
Cáceres Viejo, 230
Cádiz, 22, 292–295
Cámara Santa, 568
Ceboleiro II, 590
Cellar Ca'n Amer, 625
Cellar Pagés, 617
Center del Carmen, 364
Center of Contemporary Culture of Barcelona (CCCB), 431
Central Holidays, 35
Centro Comercial Ruta de la Plata, 231
Centro Comercial Valle Real, 555
Centro Cultural Palacio de Villardompardo, 244
Centro de Anticuarios Lagasca, 140
Centro de Investigación y Museo de Altamira, 560
Centro Gallego de Arte Contemporáneo, 582
Ceramics, 141, 163, 176, 219, 376, 575, 582
Cervecería Alemania, 125
Cervecería Santa Bárbara, 125
Cénit, 638
Chamartín, 99–100, 118–119
Chamberí, 97–98, 114–116
Charolés, 175
Chef Rivera, 591
Chez Jeanette, 469
Chez Victor, 17, 204
Chicote, 136, 151
Chigre Asturianu, 567
Chikito, 314

Chinchón, 184–185
Chinchón Castle, 184
Chueca, 79, 120, 145
Church of San Miguel, 548
Church of Santa María, 513
Church of Santiago, 231
Ciao Madrid, 117
Cimadevilla, 565
Circus Maximus, 234
Ciro's, 260
City of the Arts and Sciences, 364
Ciudad de La Coruña, 577
Ciudad de las Artes y de las Ciencias, 364
Ciudad Encantada, 191
Ciudad Rodrigo, 22, 195–198
Ciudad Universitaria, 124
Ciudadela, 659–662
Ciutat Vella, 397–403
Civera, 368
Clamores, 149
Claris, 403
Clarín, 570
Classical music, 146, 282, 445
Club El Padrastro, 340
Club La Mola, 649
Club Los Gallos, 281
Club Náutico, 544
Club Punta Prima, 649
Codina, 528
Codorníu, 451
Colegiata de Santillana, 558
Colegio Mayor de San Ildefonso, 182
Collingwood House, 656
Columbus Monument, 391
Compañía Nacional de Nuevas Tendencias Escénicas, 146
Compañía Nacional de Teatro Clásico, 146
Condal, 476
Conde Duque, 98
Conde Rodrigo I, 196

Confitería La Mora, 582
Confitería Vilas, 583
Conjunto Arqueológico Madinat Al-Zahra, 254
Conquistadors, 226
Consulates, 57
Convent of the Poor Clares, 558
Convento de las Carmelitas, 206
Convento de las Dueñas, 200
Convento de San Esteban, 201
Convento de Santa Teresa, 188
Coral Beach, 328
Corcubión, 589
Cordoníu, 10
Corme, 589
Cornucopia, 109
Corpus Christi, 32
Corral de la Morería, 150
Corte Fiel, 201
Corte Inglés, 210
Cosgaya, 564
Costa Azul, 610
Costa Blanca, 5, 23, 71, 359
Costa Brava, 5, 24, 29, 454, 472–473
Costa da Morte, 589
Costa de Garraf, 454
Costa de la Luz, 4, 295–297
Costa del Sol, 5, 23, 29, 71, 242, 318–358
Costa Dorada, 454, 463
Costa Sur, 664
Costa Vasca, 526
Costa Verde, 5, 550
Costabella, 476
Council on International Educational Exchange (CIEE), 37
Cova de Can Merca, 644
Covadonga, 563, 565
Córdoba, 22, 29, 250–262
Córdoba Gate, 284
Credit cards, 29
Crowne Plaza Madrid City Centre, 88, 96

Cruising (bar), 153
Cuenca, 3, 22, 191–194
Cueva de la Pileta, 298
Cueva de Nerja (Cave
of Nerja), 355–358
Cueva de Ses
Fontanelles, 641
Cuevas de Altamira, 559
Cuevas de Artá, 629
Cuevas del Drach, 629
Cuevas del Ham, 629
Currency, 68
    basic information
        regarding, 27–28
    conversions, 27–28
Customs, 26–27
Cuzco, 99
Cyclists' Touring Club,
35

Dalí Museum, 485, 487
Dalli's Pizza Factory,
325
Daroca, 24
Deià, 4, 620–623
Delfín, 378
Diada, 33
Dining, 1
Diplomatic, 614
Disabled travelers, 39
Disco Antigüedades,
282
Disco Caballito de Mar,
370
Disco Cahira, 262
Disco Morgana, 205
Disco Plato, 262
Divine Gorge, 563
Día de los Reyes, 30
Día de los Santos
Inocentes, 34
Día de San Antonio, 30
Domecq, 286
Domingo Pablos
Barquillo, 228
Don Carlos, 330
Don Felipe II, 176
Don Leone, 326
Don Miguel Restaurant,
301
Don Pancho, 373
Don Pé, 339
Don Quijote, 490
Don Yo, 496
Donna Donna, 371

Doña Antonia, 593
Doña Margarita, 647
Dosel, 582
Dulcinea, 419
Duques de Bergara, 401
Durán, 488

Easy Rider Tours, 34
Egaña Oriza, 276
Egipte, 413
Eixample, 392, 397, 409
El Alcázar, 6, 177
El Amparo, 17, 112
El Ancla del Laredo, 552
El Arco de la Estrella,
231
El Arco de los
Cuchilleros Artesanía
de Hoy, 141
El Arenal, 604
El Bernardino, 179
El Blasón, 260
El Bodegas Castañera,
316
El Bosque, 289
El Burladero, 277
El Buxu Cueva, 563
El Caballito Blanco, 419
El Caballo Rojo, 17, 260
El Cabo Mayor, 119
El Cardenal, 261
El Castillo de Monda,
333
El Catavinos, 169
El Cellar de Can Roca,
478
El Cenachero, 351
El Cenador del Prado,
110
El Chinitas, 352
El Churrasco, 260
El Colono, 357
El Coloso, 289
El Conquistador Hotel,
256
El Convento Hotel, 291
El Convento Restaurant,
292
El Coral, 578
El Corsario, 636, 639
El Corte Inglés, 141,
255, 269, 365, 376,
576
El Cosaco, 121
El Duc, 414

El Escorial, 22
El Espejo, 102
El Faro, 294
El Ferrol, 588
El Figón de Pedro, 193
El Figón de Eustaquio,
233
El Fuerte, 326
El Galeón, 468
El Gato Viudo, 344
El Gourmet, 369
El Grove, 596
El Jardineto, 379
El Magistral, 570
El Mentidero de la
Villa, 107
El Mesón, 379
El Naranjo, 647
El Olivo, 624
El Olivo Restaurant,
118
El Palacio de Miramar,
525
El Palma, 372
El Pardo, 183–184
El Paso, 339
El Patio Sevillano, 281
El Pescador, 112
El Plat, 17, 369
El Portalón, 333, 549,
639
El Postigo, 269
El Pote Gallego, 379
El Prat de Llobregat,
388
El Raitán, 571
El Rastro, 142, 189–190
El Refugio, 335
El Rinconcillo, 280
El Rincón de Pepe, 643
El Rodeo, 332
El Salí, 247
El Sardinero, 25
El Schotis, 121
El Simpecao, 282
El Tablao de Carmen,
446
El Timonel, 368
El Trull, 481
El Túnel, 423
El Valle de los Caídos,
173–174
El Velero, 469
El Ventorillo del Chato,
295

Eladio, 368
Elche, 4, 23, 379–380
Els Balomins, 464
Els Quatre Gats, 413, 470
Embassies, 57
Emilio Hidalgo, 10
Emperatriz, 95
Empordá, 18, 487–488
Empresa La Sepulvedana, 224
Enara, 215
Enchanted City, 191
English Bookshop, 269
Enrique Becerra, 278
Episcopal Palace, 595
Erburu, 511
Errota-Zar, 103
Es Caliu Grill, 662
Es Mercadal, 663
Es Molí, 484
Es Molí del Sal, 650
Es Parlament, 616
Es Pla, 666
Es Trull, 490
Escolanía, 457
Escuela Andaluza del Arte Ecuestre, 287
Església de Sant Feliu, 475
Església de Santa María la Major, 654
Estació de França, 388
Estación de Comes terminal, 292
Estallenchs, 619
Esteban Vicente Contemporary Art Museum, 177
Estepona, 318, 322–324
Estilo, 572
Estoril, 196
Eurobuilding, 99
Europa, 509
Explanada d'Espanya, 376
Extremadura, 22, 223–241

Fallas de Valencia, 31
Federación Española de Pesca, 162
Felipe IV, 215
Felipe Suarez, 163
Feria de Málaga, 33

Feria de Sevilla, 31
Feria del Caballo, 12, 32
Fernando Mayer, 582
Ferreiros, 596
Ferries, 360
Festival de los Patios, 31
Festival of St. James, 32
Fiesta de San Fermín, 33, 502, 507
Fiesta de San Isidro, 32
Fiestas de la Merced, 33
Figueres, 24, 485–488
Fine Arts Museum, 132
Fishing, 162, 463
Flamenco, 2, 134, 145, 149–150, 281, 317, 337, 446
Flea markets, 142, 644
Florencia, 277
Florida, 338
Formela, 212
Formentera, 647–650
Formentor, 625–627
Formentor Peninsula, 626
Fornalutx, 620
Fornells, 665–666
Foster's Hollywood, 116
Fragata, 470
Fragata Beach, 464
Fran Holuba, 376
Freixenet, 10
Frutos, 346
Fuendetodos, 498
Fuengirola, 337–339
Fuente-Dé, 562
Fuenterrabía, 24, 535–537
Fundació Antoni Tàpies, 432
Fundació Joan Miró, 430
Fundación Juan March, 144, 147
Fundación Marcellino Botín, 555
Funte-Dé, 565

Gaig, 420
Gaitán, 289
Galeria de Arte del Lubre, 140
Galería del Prado, 144
Galería Kreisler, 140
Galería Olímpica, 436

Galicia, 11, 25, 73
Gardens
  in Barcelona, 436–437
  in Córdoba, 252
  in Madrid, 135
Garduña, 414
Gay and lesbian travelers, 282, 450
  in Granada, 317
  in Madrid, 152–153
  tips for, 40
Generalife, 306
Gibraltar, 319
Gijón, 565–568
Giralda Tower, 265
Girona, 472–478
glesia de San Andrés, 304
Goizeko Kabi, 119
Golden Curry, 345
Golf, 365, 439, 605
Golf Hotel Guadalmina, 318, 324
Golf International, 35
González Byass, 10, 286
Goya's Tomb, 130
Gran Café de Gijón, 114
Gran Casino del Sardinero, 557
Gran Hotel, 201, 495
Gran Hotel Colón, 95
Gran Hotel Delfín, 373
Gran Hotel Ercilla, 543
Gran Hotel Havana, 405
Gran Hotel Lugo, 595
Gran Hotel Monterrey, 479
Gran Hotel Palacio de Valderrábanos, 188
Gran Hotel Reina Victoria, 90
Gran Hotel Son Net, 613
Gran Hotel Velázquez, 96
Gran Hotel Zurbarán, 238
Gran Meliá Don Pepe, 328
Gran Teatre del Liceu, 391, 445
Gran Vía, 78, 89, 107
Grana Vision, 317

Granada, 10, 23, 302, 304–317

Grand Hotel Reymar, 483

Granda Reconquest Festival, 30

Granja Colom, 662

Granvía, 401

Grape Harvest Festival, 34

Gràcia, 397

Green Hotel El Prado, 90

Gregal, 657

Guadalete, 287

Guadalupe, 22, 223–226

Guernica, 24, 537

Guggenheim Museum, 541

Guría, 544

Gurrea, 496

Gurriato, 176

Guzmán El Bueno, 210

Hacienda Benazuza, 276

Haro, 24, 502, 519–520

Hartza, 510

Harveys of Bristol, 286

Hernán Cortés, 566

Herrero, 142

Hesperia, 495

Hérederos de Marqués de Riscal, 11

Hijos de Agustín Blazquez, 10

Hispano Bar/Buffet, 151

Holy Chamber, 569

Holy Grotto, 458

Holy Week, 31

Horcher, 112

Horse Fair, 32

Horseback riding, 287, 606

Hospedería, 516

Hospedería Real Monasterio, 224

Hospital de la Santa Caridad, 266

Hospital de Santiago, 249

Hospital de Tavera, 161

Hostal Bahía, 528

Hostal Castilla, 171

Hostal Cervantes, 88

Hostal Chiqui, 207

Hostal Cristina, 175

Hostal de la Gavina, 477

Hostal de Los Reyes Católicos, 14, 580, 583–584

Hostal del Cardenal, 16, 165, 168

Hostal El Castillo, 332

Hostal Goya, 275

Hostal la Macarena, 91

Hostal la Perla Asturiana, 92

Hostal Laguna, 203

Hostal Los Jazmines, 343

Hostal Mena, 357

Hostal Miguel, 357

Hostal Montesol, 637

Hostal Munich, 332

Hostal Nuevo Gaos, 90

Hostal Plaza Mayor, 204

Hostal Residencia Alameda, 585

Hostal Residencia Americano, 92

Hostal Residencia Bisbal, 368

Hostal Residencia Carlos V, 351

Hostal Residencia Ciutadella, 661

Hostal Residencia Derby, 351

Hostal Residencia Don Diego, 99

Hostal Reynes, 655

Hostal S'Aguarda, 490

Hostal S'Algaret, 666

Hosteria de Bracamonte, 190

Hostería del Estudiante, 182

Hostería del Laurel, 279

Hostería del Mar, 334

Hostería Real de Zamora, 16, 207

Hotel Al-Mar, 320

Hotel Alarde, 320

Hotel Alfonso V, 210

Hotel Alfonso XIII, 15, 270

Hotel Alhambra Palace, 308

Hotel Almirante Bonifaz, 219

Hotel Almirante Farragut, 660

Hotel Altamira, 559

Hotel Amandi, 597

Hotel América, 16, 309

Hotel Anacapri, 309

Hotel Araguaney, 583

Hotel Area Central, 585

Hotel Artola Golf, 331

Hotel Arts, 408

Hotel Astari, 461

Hotel Astoria, 407

Hotel Astoria Palace, 366

Hotel Atalaya Park, 318

Hotel Atlántico, 577

Hotel Aultre Naray, 564

Hotel Avenida, 577

Hotel Avenida Jerez, 287

Hotel Averroes, 258

Hotel Ávila, 289

Hotel Balcón de Europa, 356

Hotel Balmes, 407

Hotel Bon Sol, 611

Hotel Botánico, 174

Hotel Brisa, 373

Hotel Calatayud, 500

Hotel Calípolis, 466

Hotel Canfali, 374

Hotel Cap d'Or, 483

Hotel Capri, 655

Hotel Carelmany, 476

Hotel Central, 555

Hotel Cervantes, 342

Hotel Chamartín, 100

Hotel Cimbel, 374

Hotel Ciudad de Santander, 555

Hotel Claridge, 96

Hotel Colón, 400, 404

Hotel Comercio, 592

Hotel Compostela, 584

Hotel Conde de Floridablanca, 382

Hotel Condes de Barcelona, 406

Hotel Condesable Iranzo, 245

Hotel Consul del Mar, 367

Hotel Continental, 402

Hotel Cortés, 402

Hotel Costa d'Or, 623
Hotel Dato, 549
Hotel de la Reconquista, 569
Hotel de Londres y de Inglaterra, 527
Hotel del Almirante, 656
Hotel del Cid, 219
Hotel del Oso, 564
Hotel del Peregrino, 584
Hotel Derby/Hotel Gran Derby, 407
Hotel Diana, 483
Hotel Doménico, 165
Hotel Don Curro, 350
Hotel Don Juan, 204
Hotel Don Miguel, 299
Hotel Doña María, 16, 273
Hotel El Cid, 469
Hotel El Fuerte, 331
Hotel El Mesón, 516
Hotel el Pintor El Greco, 166
Hotel El Pozo, 343
Hotel Emperatriz, 236
Hotel Es Molí, 622
Hotel Escultor, 98
Hotel Esmeralda, 661
Hotel España, 220, 402, 578
Hotel Excelsior, 481
Hotel Extremadura, 232
Hotel Fernán González, 220
Hotel Finisterre, 576
Hotel Formentor, 627
Hotel Francisco I, 92
Hotel Galeón, 645
Hotel Gaudí, 89
Hotel Gelmírez, 585
Hotel General Álava, 548
Hotel Gran Via, 496
Hotel Guadalupe, 311
Hotel Hacienda, 645
Hotel Hespería, 404, 408
Hotel Hispano 1, 382
Hotel Husa Princesa, 101
Hotel Illa d'Or, 626
Hotel Imperial Tarraco, 460

Hotel Imperio, 167
Hotel Infanta Isabel, 178
Hotel Inglaterra, 309
Hotel Inglés, 92, 367
Hotel Isabel, 342
Hotel Jorge Primeiro, 595
Hotel la Española, 300
Hotel La Fuente, 571
Hotel La Gruta, 570
Hotel la Paz, 249
Hotel La Rabida, 275
Hotel Larios, 349
Hotel Las Adelfas, 256
Hotel Las Palomas, 342
Hotel las Torres, 203
Hotel Lasa, 203
Hotel Lauria, 461
Hotel Leyre, 509
Hotel Lisboa, 238
Hotel Los Cóndores Sol, 661
Hotel Los Linajes, 179
Hotel Los Naranjos, 351
Hotel los Olivos, 291
Hotel Los Seises, 273
Hotel Louxo, 597
Hotel López de Haro, 543
Hotel Macia Alfaros, 256
Hotel Maimónides, 256
Hotel Majestic, 406
Hotel Marbella-Dinamar, 325
Hotel María Cristina, 15, 166, 526
Hotel Marisa, 258
Hotel Marquéz de Vallejo, 518
Hotel Marsol, 481
Hotel Martin, 167
Hotel Maycar, 585
Hotel Mayoral, 167
Hotel Meliá 7 Coronas, 382
Hotel Meliá Alicante, 377
Hotel Meliá Barcelona Sarrià, 406
Hotel Meliá de Mar, 611
Hotel Meliá Parque, 215
Hotel Mercátor, 93
Hotel Mezquita, 258

Hotel México, 556
Hotel Mijas, 16, 340
Hotel Miramar, 627
Hotel Monte Triana, 273
Hotel Monterrey, 202
Hotel Mónica, 355
Hotel Murrieta, 518
Hotel Neptuno, 484
Hotel NH Calderón, 400
Hotel NH Ciudad de Cuenca, 192
Hotel Norte y Londres, 220
Hotel Nuevo Chichon, 184
Hotel Occidental Porta Coeli, 271
Hotel Octavio, 320
Hotel Olid Meliá, 216
Hotel Opera, 91
Hotel Orense, 98
Hotel Palacio Santa Inés, 310
Hotel Palafox, 494
Hotel Pampinot, 17, 536
Hotel Paris, 92, 211
Hotel Parma, 528
Hotel Patricia, 660
Hotel Pelayo, 565
Hotel Peninsular, 477
Hotel Pirineos, 487
Hotel Platjador, 468
Hotel Playa Sol, 489
Hotel Plaza de Armas, 273
Hotel Pollentia, 627
Hotel Port Lligat, 489
Hotel Port Mahón, 656
Hotel President, 488
Hotel Princesa Ana, 310
Hotel Princesa Sofía, 404
Hotel Principado, 570
Hotel Puerta de Toledo, 96
Hotel Punta Negra, 614
Hotel Quindós, 211
Hotel Real, 556
Hotel Real de Toledo, 167
Hotel Rector, 202
Hotel Regencia Colón, 401

Index

Hotel Regina, 274
Hotel Reina Cristina, 310, 321
Hotel Reina Isabel, 188
Hotel Reina Victoria, 16, 299, 366
Hotel Reino de Granada, 311
Hotel Residencia Alfonso VI, 166
Hotel Residencia El Califa, 257
Hotel Residencia Gasteiz, 548
Hotel Residencia Lisboa, 93
Hotel Residencia Polo, 300
Hotel Residencia San Remo, 378
Hotel Residencía Cortezo, 93
Hotel Residencía Leuka, 377
Hotel Rhin, 556
Hotel Rice, 220
Hotel Rincón Andaluz, 332
Hotel Ritz, 15, 404
Hotel Rías Bajas, 593
Hotel Roger de Flor, 480
Hotel Roma, 216
Hotel Romàntic de Sitges, 468
Hotel Ronda, 488
Hotel Rosamar, 611
Hotel Royal Plaza, 637
Hotel Royal Sherry Park, 288
Hotel S'Argamassa Sol, 646
Hotel San Agustín, 402
Hotel San Gabriel, 300
Hotel San Polo, 203
Hotel Sancho Ramírez, 508
Hotel Santa Isabel, 167
Hotel Santa Marta, 480
Hotel Santo Domingo, 89
Hotel Santo Tomás, 664
Hotel Saratoga, 610
Hotel Serit, 289
Hotel Ses Estaques, 646

Hotel Siglo XVIII, 559
Hotel Simon, 274
Hotel Sol Inn Jaime III, 611
Hotel Subur, 469
Hotel Tonet, 484
Hotel Torrequebrada, 344
Hotel Travé, 488
Hotel Tres Reyes, 508
Hotel Tres Torres, 646
Hotel Triunfo Granada, 310
Hotel Tropical, 642
Hotel Tropicana, 341
Hotel Tryp Gran Sol, 377
Hotel Tudela, 514
Hotel Ultonia, 476
Hotel Universal, 585
Hotel Urbis, 461
Hotel Vetusta, 570
Hotel Victoria, 228
Hotel Victoria Palace, 175
Hotel Vila del Mar, 480
Hotel Villa Hermosa/Restaurant Vista Hermosa, 612
Hotel Villa Real, 85
Hotel Villacarlos, 367
Hotel Village, 642
Hotel Virgen del Camino, 593
Hotel Vora la Mar, 484
Hotel Wilson, 408
Hotel-Residencia Almudaina, 610
Hotels Cala Bona & Mar Blava, 661
House of Shells, 199
House of the Storks, 231
Huerta Honda, 240
Huerto del Cura, 16, 380
Hyatt Regency La Manga, 382

Ibáñez Bernabeu, 376
Ibiza, 25, 599, 630, 652
  accommodations, 634–638, 642–643, 645–647
  beaches, 633
  nightlife, 639–640
  restaurants, 638–639, 643, 647
  shopping, 633, 636
  sightseeing, 632, 636, 641, 644, 646
  transportation services, 631–632
  visitor information, 632
Iconos, 269
Iglesia de la Asunción, 552
Iglesia de la Magdalena, 206, 244
Iglesia de la Vera Cruz, 177
Iglesia de San Bartolomé, 598
Iglesia de San Francisco, 592, 595
Iglesia de San Ildefonso, 206
Iglesia de San Martín, 227
Iglesia de San Martín de Mondoñeda, 588
Iglesia de San Mateo, 231
Iglesia de San Nicolás, 542
Iglesia de San Pablo, 214, 248
Iglesia de San Pedro, 291
Iglesia de San Tomás, 519
Iglesia de Santa Ana, 304
Iglesia de Santa María, 228, 291, 515, 536
Iglesia de Santa María de Los Reales Alcázares, 249
Iglesia de Santa María de Palacio, 517
Iglesia de Santa María del Campo, 574
Iglesia de Santa María la Mayor, 235
Iglesia de Santa María la Nueva, 206
Iglesia de Santa Teresa, 206
Iglesia de Santiago, 304, 515
Iglesia de Santiago el Burgo, 206

Iglesia de Santo
  Domingo, 598
Iglesia de Santo Tomé,
  161
Iglesia El Salvador, 248
Igrexa de San Francisco,
  590
Igrexa de Santa María,
  590
Inca, 624
Instituto Valencia de
  Arte Moderno (IVAM),
  364
Internacional El Altet
  Airport, 375
International Film
  Festival, 34
International Music and
  Dance Festival, 32
Irún, 535
Iruña Park Hotel, 508
Isabellino
  Ayuntamiento, 293
Isbiliyya Café-Bar, 282
Ispahan, 141
Itálica, 285
Iturrimurri, 520

Jaén, 242–246
Jàgaro, 657
Jaime, 624
Jaizkibel Road, 536
Jardines de Méndez
  Núñez, 574
Jardines Neptuno, 317
Jardins d'Alfàbia, 621
Jardín de la Isla, 171
Jardín de San Carlos,
  574
Jaume de Provença, 18,
  417
Jáuregui, 536
Javier Castle, 516
Jazz, 148, 446–447
Jazzaldia, 524
Jerez, 2, 9, 285,
  287–290
Jockey, 114
José María, 180
Josetxo, 510
Joy Eslava, 150
Juanito Kojua, 531
Julio González Center,
  364

Kabutzia, 533
Kapital, 150
Koldo Royo, 614

L'Aquarium de
  Barcelona, 431
L'Armeler, 372
L'Olive, 418
La Abadia, 168
La Albahaca, 278
La Albufera, 372
La Alcaria de Ramos,
  324
La Alicantina, 281
La Almudaina, 259
La Atalaya, 123
La Balsa, 423
La Barceloneta, 392
La Bobadilla, 15, 351
La Boîte, 295
La Bola, 116
La Bóveda, 617
La Buena Brasa, 418
La Carihuela, 345
La Casa de la Judería,
  274
La Casa de los Toledo-
  Montezuma, 231
La Casita, 617
La Casona de Jovellanos,
  567
La Cazuela, 339
La Cepa, 532
La Chata, 122
La Concha, 523
La Coruña, 25,
  573–578, 589
La Cova d'en Xoroi, 663
La Cueva Park, 288
La Cuineta, 413
La Dama, 417
La Dársena, 378–379
La Dehesa, 278
La Dentellière, 415
La Esquina del Real,
  110
La Esquinita, 315
La Fidula, 147
La Fontanilla, 326
La Fragua, 216
La Fuencisla, 115
La Galiota, 490
La Gamella, 112
La Gran Taverna, 316
La Granja, 180–181

La Guerra, 371
La Hacienda, 334
La Isla, 277
La Jarra, 425
La Langosta, 339
La Línea, 320
La Llauna, 423
La Lonja de la Seda, 362
La Lubina, 615
La Manchega, 353
La Manga Club, 35
La Mar, 497
La Maresme, 454
La Masía, 470
La Muralla, 555
La Nogalera, 344
La Numantina, 518
La Oka, 531
La Palmera, 564
La Paloma, 33, 115
La Parte Vieja, 523
La Perdiz, 169
La Perla, 509
La Pescera, 335
La Posada de la Villa,
  121
La Pousada del Mar,
  597
La Rambla, 391
La Rana Verde, 172
La Rapa das Bestas, 32
La Raza, 279
La Residencía, 15, 623
La Rinconada de
  Lorenzo, 497
La Rioja, 24, 73, 502,
  513
La Rioja Alta, 11
La Rosca, 415
La Sagrada Família, 426
La Santa Cueva, 563
La Sardina de Plata, 557
La Seo del Salvador, 492
La Taberna del
  Alabardero, 326
La Tacita d'Juan, 586
La Tapería, 379
La Tarasca, 169
La Toja, 596–597
La Tomatina, 12, 33
La Traida, 579
La Trainera, 113
La Tropical, 658
La Venencia, 151
La Ventana, 637

Lainz, 555
Lambda organization, 370
Landa Palace, 219
Laredo, 25, 552–553
Largada, 478
Las Arenas de Cabrales, 563
Las Batuecas, 124
Las Campanas (Casa Marcos), 425
Las Casas de los Mercaderes, 274
Las Casas del Rey de Baeza, 272
Las Cascadas, 645
Las Cigueñas, 229
Las Cuatro Estaciones, 115
Las Dunas, 323
Las Hogueras de San Juan, 12, 32
Las Pirámides, 338
Las Sirenas, 179
Las Tinajas, 312
Las Trevedes, 353
Lasarte, 143
Lavapiés, 33
Le Goulou, 371
Le Meridien Barcelona, 397
Le Méridien Los Monteros, 331
Leather Bar, 153
Lebrija, 287
Lekeitio, 534–535
Leonor de Aquitania, 192
León, 22, 70, 195, 209, 561
  accommodations, 210–211
  nightlife, 213
  restaurants, 212
  shopping, 210
  sightseeing, 209
  transportation services, 209
  visitor information, 209
Les Jardins de Palerm, 642
Les Rambles, 391
Leyre, 516
Lhardy, 108
Libreria Seferad, 255

Libreria Vértice, 269
Little Seahorse, 616
Lladró, 366
Lloret de Mar, 24, 472, 479–482
Llotja, 607
Lluch Alcari, 620
Localidades Galicia, 131, 146
Loewe, 143
Logroño, 502, 517–518
Lonja del Pescado, 615
Los Agustinos, 520
Los Alamos, 346
Los Amarillos, 297
Los Arcos, 179
Los Blasones, 559
Los Boliches, 337–339
Los Borrachos, 497
Los Caracoles, 18, 413
Los Gabrieles, 152
Los Gavilanes Sol, 664
Los Infantes, 559
Los Molinos, 638
Los Monteros, 318
Los Omeyas, 258
Los Picos de Europa, 25, 560–561
Los Tarantos, 446
Loyola, 534
Lugo, 25, 573, 594, 596

Macía Plaza, 311
Mad Madrid, 110
Madrid, 24, 195, 217, 224, 678
  accommodations, 84–101
  city layout, 77–78
  nightlife, 144–154
  planning your trip to, 19, 22
  restaurants, 102–125
  shopping, 138–143
  sightseeing, 125–137
  transportation services, 76–79
  visitor information, 77
  Web sites, 70
Madrid Carnaval, 31
Maestranza bullring, 268
Mahón, 652–656

Maisonnave, 509
Majorca, 25, 29, 599
Mallorca, 143,
Malpica, 589
Manacor, 629
Manises, 365
Mansion, 181
Mar de Alborán, 346
Mar Menuda, 483
Marbella, 23, 318, 320–321, 324, 326
  accommodations, 328–333
  nightlife, 336–337
  restaurants, 333–336
  shopping, 327–328
  transportation services, 326
Marbella Club, 15, 328
Marbella Club Restaurant, 334
Marbella Inn, 332
Mare Nostrum, 470
María Pita, 576
Marineland, 608
Martian, 269
Martín Berasategui, 530
Matador, 270
Matxinbenta, 545
Mayton, 198
Málaga, 23, 30, 318, 347–354
Málaga Cathedral, 348
Málaga Fair, 33
Málaga Palacio, 349
Medellín, 239
Medina Sidonia, 290
Mediterráneo 1930, 615
Meliá Cáceres, 232
Meliá Castilla, 96, 100
Meliá Confort, 576
Meliá Confort Girona, 476
Meliá Confort Los Bracos, 518
Meliá Costa del Sol, 341
Meliá Gran Sitges, 466
Meliá Madrid Princesa, 101
Meliá Palacio de Los Velada, 189
Meliá Rey Don Jaime, 367
Meliá Torremolinos, 341
Méndez Núñez, 595

Mercat de Los Flors, 445

Mérida, 233–237, 239, 674

Meryan, 255

Mesa, 549

Mesa Redonda, 290

Mesón Antonio, 314

Mesón Can Pedro, 617

Mesón Casa Colgadas, 17, 193

Mesón Castilla, 16, 403

Mesón Cervantes, 216

Mesón Cuevas del Vino, 185

Mesón Danes (Faarup), 354

Mesón de Alberto, 596

Mesón de Cándido, 17, 180

Mesón de la Guitarra, 154

Mesón de los Infantes, 221

Mesón del Champiñón, 154

Mesón del Museo, 335

Mesón del Oso, 564

Mesón del Puerto, 379

Mesón Duque, 180

Mesón el Cordero, 226

Mesón el Purladero, 259

Mesón El Sol y Residencia Santa Teresa, 191

Mesón el Tronco, 239

Mesón la Troya, 229

Mesón Leonés del Racimo de Oro, 213

Mesón Panero, 217

Mesón Rio Chico, 246

Mesón Santiago, 301

Mezquita-Catedral de Córdoba, 8, 252

Miami, 343

Miguel Angel, 98

Miguel Torres, 11

Mijas, 4, 340

Minorca, 25, 599, 650–652, 657–659, 663–665

Mirador de Colomer, 625

Mirador de Colón, 434

Mirador de la Curota, 590

Mirador de Ses Animes, 619

Mirador Ricardo Roca, 619

Miranda & Suizo, 175

Missing, 379

Misteri d'Elx, 12, 379

Modas Gonzalo, 142

Modesto, 281

Mogambo, 371

Molí d'es Reco, 665

Monasterio Cartuja, 306

Monasterio de la Oliva, 513

Monasterio de la Rábida, 296

Monasterio de las Descalzas Reales, 131

Monasterio de las Huelgas, 218

Monasterio de Lluch, 621

Monasterio de Piedra, 500–501

Monasterio de San Ignacio de Loyola, 534

Monasterio de San Juan de los Reyes, 161

Monasterio de San Martín Pinario, 582

Monasterio de San Pedro, 562

Monasterio de San Salvador of Leyre, 516

Monasterio de Santo Tomás, 188

Monasterio del Parral, 178

Monastery of Santo Toribio de Liébana, 562

Moncho Vilas, 586

Moncloa, 79, 101, 145

Monecristo, 379

Monestir de Pedralbes, 433

Monestir de Poblet, 455, 462

Montblanch, 463

Monte Igueldo, 526–527

Monte Toro, 663

Montecarlo, 401

Montecastillo, 288

Montjuïc, 392

Montserrat, 9, 23, 454–458

Moorish old town, 243

Morai, 466

Morase, 514

Moros y Cristianos, 12, 31

Move it disco, 176

Muelle del Puerto, 379

Mugia, 589

Murcia, 379, 381–383

Murillo's House, 267

Muros, 590

Museo a Euska/Museo Vasco, 542

Museo Arquelógico, 284

Museo Arqueològic de Ibiza y Formentera, 636

Museo Arqueológico, 569

Museo Arqueológico de Arte Visigodo, 236

Museo Arqueológico e Histórico, 574

Museo Arqueológico Nacional, 132

Museo Arqueológico Provincial, 254, 268

Museo Art Nouveau–Art Deco, 200

Museo Bellas Artes en la Alhambra, 305

Museo Camón Aznar, 494

Museo Casa Natal de Cervantes, 182

Museo de América, 132

Museo de Arqueología, 381

Museo de Arqueología de Álava, 548

Museo de Arte Abstracto Español, 6, 192

Museo de Artes y Costumbres Populares, 268

Museo de Bellas Artes, 348, 542

Museo de Bellas Artes de Álava, 548

Museo de Bellas Artes de Córdoba, 253

Museo de Cádiz, 293

Museo de Cera de Madrid, 136
Museo de Julio Romero de Torres, 253
Museo de la Real Academia de Bellas Artes de San Fernando, 132
Museo de Navarra, 506
Museo de Salamanca, 200
Museo de Salzillo, 381
Museo de San Telmo, 524
Museo de Santa Cruz, 7, 162
Museo de Zaragoza, 494
Museo del Ejército, 132
Museo del Jamón, 111
Museo del Prado, 128
Museo Diocesano, 558
Museo Hispano-Musulman en la Alhambra, 305
Museo Lázaro Galdiano, 6, 130
Museo Municipal, 133
Museo Municipal de Arte Táurino, 253
Museo Municipal de Bellas Artes, 554
Museo Nacional Centro de Arte Reina Sofía, 129
Museo Nacional de Arte Romano, 7, 235
Museo Nacional de Artes Decorativas, 133
Museo Nacional de Escultura, 7, 214
Museo Naval, 133
Museo Oriental, 215
Museo Pablo Gargallo, 494
Museo Provincial, 244, 592, 595
Museo Provincial de Bellas Artes de Sevilla, 7, 267
Museo Regional de Prehistoria y Arqueología de Cantabria, 554
Museo Románico, 133
Museo Sorolla, 133

Museo Taurino, 134, 298
Museo Tiflológico, 134
Museo-Casa Natal de Jovellanos, 566
Museu Arqueològic, 433, 475
Museu Barbier-Mueller Art Precolombí, 431
Museu Cau Ferrat, 465
Museu Colecció Art del Segle XX, 376
Museu d'Art, 474
Museu d'Art Contemporani, 391, 433
Museu d'Art Espanyol Contemporani, Fundación Juan March, 607
Museu d'Art Modern, 433
Museu d'Història de la Ciutat, 434
Museu d'Història de la Ciutat, 475
Museu de la Ciència (Science Museum), 432
Museu de les Arts Decoratives, 433
Museu de Montserrat, 457
Museu Egipci de Barcelona, 434
Museu Frederic Marès, 431
Museu Maricel, 465
Museu Marítim, 432
Museu Nacional Arqueològic, 459
Museu Nacional d'Art de Catalunya, 427
Museu Necròpolis, 459
Museu Picasso, 7, 392, 426
Museu Romàntic, 466
Museu San Pío, 364
Museu Sant Píus V, 364
Museum of Archaeology, 636
Museum of the Americas, 132
Music and Dance Festival, 554
Mystery of Elche, 379
Mystery Play of Elche, 33

Nabucco, 120
Nájera, 502
National Museum of Sculpture, 214
Navarre, 24, 73, 502, 504, 506–511, 515
Naveta d'es Tudons, 655
Neichel, 421
Nerja, 4, 23, 355–358
Nervión River, 541
New Cathedral, 200
NH Nacional, 93
NH Palacio de Castellanos, 202
Nicole Miller, 269
Nicomedes, 122
Nito, 588
Niza, 528
Nou Manolín, 378
Nova Roma, 236
Noya, 590
Nuestra Señora de la Asunción, 184
Nuestra Señora de la Candelaria, 240
Nuestra Señora de Lebana, 561
Nuévalos, 500–501
Nuévalos/Piedra, 24

Obradoiro, 575
Old Castile, 195
Old Castille, 70
Old Cathedral, 200
Old Square, 240
Old Town Hall, 227
Olite, 511–512
Oliver's, 471
Oñatz, 532
Onda, 365
Ondárroa, 534
O'Pazo, 119
Oratorio de San Felipe Neri, 293
Oriental Perfumeries, 143
Orquesta Nacional de España, 146
Orquesta Sinfónica de Madrid, 146
Ortigueira, 588
Oscar Torrijos, 369
Oviedo, 25, 568–572

Pablo Casals Museum, 453

Pachá, 150

Paellería Valenciana, 108

Palace, 85

Palace Fesol, 369

Palacio Casa Galesa, 609

Palacio de Ayete, 525

Palacio de El Pardo, 183

Palacio de Gelmírez, 580

Palacio de Jabalquinto, 247

Palacio de la Aljafería, 493

Palacio de la Conquista, 228

Palacio de la Quinta, 184

Palacio de la Rambla, 249

Palacio de los Duques de San Carlos, 228

Palacio de Mondragón, 298

Palacio del Mar, 524, 556

Palacio Gaviria, 152

Palacio Museo de Viana, 254

Palacio Real, 5, 6, 130, 171

Palacio Real de La Granja, 181

Palau de l'Almudaina, 608

Palau de la Generalitat, 362

Palau de la Música, 371

Palau de la Música Catalána, 445

Palau del Rei Sancho, 621

Palau Reial (Royal Palace), 434

Palma de Majorca, 604–605, 652

  accommodations, 608–613

  nightlife, 618–619

  restaurants, 614–617

  sightseeing, 606–607, 619–620

  visitor information, 604

Palmera del Cura, 380

Pamplona, 2, 24, 504, 506–511

Panes, 561, 563

Panier Fleuri, 530

Panteón de Goya, 130

Panteón y Museos de San Isidoro, 210

Parador Castillo de Santa Catalina, 14, 245

Parador de Arcos de la Frontera, 292

Parador de Ávila, 13, 189

Parador de Cáceres, 13, 232

Parador de Chinchón, 185

Parador de Fuente-Dé, 565

Parador de Golf, 318

Parador de Hondarribía, 536

Parador de Málaga-Gibralfaro, 350, 353

Parador de Ronda, 299

Parador de Santillana, 14, 558

Parador de Segovia, 178

Parador de Turismo de Cuenca, 13, 193

Parador del Molino Viejo, 14, 566

Parador del Río Deva, 562

Parador Fernando de Aragón, 501

Parador Hernán Cortés, 240

Parador Hotel Atlántico, 293

Parador Nacional Casa del Barón, 14, 592

Parador Nacional Costa de la Luz, 296

Parador Nacional Cristóbal Colón, 297

Parador Nacional de Conde Orgaz, 13, 165

Parador Nacional de la Arruzafa, 257

Parador Nacional de Nerja, 356

Parador Nacional de Salamanca, 202

Parador Nacional de San Francisco, 308

Parador Nacional de San Telmo, 598

Parador Nacional de Trujillo, 14, 229

Parador Nacional del Condestabe Dávalos, 249

Parador Nacional del Golf, 351, 353

Parador Nacional Duques de Cardona, 452

Parador Nacional San Francisco, 312

Parador Nacional Zurbarán., 225

Parador Príncipe de Viana, 512

Parador Restaurante Nacional del Condestabe Dávalos, 250

Parador San Marcos, 13, 211

Parador Turístico de Zamora, 13, 207

Parador Vía de la Plata, 14, 236

Parc d'Atraccions (Tibidabo), 438

Parc Güell, 430

Parc Zoologic, 438

París, 208

Park Hyatt Villa Magna, 14, 94

Parque de Atracciones, 136

Parque de Retiro, 135

Parque Isabel la Católica, 565

Parque María Luisa, 267

Parque Municipal, 380

Pasai Donibane, 533

Pasajes de San Pedro, 533

Paseo de Colón, 268

Paseo de la Herradura, 582

Paseo de los Tristes, 304

Paseo del Prado, 79

Paseo Nuevo, 524

Passeig Arqueològic, 459

Passeig de Gràcia, 391

Paterna, 365

Patos, 370

Pedralbes, 392
Pedro Domecq, 10
Pedro Larumbe, 113
Pedro Romero, 301
Pedro Soriano, 376
Pedro's, 184
Peñalver, 244
Penedés, 10–11, 451
Pepe Rico Restaurant, 357
Perdales, 270
Performing arts
  in Barcelona, 445–446
  in Madrid, 146–149
  in Seville, 282
Perfumería Padilla, 143
Petra, 628
Pérgola, 374
PGA Travel, 35
Piano Bar Regina, 176
Picasso House-Museum, 348
Picos de Europa, 550
Piedra, 500–501
Pikes, 643
Pilar, 658
Pilgrimage of the Virgin of the Dew, 31
Pitarra, 416
Pizarro, 207, 229
Pizzeria San Marco, 280
Pla de la Garsa, 416
Plaça de Catalunya, 391, 393
Plaça de Sant Jaume, 391
Platges de Son Bou, 663
Platja Binimella, 665
Playa Benirras, 644
Playa de Mitjorn, 649
Playa de Ondarreta, 523
Playa Nova, 604
Playa San Lorenzo, 565
Playa San Sebastián, 464
Playamar, 345
Playas del Muerto, 465
Plaza Ayuntamiento, 365
Plaza Cavana, 356
Plaza de América, 268
Plaza de Armas, 264
Plaza de Ayuntamiento, 370

Plaza de España, 78, 88, 268, 548
Plaza de Isabel, 145
Plaza de la Cibeles, 103
Plaza de la Quintana, 582
Plaza de la Virgen Blanca, 547
Plaza de las Cortés, 85
Plaza de las Platerías, 582
Plaza de las Veletas, 231
Plaza de María Pita, 574
Plaza de Oriente, 145
Plaza de Ramón Pelayo, 558
Plaza de San Juan de Dios, 293
Plaza de Toros, 252, 298, 304
Plaza de Vázquez de Molina, 248
Plaza del Campo, 595
Plaza del Pópulo, 247
Plaza del San Miguel, 217
Plaza Mayor (Cáceres), 231
Plaza Mayor (Ciudad Rodrigo), 196, 198
Plaza Mayor (Guadalupe), 223–224
Plaza Mayor (León), 213
Plaza Mayor (Madrid), 77–78, 97, 120–122, 125, 139, 144
Plaza Mayor (Salamanca), 198, 200–203, 205
Plaza Mayor (Trujillo), 227–228
Plaza Mayor (Zafra), 240
Plaza Mayor (Zamora), 208
Plaza Monumental de Toros de las Ventas, 131
Plaza Nueva, 304
Plaza República Argentina, 123
Plaza San Fernando, 284
Plaza Vieja, 240

Plazuela de Santa Bárbara, 574
Poble Espanyol, 419, 434, 608
Polinario, 314
Pontevedra, 591–594
Port Aventura Amusement Park, 460
Port D'Andratx, 619
Port de Pollença, 625–627
Port d'es Canonge, 620
Port de Sóller, 620
Portinatx, 644
Porto Cristo, 629
Porto do Son, 590
Porto Pí, 615
Portugal, 378
Posada de San José, 16, 193
Poseidon, 282
Postiguet Beach, 375
Potes, 561–562
Prado, 6
Priest's Grove, 380
Priest's Palm, 380
Prince's Cottage, 174, 184
Principe de Viana, 118
Príncipe y Serrano, 123
Pub Rojo y Negro, 205
Puebla de Caramiñal, 590
Puebla Vieja, 552
Puente de Poncebos, 563
Puente del Arzobispo, 163
Puente Romano, 15, 252, 329
Puerta de Elvira, 304
Puerta de Toledo, 136
Puerta de Triana, 275
Puerta del Sol, 78, 90–92, 108–110, 144
Puerto Banús, 23, 325
Puig, 625
Pyrenees, 3

Quo Vadis, 409

Raco de l'Olla, 372
Rafael Ortíz, 269
Rail travel, 1
Raixa, 621
Ramblers Holidays, 35

Ramiro I, 496
Ramón Roteta, 537
Ramonet, 422
Rapa das Bestas, 591
Rapa das Bestas, A, 12
Read's Hotel, 612
Real Basílica de San
    Francisco el Grande,
    135
Real Fábrica de Tabacos,
    268
Real Fábrica de Tapices,
    131
Real Jardin Botánico,
    135
Real Monasterio de San
    Lorenzo de El
    Escorial, 8, 173
Real Monasterio de
    Santa María de
    Guadalupe, 224
Recoletos, 79
Refectorium, 353
Refugio, 153
Refugio de Aliva, 562
Regio 1, 294
Rekondo, 531
Renaissance, 680
Reno, 421
Residencia Eslava, 509
Residencia Finlandia,
    333
Residencia Liabeny, 89
Residencia Lima, 333
Residencia Murillo, 275
Residencia Rincón de
    Pepe, 382
Residencia San
    Cristóbal, 333
Restaurant Chapeau,
    204
Restaurant Clivia, 628
Restaurant Hoffmann,
    412
Restaurant Martín, 565
Restaurant Mirador de
    Moraima, 314
Restaurant O Caña, 315
Restaurant, best, 17
Restaurante Begoña,
    545
Restaurante Cunini,
    313
Restaurante Da Vinci,
    261

Restaurante de Miguel,
    358
Restaurante Egaña, 535
Restaurante El
    Jumillano, 378
Restaurante Hostería
    Real, 207
Restaurante Jaime, 620
Restaurante La Finca,
    380
Restaurante Nicolás,
    237
Restaurante Rey
    Alfonso, 358
Restaurante Salvador,
    120
Restaurante Santa
    Marta, 481
Restaurante Sevilla, 315
Restaurante Tendido 6,
    290
Restaurante Vilas, 586
Restaurante/Bar Rias
    Baixas, 643
Restaurants, 1
Restaurants, best, 17
Retiro, 94, 95, 111–114
Rey Alfonso I, 495
Rey Casto, 570
Rey de la Gamba, 425
Rey Juan Carlos I, 405
Rías Altas, 587–589
Rías Bajas, 589
Ribadeo, 588
Ribera del Duero, 9
Rick's, 154
Rincón de España, 221
Rincón de la Casana,
    279
Rincón de Pepe, 383
Rio Bidasoa, 537
Río de la Plata, 205
Río Grande, 280
Ríofrío, 116
Risco, 553
Ritz, 15, 94
Rivoli Ramblas, 400
Rocamar, 657
Rodilla, 122
Roig Robí, 421
Roman amphitheater,
    284
Roman Aqueduct, 178
Roman bridge, 252
Roman necropolis, 284

Romería del Rocío, 31
Ronda, 3, 297–301
Roquefer, 544
Rosalert, 418
Royal Palace, 130
Royal Tapestry Factory,
    131
Rusiñol, Santiago,
    467
Ruta del Valleta, 313

S'Algaret, 666
S'Engolidor, 665
Sa Calobra, 621
Sa Capella, 644
Sa Plaça, 665
Sa Volta, 649
Sagunto, 372
Sala la Bicicleta, 147
Salamanca, 22, 94–95,
    111–114, 196
    accommodations,
        201–204
    nightlife, 205
    restaurants, 204
    shopping, 201
    sightseeing, 198–201
    transportation
        services, 198
    visitor information,
        198
Salamanca Quarter, 78
San Antonio de
    Portmany, 640–643
San Carlo, 107
San Granja, 620
San Juan, 375
San Lluís, 656
San Lorenzo, 610
San Lorenzo de El
    Escorial, 172–176
San Mamés, 124
San Marino, 647
San Marroig, 621
San Miguel de Lillo, 569
San Pablo, 231
San Pedro de Alcántara,
    324
San Sebastián, 24–25,
    521–533
San Sebastián Interna-
    tional Film Festival,
    524
San Sebastián Jazz
    Festival, 32

San Sebastián Playa, 466
Sanctuary of Santa Catalina, 620
Sangüesa, 515–516
Sanlúcar de Barrameda, 295
Sant Agustí, 604
Santa Casa, 534
Santa Cova, 458
Santa Eulalia del Río, 645–647
Santa Maria de Regla, 209
Santa María, 196, 284
Santa María del Naranco, 569
Santa María del Sar, 582
Santa Ponça, 619
Santa Uxea de Ribeira, 590
Santander, 25, 550, 553–557, 561
Santander International Festival of Music and Dance, 33
Santiago, 3, 335
Santiago de Compostela, 25, 579, 582–587, 591
Santiago Sanchez Martín, 164
Santillana del Mar, 4, 555, 557–559
Santo Domingo de la Calzada, 221–222, 502
Santo Mauro Hotel, 97
Saranjan Tours, 35
Sargadelos, 582, 588
Sebastián, 537
Segovia, 22, 176–181
Semana Santa, 31
Senyor Parellada, 416
Serafin, 208
Ses Murteres, 620
Sesamo, 154
7 Portes, 422
Seville, 22, 29, 262
  accommodations, 270–276
  nightlife, 280–282
  restaurants, 276–280
  shopping, 269–270
  sightseeing, 265–268
  transportation services, 262
  visitor information, 264
Seville Fair, 31
Seville Gate, 284
Sidi Lago Rojo, 343
Silversmiths' Square, 582
Sinagoga, 253
Sitges, 4, 23, 454, 464–469, 471
Sitges Park Hotel, 469
Sínagoga de Santa María La Blanca, 162
Sínagoga del Tránsito, 162
Sobrino de Botín, 17, 121, 136
Sol Don Pedro, 343
Sol Elite Don Pablo, 341
Sol Inn Gallos, 257
Sol Inn Hotel, 377
Sol Palas Atenea, 610
Sol y Brisa, 637
Sóller, 620
Sol-Ric, 462
Son Marroig, 620
Son Vida, 609
Sorolla, 368
Sos del Rey Católico, 24, 501
Spanish Golf Adventures, 35
St. Anthony's Day, 30
St. John's Bonfires, 32
St. Teresa Week, 34
Stay Restaurant, 628
Subur Maritim, 468
Sultan Club, 329
Suntory, 113

Taberna Carmencita, 120
Taberna del Alabardero, 111
Taberna Toscana, 125
Tablao Flamenco Cordobés, 446
Talaia Mar, 419
Talatí de Dalt, 655
Talavera la Reina, 163
Tapas, 1
Tarazona, 24, 498
Tarifa, 322
Tarragona, 23, 454, 458, 460–461, 463
Taverna del Alabardero, 272, 279
Taverna Pil-Pil, 578
Teatre Lliure, 445
Teatre Museu Dalí, 7, 485
Teatre Nacional de Catalunya, 446
Teatriz, 116, 152
Teatro Alameda, 282
Teatro Calderón, 148
Teatro Cultural de la Villa, 147
Teatro de la Comedia, 148
Teatro de la Maestranza, 282
Teatro de la Opera, 146
Teatro Español, 148
Teatro Lírico Nacional de la Zarzuela, 148
Teatro Lope de Vega, 282
Teatro María Guerrero, 148
Teatro Nuevo Apolo, 148
Teatro Real, 147
Teatro Romano, 235
Tejidos Artisticos Fortuny, 308
Teleférico, 137
Temple of Diana, 235
Templo de Debod, 135
Tennis, 606
Terete, 520
Terramar, 468
Terraza, 108
Theater, 147
Three Kings Day, 30
Thyssen-Bornemisza Museum, 6, 128
Tibidabo, 392
Tienda Eduardo Ferrer Castillo, 308
Tienda Eduardo Ferrer Lucena, 308
Tiffany's, 374
Tirol, 96, 102
Tocororo, 106
Togar, 194

Toledo, 19, 156, 160, 172, 224
accommodations, 164–167
nightlife, 170
restaurants, 168–169
shopping, 163
sightseeing, 160–162
transportation services, 160
visitor information, 160
Toñi Vicente, 587
Torre d'en Gaumés, 655
Torre de la Calahorra, 253
Torre de Sande, 233
Torre del Oro, 266
Torre Sagrienta, 239
Torremolinos, 23, 318, 320–321, 340
accommodations, 341–343
nightlife, 346
restaurants, 344–345
transportation services, 340
Tossa de Mar, 24, 472, 482–485
Tourist Office of Spain, 25
Tours
in Barcelona, 438
in Madrid, 137
Town Hall (Cádiz), 293
Tragabuches, 301
Tragaluz, 420
Train travel
basic information regarding, 45, 50
EurailPass for, 45, 50–51
in Alcalá de Henares, 181
in Alicante, 375
in Aranjuez, 170
in Ávila, 186
in Badajoz, 237
in Baeza, 246
in Barcelona, 388, 395
in Bilbao, 540
in Burgos, 217
in Cáceres, 230
in Cádiz, 292

in Ciudad Rodrigo, 196
in Córdoba, 250–251
in Cuenca, 191
in Elche, 380
in Granada, 302
in Haro, 519
in Jaén, 243
in Jerez, 285
in La Coruña, 574
in Logroño, 517
in Lugo, 594
in Madrid, 76
in Málaga, 320, 347
in Mérida, 234
in Minorca, 652
in Murcia, 381
in Olite, 512
in Pamplona, 504
in Ronda, 297
in San Lorenzo de El Escorial, 173
in San Sebastián, 524
in Santander, 554
in Santiago, 580
in Segovia, 176
in Seville, 262
in The Balearic Islands, 602
in Toledo, 160
in Tudela, 513
in Túy, 598
in Valencia, 360
in Valladolid, 213
in Vitoria, 547
in Zamora, 206
Trajan's Arch, 234
Transporres Generales Comes, 320, 322
Transportes Los Amarillos, 292
Trento, 205
Trepucó, 655
Tristán, 616
Tritón, 344
Tropicana, 213
Trujillo, 22, 227–229
Tryp Ambassador, 91
Tryp Guadalmar, 350
Tryp Medea, 236
Tudela, 513–514
Turín, 403
Túy, 597
Txulotxo, 533

Úbeda, 242, 248–250
Ujúe, 513
Universidad de Salamanca, 201
Urepel, 531

Valderrama, 35
Valencia, 23, 71, 359, 375
accommodations, 366–368
nightlife, 370–371
restaurants, 368–369
shopping, 365–366
sightseeing, 362–365
transportation services, 360
visitor information, 360
Valladolid, 22, 195, 561
accommodations, 215–216
nightlife, 217
restaurants, 216–217
sightseeing, 214–215
transportation services, 213–214
visitor information, 214
Valldemossa, 620–623
Valley of the Fallen, 173–174
Valparaiso Palace, 613
Venial, 371
Venta de Aires, 168
Veranos de la Villa, 32
Verbena de Sant Joan, 32
Versus, 317
Vía Romana, 495
Via Veneto, 421
Viajes Arifran, 589
Vicedo, 588
Victor Montes, 546
Victorio & Lucchino, 270
Vila Olímpica, 392
Villa Tiberio, 334
Villa Vieja, 376
Villacarlos, 652–653
Villanueva, 562
Viridiana, 114
Vitoria, 521, 546–547
Viva Madrid, 152
Vivero, 588

Walls of Ávila, 186
Wax Museum, 136
Waymark Holidays, 35
Weather Vane House, 231
Wellington, 95
Williams & Humbert
    Limited, 286
Wine
        near Barcelona, 451
        in Granada, 316

list of vineyards and
    wineries, 9–11
in Madrid, 143
touring the bodegas,
    286
types of, 684
Wine Harvest Festival,
517
Wines from Spain, 9
Winetrails, 35

Xauen, 246

Yamaguchy, 515

Zafra, 3, 22, 239–241
Zalacaín, 118
Zamora, 22, 206–208
Zaragoza, 24, 491–498
Zoo Aquarium de la
    Casa de Campo, 137
Zortziko, 545

FROMMER'S® COMPLETE TRAVEL GUIDES

Alaska
Amsterdam
Arizona
Atlanta
Australia
Austria
Bahamas
Barcelona, Madrid &
  Seville
Beijing
Belgium, Holland &
  Luxembourg
Bermuda
Boston
British Columbia & the
  Canadian Rockies
Budapest & the Best of
  Hungary
California
Canada
Cancún, Cozumel &
  the Yucatán
Cape Cod, Nantucket &
  Martha's Vineyard
Caribbean
Caribbean Cruises & Ports
  of Call
Caribbean Ports of Call
Carolinas & Georgia
Chicago
China
Colorado
Costa Rica
Denmark
Denver, Boulder & Colorado
  Springs
England
Europe

European Cruises & Ports
  of Call
Florida
France
Germany
Greece
Greek Islands
Hawaii
Hong Kong
Honolulu, Waikiki & Oahu
Ireland
Israel
Italy
Jamaica
Japan
Las Vegas
London
Los Angeles
Maryland & Delaware
Maui
Mexico
Montana & Wyoming
Montréal & Québec City
Munich & the Bavarian
  Alps
Nashville & Memphis
Nepal
New England
New Mexico
New Orleans
New York City
New Zealand
Nova Scotia, New Brunswick
  & Prince Edward Island
Oregon
Paris
Philadelphia & the
  Amish Country

Portugal
Prague & the Best of the
  Czech Republic
Provence & the Riviera
Puerto Rico
Rome
San Antonio & Austin
San Diego
San Francisco
Santa Fe, Taos & Albuquerque
Scandinavia
Scotland
Seattle & Portland
Shanghai
Singapore & Malaysia
South Africa
Southeast Asia
South Florida
South Pacific
Spain
Sweden
Switzerland
Thailand
Tokyo
Toronto
Tuscany & Umbria
USA
Utah
Vancouver & Victoria
Vermont, New Hampshire
  & Maine
Vienna & the Danube Valley
Virgin Islands
Virginia
Walt Disney World &
  Orlando
Washington, D.C.
Washington State

FROMMER'S® DOLLAR-A-DAY GUIDES

Australia from $50 a Day
California from $60 a Day
Caribbean from $70 a Day
England from $70 a Day
Europe from $70 a Day

Florida from $70 a Day
Hawaii from $70 a Day
Ireland from $60 a Day
Italy from $70 a Day
London from $85 a Day

New York from $80 a Day
Paris from $80 a Day
San Francisco from $60 a Day
Washington, D.C.,
  from $70 a Day

FROMMER'S® PORTABLE GUIDES

Acapulco, Ixtapa &
  Zihuatanejo
Alaska Cruises & Ports of Call
Bahamas
Baja & Los Cabos
Berlin
California Wine Country
Charleston & Savannah
Chicago
Dublin

Hawaii: The Big Island
Las Vegas
London
Los Angeles
Maine Coast
Maui
Miami
New Orleans
New York City
Paris

Puerto Vallarta, Manzanillo
  & Guadalajara
San Diego
San Francisco
Sydney
Tampa & St. Petersburg
Venice
Washington, D.C.

FROMMER'S® NATIONAL PARK GUIDES

Family Vacations in the
   National Parks
Grand Canyon

National Parks of the
   American West
Rocky Mountain

Yellowstone & Grand Teton
Yosemite & Sequoia/
   Kings Canyon
Zion & Bryce Canyon

FROMMER'S® MEMORABLE WALKS

Chicago
London

New York
Paris

San Francisco
Washington, D.C.

FROMMER'S® GREAT OUTDOOR GUIDES

New England
Northern California

Southern California & Baja
Southern New England

Washington & Oregon

FROMMER'S® BORN TO SHOP GUIDES

Born to Shop: France
Born to Shop: Italy

Born to Shop: London
Born to Shop: New York

Born to Shop: Paris

FROMMER'S® IRREVERENT GUIDES

Amsterdam
Boston
Chicago
Las Vegas

London
Los Angeles
Manhattan
New Orleans

Paris
San Francisco
Seattle & Portland
Vancouver

Walt Disney World
Washington, D.C.

FROMMER'S® BEST-LOVED DRIVING TOURS

America
Britain
California

Florida
France
Germany

Ireland
Italy
New England

Scotland
Spain
Western Europe

THE UNOFFICIAL GUIDES®

Bed & Breakfasts in
   California
Bed & Breakfasts in
   New England
Bed & Breakfasts in
   the Northwest
Bed & Breakfasts in
   Southeast
Beyond Disney
Branson, Missouri

California with Kids
Chicago
Cruises
Disneyland
Florida with Kids
Golf Vacations in the
   Eastern U.S.
The Great Smoky &
   Blue Ridge
   Mountains

Inside Disney
Hawaii
Las Vegas
London
Miami & the Keys
Mini Las Vegas
Mini-Mickey
New Orleans
New York City
Paris

San Francisco
Skiing in the West
Southeast with Kids
Walt Disney World
Walt Disney World
   for Grown-ups
Walt Disney World
   for Kids
Washington, D.C.

SPECIAL-INTEREST TITLES

Frommer's Britain's Best Bed & Breakfasts and
   Country Inns
Frommer's Britain's Best Bike Rides
The Civil War Trust's Official Guide
   to the Civil War Discovery Trail
Frommer's Caribbean Hideaways
Frommer's Adventure Guide to Central America
Frommer's Adventure Guide to South America
Frommer's Adventure Guide to Southeast Asia
Frommer's Food Lover's Companion to France
Frommer's Gay & Lesbian Europe
Frommer's Exploring America by RV
Hanging Out in Europe

Israel Past & Present
Mad Monks' Guide to California
Mad Monks' Guide to New York City
Frommer's The Moon
Frommer's New York City with Kids
The New York Times' Unforgettable
   Weekends
Places Rated Almanac
Retirement Places Rated
Frommer's Road Atlas Britain
Frommer's Road Atlas Europe
Frommer's Washington, D.C., with Kids
Frommer's What the Airlines Never Tell You